African Americans and Criminal Justice

African Americans and Criminal Justice

An Encyclopedia

Delores D. Jones-Brown, Beverly D. Frazier, and Marvie Brooks, Editors

GREENWOOD

AN IMPRINT OF ABC-CLIO, LLC
Santa Barbara, California • Denver, Colorado • Oxford, England

Library of Congress Cataloging-in-Publication Data

African Americans and criminal justice : an encyclopedia / Delores D. Jones-Brown, Beverly D. Frazier, and Marvie Brooks, Editors.
     pages cm
  Includes index.
  ISBN 978-0-313-35716-9 (Hardcover. : alk. paper) — ISBN 978-0-313-35717-6 (ebook)
1. Criminal justice, Administration of—Moral and ethical aspects—United States.
2. Discrimination in criminal justice administration—United States. 3. Discrimination in capital punishment—United States. 4. African American criminals. 5. United States—Race relations. I. Jones-Brown, Delores D. II. Frazier, Beverly D. III. Brooks, Marvie.
  HV9950.A356 2014
  364.089'96073003—dc23   2013042831

ISBN: 978-0-313-35716-9
EISBN: 978-0-313-35717-6

18 17 16 15 14 1 2 3 4 5

This book is also available on the World Wide Web as an eBook.
Visit www.abc-clio.com for details.

Greenwood
An Imprint of ABC-CLIO, LLC

ABC-CLIO, LLC
130 Cremona Drive, P.O. Box 1911
Santa Barbara, California 93116-1911

This book is printed on acid-free paper ∞
Manufactured in the United States of America

Contents

List of Entries

Acknowledgments

It has been said that a journey of a thousand miles begins with a single step. The development of this book has been consistent with that saying. This final product is a collaborative effort among many individuals who have given their time and expertise to the creation of a comprehensive volume with content that spans three centuries. We thank the contributors for their patience and their diligence in responding to inquiries and completing their work. We also thank you for helping us solicit your colleagues, students, professional associates, and even family members to become a part of this very important effort.

Beyond the substantive entries, the logistics of pulling this volume together were made possible by the co-editors working with dedicated individuals from two schools: John Jay College of Criminal Justice and the University of Pennsylvania. At John Jay College, in addition to the many contributors, we would like to thank Petula Bailey, Cameo Christian, Mia Ramdial, Luise Pedroso-Kipler, and Cherise Bruce for the hours they spent tracking authors, editing copy, and conducting supplemental research. A special thanks to Cameo Christian and Nicole Hanson for going the extra mile by searching for photographs and other supplements to make the volume more visual and interesting. Special thanks to Professor Jose Luis' Morin for sharing his *Latinos and Criminal Justice* outline early in this process, and to Professors Matthew Johnson and Kyoo Lee (aka Q) for their editorial comments regarding the Termination of Parental Rights and Critical Race Theory entries. Logistical efforts at the University of Pennsylvania were led by head research assistants Ike Onyeado, Alisha Roman, and Fabiel Jean-Philippe. Dr. Frazier also wishes to extend a special show of gratitude to Professor John Dilulio.

Dr. Jones-Brown wishes to thank her brother, Claiborne Jones III, for his keen interest in this project and for granting access to his laptop to allow her to continue working "on the go" while dealing with serious family issues. We all extend our sincere apologies to anyone who we called on in this process but have failed to call out in this acknowledgment. We thank you for all of your efforts, nonetheless, and include you among our unsung heroes.

This project has been a labor of love that took us away from friends and family for long periods of time, so we would also like to thank them for their patience and support. A special thank you to Pamela Sims-Jones, a friend and confidante, for her editing expertise and for recognizing that "this work is really hard." To friend Jerome Wakefield, proud graduate of Seton Hall University Law School, thanks so much for your help with the law-related entries. We also wish to extend our thanks to the other publishers who granted permission to have materials reprinted in this volume. But most of all we thank Kim Kennedy-White and the other dedicated staff members at ABC-CLIO for having the patience to wait faithfully for this volume to come together. We especially thank Kim for her continued dedication to our project and her willingness to see it through to the end, and all the ways in which she supported this gargantuan effort.

Through this encyclopedia, we hoped to effectively and succinctly illuminate the complex and often painful historical and contemporary experience of people of African ancestry in relation to the system of justice in the United States. Our desire was to make this information accessible and understandable to a wide audience. Because of your combined efforts, we are confident that we have achieved our goal.

Delores D. Jones-Brown, JD, PhD
Beverly D. Frazier, MDiv, MBA, PhD
Marvie Brooks, MA

Introduction

Each year, Blacks[1] make up roughly 30 percent of those arrested for crime in the United States, while they make up 12 to 13 percent of the general population. In some locations, Blacks make up close to 50 percent of the prison population, and as a consequence many have lost important civil rights, including the right to vote. This overrepresentation of African Americans within the prison system was first formally documented via the 1890s census and has continued to be a topic of discussion in current debates about mass incarceration and the prison industrial complex.

As academics, criminal justice professionals, and ordinary people have struggled to understand the reasons for this overrepresentation, many falsehoods have developed, the primary one being that Blacks commit the most crime. This myth exists despite statistics showing that each year Whites make up roughly 70 percent of people arrested across the country. Although this 70 percent figure is far greater than the 51 percent needed to represent a majority, media and other attention tend to focus on "Black" crime that primarily takes place within urban neighborhoods marked by high levels of poverty, crowding, poor schools, poor housing, and poor prospects for employment within the legitimate job market. The "Black on Black" crime that occurs within these neighborhoods garners a great deal of attention and becomes *the* indicator of Black behavior, while "White on White" crime is rarely ever discussed, accept as aberrant conduct by particular individuals.

Many have argued that the tendency to see Blacks as a criminal collective is the primary cause of their overrepresentation within the American criminal justice system. Others argue that their representation within the criminal justice system is consistent with the amount and seriousness of their offending. Still others point to racial discrimination within the larger society and the justice system as accounting for current disparity in who has and who avoids contact with the criminal justice system. Readers of this encyclopedia should come away with a better understanding of the complex ways in which many factors have come together over time to create a contemporary system of criminal justice that disproportionately impacts racial and ethnic minorities, with perhaps its greatest negative impact on African Americans.

What follows is a collection of essays and supporting material that document both the historical and contemporary impact of the law and the justice system on people of African ancestry in the United States. The entries cover three centuries of racialized law and criminal justice practice at the local, state, and federal levels and demonstrate how such practices have contributed to the disproportionate processing of Blacks through the various components of the American system of criminal justice. The entries also describe the ways in which people of African ancestry have resisted legalized oppression and how that resistance has contributed to the perception and reality of them as criminals and violent offenders. There are entries that present the biographies of famous and infamous Black criminal suspects, victims, lawyers, and leaders from early American history to contemporary times. Some of those biographies demonstrate the fine line between villain and icon, and how frequently the path between the two involves some criminal justice system contact.

Note

1. Official crime statistics collected by the FBI and Bureau of Justice Statistics use the term "Black" to describe persons of Black racial identity whether or not they were born in the United States. This volume will use the term Black and African American interchangeably, but will at times point out the distinction between persons of African ancestry who are born within the United States and those who are born in other countries.

A

Abu-Jamal, Mumia (1954–)

Mumia Abu-Jamal is one of the most controversial figures in the American criminal justice system. In December 2011, after nearly 30 years on death row in Pennsylvania, Philadelphia, prosecutors announced that they would no longer seek the death penalty for his 1982 conviction for killing 25-year-old police officer Daniel Faulkner. The prosecutor's decision was made after nearly three decades of appeals and conflict over his original conviction and death sentence. Throughout his confinement, Abu-Jamal has contended that racism on the part of the trial judge and the prosecutors led to both his conviction and his capital sentence. A three-judge panel of the U.S. Court of Appeals for Philadelphia's Third Circuit heard an appeal of his case on May 17, 2007, and agreed with a lower court judge who had ordered that Abu-Jamal's death sentence be set aside, finding that the trial jurors may have been unduly confused and encouraged to choose a death sentence over one of life imprisonment.

Although the U.S. Supreme Court ordered the lower court to reexamine its decision, in April 2011 the decision to set aside the death sentence was reaffirmed. The prosecution was left to decide whether to request a new sentencing hearing with a new jury or allow the death sentence to be commuted to a life sentence without the possibility of parole. Citing the potential costs and possibility of additional lengthy appeals, Philadelphia prosecutor Seth Williams opted not to seek a new sentencing hearing. Over the 30 years of Abu-Jamal's imprisonment, Maureen Faulkner, the slain officer's widow, adamantly insisted that Abu-Jamal was correctly sentenced at the end of his original trial. The case garnered national and international attention in part because Abu-Jamal is African American and over time has been a member of groups that have been considered radical—including the Black Panther Party and MOVE, a Philadelphia-based organization founded by John Afrika reported as dedicated to Black liberation—while the deceased officer was a young White family man with small children.

1

Pennsylvania death row inmate Mumia Abu-Jamal, seen here in a December 13, 1995, photo from prison, was convicted in 1982 of murdering a Philadelphia policeman. Police in Washington, D.C., arrested dozens of Abu-Jamal supporters who were demanding a new trial for Abu-Jamal and the abolition of the death penalty in the United States, February 28, 2000. (Getty Images)

Philadelphia is a city with a long history of racial tensions and complaints of police brutality. The arrest, trial, conviction, and capital sentencing of Mumia Abu-Jamal during and following the early 1980s drew the attention of civil and human rights activists, among the most noteworthy South Africa's Archbishop Desmond Tutu, who has been identified as a Mumia "supporter." There is an ongoing campaign to "Free Mumia" at the same time that others identify him simply as a "cop killer." The dual identity of Abu-Jamal is complicated further by his status as a media personality, having written and produced journalistic work prior to and throughout his incarceration. He has published more than six books, including his 1995 memoir *Live from Death Row.* Additional titles include *We Want Freedom, All Things Censored, Jailhouse Lawyers,* and *Faith of Our Fathers.*

The events that propelled Mumia Abu-Jamal, who was born Wesley Cook, into the public eye began on the morning of December 9, 1981, somewhere between 3:30 and 4:00 a.m. Philadelphia police officer Daniel J. Faulkner was shot and killed, reportedly while attempting to arrest William Cook (Mumia's brother) for driving in the wrong direction, with his Volkswagen Beetle's headlights off, on a one-way street. According to reports and witness accounts, Abu-Jamal intervened in the arrest. The incident ended with an exchange of gunfire between Abu-Jamal and Faulkner, a six-year veteran of the force. Abu-Jamal was left wounded by a shot from Officer Faulkner's gun. Officer Faulkner was dead on arrival at the local hospital, having been shot multiple times, with one bullet in his back and four fired at close range. When other police arrived, Abu-Jamal's shoulder holster was found empty; he lay on the street, shot in the chest. A few feet away from him was a .38 revolver registered to him with five empty chambers.

It is reported that William Cook's sole comment at the scene of the shooting was: "I ain't got nothing to do with this." In 1982, he entered a guilty plea to the charge of physically assaulting Faulkner, after the officer hit him three times before his brother intervened. Abu-Jamal himself did not initially give his version of the events to the police. In an April 2001 affidavit, Cook states that his childhood friend, army veteran Kenneth "Poppi" Freeman, was in the passenger seat of the Volkswagen carrying a .38 revolver and later claimed that he (Freeman) planned to kill Officer Faulkner.

In July 1982, Mumia Abu-Jamal was convicted of the murder, after a trial in which he chose to defend himself. Against the recommendation of the trial judge, Albert F. Sabo, Abu-Jamal refused the legal counsel of his attorney Anthony E. Jackson and the opportunity to testify on his own behalf, citing a history of U.S. institutional racism. The president of the local chapter of the Association of Black Journalists repeatedly requested to have MOVE's founder, John Afrika, as Abu-Jamal's legal representation. These requests were denied because Mr. Afrika was not a lawyer.

During the trial, Abu-Jamal repeatedly called his alleged confession into question—a confession that was reportedly heard by a Black security officer, Priscilla Durham, at the entrance to Jefferson Hospital's emergency room, where he was treated after the shooting. The trial jury was composed of 2 African Americans and 10 Whites. They deliberated less than two hours before reaching a verdict. Subsequent courts found that once the verdict was in, the jury was never effectively informed of the option of sentencing Abu-Jamal to life in prison without parole instead of death. Originally scheduled for execution by lethal injection on August 17, 1995, Abu-Jamal continues to claim that he was framed by Philadelphia's police department. The original death sentence was declared unconstitutional by Judge William H. Yohn, Jr., in December 2001, but it would be another 10 years before Abu-Jamal's death sentence would be commuted to life.

Prior to the 1981 incident that changed his life forever, Mumia Abu-Jamal lived a life full of challenges. He was born on April 24, 1954, to an orphaned mother from North Carolina and her second husband. His father died when he was nine. He acquired the name "Mumia" in 1968, from his Kenyan teacher Timone Ombina at Benjamin Franklin High School. Abu-Jamal later dropped out of Benjamin Frankin and, disregarding his mother's concern for the family's safety, as a 15-year-old, gave out their home number as the local Black Panther Party chapter's contact information. This led to ongoing racist threats. He later left home to live in party quarters. In the winter of 1969–1970, he was transferred by the Party from its base in Philadelphia to its New York City chapter. At one time, Huey Newton was one of

Abu-Jamal's heroes. However, he left the Party after its national convention in September 1970. He returned to high school, but was suspended for attempting to change the school's name to Malcolm X High; he eventually earned his GED.

Mumia had his first son at age 17 in July 1971 and changed his surname from Cook to Abu-Jamal (Arabic for "father of Jamal"). He became a student at Goddard College in Plainfield, Vermont, where he earned his bachelor of arts degree and became exposed to radio broadcasting at its student-run station. Mumia then returned to Philadelphia, where he had his own program on Temple University's radio station, WRTI.

Abu-Jamal remains incarcerated in the State Correctional Institution at Greene, in Waynesburg, Pennsylvania, where he has authored *Live from Death Row* (May 1995), earned a master of arts degree from California State University–Dominguez Hills, and given commencement addresses to graduating college classes.

Rhodine Moreau and Delores Jones-Brown

See also: Black Panther Party; Civil Rights Movement; Police Brutality

References

Associated Press. "Execution Warrant Is Signed for a Prison Celebrity." *The New York Times,* June 3, 1995. http://www.nytimes.com/1995/06/03/us/execution-warrant-is-signed-for -a-prison-celebrity.html?ref=mumiaabujamal.

Burroughs, Todd Steven. "Ready to Party: Mumia Abu-Jamal and the Black Panther Party," 2004. http://www.tcnj.edu/~kpearson/Mumia/index.htm.

Commonwealth of Pennsylvania, Appellee, v. Mumia Abu-Jamal a.k.a. Wesley Cook, Appellant. http://justice.danielfaulkner.com/docs/Transcripts.pdf.

"Lawyers Seek New Trial for Pennsylvania Death Row Inmate, Saying Evidence Was Withheld." *The New York Times,* June 12, 1995. http://www.nytimes.com/1995/06/12/ us/lawyers-seek-new-trial-for-pennsylvania-death-row-inmate-saying-evidence-was .html?ref=mumiaabujamal.

Lopez, Steve. "Wrong Guy, Good Cause." *Time,* July 23, 2000. http://www.time.com/time/ magazine/article/0,9171,50613,00.html#ixzz1fnItix1L.

Russ, Valerie M. "Mumia's Sister Says He's 'Strong, Calm.'" *Philadelphia Daily News,* June 6, 1995. http://articles.philly.com/1995-06-06/news/25689418_1_mumia-abu-jamal -faulkner-brother.

Terry, Don. "A Fight for Life Is Waged in an Angry Courtroom." *The New York Times,* July 30, 1995.

United States Court of Appeals for the Third Circuit (5/17/2007 appeal). http://www.ca3 .usCourts.gov/opinArch/019014p2.pdf.

Williams, Lena. "Pending Execution of Former Radio Reporter Divides Organization of Black Journalists." *The New York Times,* July 17, 1995. http://www.nytimes .com/1995/07/17/us/pending-execution-former-radio-reporter-divides-organization -black-journalists.html?ref=mumiaabujamal&pagewanted=print.

Adams, The Honorable Eric L. (1960–)

Eric L. Adams is a former captain with the New York City Police Department (NYPD) and former Democratic state senator for the 20th District of New York. Adams was elected to the New York State Senate in 2006, after having spent more than two decades of public service with the city's police. He was re-elected in 2008 and 2010. His district covered the New York City neighborhoods of Borough Park, Crown Heights, Flatbush, Park Slope, Prospect Heights, Sunset Park, and Windsor Terrace. In 2013, Eric Adams became the first African American to be elected to the position of Brooklyn borough president.

Throughout his career in law enforcement, Captain Adams was extremely vocal in speaking out against police brutality and racial profiling. He co-founded 100 Blacks in Law Enforcement Who Care ("100 Blacks"), a group comprised of law enforcement personnel and their supporters that provides assistance to community-based organizations striving to improve their neighborhoods. He also chaired the Grand Council for the Guardians, an African American police fraternal organization, and served on the Board of the Eastern District Counseling Service, a nonprofit organization that assists former substance abusers with their transition back to a drug- and alcohol-free life.

In 2001, 100 Blacks sued New York City, claiming that the police department illegally monitored political activities of its members by reviewing telephone records and following members over the course of a two-year period (Flynn, 2001). Adams sought to uncover the identities of those who authorized the investigation and to discern their motives. He looked across many of the community organization leaders to determine if there was a pattern among people who were brought in for unrelated charges or who were audited by the IRS during the two-year period in question.

Outside of New York, his investigative interests also focused on policing. He sought to identify acts of overt racism by public officials in New Jersey by patrolling that state's highways equipped with a video recorder. By witnessing first-hand state troopers pulling over Black motorists, he aimed to identify whether the vehicles matched the same description as those in allegations put forth in civil suits against the state. His straightforward tactics are viewed by many as controversial, but provide a unique way of exploring various issues of social injustice.

Adams' departure from law enforcement occurred after controversy erupted in the wake of an alleged terrorist threat to the city's subway system in 2006. It was Adams' position that New York mayor Michael Bloomberg and senior NYPD officials did not respond to the threat according to proper department policies and procedures. Adams was formally reprimanded by the NYPD for publicly denouncing response tactics in a live public forum. Prior to his retirement, Adams had been considered by some as a top contender for the position of New York police commissioner (Noel, 2001).

Eric Adams is a former New York State senator, former captain in the NYPD, and former president of the organization 100 Blacks in Law Enforcement Who Care. In 2013 he became the first African American to be elected Brooklyn borough president. (Associated Press)

His expertise, developed over the course of a 22-year career in law enforcement, and his involvement with other criminal justice issues earned him numerous leadership positions within the State Senate. During the 2007 and 2008 legislative sessions he was appointed the ranking minority member on the Crime Victims, Crime, and Correction Committee and ranking minority member on the Veterans, Homeland Security, and Military Affairs Committee. He has also served as a member on the Senate's Aging, Codes, and Civil Service and Pensions Committee. During the 2009 and 2010 legislative sessions he chaired both the Veterans, Homeland Security, and Military Affairs Committee and the Racing, Gaming, and Waging Committee, and was a member of the Finance, Judiciary, Banks, Consumer Protection and Energy, and Telecommunications committees.

In May 2010, Adams introduced a bill aimed at prohibiting the NYPD's practice of retaining personal data for those who were stopped and questioned by police but not charged with a crime or issued a summons. The law was successfully passed. Adams has also been influential through his community-based lecture series. His program for providing essential educational skills to New York City's youth is presented in his annual "Cradle to College" seminar. This event is aimed at connecting parents to the resources they need in order to empower families. Adams is also widely regarded for his "stop the sag" campaign, which encourages youth to wear their pants above the waistline. Adams argues, "Sagging pants have become a degrading and self-inflict[ed] icon that follows on a long tradition of negative stereotyping" (Katz, 2011).

In addition to speaking out against police brutality and misconduct, Adams is recognized for his vigorous efforts to combat gun violence and to rid New York's streets of illegal firearms. A video he launched in January 2011 demonstrates various methods that parents can use to find illegal guns or contraband within their homes. Working with and without 100 Blacks, the former senator has addressed many criminal justice issues in the city, many of them controversial. He has served as a panelist for discussions about the death penalty. He pushed to have the NYPD reconstruct security camera monitoring teams in public housing when the NYPD video monitoring unit failed to detect the rape of a Brooklyn woman. He worked with clergy acting as crisis teams in high-crime areas. He has been a keynote speaker for Drug Treatment Alternative-to-Prison (DTAP) programs of Kings County district attorney Charles Hynes. And in November 2011, he was publicly critical of the procedures that the NYPD used to disperse Occupy Wall Street protesters from their New York City "headquarters" in Zuccotti Park. In 2013, he served as a plaintiff's witness in the historic class-action lawsuit *Floyd et al. v. the City of New York.* The suit was brought against the city and the NYPD, challenging the constitutionality of its stop, question, and frisk practices. In August 2013, a federal judge decided the case in favor of the plaintiffs.

Beyond criminal justice matters, Senator Adams has collaborated on legislation to extend rent control for over one million New Yorkers, and in February 2011, he sponsored a bill that would enable military service credit for New York City civil service pensions for all honorably discharged veterans. Eric Adams has been described as a man who has devoted his life to the least privileged in society, and who has sought to ensure that they are not further deprived by inequitable laws and policies.

A product of New York City's public and private schools, Adams completed undergraduate degrees at both New York City Technical College and John Jay College of Criminal Justice. He also received a master's degree in public administration from Marist College.

Walter Berbrick

See also: Bell, Sean; Diallo, Amadou; Louima, Abner; 100 Blacks in Law Enforcement Who Care; Police Brutality; Racial Profiling

References

Adams, Eric. "S3291-2011: Allows Military Service Credit for Retirement to All Honorably Discharged Veterans." New York State Senate. http://open.nysenate.gov/legislation/api/1.0/html/bill/S3291-2011.

Adams, Eric. "NYS Senator Eric Adams Joins NYS Senator Adriano Espaillat's Introduction of Legislation to Extend Rent Control; Strengthen Tenant Protections," New York State Senate. February 23, 2011. http://www.nysenate.gov/press-release/nys-senator-eric-adams-joins-nys-senator-adriano-espaillats-introduction-legislation-e.

Floyd et al v. the City of New York, et al. (08 Civ. 1034 [SAS] 2013).

Flynn, Kevin. "Black Police Officers Sue City, Citing Surveillance." *The New York Times,* December 13, 2001. http://www.nytimes.com/2001/12/13/nyregion/black-police-officers-sue-city-citing-surveillance.html.

Katz, Celeste. "Sen. Eric Adams: How to Police Your Own Home." *New York Daily News,* January 31, 2011. http://www.nydailynews.com/blogs/dailypolitics/2011/01/sen-eric-adams-how-to-police-your-own-home.

Noel, Peter. "Eric Adams for Police Commissioner." *The Village Voice,* July 31, 2001. http://www.villagevoice.com/2001-07-31/news/eric-adams-for-police-commissioner/.

African Diaspora, Crime, and Justice

"African American" is the term currently used to describe persons of Black racial identity who are born in the United States. The Afrocentric social movements of the twentieth century (see Black Panther Party, Civil Rights Movement, Nation of Islam, and Southern Christian Leadership Conference [SCLC]) might cause one to assume a collective sense of pride and connection between the various Black ethnic groups living within the country. Instead, there is evidence that the recent influx of African immigrants (primarily West Africans and Nigerians) has caused the American Black populations to revisit the question of Black solidarity. This question is most highly debated within areas of New York City, as volumes of West African and Nigerian immigrants have encountered unwelcoming resistance in traditionally Black neighborhoods, especially sections of both Harlem and the Bronx (Abdullah, 2009; Dolnick, 2009).

While other groups, such as Haitians and Jamaicans, have reportedly successfully integrated within and redefined modern African American culture for decades, there appears to be a stark difference between other immigrants of African ancestry and African Americans, creating substantial difficulty for some of these immigrants in identifying with and creating community between themselves and American-born Blacks. The end result is a process of fragmented assimilation rife with conflict, violence, and discrimination (Abdullah, 2009).

Pride and Prejudice: The Problem

One of the significant sociocultural issues in the divide between African immigrants, African Americans, and other Black Americans (primarily immigrants from Caribbean countries) is the underacknowledgment of the achievements and successes accomplished by those who are Black and native born and an underrecognition of the accomplishments and contributions of predominantly Black societies around the world. Images of crime, laziness, disorganization, and underachievement as the mainstay of Black populations tend to prevail. In addition, the sense of pride that many African Americans and international Blacks have struggled to obtain is hindered by "Third World" stereotypes projected upon African and many Caribbean immigrants by other groups. The end result is a desire for African Americans and other Blacks to disassociate themselves from immigrant neighbors with whom they have common ancestral roots—a desire so strongly held by some that it leads to discrimination and violence (Abdullah, 2009).

The West African Experience in Black American Society

One of the largest new immigrant groups to arrive in New York City has been West Africans, a predominantly Muslim, family-oriented, educated group seeking economic prosperity and familial achievement of the "American Dream." While West Africans can be found throughout New York's five boroughs, the majority of the population resides within two distinct ethnic pockets of the city: Little Africa in Harlem, and the Claremont section of the South Bronx (Abdullah, 2009). Although these individuals have attempted to create community and economic revitalization among their fellow African American neighbors by opening African restaurants, clothing stores, and mosques within these areas, their presence has been met with extreme cases of discrimination, vandalism, and violence. According to a 2009 article in *The New York Times,* over two dozen attacks in the Claremont section of the Bronx were carried out on West African immigrants and West African–owned businesses within a two-year period. Two of the incidents were deemed hate crimes (Dolnick, 2009).

In response to the attacks, some have asked: Why hurt what helps the neighborhood? It appears that an immense cultural and religious disconnect exists between local Black American residents and their West African neighbors, resulting in a Black caste system within these historically Black neighborhoods. Consequently, West Africans seeking personal economic prosperity and simultaneous improvement of their economically blighted communities have been subjected to violent reprisal by local residents who claim that the group's "savage attitude" in "taking over" the neighborhood justifies their response. Members of the immigrant group are also criticized for their "aloof refusal" to assimilate with Black American culture, thus causing a "great divide" among these culturally distinct Black populations.

In addition, in the post-9/11 era, West African residents, who tend to be practicing Muslims, in contrast to American and Caribbean Blacks, who tend to be Christians, have become positioned as a collective pariah in American Black culture. They often bear the brunt of terrorist suspicions from neighbors and the larger society (Dolnick, 2009).

While the fear and tension felt by West African immigrants is unfortunate and unwarranted, they continue to stay within their residential enclaves in hopes of one day bridging the gap between themselves and their American-born counterparts (Abdullah, 2009). This is not the case with the existing Nigerian population, which has experienced the divide between African immigrants and local Blacks in a different way (Oyeyemi & Sedenu, 2007).

The Nigerian Experience in Black American Society

The Nigerian experience begins with a similar story to that of the West African population: a predominantly Muslim, family-oriented, educated group who seeks economic prosperity within New York City, but is targeted and discriminated against by fellow Black neighbors. However, the differences between the Nigerian and West African populations in dealing with such conflict are significant, and include resorting to collective forms of criminal activity as a means of survival.

While many Nigerian immigrants are actively employed and earn a median income well above the poverty line, they are regarded as a lower-class group and are often isolated due to their African heritage. This has resulted in a subset of the population falling victim to the Pygmalion prophecy, in which affected Nigerian immigrants have succumbed to the world of underground crime. In recent years, news stories and Internet pop-up warnings have painted a largely negative picture of this immigrant group, largely related to crackdowns for dealing in counterfeit goods and identity theft scams, an affiliation that has had a detrimental impact on the sustainability of the population in New York City (Oyeyemi & Sedenu, 2007).

There is evidence that many Nigerians are adopting a transient outlook on their new home by transmitting any economic gains back to their homeland in hopes of soon returning. According to a 2007 survey of 177 Nigerian immigrants interviewed throughout New York City, over 88 percent of those surveyed planned on returning to Nigeria in the near future, which has serious implications for ethnic extinction of this particular group within New York City (Oyeyemi & Sedenu, 2007).

Implications for the Future

The discrimination felt by African immigrants in African American neighborhoods runs the risk of negative impacts on both social and economic levels. Further fragmentation and tension may not only cause the targeted ethnic groups to retaliate in violence, but may also remove their ethnic footprint from the area. The disappearance of ethnic enclaves can not only lead to cultural and economic dissipation; it can also result in the disappearance of a variety of African ethnics, as the rich history embodied in African heritage could be buried in bias and prejudice and made unavailable to future generations. If the American Black community is to revisit the question of being African American, African immigrants should not be dismissed, as they represent the core and foundation of today's American immigrant experience.

In addition, while there is evidence that Black ethnic groups are making distinctions among each other, American criminal justice agents see them as all the same. The shooting deaths of Amadou Diallo, Ousmane Zongo, Patrick Dorismond, and Sean Bell all indicate that New York City police officers do not distinguish among the ethnic origins of Blacks whom they see as potentially dangerous. Diallo and Zongo were from African nations. Dorismond and Bell had roots in the African Caribbean. And the sodomy of Abner Louima, one of the most publicized acts of police brutality by a member of the New York City police department, was committed against a Haitian immigrant. The one thing that these men all have in common is that they were unarmed but were perceived to be dangerous by police officers nonetheless. Hence, the physical appearance of these individuals, i.e., their Blackness, seems to have been the controlling factor in how the police responded to them. While within-group discrimination is taking place among civilians from different Black ethnic groups, it seems that law enforcement personnel are failing to make these fine distinctions, suggesting that Black solidarity may be as important in this century as it was in the last.

Ashley York-Kurtz

See also: Bell, Sean; Diallo, Amadou; Dorismond, Patrick; Zongo, Ousmane

References

Abdullah, Z. "African 'Soul Brothers' in the Hood: Immigration, Islam, and the Black Encounter." *Anthropological Quarterly* 82, no. 1 (2009): 37–62.

Dolnick, S. "For African Immigrants, Bronx Culture Clash Turns Violent." *The New York Times Online,* October 20, 2009. http://www.nytimes.com/2009/10/20/nyregion/20africans.html?_r=1.

Oyeyemi, A., and B. Sedenu. "Immigrants of Nigerian Descent in New York: Their Perception and Integration in the New Society." *Journal of Immigrant & Refugee Studies* 5, no. 3 (2007): 115–19.

Alternative Sentencing

Alternative sentencing is a sanction that redirects nonviolent offenders from prison to an alternative disposition, with the intent to rehabilitate as well as reduce prison overcrowding. These alternative sanctions take many forms, including drug and mental health treatment, creative sentencing, shaming punishments, electronic monitoring, and specialized courts (such as drug courts), to name a few. Many prisons are operating at or over capacity, leading lawmakers and activists to call for the use of alternative sentencing in an effort to relieve prison overcrowding (Hanrahan, 2007; Espejo, 2002). In addition to easing the prison overcrowding epidemic (Drucker, 2011), alternative sentencing is less expensive and focuses on the rehabilitation of the offender. According to the Bureau of Justice Statistics Web site, there are currently more than 2.2 million persons incarcerated; corrections costs have risen to over $68 billion annually, with the cost of housing one inmate at over $22,000 per year (see Bureau of Justice Statistics, 2010). In an effort to reduce the prison population and the associated costs, many states have turned to alternative sentencing.

Specialized courts are one category of alternative sentencing that focus on a particular nonviolent crime. The center of attention for such courts is offender outcomes rather than punishment. Drug courts are one such type of specialized court. They focus on drug treatment and address the problems in offenders' lives because of their addiction. Evaluations of these courts indicate that they appear to provide substantial benefits to the offender and to the larger society. Former addicts become sober and can therefore become working taxpayers. According to Everett (2000), "[P]risons do not offer drug offenders the tools to fight their addictions." The idea behind drug courts is that if the offender receives treatment, not only will drug-related crimes decrease, but the offender also gains the ability to become a contributing member of society, reducing the need to build more prisons. According to Maguire and Okada (2011), the results of multiple studies show a linkage between drug use and crime. By shifting users from criminal courts to drug courts—through which they are subject to intensive judicial supervision; mandatory drug treatment; mandatory drug testing; and rehabilitation programs that provide vocational, educational, family, and medical services—criminal behavior and recidivism can effectively be reduced. If the offender fails to complete the program, he or she is subject to the original sanctions to which he or she would have been sentenced in traditional criminal court.

The financial benefits to drug court processing as opposed to traditional criminal court processing are substantial, with the cost of drug treatment at a mere $5,000 a year per case, as compared to the $22,000 that it takes to house an inmate (Everett, 2000). Also, because stiffer sentences are applied to "poor man" drugs, such as crack cocaine versus powder cocaine, minorities and those of a low socio-economic status are grossly overrepresented within the prison system. The expectation is that drug courts will help ease this trend by altering the punishment for drug-related offenses.

Another alternative sanction is creative sentencing, in which extensive discretion is given to the presiding judge. It can entail community service, which not only gives the punishment meaning, but also benefits society and works toward diverting minor offenders from prison; for example, an adolescent who was convicted of vandalism was sentenced to guard and clean the wall he vandalized (Mulholland, 1994). A more controversial type of creative sentencing is what is known as a shaming punishment, a penalty enforced with the intention of "shaming" or "embarrassing" the wrongdoer—for example, a shoplifter having to wear a shirt stating her crime or a DWI offender having to place a placard on his car advising that he was convicted of driving while intoxicated. This method encounters opposition because total discretion is left to the judge. Many also view these punishments as demeaning and ineffective, perhaps particularly so for persons who already suffer from demeaning and oppressive circumstances related to their race, ethnicity, or economic status.

Electronic monitoring has been proposed as an effective alternate form of punishment because it allows the offender to remain within society, although subject to restrictions. Otero (2009) states that "the failure of imprisonment has not been its severity but its inefficiency regarding social rehabilitation." Inmates do not receive important social supports within the prison system and may, in fact, learn some behaviors that increase the risk of recidivism (Valentine et al., 2006). With electronic monitoring, the offender is placed under supervision to ensure public safety, but also has the ability to attend counseling and assistance programs centered on his or her rehabilitation. This promotes accountability of the offender to his or her victim, the community, and him- or herself, which increases the likelihood that the offender will become a successful participant within society rather than merely a good inmate (Valentine et al., 2006).

Societal concerns and concerns regarding victims' need for retribution accompany alternative sentencing. Although these alternatives are geared toward nonviolent offenses, the community may still feel at risk and victims may feel as though the punishment is too lenient. To help allay these concerns, alternative sanctions are developed to be responsive to the needs of the wrongdoer while maintaining public safety and ensuring that the sentence suits the crime (Valentine, Albers, & Huebner, 2006). Consequently, states have enacted sentencing laws that require financial restitution to victims as part of alternative sentencing. Some research (Cherry, 2001) indicates that financial penalties have a deterrent effect on potential offenders as well as the effect of reducing recidivism among former offenders.

Although surrounded in controversy, alternative sentencing is continuing to gain support. In June 2010, Lia Gormsen wrote that the U.S. Sentencing Commission sent Congress several amendments to the federal sentencing guidelines that included increasing the availability of alternatives to prison. These amendments would allow more offenders to be eligible for alternative sanctions based on mitigating circumstances, such as age; physical, mental, and emotional condition; and military service (Gormsen, 2010). Proponents argue that offenders deserve a second chance to become law-abiding contributors to society instead of being locked away and denied the opportunity for rehabilitation. Those in opposition feel as though the criminal made the cognitive choice to break the law, and therefore must pay the consequences.

The ultimate goal of alternative sentencing is to offer solutions to offenders with the hopes of rehabilitation and a reduction in recidivism by providing vocational skills, education, drug treatment, and medical services. Reduction of prison costs, prison overcrowding, crime, and drug-related offenses are the potential benefits. Since statistically the increasing rate of imprisonment has fallen most heavily on young African American males (Valentine et al., 2006), alternative sanctions can benefit this group most. However, some research has found that African Americans are substantially less likely than their White counterparts to receive alternative sanctions such as community service and restitution orders (Gilbert, 2000) and, due to lack of insurance coverage, are also substantially less likely to be sentenced to drug or mental health treatment as alternatives to their incarceration.

To be eligible for alternative sentences, offenders must often exhibit social characteristics that urban minority poor populations tend to lack. These include stable employment histories, promises of employment, telephone service, reputable or noncriminal references, and a single long-term residential address. The lack of these characteristics is often associated with the reasons why these individuals became involved in crime or were processed through the criminal justice system in the first place. Hence, those who need alternative sentencing most may be the least likely to receive it.

Shannon O'Brien

See also: Correctional System and African Americans; Federal Sentencing Disparity; Prisons; Sentencing Disparities

References

Bureau of Justice Statistics. "Federal Justice Statistics, 2010: Statistical Tables." Washington, DC: Office of Justice Programs, 2010. http://bjs.ojp.usdoj.gov/.

Cherry, T. L. "Financial Penalties as an Alternative Criminal Sanction: Evidence from Panel Data." *Atlantic Economic Journal* 29, no. 4 (2001): 450–58.

Drucker, E. *A Plague of Prisons: The Epidemiology of Mass Incarceration in America.* New York: The New Press, 2011.

Espejo, R., ed. *America's Prisons: Opposing Viewpoints.* San Diego: Greenhaven Press, 2002.

Everett, C. "Treatment, Not Prison, Best Solution for Drug Offenders." *Daily Bruin,* October 19, 2000.

Gilbert, E. "The Significance of Race in the Use of Restitution." In *The System in Black and White: Exploring the Connections between Race, Crime and Punishment,* edited by M. Markowitz and D. Jones, 199–212. Westport, CT: Praeger, 2000.

Gormsen, L. "Sentencing Commission Approves Guidelines on Prison Alternatives." *Corrections Today* (July 2010).

Hanrahan, C. *America's Prisons: Opposing Viewpoints.* San Diego: Greenhaven Press, 2007.

Maguire, M., and D. Okada. *Critical Issues in Crime and Justice: Thought, Policy and Practice.* Los Angeles: Sage, 2011.

Mulholland, D. "Judges Finding Creative Ways of Punishing." *The Wall Street Journal,* May 24, 1994.

Otero, P. "Electronic Monitoring, an Alternative Way of Preventing Aggression and Helping Social Rehabilitation." *Journal of Organisational Transformation and Social Change* 6, no. 2 (2009): 133–52.

Valentine, D. C., N. A. Albers, and B. Huebner. "Alternative Sentencing & Strategies for Successful Prisoner Reentry." *Institute of Public Policy* (2006): 1–13.

American Law and African Americans

In contemporary America, by most accounts, in the minds of many, Blacks are viewed as likely lawbreakers. In policing practices such as stop-and-frisk, Blacks are frequently seen as criminal suspects. In juvenile court proceedings, Black youth who are accused of crimes are often held in detention and transferred to adult court. In adult court, Blacks are disproportionately convicted, sentenced to prison, and given death sentences. And in corrections, Blacks disproportionately serve long sentences in maximum-security prisons (Alexander, 2010; Muhammad, 2010; Eberhardt, 2004; Robinson, 2000; Jones-Brown, 2000a; Russell, 1998).

This is true despite the fact that each year, nationally, 70 percent of arrests reported by the FBI involve persons who are categorized as White. Blacks do not commit the most crime in the United States, as commonly thought, not even in violent crime categories—but Black individuals are disproportionately arrested for crimes at a higher rate than Whites (see Disproportionality and Crime).

Explanations for Black overrepresentation in crime statistics often focus on differential group or individual offending. Until recently, rarely have explanations seriously examined the role of lawmaking in producing Black crime and criminal justice processing (Browne-Marshall, 2007; Robinson, 2000; Jones-Brown, 2000b). Legal socialization theory, introduced by social psychologists in the late 1970s, suggests that Black overrepresentation among lawbreakers may be due in part to a legitimate disconnection from the law itself (Cohn & White, 1990). The theory takes into account that criminal justice and injustice begins with lawmaking (Robinson, 2000), and that racialized lawmaking in the United States has spanned more than four centuries, first in overt and then more subtle forms (Alexander, 2010; Mann, 1993; McIntyre, 1993).

Early criminal and civil law specifically restricted Black life in five major areas: freedom of movement; substantive rights such as marriage, homeownership, and employment; voting rights; education; and criminal procedure. Under legal socialization theory, the fact that such restrictions did not exist for Whites, and that they existed alongside a national legal philosophy emphasizing freedom, equality, and protection from government abuse, may partially account for racial differentials in allegiance to formal law and formal legal mechanisms—such as police and courts (Tyler, 1990). In this case, informal behavioral controls such as bonds to family, peers, and religious institutions and the presence or absence of internalized guilt become more predictive of African American behavior than laws, law enforcement, or threats of government punishment.

Under legal socialization theory, the historical and contemporary use of formal law and enforcement mechanisms in racialized ways work to diminish the law's ability to consistently compel legal compliance and produces structural barriers such as limited employment opportunities, educational access, access to home-ownership, wage-earning capacity, civic participation, and access to conventional recreation. These limitations contribute to adaptive behaviors that are defined as deviant and that come to be seen as attributes of Black "culture," rather than manifestations of the impact and construction of law (Muhammad, 2010; Jones-Brown, 2000b; Sampson & Wilson, 1995; Tyler, 1990; Rawls, 1971).

Slave Codes, Black Codes, and Jim Crow Laws

In their Pulitzer Prize–winning history of New York (1999), historians Edwin Burrows and Mike Wallace document the intent to treat Blacks differently under criminal and civil law dating back to the 1600s. They note that Black slaves were prohibited from "bearing arms"—a right later embodied in the Second Amendment—and from being employed in the skilled trades, to avoid conflict with White laborers. They also include the wording from an ordinance that specifically prohibited "adulterous intercourse with heathens, blacks, or other persons" (35). In many states, Slave Codes, Black Codes, and Jim Crow laws made constitutional rights into crimes for Blacks. The creation of these laws, not differential rates of offending, began the formal connection between race and crime in the United States (Muhammad, 2010; Alexander, 2010; Robinson, 2000; Jones-Brown, 2000a, 2000b; Russell, 1998).

Historical Background

It is estimated that the first African slaves were brought to what would become the United States in 1619. While the nation would later become known for its Constitution designing a three-branch government incorporating checks and balances, and a set of amendments called the Bill of Rights designed to protect private citizens from abusive government power, the libertarian rights created by those enactments did not apply to people of Black racial identity. In fact, once African slaves were introduced to the colonies, free Blacks who had been residing in the various territories that would later become states lost many of the freedoms that others who had traveled to the "New World" continued to enjoy.

Chattel slavery, or the notion that one human could own another human much like a piece of furniture, became a staple of the "New World" economy and existed in both the North and the South. Prior to the introduction of the African slave, the need for labor had been filled in part by indentured servants who were European ethnics who agreed to work for a period without pay in exchange for their boat passage to the colonies. There were also attempts to enslave the Native Americans, which proved difficult as they were indigenous to the land and could effectively escape their captivity. In contrast, kidnapping Africans from their homeland proved to be an effective means of ensuring the availability of laborers for the largely agricultural economy that was developing at the time. Slave masters not only owned the slaves that they purchased, they also owned all of the slaves' offspring. The children of slaves could be sold for profit or retained as additional free labor. Slaves could be inherited like other assets, which meant their period of service was for their entire lives. At the beginning, this legalized human bondage system succeeded in part because the Africans were highly visible. Their dark skin and distinct language, and the fact that they were thousands of miles from their homeland, made them convenient targets to be contained and controlled through fear and intimidation (see Slavery) (Browne-Marshall, 2007; Jones-Brown, 2000a, 2000b).

Adamson (1983) notes that "[t]he existence of slavery made two separate systems of punishment necessary. Through plantation justice, masters sought to impose an absolute system of authority on their bondsmen. Like monarchial law, the Slave Codes prescribed barbaric and public punishment." Slave Codes were a set of laws enacted by several of the Southern colonies in the late 1600s, designed specifically for the discipline and control of the slaves. Under the codes, slaves could be whipped, hanged, branded, or castrated as forms of punishment. For example, to discourage slave insurrection, a South Carolina statute called for slaves to be burned alive if they murdered their masters. In Louisiana, rebellious slaves were beheaded and their heads put upon posts as a warning to others. It was not uncommon for slaves to be boiled alive or whipped to death. Masters who killed their slaves were not subject to legal punishment (Jones-Brown, 2000a).

Beyond prescribing barbaric punishments, the Slave Codes also prohibited slaves from having any legal rights or protections (Mann, 1993; Owens & Bell, 1977), including the right of self-defense (Browne-Marshall, 2007). The codes prevented slaves from carrying weapons, owning property, becoming educated, and from being off the plantation without permission. Slaves who were permitted to travel off the plantation were required to carry a pass or document verifying that they had permission to move about. Any White person could stop a Black person to determine if he or she had permission to be off the plantation. As it became more difficult to distinguish between free Blacks and slaves, Black Codes were enacted. Such codes became even more prevalent following the end of the Civil War. Black Codes limited the rights of African Americans to own or rent property. They restricted free Blacks from working as store clerks or in jobs other than those requiring manual labor. They allowed Blacks to be imprisoned for breach of employment contracts. This restriction would become particularly important following the end of the Civil War, when many Blacks would become sharecroppers. The Black Codes denied African Americans the right to bring charges or testify against Whites, to assemble in numbers greater than two, to visit in each other's homes without a White person present, and to be on public streets after dark. As late as 1835, a free Black could be whipped for teaching a slave to read or write, while a White person was subject to fine or imprisonment (Browne-Marshall, 2007; Jones-Brown, 2000a, 2000b, 2007; Mann, 1993; Owens & Bell, 1977).

By 1691, statutes in both Virginia and North Carolina made it unlawful for free Blacks to live there. In Connecticut, from 1774 to 1797, all Blacks had to have a written pass to travel outside of their hometown. Violators of the statute were subject to a fine. Restrictions on the movement of free Blacks existed in other states as well. The state of Maryland imposed a $50 fine against free Blacks who entered the state and assessed an additional $50 per week against any who remained. Free Blacks who were unable to pay their fines were arrested and enslaved. As late as 1804, in part because it was a popular destination for Blacks escaping slavery on the "underground railroad," the state of Ohio prohibited Blacks from becoming permanent residents unless they could furnish a "certificate of freedom" issued by a U.S. court (McIntyre, 1993).

To dispense with the difficulty of distinguishing between free Blacks and slaves, the legal presumption within the courts became that Black skin meant slave status unless the individual could prove otherwise. Such proof was hard to come by since Blacks could not testify in court or serve on juries. One exception to the rule about giving testimony was that Blacks would be allowed to inform on other Blacks who were guilty of violating the Slave Codes or Black Codes. In response to the legal assumption that Black skin meant slave status, over time the courts began to be flooded with "freedom suits"—cases brought by African Americans seeking to prove that they were free so that they could avoid or terminate contact with slave patrollers; move about without restriction; own property, if allowed; and enjoy the limited freedom that existed within the minor differences between the Slave Codes and Black Codes. For some, that freedom included having the right to leave the country, since liberty for Blacks had become so restricted. In *Criminalizing a Race: Free Blacks during Slavery,* Charsee McIntyre notes that many Blacks who had come to the country as free immigrants, like their European counterparts, fled to what is now Nova Scotia to avoid harsh treatment and to regain the freedoms they had enjoyed before African slavery was introduced to the American colonies. In other words, the Black experience in the colonies did not begin with enslavement.

African slavery existed as a legal practice in what would become the United States for nearly two and a half centuries, from 1619 to 1865, at the conclusion of the Civil War. In contemporary times, it is hard to imagine that in the United States people legally owned other people for nearly 250 years. This was true despite the fact that the founders of the nation recognized and demanded their own right to freedom as early as 1776. In the midst of the Revolutionary War, the founders wrote in the Declaration of Independence that "all men are created equal, that they are endowed by their Creator with certain unalienable Rights, that among these are Life, Liberty, and the Pursuit of Happiness." This declaration did nothing to improve the status of Blacks in relation to legal rights. Colonies continued to enact statutes aimed at protecting the rights of slave owners, including authorizing private citizens to be paid for capturing runaway slaves. These "slave patrols," as the groups were called, have been identified as the first form of organized policing in the United States (Williams & Murphy, 1990).

South Carolina and Georgia were among the first colonies to enact statutes creating such patrols. Other states soon followed, and in 1793, even the federal government issued a "fugitive slave" law that validated the actions of the slave patrols and made it a crime for private citizens to fail to turn over runaway slaves, to harbor them, or to otherwise assist in their escape. The federal statute provided for a fine and potential imprisonment for anyone found in violation of the law. Under this federal mandate and the statutes of the various colonies (which later became states), runaway slaves became one of the first group of black criminals. Slaves who sought the same freedom that the nation's founders fought for, and anyone who attempted to help them obtain that freedom were subject to punishment under local, state, and federal laws (Jones-Brown, 2000a; McIntyre, 1993). (See the Slavery entry for racial restrictions included in provisions of the federal constitution.)

The runaway slaves stood in sharp contrast to the slaves and free men who periodically led violent insurrections against slave owners. John Brown, a free White man, and Nat Turner, a slave, are perhaps the most well known among this group. They both led slave revolts that resulted in the deaths of Whites in the state of Virginia. These violent attacks caused legislative bodies to enact more stringent laws restricting the rights of Blacks, both free and enslaved (McIntyre, 1993; Jones-Brown, 2000a).

In 1791, when the states ratified the Bill of Rights, essentially none of the enumerated rights applied to slaves or free Blacks. In fact, to preserve the racial hierarchy enforced since 1619, a new legal rule was adopted regarding racial identity. The "one drop rule," as it came to be known, became the defining principle for access to legal rights and privileges. Under this rule, one drop of African blood made a person Black under the law, subjecting that individual to all of the restrictions that any local, state, or federal law prescribed (Davis, 1991). Liberty and civil rights in the United States became so tied to skin color that both during slavery and after emancipation Blacks who, through some degree of White ancestry, were sufficiently fair-skinned would defy the "one drop rule" by "passing" for White. In this way, they could enjoy the same freedom of movement and social access as did Whites. In states such as Louisiana, the extent of legal rights and privileges bestowed upon Black residents was determined, in part, by the degree of Whiteness in their lineage. The term "mulatto" was used to describe people of mixed-race ancestry with one Black parent and one White parent. In some places, the parsing of racial identity was more in depth, with terms like "octoroon," "quintroon," and "quadroon" used to describe Blacks who were one-eighth, one-fifth, or one-fourth Black, respectively. Many of the freedom suits mentioned previously involved plaintiffs who demanded that the courts make these determinations, long before DNA testing existed.

The Supreme Court and Racialized Laws

The U.S. Supreme Court has a mixed record of upholding and overturning racialized laws and legal practices. In the 1857 decision in *Dred Scott v. Sandford,* with only two justices dissenting, the Court upheld the right of Americans to own slaves. The Civil War began four years later. In the majority opinion, Chief Justice Roger B. Taney wrote that Blacks are "a subordinate and inferior class of beings" never intended to be included in the meaning of the phrase, "We the People of the United States" and that no one of "the negro race" was entitled to "the rights and privileges conferred by the Constitution upon citizens." To support its conclusions, the Court examined statutes in states that had abolished slavery. Many maintained statutes that restricted the lives of free Blacks—prohibiting them from military service, interracial marriage, and unrestricted use of public streets. Most of these states were in the North. A footnote in the case reveals that New Jersey had once given and then taken away free Black men's right to vote.

In 1896, the U.S. Supreme Court was again afforded the opportunity to equalize criminal laws. In the case of *Plessy v. Ferguson,* the Court was asked to strike down an 1890 Louisiana statute that prohibited Blacks and Whites from sitting in the same railcars on trains. Instead, the Court affirmed the validity of the statute with only one justice dissenting. In the majority opinion, Justice Henry B. Brown wrote:

> A statute which implies merely a legal distinction between the white and colored races—a distinction which is founded in the color of the two races and which must always exist so long as white men are distinguished from the other race by color—has no tendency to destroy the legal equality of the two races. . . .

In contrast, in the dissenting opinion, Justice John Harlan wrote:

> Our Constitution is color-blind, and neither knows nor tolerates classes among citizens. In respect of civil rights, all citizens are equal before the law. . . . [T]he judgment this day . . . in time will prove to be quite as pernicious as the decision . . . in the *Dred Scott* case . . . [and] will not only stimulate aggressions, . . . upon the admitted rights of colored citizens, but will encourage the belief that it is possible, by means of state enactments, to co-opt [constitutional amendments].

The Supreme Court's decision in *Plessy v. Ferguson* allowed the conviction of Homer Plessy to stand. Though by ancestry he was seven-eighths White, Plessy was required to pay a fine for being Black and sitting in a railcar reserved for Whites. The impact of the decision was to uphold the legality of "Jim Crow" laws that continued to punish Blacks for "crimes" that were constitutionally protected acts for Whites. These laws became popular along with Black Codes between 1865 and 1866, when the Civil War Amendments (the Thirteenth, Fourteenth, and Fifteenth) were passed in an attempt to grant Blacks the constitutional protections denied by many local, state, and federal laws. Laws that allowed so-called "separate but equal" public facilities for Blacks and Whites were called "Jim Crow" laws after a character in an old minstrel show. The character was portrayed as Black but was played by a White actor in black face paint.

The impact of the *Plessy* decision was immediate. Not only did it affect private citizens, but it also affected the hiring practices in criminal justice agencies. Black police officers, who in some agencies already had their authority restricted to arresting only Blacks, were fired or refused employment. The New Orleans police department went from 177 Black officers to none and did not hire another one for 40 years (Williams & Murphy, 1990). It was now lawful for jurisdictions to post signs refusing admittance to Blacks in facilities like hotels, requiring them to use back entrances and to use separate bathrooms, waiting rooms, schools, hospitals, and drinking fountains. Public transportation designated separate seating sections for Blacks and Whites. Anyone violating these racial restrictions was subject to arrest. The impact of Jim Crow laws was felt well into the 1970s, although multiple civil rights acts and Supreme Court rulings were intended to reverse their legality. It would take a civil rights movement involving both peaceful protests and violent resistance, both of which were in violation of the formal law, to bring about meaningful legal change. Some observers chose to interpret the movement as confirmation of Black lawlessness (Muhammad, 2010) (see Civil Rights Movement).

One of the particularly personal racialized legal restrictions that carried criminal penalties upon arrest and conviction was the ban on inter-racial marriage. In the 1967 case of *Loving v. Virginia,* the U.S. Supreme Court was willing to overturn the conviction and prison sentences imposed against Mildred Jeter and Richard Loving and to declare all statutes prohibiting inter-racial marriage unconstitutional.

The Court's 1954 ruling in *Brown v. the Board of Education of Topeka, Kansas,* is popularly recognized as the case that made racial segregation in public schools illegal. The history of laws that prohibited education for Blacks are less known. Various Southern states criminalized education for Blacks. As late as 1835, a South Carolina statute made it a crime to teach free Blacks or slaves to read or write and designated different punishments for anyone caught doing so. Whites who violated the law were subject to a fine of up to $100 and imprisonment for up to six months. Free Blacks could receive up to 50 lashes with a whip and a $50 fine. Slaves caught teaching other slaves could receive up to 50 lashes (Jones-Brown, 2000a).

Some Northern laws also prohibited education for Blacks. Though Massachusetts abolished slavery as early as 1781, Blacks were excluded from public school education. A petition filed by a Black parent in 1787 eventually led to the admission of Black students to Boston's public school system, but Black children were treated so badly by their White classmates that Black parents complained. In response, the city of Boston enacted legislation requiring racially separate schools. Blacks could then only attend the schools designated for Blacks. The Massachusetts legislature did not repeal racialized public school admissions requirements until 1855 (Browne-Marshall, 2007). Litigation over busing to achieve integrated schools in Boston and elsewhere and affirmative action admission policies in education have persisted into the twentieth and twenty-first centuries (*Palmer v. Thompson* [1971] and *Swann v.*

Charlotte-Mecklenberg Board of Education [1970]; *Grutter v. Bollinger* and *Gratz v. Bollinger* [2003]; *Meredith v. Jefferson* [2007]; *Fisher v. University of Texas* [2013]).

The voting rights of Blacks and other racial and ethnic minorities also continue to be a source of legal controversy connected to criminal and civil sanctions. Michelle Alexander begins the introduction to her book *The New Jim Crow: Mass Incarceration in the Age of Colorblindness* with the following paragraph:

> Jarvious Cotton cannot vote. Like his father, grandfather, great-grandfather, and great-great-grandfather, he has been denied the right to participate in our electoral democracy. Cotton's family tree tells the story of several generations of black men who were born in the United States but who were denied the most basic freedom that democracy promises—the freedom to vote for those who will make the rules and laws that govern one's life. Cotton's great-great-grandfather could not vote as a slave. His great-grandfather was beaten to death by the Ku Klux Klan for attempting to vote. His father was barred from voting by poll taxes and literacy tests. Today, Jarvious Cotton cannot vote because he, like many black men in the United States, has been labeled a felon and is currently on parole.

Felon disenfranchisement—the prohibition of convicted felons from voting— affects hundreds of thousands of Blacks in the United States, mostly men.

In the 1876 decision in *United States v. Reese,* the U.S. Supreme Court ruled that the Fifteenth Amendment does not confer the right to vote upon anyone, though it prevents the states from giving preference to one citizen over another based on race, color, or previous condition of servitude. The Court also determined that the right to vote is derived from the states, though the right to vote free from racial discrimination is protected by federal law. The effect of the ruling in *Reese* was to affirm that the states have their own power to enact legislation designating who is qualified to vote and under what circumstances. The *Reese* ruling has essentially been reaffirmed by the Court's 2013 ruling in *Shelby County v. Holder,* striking down the constitutionality of Section IV of the Voting Rights Act, which had provided federal oversight of state voting procedures.

The notion that convicted felons should endure "civil death" for offending against the laws of society, including loss of voting rights; the right to hold public office; the right to act as a witness or juror in court; and the right to own, inherit, or convey property has its origins outside the United States. In recognition of the disproportionate impact of criminal court convictions on Blacks and under procedures that research suggests are not always fair, contemporary activists and policy organizations such as the Sentencing Project in Washington, D.C., have advocated the abolition of voting prohibitions based on conviction status. They see this abolition as a viable means of giving Blacks more say in the political process. The movement to abolish felon disenfranchisement must not only overcome mainstream resistance to voting rights for felons but both historical and contemporary beliefs that Blacks are incapable of grasping political issues or appropriately exercising the power of the vote (Browne-Marshall, 2007).

Finally, laws surrounding criminal procedure have taken up as much or more legislative and judicial ink as laws seeking to define the substantive rights of Blacks. For decades, state and local statutes excluded Blacks from witness stands, the jury box, and employment within the criminal justice system. Lawmaking and judicial decisions related to criminal matters have both helped and hurt the case for equality under law for African Americans. In 1890, the U.S. Supreme Court found that laws restricting criminal jury participation to Whites only violate the Constitution (see Juries). The Court reaffirmed that ruling in 1986 by prohibiting prosecutors from exercising their discretion in ways that excluded all Blacks from jury panels. In 2008, in the case of *Snyder v. Louisiana,* a death penalty case, the Court again affirmed its holding that prosecutors' use of preemptory challenges to exclude all Black jurors is not constitutional. Historically, all-White juries were known to return verdicts that were inconsistent with the evidence when offenders and victims were of different races (see Scottsboro Cases and Till, Emmett).

Legislation and case law regarding the permissible boundaries of police activity, especially with regard to race, have proved to be a source of continuous and deep-seated debate. The legal limits on how law enforcement officials conduct investigations, collect evidence, use force, identify suspects, maintain evidence, and conduct surveillance have expanded and contracted over time. One source (Packer, 1968) has suggested that the legal leeway given to police can be gauged by mainstream society's concern with crime control or due process. "Mainstream society" is often defined as the racial majority, property owners, and others who have status and a confirmed stake in existing dominant social arrangements. In a capitalist society, this generally means those who have conventional access to things that are valued by the society. The conflict theory of crime suggests that lawmakers will construct the law so that access to these things is protected for those who have them. Conversely, this means that those who do not have them are perceived as a threat (Gabbidon & Greene, 2005) (see Inequality Theory and Theories of Race and Crime).

During the 1960s, the U.S. Supreme Court made many rulings involving the legality of police behavior. Many of the decisions involved incidents where African Americans were the offenders or suspects. In 1961, in the case of *Mapp v. Ohio* (see Mapp, Dollree), the Court ruled that illegally obtained evidence gathered by local police could not be introduced to convict a defendant at trial. It had previously made a similar ruling against federal law enforcement agents (*Weeks v. U.S.*). In 1964, the Court ruled that criminal suspects have a right to have a lawyer present during interrogation (*Escobedo v. Illinois*). In 1968, the Court ruled in favor of the police, allowing them to conduct brief stops or "field interrogations" of suspects based on reasonable suspicion of crime, rather than "probable cause," as specified in the Fourth Amendment. The ruling in *Terry v. Ohio* and the statutes and police policies that were enacted pursuant to that case have become one of the most contentious race and justice issues of the last three and a half decades.

In the 8 to 1 ruling, the majority of the Court authorized the use of an officer's "reasonable suspicions" as a legitimate basis for stopping a civilian on the street to inquire about his or her identity and actions in relation to a potential crime. The ruling required that the officer be able to provide a specific basis for suspecting the specific individual of criminality. It also authorized the officer to conduct a patdown of the person's outer clothing if there was evidence that he or she might be armed and dangerous. Justice William O. Douglas saw the ruling as legally problematic. In his dissenting opinion, he wrote:

> We hold today that the police have greater authority to make a seizure and conduct a search than a judge has to authorize such action . . . to give the police greater power than a magistrate is to take a long step down the totalitarian path. . . .

Noting that judges can only issue arrest and search warrants based on probable cause—evidence suggesting that criminal activity is more likely than not, or 51 percent certainty, Justice Douglas commented that the majority's opinion would diminish citizens' personal security, which would go against the distinct purpose of the Fourth Amendment. He wrote, "[I]f the police can pick him up whenever they do not like the cut of his jib, if they can seize and search him in their discretion, we have entered a new regime." He urged that if this police tactic was "desirable to cope with modern forms of lawlessness . . . ," a formal constitutional amendment was required.

Currently, most police departments conduct *Terry*-stops. In some departments, statistics regarding these stops are collected and analyzed. Two patterns have emerged. In most cases, *Terry*-stops do not lead to the detection of crime, and in most cases Blacks or other racial/ethnic minorities are stopped at a disproportionately higher rate than Whites. Research has found that the racial disproportionality in stops cannot be adequately explained by nonracial factors such as rates of crime or the racial composition of residents in the location where stops occur. Blacks are stopped more frequently than Whites in both high-crime and low-crime locations and in locations where they make up the minority or majority of the population (Gelman et al., 2007). These facts have led to numerous lawsuits and feelings of distrust between police agencies and the public.

Some officials have publicly stated that by focusing on stopping Blacks and Latinos, they can effectively control crime by deterring potential offenders from carrying guns or engaging in acts of violence (*Nightline,* 2013). This justification is tied to statistical percentages that show Black and Latino overrepresentation as suspects, perpetrators, or arrestees. But nothing in the *Terry* decision authorizes a broad-based approach to the use of a technique that was justified on the basis of its potential to apprehend suspects (Terry and his two companions) or to thwart a specific suspected crime (armed robbery). Though the *Terry* ruling was expanded in subsequent cases, the requirement for individual suspicion to justify a stop and evidence of potential danger from the suspect to justify a frisk remain intact. Because the aggressive use of *Terry*-stops coincides with the substantial crime decline in New York City, several urban cities have considered or attempted a similar policing approach: Philadelphia, Chicago, Baltimore, San Francisco, Oakland, and Los Angeles among them. But most research that has attempted to establish a causal connection between stop-and-frisk and crime decline has failed to do so or been inconclusive (Zimring, 2011; Rosenfeld & Fornango, 2014).

Courts have found that the use of *Terry*-stops can result in illegal racial profiling (*Ligon v. the City of New York, Floyd v. the City of New York, State v. Pedro Soto*). When faced with legal challenges, the Philadelphia and Baltimore police departments agreed to abandon the aggressive use of stop-and-frisk as primary policing strategies. After some consideration, Chicago and San Francisco declined to openly adopt aggressive stop-and-frisk as a uniform policing policy. Several U.S. Supreme Court decisions have been accused of leaving the law regarding the permissible use of race in police discretion unclear (*California v. Hodari, Illinois v. Wardlow, U.S. v. Broadie, Whren v. U.S.*). Such cases have failed to explicitly condemn the use of racial assumptions or racial proxies (terms such as "inner city," "high drug," or "high crime" area) as a basis for making police stops, thereby leaving the legal limits unclear for both the police and the public.

Modern Criminal Justice Policy and Law

While the inclusion of explicit race-based language in statutes is no longer legal, several current criminal justice policies and legislative mandates enacted to "promote public safety" or to impose "deserved punishment" bear a resemblance to the practices authorized by historical laws. Child welfare statutes allow children to be permanently separated from their parents, especially parents who become incarcerated (see Termination of Parental Rights). Police presence in schools has been shown to retard educational access and achievement, creating a school-to-prison-pipeline (NYCLU, 2007). Incarceration leads to brutal rape that often goes unpunished (Henriques & Jones-Brown, 2009). Police enforcement of curfews in certain neighborhoods is reminiscent of a time when Blacks were not permitted on public streets after sundown (Muhammad, 2010; Mann, 1993; McIntyre, 1993). Aggressive police sweeps for guns, drugs, or general evidence of "crime" in neighborhoods where the residents are predominantly Black, along with multiple stops and demands that residents produce identification; continuous questioning such as, "Where are you coming from?" or "Where are you going?"; and demands that youth "move along" or "clear the corner" are viewed through different racial lenses as either police harassment or "good policing." They resemble actions that were permitted under slave patrols and Jim Crow policing, typically, though not exclusively, carried out by White males (Rios, 2011; Rice & White, 2010; Crawford, 2010; Dunn & Reed, 2011; Birzer, 2013).

Then as now, Black homes were not shielded from intrusion. Laws allowed patrollers to go onto plantations and forcefully enter the cabins of Black slaves to search for weapons. Aggressive execution of search warrants today, sometimes at the wrong address, most often occur in minority neighborhoods. Statutes allow residents to be evicted from public housing for drug and other arrests, even if the offense is not committed by the leaseholder (see Public Housing). These legally sanctioned intrusions may contribute to a feeling among Blacks that they are not in control of their own destinies (Rios, 2011; Jones-Brown 2000a, 2000c).

Research reveals that many of these law-related factors may contribute to the risk of criminal behavior even though they are designed to prevent or reduce it (Wiley & Esbensen, 2013; Jones-Brown, 2000c). Undereducation, underemployment, feelings of hopelessness and helplessness, family disruption, feelings of strain and oppression, and lack of personal control are all factors that have been found to contribute to crime and aggressive behavior in the absence of counterbalancing forces (see Theories of Race and Crime). A major premise of legal socialization theory is that the law and its agents lose their legitimacy when they are the actual or perceived source of these negative feelings and conditions. Blacks who live in or visit neighborhood settings where police presence is either very high or blatantly absent run a heightened risk of criminal justice system contact, including wrongful conviction, whether they are criminals or not (see Innocence Project, Wrongful Convictions, Racial Stereotyping and Wrongful Convictions, False Confessions, and Eyewitness Misidentification).

Delores Jones-Brown

See also: Civil Rights Movement; Disproportionality and Crime; Eyewitness Misidentification; False Confessions; Inequality Theory; Innocence Project; Juries; Mapp, Dollree; Public Housing; Racial Stereotyping and Wrongful Convictions; Scottsboro Cases; Slavery; Termination of Parental Rights; Theories of Race and Crime; Till, Emmett; War on Drugs; Wrongful Convictions

References

Adamson, C. R. "Punishment after Slavery: Southern State Penal Systems, 1865–1890." *Social Problems* 30, no. 5 (1983): 555–69.

Alexander, M. *The New Jim Crow: Mass Incarceration in the Age of Colorblindness.* New York: The New Press, 2010.

Birzer, M. *Racial Profiling: They Stopped Me Because I'm _____!* New York: CRC Press, 2013.

Brown v. the Board of Education of Topeka, Kansas, 347 U. S. 483 (1954).

Browne-Marshall, G. *Race, Law, and American Society: 1607 to Present.* New York: Routledge, 2007.

Burrows, E., and M. Wallace. *Gotham: A History of New York City to 1898.* New York: Oxford University Press, 1999.

California v. Hodari, 499 U. S. 621 (1991).

Cohn, E., and S. White. *Legal Socialization: A Study of Norms and Rules.* New York: Springer, 1990.

Crawford, C. *Spatial Policing: The Influence of Time, Space, and Geography on Law Enforcement Practices.* Durham, NC: Carolina Academic Press, 2010.

Davis, F. *Who Is Black: One Nation's Definition.* State College, PA: Pennsylvania State University Press, 1991.

Dred Scott v. Sandford, 60 U.S. 393 (1856).

Dunn, R., and W. Reed. *Racial Profiling: Causes and Consequences.* Dubuque, IA: Kendall Hunt, 2011.

Eberhardt, J., V. Purdie, P. Goff, and P. Davies. "Seeing Black: Race, Crime and Visual Processing." *Journal of Personality and Social Psychology* 83 (2004): 1314–29.

Escobedo v. Illinois, 378 U.S. 478 (1964).

Fisher v. University of Texas, 570 U. S. _____ (2013).

Floyd v. the City of New York, 08 Civ. 01034 (SDNY)(2013).

Gabbidon, S., and H. T. Greene. *Race and Crime.* Thousand Oaks, CA: Sage, 2005.

Gelman, A., J. Fagan, and A. Kiss. "An Analysis of the New York City Police Department's 'Stop-and-Frisk' Policy in the Context of Claims of Racial Bias." *Journal of the American Statistical Association* 102, no. 479 (2007): 813–23.

Gratz v. Bollinger, 539 U.S. 244 (2003).

Grutter v. Bollinger, 539 U. S. 306 (2003).

Henriques, Z., and D. Jones-Brown. "A Violation of Trust and Professional Ethics: Sexual Abuse of Women Prisoners by Correctional Staff." In *Sexual Assault: The Victims, the Perpetrators, and the Criminal Justice System,* 2nd ed., edited by F. P. Reddington and B. W. Kriesel, 171–78. Durham, NC: Carolina Academic Press, 2009.

Illinois v. Wardlow, 528 U.S. 119 (2000).

Jones-Brown, D. 2000a. *Race, Crime and Punishment.* Philadelphia: Chelsea House Publishers, 2000.

Jones-Brown, D. 2000b. "Race as a Legal Construct: The Implications for American Justice." In *The System in Black and White: Exploring the Connections between Race,*

Crime and Justice, edited by M. Markowitz and D. Jones-Brown, 137–52. Westport, CT: Praeger, 2000.

Jones-Brown, D. 2000c. "Debunking the Myth of Officer Friendly: How African American Males Experience Community Policing." *Journal of Contemporary Criminal Justice* 16, no. 2 (2000): 209–29.

Jones-Brown, D. "Forever the Symbolic Assailant: The More Things Change, the More They Remain the Same. Reaction Essay to "'Police Don't Like Black People": African-American Young Men's Accumulated Police Experiences' by Rod K. Brunson." *Criminology and Public Policy* 6, no. 1 (2007): 103–22.

Jones-Brown, D., and E. King-Toler. "The Significance of Race in Contemporary Urban Policing Policy." In *U.S. Criminal Justice Policy: A Contemporary Reader,* edited by K. Ismaili, 21–48. Sudbury, MA: Jones and Bartlett, 2011.

Jones-Brown, D., and B. Maule. "Racially Biased Policing: A Review of the Judicial and Legislative Literature." In *Race, Ethnicity and Policing: New and Essential Readings,* edited by S. Rice and M. White, 140–73. New York: New York University Press, 2010.

Ligon v. the City of New York, 12 Civ. 2274 (SAS)(HBP)(2013).

Mann, C. *Unequal Justice: A Question of Color.* Bloomington: Indiana University Press, 1993.

Mapp v. Ohio, 367 U. S. 643 (1961).

McIntyre, C. *Criminalizing a Race: Free Blacks during Slavery.* Queens, NY: Kayode, 1993.

Meredith v. Jefferson, 551 U. S. _____ (2007).

Muhammad, K. G. *The Condemnation of Blackness: Race, Crime, and the Making of Modern Urban America.* Cambridge, MA: Harvard University Press, 2010.

New York Civil Liberties Union (NYCLU). *Criminalizing the Classroom: The Over-Policing of New York City Schools.* New York: NYCLU, 2007.

Nightline. "NYPD's Stop-and-Frisk: Racial Profiling or 'Proactive Policing'?" ABCNews, New York, May 1, 2013. http://abcnews.go.com/Nightline/video/nypds-stop-frisk-racial-profiling-proactive-policing-19088868.

Owens, C. E., and J. Bell. *Blacks and Criminal Justice.* Lexington, MA: D.C. Heath, 1977.

Packer, H. *The Limits of the Criminal Sanction.* Palo Alto, CA: Stanford University Press, 1968.

Palmer v. Thompson, 403 U.S. 217 (1971).

Plessy v. Ferguson, 163 U. S. 537 (1896).

Rawls, J. *A Theory of Justice.* Cambridge, MA: Harvard University Press, 1971.

Rice, S., and M. White. *Race, Ethnicity, and Policing: New and Essential Readings.* New York: New York University Press, 2010.

Rios, V. *Punished: Policing the Lives of Black and Latino Boys.* New York: New York University Press, 2011.

Robinson, M. "The Construction and Reinforcement of Myths of Race and Crime." *Journal of Contemporary Criminal Justice* 16 (2000): 133–56.

Rosenfeld, R., and R. Fornango. "The Impact of Police Stops on Precinct Robbery and Burglary Rates in New York City, 2003–2010." *Justice Quarterly* 31, no. 1 (2014). doi: 10.1080/07418825.2012.712152.

Russell, K. K. *The Color of Crime: Racial Hoaxes, White Fear, Black Protectionism, Police Harassment, and Other Macroaggressions.* New York: New York University Press, 1998.

Sampson, R., and W. J. Wilson. "Toward a Theory of Race, Crime and Urban Inequality." In *Crime and Inequality,* edited by J. Hagan and R. Peterson, 37–54. Palo Alto, CA: Stanford University Press, 1995.

Shelby County v. Holder, 570 U. S. _____ (2013).

Snyder v. Louisiana, 552 U.S. 472 (2008).

State v. Pedro Soto, 732 a. 2D 350 (1996).

Swann v. Charlotte-Mecklenberg Board of Education, 402 U. S. 1 (1970).

Terry v. Ohio, 392 U.S. 1 (1968).

Tyler, T. *Why People Obey the Law.* New Haven, CT: Yale University Press, 1990.

United States v. Reese, 92 U. S. 214 (1876).

U.S. v. Broadie, 452 F.3d 875 (2006).

Weeks v. U.S., 232 U.S. 383 (1914).

Whren v. U.S., 517 U.S. 806 (1996).

Wiley, S., and F. Esbensen. "The Effect of Police Contact: Does Official Intervention Result in Deviance Amplification?" *Crime and Delinquency* 59, no. 7 (2013): 1–25.

Williams, H., and P. Murphy. *The Evolving Strategy of the Police: A Minority View.* Washington, DC: National Institute of Justice, 1990.

Zimring, F. *The City That Became Safe: New York's Lessons for Urban Crime and Its Control.* New York: Oxford University Press, 2011.

B

Barry, Jr., Marion S. (1936–)

Born on March 6, 1936, in Itta Bena, a small town in Leflore County, Mississippi, Marion S. Barry, Jr., was the third of 10 children. His early years were marked by personal tragedy, including the passing of his father, a handyman, when Barry was four. Shortly thereafter, his mother married a butcher and relocated the family to Memphis, Tennessee. Barry possessed a profound commitment to hard work, and his employment history includes jobs as a waiter, grocery store clerk, newspaper deliveryman, and textile worker. His perseverance allowed him to attain the rank of Eagle Scout, and afforded him entry into the highly respected LeMoyne-Owen College in Memphis.

During his undergraduate years from 1954 to1958, Barry was outspoken, with a penchant for addressing what he perceived as social injustice. For example, he rebuked a member of his college's board of trustees for what he considered racially insensitive comments, nearly resulting in his expulsion. Much of his desire to address social inequity led him to the Civil Rights Movement, and his passion for effectively communicating his concerns yielded him the nickname "Shep," a variant of the Soviet propagandist Dmitri Shepilov, which Barry ultimately took as his middle name. He continued to champion civil rights issues during his master's studies in organic chemistry at Fisk University, where he received his degree in 1960. He then pursued a doctoral education at the University of Kansas and University of Tennessee–Knoxville, but discontinued his studies at both institutions because neither would allow him to tutor White students.

Barry's foray into public service can be attributed largely to his commitment to the Civil Rights Movement, especially to ending racial segregation. This included his election as the first national chairman of the Student Nonviolent Coordinating Committee (SNCC). Barry was actively involved in protesting transportation issues that disproportionately affected Black Americans, including successfully organizing a boycott of the Washington (D.C.) Metropolitan Area Transit Authority

District of Columbia's mayor Marion S. Barry, Jr., testifying in front of the House Select Committee on Narcotics Abuse and Control regarding the legalization of drugs in 1988. Barry was convicted of possessing crack cocaine in 1990 and sent to prison. He was re-elected as mayor upon his release. (Time & Life Pictures/Getty Images)

when a proposed bus fare hike was announced. During much of the late 1960s and early 1970s, Barry established programs through his Pride, Inc., program, which capitalized on federal grants and partnerships with local businesses to train and employ Black men. He was also instrumental in ensuring that adequate food supplies were delivered to low-income neighborhoods during the 1968 riots, convincing supermarket chains to deliver food despite the social upheaval and amid physical violence.

Barry was appointed to the board of the Washington, D.C., Model Police Precinct project, a $3 million effort from 1968 to 1972 that sought to improve relationships between the local law enforcement in Washington, D.C., and the Black community. He was considered "militant" by some involved with the program (Lemann, 1979), and resigned in 1971 to seek a position on the Washington, D.C., School Board. Barry had also been appointed to serve as a member of the city's Economic Development Committee, which had the task of helping to route federal funds and venture capital to Black-owned businesses as they struggled to recover from the riots.

While serving on the Washington, D.C., City Council, on March 9, 1977, Barry was shot near the heart by radical Hanafi Muslims (a breakaway from the Nation of Islam) during a two-day siege. The fact that he had survived a shooting, along with his campaign slogan "Take a Stand," may help account for the political success that followed. In 1979, Barry successfully realized his dream of higher political office with his landslide election to the position of mayor of the District of Columbia. He was only the second person to hold that office after a 1974 law, the Home Rule Act, allowed Washington, D.C., residents to elect their own mayor. During his first term, despite early successes in improving the efficiency of the

Sanitation Department and developing a youth summer jobs program, unemployment continued to rise within the district. He garnered criticism because the majority of cuts that he made in government personnel were borne predominantly by the D.C. Metropolitan Police Department, including a reduction of more than 1,500 officers. By 1981, the increases in unemployment, heightened use of crack cocaine, and lack of a crime control response placed Washington, D.C., among the most dangerous cities in the nation. It held this distinction for nearly 25 years and became known as the "murder capital of the country" in 1990, and for much of the period from 1988 to 1998 (Pan, 1999; Urbina, 2006).

In addition to the economic and public safety challenges that Barry faced during his first term, less than 100 days into his tenure, his personal ethics began to be called into question. From an extravagant "100 days in office" party at Club La Serre during which he allegedly used cocaine, to an "adulation-filled trip to Africa whose relevance to the governance of the city he has never convincingly explained" (Lemann, 1979: 1), Barry's commitment to effective stewardship began to raise doubts within political circles. His second term, from 1983 to 1987, proved even more problematic, including a federal indictment and subsequent conviction handed down against Deputy Mayor Alphonse G. Hill for "steering contracts to a friend in exchange for kickbacks" (Franklin, 1987: 1); in addition, Barry's most trusted advisor, Ivanhoe Donaldson, pled guilty to stealing more than $200,000 from the city, obstructing justice, and engaging in income tax evasion in order to fuel his lavish lifestyle (Stone, 1986). In all, 11 members of the Barry administration, including Hill and Donaldson, were convicted of federal crimes.

During his third term, starting in 1987, as the city fell further into economic despair, Barry's purported drug use and alleged sexual improprieties continued to raise eyebrows. Allegations of widespread cocaine use had dogged him since late into his first term. These allegations served as the catalyst for a six-year federal investigation for drug possession. On January 18, 1990, Barry, along with his former girlfriend and ex-model Hazel Diane "Rasheeda" Moore, were arrested in Washington's Vista Hotel in a sting operation conducted by the D.C. Metropolitan Police and the Federal Bureau of Investigation. Barry was charged with 10 counts of misdemeanor illicit drug possession and an additional count of conspiracy to possess cocaine. Ultimately, he was convicted on only one count of drug possession and sentenced to six months in federal prison in October 1990. Throughout the trial, he continued to serve as mayor.

Upon his release from prison in 1992, Barry ran for the office of D.C. councilman for the Eighth Ward, easily winning 70 percent of the vote. In 1994, he successfully sought a fourth term as city mayor, and was sworn into office in 1995. However, so pronounced was the economic crisis in the District of Columbia that the U.S. Congress placed the city under the authority of a financial control board with day-to-day oversight of its operations. Barry was stripped of all of his authority as mayor, except for managing the city's parks and libraries, and the Office of Tourism. After completing his final term as mayor in 1999, Barry worked briefly for a financial investment firm and was involved in a 2002 incident during which the U.S. Park Police allegedly found marijuana and traces of cocaine in his vehicle.

Seeking a return to political office, in 2004 he was elected councilman for the Eighth Ward with 95 percent of the vote. Again accompanying his political success were legal issues, including a difficult (yet unresolved) divorce from third wife Cora Masters Barry (Harris & Smith, 2009), entering a guilty plea to misdemeanor federal tax evasion charges in 2005, three years' probation for failing drug testing due to the presence of cocaine and marijuana in 2006, and failure to file a 2007 tax return. He was also arrested in 2009 on a stalking charge in connection with alleged threats against ex-girlfriend and political consultant Donna Watts-Brighthaupt (DeBonis, 2009), although Watts-Brighthaupt, whom Barry had hired and ultimately paid more than $20,000 for work on his campaign, ultimately dropped the charges (Craig & Johnson, 2009).

Reports indicate that Watts-Brighthaupt had also been responsible for plagiarizing much of a research contract that Barry had awarded her, which was slated to explore education issues in the district. Barry also allegedly sought to distribute nearly $8.4 million in earmarks to vendors and organizations whose credentials or qualifications to perform specific functions appeared tenuous at best, and who allegedly had connections to his campaign (Weber, 2010).

Chuck Stone (1986) notes,

> [T]he story of Marion Barry is particularly tragic because it involves a man who abandoned the principles of the civil rights struggle for which he fought so valiantly. Barry did more good for his people when he was working in the Civil Rights Movement to gain power than he did after he had that power. . . . [C]onstant bouts with petty corruption have diverted attention from Barry's policy failures and from the larger agenda of reforms that black voters might demand.

Despite his personal foibles, Barry continues to serve as a councilman for the Eighth Ward of the District of Columbia. It seems that his personal tribulations have not tarnished his civil rights legacy to the point where voters are unwilling to support him. Barry has continued to win public office but also continues to engage in questionable conduct as a public official. In September 2013 he was censured and removed from his position of committee chair on the D.C. City Council for accepting cash payments from city contractors. In 2010 he was similarly censured and removed from a chairman's position for giving council contracts to a girlfriend (Davis & DeBonis, 2013).

A Washington, D.C., alternative weekly, *Washington City Paper,* has dubbed Barry "Mayor for Life." His reality show, which uses this title, launched on YouTube in December 2010. Moreover, *The Washington Post* has noted that in order to understand the District of Columbia, one must understand Marion Barry. He was recently immortalized as a figure in Madame Tussaud's Wax Museum, "joining 49 others, including civil rights leaders Martin Luther King Jr., Rosa Parks and Malcolm X" (Johnson & Roberts, 2007: 1).

Hank Brightman

See also: Civil Rights Movement; Student Nonviolent Coordinating Committee (SNCC); War on Drugs

References

Cohon, R. "Hume's Moral Philosophy." In *Stanford Encyclopedia of Philosophy.* Stanford University, 2010–. http://plato.stanford.edu/entries/hume-moral/.

Craig, T., and J. Johnson. "Barry Arrested, Accused of Stalking Ex-Girlfriend." *The Washington Post,* July 5, 2009. http://www.washingtonpost.com/wpdyn/content/article/2009/07/05/AR2009070501056.html.

Davis, A., and M. DeBonis. "D.C. Council Censures Marion Barry for Taking Cash Payments from City Contractors." *The Washington Post,* September 17, 2013. http://www.washingtonpost.com/local/dc-politics/dc-council-censures-marion-barry-for-taking-cash-payments-from-city-contractors/2013/09/17/02f22d06-1fba-11e3-b7d1-7153ad47b549_story.html.

DeBonis, Mike. "The Barry Archives: Voicemails Reveal Depths of Councilmember's Obsession with Girlfriend." *Washingtoncitypaper.com,* July 10, 2009. http://www.washingtoncitypaper.com/articles/37514/marion-barrys-voicemails-reveal-depths-of-his-obsession-with-girlfriend.

Franklin, B. A. "2d Washington Deputy Mayor Gets Prison Term." *The New York Times,* June 24, 1987. http://www.nytimes.com/1987/06/24/us/2d-washington-deputy-mayor-gets-prison-term.html.

Harris, H. R., and M. Smith. "Many Women in Marion Barry's Life." *The Washington Post,* July 7, 2009. http://www.washingtonpost.com/wp-srv/local/longterm/library/dc/barry/79prof.htm.

Jaffe, H. S. *Dream City: Race, Power and the Decline of Washington, D.C.* New York: Simon and Schuster, 1994.

Johnson, D., and R. Roberts. "Washington's Mayor for Life to Be Truly Immortalized—In Wax." *The Washington Post,* July 18, 2007. http://www.washingtonpost.com/wp-dyn/content/article/2007/07/17/AR2007071701643.html.

Lemann, N. "The Question Is: Will He Deliver?" *The Washington Post,* December 16, 1979. http://www.washingtonpost.com/wp-srv/local/longterm/library/dc/barry/79prof.htm.

Pan, P. P. "D.C. Murders Down; Suburban Killings Up." *The Washington Post,* January 1, 1999. http://www.washingtonpost.com/wp-srv/local/longterm/crime/homicides0101.htm.

Stone, C. "A Dream Deferred: A Black Mayor Betrays the Faith." *Washington Monthly,* July 1, 1986. http://www.thefreelibrary.com/A+dream+deferred%3B+a+black+mayor+betrays+the+faith.-a04330756.

Urbina, I. "Washington Officials Try to Ease Crime Fear." *The New York Times,* July 13, 2006. http://www.nytimes.com/2006/07/13/us/13deecee.html?_r=1&n=Top%2F-Reference%2FTimes%20Topics%2FPeople%2FW%2FWilliams%2C%20Anthony%20A.

Weber, J. "Report: Barry Violated City Contract Law." *The Washington Times,* February 16, 2010. http://www.washingtontimes.com/news/2010/feb/16/report-barry-violated-city-contract-law/?feat=home_top5_read.

Bell, Sean (1983–2006)

Sean Bell was a 23-year-old African American father of two who was shot and killed by undercover detectives on the day that he was due to be married. The shooting took place on November 25, 2006, in Jamaica, Queens, New York. Two of Bell's friends, 23-year-old Trent Benefield and 21-year-old Joseph Guzman, were also injured during the incident. Though the events that led to Bell's death have been disputed both in the media and in criminal and civil courts over the past several years, the event became newsworthy in part because of the facts that are not in dispute. Police officers fired a total of 50 bullets on a public street during an encounter with three civilians who were later determined to be unarmed.

The incident also had racial overtones. The victims of the shooting were young males, two Black and one Hispanic. Thirty-one of the 50 police bullets were fired by Detective Michael Oliver, a White 12-year veteran of the force. Eleven of the bullets were fired by Detective Gescard Isnora, who has been alternately described as mixed race (Mexican and Haitian), or Black, or Hispanic, and who was a member of the department for five and a half years. Marc Cooper, an African American detective, fired four times. Michael Carey, who has been identified as White, fired three times. A fifth detective, Paul Headley, who was also African American, fired once (Iverac, 2011). During the incident, Detective Oliver fired his semi-automatic weapon until it was empty, then reloaded and continued to fire (Plocienniczak, 2008). He fired nearly three times the number of bullets as Detective Isnora, who, according to testimony, was struck by Sean Bell's car, which precipitated the shooting. Detectives Oliver, Isnora, and Cooper were indicted, tried, and acquitted of all criminal charges related to the case.

Prior to the shooting, Sean Bell and his friends had been celebrating his bachelor party at Club Kalua, a reported strip club. Police reports indicate that at the time of the shooting, the establishment was under surveillance by NYPD

Anti-police brutality supporters and members of the New Black Panther Party march along Jamaica Avenue in the Queens borough of New York, on December 2, 2006. The rally protested the killing of 23-year-old Sean Bell on November 25, 2006, hours before he was to have married the mother of his two children, Nicole Paultre. (Associated Press)

narcotics and vice units (Wilson & McLean, 2008). According to police records, the officers were in the club as part of a sting operation to detect prostitution. As part of this investigation, nine officers, including seven detectives, were either in or outside of the club.

Witness accounts seem consistent that around 4:00 a.m., Sean Bell and seven other individuals began arguing with a man, later identified as Fabio Coicou, just outside the club (Wilson & McLean, 2008). Coicou was reportedly waiting for his girlfriend, who worked at the club. According to police, someone in Bell's party was alleged to have said, "Go get my gun" (Wilson, 2008d), at which time Sean Bell and his friends left the front of Club Kalua and started walking toward Bell's car.

Detective Isnora, who was in plainclothes as part of the undercover team, followed the group on foot and reported to his superior, Lieutenant Gary Napoli, that it was "[g]etting hot on Liverpool, for real, I think there's a gun" (Wilson & McLean, 2008). Bell's car was parked on Liverpool Street. According to testimony, the lieutenant then commanded that the undercover detectives apprehend the group (Wilson & McLean, 2008). Many facts are in dispute regarding what happened once Bell, Benefield, and Guzman reached the car. While the police claimed that Joseph Guzman made the statement about getting a gun, no gun was recovered from the car and other witnesses deny that the statement was ever made. In the immediate aftermath of the shooting, the police department claimed that there had been a fourth man at the car and who might have been in possession of a gun. After days of looking for this fourth person, the department recanted and said there was no proof of a fourth man and no proof that the trio had access to a gun during the early morning hours of March 25.

Once the three were inside the car, Detective Isnora approached the driver's side window with his gun drawn. Whether the police identified themselves and whether Bell understood he was being stopped by police are not clear. Bell was in the driver's seat and attempted to pull away from the curb. His vehicle struck the unmarked police minivan that was being used as part of the undercover operation at the club. It also struck Detective Isnora. Detective Isnora fired his weapon first. Detective Oliver is reported to have fired his weapon from atop the hood of Bell's car (Wilson, 2008a). Oliver testified that he was firing at Guzman, the person he thought had a gun. Sean Bell was struck by four bullets. Trent Benefield was struck by three bullets. Joseph Guzman was struck by 19 bullets but managed to survive.

The shooting became a lightning rod for the community and garnered considerable attention from the media. Unanswered questions were raised as to whether the officers had been drinking while working undercover in the club prior to the shooting, while test results were released indicating that Sean Bell was legally drunk when he attempted to drive away from the officers. Several nonviolent protests occurred in the wake of the shooting, demanding justice be served in the case. Protesters held signs that said, "Justice for Sean Bell," and "I am Sean Bell" (Bedford, 2006). Family members of all three victims pleaded for peace and justice.

Mayor Michael Bloomberg joined forces with religious leaders and elected officials to calm residents, but called the circumstances "inexplicable" and "unacceptable" (Cardwell & Chan, 2006). During a press conference, Reverend Al Sharpton referenced two racially motivated crimes from the past—the 1986 death of Michael Griffith in Howard Beach and the 2005 beating of Glenn Moore in the same community. Though the incidents had involved White civilian offenders, the cases came before the same court where justice was being sought for Sean Bell. New York City Council member Charles Barron was quoted as noting, "[T]his is the last opportunity for this system to show that they value black life, the same as they value white life" (Wilson, 2008c).

In the Queens neighborhood where the shooting occurred, many residents saw it as yet another example of unfair and abusive treatment of Blacks by police (Cardwell & Chan, 2006), despite the fact that some of the police involved in the incident were African American. Many private citizens, religious leaders, and public officials, as well as several celebrities, were involved with, and arrested during, protests demanding that the officers be arrested and indicted. On March 16, 2007, a Queens grand jury voted to indict the three detectives.

In February 2008, Oliver, Isnora, and Cooper were placed on trial. For firing 31 of the 50 shots, Oliver faced charges of first- and second-degree manslaughter and two counts of first-degree assault. Isnora, who was the first to fire, faced charges of first- and second-degree manslaughter, felony assault, and misdemeanor reckless endangerment. Cooper faced two counts of reckless endangerment for a shot he fired that hit a nearby Air Train platform. Video footage showed the bullet barely missing a waiting commuter (Wilson, 2008b). After an unsuccessful motion for change of venue, the three detectives waived their rights to a jury trial, choosing instead to have their cased heard only by a judge (Wilson, 2008c). If convicted, Oliver and Isnora could have received up to 25 years in prison (New York 1 News, 2008).

During the trial, prosecutors and defense lawyers presented different narratives of the events that occurred during the early morning hours of November 25, 2006. Assistant District Attorney Charles A. Testagrossa called the shooting unjustified (Wilson, 2008c). "The story of how this tragedy occurred is a tale of carelessness," he said, adding that the shooting "can only be characterized as criminal." Testagrossa pointed out that detectives Oliver and Isnora should have paused as they fired to assess the effects of the first shots (Wilson, 2008c). On this topic, Police Commissioner Raymond Kelly commented, "Officers are trained to shoot no more than three bullets before pausing to assess the situation." Moreover, "[d]epartment policy also largely prohibits officers from firing at vehicles, even when they are being used as weapons" (Cardwell & Chan, 2006). Prosecutors tried to convince the judge that the detectives were "inept and trigger-happy" (NPR, 2008). "We ask police to risk their lives to protect ours," said Assistant District Attorney Testagrossa in his closing arguments, "not to risk our lives to protect their own" (Wilson, 2008b).

On the opposite side, the defense described Sean Bell's killing as "the tragic end to a nonetheless justified confrontation" (Wilson, 2008b). It claimed that "Detective Isnora had solid reasons to believe his life was in danger when Mr. Bell [drove] the car directly at him" (Wilson, 2008b). In the trial, defense attorneys (James Culleton for Oliver, Phillip Karasyk for Isnora, and Paul Martin for Cooper) characterized the victims as "drunken and unruly," and stated that the detectives had reason to believe they were armed (NPR, 2008).

In a decision that stunned many who had heard the facts of the case, New York criminal court judge Arthur Cooperman acquitted all three detectives of all charges. In his decision, Justice Cooperman noted, "Inconsistent testimony and other problems . . . had the effect of eviscerating the credibility" of critical prosecution witnesses, and that some of their testimony simply "didn't make sense" (Plocienniczak, 2008).

Despite the criminal court acquittals, in May 2008, departmental disciplinary charges were filed against Detectives Isnora, Oliver, and Cooper. Each was charged with discharging their firearms outside of departmental guidelines. Michael Carey was similarly charged but later cleared. Detective Isnora was also charged with taking enforcement action while working undercover rather than letting officers who were not undercover take control (Baker, 2008). Lieutenant Napoli received departmental charges for failing to properly supervise the operation. Paul Headley was not charged by the department but gave up his position with the agency. Both Oliver and Cooper resigned from the department in conjunction with the settlement of their disciplinary charges. In 2012, Detective Isnora was fired from the department after exhausting all appeals regarding the disciplinary claims. He has sued to be reinstated. After being named in the wrongful death suit filed by the family of Sean Bell, Michael Carey filed a counterclaim against the Sean Bell estate claiming he was injured when the van he was in was struck by Bell's car while Bell was driving intoxicated. The status of that suit is unknown.

After deliberation, federal prosecutors passed on filing civil rights charges against the detectives, citing "insufficient evidence" (Baker & Eligon, 2010). After declining to prosecute the case, the Justice Department stated, "Neither accident, mistake, fear, negligence nor bad judgment is sufficient to establish a federal criminal civil rights violation" (Baker & Eligon, 2010).

In May 2010, the Bell family settled a civil suit against New York City and the NYPD for Sean Bell's death (New York 1 News, 2008). The $7 million dollar settlement included $3.25 million to the estate of Sean Bell, $3 million to Joseph Guzman (who suffered several gunshot wounds that left him partially disabled), and $900,000 to Trent Benefield (Messana, 2010). Bell's fiancée, Nicole Paultre Bell, has begun a career in politics to try to effect change in the community. In May 2011, the Sean Elijah Bell Community Center was opened on Sutphin Boulevard in Jamaica, Queens, at an intersection that has been renamed Sean Bell Way.

The killing of Sean Bell in a shower of bullets by New York City police officers was eerily reminiscent of the Amadou Diallo shooting just a few years earlier in 1999. Like Bell, Diallo was also unarmed, and killed when four White officers fired 41 shots as he stood in front of the Bronx building where he lived. Both incidents prompted significant questions about minority relations with the police department and the role of race in the justice system overall. Both incidents brought to the forefront a groundswell of community discontent with the police. Protest "pray ins" that stopped traffic were staged at six different locations in the city shortly after the acquittals in the Bell case. These were largely peaceful events (Buckley & Lueck, 2008). Several rappers, including Nicki Minaj and Swizz Beatz, wrote about Sean Bell, either in tribute or to use the incident as a call to stand up to police oppression. Although the criminal trial and civil proceedings have

Unpublished Op-ed to *The New York Times*

March 21, 2007

In Tuesday's Metro section, the attorney for Detective Gescard Isnora is quoted as stating that his client "didn't do anything wrong." Similar statements have reportedly been made by the representative for the Detectives' Benevolent Association. If they believe their own statements, this is a sad time in American history.

For several years I have taught New York Penal Code, Article 35—the portion of New York State law that defines the defense of justification. Nothing in it authorizes police or civilians to recklessly endanger the lives of innocent others in order to save their own.

In fact, the statute expressly negates a justification defense for police officers who act recklessly. Hence, the firing of 50 unanswered bullets into public space is unlawful behavior, no matter who is doing the shooting. At least in the Amadou Diallo case, the agency had the decency to say that the officers "made a mistake."

Here, there are claims that the officers "did nothing wrong" when their own department guidelines: prohibit shooting at cars; require a reassessment of the perceived threat after three bullets are fired; and, since the 1970s, have made "the preservation of life" a priority. The "preservation of life" requirement is not limited to preserving the lives of police officers.

If, as Detective Isnora has claimed, he overheard one of the men say, "Get my gun from the car," why allow the men to make it to the car at all? Why not intervene before the car was reached? By first going to retrieve his own gun from a vehicle before approaching the group, it seems that Detective Isnora was setting the stage for a potential gun battle on a public street. My 10-year-old son has commented, "Maybe it was because he wanted to see some action."

Despite the fact that he had significant back-up, was Detective Isnora afraid to approach these young men while (by his own admission) they were unarmed? If so, what was the source of that tremendous fear? For those who claim that this case isn't about race, they are missing the point entirely. For this case to not be about race, at least one of the victims in Sean Bell's car would have to have been White.

As for Detective Oliver, if there is "nothing wrong" with shooting more than 10 times the number of bullets than the guidelines allow, without ever stopping to reassess the "threat," then the entire Patrol Guide should be discarded. If that's not "depraved indifference" to the position of trust that he holds and the harm that he caused, certainly enjoying a $4,200 dinner while waiting to be indicted exhibits a level of arrogance commensurate with the number of bullets he fired.

Police condemn gangbangers and drive-by shooters when they carelessly discharge their illegal firearms in residential neighborhoods and occasionally hit innocent bystanders. Should the police be rewarded because their guns are legal and some of the folks within their zone of danger have the wherewithal to duck?

Delores Jones-Brown

ended, the case is likely to live on in this community for many years. As a result of the Bell case, Commissioner Kelly conducted an investigation into the department's undercover operations and announced a list of 19 recommendations, among them mandatory alcohol testing of officers who are involved in shootings with fatalities or injuries.

Natalie Petit and Jennifer Balboni

See also: Diallo, Amadou; 100 Blacks in Law Enforcement Who Care; Police Brutality; Sharpton, Jr., Alfred Charles

References

Baker, A. "Officers Face Department Charges in Bell Killing." *The New York Times,* May 21, 2008. http://panafricannews.blogs.com/2008/05/police-brutality-update-officers_21.html.

Baker, A., and J. Eligon. "Officers Won't Face Charges in Sean Bell Killing." *The New York Times,* December 22, 2010. http://topics.nytimes.com/top/reference/timestopics/people/b/sean_bell/index.html.

Bedford, K. "NYC Shooting Victim's Funeral Held at Church Where He Was to Be Married." *USA Today,* December 1, 2006. http://www.usatoday.com/news/nation/2006-12-01-ny-shooting_x.htm.

Buckley, C., and T. Lueck. "Verdict in Sean Bell Case Draws a Peaceful Protest, but Some Demand More." *The New York Times,* April 28, 2008. http://www.nytimes.com/2008/04/28/nyregion/28bell.html.

Cardwell, D., and S. Chan. "Mayor Calls 50 Shots by the Police 'Unacceptable.'" *The New York Times,* November 28, 2006. http://www.nytimes.com/2006/11/28/nyregion/28shoot.html?_r=1&pagewanted=print.

Celona, L. "Cops Will Be Riot Ready." *The New York Post,* April 14, 2008. http://www.nypost.com/p/news/regional/item_aMnsQRgdeAW0gATjY5LKMJ.

Iverac, M. "Sean Bell Fiance Says Trial Is Like Reliving a 'Nightmare.'" WNYC News Blog, October 25, 2011. http://www.wnyc.org.

Messana, P. (2010). "Plaintiffs: NYC Settlement on Sean Bell Case Is Far." *USA Today,* July 28, 2010. http://www.usatoday.com/news/nation/2010-07-28-police-sean-bell-settlement_N.htm.

National Public Radio (NPR). "Trial Verdict: Officers Acquitted in Sean Bell Case." April 25, 2008. http://www.npr.org/templates/story/story.php?storyId=89938081.

New York 1 News. "Not Guilty: Detectives Charged in Sean Bell Shooting Acquitted on All Charges." April 25, 2008. http://www.ny1.com/?SecID=1000&ArID=80881.

Plocienniczak, M. "Civil Suit: New York City Settles Sean Bell Lawsuit. *The New York Times,* April 28, 2008. http://www.nytimes.com/2008/04/28/nyregion/28bell.html.

Spence, L. "Race and the Sean Bell Shooting." December 8, 2006. http://www.npr.org/templates/story/story.php?storyId=6597713&ps=rs.

Wilson, M. "Nightclub Parting Shots Kill a Bridegroom." 2008a. *The New York Times,* 2008a. http://proquest.umi.com/pqdweb?index=12&did=1304486321&SrchMode=1&

sid=1&Fmt=6&VInst=PROD&VType=PQD&RQT=309&VName=PQD&TS=129357
0746&clientId=15327.

Wilson, M. 2008b. "3 Detectives Acquitted in Bell Shooting." *The New York Times,* April 26, 2008. http://www.nytimes.com/2008/04/26/nyregion/26BELL.html.

Wilson, M. 2008c. "Trial Starts for Detective in Bell Shooting." *The New York Times,* February 25, 2008. http://cityroom.blogs.nytimes.com/2008/02/25/trial-starts-for-detectives-in-bell-shooting/.

Wilson, M. 2008d. "Figure in Sean Bell Shooting Disputes Detectives' Version." *The New York Times,* March 20, 2008. http://www.nytimes.com/2008/03/20/nyregion/20bell.html.

Wilson, M., and A. McLean. "Actual Trial: Inside the Sean Bell Case." *The New York Times,* April 24, 2008. http://www.nytimes.com/interactive/2008/04/24/nyregiton/20080424_BELL_GRAPHIC.html.

Black Panther Party

The Black Panther Party (BPP), originally known as the Black Panther Party for Self-Defense, was created in October 1966 by Huey Newton, Bobby Seale, and David Hilliard, all students at Merritt College in Oakland, California. They named the new organization after the panther emblem adopted by the Lowndes County Freedom Organization, which was founded by Stokely Carmichael in Alabama in 1964. The Black Panthers were initially formed to protect local communities from police brutality and racism. The party began to develop a series of social programs to provide needed services to Black and poor people. These programs, which included free breakfasts and medical care, were eventually referred to as survival programs, and were operated by party members under the slogan "survival pending revolution."

The leaders of the Black Panthers were influenced by the ideas expressed by Malcolm X in the final months of his life. The Panthers therefore argued for international working class unity and supported joint action with White revolutionary groups. The Panthers eventually developed into a Marxist revolutionary group. Prominent members of the group were Elaine Brown, Stokely Carmichael, H. Rap Brown, Fred Hampton, Fredrika Newton, Eldridge Cleaver, Kathleen Cleaver, Angela Davis, and Bobby Hutton. Indeed, any doubt as to the motivation and driving force of the party was dispelled by its motto, which noted that "we are advocates of the abolition of war, we do not want war, but war can only be abolished through war and in order to get rid of the gun it is necessary to pick up the gun."

In October 1966, the BPP created a 10-point platform and program: "What We Want, What We Believe" (it was revised in 1972). This platform and program was a manifesto that included demands for basic rights that ran alongside criticisms of capitalist society that reflected a Marxist influence. In fact, early fundraising for the BPP included the resale of Mao Tse Tung's *Little Red Book,* which the BPP bought for 30 cents and resold for one dollar, mostly on the campus of the University of California–Berkeley (George & Wilcox, 1996). Mao Tse Tung was the first chairman of the Central Committee of the Communist Party of China. The book contained a compilation of his quotes. The Black Panthers had chapters in several major cities and estimates place its peak membership at nearly 10,000 in 1969.

In 1967, Eldridge Cleaver joined the party, and together with Newton and Seale, published the first issue of the party's tabloid, *The Black Panther.* An extract from the issue dated May 11, 1969, in which Bobby Seale addresses a rally to free Huey Newton, provides an indication of the contempt with which the power base of White society was viewed:

> It's about 12:00 and if you look in the back of you, you will see Reagan's state building, with his state pigs observing the people. And, of course, if you look in front of you, you will see Nixon's U.S. federal building, with the pigs inside, observing the people. And if later on you decide to leave here and go on down Polk Street, you'll walk in front of pig mayor Alioto's office, and they'll be observing the people. (Seale, 1969)

At the time of this speech, Ronald Reagan, who would later become president of the United States, was the governor of California. Richard Nixon was the nation's president. The BPP used the term "pig" to refer to government officials, especially the police. By BBP's definition a "pig" is a "low natured beast that has no regard for law, justice, or the rights of people; a creature that bites the hand that feeds it; a foul traducer, usually found masquerading as the victim of an unprovoked attack" (cited in Foner, 1995).

The ideology and tactics of the BPP often brought its members into conflict with law enforcement officials. The conflicts included multiple shoot-outs during which founding members were seriously injured or killed. Though the BPP became known in some circles as a militant Black hate group, the evidence from several incidents revealed that the police typically did most of the shooting, and there are allegations that various BPP members were targeted for assassination by the Federal Bureau of Investigation (FBI) and local police departments.

In August 1967, the FBI initiated a covert action program known as COIN-TELPRO (Counter-Intelligence Program) to disrupt and neutralize organizations deemed "Black Nationalist Hate Groups." The stated aims of COINTELPRO included the prevention of the formation of a coalition of militant Black Nationalist groups and the prevention of such groups and their leaders from gaining respectability by attempting to discredit them. The BPP was not among the original Black Nationalist groups targeted, but in September 1968, FBI director J. Edgar Hoover argued that the Black Panther Party constituted "the greatest threat to the internal security of the country" (Select Committee to Study Governmental Operations, 1976). Through COINTELPRO, he supervised an extensive operation of surveillance, infiltration, perjury, police harassment, reported assassinations, assassination attempts, and other tactics designed to undermine BPP leadership, incriminate party members, and drain the organization of resources and manpower. A 1975 investigation of alleged CIA and FBI abuses of power by the Select Committee to Study Governmental Operations with Respect to Intelligence Activities, chaired by Frank Church, confirmed FBI involvement in at least one attack on BPP headquarters in Chicago. In that incident, it is reported that a single bullet was fired by a BPP member while nearly 100 bullets came from guns issued to the police.

In 1971, the Black Panther Party split with Huey Newton on one side and Eldridge Cleaver on the other. It is reported that Cleaver doubted the leadership ability of Newton. Newton argued that the Black Panther Party had been operating incorrectly and that from that point forward it would focus upon church and community affairs and work within rather than against the system. Consequently, during the mid to late 1970s, party members Elaine Brown and Bobby Seale ran for public office but lost, and most of the BPP activities centered around the national headquarters and a school in Oakland. The party continued to influence local politics, but most of the original leadership was gone. By 1980, BPP membership was estimated at less than 30 members.

There has been a great deal written about the Black Panther Party, but much of this has consisted of historical overviews of the origins of the party and/or its organization and the ultimate demise of the founding Oakland chapter. In addition, the majority of literature is a compilation of either the autobiographies of party members or revelatory tracts by other observers. In both cases, there is arguably a degree of subjectivity (witting or otherwise) throughout. Moreover, the substance of the literature tends to focus not upon the operations of the Black Panther Party but rather upon attempts made to persecute and discredit the party and its members (Jeffries, 2002). Interestingly, alleged nonpartisan works tend to deal with the BPP within the context of terrorism rather than politics (Martin, 2003).

Clayborne Carson (1995) argued that "[t]he rapid rise and decline of the Panthers reflected the general course of black political militancy during the late 1960s and 1970s." During its brief presence, however, he suggested that the movement "demonstrated the ability of urban, grassroots, political activists to offer intellectual and tactical guidance for the on-going African-American freedom struggle" (Carson, 1995: xvii) and that "at its best offers a historical example of brave activists willing to 'die for the people' and thus continues to provide

---

The New Black Panther Party

The New Black Panther Party (NBPP), whose formal name is the New Black Panther Party for Self Defense, was founded in Dallas, Texas, in 1989. Despite its name, the NBPP is not an official successor to the Black Panther Party. Members of the original Black Panther Party have insisted that the newer party is illegitimate and have strongly objected that there "is no new Black Panther Party." The Anti-Defamation League, the Southern Poverty Law Center, and the U.S. Commission on Civil Rights consider the NBPP to be a hate group. When former Nation of Islam minister Khalid Abdul Muhammad became the NBPP national chairman in the late 1990s, a position he retained until his death in 2001, the NBPP attracted many former Nation of Islam members. The NBPP is currently led by Malik Zulu Shabazz, and members consider Khalid Abdul Muhammad as the "father of the movement."

---

discontented African-American youth an alternative to self-destructive despair" (Carson, 1995: xviii).

Rob McCusker

See also: Brown, H. Rap (aka Jamil Abdullah Al-Amin); Carmichael, Stokely; Davis, Angela Yvonne

References

Anti-Defamation League. "New Black Panther Party for Self Defense." http://www.adl.org/assets/pdf/anti-semitism/New-Black-Panther-Party.pdf.

Black Panther Party Official Web Site. 2012. http://www.blackpanther.org//html.

Black Panther Research Project. 1997. http://www.stanforduniv.edu/group/blackpanthers.

Bukhri-Alston, S. "Notes on the Black Panther Party: Its Basic Working Papers and Policy Statements," 1968. http://www.peopleofcolororganize.com/wp-content/uploads/pdf/notes_on_the_black_panther_party_its_basic_working_papers_and_policy_statements.pdf.

Carson, C. "Foreword." In *The Black Panthers Speak,* edited by P. S. Foner, ix–xviii. New York: Da Capo Press, 1995.

Dr. Huey P. Newton Foundation. *There Is No New Black Panther Party.* 2011. http://www.blackpanthers.org/html.

Foner, P. S., ed. *The Black Panthers Speak.* New York: Da Capo Press, 1995.

George, J., and L. Wilcox. *American Extremists: Militias, Supremacists, Klansmen, Communists, & Others.* New York: Prometheus Books, 1996.

Jeffries, J. L. "Black Radicalism and Political Repression in Baltimore: The Case of the Black Panther Party." *Ethnic and Racial Studies* 25, no. 1 (January 2002): 64–98.

Martin, G. *Understanding Terrorism: Challenges, Perspectives, and Issues.* Thousand Oaks, CA: Sage, 2003.

Newton, Huey. "The Ten-Point Program." In *War against the Panthers.* Marxist.org, October 15, 1966. http://www.marxists.org/history/usa/workers/black-panthers/1966/10/15.htm.

Pearson, Hugh. *In the Shadow of the Panther: Huey Newton and the Price of Black Power in America.* Reading, MA: Perseus Books, 1994.

Seale, B. "Chairman Bobby Speaks at May Day Rally to Free Huey." *The Black Panther,* May 11, 1969. http://www.mimdown.org/bpp/bpp110569_11.htm.

Select Committee to Study Governmental Operations. *Supplementary Detailed Staff Reports on Intelligence Activities and the Rights of Americans, Book III, Final Report of the Select Committee to Study Governmental Operations with Respect to Intelligence Activities.* United States Senate, Washington, DC, April 23, 1976. http://www.icdc.com/~paulwolf/cointelpro/churchfinalreportIIIb.htm.

Southern Poverty Law Center. "New Black Panther Party." http://www.splcenter.org/get-informed/intelligence-files/groups/new-black-panther-party#.UYQaNaI6NXc.

Black Protectionism

Black protectionism is a phenomenon that takes place in the African American community when a fellow member, usually of reputable standing and high-profile status, is alleged to have committed a crime or other type of deviance or wrongdoing. Depending on the individual and circumstances, the accused quickly becomes enshrined and defended by the Black community in a form of group protection, which occurs automatically and in some cases, even in the face of compelling evidence of guilt. The term "Black protectionism" was developed by Katheryn Russell-Brown, an African American law professor, who has extensively observed, researched, and documented the origins, mechanisms, cases, prevalence, and applications of this strategy among African Americans (2005). In her 1998 book *The Color of Crime,* she defines Black protectionism as:

> what happens when the credentials, past history, or behavior of a well-known, successful Black person is called into question. In these instances, the Black community's reaction is protective, almost material. The Black community builds a fortress around its fallen hero and begins to offer explanations and defenses. Whenever . . . Blacks fall into national disgrace and scandal, they are picked up and brushed off by the Black community. Like a good wife, Black people "stand by their man." (57)

As such, this protective strategy, intertwined with the group dynamics, along with the community responses and media attention given to applicable Black individuals, may pose new difficulties, challenges, and opportunities to society, law, and justice.

Clarence Thomas

Clarence Thomas is an associate Supreme Court Justice, having held the position since 1991. He has written over 350 opinions throughout his tenure, most of which are revealing of his widely affirmed "conservative" jurisprudence. He is known for his commitment to an originalist interpretation of the Constitution and federal statutes; his focus on the Constitution's structural pillars of federalism and separation of power; and to his strong belief in judicial self-restraint (Holzer, 2007). Two cases that highlight Thomas' conservative approach are *Hudson v. McMillian* and *Georgia v. McCollum.*

In 1991, Hudson testified to the court that he had suffered loosened teeth, a cracked dental plate, facial swelling, and minor bruises during a beating by prison guards McMillian and Woods while handcuffed and shackled. The beating occurred as the result of an argument between the petitioner and McMillian. The magistrate trying the case found that although Hudson's injuries were "minor," the officers had used excessive force when such was not necessary, and thus, had violated the Eighth Amendment's prohibition against cruel and unusual punishment. This decision ultimately held that use of excessive force against an incarcerated prisoner may constitute cruel and unusual punishment even if the prisoner does not suffer from any serious physical injury (503 U.S. 1). Thomas wrote a dissenting opinion, stating that the use of excessive force that causes only insignificant harm, though immoral and scarring, should not be viewed as a violation of the Eighth Amendment as it is not "cruel and unusual punishment." Thomas further stated that in the past, the Court had limited the application of the Eighth Amendment so that it played a very limited role in prison regulations. Generally, precedent cases are considered the foundation of subsequent decisions. Accordingly, Thomas noted in his dissent that the Court should maintain this precedent and not widen the application of the Eighth Amendment to prisoners (503 U.S. 1).

Georgia v. McCollum was a case that held that a criminal defendant could not make peremptory challenges based solely on race. The case first arose after two White males were charged in 1992 of assaulting two African Americans. During the jury selection process, the prosecution's motion to prohibit the defendants from exercising peremptory challenges on the grounds of race was denied by the trial judge. Upon further consideration, the Georgia Supreme Court ruled that the Constitution prohibits criminal defendants from intentionally discriminating against others on the ground of race during the process of peremptory challenges (505 U.S. 42). This ruling was an extension of a previous ruling in *Edmonson v. Leesville Concrete Company,* which held that private litigants in civil cases may not use peremptory challenges to exclude jurors on the basis of race (500 U.S. 614). Thomas wrote a concurring opinion, arguing that although he initially shared the perspective of the dissenting opinions, he believed that the decision in a previous case, *Edmonson v. Leeville Concrete Company,* had set the precedent for the current case, thereby forcing him to change his opinion. Though Thomas disagreed with the use of the Constitution in regulating peremptory challenges altogether, he gave a concurring opinion on the ground that he believed it paramount to abide by the existing case law precedents (505 U.S. 42).

Black protectionism is a shield of protection provided freely by the Black community to those they see as representative of Black power and popularity. Generally, recipients of Black protectionism are notable Blacks who have made a major contribution to society, usually in the area of civil rights, or who have otherwise helped improve, or at least are perceived as having helped to improve, the quality of life for African Americans. Given this, when such individuals come under attack, the question arises: Would an accomplished person who has achieved the American Dream really throw all of it away for the crime or deviance they are alleged to have committed? Any rational mind would argue no, and would therefore scrutinize the nature of such allegations carefully. Interestingly, Black protectionism is afforded to individuals who are only part Black, and to those who have taken steps to actively leave behind the Black community, their roots—and their color—for acceptance into White society. Michael Jackson, O. J. Simpson, Clarence Thomas, Condoleezza Rice, and Colin Powell might be thought by some to fit this description. However, when such individuals find themselves in trouble, Black protectionism automatically swings into action, even if unwanted by the beneficiary. Interestingly, this shield may also be given to people of other races, usually for those who have in some way helped to improve, or who are perceived as having helped to improve, the lives of Black people. Former president Bill Clinton might be seen in this light. It has been suggested that Clinton was viewed favorably by African Americans because he shared a background akin to that of many Blacks, and because of his public appearances, where he appeared genuinely comfortable while speaking and interacting with Blacks.

In her 2004 book *Underground Codes,* Katheryn Russell-Brown identified four operating mechanisms behind Black protectionism, which are shown in Figure 1. First, there has to be some type of allegation of wrongdoing, which either can be a serious crime (e.g., murder, rape, etc.) or other wrongdoing (e.g., inappropriate remarks, questionable behavior, etc.) sufficient to bring large-scale negative attention to the accused. Secondly, the accusations have to be against someone Black; however, even those who have assimilated into White society

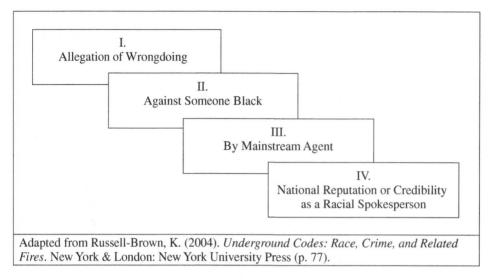

Adapted from Russell-Brown, K. (2004). *Underground Codes: Race, Crime, and Related Fires*. New York & London: New York University Press (p. 77).

Figure 1   Operating Mechanisms for Black Protectionism

(and other unique exceptions as mentioned above) are still eligible. Thirdly, the accusations should originate from a mainstream agent outside the Black community, for example, the police, district attorney, or public office, or generally an area in society typically dominated by Whites. Lastly, the individual accused should be one of credible character and recognized nationally, such as a politician, athlete, celebrity, scholar, or corporate executive previously in good standing—in other words, "the targeted person has something valuable to lose" (2004: 78). Those who fulfill the criteria may be eligible for Black protectionism.

In her book, Katheryn Russell-Brown provides a number of trigger questions for Black protectionism (see Table 1). These are questions that are often asked by Blacks when accusations of wrongdoing are levied against a well-known Black. These multiple questions are in contrast to the single question:

1. "Did he or she commit the offense?"

This question would be asked by and about a White person who was similarly accused. For African Americans, Black protectionism is afforded to Blacks who are accused whether the answer to this question is yes or no, and the Black community will initiate its own investigation to seek answers to a number of other questions—those listed in Table 1.

Typically, an answer of "Yes" to questions 2 and 6 and an answer of "No" to questions 3, 4, and 5 can trigger Black protectionism to help shield the accused from further defamation.

Table 1 Trigger Questions for Black Protectionism

Whites	Blacks
1. Did he or she commit the offense?	1. Did he or she commit the offense?
	2. Even if he or she did, was he or she set up?
	3. Would he or she risk everything (e.g., wealth, fame, material possessions) to commit an offense?
	4. Is he or she the only person who has committed this offense?
	5. Do Whites accused of the same offense receive the same scrutiny and treatment?
	6. Is this accusation part of a government conspiracy to destroy the Black race?

Adapted from K. Russell-Brown, "Black Protectionism as a Civil Rights Strategy." *Buffalo Law Review* 53, no. 1 (2005): 1–64, p. 22, and K. K. Russell, *The Color of Crime: Racial Hoaxes, White Fear, Black Protectionism, Police Harassment, and Other Macroaggressions* (New York: New York University Press, 1998), p. 60.

Table 2 includes individuals who were likely candidates for Black protectionism, while Table 3 contrasts these names to show whether the protective shield will be fully applied. As shown in Table 3, the names of a few women—Joycelyn Elders, Lani Guinier, and Alexis Herman—appear in the "No" category, while all the names of those who have received protection are exclusively male. When accusations involve both Black men and Black women, Black men seem to get the benefit of protection over Black women. For example, in July 1991, U.S. Supreme Court nominee Clarence Thomas was accused of sexually inappropriate behavior toward his former colleague Anita Hill, who had gone on to a career as a law school professor. During the course of the investigation, it was Hill who was portrayed in the most negative light, as a Black woman eager for 15 minutes of fame and angry that her former lover had married a White woman. Similarly, in 1992, when Mike Tyson was sent to prison after being accused and convicted of raping college student Desiree Washington, Washington was viewed by many as a gold-digger looking to cash in on the incident. In other cases involving women, for example, with O. J. Simpson, Jesse Jackson, Marion Barry, and Bill Clinton, Black protectionism was afforded the men despite strong evidence against them and in favor of the claims of the women.

Table 2 Potential Recipients of Black Protectionism, 1990–2003

Name	Allegation	Position
Marion Barry	Drug use	Mayor of Washington, D.C.
Ron Brown	Bribery	U.S. Secretary of Commerce
Kobe Bryant	Sexual assault	NBA
Rae Carruth	Murder	NFL
Ben Chavis	Fraud; extramarital affair with NAACP coworker	NAACP Executive
Sean "P. Diddy" Combs	Illegal possession of a firearm; assault	Music entrepreneur and rapper
Joycelyn Elders	Inappropriate remarks	U.S. Surgeon General
Mike Espy	Bribery	Secretary of Agriculture
Lani Guinier	Inappropriate writings	Law professor
Alcee Hastings		
Alexis Herman	Bribery	Secretary of Labor
Allen Iverson	Assault	NBA
Jesse Jackson	Extramarital affair; embezzlement	Director, Rainbow/PUSH
Michael Jackson	Child sexual assault	Entertainer
R. Kelly	Sex with minor; child pornography	Entertainer
Ray Lewis	Murder	NFL
Henry Lyons	Extramarital affair; corruption	Reverend, National Baptist Convention
Carol Moseley-Braun	Mismanagement of public funds	U.S. Congress
Hazel O'Leary	Excessive speeding	Secretary of Energy
Melvin Reynolds	Sex with minor; child pornography; phone sex	U.S. Congress
Carl Rowan	Unlawful possession of a firearm	Public servant and journalist
O. J. Simpson	Murder	NFL
John Street	Corruption	Mayor of Philadelphia
Clarence Thomas	Sexual harassment	Supreme Court nominee
Mike Tyson	Rape; aggravated assault	Boxer
Rasheed Wallace	Drugs	NBA
Chris Webber	Speeding; marijuana possession; gambling	NBA
Jayson Williams	Involuntary manslaughter	NBA

Adapted from K. Russell-Brown, "Black Protectionism as a Civil Rights Strategy." *Buffalo Law Review* 53, no. 1 (2005): 1–64, pp. 23–26, and K. Russell-Brown, *Underground Codes: Race, Crime, and Related Fires* (New York: New York University Press, 2004), p. 80.

Table 3 Whether Black Protectionism Applies: Select Cases

Yes	No
Marion Barry	Rae Carruth
[Bill Clinton]	Joycelyn Elders
Jesse Jackson	Lani Guinier
R. Kelly	Alexis Herman
Melvin Reynolds	Chris Webber
O. J. Simpson	Jayson Williams
Clarence Thomas	
Mike Tyson	

Adapted from K. Russell-Brown, *Underground Codes: Race, Crime, and Related Fires* (New York: New York University Press, 2004), p. 81.

Historically, the origins of Black protectionism can be traced to the slavery period in the United States. In order to survive during this time, Blacks living on slave plantations often relied on one another for safety and protection from potentially abusive slave owners. Relatively minor infractions could mean harsh penalties, during which violators could be verbally reprimanded or more seriously, whipped, tortured, or executed by their masters. In some cases, a decision might be made to sell the slave, which would in turn have devastating effects on the slave group, or family. As Russell-Brown notes, the legacy of the slavery era helped lay the foundation for Black protectionism:

> Denial of wrongdoing [by slaves] became a form of group protection against an irrational, racist system of formal and informal laws. A slave's acknowledgement to someone White that another slave had done something unlawful (e.g. learning to read) could forever seal the other slave's fate. The brutality of slavery created a strong bond between Blacks. Any slave who broke racial ranks and informed the slave master was viewed as selling out the race. (1998: 59)

Some Blacks know this history well and recognize the connection between how they are currently perceived and their previous treatment by White society. This recognition comes through stories handed down across the generations as well as through media representations and life experiences. As such, Black protectionism is essentially a reactive defense strategy exhibited by historically marginalized groups in society, which can easily extend to other ethnicities.

There are a few limitations and disadvantages to Black protectionism. Mainly, even in cases where there is compelling evidence of wrongdoing, Black protectionism still operates and fails to distinguish truthful from false accusations. Similarly, no sanction is given if the allegations are true, as many would argue that the negative attention and public shaming serves as sanction enough in and of themselves. Secondly, a type of apolitical Black protectionism may occur when afforded to an individual who is seen as a leader in the African American community, even when the person has previously behaved or made decisions (while in a position of power) in a manner that impedes Black progress (e.g., a judge failing to uphold civil rights laws). Thirdly, Black protectionism may provide a biased picture of the case in question and leave no room for opposing views, even from the Black community itself, and therefore may become regarded as the thinking for the entire group. Fourthly, Black protectionism operates with a type of blind loyalty, for example by giving cover to those, usually of another race, who are well liked and respected by Blacks, though their true interests lie elsewhere. Finally, although only a few reputable Black women have been accused of wrongdoing over the years, rarely do they actually receive this cover, which may be indicative of a Black protectionism gender bias.

While centuries old, Black protectionism serves many functions today, mainly by providing an oppressed and marginalized group of people with a more positive way to view themselves and a way to debunk stereotypes of Black deviance and criminality. Black protectionism can help foster group solidarity within the Black community by providing common ground to create a unified force for a politically, legally, economically, and socially diverse group of people. In turn, this device helps to send a strong message to mainstream society; works to keep race relations in a certain kind of balance; and acts as a type of barometer on where the Black and White community stands on race and racism. As a grim reminder of the dark side of American history—slavery, lynching, Black codes, segregation—and of contemporary examples of continuing racial discrimination, police brutality, and racial profiling, Black protectionism serves a variety of sociopolitical functions and a reality check of sorts on whether race relations and the lives of Blacks today have improved as substantially as some would like to believe. This protective behavior helps society to analyze the circumstances of the accused more carefully, and begs the question of whether the "moral lapse" outweighs the positive contributions the person has made to society. In turn, this helps to distinguish between public and private life, and offers a means of "resurrecting" fallen members who, while factually guilty in the instant moment, should not have their positive contributions to African American life ignored or dismissed.

Michael Puniskis

See also: Adams, The Honorable Eric L.; Barry, Jr., Marion S.; Jefferson, The Honorable William Jennings; Simpson, Orenthal James "O. J."

References

Edmonson v. Leesville Concrete Company, 500 U.S. 614 (1991).

Georgia v. McCollum, 505 U.S. 42 (1992).

Georgia v. McCollum, 505 U.S. 42 (1992) (Thomas, Clarence, J.J., concurring).

Holzer, Henry. *The Supreme Court Opinions of Clarence Thomas, 1991–2006.* Jefferson, NC: McFarland & Company, 2007.

Hudson v. McMillian, 503 U.S. 1 (1991).

Hudson v. McMillian, 503 U.S. 1 (1991) (Thomas, Clarence, J.J., dissenting).

Russell, K. K. *The Color of Crime: Racial Hoaxes, White Fear, Black Protectionism, Police Harassment, and Other Macroaggressions.* New York: New York University Press, 1998.

Russell-Brown, K. "Black Protectionism as a Civil Rights Strategy." *Buffalo Law Review* 53, no. 1 (2005): 1–64.

Russell-Brown, K. *Underground Codes: Race, Crime, and Related Fires.* New York: New York University Press, 2004.

Brown, H. Rap (aka Jamil Abdullah Al-Amin) (1943–)

Hubert Gerold Brown, aka Jamil Abdullah Al-Amin, was born on October 4, 1943, in Baton Rouge, Louisiana, less than 15 minutes from Louisiana State University. He and his older brother and sister were born into a low-income family. Their father served in World War II and worked as a laborer for the Standard Oil Company for 30 years.

Brown was popularly known as H. Rap Brown because he could defend himself with words, signifying and "playing the dozens." Signifying refers to a way of expressing one's feelings very similar to open microphone poetry or rap music. "Playing the dozens" is a verbal competition of boasting and exchanging insults. Having a way with words and having a fast mouth got Brown into a great deal of trouble with his teachers, the police, and others in authority. Brown was also a very gifted athlete. Standing six feet five inches tall, he played quarterback on the football team and point guard in basketball. It would be safe to say that all of the aforementioned made him a target in and out of school. Although he was drawn into "street corner" activity, under his mother's tutelage, he managed to transfer from a poor high school (McKinley) to Southern High, which was connected to the historically Black Southern University in Baton Rouge. According to Brown, "[T]his is where all of the bourgeois Negroes were supposed to go" (Brown, 1969: 22). He went on:

> But I stayed in school, 'cause I wasn't willing to get caught in another trick that eventually led to long sentences in jail or ending up in the gutter one night with a knife in your back. A lot of bloods, though, couldn't cut school. When they came, it was to practice the education they'd been getting out in the street. (Brown, 1969: 23)

After he graduated from Southern High School in June 1960, Brown entered Southern University. He was 15 years old, and stayed in constant conflict with the administration, including the president, dean, and other administrators, as well as professors. By 1965, he was living in Washington, D.C., serving as the chairperson of the Nonviolent Action Group (NAG). This was during the same time when Dr. Martin Luther King, Jr., was leading the Selma, Alabama, march when people were beaten by police on the Edmund Pettis Bridge. In May 1967, Brown succeeded Kwame Toure (formerly known as Stokely Carmichael) as the leader of the Student Nonviolent Coordinating Committee (SNCC), a civil rights and anti–Vietnam War student organization that had emerged seven years earlier under the leadership of Dr. Martin Luther King, Jr., when King was the leader of the Southern Christian Leadership Conference (SCLC). (Current congressman John Lewis was the leader of SNCC before Kwame Toure, and attorney Victor Goode, a graduate of Howard University Law School, was the leader after Brown.)

H. Rap Brown, chairman of the Student Nonviolent Coordinating Committee, at a news conference, ca. 1967. (Library of Congress)

Brown and Stokely Carmichael (Kwame Toure) together were key activists in the Alabama Freedom Organization, which sported a black panther on its flag. The two men, unimpressed by the nonviolent and integrationist politics linked most often to Dr. Martin Luther King, Jr.'s, movement, rallied instead to support "Black Power," making statements such as, "Violence is as American as apple pie." In 1967, a *Newsweek* article described Brown as a man who supported an "eye for an eye violence as a form of self-defense for Negroes and packs a 12-gauge 'cracker gun' in his own dusty Plymouth" (*Newsweek*, February 12, 1973, as cited in Rashad, 1995: 214). Consequently, during the 1960s and 1970s Brown would become involved with several violent confrontations with the police.

In July 1967, Brown was arrested for inciting a riot at a civil rights rally in Cambridge, Maryland. During the riot Brown was quoted as saying, "Black folks built America, and if America don't come around, we're going to burn America down." The Blank Panther Party of California named Brown their minister of justice. In his 1969 book *Die Nigger Die!*, Brown claimed that White people wanted all Blacks dead. In an effort to evade the charges stemming from the Cambridge, Maryland, incident, he jumped bail in 1967 and disappeared for two years. This resulted in his name being placed on the FBI's "Top Ten Most Wanted List."

Eventually, Brown was apprehended and convicted for a 1971 shootout with police in New York City and was sent to prison for five years. He retained the radical/activist New York attorney William Kunstler, who had previously represented Stokely Carmichael and Communist history/philosophy professor Dr. Angela Davis of the University of California–San Diego. While serving his sentence, Brown converted to Islam and changed his name to "Al-Amin," which means "the trustworthy" in Arabic.

Paroled in 1976, Brown (Al-Amin) became an imam (pastor/cleric) of the Atlanta, Georgia, Community Mosque, and in 1983, he established the Imam Jamil Al-Amin's National Community, a coalition of 30 mosques that fell under his guidance (DiscoverTheNetworks.org). In 1990, he was elected vice president of the American Muslim Council and member of the Bosnia Task Force (which supported Muslims affected by the Bosnian War). He also helped to organize the Islamic Shura Council of North America, along with Imam Wallace Deen Muhammad (the son of deceased leader Honorable Elijah Muhammad of the Nation of Islam). Brown (Al-Amin) was involved in countless other Muslim activities.

Brown (Al-Amin) continued to have troubles with the law. On May 31, 1999, he was charged with possessing a stolen car, driving without insurance, and impersonating a police officer in Cobb County, Georgia. On March 16, 2000, during the Muslim holiday Eid ul-Adha, when two Atlanta, Georgia, sheriff's deputies tried to serve a bench warrant on him at his grocery store shortly before 10:00 p.m., they were shot. Deputy Rickey Kinchen was killed and his partner, Aldranon English, was wounded. Deputy English later identified Brown (Al-Amin) as the shooter. On March 20, 2000, after a five-day police manhunt, Brown (Al-Amin) was captured and arrested in a wooded area near the small town of White Hall, Alabama. Though questions were raised about the true intent of the reportedly heavily armed law enforcement officers and the identification of Brown (Al-Amin) as the shooter, after considerable legal battles over extradition and jurisdiction, on March 9, 2002, he was tried and found guilty of Deputy Kinchen's murder and sentenced to life imprisonment without parole. He is serving his sentence in a super-maximum-security prison in Florence, Colorado (Hart, 2004; Sanusi, 2009).

Ekwueme Michael Thelwell, a former SNCC field secretary and a professor in the W. E. B. Du Bois Department of Afro-American Studies at the University of Massachusetts–Amherst, notes in the foreword to the 2002 reprint of *Die Nigger Die*:

> Imam Al-Amin has been incarcerated since March 2000 under conditions that seem unnecessarily draconian. In solitary confinement, he was for a time deprived of his Holy Koran, and he has never been permitted to participate in weekly Jumu'ah services with other members of his faith. (xxxvi–xxxvii)

Former members of the civil rights organization SNCC and many friends and associates have questioned the circumstances related to Brown (Al-Amin)'s final arrest and have rallied for his release. The hopes of Thelwell and other supporters were dashed when on May 21, 2004, in a unanimous decision, the Georgia Supreme Court upheld the 2002 conviction of the 68-year-old (Hart, 2004). Subsequent to his trial and conviction, the Muslim community in the United States and other people around the world have been crying out for his vindication and release. They believe that his militant activist history and not his behavior resulted in his arrest and conviction.

Robert C. Butler

See also: Carmichael, Stokely; Davis, Angela Yvonne; Nation of Islam; Southern Christian Leadership Conference (SCLC); Student Nonviolent Coordinating Committee (SNCC)

References

Brown, H. Rap. *Die Nigger Die!* New York: Dial Press, 1969.

DiscoverTheNetworks.Org: A Guide to the Political Left. "Jamil Abdullah Al-Amin (aka H. Rap Brown)." © 2003–2012. http://www.discoverthenetworks.org/individualProfile.asp?indid=1308.

Hart, Ariel. "Court in Georgia Upholds Former Militant's Conviction." *The New York Times,* May 25, 2004, A16. http://ez.lib.jjay.cuny.edu/docview/92805184?accountid=11724

Rashad, A. *Islam, Black Nationalism and Slavery: A Detailed History.* Beltsville, MD: Writers Inc. International, 1995.

Sanusi, Daa'iya L. "Protest for Jamil Al-Amin, a.k.a. H. Rap Brown." *The New York Amsterdam News,* March 26, 2009.

Thelwell, E. M. Foreword to *Die, Nigger, Die!* by H. Rap Brown, vii–xxxviii. Brooklyn, NY: Lawrence Hill Books, 2002.

Brown, James Joseph (1933–2006)

James Brown was one of the most prolific and influential African American rhythm and blues singers, dancers, and songwriters of the twentieth century. Brown was born on May 3, 1933, in Barnwell, South Carolina, to Joe Gardner and Susan Brown. He died on December 25, 2006, in Atlanta, Georgia, at the age of 73.

Brown experienced numerous hardships during his childhood. When he was about four years old, his parents divorced. About two years after the divorce, his father moved him to Augusta, Georgia, to live with his aunt, Minnie Walker, who managed a brothel. This environment exposed young James Brown to situations beyond his age. Poverty, segregation, and the Great Depression compounded his problems. For example, Brown was sent home from grade school because his clothing was inappropriate for a school setting. Brown also spent a great deal of time on the streets hustling to make ends meet. His efforts to make extra money included tap dancing in the streets, selling and buying stamps, sweeping floors in stores, delivering groceries, and playing a harmonica, which was given to him by his father. At the age of eight, he learned to play an organ and progressed to other instruments (e.g., piano, guitar, trumpet, saxophone, drums). At the age of 11, Brown won his first talent show for singing.

Brown not only hustled in the streets, he also engaged in petty crime in the Augusta area, such as shoplifting and stealing car batteries and hubcaps. In 1949, at the age of 16, he was convicted of a second auto theft offense and was sentenced to 8 to 16 years in the juvenile detention center in Georgia, thus dropping out of school in the seventh grade. While at the detention center, he met Bobby Byrd during a baseball game. Bobby Byrd had a gospel group called the Gospel Starlighters. After a while, the group started singing rhythm and blues instead. It later changed its name to the Avons. Byrd had observed Brown singing and dancing while he was in reform school and was very pleased with his performance. The relationship Brown had with Bobby Byrd, coupled with his good behavior, led to his early release; after serving less than 4 years of a potential 16-year sentence, Brown was released under the condition that he would not return to Augusta or Richmond County, Georgia. Upon his release, Brown joined the Avon musical group.

Brown became a pivotal figure in the music industry. His contribution to the music industry and the pride and emancipation of African Americans is unparalleled. In the early 1950s, Brown had joined the Avons; the group became known as the Flames and later as James Brown and the Famous Flames. The group's energetic performances made it popular throughout the South. The group signed a contract with a Cincinnati, Ohio–based record label, Federal Records. With a mixture of gospel, R&B, and soul, and collaboration with other musical superstars of the time such as Ray Charles and Little Richard, the group's first release, "Please, Please, Please," sold over a million copies in 1956. Other top hits included "Try Me," which was the bestselling R&B single in 1958. In 1959, Brown and the Famous Flames changed to a more prestigious label, King Records. However, over time Brown and Syd Nathan, who was the president of King Records, became estranged. As a result of the estrangement, in 1962 Nathan refused to finance a live recording of Brown at the Apollo Theater in New York. This forced Brown to start exploring other ways to promote his music. With no promoter available, Brown financed the show himself. He was assured that a recorded version of his show would be financially rewarding. In 1963, *Live at the Apollo,* the recording of his show, skyrocketed to number two on the Billboard LP chart, a success that was unprecedented for African American musicians at the time. Spurred by this success, Brown and Bobby Byrd formed Fair Deal, their own production company, to promote Brown's music to White audiences. In the early 1960s, Smash Records, a subsidiary of Mercury Records, was used as an avenue to distribute Brown's music. In 1964, Brown released a popular hit through Smash entitled "Out of Sight," which climbed to number 24 on the pop charts. This record exposed Brown's music not only to African American audiences but also to the White community. Brown's popularity as a "funk" music artist soared.

Brown was a powerful voice during the Civil Rights Movement and the struggle for the legal desegregation of America. His voice was also a soothing balm during the difficult times following the assassinations of John F. Kennedy and Martin Luther King, Jr., prominent advocates of civil rights. Brown's contribution to African Americans is immeasurable and goes beyond music. Through his music, he fostered self-worth and pride among African Americans. Brown was an American musical and cultural icon. He produced a string of hits such as "Papa's Got a Brand New Bag," "I Got You (I Feel Good)," "It's a Man's World," and "Say It Loud—I'm Black and I'm Proud," Cold Sweat," and "I Got the Feelin'." His music brought racial pride and African consciousness to the African American community. For example, in one of Brown's songs, "Cold Sweat," rather than singing the chords, he spoke the lyrics, thereby re-Africanizing his music. Brown's Black consciousness, social and political enlightenment, and emancipation were further demonstrated through such lyrics in "Say It Loud—I'm Black and I'm

Proud." He has been credited with preventing a riot in Boston, Massachusetts, with his performance on April 5, 1968, following the assassination of Dr. Martin Luther King, Jr. In 1972, Brown supported Richard Nixon, whose presidential platform was supportive of "black capitalism," a movement among African Americans aimed at building wealth through ownership and development of businesses.

However, in the late 1970s, Brown's career began to wane. The emergence of hip-hop music is viewed as a significant contributor to the decline of his musical influence. He also had to contend with other problems, such as unpaid taxes and drug addiction. On December 15, 1988, James Brown became inmate number 155413 at the State Park Correctional Institute in State Park, South Carolina. The six-year, six-month sentence that he began serving stemmed from a September 24 incident where he possessed a firearm and fled from the police. He was charged with multiple offenses, including assault and battery with the intent to kill. Brown was already on probation for drug charges at the time of the events that led to his imprisonment. He was released after serving three years. A subsequent arrest in 1998 resulted in a 90-day sentence to a drug treatment program.

Despite his troubles with the law, Brown was a world-renowned musical prodigy. Many still fondly refer to him as "Soul Brother Number One," "The Godfather of Soul," "The Hardest-Working Man in Show Business," "The King of Soul," or "The King of Funk." Brown was an exceptionally talented and self-motivated figure in the music industry. He was unique in his vocals and his intense and energetic choreography. Prior to Brown coming onto the music scene, traditional pop dominated rhythm and blues, but Brown changed all that by combining blues and gospel elements, giving soul a new identity. Rhythm and blues became soul and funk. Brown influenced and inspired a host of other popular superstars, such as Prince and Michael Jackson. Brown is also credited with being the musical artist who produced and charted the most singles on the Billboard Hot 100. His contribution to African American pride and emancipation is immeasurable.

Rochelle Cobbs and O. Oko Elechi

See also: Civil Rights Movement

References

Brown, J., and B. Tucker. *James Brown: The Godfather of Soul.* New York: Thunder's Mouth Press, 1997.

Gates, H. L., Jr., and E. B. Higginbotham. *African American Lives.* New York: Oxford University Press, 2004.

Guralnick, P. *Sweet Soul Music: Rhythm and Blues and the Southern Dream of Freedom.* New York: Back Bay Books, 1986.

Rose, C. *Living in America: The Soul Saga of James Brown.* New York: Serpent's Tail, 1990.

White, C. *The Life and Times of Little Richard: The Authorized Biography.* London: Omnibus Press, 2003.

Bumpurs, Eleanor (1918–1984)

Eleanor Bumpurs was a mentally ill 66-year-old African American woman who died after being shot on October 29, 1984, in her New York City (NYC) Housing Authority apartment at 1551 University Avenue in the Bronx. She was shot by a White police officer, Stephen Sullivan, a member of the New York Police Department (NYPD) Emergency Services Unit (ESU). The confrontation that resulted in the death of Mrs. Bumpurs was controversial and racially divisive.

Mrs. Bumpurs was being evicted from her apartment for nonpayment of rent. Prior to the eviction, a psychiatrist interviewed Mrs. Bumpurs in her apartment. He concluded that she was psychotic and not capable of properly handling activities of daily living, and that she should be hospitalized. He also reported that she held a knife during the interview. Subsequently, a supervisor from the NYC Human Resources Administration decided that the best way to obtain help for Mrs. Bumpurs was to have her evicted from the apartment and then hospitalized.

Officer Sullivan and several other ESU officers had gone to the apartment at the request of the NYC Housing Authority because Mrs. Bumpurs refused to allow them to enter the apartment and because Mrs. Bumpurs reportedly had a history of mental illness and irrational behavior. For several years prior to this incident, the NYPD had regularly dispatched officers from the ESU to assist local patrol officers when it appeared potentially necessary to subdue or arrest an armed person believed to be emotionally disturbed.

After a period of time during which the ESU officers unsuccessfully attempted to persuade Mrs. Bumpurs to allow them to enter the apartment, they forced entry; they were met by Mrs. Bumpurs, armed with a knife. The officers, who had arrived equipped with riot-type gear, including a protective shield, attempted to convince Mrs. Bumpurs to surrender the knife. A confrontation followed that resulted in one officer slipping and falling and with Mrs. Bumpurs advancing. According to his statements, Officer Sullivan, observing that his fellow officer's life was in danger, fired a single shot from a 12-gauge shotgun. One source notes that the first shot severed the hand in which Mrs. Bumpurs had been holding the knife. But according to his statements, Officer Sullivan, believing that the first shot had not stopped Mrs. Bumpurs, fired a second shot, which proved fatal.

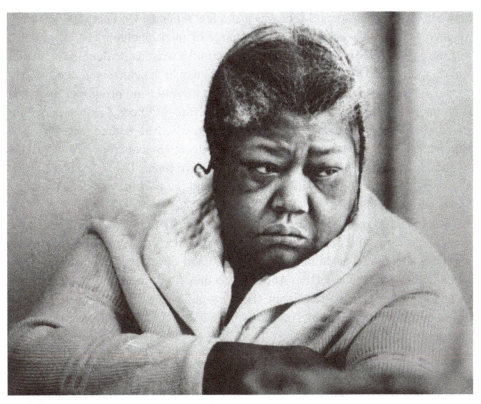

Sixty-six-year-old Eleanor Bumpurs was shot and killed by NYPD Officer Stephen Sullivan during an eviction attempt in 1984. (Associated Press)

As with all fatal shootings by police, the Bronx County district attorney conducted an investigation and presented evidence to a grand jury. On January 30, 1985, the grand jury indicted Police Officer Sullivan on the charge of second-degree manslaughter. Ten thousand police officers staged a protest against the Bronx district attorney for presenting the case to the grand jury. Sullivan pleaded not guilty and was suspended by the NYPD. On April 12, 1985, the indictment was dismissed in State Supreme Court, Bronx County. The district attorney appealed the Supreme Court ruling and on November 25, 1986, the New York Court of Appeals reinstated Sullivan's second-degree manslaughter indictment. Sullivan was once again removed from active police duty pending further legal action.

Officer Sullivan waived his constitutional right to a trial by a jury of his peers and opted for a bench (nonjury) trial before a judge. On January 12, 1987, the trial started. Central to the prosecutor's case was proving that Sullivan had used excessive force in firing the second shot. The defense contended that the first shot did not stop Mrs. Bumpurs from advancing with the knife and that the time between the first and second shot was just a few seconds. On February 26, 1987, Stephen Sullivan was acquitted of the charge of manslaughter. The judge ruled that the prosecutor did not prove the case beyond a reasonable doubt. The matter was then reviewed by the U.S. Attorney's Office, which determined that the proceedings had been fair and competent and that there was no proof that there had been intent to inflict excessive and unjustified force. Officer Sullivan was reinstated to full duty and later promoted to detective; he retired in 1990. The Bumpurs shooting continues to be a source of disagreement among New Yorkers in discussions about police brutality and excessive force. The assessment of the appropriateness of Officer Sullivan's actions and the trial judge's decision often varies across racial lines.

Less than 30 days after the shooting, the NYPD publicized changes in the way the police would deal with emotionally disturbed persons (EDPs). The department announced an initiative to research and develop additional less-than-lethal means to subdue EDPs. And for the first time, members of the department's Hostage Negotiation Team (HNT) would be dispatched to the scene. Starting in 1973, the HNT had primarily been dispatched to confirmed reports of hostages being held.

The NYC Human Resources Administration (HRA) determined that two supervisors in the city's Social Services Department were slow in arranging psychiatric aid and rent assistance for Mrs. Bumpurs, which may have contributed to the volatility of the situation that the police encountered at her apartment. The HRA supervisors were demoted.

In 1985, the New York State Division of Criminal Justice Services prepared a report for the governor on use of deadly force by the police. This report served as the basis for revised training as well as for the initiation of a new program for police throughout New York in dealing with mentally ill persons. Currently all police recruits in NYC receive a minimum of 14 hours of this training. And a collaborative program between the NYPD and John Jay College of Criminal Justice provides a 40-hour training program, Emergency Psychological Technician, which is given to all new ESU and HNT officers. Variations on this program have been presented to corrections personnel, transit officers, and police officers assigned to the Long Island Railroad (LIR). The training for LIR officers was instituted following a 1993 incident when an emotionally disturbed rider of Caribbean descent, Colin Ferguson, shot several commuters on a LIR train. In 1990, the Bumpurs family accepted a $200,000 settlement in response to the $10 million civil suit that they had initiated against NYC.

Robert Louden

See also: Ferguson, Colin; Police Brutality

References

Barbanel, Josh. "Officer Plans to Ask for Nonjury Trial in Bumpurs Killing." *The New York Times,* February 11, 1985.

Condom, Richard J. *Police Use of Deadly Force in New York State: A Report to Governor Mario M. Cuomo.* Albany, NY: Division of Criminal Justice Services, 1985.

O'Donnell, Eugene. "Cops and the Mentally Ill: How Police Can Better Handle Emotionally Disturbed Citizens." *Newsweek,* July 31, 2008.

Panzarella, Robert, and Justin O. Alicea. "Police Tactics in Incidents with Mentally Disturbed Persons." *Policing: An International Journal of Police Strategies and Management* 20, no. 2 (1997): 326–38.

United States Department of Justice, Community Relations Service. *Principles of Good Policing: Avoiding Violence between Police and Citizens.* Washington, DC: Government Printing Office, 1993.

Williams, Patricia. *Alchemy of Race and Rights: Diary of a Law Professor.* Cambridge, MA: Harvard University Press, 1991.

Williams, Patricia. "The Bumpurs Case Endures." *The New York Times,* February 27, 1987.

Williams, Patricia. "Officer Sullivan's Second Shot." *The New York Times,* November 27, 1986.

Williams, Patricia. "Officer Upheld in Shooting." *The New York Times,* April 2, 1986.

Byrd, Jr., James (1949–1998)

It has been over 10 years since the dragging death of James Byrd, Jr. The dragging death of an African American man by three White men caused many to reflect on the racism that still exists in modern America. Before Byrd's death, instances such as this were viewed as a thing of the distant past. However, the 1999 murder suggests that racism is, indeed, a reality. On June 7, 1998, 49-year-old James Byrd, Jr., was walking down a road in Jasper, Texas, when he was approached by a truck carrying three White men. Byrd was on his way home after attending a gathering. The three men offered Byrd a ride; then, at some point, they pulled over to the side of an east Jasper rural road. Witness testimony suggests that Lawrence Brewer was the driver of the truck that picked up Byrd. It is unclear what led to a fight between Byrd and at least one of the three White men, but Byrd was beaten, and by most accounts stabbed, by at least one of them. Byrd was then chained by the ankles to the truck and dragged for approximately three miles down the rural road. Expert medical testimony suggests that Byrd was alive for some time during the dragging and was probably conscious until the truck hit a drain (*King v. State*). Byrd's head was severed from his body by the impact. An investigation determined that other body parts lay along the three-mile drag site (Sherr, 2009; King, 2002).

The three White men responsible for the dragging were John William King, Lawrence Russell Brewer, and Shawn Allen Berry. The men, apparently friends, were strangers to Byrd. The dragging death is considered one of the most heinous race crimes in recent American history (Graczyk, 2011). King, an ex-convict, has been tied to at least one racist group (the Confederate Knights of America), and court testimony suggested that his body was covered with numerous racists tattoos—a Black man hanging from a tree, Nazi symbols, and the words "Aryan pride" (Ainslie, 2004). Brewer has also been determined to have ties with racist groups, in particular the Confederate Knights of America, a prison gang that he and King are reported to have joined together for protection from other inmates (Brookfield, 1999). There is no clear evidence that Berry was affiliated with hate groups. It appears that he was just out for the night with King and Brewer. At trial, Brewer testified that he was innocent of the charges in James Byrd's death and that his participation was limited to sitting inside the pickup truck and looking out of the window as Berry sliced James Byrd's throat (Miller, 2011). However, investigating authorities determined that Brewer's testimony concerning his nonparticipation in James Byrd's murder was not consistent with forensic evidence (Miller, 2011). Berry was found to be the least active in the dragging death of Byrd. In November 1999, Berry was sentenced to life in prison and must serve at least 40 years before he has a chance of parole. He is currently housed in the Ramsey Unit in Brazonia County, Texas, and is eligible for parole in 2038 (England, 2011). In February and September 1999, both King and Brewer were sentenced to death for their roles in the killing (Lyman, 1999). King remains on death row at the Allan B. Polunsky Unit in Polk County, Texas. Brewer was executed by lethal injection on September 21, 2011.

The immediate response following the dragging death of Byrd was one of disbelief that something so reprehensible could occur in late-twentieth-century America (Petersen, 2011). In June 1998, soon after the death, members of both the New Black Panther Party (NBPP) and the Ku Klux Klan arrived in Jasper, Texas, to protest and demonstrate. Dr. Khalid Abdul Muhammad, leader of the NBPP and former national spokesman for the Nation of Islam, led a group of 50 NBPP members to Jasper, Texas—including a dozen carrying shotguns and rifles—to "protect" the streets in the wake of the Byrd murder (Taharka, 2001). In the small town two weeks later, Muhammad and his followers, many wearing black berets like the original Black Panthers, showed up to counter-demonstrate in protest against a rally organized by Klansmen. When members of the NBPP tried and failed to get past police separating them from the Klan, several minor scuffles between supporters on both sides broke out, resulting in two arrests (Anti-Defamation League).

There has been both a social and political response to the senseless death. In 1998, the James Byrd Foundation for Racial Healing was created to focus on healing racial tension. In 1999, the James Byrd Jr. Act was approved by the Texas House Committee but died when then Governor George W. Bush did not support the bill, which cited race, religion, color, sex, disability, sexual orientation, age, and national origin as the statute's protected classes. Reportedly, Bush did not support the bill because of its inclusion of lesbians and gays among the protected groups. Bush was also accused of displaying racism indirectly by not attending James Byrd's funeral and maintaining that the outcome of the trial demonstrated that there was no need for tougher hate crime legislation (Tapper, 2000). The James Byrd Hate Crimes Act was subsequently signed into law in May 2001 by Texas governor Rick Perry. In October 2010, Byrd's mother, Stella Byrd, passed away. A matriarch of the family, Stella Byrd played a key role in getting the hate crime legislation passed and signed into law.

Congress has enacted the Matthew Shepard and James Byrd, Jr. Hate Crimes Prevention Act S. 909 to combat the prevalence of hate crime victimization in America (Matthew Shepard Hate Crimes Prevention Act of 2009 [S. 909]). The brutal deaths of Matthew Shepard in Wyoming and James Byrd, Jr., in Texas impacted the nation and brought to the forefront the realities of bias crimes. Since 1991, FBI statistics report an increase in hate crimes against minorities; immigrant groups; and the lesbian, gay, bisexual, and transgender community (LGBT). In recent years religious fervor, racial disparities, anti-Semitism, and stringent immigration policies have also helped increase the prevalence of hate crimes in America (Sherr, 2009). The Matthew Shepard and James Byrd, Jr. Hate Crimes Prevention Act was enacted to amend previous legislation. It is reported to be an expansion of the 1969 U.S. federal hate crime law that encompasses crimes that are committed because of a victim's gender or appearance, sexual orientation, gender identity, or disability.

The act extends protection from hate crimes committed based on race, color, religion, or national origin, ethnicity, gender, gender identity, sexual orientation, or disability. The act also provides for coordinated collaborative efforts between the federal, state, and local law enforcement agencies when addressing and investigating such crimes. It provides funding to enhance the resources of state and local law enforcement to prevent and prosecute hate crimes. In addition, the act amends the Hate Crimes Statistics Act to expand data collection regarding crimes manifesting prejudice based on gender and gender identity and crimes committed by and against juveniles. This law does not limit an individual's First Amendment right of free speech with regard to hate speech propaganda.

The town of Jasper, Texas, was known to be racially divided before the dragging death of James Byrd, Jr. (Temple-Raston, 2002; King, 2002). For example, there was an iron fence separating African American graves from those of Whites. Since the incident, the fence has come down. The James Byrd Jr. Memorial Park was constructed in 1999 to help ease racial tensions and erase the racial divide between African Americans and Whites in Jasper. Although there have been signs of change within the city, Byrd's grave has been desecrated at least twice. Nevertheless, many are hopeful that racial tension is on the decline.

Traqina Q. Emeka

See also: Death Penalty; Hate Crimes; Inter-Racial Offending; Lynching; Prisons

References

Ainslie, Ricardo. *Long Dark Road: Bill King and Murder in Jasper, Texas.* Austin: University of Texas Press, 2004.

Anti-Defamation League. "New Black Panther Party for Self Defense: Early Expansion." http://www.adl.org/main_Extremism/new_black_panther_party.htm?Multi_page_sections=sHeading_7.

Brookfield, James. "Trial Opens in Racist Dragging Death in Jasper, Texas." International Committee of the Fourth International, World Socialist Web site, February 18, 1999.

England, Kenzy. "Three Men Arrested for Hill County, Texas Dragging Death: Dragging Deaths Are Nothing New in Texas." Yahoo News, February 14, 2011. http://news.yahoo.com/three-men-arrested-hill-county-texas-dragging-death-20110214-145900-291.html.

Graczyk, Michael. "Lawrence Brewer Executed: White Supremacist Executed for Texas Dragging Murder." *The Huffington Post,* September 21, 2011.

John William King v. The State of Texas. 29 S.W.3d 556. Court of Criminal Appeals of Texas. 2000.

King, Joyce. *Hate Crime: The Story of a Dragging in Jasper, Texas.* New York: Pantheon, 2002.

Lyman, Rick. "Man Guilty of Murder in Texas Dragging Death." *The New York Times,* February 24, 1999.

Matthew Shepard Hate Crimes Prevention Act of 2009 (S. 909). Thomas Library of Congress. http://thomas.loc.gov/cgi-bin/bdquery/D?d111:2:./temp/~bdScgj::l/home/LegislativeData.php?n=BSS;c=111l.

Miller, Doug. "James Byrd's Killer: 'I'd Do It All Over Again.'" KHOU 11 News, September 21, 2011. http://www.khou.com/news/The-Texas-murder-that-shook-America--130176288.html.

Petersen, Jennifer. *Murder, the Media, and the Politics of Public Feelings: Remembering Matthew Shepard and James Byrd Jr.* Bloomington: Indiana University Press, 2011.

Sherr, Mitchell. "Hate Crimes Based on Ethnicity and Religion: A Description of the Phenomenon in the United States since 2000." *The International Journal of Diversity in Organizations, Communities, and Nations* 9, no. 4 (2009): 23–37.

Taharka, Kofi. "A Black Power Salute to Dr. Khallid Abdul Muhammad." February, 17, 2001. http://www.ag-east.org/archives/AA25.htm.

Tapper, Jake. (2000). "Bush Angers Slain Man's Family." *Salon.com,* October 16, 2000. http://www.salon.com/2000.10.16/byrds/.

Temple-Raston, Dina. *A Death in Texas: A Story of Race, Murder, and a Small Town's Struggle for Redemption.* New York: Henry Holt and Company, 2002.

C

Carmichael, Stokely (1941–1998)

Stokely Standiford Churchill Carmichael, also known as Kwame Toure, was born in the Port of Spain, Trinidad, on June 29, 1941. He died at the age of 57 on November 15, 1998, in Conakry, Guinea. A Trinidadian American, he was a major Black activist, extremely active and influential in the United States in the 1960s. During this time he became an important proponent of the U.S. Civil Rights Movement.

Stokely Carmichael first rose to prominence as a leader of the Student Nonviolent Coordinating Committee (SNCC), a group that originated in student meetings at Shaw University in Raleigh, North Carolina, in April 1960. He later became the honorary prime minister of the Black Panther Party. Historically, one would argue that his initial philosophy was that of an integrationist, but due to his experiences in the civil rights struggle, he would later become affiliated with Black Nationalist and Pan-Africanist beliefs and movements.

Black Power: Struggles in the American Civil Rights Movement

In the early 1960s, Stokely Carmichael became very disillusioned with the National Democratic Party when the party refused to seat a member of the newly organized multiracial Mississippi Freedom Democratic Party (MFDP) delegation (a group he had helped organize). He and others wanted the MFDP to be represented instead of the standing official all-White, pro-segregation Mississippi Democratic Party during the 1964 National Convention in Atlantic City, New Jersey. During this time, Carmichael began to seek alternative means for the political empowerment of African Americans. He would eventually become heavily influenced by the ideologies of Malcolm X and Kwame Nkrumah.

In 1966, Carmichael became chairman of the Student Nonviolent Coordinating Committee (SNCC) and gave his very first "Black Power" speech. He used this phrase as a salute to the Black Panther Movement, but more so to urge Black pride and socioeconomic independence. While this term was not a new concept, this speech placed it in a spotlight that allowed it to become the rallying cry for many young African Americans across the United States. During the rest of the 1960s, he gradually became more radical and focused more and more on Black Power as his core goal and ideology. Also, during this time, many of Carmichael's actions would become controversial, in that he urged that all Whites should be expelled from all Black activist groups. He felt that this should be done to encourage Whites to begin organizing poor White Southern communities while Black groups should focus on promoting African American self-reliance through Black Power.

In contrast to Dr. Martin Luther King, Jr., Carmichael saw nonviolence as a tactic as opposed to a principle. He became very critical of civil rights leaders whom he saw as simply calling for the integration of African Americans into existing institutions of the White middle-class mainstream. Like Malcolm X, Carmichael believed that in order to genuinely integrate, Blacks first had to unite in solidarity and become self-reliant.

Travels and Name Change

Stokely Carmichael did a great deal of traveling nationally and internationally over the course of his life. In 1969, he traveled to Conakry, Guinea, where he became an aide to Guinean prime minister Ahmed Sékou Touré and the student of exiled Ghanaian president Kwame Nkrumah. During this time, he would change his name to Kwame Toure to honor the African leaders Nkrumah and Touré who had become his patrons. Throughout the rest of his life, close friends would refer to him interchangeably by both names.

Carmichael would eventually separate from the Black Panther Party and remain in Guinea. He would continue to travel, write, and speak out in support of international leftist movements. During these years he would write two books, *Black Power: The Politics of Liberation,* and *Stokely Speaks: From Black Power to Pan-Africanism.* These books contain a very strong socialist Pan-African vision. This was a vision that he would maintain until his death.

End of Life, Beginning of Legacy

In the mid 1990s, Stokely Carmichael received several years of treatment at the Columbia Presbyterian Medical Center in New York, New York, for prostate cancer. He would eventually die of this disease on November 15, 1998, at the age of 57 in Conakry, Guinea. For many years he claimed that his illness was actually caused by the U.S. Federal Bureau of Investigation. He believed that they had introduced this cancer to his body as an assassination attempt. It was revealed almost 10 years after his death (in 2007), through the release of previously secret federal documents, that the U.S. Central Intelligence Agency had tracked and monitored him. This apparently had begun in 1968 as part of a program that was initiated to conduct surveillance of Black activists of the time.

During Stokely Carmichael's final years, he often spoke of his contempt for the lack of progress made by Blacks during his time in the American economic and electoral arenas. He often acknowledged their progress, but insisted that a great deal of it still had its power diminished and much of it was meaningless.

One of Stokely Carmichael's most significant legacies comes from a term he coined in the late 1960s—"institutional racism," which he defined as a form of racism that occurs in institutions such as public bodies and corporations. He viewed it as a serious problem in that he felt there was a collective failure of many organizations to provide appropriate and professional service to people because of their color, culture, or ethnic origin.

Gordon Crews

See also: Black Panther Party; Malcolm X (aka El-Hajj Malik El-Shabazz); Student Nonviolent Coordinating Committee (SNCC)

References

Asante, M. K. *100 Greatest African Americans: A Biographical Encyclopedia.* Amherst, NY: Prometheus Books, 2002.

Carmichael, S. *Ready for Revolution: The Life and Struggles of Stokely Carmichael (Kwame Toure).* New York: Scribner Publishers, 2005.

Carmichael, S., and M. Abu-Jamal. *Stokely Speaks: From Black Power to Pan-Africanism.* New York: Lawrence Hill Books, 2007.

Hamilton, C., and S. Carmichael. *Black Power: The Politics of Liberation.* New York: Vintage Press, 1992.

Citizenship

Citizenship is the state of being a legally recognized member of a particular country with rights, privileges, and duties. It demands allegiance to the government by each citizen, and (ideally) in turn it provides protection and legal status in a political community. In the United States, citizenship is a civil status that has traditionally been overseen by the federal government. However, particularly in the aftermath of the terror attacks of September 11, 2001, state and local law enforcement agencies have been recruited by the federal government to help monitor the citizenship status of those found within U.S. borders.

Today, in the United States and elsewhere, a great deal of time and resources go into determining and confirming individuals' citizenship status. Numerous agencies and many work hours are dedicated to this function. (See, for example, the tasks performed by the U.S. Immigration and Customs Enforcement Bureau [ICE], U.S. Customs and Border Protection [CBP], and the Department of Homeland Security [DHS]). However, there was no citizenship in the beginning of the human race. People were free to move from one place to another and settle down anywhere they preferred. As human populations increased and numerous nations and kingdoms were formed, the granting or denial of citizenship status became a powerful form of government control.

For African Americans, the still-controversial 1857 U.S. Supreme Court decision *Dred Scott v. Sanford* (misspelled Sandford in the opinion) stands as a profound reminder of the government's ability to determine the rights and protections to which individuals or groups are or are not entitled. In the decision, supported by seven of the nine Supreme Court judges, Chief Justice Roger B. Taney delivered the opinion of the Court, writing:

> The descendants of Africans who were imported into this country and sold as slaves, when they shall become emancipated, or who are born of parents who had become free before their birth, are not citizens of the state in the sense which the word "citizens" is used in the Constitution of the United States.

Though the decision may seem contrary to many of the principles outlined in the U.S. Constitution, it was consistent with the practices of other governments, including those of ancient Greece and Rome, where the term "citizen" is said to have originated. In ancient Greece, citizenship was granted only to property owners. Consequently, slaves were not recognized as citizens or afforded any of the special rights occasioned by citizenship. Similarly, in 212 AD, the Roman government granted citizenship to most of the people throughout the empire, except slaves. For political and other reasons, especially those related to the desire for social dominance, many nations continued to follow the practice of limiting citizenship to only a portion of their population. Several sources have credited the *Dred Scott* decision with being one of the factors that propelled the United States into civil war four years later.

Even prior to the *Dred Scott* decision, the U.S. government demonstrated its intent to limit the rights and status of people of African ancestry. In article 1, section 2 of the Constitution, an African slave was counted as three-fifths of a human being, instead of as a whole person, in determining the number of congressional representatives each Southern state would have; and, in article 1, section 9, the importation of African slaves to the United States was allowed to continue until 1808. The Constitution itself was ratified in 1789. The following year, a federal law excluded people of African ancestry from becoming citizens through the process of naturalization by limiting the eligibility for such citizenship to "free white persons." This limitation was reconfirmed in the revision of the law in 1795.

Nearly 75 years after the revised "act to establish a uniform rule of naturalization" and 11 years after *Dred Scott,* the enactment of the Fourteenth Amendment, in 1868, was designed to grant citizenship to the former African slaves and their descendants. Slavery had been abolished three years prior, in 1865, under the Thirteenth Amendment. An exception in the Thirteenth Amendment's prohibition against slavery allowed involuntary servitude and consequent restrictions on citizenship rights for those convicted of a crime. This exception would prove to be a major mechanism for continuing to restrict the rights of African Americans in years to come (Alexander, 2010).

Section one of the Fourteenth Amendment, which begins, "All persons born or naturalized in the United States, and subject to the Jurisdiction thereof, are citizens of the United States and the state wherein they reside," immediately became controversial to the extent that it defined the terms of both national and state citizenship. The Southern states resisted being told who they should consider as entitled to government recognition and the rights and privileges (such as voting) that came with that recognition. Southern states reluctantly ratified the Fourteenth Amendment in order to retain their political participation in the national government.

The Fourteenth Amendment provides U.S. citizenship by birth and through naturalization. Ironically, the 2008 election of President Barack Obama, the nation's first visibly Black president, raised factual questions about "birthright" citizenship, authorized 140 years earlier. Opponents of his election challenged his citizenship status, claiming that he had been born outside the United States. Article 2, section 1 of the Constitution states, "[N]o person except a natural born citizen . . . shall be eligible to [for] the office of President. . . ." Although the president has produced a birth certificate documenting that he was born in the state of Hawaii, some of his opponents insist that he was born in Kenya, the birthplace of his father, which would make him ineligible for his post.

Recently, increased waves of immigration, particularly among those without the proper documents, have caused some Americans to push to eliminate or limit "birthright" citizenship. Under current law, regardless of the legality of the parents' immigration status, any child born in the United States is a U.S. citizen. In the 1982 case of *Plyer v. Doe,* the U.S. Supreme Court has declared that even the children of illegal immigrants are entitled to free elementary school education.

Afraid of competition for jobs and alleged immigrant criminality, Americans have become more and more intolerant of illegal immigrants. Some evidence suggests that such fears are primarily focused on immigrants who are non-White. Under Arizona law SB1070, police officers are required to inquire about the immigration status of people they encounter or run the risk of professional sanctions or civil liability. Section 287(g) of the federal Immigration and Nationality Act gives state and local police agencies the authority to enforce immigration laws within their jurisdictions. The past history of racial discrimination in granting citizenship suggests that non-Whites are those most likely to be targeted for such enforcement.

During the 1980s and 1990s, as part of the war on drugs, immigrants from the Afro-Caribbean became particularly susceptible to checks of their citizenship status. Media accounts that associated drug trafficking with Jamaican drug posses, and which tied drug activity to violence, subjected foreign-born Blacks to heightened police scrutiny. Being viewed by police as "the" public enemy during the 1950s, 1960s, and 1970s had led African Americans to join separatist and nationalist groups, a few of which advocated violent resistance to government oppression (see Black Panther Party).

Nationality is another term given for citizenship. The concept of citizenship is seen as essential for the legal approval of a person's nationality. Nationality is often used to signify membership in a community on the basis of common cultural characteristics. Each nation defines the nationality status of its own citizens. The slave ancestry of African Americans has had significant impact on their recognition as full-fledged citizens of the United States, and their denial of full citizenship status has at times led to efforts by them to declare a separate national identity. These have included the Pan-African Movement, the Black Nationalist Movement, the Black Power Movement, and others.

In 1892, Homer Plessy faced jail time for daring to attempt to assert full citizenship by sitting in a Louisiana railcar that had been designated "white only." By appearance, Plessy was White; in the opinion ultimately issued by the U.S. Supreme Court, his lineage is described as seven-eighths White. At the time of his case, the American standard for determining race was called the "one drop" rule, meaning that any proof of African ancestry was sufficient to categorize a person as Black. Plessy purposely bought a first-class ticket, purposely sat in the "white only," car and the conductor was purposely notified that Plessy was not a White man despite his appearance. Plessy and the civil rights organization to which he belonged hoped that a court would rule that Black citizens could no longer legally be made to lead lives that were segregated from those of White citizens.

Plessy and his colleagues were wrong. In an 8 to 1 decision, the Supreme Court created a legal rule that came to be known as the "separate but equal" doctrine, permitting states to separate their populations by race and allowing criminal sanctions to be imposed against anyone who failed to abide by segregation laws. Justice John Marshall Harlan was the sole dissenter in the case. In his dissent to the Court's 1896 decision in *Plessy v. Ferguson,* Justice Harlan wrote:

> Our Constitution is color-blind, and neither knows nor tolerates classes among Citizens. In respect to civil rights, all citizens are equal before the law. . . . In my opinion, the judgment this day rendered will, in time prove to be quite as pernicious as the decision made by this tribunal in the *Dred Scott* case. . . . The present decision . . . will not only stimulate aggressions, more or less brutal and irritating, upon the admitted rights of colored citizens, but will encourage the belief that it is possible, by means of state enactments, to co-opt recent amendments to the Constitution.

Though the Fourteenth Amendment had been designed to give full citizenship to Blacks, the *Plessy* decision validated a status of second-class citizenship similar to the restricted lives they had led under the Slave Codes and Black Codes of previous periods. As Justice Harlan predicted, following the Court's ruling, many states enacted segregationist legislation later termed "Jim Crow" laws that denied Blacks full access to the benefits of national citizenship. By some accounts these restrictions were abandoned following the successes of the Civil Rights Movement of the 1950s and 1960s. By others, they persist to this day (see for example, *The New Jim Crow: Mass Incarceration in the Age of Colorblindness*).

Delores Jones-Brown and Mathew Vairamon

See also: Black Panther Party; Civil Rights Movement; Criminal Deportation

References

Alexander, M. *The New Jim Crow: Mass Incarceration in the Age of Color-Blindness.* New York: The New Press, 2010.

Atkinson, L. *Your Legal Rights.* New York: Watts, 1982.

Baubock, R. *Stakeholder Citizenship: An Idea Whose Time Has Come?* Trans Atlantic Council on Migration. European University Institute, 2008.

Citizenship in the United States. Washington, DC: U.S. Department of Homeland Security, 2004.

Dred Scott v. Sandford (60 U.S. 393, 1857).

Heater, D. *What Is Citizenship?* Cambridge, England: Polity Press, 1999.

Jafri, S. I., and K. N. Seth. *Seth's Law of Citizenship Foreigners and Passports with Allied Laws.* Allahabad, India: Law Publishers (India) Pvt. Ltd, 2007.

Jones-Brown, D. *Race, Crime, and Punishment.* Philadelphia: Chelsea House, 2000.

Jones-Brown, D. "Race as a Legal Construct: The Implications for American Justice." In *The System in Black and White: Exploring the Connections between Race, Crime and Justice,* edited by M. Markowitz and D. Jones-Brown, 137–52. Westport, CT: Praeger, 2000.

Marshall, T. H. *Citizenship and Social Class and Other Essays*. Cambridge, UK: University of Cambridge Press, 1950.

Plessy v. Ferguson (163 U.S. 537, 1896).

Plyer v. Doe (457 U.S. 202, 1982).

Shachar, A. *The Birth Right Lottery: Citizenship and Global Inequality.* Cambridge, MA: Harvard University Press, 2008.

Sklansky, D. "Cocaine, Race and Equal Protection." *Stanford Law Review* 47 (1995): 1283–1322. United States Office of Personal Management Investigations. Citizenship Laws of the World. Washington, DC: International Law Division, Library of Congress, 2001.

Civil Rights Movement

Not the first forcibly displaced and enslaved African to defend her rights in a hostile society, Mum Bett received an arm wound in 1781 when she attempted to protect her sister from her owner's wife, who attacked both of them with a hot kitchen shovel. Outraged by the attack, Bett left the owner's house and obtained legal assistance for her freedom on the basis of Massachusetts' new bill of rights. A jury decided in Bett's favor and the owner was forced to pay damages. At this point Mum Bett changed her name legally to Elizabeth Freemen, and a short time afterwards the Massachusetts Supreme Court declared slavery unconstitutional (Kinshasa, 2006: 17).

The history of civil disobedience and acting in defiance of unjust laws by people of African ancestry that was demonstrated by Mum Bett is continuous, and underscores the struggle to construct a society premised upon human and civil rights. Significant in this respect were organizations such as the National Association for the Advancement of Colored People (NAACP) (1909), which traditionally favored a judicial approach to civil and human rights abuses, while other organizations, such as the Montgomery Improvement Association (MIA), Southern Christian Leadership Conference (SCLC), Student Nonviolent Coordinating Committee (SNCC), the Congress on Racial Equality (CORE), and the Mississippi Freedom Democratic Party (MFDP) favored direct action approaches involving "sit-ins" and economic boycotts.

In the mid twentieth century, a centerpiece for most civil rights organizations and the movement itself was the overturning of the *Plessy v. Ferguson* (1896) case, which previously institutionalized a societal racial doctrine of separate but equal, i.e., the official segregating of the races. This doctrine was judicially overturned in *Brown v. Board of Education of Topeka, Kansas* (1954). However, the relevance of *Brown* in alleviating the criminalizing effect of racial segregation upon African Americans was tested by thousands of Black protestors one year later in the historic Montgomery, Alabama, bus boycott. For 382 days beginning in December 1955, thousands of Black Montgomery residents boycotted a privately run Chicago-based bus company that maintained a racially biased seating arrangement on its buses as well as an exploitative economic relationship toward the Black community. At the heart of the matter, the criminal act of financially taxing African American citizens while depriving them by law of the right to fully and equally enjoy the benefits of their own labor became the driving force to challenge a series of contrived unjust laws, segregated busing being but one of a multitude of social anomalies.

Civil rights activist Ella Baker, ca. 1942. (Library of Congress)

With relative success, civil rights organizations such as the Montgomery Improvement Association (MIA) under the leadership of Rev. Dr. Martin Luther King, Jr., emerged to organize a Christian-based organization labeled the Southern Christian Leadership Conference (SCLC) that would challenge Southern segregation policies and their accompanying White racial violence of resistance. Formed in New Orleans, Louisiana, in February 1957, the SCLC cultivated a diverse leadership with individuals such as Ella Baker, Baynard Rustin, and Stanley Levinson (Kinshasa, 2006: 122).

Mississippi sharecropper Fannie Lou Hamer became a major spokesperson and organizer of marginalized Black sharecroppers and farm workers. In 1961, Hamer was one of the first volunteers to work with the Student Nonviolent Coordinating Committee (SNCC) on a statewide voter registration plan and attended the SCLC Citizenship Schools (Morris, 1984: 239). By 1962, Fannie Hamer became the field secretary for SNCC's voter education project. Targeted and harassed by local police, she continually articulated that the Civil Rights Movement was actually an international human rights struggle that extended beyond the limits of local or federal government. On June 9, 1963, Hamer and eight other women returning from a workshop in South Carolina were stopped and arrested by police in Winona, Mississippi. Two Black deputy sheriffs, following the orders of a White sheriff, beat Hamer to the extent that she never fully recovered from her injuries. Hamer's account of her beating underscores the pathological and violent criminality that racism breeds:

> The first Negro began to beat, and I was beat until I was exhausted. . . . After the first Negro . . . was exhausted, the State Highway Patrolman ordered the second Negro to take the blackjack. The second began to beat. . . . I began to scream, and one white man got up and began to beat me on my head and tell me to "hush."
>
> One white man—my dress had worked up high—he walked over and pulled my dress down and he pulled my dress back, back up. . . . All of this is on account we want to register [to vote], to become first-class citizens, and if the Freedom Democratic Party is not seated now, I question America. (White, 1965: 333)

Partially recovering from her injuries, in 1964 Hamer led a delegation of Blacks to the National Democratic Party convention in Atlantic City, New Jersey, that challenged an all-White Mississippian delegation's right to represent the state. Identifying themselves as the Mississippi Democratic Freedom Party (MFDP), they successfully gained two seats on the convention floor (Sherrod, 1964: 9).

Despite overtures to nonviolence and pacifism by civil rights activists during the 1950s and 1960s, this era in U.S. history was extremely violent. The killings of Emmett Till; Mack Charles Parker; Medgar Evers; James Chaney and two Whites, Michael Schwerner and Andrew Goodman; four girls in Birmingham, Alabama, at the 16th Street Baptist Church—Addie Mae Collins, Denise McNair, Carole Robertson, and Cynthia Wesley—and countless thousands more are a testament to American racism as well as judicial duplicity.

As intimidation and direct violence by those opposed to civil rights intensified, SCLC leader Ella Baker proclaimed in an April 1960 speech entitled "More Than a Hamburger" that the movement now required a new set of goals and strategies (Baker, 1960: 4; Kinshasa, 2006: 124). Concerned with how to obtain greater levels of militancy beyond what was presently being utilized by SCLC leadership, Baker announced the formation of the SNCC. In effect, the development of SNCC was in direct response to student demands for "an organization that would expand black militancy rather than restrain or control it" (Carson, 1981: 18).

In this heightened and violent political atmosphere, rural Black farmers knew fairly well that the ability to defend oneself in the face of White racist violence was paramount. In 1965, one group of armed and dedicated religious Louisiana civil rights activists had few qualms about organizing themselves into the Deacons for Defense and Justice, an organization sworn to protect civil rights workers. Unfortunately, they were not with James Meredith, the first African American to graduate from the University of Mississippi, when he was ambushed and shot in June 1966 while walking some 220 miles from Memphis, Tennessee, to Jackson, Mississippi, to underscore the importance of Black voter registration. However, Meredith's walk was later completed by 30,000 civil rights activists on July 26 under the protection of the Deacons of Defense and Justice, who on more than one occasion fought armed battles at night with racist elements (Carson, 1981: 207–8; Kinshasa, 2006: 136).

By 1968, the civil rights philosophy of racial and social inclusiveness, as personified by the slogan "Freedom Now," reached its apex when "Black Power" as a movement slogan, advocated by Willie Ricks of SNCC, was popularized (Carson, 1981: 209–10). Supporting this far-reaching slogan, SNCC chairman Stokely Carmichael noted that "'Self-power' as in 'Black Power' seemed the most natural desire for any group" (Kinshasa, 2006: 136). However, many civil rights leaders and activists within the movement, such as Roy Wilkins, Bayard Rustin, and Dr. Martin Luther King, Jr., railed against this new clarion call as being excessively militant, implying violence and being anti-White in sentiment. For many other activists, this development signaled the end of the civil rights era and the beginning of the Black Power movement (Kinshasa, 2006: 136–7).

Kwando M. Kinshasa

See also: Black Panther Party; Carmichael, Stokely; Southern Christian Leadership Conference (SCLC); Student Nonviolent Coordinating Committee (SNCC)

References

Baker, Ella. "Bigger Than a Hamburger." *Southern Patriot,* June 1960: 4.

Carson, Clayborne. *In Struggle: SNCC and the Black Awakening of the 1960s.* Cambridge, MA: Harvard University Press, 1981.

Kinshasa, Kwando M. *African American Chronology: Chronologies of the American Mosaic.* Westport, CT: Greenwood Press, 2006.

Morris, Aldon D. *The Origins of the Civil Rights Movement: Black Communities Organizing for Change.* New York: The Free Press, 1984.

Sherrod, Charles. "Mississippi at Atlantic City." *Grain of Salt (Union Theological Seminary),* 1964.

White, Theodore H. *The Making of the President 1964.* New York: New American Library, 1965.

Cochran, Jr., Johnnie L. (1937–2005)

Johnnie L. Cochran, Jr., born in Shreveport, Louisiana, on October 2, 1937, has been recognized as a seasoned litigator, philanthropist, and outstanding trial

Acclaimed civil rights attorney, Johnnie Cochran, Jr., was lead defense attorney for former NFL player O. J. Simpson during his 1995 trial and controversial acquittal for the deaths of his former wife and her acquaintance. (Getty Images)

lawyer, and considered a leading authority on the criminal and civil justice system. Cochran earned his bachelor's in business administration from UCLA in 1959 and his JD from Loyola Marymount University School of Law (now Loyola Law School) in 1962. In 1963, he passed the California bar and began working in Los Angeles as a prosecutor and deputy city attorney general in the criminal division. Cochran worked his way through the ranks to accept a position as assistant district attorney for Los Angeles County. As the third-ranking lawyer in the nation's largest law office, he had general administrative responsibility for 600 lawyers. In 1965, he worked with criminal lawyer Gerald Lenoir and later founded his own firm, Cochran, Atkins and Evans, where he handled civil and criminal cases. The practice is now known simply as the Cochran Firm (Biography.com, 2012; Cochran Firm, 2012).

During his life, Cochran wrote two autobiographies and received many honors and awards, including the Los Angeles Criminal Trial Lawyer of the Year, Los Angeles Civil Trial Lawyer of the Year, and *National Law Journal*'s America's Trial Lawyer of the Year. Cochran died of a brain tumor on March 29, 2005 (Biography.com, 2012).

Through personal injury lawsuits and through filing and pursuing many civil and civil rights cases on behalf of his clients, Cochran forced changes in case processing and both criminal and civil procedure. In many cases, his work led to official changes in the way minorities are treated by the police. He also defended celebrity clients such as Michael Jackson, Todd Bridges, O. J. Simpson, Jim Brown, and Sean Combs. Cochran arranged an out-of-court settlement with a boy who claimed that Michael Jackson molested him. He also engineered an acquittal for television's *Diff'rent Strokes* star Todd Bridges, who stood accused of attempted murder (Cochran Firm, 2012). He represented NFL player Jim Brown to an acquittal on a rape charge. And in 2001, Cochran represented Sean "P. Diddy" Combs against charges of gun possession and for purportedly bribing a witness to change his testimony. Cochran was able to convince a jury that Combs had not broken any laws (*Biography.com,* 2012).

In May 1966, Leonard Deadwyler was shot and killed by Los Angeles police when he was stopped for speeding. He was rushing his pregnant wife to the hospital. Cochran represented the Deadwyler family, who accused the Los Angeles Police Department (LAPD) of brutality in their son's murder while the police claimed that they acted in self-defense. The sensational proceedings featured an audiotape of police actions, which was turned over to Cochran. Officer Jerold M. Bova, who had leaned into the car to get Deadwyler to stop, said his gun went off when Deadwyler's car lurched, killing him. Officer Bova was exonerated. Though Cochran's firm filed and lost a civil lawsuit in the matter, because of the Deadwyler case and others, the LAPD changed its tactics to advise officers not to put any part of their bodies into a car that is under the suspect's control (Johnson & Shuster, 1996).

Along with Stuart Hanlon, Cochran defended former Black Panther Party leader and decorated Vietnam veteran Elmer "Geronimo" Pratt, who was charged with robbing and shooting a young White couple, Caroline and Kenneth Olsen, on December 18, 1968, in Santa Monica, California. Caroline Olsen died 10 days later. Pratt was convicted of first-degree murder on July 28, 1972, and sentenced to life imprisonment a month later. Cochran and Hanlon continued to file motions to have Pratt's conviction overturned. Between 1972 and 1997, the parole board denied parole to Pratt 16 times. In 1997, California Superior Court judge Everett W. Dickey granted Pratt a new trial and vacated Pratt's conviction based on the fact that prosecutors had withheld crucial evidence during the first trial. A key prosecution witness, Julius Butler, who claimed that Pratt confessed to him, lied about being a government informant. The LAPD, the FBI, and prosecutors had not shared with the defense the fact that Butler was an informant. Upon his release, Cochran helped Pratt file a civil lawsuit for false imprisonment. The suit resulted in a judgment for Pratt in the amount of $4.5 million. Over his 27-year confinement, Pratt had garnered support of civil rights and international humanitarian groups such as Amnesty International, the American Civil Liberties Union, and the NAACP. He died in June 2011 at the age of 63 in his adopted country of Tanzania (Deutsch, 2011; Martin, 2011).

In 1981, Cochran represented the family of Ron Settles. Settles was a college football player who was picked up for speeding, and the LAPD said he hanged himself in a jail cell. On behalf of the Settles family, Cochran demanded that the athlete's body be exhumed and examined. A coroner determined that Settles had been strangled by a police chokehold, and a pretrial settlement of $760,000 was awarded to the family.

Cochran also represented White truck driver Reginald Denny in a lawsuit against the LAPD. Reginald Denny was pulled from his truck and beaten at the start of the 1992 riots that were sparked by the acquittal of officers in the Rodney King beating. In the criminal trial, where Denny was the victim, the brick-throwing defendant, Damian Williams, was found not guilty of attempted murder and guilty only of simple mayhem and simple assault. Antoine Miller, another defendant involved in the attack, had pleaded guilty earlier to grand theft for going through Denny's pockets (Williams, 1993).

Cochran was also able to secure a substantial financial award for a teenager who reported that she was molested by an off-duty police officer who then threatened her with bodily harm if she told anyone. Cochran refused an out-of-court settlement and went to trial, where a jury awarded his client $9.4 million. A postverdict settlement paid the young woman $4.6 million (Cochran & Fisher, 2003).

One of Cochran's biggest celebrity trials was that of O. J. Simpson. In the summer of 1994, Simpson was arrested and charged with the murders of his ex-wife, Nicole Brown Simpson, and her friend Ron Goldman. After months of trial, Simpson was found not guilty. He had hired Cochran, Robert Shapiro, and a "dream team" of lawyers. Cochran replaced Robert Shapiro as lead counsel in what was termed the "trial of the century" (Cochran & Fisher, 2006). Cochran vowed to win an acquittal for Simpson. Cochran was controversial and confident in his closing arguments in defense of Simpson. He challenged the evidence presented by the district attorneys, Marcia Clark and Christopher Darden, and claimed Simpson had been framed by a racist Los Angeles police officer, Mark Fuhrman (Bugliosi, 1996). Many, including his co-counsel Shapiro, criticized Cochran for using the race card. Cochran did not apologize for his strategy and explained that his scenario presented the truth as he saw it. After deliberating for only four hours, the majority-Black jury rendered a not guilty verdict on all counts (Biography.com, 2012; Deutsch, 2011; Bernstein, 2005; Spence, 1997; Toobin, 1996).

Cochran successfully sued police departments on both coasts. He sued the New York City Police Department (NYPD) after half a dozen New York police officers tortured and brutalized Haitian immigrant Abner Louima in 1997. The settlement in the case was one of the largest in the history of the department. In 1999, he prosecuted another successful six-figure civil lawsuit against the NYPD, for the shooting death of 22-year-old Amadou Diallo, an immigrant from Guinea, West Africa (Cochran Firm, 2012). During his lifetime, Johnnie Cochran seemed to never lose his zeal for justice. The Cochran Firm is charged with continuing his crusade against injustice.

Edward J. Schauer

See also: Black Panther Party; Diallo, Amadou; King, Rodney; Los Angeles Riots of 1992; Louima, Abner; Police Brutality; Simpson, Orenthal James "O. J."

References

Bernstein, A. "Showy, Tenacious Lawyer Rode Simpson Murder Trial to Fame." *Washington Post,* March 30, 2005. http://www.washingtonpost.com/wp-dyn/articles/A10668-2005Mar29.html.

Biography.com. "Cochran, Johnnie." 2012. http://www.biography.com/people/johnnie-cochran-9542444.

Bugliosi, Vincent T. *Outrage: The Five Reasons Why O. J. Simpson Got Away with Murder.* New York: W.W. Norton, 1996.

Cochran Firm (2012). "About Johnnie Cochran." http://cochranfirmlaw.com/.

Cochran, J. L., Jr., and D. Fisher. *A Lawyer's Life.* New York: St. Martin's Press, 2003.

Cochran, J. L., Jr., and T. Rutten. *Journey to Justice.* New York: One World/Ballantine Books, 1996.

Deutsch, L. "Geronimo Pratt Dead at 63." *The Huffington Post,* June 3, 2011. http://www.huffingtonpost.com/2011/06/03/geronimo-pratt-dead-at-63_n_870910.html.

Johnson, J., and B. Shuster. "Shooting Recalls Dangers of Traffic Stops." *The Los Angeles Times,* March 16, 1996. http://articles.latimes.com/1996-03-16/news/mn-47676_1_traffic-stop.

Martin, D. "Elmer G. Pratt, Jailed Panther Leader, Dies at 63" *The New York Times,* June 3, 2011. http://www.nytimes.com/2011/06/04/us/04pratt.html?_r=1.

Spence, Gerry. *O. J.: The Last Word.* New York: St. Martin's Press, 1997.

Toobin, Jeffrey. *The Run of His Life: The People v. O. J. Simpson.* New York: Random House, 1996.

Williams, D. "The Denny Beating Trial: Justice in the Balance." *The Chicago Tribune,* November 3, 1993. http://articles.chicagotribune.com/keyword/reginald-denny.

Code of the Street

Code of the Street: Decency, Violence and the Moral Life of the Inner City, by Elijah Anderson (1999), winner of the Eastern Sociological Association's Komarovsky Book Award and the 1999 Critic's Choice Award given by the *Washington Post,* is the result of four years of participant observation work in inner-city Philadelphia neighborhoods. Anderson examines the social and cultural dynamics behind the prevalence of a style of interaction involving the ever-present threat of interpersonal violence among those living in inner cities of the United States. Residents experience a profound level of alienation from the dominant structure and its representatives. Residents do not believe the system will bring justice. Calls for police may not even be responded to. Residents face the stigma of daily racism, a lack of jobs providing a living wage, rampant drug use, and high crime rates. In response to these conditions and a lack of faith in the justice system, a "code of the street" has developed, where people earn or lose respect through following a set of informal rules for behavior when challenged. Residents may take matters into their own hands if necessary, with the threat of violence as a constant possibility. Earning respect is important for assuring one's ability to move freely within the neighborhood. One's "juice," or respect, must be constantly guarded and often defended. Both "decent" and "street" families must respond when challenged, even if they do not believe in violence as a way of resolving problems.

According to Anderson, "the code of the street thus emerges where the influence of the police ends" and where the ability to prove one's own ability to defend oneself begins. Such personal ability may be challenged in "staging areas," which are places where young adults tend to hang out together. Anderson provides a good understanding of the diversity and complexity of families and people within such neighborhoods in his description of "decent" and "street" families, and the "decent daddy." Using terms that people in this neighborhood use to describe themselves, Anderson describes "decent" families as those with one or two parents who work mainstream jobs and identify with a value system that more closely follows mainstream culture. "Decent" parents do not participate in the drug culture, usually attend church, do their best to keep their children in school, and see education as the best possibility for their children's success in life. "Street" families, on the other hand, do participate in the drug or prostitution culture, do not hold mainstream jobs, and often leave their children unsupervised. One family can have a mixture of "decent" and "street" family members. One person may have to "code-switch," behaving consistent with a "decent" or "street" culture depending on the situation he or she faces. Both types of families love their children. Both are the result of an inner-city culture that has developed in response to a system that offers them few legitimate options for financial success.

Carol F. Black

Reference

Anderson, Elijah. *Code of the Street: Decency, Violence and the Moral Life of the Inner City.* New York: W.W. Norton and Company, 1999.

Community-Based Crime and Reentry Theory

The theoretical framework for this discussion connects community capacity to collective efficacy, and collective efficacy to reducing crime and pro-social reintegration or successful prisoner reentry in urban, predominantly African American communities. This is important when examining the role of religious institutions in reducing crime and improving reentry. Most would agree that social disorganization theory has been one of the prevailing theoretical underpinnings for research on crime, and more recently prisoner reentry, particularly as it relates to visible crimes, which are often associated with predominantly African American communities. This framework is predominant in criminology and related bodies of literature and does not reinforce an understanding of strengths and assets within disadvantaged neighborhoods, such as many urban African American contexts. While the relevance of social disorganization theory cannot be denied, it is helpful to consider alternative ways of understanding the relationship of the social environment of crime and reentry that is provided by collective efficacy theory, and how that understanding can translate into a framework for addressing both.

Research has found that the strength of organizations and institutions within a neighborhood and its surrounding community represents a force that can be mobilized for action to effect change beyond what an individual is able to do alone (see Backer, 2001; Stone, Hager, & Griffin, 2001; Roman & Moore, 2004; Sampson et al., 1997). This may be particularly true of religious and social organizations in African American communities, where these institutions have been the historic center of social change. This strategic networking of organizations in a neighborhood should, at least in principle, produce collective efficacy (Sampson, 2006). In addition, the density of local organizations and voluntary associations predicts higher levels of collective efficacy, controlling for prior crime, poverty, and social composition of the population (Morenoff et al., 2001). Social disorganization theory, which begins with socioeconomic disadvantage, residential instability, and racial/ethnic heterogeneity, is often associated with inner-city communities. In comparison, the framework presented by Frazier (2007) corresponds with the conceptual framework of an asset-based approach and assumes "social organization," which is conceptualized by a number of community characteristics, including the density and range of local social networks (see figure 8, Roman & Moore, 2004: 57).

The framework combines capacity building and community development literature, which provide the dimensions of community capacity, with criminology literature, which seeks to predict, explain, and reveal the causes of crime or criminal behavior in African American communities.

The prevailing traditional approach to addressing crime at the neighborhood level has been social disorganization theory, which starts with a need and corresponds with the deficit-based approach to neighborhood-level analysis of crime. Social disorganization theory, for at least a hundred years, has shaped criminological research in an ecological tradition that recognizes the existence of crime in high poverty, racially segregated neighborhoods primarily consisting of minority groups and with a high percentage of single-parent families (Sampson, 2006). Sampson (2006) questions this approach and lays out a compelling argument for researchers to begin to focus more on networks within neighborhoods and less on markers such as poverty and race as risk factors for crime rates. He asserts that "by focusing primarily on correlates of crime at the level of community social composition—especially poverty and race—traditional neighborhood research has tended toward a risk-factor rather than an explanatory approach" and suggests a "move away from community-level corrections, or markers, to a theory of the underlying *social mechanisms* theoretically at work" (149). Specifically, Sampson conceptualized the social-mechanistic theory of collective efficacy as a theoretically plausible contextual process that accounts for or explains the phenomena of crime rates and by extension makes the link to pro-social reintegration or successful prisoner reentry as well.

There is growing evidence that an increase in crime in predominantly African American communities is one aggregate effect of the cycle of individuals returning from periods of incarceration to the community (Clear et al., 2001). Research also shows that first-time parolees have a recidivism rate of approximately 60 percent, which increases in subsequent parole terms. This research provides empirical evidence for the logical assumption that models that seek to explain, predict, and describe crime phenomena can be used to do the same for prisoner reentry. This is particularly important to addressing issues of crime and reentry in high concentrations in predominantly African American communities.

Social Disorganization and the Deficit-Based Approach

Social disorganization is based on the premise of the inability of informal community rules and social control systems to regulate conduct and is theoretically aligned with the needs- or deficit-based model of capacity building, in that they both begin with dysfunction. Essentially, the social disorganization theory postulates that some communities experience more crime than others because of qualities of the neighborhood rather than qualities of the individuals who live there (Shaw & McKay, 1942). From an ecological perspective, three factors are the primary focus of the social disorganization tradition: poverty, ethnic heterogeneity, and residential mobility. Decades later, theorists would add joblessness, single-parent families, structural density, and other variables that are thought to impact community structure by reducing capacity for informal social control so that crime flourishes (see Sampson et al., 1997; Sampson & Groves, 1989). Such factors have been significantly linked to urban contexts and predominantly African American communities. Merging social disorganization and community capacity theories provides a framework for assessing community institutional capacity for reducing visible crime and improving prisoner reentry outcomes.

As seen in the social organization model above, social disorganization begins with unfavorable community characteristics as the genesis of other relationships in the model. The primary assumption of the deficit-based model is social disorder. It begins with deficiencies, needs, and deficits at the neighborhood level. Social disorganization theory has a long history in both criminology and sociological literature, although the latter employs different concepts, such as the cultural deviance and strain traditions.

It was hypothesized in an early-twentieth-century work by the Chicago School of Urban Sociology that population density, low economic status, ethnic heterogeneity, and residential instability were precursors to high rates of crime and disorder (Sampson, 2006). Shaw and McKay and their predecessors were able to show that areas with a high degree of such problems (crime, delinquency, truancy, mental disorder, etc.) were also marked by low educational attainment, a high proportion of families on welfare, low rental property values, a high percentage of the work force at low occupational levels, and poor community organization. The social disorganization interpretation of crime rate differences assumes that people will commit criminal acts when the surrounding society is unable to prevent them from doing so. Society would need to control the behavior of these offending individuals if they were to remain law abiding.

This hypothesis supports the contention that postmodernity, and by extension urbanization, negatively impacts primary relationships. Walsh and Ellis (2007) argue that the continuous redistribution of populations within neighborhoods leads to disorganization, supporting the early work by Durkheim, which concluded that rapid social change, as seen in the 1960s, weakens social controls. Further, scholars asserted that when people of limited resources and divergent values are not in step with traditional American middle-class norms, the sense of a productive, cohesive community is lost. This clash of values among culturally heterogeneous groups breeds social disorganization and results in crime. Gabbidon and Green (2005) resurrected Shaw and McKay's detailed work in Chicago. Identifying concentric circles, or high-crime "capital zones in transition" previously delineated by Park and Burgess, the new work showed that the farther one moves away from the slums or "the capital zone in transition," the more crime decreases (see Bursik & Grasmick, 1993: 39).

Sampson (2006) defines the concept of social disorganization as "the inability of a community to realize the common values of its residents and maintain effective social order. Thus the "disorganized community" is characterized by a weakened network of relationships (i.e., friends and acquaintances) as a consequence of its unique socialization process. In the predominant research on communities, the idea of "social capital" has become increasingly popular (see Schneider, 2006). It is widely accepted that social capital has many definitions and instantiations (Putman, 2000). Roman and Moore suggested that social capital can be defined as "the activation of actual or potential resources embodied in communities stemming from a durable network of relationships or structures of social organization" (2004: ii). On the connection of social disorganization to social capital theory, Bursik (1999) suggested that neighborhoods without social capital, which is evident in a reduction of social networks, are less able to realize common values and maintain the social controls that foster safety. Dense social ties thus play a key role in social controls that foster safety.

The notions associated with the deficit-based model are aligned with social disorganization theory. Although social disorganization theory explains, predicts, and shows causal relationships for crime in neighborhoods and the deficit-based approach is a conceptual approach used to solve community problems like crime, they are not dissimilar. The way a problem is defined governs how it is approached. If crime or prisoner reentry was seen from a deficiency perspective—that is, beginning with the needs, deficiencies, and "disadvantages" of urban neighborhoods—it stands that the response will be framed only in the context of lack and inadequacy. On the other hand, if the problem is defined beginning with what is available in communities—their assets—then the approach to solving the problem or improving outcomes for those returning from prison or jail would be framed in the context of potential and some sense of sufficiency.

Deficit-Based Model

The widely accepted "needs" map determines how problems are to be addressed through deficiency-oriented policies and programs (Kretzman & McKnight, 1993). The map outlines a neighborhood's deficiencies, including high unemployment and dropout rates, illiteracy, the menace of gangs, lead poisoning, broken homes, etc., which often is the only information reported by news media. In addition, much of the funded research in the public and private sector is needs oriented. Commonly accepted deficiencies in social disorganization theory encompass the following areas: lack or absence of informal social control; absence of social control as taught and enforced by parents; greater opportunities for delinquent behavior; economic disinvestment, resulting in low employment opportunities; social isolation; residential mobility, or high concentrations of the cycle of incarceration and return; and a considerable number of disrupted families and broken homes (Sampson & Groves, 1989). The existence of these problems in many urban areas is unquestioned; however, there are differences of opinion as to whether these problems should be the only basis for seeking solutions.

Kretzman and McKnight (1993) argue that public, private, and nonprofit human service systems transform problems into local activities that teach people the nature and extent of their problems and the value of services as the answer to their problems. While the present study assesses the capacity of organizations within the community to reduce crime and provide services to returning ex-offenders, many of these organizations are not purely service organizations. They include congregations, advocacy and legal service organizations, recreation centers, schools, hospitals, homeless shelters, and other community-based organizations that also offer products, services, and support. The initiatives of these community-based organizations allow opportunities for the ex-offender or the community to create new and better ways to improve the reintegration process. These supplemental services are an added benefit for those individuals and their families who struggle to triumph over the unintended consequences of incarceration in neighborhoods already overrepresented in many areas cited on neighborhood needs maps. Kretzman and McKnight (1993) recognized that the prevailing deficiency orientation represented by the needs map constituted the only guide to lower-income neighborhoods, and they contend that the consequences of that limitation are devastating.

One of the most tragic consequences is that the residents of African American communities themselves begin to accept the needs map as the only guide to the reality of their lives. They think of themselves and their neighbors as fundamentally deficient victims incapable of taking charge of their lives and their community's future.

Criticisms of Social Disorganization—A Move toward Alternative Theories

Despite its prolific use, social disorganization theory has been questioned because of the role played by social networks, especially the effect of density of social ties in generating a low crime rate, in its conceptual definition (Sampson, 2006). Sampson questions the tendency to label a neighborhood as unable to achieve social order simply because disorder exists within it: "[I]f the cause is defined in terms of the outcome, we really have no explanation at all. Further, if crime and disorder both are indicators of lack of order, a 'matrix of risk' is described but not 'independent causal mechanisms' of the processes" (2006: 151). Consequently, social disorganization research has moved toward a conceptualization in systemic terms, particularly with regard to density of social ties (Bursik, 1999; Warner & Rountree, 1997; Sampson & Groves, 1989).

Sampson (2006) outlined the primary problems with social disorganization theory that he associated with the issues of networks. First, he contends that the environment of some neighborhoods actually impedes efforts to establish social control. Impoverished residents of the same neighborhood may have strong social ties through various networks, but the connections do not produce collective resources such as social control. These same networks connect both those individuals who are engaged in pro-social activities and those who are criminals; that is, networks are not inherently egalitarian or pro-social in nature. Further, loose ties among neighbors neither preclude shared expectations of social control nor the connections that yield collective action. Evidence shows that even weak ties among neighbors are predictive of lower crime rates (Bellair, 1997).

The most common criticism of the social disorganization theory is the so-called "ecological fallacy," which alleges that researchers erroneously apply data peculiar to the aggregate at the individual level. Robinson (1980) purports that inferences about individuals and groups cannot be made on the basis of information derived from the larger community. Social disorganization theory does not explain the phenomenon of low crime levels being maintained in high crime areas among certain groups, such as Asian and Jewish sub-communities. Further, we must consider the possibility that the characteristics individuals bring to communities more accurately predict crime than aggregate community characteristics.

As Roman and Moore (2004) observe, the social disorganization framework is limited in articulating the role of organizations. The theory asserts that organizations increase secondary relational networks, which as a socialization tool is important in generating social control. Exactly how organizations socialize individuals is not explained. Similarly, social disorganization literature does not discuss which organizations are relevant for positive community outcomes or how neighborhood organizations provide direct services.

Although these issues of social disorganization have more to do with methodological problems than with empirical research or theoretical and conceptual frameworks, they eliminate some of the fundamental aspects of the deficit model of approaching community problems. Specifically, they challenge the notion that these communities are defined by their challenges. Mapping communities as lists of problems hinders attempts to find solutions. Further, it creates yet another problem, specifically a sense within the community that it is unable to solve its own problems (Kretzman & McKnight, 1993). It is more reasonable to develop an approach to crime and reentry problem solving that is based on the capabilities, skills, and assets of neighborhoods.

Collective Efficacy, Social Organization, and an Asset-Based Approach

Walsh and Ellis (2007) argue that social disorganization is in truth a loss of collective efficacy. Collective efficacy refers to the power of a group to achieve a mutually desired outcome, whereas personal efficacy is defined as the capability of individuals to achieve personally desirable outcomes. Informal social control involves residents behaving proactively (calling police, aiding the wounded, etc.) when they observe troublesome behavior. Neighbors, however, vary in their ability to activate this informal social control. Mutual trust among neighbors is essential for residents to engage proactively. As a result, in neighborhoods where such cohesiveness exists, residents can depend on each other to enforce rules of good behavior, and in so doing exhibit collective efficacy. Although collective efficacy is seen in terms of individual participation in collective action, research shows that collective efficacy is increased by community institutions and organizations; therefore, increasing community institutional capacity increases collective efficacy (see Sampson, 2006: 56).

By delineating collective efficacy, Sampson, Raudenbush, and Earls (1997) extended the traditional paradigm set forth by Shaw and McKay that the degree of informal social control exercised by residents will affect the extent of a community's crime problem. Research suggests that informal social controls, which include local organizations, can be a source of increased collective efficacy that in turn reduces crime. To address the new challenges of urban areas, Sampson and colleagues proposed focusing on aspects of social organization that may be aided by, but do not necessarily require, strong associations. Rather than maintaining the model that ideal neighborhoods by necessity must possess ties, the focus is on defining the terms that allow for variance in the analysis of social organizations (see figure 5.1, Sampson, 2006: 156).

Asset-Based Community Development

Asset-based community development assumes some degree of social organization, social order, and social cohesion within troubled neighborhoods. It assumes that communities with concentrated poverty, high unemployment, and high crime and reentry rates have social mechanisms that allow them to exist in the midst of all of their disadvantages and problems. The key to the asset-based approach is to identify those strengths and assets in individuals, families, associations, and institutions within communities as a way to increase the community's capacity to improve its own well-being. Asset-based community development can be defined by three interrelated characteristics.

First, it begins with what already exists in the community. Instead of focusing on what is absent, the emphasis is on exploring the capacity of the residents, associations, organizations, and institutions. The study focused on the assets or capacity of institutions and organizations within the community and not on individuals, families, and small voluntary associations. Its primary aim is to map the organizations that are present in the community; look at what products, services, and support are provided; and determine the capacity to address problems of crime and serve residents returning from prisons and jails. Businesses, schools, libraries, parks, police stations, fire stations, hospitals, congregations, and social services agencies and programs comprise the front-line organizations available to meet this charge. These organizations make up the most visible and formal part of a community's fabric. Accounting for them in full and enlisting them in the process of community development is essential to the success of the process. Mapping the institutional assets of the community includes assessing the relationships between organizations and with the criminal justice system.

Second, the asset-based approach incorporates the community's own definition of itself in any attempt to articulate goals, hopes, and dreams, or to establish internal governance. It does not negate the role external forces may have played in creating the conditions that exist, or ignore the need to attract additional resources. Although the focus is internal, it is understood that while assets within challenged neighborhoods are central to improving outcomes, they are usually not sufficient to meet the enormous challenges they face. Additional resources are more effective when the community itself is mobilized and participates in defining the terms under which the additional resources were acquired (Kretzman & McKnight, 1993).

Third, the asset-based approach is "relationship driven." Asset-based community developers are constantly challenged to nurture existing relationships and foster new ones between the neighborhood's local residents and its local associations, organizations, and institutions. Community organizers are not unaware of the importance of relationship building, but they are challenged in this endeavor by longer travel times between work and home, racial and generational segregation, and media influences. Consequently, the sense of efficacy must be based on interdependence, the idea that people can count on their neighbors and neighborhood resources for support and strength. For all stakeholders (individuals and families, policymakers, criminal justice agencies, institutions, and community organizations) who seek a promising route to reduce visible crime and improving the pro-social reintegration of the thousands of individuals returning from prisons and jails to their already challenged neighborhoods, focusing on assets and rebuilding local relationships, that will increase collective efficacy, seems the path to take.

Reentry and Community Capacity Assessment/ Measurement Research

The merging of community capacity and reentry literature provides a profound critical lens from which to review earlier studies that first defined and analyzed communities and neighborhoods. In general, conceptualizations of community capacity have been incorporated to deal practically with an array of community issues. The scope of community capacity, which has brought the analysis to this point, is inclusive of the criminal justice and criminological issues of reentry. When linking community and reentry, the discussion leans toward formal and informal agents, agencies, and social control—concepts found in criminology, corrections, and criminal justice literature. More research is needed to understand the implications of communities, especially when identifying assessment as a model for community capacity. Despite the dearth of research in the literature, there is evidence of community-level outcome studies, as discussed below, which can provide a basis for review.

Emerging Criminal Justice Community Capacity Research in Urban Contexts

Practitioners and lawmakers alike have begun to make the link between community capacity and controlling crime, as seen in the Community Oriented Policing Services (COPS) initiative in the 1990s and other community justice applications, and the subsequent research. More recent studies have extended this research to assessing the ability of community organizations, including criminal justice organizations, to partner and build stronger networks and collaborations (Roman el al., 2002); and the role organizations are playing in the reentry efforts to reduce reentry and create safer and healthier communities (Solomon el al., 2006). Few studies, however, assess community institutional capacity research for prisoner reentry.

Frazier (2007) is one of a few studies that make the conceptual link between community institutional capacity, collective efficacy, and prisoner reentry, and the only one that does so from an asset-based approach found in community capacity literature. From a social disorganization framework, criminological research has rarely gone beyond asking individuals about participation in secondary networks when looking at mediating variables that impact social capital or collective efficacy. In contrast, community development literature, which explores *capacity* as an important feature for organizations *and* neighborhoods, discusses how organizations can mobilize communities around collective action to impact community change to improve well-being. Characteristics of services and organizations that embody capacity become important variables in this literature. The merging of criminology and community development literature provides a conceptual framework that shows the relevance of collective efficacy in improving a community's capacity to aid in the pro-social reintegration of individuals returning from prisons and jails.

Second, Frazier's Philadelphia-based research examines the community institutional capacity (CIC) of an entire city and includes all institutions and organizations that provide social services, products, or support to ex-offenders. In their study, Roman and Moore (2004) examine CIC and its relationship to social capital. Their cross-sectional, exploratory study investigated the dimensions of CIC and was viewed as "a first step towards understanding not only the dimensions of institutional capacity, but also systematically assessing its presence in a community." Using existing measures of institutional capacity, the researchers assessed where CIC existed and where it did not within Ward 8, a

29-block neighborhood in Washington, D.C. The study also evaluated the practicality of building social capital through organizations and the larger community infrastructure. The intent provided scores for various community institutional capacity dimensions (organizational stability, leadership, human resources, financial resources, technical resources, community outreach, services and related service capacity, and products); its goal was to create a measure for CIC. This D.C. study measured CIC *at the community level,* primarily utilizing publicly available information that would also be available to organizations in their own efforts to measure social capital. In addition, Roman and Moore (2004) examined whether the *presence* (the number or density) of organizations, institutions, and businesses is related to neighborhood well-being; if the *location* (distance) of community-based organizations has a role in neighborhood well-being; and whether the *capacity* of community organizations factors into neighborhood well-being.

Third, the Philadelphia-based study examines the collective capacity of organizations providing products, services, and support in all major areas of need (housing, employment, alcohol and substance abuse treatment, HIV/AIDS and health treatment, education and training, etc.) not in just one of these areas (Frazier, 2007). Roman, Kane, and Giridharadas (2006) sought, among other research objectives, to develop an assessment of housing and community-based capacity. Using survey data that included several dimensions of community capacity, Roman and colleagues provided an overview of the community capacity for housing, as well as attitudes of housing providers with regard to the housing needs of ex-prisoners in the District of Columbia, and the barriers within the community to meeting those needs. Although this was not a "community capacity" study, the research assessed the community institutional capacity for housing in support of prisoner reentry.

Fourth, the Philadelphia-based study specifically addresses community institutional capacity for prisoner reentry as opposed to other criminal justice applications, such as those seen in community justice. Community justice is "a participatory process in which stakeholders join in collective problem solving with the goals of improving community safety, promoting community capacity for collective action, and healing the harms imposed by crime" (Roman et al., 2002). Roman and colleagues (2002) assessed the capacity of community organizations to engage as partners in strategies to prevent crime—and in doing so, discuss the role of community capacity in community justice outcomes. The goal of the project was to review what is known about the role of community organizations in partnerships, and to explore the myriad contextual issues—social, economic, political, and spatial—that challenge or foster their ability to effect positive change within partnership initiatives. Their report synthesizes key dimensions and characteristics that embody partnership capacity.

The capacity of organizations and partnerships to pursue community justice, according to Karp and Clear (2000), is an example of community capacity directed at the joint goals of enhancing social control and improving quality of community life. Stakeholders are brought together to collaborate on plans to increase safety and strengthen the community.

Lastly, Frazier (2007) examined the density of those returning from jail, as well as state and federal prisons. Mapping, originally used for crime statistics, is increasingly also being used for prisoner reentry in order to provide a visual depiction of the organizations and services available for pro-social reintegration. It is also used to provide a visual of those returning from prison and jail. This mapping provides a means to observe patterns of concentration within neighborhoods, of both the availability of reintegration services and the number of reentering individuals in proximity to those services. Roman, Kane, Turner, and Frazier (2006) mapped returning prisoners from the Philadelphia prison system, which is the county jail. Unlike most studies, it included those returning from federal, state, and local correctional facilities.

The results of the Philadelphia study were striking. Of organizations within the community that presently serve individuals returning from prison or jail, most of them said they had the capacity to serve more ex-offenders. Of those that do not currently serve ex-offenders but do not have any restrictions to serving them, 60 percent say they have the capacity to serve more. The locations of the serving organizations were found to be a barrier to enhanced utilization. Furthermore, overnight care was found to be in extremely short supply. Services were found to be uncoordinated and fragmented. The challenge, then, is to connect the tens of thousands of ex-prisoners with the much-needed services available, to develop new services, and to coordinate the service delivery system.

While there is no doubt that many predominantly African American urban communities need help in their struggle to reduce crime and improve the outcomes of those returning from prison and jails, they have extraordinary resilience and fortitude among their institutions and families. One approach, outlined here, is that in addition to providing such help, that coordinated and strategic efforts be made to build the capacities of these communities to better help solve their challenges.

Beverly D. Frazier

See also: Correctional System and African Americans; Disproportionality and Crime; Drug Treatment Strategies; Education; Faith-Based Prisoner Reentry; Inequality Theory; Institutional Racism; Legal Socialization and Race; Prisoner Reentry and African Americans; Prisoner Reentry Models: A Focus on Arkansas; Prisons; Socioeconomic Factors; Theories of Race and Crime

References

Backer, T. E. "Strengthening Nonprofits: Foundation Initiatives for Nonprofit Organizations." In *Building Capacity in Nonprofit Organizations,* edited by C. J. DeVita and C. Fleming, 33–84. Washington, DC: The Urban Institute Press, 2001.

Bellair, P. E. "Social Incarceration and Community Crime: Examining the Importance of Neighbor Networks." *Criminology* 35 (1997): 677–703.

Bursik, R. J. "The Informal Control of Crime through Neighborhood Networks." *Sociological Focus* 32 (1999): 85–97.

Bursik, R. J., and H. G. Grasmick. *Neighborhoods and Crime: The Dimensions of Effective Community Control.* Lanham, MD: Lexington Books, 1993.

Clear, T. R., D. R. Rose, and J. A. Ryder. "Incarceration and the Community: The Problem of Removing and Returning Offenders." *Crime & Delinquency* 47 (2001): 335–51.

Frazier, B. D. "Assessing Philadelphia's Community Capacity for Prisoner Reentry." PhD diss., University of Pennsylvania, 2007.

Gabbidon, S., and H. Greene. *Race and Crime.* Thousand Oaks, CA: Sage, 2005.

Karp, D. R., and T. R. Clear. "Community Justice: A Conceptual Framework." In *Boundaries Changes in Criminal Justice Organizations.* Vol. 2, *Criminal Justice,* edited by C. M. Friel, 323–68. Washington, DC: National Institute of Justice, 2000.

Kretzmann, J. P., and J. L. McKnight. *Building Communities from the Inside Out: A Path toward Finding and Mobilizing a Community's Assets.* Evanston, IL: Center for Urban Affairs and Policy Research, 1993.

Morenoff, J. D., R. J. Sampson, and S. Raudenbush. "Neighborhood Inequality, Collective Efficacy, and the Spatial Dynamics of Urban Violence." *Criminology* 39 (2001): 517–60.

Putman, R. D. *Bowling Alone: The Collapse and Revival of American Community.* New York: Simon & Schuster, 2000.

Robinson, J. W., Jr. "The Conflict Approach." In *Community Development in the United States,* edited by J. A. Christenson and J. W. Robinson, Jr., 73–95. Ames: Iowa State University Press, 1980.

Roman, C., M. J. Kane, and R. Giridharadas. *The Housing Landscape for Returning Prisoners in the District of Columbia.* Washington, DC: The Urban Institute Press, 2006.

Roman, J., M. Kane, E. Turner, and B. Frazier. *An Assessment of Prisoner Preparation for Reentry in Philadelphia.* Washington, DC: The Urban Institute Press, 2006.

Roman, C., and G. E. Moore. *Measuring Local Institutions and Organizations: The Role of Community Institutional Capacity in Social Capital.* Washington, DC: The Urban Institute, 2004.

Roman, C., G. E. Moore, S. Jenkins, and K. M. Small. *Assessing the Capacity to Partner: Community Justice Partnerships.* Washington, DC: The Urban Institute Press, 2002.

Sampson, R. J. "Collective Efficacy Theory: Lessons Learned and Directions for Future Inquiry." In *Taking Stock: The Status of Criminal Justice Theory,* edited by F. Cullen, J. P. Wright, and K. R. Blevins, 149–67. New Brunswick, NJ: Transaction, 2006.

Sampson, R. J., and B. W. Groves. "Community Structure and Crime: Testing Social-Disorganization Theory." *American Journal of Sociology* 94 (1989): 774–802.

Sampson, R. J., S. W. Raudenbush, and F. Earls. "Neighborhoods and Violent Crime: A Multilevel Study of Collective Efficacy." *Science* 277 (1997): 918–24.

Schneider, J. *Social Capital and Welfare Reform: Organizations, Congregations, and Communities.* New York: Columbia University Press, 2006.

Shaw, C. R., and H. D. McKay. *Juvenile Delinquency and Urban Areas.* Chicago: University of Chicago Press, 1942.

Solomon, A., T. Palmer, A. Atkinson, J. Davidson, and L. Harvey. *Prisoner Reentry: Addressing the Challenges of Weed and Seed Communities.* Washington, DC: The Urban Institute Press, 2006.

Stone, M. M., M. A Hager, and J. J. Griffin. "Organizational Characteristics and Funding Environments: A Study of a Population of United Way–Affiliated Nonprofits." *Public Administration Review* 61, no. 3 (May/June 2001): 276–89.

Walsh, A., and L. Ellis. *Criminology: An Interdisciplinary Approach.* Thousand Oaks, CA: Sage, 2007.

Warner, B., and P. Roundtree. "Local Social Ties in a Community and Crime Model: Questioning the Systematic Nature of Informal Social Control." *Social Problems* 44 (1997): 520.

Conyers, Jr., John (1929–)

Representative John Conyers, Jr., a Democrat, has represented a Michigan congressional district that includes parts of Detroit since 1965. He has never faced significant opposition. He is a founding member of the Congressional Black Caucus, designed to strengthen African American lawmakers' ability to address concerns of Black and minority citizens. He was elected to serve as chair of the House Judiciary Committee for the 110th and 111th Congresses. This responsibility fell to him in 2006. The position entails overseeing the Department of Justice (including the FBI) and the federal courts. The Judiciary Committee also has jurisdiction over copyright, civil rights, consumer protection, and constitutional issues (U.S. House of Representatives, n.d; Project Vote Smart). Congressman Conyers has been the committee's ranking Democrat since 1997, and is one of the most senior members of the House of Representatives.

Considered one of the most liberal members of Congress, in November 2010, Conyers was elected to his twenty-fourth term (U.S. House of Representatives, n.d.). His positions on criminal justice bills have reflected the concerns of his constituents and minorities throughout America, and his liberal beliefs. In 2007, Rep. Conyers sponsored a bill to expand the definition of hate crimes to include offenses that target victims based on their sexual orientation. The bill was co-sponsored by a large number of representatives and passed in the House, but was later dropped (U.S. House of Representatives, n.d.).

Representative John Conyers, Jr., is one of the longest serving congressmen. A Democrat, he has served Detroit, Michigan's, congressional district since 1965. He is a founding member of the Congressional Black Caucus and sponsor of the End Racial Profiling Now Act, better known as ERPA. (U.S. House of Representatives)

Conyers has demonstrated that he is a public official who has his own ideas and ideologies. On more than one occasion he has gone against his party's leadership, including voting against the massive 1994 Violent Crime Control and Law Enforcement Act, otherwise known as Omnibus Crime Control Bill, a bill that was strongly supported by President Clinton. The bill provided federal funding for more police officers and programs to reduce violence against women, but also expanded the death penalty. His amendment to that law, the Racial Justice Act, would have allowed persons convicted of capital crimes to challenge the death penalty on the basis of racial bias. Conyers' proposed amendment passed in the House but was defeated in the Senate.

Rep. Conyers' leadership in efforts to enact a federal law banning racial profiling spans more than 10 years. In 1997, he proposed the Traffic Stops Statistics Act (known early as H.R. 118) requiring the U.S. attorney general to conduct a study to determine if racial and ethnic minorities were being targeted for selective enforcement of traffic laws. He has also introduced the End Racial Profiling Act (ERPA) multiple times. Though these proposals have failed to garner the congressional votes they need to become law, his efforts do seem to have influenced some changes in policy (Iwabu, 2011). His activism has been credited with spurring the Bush administration to issue guidelines banning racial profiling in domestic law enforcement practice, and led many states to pass legislation designed to curb the practice of police stopping motorists on the basis of race. The requirement that patrol cars be equipped with video cameras has also been identified as due in part to the efforts of Rep. Conyers (Laney, 2004; Jones-Brown & Maule, 2010).

In his role as chair of the House Judiciary Committee, Rep. Conyers has had other occasions to challenge law enforcement practices. As part of his oversight function, he has called the sheriff of Maricopa County (Phoenix, Arizona) to testify before Congress about possible racial profiling in enforcing immigration laws. The call to testify coincided with an investigation of that county's Sheriff's Department by the Obama administration (Ballasy, 2009). Throughout his time in public office, Rep. Conyers' voting record has reflected his concern for justice and the rights of "the people." His legislative work has been vast and productive. Among that work has been securing $2.75 million in funding for various infrastructure improvements in Detroit and providing unemployed individuals with training programs and jobs through his bill H.R. 870. This bill, known as the Humphrey-Hawkins 21st Century Full Employment and Training Act, was designed to create a new tax on Wall Street speculators "that would pour billions of dollars a year into the Workforce Investment Act training programs and innovative public and private sector jobs programs across the country" (U.S. House of Representatives, n.d.). Rep. Conyers' legislative work also includes the authorship of the Helping Families Save Their Homes Act (H.R. 1106), which allows "bankruptcy court judges to reduce the principal and interest rates for homeowners facing foreclosures and help them remain in their homes" (U.S. House of Representatives, n.d.). Furthermore, he aided in efforts to oppose any legislation designed to cut Social Security benefits or raise the retirement age. He has also taken part in many efforts to reform the health care system (U.S. House of Representatives, n.d.). This list of accomplishments is far from exhaustive, as Rep. Conyers has made it his mission to work to improve public safety and increase productivity and benefits for all citizens.

In criminal justice, this has meant many years opposing numerous laws that have increased prison populations through harsher penalties and mandatory minimum sentences. After decades of opposition, national policy is beginning to swing sharply toward his views, mandating a reduction in such penalties, especially for drug offenses, and withholding prison penalties in favor of greater rehabilitation and support for reentry programs (Marion & Oliver, 2006). The following are some of the other criminal justice policies and legislation that Conyers has backed since 1965.

Violence Against Women Act (1994, 2000, 2005, 2012)
Domestic Violence Connections Campaign Act (2011)
Fair Sentencing Act (2010)
Hate Crimes Prevention Act (2009)
Second Chance Act (2008)
Emmett Till Unsolved Civil Rights Crime Act (2008)
Court Security Improvement Act (2008)
Church Arson Prevention Act (1996)
Pattern and Practice Violations (1994)

Hate Crimes Statistics Act (1990)
Racial Justice Act/Innocence Protection Act (1988)
Sexual Abuse Act (1986)
Law Enforcement Assistance Administration (1976)
End Racial Profiling Act (H.R. 3618)
Shield Our Streets Act (H.R. 4098)
Cyber Privacy Fortification Act (H.R. 6143)

Marvin Zalman

See also: Alternative Sentencing; Correctional System and African Americans; Criminal Deportation; Dating Violence (H.R. 789); Death Penalty; Domestic Violence and African American Females; Environmental Justice; Fair Sentencing Act of 2010; Federal Death Penalty Abolition Act of 2009 (S. 650); Federal Sentencing Disparity; Habitual Offender Laws; Sentencing Disparities; Three Strikes Legislation

References

Ballasy, N. "Sheriff Arpaio Has 'No Intention' of Testifying before Conyers Committee on Alleged Immigration Enforcement Abuses." CBS News, March 16, 2009. http://www .cnsnews.com/PUBLIC/Content/Article.aspx?rsrcid=45078.

Iwabu, T. "Senate Derails Racial Justice Act." *News Observer,* November 29, 2011. http:// www.newsobserver.com/2011/11/29/1677606/senate-derails-racial-justice.html.

Jones-Brown, D., and B. Maule. "Racially Biased Policing: A Review of the Judicial and Legislative Literature." In *Race, Ethnicity and Policing: New and Essential Readings,* edited by S. Rice and M. White, 140–73. New York: New York University Press, 2010.

Laney, G. "Racial Profiling: Issues and Federal Legislative Proposals and Options." Washington, DC: Congressional Research Service, February 17, 2004. http://www.law .umaryland.edu/marshall/crsreports/crsdocuments/RL32231_02172004.pdf.

Marion, Nancy E., and Willard M. Oliver. *The Public Policy of Crime and Criminal Justice.* Upper Saddle River, NJ: Prentice Hall, 2006.

Project Vote Smart. http://www.votesmart.org/search.php?search=john+conyers.

U.S. House of Representatives. "Biography on United States Congressman John Conyers, Jr.," n.d. http://conyers.house.gov/index.cfm?FuseAction=About.Biography.

Correctional System and African Americans

The correctional authority in the United States includes the use of capital punishment, institutional confinement, and community-based alternatives. Death sentences are authorized by federal statutes and by statutes in a majority of states (see Death

Penalty). Confinement in correctional institutions may occur for violations of federal, state, or local laws, both while awaiting trial and after conviction (see Prisons). Federal and state prisons house individuals who have been convicted of felonies, while local jails and detention centers house individuals awaiting trial or serving short sentences. Increasingly, correctional facilities also house individuals awaiting deportation and those who are being detained on suspicion of terrorism.

Community-based supervision is available as an alternative to confinement, typically for those convicted of less serious crimes and for non-dangerous offenders (see Alternative Sentencing). Probation, parole, pretrial detention, diversionary programs, community service, restitution, and fines are all examples of such alternatives. Collectively the agencies, programs, officials, and staff that carry out these functions are considered part of the correctional or corrections system. Blacks, both native and foreign born (see Criminal Deportation), are disproportionately impacted by the workings of the correctional system, especially with regard to death sentences and imprisonment (Alexander, 2010; Loury, 2008; Western, 2006; Miller, 1996; Sklansky, 1995) (see Disproportionality and Crime; Sentencing Disparities).

Race and Executions

Federal

Though not all death penalty cases result in the sentence being carried out, studies have consistently found that the likelihood is greater that a prosecutor will seek and secure a death sentence against a Black defendant than a similarly situated White defendant and that the sentence will result in a completed execution (Baldus et al., 1990). This is particularly true in cases involving White victims (Baldus et al., 1990; Eckholm, 1995; Kansal, 2005; Williams & Holcomb, 2004). A 1994 congressional report prepared in conjunction with the Death Penalty Information Center (DPIC) examined racial disparities in federal death penalty cases from 1988 to 1994. It found that racial minorities were prosecuted under federal death penalty laws "far beyond their proportion in the general population or the population of criminal offenders (Subcommittee on Civil and Constitutional Rights, 1994: 1). An analysis of death-eligible drug cases for that period revealed that 89 percent of defendants against whom federal prosecutors sought death sentences were either African American or Mexican American. The report went on to note that, consistent with a two-year pattern that seemed to be increasing steadily, all 10 of the then recently approved federal capital drug cases involved Blacks. Black defendants' risk of execution was heightened by a section of the federal drug statutes that authorized death sentences for anyone involved with a "continuing criminal enterprise," i.e., drug ring, whose activities resulted in a killing. In the late 1980s and early 1990s, while three-quarters of defendants convicted under that section of the statute were White and about 24 percent were Black (BJS, 1993), 78 percent of those chosen for death penalty prosecutions were Black and only 11 percent were White (Subcommittee on Civil and Constitutional Rights, 1994).

Nearly 10 years later, an Amnesty International report found that "African Americans are disproportionately represented among people condemned to death in the USA" (2003: 1). The report emphasized this point by noting, "While they [African Americans] make up 12 percent of the national population, they account for more than 40 percent of the country's current death row inmates, and one in three of those executed since 1977."

The report also noted that "the United States resorts to the death penalty more than most countries" in the world. It condemned the fact that "the USA will soon carry out its 300th execution of an African American prisoner since resuming judicial killing in 1977" (1). The practice had been suspended nationwide following the U.S. Supreme Court's 1972 decision in *Furman v. Georgia*, but was reinstated with the Court's 1976 decision of *Gregg v. Georgia*. At the time the report was published (April 10, 2003) 290 Blacks had been executed by the federal authorities and an additional 10 were slated for execution by that July (Amnesty International, 2003). U.S. senator Russ Feingold is quoted at the beginning of the report advising the 108th Congress, "We simply cannot say we live in a country that offers equal justice to all Americans when racial disparities plague the system by which our society imposes the ultimate punishment" (Amnesty International, 2003: 1).

Evidence that this racial disparity persists can be found in the fact that, as reported on July 1, 2013, nearly half of the non-military federal death row inmates were Black (28 out of 59). An additional three Blacks on death row at that time had been sentenced by the U.S. military, compared to two Whites. As of February 26, 2014, Black defendants, numbering 470, represented 34 percent of those executed under federal authority since 1976 (DPIC, 2014a).

State

Before being executed, defendants typically spend a considerable number of years confined on death row in correctional institutions. Statistics for executions conducted during the first two months of 2014 demonstrate that, as within the federal correctional system, capital punishment within states disproportionately involves Black defendants, and disproportionally involves White victims, and executions occur after many years of confinement. The DPIC reports that between January 7 and February 26, 2014, 10 executions occurred across five states. The state of Florida led with three. Ohio carried out the lowest number with one. Oklahoma,

Texas, and Missouri each performed two. Among those executed, the longest time spent on death row after being sentenced was 30 years, served by a Black defendant. The shortest time spent was 11 years, served by a White defendant. Five out of the 10 people executed were Black, compared to three Whites and two Latinos. All of the victims in these capital cases were White (DPIC, 2014b).

Research, litigation, and DNA testing have confirmed that Blacks are disproportionately wrongfully convicted of capital crimes (see Innocence Project; Wrongful Convictions) and wrongfully executed. Black defendants often serve long terms on death row as their cases wind through the capital appeals process. Infrequently, appeals result in death sentences being overturned or commuted to life imprisonment (see Abu-Jamal, Mumia). More often, after many years of litigation and requests for clemency, time spent on death row ends with an execution (see the entries on Troy Anthony Davis and Stanley "Tookie" Williams). As with non-capital cases, capital juries have been found to convict Black defendants of capital crimes on lesser evidence than that presented against White defendants (Eberhardt et al., 2006), particularly in cases involving White victims (see Death Penalty; Juries; Racial Stereotyping and Wrongful Convictions).

The increased likelihood of being charged with a capital crime and sentenced to death when the victim is White as opposed to Black is commonly referred to as the "race of victim effect" (Baldus et al., 1990). In 1994, the consistent strength of this finding in death penalty cases led U.S. Supreme Court Justice Harry Blackmun to announce his intent to oppose the death penalty in every case. In a dissenting opinion, he noted, "Even under the most sophisticated death penalty statutes, race continues to play a major role in determining who shall live and who shall die" (*Callins v. Collins,* 1994: 153).

Four correctional systems that currently carry out death sentences have the dubious reputation of being the "top execution states." They are Virginia, Texas, Pennsylvania, and Georgia. Since 1608 they are on record as having completed 1,385, 1,221, 1,043, and 999 executions respectively. A fifth state, New York, which abolished its death penalty for the second time in 2007, had amassed 1,130 executions (DPIC, 2014c). Combined, these figures make up more than a third of the 15,269 executions recorded in the United States between 1608 and 2002. Some statistics suggest that the Supreme Court's *Furman* decision may have helped to reduce the racial disparity in state executions somewhat. Between 1608 and 1972, Whites made up 41 percent of persons executed, while Blacks made up 49 percent. In raw numbers, 7,084 Blacks were executed in comparison to 5,902 Whites—a difference of nearly 1,200. By comparison, Whites represented nearly 80 percent of the general population compared to the 12 to 13 percent represented by Blacks (DPIC, 2014c).

Between 1976 and 2011, there was a downward shift in the percentage of Blacks executed. DPIC reports that during that period 35 percent of executions (432) involved Black defendants, compared to the 56 percent (696) that involved Whites (DPIC, 2014a). This downward shift is more attributable to reductions in state rather than federal capital sentencing, in part because under drug "kingpin" laws nearly all of the capital prosecutions approved by U.S. attorney generals Richard Thornburgh (1988), William Barr (1991), and Janet Reno (1993) were of Black and Latino defendants, amounting to a federal capital prosecution rate of racial/ethnic minorities of nearly 90 percent (Subcommittee on Civil and Constitutional Rights, 1994; Reiman, 1998). Black defendants make up the majority of that 90 percent.

Race and Incarceration

As with capital punishment, the United States has become the world leader in the use of incarceration. Though declines have been reported recently (Carson & Golinelli, 2013), with only 5 percent of the world's population, the United States houses 25 percent of the world's inmates (Loury, 2008; NAACP, 2014). In 2005, with an incarceration rate of 714 per 100,000 residents, the U.S. rate of incarceration was almost 40 percent greater than that of Russia and was 6.2 times that of Canada, 7.8 times that of France, and 12.3 times that of Japan (Loury, 2008: 5). The size of the U.S. incarcerated population has grown exponentially over time from a low of roughly 200,000 in 1970 to 2.3 million in 2008. Consequently, the rate of incarceration increased to more than 762 per 100,000 residents (Carson & Golinelli, 2013).

Since the earliest recording of the prison population, Blacks have been over-represented. Muhammad (2010: 3–4) notes that:

> With the publication of the 1890 census, prison statistics for the first time became the basis of a national discussion about blacks as a distinct and dangerous criminal population. . . . The census marked twenty-five years of freedom and was, consequently, a much anticipated data source for assessing black's status in a post-slavery era. . . . [The] New statistical data and racial identities forged out of raw census data showed that African Americans, as 12 percent of the population, made up 30 percent of the nation's prison population.

The overrepresentation of Blacks among state prison inmates has been continuous, making up 30 percent of individuals admitted to state prison in 1950, 34 percent in 1960, roughly 40 percent in 1970, and 42 percent in 1980 (Petrella, 2014: 83). Even amid reports that the Black incarceration rate fell sharply between 2000 and 2009, Blacks continued to represent 38 percent of state and federal inmates (Goode, 2013). The history of racial disparity has resulted in the following comparative rates of incarceration across race (Sabol et al., 2007: 9, Table 14):

Black men	4,789 per 100,000 residents
White men	736 per 100,000 residents
Latino men	1,862 per 100,000 residents
Black women	358 per 100,000 residents
White women	94 per 100,000 residents
Latina women	152 per 100,000 residents

Of the 2.3 million incarcerated Americans, it is estimated that nearly 1 million are Black. Mid-year 2012 statistics place the number of Blacks confined in jails alone at 274,600 (Minton, 2013). According to Bonzcar (2003), although the increase in incarceration has disproportionately impacted Blacks generally, Black men continue to remain the group most widely affected.

Though males make up the overwhelming majority of Blacks who are incarcerated, in 2005 Black women represented 30 percent of the females who were confined in state and federal prisons, and they were three times as likely as White women to be incarcerated in a prison or jail (Harrison & Beck, 2006: 8). After growing by more than 800 percent (*ABS* Staff, 2012), in 2013 it was reported that the rate of prison incarceration for Black women fell 30.7 percent between 2000 and 2009 (Goode, 2013). Comparatively, in 2009, Black women were 2.8 times more likely to be in prison than White women, as opposed to 6 times more likely in 2000. Changes in drug sentencing statutes have been credited with these recent reductions in Black incarceration rates. But in 2011, young Black women and Black girls were nonetheless noted as the fastest growing population of incarcerated young people (Pfeffer, 2011). Harsh drug laws and zero tolerance policies rather than increased crime are seen as the major contributors to the level of incarceration for Black women and girls over time (Goode, 2013; Pfeffer, 2011).

The racial disparities in incarceration are not explained by differential rates of offending across the races. For example, one source notes that while African American juveniles represent 26 percent of arrests nationwide, they represent "44 percent of youth who are detained pretrial, 46 percent of youth who are waived to adult criminal court and 58 percent of youth admitted to state prisons" (NAACP, 2014). Similarly, while roughly 14 million Whites report using illicit drugs compared to 2.6 million African Americans, Blacks are sent to prison for drug offenses at 10 times the rate of Whites (NAACP, 2014). Before changes were made in the law (see Fair Sentencing Act of 2010), statistics revealed that Blacks made up 80 percent of people sentenced for violating federal crack cocaine laws, despite evidence that two-thirds of crack cocaine users in the United States are White or Latino (NAACP, 2014) (see Disproportionality and Crime; Federal Sentencing Disparity; Sentencing Disparities).

The disparity in the rates of incarceration for drug violations between Blacks and Whites is greatest among males over the age of 18. The drug offender admissions rate for Blacks over age 18 ranges from 60 to 1,146 per 100,000 Black men, whereas for White men it ranges from 6 to 139 per 100,000 (Fellner, 2000). On average, Black men are sent to prison on drug charges at 13 times the rate of White men (Fellner, 2000). In 2008, Black males aged 25 to 29 were incarcerated at a rate of 1 in 10, in comparison to Hispanic males at 1 in 26, and White males at 1 in 63. Black women are also disproportionately sentenced for drug crimes (Harrison & Beck, 2005). Statistics as recent as 2012 confirm that overall, more Black inmates were sentenced for drug offenses than inmates of other races or ethnic backgrounds. Though they do not make up the greatest number of drug users, Blacks represent 59 percent of state prison inmates for drug offenses and serve nearly as much time in prison for a drug offense (58.7 months) as Whites do for a violent crime (61.7 months) (NAACP, 2014).

For more than two decades, Whites have represented nearly 70 percent of the nation's total arrests, while Black arrests comprise much of the remaining 30 percent. Studies find that Blacks are more likely than their White counterparts to be sentenced to time in jail or prison even when they commit comparable crimes (Miller, 1996; Heaney, 1991). Though nationally, the number of Black arrests for homicide and robbery are disproportionately high (see Homicide), Blacks are not arrested for the greatest number of violent crimes, which for federal reporting includes homicides, robberies, forcible rapes, and aggravated assaults. In 2009, for example, according to the *Sourcebook of Criminal Justice Statistics,* Table 2.10, figures for Black violent crime arrests compared to White violent crime arrests were reported as follows:

	Black	White
Murder/Non-negligent Manslaughter	4,801 (49.3%)	4,741 (48.7%)
Robbery	55,742 (55.5%)	43,039 (42.8%)
Forcible Rape	5,319 (32.5%)	10,039 (65.1%)
Aggravated Assault	111,904 (33.9%)	209,922 (63.5%)

(More recent numbers were not available. Due to federal budget cuts, this resource was defunded in August 2012.) These numbers are typical of the statistics from previous and subsequent years. But statistics from 2011 report the percentage of non-Hispanic Black inmates sentenced for violent crimes at 56 percent, compared to 49 percent for non-Hispanic Whites.

Once incarcerated, records indicate that Blacks continue to have a different experience from Whites. They serve longer periods of confinement before release, even when sentenced for comparable offenses. They are more likely than their White counterparts to serve their time in medium- or maximum-security facilities, as compared to minimum security. They are subjected to disciplinary action more often, including time spent in solitary confinement. A recent study found that

Blacks are more likely to be housed in private prisons than are their White counterparts (Petrella, 2014). Such prisons have higher levels of violence and recidivism and the quality of healthcare and educational programs is below that of comparable government-run facilities (Quandt, 2014).

Mass Incarceration and the Prison Industrial Complex

The term "mass incarceration" has been used to describe the United States' expanded use of confinement as a primary criminal justice sanction. The impact of mass incarceration on American life, particularly the lives of African Americans, has become the subject of many books, articles, documentaries, and artistic productions. In her widely read book *The New Jim Crow: Mass Incarceration in the Age of Colorblindness,* civil rights advocate and law professor Michelle Alexander describes the plight of a majority of young Black men living in America's major cities. She notes that despite the election of the nation's first visibly Black president, many of these young men are locked behind bars or have been labeled felons for life. In his book *Race to Incarcerate,* first published in 1999 and updated in 2006 and 2013, executive director of the Sentencing Project Marc Mauer chronicles the massive harm done to generations of Americans, mostly Black, caused by four decades of prison expansion and its collateral consequences. Cornel West, a former professor of African American Studies at Harvard University, is co-organizer of a New York–based activist group called the Stop Mass Incarceration Network, a group that advocates for prison reform and even abolition.

Reports that the incarceration rate for Blacks has begun to drop are encouraging (Goode, 2013), but they fail to address the question of what will become of the hundreds of thousands of individuals who have already been processed through the confinement system (see Prisoner Reentry and African Americans) or who remain locked behind bars because of "get tough" sentencing measures that were intentionally designed to send more offenders to prison and for longer periods of time (see Habitual Offender Laws; Rockefeller Drug Laws: Policy Review; Three Strikes Legislation). Though it is reported that Black incarceration rates began to decrease as early as 2000, figures from mid-year 2006 documented that more than 836,800 Black men were confined in roughly 5,000 state and federal prisons or local jails—nearly 120,000 (118,700) more than White males and 409,900 more than Latino males (Sabol et al., 2007: 9; Loury, 2008: 6). When figures for incarcerated women and juveniles are included, the number of Blacks behind bars in a given year exceeds one million, causing many social commentators to define mass incarceration as a "crisis" in the Black community (Mauer, 1999).

The cost of confinement is extremely high. Estimates range from $60 to $70 billion annually, or roughly one-third of the nation's total yearly public safety budget (NAACP, 2014).

In a speech recorded in 1997, social activist and University of California–Santa Cruz professor Angela Davis (see Davis, Angela Yvonne) used the term "prison industrial complex" (PIC) to describe the network of public and private resources sustaining and profiting from mass incarceration (see *The Prison Industrial Complex,* 1999). The next year, an article in the *Atlantic Monthly* written by investigative journalist Eric Schlosser had the following lead-in: "Correctional officials see danger in prison overcrowding. Others see opportunity. The nearly two million Americans behind bars—the majority of them nonviolent offenders—mean jobs for depressed regions and windfalls for profiteers" (1998: 51).

Angela Davis would go on to describe the PIC as a form of modern-day slavery with both government and private businesses profiting from the labor and services of the disproportionately Black inmates. Many social commentators saw the parallels between the PIC and the "military industrial complex" of the 1950s. In his article, Schlosser specifically stated, "The lure of big money is corrupting the nation's criminal-justice system, replacing notions of safety and public service with a drive for higher profits." He went on to define the PIC as "a set of bureaucratic, political and economic interests that encourage increased spending on imprisonment, regardless of the actual need."

Davis also saw the PIC as the government's attempt to remove the socially undesirable from public view by incarcerating them rather than assisting them. In a 1998 *Colorlines* article she notes, "Homelessness, unemployment, drug addiction, mental illness, and illiteracy are only a few of the problems that disappear . . . when human beings contending with them are relegated to cages." A May 2007 report by the Sentencing Project, a criminal justice research and advocacy nonprofit in Washington, D.C., confirms that these are still the primary issues confronting incarcerated African Americans.

Race and Correctional Control

In addition to the incarcerated population, statistics for 2003 document an additional 4.7 million individuals under correctional supervision by means of probation or parole (Pastore & Maguire, 2005), bringing the correctional population—the incarcerated and those under correctional supervision in the community—to nearly 7 million. In 1990, the Sentencing Project reported that one in four (23 percent) of young Black men between the ages of 20 and 29 was in prison or jail or on probation or parole (Mauer, 1990). Five years later the ratio had shifted to one in three or 32.2 percent (Mauer & Huling, 1995). By 2013, the Sentencing Project warned that "if current trends continue, one of every three Black American males born today can expect to go to prison in his lifetime (Sentencing Project, 2013: 1, citing Mauer, 2011: 8). This 1:3 ratio is exclusive of estimates for probation and parole supervision.

In a 2011 interview, Michelle Alexander pointed out that there are more Black men in prison or jail and on probation and parole than were enslaved in 1850 (Lu, 2011). The number of adult Blacks on probation is estimated to be 1.26 million out of a total of just over 4 million. Adult Blacks on parole number 336,239, or roughly 40 percent of all adult parolees. These figures do not include Black juveniles that come into contact with the criminal justice system or individuals who are awaiting trial on open charges. For a host of reasons not related to their charges or criminal history—called extralegal factors—Blacks are less likely than others to receive pretrial supervised release in the community; and, once convicted, even for relatively minor charges they are likely to receive more restrictive punishments than their White counterparts (Miller, 1996; Heaney, 1991; Gilbert, 2000). For juvenile offenders, Black youth are more likely to receive some form of punishment, while White youth are more likely to receive treatment as a sentencing option (Sheppard & Benjamin-Coleman, 2001).

Collateral Consequences

Racial disparity, in which people of color are overrepresented in the prison and jail systems compared to their portion of the general population, has been termed "disproportionate minority confinement (DMC)."[1] Use of the word "correction" to describe the confinement system in the United States presupposes that, through confinement, people who commit crime can somehow be reformed into law-abiding citizens—an idea that stems from the medical model of criminology (see Prisons). But work by criminal justice professor and corrections expert Todd Clear indicates little evidence of Black inmates being "corrected" by their imprisonment experience. Instead, his 2007 book *Imprisoning Communities: How Mass Incarceration Makes Disadvantaged Neighborhoods Worse* documents the ways in which the growth in the use of incarceration as a primary criminal sanction caused greater harm to Black communities that were already socially and economically deprived. He notes that the removal of many of the men from these communities made them more vulnerable to crime, and deprived young men of adult male role models and women of marriage partners. The increased presence of single-female headed households increased young people's risk of living in poverty and becoming involved with the criminal justice system. This is true despite the fact that the strict sentences for drug offenses (like crack cocaine possession) and for crimes of violence were reportedly enacted by legislators specifically to provide greater protection to those living in low income urban areas—areas where, in most states, the residential population is predominantly Black or Latino (Jones-Brown, 2000).

"Collateral consequences" is a term that has been developed to address the multiple negative residual effects caused by increased correctional control in the United States, especially through prison and jail confinement. Social commentators have argued over whether these consequences are intentional or unintentional (Sklansky, 1995) and the extent to which they stem from or reestablish patterns of racial discrimination dating back to precolonial and colonial America (Browne-Marshall, 2007, Loury, 2008) (see American Law and African Americans; Slavery). Whether collateral consequences are unintended or consequences that should have been anticipated by legislators before enacting various criminal justice statutes, the Sentencing Project has proposed that lawmakers conduct "racial impact" reviews before approving of criminal justice policies or practices. A few states have adopted this approach. For Blacks, the collateral consequences of correctional policies and practices fall into three major areas: family relations, voting rights, and employability.

The mass incarceration of Black parents, especially mothers, left Black children to be raised by friends, relatives, or the foster care system. While 28 percent of mothers reported that their children lived with their fathers during the mother's incarceration, research reveals that in most instances the custodial relatives tended to be grandparents, many of whom were older and on fixed incomes (Sentencing Project, 2007). Being raised by older low-income caregivers and being in the foster care system increased young people's risk for contact with the criminal justice system. Presence within the foster care system increased Black children's risk of suffering various forms of abuse and their risk for contact with the juvenile justice and child welfare systems. The data regarding parental incarceration and correctional control are staggering and disproportionately linked to race. In 2007, the Sentencing Project reported: "In 1999, one in every 14 Black children had a parent in prison, compared with one in every 125 White children. Black children are almost 9 times more likely than White children to have a parent in prison and Hispanic children are 3 times more likely" (2007: 2). In raw numbers, over 1.5 million children had a parent in prison and more than 8.3 million children had a parent under some form of correctional control. More than one in five of such children were under age five (Mumola, 2000). Black children made up a substantial portion of these children.

A majority of all incarcerated parents are housed in prisons 100 to 500 miles from home. Most children with incarcerated parents lived with their mother before she was sentenced to prison. Half of all female prisoners reported that they never had a visit from their children while confined, and one in three mothers reported that they had no telephone contact with their children during their prison stay.

More than 60 percent of mothers expected to serve more than two years in prison on their current sentence (Mumola, 2000: 6). This lack of contact poses the greatest threat to parent-child relationships. The Adoption of Safe Families Act of 1997, which was designed to reduce long stays in the foster care system, allows states to permanently terminate the parental rights to any child who has been living in foster care for 15 of the last 22 months (see Termination of Parental Rights). This means that a substantial portion of Black parents in prison, especially women, run the risk of losing the legal bond to their children forever because the statute allows them to be permanently adopted by others.

Felony disenfranchisement or loss of the right to vote is one of the oldest collateral consequences of being convicted of a crime, whether or not one is incarcerated (see American Law and African Americans). Because it took years of political struggle at great cost, including victimization through lethal violence, for Blacks to obtain that right, its loss by convicted African Americans has a significant historic and political impact (see Civil Rights Movement; Lynching; Slavery). An estimated 1.6 million Blacks are either temporarily or permanently ineligible to vote due to a felony conviction. The Brennan Center for Justice reports that 13 percent of African American males have lost their right to vote, which is seven times the national average. Without voting rights, they are not able to vote for any political leaders or legislative changes, even those that might help curb the tide of mass incarceration and correctional control.

A substantial body of research has documented the difficulties that Blacks experience in the job market. One study found that White males with criminal records have a better chance of being hired than do Black males without criminal records (Pager, 2004; 2007). Another study found that unemployed White males are more likely to receive pretrial release and probation than are employed Black males (Miller, 1996). Once convicted, particularly of a felony, the employability of African Americans decreases significantly, exacerbating an already less-than-optimal situation. In addition to the loss of voting rights, in many jurisdictions, felony disenfranchisement includes the automatic and temporary or permanent ineligibility for certain private and public positions. Answering truthfully to questions regarding arrests or convictions on employment applications often leads to not being hired. Answering falsely or leaving the response blank can lead to being fired if hired. In response to mass incarceration, the needs of the millions of formerly incarcerated prisoners (see Prisoner Reentry and African Americans) and their families and the even greater number of convicted persons under supervision in the community seeking employment, currently there is a "ban the box" movement in place (National Employment Law Project, 2014). This movement is aimed at making employers remove questions about one's criminal history from standard job applications, but would not preclude discussion of such a history in an interview if there are charges that might be relevant to the position the applicant is seeking (e.g., sex abuse charges if the applicant is applying for a position at a school or embezzlement charges if the applicant if applying for a position at a bank).

Other collateral consequences of felony conviction or incarceration that substantially impact African Americans are loss of public housing (see Public Housing); ineligibility for student loans (see Education); and loss of eligibility for food stamps or subsidized medical care (Allard, 2002). The cumulative effects of these collateral consequences are a Black population that is at greater risk of homelessness, undereducation, hunger, poor health, and early death. Gang violence in correctional institutions may also negatively impact community relations on the streets (see Gangs). And the high rate of HIV infection in corrections facilities and the high rate of Black incarceration have combined to substantially increase the rate of HIV infection in the communities to which Black inmates return.

It is noted that corrections, both private and public, is an area of the criminal justice system where a substantial number of Blacks have been able to secure employment. Until recently, employment with departments of corrections has meant steady work, often with overtime, at competitive wages with medical and other benefits. The emergence of private prisons has led to the closing of many public correctional institutions and the opening of private facilities paying minimum wage, with some offering no benefits. In some locations, the portion of the non-inmate workforce is reported as nearly 90 percent Black (Robinson, 2014).

Reducing the Incarceration Rates of African Americans

Though young Black men's overrepresentation in crimes of violence cannot be understated (see Homicide; Gangs), drug crimes, not violent crimes, have been the primary charges leading to African American incarceration for more than two decades. Since drug crimes generally begin with detection by law enforcement agencies, close attention must be paid to the role of police practices as a feeder to the correctional system (see Racial Profiling). Empirical research has shown that Blacks and Latinos are consistently overrepresented among police stops, searches, and arrests (Miller, 1996; Harris, 2002; Weitzur & Tuch, 2002), and that this overrepresentation may be based on the conscious or unconscious use of racial stereotypes when police exercise their discretion (Smith & Alpert, 2007; Eberhardt et al., 2004; Alpert Group, 2004; Engel & Calnon, 2004; Farrell et al., 2003; Smith & Petrocelli, 2001). Based on racial stereotypes, the police may form impressions that various racial groups are most likely to commit crime or certain crimes (for example, violence or drug crimes) (Radosh, 2008; Graham & Lowery, 2004;

Fishman, 1956; Allport, 1954). As a result of these impressions, police in some communities may exhibit patterns of racial discrimination and increased suspiciouson of racial/ethnic minority groups (Walker et al., 2004; Williams & Murphy, 1990; Smith et al., 1984). Consequently, in order to address disproportionate minority confinement and associated racial discrimination, there needs to be an ongoing, comprehensive approach that extends to all components of the criminal justice system.

Joseph, Henriques, and Ekeh (2003) have outlined several areas of reform including revision to the drug laws, which as noted earlier, have already begun. The following are some of their additional recommendations:

Legislative Reform

- Mandatory sentences should be abolished because of their ineffectiveness. They create prison overcrowding, a high cost of imprisonment, and a growing number of (Black) elderly and geriatric inmates in prison. Mandatory sentencing laws should be repealed.
- Governments should examine all sentencing policies and practices with the goal of reducing the use of incarceration, and should develop effective alternatives.

Criminal Justice Reform

- Law enforcement should redirect antidrug efforts toward catching higher-level dealers while providing alternatives for nonviolent offenders (Fellner, 2000).
- Prison and prison programs should be designed to provide rehabilitative opportunities for African American prisoners, and reduce the likelihood that they will return to the system.
- States need to use more front-end strategies with African Americans, such as probation, fines, community service, electronic monitoring, shock incarceration, and diversion. These sanctions promote rehabilitation and reintegration of the offenders.
- Judges should refer more African Americans who are convicted of nonviolent drug violations to community-based corrections and expand the use of treatment programs for African Americans with drug problems. Drug addiction should be seen as a public health problem rather than a criminal justice problem (SAMHSA, 2007; Fellner, 2000).
- States and the federal government should create a formal mandate to eliminate unwarranted sentencing disparity in the criminal justice system.
- It is critical that policymakers, law enforcement, and all criminal justice staff receive training geared toward addressing racial attitudes, discriminatory behavior, and stereotypes.

Delores Jones-Brown, Zelma W. Henriques, and Lorie A. L. Nicholas

Note

1. Closer examination of Black people's experience with policing, courts, and corrections revealed that they are overrepresented in each stage of the criminal justice system process. This recognition resulted in the term being broadened to "disproportionate minority contact" (retaining the acronym DMC).

References

ABS Staff. "Rate of Incarceration for Black Women on the Rise." *Atlanta Black Star,* May 4, 2012. http://atlantablackstar.com/2012/05/04rate-of-incarceration-for-black-women-on-the-rise/.

Alexander, M. *The New Jim Crow: Mass Incarceration in the Age of Colorblindness.* New York: The New Press, 2010.

Allard, P. *Life Sentences: Denying Welfare Benefits to Women Convicted of Drug Offenses.* Washington, DC: The Sentencing Project, 2002.

Allport, G. W. *The Nature of Prejudice.* Reading, MA: Addison-Wesley, 1954.

Alpert Group. *Miami-Dade Racial Profiling Study.* Columbia, SC: Alpert Group, 2004.

Amnesty International. *United States of America: Death by Discrimination: The Continuing Role of Race in Capital Cases.* AI Index: AMR 51/046/2003, 2003.

Baldus, D. C., G. Woodworth, and C. Pulaski. *Equal Justice and the Death Penalty: A Legal and Emprical Analysis.* Boston: Northeastern University Press, 1990.

Bonzcar, T. P. *Prevalence of Imprisonment in the U.S. Population, 1974–2001.* Bureau of Justice Statistics Special Report, NCJ 197976. Washington, DC: Department of Justice, 2003.

Brennan Center for Justice, New York University Law School, New York. https://www.brennancenter.org/issues/restoring-voting-rights.

Browne-Marshall, G. *Race, Law and American Society: 1607 to Present.* New York: Routledge, 2007.

Bureau of Justice Statistics (BJS). *Special Report: Prosecuting Criminal Enterprises.* Washington, DC: U.S. Department of Justice. Table 10 (Convictions 1987–90), 1993.

Bureau of Justice Statistics (BJS). *Correctional Populations in the United States, 2011.* Washington, DC: U.S. Department of Justice, November 2012.

Callins v. Collins, 510 U.S. 1141 (1994).

Carson, E., and D. Golinelli. *Prisoners in 2012: Advance Counts,* Bureau of Justice Statistics. Washington, DC: U.S. Department of Justice, 2013.

Clear, T. *Imprisoning Communities: How Mass Incarceration Makes Disadvantaged Neighborhoods Worse.* New York: Oxford University Press, 2007.

Davis, A. *The Prison Industrial Complex.* CD-ROM (Audiobook). Oakland, CA: AK Press, 1999.

Davis, A. "Masked Racism: Reflections on the Prison Industrial Complex." *Colorlines,* September 10, 1998. http://colorlines.com/archives/author/angela-davis/.

Death Penalty Information Center (DPIC). 2014a. *Race of Death Row Inmates Executed since 1976.* Washington, DC: DPIC, 2014. http://www.deathpenaltyinfo.org/race-death-row-inmates-executed-1976.

Death Penalty Information Center (DPIC). 2014b. *Execution List 2014.* Washington, DC: DPIC, 2014. http://:www.deathpnealtyinfo.org/execution-list-2014.

Death Penalty Information Center (DPIC). 2014c. *Executions in the U.S. 1608–2002: The Espy File.* Washington, DPIC, 2014. http://www.deathpenaltyinfo.org/executions-us-1608-2002-espy-file?scid=8&did=269.

Eberhardt, J., P. Davies, V. Purdie-Vaughns, and S. Johnson. "Looking Deathworthy: Perceived Stereotypicality of Black Defendants Predicts Capital Sentencing Outcomes." *Journal of Psychological Science* 17, no. 5 (2006): 383–86.

Eberhardt, J., P. Goff, V. Purdie, and P. Davies. "Seeing Black: Race, Crime and Visual Processing." *Journal of Personality and Social Psychology* 87, no. 6 (2004): 876–93.

Eckholm, E. "Studies Find Death Penalty Tied to Race of the Victims." *The New York Times,* February 17, 1995. http://www.nytimes.com/1995/02/24/nyregion/studies-find-death-penalty-tied-to-race-of-the-victims.html.

Engel, R., and J. Calnon. "Examining the Influence of Driver's Characteristics during Traffic Stops with Police: Results from a National Survey." *Justice Quarterly* 21 (2004): 702–42.

Farrell, A., J. McDevitt, S. Cronin, and E. Pierce. *Rhode Island Traffic Stop Statistics Act Final Report.* Boston: Northeastern University Institute on Race and Justice, 2003.

Fellner, J. "United States: Punishment and Prejudice: Racial Disparities in the War on Drugs." *Human Rights Watch* 12, no. 2 (May 2000): 1–28.

Fishman, J. A. "An Examination of the Process and Function of Social Stereotyping." *Journal of Social Psychology* 43 (1956): 27–64.

Furman v. Georgia, 408 U.S. 238 (1972).

Gilbert, E. "The Significance of Race in the Use of Restitution." In *The System in Black and White: Exploring the Connections between Race, Crime and Punishment,* edited by M. Markowitz and D. Jones, 199–212. Westport, CT: Praeger, 2000.

Goode, E. "Incarceration Rates for Blacks Have Fallen Sharply, Report Shows." *The New York Times,* February 27, 2013. http://www.nytimes.com/2013/02/28/us/incarceration-rates-for blacks-dropped-report-shows.

Graham, S., and B. S. Lowery. "Priming Unconscious Racial Stereotypes about Adolescent Offenders." *Law and Human Behavior* 28 (2004): 483–504.

Gregg v. Georgia, 428 U.S. 153 (1976).

Harris, D. A. *Profiles in Justice.* New York: New Press, 2002.

Harrison, P. M., and A. J. Beck. *Prison and Jail Inmates at Midyear 2005.* Bureau of Justice Statistics. Washington, DC: U.S. Department of Justice, November 2006.

Harrison, P. M., and A. J. Beck. *Prison and Jail Inmates at Midyear 2004.* Bureau of Justice Statistics. Washington, DC: U.S. Department of Justice, NCJ# 208801, April 2005.

Heaney, G. "The Reality of Guidelines Sentencing: No End to Disparity." *American Criminal Law Review* 28, no. 2 (Fall 1991): 161–232.

Jones-Brown, D. *Race, Crime and Punishment.* Philadelphia: Chelsea House Publishers, 2000.

Joseph, J., Z. W. Henriques, and K. R. Ekeh. "Get Tough Policies and the Incarceration of African Americans." In *With Justice for All: Minorities and Women in Criminal Justice,* edited by J. Joseph and D. Taylor, 149–60. Upper Saddle River, NJ: Prentice Hall, 2003.

Joseph, J., and D. Taylor, eds. *With Justice for All: Minorities and Women in Criminal Justice.* Upper Saddle River, NJ: Prentice Hall, 2003.

Kansal, T. *Racial Disparity in Sentencing: A Review of the Literature.* Washington, DC: The Sentencing Project, January 2005.

Loury, G. *Race, Incarceration and American Values.* Cambridge, MA: MIT Press, 2008.

Lu, T. "Michelle Alexander: More Black Men in Prison Than Were Enslaved in 1850." *Colorlines,* March 30, 2011. http://colorlines.com/archives/2011/03/prison_system _more_black_men_slavery_did.html.

Mauer, M. *Race to Incarcerate.* New York: The New Press, 1999. Updated 2006 and 2013.

Mauer, M. "Addressing Racial Disparities in Incarceration." *The Prison Journal* 91, no. 3 (September 2011): 87S–101S.

Mauer, M. *The Crisis of the Young African American Male and the Criminal Justice System.* Washington, DC: The Sentencing Project for the U.S. Commission on Civil Rights, April 1999.

Mauer, M. *Young Black Men and the Criminal Justice System: A Growing National Problem.* Washington, DC: The Sentencing Project, 1990.

Mauer, M., and T. Huling. *Young Black Americans and the Criminal Justice System: Five Years Later.* Washington, DC: The Sentencing Project, October 1995.

Miller, J. *Search and Destroy: African-American Males in the Criminal Justice System.* New York: Cambridge University Press, 1996.

Minton, Todd D. "Jail Inmates at Midyear 2012: Statistical Tables." Bureau of Justice Statistics, NCJ 241264, Table M. Washington, DC: Department of Justice, 2013. http:// www.bjs.gov/content/pub/pdf/jim12st.pdf.

Muhammad, K. G. *The Condemnation of Blackness: Race, Crime and the Making of Modern Urban America.* Cambridge, MA: Harvard University Press, 2010.

Mumola, C. *Incarcerated Parents and Their Children.* Bureau of Justice Statistics, August. Washington, DC: U.S. Department of Justice, 2000.

NAACP. *Criminal Justice Fact Sheet.* Baltimore: NAACP, 2014. http://www.naacp.org/ pages/criminal-justice-fact-sheet.

National Employment Law Project. *Ban the Box: Resource Guide.* New York: National Employment Law Project, January 2014. http://www.nelp.org/page/-/SCLP/Cityand -CountyHiringInitiatives.pdf?nocdn=1.

Pager, D. *Marked: Race, Crime and Finding Work in an Era of Mass Incarceration.* Chicago: University of Chicago Press, 2007.

Pager, D. "The Mark of a Criminal Record." *Focus* 23, no. 2 (Summer 2004): 44–6.

Pastore, A., and K. Maguire. *Sourcebook of Criminal Justice Statistics* online, Tables 6.1 and 6.2, 2005. http://www.albany.edu/sourcebook/.

Petrella, C. "The Color of Corporate Corrections, Part II: Contractual Exemptions and the Overrepresentation of People of Color in Private Prisons." *Radical Criminology* 3 (2014): 81–100.

Pfeffer, R. "In Post Racial America Prisons Feast on Black Girls." *Ethnoblog, New America Media,* March 15, 2011. http://ethnoblog.newamericamedia.org/2011/03/ in-post-racial-america-prisons-feast-on-black-girls.

Quandt, K. R. "Why There's an Even Larger Racial Disparity in Private Prisons Than in Public Ones." *Mother Jones,* February 17, 2014. http://www.motherjones.com/mojo/2014/01/even-larger-racial-disparity-private-prisons-public-prisons.

Radosh, P. F. "War on Drugs: Gender and Race Inequities in Crime Control Strategies." *Criminal Justice Studies* 21, no. 2 (2008): 167–78.

Reiman, J. *The Rich Get Richer and the Poor Get Prison.* Boston: Allyn and Bacon, 1998.

Robinson, Jr., A. "Inside a CCA Private Prison: Two Slaves for the Price of One." *Bayview,* March 3, 2014. http://sfbayview.com/2014/inside-a-cca-private-prison-two-slaves-for-the-price-of-one/.

Sabol, W., T. Minton, and P. Harrison. *Prison and Jail Inmates at Midyear 2006.* Bureau of Justice Statistics, Table 14. Washington, D.C.: U.S. Department of Justice, NCJ217675, June, 2007.

Schlosser, E. "The Prison-Industrial Complex." *The Atlantic Monthly,* December 1998: 51–77.

Sentencing Project, The. *Report to the United Nations Human Rights Committee: Regarding Racial Disparities in the United States Criminal Justice System,* August. Washington, DC: 2013.

Sentencing Project, The. *Women in the Criminal Justice System: Briefing Sheets,* May. Washington, DC: The Sentencing Project, 2007.

Sheppard, V. B., and R. Benjamin-Coleman. "Determinants of Service Placements for Youth with Serious Emotional and Behavioral Disorders." *Community Mental Health Journal* 37, no. 1 (2001): 53–65.

Sklansky, D. A. "Cocaine, Race and Equal Protection." *Stanford Law Review* 47, no. 6 (1995): 1238–1322.

Smith, M. R., and G. P. Alpert. "Explaining Police Bias: A Theory of Social Conditioning and Illusory Correlation." *Criminal Justice and Behavior* 34, no. 10 (October 2007): 1262–83.

Smith, M. R., and M. Petrocelli. "Racial Profiling? A Multivariate Analysis of Police Traffic Stop Data." *Police Quarterly* 4 (2001): 4–27.

Smith, D., C. Visher, and L. Davidson. "Equity and Discretionary Justice: The Influence of Race on Police Arrest Decisions." *Journal of Criminal Law and Criminology* 75 (1984): 234–49.

Sourcebook of Criminal Justice Statistics Online, Table 4.10, 2009. http://www.albany.edu/sourcebook/pdf/4102009.pdf.

Stop Mass Incarceration Network. http://www.stopmassincarceration.net/.

Subcommittee on Civil and Constitutional Rights. Staff Report. *Racial Disparities in Federal Death Penalty Prosecutions 1988–1994.* Washington, DC, Committee on the Judiciary, 103rd Congress, Second Session, March 1994.

Substance Abuse and Mental Health Services Administration (SAMHSA). *Results from the 2006 National Survey on Drug Use and Health: National Findings.* NSDUH Series H-32, DHHS Publication No. SMA 07-4293 Rockville, MD: Office of Applied Studies, 2007.

Walker, S., C. Spohn, and M. DeLone. *The Color of Justice,* 3rd ed. Belmont, CA: Thomson-Wadsworth, 2004.

Weitzur, R., and S. A. Tuch. "Perception of Racial Profiling: Race, Class, and Personal Experience." *Criminology* 40 (2002): 435–56.

Western, B. *Punishment and Inequality in America*. New York: Russell Sage Foundation, 2006.

Williams, H., and P. V. Murphy. "The Evolving Strategy of Police: A Minority View." Paper 13 in the Perspectives on Policing series, National Institute of Justice, Washington, DC, January 1990.

Williams, M., and J. Holcomb. "The Interactive Effects of Victim Race and Gender on Death Sentence Disparity Findings." *Homicide Studies* 8, no. 4 (November 1, 2004): 350–76.

Criminal Deportation

Criminal deportation is the act or instance of ordering, removing, and/or transporting a person out of the state or country due to his or her involvement in criminal activity or violation of the immigration laws. Under the federal Immigration and Nationality Act (INA), individuals who are not citizens of the United States can be deported on the following criminal grounds: commission of an aggravated felony; domestic violence, including child abuse; weapons offenses, particularly involving firearms or explosives; drug offenses; and crimes involving moral turpitude (CIMT).

These grounds for deportation apply to all noncitizens, even those who are present in the country as permanent residents, or holders of "green cards." A person who holds a green card can be subject to criminal deportation even if that person has been in the country for many years, including close to his or her entire life. Birthright citizenship prevents a person from being deported if he or she is born within a U.S. state or territory, even if his or her parents were in the country illegally (see Citizenship).

Conviction of an aggravated felony as a basis for deportation includes some obvious crimes: any violent crime subject to imprisonment of one year or more, murder, rape, drug trafficking, and sex involving minors. But they also include some not-so-obvious crimes—prostitution-related offenses like pimping or pandering, forgery, fraud, burglary, theft, writing bad checks, shoplifting, and driving while intoxicated. In addition, domestic violence, violating a restraining order, stalking, and child abuse are common grounds for criminal deportation. Individuals can be deported for the violation of immigration laws, though technically one's immigration status is a civil matter.

Noncitizens who are found to illegally possess firearms or explosives (which can include fireworks) or those who are convicted of an assault with a deadly weapon, even if not a firearm, are also subject to deportation. For drug offenses, even those who possess drugs for personal use can be subject to deportation, along with drug traffickers. The catch-all phrase "crimes involving moral turpitude," or CIMT, has been the most controversial basis for criminal deportation because it may allow a person to be deported or "removed" from the United States for crimes that are considered minor by many standards. Whether a crime involves moral turpitude is determined by an immigration judge on a case-by-case basis. Only simple assault has been ruled to not constitute a CIMT offense, barring extenuating circumstances.

There is no statutory definition of CIMT. CIMT can encompass a felony or misdemeanor that manifests an element of "baseness or depravity," or that exhibits "evil or predatory intent." For all offenses, including CIMTs, an individual is subject to criminal deportation whether he or she commits one of the eligible offenses or is convicted of having attempted or conspired to commit one of the offenses. For CIMT, conviction of two or more crimes, or one conviction that occurs within five years of having been admitted to the United States, is required before removal. The INA makes the lives of noncitizens subject to highly discretionary decisions by criminal justice personnel (Brotherton & Kretsedemas, 2008; Hing, 2004; Harris, 2007; Human Rights Watch, 2010).

Although the U.S. government has exercised its right to protect itself from the criminality of noncitizens since at least the 1700s (the Alien and Sedition Laws of 1798 authorized the president to deport any alien or resident noncitizen deemed a threat or danger to the well-being of the country), following the terrorist attacks of September 11, 2001, the criminal deportation laws were expanded and their authority increased. In line with the perceived urgency and renewed interest in the protection of the country from foreign-born terrorists, Congress passed the USA Patriot Act and ordered the reorganization of the Immigration and Naturalization Service (INS). The new department charged with the regulation and enforcement of the immigration laws is the Bureau of Immigration and Customs Enforcement (ICE) formed in 2003.

In the aftermath of the 2001 terrorist attacks, even prior to the formation of ICE, the arrest and deportation or "removal" of noncitizens accused of criminal activities became more intense. By the end of fiscal year 2001, the number of criminal deportees had reached 70,000, in contrast to 1980, when the figure was less than 500, despite the existence of 31,000 people who were known to be eligible for criminal deportation (Harris, 2007). In 2005, the number of aliens sent out of the country reached 89,406 (Dougherty et al., 2006). Records from the U.S. Department of Homeland Security (DHS) show that 128,000 convicted alien (e.g., noncitizen) criminals were deported in 2009 (DHS, Office of Immigration Statistics, 2010). These figures more than doubled by 2011 (Simanski & Sapp, 2011).

In 2011, the then director of ICE, John Morton, announced that the agency had developed certain priorities for individuals whom it would target for removal.

These included those who had broken criminal laws, those who represented threats to national security, recent border crossers, repeat violators of immigration laws, and fugitives from immigration court. This array of priority deportees resulted in the removal of nearly 400,000 (396,906) individuals by ICE's Office of Enforcement and Removal Operations in a single year, the largest number in the agency's nine-year history (Inda, 2013). Of those removed, nearly 55 percent (216,698) were convicted of felonies or misdemeanors. This represented an 89 percent increase in criminal removals since 2008 (DHS, 2011).

Among the criminal deportees in 2011, there were 1,119 individuals who had been convicted of homicide, 5,848 who were convicted of sexual offenses, nearly 45,000 (44,653) who were convicted of drug-related crimes, and 35,927 who were convicted of driving under the influence (DHS, 2011). The result was that 90 percent of ICE's removals in 2011 fell into a priority category. And these criminal deportees had dual targeted identities. More than two-thirds were either recent border crossers or repeat immigration law violators (Goodson, 2011).

There is a historical irony to the enforcement of criminal deportation laws in the United States. During the precolonial and colonial period, England had a practice of transporting convicts to the land that eventually became the United States. Many of those transported were European ethnics who were granted the opportunity to choose between the dungeon or the "New World." Under modern criminal deportation practice, many of those who are deported based on criminal convictions are people of color (Brotherton & Kretsedemas, 2008). According to a report issued by the Department of Homeland Security (DHS), in 2009, 76 percent of the deportees were from Mexico (Simanski & Sapp, 2012). Agency statistics also indicate that individuals from Africa and the Afro-Caribbean make up a substantial portion of those who are subject to criminal removal. Statistics for 1998 to 2005 indicate that criminal removal for individuals from Africa totaled 5,551 for the seven-year period. Criminal deportations of those from other parts of North America (outside the United States) totaled more than 500,000 (557,964), by far the majority of all criminal deportations (DHS, 2006).

Beyond Mexico, there were substantial North American deportations to the Caribbean, including more than 20 countries where the residential population is predominantly Black (of African ancestry). These locations included Anguilla, Antigua and Barbuda, Bahamas, Barbados, Bermuda, British Virgin Islands, Cayman Islands, Grenada, Guadeloupe, Haiti, Jamaica, Martinique, Montserrat, Netherlands Antilles, Saint Kitts and Nevis, Saint Lucia, Saint Vincent and the Grenadines, Trinidad and Tobago, Turks and Caicos, and the U.S. Virgin Islands (DHS, 2006). In comparison, the number of criminal deportations to nations where the residential population is predominantly White (for example, Canada and the European Union) tends to be very low, though the number of illegal immigrants from these nations collectively may exceed one million (Passel, 2005; Passel et al., 2004; Hoeffer et al., 2012).

Table 1 Criminal Deportations Worldwide

Region & Country of Nationality	2002	2003	2004	2005	2006	2007	2008	2009	2010	2011
Africa	687	854	838	761	704	805	647	718	666	635
Asia	1,211	1,442	1,518	1,445	1,206	1,217	1,339	1,334	1,559	1,535
Caribbean	4,340	4,685	4,936	5,309	4,242	4,207	4,216	4,543	4,129	4,148
Central America	5,144	6,487	8,241	8,352	14,370	14,913	17,045	20,839	29,461	32,090
Europe	938	1,058	1,198	1,107	1,054	953	1,076	1,078	1,226	1,221
North America	58,471	66,551	72,090	71,241	73,594	77,378	77,878	100,034	128,853	145,157
Oceania	133	133	152	123	113	143	165	160	203	217
South America	2,503	2,513	3,400	4,152	3,199	2,774	2,890	3,118	3,500	3,366
Unknown	2	8	7	1	8	4	10	13	19	13

- *Africa* includes Algeria, Angola, Benin, Botswana, Burkina Faso, Burundi, Cameroon, Cape Verde, Central African Republic, Chad, Comoros, Cote d'Ivoire, Democratic Republic of the Congo, Djibouti, Egypt, Equatorial Guinea, Eritrea, Ethiopia, Gabon, Gambia, Ghana, Guinea, Guinea-Bissau, Kenya, Lesotho, Liberia, Libya, Madagascar, Malawi, Mali, Mauritania, Mauritius, Morocco, Mozambique, Namibia, Niger, Nigeria, Republic of the Congo, Reunion, Rwanda, Saint Helena, Sao Tome and Principe, Senegal, Seychelles, Sierra Leone, Somalia, South Africa, Sudan, Swaziland, Tanzania, Togo, Tunisia, Uganda, Western Sahara, Zambia, and Zimbabwe.

- *Asia* includes Afghanistan, Bahrain, Bangladesh, Bhutan, Brunei, Burma, Cambodia, China, Cyprus, East Timor, Hong Kong, India, Indonesia, Iran, Iraq, Israel, Japan, Jordan, Kuwait, Laos, Lebanon, Macau, Malaysia, Maldives, Mongolia, Nepal, North Korea, Oman, Pakistan, Philippines, Qatar, Saudi Arabia, Singapore, South Korea, Sri Lanka, Syria, Taiwan, Thailand, Turkey, United Arab Emirates, Vietnam, and Yemen.

- *Europe* includes Albania, Andorra, Armenia, Austria, Azerbaijan, Belarus, Belgium, Bosnia and Herzegovina, Bulgaria, Croatia, Czech Republic, Denmark, Estonia, Finland, France, Georgia, Germany, Gibraltar, Greece, Holy See, Hungary, Iceland, Ireland, Italy, Kazakhstan, Kyrgyzstan, Latvia, Liechtenstein, Lithuania, Luxembourg, Macedonia, Malta, Moldova, Monaco, Netherlands, Norway, Poland, Portugal, Romania, Russia, San Marino, Slovak Republic, Slovenia, Spain, Serbia and Montenegro, Switzerland, Tajikistan, Turkmenistan, Ukraine, United Kingdom, and Uzbekistan.

- *North America* includes Canada, Greenland, Mexico, Saint Pierre and Miquelon, United States, and the countries within the regions of the Caribbean and Central America.

(Continued)

- *Caribbean* includes Anguilla, Antigua and Barbuda, Aruba, Bahamas, Barbados, Bermuda, British Virgin Islands, Cayman Islands, Cuba, Dominica, Dominican Republic, Grenada, Guadeloupe, Haiti, Jamaica, Martinique, Montserrat, Netherlands Antilles, Puerto Rico, Saint Kitts and Nevis, Saint Lucia, Saint Vincent and the Grenadines, Trinidad and Tobago, Turks and Caicos Islands, and U.S. Virgin Islands.

- *Central America* includes Belize, Costa Rica, El Salvador, Guatemala, Honduras, Nicaragua, and Panama.

- *Oceania* includes American Samoa, Australia, Christmas Island, Cocos (Keeling) Islands, Cook Islands, Federated States of Micronesia, Fiji, French Polynesia, Guam, Kiribati, Marshall Islands, Nauru, New Caledonia, New Zealand, Niue, Northern Mariana Islands, Palau, Papua New Guinea, Pitcairn Islands, Samoa, Solomon Islands, Tokelau, Tonga, Tuvalu, Vanuatu, and Wallis and Futuna Islands.

- *South America* includes Argentina, Bolivia, Brazil, Chile, Colombia, Ecuador, Falkland Islands, French Guiana, Guyana, Paraguay, Peru, Suriname, Uruguay, and Venezuela.

NOTE: THIS TABLE IS A MODIFICATION OF THE ORIGINAL, WHICH SHOWED BOTH CRIMINAL AND NONCRIMINAL DEPORTATIONS BY REGION. FOR EACH REGION, THIS TABLE PRESENTS THE NUMBER OF CRIMINAL DEPORTATIONS ONLY.

Source: U.S. Department of Homeland Security. *Yearbook of Immigration Statistics: 2011.* Washington, DC: U.S. Department of Homeland Security, Office of Immigration Statistics (Table 41), 2012.

Estimating that roughly two-thirds of North American criminal deportations involve Mexicans leaves nearly 150,000 criminal deportations to Africa and the Afro-Caribbean (exclusive of Cuba and the Dominican Republic) over the seven-year period.

It has been suggested that War on Drugs rhetoric that associated Jamaican posses with drug dealing and marijuana use (Sklansky, 1995), and the general stereotyping of Blacks as violent, contributed to Blacks being targeted for criminal deportation. Criminal deportees are forced to leave their families, friends, personal possessions, and jobs behind often to return to countries where they no longer have familial, emotional, or other ties. Being deported from the United States does not guarantee that these persons deported will be returned to their native country. They are simply removed from the United States. Many Caribbean countries have complained that the arrival of criminal deportees from the United States has driven up their crime rates because the natives and non-natives arrive in the country without any financial support or community ties (Brotherton & Kretsedemas, 2008).

Although the term "alien" has long been used to describe noncitizens and "illegal alien" has been used to describe those who are in the country without proper documents (such as visit, education, or work visas), the recognition that in modern times such terms are being applied to children who have little or no control over their citizenship status has led to the development of terms such as "foreign-born," "undocumented," or "out of status" to describe individuals who otherwise would fall within one of the "alien" groups.

But old traditions die hard, and especially with regard to criminal deportations the word "alien" continues to be used in government reporting (DREAM Act, 2001–2002).

According to one report, most of the aliens deported in 2009 were convicted of crimes involving illegal drugs, traffic offenses, and immigration-related offenses (DHS, 2010). It should be noted that a person who actively interferes with an investigation into the immigration status of a loved one, or conceals that person to prevent his or her apprehension and deportation, can be charged with obstructing justice. Felony obstruction, an obstruction charge that can result in a year or more of imprisonment, can amount to an aggravated felony and subject the loved one to deportation. Conviction of an aggravated felony has dire procedural consequences. Aliens convicted of aggravated felonies are not eligible to invoke the "waivers" or exceptions laws to stop their deportation. Unlike other criminal aliens, aliens convicted of aggravated felonies are not eligible to apply for asylum or permanent residence. Aliens charged with aggravated felonies are not entitled to bail. They must remain in detention until the Department of Homeland Security is able to carry out their deportation order. Such felons are technically ineligible for the provision of the INA that allows for waiver of deportation if the defendant is willing to cooperate with the government and provide information (i.e., snitch) about other criminals (Cook, 2003; TRAC Immigration, 2006).

Provisions of the immigration law allow an immigration judge to hear deportation cases and decide whether or not to sign a deportation order before a criminal alien is removed from the country. However, aliens involved in aggravated felony offenses are not entitled to judicial determination or review of their cases before removal. Their removal from the country can be administratively effected through the immigration agency. Furthermore, aliens involved in aggravated felony offenses are not entitled to an appeal of the deportation decision. Generally, aliens convicted of criminal acts and deported from the United States may legally apply to return to the country after about 5 to 20 years, depending on their circumstances and the conditions under which they were deported. However, aliens accused of aggravated felonies are permanently expelled (Cook, 2003).

In conclusion, noncitizens residing in the United States have limited rights and privileges. Their rights and privileges are further diminished if they become involved in criminal activities. Like those of Mexican appearance, immigrants of African ancestry may be targeted for immigration enforcement based on criminal stereotypes or their residence in locations where there is high police presence (Seghetti et al., 2009; Brotherton & Kretsedemas, 2008). In addition to other sanctions, aliens involved in even minor criminal activities can be temporarily deported. However, aliens engaging in aggravated felonies have limited legal recourse and their ejection from the country is permanent. Attempts to return to the country in order to maintain contact with loved ones left behind will again subject them to deportation. Thus, current immigration law may serve to keep some members of the Black community in a vicious cycle of government confinement and control.

Rochelle Cobbs and O. Oko Elechi, with Delores Jones-Brown

See also: Citizenship; Disproportionality and Crime; Federal Sentencing Disparity; Sentencing Disparities; Socioeconomic Factors; Stop Snitching Campaign; War on Drugs

References

Brotherton, D. C., and P. Kretsedemas. *Keeping Out the Other: A Critical Introduction to Immigration Enforcement Today.* New York: Columbia University Press, 2008.

Cook, M. "Banished for Minor Crimes: The Aggravated Felony Provision of the Immigration and Nationality Act as a Human Rights Violation." *Boston College Third World Journal* 23, no. 2 (2003): 293–329.

Dougherty, M., D. Wilson, and A. Wu. "Immigration Enforcement Actions: 2006." 2006. http://http://www.dhs.gov/xlibrary/assets/statistics/yearbook/2005/Enforcement_AR_05.pdf.

DREAM Act (Development, Relief and Education for Alien Minors). 2001–2002. 107th Congress, S. 1291.

Goodson, H. N. "ICE Reports FY2011 Removal Totals of Illegal Aliens from the U.S." Hispanic News Network USA Blog. October 18, 2011. https://hngwiusa.wordpress.com/2011/10/18/ice-reports-fy2011-removal-totals-of-illegal-aliens-from-the-u-s/.

Harris, C. "A Problem of Proof: How Routine Destruction of Court Records Routinely Destroys a Statutory Remedy." *Stanford Law Review* 59, no. 6 (2007): 1791–1820.

Hing, B. O. *Defining America through Immigration Policy.* Philadelphia: Temple University Press, 2004.

Hoeffer, M., N. Rytina, and B. Baker. "Estimates of the Unauthorized Immigrant Population Residing in the United States." U.S. Department of Homeland Security, Office of Immigration Statistics, Washington, DC, March 2012.

Human Rights Watch. *Deportation by Default: Mental Disability, Unfair Hearings, and Indefinite Detention in the U.S. Immigration System.* New York, 2010. http://www.hrw.org.

Inda, J. X. "Subject to Deportation: IRCA, 'Criminal Aliens,' and the Policing of Immigration." *Migration Studies* 1, no. 3 (2013): 292–310. http://migration.oxfordjournals.org/content/early/2013/02/13/migration.mns003.full.pdf+html.

Passel, J. "Estimates of the Size and Characteristics of the Undocumented Population." Pew Hispanic Center, Washington, DC, March 21, 2005.

Passel, J., J. Van Hook, and F. Dean. "Estimates of Legal and Unauthorized Foreign Born Population for the U.S. and Selected States, Based on Census 2000." Report to the Census Bureau. Urban Institute, Washington, DC, June 1, 2004.

Seghetti, L. M., K. Ester, and M. J. Garcia. *Enforcing Immigration Law: The Role of State and Local Law Enforcement.* Washington, DC: Congressional Research Service, 2009.

Simanski, J., and M. Sapp. M. *Immigration Enforcement Actions: 2011.* 2012. http://www.dhs.gov/sites/default/files/publications/immigration-statistics/enforcement_ar_2011.pdf.

Sklansky, D. "Cocaine, Race, and Equal Protection." *Stanford Law Review* 47, no. 6 (1995): 1283–1322.

TRAC Immigration: Aggravated Felonies and Deportation. Syracuse, NY: Trac Reports Inc., 2006. http://trac.syr.edu/immigration/reports/155/.

U.S. Department of Homeland Security. *Yearbook of Immigration Statistics: 2011.* Washington, DC: U.S. Department of Homeland Security, Office of Immigration Statistics, 2012.

U.S. Department of Homeland Security. *FY 2011: ICE Announces Year-End Removal Numbers, Highlights Focus on Key Priorities Including Threats to Public Safety and National Security.* Washington, DC: U.S. Department of Homeland Security, 2011. www.ice.gov/news/releases/1110/111018washingtondc.htm.

U.S. Department of Homeland Security. *Immigration Enforcement Actions: 2009.* Washington, DC: U.S. Department of Homeland Security, Office of Immigration Statistics, 2010. http://www.dhs.gov/xlibrary/assets/statistics/publications/enforcement _ar_2009.pdf.

U.S. Department of Homeland Security. *Yearbook of Immigration Statistics: 2005.* Washington, DC: U.S. Department of Homeland Security, Office of Immigration Statistics (Table 41), 2006.

Critical Race Theory

Critical race theory (CRT) is a form of legal analysis that places race and racism at the center of American lawmaking. It takes into consideration how racism affects individuals and groups in regards to the law. CRT originated in two prominent law schools, Harvard and the University of California–Berkeley, during the late 1960s and early 1970s, as lawyers and law professors began to recognize that the "gains of the civil rights era had stalled and in many cases were being rolled back" (Delgado & Stefancic, 2005: 2). At a keynote address for the founding of the Center on Race, Crime and Justice at John Jay College of Criminal Justice in New York, CRT cofounders Richard Delgado and Jean Stefancic (2005) went on to suggest that CRT grew out of the understanding that "[n]ew approaches were needed to deal with the new types of colorblind, subtle, or institutional racism that were developing, and a public that seemed increasingly tired of hearing about race."

Derrick Bell, one of the best-known founders of CRT originating from Harvard Law School, was not afraid to express his anger over what he saw as the slow progress of racial reform in the United States. He believed that Whites support civil rights protections for Blacks only if those protections also promote White self-interest and social status (Bell, 1980). Bell maintained that racial minorities are a permanently oppressed caste and that the concept of equality before the law is unfair to Blacks because the moral claims of Blacks are superior to those of Whites. Other CRT scholars include Kimberle Crenshaw, Patricia Williams, Charles Ogletree, Charles Lawrence, Alan Freeman, Girardeau Spann, Mari Matsuda, Ian Haney Lopez, Michelle Alexander, and the late Haywood Burns, former dean of City University of New York (CUNY) Law School.

Since its inception, CRT analysis has expanded into broader fields, most notably education (American Educational Association, 2006; Dixson & Rousseau, 2005; Laurence et al., 1998; Yosso, 2005; Parker et al., 1999). There are sociologists, psychologists, philosophers, and others who also identify themselves as critical race theorists. Many of them use CRT to understand and explain the overrepresentation of African Americans within the criminal justice system and their continually oppressed status within the wider society.

Schaeffer (2011) defines racism as a belief that one's race is superior to another. One of the primary tenets of CRT is that racism is ordinary, not exceptional; "that it is the usual way that society does business and thus represents the common, everyday experience of most people of color in this country [the United States]. Its ordinariness [sometimes] makes racism hard to recognize, much less address . . ." (Delgado & Stefancic, 2005: 5–6). According to Derrick Bell, existing legal structures are, like American society at large, racist in their very construction (Bell, 2008). CRT suggests that to combat "institutional racism," oppressed racial groups have both the right and the duty to decide for themselves which laws are valid and are worth observing. The work of George Washington University law professor Paul Butler speaks to these issues. A former prosecutor and CRT scholar, he has written about Black jury nullification (Butler, 1995) (see Juries) and put forth a hip-hop theory of justice (Butler, 2008) in which he maintains that "in order to fight for justice, Americans must sometimes fight the power of the justice system" (NPR, 2009).

Another CRT scholar, Professor Charles Lawrence of Georgetown Law School, has argued that much discrimination is unconscious—that is, devoid of any intent on the part of the actor to harm or disadvantage a particular Black victim. Yet legal doctrine for the most part requires demonstration of intent. In "The Id, the Ego and the Equal Protection" (1987), Lawrence argued that the Supreme Court's approach in *Washington v. Davis* (a 1976 U.S. Supreme Court case on discriminatory intent versus racially disparate effects of a written test for applicants to the police department in Washington, D.C.) is inadequate to deal with the racism that is implicit, or latent, rather than explicit. He proposed a new "cultural meaning" test, according to which courts would look to cultural symbols to decide whether an act's meaning is racially discriminatory. The article constituted an important early use of social science to expose the deficiencies of legal doctrine.

"Interest convergence" or "material determinism" (Bell, 1980) is a second feature of CRT. These concepts recognize that racism can advance the interests of both White elites and the White working class; as such, a large segment of society has little incentive to work to eradicate it. For example, through racism, White elites are in a position to manipulate the labor pool, and working-class Whites can have a reason to feel superior to Blacks (and other visible minorities). This feature of CRT counters common social science approaches that seek to place class ahead of race as the leading cause of social oppression and contact with the criminal justice system (Delgado & Stephancic, 2005).

A third principle of CRT is the notion that race is socially constructed and the social identity of racial groups are constructed differently at different times based on what Whites see as being in their best interest. Many CRT scholars have written about the concept of "whiteness" (see Delgado & Stephancic, 1997; Haney Lopez, 1996; Harris, 1993). Jean Stefancic was a prolific Whiteness author, and Derrick Bell endorsed a journal dedicated to the abolition of Whiteness. The journal was called *Race Traitor,* and its motto was "Treason to the White race is loyalty to humanity." In her 1993 article "Whiteness as Property," CRT scholar Cheryl Harris argues that while Whiteness was initially constructed as a form of racial identity, it has evolved into a form of property, both historically and currently acknowledged and protected by American laws.

CRT scholars have termed this "differential racialization," and it has an impact on how members of different racial groups are seen based on shifting needs of the White majority. Labor market needs and concerns about crime are primary areas where differential racialization occurs and laws are adjusted accordingly (Delgado, 2000). When labor needs are high, laws are adjusted to address those needs; for example, allowing more immigrants of color into the country to serve as low-wage laborers, but restricting such immigration when perceived labor needs are low or perceived as in competition with the White working-class. The federal, state, and local statutes that supported African slavery for nearly 250 years in a country professing adherence to principles dedicated to recognizing the inalienable right to freedom, equality, and liberty is another labor needs example (see American Law and African Americans).

The current practice of allowing the police to aggressively use stop-and-frisk tactics almost exclusively against young Black and Latino males, in order to keep crime down in major cities like New York, is an example of differential racialization in the crime concern context. CRT also looks at the ways in which different identities and various stereotypes and assumptions about them intersect to increase the likelihood of oppression for individuals and groups of color. For example, aggressive stop-and-frisk policing tactics are used and justified as legitimate more often in urban poor communities than in suburban more affluent communities, meaning that boys and men of color and who are economically disadvantaged are more likely to be harassed by such tactics. However, by virtue of the focus on urban poor communities, women of color in such spaces also find themselves subject to more police contact than do White women of comparable status.

By some accounts, the recognition of the intersectionality of different identities, and the differential racialization of those identities by Whites, has led to the splintering of CRT perspectives over time. For example, there are now LatCrits, those who study and write about the intersectionality of immigration status, language, and nationality for Latinos, and FemCrits, who study the intersectionality of one's status as a woman or girl with being middle-class versus poor and Black versus White. TribalCrits examine various identities that intersect with being Native American. Critics of all forms of critical legal theory claim that it lacks neutrality and is merely a form of advocacy rather than intellectual examination of "truths."

These criticisms may stem in part from two additional mainstays of the CRT approach, the critique of liberalism and the use of storytelling and counter-storytelling as a main approach to setting forth CRT analysis and ideas. Many CRT scholars take exception to liberal ideologies such as equal opportunity, color-blindness, merit systems, and a role model approach to affirmative action (Delgado & Stefancic, 2005). For example, in "Race, Reform and Retrenchment," Critical Race Theory co-founder Kimberle Crenshaw (1988) critiqued the conservative right's and the liberal left's approaches to antidiscrimination law. She argued that "color-blind" race reform law, espoused by the conservative right, can make only modest inroads into institutionalized racism. But she also pointed out that the left's harsh criticism of such measures ignores the benefits they can provide while downplaying the role of racism in legitimizing oppression. Her article constituted an influential attempt to delineate the difference between the critical and noncritical approaches to racial justice.

CRT scholars believe that classic liberal jurisprudence fixated on colorblindness is unlikely to produce much meaningful change given America's lengthy history of enormously exploitative and debilitating racialized oppression, especially as it continues to play out in criminal justice processes that different groups simultaneously see as fair and unfair—for example, prison admissions and stop-and-frisk practices. Many Whites see the overrepresentation of Blacks in the prison population and among people getting stopped by police as reflective of the amount of Black criminal behavior. They fail to note that Whites engaged in similar or worse behavior may go undetected or unpunished for years because they do not fit racial criminal stereotypes.

Though the storytelling approach of CRT scholars is highly criticized by "traditional" mainstream scholars, early on, CRT scholars saw the need to develop a "voice of color" as a means of "naming one's own reality" (Delgado & Stefancic, 2005: 10). CRT uses the storytelling approach to reinforce legal points and propositions in a vivid manner; it was an approach pioneered by Derrick Bell, who saw the use of storytelling narratives in law review articles as a better reflection of the "oral traditions" of the Black experience. Instead of the doctrine-laden, citation-heavy traditional law review pieces (Hayman, 1995), Bell used the technique of placing legal and social commentary into the mouths of invented characters. In general, CRT is the theoretical challenge to racial oppression and the status quo by analyzing the myths, presuppositions, and received wisdoms that make up the common culture about race and that typically renders Blacks and other non-White racial/ethnic minorities subordinate to Whites. Starting with the proposition that a culture constructs its own social reality in ways that promote its own self-interest,

The late Derrick Bell is among the most well known of the founders of critical race theory (CRT), in part for his stories that provide a searing critique of American constitutional law development and strongly question accepted notions of equal justice. His 1987 book *And We Are Not Saved: The Elusive Quest for Racial Justice* includes the story of a fictional African American female character named Geneva Crenshaw who appears on the floor of the Constitutional Convention in the form of a hologram and unsuccessfully attempts to convince the founders not to include the provisions that supported slavery (see Slavery).

In his story "The Space Traders," which first appeared in his 1992 book *Faces at the Bottom of the Well* and two years later was produced as an HBO film, Bell suggests that America would accept an offer from extraterrestrial aliens to exchange all of its African Americans for an unlimited supply of gold and other natural resources. In the story, the nation accepts the offer and passes a law to enable the exchange. In 2012, this allegory was still stirring political debate because its author had once hugged President Barack Obama while they were both at Harvard University (Friedersdorf, 2012).

As a nonfictional critique, his 1980 *Harvard Law Review* article suggests that the 1954 *Brown v. Board of Education* decision by the U.S. Supreme Court was less about the moral stance of ending racial segregation in public schools and more about elite Whites wanting to improve the image of the United States in comparison to that of the Soviet Union during the Cold War.

Professor Bell is also known for his 1990 decision to leave his tenured faculty position at Harvard Law School to protest the fact that the school had not tenured any Black women. Bell had become the first Black tenured faculty member in 1971. Among his students was President Barack Obama. In 1998, Lani Guinier, President Bill Clinton's nominee for U.S. attorney general, became the first Black female to receive tenure at Harvard Law. By that time, Professor Bell was in the seventh year of a visiting professorship at New York University Law School, where he remained until his death in 2011.

Professor Bell's casebook *Race, Racism and American Law* became a classic within CRT legal resources, and though he published many law review articles, he was criticized by other legal scholars for his use of the storytelling approach. A White male colleague called the approach less rigorous than "traditional" legal writing and analysis and suggested that Bell's use of it served as proof that Blacks were less capable of performing at the level of Whites in similar positions. Bell's decision to leave Harvard was seen by some as principled and by others as counterproductive, distracting to students and divisive among the faculty. Before joining the law faculty at Harvard, Derrick Bell had spent more than 10 years as an active civil rights lawyer. Throughout his life, he stood on principle, even resigning from his first job as an attorney for the U.S. Department of Justice rather than give up his membership in the NAACP.

CRT scholars set out to construct a different reality. CRT scholars believe that with its rules, practices, and assignments of prestige and power, reality is not fixed but rather constructed by the populace with words, stories, and silence. But humans need not acquiesce in arrangements that are unfair and one-sided. Writing and speaking against them is expected to contribute to a better, fairer world (Delgado & Stefancic, 2005).

CRT scholars see the majority White mindset, which comes with its own set of presuppositions, perceived/received wisdoms, and shared understandings (many involving race and racial hierarchy), as a major impediment to racial reform (Hayman, 1995). CRT writers employ stories and parables to reveal the cruel and self-serving nature of the majoritarian mindset. For a while their work seemed to gain acceptance, but in 2012 CRT began to experience formal resistance. The Tucson, Arizona, public school system banned the use of CRT in its classes based on a recently passed state statute prohibiting schools from offering any courses that "advocate ethnic solidarity" instead of treating students as individuals. The school system also dissolved its Mexican-American Studies program (Winerip, 2012; Seitz-Wald, 2012).

Deidre Tyler with Delores Jones-Brown

See also: American Law and African Americans; Civil Rights Movement; Institutional Racism; Juries; Slavery; Structural Racism and Violence

References

American Educational Research Association. Education Research in the Public Interest, Annual Meeting. San Francisco, CA, April 7–11, 2006.

Bell, D. R., Jr. "*Brown v. Board of Education* and the Interest Convergence Dilemma." *Harvard Law Review,* 93 (1980): 518–33.

Bell, D. R., Jr. *And We Are Not Saved: The Elusive Quest for Racial Justice.* New York: Basic Books, 1987.

Bell, D. R., Jr. *Race, Racism and American Law.* 6th ed. New York: Little, Brown and Company, 2008. First published 1973 by Little, Brown and Company.

Butler, P. *Let's Get Free: A Hip Hop Theory of Justice.* New York: The New Press, 2008.

Butler, P. "Racially Based Jury Nullification: Black Power in the Criminal Justice System." *Yale Law Journal* 105, no. 3 (1995): 677–725.

Crenshaw, K. "Race, Reform and Retrenchment: Transformation and Legitimation in Anti-discrimination Law." *Harvard Law Review* 101, no. 7 (1988): 1331–87.

Delgado, R. "Derrick Bell's Toolkit: Fit to Dismantle that Famous House?" *New York University Law Review* 75, no. 2 (2000): 283–307.

Delgado, R., and J. Stefancic. "The Role of Critical Race Theory in Understanding Race, Crime and Justice Issues." Keynote address at John Jay College of Criminal Justice,

City University of New York, on the occasion of the launch of the Center on Race, Crime and Justice. New York, NY, October 5, 2005. http://www.jjay.cuny.edu/crcj.

Delgado, R. and Stefancic, J., eds. *Critical White Studies: Looking Behind the Mirror.* Philadelphia: Temple University Press, 1997.

Dixson, A. D., and C. K. Rousseau, eds. "Critical Race Theory in Education." Special Issue, *Race, Ethnicity and Education* 8, no. 1 (March 2005).

Friedersdorf, C. "The Sci-Fi Story That Offends Oversensitive White Conservatives." *The Atlantic,* March 8, 2012.

Haney Lopez, I. *White by Law: The Legal Construction of Race.* New York: New York University Press, 1996.

Harris, C. "Whiteness as Property." *Harvard Law Review* 101, no. 8 (1993): 1709–95.

Hayman, Jr., R. L. "The Color of Tradition: the Critical Race Theory and Postmodern Constitutional Traditionalism." *Harvard Civil Rights-Civil Liberties Law Review* 30 (January 1995): 57–108.

Laurence, P., D. Deyhle, S. Villenas, and K. C. Nebeker, eds. "Critical Race Theory in Education." Special Issue, *International Journal of Qualitative Studies in Education* 11, no. 1 (1998).

Lawrence, C., III. "The Id, the Ego and Equal Protection: Reckoning with Unconscious Racism." *Stanford Law Review* 39, no. 2 (1987) 317–88.

National Public Radio (NPR). "Former Prosecutor Pens a Hip-Hop Theory of Justice." "NPR News, Tell Me More," hosted by Michel Martin (Interview with Paul Butler), November 19, 2009. http://www.npr.org/templates/story/story.php?storyId=120567780.

Parker, L., D. Deyle, and S. Villenas, eds. *Race Is—Race Isn't: Critical Race Theory and Qualitative Studies in Education.* Boulder, CO: Westview, 1999.

Schaeffer, R. *Racial and Ethnic Groups.* Boston: Prentice Hall, 2011.

Seitz-Wald, A. "How Breitbart and Arizona Seized on "Critical Race Theory." *Salon .com,* March 21, 2012. http://www.salon.com/2012/03/21/how_breitbart_and_arizona _seized_on_critical_race_theory/singleton/.

Winerip, M. "Racial Lens Used to Cull Curriculum in Arizona." *The New York Times,* March 19, 2012.

Yosso, T. *Critical Race Counterstories along the Chicana/Chicano Educational Pipeline.* New York: Routledge, 2005.

D

Dahmer, Jeffrey Lionel (1960–1994)

Jeffrey Lionel Dahmer was one of the most notorious serial killers in the twentieth century, causing the death of 17 persons from 1978 to 1991. Of Dahmer's 17 victims, only 3 were White (the first, second, and last). Of the remaining victims, 10 were black, 2 were Hispanic, 1 was Asian, and 1 was American Indian. Their ages ranged from 14 to 33, and most of them (12) had a criminal record. This racial spread is unusual for serial killers, who usually kill within their own racial group or have a particular victim type.

The handling of the Dahmer case by the Milwaukee, Wisconsin, Police Department prompted strong minority resentment of the local police. Representatives of the Black and homosexual communities cited the department's inadequate handling of the Jeffrey Dahmer killings as an example of the prejudice that members of the police department harbored toward homosexuals, racial/ethnic minorities, and persons with criminal records. As the investigation unfolded, rallies were held to force the then mayor of Milwaukee, John O. Norquist, to create the Citizen Commission on Police Community Relations. Walter Farrell, a Black professor from the University of Wisconsin and a prominent member of the Black community, emphasized how Dahmer, who was White, not only targeted males or homosexuals, but also "black males or males of color." Professor Norquist agreed with the opinions of minority members of the general public that Dahmer's victims had received differential or indifferent police treatment as compared to White victims of serial violence (*Christian Science Monitor,* 1991).

In consequence, a report issued in October 1991 advocated for the recruitment of minorities to the police department to counteract the great racial polarization between Whites and Blacks, and to a lesser extent, between Hispanics and Whites as well.

The poor handling of the Dahmer murders was quoted frequently in the 1992 local elections in Milwaukee as a main source of racial controversy. Gregory

Gracz, one of the aspiring candidates, alleged that a clear indication that the police action and inaction in the case had been influenced by racial bias could be found in the fact that two officers who encountered one of Dahmer's victims, a Laotian named Konerak Sinthasomphone who had managed to escape from Dahmer's home in May 1991, had returned Sinthasomphone to Dahmer's home and left him there when Dahmer claimed that the teenager was his 19-year-old drunk lover. Sinthasomphone, who was 14 years old, and who had been drugged by Dahmer, was subsequently murdered and dismembered. Dahmer would not be arrested until July, when another victim, an adult Black male, would escape wearing a handcuff on one wrist. This time the police would investigate and find a "house of horrors" in Dahmer's neat but smelly apartment, which contained remnants of multiple decomposing bodies and graphic photographs of the men and boys he had killed.

Though raised in several places due to his father's studies in chemistry, Dahmer was a Milwaukee native. In his early years he was considered a shy child, with few friends. There is some indication that the serial murders may have been a result of mental illness associated with Dahmer's shame and attempts at repressing his own homosexuality.

The Dahmer murders garnered media attention not simply because of the number. He had also dismembered his victims and eaten various parts of their bodies and organs. Dahmer is noted as having attributed his cannibalism to wanting to feel closer to his victims; to keeping them with him always; or, the belief that they would live on inside him. He kept heads, skulls, and other body parts as souvenirs; had sex with the corpses; and strangled most by hand or with a leather strap. Ironically, Dahmer was on probation for child molestation at the time the two officers gave him back Konerak Sinthasomphone. Some of his bizarre behavior may be attributable to the fact that while living in Ames, Iowa, he often frequented a research center where different animals were held for study, thus raising his interest in the variations of different species; and that while living in a rural environment he had favored the finding of old animal bones, which he found fascinating.

At the age of eight, the whole family moved to Bath, Ohio, where Dahmer attended Eastview Junior High School. There, his peers perceived him as smart, but rather odd. While attending Senior High in Revere, Ohio, Dahmer began drinking heavily and became isolated and apathetic. His first homosexual encounter, limited to caressing and kissing with a friend, happened when he was 13. His curiosity about animals also grew stronger; Dahmer performed several experiments with dead animals in order to see the process of decomposition. At 17, he experimented with drugs due to his friendship with a student who was a known supplier of marijuana at his school.

A sexual fantasy about a jogger who routinely passed Dahmer's house prompted his first killing. On June 18, 1978, he met a jogger on the road. The jogger's name was Steven Hicks. He was 18 years old. Dahmer invited Hicks to his house, where they both drank, and where Dahmer later killed Hicks, dismembering the body and hiding it in his backyard.

Due to his alcoholism, Dahmer never finished his studies at Ohio State University. The same problem caused him to be discharged from the Army in 1981. The next year he moved in with his grandmother in West Allis, Wisconsin. In this period of his life he was arrested several times for drunk and disorderly conduct and indecent exposure.

The next killings would not occur until nine years later. Dahmer murdered four men (Steven Toumi, James Doxtator, Richard Guerrero, and Anthony Lee Sears) over the course of two years, ranging from September 15, 1987, to March 25, 1989. The first death in this period occurred in Ontagon, Michigan, while the rest would happen in Milwaukee, Wisconsin, where he killed most of his victims (the exceptions being Matt Turner on June 30, 1991, in Flint, Michigan; Jeremiah Weinberger, on July 5, 1991, in Chicago, Illinois; and Joseph Bradehoft, his last victim, on July 19, 1991, in Minnesota).

After the death of Anthony Lee Sears, Dahmer's fifth victim, Dahmer began killing far more frequently, killing a total of 12 persons between June 14, 1990, and his arrest on July 22, 1991. Between May and July 1991, 31-year-old Dahmer was killing at a rate of nearly one person per week. He was subsequently charged, tried, and found guilty of 15 murders. His trial included a reading of his 160-page confession; although Dahmer used an insanity defense, the jury rejected it and he was sentenced to 15 consecutive life sentences for a total of 957 years in prison. On November 28, 1994, Dahmer was killed by a Black inmate named Christopher J. Scarver at the Columbia Correctional Institution, where both men were serving time for murder.

In March 2012, documentary director Chris James Thompson created a documentary centered on the arrest of Dahmer. Consisting mostly of interviews with the people involved in and affected by his arrest (the lead detective, the medical examiner, etc.), the film focuses on the arrest and interrogation of Dahmer that occurred in the summer of 1991.

Marc Balcells Magrans

References

Baumann, E. *Step into My Parlor: The Chilling Story of Serial Killer Jeffrey Dahmer.* Los Angeles, CA: Bonus Books, 1991.

Castoulis, J. "Getting to Know a Serial Killer: 'The Jeffrey Dahmer Files,' by Chris James Thompson." *The New York Times,* February 15, 2013. http://movies.nytimes .com/2013/02/15/movies/the-jeffrey-dahmer-files-by-chris-james-thompson.html?_r=0.

Christian Science Monitor. "Dahmer Case Unleashes Black Anger in Milwaukee," 1991. http://www.csmonitor.com/1991/0816/16041.html/(page)/2.

Masters, B. *The Shrine of Jeffrey Dahmer.* London: Hodder & Houghton, 1993.

Ressler, R. K., and T. Schachtman. *I Have Lived in the Monster.* New York: St. Martin's Press, 1997.

Schwartz, A. E. *The Man Who Could Not Kill Enough: The Secret Killings of Milwaukee's Jeffrey Dahmer.* Secaucus, NJ: Carol Publishing Group, 1992.

Tithecott, R. *Of Men and Monsters: Jeffrey Dahmer and the Construction of the Serial Killer.* Madison: University of Wisconsin Press, 1997.

Dating Violence (H.R. 789)

Research reveals a high rate of teen dating violence (CDC, 2010; NCVC, 2007). According to the CDC (2010), 72 percent of eighth and ninth graders date, and one in four teens reveal "verbal, physical, emotional, or sexual abuse from a dating partner each year." The true extent of teen dating violence is difficult to assess. Victims may fail to report their victimization out of fear, and such underreporting may mean that the problem of teen dating violence is more pervasive than is reflected in official statistics (CDC, 2010).

Females have a 10 times greater chance than males of experiencing dating violence (NCVC, 2007). The *Criminal Victimization Report* (2009), compiled by the Bureau of Justice Statistics (Truman & Rand, 2010), reveals that for youth ages 12 to 24, 79 percent of female rape or sexual assault victims were attacked by a known person. In contrast, 74 percent of male rape and sexual assault victims report being assaulted by a stranger, and only 26 percent are reported to involve a known person (Truman & Rand, 2010). Like domestic violence, teen dating violence crosses all social and economic classes, races, and cultures, but African American teens may be at an elevated risk for dating violence as compared to Whites or persons of other races (American Indian, Alaska Native, Asian, Native Hawaiian, and other Pacific Islander) since annual statistics from the Bureau of Justice Statistics (BJS) reveal higher Black victimization rates for overall violent crime in comparison to other racial groups.

The Teen Dating Violence Prevention Act of 2009, also referred to as House Bill 789, was presented to Congress on February 2, 2009, with the primary goal of reducing and preventing violence among the teen dating population. H.R. 789 is a direct descendant of the Title IV Violence Against Women Act of 1994, found within the Violent Crime Control and Law Enforcement Act of 1994. (Title IV of H.R. 3355, the Violent Crime Control and Law Enforcement Act of 1994, provides a more detailed explanation of specific terms found within House Bill 789, including what constitutes domestic violence crimes and victims.)

The act proposed the appropriation of $3 million a year for five years for grants to be awarded to state, local, or tribal governments, the nonprofit community, faith-based

People of the State of California v. Christopher Brown

On June 22, 2009, music artist Chris Brown pled guilty to a felony charge for assaulting his girlfriend, music artist Rihanna (Robyn Rihanna Fenty). On March 5, 2009, just before they were both scheduled to perform at the Grammy Awards, the two got into a verbal argument that escalated into physical violence and resulted in Brown being charged with one count of "assault by means likely to produce great bodily injury" and one count of "criminal threats" under Case No. BA353571, in Los Angeles County. At the time of the incident, Chris Brown was 19 and Rihanna, who is referred to in the complaint as Robyn F., was 20. During the attack Rihanna sustained visible injuries to her face and required hospital treatment. According to police sources, Brown had no visible injuries when he turned himself in to the police following the incident.

Chris Brown received a sentence of five years' probation and 180 hours of community service. The sentence also required that he undergo domestic violence counseling. In the aftermath of the incident, Brown released a YouTube video apologizing to Rihanna and his fans. Brown and Rihanna continue to be in an on-again-off-again dating relationship.

organizations, or victim services organizations. The money was designated for use as a funding source for social-based programs that directly address the problem of youth dating violence.

As originally proposed, H.R. 789 was designed to target youth ages 11 to 25, including runaways, homeless youth, youth in foster care, and teens in the juvenile justice system who were victims of domestic or dating violence, sexual assault, or stalking, and sought to prevent both future victimization and offending. The bill sought to establish programs aimed at preventing and reducing teen dating violence, and increasing awareness for potential victims and offenders, as well as parents, caretakers, and school officials.

A modified version of House Bill 789 was introduced in 2011 as the SMART Teen Dating Violence Awareness and Prevention Act or H.R. 3515 and S. 1920 by Democratic congressmen John Lewis and Sheldon Whitehouse. The modified version of the act also includes the development of services for children exposed to violence, thus expanding the act's scope and relevance for youth who are African American, especially those living in urban areas. The new act targets youth ages 11 through 19, with a special focus on ages 11 through 14.

Jessica Melain Boyd

See also: Domestic Violence and African American Females

References

Centers for Disease Control and Prevention (CDC). *Understanding Teen Dating Violence: Fact Sheet.* Atlanta, GA: National Center for Injury Prevention and Control, 2010. http://www.cdc.gov/violenceprevention/pdf/TeenDatingViolence_2010-a.pdf.

H.R. 3355. 103rd Congress. 1994. http://frwebgate.access.gpo.gov/cgi-bin/getdoc.cgi?dbname=103_cong_bills&docid=f:h3355enr.txt.pdf.

H.R. 789. 111th Congress. 2009.

The National Center for Victims of Crime (NCVC). *Teen Dating Violence Fact Sheet.* Atlanta, GA: Center for Disease Control and Prevention, 2007. http://www.ncvc.org/ncvc/AGP.Net/Components/documentViewer/Download.aspxnz?DocumentID=42307.

Truman, J. L., and M. R. Rand. *Criminal Victimization, 2009.* Washington, DC: U.S. Department of Justice, October 2010. http://bjs.ojp.usdoj.gov/content/pub/pdf/cv09.pdf.

Davis, Angela Yvonne (1944–)

Angela Yvonne Davis was born in Birmingham, Alabama, on January 26, 1944. She is the daughter of Frank Davis and Sally Davis. Frank was a college graduate of St. Augustine's College, a historically Black college in Raleigh, North Carolina. For a brief time he was a high school history teacher and later owned and operated a service station in Birmingham. Sally was a graduate of Miles College in Birmingham, and was an elementary school teacher. Angela Davis' parents made sure that at an early age she became aware and was educated about the racial injustices and class oppressions against minorities. Her parents joined the NAACP and befriended members of the Communist Party USA (Davis, 1974; Purple Wolf, 2009).

At a very young age Davis was exposed to many unnerving events in the city of Birmingham. The political and racial climate in Birmingham during the 1950s and 1960s was extremely intimidating toward Blacks. As Black families moved near the Davis residence, many Whites became infuriated and they retaliated by bombing houses owned by Blacks. For many years several homes in the neighborhood owned by Blacks were continuously bombed, and eventually that section of town was known as "Dynamite Hill" (O'Brien, 2013). This hostile environment in the segregated South affected Davis and she was eager to find a way to leave Birmingham (Davis, 1974; Purple Wolf, 2009).

Davis attended the Carrie A. Tuggle Elementary School in Birmingham during a time when all schools in the area were racially segregated. Most Black schools had poor facilities and outdated material and books, but Davis' parents went out of their way to obtain books for her to read as they knew the importance of a good education. After graduating from Carrie A. Tuggle she attended Parker Annex, a

University of California professor Angela Davis in 1973. (Associated Press)

middle school branch of Parker High School in Birmingham (Davis, 1974). Eager to become a pediatrician, she found two programs of interest, one in Nashville, Tennessee, and the other in New York City. Davis applied to both programs and was accepted to both but chose Elizabeth Irwin High School in Greenwich Village in New York City since she wanted to be as far north as she could go (Purple Wolf, 1989). At Elizabeth Irwin, she was introduced to socialism and communism and became a member of a communist youth group as she became very interested in studying the *Communist Manifesto* (Davis, 1974).

After graduating from Elizabeth Irwin, she attended Brandeis University in Waltham, Massachusetts. During her freshman year she was given the opportunity to visit Helsinki, Finland, for the eighth World's Festival for Youth and Students. She also visited the European cities of Paris, London, and Geneva. This trip encouraged her to learn more about foreign affairs and diverse cultures, which eventually led her to apply to the Hamilton College French Program, and she spent a year studying French. While in France, she became involved in political movements and several protests (Davis, 1974).

In Biarritz, France, Davis stumbled across the *International Herald Tribune* in which she read the news of the 1963 Birmingham church bombing committed by members of the Ku Klux Klan, an experience that changed and affected her life forever. As Davis continued to read the news of the bombing that took place at the 16th Street Baptist Church, she was moved by the loss of the four innocent children that were murdered by the White supremacy group (Davis, 1974).

In 1960, she spent two years on a $100-a-month stipend in Germany at the Frankfurt School under the tutelage of acclaimed teacher Theodor Adorno. Davis also attended the University of Paris from 1963 through 1964, and later returned to the United States to finish her studies at Brandeis University in Waltham, Massachusetts. She earned her bachelor of arts magna cum laude in 1965. Upon graduation she flew to Germany, where she conducted graduate research in one of the best philosophy programs in the world. Davis was proud of her studies in philosophy, but felt isolated and returned to the United States to become involved in the political struggles of her people.

In the United States, Davis enrolled at the University of California–San Diego in pursuit of her master's degree under the tutelage of Herbert Marcuse, author of the book *One-Dimensional Man*. Upon receiving her degree in 1968, she continued her lifelong dedication to the quest for human rights. Davis was involved in many organizations, including the Black Student Union at the University of California–San Diego, the Student Nonviolent Coordinating Committee, the Black Panther Party on educational programs, and organizations advocating for the civil rights of Chicanos (Davis, 1974). In 1969, Davis was a visiting assistant professor in the philosophy department at UCLA, while at the same time she was known as a radical feminist and activist, a member of the Communist Party USA, and an associate of the Black Panther Party. The affiliation with radical associations resulted in the loss of her teaching position as assistant professor of philosophy at UCLA in 1970.

Davis became a national figure as she fought to keep her teaching position. The California Board of Regents refused to renew her academic appointment, despite her qualifications and excellent teaching record (Davis, 1974). On June 19, 1970, then California governor Ronald Reagan sent a memorandum addressed to all UCLA faculty advising that:

> Angela Davis, Professor of Philosophy, will no longer be a part of the UCLA staff. As head of the Board of Regents, I, nor the board will tolerate any Communist activities at any state institution . . . any member of the Communist Party is barred from teaching at this institution. (Reagan, 1970)

The Board of Regents was censured by the American Association of University Professors for its failure to reappoint Angela Davis after her teaching contract expired. As a consequence of her legal actions, she was later rehired.

People began to contact Davis for advice with different situations. One such person was a young Black inmate at a corrections facility. Davis soon learned the injustices surrounding the corrections systems of California and became engrossed in a prison case that involved three Black inmates in Soledad prison who came to be known as the "Soledad Brothers." Davis devoted most of her free time to helping the three prove their innocence (Davis, 1974). Without warning, on August 7, 1970, in the Marin County Hall of Justice Courtroom, Marin County, California, four men were left dead: Superior Court Judge Harold Haley, two San Quentin prisoners, and Jonathan Jackson, a 17-year-old civilian (Davis, 1974). The 17-year-old was a very close friend of Angela's and he was the younger brother of one of the Soledad Brothers. The deaths occurred as part of an escape attempt during which Judge Haley and three female jurors were taken hostage. The guns used in the incident were all registered to Davis. Although Davis was not present at the killings, she was placed on the FBI's Top 10 Most Wanted List (Davis, 1974). The California warrant issued for Davis charged her as an accomplice to conspiracy, kidnapping, and homicide.

Davis managed to evade arrest for two months in Greenwich Village, New York, but was arrested and formally charged in New York City (Davis, 1974). The state of New York dropped the charges for evading arrest and she was released, but seconds later she was re-arrested by federal agents for murder and kidnapping in California (Davis, 1974). Angela was extradited to a jail in San Jose, California, after spending several months in the New York Women's House of Detention (Davis, 1974; James, 1998). During her incarceration, a massive international "Free Angela Davis" campaign was organized. Her trial has been described as one of the most famous in recent U.S. history. After spending a total of 18 months in jail, on June 4, 1972, Davis was acquitted of all charges by an all-White jury (Davis, 1974).

To this day Davis is an advocate and continues to fight for the freedom and liberty of wrongfully held prisoners throughout the country. She continues her career of activism and has written several books. She taught at San Francisco State from 1979 to 1991 and later became the first Black woman in her department at the University of California–Santa Cruz to receive tenure. She is currently Distinguished Professor Emerita in the History of Consciousness and Feminist Studies Departments at the University of California–Santa Cruz (Purple Wolf, 2009). She remains committed to advocating for prisoners' rights and the abolition of prisons (James, 1998). In her scholarly work she has developed a poignant critique of racism and the criminal justice system, including her description of the "prison industrial complex" (Davis, 2003a; 2003b). She has continued her activism, including appearing in November 2011 at the controversial Occupy Wall Street demonstrations in New York City.

Frank Anthony Rodriguez

See also: Black Panther Party; Civil Rights Movement; Hate Crimes; Police Brutality; Shakur, Assata (aka Joanne Chesimard); Student Nonviolent Coordinating Committee (SNCC)

References

Davis, A. Y. "Slavery and the Prison Industrial Complex." 2003a. Fifth Annual Eric Williams Lecture, Florida International University, September 19, 2003. www.youtube.com.

Davis, A. Y. *Are Prisons Obsolete?* 2003b. New York: Seven Stories Press, 2003.

Davis, A. Y. *Angela Davis: An Autobiography.* New York: Random House, 1974.

James, J., ed. *The Angela Y. Davis Reader.* Malden, MA: Blackwell Publishers, 1998.

O'Brien, Matt. "Angela Davis Commemorates 50th Anniversary of Alabama Church Bombing." *San Jose Mercury News,* September 12, 2013. http://www.mercurynews.com/breaking-news/ci_24078761/angela-davis-commemorates-50th-anniversary-alabama-church-bombing.

Purple Wolf, Jaye. "Angela Davis Biography." Midnight/Dawn Production Designs, 2009. http://www.jayepurplewolf.com/PASSION/ANGELADAVIS/index.html.

Reagan, R. "Memorandum to All Faculty." Los Angeles, June 19, 1970. http://www.clas.ufl.edu/users/ssmith/davisbio.html.

Davis, Larry (1966–2008)

Larry Davis, who changed his name to Adam Abdul-Hakeem in 1989, was born on May 28, 1966. He was stabbed to death at the age of 41, on February 20, 2008, in Shawangunk Correctional Facility in Ulster County, New York, by a fellow inmate who assaulted him multiple times with a metal shank. Davis had been incarcerated for almost 20 years after a 1989 conviction for the homicide of a drug dealer. But that is not the main reason that Larry Davis is noteworthy. His fame and infamy date back to the 1980s in Bronx, New York.

In 1986 Larry Davis was an aspiring rap artist, a suspected drug dealer, and one more individual being sought by New York Police Department (NYPD) investigators assigned to the Bronx Homicide Task Force. He had a history of criminal activity and was being sought for questioning in connection with the death of five other alleged drug dealers. In early November 1986, a group of detectives developed information that led them to believe that they had located Davis at the home of his sister. By the time police arrived at that location, he apparently had been there, but had gotten away.

On November 19, 1986, he was again located at his sister's apartment, but was not able to immediately escape. This time the nine-member team seeking to take him into custody included investigative personnel, a uniformed Emergency Service Unit (ESU), and a tactical team (otherwise known as a SWAT unit). Apparently seeing no safe way out, Davis engaged in a gunfight with the officers and managed to get away. He left behind six wounded NYPD officers, among them

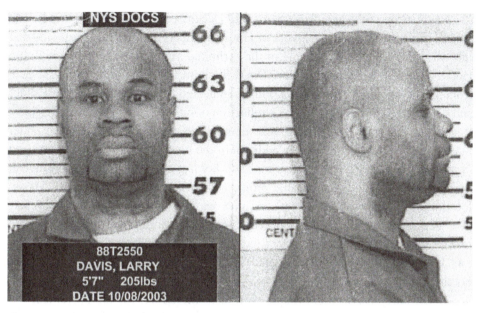

The New York State Department of Correctional Services shows convict Larry Davis on October 8, 2003. Corrections officials say Davis, who wounded six police officers in a 1986 gunfight that led to a nationwide manhunt, was killed in prison at the Shawangunk Correctional Facility in Wallkill, New York. (Associated Press)

detectives, SWAT team members, a captain, a sergeant, and one of the first female officers assigned to the NYPD ESU. The officers stated that Davis fired first and that they only returned fire. They also indicated that they were especially cautious during the apprehension attempt because a young child was present. Later, Larry Davis would tell a different story about this raid on his sister's apartment. The wounded officers were transported to hospitals and a manhunt began for Davis.

At the time, the search for Davis was reported to be the largest manhunt for a single suspect in the history of the NYPD. Coordinated operational command posts were established at police headquarters in downtown Manhattan and the Bronx. Hundreds of police personnel including uniformed patrol, ESU, investigators, surveillance experts, and hostage negotiators were assigned around the clock. Contrary to the police account of the events, it was reported that Davis had put the word out on the street that the apprehension team that came to his sister's apartment was actually a police "hit" team that sought to silence him because he claimed to have knowledge about police corruption. The corruption involved drug dealing by and with police officers. It was also reported that Davis had bragged that he would not be taken alive. New York City mayor Ed Koch and the police commissioner, Benjamin Ward, decided that it was crucial that Davis be safely taken into custody, in part to dispel the "hit" team and corruption allegations and to minimize the probability of additional officers being wounded.

Davis successfully avoided capture until December 6, 1986. During this 18-day search, he was assisted by a network of family members and friends. Some said that this was almost a classic example of the "criminal as hero" in the genre of Robin Hood. Before he went underground, Davis sometimes dressed in the style of Mr. T from the TV program *The A-Team*. Others indicated that his ability to move about and be sheltered in safehouses was a reflection of citizen distrust of the authorities. Regardless, the police conducted an extensive and expansive search, often under intense media attention. The early addition of the hostage negotiation team proved prophetic. The police reported locating Davis holding a woman and child hostage in their apartment in a Bronx housing project. Other accounts suggested that Davis' location was discovered when he placed an order for a Chinese food delivery. Whatever the facts, after several hours of tense negotiation during which Davis claimed to have both guns and hand grenades, he surrendered quietly to a team of negotiators and ESU officers. No hand grenades were found. The manhunt was over, but not the story.

When Larry Davis was brought to trial in the Bronx for the November 19, 1986, attempted murder of the police officers he wounded in his sister's apartment, he was able to secure the services of well-known radical defense attorney William Kunstler. The prosecution's case was based on the notion that Davis was a drug dealer who engaged in the armed robbery and murder of rival dealers. The defense case was that Davis had been co-opted by rogue cops who wanted to silence him. The defense version of the story indicated that members of the NYPD were involved in drug deals and forced a teenage Larry Davis to participate as well. The execution attempt was to be retaliation for backing out of a deal.

Larry Davis holds a prominent place in the annals of African Americans and criminal justice because in an unprecedented decision and one that has not been seen again, the jury decided that William Kunstler had successfully made a case for self-defense in favor of Davis and against the police officers who attempted to arrest him on November 19, 1986, and only convicted Davis of illegally possessing the gun that he had used to shoot the six officers on the police apprehension team. Some members of the community praised the verdict, while more than 1,000 police officers held a protest demonstration.

Although essentially acquitted in this case, subsequent trials for other drug- and homicide-related crimes followed for Davis. He was acquitted several times until he and his brother were convicted of murder in 1989. That conviction, coupled with the gun charge from the police shooting, placed him in the custody of the New York State Department of Corrections in Shawangunk. The NYPD and the Bronx district attorney's office investigated the allegations of police corruption but did not substantiate the charges. Early in 2008, the Black Entertainment Television (BET) cable channel show *American Gangster* came to an agreement with Davis to interview him about his life. Davis was killed before the interview took place, but the BET producers decided to continue with the project and in the fall of 2008, aired "Larry Davis: He Fought the Law, and the Law Won."

The Larry Davis story continues to divide perceptions of the police in New York City. In a 2003 independent documentary titled "The Larry Davis Story," Davis continued to claim that the attempted arrest at his sister's apartment was a planned execution and that he merely acted in self-defense. He also maintained his innocence in the case that sent him and his brother to prison, claiming that it was a "frame-up" in retaliation for the shootout and for revealing the corruption associated with it. In the documentary, witnesses provide information that calls the police version of Davis' criminal activity into question.

Robert Louden

References

Chan, Sewell. "The Death of Larry Davis." *The New York Times,* February 21, 2008. http://cityroom.blogs.nytimes.com/2008/02/21/the-death-of-larry-davis.

Esposito, Richard. "Cop Shooter 'Loco Larry' Slain in Jail." *ABC News,* February 21, 2008. http://abcnews.go.com/blogs/headlines/2008/cop-shooter-loc/.

Langum, David. *William M. Kunstler: The Most Hated Lawyer in America.* New York: New York University Press, 1999.

McFadden, Robert, A. Hartocollis, D. Kiper, C. Moynihan, and A. O'Connor. "Slain in Prison, but Once Celebrated as a Fugitive." *The New York Times,* February 22, 2002: A1.

Reed, Troy. *The Larry Davis Story: A Routine Typical Hit.* Documentary, Street Stars, Inc, 2003.

Verhouek, Sam. "Larry Davis Cleared in the 1986 Slaying of 4 Drug Suspects." *The New York Times,* March 4, 1988.

Wolff, Craig. "Defiant Larry Davis Gets 25 Years to Life in Killing." *The New York Times,* April 26, 1991: A1.

Davis, Troy Anthony (1968–2011)

Troy Davis was executed by the state of Georgia on September 21, 2011, two and a half weeks before his forty-third birthday. At age 20, he had been accused of shooting off-duty police officer Mark Allen MacPhail twice in the early morning of August 19, 1989. The shooting took place in a Burger King parking lot in Savannah, Georgia. For more than 20 years, Davis' involvement in the shooting was contested. According to testimony, at the time of his death, MacPhail, who had been moonlighting as a security guard, was coming to the aid of a homeless man, Larry Young, when he was shot with a .38 caliber gun at close range, first in the heart, then in the face. Young's attacker was described as "a man in a white shirt." In addition to being a White police officer, MacPhail was a married father of two small children. Davis was African American.

What makes the Troy Davis case unique is the fact that his execution was opposed by some of the world's most prominent people, Pope Benedict XVI and Archbishop Desmond Tutu among them. In the United States, former president Jimmy Carter, Rev. Al Sharpton, and former FBI director and judge William Sessions were among his supporters. Presidential candidate and former U.S. congressman Robert Barr called for the state of Georgia to give Troy Davis a new trial. Almost a million people signed petitions asking that Davis be granted clemency. Seven of nine important witnesses in the case recanted their testimony, alleging that they had been pressured by law enforcement to testify against Davis. Prior to the execution, even jurors in the original trial stated that they believed he was innocent.

None of this convinced Georgia officials to revoke the death sentence that had been issued in August 1991. Although Davis was convicted as the killer, he contended that another man, Sylvester Coles, whom witnesses place at the scene of the shooting, was the actual perpetrator.

Through the course of his appeals, Troy Davis was supported by his sister, Martina Davis-Correia, who died of cancer in late November, two months after his execution. For the anti–death penalty work on her brother's case, Davis-Correia, who had served as an army flight nurse in the Gulf War, received awards from the America Civil Liberties Union of Georgia and the Southern Center for Human Rights. Davis' mother, hospital worker Virginia Davis, had also fought against his execution until her death in April of that same year. Before the events leading to his execution, the Davis family had lived in a predominantly Black, middle-class neighborhood in the Cloverdale section of Savannah. Troy Davis' father, Joseph Davis, was a Korean War veteran.

Rhodine Moreau with Delores Jones-Brown

See also: Death Penalty; Innocence Project; Inter-Racial Offending; Wrongful Convictions

References

Amnesty International USA affidavits. http://www.amnestyusa.org/sites/default/files/pdfs/affadavits.pdf.

Appendix of Petition for a Writ of Certiorari, http://sblog.s3.amazonaws.com/wp-content/uploads/2011/01/10-949-appendix.pdf.

Davis, Troy A. V. Humphrey, Warden. Petition for a Writ of Certiorari. 10-949 & 10-950. http://www.supremecourt.gov/orders/courtorders/032811zr.pdf.

Bluestein, Greg. "Ga. High Court Rejects Plea to Stop Davis Execution." AP via Forbes. September 21, 2011.

Davis, 565 F.3d 810 (11th Cir. 2009).

Davis v. Georgia, 510 U.S. 950, 114 S.Ct. 396, 126 L.Ed.2d 344 (1993).

Davis v. Georgia, 510 U.S. 1066, 114 S.Ct. 745 (1994).

Davis v. State, 263 Ga. 5, 426 S.E.2d 844, cert. denied, 510 U.S. 950, 114 S. Ct. 396 (1993). Direct Appeal. http://174.123.24.242/leagle/xmlResult.aspx?xmldoc=1993268263Ga5_1267.xml&docbase=CSLWAR2-1986-2006.

Davis v. State, 282 Ga. 368, 651 S.E.2d 10 (2007). Application for Leave to File a Second or Successive Habeas Corpus Petition, 28 U.S.C. § 2244(b). http://www.ca11.UScourts.gov/opinions/ops/200816009ord.pdf.

Davis v. State, 283 Ga. 438, 441–447, 660 S.E.2d 354 (2008). http://caselaw.findlaw.com/ga-supreme-court/1094841.html.

Davis v. Terry, 465 F.3d 1249 (11th Cir. 2006). Federal Habeas.

Davis v. Turpin, 273 Ga. 244, 539 S.E.2d 129 (2000). State Habeas, Cert. Denied, 534 U.S. 842, 122 S. Ct. 100 (2001). http://caselaw.findlaw.com/us-11th-circuit/1544139.html.

Davis v. Turpin, 534 U.S. 842, 122 S.Ct. 100, 151 L.Ed.2d 59 (2001).

MacPhail Family Rebuttals, http://www.fop9.net/MarkMacPhail/debunkingthemyths.cfm.

Motion for Certificate of Appealability. United States District Court for the Southern District of Georgia Savannah Division. "Troy Anthony Davis Case No. CV409-130." http://sblog.s3.amazonaws.com/wp-content/uploads/2010/10/Troy-Davis-DCt-decision-on-appeal-10-8-10.pdf.

Petition for a Writ of Certiorari. http://sblog.s3.amazonaws.com/wp-content/uploads/2011/01/10-949-Troy-Davis-cert-petition.pdf.

Petition for a Writ of Habeas Corpus. United States District Court for the Southern District of Georgia Savannah Division. Troy Anthony Davis Case No. CV409-130, 2010 WL 3385081, *1, 61 (S.D.Ga. August 24, 2010). http://multimedia.savannahnow.com/media/pdfs/DavisRuling082410.pdf.

Sessions, William. http://m.ajc.com/opinion/should-davis-be-executed-1181530.html.

"The Shooting of Officer Mark MacPhail." http://crime.about.com/od/murder/a/The-Shooting-Of-Officer-Mark-Macphail.htm?p=1.

Skutch, Jan. "Testimony to Begin in '89 Murder Case." *Savannah Morning News,* August 23, 1991. http://multimedia.savannahnow.com/media/DavisMcPhail/1991/08231991op eningstatement1.pdf.

"Troy Davis Execution: Former FBI Chief William S. Sessions Calls on Georgia to Stay Order." *Huffington* Post, September 15, 2011. http://www.huffingtonpost.com/2011/09/15/troy-davis-execution-william-sessions_n_963366.html.

"Troy Davis Heads Back to Savannah." *Savannah Now,* June 20, 2010. http://savannahnow.com/troy-davis/2010-06-20/troy-davis-heads-back-savannah.

"UCC Minister Offers to Die for Troy Davis, Death Row Inmate," December 2, 2008. http://chuckcurrie.blogs.com/chuck_currie/2008/12/ucc-minister-of.html.

D.C. Snipers

In October 2002, John Allen Muhammad and Lee Boyd Malvo, known as the D.C. Snipers, carried out a three-week shooting spree leaving 10 people dead and three others critically wounded in Maryland, Washington, D.C., and Virginia. The shootings occurred in ordinary places, including gas stations, grocery stores, restaurants, and parking lots, in addition to shooting victims being dropped off at school, mowing a lawn, and walking down a street. Some of these shootings took place in broad daylight and on major streets or at busy intersections. The victims were chosen at random, crossing all racial, gender, age, and socioeconomic boundaries. The random selection of victims in public places over three weeks terrified residents of the Washington, D.C., metropolitan area, leading the D.C. Snipers to be labeled as terrorists (Erickson, 2003).

John Allen Muhammad, previously known as John Allen Williams before converting to Islam years prior to the shootings, was a former U.S. Army soldier who served in the Gulf War. The U.S. Department of Defense indicated that Muhammad was considered an expert marksman and received awards for his rifle skills during his service (BBC News, 2006). He had been stationed at Fort Lewis in Washington State, which is home to the U.S. Army's sniper training grounds. The snipers are trained in teams of two, one shooter and one spotter, much like the way Muhammad and Malvo operated when they carried out their attacks.

Muhammad had four children from at least two prior marriages. In his early years, he appeared to have been a dedicated soldier and father. His first wife stated that he was an outgoing individual who was not violent. The experiences of his second wife paint a different picture. She was awarded a permanent restraining order after he allegedly threatened to kill her (BBC News, 2006).

Lee Boyd Malvo, also known as John Lee Malvo, was born into poverty in Jamaica. His early life was unstable. His unmarried parents split when he was very young. His mother often traveled for work and left him in the care of friends or relatives for extended periods of time. When he was in his early teens, Malvo and his mother moved to Antigua. According to his mother, Malvo met Muhammad in Antigua in 2000 and formed a strong relationship with Muhammad, who served as a father figure (BBC News, 2003). Malvo's mother moved to Florida illegally, and left Malvo in the care of Muhammad until he could join her in the United States. In 2001, Malvo briefly lived in Florida with his mother before moving to Bellingham, Washington, where he lived with Muhammad in a homeless shelter for a period of time. Malvo left Washington with Muhammad in the summer of 2002 and traveled to Baton Rouge, Louisiana, near the residence of one of Muhammad's ex-wives (BBC News, 2003).

The pair began their D.C. shooting spree on October 2, 2002, in Maryland, where they claimed the life of their first victim. Over the three weeks they were active in the D.C. area, they left cryptic messages and notes at crime scenes, attempted to communicate with police, and demanded a $10 million ransom (Mueller & Lanterman, 2004). After a deluge of inaccurate and misleading tips, police finally captured Muhammad and Malvo as they slept in their 1990 blue Chevrolet Caprice at a rest stop in Maryland. The car had been modified so that they could shoot from inside the car without detection. Police also found a Bushmaster XM-15 semi-automatic .223-caliber rifle in their possession. This weapon is accurate up to 500 meters for a point target and 800 meters for an area target (Federation of American Scientists, 2000), and is the civilian equivalent of the M-16 rifle used by the U.S. military. Ballistics and DNA evidence conclusively linked the pair to 11 of the shootings.

There was a debate as to where the snipers should be prosecuted first due to murders in multiple jurisdictions. U.S. Attorney General John Ashcroft spoke openly regarding his belief that the snipers should be prosecuted in a jurisdiction that allowed capital punishment for both adults and juveniles because Malvo was 17 years old at the time of the shootings (Lichtblau & Blair, 2002). At the time, Virginia allowed the execution of individuals who were minors at the time of their crimes and Maryland did not. Malvo's defense attorneys also argued that he should be considered temporarily insane during the shootings, as they argued that Muhammad brainwashed him.

Muhammad and Malvo were first brought to trial in Virginia. They were both found guilty of murder and weapons offenses. Muhammad was sentenced to death and Malvo received life in prison without parole. Both were extradited to Maryland to face trial for six murders. Malvo pled guilty to the six murders and agreed to testify against Muhammad at trial in exchange for additional life sentences without parole. Muhammad was convicted of six counts of murder and received six life sentences without parole. Muhammad was executed by lethal injection at Greensville Correctional Center in Virginia on November 10, 2009.

The snipers are thought to have been involved in robbery-related shootings in Antigua, Washington State, Louisiana, and Alabama in the months preceding the shootings in the Washington, D.C., area.

Jennifer Lanterman

References

BBC News. "Profile: John Allen Muhammad." May 31, 2006. http://news.bbc.co.uk/2/hi/americas/2357393.stm.

BBC News. "Profile: Lee Boyd Malvo." October 10, 2003. http://news.bbc.co.uk/2/hi/americas/3178504.stm.

Erickson, Dave. *D.C. Sniper: 23 Days of Fear.* Directed by Tom McLoughlin. U.S.A Network, New York, NY, 2003.

Federation of American Scientists Military Analysis Network. "M16A2 5.56mm semi-automatic rifle." February 22, 2000. http://www.fas.org/man/dod-101/sys/land/m16.htm.

Lichtblau, E., and J. Blair. "Ashcroft Decided Virginia Will Try Sniper Cases First." *The New York Times,* November 8, 2002, A-1.

Mueller, G.O.W., and J. L. Lanterman. "Terrorism and Media Deceit: A Study in Criminological Education and Research." In *Festschrift Fur Professor Manfred Burgstaller zum 65 Geburtstag,* edited by C. Grafl and U. Medigovic, 337–51. Wien-Graz: Neuer Wissenschaftlicher Verlag GmbH, 2004.

Death Penalty

Of all sentencing disparities across race, research has found that death penalty sentencing has consistently demonstrated disproportionate impact on African Americans (see Disproportionality and Crime and Sentencing Disparities). During the 1800s, racially different punishments were expressly written into criminal statutes. For example, in 1861, a Georgia rape statute authorized a mandatory death sentence for the rape of a White woman by a Black man and a prison sentence of 2 to 20 years if the rapist was White. The rape of a Black woman was not punishable by death at all (Jones-Brown, 2000).

Although such blatant racial distinctions in punishment were eventually removed from criminal statutes, national statistics for the period 1930 to 1964 reveal that more than eight times as many Black defendants were executed for the offense of rape in comparison to White defendants. The numerical difference was 405 to 48 (Jones-Brown, 2000). This difference did not reflect a difference in the number of Blacks versus Whites arrested for rape during the time period. The U.S. Supreme Court did not outlaw the use of the death penalty in rape cases until 1977. Blacks were also more likely to receive a death sentence for nonlethal felonies such as robbery, burglary, kidnapping, and some thefts.

By today's laws, use of the death penalty is almost exclusively limited to cases involving first-degree murder, but within the realm of homicide cases, racial disparities also exist. The disparity has not simply meant that Black defendants are more likely to receive death sentences than White defendants. Research has found that Blacks who kill other Blacks are more likely to receive lenient non–death penalty sentences in some jurisdictions; that Whites who kill Blacks are less likely to receive death sentences; and that both Whites and Blacks who kill Whites are more likely to receive a death sentence, though the likelihood is greater for Black defendants. This latter race-of-victim effect was revealed in a groundbreaking statistical analysis by the late Professor David Baldus in preparing the U.S. Supreme Court case *McCleskey v. Kemp*. The study looked at over 2,000 murder cases that occurred in Georgia in the 1970s (Baldus et al., 2007; Baldus et al., 1990).

Though the data from Georgia's death penalty cases showed that prosecutors were more likely to request and secure death sentences in homicide cases where the victims were White, in a 1987, 5 to 4 decision, the U.S. Supreme Court ruled that such evidence was not sufficient to overturn a death sentences on race discrimination grounds. Warren McCleskey, an African American man accused of being involved with the murder of a White police officer, had been sentenced to death. The statistical analysis conducted by Baldus and his colleagues showed that Georgia courts had a pattern of sentencing Blacks to death for the murder of White victims more often than in cases where Whites killed White victims. Despite the evidence, the majority of the justices ruled that proof of intentional discrimination directed at McCleskey himself was necessary to overturn the capital sentence. Absent such proof, the Court upheld the sentence, and Warren McCleskey was executed in 1991.

The findings in the Baldus study included that Georgia courts were 4.3 times more likely to hand out a death sentence when victims were White as opposed to Black. Black defendants received death sentences in 22 percent of cases, as compared to 8 percent of cases for Whites. In cases involving Black defendants and Black victims, death sentences were imposed in only 1 percent of cases, and in 3 percent of cases in which Whites killed Blacks.

Subsequent research has revealed additional disparities, including the fact that prosecutors in jurisdictions other than and including Georgia are more likely to seek a death sentence in Black on White homicide cases; once death sentences are pronounced, Whites stand a greater chance of having their sentences overturned or commuted to life imprisonment than do their Black counterparts; and that consequently, death sentences imposed against Black defendants stand a greater chance of actually resulting in an execution.

Georgia, Texas, Florida, and Illinois have been among the leading states named in death penalty litigation reviewed by the U.S. Supreme Court. Alabama and Mississippi have also had their fair share. A landmark death penalty case with a decision that was later reversed on non–death penalty grounds, but too late to prevent the execution of the defendant, involved the state of Connecticut (*Palko v. Connecticut* [1932]). In the majority of cases the defendants were Black.

Despite evidence of continued racial disparity in seeking, imposing, and carrying out death sentences, the U.S. Supreme Court and the high courts of 32 states have refused to find death sentences unconstitutional under all circumstances. New York (2004, 2007), New Jersey (2007), New Mexico (2009), Illinois (2011), Connecticut (2012), and Maryland (2013) have joined the ranks of states discontinuing the use of the death penalty within the last 10 years. (New York discontinued the death penalty in 2004, reinstated it, and then discontinued it again in 2007.) Illinois governor Pat Quinn commuted all death sentences to life imprisonment in 2011 based on the evidence of racial disparities and wrongful convictions (see Wrongful Convictions). In both *Furman v. Georgia* (1972) and *Gregg v. Georgia* (1976), the U.S. Supreme Court has attempted to resolve issues of bias involved in death sentencing such as that reflected in the 1861 statute. But for the 32 states that still authorize death as a sentence for homicide cases, racial bias continues to be a matter of significant concern. It should be noted that the U.S. Supreme Court case that led to the elimination of the juvenile death penalty, *Roper v. Simmons,* involved a White defendant, but some researchers continue to claim that racial differences in death sentencing can be explained by differential rates of capital offending by different racial groups instead of racial biases.

U.S. criminal procedure has come a long way from the time when executions came in the form of lynchings, which were the result of unofficial accusations and summary "trials" involving unqualified laymen and some law enforcement officials (Ifill, 2003; Raper, 2003) (see Lynching), but statistical evidence continues to reveal racial influences in capital sentencing that a majority of researchers find cannot be accounted for by nonracial factors.

Beth Ellefson and Delores Jones-Brown

See also: Abu-Jamal, Mumia; Byrd, Jr., James; Davis, Troy Anthony; Disproportionality and Crime; Federal Death Penalty Abolition Act of 2009 (S. 650); Lynching; Sentencing Disparities; Wells-Barnett, Ida B.; White, Walter Francis; Wrongful Convictions

References

Baldus, D. C., G. Woodworth, and C. M. Grosso. "Race and Proportionality Since *McCleskey v. Kemp* (1987): Different Actors with Mixed Strategies of Denial and Avoidance." *Columbia Human Rights Law Review* (2007): 143–77.

Baldus, D. C., G. Woodworth, and C. Pulaski. *Equal Justice and the Death Penalty: A Legal and Emprical Analysis.* Boston: Northeastern University Press, 1990.

Furman v. Georgia, 408 U.S. 238 (1972).

Gregg v. Georgia, 428 U.S. 153 (1976).

Ifill, S. A. "Creating a Truth and Reconciliation for Lynching." *Law and Inequality* 21 (2003): 263–311.

Jones-Brown, D. *Race, Crime and Punishment.* Philadelphia: Chelsea House, 2000.

McCleskey v. Kemp, 481 U.S. 279 (1987).

Palko v. Connecticut, 302 U.S. 319 (1937).

Raper, A. F. *The Tragedy of Lynching.* Chapel Hill, NC: Dover, 2003.

Roper v. Simmons, 543 U.S. 551 (2005).

Diallo, Amadou (1975–1999)

Amadou Bailo Diallo was a 23-year-old immigrant from the West African country of Guinea who was killed by four undercover New York City police officers in the borough of the Bronx during the early morning hours of February 4, 1999. The killing was highly controversial given the amount of force used by the police officers, who were all White, against Diallo, who was Black, unarmed, not involved in a crime at the time of the shooting, and had no previous criminal record. For many New Yorkers, particularly those living in minority communities, the incident reinforced their perceptions of a hostile and overaggressive police

Twenty-three-year-old Amadou Diallo was gunned down in his Bronx home by four white police officers on February 4, 1999. (Associated Press)

department (Yardley, 1999). The officers fired 41 bullets, striking Diallo 19 times (Cooper, 1999a; Flynn, 1999). Two officers, Sean Carroll and Edward McMellon, fired 16 bullets each, completely emptying their weapons, while officers Kenneth Boss and Richard Murphy fired five times and four times, respectively.

After an investigation and several public protests, the four police officers were indicted for second-degree murder (McFadden, 1999). The indictment was issued in Bronx County, New York, where the shooting occurred, but a successful request for a change of venue resulted in the case being tried in Albany County, where the four officers were eventually found not guilty of all charges (Perez-Pena, 1999). The killing of Amadou Diallo and the subsequent not-guilty verdicts had a divisive effect (Connelly, 2000) throughout New York State. The indictments had been issued in Bronx County, where the district attorney, Robert Johnson, was African American. The acquittals had occurred in Albany County, where the jurors and residents were predominantly White. The incident and its aftermath led to numerous protests against police brutality and to policy changes within the New York City Police Department (NYPD) regarding undercover policing (Roane, 1999).

The Incident

At the time of his death, Amadou Diallo had lived in the United States for approximately two years (Waldman, 1999; Weill, 2001). On February 4, 1999, he had returned to his home from his job as a street vendor in Manhattan to his apartment on Wheeler Avenue in the working-class neighborhood of Soundview (Flynn, 1999). According to his roommates at the time, he entered his apartment briefly, then went downstairs toward the lobby area. At approximately 12:40 a.m., he was standing in the vestibule in front of his apartment building. The four police officers, who were on patrol in unmarked vehicles and in plainclothes, saw him. According to the accounts given by the police, the officers thought Diallo fit the composite sketch of a serial rapist who had been operating in the area. As Amadou Diallo was standing in the doorway of his apartment building, the team of four undercover officers—two officers in each of two cars—pulled up in front of Amadou Diallo's residence and double-parked. The first of the two officers began climbing a set of stairs in front of the apartment building (Flynn, 1999). What happened next will never be known conclusively. The investigation of the incident failed to produce any civilian witnesses to the actual shooting, which left the Albany jury with only the police version of events to consider in its deliberations.

According to police accounts, one of the officers verbally identified himself as a police officer and displayed his badge. The officer then asked Diallo, "Can we have a word?," at which time it is reported that Diallo began to back up into the vestibule of the building and also began reaching into his pocket. The officers testified that they ordered Diallo to show his hands because of their fear that he was attempting to access a weapon. They further testified that during this exchange, Diallo's body was turned askew to them as he began removing a black object from his pocket. They stated that they thought they were seeing the slide portion of a small automatic weapon and that it was being raised into the firing position. Sean Carroll, the officer closest to Diallo, yelled: "Gun, he's got a gun!" Carroll then drew his own 9-mm semiautomatic duty weapon and began firing it at Diallo. In an effort to avoid the shots that he imagined were coming from Diallo, the officer who was behind Carroll, Edward McMellon, backed up quickly and fell rearward down the stairs, firing his gun as he did so. Carroll, still in the vestibule with Diallo, thought that McMellon's bullets had been fired by Diallo and that McMellon was falling backward because Diallo had shot him. He continued firing at Diallo, aiming for his chest and torso, as he had been trained to do by the department. When the shooting began, Ken Boss and Richard Murphy were still in their unmarked car. When they heard the shots, they ran toward the building, looked up and saw Diallo with his hand outstretched and also began shooting at him.

According to witness accounts, the four police officers shot a total of 41 times within 10 seconds (Flynn, 1999; Cooper, 1999a). Diallo died at the scene. There were no weapons recovered from where he was standing, only a beeper and wallet. It was later determined that Amadou Diallo was not involved in any crime, and by all accounts he was a hardworking, decent person (Waldman, 1999). The NYPD was criticized for the extensive search that they conducted of Diallo's apartment after he was shot, some believed in an effort to justify the shooting after the fact. The police officers who killed Diallo were working for an undercover division known as the Street Crimes Unit (Flynn, 1999), which has been described as an "elite" unit and was tasked with investigating patterns of violent crime and with recovering guns, thought to be the primary source of violent crime within the city (Roane, 1999). Prior to the Diallo shooting, the four police officers had amassed over 300 felony arrests during their careers (Chua-Eoan et al., 2000). Under the Rudolf Giuliani mayoral administration in New York City, the unit expanded to four times its original size, from approximately 100 officers to approximately 400 officers (Flynn, 1999). The four police officers who shot and killed Amadou Diallo did not have a supervisor with them during the confrontation.

Protests, the Trial, and the Aftermath

Within days of the killing of Amadou Diallo, large demonstrations organized by activist Rev. Al Sharpton began to form, first in front of Diallo's home in the Bronx (Thompson, 1999; Goodnough, 2000; Lipton, 2000), and then in front of city hall, One Police Plaza, Federal Plaza, and other locations throughout New York City (Wakin, 2000). Protests continued after the incident and throughout the trial, leading to numerous arrests, including those of notable politicians such as the former mayor of New York City, David Dinkins, and U.S. congressman Charles Rangel (Cooper, 1999b). The musician Bruce Springsteen wrote a song about the incident entitled "American Skin (41 Shots)" (Springsteen, 2011). Police protests were formed criticizing the song and calling for a boycott of Springsteen's concert at Madison Square Garden.

When the case against the police officers was presented to the Bronx County grand jury, the police officers did not testify about their version of events and were indicted for second-degree murder, the most serious charge alleged (McFadden, 1999). Given the protests and extensive publicity surrounding the incident, a motion for a change of venue was granted. Granting the change of venue motion also prompted protests and additional media coverage (Harring, 2000). Many believed that the case was moved out of the Bronx because there was a history of jury distrust of police witnesses, which had resulted in many acquittals in the past (Levine, 2000). It was felt that the Albany County jury would be more sympathetic to officer testimony, which apparently proved to be true (Fritsch, 2000a; 2000b). There were additional protests once the officers were acquitted, but not the outbreak of violence that the department had prepared for. Many have attributed this to the fact that the trial had taken place so far away from the city and so far away from the borough of the Bronx in particular.

After the Diallo shooting, the controversial Street Crimes Unit was decentralized and placed under the supervision of local patrol commanders. It was eventually disbanded altogether by Police Commissioner Raymond Kelly shortly after he was appointed in 2002 (Rashbaum & Baker, 2002). In 2004, New York City settled a wrongful death suit with the family of Amadou Diallo for 3 million dollars (Feuer, 2004). His mother, Kadiatou Diallo, became a civil rights activist and an activist against police brutality. Her book *My Heart Will Cross This Ocean: My Story, My Son, Amadou* was published by Ballantine Books that same year. Also in 2004, the shooting of Amadou Diallo and two other controversial police killings were featured in the award-winning film *Every Mother's Son* produced by Kelly Anderson and Tami Gold. The story of Amadou Diallo's life and death is also featured in the 2007 film *Death of Two Sons,* directed by Micah Schaffer.

Despite the fact that they were found not guilty in state court, that the federal authorities chose not to prosecute, and that they were not disciplined by the police department, Sean Carroll, Richard Murphy, and Edward McMellon each left the force. Amid some controversy, both Murphy and McMellon were hired by the New York City Fire Department. After years of being assigned to the automotive unit, and both a state and a federal suit, on October 1, 2012, Kenneth Boss was allowed to carry a gun again by the NYPD. In the previous suits, the courts had sided with the police commissioner, upholding the agency's right to refuse to let Boss carry a gun. As of October 2, 2012, media outlets had not been informed of why Commissioner Raymond Kelly changed his mind in this matter.

Joseph Pascarella and John DeCarlo

See also: Bell, Sean; Bumpurs, Eleanor; Davis, Larry; Dorismond, Patrick; Louima, Abner; Police Brutality

References

Chua-Eoan, H., E. Rivera, E. Barnes, E. Pooley, and W. Dowell. "Black and Blue." *Time* 155, no. 9 (2000), 24.

Connelly, M. "Poll Finds That Half in State Disagree with Diallo Verdict." *The New York Times,* February 29, 2000. http://www.nytimes.com/2000/02/29/nyregion/poll-finds -that-half-in-state-disagree-with-diallo-verdict.html?ref=amadoudiallo.

Cooper, M. 1999a. "Officers in Bronx Fire 41 Shots, and an Unarmed Man Is Killed. *The New York Times,* February 5, 1999. http://www.nytimes.com/1999/02/05/nyregion/ officers-in-bronx-fire-41-shots-and-an-unarmed-man-is-killed.html?ref=amadoudiallo.

Cooper, M. 1999b. "Dinkins among 14 Arrested in Protest of Police Shooting." *The New York Times,* March 16, 1999. http://www.nytimes.com/1999/03/16/nyregion/dinkins-among-14-arrested-in-protest-of-police-shooting.html?ref=amadoudiallo.

Diallo, Kadiatou, and Craig Wolff. *My Heart Will Cross This Ocean: My Story, My Son, Amadou.* One World/Ballantine: New York, 2004.

Feuer, A. "$3 Million Deal in Police Killing of Diallo in '99." *The New York Times,* January 7, 2004. http://www.nytimes.com/2004/01/07/nyregion/3-million-deal-in-police-killing-of-diallo-in-99.html?ref=amadoudiallo.

Flynn, K. "Shooting in the Bronx: The Overview; Revisiting a Killing: Many Details, but a Mystery Remains." *The New York Times,* February 14, 1999. http://www.nytimes.com/1999/02/14/nyregion/shooting-bronx-overview-revisiting-killing-many-details-but-mystery-remains.html?ref=amadoudiallo.

Fritsch, J. 2000a. "Officer Recounts Diallo's Shooting in Day on Stand." *The New York Times,* February 15, 2000. http://www.nytimes.com/2000/02/15/nyregion/officer-recounts-diallo-s-shooting-in-day-on-stand.html?ref=amadoudiallo.

Fritsch, J. 2000b. "Two Officers Back Story of Partners." *The New York Times,* February 16, 2000. http://www.nytimes.com/2000/02/16/nyregion/two-officers-back-story-of-partners.html?ref=amadoudiallo.

Goodnough, A. "Hundreds of Students March against Diallo Verdict." *The New York Times,* March 4, 2000. http://www.nytimes.com/2000/03/04/nyregion/hundreds-of-students-march-against-diallo-verdict.html?ref=amadoudiallo.

Harring, S. L. "The Diallo Verdict: Another 'Tragic Accident' in New York's War on Street Crime?" *Social Justice* 27, no. 1 (2000): 9–18.

Levine, J. "The Impact of Racial Demography on Jury Verdicts in Routine Adjudication." In *The System in Black and White: Exploring the Connections between Race, Crime and Justice,* edited by M. Markowitz and D. Jones-Brown, 153–69. Westport, CT: Praeger, 2000.

Lipton, E. "The Diallo Case: The Overview; From Pulpits to Politics, Angry Voices on Diallo." *The New York Times,* February 28, 2000. http://www.nytimes.com/2000/02/28/nyregion/the-diallo-case-the-overview-from-pulpits-to-politics-angry-voices-on-diallo.html.

McFadden, R. "Four Officers Indicted for Murder in Killing of Diallo, Lawyer Says." *The New York Times,* March 26, 1999. http://www.nytimes.com/1999/03/26/nyregion/four-officers-indicted-for-murder-in-killing-of-diallo-lawyer-says.html?ref=amadoudiallo.

Perez-Pena, R. "Albany County Is Friendly Place for Police Officers on Trial." *The New York Times,* December 18, 1999. http://www.nytimes.com/1999/12/18/nyregion/albany-county-is-friendly-place-for-police-officers-on-trial.html?scp=6&sq=change%20of%20venue%20amadou%20diallo&st=cse.

Rashbaum, W., and A. Baker. "Police Commissioner Closing Controversial Street Crime Unit." *The New York Times,* April 10, 2002. http://www.nytimes.com/2002/04/10/nyregion/police-commissioner-closing-controversial-street-crime-unit.html?ref=amadoudiallo.

Roane, K. R. "Elite Force Quells Crime, but at a Cost, Critics Say." *The New York Times,* February 6, 1999. http://www.nytimes.com/1999/02/06/nyregion/elite-force-quells-crime-but-at-a-cost-critics-say.html?ref=amadoudiallo.

Springsteen, Bruce. "American Skin (41 Shots)." 2011. http://brucespringsteen.net/songs/AmericanSkin.html.

Thompson, G. "1,000 Rally to Condemn Shooting of Unarmed Man by Police." *The New York Times,* February 8, 1999. http://www.nytimes.com/1999/02/08/nyregion/1000-rally-to-condemn-shooting-of-unarmed-man-by-police.html?ref=amadoudiallo.

Wakin, D. "15 Arrested after Protest against Police." *The New York Times,* April 18, 2000. http://www.nytimes.com/2000/04/18/nyregion/15-arrested-after-protest-against-police.html?ref=amadoudiallo.

Waldman, A. "A Hard Worker with a Gentle Smile." *The New York Times,* February 5, 1999. http://www.nytimes.com/1999/02/05/nyregion/a-hard-worker-with-a-gentle-smile.html?ref=amadoudiallo.

Weill, J. "Amadou Bailo Diallo's Life Story." *New York Amsterdam News,* February 22–28, 2001.

Yardley, J. "The Diallo Shooting: The Community; In 2 Minority Neighborhoods, Residents See a Pattern of Hostile Street Searches." *The New York Times,* March 29, 1999. http://www.nytimes.com/1999/03/29/nyregion/diallo-shooting-community-2-minority-neighborhoods-residents-see-pattern-hostile.html?ref=amadoudiallo.

Disproportionality and Crime

The shaping of public perception of crime, and Black participation in it, is based on officially reported proportional rates of offending for the group and typically in comparison to the rates of offending for Whites as a group. Official reports are those that are released by government agencies such as the Federal Bureau of Investigation (FBI) in its annual *Uniform Crime Reports* (UCR). The UCR reports criminal activity across the United States based on information that the FBI receives from state and local police agencies. It primarily reports the number of arrests for various criminal offenses across four racial categories: White, Black, American Indian/Alaskan Native, or Asian/Pacific Islander.

Typically, these arrest figures are then compared to the proportion of the general population that each group represents. For Blacks, the figures typically run between 12 to 13 percent of the general population and 30 percent of reported crime (as measured by arrests). For Whites, the figures typically run around 80 percent of the general population and 70 percent of reported crime (as measured by arrests). While it is clear when looking at the difference between 70 percent and 30 percent that Blacks make up the minority of criminal offenders, rather than focusing on this difference, sociologists, criminologists, and the public are trained to look at the fact that Blacks, as 12 or 13 percent of the general public, commit 30 percent of overall crime, and thus are disproportionately represented among individuals arrested for crime. Conversely, while they make up the majority of offenders, Whites are under-represented in crime because they make up 80 percent of the general population and 70 percent of overall crime.

This racial proportion analysis becomes more stark when the focus is on violent crime. Federal statistics report violent crime under the figures for four offenses: homicide (reported as murder and non-negligent manslaughter), forcible rape, robbery, and aggravated assault. In 2011, when the U.S. Black population was estimated as 13.7 percent, the Black percentage of arrestees for each violent crime category greatly exceeded that number. For homicide, the figure was 49.7 percent. For forcible rape it was 32.9 percent. For robbery it was 55.6 percent, and for aggravated assault the figure was 33.6 percent (*Sourcebook of Criminal Justice Statistics,* 2011).

Reporting crime using group arrest proportions compared to the general population masks the fact that for two of the offense categories, forcible rape and aggravated assault, the majority of arrestees were White, at 65 and 63.9 percent, respectively. It also masks the fact that even where the reported percentage of Black arrestees is highest, for homicide and robbery, the raw number of Whites arrested in these offense categories is closer to that of Black arrestees than one might think. For homicide, the numbers were 4,000 White arrestees compared to 4,149 Black arrestees. For robbery, the difference in raw numbers is more substantial: 35,443 for Whites arrested and 45,827 for Blacks arrested, a difference of just over 10,000. However, in the offense categories where Whites make up the greatest proportion of those arrested—forcible rape and aggravated assault—the arrest numbers are roughly twice that of Blacks: 9,504 versus 4,811 and 194,981 versus 102,597, respectively (*Sourcebook of Criminal Justice Statistics,* 2011).

For 2011, Whites were estimated as making up 78.1 percent of the U.S. population. So despite these raw number differences in offending (measured as the number of arrests) and the fact that they make up a substantial majority of those arrested in two of the violent crime categories, Whites are considered as underrepresented in violent crime and Blacks are considered as overrepresented. This Black overrepresentation is often confused to mean that Blacks commit the "most" crime in the United States. The term "most" implies greater than 50 percent. The inaccuracy of the belief that Blacks commit the most crime can be confirmed by examining the percentage of Black versus White arrests for *UCR* index crimes.

The FBI identifies eight serious offenses as Part 1 Index crimes. They include the four violent crime categories already discussed and four property crimes: burglary, larceny, motor vehicle theft, and arson. For each of these property crime categories, the highest percentage and raw number of those arrested for them are White, and each percentage exceeds 50 percent. For burglary, the percentage is 66.7 percent White. For larceny the figure is 68.6 percent White. For motor vehicle theft, the percentage is 64 percent White, and for arson, the figure is 72.3 percent White. However, when these high percentages are compared to the general population of Whites, estimated as 78.1 percent, Whites are considered underrepresented in crime. The comparable figures for Black arrests for the offenses are 31.7 percent, 28.8 percent, 33.9 percent, and 25.7 percent, respectively. Since these numbers exceed 13.7, Blacks are disproportionately overrepresented in these crimes, although they are the minority of those arrested for them.

For the 21 less serious crimes that make up Part II Index crimes, with the exception of gambling, White arrests make up the greatest percentage and raw number of those arrested as well. However, in any offense category for which the percentage of Black arrests exceeds 13.7, Black participation is considered disproportionately high. For 2011, only driving under the influence and liquor law violations would be excluded from Black disproportionality using these standards. This method of reporting and interpreting crime statistics has been challenged (see Muhammad, 2010; Knepper, 2000).

One proponent of this challenge is Katheryn Russell-Brown, a professor of law and director of the Center for the Study of Race and Race Relations at the University of Florida, Levin College of Law. In her book *The Color of Crime* (1998), Russell-Brown presents her study of how crime is colored Black. She questions the use of racial disproportionality as the measure of crime occurrence in the United States because it inevitably places Blacks at a disadvantage, given the tremendous difference in the size of the Black and White U.S. populations (see also Young, 1994).

In his book *The Condemnation of Blackness: Race, Crime and the Making of Modern Urban America* (2010), Khalil Gibran Muhammad, the director of the Schomburg Center for Research in Black Culture, traces this practice of crime reporting back to 1890 and suggests that its use may have been intentionally designed to diminish any focus on crime among White ethnics and as a means of declaring the newly emancipated Blacks as "unfit" for modern life. The reporting of crime in this way denies Black individuality and agency and greatly overstates Black involvement in crime (see Young, 1994).

Russell-Brown (1998) notes that the 70/30 split in White versus Black arrests has persisted for more than 20 years. Muhammad (2010) traces the same 70/30 racial split to prison populations at the end of 1890. The focus on rates and proportions of crime across racial categories and in comparison to general population figures distorts the representation of crime to the point that changes in raw numbers in serious offending may go unnoticed. For example, for more than 20 years, the majority of raw numbers of arrests for homicide have been of Black arrestees. Even with these raw number differences, the percentage of such arrests across Black and White racial categories has been roughly 50/50. For three consecutive years—2003, 2004, and 2005—the raw number of White arrests for homicide exceeded that of Blacks, representing a break from a long-standing pattern. Although in total this amounts to 311 more White arrests for homicide than Blacks, little to no attention was shown to this change. In 2010, the number of White arrests for homicide again exceeded the number of Blacks arrested for the offense, this time by 52. The focus on racial proportions rather than raw numbers allowed these shifts to essentially go unnoticed (*Sourcebook of Criminal Justice Statistics,* 2011).

Comparative offending is also reported using rates. Rates of offending are calculated per 100,000 of the general population represented by different racial groups. Again, in comparison to Whites, Blacks are at a disadvantage given the substantial difference in population size, though for some offenses, their numbers are also disproportionately high in comparison to other smaller racial groups. For example, cumulative statistics from 1993–2011 show that for Blacks, the rate of firearm homicide offending was 14.6 per 100,000, compared to 1.9 for Whites; 2.7 for American Indians/Native Alaskans; and 1.0 for Asian/Pacific Islanders (Planty & Truman, 2013). For overall homicides in 2008, Black offending rates were 24.7 per 100,000, seven times higher than that of Whites (Cooper & Smith, 2011).

In response to complaints that proportional comparisons and reported rates of offending create impressions that overstate Black offending and ignore Black victimization, official statistics began reporting crime based on the race of victims. In 2008, Black victimization rates were 19.6 per 100,000, 6 times higher than that of Whites (Cooper & Smith, 2011). Even this focus on Black rates of victimization obscures the fact that only a very small proportion of the roughly 33 million Blacks who make up the U.S. population are engaged in serious crime in any given year. It also detracts from the fact that a significant decrease in Black crime, as well as crime committed by others, has been occurring over roughly the last 10 years. Some scholars have suggested that racial categories be eliminated from the reporting of crime statistics altogether to avoid inappropriate attribution of criminal activity to one's racial identity (Knepper, 2000). Such categories have been eliminated in the Canadian crime reporting system and the crime statistics of many other countries.

The use of crime rates can be traced to studies by Durkheim and Du Bois. Durkheim's study (1897) of suicide rates among religious denominations in Europe and Du Bois' (1898) study of crime among Blacks in Philadelphia have been sociological models for determining proportional crime participation of groups of people. Du Bois studied the rates of crime among Blacks in Philadelphia and determined that they were high compared to the overall Black population. Subsequent studies of other social issues not only use rates but also select certain variables over others to show evidence of crime participation. This is evident in Gilens' study of welfare, in which he chose, among other variables, laziness as explanatory of Blacks' disproportionate inclusion among welfare recipients. The title of his book *Why Americans Hate Welfare* reflects his findings. His study is based primarily on perceived laziness among Blacks. Had Gilens selected other variables or compared the laziness of Whites and others, the resulting information might have differed.

In a May 1, 2013, national television interview with the American Broadcasting Company (ABC), the New York City Police Department commissioner Raymond Kelly repeated a proportional analysis that is the source of great controversy. He claimed that 75 percent of violent crime suspects describe their attackers as African American, and since only 53 percent of the population being stopped in the city is African American, African Americans are "under-stopped." He went on to claim that the disproportionate stopping of African Americans is justified because "crime happens in communities of color" and that "they are being disproportionately victimized." His justification for disproportionately stopping African Americans compared to other groups was that he was saving the lives of young people, who are disproportionately victimized in New York and in other cities.

A close look at the raw numbers behind the commissioner's proportional analysis using figures from 2012 reveals the primary problem in looking at crime statistics in this way. In New York City in 2012, 288,584 persons of Black racial identity were stopped on suspicion of crime; 254,229 or 88 percent of those stopped were not charged with criminal activity. According to police data, 66 (not 75) percent of violent crime suspects are recorded as Black (NYPD, 2012). The raw number of Blacks suspected of violent crime was 19,184 out of a total estimated Black population of 1,861,295, or 1.03 percent. Even when the potentially criminal Black population is limited to young Black males, the percentage of stops compared to crime suspects is low. If all of the violent crime in New York City were committed by the young Black male population (those between ages 14 and 24), violent crime suspects would only represent 12 percent of that population (Gardiner, 2012). In fact, the raw number of homicides involving a Black suspect in 2012 was 154, hardly warranting almost exclusive attention to a population of nearly 2 million people, or its male youth, who number just under 200,000 (Gardiner, 2012).

The disproportionate involvement of Blacks in crime and especially crimes of violence does warrant attention. Shifting the focus away from race and toward other social factors might better help continue the crime decline among Blacks that has been occurring since the early 2000s. In addition to reporting national crime trends, the Bureau of Justice Statistics (BJS) reports crime by race across different demographic contexts; that is, across areas that are urban, suburban, and rural. It is the case that Black crime, especially violent crime, occurs most in urban settings. Sampson and Wilson (1995) document that urban cities are socially isolated; underresourced; and culturally, economically, and racially segregated in ways that White communities are not. They also note that structural changes in employment opportunities and wages have impacted Blacks more negatively than Whites, in part because of Blacks' slave ancestry and postslavery discrimination in employment, housing, and education.

The work of Sampson and Wilson in Chicago (1995) and Robert Agnew's general strain theory (1992) suggest that Blacks' disproportionate involvement in crimes of violence can be explained by the multiple stressors they experience in daily life and that racial discrimination and racially disparate treatment are among those stressors (see Inequality Theory). Media images that continuously associate Blacks with deviance and violence reinforce the factually inaccurate notion that Blacks commit the most crime and increase the likelihood that Blacks will be feared and treated as dangerous and criminal, even when they are not, which is most of the time. These and other social reactions, especially in urban settings, increase stress and anxiety for Blacks and contribute to levels of agitation associated with aggressive behavior. Sampson and Wilson (1995) also note that feelings of hopelessness and helplessness that emerge from urban settings are contributors to the adoption of illegal behavior as adaptions to challenging environmental circumstances. Because these adaptions are often transferred from generation to generation, they are seen as cultural as opposed to environmental traits. That is, rather than seeing aggressive behavior and/or gang involvement as an adaptation to living in fearful urban settings, such behavior is seen as "the way Black people are." Media, police, and the public often fail to realize that only a minority of urban or other Black residents adopt these modes of behavior.

Blacks' disproportionate involvement in crime is often linked to their disproportionate representation in poverty statistics as well. In a 2011 report, *Income, Poverty and Health Insurance Coverage: 2010,* the figure for African Americans living below the poverty level was reported as 27.4 percent. It is noted that the Census Bureau did not record the poverty status of Blacks in the Statistical Abstract of the United States until after 1965. Before that time the images of poverty transitioned between the 1950s and early 1960s from White to Black. This shift is referred to as the "racialization of poverty," and occurred between 1965 and 1967, after the War on Poverty was declared by President Lyndon Baines Johnson. Gilens (2000) notes that during periods when stories of poverty were most negative, e.g., when associated with the root causes of crime, images of poverty were most closely associated with Blacks. However, Blacks were less frequently represented among more sympathetic images of the poor (Gilens, 2000).

Finally, the disproportionality of Black participation in crime may be exaggerated by statistics that fail to separate Hispanics into their own racial category. Under the federal system, Hispanics are an ethnic group, not a race, and thus may be counted among any of the four racial groups based on appearance or self-identification. State and local police departments may designate Hispanics as a racial group but then typically report the group by two categories, White-Hispanic and Black-Hispanic.

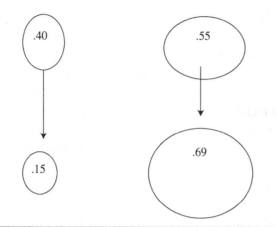

Concept by Johnnie Griffin 2000, 2011.

Figure 1 *Mis*perception by Disproportionality

Such is the case with the NYPD. These different reporting systems may unintentionally skew the racial proportions of offenders in different sets of statistics. Using arrests as the measure of offending is also problematic since not everyone who is arrested is guilty of having committed a crime. Moreover, the fact that police tend to be assigned to conduct surveillance in and patrol poor communities of color more than middle-class and affluent White ones increases the likelihood that Blacks will be arrested more than Whites who are engaged in the same behavior. The issues raised in this essay should cause one to question why "the concept of disproportionality has been used almost exclusively to discuss race and crime in the United States" (Young, 1994: 74).

Delores Jones-Brown and Johnnie Griffin

See also: Du Bois, W. E. B.; Gangs; Homicide; Inequality Theory; Institutional Racism; Intra-Racial Offending; Racial Profiling; Racial Stereotyping and Wrongful Conviction; Sex Crimes and Race; Socioeconomic Factors; Theories of Race and Crime; Wolfgang, Marvin

References

Agnew, R. "Foundation for a General Strain Theory of Crime and Delinquency." *Criminology* 30, no. 1 (1992): 47–87.

Cooper, A., and E. Smith. *Homicide Trends in the United States: 1980–2008.* Office of Justice Programs, Bureau of Justice Statistics. Washington, DC: U.S. Department of Justice, 2011.

DeNavas, C., B. Proctor, B., and J. Smith. *Income, Poverty and Health Insurance Coverage: 2010.* U.S. Census Bureau. Washington, DC: Government Printing Office, 2011.

Du Bois, W. E. B. *The Philadelphia Negro: A Social Study.* Philadelphia: University of Pennsylvania Press, 1898.

Durkheim, E. *Suicide and Study in Sociology.* Paris: Felix Alcan, 1897.

Gardiner, S. "Report Finds Stop-and-Frisk Focused on Black Youth." *The Wall Street Journal,* May 9, 2012.

Gilens, Martin. *Why Americans Hate Welfare: Race, Media, and the Politics of Antipoverty Policy.* Chicago: University of Chicago Press, 1999.

Knepper, P. "The Alchemy of Race and Crime Research." In *The System in Black and White: Exploring the Connections between Race, Crime and Justice,* edited by M. Markowitz and D. Jones-Brown, 15–29. Westport, CT: Praeger, 2000.

Muhammad, K. G. *The Condemnation of Blackness: Race, Crime and the Making of Modern Urban America.* Cambridge, MA: Harvard University Press, 2010.

New York City Police Department (NYPD). *Crime and Enforcement Activity in New York City.* New York: NYPD, 2012. http://www.nyc.gov/html/nypd/html/analysis_and_planning/crime_and_enforcement_activity.shtml.

Planty, M., and J. Truman. *Firearm Violence, 1993–2011.* Special Report, Office of Justice Programs, Bureau of Justice Statistics. Washington, DC: U.S. Department of Justice, 2013.

Russell, K. K. *The Color of Crime.* New York: New York University Press, 1998.

Sampson, R., and W. J. Wilson. "Toward a Theory of Race, Crime and Urban Inequality." In *Crime and Inequality,* edited by J. Hagan and R. Peterson, 37–54. Palo Alto, CA: Stanford University Press, 1995.

Sourcebook of Criminal Justice Statistics Online. Washington, DC: Bureau of Justice Statistics, 2011. http://www.albany.edu/sourcebook/.

Young, V. "The Politics of Disproportionality." In *African-American Perspectives on Crime Causation, Criminal Justice Administration and Crime Prevention,* edited by A. Sulton, 69–81. Englewood, CO: Sulton Books, 1994.

DNA Testing

Introduction

In the last 35 years, DNA testing has become a staple in criminal investigations and prosecutions within the United States, and despite concerns over issues of privacy, on June 3, 2013, in the case of *Maryland v. King,* the U.S. Supreme Court ruled that criminal suspects can be made to submit to a police DNA test after they have been arrested. In the 5 to 4 decision, the majority found that a DNA swab during an arrest for a serious crime is a legitimate and reasonable search. The case involved a DNA sample from a man accused of menacing with a shotgun in 2009. The sample in the menacing case led to his conviction for a rape that occurred in 2003. The sample had been taken in accordance with the provisions of the Maryland DNA Collection Act. The defendant claimed that the sample was taken unlawfully.

The Basics of DNA

Each individual has unique DNA inherited from his or her parents that may be likened to a person's own specific blueprint. This DNA contains information that codes for proteins that directly and indirectly influence physical, psychological, emotional, and behavioral traits (see Guo et al., 2008). DNA exists in the nucleus of almost every cell in the body and is composed of two long polynucleotide chains wrapped around one another in the form of a double helix. Each of these polynucleotide chains is composed of a series of simple nucleotides, each of which possesses one of the four distinct bases: adenine, thymine, guanine, or cytosine (Thomas, 2010).

Every individual has a unique series of bases on each of his or her 23 pairs of chromosomes (totaling billions of base pairs) that serve as the chemical instructional code for all the components of that individual's body. Some series of sequential base pairs that are hundreds or thousands of bases long, called genes, code for specific proteins and may vary from individual to individual. The majority of genes, however, do not vary in the population. Those genes that do exist in multiple forms are considered to have polymorphisms, with the differing versions called alleles. Genes with polymorphisms are responsible for much of the variation in the physical and behavioral characteristics of a population (Thomas, 2010).

DNA and Multiracial Identity

While DNA characteristics are often used to identify the likely racial identity of criminal suspects, DNA testing has also been instrumental in revealing the multiracial identity of most people. In an editorial entitled "Why Race Isn't as 'Black' and 'White' as We Think," *New York Times* journalist Brent Staples (2005) describes submitting to DNA testing after years of being accused of having a "White" name that many people thought he had made up. In fact, the name had been given to him by his parents, who were African American, with slave ancestry that they could trace back to the state of Virginia. The DNA test results for Brent Staples revealed that he is of mixed-race ancestry, with roughly half of his genetic material coming from sub-Saharan Africa, a quarter coming from Europe, and one-fifth from Asia. His Asian ancestry was a big surprise and his article makes the point that the sharp distinctions made among racial groups are not warranted. These would include the sharp distinctions made and used in crime statistics.

The work of African American professor Henry Louis Gates, Jr., at Harvard University also confirms most people's mixed-race origins. In 2006, Professor Gates hosted a critically acclaimed PBS series called *African American Lives* on which he revealed the mixed-race identity of many Black celebrities through DNA testing. His work can be followed at AfricanDNA.com. For the most part, the U.S. criminal justice system continues to treat people as if they belong to discrete racial groups and uses DNA samples to identify particular individuals or exclude them from suspicion.

The Use of DNA Testing

DNA testing was first used as a forensic tool to identify individuals in the United Kingdom in 1985, and within three years was used by the U.S. justice system (Murphy, 2008). RFLP testing was the initial standard, but due to its cost and sample requirements it has for the most part been replaced by the PCR/STR technique. At its inception, DNA testing was simply used to prove paternity and link biological samples at a crime scene to a particular suspect. However, it would be later utilized as a screening tool, with numerous members of a community being tested for DNA matching that left at a crime scene. Within 10 years of its initial use, most states allowed DNA evidence to be presented at trial, and now all states utilize DNA testing in some form to assist in criminal investigations and prosecutions (Thomas, 2010; Murphy, 2008; Krimsky & Simoncelli, 2011).

In 1990, the FBI piloted a DNA database program that evolved into what is now referred to as CODIS (Combined DNA Index System). It was designed to collect DNA information from convicted offenders so that biological samples present at future crimes could be compared to these known offenders. CODIS was fully adopted in 1993 and now each state maintains its own criteria for inclusion in the database. The majority require only convicted violent offenders to be included, but the database also includes some nonviolent offenders and arrestees. It has expanded to include over 9 million offenders and also includes forensic samples from unsolved crimes, unidentified remains, and missing persons. This database has been useful in solving new crimes when a released offender leaves a biological specimen at a new crime scene, solving cold cases in which biological samples were gathered, and clearing potential suspects. In all, CODIS has been used to successfully identify those responsible for over 130,000 other crimes (FBI, 2010).

Due to the work of several key organizations, DNA testing has been responsible for overturning a number of wrongful convictions. The Innocence Project, founded at the Cardozo School of Law, is one of the leaders in utilizing this technology to free those convicted of crimes they did not commit. Since its founding in 1992, the Innocence Project has helped overturn more than 265 convictions, including several death sentences. Of these, 158 were African Americans incorrectly convicted due to eyewitness misidentification, false confessions, the use of informants, or weak forensics (Innocence Project, 2010).

Issues Related to DNA Testing

While DNA testing has revolutionized police work and the accuracy of the criminal justice system, it has also created a number of issues. First, the view that DNA evidence is now the "gold standard" of forensics may hinder the prosecution's ability to convince jurors that a defendant is guilty in a case without DNA evidence. Even for the most severe crimes, DNA evidence is not available or relevant in the majority of cases. The Innocence Project estimates that DNA evidence is only critical to 10 percent of severe cases, yet the lack of this type of evidence in other trials may bias jurors toward acquittals (Thomas, 2010).

Secondly, there is a great deal of concern over the privacy of individuals. DNA is extremely personal information, leading some to question whether it is appropriate to record an individual's DNA even if he or she has been convicted of an offense, whether those found to be innocent or ruled not guilty should be removed from the database, whether those committing adolescent offenses should be placed in the databases, whether the information is secure, and if it is appropriate to use a near match from a relative as the rationale for investigating the potential guilt of an individual not in the database. The familial issue is an interesting concern. Sins of a father may make a son or daughter more likely to be identified, arrested, and convicted for his or her crimes than individuals who commit the same crime but whose relatives have not previously been convicted. This may serve to perpetuate discrimination between families who have members with criminal histories from those that do not. This issue is of particular concern for African Americans since they are already severely overrepresented in the criminal justice system (Murphy, 2008; Kahn, 2008; Krimsky & Simoncelli, 2011).

Finally and perhaps most importantly, the existence of DNA databases in their present form may serve to further perpetuate racial imbalances within the criminal justice system. There are few who would argue that African Americans are not disproportionately represented in the criminal justice system or that this overrepresentation does not indicate a significant degree of bias within the system as a whole. Many would suggest that the use of DNA evidence in trials helps to level the playing field and that postconviction exonerations using DNA evidence are likely to release those imprisoned due to bias, but this may not be the case (see Cole, 2007). Actors within the criminal justice system still have the ability to choose which cases to investigate and prosecute. Tools such as DNA evidence may serve as a way for police and prosecutors to more successfully solve crimes committed by individuals from groups or communities they already target without affecting overall imbalances since members of different groups are not equally targeted. One must consider the racial composition of DNA databases. As the criminal justice system has been overrepresented by minorities in the past, CODIS and other databases are likely to include a disproportionate number of minorities. This makes it more likely that minorities are arrested for their future crimes as they, or a relative, are more likely to have DNA in the database than others. Put another way, DNA testing in many cases will help to correctly identify the offender, but because of the composition of DNA databases and investigational decisions of law enforcement, its overall effect may be to perpetuate racial imbalance in the criminal justice system (Murphy, 2008; Kahn, 2008; Krimsky & Simoncelli, 2011). It remains to be seen whether the decision in *Maryland v. King* will work to make the racial imbalance better or worse.

John Stogner with Delores Jones-Brown

See also: Disproportionality and Crime; False Confessions; Gates, Jr., Henry Louis; Innocence Project; Racial Stereotyping and Wrongful Convictions; Theories of Race and Crime; Wrongful Convictions

References

Cole, S. A. "How Much Justice Can Technology Afford? The Impact of DNA Technology on Equal Criminal Justice." *Science and Public Policy* 34, no. 2 (2007): 95–107.

Federal Bureau of Investigation (FBI). Combined DNA Index System (CODIS), 2010. http://www.fbi.gov/about-us/lab/codis/codis.

Guo, G., X.-M. Ou, M. Roettger, and J. C. Shih. "The VNTR 2 Repeat in MAOA and Delinquent Behavior in Adolescence and Young Adulthood: Associations and MAOA Promoter Activity." *European Journal of Human Genetics* 16, no. 5 (2008): 626–34.

Innocence Project, The. The Innocence Project Home, 2010. http://www.innocenceproject.org.

Kahn, J. "Race, Genes, and Justice: A Call to Reform the Presentation of Forensic DNA Evidence in Criminal Trials." *Brooklyn Law Review* 74, no. 2 (2008): 325–75.

Krimsky, S., and T. Simoncelli. *Genetic Justice: DNA Data Banks, Criminal Investigations, and Civil Liberties.* New York: Columbia University Press, 2011.

Maryland v. King, 569 U.S. _____, No. 12–207 argued February 26, 2013, decided June 3, 2013.

Murphy, E. "The Art in the Science of DNA: A Layperson's Guide to the Subjectivity Inherent in Forensic DNA Typing." *Emory Law Journal* 58 (2008): 489–512.

Staples, B. "Why Race Isn't as 'Black' and 'White' as We Think." *The New York Times,* October 31, 2005.

Thomas, T. R. *DNA Evidence.* Costa Mesa, CA: Saddleback Educational Publishing, 2010.

Suggested Links

http://www.AfricanDNA.com
http://www.fbi.gov/about-us/lab/codis/codis
http://www.innocenceproject.org

Domestic Violence and African American Females

Some research has found that domestic violence victimization rates do not differ between African American females and other races (Rennison & Planty, 2003). Joseph's (1997) personal interviews with 204 battered women who were legally married or cohabitating with men revealed no significant differences between Black and White women with regards to the nature and extent of the abuse. In contrast, research with larger samples and several statistical sources reveal that African American females do experience higher rates of domestic violence victimization (Catalano, 2006; Fox & Zawitz, 2006; Greenfeld et al., 1998; Tjaden & Thoennes, 2000; West, 2004). For example, Greenfeld and colleagues (1998) found that race was a significant factor in nonlethal intimate violence; Black females were more likely to experience this form of violence compared to White females. In addition, Catalano's (2006) examination of National Crime Victimization Survey (NCVS) data from 1993–2004 revealed that only American Indian females experience higher rates of intimate partner violence (18.2%) than do African American females (8.2%). White females (6.3%) and Hispanic females (6%) experience lower rates.

In particular, statistical data reveal that African American females are at greater risk of domestic violence–related homicide. When Fox and Zawitz (2006) examined Bureau of Justice Statistics (BJS) homicide trends, their findings revealed that Black females experience the highest rate of homicide within the context of intimate partner violence. When comparing the category of spouse or ex-spouse, Black females had a homicide rate of 2.76 per 100,000 as compared to White females, who experienced homicide at a rate of 0.98 per 100,000. When comparing the category of "girlfriend," the disparity remains. Black females are killed at a rate of 3.49 per 100,000, compared to White females at a rate of 1.62. In addition, Grisso et al. (1999) found femicide, the killing of a woman or girl, was the leading cause of death for African American females ages 15 to 34.

Intersections of Race and Socioeconomic Variables

Although much research illuminates the disproportionate occurrences of domestic violence by race, West (2004) and Rennison and Planty (2003) stress the need to look beyond race alone when discussing African American female victims of domestic violence. They assert that the intersectionality of socioeconomic variables and race must be considered. Rennison and Planty's dissection of National Crime Victimization Survey (NCVS) data reveals that the "failure to account for the role of income leads to the use of race as an oversimplified proxy" (2003: 440). Their analysis revealed that Black and White females experience similar rates of intimate partner violence when controlling for income. According to their findings, poverty, as opposed to race, is the greatest risk factor. Black females in the lowest income category reported the highest rates of intimate partner violence (14.4%) compared to White females (13.5%) and females of other races/ethnicities (5.0%).

Sokoloff and Dupont's review of various empirical evidence also suggests that "the most severe and lethal domestic violence occurs disproportionately among low-income women of color" (2005: 44). This assertion is supported by the findings of a study by McFarlane, Campbell, and Watson (2002) that examined the correlation between femicide and stalking. Overall findings revealed that the occurrence of stalking was significantly higher among the attempted/actual femicides (68%) than those who experienced less life-threatening forms of violence. In addition, demographic differences existed between the two groups. Specifically, the largest ethnic group of the attempted/actual femicide group was African Americans (46%), and almost twice as many females in the attempted/actual femicide group as victims did not graduate from high school. For femicide defendants, Campbell et al. (2003) found the strongest socioeconomic risk factor was the perpetrator's lack of employment.

While Rennison and Planty (2004) and McFarlane et al. (2002) stress the need to consider socioeconomic variables when examining domestic violence rates within the African American community, West (2004) posits that even more complex layers of intersectionality need to be addressed. She asserts that the African American/Black community is ethnically diverse; therefore, consideration should be given to sub-groups (e.g., Caribbeans and Africans).

African American Females and Domestic Violence Services

A discussion of domestic violence and African American females would not be complete without mention of the services offered to and utilized by this population. It should first be understood that many authors have noted the reluctance of African American female victims of domestic violence to seek out services (Rasche, 1988; Incite! Critical Resistance & Sudbury, 2005; Richie, 2000; Websdale, 1999). Richie (2000) and Rasche (1988) note the reluctance of battered African American females to seek protection from law enforcement in particular, due to a history of oppressive criminal justice practices targeted at and utilized against

African American men and a distrust of law enforcement in general. In addition, recent research has found that reports of domestic violence to law enforcement may be hindered by shame. Lichtenstein and Johnson's (2009) interviews with older, rural, Southern African American women revealed that overall reporting of domestic violence to law enforcement was hindered because of fear of stigmatization from their church, family, and community.

Seeking services extends beyond the protections that law enforcement can afford; community programs, shelters, court advocacy, and counseling services are all available nationwide. While services may not blatantly discriminate, authors have noted that services operate via a White middle-class lens (Bograd, 2005; Coker, 2005; Das Dasgupta, 2005; Bui, 2003; Incite! Critical Resistance & Sudbury, 2005; Richie, 2000; Sokoloff & Pratt, 2005); therefore, the needs of African American women seeking services may be unmet. For instance, Incite! Critical Resistance and Sudbury (2005) critique the women's antiviolence movement for discounting the needs and experiences of women of color; they suggest a more inclusive, critically conscious approach that recognizes that institutional racism and poverty differentially affect Black women. In addition, Gillum (2008), Weisz (2005), and Sullivan and Rumptz (1994) point out that research has underrepresented the experiences of African American females who utilize domestic violence services. Despite these noteworthy critiques, African American female victims of domestic violence do utilize domestic violence services nationwide.

A review of the literature that measures battered African Americans' perceptions of services yields mixed results. Weisz's examination of 242 primarily (97%) African American women revealed that most of the women rated domestic violence advocacy as at least somewhat helpful, and "satisfaction with police and receiving referrals from the legal system were significantly associated with ratings of advocates' helpfulness" (91). Sullivan and Rumptz found that domestic violence shelter stays may be beneficial for African American women; their sample reported "a decrease in abuse, fear, anxiety, depression, and emotional attachment to their assailants, as well as an increase in social support, sense of personal control, and quality of life" (1994: 283). In contrast, Gillum (2008) found that African American female survivors of domestic violence were dissatisfied with community services and support systems available to them. Findings revealed that their "dissatisfaction was in part due to racism and of a lack of cultural competence. The other part was due to general insensitivity and inadequate service provision to women who have been victimized by an intimate partner" (51).

Particularly for African American women, Rasche (1988) and Potter (2007) note the importance of the church in addressing domestic violence. These authors note specifically the role that the African American Christian church structure can have in sustaining domestic violence by encouraging Black women to remain in abusive relationships as a means of honoring their wedding vows. By contrast, while the church may send a message that can be harmful, some research has found that for battered African American women, religion and prayer can also be a source of assistance and coping (Short et al., 2000). In this regard, a distinction may be made between prayer and faith versus church figures and doctrine. Potter (2007) has noted that when examining the effect of religion on battered African American women, religions beyond Christianity should be considered.

Findings regarding domestic violence rates, including homicide, collectively suggest that African American women are disproportionately affected. The University of Minnesota maintains an Institute on Domestic Violence in the African-American Community (IDVAAC) and national data and resources are available specific to the needs of African American (and other) females through AARDVARC (An Abuse, Rape, and Domestic Violence Aid and Resource Collection). However, race alone is not the determining factor. An intersection of race and socioeconomic variables needs to be explored. As noted by West, research must include more diverse Black samples, and consider "how living at the intersection of multiple forms of oppression shapes Black women's experience with violence" (2004: 1487) in their homes and interpersonal relationships.

Tracy Tamborra

See also: Dating Violence (H.R. 789); Disproportionality and Crime; Drug Treatment Strategies; Education; Homicide; Institutional Racism; Socioeconomic Factors; Structural Racism and Violence; *When Work Disappears: The World of the New Urban Poor*

References

AARDVARC: African-American Domestic Violence Resources. http://www.aardvarc.org/dv/africanamerican.shtml.

Bograd, M. "Strengthening Domestic Violence Theories: Intersections of Race, Class, Sexual Orientation, and Gender." In *Domestic Violence at the Margins,* edited by N. Sokoloff and C. Pratt, 25–38. New Brunswick, NJ: Rutgers University Press, 2005.

Bui, H. N. "Help-Seeking Behavior among Abused Immigrant Women: A Case of Vietnamese American Women." *Violence against Women* 9, no. 2 (2003): 207–39.

Campbell, J. C., D. Webster, J. Koziol-McLain, C. Block, D. Campbell, M. A. Curry, F. Gary, N. Glass, J. McFarlane, C. Sachs, P. Sharps, Y. Ulrich, S. A. Wilt, J. Manganello, X. Xu, J. Schollenberger, V. Frye, and K. Laughon. "Risk Factors for Femicide in Abusive Relationships: Results from a Multisite Case Control Study." *American Journal of Public Health* 93, no. 7 (2003): 1089–97.

Catalano, S. Intimate Partner Violence in the United States. Bureau of Justice Statistics Report (Report No. NCJ 210675). Washington, DC: U.S. Department of Justice, 2006.

Coker, D. "Shifting Power for Battered Women: Law, Material Resources and Poor Women of Color." In *Domestic Violence at the Margins,* edited by N. Sokoloff and C. Pratt, 369–88. New Brunswick, NJ: Rutgers University Press, 2005.

Das Dasgupta, S. "Women's Realities: Defining Violence against Women by Immigration, Race and Class." In *Domestic Violence at the Margins,* edited by N. Sokoloff and C. Pratt, 56–70. New Brunswick, NJ: Rutgers University Press, 2005.

Fox, J. A., and M. W. Zawitz. *Homicide Trends in the United States.* Washington, DC: Government Printing Office, 2006.

Gillum, T. "The Benefits of a Culturally Specific Intimate Partner Violence Intervention for African-American Survivors." *Violence against Women* 14, no. 8 (2008): 917–43.

Greenfeld, L., M. Rand, D. Craven, P. Klaus, C. Perkins, C. Ringel, G. Warchol, C. Maston, and J. Fox. *Violence by Intimates: Bureau of Justice Statistics Factbook* (Report No. NCJ-167237). Washington, DC: U.S. Department of Justice, 1998.

Grisso, J. A., D. F. Schwartz, N. Hirschinger, M. Sammel, C. Brensinger, J. Santanna, and L. Teeple. "Violent Injuries among Women in an Urban Area." *New England Journal of Medicine* 341 (1999): 1899–1905.

Incite! Critical Resistance and J. Sudbury. "Gender Violence and the Prison Industrial Complex: Interpersonal and State Violence against Women of Color." In *Domestic Violence at the Margins,* edited by N. Sokoloff and C. Pratt, 102–14. New Brunswick, NJ: Rutgers University Press, 2005.

Institute on Domestic Violence in the African-American Community. http://www.dvinstitute.org/.

Joseph, J. "Woman Battering: A Comparative Analysis of Black and White Women." In *Out of the Darkness: Contemporary Perspectives in Family Violence,* edited by G. K. Kantor and J. L. Janinski, 161–69. Thousand Oaks, CA: Sage Publications, 1997.

Lichtenstein, B., and I. M. Johnson. "Older African-American Women and Barriers to Reporting Domestic Violence to Law Enforcement in the Rural Deep South." *Women and Criminal Justice* 19, no. 4 (2009): 286–305.

McFarlane, J., J. C. Campbell, and K. Watson. "Intimate Partner Stalking and Femicide: Urgent Implications for Women's Safety." *Behavioral Sciences and the Law* 20 (2002): 51–68.

Potter, H. "Battered Black Women's Use of Religious Services and Spirituality for Assistance in Leaving Abusive Relationships." *Violence against Women* 13, no. 3 (2007): 262–84.

Rasche, C. E. "Minority Women and Domestic Violence: The Unique Dilemmas of Battered Women of Color." *Journal of Contemporary Criminal Justice* 4 (1988): 150–71.

Rennison, C., and M. Planty. "Nonlethal Intimate Partner Violence: Examining Race, Gender, and Income Patterns." *Violence and Victims* 18, no. 4 (2003): 433–43.

Richie, B. "Black Feminist Reflection on the Antiviolence Movement." *Signs* 25, no. 4 (2000): 1127–33.

Short, L. M., P. M. McMahon, D. D. Chervin, G. A. Shelley, N. Lezin, K. S. Sloop et al. "Survivors' Identification of Protective Factors and Early Warning Signs for Intimate Partner Violence." *Violence against Women* 6 (2000): 272–85.

Sokoloff, N. J., and I. Dupont. "Domestic Violence at the Intersection of Race, Class and Gender: Challenges and Contributions to Understanding Violence against Marginalized Women in Diverse Communities." *Violence against Women* 11, no. 1 (2005): 38–64.

Sokoloff, N., and C. Pratt. *Domestic Violence at the Margins.* New Brunswick, NJ: Rutgers University Press, 2005.

Sullivan, C. M., and M. H. Rumptz. "Adjustment Needs of African-American Women Who Utilized a Domestic Violence Shelter." *Violence and Victims* 9, no. 3 (1994): 275–86.

Tjaden, P., and M. Thoennes. "Prevalence and Consequences of Male-to-Female and Female-to-Male Intimate Partner Violence as Measured by the National Violence against Women Survey." *Violence against Women* 6, no. 2 (2000): 142–61.

Websdale, N. *Understanding Domestic Violence.* Boston: Northeastern University Press, 1999.

Weisz, A. N. "Reaching African-American Battered Women: Increasing the Effectiveness of Advocacy." *Journal of Family Violence* 20, no. 2 (2005): 91–9.

West, C. M. "Black Women and Intimate Partner Violence: New Directions for Research." *Journal of Interpersonal Violence* 19 (2004): 1487–93.

Dorismond, Patrick (1974–2000)

Patrick Dorismond was a 26-year-old Haitian immigrant who was shot and killed by a New York City police officer on March 16, 2000, shortly after he got off work at the Wakamba Cocktail Lounge on 8th Avenue in Manhattan. At the time of his death, Dorismond was the father of two small daughters, ages five and one. Dorismond, who worked as a security guard at the lounge, was shot by a Latino police officer, Anthony Vasquez, aged 29. Only three weeks prior, four White NYPD police officers had been acquitted of illegally shooting West African immigrant Amadou Diallo as he stood in front of his apartment building in the Bronx. Dorismond's shooting was the third shooting of an unarmed person by plainclothes police in 13 months. In each incident, the victim was Black (Chivers, 2000; Rashbaum, 2000a). Three years earlier, a Haitian immigrant, Abner Louima, had been brutally assaulted by officers in a Brooklyn precinct bathroom, leading to the trial and conviction of more than one officer.

Some have described Patrick Dorismond as a casualty of the war on drugs. According to reports in *The New York Times* (2000), Dorismond, who was unarmed, was approached by undercover officers, Vasquez among them, and asked if he had drugs. Accounts differ as to whether he was asked to sell the officers crack or marijuana. Dorismond is said to have responded angrily to the suggestion that he was a drug dealer. Subsequently, a scuffle ensued between Dorismond and the officers, during which Dorismond was shot. There are conflicting stories regarding whether Vasquez ever identified himself as a cop. According to some accounts, someone yelled "gun" before Officer Vasquez fired (Rashbaum, 2000b).

In the African American community, Dorismond's death at the hands of an undercover police officer led to an immediate outcry against racism. As if to somehow explain or excuse the shooting, then Mayor Rudolf Giuliani made a statement that Dorismond was "no altar boy," after having investigated him as though he were the shooter rather than the victim. The investigation revealed that as an adult, Dorismond had twice been arrested for disorderly conduct. The last time had been in 1996. The mayor received severe criticism when he authorized the police commissioner to release information from Dorismond's sealed juvenile record (*The New York Times,* 2000).

At age 13, Dorismond had been arrested for robbery and assault in an incident that has been described as a fistfight over a dropped quarter (Amato, 2012). To antidiscrimination activists, the release of Dorismond's private juvenile record was an attempt to sully the image of the victim, who had indeed been an altar boy and who had attended the same elite Catholic school as Guiliani (Newfield, 2002). In a March 2012 article for *The Huffington Post,* journalist Mike Amato compared the postdeath treatment of Patrick Dorismond to that of Trayvon Martin, killed by a Florida civilian a dozen years later (see Martin, Trayvon). The article, titled "Trayvon Martin, Patrick Dorismond and the Defiling of Dead Black Men," describes the similarity of the circumstances under which both had been shot, including the fact that they both died from chest wounds. Following both deaths, attempts were made to paint the victims as villains. In New York in 2000, the decision by Mayor Guiliani infuriated the Black community. The funeral of Dorismond drew 5,000 people, and resulted in a physical confrontation between the police and protestors. As a result, about 23 police officers were injured and many protestors were arrested (Crouch, 2000).

The case was reviewed by a grand jury, but Officer Vasquez was not indicted because the grand jurors found insufficient evidence that the shooting was deliberate. Many in the Black community were deeply disappointed that the case did not go to trial. Even Officer Vasquez issued a statement noting that as "a Hispanic American he was personally aware of the skepticism that some members of the minority community feel toward the criminal justice system" (Rashbaum, 2000b). The death of Patrick Dorismond bears the marks of a tragedy born from selective enforcement of drug laws based on racism in the criminal justice system (Free, 1996). The family of Patrick Dorismond filed a civil suit, and in 2003, the city of New York agreed to pay a $2.25 million settlement (Glaberson, 2003).

Marika Dawkins

See also: Bell, Sean; Diallo, Amadou; Louima, Abner; Martin, Trayvon; Petit Apartheid; Police Brutality; War on Drugs

References

Amato, M. "Trayvon Martin, Patrick Dorismond and the Defiling of Dead Black Men." *The Huffington Post,* March 29, 2012. http://www.huffingtonpost.com/mike-amato/trayvon-martin-patrick-dorismond-comparison_b_1382665.html.

Chivers, C. J. "Grand Jury Clears Detective in Killing of Unarmed Guard." *The New York Times,* July 28, 2000. http://www.nytimes.com/2000/07/28/nyregion/grand-jury-clears-detective-in-killing-of-unarmed-guard.html.

Crouch, S. "What the NYPD Did Right: By Exercising Restraint against Rioters after Patrick Dorismond's Funeral, the Police Gave Giuliani a Chance to Regain the Moral High Ground—But Will He Take It?" *Salon.com,* March 29, 2000. http://www.salon.com/news/col/crouch/2000/03/29/dorismond/index.html.

Free, M. D. *African Americans and the Criminal Justice System.* New York: Taylor & Francis, 1996.

Glaberson, W. "City Settles Suit in Guard's Death by Police Bullet." *The New York Times,* March 13, 2003. http://www.nytimes.com/2003/03/13/nyregion/city-settles-suit-in-guard-s-death-by-police-bullet.html.

Newfield, J. "The Full Rudy: The Man, the Mayor, the Myth." *The Nation,* June 17, 2002. http://www.thenation.com/article/full-rudy-man-mayor-myth#axzz2XTCPJefs.

The New York Times. "The Patrick Dorismond Case." March 21, 2000. http://www.nytimes.com/2000/03/21/opinion/the-patrick-dorismond-case.html.

Rashbaum, W. K. "Undercover Police in Manhattan Kill an Unarmed Man in a Scuffle." 2000a. *The New York Times,* March 17, 2000. http://www.nytimes.com/2000/03/17/nyregion/undercover-police-in-manhattan-kill-an-unarmed-man-in-a-scuffle.html?pagewanted=1.

Rashbaum, W. K. "Officer Denies Race Played Role in Killing of Unarmed Black Man." 2000b. *The New York Times,* July 30, 2000. http://www.nytimes.com/2000/07/30/nyregion/officer-denies-race-played-role-in-killing-of-unarmed-black-man.html.

Drug Treatment Strategies

The African American population in the United States is disproportionately exposed to risk factors for substance use and abuse. Research suggests that such factors exist at both the individual and community level. Among them are high rates of concentrated poverty, unemployment, residence in urban settings, and involvement with the criminal justice system (SAMHSA, 2011; NIDA, 2011a; NIH, 1998).

In 2010, an estimated 22.1 million people age 12 and older were classified with substance dependence or abuse. The rate of illicit drug use among Blacks was reported as 10.7 percent (SAMHSA, 2011: 21). The use of cocaine and heroin has been most problematic, with cocaine being responsible for more than half of drug-related emergency room treatments among Blacks, and heroin being responsible for nearly 20 percent (NIH, 1998). In 2008, African Americans constituted 20.9 percent of admissions to publicly funded substance abuse programs (NIDA, 2011b). However, it is estimated that such programs exist for less than half of all persons who have drug treatment needs (SAMHSA, 2011).

Research conducted on the detoxification and rehabilitation of substance abusers distinguishes between four main models of substance-abuse treatment: 1) detoxification; 2) methadone maintenance (Strain et al., 1999; Falk & Tonkin, 2001; Kelley, 2001: 3) outpatient drug-free setting (Hubbard et al., 1989; Haines, 1991; Borkman et al., 1998); and 4) therapeutic community (TC) (Manning, 1990; Kennard, 1998a, 1998b; Pearson & Lipton, 1999; Gideon, 2002; Vandevelde et al., 2004).

Detoxification is designed to help the addicted individual physically rid him- or herself of the substance dependency. These programs usually take between 21 to 30 days, but there are cases where longer periods of detoxification were recorded. Different from detoxification programs that require the addicted individual to stop using substances upon admission to the program, methadone maintenance is designed to help addicted individuals reduce their dependency on substances in increments. Methadone is administered to addicted individuals in the same fashion as regular prescription drugs, with a reduction in dosage after each increment until no medication is needed. Under this strategy, methadone is a synthetic substance that is considered to be "medicine" for the abuse, particularly for those who are addicted to heroin.

Outpatient drug-free settings may combine the previous two approaches while taking the approach of an outpatient clinic. Similar to the medical model, according to which patients admit themselves for treatment, substance-abusing individuals are being admitted to such settings, which are located in the community, and where they can receive an array of treatments; these settings may also combine detoxification with counseling and supervision.

Finally, the TC model is by far the most intensive method to address addiction, as individuals are admitted to a therapeutic surrounding that is active 24/7 and provides detoxification, counseling, and peer pressure. Many evaluation studies conducted on TCs found favorable results that support the ability of TCs to reduce substance-abuse relapse. Length of stay in a TC program may range from a few months to a year (see Berg, 1992; De Leon, 1989). Each of the above models uses a different approach to help the abuser abstain from substance use while bettering his or her life and the life of those surrounding him or her (De Leon, 1989; Hubbard et al., 1989; Rosental, 1989).

The above models can be viewed in contrast to punitive trends in the social response to deviance and criminality. They focus on treatment rather than punishment of substance abusers. Detoxification corresponds with the view that substance abuse is purely a physiological problem, and thus needs to be treated by administering medication—hence the use of methadone maintenance. Outpatient and TC programs were added to the treatment repertoire as behavioral and sociological theories gained dominance among the explanations of delinquency and criminality, emphasizing that such behavior is as a result of one's surroundings and lifestyle.

The main goal of all four substance-abuse treatment programs is to reduce abuse, or optimally, to bring the abuser to total discontinuance of abuse (Lipton et al., 1992). An additional goal of many programs is to reduce and eliminate as much as possible the criminal activity that relates to and supports the addiction. In fact, this last goal is the reason many policymakers give for supporting these high-cost treatment alternatives (Courtwright, 1982; Musto, 1987; Jaffe, 1987; Lipton et al., 1992).

Other treatment programs—mainly those associated with outpatient treatment and TC—are aimed at rehabilitating addicted individuals while helping them to reintegrate into the normative, noncriminal community. One example of this type of program is the CREST model, implemented in Delaware (Nielsen & Scarpitti, 1997; Mello et al., 1997; Inciardi et al., 1997). The aim of transforming recovered addicts into functioning members of the society has driven many governments around the world to allocate treatment funds for decades (beginning at the end of the 1950s).

Despite significant evidence to support the effectiveness of substance abuse treatment, there are still numerous questions as to the efficiency of the different models (Berg, 1992; Gerstein, 1992; Hubbard, 1992; Ortmann, 2000). Addressing complex questions about substance abuse and how to effectively target and treat it requires an understanding of the factors associated with the addiction and those associated with successful programming. It is at this juncture that culturally competent substance abuse treatment is needed. Unfortunately, very few studies have been conducted regarding cultural competence in the context of substance abuse treatment. In fact, in a content analysis of clinical psychological intervention, it was found that less than 6 percent of the studies examined over a period of 17 years dealt with ethnic minority populations (Iwamasa et al., 2002). This is in spite of the fact that the demographics of the United States are becoming more diverse, and that the majority of incarcerated inmates that suffer from addiction are predominantly from the inner city and belong to ethnic minority groups.

Studies have found that socio- and ethnocultural differences have an effect on one's life experiences (Fowler et al., 2004), and hence on substance abuse treatment experiences as well. In examining ethnic differences in treatment outcomes, Jerrell and Wilson (1996) found greater reduction in alcohol and other drug symptoms after six months of intervention for African Americans, Hispanics, Native Americans, and Asian Americans in comparison to White males. Similar results were found by Fowler and her colleagues (2004) in regard to minority women in Austin, Texas. Specifically, they found a significant difference in the overall decrease in alcohol and substance abuse for African American and Hispanic women in comparison to Anglo (White) women, although the greatest decrease was observed for Anglo (White) participants as a whole.

Consequently, culturally competent treatment that is designed to treat racial/ethnic minorities is desirable, although socio- and ethnocultural differences pose challenges to an effective execution of such treatment. Mallow and Cameron-Kelly argue that a culturally competent substance-abuse approach within a therapeutic community "can seem counter-intuitive to program staff [who are many times educated counselors that did not mature from the TC itself] and are subsequently not administered or administered in a way that sabotage the integrity of the intervention" (2006: 63). Nevertheless, TCs are adequate environments for culturally competent substance abuse treatment as they are responsive to diverse populations (Manning, 1990). With that in mind, it is evident that compliance with and completion of the treatment are essential factors in, and precursors to, successful recovery.

Lior Gideon

See also: *Code of the Street*; Fair Sentencing Act of 2010; Inequality Theory; Institutional Racism; Socioeconomic Factors; War on Drugs

References

Berg, W. "Evaluation of Community-Based Drug Abuse Treatment Programs: A Review of the Research Literature." In *The Addiction Process: Effective Social Work Approaches,* edited by E. Freeman, 81–95. White Plains, NY: Longman, 1992.

Borkman, T. J., L. A. Kaskutas, J. Room, K. Bryan, and D. Barrows. "An Historical and Developmental Analysis of Social Model Programs." *Journal of Substance Abuse Treatment* 15, no. 1 (1998): 7–17.

Courtwright, D. T. *Dark Paradise.* Cambridge, MA: Harvard University Press, 1982.

De Leon, G. "Therapeutic Communities for Substance Abuse: Overview of Approach and Effectiveness." *Psychology of Addictive Behavior* 3 (1989): 140–47.

Falk, R. F., and P. Tonkin. "Soft Modelling the Predictors of Drug Treatment Use." *Social Research Update* 32 (2001): 1–4.

Fowler, D. N., D. M. DiNitto, and D. K. Webb. "Racial/Ethnic Differences in Dually Diagnosed Anglo and Ethnic Minority Women Receiving Chemical Dependency Treatment." *Journal of Ethnicity in Substance Abuse* 3, no. 3 (2004): 1–16.

Gerstein, D. "The Effectiveness of Drug Treatment." *Research Publications: Association for Research in Nervous and Mental Disease* 70 (1992): 253–82.

Gideon, L. "Detoxification and Rehabilitation Programs in Prison and Community Support Systems: Their Contribution in Reducing Recidivism and Drug Use among Released Prisoners." PhD diss., The Hebrew University, Jerusalem, Israel, 2002.

Haines, K. "Issues for After-care Services for Released Prisoners." *Research Bulletin Number 30.* Cambridge: Home Office Research and Statistics Department, 1991.

Hubbard, R. L. "Evaluation and Treatment Outcome." In *Substance Abuse: A Comprehensive Textbook,* 2nd ed., edited by J. Lowinson, P. Ruiz, R. Millman, and J. Langrod, 596–611. Baltimore, MD: Williams and Wilkins, 1992.

Hubbard, R. L., M. E. Marsden, J. V. Rachal, H. J. Harwood, E. R. Cavanaugh, and H. M. Ginzburg. *Drug Abuse Treatment: A National Study of Effectiveness.* Chapel Hill: University of North Carolina Press, 1989.

Inciardi, J. A., S. S. Martin, C. A. Butzin, R. M. Hooper, and L. D. Harrison. "An Effective Model of Prison-Based Treatment for Drug-involved Offenders." *Journal of Drug Issues* 27, no. 2 (1997): 261–78.

Iwamasa, G. Y., K. H. Sorocco, and D. A. Koonce. "Ethnicity and Clinical Psychology: A Content Analysis of the Literature." *Clinical Psychology Review* 22, no. 6 (2002): 931–45.

Jaffe, J. H. "Footnotes in the Evaluation of the American National Response: Some Little Known Aspects of the First American Strategy for Drug Abuse and Drug Traffic Prevention." *British Journal of Addiction* 82 (1987): 587–600.

Jerrell, J. M., and J. L. Wilson. "Ethnic Differences in the Treatment of Dual Mental and Substance Disorders: A Preliminary Analysis. *Journal of Substance Abuse Treatment* 14, no. 2 (1996): 133–140.

Kelley, M. S. "Toward an Understanding of Responses to Methadone Maintenance Treatment Organizational Style." *Research in Social Problems and Public Policy: The Organizational Response to Social Problems* 8 (2001): 247–73.

Kennard, D. 1998a. *An Introduction to Therapeutic Communities.* London: Jessica Kingsley Publishers, 1998.

Kennard, D. 1998b. "Therapeutic Communities Are Back—And There Is Something a Little Different about Them." *Therapeutic Communities: The International Journal for Therapeutic and Supportive Organizations* 19 (1998): 323–29.

Lipton, D.S., G. P. Falkin, and H. K. Wexler. "Correctional Drug Abuse Treatment in the United States: An Overview." In *Drug Abuse Treatment in Prisons and Jails,* edited by F. M. Tims and C. G. Leukefeld, 8–29. New York: NIDA, 1992.

Mallow, A., and D. Cameron-Kelly. "Unraveling the Layers of Cultural Competence: Exploring the Meaning of Meta-Cultural Competence in the Therapeutic Community." *Journal of Ethnicity in Substance Abuse* 5, no. 3 (2006): 63–74.

Manning, N. *The Therapeutic Community Movement: Charisma and Routinization.* New York: Routledge, 1990.

Mello, C. O., F. Penchansky, J. A. Inciardi, and H. L. Surratt. "Participant Observation of a Therapeutic Community Model for Offenders in Drug Treatment." *Journal of Drug Issues* 27, no. 2 (1997): 299–314.

Musto, D. M. *The American Disease: Origin of Narcotic Control.* New York: Oxford University Press, 1987.

National Institute on Drug Abuse (NIDA). 2011a. *Info Facts: Lessons from Prevention Research,* 2011. http://www.drugabuse.gov/publications/infofacts/lessons-prevention-research.

National Institute on Drug Abuse (NIDA). 2011b. *Info Facts: Treatment Statistics,* 2011. http://www.drugabuse.gov/publications/infofacts/treatment-statistics.

National Institutes of Health (NIH). *Drug Use among Racial/Ethnic Minorities.* Washington, DC: National Institute on Drug Abuse, 1998.

Nielsen, A. L., and F. R. Scarpitti. "Changing the Behavior of Substance Abusers: Factors Influencing the Effectiveness of Therapeutic Communities." *Journal of Drug Issues* 27, no. 2 (1997): 279–98.

Ortmann, R. "The Effectiveness of Social Therapy in Prison: A Randomized Experiment." *Crime and Delinquency* 46, no. 2 (2000): 214–32.

Pearson, F. S., and D. S. Lipton. "A Meta-Analytic Review of the Effectiveness of Corrections-Based Treatment for Drug Abuse." *Prison Journal* 79, no. 4 (1999): 384.

Rosental, M. S. "The Therapeutic Community: Exploring Boundaries." *Journal of Addiction* 84 (1989): 141–50.

Strain, E. C., G. E. Bigelow, I. A. Liebson, and M. L. Stitzer. "Moderate versus High-Dose Methadone in the Treatment of Opioid Dependence: A Randomized Trial." *The Journal of the American Medical Association* 281 (1999): 1000–1005.

Substance Abuse and Mental Health Services Administration (SAMHSA). *Results from the 2010 National Survey on Drug Use and Health: Summary of National Findings,* NSDUH Series H-41, HHS Publication No. (SMA) 11-4658. Rockville, MD: Substance Abuse and Mental Health Services Administration, 2011.

Vandevelde, S., E. Broekaert, R. Yates, and M. Kooyman. "The Development of the Therapeutic Community in Correctional Establishments: A Comparative Retrospective Account of the 'Democratic' Maxwell Jones TC and the Hierarchical Concept-Based TC in Prison." *International Journal of Social Psychiatry* 50, no. 1 (2004): 66–79.

Du Bois, W. E. B. (1868–1963)

William Edward Burghardt Du Bois was one of the leading intellectuals of the twentieth century. He was born in Great Barrington, Massachusetts, on February 23, 1868, five years after the abolition of slavery. He was of African, French, and Dutch parentage. Du Bois was a prolific writer, an outstanding scholar, poet, and political activist who devoted his life to the fight for racial equality and the promotion of Pan-Africanism. He was a pioneering advocate for racial equity and the respectful treatment of African Americans. A man of enormous talent and versatile ability, he excelled in almost everything he did during his more than 70-year career. His professionalism was displayed in his roles as historian, sociologist, professor, and journalist (Hanson, 2010; Lewis, 2000).

During the post–Civil War Reconstruction period, Great Barrington was an affluent area with a racial harmony that enabled Du Bois to escape the conditioning that was the lot of many African American males of that period. Having had little experience with racial discrimination, Du Bois attended a racially integrated school, which was a rare experience for his time. At the time that Du Bois was growing up, Great Barrington was a city of about 5,000 people. Fewer than 50 of them were of African American descent (Hanson, 2010; Lewis, 2000).

Du Bois' illustrious academic career started in high school; he graduated in 1884 as his class valedictorian. Due to financial constraints, Du Bois could not go to Harvard for his undergraduate degree. Some members of his community, realizing his enormous academic potential, raised money through local churches to sponsor his education at Fisk University. Fisk was a historically Black college founded in 1866 in Nashville, Tennessee. It was at Fisk that he literally came face to face with the plight of the Black person in America and vowed to devote the rest of his life to the

W. E. B. Du Bois (1868–1963), called the father of Pan-Africanism for his work on behalf of the emerging African nations, devoted his life to the struggle for equality for African Americans and all people of color. He was among the first criminologists in the United States with his seminal study of crimes committed by African Americans in Philadelphia, Pennsylvania. (Library of Congress)

emancipation of his people. Du Bois received his bachelor of arts degree from Fisk in 1888. He subsequently won a scholarship to Harvard, where he completed a bachelor's degree in 1890, a master's in 1891, and a doctorate in sociology in 1895. He was the first African American to earn a PhD from Harvard. Upon his return from the University of Berlin, Germany, where he carried out his postdoctoral work, Du Bois accepted his first job as a professor at Wilberforce University in Ohio. He also held teaching positions at both the University of Pennsylvania and Atlanta University (Hanson, 2010; Lewis, 2000).

One of Du Bois' most lasting legacies to civil rights advocacy was his co-founding of the NAACP (National Association for the Advancement of Colored People) in 1905. The NAACP, which began initially as the Niagara Movement, is the oldest civil rights organization in the world. Its purpose is to promote the civil and human rights of minority groups. Furthermore, through his writings, Du Bois put the African American people's condition and character into historical, socio-logical, political, and religious context (Hanson, 2010; Lewis, 2000).

Du Bois' professional contribution to the study of criminology, crime, and criminal justice is finally receiving the attention it deserves. In one of his seminal works, "The Negro Criminal," a chapter in his book *The Philadelphia Negro* (1899), Du Bois studied, identified, and explained the apparent involvement of African Americans in criminal activities in Philadelphia from the post–Civil War period to the last decade of the 1800s. From his research on the criminal data from Philadelphia, he concluded that social exclusion and environmental factors explain the criminality of African Americans. Consequently, he challenged the ideas espoused by the eugenics movement propagandists that African Americans were inferior and prone to criminal behavior. He argued that the economic and political marginalization of African Americans partly accounts for their involvement in crime. He posited that the majority of African Americans who committed crimes acted out of desperation, as crime became their only option for survival (Gross, 2006). Many resorted to drunkenness and debauchery as escape from their deplorable circumstances and environment. In addition, Du Bois observed that some of the criminal acts of African Americans bore the hallmarks of protests against their oppression, a conclusion strongly supported by twenty-first-century research findings (Du Bois, 1904; Gabbidon, 2007).

Du Bois also made a case against the discriminatory treatment of African Americans by the criminal justice system, for instance noting that African American neighborhoods were overpoliced. The overpolicing of African American communities in turn accounted for their overrepresentation in the criminal justice system. He also pointed out that the minor deviant behavior of African Americans attracted very harsh punishment by the system. Whipping as a form of punishment was frequently used against African Americans; the whipping was so harsh and the humiliation so intense that some, especially during the slave era, preferred suicide (Du Bois, 1904; Gabbidon, 2007).

Hanging as a form of punishment for more serious offenses was also widely used against African Americans. Curfew as a form of social control was frequently used to limit the movement and freedoms of African Americans since they were perceived as a threat to the life and property of the powerful classes. To modulate the racial discrimination against African Americans, Du Bois made a case for the hiring of African American police officers and for the inclusion of African Americans on juries (Gabbidon, 2007).

Du Bois noted that while minor infractions attracted very harsh punishment, white-collar crimes such as embezzlement and fraud were leniently treated. He insisted that this was because the perpetrators of the latter crimes were people who belonged to the dominant group and also people who wielded significant influence and power in the society. In his work on the convict-lease system in the South (1901), Du Bois highlighted how the governments of the Southern states colluded with the Southern plantation owners to exploit the labor of African Americans through the vagrancy laws. African Americans arrested for violation of the vagrancy laws who failed to pay the hefty fines imposed on them were blatantly leased out to the plantation owners to work off their fines. Du Bois' ideas very much implicated the role of power in the definition of crime and the selective societal response to deviance. His criminological ideas laid the foundation for some of the contemporary criminological theories, including white-collar crime, conflict, strain, anomie, and social disorganization theories, among others. His research on the "Philadelphia Negro" was the first study of its kind. It was among the first scientific urban studies of African Americans, and established Du Bois as one of the leading scholars of his day (Gabbidon, 2007; Hanson, 2010; Lewis, 2000).

O. Oko Elechi and Edward J. Schauer

See also: Institutional Racism; Lynching; 100 Blacks in Law Enforcement Who Care; Police Brutality; Slavery; Socioeconomic Factors; Wells-Barnett, Ida B.; White, Walter Francis

References

Du Bois, W. E. B. *The Souls of Black Folk: Essays and Sketches.* Chicago: A.C. McClurg and Company, 1904.

Du Bois, W. E. B. "The Spawn of Slavery: The Convict-Lease System in the South." *The Missionary Review of the World* 24 (October 1901): 737–45.

Du Bois, W. E. B. "The Negro Criminal." In *The Philadelphia Negro: A Social Study,* 235–68. Philadelphia: University of Pennsylvania Press, 1899.

Gabbidon, S. L. *W. E. B. Du Bois on Crime and Justice: Laying the Foundations of Sociological Criminology.* Burlington, VT: Ashgate Publishing, 2007.

Gross, K. N. *Colored Amazons: Crime, Violence, and Black Women in the City of Brotherly Love, 1880–1910.* Durham, NC: Duke University Press, 2006.

Hanson, L. J. "W. E. B. Du Bois (1868–1963)." In *Fifty Key Thinkers in Criminology,* edited by K. Hayward, S. Maruna, and J. Mooney, 53–5. New York: Routledge, 2010.

Lewis, D. L. *W. E. B. Du Bois: The Fight for Equality and the American Century, 1919–1963.* New York: Henry Holt and Company, 2000.

Dutton, Charles Stanley (1951–)

Charles Stanley Dutton was born on January 30, 1951, and began his life in a public housing project in Maryland (Mallegg, 2009). Violence and drug use were common in his neighborhood, and had a direct impact on his family. Dutton has

Charles Dutton, once an imprisoned felon, is now a successful actor and former director of the HBO series *The Corner* depicting Black life on the streets of Baltimore, Maryland. (Associated Press)

one sister, a recovering cocaine addict, and one brother who had been addicted to heroin and who died of AIDS in 1993 (Scott, 2000). He spent time on the streets during his youth, and earned the nickname "Roc" as a result of engaging in rock fights in the neighborhood, in which his gang would line one side of the street and throw rocks at another gang (Clark, 1991). He believed, similar to many other youths in his neighborhood, that he would ultimately find himself in prison.

At 12 years old, Dutton dropped out of school, claiming that the streets were more interesting. This marked the beginning of his interaction with the criminal justice system. He was in and out of a variety of state and federal institutions until the age of 26 (Sparrow, 2009). His life took a drastic turn at the age of 17 when he pled guilty to manslaughter. Dutton had been in a fight and stabbed a man who had pulled a knife on him (Scott, 2000). After serving two years in prison, he was released on parole.

In 1969, Dutton was sent back to prison for possession of a deadly weapon when he was caught with a handgun (*USA Today*, 2009). While serving a three-year sentence, he was convicted of assaulting a prison guard. He spent more than seven years in the Maryland State Penitentiary. Dutton was sent to solitary confinement, a dark five-by-seven-foot cell with no bed or toilet, on several occasions (Clark, 1991). Prisoners were held without clothes and fed once every three days. Prisoners were permitted a single piece of reading material. During one stay in solitary confinement, he took with him a compilation of plays written by African American playwrights, which he read by the light that shone beneath the door. He was inspired by *Day of Absence* by Douglas Turner Ward (Scott, 2000). He convinced the warden to allow him to organize a theatre group, which Dutton directed;

he also performed the lead role in the play. He claims that the experiences in prison led him to discover his purpose in life (Sparrow, 2009).

The transformation of Dutton's life was evident during his incarceration. After organizing the theatre group, Dutton was stabbed in the neck with an ice pick by another inmate (Donlon, 1991). During his recovery he made the decision to change his life and not retaliate against his attacker, violating the "code" of prison. He also earned his high school equivalency certificate and an associate's degree in college prior to his release from the penitentiary (Scott, 2000). He went on to Towson State University in Maryland, where he was a drama major, earning a bachelor of arts in 1978. During his studies at Towson State, a drama teacher encouraged him to apply to the Yale University School of Drama. He was accepted and graduated from Yale in 1983.

Since his graduation from Yale, Dutton has had a successful acting career in theater, television, and cinema. He has been nominated for countless awards, and has won several. Dutton revisited the streets of Maryland while directing HBO's documentary series *The Corner* (Scott, 2000). He has also shared his story in his live show "From Jail to Yale . . . Serving Time on Stage."

Jamie Newsome

References

Clark, K. R. "After a Rocky Start, Dutton's Life Now 'Roc'-Solid." *The Chicago Tribune,* August 25, 1991.

Donlon, B. "Dutton Is a Solid 'Roc.'" *USA Today*, August 30, 1991.

Mallegg, K., ed. *Who's Who among African Americans.* 23rd ed. Farmington Hills, MI: Gale, 2009.

Scott, J. "Who Gets to Tell a Black Story?" *The New York Times,* June 11, 2000.

Sparrow, K. (producer). "Charles S. Dutton Interview Part 2 [Connecticut Style]." WTNH, New Haven, CT, May 8, 2009.

USA Today. "Should a 13-Year-Old Be Locked Away for Life?" November 10, 2009.

E

Early Intervention for African Americans

Those of lower socioeconomic status within the United States are disproportionately exposed to numerous health risks (Griffin, 2005). They are also more likely to be exposed to criminal activity as perpetrators, victims, and/or bystanders. To be an ethnic minority in a lower-class area—in particular, to be African American—is to be further at risk of becoming involved in the criminal justice system and encountering health issues (Griffin, 2005; Carswell et al., 2009).

In 2008, Black youth accounted for 16 percent of the juvenile population aged 10 to 17, yet they were involved in 52 percent of juvenile arrests for Violent Crime Index offenses, and 33 percent of arrests for juvenile Property Crime Index offenses (Puzzanchera, 2009). In an effort to combat the disproportionate numbers of African Americans within the criminal justice system, several forms of intervention programs have emerged (Forster & Rehner, 1999). The primary purpose of these programs is to intervene in the lives of African American youth *before* they are exposed to the justice system and to improve their resiliency to delinquent behaviors (Clarke & Campbell, 1998; Mann & Reynolds, 2006). Early intervention takes numerous forms, including preschool curricula, mentoring, family skills training, and substance abuse prevention programs. Each works to address some risk factor for delinquency, thereby building a youth's resiliency. The programs affect the child and the child's environment simultaneously (Clarke & Campbell, 1998; Forster & Rehner, 1999). These programs have great appeal for those interested in preventing delinquency, as postadmission intervention to the justice system has not been as successful as originally hoped (Clarke & Campbell, 1998; Mann & Reynolds, 2006). The empirical research into these ethnically or culturally limited programs is rare; many programs instead are largely comprised of African Americans but also contain participants of other races (Forster & Rehner, 1999; Kumpfer & Tait, 2000; Reynolds et al., 2003; Brody et al., 2004; Mann & Reynolds, 2006).

Two distinct categories of early intervention are easy to discern when reviewing the literature. Educational intervention programs may refer to prescribed preschool curricula and family relationship building (known as early childhood intervention) or alternative educational settings for school-age youth (Clarke & Campbell, 1998; Mann & Reynolds, 2006). Community programming interventions seek to affect not only at-risk youth but their neighborhoods as well, providing intervention on a multigenerational level (Piquero et al., 2009; Kumpfer & Tait, 2000; Brody et al., 2004). These two categories of early intervention often share techniques or target the same risk factors, including poor school performance, poor family relations, and impoverished neighborhoods (Smith & Stern, 1997; Kumpfer & Tait, 2000; Brody et al., 2004).

The original goal of early educational intervention efforts in the 1960s and the 1970s was to improve the academic chances for disadvantaged and minority youth (Carswell et al., 2009). The two main methods of achieving this goal were in the form of preschool intervention or alternative education programming. It is only more recently that the potential for building delinquency resilience in youth has been examined (Cox et al., 1995; Clarke & Campbell, 1998; Tobin & Sprague, 2000; Carswell et al., 2009). School-related behavior complaints and poor academic performance are both acknowledged risk factors for delinquent behavior later in life (Cox et al., 1995; Mann & Reynolds, 2006). African American youth are more likely to exhibit problem behaviors within the school setting, and are more likely to be suspended and for lengthier periods of time. If such problems continue, dropping out is a serious risk, which further increases a youth's likelihood of becoming delinquent (Carswell et al., 2009). By either intervening in preschool or kindergarten, or working to rebuild ties to the educational system through alternative programming, it is hoped that youth will build resiliency to these particular risk factors (Cox et al., 1995; Reynolds et al., 2003).

Early childhood interventions are theorized to have their impact on crime and delinquency by improving early cognitive abilities and scholastic achievement and improving parenting techniques (Clarke & Campbell, 1998; Reynolds et al., 2004; Piquero et al., 2009). A prescribed curriculum readies the participants for their formal education to come. At the same time, programming is made available to a child's parents. This may include pediatric care, skill-building opportunities, and home visits (Clarke & Campbell, 1998; Reynolds et al., 2003; Piquero et al., 2009).

An examination of early childhood programs warrants the inclusion of a discussion of the Chicago Longitudinal Study. The study investigated the long-term outcomes of a largely African American cohort of 1,539 disadvantaged youth. The study began with the cohort's participation in the Chicago Child-Parent Center (CPC) Program in 1985–1986. The CPC program is a federally funded early education program that provides preschool and kindergarten resources to children in at-risk neighborhoods. After participants completed the CPC program, they were monitored for several years to determine whether their experiences had any impact on their later social and academic lives (Reynolds et al., 1998; Reynolds et al., 2004; Smokowski et al., 2004; Mann & Reynolds, 2006).

The results of the Chicago Longitudinal Study indicated that participation in the CPC program had significant impact on school achievement and parental involvement in education, as well as lower delinquency and dropout rates among participants (Reynolds et al., 1998; Reynolds et al., 2004). Youth involved in the CPC program had significantly lower rates of delinquency than a comparison group who did not participate in CPC programs (Reynolds et al., 1998; Smokowski et al., 2004; Mann & Reynolds, 2006). Depending on type of delinquency, CPC preschool education was associated with a 40 to 50 percent decrease (Mann & Reynolds, 2006). Although research into other preschool programs has not always been so conclusive, the success of the CPC program indicates that by alleviating some school-related stressors in a youth's life, he or she may then be more resilient to delinquent behavior (Clarke & Campbell, 1998; Reynolds et al., 1998; Reynolds et al., 2003).

The other form of intervention through education involves alternative education programs. Although today the phrase "alternative education" may also mean "charter school" or "home school," it has also long referred to the type of schooling available to youth who are unable to perform well, academically and/or behaviorally, in the traditional school system (Tobin & Sprague, 2000). There is no one particular model that is followed by alternative education, despite its widespread use. Students may be of any age within the school system. Specific populations, such as minority or at-risk youth, have often been targeted. No matter what the student background, there are some elements that are common to the more successful programs. Low student-teacher ratios, supportive environments, and student-centered curricula have been found to be common to more successful programs (Cox et al., 1995; Tobin & Sprague, 2000; Carswell et al., 2009).

Often, the purpose of this type of program is to reduce a student's instances of problematic behavior and to improve his or her academic capabilities. The link between problems within school and delinquent behavior has been well documented, and some programs also claim to increase a youth's resiliency to delinquent behavior (Reynolds et al., 2003; Carswell et al., 2009; Piquero et al., 2009). Whether educational programs are successful in their aims has been a matter of debate for decades (Cox et al., 1995; Tobin & Sprague, 2000; Reynolds et al., 2003). In contrast to the findings for the CPC, some research suggest that the impact on delinquent behavior, when it occurs, appears to be minimal and temporary (Cox et al., 1995; Tobin & Sprague, 2000).

As mentioned earlier, early educational intervention sometimes shares aspects of the second category of interventions: community programming. For example, substance abuse and violence prevention programming have occurred in educational settings either as after-school programs or lessons during the regular school day. In community programming, classes may be offered in a community center or a mentoring program to provide a more personal approach (Kumpfer & Tait, 2000; Hanlon et al., 2002; Brody et al., 2004; Griffin, 2005). Both community and educational interventions have offered programming opportunities for parents in the past. In educational settings, this might be in the form of tutoring to improve a parent's academic abilities or allowing parents to be involved by participating with their children in educational events such as field trips (Reynolds et al., 1998; Reynolds et al., 2003; Carswell et al., 2009; Piquero et al., 2009).

In a community-based approach, the services for parents often extend beyond the borders of education to other aspects of life (Smith & Stern, 1997; Kumpfer & Tait, 2000; Brody et al., 2004). For example, the Strong Families Program, which has been adapted to serve families of numerous ethnicities including African Americans, works with parents to understand their roles in building a child's resiliency. Lessons in disciplining children, rewarding them for positive behaviors, stress management, and communications are all offered. These are reinforced for the whole family through simultaneous lessons for children, as well as later lessons for children and parents together (Kumpfer & Tait, 2000; Brody et al., 2004; Piquero et al., 2009).

Other services offered through community interventions may include mentoring and role model programs for youth who perhaps lack a strong parental figure within the community. These mentors, as mentioned earlier, might focus only on delinquency prevention, or they may work with youth to improve skills in social engagement and life skills such as finding gainful employment (Forster & Rehner, 1999; Hanlon et al., 2002; Griffin, 2005). Community employment and financial workshops allow participants to obtain knowledge about properly filing tax refunds or how to complete a job application and prepare for an interview. Childcare options, transportation services for those who qualify, and lessons in artistic expression have also been featured in community programming. Unlike educational interventions, that seek mainly to address school-related risk factors for delinquency, community interventions seek to improve a community as a whole (Forster & Rehner, 2003). By assisting participants in taking charge of their own lives and improving their own communities, not only are services available for current at-risk youth, but the groundwork is laid to build resiliency in future generations (Forster & Rehner, 1999; Brody et al., 2004). By some reports, community programming has shown more positive results and lasting results than educational intervention (Clarke & Campbell, 1998; Kumpfer & Tait, 2000; Hanlon et al., 2002; Brody et al., 2004).

Since the 1960s, these two categories of intervention for at-risk youth have been gaining in popularity and spreading across the United States. Designed to address different delinquency factors, they nevertheless occasionally overlap in the services offered to the children and families who participate. Empirical research has indicated that some success may be had by these programs, though the tailoring necessary to meet a specific population's needs may make it difficult to create results that may be generalized to larger populations. Community programming is able to offset this somewhat more than educational programming when national models such as the Safe Families Program are followed and tested, but results remain difficult to generalize. The existence of some data suggesting that these programs have an impact cannot be ignored and are useful in the evolution of more effective future programs and processes to combat juvenile delinquency.

Katherine Grady

See also: Education

References

Brody, G. H., V. M. Murry, M. Gerrard, F. X. Gibbons, V. Molgaard, L. McNair, . . . E. Carlan-Neubaum. "The Strong African American Families Program: Translating Research into Preventative Programming." *Child Development* 73, no. 3 (2004): 900–17.

Carswell, S. B., T. E. Hanlon, K. E. O'Grady, A. M. Watts, and P. Pothong. "A Preventive Intervention Program for Urban African American Youth Attending an Alternative Education Program: Background, Implementation, and Feasibility." *Education and Treatment of Children* 32, no. 3 (2009): 445–69.

Clarke, S. H., and F. A. Campbell. "Can Intervention Early Prevent Crime Later? The Abecedarian Project Compared with Other Programs." *Early Childhood Research Quarterly* 13, no. 2 (1998): 319–43.

Cox, S. M., W. S. Davidson, and T. S. Bynum. "A Meta-Analysis Assessment of Delinquency-Related Outcomes of Alternative Education Programs." *Crime & Delinquency* 41, no. 2 (1995): 219–34.

Forster, M., and T. Rehner. "Delinquency Prevention in Poor and At-Risk African-American Youth: A Social Work Practice Innovation." *Social Thought* 19, no. 2 (1999): 37–52.

Forster, M., and T. Rehner. "Delinquency Prevention as Empowerment Practice: A Community-Based Social Work Approach." *Race, Gender, & Class* 10, no. 2 (2003): 109–20.

Griffin, J. P. "The Building Resiliency and Vocational Excellence (BRAVE) Program: A Violence-Prevention and Role Model Program for Young, African American Males." *Journal of Health Care for the Poor and Underserved* 16 (2005): 78–88.

Hanlon, T. E., R. W. Bateman, B. D. Simon, K. E. O'Grady, and S. B. Carswell. "An Early Community-Based Intervention for the Prevention of Substance Abuse and Other Delinquent Behavior." *Journal of Youth and Adolescence* 31, no. 6 (2002): 459–71.

Kumpfer, K. L., and C. M. Tait. *Family Skills Training for Parents and Children* (OJJDP Publication No. NCJ 180140). Washington, DC: Government Printing Office, 2000.

Mann, E. A., and A. J. Reynolds. "Early Intervention and Juvenile Delinquency Prevention: Evidence from the Chicago Longitudinal Study." *Social Work Research* 30, no. 3 (2006): 153–67.

Piquero, A. R., D. P. Farrington, B. C. Welsh, R. Tremblay, and W. G. Jennings. "Effects of Early Family/Parent Training Programs on Antisocial Behavior and Delinquency." *Journal of Experimental Criminology* 5, no. 2 (2009): 83–120.

Puzzanchera, C. *Juvenile Arrests 2008* (OJJDP Publication No. NCJ 228479). Washington, DC: Government Printing Office, 2009.

Reynolds, A. J., H. Chan, and J. A. Temple. "Early Childhood Intervention and Delinquency: An Exploratory Analysis of the Chicago Child-Parent Centers." *Evaluation Review* 22, no. 3 (1998): 341–72.

Reynolds, A. J., J. A. Temple, and S. Ou. "School-Based Early Intervention and Child Well-Being in the Chicago Longitudinal Study." *Child Welfare* 82, no. 5 (2003): 633–56.

Reynolds, A. J., S. Ou, and J. W. Topitzes. "Paths of Effects of Early Childhood Intervention on Educational Attainment and Delinquency: A Confirmatory Analysis of the Chicago Child-Parent Centers." *Child Development* 75, no. 5 (2004): 1299–1328.

Smith, C. A., and S. B. Stern. "Delinquency and Antisocial Behavior: A Review of Family Processes and Intervention Research." *Social Service Review* 71, no. 3 (1997): 382–420.

Smokowski, P. R., E. A. Mann, A. J. Reynolds, and M. W. Fraser. "Childhood Risk and Protective Factors and Late Adolescent Adjustment in Inner City Minority Youth." *Children and Youth Services Review* 26 (2004): 63–91.

Tobin, T., and J. Sprague. "Alternative Education Strategies: Reducing Violence in School and the Community." *Journal of Emotional and Behavioral Disorders* 8, no. 3 (2000): 177–86.

Education

The link between education and criminal involvement among African Americans is well documented and stems from both historical and current contexts. Despite the elimination of formal segregation based on the ruling in *Brown v. Board of Education of Topeka, Kansas* (1954) (Skiba et al., 2011), African Americans continue to experience unequal access to quality education as manifested through a fractured educational infrastructure and poor academic achievement (James, 2011). These factors play a role in reinforcing antisocial and delinquent behaviors that create pathways into the juvenile justice and adult criminal justice systems. Over the past two decades, there has been considerable inquiry about such factors, which have come to be called "the-school-to-prison-pipeline" (James, 2011). In many respects, the educational system has been largely responsible for implementing policies and practices that perpetuate the criminalization of socially disenfranchised children and have ultimately led to the overrepresentation of African American children in the juvenile justice system (Nicholson-Crotty et al., 2009; Puzzanchera & Adams, 2011; Thompson, 2011).

Schools in predominantly African American communities face greater challenges than schools in other locations (Noguera & Akom, 2000). Such schools are situated in areas of high unemployment and significant criminal activity, and locations where a significant portion of the population is under criminal justice supervision (Boggess & Hipp, 2010). Teachers in schools with predominantly African American students are generally likely to be newer and less experienced. Within these schools, there are higher rates of teacher and administrator attrition within shorter periods of time (Boyd et al., 2009). Moreover, both teachers and students report that race plays a role in how students' academic capabilities are perceived (Pringle et al., 2010; DeCastro-Ambrosetti & Cho, 2011).

The culture and physical environment of a school also plays a significant role in criminalizing inner-city students (Thompson, 2011). Despite the reduction of school-related violent incidents across the country (Cole & Helig, 2011), zero-tolerance policies remain disproportionately enforced in schools with predominantly minority students (Thompson, 2011). Students (specifically males) within these schools are more likely to experience higher-than-average rates of suspension, expulsion (Krezmien et al., 2006; Rocque, 2010; Skiba et al., 2011), and student arrests, and are more likely to experience probation or juvenile court activity due to truancy (Thompson, 2011).

In regards to academic achievement, over the past two decades, African American students nationally yield lower test scores in math and reading compared to their White and Asian counterparts on fourth- and eighth-grade assessments (U.S. Department of Education, 2009a and 2009b). African American children have a higher propensity of being misclassified with mild mental retardation or emotional disturbance (Barbarin, 2010; Fowler, 2011). Moreover, African American high school students drop out of school at twice the rate of White students (U.S. Department of Education, 2011). In fact, the majority of high schools with higher-than-national-average dropout rates are located in either predominantly African American or Hispanic communities (Balfanz & Legters, 2004).

The impact of educational failure upon African American students is profound. African American students who drop out or leave high school with poor academic preparation are disenfranchised from economic opportunities and are more likely to engage in criminal activities than students who have had successful academic careers (Stewart, 2007; Tobler et al., 2011). Additionally, students who emerge from schools with draconian zero-tolerance policies, high police involvement, and metal detector use draw the conclusion that they are not to be trusted (Mukherjee,

Margaret Munnerlyn Mitchell
(November 8, 1900–August 16, 1949)

Margaret Munnerlyn Mitchell was born in Atlanta, Georgia, on November 8, 1900. A fourth-generation Atlantan, she was the daughter of Mary Isabelle, an Irish suffragette, and Eugene, an attorney. Mitchell began writing early before she actually could write by dictating to her mother. Growing up around Civil War veterans as she attended Atlanta public schools influenced her childhood stories as well as her later work (Edwards, 1983).

Mitchell graduated from Washington Seminary, an Atlanta preparatory school. After a brief engagement to a young soldier killed in battle shortly after their engagement, she enrolled in Smith College in Northampton, Massachusetts, but attended classes for about a year until her mother died and she had to return to Atlanta to run the household (Thomas, 2011).

In 1922, she married Berrien "Red" Upshaw. Shortly afterward, the *Atlanta Journal* hired her to write a weekly column in their *Sunday Magazine* under the name "Peggy" (Allen, 2000). Although her career with the *Atlanta Journal* lasted from 1922 to 1926, her marriage to Upshaw was annulled in 1924 amid allegations of spousal rape, abuse, and alcoholism. In 1925, she married John R. Marsh, Upshaw's best friend and the best man at their wedding.

Ankle problems ended Mitchell's journalism career. Confined to her home and consumed with wifely duties, she began writing a Civil War drama. The manuscript was haphazardly compiled over nine years, typewritten, jotted on grocery and laundry lists, shoved in desk drawers and on closet shelves, with sections randomly crammed into envelopes. She wrote the last chapters first, preferring to work backwards. Although she let friends read parts of the manuscript, she had never shared it with any publishers.

In late 1935, H. S. Latham, a Macmillan Company vice president, traveled throughout the South searching for new authors. Mitchell and a former co-worker met Latham to suggest potential authors he should contact when the co-worker told him that Mitchell had written a book. Reluctant, Mitchell demurred and told Latham she did not want the material considered for publication. Later that evening, however, she reconsidered, and took her materials to Latham in his hotel room. The material was so voluminous, Latham had to purchase a suitcase (Brown & Wiley, 2011) to contain it all.

Macmillan agreed to publish the book, subject to revisions that took Mitchell six months. The 1,037-page novel, *Gone with the Wind* (GWTW), was published in June 1936 and sold more than 50,000 copies on just one day that summer. Although some critics viewed it as racist and as promoting slavery, it won the Pulitzer Prize in 1937 (Brown & Wiley, 2011; Glanton, 2002; Dixon, 2000).

(Continued)

The fame and accompanying adoration and curiosity caused major disruption to Mitchell's privacy. She was so frustrated at one point she vowed to never write another word, and with the exception of personal letters, she did not. Her only other publication, *Lost Laysen,* a romantic adventure set in the South Pacific, was written when she was 16 but not published until 1996.

In 1936, David O. Selznick gave Mitchell $50,000 for the film rights to GWTW (but paid her another $50,000 later). The film premiered in Atlanta on December 15, 1939, and received a record-breaking 10 Academy Awards. Although the performance of the film's Black cast was one reason for its success, and Hattie McDaniel (who played the character Mammy) was the first African American to win an Oscar, they were banned from the premiere. Clark Gable, who played Rhett Butler, was so outraged that he was going to boycott the event until McDaniel encouraged him to attend (Brown & Wiley, 2011).

After the film, Mitchell, a White writer often perceived as racist, wrote McDaniel, a Black actress often accused as portraying characters that perpetuated racist stereotypes, and applauded her performance. Mitchell established a friendship with McDaniel through written correspondence that lasted the remainder of her life (Glanton, 2002).

The letters between Mitchell and McDaniel inspired Andrew Young, a filmmaker and former mayor of Atlanta, to make a documentary, *Change in the Wind,* about a seven-year friendship between Mitchell and Dr. Benjamin Mays, the president of Morehouse College from 1940 to 1967. Young speculates that Mitchell-McDaniel friendship influenced Mitchell's subsequent friendship with Mays, as well as her financial contributions to Morehouse, a traditionally Black college in Atlanta (Hackwork, 2010).

Mays' and Mitchell's unusual friendship began in 1942, when he approached her for scholarship money for struggling students. Mitchell did not respond to these requests and her husband politely turned them down. However, when illness and death took one of Mitchell's beloved servants after she could not find adequate medical care, she became incensed over the racial inequalities in basic services. After this, she gave money for a scholarship in the maid's name. Eventually, Mitchell anonymously paid the tuitions for 50 Black men to attend colleges and medical schools in several states. Mays protected her anonymity even after her death but eventually revealed to Georgia's first Black pediatrician that the famous author had funded his education (Hackworth, 2010).

Mitchell died at the age of 48 on August 16, 1949, five days after being struck by an off-duty cab driver as she crossed Peachtree Street with her husband to see *A Canterbury Tale* at the Peachtree Art Theater (*New York Times,* 1949). The book she was hesitant to publish is one of the best-selling novels of all time. To date, it has sold more than 30 million copies and has been translated into more than 30 languages in more than 40 countries (*New York Times,* 1949).

(Continued)

Mitchell's legacy at Morehouse College did not end with her death. On Monday, March 18, 2002, her nephew, Eugene Mitchell, gave the college $1.5 million dollars to celebrate Mitchell's lifelong commitment to scholarship, literature, and humanity by endowing the "Margaret Mitchell Marsh" Dean's Chair for the Humanities and Social Sciences (*Atlanta Inquirer*, 2002).

Although Mitchell spent her life in a racially segregated South where old perceptions about race relations dominated, she still managed to quietly and effectively help dozens of Black citizens to achieve their educational and career goals (Hackwork, 2010; Glanton, 2002). As a result, medical care and treatment for Blacks throughout the South improved. Her contributions continue with this most recent gift and will help assure continued progress toward the ultimate goal of racial equality. A continuous line of research finds that higher education is a primary tool for African American men to avoid the criminal justice system.

Angela West Crews

2007; Sealey-Ruiz, 2010; James, 2011). Students internalize the treatment that they routinely experience within the educational system, which may in turn lead to or increase delinquency and criminal activity (Thompson, 2011).

African American youth who enter the juvenile justice or criminal justice system are generally two to three years below grade level in reading and math, tend to have a learning disability, and have had a history of truancy and behavioral problems in the school system (Foley, 2001; Harris et al., 2009). Within the correctional setting, educational quality and the youth's commitment to school are varied (Foley, 2001). In fact, in one study, less than half (45%) of the youth reported attending school for a full day while incarcerated (Sedlak & McPherson, 2010: 6). Consequently, such youth who return to their communities from incarceration may continue to experience significant educational gaps that were not addressed while they were detained, thus reducing their odds of graduating from high school.

Addressing the school-to-prison-pipeline involves both structural and pedagogical changes (Barbarin, 2010). Within the educational realm, the most significant mandate to address the achievement gap between White and minority students has been the legislation No Child Left Behind (NCLB) (2002), which requires certified and qualified teachers within all classrooms and proficiency in math and reading for all students. Despite its ambitious aims, critics argue that NCLB fails to address the disparity of resources between affluent and disadvantaged communities as well as the lack of seasoned teachers, who are needed within struggling communities (Darling-Hammond, 2007). Other efforts have included attempts to strengthen the role of pre-kindergarten teachers and early intervention within these communities (Barbarin, 2010). There have also been greater efforts to reinforce the school counselors' role in identifying students who are at risk for delinquency (Bemak et al., 2005). Mentoring and tutoring programs for young African American males have been shown to reinforce confidence, pro-social values, and educational achievement (Campbell-Whatley & Algozzine, 1997; Martin et al., 2007). Single-sex education has also shown promise for positively impacting the development of African American male students (Noguera, 2012). To break the negative connection between African American students and schools, multiple studies have found that both teachers and administrators within high-minority schools must adapt their pedagogical practices to be more sensitive to the needs of the students and the community (Cartledge et al., 2008; James, 2011; Thompson, 2011).

Mia Green

See also: Early Intervention for African Americans; Inequality Theory; Legal Socialization and Race; Theories of Race and Crime

References

Allen, P., ed. *Margaret Mitchell, Reporter.* Athens, GA: Hill Street Press, 2000.

Atlanta Inquirer. "Morehouse College Gets $1.5 Million Gift in the Name of Pulitzer Prize–Winning Author Margaret Mitchell." April 20, 2002.

Balfanz, R., and N. Legters. *Locating the Dropout Crisis: Which High Schools Produce the Nation's Dropouts? Where Are They Located? Who Attends Them?* Center for Research on the Education of Students Placed at Risk (CRESPAR). U.S. Department of Education grant (No. R117-D40005), 2004.

Barbarin, O. A. "Halting African American Boys' Progression from Pre-K to Prison: What Families, Schools, and Communities Can Do!" *American Journal of Orthopsychiatry* 80, no. 1 (2010): 81–88. doi:10.1111/j.1939-0025.2010.01009.x.

Bemak, F., R. Chi-Ying, and L. A. Siroskey-Sabdo. "Empowerment Groups for Academic Success: An Innovative Approach to Prevent High School Failure for At-Risk, Urban African Americans." *Professional School Counseling* 8, no. 5 (2005): 377–89.

Boggess, L., and J. Hipp. "Violent Crime, Residential Instability and Mobility: Does the Relationship Differ in Minority Neighborhoods?" *Journal of Quantitative Criminology* 26, no. 3 (2010): 351–70. doi:10.1007/s10940-010-9093-7.

Boyd, D., P. Grossman, M. Ing, H. Lankford, S. Loeb, and J. Wyckoff. "The Influence of School Administrators on Teacher Retention Decisions." May 2009. http://www.stanford.edu/~sloeb/papers/Admin%20and%20Retention%2012_12_09.pdf

Brown v. Board of Education of Topeka, Kansas, 347 U.S. 483 (1954).

Brown, E. F., and J. Wiley, Jr. *Margaret Mitchell's* Gone with the Wind: *A Bestseller's Odyssey from Atlanta to Hollywood.* Lanham, MD: Taylor Trade Publishing, 2011.

Campbell-Whatley, G. D., and B. Algozzine. "Using Mentoring to Improve Academic Programming for African American Male Youths with Mild Retardation." *School Counselor* 44, no. 5 (1997): 362.

Cartledge, G., A. Singh, and L. Gibson. "Practical Behavior-Management Techniques to Close the Accessibility Gap for Students Who Are Culturally and Linguistically Diverse." *Preventing School Failure* 52, no. 3 (2008): 29–38.

Cole, H. A., and J. Heilig. "Developing a School-Based Youth Court: A Potential Alternative to the School to Prison Pipeline." *Journal of Law & Education* 40, no. 2 (2011): 305–21.

Darling-Hammond, L. "Race, Inequality and Educational Accountability: The Irony of 'No Child Left Behind.'" *Race, Ethnicity & Education* 10, no. 3 (2007): 245–60. doi:10.1080/13613320701503207.

DeCastro-Ambrosetti, D., and G. Cho. "A Look at 'Lookism': A Critical Analysis of Teachers' Expectations Based on Students' Appearance." *Multicultural Education* 18, no. 2 (2011): 51–4.

Dixon, J. "Fiddle-dee-dee! Margaret Mitchell Turns 100." *Southern Scribe Literary Classics,* 2000. http://www.southernscribe.com/zine/lit_classics/Mitchell_Margaret.htm.

Edwards, A. *Road to Tara: The Life of Margaret Mitchell.* New Haven, CT: Ticknor and Fields, 1983.

Foley, R. M. "Academic Characteristics of Incarcerated Youth and Correctional Educational Programs." *Journal of Emotional & Behavioral Disorders* 9, no. 4 (2001): 248.

Fowler, D. "School Discipline Feeds the 'Pipeline to Prison.'" *Phi Delta Kappan* 93, no. 2 (2011): 14–19.

Glanton, D. "Of Race and a Southern Novel: Mitchell Family, Black College Renew Alliance." *Chicago Tribune,* March 31, 2002. http://articles.chicagotribune.com/2002-03-31/news/0203310407_1_morehouse-college-black-men-mrs-mitchell/3.

Hackworth, C. B. "Morehouse Friendship: Mitchell and Mays." *Atlanta Magazine,* December 1, 2010. http://www.atlantamagazine.com/history/story.aspx?ID=1320095

Harris, P. J., H. M. Baltodano, A. Bal, K. Jolivette, and C. Malcahy. "Reading Achievement of Incarcerated Youth in Three Regions." *Journal of Correctional Education* 60, no. 2 (2009): 120–45.

James, M. C. "Toward Systems of Opportunity: How to Cap Pipelines to Prisons in Schools." *Journal of Curriculum & Pedagogy* 8, no. 2 (2011): 123–27. doi:10.1080/15505170.2011.624894.

Krezmien, M. P., P. E. Leone, and G. M. Achilles. "Suspension, Race, and Disability: Analysis of Statewide Practices and Reporting." *Journal of Emotional & Behavioral Disorders* 14, no. 4 (2006): 217–26.

Martin, D., M. Martin, S. Gibson, and J. Wilkins. "Increasing Prosocial Behavior and Academic Achievement among Adolescent African American Males." *Adolescence* 42, no. 168 (2007): 689–98.

Mukherjee, E. *Criminalizing the Classroom: The Over-Policing of New York City Schools.* New York: New York Civil Liberties Union, 2007.

New York Times. "Miss Mitchell, 49, Dead of Injuries." August 17, 1949. http://www.nytimes.com/learning/general/onthisday/bday/1108.html.

Nicholson-Crotty, S., Z. Birchmeire, and D. Valentine. "Exploring the Impact of School Discipline on Racial Disproportion in the Juvenile Justice System." *Social Science Quarterly* 90, no. 4 (2009): 1003–18. doi:10.1111/j.1540-6237.2009.00674.

No Child Left Behind (NCLB) Act of 2001, Pub. L. No. 107–110, § 115, Stat. 1425 (2002).

Noguera, P. A. "Saving Black and Latino Boys." *Phi Delta Kappan* 93, no. 5 (2012): 8–12.

Noguera, P. A., and A. Akom. "Disparities Demystified." *The Nation* 270, no. 22 (2000), 29–31.

Pringle, B. E., J. E. Lyons, and K. C. Booker. "Perceptions of Teacher Expectations by African American High School Students." *Journal of Negro Education* 79, no. 1 (2010): 33–40.

Puzzanchera, C., and B. Adams. *National Disproportionate Minority Contact Databook.* Washington, DC: National Center for Juvenile Justice, Office of Juvenile Justice and Delinquency Prevention, 2011.

Rocque, M. "Office Discipline and Student Behavior: Does Race Matter?" *American Journal of Education* 116, no. 4 (2010): 557–81.

Sealey-Ruiz, Y. "Dismantling the School-to-Prison Pipeline through Racial Literacy Development in Teacher Education." *Journal of Curriculum & Pedagogy* 8, no. 2 (2011): 116–20. doi:10.1080/15505170.2011.624892.

Sedlak, A. J., and K. S. McPherson. "Youth's Needs and Services: Findings from the Survey of Youth Placement." 2001–JR–BX–K001 Juvenile Justice and Delinquency Prevention. Washington, DC: U.S. Department of Justice, 2010.

Skiba, R. J., R. H. Horner, C. Choong-Geun, M. Rausch, S. L. May, and T. Tobin. "Race Is Not Neutral: A National Investigation of African American and Latino Disproportionality in School Discipline." *School Psychology Review* 40, no. 1 (2011): 85–107.

Stewart, E. B. "Individual and School Structural Effects on African American High School Students' Academic Achievement." *The High School Journal* 91, no. 2 (2007): 16–34.

Thomas, J. "Margaret Mitchell (1900–1949)." *The New Georgia Encyclopedia,* 2011. http://www.georgiaencyclopedia.org/nge/Article.jsp?id=h-2566.

Thompson, H. "Criminalizing Kids: The Overlooked Reason for Failing Schools." *Dissent (00123846)* 58, no. 4 (2011): 23–7.

Tobler, A., K. Komro, A. Dabroski, P. Aveyard, and W. Markham. "Preventing the Link between SES and High-Risk Behaviors: 'Value-Added' Education, Drug Use and Delinquency in High-Risk, Urban Schools." *Prevention Science* 12, no. 2 (2011): 211–21. doi:10.1007/s11121-011-0206-9.

U.S. Department of Education, Institute of Education Sciences, National Center for Education Statistics, National Assessment of Educational Progress (NAEP). 2009a. Mathematics Assessment, 2009a.

U.S. Department of Education, Institute of Education Sciences, National Center for Education Statistics, National Assessment of Educational Progress (NAEP). 2009b. Reading Assessment, 2009b.

U.S. Department of Education, National Center for Education Statistics. *The Condition of Education 2011* (NCES 2011-033), Indicator 20. Washington, DC, 2011.

Environmental Justice

Environmental justice is a term of art referring to the unequal geographic and spatial distribution of environmental benefits and hazards based on race. Environmental justice is synonymous with the concepts of "environmental racism" and "environmental equity" and speaks of an activist movement, a body of law, and sociological literature.

The watershed moment in the history of the environmental justice movement came in Warren County, North Carolina, during 1982. Following the clean-up of a massive unlawful disposal of polychlorinated biphenyls (PCBs) along its highways, North Carolina permitted a landfill facility in a predominantly African American area to store the recovered PCBs. PCBs are a known carcinogen and a hormone and autoimmune system disruptor, and are regulated by the Toxic Substances Control Act. In the aftermath of this decision, over 500 nonviolent protestors were arrested as they demonstrated in resistance to having the hazardous materials stored at the site. While the protests and arrests did not result in the removal of the hazard, they did call attention to this previously ignored issue (McGurty, 2000).

Problems regarding hazardous waste disposal persist in Warren County to this day. But this citizen activism convinced the U.S. General Accounting Office (GAO) to conduct a 1983 study documenting the disproportionate locating of hazardous waste sites in and near predominantly African American and other minority residential areas. The GAO study was followed by a United Church of Christ Commission for Racial Justice (UCCCRJ) study in 1987, which concluded that commercial hazardous waste facilities tend to be disproportionately located in minority areas, and that race, not poverty, was the most significant factor associated with the location of such sites. The UCCCRJ study found that 66 percent of African Americans and Hispanics and half of Native Americans live near uncontrolled toxic waste sites. In response to the findings of additional similar studies, civil rights leader Rev. Benjamin Chavis, Jr., who would later become NAACP president, coined the term "environmental racism" to account for the decisionmaking that resulted in these dangerous disproportionate placements (Lazarus, 2000).

In 1990, sociologist Robert Bullard released his influential book *Dumping in Dixie: Race, Class and Environmental Quality.* In 1994, President Clinton issued Executive Order (EO) #12898, which required all federal agencies to "make achieving environmental justice a part of [their] mission." The EO had the effect of creating a number of federal offices to help implement it. These offices included the Office of Environmental Justice (OEJ); the EPA's (Environmental Protection Agency's) own Office of Civil Rights; the National Environmental Justice Advisory Committee (NEJAC); and the Federal Interagency Working Group on Environmental Justice (IWG), which created liaison offices in the EPA, the Department of

Justice, the Department of Defense, the Department of Labor, the Department of Agriculture, and many other federal, state, and local agencies.

The EO has not been as effective as hoped. This is due in large part to a line of conservative federal court rulings tending to close off legal claims that attempt to compel government agencies to consider environmental justice concerns under Title VI of the Civil Rights Act of 1964. The courts reason that forcing governments to take environmental justice concerns into account without a showing of racial animus would potentially force governments into "unlawful race-based affirmative action"—meaning that such considerations may be in violation of current law that requires intentional race discrimination rather than only a showing of racially disparate impact before such matters become legally actionable. The 2001 U.S. Supreme Court decision in *Alexander v. Sandoval* effectively solidifies the requirement for proof of intentional race-based discrimination in order to be successful in such challenges. This means that "disparate impact" discrimination claims in the environmental justice area are not sustainable in the courts (Anderson & Hirsch, 2003). This state of affairs remains even after Congress proposed the Environmental Justice Enforcement Act of 2008, which was intended to codify EO 12898 into law. The act as originally proposed intended to reverse the impact of *Sandoval* on environmental justice claims, but that version did not receive enough votes to become law. All doors are not closed, however, and environmental justice activism most strongly persists under an ameliorative approach involving public relations, agency hearings, mediation, local grassroots organizing, boycotts, protests, and research (Davis, 2002; Hill & Targ, 2000).

Environmental justice as a movement proceeds along this ameliorative but increasingly intense approach today predominantly through a wide number of local grassroots minority nongovernmental organizations (NGOs). Examples of these can be seen in the activities of such groups as Re-Genesis: Environmental Cleanup and Community Revitalization in Spartanburg, South Carolina; Protecting Children's Health & Reducing Lead Exposure through Collaborative Partnerships in East St. Louis, Illinois; New York City's Alternative Fuels Summit; and the Easing Troubled Waters: Farm Worker Safe Drinking Water Project in Colorado. The movement is also driven through vigorous sociological research, where accepted academic approaches include activism. Environmental justice has become a global issue, and pressure to involve international tribunals and commissions to rectify documented problems has steadily grown. Such a trend is exemplified by the recent attention residents of Mossville, Louisiana (a small, predominantly African American, community near Lake Charles facing large-scale pollution), have received in the United Nations and through the Inter-American Commission on Human Rights.

A fairly large body of both objective and subjective evidence exists purporting to prove or disprove the existence of race-based environmental injustices or inequities.

This evidence is found in studies based on zip codes, census tracts, demographics, air and water pollution, visual inspections, case studies, case law, agency records, human rights petitions, and global calls for environmental constitutional provisions. The evidence points to the frequency with which hazardous chemicals are produced, consumed, treated, stored, and disposed near communities of color. It also points to the differential infrequency and intensity of environmental cleanups and enforcements in these communities compared to White communities. Those trying to refute the claims of environmental justice point to methodological difficulties in proving intentional race-based animus regarding site locations, cleanups, and discriminatory enforcement habits by focusing on whether the proper units of analysis (e.g., whether zip codes, census tracts, governmental boundaries, geographical markers, visual observation of communities, or some other parameter of measurement) are being used to determine when a race, ethnicity, or sub-group is being unfairly burdened. Critics also look to control variables such as the price of real estate, cultural influences, or other competing interests such as agriculture, industry, or tourism that might explain the conduct without regard to race.

Also debated is the issue of causal ordering; for example, which came first, the minority community and then the pollution, or the pollution and then the minority community. Denying the influence of race on site location decisionmaking, opponents of environmental justice approaches also cite free-market arguments (e.g., it's not racism, the real estate is just cheaper); community efficacy arguments (e.g., most NGOs tend to have White middle-class membership structures, and historically have been little concerned with racial issues); and the Not-In-My-Backyard (NIMBY) phenomenon (e.g., hazardous facility sitings being sold to the community as job producers, while other communities without employment concerns naturally resist the location of such hazards within proximity to its residents) (Hill & Targ, 2000). A number of studies have revealed that financial elites, who do not want the hazardous facilities sited in their own backyards, profit significantly from these sitings in other locations. These studies have also found that very little local employment is actually gained from the facilities in the communities where the facilities end up (Davis, 2002). The evidence indicates that White middle-class communities tend to have more political capital and are thereby more effective than communities of color in keeping out environmentally undesirable land uses (Been, 1993).

The infamous Cerrell Report of 1984 further documents the insidious modus operandi of many major industrial polluters' siting strategies. The Cerrell Report was a metaphoric "smoking gun," discussed by Cole and Foster (2001) and Rechtschaffen and Gauna (2003), whereby a confidential consulting group report was leaked showing that corporations were being advised to locate hazardous sites in poorer communities based on a list of demographic, community, and lifestyle factors. These factors included race, ethnicity, religion, living habits, cultural factors relating to extraction industries, and levels of social disorganization. The goal of the Cerrell group was to help profit-maximizing corporations look for and find sites for their hazardous facilities cheaply, quickly, and with minimal political opposition and bad publicity.

While environmental justice legal claims under either the equal protection clause of the Fourteenth Amendment, Title VI of the Civil Rights Act of 1964, or even 42 U.S.C. §1983 seem to require the difficult proof of racial intent or animus (rather than a lower "disparate impact" standard), ultimately environmental justice sociological studies tend to conclude that demonstrated racist motives are not an essential element for one to be concerned about the problem in light of long-standing institutionalized inequities. What matters more is not whether such environmentally noxious sitings and/or lack of enforcement and cleanup are race based; rather, it is that such inequities are so demonstrable. Probably Ringquist (2005) more than any other scholar has effectively demonstrated that the weight of sociological authority indicates environmental justice issues and concerns are very real.

The topic of environmental justice is slowly but steadily making its way into criminology, particularly the areas of social disorganization, community efficacy, victimology, conflict, state-corporate crime, and bio-social theories. Some criminologists now see environmental degradation as part of the physical and social deterioration of inner cities, and the ability or inability of the community to rectify these environmental harms as critical to proper community functioning as a means of social control. Some criminologists are examining how differential meanings given to environmental harms tend to favor elites and negatively impact minorities, turning the latter into "environmental victims" (Lazarus, 2000).

Other criminologists look to abuses of discretion in the enforcement and implementation of environmental laws. The process of decriminalization of environmental harms is said to serve the interest of the powerful, who tend to dominate conflicts between the environment and capital, health and technology, stability and growth. This dominance leads to state failures to protect demographically identifiable minorities from serious environmental harms and serves to highlight another palpable form of law enforcement: racial bias. Still other criminologists are examining how environmental toxins cause developmental and neurological damage and increase the likelihood of criminal behavior. A number of studies focusing on lead, cadmium, and mercury in the environment have demonstrated very significant increases of aggression and antisocial behavior in demographic populations where such toxicity levels in the body are higher. There are many reasons why places with high levels of pollution tend to be places with high crime rates, and much criminological work that looks into these connections remains to be done

(Lynch & Stretesky, 2003; Lynch et al., 2004, 2008; White, 2003; Zilney et al., 2006).

Andrew Franz

See also: Institutional Racism; Socioeconomic Factors; Structural Racism and Violence

References

42 U.S.C. Sect. 1983.

Alexander v. Sandoval, 532 U.S. 275 (2001).

Anderson, J. L., and D. D. Hirsch. *Environmental Law Practice: Problems and Exercises for Skills Development.* 2nd ed. Durham, NC: Carolina Academic Press, 2003.

Been, V. "What's Fairness Got to Do with It? Environmental Justice and the Siting of Locally Undesirable Land Uses." *Cornell Law Review* 78 (1993): 1001–85.

Bullard, R. D. *Dumping in Dixie: Race, Class and Environmental Quality.* 3rd ed. Boulder, CO: Westview Press, 2000.

Clinton, W. J. "Federal Actions to Address Environmental Justice in Minority Populations and Low-Income Populations." Executive Order 12898, February 11, 1994.

Cole, L. W., and S. R. Foster. *From the Ground Up: Environmental Racism and the Rise of the Environmental Justice Movement.* New York: New York University Press, 2001.

Davis, D. *When Smoke Ran Like Water: Tales of Environmental Deception and the Battle against Pollution.* New York: Basic Books, 2002.

Hill, B. E., and N. Targ. "The Link between Protecting Natural Resources and the Issue of Environmental Justice." *Boston College Environmental Affairs Law Review* 28 (2000): 1–38.

Lazarus, R. J. "Environmental Racism! That's What It Is." *University of Illinois Law Review* (2000): 255–74.

Lynch, M. J., and P. B. Strestesky. "The Meaning of Green: Contrasting Criminological Perspectives." *Theoretical Criminology* 7 (2003): 217–38.

Lynch, M. J., P. B. Stretesky, and R. G. Burns. *Environmental Law, Crime, and Justice.* El Paso, TX: LFB Scholarly Publishing, 2008.

Lynch, M. J., P. B. Stretesky, and R. G. Burns. "Determinants of Environmental Law Violation Fines against Petroleum Refineries: Race, Ethnicity, Income, and Aggregation Effects." *Society & Natural Resources* 17 (2004): 333–47.

McGurty, E. M. "Warren County, NC and the Emergence of the Environmental Justice Movement: Unlikely Coalitions and Shared Meanings in Local Collective Action." *Society & Natural Resources* 13 (2000): 373–87.

Rechtschaffen, C., and E. Gauna. *Environmental Justice: Law, Policy & Regulation.* Durham, NC: Carolina Academic Press, 2003.

Ringquist, E. "Assessing Evidence of Environmental Inequities: A Meta-Analysis." *Journal of Policy Analysis and Management* 24 (2005): 223–47.

Title VI, Civil Rights Act of 1964.

U.S. Const. amend. XIV, sec. 1 (Equal Protection Clause).

U.S. General Accounting Office. *Siting of Hazardous Waste Landfills and Their Correlation with Racial and Economic Status of Surrounding Communities.* Washington, DC: Government Printing Office, 1983.

White, R. "Environmental Issues and the Criminological Imagination." *Theoretical Criminology* 7 (2003): 483–506.

Zilney, L. A., D. McGurrin, and S. Zahran. "Environmental Justice and the Role of Criminology: An Analytical Review of 33 Years of Environmental Justice Research." *Criminal Justice Review* 31 (2006): 47–62.

Eugenics

The American Heritage Dictionary defines *eugenics* as the study of hereditary improvement of the human race by controlled selective breeding. The term itself dates back to the late nineteenth century and the British psychologist Sir Francis Galton, cousin of Charles Darwin, who coined the term and proposed the science of eugenics in order to produce a highly gifted race. Galton's theory of Social Darwinism and the creation of a superior race were widely supported in the United States during the early twentieth century. Indeed, the concept of White supremacy in the United States dates back to its early history with the long-held concept of *manifest destiny,* the belief that White males were predestined by God to be superior to all others. Nazi Germany later followed the United States in supporting the social engineering of a superior Aryan race. Clearly eugenics and racism are closely associated, providing a seemingly objective rationale for social discrimination along lines of race, class, caste, and even gender. The concept of eugenics fostered such practices as apartheid, ethnic cleansing, and genocide (a concept coined in 1947 following the Nazi war trials).

Blacks, American Indians, Asians, and other non-Whites and even non-Protestant Whites, as well as the mentally deficient, were quickly labeled as being *genetically defective* and in need of purging from the U.S. population. In Nazi-influenced Europe, the classes of human defectives included Jews, Gypsies (Roma), non-Whites, and even Whites not considered the genetic equivalent of Northern and Western European Whites. The Nazi atrocities were widely publicized due largely to the extremes taken in the *final solution.* What is less known is America's well-kept secret of sterilization, institutionalization, and execution of those deemed genetically inferior to the dominant White society. The White elite in U.S. society found a champion for their cause at Stanford University with psychologist Lewis M. Terman and his revision of the original 1908 French Binet-Simon IQ test.

Lewis Terman was influenced by his mentor Francis Galton, who was considered to be the founder of scientific psychology, setting the stage for the use of psychological tests to implement the dictates of Social Darwinism. Eugenics, implemented partly through involuntary sterilization, was seen as the means for achieving successful Social Darwinism in the United States. The goal of eugenics was the improvement of the human race through the elimination of what were considered to be defective gene pools. It was Terman who provided the seemingly objective measure of determining who was unfit. Terman was confident that his version of the IQ test would accurately weed out the genetically deficient members of American society, those he termed the serious deviant. His solution included plans for eliminating these genetic inferiors through institutionalization and sterilization. Terman proposed his 1916 IQ test, the Stanford Binet, as a scientific tool for determining those in society who needed to be controlled and eventually taken out of the gene pool. What was not factored into this test was the racial and class bias of his sample—the upper-middle-class White faculty and families at Stanford University.

By 1926, 23 states had enacted compulsory sterilization laws and this practice was condoned by the U.S. Supreme Court in 1927 in its decision *Buck v. Bell,* based mainly on Terman's contention:

It is safe to predict that in the near future intelligence tests will bring tens of thousands of these high-grade defectives under the surveillance and protection of society. This will ultimately result in curtailing the reproduction of feeble-mindedness and in the elimination of an enormous amount of crime, pauperism, and industrial inefficiency. . . . Not all criminals are feeble-minded, but all feeble-minded are at least potential criminals. That every feeble-minded woman is a potential prostitute would hardly be disputed by anyone. . . . Considering the tremendous cost of vice and crime . . . it is evident that psychological testing has found here one of its richest applications. (1916: 26)

Of course this assessment did not take into account the poor educational opportunities afforded Blacks and other minorities in U.S. society under de jure and de facto segregation, hence further fueling existing discriminatory practices that not only produced substandard education but a biased measurement of someone's true intelligence. Also, the stigma associated with being genetically inferior led to harsh solutions for those falling into this category, even if their only "societal offense" was procreation. It is estimated that some 40,000 individuals, mainly African American and American Indian females, were involuntarily sterilized in the United States at both the state and federal levels (Indian Country is federally administered) until this practice was challenged during the Civil Rights era of the 1960s, when it was disclosed that those most likely to be subjected to this practice were poor minorities. While the practice of compulsory sterilization began to wane in the late 1960s and early 1970s, the practice of genetic cleansing continued in U.S. society through other avenues, most notably incarceration and the death penalty.

The controversy over the stigma associated with psychological testing came to a head in 1972 with the use of standardized tests to label students within the California public schools as being mentally deficient and hence stigmatized within society. Terman and his Stanford-Binet test played a role in this controversy. The legal case *Larry P. v. Riles* began in 1972 at about the same time that forced sterilization was coming to an end and school integration was being forcefully implemented throughout the United States. In this case, a class of Black California elementary school children challenged the use of standardized IQ tests for labeling children as being *educable mentally retarded* (EMR), and subsequently placed in special education classes. The lawsuit was filed primarily on the ground that this process resulted in placement of a disproportionate number of Black children in these special education classes. Petitioners contended that this was in violation of Title IV of the 1964 Civil Rights Act, the 1973 Rehabilitation Act, and the 1975 Education for All Handicapped Children Act. They argued that the stigma associated with a special education curriculum placed Blacks at a disadvantage in the job market once they left school. Since the main criterion for placement was the score generated in the IQ tests, the validity of the standardization on which these instruments are based was questioned—especially their sensitivity to cultural differences within the United States.

Another issue that surfaced during this era was that of the fairness of capital punishment in the United States. In *Furman v. Georgia* (1972), the U.S. Supreme Court found capital punishment in the United States to be unconstitutional due to its discriminatory practice up to that time. The data on executions clearly showed that Blacks were executed at a far greater rate than Whites and for lesser crimes. And, while Western societies (Europe and Canada) were doing away with capital punishment, the United States, notably in the South, insisted on carrying on this effective form of eugenics. Hence, in 1976, three states—Georgia, Texas, and Florida—successfully had their revised death penalty codes approved by the U.S. Supreme Court, setting the stage for a resumption of capital punishment in the United States. Capital punishment was now restricted to *capital murder* and could no longer be used for arson, burglary, robbery, or rape, offenses often used to death qualify Blacks in the past. Still, it took another 30 years for the U.S. Supreme Court to disallow the execution of the mentally retarded, a practice long abandoned by most other societies. As in the past, most of the mentally deficient who were deemed "death qualified" by state juries, were poor minorities, mainly Blacks.

Daryl Renard Atkins' case found its way to the U.S. Supreme Court, where in June 2002, the Court ruled against Virginia's law allowing the execution of mentally handicapped individuals, stating that this violated the Eighth Amendment's prohibition of cruel and unusual punishment. IQ testing became a tool for death qualifying what Virginia considered to be its genetically inferior class, notably poor minorities. Following the U.S. Supreme Court decision, Virginia shopped around for pro–death penalty psychologists who would challenge Atkins' 59 IQ, providing one that was above 70 and thus allowing the state to reinstate Atkins' death sentence in August 2005 and setting his execution date for that December. Atkins' life was spared due to prosecutorial misconduct when it was revealed that his co-defendant's testimony was rehearsed in order to implicate Atkins as the triggerman. A judge commuted his sentence to life imprisonment in 2008.

Other milestones in death penalty law further weakened the eugenic options for ethnic cleansing in the United States. In *Roper v. Simmons* (2005), the U.S. Supreme Court ruled against the execution of individuals who committed their offense prior to age 18, again making the United States one of the last societies to do so. The role of eugenics in maintaining racism and social and legal discrimination in the United States was a costly experiment during the twentieth century in terms of human lives and social control. It is proof that well-educated scholars and popular politicians can be blind to the complexities of human beings, and most importantly, to their own prejudices.

Laurence French

See also: Death Penalty; Institutional Racism

References

Atkins v. Virginia, 536 U.S. 304 122 S. Ct. 2242 (2002).

Black, E. *War against the Weak: Eugenics and America's Campaign to Create a Master Race.* New York: Four Walls Eight Windows, 2003.

Braddock, D. "Deinstitutionalization of the Retarded." *Hospital and Community Psychiatry* 32 (1981): 607–15.

Brantlinger, E. *Sterilization of People with Mental Disabilities: Issues, Perspectives, and Cases.* Westport, CT: Auburn House, 1995.

Buck v. Bell, 274 U.S. 200, 205. No. 292 U.S. Supreme Ct. (1927).

EAHCA. *The Education for All Handicapped Children Act of 1975.* P.L. 94–142, 1975.

French, L. A. "Mental Retardation and the Death Penalty: The Clinical and Legal Legacy." *Federal Probation* (June 2005): 15–20.

French, L. A. "Minority and Mentally Retarded: Double Stigma by School Labeling." *Free Inquiry in Creative Sociology* 14 (1986): 213–16.

French, L. A. "The Mentally Retarded and Pseudoretarded Offender: A Clinical/Legal Dilemma." *Federal Probation* XXXVI (1983): 55–61.

Furman v. Georgia, 408 U.S. 238, 345 (1972).

Galton, F. *Hereditary Genius: An Inquiry into Its Laws and Consequences.* London: Macmillan, 1869.

Larry P. v. Riles, 502 Fed 963 (9th Cir.) (1979; 1984) *Affirmed; final order.*

Larry P. v. Riles, 343 F Supp. 1308 N.D. Cal. (1972) *Preliminary Injunction.*

Larson, E. *Sex, Race, and Science: Eugenics in the Deep South.* Baltimore: Johns Hopkins University Press, 1995.

Roper v. Simmons, 543 U.S. 551 (2005).

Terman, L. M. *The Measurement of Intelligence.* Boston: Houghton Mifflin, 1916.

Evers, Medgar (1925–1963)

Twenty minutes past midnight on June 12, 1963, Medgar Evers pulled his family Oldsmobile into the carport of his house. After a long day of work, the 37-year-old field secretary for the National Association for the Advancement of Colored People (NAACP) was awaited by his wife and three children. Carrying paperwork and sweatshirts that read "Jim Crow Must Go," he stepped into the light of the carport, unaware that Ku Klux Klansman Byron de la Beckwith was hiding in the bushes of a vacant lot across the street. Beckwith aimed his rifle and fired. Fifteen minutes after arriving at the University of Mississippi Hospital, Evers was pronounced dead.

Medgar Evers, Mississippi field secretary for the National Association for the Advancement of Colored People, was shot and killed outside his home after returning from an integration rally in Jackson, Mississippi, on June 12, 1963. His killer, Byron de la Beckwith, was not convicted of the murder until 1994. (Associated Press)

Beckwith dropped the murder weapon at the scene, and it had his fingerprints on it. He had earlier spoken of his desire to kill Evers, and after the murder was even said to have bragged that he was the killer. Yet at two trials in 1964, the all-White male juries deadlocked, and Beckwith remained a free man.

In 1989, however, evidence surfaced of jury tampering in the earlier trials, and the district attorney filed new charges against Beckwith. He was rearrested in 1990. In 1994, more than 30 years after the crime, Beckwith was found guilty of murdering Medgar Evers and sentenced to life imprisonment without the possibility of parole. The third jury was composed of six men and six women, eight of whom were Black (Jones-Brown, 2000).

The memory of Medgar Evers is preserved in a City University of New York college that bears his name. *Ghosts of Mississippi,* a 1996 film by director Rob Reiner, follows the retrial and conviction of Byron de la Beckwith. Well-known African American actor Whoopi Goldberg plays the role of Evers' courageous wife Myrlie Evers in the film. Byron de la Beckwith died in 2001 at the age of 80, while serving a life sentence for the 1963 killing.

Delores Jones-Brown

See also: Civil Rights Movement

Reference

Jones-Brown, D. *Race, Crime and Punishment.* Philadelphia: Chelsea House Publishers, 2000.

Eyewitness Misidentification

Eyewitness testimony is typically considered the most influential evidence presented in a criminal trial, but a growing body of recent research suggests that jurors tend to be insensitive to factors influencing eyewitness accuracy (Abshire & Bornstein, 2003; Cutler et al., 1990). Moreover, eyewitness misidentification has come to be recognized as the number one cause of wrongful convictions. Out of all convictions overturned by DNA testing, 75 percent of the cases involve situations where the defendants were the victims of eyewitness misidentification (Innocence Project, 2011).

Significant race effects have been found in reference to the accuracy of eyewitness identifications (Abshire & Bornstein, 2003). Cross-racial identifications have been found to be the most problematic (Eberhardt et al., 2004; Meissner & Brigham, 2001; Wells & Olson, 2001). This means that researchers have found a cross-race effect (or *own race bias*) that suggests individuals are better at identifying faces of their own race and have a more difficult time accurately identifying or recognizing faces outside their own racial group (Eberhardt et al., 2004). Extensive empirical and archival data suggest that minorities are most vulnerable to misidentification.

In fact, the majority of eyewitness experts are willing to testify to the relative strength of this effect. Specifically, a meta-analysis conducted by Meissner and Brigham (2001) found that Blacks are 1.56 times more likely to be misidentified by a White eyewitness than a Black eyewitness. They also found that Whites are more likely to misidentify Black faces than Blacks are to misidentify White faces.

For the benefit of African Americans and others, researchers have suggested ways to attempt to reduce the likelihood of eyewitness misidentification (Wells et al., 1998). For practical purposes in eyewitness research, Wells (1978) first introduced the concepts of *system* and *estimator variables*. System variables mainly concern the actual identification, such as a lineup's construction, method, administration, and instructions, as well as any postidentification feedback. In contrast, *estimator variables* describe factors that are beyond the control of the criminal justice system (Wells & Olson, 2003; Cutler et al., 1987).

Estimator variables are any variety of characteristics related to the criminal event, perpetrator, or witness. These can include exposure time, lighting, and distance from crime, as well as the presence of a weapon and the race of the individuals involved (see Eberhardt et al., 2004). While estimator variables cannot be controlled by the criminal justice system, it is important to understand that these factors can affect accuracy of an eyewitness's identification of a perpetrator. For example, research on exposure time has found that the less time an eyewitness is exposed to an event, the less able he or she is to encode all relevant information, especially the appearance of the perpetrator, in order to correctly remember it. This will also be influenced by the lighting and distance from the crime as well as any distracters, such as a weapon. The weapon focus effect is considered a well-established phenomenon in the eyewitness literature, with findings demonstrating that the presence of a weapon significantly reduces the likelihood of a correct identification (Wells & Olson, 2003; Cutler et al., 1987).

While pre-crime interracial contact appears to slightly reduce the likelihood of misidentification in situations involving witnesses and perpetrators of different races, examination of the past 30 years of this research does not show much relative improvement in performance across races. In response to this problem, Wells and Olson (2001) propose a system variable approach, wherein such variables can be utilized as preventive measures against cross-race misidentifications. Specifically, they suggest that when conducting a lineup, all members should be of the same race; there should be more foils (foils are members of the lineup known to be innocent) in the lineup than are used for intra-race identifications; and the lineup constructor should be of the same race as lineup members. Furthermore, the use of a blank lineup (a lineup in which all the members are known to be innocent by the constructor) before an actual lineup is recommended so that those eyewitnesses who are eager to choose, whether accurately or not, can be discredited without wrongly identifying an innocent suspect.

There are additional system variables that can influence the likelihood of a misidentification, but can also be changed by the criminal justice system. Research has indicated that more misidentifications occur when the suspect stands out from the foils than when the lineup construction is such that foils are similar to one another and to the witness's description of the perpetrator. Additionally, research has established that a sequential lineup (a sequential lineup is one in which the witness is shown only one person at a time but with the expectation that there are several lineup members to be shown) is preferable to a simultaneous lineup (one in which all lineup members are presented to the witness at once, the most common lineup in use by law enforcement) as the former results in the use of absolute judgment. This forces eyewitnesses to compare each lineup member to their memory and not to one another. Comparing members to each other, which is termed relative judgment, can result in an eyewitness picking someone who most resembles the perpetrator, whether or not the actual perpetrator is present in the lineup.

As with scientific experiments, it is important to maintain objectivity through the use of double-blind administration. That is, the person conducting the lineup should not know which member, if any, is the suspect. This will prevent pressure to choose, or leading the eyewitness toward any particular person by the lineup administrator. Double-blind administration will also eliminate the possibility of postidentification feedback, which can serve to confirm an eyewitness identification and increase confidence in an identification that is incorrect. Lastly, a blind administrator should inform an eyewitness that he or she is indeed unaware of who is in the lineup, as well as instructing the eyewitness that a suspect may or may not be present in a lineup. Neglecting to inform the eyewitness that the suspect may or may not be present has been demonstrated to increase reliance on relative judgments, resulting in significantly more misidentifications (Wells et al., 1998).

Performing any of these biased lineup procedures can inflate the confidence of a witness. This can be problematic, as several studies have found that when jurors are determining the credibility of a witness, they largely rely on witness confidence despite evidence that confidence can be very malleable. Moreover, other witnessing and identification conditions, such as poor lighting, distance from crime, and distraction by a weapon, tend to be ignored when an eyewitness displays high confidence (Wells & Olson, 2003).

The traditional safeguards used in court to protect defendants against eyewitness misidentifications may not be effective at pinpointing the aforementioned issues. For instance, research has demonstrated that judicial instructions are often misunderstood or ignored. Cross-examination is utilized as a tool to decipher lies from the truth, but may be useless with mistaken eyewitnesses who are not intentionally lying.

The number of DNA exonerations speaks directly to the failure of cross-examination as a safeguard against misidentification. Another court remedy, expert testimony, may sensitize jurors to witnessing and identification conditions, but at best can only attempt to address issues of identification accuracy after the fact, once an innocent defendant has already been drawn into the criminal justice system (Cutler et al., 1990). Any influence is diminished, if not eliminated, when both sides have experts testifying both for and against the accuracy of what a witness claims to have seen. In addition, defendants who are poor—and these are disproportionately Blacks and Latinos—are more likely to be represented by public defenders or other state-appointed attorneys whose agencies may not have adequate budgets to hire expert witnesses. This lack of funding reduces the likelihood that such a corrective measure would be available or effective for defendants of color who, as the research notes, run the greatest risk of being misidentified (Meissner & Brigham, 2001).

Angela Yarbrough

References

Abshire, J., and B. H. Bornstein. "Juror Sensitivity to the Cross-Race Effect." *Law and Human Behavior* 27 (2003): 471–80. doi:10.1023/A:1025481905861.

Cutler, B. L., S. D. Penrod, and H. R. Dexter. "Juror Sensitivity to Eyewitness Identification Evidence." *Law and Human Behavior* 14 (1990): 185–91. http://www.jstor.org/stable/1393598.

Cutler, B. L., S. D. Penrod, and T. K. Martens. "The Reliability of Eyewitness Identification: The Role of System and Estimator Variables." *Law and Human Behavior* 11 (1987): 233–58. doi:10.1007/BF01044644.

Eberhardt, J., V. Purdie, P. Goff, and P. Davies. "Seeing Black: Race, Crime, and Visual Processing." *Journal of Personality and Social Psychology* 87, no. 6 (2004): 876–93.

Innocence Project. "Understand the Causes: Eyewitness Misidentification." New York: Innocence Project, 2011. www.innocenceproject.org.

Meissner, C. A., and J. C. Brigham. "Thirty Years of Investigating the Own-Race Bias in Memory for Faces: A Meta-Analytic Review." *Psychology, Public Policy, and Law* 7 (2001): 3–35. doi:10.1037//1076-8971.7.1.3.

Wells, G. L. "Applied Eyewitness Testimony Research: System Variables and Estimator Variables." *Journal of Personality and Social Psychology* 36 (1978): 1546–57. doi:10.1037/0022-3514.36.12.1546.

Wells, G. L., and E. A. Olson. "Eyewitness Testimony." *Annual Review of Psychology* 54 (2003): 277–95. doi:10.1146/annurev.psych.54.101601.145028.

Wells, G. L., and E. A. Olson. "The Other-Race Effect in Eyewitness Identification: What Do We Do about It?" *Psychology, Public Policy, and Law* 7 (2001): 230–46. doi:10.1037//1076-8971.7.1.230.

Wells, G. L., M. Small, S. D. Penrod, R. S. Malpass, S. M. Fulero, and C.A.E. Brimacombe. "Eyewitness Identification Procedures: Recommendations for Lineups and Photospreads." *Law and Human Behavior* 22 (1998): 603–47. doi:10.1023/A:1025750605807.

F

Fair Sentencing Act of 2010

The Fair Sentencing Act of 2010 (also known as Public Law 111–220) embodies one of the most dramatic shifts in federal drug policy since the 1970 Controlled Substances Act was amended in 1986 and 1988 by the Anti-Drug Abuse Act to include harsher sentences for the possession, sale, transport, and manufacturing of crack cocaine versus powder cocaine. The Fair Sentencing Act of 2010 (FSA 2010), signed by President Barack Obama on August 3, reduced the disparity in sentences for cocaine-related offenses. Prior to the passing of this act, an individual would have to possess 100 times the amount of powder cocaine to receive the same sentence as someone possessing crack cocaine. That is, an individual possessing 500 grams of powder cocaine would receive the same sentence as an individual possessing 5 grams of crack cocaine. FSA 2010 amends that disparity to a point that is still not equal, but is greatly reduced. The bill not only reduces the disparity but provides a multitude of additional measures to ensure that nonviolent offenders are sentenced less harshly than violent offenders (S. 1789, 2010). The provisions of the FSA 2010 represent a bipartisan compromise among lawmakers. The Fairness in Cocaine Sentencing Act (H.R. 3245), proposed previously by Representative Bobby Scott (D-VA), called for complete parity, a 1:1 weight ratio between crack and powder cocaine offenses. The language in FSA 2010 was drafted in order to gain a unanimous congressional vote (Piper & Tyler, 2010).

In matters of public policy, an understanding of the historical context in which the policy or legislation was enacted is important to ensure that changes address the problem. In this instance, the time period and environment in which the 1986 and 1988 drug sentencing laws were passed are central to understanding the racial disparity that grew out of them. The amendments to the Anti-Drug Abuse Act that caused the disparities were passed amid a media-induced drug panic in the 1980s, spurred in part by sensationalist reporting of the death of National Basketball Association draftee Len Bias in 1986, under the mistaken belief that he had died from a crack cocaine instead of a powder cocaine overdose (Vagins & McCurdy, 2006). It was during that time that crack cocaine, a cheaper smokable form of powder cocaine, became popular nationwide among drug users. The media fanned the flames of fear by overreporting instances of violence in which the offenders were under the influence of crack cocaine, and associated its distribution with Jamaican drug posses (Sklansky, 1995). As a result, voters, and even nonvoting members of urban communities plagued by the violence associated with crack drug markets and the devastation caused to the lives of those in contact with addicts, demanded harsher sentences for users of crack cocaine. These harsher sentences resulted in a sentencing differential based on a weight ratio of 100:1. That is, an individual arrested for possessing 5 grams/50 grams of crack cocaine would receive the same sentence (5 years/10 years prison) as an individual arrested for possession of 500 grams/5,000 grams of powder cocaine. Such prison sentences were mandatory; that is, judges had no discretion to impose a lesser sentence, and it was mandatory that they be served without eligibility for parole.

It is commonly believed that African Americans were overwhelmingly affected by this change in the drug laws because they had greater accessibility to this cheaper form of the drug than they had to the more expensive powder cocaine. With a greater number of African Americans (than Whites) in lower socioeconomic brackets, it was believed that the low cost of the drug meant more involvement in use, manufacturing, and sales. Crack could be easily produced by mixing powder cocaine with water and baking soda and bringing the concoction to a boil. The more intense high achieved by smoking a small amount of crack than ingesting similar amounts of powder cocaine was believed to be its attraction, but crack and powder cocaine are the same substance, just with different methods of preparation and ingestion.

Some have suggested that punishing individuals more severely for ingesting a cheaper form of the same drug is an obvious form of systemic discrimination. Statistics confirm that within five years of the enactment of the law that imposed this different sentencing scheme for crack versus powder cocaine, 88 percent of those sentenced under it were Black. This was true despite a Sentencing Commission Survey that showed that 52 percent of crack users were White.

In the 24-year period between the enactment of the law that created this sentencing disparity and the signing of the FSA 2010, there were many failed legislative attempts to change the law (for example, the Crack Cocaine Equitable Sentencing Act of 1995, introduced by African American House of Representatives member Charles Rangel of New York) and a U.S. Supreme Court decision (*U.S. v. Armstrong* [1996]) that tacitly upheld it. Not until 2005, in the case of *U.S. v. Booker*, did the U.S. Supreme Court rule that judges could grant sentences other than mandatory prison in crack cocaine cases. They reconfirmed that ruling in *Kimbrough v. U.S.*

in 2007, but the 100:1 weight ratio for the possession of crack versus powder co- caine remained an enforceable part of the law, meaning those who possessed small amounts of crack cocaine could receive much harsher sentences than those who possessed greater amounts of powder. The FSA 2010 in large part addresses this discrepancy.

The Act

The FSA 2010 or Public Law 111–220 begins with the caption, "An Act to restore fairness to federal cocaine sentencing." The legislation is made up of 10 different sections. The first section names the act the Fair Sentencing Act of 2010. The second section addresses some of the inequities that were in place prior to its passage. The act does not eliminate the weight disparity between possessing crack versus powder cocaine for sentencing purposes, but it does reduce the ratio from 100:1 to 18:1. Now, it would take 280 grams of crack cocaine to receive a mandatory minimum 10-year sentence, or 28 grams of crack cocaine to receive a mandatory minimum 5-year sentence (S. 1789, 2010). This section also applies the same ratios for the importation or exportation of powder cocaine. The third section eliminates mandatory minimum sentences for simple possession, defined as anything less than 28 grams of crack cocaine or 500 grams of powder cocaine (Sabet, 2005). Mandatory minimums still exist for possession of a large amount of the drugs.

Per its title, the aim of the fourth section is to increase the penalties for major drug traffickers of both powder and crack cocaine. The act greatly increases the possible fines for offenders believed to be manufacturing, distributing, or possess- ing with the intent to distribute or manufacture the drugs. The fine amounts are based on whether offenders acted alone or as part of an organization. Fines that once ranged from $2 million to $20 million were increased to a range of $5 mil- lion to $75 million. The same adjustments have been made to the fines for acts of importation and exportation. Section 5 provides additional penalties for defen- dants who use, threaten to use, or direct the use of violence during a trafficking offense (S. 1789, 2010).

Sections 6 and 7 take into consideration the defendant's role during the offense as aggravating or mitigating factors to be considered during sentencing. For sec- tion six, aggravating factors can include the attempted bribe of a law enforcement official, the maintenance of an establishment for the manufacture or distribution of substances, or the hierarchal position of an offender within a wider drug network (S. 1789, 2010). This section also creates super-aggravating factors, which include the use of another person to buy, sell, transport, or store a substance; the involvement of a person under the age of 18, over the age of 64, or who is pregnant; or the involvement of a person of diminished mental or physical ability (S. 1789, 2010). Similarly, section 7 recognizes mitigating factors to be considered in sentencing, such as the minimal role a defendant may have played; whether or not the defendant received monetary compensation for his or her involvement, or if the defendant was motivated by an intimate or familial relationship to become involved in the drug activity (S. 1789, 2010).

The remaining three sections are administrative in nature but have considerable significance for the direction of future federal drug policy. Section 8 specifies that the provisions of the act must be implemented within 90 days of its signing. Section 9 calls for an evaluation of the effectiveness of drug courts one year after the implementation of the Act (S. 1789, 2010). The final section directs the U.S. Sentencing Commission to conduct a study of the impact of the act within five years of its adoption and to submit a report to Congress regarding its impact on Federal Sentencing Law (S. 1789, 2010). After nearly 25 years of requesting that the law be changed, primarily because of its racially disparate impact, Congress voted unanimously to approve this act. Its impact on the incarceration rate for African Americans remains to be determined.

Peter Donna

See also: Drug Treatment Strategies; Rockefeller Drug Laws: Policy Review; Sentencing Disparities; War on Drugs

References

Piper, B., and J. Tyler. "Change Cocaine, Crack Sentencing." *The Detroit News,* April 1, 2010.

S. 1789, 111th Congress (2009–2010).

Sabet, K. A. "Making It Happen: The Case for Compromise in the Federal Cocaine Law Debate." *Social Policy & Administration* 39, no. 2 (2005): 181–91.

Sklansky, D. A. "Cocaine, Race and Equal Protection." *Stanford Law Review* 47, no. 6 (1995): 1238–1322.

Vagins, D., and J. McCurdy. "Cracks in the System: Twenty Years of Unjust Federal Crack Cocaine Law." Washington, DC: American Civil Liberties Union, 2006. http://www.aclu.org/pdfs/drugpolicy/cracksinsystem_20061025.pdf.

Faith-Based Prisoner Reentry

The challenges of reentry are many, and so are the social implications. There are, therefore, enormous opportunities for programs and interventions to enhance the public safety, health, and cohesion of the communities that are at the center of this cycle by improving reentry outcomes for ex-prisoners. The literature has shown that institutions of faith can and do play a significant role in easing what proves to be a very complicated problem in America.

Faith-Based Response

Some theorize that since faith-based and community-level organizations typically have close ties to the communities they serve, they can be more efficient than traditional government agencies in helping those in need, and should therefore have increased access to federal social service funds. This rationale supported the federal government's establishment and expansion of the White House Office of Faith-Based and Community Initiatives (OFBCI), which created centers in five cabinet departments, including the U.S. Department of Justice, paving the way for faith-based organizations to provide prisoner reentry programming and services.

Faith-based organizations (FBOs) and other community groups have historically played a critical role in supporting both incarcerated and paroled prisoner populations. Rossman averred, "currently, thousands of faith-based and community organizations provide emergency and long-term shelter, job training, substance abuse treatment, and mentoring for ex-offenders and their families, all of which may ease the former prisoner's reintegration into the community" (2002: 164). While there has been recent emphasis on expanding the opportunities of churches, temples, mosques, and other faith institutions to provide a wide range of social services, there has been growing interest in the systematic study of the effectiveness of faith-based reentry programs and other services.

Faith-Based Organizations and Prisoner Reentry

Partnerships between government and faith-based organizations in America are hardly new. In one form or another, such partnerships have existed for hundreds of years. However, broader participation of FBOs in the delivery of public service has been advancing over the past two decades by program devolution. Program devolution, a component of the "New Federalism," is used to describe the shifting of responsibility for social programs from the federal government to the states. It reflects the view that placing program authority closer to the point of service will permit locally tailored, more effective services for poor families than standardized, uniform efforts controlled from Washington. As program administrators look outside the capitol for solutions, nongovernmental organizations, such as communitybased organizations and FBOs, are seen as valuable resources that can address a variety of social needs, and that should be financially supported in their work.

Faith-Based Organizations and Interventions

To be considered a FBO, an organization must, at a minimum, be connected with an organized *faith* community, such as an organized religion. The terms "faith-based" and "spiritually based" are used interchangeably, as here they both refer to personal and public practice of religious activities and acts of worship, such as prayer, reading of sacred texts, and belief in religious dogma and/or theology. According to one school of thought, the connections of organizations to a faith community or organized religion occur when a FBO is based on a particular religious ideology and draws staff, volunteers, or leadership from a particular religious group. Other characteristics that qualify an organization as faith-based are its religiously oriented mission statements, receipt of substantial support from a religious organization, or initiation by a religious institution. Spiritually or faith-based interventions are also religiously oriented and usually involve some religious practices (e.g., prayer, meditation, reading of sacred texts, and other acts of worship). Such defining characteristics are valuable because they help to distinguish FBOs from secular organizations, yet they also mask the numerous distinctions that can be found among faith-based organizations. A small local congregation and the national Salvation Army, for example, are both FBOs that draw staff and volunteers from a particular religious group. However, these FBOs differ substantially in the scope and scale of their service provision (Frazier, 2009).

Although these typologies help in understanding how differentiated FBOs are based on a number of factors, the basic definition that binds them together and separates them from secular organizations is the presence of religion, either in its organizational affiliation, funding source, and/or mission statement, and in their provision of interventions. Recent studies have demonstrated that FBOs and religious congregations, which typically use spiritually or faith-based interventions, have already been an essential part of the social welfare net for decades, providing food and clothing pantries, financial aid, job referrals, tutoring, childcare, language classes, self-help programs, and services to prisoners.

Faith-Based Prisoner Reentry

Religious education and training programs have always been a part of state prison systems, which offer different levels of religious and rehabilitative services to offenders. Until recently, however, these rehabilitative programs received very little attention and resources because of constitutional restrictions concerning the separation of church and state and because of widely held perceptions of religion. Lukoff, Turner, and Lu (1992) pointed out that in theory, research, and practice, mental health professionals have tended to ignore or pathologize the religious and spiritual dimensions of life. This is a trend that has begun to reverse somewhat with the deletion of "religiosity" as a pathology in the *Diagnostic and Statistical Manual of Mental Disorders* version four (*DSM-IV*), and the move to increase the competence and sensitivity of mental health professionals in dealing with spiritual issues. In the past, religious programs also did not receive much attention because of the lack of research evaluations about such programs. Although there have been greater levels of scientific research and data over the past decade, policy changes at the federal level and federal funding to support state-level efforts require a closer examination of faith-based partnerships as they begin to serve as alternatives to traditional, secular efforts.

Faith-based organizations are increasingly given the opportunity to provide a variety of rehabilitative services to corrections facilities, either voluntarily or contractually. These services often include religious and moral teachings that incorporate religious practices such as reading of sacred texts, meditation, and prayer. In addition, they may include the more commonly offered anger management classes, substance abuse counseling, job and life skill education and training, and housing assistance. Religious practices, which research suggests may be associated with fewer in-prison disciplinary problems, may also be associated with better physical and mental health among prisoners.

Many of those incarcerated, nearly one-third, are reported to have serious physical or mental illnesses (Frazier, 2009). However, some studies show that prisoners who identify themselves as religious have fewer physical and mental health problems overall than those who do not identify themselves as religious (see Johnson & Larson, 2003). Since mental and physical illnesses can prevent ex-offenders from successfully reintegrating into society after their release, the connection between religion and health is an important avenue for research. Mental and physical challenges are only two of the primary obstacles for ex-prisoners.

Beyond their mental and physical health status, overcoming substance abuse, finding employment, securing housing and other needed social services make successful reentry difficult for many ex-prisoners. As a consequence of a growing trend that began with devolution and continued with the creation and expansion of the OFBCI, there are many examples of faith-based organizations providing and partnering with governments to provide reentry services. Prisons and jails are increasingly looking at faith-based programs to cut costs, help reduce recidivism and address the problems associated with the record number of offenders who have been incarcerated over the last decade. This, coupled with the growing political and social demands to address the issue of prisoner reentry has led all levels of governments (local, state, and federal) to consider faith-based providers for reentry programming.

While there are still many questions about the effectiveness of and processes used in faith-based interventions and service delivery, African American ex-offenders may find working with these nongovernmental organizations and institutions more appealing than being under the direction of traditional corrections agencies. Historically, the Black church has been at the center of the attempts to bring about political and social progress for African Americans (see Southern Christian Leadership Conference; Community-Based Crime and Reentry Theory and Healing Communities). Faith-based organizations may provide the prime means of providing needed services and supports within the ex-offenders' local community; and, may stand in stark contrast to the racially discriminatory treatment that offenders have experienced in prisons and jails or while under traditional probation or parole supervision.

Beverly D. Frazier

See also: American Law and African Americans; Citizenship; *Code of the Street*; Community-Based Crime and Reentry Theory; Correctional System and African Americans; Drug Treatment Strategies; Healing Communities; Institutional Racism; Prisoner Reentry and African Americans; Prisoner Reentry Models: A Focus on Arkansas; Prisons; Sentencing Disparities; Socioeconomic Factors; War on Drugs

References

Frazier, B. "Faith-Based Programs." In *Rethinking Corrections,* edited by L. Gideon and S. Hung-En. Thousand Oaks, CA: Sage, 2009.

Johnson, B. R., and D. B. Larson. *The InnerChange Freedom Initiative.* Philadelphia: University of Pennsylvania, Center for Research on Religion and Urban Civil Society, 2003.

Lukoff, D., R. Turner, and F. Lu. "Toward a More Culturally Sensitive DSM-IV: Psychoreligious and Psychospiritual Problems." *Journal of Nervous and Mental Disease* 180 (1992): 673–82.

Rossman, S. *Building Partnerships to Strengthen Offenders, Families and Communities.* Washington, DC: The Urban Institute, 2002.

False Confessions

False confessions are defined as admittance to the commission of a crime when the confessor is not responsible for the crime. Confession plays an important role in securing convictions. Estimates are that confessions account for 70 percent of convictions (Brandon & Davies, 1973). In addition to securing convictions, confessions are considered one of the "most attractive ways of solving crimes" (Brandon & Davies, 1973). The rate of convictions secured by a false confession is unknown, but DNA evidence has exonerated up to 25 percent of known false confession cases (Kassin, 2008a). Given that confessions are a very important and powerful form of evidence (Conti, 1999), the police invest considerable time and resources in securing confessions through training and interrogations. Law enforcement interrogations play a major role in eliciting false confessions in a variety of ways. Factors that contribute to false confessions are duress, coercion, intoxication, diminished capacity, mental impairment, ignorance of the law, fear of violence, the actual infliction of harm, the threat of a harsh sentence, and misunderstanding of the situation (Innocence Project, 2010; Kassin, 1998).

Types of False Confessions

Theories of social influence and American history suggest that three types of false confession exist: compliant false confessions, internalized false confessions, and voluntary false confessions (Kassin & Wrightsman, 1985). Compliant false confessions are when individuals are persuaded to confess through the process of police questioning. Internalized false confessions refer to situations where vulnerable or highly impressionable suspects succumb to investigative interrogation tactics to the point where they come to believe that they have committed the crime, and so they eventually confess (Kassin, 2008b). Although police interrogations substantially contribute to false confession, they are not the only cause of false confessions; individuals also make voluntary false confessions. Voluntary false confessions are those where individuals claim to be responsible for crimes that they did not commit. These individuals confess without any police influence. Voluntary false confessions are typically influenced by an internal desire to become famous in a celebrated case, feelings of guilt from previous transgressions, mental impairment, or a desire to help protect the real criminal (Montaldo, 2010). Voluntary false confessions do not account for the bulk of false confessions.

Police Interrogations

Police interrogative practices account for the most false confessions. Compliant false confessions and internalized false confessions are outcomes of police interrogations. Police interrogations may evoke false confessions when some individuals see the confession as the only way out of a negative situation. The compliant false confession is about escaping an implied or perceived danger with some implied benefit from the confession (Kassin & Gudjonsson, 2004). The 10 most frequent interrogation practices that influence innocent people to confess falsely are:

1) isolating the suspect from family and friends; 2) conducting interrogation in a small private room; 3) identifying contradictions in the suspect's story; 4) establishing rapport and gaining the suspect's trust; 5) confronting the suspect with evidence of guilt; 6) appealing to the suspect's self-interest; 7) offering sympathy, moral justifications, and excuses; 8) interrupting the suspect's denials and objections; 9) pretending to have independent evidence of guilt; and 10) minimizing the moral seriousness of the offense (Kassin et al., 2007).

Internalized false confessions occur when an interrogator convinces the suspect that he or she has committed a crime that the person has not in fact committed. Individuals who usually internalize false confessions tend to be young, tired, and confused by the interrogator, suggestible, and/or people who have been exposed to or misled by false information during the interrogation (Kassin, 2005). In short, malleable individuals often falsely confess. Malleable individuals include children/ juveniles; those with low intelligence, poor memory, low self-esteem, lack of assertiveness, and/or anxiousness; and introverts (Gudjonsson, 1999). Whether the individual is inclined to confess because of police tactics or internalized factors, the mental state of the suspect is important.

Historical and Celebrated Cases of False Confessions

Historically, it was not uncommon for law enforcement officers to beat Blacks to get confessions from them. Blacks in the early 1900s routinely confessed to crimes that they did not commit after acts of police brutality (Kassin & Sukel, 1997; Kassin & Wrightsman, 1985; Wrightsman & Kassin, 1993; Wrightsman et al., 1994). *Brown v. Mississippi* (1936) is an example of physical police brutality to elicit a confession. In this case, three Black men were arrested by the police for the murder of a White man; the three Black suspects were beaten until they confessed to the murder of the White planter in Mississippi. The men were convicted of murder and the U.S. Supreme Court reversed the convictions. The Supreme Court decided that physical coercion through brutality or violence is a violation of an individual's right to due process of the law (Conti, 1999).

In addition to physical torture and threats, mental coercion was also commonplace in the production of false confessions. *Chambers v. Florida* (1940) is an example of psychological coercion that influenced a false confession. In this case, the Black defendant, along with three Black co-defendants, falsely confessed to the murder of a White man in Florida. Chambers was transported to different cities in Florida, including Miami and Ft. Lauderdale, and held for police interrogation for approximately a week. He was subjected to random questioning by numerous police officers and community members before he finally signed a written confession to the murder. In the *Chambers* case, the Court decided that five or more days of

In the U.S. criminal justice system, confessions are viewed as damning evidence of guilt against a defendant, and they often override exculpatory evidence or even the total lack of corroboration. Recantations (attempts to take back a confession) are nearly always considered dubious, regardless of the fact that forceful or coercive interrogation techniques were used and despite extensive research showing that true confessions can be distinguished from false ones by specific corroborating facts.

Although the frequency of false and forced confessions in the United States is uncertain, contemporary statistics and historical data reflect a long connection between forced confessions and African American defendants, who are overrepresented generally in the criminal justice system and in populations considered highly vulnerable to the law enforcement techniques that lead to false confessions, especially if they are juveniles, socially disadvantaged, and/or undereducated.

Historically, false confessions were elicited through physical abuse, including torture techniques such as waterboarding (known as "the water cure"), which were used in the South to force confessions from African Americans accused of crimes (see, e.g., *Fisher v. State,* 110 So. 361, 362 [Miss. 1926] and *White v. State,* 91 So. 903, 904 [Miss. 1922]). Since the courts began requiring video or tape recording of police interrogations in the mid twentieth century, physical abuse of suspects has significantly diminished, along with the estimated number of false confessions.

In place of physical coercion, police interrogators developed psychological techniques designed to encourage suspects to confess. Elements of this coercive persuasion include the following:

- Destabilization of the individual's sense of reality and identity through forceful psychological (as opposed to physical) threats and manipulation
- Intense, prolonged, unavoidable questioning accompanied by obsessive demands for a confession
- Control of the individual's environment, such as minimizing communications with others and increasing physical discomfort (exhaustion, anxiety, hunger, sleep deprivation)
- The promise of a respite if the individual "allows" him- or herself to confess

An individual susceptible to this form of coercion is likely to experience two phases prior to falsely confessing:

1. Unfreezing, during which the individual's resistance to the narrative promoted by the interrogators is softened. During this phase, his or her confidence and sense of reality falters, and feelings of powerlessness, hopelessness, and guilt and emotional turmoil take over.

(Continued)

> 2. Change, during which the individual is encouraged to comply by the potential "reward" of release from the interrogation if he or she offers a confession compatible with the information the interrogators supplied during questioning.
>
> These phases can bring about a transient acceptance by the individual of the crime as described by the interrogators. The individual submits to the desired narrative, in which he or she is the culpable actor, as a means to end the tensions created by the interrogation. The change, however, is situationally adaptive, unstable, and circumstantial, such that the "confession" is likely to be recanted once the coercion desists.
>
> *Roz Myers*

prolonged questioning that resulted in a confession made the confession highly suspect (Conti, 1999).

To conclude, internal and situational factors contribute to false confessions. The most influential factor appears to be police interrogations. Police questioning and police strategies and suggestive techniques are highly influential in individuals confessing to crimes that they did not commit. Historically, the police target groups of people (Blacks) based on erroneous judgments of guilt. Whether the accused internalizes the false confession or is confessing out of a sense of compliance, the interrogation generates the confession. Interrogation tactics coupled with the suspect's vulnerabilities account for the bulk of false confessions.

Doshie Piper

See also: DNA Testing; Innocence Project

References

Bailey, J. "The Central Park Jogger Case Had Six Victims, and Only One Was the Jogger." *The Atlantic*, November 27, 2012. http://www.theatlantic.com/entertainment/archive/2012/11/the-central-park-jogger-case-had-six-victims-and-only-one-was-the-jogger/265609/.

Brandon, R. R., and C. C. Davies. *Wrongful Imprisonment: Mistaken Convictions & Their Consequences.* London: Allen and Unwin, 1973.

Brown v. Mississippi, 297 U.S. 278 (1936).

Chambers v. Florida, 309 U.S. 277 (1940).

The Central Park Jogger Case

The Central Park Jogger case involved the brutal rape and assault of Trisha Meili, a 28-year-old White female from an affluent background who worked for an investment banking firm. The crime took place while she was jogging in New York City's Central Park on April 19, 1989. Five minority juveniles from Harlem, four Blacks and one Latino, were picked up by the police, questioned for hours without their parents or attorneys present, and eventually charged with the crime. Their names were Antron McCray, age 15; Kevin Richardson, age 14; Raymond Santana, age 14; Yusef Salaam, age 15; and Kharey Wise, age 16. In stark contrast to the victim, the young men were from working-class backgrounds and lived in a predominantly Black and Latino neighborhood. Media accounts portrayed them as part of a group of youngsters roaming through the park "wilding," or "acting like wild animals," who also attacked nine other people.

The case received a great deal of media attention in which many of the stories used animal imagery, referring to the group as a "wolf pack" or "herd." The incident was often referred to as a "savage" attack by teenagers who were portrayed as beast-like. In contrast, the race and social status of the victim were emphasized as factors that made her a clearly sympathetic victim about whom the entire city should be concerned. Millionaire Donald Trump ran full-page ads in four major New York newspapers calling for the arrest of the teenagers and reinstatement of the death penalty to address the case.

Despite the fact that DNA testing revealed a semen sample that did not match any of the boys, prosecutors moved forward with the case. Inconsistent and equivocal statements made by four of them on videotape were characterized as confessions, even though they retracted the statements soon thereafter, stating that they had been intimidated, lied to, and coerced into making them (*New York Daily News*, 2013). All five were tried and convicted. They served prison sentences ranging from 5 to 13 years (*NYMag.com*, 2013).

In 2002, Matias Reyes, a convicted rapist and murderer serving a life sentence for other crimes, confessed to single-handedly committing the brutal attack. His DNA confirmed his involvement. Though some of the investigating officers stood by their belief in the young men's guilt, the convictions were vacated at the request of the Manhattan district attorney (*New York Daily News*, 2013). *The Central Park Five*, a documentary that portrays the events from the perspective of the young men who were convicted, was released by Ken Burns, David McMahon, and Sarah Burns in 2012. The five are still seeking a civil judgment against the city in a $250 million lawsuit (Bailey, 2012).

Delores Jones-Brown and Allana Beddoe

Conti, R. P. "The Psychology of False Confessions." *The Journal of Credibility Assessment and Witness Psychology* 2, no. 1 (1999): 14–36.

Gudjonnson, Gisli. *The Psychology of Interrogation and Confession: A Handbook.* Hoboken, NJ: John Wiley, 2003.

Gudjonsson, G. "The Making of a Serial False Confessor: The Confessions of Henry Lee Lucas." *Journal of Forensic Psychiatry* 10, no. 2 (1999): 416–26.

Inbau, Fred, John Reid, and Joseph Buckley. *Criminal Interrogation and Confessions.* 3rd ed. Baltimore: Williams and Wilkins, 1986.

Innocence Project. "Understanding the Causes: False Confessions." New York: Innocence Project, 2010. http://www.innocenceproject.org/understand/False-Confessions.php.

Kassin, S. M. 2008a. "Confession Evidence: Commonsense Myths and Misconceptions." *Criminal Justice and Behavior* 35, no. 10 (2008): 1309–22.

Kassin, S. M. 2008b. "False Confessions: Causes, Consequences, and Implications for Reform." *Current Directions in Psychological Science* 17, no. 4 (2008): 249–53.

Kassin, S. M. "True Crimes False Confessions." *Scientific American Mind* 16, no. 2 (2005): 24.

Kassin, S. M. "More on the Psychology of False Confessions." *American Psychologist* 53, no. 3 (1998): 320–21.

Kassin, S. M., et al. "Police Interviewing and Interrogation: A Self-Report Survey of Police Practices and Beliefs." *Law and Human Behavior* 31 (2007): 381–400.

Kassin, S. M., and G. H. Gudjonsson. "The Psychology of Confessions: A Review of the Literature and Issues." *Psychological Science in the Public Interest* 5, no. 2 (2004): 33–67.

Kassin, S. M., and H. Sukel. "Coerced Confessions and the Jury: An Experimental Test of the 'Harmless Error' Rule." *Law and Human Behavior* 21, no. 1 (1997): 27–46.

Kassin, S. M., and L. S. Wrightsman. "Confession Evidence." In *The Psychology of Evidence & Trial Procedure,* edited by S. M. Kassin and L. S. Wrightsman, 67–94. Beverly Hills, CA: Sage, 1985.

Montaldo, C. "Why Do Innocent People Make False Confessions?" *Crime/Punishment,* 2010. http://crime.about.com/od/issues/a/false.htm.

New York Daily News. "The Central Park Five." 2013 http://www.nydailynews.com/services/central-park-five.

NYMag.com. "Central Park Revisited." N.d. http://nymag.com/nymetro/news/crimelaw/features/n_7836/.

Ofshe, Richard J., and Richard A. Leo. "The Social Psychology of Police Interrogation: The Theory and Classification of True and False Confessions." *Studies in Law, Politics, and Society* 16 (1997): 189–251.

Schein, Edgar H., with Inge Schneier and Curtis H. Barker. *Coercive Persuasion.* New York: W.W. Norton, 1961.

Wrightsman, L. S., and S. M. Kassin. *Confessions in the Courtroom.* Newbury Park, CA: Sage, 1993.

Wrightsman, L. S., M. T. Nietzel, and W. H. Fortune. *Psychology and the Legal System.* 3rd ed. Belmont, CA: Thomson Brooks/Cole, 1994.

Federal Death Penalty Abolition Act of 2009 (S. 650)

Executive Summary

Introduced in the Senate of the United States on March 9, 2009, the Federal Death Penalty Abolition Act of 2009 (S. 650) is the first step in abolishing the death penalty in the United States. The proposed bill prohibits the death penalty for violation of federal law, and commutes death penalties already imposed to life imprisonment without the possibility of parole.

Background

The death penalty stirs much controversy in the United States because each state as well as the federal government has differing opinions on what are, if any, the "right" goals and values of capital punishment. Examining the flaws in the death penalty system at both the state and the federal level, one cannot help but see that any use of the death penalty in the United States stands in bleak contrast to the majority of nations, 123 to be exact, which have abolished the death penalty in law or practice (Feingold, 2009; Amnesty International, 2007). In 2007, only China, Iran, Saudi Arabia, and Pakistan executed more people than did the United States. Those countries are the ones criticized most often for human rights abuses. The European Union denies membership to nations that use the death penalty and even passed a resolution calling for the immediate and unconditional global abolition of the death penalty, and it specifically called on all states within the United States to abolish the death penalty (Feingold, 2009; Amnesty International, 2007).

   S. 650 was primarily constructed to bring an end to the serious problems that the federal capital punishment system incurs, such as wrongful convictions, racial disparities, issues related to the right to counsel, and the monetary costs associated with capital prosecutions. These also happen to be some of the same problems that many state capital punishment systems face. Addressing these problems at the federal level can set a precedent to be followed by the 32 states that still use the death penalty. Serious mistakes do occur in the criminal justice system, and as for the death penalty, Hugo Bedau and Michael Radelet estimated that for every 20 persons executed in this country since 1900, at least one innocent person was convicted of a capital crime (Walker, 2008).

   By 2008, a total of 343 persons had been mistakenly convicted of capital crimes; 25 were actually executed, while many of the others served prison terms of up to 25 years (Walker, 2008). The Innocence Project has found that an innocent person can be convicted of murder and sentenced to death because of false identification, police or prosecutor misconduct, bad lawyering by defense counsel, and incorrect scientific analysis of evidence (Walker, 2008). Clearly, the United States' capital punishment system is in need of repair.

Another controversial issue is the notion that there are racial disparities when it comes to the use of the death penalty. For example, in 96 percent of the states where there have been reviews of race and the death penalty, there was a pattern of either race-of-victim or race-of-defendant discrimination, or both (Baldus, 1998). It is often the poor, the uneducated, and minority group members who die, not the worst offenders.

There are enormous problems with the right to counsel in death penalty cases. For example, in Alabama, 60 percent of people on death row were defended by lawyers appointed by courts who, by statute, could not be paid more than $1,000 for their out-of-court time to prepare the case for trial (Feingold, 2009). In Texas, hundreds of death row inmates are awaiting execution after being represented by lawyers who could not receive more than $500 for experts or mitigation evidence. Across the country, there are hundreds of death row inmates whose lawyers had their compensation capped at levels that make effective assistance impossible (Feingold, 2009). This problem clearly affects the poor, who in many cases are also minorities.

There is also evidence that seeking capital punishment comes at great monetary cost to taxpayers. The Urban Institute examined 162 capital cases that were prosecuted between 1978 and 1999 and found that seeking the death penalty in those cases cost $186 million more than what those cases would have cost had the death penalty not been sought (Chaflin et al., 2008). Apparently, the Department of Justice does not track the monetary costs of the federal death penalty (Feingold, 2009).

Many people believe that the death penalty is a deterrent and may stop some people from committing violent crimes, especially murder. However, according to a survey of the former and current presidents of the country's top academic criminological societies, 88 percent of these experts rejected the notion that the death penalty acts as a deterrent to murder (Walker, 2008). Consistent with previous years, the 2009 FBI Uniform Crime Report showed that the South had the highest murder rate. The South accounts for over 80 percent of executions. The Northeast, which has less than 1 percent of all executions, has the lowest murder rate (FBI Uniform Crime Report, 2009).

Policy Background

In 2007, Senator Feingold held a hearing on oversight of the federal death penalty, which was the first such oversight hearing in the Senate Judiciary Committee in six years. The purpose of the hearing was to highlight the Department of

Justices lack of transparency about death penalty decisionmaking and to address the racial disparities in the federal system. The Federal Death Penalty Abolition Act (S. 650) was re-introduced in the 111th Congress of the United States, at its first session on March 19, 2009. The purpose of the act, to abolish the death penalty under federal law, was read twice by Senator Feingold and referred to the Committee on the Judiciary. This legislation would impact those currently on federal death row as well as those on trial for all federal convictions that could potentially lead to death sentences.

Capital punishment at the federal level was reinstated in 1988 in a federal law that provided for the death penalty for murder in the course of a drug kingpin conspiracy. It was then expanded significantly in 1994, when a compilation crime bill expanded its use to a total of some 60 federal offenses (Feingold, 2009). By 2009, three individuals had been executed under the federal system, and there were 55 inmates on federal death row (Feingold, 2009).

In 2008, there were 3,261 people on death row in the United States. Of those people, 1,351 (41.43%) were Black, 1,448 (44.4%) were White, 383 (11.74%) were Latino, and 79 (2.42%) were of another race (Phillips, 2008). According to these statistics, nearly half of the prisoners on death row in 2008 were Black; however, 2009 U.S census data indicated that Blacks only made up 12.9 percent of the United States' population. The racial disparity in the data is clear. Since 1995, some 80 percent of the 682 defendants who have faced capital charges in the federal courts have been minorities (Phillips, 2008). After conviction, U.S. attorneys recommended the death penalty for 183 of these defendants, 74 percent of whom were minorities (Phillips, 2008). This is even more racially unbalanced than the death sentencing record in states with high execution rates, like Texas and Mississippi.

Policy Description

The Federal Death Penalty Abolition Act of 2009 (S. 650) repeals death penalty provisions for a wide range of homicide-related offenses under the Immigration and Nationality Act; the federal criminal code; the Controlled Substances Act and other statutes relating to aircraft hijacking, espionage, and treason; and offenses punished under the Uniform Code of Military Justice. It prohibits the sentencing to death or execution of any person for any violation of federal law after its enactment. It also commutes death penalties imposed prior to its enactment to life imprisonment without the possibility of parole. However, in 2009, to combat the prevalence of hate crime victimization in America, Congress also enacted the Matthew Shepard and James Byrd, Jr. Hate Crimes Prevention Act (S. 909). This act authorizes use of the death penalty as a possible punishment for hate crimes.

Conclusion

At the federal level and in 32 of the 50 states, the death penalty is an example of the use of two criminal sanctions, retribution and deterrence. If the punishment involves only retribution, no future good for society is intended, and the rightful purpose of punishment is to assign blame and punishment to the wrongdoer. If the primary goal of the punishment is deterrence, the purpose of punishment is to send a message to other potential lawbreakers that the specific offense being punished will not be tolerated. Both retribution and deterrence have proven to be unsuccessful punishments for violent crimes at both the state and federal level. By first enacting legislation to do away with the federal death penalty, the federal government can then call on each state that authorizes the use of the death penalty to end the practice.

Anne Gregory

See also: Byrd, Jr., James; Death Penalty; Disproportionality and Crime; Federal Sentencing Disparity; Hate Crimes; Sentencing Disparities

References

Amnesty International. *Execution by Lethal Injection: A Quarter Century of State Poisoning.* New York: Amnesty International, 2007. http://www.amnesty.org.

Baldus, David. *Report to American Bar Association.* Washington, DC: Death Penalty Information Center, 1998. http://www.deathpenaltyinfo.org/.

Chaflin, Aaron, Askar Darmenov, Carly Knight, John Roman, and Aaron Sundquist. *The Cost of the Death Penalty in Maryland.* Washington, DC: Urban Institute, 2008. http://www.urban.org/publications/411625.html.

FBI Uniform Crime Report. FBI: Washington, DC: 2009. http://www.fbi.gov/publications.htm.

Feingold, Russ. Congressional Record, 111th Congress, 2009–2010. http://thomas.loc.gov.

Phillips, Scott. *Racial Disparities in the Capital of Capital Punishment.* Denver, CO: University of Denver Press, 2008. U.S. Census Bureau. 2009. http://quickfacts.census.gov.

Walker, Samuel. *Sense and Nonsense about Crime, Drugs, and Communities: A Policy Guide.* Belmont, CA: Wadsworth/Cengage Learning, 2008.

Federal Sentencing Disparity

Suspicion of unfairness in sentencing has led to some research concluding that extralegal factors such as race influence sentencing. Race does not account for disparity in sentencing alone, but the confluence of race and other factors intensify one's disadvantages in sentencing (Farrell, 2001). The assistant U.S. attorney (AUSA) has tremendous indirect control when determining the sentences of federal offenders (Spohn & Fornango, 2009). Not only does the AUSA determine the charge, but through the 5k1.1 substantial assistance clause of the Federal Sentencing Guidelines, the AUSA is also able to significantly reduce an offender's sentence for cause. Through this clause, the prosecutor is able to ask a federal judge to lower a sentence if she or he determines that the offender "substantially assisted" the government in investigating a case, building a case, or prosecuting another person (Spohn & Fornango, 2009).

The 1984 Sentencing Reform Act was designed to reduce judicial disparity in sentencing when it came to similar offenders who committed similar crimes (Spohn & Fornango, 2009). This law was supposed to make sentences more uniform and fair (Spohn & Fornango, 2009). However, disparities in sentencing still exist (Spohn & Fornango, 2009), in part because prosecutors have broad discretion that can affect the sentencing process. Specifically, the prosecutor decides how the offender will be charged; the parameters of plea agreements; whether to increase the sentence or not by including certain charges, such as possessing a firearm; or filing for a downward departure because of a defendant's "substantial assistance." All of these factors may work to decrease a defendant's sentence (Spohn & Fornango, 2009). While most "downward departures" from the federal sentencing guidelines involve mitigating circumstances, 5k1.1 downward departures are awarded to offenders who reveal information about other people (Farrell, 2001). The prosecutor is able to choose what offense to charge a cooperating offender with; and, while once a defendant is convicted, the judge must sentence within certain guidelines, the prosecutor can still influence the sentence, within statutory limits (Spohn & Fornango, 2009). Through all of the avenues that prosecutors have that impact sentencing, disparities still occur, despite legislative attempts to eliminate them. Some researchers have found that not only do disparities in sentencing still exist, they may be partly attributable to offender characteristics such as race (Spohn & Fornango, 2009).

The offender that is granted a downward departure through substantial assistance may have her or his sentence reduced, but the sentencing judge determines how much it is reduced (Spohn & Fornango, 2009). The judge makes this decision after careful consideration. The usefulness and importance of the assistance are analyzed. Some important considerations are the reliability of the offender and the information provided, the nature and timeliness of assistance, and any personal risk the offender has experienced due to her or his assistance (Spohn & Fornango, 2009). If the sentencing judge finds that the assistance was very useful, the sentence can be lower than the mandatory minimum sentence designated under the sentencing guidelines (Spohn & Fornango, 2009). Consequently, both the judge and the prosecutor determine the sentence that an offender receives (Spohn & Fornango, 2009).

One dimension that may lead to sentencing disparities is that substantial assistance does not have a simple or uniform definition (Spohn & Fornango, 2009). Jurisdictions differ in what is considered substantial assistance; in one jurisdiction, prosecutors may require that the offender be a witness during trial. In another, the prosecutor may only require information that may potentially lead to another prosecution (Spohn & Fornango, 2009). These differences across jurisdictions and prosecutors often manifest themselves in disparate sentencing outcomes.

In recent research examining substantial assistance downward departures, racial disparities existed, both in regard to *which* offenders received downward departures and in the *length* of the sentence imposed in exchange for individual defendant's assistance (Spohn & Fornango, 2009). This research is consistent with earlier research, where Mustard (2001) found that from 1991–1994, downward sentencing departures were granted with great disparity (Spohn & Fornango, 2009): "He found that downward departures accounted for 56 percent of the racial ethnic disparity . . . in sentence length. . . . He also found that nearly two thirds of the black-white sentence disparity for drug trafficking cases could be attributed to downward departures" (Spohn & Fornango, 2009: 817).

More recently, Spohn and Fornango (2009) found that on average, a prosecutor seeks a downward departure through substantial assistance in about 27 percent of her or his cases. However, this varies greatly by prosecutor. Prosecutors have been found to seek such departures in 0 to 67 percent of their cases (Spohn & Fornango, 2009). In addition to inter-prosecutor differences, there were differences by the type of offense as well. Offenders presented with drug charges were found to receive downward departures about four times as often as offenders with other charges (Spohn & Fornango, 2009).

Spohn and Fornango (2009) found that White offenders were more likely than Black offenders to be granted a downward departure through substantial assistance. Researcher Amy Farrell (2001) found that White women received a departure from a prosecutor at a rate of 49 percent, while minority women did 32 percent of the time. When controlling for offense type, White men were granted a departure 42 percent of the time, but minority men were granted them at a rate of 27 percent (Farrell, 2001). This research suggests that the race of a defendant may be playing some role in determining who receives substantial assistance downward departures, although legally, for purposes of sentencing, a defendant's race should not matter.

This racial disparity in sentencing that remains after guidelines were developed to eliminate it suggests that prosecutors are unable to be totally objective when recommending substantial assistance downward departures (Farrell, 2001).

However, other research suggests that Black defendants may also be less willing to cooperate with prosecutors than are members of other groups. That is, they are less likely to plead guilty and they are more reluctant to provide incriminating evidence against others (Mustard, 2001). The Sentencing Reform Act of 1984 was designed to reduce sentencing disparities in the federal system. However, the 5k1.1 substantial assistance clause appears to have created a new avenue for disparities (Farrell, 2001). These disparities may be due to many factors, but the race of the defendant still appears to be one of them.

Ashley Derome

See also: Institutional Racism; Sentencing Disparities; Socioeconomic Factors; War on Drugs

References

Farrell, A. "The Effect of Gender and Family Status on Downward Departures in Federal Criminal Sentences." PhD diss., Northeastern University, 2001.

Mustard, D. "Racial, Ethnic, and Gender Disparities in Sentencing Evidence from the U.S. Federal Courts." *Journal of Law and Economics* 44 (2001): 285–314.

Spohn, C., and R. Fornango. "U.S. Attorneys and Substantial Assistance Departures: Testing for Interprosecutor Disparity." *Criminology* 47, no. 3 (2009): 813–46.

Ferguson, Colin (1958–)

On the evening of December 7, 1993, divorced Brooklynite Colin Ferguson shot and killed passengers on the 5:33 evening commuter Long Island Rail Road train to Hicksville, New York. His three-minute rampage was ended by three men, who tackled and restrained him as he attempted to reload his 9-mm Ruger P-89 weapon for the third time. During the episode, Ferguson killed six people and wounded 19 (Schemo, 1993).

Formerly accustomed to a comfortable middle-class life in the Caribbean, the well-educated 36-year-old immigrant from Jamaica became obsessed with the racism he experienced in the United States. According to notes found in his pockets after the shooting, Ferguson felt that American racism was pervasive and extended to all Whites, as well as Asians and "Uncle Tom" Black people (McFadden, 1993).

Before being fired as Ferguson's attorneys, famed trial lawyers William Kunstler and Ronald Kuby announced their intentions to take a novel approach to their legal representation of him. They proposed to mount what they termed a "Black Rage" defense as explanation for their client's actions. Under the approach, they would

Colin Ferguson is charged with the shooting deaths of six people during a shooting rampage on the Long Island, New York, railroad commuter train on December 10, 1993. (AFP/Getty Images)

argue that at the time of the shootings, Ferguson had been driven legally insane by racist treatment and therefore should not be held responsible for his actions. The announcement engendered major racial vitriol, as the majority of the victims in the case were White and middle- to upper-middle class (Toufexis et al., 1993).

Before Kunstler and Kuby could pursue the controversial defense, Ferguson fired them as his lawyers, opting to exercise his right to defend himself in court instead (Rabinovitz, 1993b). Kunstler and Kuby remained available to give legal advice to Ferguson, who rejected their representation because he did not want to be declared insane (Van Biema & Cohen, 1995; Rabinovitz, 1993a). Ferguson was declared competent to stand trial and appeared in court each day, well-dressed and prepared to question witnesses. As his defense tactic, Ferguson decided to deny being the shooter. Instead he claimed that an unknown person stole his gun while he slept and apparently committed the crime for which he was charged in a 93-count indictment (McQuiston, 1995).

During the trial, Ferguson repeatedly questioned the arresting officers, witnesses to the shootings, and the surviving victims. The case was televised on *Court TV*

Sociological Defenses

Sociological defenses are those that rely on defendants' claims that their life experiences or environment caused them to commit a crime.

Black Rage. Though raised in defense of Colin Ferguson in 1993, the basis for the "Black Rage" defense is outlined in a 1968 book, *Black Rage* (Basic Books), written by two Black psychiatrists, William Grier and Price Cobbs. They describe the book as revealing "the full dimensions of the inner conflicts and the desperation of the black man's life in America." See also *Black Rage Confronts the Law* by Paul Harris (New York University Press, 1997).

Rotten Social Background (RSB). This defense was unsuccessfully offered in the trial of Gordon Alexander, an African American male who shot and killed a White Marine for using a racial epithet. Alexander said the shooting was the result of an irresistible impulse that stemmed from his deprived childhood, during which he experienced abandonment, poverty, discrimination, and a lack of love. Although the appellate court upheld the trial court's refusal to submit such an instruction to the jury, one judge did question whether society had the right to sit in judgment of a defendant who had been so thoroughly mistreated.

Media Intoxication. This defense was used unsuccessfully by 19-year-old Ronald Ray Howard to support his claim that he should not receive a death sentence for killing a police officer while listening to gangsta rap. His claim was that his criminal conduct was caused by "intoxication" from television and pornography.

Urban Survivor Syndrome. This defense contends that young people living in poor and violent neighborhoods do not receive adequate police protection and therefore develop a heightened awareness and fear of threats. It was blocked from being introduced in the trial of 17-year-old Daimon Osby after he was accused of shooting and killing two unarmed cousins after a gambling dispute.

Adapted from Matthew Lippman, *Contemporary Criminal Law: Concepts, Cases and Controversies*. Thousand Oaks, CA: Sage, 2009.

in a broadcast that showed that in presenting his defense, Ferguson would ramble for hours in the courtroom, claiming that there was a vast conspiracy of racism that prevented him from receiving a fair trial.

On February 17, 1995, after 10 hours of deliberation, jurors found Ferguson guilty of 68 out of 93 charges against him. Ferguson received 25 years to life for each of his six murdered victims and for each of the 19 wounded. During the course of his trial, the state of New York reinstated the death penalty, but it could not be retroactively applied to him (Bardwell & Arrigo, 2002). Ferguson's unusual behavior in the courtroom caused some to question whether he was paranoid and delusional or simply pretending to be insane so that he might appeal his conviction (Marks, 1994). Colin Ferguson is currently serving what amounts to a 315-year, 8-month sentence in New York's correctional system. With his earliest parole eligibility date in 2309, barring a successful postconviction appeal, Ferguson will not be released in his lifetime. A previous request for retrial was rejected by the Court of Appeals in December 1998 (*Newsday*, 1993).

Rhodine Moreau

References

Bardwell, Mark C., and Bruce A. Arrigo. *Criminal Competency on Trial: The Case of Colin Ferguson.* Durham, NC: Carolina Academic Press, 2002.

Grier, William, and Price Cobbs. *Black Rage.* New York: Basic Books, 1968.

Harris, Paul. *Black Rage Confronts the Law.* New York: New York University Press, 1997.

Marks, Peter. "L.I.R.R. Case Again Raises Sanity Issue." *The New York Times,* August 12, 1994. http://www.nytimes.com/1994/08/12/nyregion/lirr-case-again-raises-sanity-issue.html.

McFadden, Robert D. "A Tormented Life: A Special Report; A Long Slide from Privilege Ends in Slaughter on a Train." *The New York Times,* December 12, 1993. http://www.nytimes.com/1993/12/12/nyregion/tormented-life-special-report-long-slide-privilege-ends-slaughter-train.html.

McQuiston, John T. "Abrupt End to Defense in Rail Case." *The New York Times,* February 16, 1995. http://www.nytimes.com/1995/02/16/nyregion/abrupt-end-to-defense-in-rail-case.html.

Newsday (Long Island, New York). "Judge Decries Cap on Penalty." March 23, 1995, A3.

Rabinovitz, Jonathan. "Death on the L.I.R.R.; Lawyer Seeks Sanity Inquiry in L.I. Killings." 1993a. *The New York Times,* December 11, 1993. http://www.nytimes.com/1993/12/11/nyregion/death-on-the-lirr-lawyer-seeks-sanity-inquiry-in-li-killings.html?pagewanted=2.

Rabinovitz, Jonathan. "Man Accused in L.I.R.R. Shootings Requests a Different Lawyer." 1993b. *The New York Times,* December 18, 1993. http://www.nytimes.com/1993/12/18/nyregion/man-accused-in-lirr-shootings-requests-a-different-lawyer.html.

Schemo, Diana Jean. "Death on the L.I.R.R.: The Confrontation; 3 Credited in Capture of Gunman." *The New York Times,* December 9, 1993. http://www.nytimes.com/1993/12/09/nyregion/death-on-the-lirr-the-confrontation-3-credited-in-capture-of-gunman.html.

Toufexis, Anastasia, and Patrick E. Cole. "Crime: Colin Ferguson: A Mass Murderer's Journey toward Madness." *Time,* December 20, 1993. http://www.time.com/time/magazine/article/0,9171,979847,00.html.

Van Biema, David, and Adam Cohen. "A Fool for a Client." *Time,* February 6, 1995. http://www.time.com/time/magazine/article/0,9171,982445,00.html.

Francois, Kendall (1971–)

Since the publication of the FBI's *Crime Classification Manual* in 1992, it has been well established in multicide research that about 90 percent of all serial murder is intra-racial; that is, the murderer kills victims that are within his or her own race or ethnicity.

Exceptions to this pattern were historically few, but appear to be increasing since the 1990s. Andrew Cunanan, Charles Ng, Angel Resendez-Ramirez, Carlton Gary, and Coral Eugene Watts are all serial killers who murdered people outside of their race. One of the most noteworthy exceptions to this intra-racial crime pattern is that of serial killer Kendall Francois.

Kendall Francois, an African American man of Haitian heritage, was born on June 26, 1971, and raised from the age of four in a simple frame house on Fulton Street in Poughkeepsie, New York, in a middle-class, mostly White neighborhood. His mother worked as a psychiatric nurse in a juvenile facility, and his father was employed as an engineer at the Duracell headquarters in nearby Danbury, Connecticut. Francois was a middle child with one older sister, one younger sister, and a younger brother.

Francois graduated from Arlington High School in Poughkeepsie in 1989 and joined the army, completing basic training in 1990. He was stationed in Texas, Hawaii, and Germany, but was honorably discharged after three years, reportedly because his obesity kept him from fulfilling the physical requirements of the job. In 1993, he returned to the ramshackle house on Fulton Street where his parents and younger sister still lived. He spent the next several years working a series of menial jobs, including custodian and hall monitor at the local middle school. He sporadically took random classes at Dutchess Community College between 1993 and 1996, usually earning Bs.

It was during this period that Francois began frequenting prostitutes. A self-described sex addict, Francois estimates that he had more than 1,000 sexual encounters with prostitutes between 1993 and 1998. In February 1995 he was convicted of soliciting a prostitute. During the summer of that same year, he tested positive for the HIV virus. According to Francois, this news represented a death knell in his life, as there was no known cure for AIDS at that time. He did not disclose his HIV status and continued to frequent prostitutes, while he described his emotional state as depressed, uncaring, fatalistic, angry, and obsessed with issues of power and control. In January 1998, Francois was again convicted of soliciting a prostitute. This time the complaint also involved allegations of severe abuse and assault of a local sex worker. By the time of his second arrest, Francois had already killed five women.

Francois' first murder victim was Wendy Meyers, reported missing in October 1996. In December 1996, Gina Barone was reported missing by her mother when she did not come home for her birthday. One month later, in January 1997, Kathleen Hurley left her apartment on Super Bowl Sunday to buy cigarettes and was never seen again. In March 1997, Catherine Marsh—who was pregnant when she was last seen in November 1996—was reported missing by her family.

These four women were White, ages 27 through 42, but there was no consistency in their appearance or build. The one constant variable, however, was that each had a history of drug and/or alcohol addiction that led to a high-risk lifestyle and itinerant living. In most instances, their families had not seen them for months, even years, and had no idea where these women were living. Because all the women were *missing* but no bodies had been found, there could be no immediate conclusion that they were dead—no crime scene, no weapon, no dump site, no forensic evidence, not even a witness to abduction. The police were therefore hesitant to pursue the theory that a serial killer was in their midst.

No more women disappeared until October 1997, when another White woman, Mary Giaccone, was reported missing. Her family admitted they had not seen her since February 1997, shortly after Kathleen Hurley had gone missing.

The profile of the missing women was complicated when in October 1997, another woman besides Mary Giaccone was reported missing. Michelle Eason, an African American woman also known to live on the streets and to have a history of drug problems, was reported missing by her pimp-boyfriend, who said he had not seen her since September.

Though the disappearance of Michelle Eason represented a racial anomaly in the victims' profile, police used investigative profiles of known offenders and similar crime patterns to conclude that they were looking for a White male, 30 to 35 years of age, who would live alone and possibly have a girlfriend or ex-wife. Based on the range of body types of the missing women, they predicted the culprit would "blend," have a medium build, be normal or average looking, and appear very "street smart" (high school dropout, perhaps menially employed). Their "unsub" (unknown subject) would most likely be a drug dealer, pimp, or other street character who regularly used drugs and alcohol, someone who would go unnoticed in the deviant circles in which these women traveled.

Despite the fact that he did not fit the profile that investigators had developed, in mid January 1998, the police interviewed Francois about the missing women. He admitted he had known some of them and had used them for sexual services in the past. Because he did not fit the investigative profile and there was nothing to link him to their disappearances, the police dismissed him as a suspect. A week later, he was arrested for assaulting and physically beating a prostitute. He was ordered to serve 14 days for the assault in May 1998, but only served one week. As part of his sentence, he was ordered to attend anger management workshops.

By the summer of 1998, it had been several months since any women had been reported missing, a welcome change from the previous pattern of nearly one disappearance a month. Then in June 1998, Sandra French, 52, was reported missing. Two months later, in August 1998, Catina Newmaster, a 25-year-old mother of five, was reported missing. Both women were White and had histories of drug addiction, but the divergence in their ages complicated the victim profile further. Other than the fact that seven of the eight missing women were White and all were drug addicts, there were no consistent similarities in their age or appearance. The police resumed their investigation, understanding that it was the vulnerability of these victims' lifestyle and drug addiction that made them most appealing to the culprit. Counting on the well-established fact that the vast majority of serial murder is intra-racial, they focused almost exclusively on White suspects.

In September 1998, Francois picked up a 21-year-old White girl on the streets who was suffering from drug withdrawal. Promising to take her to breakfast and help her get cleaned up, he instead took her to his house where he drove the car into the garage, lowered the door with the remote control, and proceeded to rape her. Strangling her during sex, he assumed he had killed her, but she eventually opened her eyes. Disoriented, but understanding that she needed to think quickly in order to survive, she convinced Francois that she was not upset about the attack and persuaded him to take her to breakfast. Along the way, she asked to stop at a gas station to buy cigarettes, and once inside the convenience store, the clerk noticed her distress and summoned police. Francois became alarmed when she did not come out of the store after several minutes, and he left the gas station and returned to his family home, which he still occupied with his parents and one sister.

Detectives who responded to the report of the assault on the young woman immediately went to Francois' home to interview him about the alleged crime. Once inside, they discovered the bodies of five missing women in his attic, and another three missing women in his basement.

What police had not anticipated was finding the body of Audrey Pugliese, a 34-year-old White woman who had not yet been reported missing by her family. Francois had killed her in early August 1998 in the basement of his home, just a week before killing his final victim, Catina Newmaster.

Though police had been looking for eight missing women, and indeed found the bodies of eight White women, one of them (Pugliese) was completely unanticipated. The one African American woman, Michelle Eason, whom police had assumed was also a victim of Francois, has never been found nor her body recovered. Her disappearance remains a mystery, with Francois insisting that he did not kill her and has no idea of her whereabouts.

The case of African American serial killer Kendall Francois is fascinating to criminologists because of the inter-racial nature of his killing. Other than being menially employed, Francois did not fit the police profile of the suspect, which was particularly errant with regard to race. The final analysis of his victims showed an unusual age range of 25 to 52, with a median age of 34, meaning Francois, at age 27 in 1998, was much younger than the profile would have suggested. With his giant stature (at more than 6 feet 4 inches tall and around 300 pounds), college education, cohabitation with his immediate family, and African American race, Francois was a most unlikely suspect in this case.

Many have hypothesized that Francois targeted prostitutes as a "mission-oriented" killer, trying to rid the world of immoral women or to seek revenge on the woman who might have given him the HIV virus. Some believe he targeted White women as a result of anger and retaliation against White society, symbolically killing members of the race that he blamed for his lack of success in life.

Interviews with Francois, however, reveal a far more simplistic explanation. Francois grew up in a White neighborhood, going to a mostly White school and surrounded by mostly White neighbors. He indicates that he simply wasn't raised to be race conscious, that White people were his peers and treated him as an equal, and that he never felt subjected to racism. Though he clearly was aware that he is a Black man, he was always most attracted to White women—perhaps due to his early sexual experience (at age 12) with a White babysitter and friend of his older sister, or simply because White females were the most common friends he had in his age and peer group growing up. When asked why he killed only White women, Francois said, "I didn't kill them because they were white, I sought them out for sex because I just prefer white women."

Francois most closely fits the profile of a power-control serial killer. Believing he was going to die early because of his HIV-positive status, he has reported that his need for relief from depression and dread, or a craving for any sort of "good feeling," became an obsession. Although the police profile suggested the killer would be involved in drugs and alcohol, there is no indication that Kendall ever used drugs. He insists that because of his weight and size (more than 300 pounds at the time of his arrest), "it would take so many beers to get someone as big as me drunk, that I'd rather spend the money on sex." He insists he never did drugs or alcohol because he viewed it as a waste of money, and he never felt anything from drinking. For Francois, the chronic need for sexual orgasm became his "drug," and eventually led to the death of at least eight innocent women.

Francois insists that the killings were never planned or anticipated. Many of the women he killed had been hired repeatedly for sexual services in the past, and hundreds of prostitutes that Francois frequented over the years were obviously never murdered by him. According to Francois, during a sex act the women he killed would start to complain or talk back to him, often refusing to provide the sexual services for which he believed he had hired them. Some would offer his money back, but Francois would become enraged by their refusal to do his bidding, and says that "the dark side" would envelop him as he forced them to have sex. When he surfaced from the fugue of anger and control, the woman he was with would be dead.

It is believed that all of Francois' victims were strangled except for Audrey Pugliese. It appears that Pugliese, who was beaten to death, fought ferociously with Francois for more than an hour when he attacked her during a sexual encounter in his basement.

In some cases, Francois dismembered bodies postmortem in order to better hide them (one he fit into a barrel in his garage until he could move it into his house), but the dismemberment was not part of his modus operandi nor sexually motivated. Perhaps the biggest mystery for criminologists is how his family could live in the same house in which the eight bodies were stored and *not know*. Some criminologists suggest that the pall of denial and level of extreme dysfunction that marked his family enabled Francois to kill and hide his victims in the house with the confidence that they would never be discovered. By secreting the bodies in his house, he was able to continue killing undetected for two years because police had absolutely no evidence that the missing women were murdered.

Kendall Francois was arrested and charged with eight counts of murder in September 1998. The victims' families were divided on whether the state of New York should pursue the death penalty, particularly because this would keep the case in the spotlight for many years and inevitably have long-lasting negative effects on the 14 children of his eight victims. Because of his HIV-positive status and pressure from the families for a quick sentencing, Francois was allowed to plead guilty to eight consecutive life sentences and was sentenced to life in prison in August 2000 (2 U.S. 46, 2000). He remains in Attica Correctional Facility in New York State.

Casey Jordan

See also: Inter-Racial Offending; Sex Crimes and Race

References

Associated Press. "Killer of 8 to Spend Life in Prison." *Times Union* (Albany, New York), August 8, 2000.

Associated Press. "Killer of Eight Women Gets Life Term; Man Had Confessed to 22-Month Spree." *The Record* (Northern New Jersey), August 8, 2000.

Beassimer, Jessica. *Poughkeepsie Beat.* News coverage from June 1997 through November 2000.

Courtroom Television Network. *Court TV's Crime Library,* 2003. http://www.trutv.com/library/crime/serial_killers/predators/francois/disappeared_1.html.

Jordan, Casey. Personal Interviews with Kendall Francois. Attica Correctional Facility, October 2000–December 2002.

Kendall Francois v. Thomas J. Dolan. 2 U.S. 46. Supreme Court of the State of New York. http://www.legalcases.docs.com/120/248/467.html.

Montero, D. "Remorse of a Serial Killer; Shocking Words: 'I Don't Feel Evil.'" *New York Post,* September 23, 2003.

G

Gangs

The definition of a gang is a debatable topic in the field of criminal justice. Nevertheless, Klein and Maxson define street gang as "any durable, street-oriented youth group whose involvement in illegal activity is part of its group identity" (2006: 4). Durability signifies a "group [that] continues despite turnover of members" (Klein & Maxson, 2006: 4). This characteristic is one of the few that differentiates street gang membership from organized crime syndicates. Organized crime groups mirror a structural organization that is more formal and lasts for longer periods compared to street gangs. There are street gangs that are durable, but they tend to dissipate quicker than organized crime groups. The characteristic of "street oriented" is inevitable because of a gang's territorial domain. Klein and Maxson argue that street orientation in street gangs implies "spending a lot of group time outside home, work and school—often on streets . . . parks . . . and so on" (2006: 4). Youth involvement is self-explanatory where it is proven that most street gangs consist of adolescents and young adults ranging from age 16 to 30 (Klein & Maxson, 2006). "Illegal activities" comprise any act that is delinquent or criminal, "not just bothersome" (Klein & Maxson, 2006: 4). The identity of the gang involves the group's identity and not individual self-image. These characteristics of street gangs are argued as sufficient elements to recognize such groups and to identify their difference from organized crime or other informal groups. Other characteristics of a gang may include having a name; controlling a specific territory; participating in criminal acts; having some form of leadership, whether formal or informal; and regular meetings among members.

Street gangs have a common identity. Identifiers include, but are not limited to, common race or ethnicity, members being of a similar age, and close territorial proximity. Gangs generally group together by specific races—White, Black, Asian, and Hispanic. A few multiracial or multiethnic gangs exist. However, society tends to focus its attention on the street gangs with members of a single race or ethnicity, particularly Black or Hispanic (Shelden et al., 2004). These gangs generally have identifiers that may reflect a hand sign, specific member colors, graffiti, tattoos, or trademark clothing. Much like the creation of White gangs, the creation of Black gangs has occurred primarily to protect members from opposing groups and racial and class violence (Anbinder, 2002; Sante, 1991). Today, gang membership provides access to desirable social commodities that residents of various communities might not otherwise be able to afford (Peralta, 2009).

Gang Formation

General strain theory represents one possible explanation for involvement in modern street gangs. Stressors or negative stimuli found within the environment may result in the pursuance of criminal activities to "make ends meet." Broidy and Agnew (1997) postulated that there are three main strains in society: the failure to achieve positively valued goals, the loss of positively valued stimuli, and the presentation of negative stimuli. The presence of these three stressors may lead an individual to make "unconventional" life decisions. These decisions may include leading a life of crime and connecting to a common bond of individuals who can relate to the stressors being faced. Some sources believe that many racial and ethnic minority males join gangs because society does not give them the same respect and standing as White males (Broidy & Agnew, 1997). The majority of Black gang members come from the inner city, where unemployment is prominent, and many communities are impoverished. Gang membership provides access to items like cash and material possessions that residents might not be able to obtain legitimately. It also provides a measure of protection in otherwise unpredictable and unsafe street environments. Being part of a gang gives people a sense of identity by allowing them to experience things like control, belonging, and unity that they have not experienced before. In prisons, gang membership has proved to be an effective means of avoiding serious violent victimization at the hands of other inmates or staff (Shelden et al., 2004; Decker & Van Winkle, 1996; Landre et al., 1997).

Overview and History

Though today the term "gang" conjures images of racial and ethnic minority males flashing hand signs and wearing specific colors, the original American street gangs were composed of European ethnics. According to one source, the history of street gangs in the United States began with their emergence on the East Coast around 1783, as the American Revolution ended (Sante, 1991). However, Howell and Moore argue that there was "considerable justification for questioning the seriousness of these early gangs" (2010: 1). They postulate that "the best available evidence suggests that the more serious street gangs likely did not emerge until the early part of the nineteenth century" (2010: 1; see also Sante, 1991). As depicted in the 2002 Martin Scorsese film *Gangs of New York,* gang emergence in places such as the Northeast and Midwest was fueled by immigration and poverty (Howell & Moore, 2010; Sante, 1991). The Five Points section of New York City was home to some of those original gangs, now mostly forgotten in favor of gang images with Black, brown, or Asian faces (Anbinder, 2002).

Researchers argue that, as a way to seek a better life, these early White immigrants "mainly settled in urban areas and formed communities to join each other in the economic struggle":

> Difficulties in finding work and a place to live and adjusting to urban life were equally common among the European immigrants. Anglo native-born Americans discriminated against these immigrants as well. Conflict was therefore imminent, and gangs grew in such environments. (Howell & Moore, 2010)

With the emergence of immigrant-based gangs to the varying regions of the country over a period of time, Howell and Moore posit that African Americans then migrated northward and westward from the Deep South. With increased migration and immigration, other gang mixtures including Hispanic/Latino (from Puerto Rico, Mexico, the Dominican Republic, Cuba); Asian (from Cambodia, China, the Philippines, Korea, Samoa, Thailand, Vietnam, and others); and Latin American (from Colombia, Cuba, the Dominican Republic, Ecuador, Panama, Puerto Rico, and other nations) later populated the gang landscape (Miller, 2001). Howell and Moore (2010) note that internal migration of Blacks motivated the emergence of another distinct wave of gang activity: "The end result was a mixture of predominantly white, Mexican, and black gangs—with varying degrees of influence—in each of the three early gang regions in the United States" (2).

With this historical background, many racial groups, including African Americans, settled into their own areas or communities where they held on to specific cultural values and behaviors. The street gangs that developed from these communities are usually of one race. According to the FBI's intelligence reports, currently "the most significant gangs operating in the East Region of the country are Crips, Latin Kings, MS-13, Ñeta, and United Blood Nation" (2008: 16). Membership in these groups tends to be exclusively of one racial or ethnic identity. Some Black gangs are open to letting other races into their membership, but given the prevalence of racially segregated residential communities in the United States, inter-racial mixing is not often an option.

Monster: The Autobiography of an L.A. Gang Member

Monster: The Autobiography of an L.A. Gang Member is a book 1993 about the life and times of Kody DeJohn "Monster" Scott, also known as Sanyika Shakur. One of six children, Scott grew up in South Central Los Angeles, where he became attracted to the gang life and addicted to drugs. At age 13, Kody and other members of his Crips gang attempted to rob a Black man (who resisted). Scott writes that he proudly earned the nickname "Monster" by beating their victim into a coma. As he approached 16, Monster was sent to Camp Munz in Lake Hughes, California, where he was held for nine months for grand theft auto and assault. The next year, he was shot in the face as a result of one of the many inter-gang feuds between Crips subsets. Scott was a member of the Eight Trays Crips set. The internal violence among Crips is said to have begun with a conflict between the Eight Trays Crips and the Rollin 60s Crips.

Scott's mother, Birdy, is criticized for having enabled his criminality because she did not try to move her children out of their violent surroundings or separate the others from their gang-involved sibling, Kody. Instead she dutifully visited him in prison and drove him to the hospital after being shot. Eventually, Kody's younger brother joined him in his violent lifestyle.

Scott spent three years incarcerated at San Quentin State Prison and five years at Pelican Bay, mostly in solitary confinement. During his time in prison he converted to Islam, renaming himself Sanyika Shakur. With the publication of *Monster* in 1993, Scott became a criminal celebrity. At that time, he no longer engaged in political activism or spoke of Black empowerment. Eventually he would return to Black activism, becoming a member of the Republic of New Afrika (see Gangs). Scott made the list of Los Angeles' most wanted gang members. In 2008, he was again sentenced to prison for assaulting a former acquaintance during an attempted carjacking. He was paroled in 2012.

Scott's first fictional work, *T.H.U.G. L.I.F.E,* was published in 2008. African American producer/director Antoine Fuqua has expressed interest in directing a movie about Scott's life. Although he is chronicled as having killed numerous rival gangsters, Kody Scott has never been tried for or convicted of murder.

Rhodine Moreau

Like their White counterparts, there is some indication that Black gangs in the United States date back to the 1700s in New York City. Many of these gangs were involved with crimes like robbery, assault, and violent conflicts with other neighborhood gangs. The Fly Boys and the Long Bridge Boys have been identified as the first of such African American gangs. In the 1970s, gangs started to pose more of a threat to the general public in various metropolitan areas by getting involved in drug sales and crimes related to supporting their drug enterprises. This led to them becoming more territorial and focused on earning money. Many Black gangs today identify as either Crips or Bloods or People Nation or Folk Nation. Black street gangs or "sets," meaning they affiliate with a larger gang organization such as Crips or Bloods, can be very small, with only a dozen or so members, as well as very large, with hundreds of members (Peralta, 2009; Miller, 2001).

Most of what is known about gang activity in the United States comes from the reports of law enforcement agencies, which may affect the accuracy of the information. According to these reports, African Americans and Hispanics make up the majority of gang members in the country, though other races continue to increase in gang membership as well. Black gangs tend to be part of an urban minority underclass, which means that people usually join young and stay involved with a gang into their adult life. Gang membership is reinforced by a lack of jobs and social resources. A 2011 FBI report estimates that there are 1.4 million gang members operating within 33,000 gangs across the country, an increase of 40 percent above 2009. The report also estimates that gangs are responsible for roughly 48 percent of violent crime in most jurisdictions and 90 percent of violent crime in several. Though they currently garner a significant amount of media coverage and law enforcement attention, African American gangs demonstrated a decrease in activity from 1965 to 1969 during the Vietnam War, the draft, the Civil Rights Movement, and the Black Awareness Movement (Miller, 2001; Landre et al., 1997; Leet et al., 2000).

African American Gangs

Crips and Bloods

The two major divisions of African American gangs today are the Crips and Bloods, with many sets that affiliate with one or the other. Law enforcement agencies estimate national membership in the Crips at 30,000 to 35,000, spread across more than 800 sets. Membership in the Bloods is estimated at 15,000 to 20,000. Subgroups of each of these street gangs are scattered across the country.

The Department of State Police in Virginia (2008) reported that the Bloods gang sets today are influenced by the organizations founded in Los Angeles, New York City, and Chicago. Initially, the Bloods originated on the West Coast, more specifically in Los Angeles; "however, their rise to power on the East has undoubtedly surpassed their presence on the West" (2008: 3).

> The Bloods are part of the People Nation, a street gang alliance that includes the Latin Kings, Vice Lord Nation, and the Black P-Stone Nation. Although the

Bloods may appear to be a large umbrella organization, each set has different rules, codes, alliances, and rivals. Therefore, what is true for one set may not be true for another. Understanding the gang set's culture and symbology may indicate a great deal about the group's structure, history, and operational scope. (Department of State Police, 2008: 4)

The Bloods reportedly emerged as a street gang in the early 1970s for protection against the larger more domineering gang, the Crips (Department of State Police, 2008). The Crips street gang is said to have formed following the dismantling of the Black Panther Party in the late 1960s and quickly grew in numbers by absorbing other local street gangs. The report suggests that several local gangs that refused to join the Crips or submit to their takeover formed what was called an "anti-Crip alliance." The alliance included the Piru Street Boys, the LA Brims, the Denver Lanes, the Inglewood Family, the Swans, and the Pueblo Bishops (Department of State Police, 2008). According to the report, "members of these anti-Crips alliance groups began calling each other 'Blood' leading to the united sets becoming known as the Bloods" (2008: 4). As time passed both gangs increased in numbers, with the Crips typically outnumbering the Bloods. The division between sets became very strong, leading to frequent and brutal fights between the two. Over time, the Bloods developed a reputation for being one of the most violent and ruthless street gangs. During the 1980s, the Bloods became heavily involved with the emerging crack cocaine market. Success in narcotics distribution fueled their expansion eastward.

The Crips and Bloods gangs started in California in the Watts, Willowbrook, and Compton sections of Los Angeles. Reportedly, original members were high school students who mainly robbed students and beat them up if anyone defied them. Former death row inmate Stanley "Tookie" Williams is largely credited with founding the Crips. In 2005 he was executed by the state of California for quadruple murder. Membership in both gangs is predominantly African American, but White and Asian members of the Crips have been reported in Maryland and Virginia. Typically members are males from their early teens to their mid-twenties. In more organized sets, members may hold leadership roles until their late twenties to early thirties, with a focus on protecting the business and drug territory of the set from rival gangs. As early as 1991, law enforcement agencies determined that Crips and Bloods sets were operating in 32 states and 69 cities, including Tucson, Las Vegas, Denver, and Des Moines (Landre et al., 1997).

In addition to drug distribution and violent rivalries with each other, the criminal activities of the Crips and Bloods have included well-organized bank and jewelry store robberies and other robberies, as well as car theft. Recently, law enforcement agencies have found multiple gangs involved with nontraditional gang-related crime such as prostitution, human trafficking, counterfeiting, identity theft, and even mortgage fraud. It is not known whether these two groups have

Books by Stanley Tookie Williams, Co-Founder of the Crips

Blue Rage, Black Redemption: A Memoir. Touchstone, 2007.

Gangs and Drugs (Williams, Stanley. Tookie Speaks Out against Gang Violence) by Stanley Williams, Barbara Cottman Becnel, 1997, (PB) ISBN 1-56838-135-2, 24 pages, Reading level: Ages 9–12.

Gangs and Self-Esteem: Tookie Speaks Out against Gang Violence (Tookie Speaks Out against Gang Violence) by Stanley Williams, Barbara Cottman Becnel, 1999, (PB) ISBN 0-613-02690-X, 24 pages, Reading level: Ages 4–8.

Gangs and the Abuse of Power (Williams, Stanley. Tookie Speaks Out against Gang Violence) by Stanley Williams, Barbara Cottman Becnel, 1997, ISBN 1-56838-130-1, 24 pages, Reading level: Ages 9–12.

Gangs and Violence (Williams, Stanley. Tookie Speaks Out against Gangs) by Stanley Williams, Barbara Cottman Becnel, 1997, (PB) ISBN 1-56838-134-4 (HB) ISBN 0-8239-2345-2, 24 pages, Reading level: Ages 4–8.

Gangs and Wanting to Belong (Williams, Stanley. Tookie Speaks Out against Gang Violence) by Stanley Williams, Barbara Cottman Becnel, 1997, (PB) ISBN 1-56838-131-X, 24 pages, Reading level: Ages 9–12.

Gangs and Weapons (Tookie Speaks Out against Gang Violence) by Stanley Tookie Williams, Barbara Cottman Becnel, 1997, (PB) ISBN 1-56838-132-8, 24 pages, Reading level: Ages 9–12.

Gangs and Your Friends (Williams, Stanley. Tookie Speaks Out against Gangs) by Stanley Williams, Barbara Cottman Becnel, 1997, (PB) ISBN 1-56838-136-0, 24 pages, Reading level: Ages 4–8.

Gangs and Your Neighborhood (Williams, Stanley. Tookie Speaks Out against Gang Violence) by Stanley Williams, Barbara Cottman Becnel, 1997, (PB) ISBN 1-56838-137-9, 24 pages, Reading level: Ages 4–8.

Life in Prison by Stanley Tookie Williams, Barbara Cottman Becnel, 1998, (PB) ISBN 1-58717-094-9, 80 pages, Reading level: Ages 4–8 (royalties donated to the Institute for the Prevention of Youth Violence).

Redemption: From Original Gangster to Nobel Prize Nominee; The Extraordinary Life Story of Stanley Tookie Williams. Maverick House, 2004, (HB) ISBN 1-903854-34-2.

ventured into these areas. Moving drug sales outside of Los Angeles proved to be significantly more profitable and may have led to involvement in international drug trafficking as well. As profits grew, the gangs' activities became more violent; increased revenue allowed them to purchase more advanced weaponry. Reports indicate that there is very little fighting between Blood gang sets, while Crip gang sets are often at war with each other (Landre et al., 1997).

Some examples of Crip sets in Los Angeles in the 1980s and 1990s include the Playboy Gangsters, Front Street, and 99 Mafia. Examples of Blood sets include Black P Stones, Be-Bop Watts, and Swans. Typically, Black gang members make a street name for themselves through certain physical traits or specific weapons. Specific types of clothing or colors may be worn, such as blue for Crips and red for Bloods, and what is becoming more common is the wearing of specific jewelry. For Crips it is the six-point star and the six-point crown. Hand signs are common and popular among the Crips and Bloods and other Black gangs (Landre et al., 1997). They are used as means of identification, getting attention, and issuing challenges. In 2009, filmmaker Stacy Peralta released a critically acclaimed documentary titled *Crips and Bloods: Made in America* that chronicled the story of these two notorious groups.

People Nation and Folk Nation

Although more racially diverse than the Crips and Bloods, the activities of the People Nation and Folk Nation are very similar to the activities of the Crips and Bloods. They are alliances of gangs formed within and outside of correctional institutions for protection. Black Gangster Disciples joined with the Simon City Royals as well as many others in the Chicago area to form the alliance known as Folk Nation. In opposition, the Vice Lords aligned with the Latin Kings to form the People Nation. People Nation members represent themselves with the left side of their body, meaning with hats to the left, left hand use for symbols, jewelry on the left, and so forth. Folk Nation members use the right side of their bodies. Examples of Folk Nation gangs include Black Disciples, Black Gangster Disciples, and Black P Stones. Examples of People Nation gangs include Blackstone Rangers, Vice Lords, and Cobra Stones (Landre et al., 1997).

Republic of New Africa (RNA)

The Republic of New Africa is a Black separatist group that was formed with the desire to take over the Southeastern United States, specifically the states of Louisiana, Mississippi, Alabama, Georgia, and South Carolina. In 2000, this was the area of the country where the highest percentage of Blacks was located. Since 1968, their intent has been to establish a Black nation separate from the United States. Started in Detroit in 1971, the organization then moved to Hinds County, Mississippi. Its efforts led the FBI to label the organization a seditious group, resulting in violent confrontations where many civilians and law enforcement officers were injured or killed (Leet et al., 2000).

Black Gangster Disciples (Birmingham, Alabama)

The Black Gangster Disciples is one of the primary street gangs of the South, and consists of mostly young males in their teens and twenties. This expanding gang has spread into various parts of Mississippi. It hopes to create a separate nation for the progress of African American Brotherhood. The gang has a king who is the most wealthy and feared of the gang, a prince who is second to the king and assists in the distribution of drugs and cash, and foot soldiers who report to the prince and are the salesmen in drug dealings. The drug dealing mainly involves crack cocaine and powder cocaine distribution networks. Ringleaders of the gang launder the money. There is no known connection between this gang of Black Gangster Disciples and the Chicago-based Black Gangster Disciples (Leet et al., 2000).

The Nation of Gods and Earths (5%ers)

Another well-known African American street gang is the Nation of Gods and Earths, otherwise known as the 5%ers. Not much formal scholarship has been written about this street gang. However, sources note that it was founded in Harlem in 1964 by Clarence Smith (Chandler, 2012). Smith, who would later be known as Clarence 13X, "Allah," or "the Father," is said to have created the group for the purpose of seeking justice, equality, and freedom from economic, political, social, educational, and religious injustice in the United States (Allah, 2007).

Smith's background included membership in the Nation of Islam (NOI), from which he was expelled by Minister Malcolm X Shabazz for what was reported as "ideological differences." It was also reported that Smith believed not only that he was God, but that the Black man is the original man of God. He coined the name "5%ers" under the assumption that the world's population comprises the 85 percent of those who follow a "mystery God" and "worship that which does not exist." He claimed that "this 85% have been subjugated by 10% of the population" (Chandler, 2012; Allah, 2007). This 10 percent, he believed, comprises political leaders, priests, and pastors. Smith argued that this 10 percent kept the 85 percent ignorant by teaching them to believe in a "mystery God." However, the remaining 5 percent are considered the "poor righteous teachers," whose role involves educating the "ignorant" 85 percent in order that they may stand against the domineering 10 percent.

The article reported that the Nation of Gods and Earths' teachings are mostly derived from those of Elijah Muhammad (see Nation of Islam). This group, though emerging from a religious background, does not claim to be religious in nature. It proclaims that "the blame should not fall on the organization for crimes or other anti-social activities committed by a few." Among the "poor righteous teachers"

Stanley "Tookie" Williams, III (1953–2005)

Stanley "Tookie" Williams was the co-founder of the Crips street gang in South Central Los Angeles. On December 13, 2005, two weeks before his fifty-second birthday, he was executed by lethal injection after spending 24 years on death row. He was the second person to be executed in California that year. Then Governor Arnold Schwarzenegger refused to commute his sentence to life imprisonment or to grant him clemency or a stay of execution, despite his claims of innocence, intense efforts by his defense attorneys, and strong public advocacy on his behalf.

The capital charges against Williams stemmed from an arrest in March 1979 for the February 28 murder of Albert Owens, a 7-Eleven store clerk, and the deaths of Tsai-Shai Chen Yang, Yen-I Yang, and Yu-Chin Yang at their family-owned Brookhaven Motel on South Vermont Street in Los Angeles. According to the charges, 26-year-old Owens was followed into the store by Williams and his friends, then shot to death. The sole eyewitness against Williams for the 7-Eleven murder was an alleged accomplice, Alfred "Blackie" Coward (currently imprisoned in Canada for manslaughter), who testified under a grant of immunity. Other witnesses claimed to have heard postcrime confessions from Williams about the motel murders. In 1981, even though there were no eyewitnesses to the Korean family's killings and only a single shell casing allegedly tying him to the hotel scene, Williams was convicted and sentenced to death for all four murders. In the clemency petition, Williams' attorneys raised the fact that all known Black jurors were excluded from sitting for the case. There was considerable disagreement as to whether the sole non-White juror was Black or Filipino (see Juries).

Stanley Tookie Williams III was born to a 17-year-old, single, teenaged mother in Louisiana on December 29, 1953. Hoping to improve her economic situation and to escape the South's pervasive racism, his mother left for California when Williams was five years old. Williams reported initially being surprised by the violence he experienced in South Central, but that he eventually became desensitized to it. He developed a reputation for fearlessly fighting tough gang members, until at age 17 he helped to co-found his own (with Raymond Lee Washington). Williams noted that the Crips were originally intended to unite the various existing gangs into one organization. Instead, it became like the independently operating cells of a terrorist group, with intra-gang rival factions attacking each other.

At one point prior to his conviction and incarceration, Williams worked as a youth counselor in a halfway house while simultaneously leading the Crips gang. He was also a student of sociology at Compton College. While inside San Quentin State Prison, Williams refused to help the police investigate the gang, even after being stabbed by a member of the Rollin 60s set of the Crips in

October 1989. After spending nearly six and a half years in solitary confinement for prison violence, Williams made a decision to change. He expressed regret for having co-founded the Crips and was instrumental in brokering gang truces. He authored autobiographies and seven children's books (all published in 1997) aimed at deterring youngsters from joining gangs. His efforts resulted in Nobel Peace Prize nominations, though some questioned whether his antigang efforts were sincere or merely aimed at avoiding the death penalty.

In 1998 and again in 2002, although they expressed doubt about the veracity of the witness accounts, the courts upheld his conviction. His famous supporters included Jamie Foxx, who played Williams in the televised 2004 movie *Redemption: The Stan Tookie Williams Story*; ex-Crip gang member and rapper Snoop Dogg; civil rights activist Jesse Jackson; and acclaimed actor Danny Glover. On December 12, 2005, Williams' final request for clemency was denied by well-known actor and then California state governor Arnold Schwarzenegger. After his execution, Williams was cremated and his ashes were scattered in South Africa. He is survived by his mother, sister, and two sons, Travon and Stanley "Little Tookie" Williams IV, a Neighborhood Crip, found guilty of shooting a 20-year-old woman to death in a Hollywood alley. As a consequence, Stanley Williams IV was sentenced to 16 years in prison for second-degree murder.

Rhodine Moreau

are many incarcerated members who are considered "threats . . . to the security of correctional institutions, their staff and other prisoners" (Chandler, 2012; Allah, 2007). In the late 1990s, the U.S. District Court ruled that the Nation of Gods and Earths (5%ers) should in fact be considered a threat, noting that "though the Nation of Gods and Earths do not claim to be a gang, members in prison identify themselves as such." In 2003, the courts recognized the religious rights of prison inmates who are members of this group.

Daniel Scott and Cherise Bruce with Delores Jones-Brown

See also: Black Panther Party; Inequality Theory; Institutional Racism; Malcolm X (aka El-Hajj Malik El-Shabazz); Nation of Islam; Organized Crime; Theories of Race and Crime; *When Work Disappears: The World of the New Urban Poor*

References

Allah, W. *In the Name of Allah: A History of Clarence 13X and the Five Percenters.* Atlanta, GA: A-Team Publishers.

Anbinder, T. *Five Points: The 19th-Century New York City Neighborhood That Invented Tap Dance, Stole Elections, and Became the World's Most Notorious Slum.* New York: Penguin, 2002.

Biography.com. "Kody DeJohn Scott." A&E Television Network, December 28, 2011. http://www.Biography.com/people/kody-scott-531202.

Broidy, L., and R. Agnew. "Gender and Crime: A General Strain Theory Perspective." *Journal of Research in Crime and Delinquency* 34 (1997): 275–306.

Chandler, D. L. "The Meaning of the 5%: A Look at the Nation of Gods and Earths." *Hip-Hop Wired,* June 28, 2012. http://hiphopwired.com/2012/06/28/the-meaning-of -the-5-a-look-at-the-nation-of-gods-and-earths/3/.

Decker, S., and B. Van Winkle. *Life in the Gangs: Family, Friends and Violence.* Cambridge, UK: Cambridge University Press, 1996.

Del Barco, Mandalit. "Gang Member Turned Author Arrested in L.A." NPR, March 9, 2007. http://www.npr.org/templates/story/story.php?storyId=7793148.

Department of State Police, Commonwealth of Virginia. *Bloods Street Gang Intelligence Report.* Virginia Fusion Center, November 2008.

District Attorney's Office of Los Angeles. http://da.lacounty.gov/mr/archive/2008/050508b .htm?zoom_highlight=SANYIKA+SHAKUR.

Egelko, Bob. "A Question of Evidence: Stanley Tookie Williams' Best Hope for Clemency May Depend More on Raising Doubt about His Guilt Than on His Redemption." *San Francisco Chronicle,* December 7, 2005. http://sfgate.com/cgi-bin/article.cgi?file=/ c/a/2005/12/07/MNG60G468I1.DTL.

Federal Bureau of Investigation (FBI). *National Gang Threat Assessment: 2011.* National Press Releases. Washington, DC: U.S. Department of Justice, Federal Bureau of Investigation, 2011.

Federal Bureau of Investigation (FBI). *National Gang Threat Assessment: 2009.* Washington, DC: U.S. Department of Justice, Federal Bureau of Investigation, 2008.

Hawkins, Shirley. "Kody 'Monster' Scott Receives Six Years in State Prison." *Our Weekly* (Los Angeles), April 30, 2008. http://ourweekly.com/los-angeles/kody-monster -scott-receives-six-years-state-prison.

Howell, J. D., and J. P. Moore. *History of Street Gangs in the United States.* National Gang Center Bulletin No. 4. Tallahassee, FL: Institute for Intergovernmental Research, National Gang Center, 2010.

Klein, M. W., and C. L. Maxson. *Street Gang Patterns and Policies.* New York: Oxford University Press, 2006.

Landre, R., M. Miller, and D. Porter. *Gangs: A Handbook for Community Awareness.* New York: Facts on File, Inc., 1997.

Leet, D., F. Rush, and A. Smith. *Gangs, Graffiti and Violence: A Realistic Guide to the Scope and Nature of Gangs in America.* Incline Village, NV: Copperhouse Publishing Company, 2000.

"Local Capture of Top-10 Gangster." http://www.streetgangs.com/topics/2007/030807 kodyscott.html.

"Los Angeles County District Attorney's Response to Stanley Williams' Petition for Executive Clemency." November 16, 2005. http://da.co.la.ca.us/pdf/swilliams.pdf.

Los Angeles Times. "Throwing the Book at "Monster."" February 15, 2007. http://articles.latimes.com/2007/feb/15/local/me-monster15.

Miller, W. B. *The Growth of Youth Gang Problems in the United States: 1970–1998.* Washington, DC: Office of Juvenile Justice and Delinquency Prevention, 2001.

North County Times–The Californian. "Kody 'Monster' Scott Arrested after Another Run-In with Police." July 18, 2004. http://www.nctimes.com/news/state-and-regional/article_27459670-b064-5c89-9935-32cbdc6c805b.html.

The People, Plaintiff and Respondent, v. STANLEY WILLIAMS, Defendant and Appellant. In re STANLEY WILLIAMS on Habeas Corpus. http://www.streetgangs.com/magazine/tookie1127_88.html.

People v. Williams (Cal Sup Ct Apr., 11, 1988). http://online.ceb.com/calcases/C3/44C3d1127.htm.

Peralta, Stacy, director. *Crips and Bloods: Made in America.* The Gang Documentary, Balance Vector Productions, and Verso Entertainment, 2009.

Sante, L. *Low Life: Lures and Snares of Old of New York.* New York: Vintage Books, 1991.

Schwarzenegger, Arnold. "Statement of Decision: Request for Clemency by Stanley Williams." December 12, 2005: 1. http://graphics8.nytimes.com/packages/pdf/national/Williams_Clemency_Decision.pdf.

Scorsese, Martin, director. *Gangs of New York.* Miramax Film Corp., 2002.

Shakur, Sanyika (aka Kody DeJohn Scott). *Monster: Autobiography of an L.A. Gang Member.* New York: Grove Press, 1993.

Shelden, R., S. Tracy, and W. Brown. *Youth Gangs in American Society.* Belmont, CA: Thompson Wadsworth, 2004.

Smith, Andrew. "Shakur, Sanyika." African American National Biography, edited by Henry Louis Gates, Jr., and Evelyn Brooks-Higginbotham. Oxford African American Studies Center, http://www2.oxfordaasc.com/article/print/opr/t0001/e3696?image_size=inline.

"Wanted Gang Member-Turned-Writer Arrested in Los Angeles." KABC-TV/DT, Thursday, March 8, 2007. http://ABClocal.go.com/kabc/story?section=news/local&id=5104067.

Gates, Jr., Henry Louis (1950–)

Henry Louis Gates, Jr., was born on September 16, 1950, in Keyser, West Virginia. Born into a humble, hardworking family, both of Gates' parents worked to support him and his brother. In addition to working, Gates' mother, Pauline, was involved in her children's education, and was the first Black PTA member in their community.

After graduating from Piedmont High School in 1968, Henry Louis Gates, Jr., went on to attend Potomac State College in his hometown before transferring to

Harvard University professor Henry Louis Gates, Jr., whose arrest on the porch of his Cambridge home on July 16, 2009, sparked a renewed debate about racial profiling by police in the United States. (Associated Press)

Yale University, where he graduated summa cum laude with a degree in history. For his academic achievements at Yale, Gates was rewarded with a fellowship to study at Clare College of Cambridge University in England. It was there that he met the Nigerian playwright and Nobel laureate Wole Soyinka, who helped spark his interest in African American studies.

After studying English literature at Clare College, Gates studied law at Yale Law School before withdrawing one month into the program. He began his academic career as a secretary in the Afro-American Studies Department at Yale, and went on to serve as a lecturer before completing his doctorate in English language and literature in 1979. After completing his PhD, Gates was hired by Yale as an assistant professor, and taught in both the English and Afro-American Studies departments. He has served as a faculty member at other universities, including Cornell University, Duke University, and Harvard University, where he currently serves as the Alphonse Fletcher University Professor and Director of the W. E. B. Du Bois Institute for African and African American Research. Additionally, Professor Gates is editor-in-chief of the Oxford African American Studies Center, an online resource that describes itself as "the online authority on the African American experience."

Already a prominent figure in academia, Henry Louis Gates, Jr., became a household name following an incident that led to his arrest outside of his home in Cambridge, Massachusetts. On July 16, 2009, following a lead from a woman who reported seeing two African American males on Gates' porch who appeared to be forcing their way into the house, Cambridge Police Sgt. Joseph Crowley arrested Henry Louis Gates, Jr. The arrest report stated that Gates was arrested for disorderly conduct after "exhibiting loud and tumultuous behavior." Gates maintains that he was arrested because of his race.

The incident led to criticism of the police from African American faculty and students at Harvard. Before the police dropped the charge against Gates, he retained Charles Ogletree as his attorney, a famous Harvard Law School professor who has worked on prior cases with racial implications. The publicity of the case ignited a firestorm of racial tension and rekindled the racial profiling debate. President Barack Obama stated that Sgt. Crowley "acted stupidly" in arresting Gates, which drew ire from members of the policing community nationwide. In hopes of calming the situation, President Obama called for a Beer Summit to bring the two men together. On July 30, 2009, Gates and Crowley sat down with President Obama and spoke about the incident face to face. Following the summit, the two men "agreed to disagree" on the issue and pledged to have future talks to foster awareness of the dangers police officers face, as well as the concerns some African Americans have about racial profiling. On June 30, 2010, an independent panel published a report stating "Sergeant Crowley and Professor Gates each missed opportunities to 'ratchet down' the situation and end it peacefully," suggesting that both men shared responsibility in the incident. A few months after the Beer Summit, Gates and Crowley met on their own at a pub in Cambridge, where they continued to work on resolving their differences. Sgt. Crowley gave Gates the handcuffs he used to arrest him as a souvenir of sorts, and Gates donated them to the National Museum of African American History and Culture at the Smithsonian.

Beau Shine

See also: Du Bois, W. E. B.; Police Brutality; Racial Profiling

References

Associated Press. "Cop, Scholar to Meet Again after Obama Chat," July 31, 2009. http://www.msnbc.msn.com/id/32210408/ns/politics-white_house/.

Gates, Jr., H. "Personal Bio." Program in the History of American Civilization, Harvard University, 2011. http://www.fas.harvard.edu/~amciv/faculty/gates.shtml.

Jan, T. (2009). "Harvard Professor Gates Arrested at Cambridge Home." *Boston Globe,* July 20, 2009. http://www.boston.com/news/local/breaking_news/2009/07/harvard.html.

Kellogg, C. (2009). "Henry Louis Gates, Jr. Arrested. Seriously, Cambridge?" *Los Angeles Times,* July 21, 2009. http://latimesblogs.latimes.com/jacketcopy/2009/07/henry-louis-gates-jr-arrested-seriously-cambridge.html.

Oxford African American Studies Center. http://www.oxfordaasc.com/public/index.jsp?url=%2F&failReason=.

Solomon, D. "After the Beer Summit." *New York Times Magazine,* February 14, 2010. http://www.nytimes.com/2010/02/14/magazine/14fob-q4-t.html.

Grant, Oscar (1986–2009)

New Year's celebrants in Oakland, California, watched as a 22-year-old unarmed train passenger, Oscar Julius Grant III, was shot in the back by German-born Bay Area Rapid Transit (BART) police officer Johannes Sebastian Mehserle with a .40-caliber bullet from his SIG Sauer P226 semi-automatic handgun in the early morning hours of January 1, 2009. Many who have viewed the YouTube video recorded on the cell phone of another passenger on the train platform described the shooting as an execution. Officer Mehserle, who fled the jurisdiction when he was first accused of a crime for the shooting, claiming fear for his life, said he thought he was reaching for his Taser when he shot Grant, who was lying face down on the platform at the time. Grant died at Highland Hospital in Oakland seven hours later.

Oscar Grant was shot by former San Francisco Bay Area Rapid Transit police officer Johannes Mehserle on New Year's Day 2009. Mehserle was tried for manslaughter and testified at trial that he mistakenly pulled out his pistol instead of a stun gun. The incident is depicted in the critically acclaimed film *Fruitvale Station*. (Associated Press)

The very public shooting of Grant and the initial failure to arrest Mehserle brought protesters to the streets of Oakland, some violent, some less so. The shooting of Oscar Grant occurred just two hours into 2009. The BART police had been summoned to the Fruitvale Rapid Transit Station on reports that a fight had broken out on one of the trains. Many digital video and cell phone cameras recorded the incidents leading up to the shooting. One video begins with Mehserle and other officers talking to Grant while he and another passenger are sitting against a wall on the platform. Many passengers can be seen and heard on the platform when Grant is directed to lie face down. Though Grant complies, some media coverage describes him as "resisting." Mehserle bends over Grant and fires a single round into his back. The shooting is so loud and sudden that it quiets the crowd into stunned silence. Though former officer Mehserle claims that he thought he was reaching for his Taser, there are questions as to whether the use of even a Taser was warranted at the time.

Under mounting pressure from local protests and the mounting number of viewings the video received on the Internet, prosecutors charged Mehserle with murder. A jury returned an involuntary manslaughter conviction and a judge sentenced Mehserle to two years in prison. Family and community members protested the leniency of the sentence, but Mehserle went on to serve the time in the county jail isolated from the other inmates. With time served and good time credits he was released after 11 months. Again protesters registered their disapproval. Although Mehserle resigned from the police department, his legal troubles were not over. Upon his release, he was again on trial for using excessive force in a beating incident that predated the Grant shooting. In that situation, Mehserle and other members of the force are accused of having beaten and restrained a 43-year-old Black man when he said the police were "useless" to assist him with a situation in which his car had been vandalized. It is alleged that Mehserle knocked the civilian to the ground, then punched and kicked him while he was on the pavement. With the assistance of other cops, he is alleged to have tied the victim's arms and legs while stating, "Well, have you learned not to mess with police officers?" The victim in that case is Kenneth Carrethers. He says he was attacked by the police, including Mehserle, on November 15, 2008, six weeks prior to the Grant shooting.

Grant's family retained Oakland civil rights attorney John Anthony Burris to file a $25 million wrongful death claim against BART. A settlement valued at $5.1 million dollars was reached on behalf of his 5-year-old daughter. A film titled *Fruitvale Station* depicting events during the last day of Oscar Grant's life, directed by Ryan Coogler, was released to theaters on July 12, 2013. The film received the Grand Jury Prize for dramatic feature and the Audience Award for U.S. dramatic film at the 2013 Sundance Film Festival.

Rhodine Moreau with Delores Jones-Brown

See also: Bell, Sean; Diallo, Amadou; Jones, Jr., Prince Carmen; Lee, Anthony Dwain/Dwayne; Racial Profiling; Young, Jr., Cornel

References

"Attorneys Spar over Whether Grant Was Resisting Arrest." KTVU, May 20, 2009.
"BART Police Officer Who Fatally Shot Man Resigns." *San Jose Mercury News,* 2009.
"BART Shooting: Family Suing BART for $25 Million." KTVU, 2009.
Bender, Kristin. "BART Police Badly Botched Call That Led to Oscar Grant Killing, Report Finds." *San Jose Mercury News,* August 18, 2009.

Bulwa, Demian. "Johannes Mehserle, Ex-BART Officer, Leaves Jail." *San Francisco Chronicle,* July 13, 2011.

Bulwa, Demian. "BART Appeals for Calm as Footage Shows Shooting." *San Francisco Chronicle,* January 9, 2011.

Bulwa, Demian. "Johannes Mehserle Sentenced to 2-Year Minimum Term." *San Francisco Chronicle,* January 7, 2011.

Bulwa, Demian. "Mehserle Convicted of Involuntary Manslaughter." *San Francisco Chronicle,* July 8, 2010.

Bulwa, Demian. "BART Pays $1.5 Million to Aid Grant's Daughter." *San Francisco Chronicle,* January 28, 2010.

Bulwa, Demian. "BART Hit with More Claims from New Year's Chaos." *San Francisco Chronicle,* February 5, 2009.

Bulwa, Damien, Wyatt Buchanan, and Matthew Yi. "Behind Murder Charge against Ex-BART Officer." *San Francisco Chronicle,* January 9, 2011.

Bulwa, Demian, and Henry K. Lee. "BART Shooting Victim's Family Decries Violence." *San Francisco Chronicle,* January 9, 2009.

Bulwa, Demian, and Henry K. Lee. "BART Shooting Victim's Family Files Claim." *San Francisco Chronicle,* January 7, 2009.

Collins, Terry. "Ex-Cop Charged with Murder in Calif. Shooting." Associated Press, January 14, 2009.

"Conflicting Stories Surround Fruitvale BART Shooting." KTVU, 2009.

"Court Releases Dramatic Video of BART Shooting." YouTube, June 24, 2010.

"D.A.: Facts in BART Shooting Case Justify Murder Charges against Former Officer." KRON 4, 2009.

"Defense Use of Force Expert Falters during Cross Examination." *California Beat,* June 28, 2010. Californiabeat.org.

Drummond, Tammerlin. "Absence of Blacks on Mehserle Jury No Guarantee of Acquittal for Former BART Officer." *Contra Costa Times,* June 13, 2010.

Egelko, Bob. "BART Shooting Draws Rodney King Case Parallels." *San Francisco Chronicle,* January 15, 2009.

"Family of Man Shot in Back by Police Sue for $25m." *The (London) Daily Telegraph,* January 7, 2009.

"Former BART Officer Johannes Mehserle Will Be Tried for Murder." KRON-4, June 4, 2009.

Fulbright, Leslie. "Many See Race as Central to BART Killing." *San Francisco Chronicle,* January 11, 2009.

Harvey, Mike. "YouTube Video Fuels U.S. Riots over Killing of Oscar Grant." *The (London) Times,* January 9, 2009.

Hill, Angela, Harry Harris, and Kelly Rayburn. "Grant's Family Pleads for Peace." *San Jose Mercury News,* January 8, 2009.

Kiss, Jemima. "Fatal Police Shooting Posted on YouTube." *The (London) Guardian,* January 9, 2009.

Lee, Henry K. "83 Arrests in Oakland Follow Mehserle Verdict." *San Francisco Chronicle,* July 9, 2010.

Matier, Phillip, and Andrew Ross. "M&R: Death Threats against BART Officer." *San Francisco Chronicle,* January 7, 2009.

McKinley, Jesse. "In California, Protests after Man Dies at Hands of Transit Police." *The New York Times,* January 9, 2009.

McKinley, Jesse. "Oakland Turns Violent over Shooting." *The New York Times,* January 9, 2009.

McLaughlin, Eliott C., Augie Martin, and Dan Simon. "Spokesman: Officer in Subway Shooting Has Resigned." *CNN.com,* January 7, 2009.

McLaughlin, Eliott C., Augie Martin, and Randi Kaye. "Video of California Police Shooting Spurs Investigation." *CNN,* January 7, 2009.

"Mehserle Jury Selected; Grant Family Angry with Makeup." KTVU, June 8, 2010.

"Mehserle Verdict Protest Turns Ugly; 78 People Arrested." KTVU.com, July 9, 2010.

Mills, Elinor. "Web Videos of Oakland Shooting Fuel Emotions, Protests." CNET Networks, 2009.

"Officer in Fatal Shooting Resigns from BART Police." KTVU, 2009.

"Oscar Grant's Killer on Trial Again for Police Brutality." RT-USA, November 23, 2011.

People v. Mehserle. A130654 (June 8, 2012).

"Police Crack Down after Train Shooting Protests, Businesses Smashed, Cars Set Blaze in Oakland after Transit Cop Killed Man." Associated Press, January 8, 2009.

Rosynsky, Paul. "Videos Spur Emotion in First Day of Hearing for BART Killing." *Bay Area News Group,* May 19, 2009.

Rosynsky, Paul T., and Chris Metinko. "Mehserle Guilty of Involuntary Manslaughter." *Oakland Tribune,* July 8, 2010.

Smith, Dave. "BART Shooting Raises Issue of TASER Confusion." *PoliceOne.com,* January 6, 2009.

"$25 Million Claim by Family of Man Killed by BART Police." *San Jose Mercury News,* January 6, 2009.

Woodall, Angela. "Police Prevent Repeat of Earlier Rioting." *Oakland Tribune,* January 31, 2009.

Habitual Offender Laws

Also called "Three Strikes laws" and "repeat offender laws," habitual offender laws require stricter punishments for individuals with prior criminal histories. These recidivist statutes mandate that enhanced sentencing measures be imposed on career criminals. New York passed habitual offender statutes as early as 1797. Alabama passed the Habitual Felony Offender Act in 1980 (Mentor, 2002).

These laws work on deterrence theory, which argues that offenders will not commit crimes that carry heavy costs or punishments. The way to decrease or eliminate crime is to increase the severity of the punishment so that any rewards obtained by the criminal are outweighed by the punishments. Three Strikes laws often require that criminals with two prior felony offenses be convicted for a mandatory sentence of 25 years to life. Offenses that are typically considered "strikes" are murder, robbery with a weapon, rape and other sex offenses, burglary, and assault. However, each state defines which offenses are considered strikes (Benavides, 2002; Mentor, 2002).

The most widely publicized discussion of habitual offender laws and Three Strikes laws came in March of 1994 when California implemented strict sentencing guidelines on repeat offenders. Outrage over the vicious murder of Polly Klass, age 12, by a man with an established violent criminal record sparked renewed calls for harsher penalties for violent offenders (RAND, 2005).

California laws require that any criminal who has two prior serious felony convictions, or strikes, be sentenced to a minimum of 25 years to life for a third felony. Other consequences, such as doubled bail amounts and sentence lengths for second felony offenses, and the removal of options for nonincarcerative sentences (such as probation and parole) have been enacted as well (RAND, 2005; Legislative Analyst's Office, 1995). About half of the states now have similar laws, and Congress has ratified national legislation regarding repeat offenders (Benavides, 2002).

Supporters for habitual offender laws, such as the Three Strikes laws, cite a decrease in crime rates as indications of the effectiveness of the statutes. However, crime rates were decreasing before their implementation. Proponents also cite the need to put away career criminals in order to make society safer, and that the "tough on crime" stance will help deter offenders from committing more crime. Supporters also cite the legality of such statutes as states having the right to strengthen their crime control efforts (Mentor, 2002).

Opponents to Three Strikes and other habitual offender laws cite numerous reasons why the laws should be reformulated. One such reason is the consideration of the policy as reasonably achieving the intended goal of crime reduction at reasonable cost to society. The financial burden on government budgets related to the increased numbers of individuals being sentenced to prison, and for longer periods, is heavy. There are added costs associated with building new prisons and jails, staffing these facilities, and housing and caring for the inmates. Additionally, the serious implications involved with accruing strikes has pressured many defendants to demand a trial instead of taking a plea bargain, resulting in dramatically larger numbers of individuals in jails awaiting trial (Legislative Analyst's Office, 1995).

Critics of habitual offender laws also point out the laws are not working as intended. Criminological theorists cite research that stricter penalties do not always serve as a deterrent, as offenders do not always make fully rational choices. There are instances where an individual earns his or her third strike for minor or nonviolent offenses and is sentenced to life (see Three Strikes Legislation), when the law was intended to reduce violent and serious crime (Mentor, 2002; Benavides, 2002).

Additionally, the laws and policies aimed at habitual offenders disproportionally impact Blacks and other non-Whites. Statistics have long shown that young Black males are more likely to be arrested, sentenced, and incarcerated than Whites. These statistics are mirrored in data on "third strikers," who are more likely to be a minority and poor. The racial differences in third-strike inmates cannot be fully, or even predominantly, accounted for by differences in the commission of crime, past criminal history, and other legal factors. As a result, there are disparities in sentencing and incarceration by race that extralegal factors, such as race/ethnicity and social class, have long been argued as explaining (Benavides, 2002). Further, the more limited resources that Blacks and other minorities have, the more difficulty they face in posting bail—bail amounts for repeat offenders are often double that of first-time offenders. These same offenders may have financial difficulty securing private legal representation and thereby be less likely to secure pretrial release.

While the underlying aim of these policies has been to reduce serious and violent crime, the effectiveness and cost of habitual offender laws has been called into question. Scholars call for revisions to the existing laws to narrow the scope of offenses considered strikes, as many states apply the law widely (see Three Strikes Legislation). There is also a demand for treatment and other forms of help for non-violent offenders. For example, many argue that drug offenders would be better served with a substance abuse treatment program, which can assist individuals in dealing with addiction, rather than punitive nonrehabilitative incarceration, which often leads to recidivism. But some opponents also argue for stiffer penalties for first and second offenses and not waiting for the third offense to mandate lengthy prison sentences.

Contrary to supporters of habitual offender laws, which cite the effectiveness of these statutes, there is a very high social and financial cost to these policies. Inmates who are confined longer must be cared for long term by the state or federal government. This care is costly. Upon release they are less likely to be employable, which may lead to costly new crimes or the need for public welfare. Consequently, habitual offender laws are being reconsidered and revised in an attempt to make them demonstratively more effective at reducing crime and less costly to society.

Valerie Stackman

See also: Alternative Sentencing; Community-Based Crime and Reentry Theory; Prisoner Reentry and African Americans; Three Strikes Legislation

References

Benavides, Amy J. "Three Strikes and You're Out." In *Encyclopedia of Crime and Punishment,* edited by David Levinson. Thousand Oaks, CA: Sage Publications, 2002.

Legislative Analyst's Office. "The Three Strikes and You're Out Law," 1995. http://wwwlao.ca.gov/analysis_1995/3strikes.html.

Mentor, Keith. "Habitual Offender Laws: Three Strikes and You're Out." In *Encyclopedia of Crime and Punishment,* edited by David Levinson. Thousand Oaks, CA: Sage Publications, 2002.

RAND Corporation. "California's New Three Strikes Law: Benefits, Costs, and Alternatives." Research Brief, 2005. http://www.rand.org/pubs/research_briefs/RB4009/index1.html.

Hate Crimes

The definition of hate crime varies from state to state, but generally includes the notion that it is a criminal act that is motivated by hatred, bias, or prejudice, based on the actual or perceived race, color, religion, national origin, ethnicity, gender, or sexual orientation of the victim. Hate crime statutes typically increase the penalty for such acts above that normally prescribed for similar criminal behavior that is not motivated by hate, and may include longer terms of incarceration for defendants who are convicted of such crimes more than once (Tolnay et al., 2001).

According to the American Psychological Association, people generally commit hate crimes for two distinct reasons (Lyons, 2008). The first is that they fear anyone who appears or seems different from them. The most obvious manifestation of this is skin color or facial features, which explains hate crimes based on race. The second reason that people may commit these crimes is that they wish to find a scapegoat for their troubles, and it is easier to blame someone other than oneself. Though the United States has a reputation for racial tolerance, particularly in comparison to some other countries, its history is filled with private and government-sanctioned prejudice against and between various racial and ethnic groups. For African Americans, these prejudices are largely traceable back to its roots in African slavery.

The formal collection of hate crimes statistics is fairly new and the designation of some behaviors as criminal offenses with more severe punishments than others is often thought of as raising some serious questions about defendants' First Amendment rights. The fact that constitutional mandates require that all victims and perpetrators of hate crimes be treated the same has raised the question of whether those who have historically been the victims of hate crimes, for example African Americans, actually suffer greater harm than others when prosecuted for offenses that long went unaddressed when perpetrated against them (see Black Panther Party, Civil Rights Movement, Lynching, and Nation of Islam).

Contemporary federal criminal hate crimes law has its origins in civil rights legislation. The 1964 Federal Civil Rights Law allows for federal prosecution of an individual who "willingly injures, intimidates or interferes with another person by force due to a person's race, color, religion or national origin." The 1969 Federal Hate Crimes Law indicates that an individual who commits a hate crime faces a fine or imprisonment of up to one year at the least. The Violent Crime Control and Law Enforcement Act of 1994 increased the penalties for individuals committing hate crimes. And in 2009, recognition of two horrendous hate-motivated killings, the dragging death of African American James Byrd and the torture of a gay White teen, Matthew Shepard, led to federal legislation that expanded the potential punishment for hate crime to include the death penalty.

A formal record of official data, or data gathered and reported by the government, was made possible by the Hate Crime Statistics Act of 1990. This act tasked the U.S. attorney general with collecting statistics on the number of hate crimes committed in the country annually. The data were collected by the FBI and reported to the public in the Uniformed Crime Reports (UCR). This, along with the National Incident-Based Reporting System (NIBRS), which collects an array of information on both hate crime victims and offenders, allows law enforcement and the nation at large to gauge the prevalence and patterns of hate crimes in the country (see Chilton & Jarvis, 1999).

In 1993, the FBI released the hate crime statistics for 1991, the first year that these statistics were compiled. Not all states and law enforcement agencies were required to provide data, and in fact only 32 states complied. Seventy-three percent of agencies reported that no hate crimes had been committed in their districts. These reports were treated with great skepticism and led to complaints that the law was not being taken seriously. Over the years, the percentage of agencies participating in gathering and reporting hate crime statistics has grown, as has the number of hate crimes reported. The number of reported hate crimes increased from 1991 through 1996, at which point they stabilized. It is speculated that the initial increases were more due to increased agency reporting rather than spikes in the occurrence of hate crime. And it has been difficult to measure if the reduction in reported incidents is as the result of increased criminal sanctions or not (Torres, 1999).

In 2009, there were 6,604 hate crimes reported by 2,034 law enforcement agencies. Of those, 48.5 percent were reported as motivated by racial bias, with the next closest reason, religious bias, reported for 19.7 percent of the crimes. The vast majority of hate crimes motivated by race, 71.4 percent of them, were crimes committed against African Americans, with the next closest amount, 17.1 percent, being reported as having been committed against Whites. Vandalism accounted for 31.6 percent of all hate crimes and 33 percent involved assaults. These percentages represent a slight decrease from 2008, during which 72.6 percent of racially motivated crimes were committed against African Americans. The overall number of reported hate crimes in 2008 was 7,780, from which 2009 figures represent a substantial decrease overall (FBI, 2009).

There is a debate over whether hate crime statutes actually help curb the problem, are useless, or even work to make racial tensions worse. Supporters of hate crime legislation believe that creating these laws helps shed light on a significant social problem and deters others from committing hate crimes via the enhanced punishments. From another perspective, it is argued that, at the very least, hate crime statutes serve an important symbolic purpose—sending the message that racial and other forms of intolerance or hate will not be accepted or condoned.

The opposition to hate crime laws comes from a variety of perspectives. The most prominent thought is that hate crime statutes infringe on an American's First Amendment right to free speech and concerns that criminalizing hateful language may actually contribute to more hate crime rather than diminish it among those

16th Street Baptist Church Bombing

On the morning of September 15, 1963, 22 parishioners were injured and four Black girls died when a bomb exploded at the 16th Street Baptist Church in Birmingham, Alabama. Four White supremacists were suspected of planting the device that killed Addie Mae Collins, Denise McNair, Carole Robertson, and Cynthia Wesley at the house of worship, which also served as a civil rights meeting place. Three of the girls were age 14. One of them was 11. The suspected bombers were Thomas Edwin Blanton, Jr., Bobby Frank Cherry, Robert Edward Chambliss, and Herman Frank Cash. The bombing came soon after Birmingham was ordered to desegregate its city schools.

The Ku Klux Klan (KKK) was immediately suspected of being involved with the bombing and the four were identified as being Klan members. The Federal Bureau of Investigation (FBI) assigned more than 50 agents to investigate the incident but did not file charges at the time. Nearly 10 years later, Alabama's attorney general, William Joseph Baxley, began efforts to reopen the case. The efforts ultimately resulted in the conviction of three out of the four men and an official FBI announcement in 2000 that the KKK was indeed involved in the bombing.

The evidence used to convict Thomas Blanton included his secretly recorded admission made on June 28, 1964, that "we planned the bomb." The statement was recorded by the FBI. Though Blanton was not tried until 2001, despite advanced age and poor health retired FBI agent Frank Spencer took the stand to testify against Blanton. Spencer had assisted in the original investigation. Blanton was found guilty and given a life sentence.

Partly due to boastful comments reported by his own niece, Robert Chambliss, also known as "Dynamite Bob" and considered the main person responsible for the bombing, was arrested and convicted in 1977. He died in prison on October 29, 1985, having been sentenced to four consecutive life sentences. Bobby Cherry was convicted on May 22, 2002, and died of cancer in prison on November 18, 2004. Herman Cash was never tried for the bombing and died in 1994. Chambliss, Blanton, and Cherry were in their sixties and seventies by the time they were convicted.

The 16th Street Baptist Church bombing is described by the Civil Rights Digital Library as "one of the deadliest acts of violence to take place during the Civil Rights Movement." It has also been described as "a rallying point" for the movement. In 1997, filmmaker Spike Lee produced a documentary titled *4 Little Girls* depicting the details of the incident. Though the documentary was co-produced by Home Box Office at a substantial financial loss, it was nominated for an Academy Award for best documentary.

Rhodine Moreau

(Continued)

References

Anderson, S. W. "The Past on Trial: Birmingham, the Bombing and Restorative Justice." *California Law Review* 96, no. 2 (2008): 471–504.

Associated Press. "Frank Spencer, 87, F.B.I. Agent Who Investigated Klan Bombing, Dies." *The New York Times,* June 8, 2006.

Barber, G. "Pursuing the Past—A Mississippi Newspaper Investigates Crimes of the Civil Rights Era: The Birmingham Church Bombing." *PBSNewshour,* April 18, 2004. http://www.pbs.org/newshour/updates/media-jan-june02-birmingham_04-18/.

Bobby Frank Cherry v. State of Alabama. 10/1/2004 CR-02-0374. http://caselaw.findlaw.com/al-court-of-criminal-appeals/1453590.html.

Bragg, Rick. "More Than Just a Racist? Now the Jury Must Decide." *The New York Times,* May 22, 2002.

Ex parte Bobby Frank Cherry v. State of Alabama. 1040646 and 1040474. 933 So.2d393(Ala.2006).http://caselaw.findlaw.com/al-supreme-court/1054904.html.

Farley, Christopher John, Hilary Hylton, Timothy Roche, and Greg Fulton. "The Ghosts of Alabama." *Time,* May 29, 2000.

The Wales Window for Alabama. Wiki. http://www.bhamwiki.com/w/Wales_Window_for_Alabama.

The Washington Post. "Six Dead After Church Bombing Blast Kills Four Children; Riots Follow Two Youths Slain; State Reinforces Birmingham Police." September 16, 1963.

Wiener, Jon. "Southern Exposure." *The Nation,* June 11, 2001. http://www.thenation.com/article/southern-exposure?page=0,3.

who see their rights as unfairly constrained by "political correctness." On a similar note, it has proved difficult to define or prove a hate crime in some cases and several state statutes have been struck down by higher courts as either constitutionally vague, overbroad, or impermissibly punitive. In such instances, it has been argued that such laws lead to the wasting of resources and that, when appropriate, defendants can as easily be prosecuted under applicable regular criminal statutes. Proponents of a smaller federal government dislike the fact that with hate crimes legislation, the federal government is taking a national role in criminal law and procedure, which might be better served by individual states. The last and perhaps most thought-provoking opposition is that the enforcement of hate crime laws may in fact divide and alienate the races, thereby doing the exact opposite of what was originally intended (Torres, 1999). Determining whether hate crime legislation provides more protection to African Americans and other targeted groups than existed prior to their enactment remains a question for ongoing research.

Benjamin Wilbur

See also: Black Panther Party; Byrd, Jr., James; Civil Rights Movement; Lynching; Nation of Islam

References

Chilton, R., and J. Jarvis. "Victims and Offenders in Two Crime Statistic Programs: A Comparison of the National Incident-Based Reporting System (NIBRS) and the National Crime Victimization Survey (NCVS)." *Journal of Quantitative Criminology* 15, no. 2 (1999): 193–205.

FBI. *Uniform Crime Reports,* 2009. FBI homepage. http://www.fbi.gov/about-us/cjis/ucr/ucr.

Lyons, C. J. "Defending Turf: Racial Demographics and Hate Crime against Blacks and Whites." *Social Force* 87, no. 1 (2008): 357–85.

Tolnay, S. E., E. Black, and J. L. Massey. "Black Lynchings: The Power Threat Hypothesis Revisited." *Social Force* 67, no. 3 (2001): 605–23.

Torres, S. "Hate Crimes against African Americans: The Extent of the Problem." *Journal of Contemporary Criminal Justice* 15, no. 1 (1999): 48–63.

Healing Communities

Healing Communities are places where loving, healthy relationships of support exist and values of forgiveness and reconciliation, together with the commitment to redemption, can be shared with men and women returning from prison. The concept was developed by the Annie E. Casey Foundation under the leadership of Chief Administrative Officer for the Executive Vice President Carole Thompson and key consultants Dr. Robert Franklin, Dr. Harold Dean Trulear, and Dr. Stephanie Boddie with support from Rev. Addie Richburg of the National Alliance of Faith and Justice. These communities reject the stigma and shame typically associated with incarceration. Instead, Healing Communities welcome formerly incarcerated men and women home as "returning citizens." Healing Communities are also places of hope, providing formal and informal networks of support for families, victims, and others seeking to forgive and even assist those returning from prison. These communities express a commitment to be people extending another chance. Some may refer to the process that must take place to experience a Healing Community as "restorative justice" (Mills, 2008a). In this process, formerly incarcerated men and women recognize the need to take responsibility for their crime, and the community also plays a part in restoring the identity of those involved as well as fostering meaningful relationships. Ultimately, these communities create an atmosphere that can complement the best efforts of secular and religious reentry programs and related referral networks (Boddie et al., 2010).

The nation's 400,000 congregations and other faith-based organizations serve as the primary catalyst for Healing Communities. Why congregations and other faith-based organizations? In general, these voluntary organizations embody the values of forgiveness, redemption, reconciliation, and healing. They are also repositories of strong relational networks that complement direct service delivery for persons returning from incarceration. In many cases, faith leaders have the reputational capital to challenge others to take a chance on helping those returning from prison and their families (Mills, 2008c).

Since 2008, several faith communities have adopted the Healing Communities model. First, the Progressive National Baptist Convention (PBNC) began working with the Annie E. Casey Foundation, Prison Fellowship, and Howard University's School of Divinity to introduce this model to their churches. A cluster of prayer circles in Detroit, Michigan, Richmond, Virginia, and Houston, Texas, met regularly to discover ways to make their congregations and neighborhoods safe places for returning citizens and their families (Goode et al., 2011).

From 2009 to 2010, the Michigan Department of Corrections sponsored the Michigan Prisoner Re-entry Initiative (MPRI), based upon the Healing Communities model, and also organized a Faith and Justice Council of religious leaders. However, due to budget cuts, the MPRI was suspended in 2011. The Community Resurrection Partnership (CRP) of Indianapolis began organizing congregations in 2009 to introduce this model. Both the Christian Association for Prison Aftercare and the American Baptist Churches also promoted this model in several cities, including Baltimore, San Diego, and Cleveland. In Philadelphia, a regional group of Sunni Muslims adopted the model and in Trenton, New Jersey, congregations have translated the training material into Spanish. In 2011, the Oklahoma Department of Correction established a prisoner reentry initiative based upon the Healing Communities model. As of 2011, Healing Communities exist in 20 cities through 120 congregations and have served over 1,000 returning citizens and their families (Mills, 2008b).

In 2010, the Philadelphia Leadership Foundation (PLF) was established as an intermediary to support the work of faith-based organizations that adopt the Healing Communities model. PLF continues to advance the concept of Healing Communities. Resources for starting Healing Communities can be found at www.healingcommunitiesusa.org. The Healing Communities model for reentry is particularly important for

African Americans who have experienced mass incarceration and punitive correctional policies in an era of shrinking governmental resources.

Stephanie Boddie, Harold Dean Trulear, and Robert Franklin

References

Boddie, S., R. Franklin, and H. D. Trulear. *Healing Communities: A Framework for Congregations in Their Ministry to Families Affected by Incarceration.* Baltimore: The Annie E. Casey Foundation, 2010.

Goode, W. W., C. E. Lewis, and H. D. Trulear. *Ministry with Prisoners & Families: The Way Forward.* Valley Forge, PA: Judson Press, 2011.

Mills, L. *What Shall We Then Do? A Family Freedom Kit for Creating Healing Communities.* 2008a. Washington, DC: Progressive National Baptist Convention, 2008.

Mills, L. *What Shall We Then Do? An Interdenominational Guide and Kit for Creating Healing Communities.* 2008b. Baltimore: The Annie Casey Foundation, 2008.

Mills, L. 2008c. *Balancing Justice with Mercy: An Interfaith Guide for Creating Healing Communities.* Baltimore: The Annie Casey Foundation, 2008.

Hip-Hop Culture

Over the last three decades, scholars such as Juliana Chang have posed the question: What is hip-hop (Chang, 2006)? Hip-hop is defined as rap music that is lyrical poetry generally spoken or rapped accompanied by sampled repetitive beats (Chang, 2006). Hip-hop comprises four elements: b-boying (also known as breaking or break dancing); dj-ing; graffiti art; and mc-ing or rapping (Forman & Neal, 2004). This popular and dynamic genre of music was created in the South Bronx during the 1970s and comprises cultural and musical elements of the African diaspora, including the Caribbean (Chang, 2006). It is said to have first emerged in New York City as a celebration of Black survival in the face of Reagan/Bush-era economic policies (Scherpf, 2001, quoted in in Au, 2005). The time period during which hip-hop emerged as an art form was also marked by the booming crack trade, falling wages, and disappearing jobs (Kitwana, 2002). Hence, rap artists such as the late Tupac Shakur are credited with artfully exposing the harsh living conditions of the culture of poverty left in the wake of political callousness and the associated economic changes and shifts.

According to Rose (1994), the intensity of these conditions sparked creative modes of sharing with the rest of the world what was happening not only in the Bronx, but also in other urban areas across the country. Some see hip-hop music and culture as a form of resistance to the social injustice that formed the pockets of devastatingly poor and racially segregated urban communities. Education scholars Roderic Land and David Stovall (2009) make a distinct connection between hip-hop and issues of social justice and note that hip-hop lyrics range from words that may be considered "the most righteous" to those that may be considered "the most virulent." As such, they note that hip-hop is at least two things—a social critique that highlights disparities in the school system, the jail system, the political system, and the social system as a whole; and, in some of its forms, such as gangster or "gangsta" rap, a form of social commentary that often hypersexualizes and objectifies people. In the latter form, hip-hop music and culture has been strongly criticized, and politicians, legislators, and private citizens have attempted to censor its use and distribution by railing against the ways in which it appears to promote violence, the use of profanity, drinking and drug use, and disrespect for women and government entities such as the police.

Another controversial form of hip-hop expression involves the use of the racist word "nigger," most often spelled "nigga" (Chang, 2006). There is continuous debate among academic scholars and various sectors of society regarding the appropriateness of such use. The use of the term "nigga" in hip-hop music is said to have a dichotomous meaning (Chang, 2006). It is viewed by some as a term of endearment that empowers those who choose to use it because its usage dissolves the "social sting" of its negative history of psychosocial labeling. Others contend that the use of the word detracts from the positive forms of hip-hop music, and perpetuates or reinforces negative stereotypes that damage young populations in (already) challenged urban communities where there are few positive role models (Chang, 2006; Jenkins, 2006).

Others note that since the early days of rhyming on the street corners of the South Bronx in the mid to late 1970s, hip-hop has also become a third thing: a confirmed U.S. national commodity that can bring in over a billion dollars a year in sales (Au, 2005). Thus many otherwise unemployed or unemployable youth aspire to become rich rap artists. Though most fail, they continue to see the existing rap icons as evidence of their ticket out of neighborhoods with little to offer.

Gladney (1995) recognizes that hip-hop is much more than a form of art, dance, and music; it is also a culture that maintains many of the convictions and aesthetic criteria that evolved out of the Black Arts Movement of the 1960s. It includes a call for social relevance, originality, and dedication to producing art that challenges mainstream American artistic expression. Scholars have also described it as "a constructive and contested space for the historically oppressed and marginalized to both resist and challenge social ideologies, practices, and structures that have caused and maintained their subordinate position" (Land & Stovall, 2009: 2); in other words, hip-hop tells the story of the "other America" (Land & Stovall, 2009: 2).

Hip-Hop and Crime

Throughout the last several decades, there have been many incidents of hip-hop artists becoming involved in criminal justice cases. The following are examples of hip-hop artists involved in legal issues.

P. Diddy (Sean Combs) was arrested in 1999 on gun possession charges after a stolen gun was found in his vehicle. The arrest came about immediately after a shooting had taken place at a Times Square dance club (Rashbaum, 1999). Though claiming he wasn't involved in the shooting, P. Diddy was charged with illegal gun possession. He was later acquitted of all charges in 2001 (Finkelstein, 2001).

In 1999, Jay-Z (Shawn Carter) was arrested after the stabbing of a record promoter during a hip-hop party in a Manhattan club. Though he denied involvement in the incident, he was charged with felony assault and was facing a possible 15-year prison sentence (Forero, 1999). Jay-Z ultimately accepted a plea deal, pleading guilty to a misdemeanor assault charge in 2001. He received three years of probation (BBC, 2001).

Lil' Kim (Kimberly Jones) was sentenced to a year and one day in prison after lying on the witness stand in 2005. She had lied about not remembering seeing her bodyguard at the scene of a crime when, in fact, security cameras had caught her standing beside him at the time. Lil' Kim served 10 months of her sentence in the Federal Detention Center in Philadelphia. She was released in July 2006 (Hess, 2007).

Snoop Dogg (Calvin Broadus, Jr.) has been arrested multiple times for a variety of charges from 1989 through 2012. In 1993, Snoop Dogg was arrested in connection with the death of a rival gang member. He was charged with murder and conspiracy to commit assault. He was acquitted of both charges in 1996 (Daunt, 1996).

In 2007, Lil Wayne (Dwayne Carter) was arrested for possession of an illegal weapon. After initially pleading not guilty to the charges, Lil Wayne entered a guilty plea for a reduced sentence in February 2008 (Juarez, 2009). He was sentenced to one year in prison. Lil Wayne was released from New York City's Riker's Island after serving eight months (BBC, 2010).

Rapper T.I. (Clifford Harris) was arrested in October 2007 on federal gun charges. Harris, who is not permitted to own guns because he is a convicted felon, attempted to buy $12,000 in weapons through his bodyguard. Further investigation by authorities led to the discovery of three firearms in his car and six more in his home (CNN, 2007). He was sentenced to one year and one day in prison, one year of house arrest, and 1,500 hours of community service. In addition, he was ordered to pay a fine of $100,300. He served his prison sentence in a federal prison in Atlanta, Georgia (CNN, 2009). Shortly after his release, T.I. and his wife, Tameka Cottle, were arrested for drug possession charges in September 2010 (BBC, 2010). Though the drug possession charges were eventually dropped, T.I. was sentenced to 11 months in prison for violating the terms of his probation. He was released after serving 10 months (McKinley, 2011).

Fabiel Jean-Philippe

Scholars of African American Studies have had intense debates about hip-hop, in particular about gangsta rap's damage to the cause of African Americans (McWhorter, 2003). The debates revolve around whether the violent and often misogynistic scenes and lyrics that play out in gangsta rap become self-fulfilling prophecies of the violence found in the culture of the inner city. John McWhorter (2003), one of hip-hop's staunchest critics, contends that "[b]y reinforcing the stereotypes that long hindered blacks, and by teaching young blacks that a thuggish adversarial stance is the properly 'authentic' response to a presumptively racist society, rap retards black success" (Kitwana, 2003: 75). While McWhorter claims that the anti-authority and anti-intellectual persona that dominates hip-hop lyrics holds Blacks back, supporters of hip-hop art and culture contend that hip-hop serves as a vehicle to express the frustrations and desires, the pains and triumphs, and the oppressions and dreams of young people of color and the older hip-hop generation around the world (Land & Stovall, 2009).

Despite its critics, hip-hop at its core has proven to be a considerable force for social change; at the very least, hip-hop has brought much needed dialogue to issues affecting America's Black community like no other popular art form since perhaps jazz and blues (Land & Stoval, 2009; Gladney, 1995). Despite its critics and split opinions about its influence and utility, it seems that hip-hop music and its supporting culture, which includes styles of dress that some attribute to emulating prison culture, are here to stay.

Cory Feldman

See also: Jena Six; Shakur, Tupac Amaru

References

Au, W. "Fresh out of School: Rap Music's Discursive Battle with Education." *The Journal of Negro Education* 74, no. 3 (2005): 210–21.

BBC News. "US Rapper Lil Wayne Sentenced to a Year in Prison." March 9, 2010.

BBC News. "Rapper Jay-Z Admits to Stabbing." October 18, 2001.

Chang, J. "Keeping It Real: Interpreting Hip Hop." *College English* 68, no. 5 (May 2006): 545–54.

CNN. "Rapper T.I. Sentenced to Year and a Day in Prison, Fined." March 27, 2009.

CNN. "Rapper T.I. Arrested on Machine Gun Charges, Misses BET Show." October 14, 2007.

Daunt, T. "Rapper Snoop Doggy Dog Is Acquitted of Murder." *The Los Angeles Times,* February 21, 1996.

Finkelstein, K. "Hip-Hop Star Cleared of Charges in Shooting at a Manhattan Club." *The New York Times,* March 17, 2001.

Forero, J. "Police Arrest Hip-Hop Star in a Stabbing at a Nightclub." *The New York Times,* December 3, 1999.

Forman, M., and M. A. Neal. *That's the Joint: The Hip-Hop Studies Reader.* New York: Routledge, 2004.

Gladney, M. J. "The Black Arts Movement and Hip-Hop." *African American Review* (Summer 1995): 291–301.

Hess, M. *Icons of Hip Hop.* Vol. 2. Westport, CT: Greenwood Press, 2007.

Jenkins, T. S. "Mr. Nigger: The Challenges of Educating Black Males within American Society." *Journal of Black Studies* 37, no. 1 (September 2006): 127–55.

Juarez, V. "Lil Wayne Pleads Guilty to Weapons Charge." CNN, October 22, 2009.

Kitwana, B. *The Hip Hop Generation.* New York: Basic Civitas Books, 2003.

Kitwana, B. *The Hip Hop Generation: Young Blacks and the Crisis in African American Culture.* New York: Basic Books, 2002.

Land, R. R., and D. O. Stovall. "Hip Hop and Social Justice Education: A Brief Introduction." *Equity & Excellence in Education* 42, no. 1 (2009): 1–5.

McKinley, J. "T.I. Released from Halfway House." *The New York Times,* September 29, 2011.

McWhorter, J. H. "How Hip-Hop Holds Blacks Back." *City Journal* (Summer 2003).

Rashbaum, W. "Rap Performer Puffy Combs Is Arrested after Shootings at Times Square Nightclub." *The New York Times,* December 28, 1999.

Rose, T. *Black Noise: Rap Music and Black Culture in Contemporary America.* Middletown, CT: Wesleyan University Press, 1994.

Scherpf, S. "Rap Pedagogy: The Potential for Democratization." *The Review of Education/Pedagogy/Cultural Studies* 23 (2001): 73–110.

Homicide

Homicide is the killing of one person by another. For most government reporting, the commission of homicide is typically classified as either murder or non-negligent manslaughter. The phenomenon and reality of homicide in the United States are disproportionately felt by African Americans, particularly African American males. A recent report from *The American Journal of Medicine* had the following stark facts to report about homicides and African Americans:

> Homicide . . . is the leading cause of death of young black men in the United States. Black men are 6 times more likely to die as the result of homicide; And, 7 times more likely to commit murder than their white counterparts One eighth of the population is black, but one half of all homicide victims are black. (Hennekens et al., 2013: 282)

Though the article is titled "A New American Tragedy," the Centers for Disease Control and Prevention in Atlanta have been reporting homicide and particularly gun homicide as an epidemic among young Black men ages 15 to 24 for many years

(CDC, 2012). The recent study examined homicide statistics for the 10-year period 1999 to 2009. Another study published in *The Journal of the American Medical Association* in 1990 similarly reported that the leading cause of death among young Black males was homicide (Fingerhut & Kleinman, 1990; 3292); and in 1985, the U.S. Department of Justice (DOJ) reported the possibility of becoming a homicide victim was 1 in 21 for Black males, compared to 1 in 131 for White males (DOJ, 1985). Statistics from the 1980s revealed that the rate of firearm deaths among young Black males more than doubled between 1984 and 1988 (Fingerhut et al., 1991), leading a pair of researchers to conclude that "a resident of rural Bangladesh [India] has a greater chance of surviving to age 40 than does a black male in Harlem" (McCord & Freeman, 1990, cited in Sampson & Wilson, 1995: 38).

While serious crime has declined in the United States for all offense categories, Blacks have experienced serious violent crime at a higher rate than other demographic groups, dating back to at least 1973 (see Fox & Zawitz, 2007). A substantial gap between Black and White rates of homicide victimization and offending has been shown dating back to 1976 (Fox & Zawitz, 2007). Though not new, the tragedy is that these statistics from the 1970s, 1980s, and 1990s are not improving, even as crime, including homicide, is declining for other demographic groups. Hennekens, Drowos, and Levine (2013) report that of the 106,271 homicides that occurred between 1999 to 2009, for victims age 15 to 34, 52,265 were Black men and boys. They also report that during that period, 81 percent of all homicides involved firearms, and 91 percent (47,513) of firearm homicides involved Black men and boys. Overall, they report that firearm homicides in the United States in the 15- to 24-year-old age group are 43 times higher than in any other developed country (see also Levine & Kilbourne, 2013; Potter, 2001). Another study of homicides during the same time period noted a 31 percent increase in firearm homicide for Black men ages 25 to 44, compared to a 12 percent increase for White men of the same age (Hu et al., 2008).

The disproportionality in the number of Blacks versus Whites who fall victim to homicide in the United States is a cause for great concern. In 2009 alone, across the nation there were an estimated 15,000 people murdered (FBI, 2009). While African Americans made up 12.9 percent of the U.S. population (U.S. Census, 2008) they accounted for 48.1 percent of the victims of murder (FBI, 2009). By comparison, White Americans represented 79.5 percent of the population and 48.2 percent of those murdered. For both groups, the majority of murders were intra-racial, meaning the victim and offender were of the same race. Cumulative statistics from 1976–2005 show that 86 percent of White victims were killed by Whites and 94 percent of Black victims were killed by Blacks (Fox & Zawitz, 2007). In instances of homicide committed by a friend or acquaintance, more than 90 percent were intra-racial. Victims and offenders are also typically similar in age.

Disproportionately high homicide victimization and offending rates hold true for both Black males and Black females, but not on the same scale. In contrast to males, the Bureau of Justice Statistics reports that females are typically murdered by people they know, including family members or intimate partners, rather than mere acquaintances or strangers. In 2007, Black females were twice as likely as White females to be killed by a spouse and four times as likely to be murdered by a boyfriend or girlfriend (Catalano et al., 2009). But between 1993 and 2007, there was substantial improvement in the reported statistics for Black female homicide victims. The number of Black females killed by intimate partners fell by 39 percent. The rate of Black females killed by spouses declined 58 percent and the rate of Black females killed by a boyfriend or girlfriend declined 36 percent (Catalano et al., 2009).

Statistics for Black female homicide offenders are sparse. Black female homicide offenders are more prevalent than White female homicide offenders, but the numbers have been declining since the early 1990s (Cooper & Smith, 2011). Specifically, Black female teens are reported to have experienced a significant reduction in their homicide offending rate, from 11 per 100,000 in 1992 to 3 per 100,000 in 2008. White females of all ages are reported as having the lowest homicide offending rates (Cooper & Smith, 2011). Part of the reduction in Black female homicide offending appears directly connected to a reduction in the killing of spouses or intimate partners outside of marriage and the reduction in teen homicide offending.

Criminologists know that even with national crime reductions, there are places that are more dangerous in the United States than others. An examination of Black homicide offending verifies that while not exclusively an urban phenomenon, homicide offending and victimization among Blacks, especially Black males, is largely an issue within cities. The significant increase in firearm homicides for Black males ages 25 to 44 that occurred between 1999 and 2005 occurred primarily within the cities of 11 states: Alabama, California, Michigan, Minnesota, Nebraska, Nevada, New Jersey, Ohio, Pennsylvania, Texas, and Washington—with 32 percent of the homicide rate increase occurring in large central metropolitan areas and 30 percent in large fringe metropolitan areas (Hu et al., 2008). For example, statistics for the period 2006 to 2010 show a homicide rate for the city of New Orleans of 426 per 100,000 young Black men compared to a national rate of 77 per 100,000 (Travis, 2013). Of the 4,209 Black arrests for homicide in 2010, 167 occurred in nonmetropolitan areas; 1,075 occurred in suburban areas; and 3,406 occurred in cities. Among arrestees under age 18, only 7 homicides occurred in nonmetropolitan areas; 108 in suburban areas; and 365 in cities (BJS, 2011).

These staggering statistics beg the question of why these rates of homicide are so high. Crime in general cannot be easily explained, let alone crime as complex and permanent as criminal homicide. While homicide is frequently among the crimes with the highest rate of being solved, more than one-third of homicides have unknown perpetrators. This leaves researchers and law enforcement personnel speculating as to the cause of many killings. A half-century ago Marvin Wolfgang provided the description of what he called "victim precipitated" homicides as the category for a fourth of murders in his large Philadelphia study (Wolfgang, 1958). Later studies by various researchers examined the role of interpersonal conflict. Figures available through the Uniform Crime Report (UCR), a database maintained by the FBI that tracks reported crime, finds that arguments can be identified as the starting point of more than 40 percent of murders (Robinson et al., 2009).

While these dynamics describe the beginning of many ultimately lethal encounters, they suggest only one area to address in reducing or preventing homicides. Other factors, such as population density, street gang density, high school dropout rates, and unemployment, are all statistically significant in examining the relationships influencing homicide in racial and ethnic groups (Robinson et al., 2009). A Florida public defender has suggested that young Black men are likely to distrust the police and to have little confidence that the police can protect them. Consequently, when there is a problem that causes them to fear for their safety, they may be more likely to take matters into their own hands than to call the police (Travis, 2013; see also O'Flaherty & Sethi, 2010).

Why a person is a victim of crime has almost as many explanations as why a person commits a crime. Two theories that share a focus on the victim are the routine activities theory (Cohen & Felson, 1979) and the lifestyle approach (Hindelang et al., 1970). Routine activities theory looks at the suitable target joined with both a motivated offender, and the absence of a capable guardian. Lifestyle approach addresses the correlates in a person's patterns of interaction with others and the environment to identify risk factors for violence or crime. The setting, available weapons, and the interaction between two people combine in complex ways to arrive at a lethal outcome. It is noted that when the lethal outcome is deemed to be a murder, African Americans hold the dubious distinction of being sentenced to capital punishment at a higher rate than other groups—suggesting yet another reason why such outcomes must be prevented and reduced.

Legislation and programs aimed at addressing factors that impact violence between and among (specifically) young Black males are critical. A number of cities have pursued "hot spots" policing and gun reduction programs to combat homicide and other violent crime. Issues such as employability, education, and mentoring are long-term initiatives that do not always fit with the attention span of politicians or the public but have demonstrated violence-reduction effects. Since 9/11 there has been a shift of resources away from community-oriented policing (COPS) programs that also may have helped reduce the risk of homicide to African Americans. This mix of enforcement activities and social programs is important. Factors such as high school dropout rates, street gang activity, and negative experiences in homes and in education are all seen as factors in community and individual violence that can be changed through appropriate interventions.

Stating with confidence why an individual kills another person is impossible given the many factors discussed previously. Accepting explanations that seem "common sense" will likely fail to account for some complexities. At the individual level, being poor, hanging around with people already leading a criminal lifestyle, or the use of and involvement with drugs may all seem plausible, especially in relation to African Americans who have been economically disadvantaged over time. But while Blacks are disproportionately both victims and perpetrators of homicide in comparison to other groups and their percentage in the general population, their homicide involvement is nowhere near the level of social and economic disadvantage they experience as a group.

Richard Hough with Delores Jones-Brown

See also: Death Penalty; Intra-Racial Offending; Martin, Trayvon; Racial Profiling; Theories of Race and Crime; Wolfgang, Marvin; Youth Violence

References

Bureau of Justice Statistics (BJS). *Sourcebook of Criminal Justice Statistics Online,* 2011. http://www.albany.edu/sourcebook/pdf/4102011.pdf.

Catalano, S., E. Smith, H. Snyder, and M. Rand. "Female Victims of Violence." Bureau of Justice Statistics: Selected Findings (September) NCJ 228356, 2009.

Centers for Disease Control and Prevention, National Center for Health Statistics (CDC). Compressed Mortality File 1999-2009. CDC WONDER Online Database, compiled from Compressed Mortality File 1999-2009 Series 20 No. 20, 2012. http://wonder.cdc.gov/cmf-icd10.html.

Cohen, L. E., and M. Felson. "Social Change and Crime Rate Trends: A Routine Activities Approach." *American Sociological Review* 33 (1979): 588–608.

Cooper, A., and E. Smith. *Homicide Trends in the United States, 1980–2008.* Bureau of Justice Statistics. Washington, DC: U.S. Department of Justice, 2011.

Federal Bureau of Investigation (FBI). Expanded Homicide Data Table 2. Washington, DC, *Crime in the United States,* 2009. http://www2.fbi.gov/ucr/cius2009/offenses/expanded_information/data/shrtable_02.html.

Fingerhut, L., J. Kleinman, E. Godfrey, and H. Rosenberg. "Firearms Mortality among Children, Youth, and Young Adults 1–34 Years of Age, Trends and Current Status: United States, 1979–88." *Monthly Vital Stastistics Report* 39, no. 11 (1991): 1–16.

Fingerhut, L. A., and J. C. Kleinman. "International and Interstate Comparisons of Homicide among Young Males." *Journal of the American Medical Association* 263 (1990): 3292–95.

Fox, J. A., and M. Zawitz. *Homicide Trends in the United States (Since 1976)*. Washington, DC: Bureau of Justice Statistics, 2007. http://bjs.ojp.usdoj.gov/content/homocide/race.cfm.

Hennekens, C., J. Drowos, and R. Levine. "Mortality from Homicide among Young Black Men: A New American Tragedy." *The American Journal of Medicine* 126, no. 4 (2013): 282–83.

Hindelang, M. J., M. R. Gottfredson, and J. Garofalo. *Victims of Personal Crime: An Empirical Foundation for a Theory of Personal Crime Vicitimization*. Cambridge, MA: Ballinger, 1970.

Hu, G., D. Webster, and S. Baker. "Hidden Homicide Increases in the USA, 1999–2005." *Journal of Urban Health: Bulletin of the New York Academy of Medicine* 85, no. 4 (2008): 597–606.

Levine R. S., G. Rust, B. Kilbourne, et al. "United States Counties with Low Black Male Mortality Rates." *American Journal of Medicine* 126 (2013): 76–80.

McCord, M., and H. Freeman. "Excess Mortality in Harlem." *New England Journal of Medicine* 322 (1990): 173–75.

O'Flaherty, B., and R. Sethi. "Homicide in Black and White." *Journal of Urban Economics* 68, no. 3 (2010): 215–30.

Potter, L. "Influence of Homicide on Racial Disparity in Life Expectancy–United States, 1998." *Morbidity and Mortality Weekly Report*. Atlanta: Centers for Disease Control and Prevention 50 (2001): 780–82.

Robinson, P., W. J. Boscardin, S. M. George, et al. "The Effects of Urban Street Gang Densities on Small Area Homicide Incidence in a Large Metropolitan County, 1994–2002." *Journal of Urban Health* 86, no. 4 (July 2009): 511–23. doi:10.1007/s11524-009-9343-x.

Sampson, R., and W. J. Wilson. "Toward a Theory of Race, Crime and Urban Inequality." In *Crime and Inequality*, edited by J. Hagan and R. Peterson, 37–54. Palo Alto, CA: Stanford University Press, 1995.

Travis, S. "Homicide Leading Cause of Death of Young Black Men, Says FAU Researchers." *Sun Sentinel*, April 10, 2013.

U.S. Census Bureau. Table 4. Projections of the Population by Sex, Race and Hispanic Origin for the United States: 2010–2050 (NP2008-T4). Population Division. August 14, 2008. www.census.gov/population/projections/files/summary/np2008-t4.xls.

U.S. Department of Justice (DOJ). *The Risk of Violent Crime*. Washington, DC: Bureau of Justice Statistics, 1985.

Wolfgang, M. *Patterns in Criminal Homicide*. Philadelphia: University of Pennsylvania Press, 1958.

Hurricane Katrina

Hurricane Katrina began as Tropical Depression 12 on August 23, 2005, off the coast of the Bahamas. One day later it was the eleventh-named storm of the 2005 hurricane season. It moved over Alabama, Louisiana, and Mississippi with hurricane-strength winds. The citizens of New Orleans were warned by the National Hurricane Center that the levees in New Orleans could be overtopped by Lake Ponchartrain. Warnings about New Orleans stated: "Most of New Orleans will be uninhabitable for weeks . . . perhaps longer. . . . Water shortages will make human suffering incredible by modern standards" (Reed & Theiss, 2005: 3). Heeding these and other warnings, 1.2 million people evacuated from Louisiana and Mississippi, accounting for 92 percent of the people in the path of the storm the day before Hurricane Katrina struck. Those who remained were the most economically distressed residents.

At 6:10 a.m. Central Daylight Time on Monday, August 29, 2005, in Plaquemines Parish (just east of New Orleans), Hurricane Katrina made landfall as a Category III storm with winds of 111 to 130 miles per hour. A storm surge of 27 feet was created in Louisiana and Mississippi, causing 6 to 12 miles of inland flooding. The surge of water caused the overtopping and breaching of the massive 350-mile levee system that surrounds New Orleans. *The Federal Response to Hurricane Katrina: Lessons Learned* was published in 2006. It stated that it was the overtopping and breaching of the levee system that led to the catastrophic flooding of New Orleans.

Leaving $96 billion in damage, Hurricane Katrina was the most destructive natural disaster to ever take place on U.S. soil. Due to technological advances, such as better forecasting science and better communication channels to assist in the evacuation process, the death toll for Hurricane Katrina was 1,330, far below the devastation of the 1900 Galveston Hurricane, which left 8,000 dead (Weems, 1956). The advances were recent and saved an unknown number of lives. It is important to note that the death toll of Katrina was largely a result of the breaching of the 350-mile levee after the hurricane and not a direct result of the hurricane itself (Townsend, 2006).

Hurricane Katrina left over 300,000 homes destroyed and 770,000 people displaced (Davis, 2007: 2). As Americans saw the devastation of the storm, issues of race and class emerged. Prior to Hurricane Katrina, New Orleans was a city that was 67 percent Black, with the lowest median income for a metropolitan area and the sixth-highest poverty rate among United States counties. Additionally 27 percent of the population (120,000) had no private vehicle belonging to their household. Images of Americans on top of roofs waving American flags for help and thousands in the Superdome and the New Orleans Convention Center raised the question of how this had occurred in the United States. The international response was overwhelming, as countries such as Venezuela, Russia, France, Germany, and even Cuba offered assistance. Most of these offers were rejected by the Bush administration, as President Bush said the United States could fend for itself.

There were serious racial tensions surrounding the Bush administration's response to the disaster and the media coverage of those affected by the powerful storm. During a telethon and concert for hurricane relief, rapper Kanye West is reported to have made the following statement: "I hate the way they portray us in the media. You see a Black family, it says 'They're looting.' You see a White family, it says, 'They are looking for food.' . . . George Bush doesn't care about Black people." Additionally, a few days after the tragedy, Wolf Blitzer, a commentator from CNN, stated, "You simply get chills every time you see these poor individuals. . . . [S]o many of these people . . . are so poor and they are so Black, and this is going to raise lots of questions for people who are watching this story unfold."

For those thousands who were displaced, the majority went to Atlanta, Baton Rouge, or Houston. The city of Houston received over 200,000 displaced New Orleans residents. Mostly Black and poor, these Houston guests soon became the brunt of hostility and racial jokes as Houston residents linked a rise in crime to the arrival of the former New Orleanians. Houston radio programs labeled them "FEMA [Federal Emergency Management Agency] Rats" and aired comments such as "Killers: I hear they kill like 10–15 people a night," "Go home niggers," and "Go home and drown in some Katrina water." Research findings indicate that crime did rise in Houston around the time of the Hurricane Katrina guests' arrival, but the cause of the rise has been identified as a combination of many variables, including population increase, reduced police presence, an annual November and December crime spike, and an existing rise in crime that had begun before Fall 2005 (Varano et al., 2010).

In his 2006 State of the Union Address just a few months after Hurricane Katrina made landfall, President Bush stated, "As we recover from a disaster, let us also work for the day when all Americans are protected by justice, equal in hope, and rich in opportunity" (Bush, 2006). To help Americans better understand what happened in New Orleans and its devastating impact, African American filmmaker Spike Lee (2006) produced an award-winning documentary titled *When the Levees Broke: A Requiem in Four Acts*. The film gives its audience an insider's view of the devastation and the multiple failures by government and other entities that served to make a terrible situation worse. Lee's film won five awards from the film industry, including the American Cinema Editors Guild, the Broadcast Film Critics Association, the International Documentary Association, the Toronto International Film Festival, and the Venice International Film Festival.

The Federal Response to Hurricane Katrina: Lessons Learned listed 125 specific recommendations from its four-month review (Townsend, 2006). Overall, the five most prominent lessons learned include:

- lack of planning and coordination at the local, state, and federal levels;
- lack of operability and inoperability of communications;
- lack of plans, procedures, and policies to maintain order and civility;

- a need for improved coordination between business, nongovernmental organizations, citizen groups, and government agencies responsible for emergency response; and
- lack of plans, procedures, and policies to coordinate the best use of foreign aid and support.

The resounding conclusion was that the response to Hurricane Katrina fell short of the seamless coordination stipulated in the National Response Plan (NRP) created by the newly formed Department of Homeland Security. Hurricane Katrina moved the Department of Homeland Security from a narrow view of terrorism as the primary threat to national safety and security to a broader view encompassing the significant threat presented by natural disasters and the accompanying multifaceted harm.

Arguably, Hurricane Karina resulted in a disturbing disruption of both the physical and social structures of the affected communities. One of the most devastating consequences was the displacement of scores of New Orleanians to cities across the state and the country, including Houston, San Antonio, and Phoenix. In response to speculation that such a grand-scale population displacement would lead to an increase in crime in the recipient cities, Varano et al. (2010) conducted a time series analysis to examine the pre- and post-Katrina trends in six Uniform Crime Report (UCR) Part I offenses (murder, robbery, aggravated assault, rape, burglary, and auto theft) to assess any impact of resettlement on crime in host communities. Contrary to much popular speculation, only modest effects were found on crime. In other words, widespread reports of crime committed by the displaced residents of New Orleans were largely not supported by the factual evidence.

Today there is the National Response Framework (NRF), which incorporates the lessons learned from Katrina and encourages citizens' emergency preparedness and coordination between local, state, and national emergency services' organizations. To address the lack of planning and coordination in response to Hurricane Katrina, all citizens are urged to have a plan so that the horrific events of New Orleans in the wake of Hurricane Katrina never happen again. The significance of Hurricane Katrina goes beyond it being the most destructive natural disaster in United States history. Hurricane Katrina brought issues of race and class to the national and international forefront and exposed levels of inequality that many thought were a thing of the past.

Everette Penn

References

Bush, George W. "State of the Union Address 2006." The White House, Washington, DC. January 31, 2006.

Davis, Lynn Etheridge. *Hurricane Katrina: Lessons for Army Planning and Operations.* Santa Monica, CA: RAND Corporation, 2007.

Lee, Spike. *When the Levees Broke: A Requiem in Four Acts.* HBO Documentary, 2006.

Reed, Jim, and Mike Theiss. *Hurricane Katrina: Through the Eyes of Storm Chasers.* Helena, MT: Farcountry Press, 2005.

Townsend, Frances Fragos. "The Federal Response to Hurricane Katrina: Lessons Learned." Washington, DC: The White House Archives, 2006.

Varano, Sean, Joseph Schafer, Jeffrey Cancino, Scott Decker, and Jack Greene. "A Tale of Three Cities: Crime and Displacement after Hurricane Katrina." *Journal of Criminal Justice* 38, no. 1 (2010): 42–50.

Weems, John Edward. "The Galveston Storm of 1990." *The Southwestern Historical Quarterly* 61, no. 4 (1956): 494–507.

I

Inequality Theory

In American society, racial and ethnic minority groups have long endured a history of disparities, leading to instances of racism, discrimination, and prejudice. Many of these occurrences have stemmed from inequality, which arises when individuals or groups experience situations of unequal social status and treatment due to a number of factors, such as race or ethnicity. As Katz and Stern have noted, "[T]he history of African American experience reflects the paradox of inequality in twentieth-century America" (2008: 63). For example, in his 2004 book *The Hidden Cost of Being African American,* one such example of inequality among many that Thomas M. Shapiro notes is how an African American family was denied a mortgage while a similar White family was approved. Consequently, such examples and occurrences create fewer opportunities for subordinated groups, thus further contributing to inequality. In inequality theory, three differing perspectives may provide a useful approach to explain such inequalities facing African Americans and their connections to crime and contact with the criminal justice system.

The first perspective of inequality theory—structural-functionalism—argues society functions similar to an organism, requiring all parts (e.g., social institutions and structures) to work in harmony in order to achieve stability and equilibrium. As such, this perspective requires consensus among members in society, which may be threatened when conflicts and struggles occur between groups. Consequently, this may lead to instances of crime and deviance, which, from this perspective, serve a function for society by clarifying and reaffirming socially defined norms, promoting unity in society while challenging the status quo. In turn, society is forced to reconsider and question acts and behaviors previously labeled as crimes and deviance, and therefore introduce change. Prior to the 1960s, things once regarded as a crime or violation of social norms, such as sitting in the wrong area of a restaurant or bus or using a water fountain intended for "Whites only," were eventually reconsidered and thus played a key role in establishing more equal

On February 1, 1960, four young African American college students walked into the Woolworth Company, sat down at a Whites-only lunch counter, and triggered the civil rights movement that spread across the nation. Shown here on February 2, 1960, are (left to right) Joseph McNeil, Franklin McCain, Billy Smith, and Clarence Henderson. (Library of Congress)

rights for African Americans and reducing the number of acts considered to be criminal. In other words, such instances of prejudice and discrimination were necessary to introduce equality, as they led to the questioning of how oppressed groups were treated by society.

The second perspective of inequality theory—conflict theory—argues conflicting groups with competing interests are the source of inequality. Here, groups holding authority in society control and subordinate groups through power, influence, and coercion. The tension between such divisions provides the basis for prejudice, racism, and discrimination to thrive in society. For historically disadvantaged groups such as African Americans, conflict theory provides a theoretically attractive explanation of inequality. From this perspective, law becomes the tool of control used by powerful groups in order to maintain a privileged position and social control over subordinate groups. Usually, those in power tend to be White, wealthy, and politically powerful, while the latter group tends to include minority races, which are financially disadvantaged, politically neglected, and typically regarded to threaten society through their mere existence. Consequently, certain behaviors associated with such groups are often criminalized. For example, since the creation of crack, this form of cocaine has been believed to be the drug of choice for African Americans due to its affordability compared to powder cocaine, which has a higher purity, and potency. Consequently, the law—created by groups in

Features	Perspectives in Inequality Theory		
	Structural Functionalism	**Conflict Theory**	**Symbolic Interactionism**
Proponents	• Emily Durkheim • Robert Merton • Alfred Radcliffe-Brown • Auguste Comte • Talcott Parsons	• Karl Marx • Ludwig Gumplowicz • Lester F. Ward • C. Wright Mills	• George H. Mead • Max Weber • Herbert Blumer • Charles Cooley
Defining Characteristics	• Society functions similar to an organism, requiring various parts to work together and rely on one another	• Ongoing competition over limited resources among unequal groups • Social structures controlled by power and reward, which ensures separation	• Importance and interpretation of symbols and interactions in everyday life • People think, behave, and respond accordingly to these meanings
Time Period of Popularity	• World War II • 1940s–1950s up until Vietnam War	• 1960s due to events of this time period, such as civil rights	• Introduced in 1920s–1930s; declined in 1960s–1970s
Worldview and Features of Society	• Macro and objective • Stable and cohesive • Interdependence required between structures for balance	• Macro and objective • Competitive and competing • Dominated by hierarchies and conflicts	• Micro and subjective • Socially constructed • Interactions and tangible objects having symbolic meanings
Methods for Maintaining Social Order	• Social consensus developed among members in society on shared values	• Power, influence, and coercion used to dominate subordinate groups	• Created and defined through collective meaning associated with symbols, events, and interactions
Means for Introducing Social Change	• Adaptation necessary to achieve stability in society, democratic order, and productivity among members	• Members in conflicting groups with competing interests struggle over limited resources	• Constantly changing meaning of symbols and interactions between people over time

(Continued)

Features	Perspectives in Inequality Theory		
	Structural Functionalism	Conflict Theory	Symbolic Interactionism
	• Change happens gradually	• Challenges the status quo	
Position of the Individual in Society	• Individuals fulfill fixed roles in society, working together to achieve equilibrium	• Subordination of individuals in society through the existence of divided groups	• Interdependence of individuals and society
Perspective on Inequalities of Race and Ethnicity	• Ethnic discrimination is inevitable, which reduces consensus and increases conflicts and threatens stability in society; distinctive groups formed in response to inequality	• Tension among conflicting and competing groups may lead to instances of prejudice, racism, and discrimination	• Experiences of inequality are individually perceived, depending on meanings given to language, interaction, rituals, and symbols
Limitations	• Focused on social order, solidarity, and equilibrium to account for social change • Does not actively encourage individuals to introduce social change, as this is considered to happen naturally when various parts of society respond to deal with problems • Overlooks power differences between groups by supporting and justifying a status quo in society and satisfaction among members	• Portrays an overall negative view on society, with attention focused on change, struggle, and conflict, rather than on cohesion and stability of societies • Positive events (e.g., democratic reform, humanitarian efforts, altruistic behaviors) are viewed as capitalistic strategies to maintain control on society rather than to preserve society and social order	• Focused on micro-level interactions and interpretations and neglects macro-level features, such as culture, norms, or overall picture of society • The same symbols and actions can have different meanings to different individuals, who may be influenced by other social forces or structures • Quantitatively weak approach to explain inequality due to a qualitative and subjective orientation

(Continued)

Features	Perspectives in Inequality Theory		
	Structural Functionalism	Conflict Theory	Symbolic Interactionism
Key Work(s)	• Merton (1957) *Social Theory and Social Structure* • Radcliffe-Brown (1965) *Structure and Function in Primitive Society* • Parsons (1937) *The Structure of Social Action;* (1951) *The Social System*	• Marx & Engels (1848) *The Communist Manifesto* • Gumplowicz (1884) *Outlines of Sociology* • Ward (1883) *Dynamic Sociology*	• Blumer (1969) *Symbolic Interactionism: Perspective and Method*

This chart is adapted in part from two created by Don Stewart, University of Nevada–Las Vegas, retrieved from http://nvsocioman.com and http://faculty.unlv.edu/stewart/Comparison%20%of20 Theories.pdf.

Crime and Inequality

In 1995, John Hagan and Ruth Peterson edited a collection of essays aimed at addressing the multiple ways in which inequality relates to an increased risk of criminality. The 12-chapter volume remains one of the most comprehensive books on the topic.

In chapter 2, Robert Sampson and William Julius Wilson present a compelling explanation for the elevated levels of violent crime that occur in urban neighborhoods where the residents are predominantly Black. In "Toward a Theory of Race, Crime and Urban Inequality," Sampson and Wilson artfully lay out an explanation of criminality that is both complex and understandable; and, unlike many individual-level theories of crime, point to multiple aspects of the physical and structural environment as main factors in a seemingly inescapable pattern of poverty, race, and violence.

The chapter opens noting that research published in 1990 found that the leading cause of death for young Black males was homicide. Sampson and Wilson cite a 1985 Department of Justice (DOJ) report as placing the lifetime risk of being murdered for Black males at 1 in 21 compared to a 1 in 131 risk for White males. They point out the role of gun violence in the risk of homicide for Black males as compared to White males, noting that between 1984 and 1988 the rate of death from firearms doubled for Black males but remained stable for Whites. A particularly somber note in the chapter's introduction is a suggestion

(Continued)

from the medical community that "a resident from rural Bangladesh has a greater chance of surviving to age 40 than does a black male in Harlem" (38).

In attempting to determine how community structure affects crime, Sampson and Wilson tried to compare rates of crime in similar Black and White communities. Despite their efforts, they could not find Black and White communities that were comparable to each other, leading them to conclude: "we still cannot say that Blacks and Whites share a similar environment" (41). For Blacks, they found what they term high levels of "concentrated poverty" that were not being experienced by Whites. Specifically, they noted that 70 percent of poor Blacks live in poverty neighborhoods, while 70 percent of poor Whites live in nonpoverty neighborhoods. They contend that the concentration of poor Blacks into socially isolated and racially segregated communities with few opportunities for legitimate employment or middle-class role models has contributed significantly to two factors associated with violent crime: family disruption and joblessness. They note that these factors are also associated with higher rates of violence among Whites, but fewer Whites experience them than do Blacks. They point to the history of racism, particularly housing discrimination, deindustrialization, and shifts in the wage structure as major contributors to the funneling of Blacks into urban areas where they are now trapped. They note that the war on drugs has disproportionally taken its toll on such communities by increasing the risk of incarceration and its consequent disadvantages. While both violent and property crime have considerably decreased since the early 1990s, Black urban communities still substantially outpace others in rates of crime.

power—has imposed harsher sentences for possession of crack cocaine, leading to the disproportionate incarceration of African Americans (Alexander, 2010; Katz et al., 2005).

Finally, the third perspective of inequality theory—symbolic interactionism—argues that the world is socially constructed through meanings and labels attached to interactions, language, conditions, and symbols. According to this perspective, certain variables have become associated with—or have symbolic meaning associated with crime and deviance; for example, poverty, low education, or in the case of African Americans, race. In their textbook *Understanding Social Problems,* authors Mooney, Knox, and Schacht explain how members of a society "learn conceptions and meanings of racial and ethnic distinctions through interactions with others and how meanings, labels, and definitions affect racial and ethnic groups" (2007: 176). For instance, they provide the example of the word "black" and the negative connotation attached in words and phrases like "blacklist," "blackball," "black sheep," and "black market." The same could be said of associating

African Americans/"Blacks" with instances of crime. Such labels and associations only serve to perpetuate inequality and subordination among this group. Similarly, history and culture for African Americans may play an imperative role in symbolic interactionism; for example, one's perceptions of being denied a job on the basis of race may be influenced by legacies of the slavery era, racism, and "Jim Crow" segregation (Alexander, 2010; Sigelman & Welch, 1991), which are each a major piece of American history and culture.

Michael Puniskis

See also: Civil Rights Movement; Critical Race Theory; Disproportionality and Crime; Environmental Justice; Institutional Racism; Petit Apartheid; Socioeconomic Factors; Structural Racism and Violence; Theories of Race and Crime

References

Alexander, M. *The New Jim Crow: Mass Incarceration in the Age of Colorblindness.* New York: The New Press, 2010.

Hagan, J., and R. Peterson. *Crime and Inequality.* Palo Alto, CA: Stanford University Press, 1995.

Katz, M. B., and M. J. Stern. "Beyond Discrimination: Understanding African American Inequality in the Twenty-First Century." *Dissent* 70 (2008): 61–5.

Katz, M. B., M. J. Stern, and J. J. Fader. "The New African American Inequality." *Journal of American History,* 92 (1) (2005): 75–108.

Mooney, L. A., D. Knox, and C. Schacht. *Understanding Social Problems.* 5th ed. Belmont, CA: Thompson/Wadsworth Publishers, 2007.

Shapiro, T. M. *The Hidden Cost of Being African American.* Oxford, UK: Oxford University Press, 2004.

Sigelman, L., and S. Welch. *Black Americans' Views of Racial Inequality: The Dream Deferred.* Cambridge, UK: Cambridge University Press, 1991.

Innocence Project

The Innocence Project is a nonprofit legal clinic closely affiliated with the Benjamin N. Cardozo School of Law at Yeshiva University in New York that works to overturn wrongful convictions based upon DNA evidence. It was founded by attorneys Barry C. Scheck and Peter J. Neufeld in 1992 and was originally part of the law school before becoming independent in 2004. In addition to its efforts on behalf of individual prisoners to overturn their wrongful convictions, the Innocence Project works to reform the criminal justice system and prevent future miscarriages of justice.

The Innocence Project represents only individuals who have a claim of actual innocence and whose cases can be proven through DNA evidence. It works to secure the prison release of individuals who have been convicted of a crime they did not commit. DNA testing proved the innocence of 43 percent of Innocence Project clients tested and the guilt of 42 percent of those tested. Test results were inconclusive in approximately 15 percent of cases. The Innocence Project does not accept cases based solely on technical grounds, such as Fourth Amendment arrest, search and seizure issues, or Fifth Amendment Miranda issues. Individuals who have a claim of actual innocence that can be proven by means other than DNA evidence are referred to organizations affiliated with the Innocence Network, which the Innocence Project helped to found.

The Innocence Network is an affiliation of more than 62 local, state, regional, national, and international independent organizations that share information and expertise and work to overturn wrongful convictions and improve the criminal justice system. Criteria for case acceptance vary among the member institutions. In addition to the United States, Innocence Projects have been established in Australia, Canada, New Zealand, and the United Kingdom. In 2012, the work of the Innocence Network helped to exonerate 22 people around the world.

The Innocence Project reported that from 1989 up until late December 2013, there had been 312 postconviction DNA exonerations through its work in the United States. Two hundred and forty-five of those exonerations occurred after 2000. The reported racial breakdown of the exonerations includes: 194 African Americans, or approximately 61 percent; 94 Whites, or 30 percent; 22 Latinos, or 8 percent; and 2 Asian Americans, or 1 percent.

Postconviction DNA exonerations have been won in 36 of the 50 states and Washington, D.C. Eighteen of the exonerees had been sentenced to death in 11 different states and had spent time on death row (202 years collectively) before DNA evidence proved their innocence and led to their release. Collectively, the Innocence Project's exonerees served an average of 13 years in prison prior to their release. The cumulative total for the number of years served by the 312 individuals released is estimated to be about 4,056. The vast majority of the exonerees were men; only four of the first 250 exonerations involved women. Most of the cases involved sex crimes or physical struggles, which increased the likelihood of finding DNA evidence. (See Wrongful Convictions for more information about how their confinement came about.)

On its Web site, the Innocence Project notes that while exoneration stories "are becoming more familiar as more innocent people gain their freedom through post conviction testing," this should not be taken as proof that the criminal justice system is "righting" itself. The organization notes that the common themes that run through wrongful conviction cases globally involve issues of poverty and race and systemic practices such as eyewitness misidentification, invalid or improper forensic science, overzealous police and prosecutors, and inept defense attorneys. The site notes further that these issues are not just things of the past, and they cannot be ignored because they "continue to plague our criminal justice system."

Michael M. Berlin

See also: Eyewitness Misidentification; False Confessions; Wrongful Convictions

References

The Innocence Project. www.innocenceproject.org.
The Innocence Network. www.innocencenetwork.org.

Institutional Racism

Although institutional racism may manifest itself within the workings of any formal social structure, within the criminal justice system it refers to racially differentiated outcomes of cases unrelated to criminal culpability, prior record, or other *race neutral* factors (Walker et al., 2007: 19). As one of a number of forms of racism, institutional racism can be distinguished from individual racism by the manner in which it occurs. It is an outcome of institutional policies, procedures, and statutes rather than of racially biased individual decisions. It can also be distinguished from systematic racism, which occurs across the entire criminal justice system at all times (Walker et al., 2007). Institutional racism is often used interchangeably with structural racism in that both focus on embedded components of discrimination. The latter concept is often applied more broadly to racism occurring in everyday life, while the former focuses on that which occurs within and between social institutions and networks.

There has been a long-standing debate about just how pervasive institutional racism is within the criminal justice system and how to isolate it from other forms of racism. One position holds that any racial disparity in outcomes is a result of racial differences in offending and other factors that are not race related. If racism or discrimination exists in criminal justice institutions, it is individualistic, not institutional or systematic (Wilbanks, 1987). The other position suggests that given the pervasive and historical roots of racism in society, it would follow that criminal justice institutions are reflections of these roots. The marked racial and ethnic disparities in criminal justice outcomes, which harm minorities, particularly African Americans and Hispanics/Latinos, alternately benefit White Americans. The criminal justice system's disparate impact on African American and Hispanic/Latino populations is considered evidence of institutional racism (Mauer, 1999). Within these two poles, however, there are various other positions. This variability is indicative of the controversial nature of racism and discrimination and the complicated way the existence of these social dynamics are negotiated within American social institutions.

Empirical findings regarding the existence of institutional racism within the American criminal justice system tend to vary depending upon whether those studies focus on policing, courts, corrections, or other criminal justice components, and they are confounded by the fact that while showing disproportionate minority contact with the criminal justice system may be problematic in some way, such showings do not automatically justify an inference that unwarranted intentional racial discrimination is taking place (Reitzel & Piquero, 2006).

Police

There are a number of ways in which police have contact with citizens and where institutional racism can play a role. This includes during police stops, searches, and arrests on the street; in drug- and gang-related enforcement; and even in calls for service that are not related to a crime. Differences in police stop, search, and arrest rates, for example, regularly show overrepresentation of African Americans and Hispanics/Latinos and have come to be a contentious issue over the past two decades (Reitzel, 2011). One form of institutional racism alleged to be practiced by the police is racial profiling, an issue that gained national prominence beginning in the late 1990s and is considered by many to be evidence of both institutional and individual racism.

As shown in Figure 1, since at least 1973 there has been a large disparity in arrests by race, which is believed to be an effect of factors beyond any race-differentiated crime rates, and therefore a result of racial profiling. This is principally relevant for drug-enforcement policies, which have led to perhaps the most striking racial disparities within policing (Reitzel, 2011). Institutional racism can also occur in calls for service. According to Walker et al. (2007), many Hispanic/Latino neighborhoods refuse to call police because they fear that it will lead to checks on their immigration status. Likewise, there is a great deal of anecdotal evidence that police seem to take longer responding to service calls in predominantly African American and other minority neighborhoods.

Courts and Imprisonment

According to Walker and colleagues (2007: 107), racial profiling is only one component of a "larger pattern of racial disparities in the criminal justice system." Since 1986, when Congress passed the Anti-Drug Abuse Act, courts began sentencing

Figure 1. African American & White Arrest Rates per 1,000 people from 1973-2005

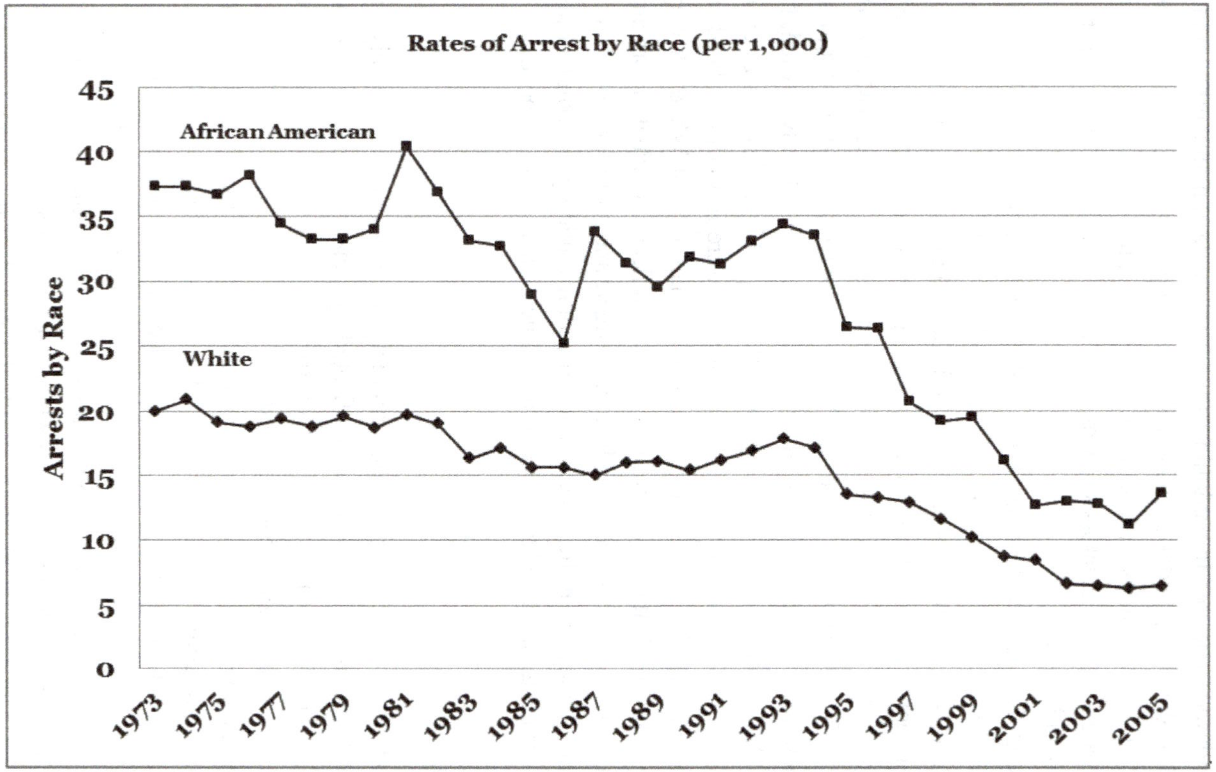

Rates of Arrest by Race (per 1,000)

* Data for Figure 1 obtained from the Bureau of Justice Statistics (http://bjs.ojp.usdoj.gov/index.cfm)

drug defendants to much more punitive penalties, which led to an *imprisonment boom* (Mauer, 1999). This legislation also created a 100:1 sentencing disparity for crack versus powder forms of cocaine.[1] Indeed, the crack cocaine disparity is clearly a primary form of institutional racism since the penalties were greater for crack cocaine, believed to be sold in predominantly lower socioeconomic urban minority communities, than for powder cocaine, believed to be sold and used among more affluent White communities. Michael Tonry (1995) called the legislation *malign neglect* and argued that legislators knew of the potential racialized outcomes that the legislation would have.

Bureau of Justice Statistics data show that the biggest contributor to imprisonment rates has been increases in prison sentences for violent crimes. However, since the 1980s, drug-related imprisonment grew at the fastest rate among all crimes. Drug-related imprisonment now comprises the second largest number of offenders in prison. Most of those offenders were arrested for nonviolent drug offenses (Mauer, 1999; Kennedy, 1997). As shown in Figure 2, by 1986 a racial disparity in drug-related imprisonment rates between Whites and African Americans already existed, but it increased substantially after the legislation was passed. As Figure 3 shows, a considerable proportion of the increasing imprisonment rates were from drug-related crime arrests, which affected poor minorities much more than affluent Whites. It may be impossible to know whether some of these statistics reflect individual racism among police, who make the decisions about who to investigate and arrest for drug offending; it does clearly indicate that the policies and procedures guiding the criminal justice system contribute to racialized differences in sentencing and imprisonment.

Summary

The racism that exists within the current criminal justice system is not simply a matter of individual criminal justice agents motivated by racial bias or individual politicians bent on destroying minorities. Rather, the racism driving inequalities in the criminal justice system stems from a combination of long-held racialized and stereotypical thinking about criminal behavior and misconceptions regarding demographic factors, which are commonly associated with drug use and sales that led to racial biases being built into the very policies and procedures guiding decisionmaking in the criminal justice system (Alexander, 2010). The racism is therefore endemic—embedded in the operation of the formal institutions and reinforced by both formal and informal decisionmaking associated with those institutions. This much is clearly evident when examining the effects of criminal justice policies, which have a wide-ranging impact on decisionmaking throughout the criminal justice system.

In sum, institutional racism continues to play a role within the criminal justice system. Policies and procedures guiding decisionmaking in criminal justice can

Figure 2. Imprisonment by Race in the United States from 1986-1997

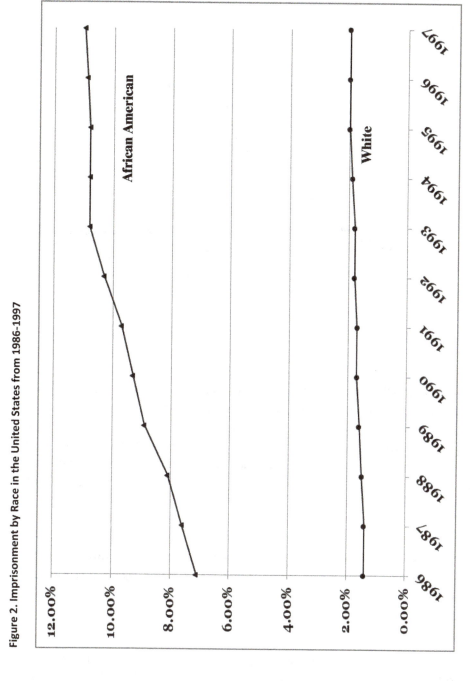

African American

White

* Data for Figure 2 obtained from the Bureau of Justice Statistics (http://bjs.ojp.usdoj.gov/index.cfm)

Figure 3. Arrests for Drug Related Crimes Nationally 1970-2008

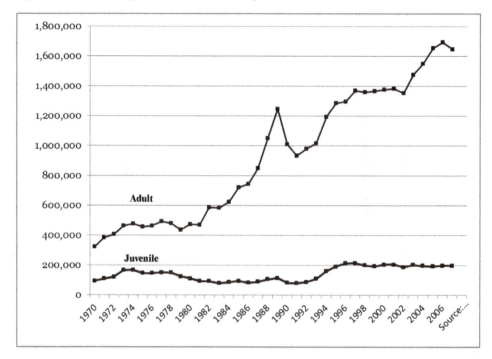

* Data for the table obtained from the Bureau of Justice Statistics (http://bjs.ojp.usdoj.gov/index.cfm)

very well be racist even when those policies were not intended to negatively affect minorities. However, what distinguishes institutional racism from individual racism is not intent but outcomes. Well-meaning policies and even policies designed explicitly to tackle existing crime problems in a race-neutral manner can and have led to institutionalizing racism. Consequently, institutional racism cannot simply be eliminated until future policies explicitly address the racial impact and influences that already exist.

John David Reitzel

See also: Carmichael, Stokely; Fair Sentencing Act of 2010; Institutional Racism: A United Kingdom Perspective; Racial Profiling; Rockefeller Drug Laws: Policy Review; Structural Racism and Violence

Note

1. On July 28, 2010, Congress passed legislation reducing the crack vs. powder cocaine disparity from 100:1 to 18:1, which substantially reduced but did not eliminate the racial disparity.

References

Alexander, M. *The New Jim Crow: Mass Incarceration in the Age of Colorblindness.* New York: The New Press, 2010.

Kennedy, R. *Race, Crime and the Law.* New York: Pantheon, 1997.

Mauer, M. *Race to Incarcerate.* New York: The New Press, 1999.

Reitzel, J., and A. Piquero. "Does It Exist? Studying Citizens' Attitudes of Racial Profiling." *Police Quarterly* 9 (2006): 161–83.

Reitzel, J. D. "Race, Crime, and Policing: The Impact of Law Enforcement on Persistent-Race Differentiated Arrest Rates." In *Disproportionate Minority Contact: Ending Differential Treatment and Creating Change through Procedural Justice,* edited by Nicolle Parsons-Pollard, 159–78. Durham, NC: Carolina Academic Press, 2011.

Tonry, M. *Malign Neglect.* New York: Oxford University Press, 1995.

Walker, S., C. Spohn, and M. Delone. *The Color of Justice: Race, Ethnicity, and Crime in America.* Belmont, CA: Wadsworth, 2007.

Wilbanks, W. *The Myth of a Racist Criminal Justice System.* Belmont, CA: Wadsworth, 1987.

Institutional Racism: A United Kingdom Perspective

Racism against Black ethnic minorities within the United Kingdom's criminal justice system is well catalogued and consists of disproportionate arrests, convictions, and prison sentences. Historically, racism within the police service has been explained using a number of theories. The "bad apple" thesis proposed that racial prejudice and discrimination could be explained by the presence of a few racist police officers' individual actions. The "reflection of society" thesis suggested that because the police service was a cross-section of society, it was inevitable that some police officers drawn from that society would be racist. A third concept was the "canteen culture" thesis, which argues that new police officers become indoctrinated with the racist and/or stereotypical views held by senior officers (Bowling & Phillips, 2002).

The degree and level of racist behavior soon outgrew such concepts, however, and the concept of "institutional racism" began to resonate. The concept of institutional racism was introduced in the United States by Carmichael and Hamilton in 1967. They argued that racism could consist of individual racism in which explicit racism is expressed and practiced by individuals or institutional racism in which "anti-black attitudes and practices, which are woven throughout all of the major institutions of society . . . have the effect of maintaining 'black' disadvantage" (Singh, 2000). As Carmichael and Hamilton express it, institutional racism originates in the operation of established and respected forces in the society. It relies on the active and pervasive operation of anti-black attitudes and practices. A sense of superior group position prevails: whites are "better" than blacks and therefore blacks should be subordinated to whites. This is a racist attitude and it permeates society on both the individual and institutional level, covertly or overtly. (Carmichael & Hamilton, 1967)

Although the concept of institutionalized racism has been applied in the United Kingdom to a range of institutions including the health service, housing, and social services, its connection with the operation of the criminal justice system has gained the greatest prominence. In the 1980s, a series of riots in Brixton, London, and Toxteth in Liverpool occurred, involving disaffected Black youths who had been stopped and searched repeatedly under controversial police powers. Those riots led to an inquiry by Lord Scarman, who noted the "ill-considered, immature and racially prejudiced actions of some officers in their dealings on the streets with young black people" but firmly rejected the notion of institutional racism in relation to the actions of police officers during those riots. He argued that "[i]f by [institutionally racist] it is meant that it is . . . a society which knowingly, as a matter of policy, discriminates against black people, I reject the allegation" (Scarman, 1981).

On April 22, 1993, Stephen Lawrence, a black British teenager, was attacked by five White youths and stabbed twice, and subsequently died of his injuries. It was not his death that proved the turning point in the United Kingdom's reassessment of the nature of racial prejudice within its police service, but rather the manner in which the murder was dealt with by the police service. The MacPherson Inquiry, created to investigate the murder, argued that there were fundamental errors in how the case was handled by the police service. In summary, the report noted that "[t]he investigation was marred by a combination of professional incompetence, institutional racism and a failure of leadership by senior officers." Furthermore, "[a] flawed [Metropolitan Police Service] review failed to expose these inadequacies [and] [t]he second investigation could not salvage the faults of the first investigation" (MacPherson, 1999). The initial police response was criticized for its apparent lack of direction and organization during the crucial hours following the murder. No officers at the scene took adequate steps to pursue the suspects because it was a commonly held view that the incident had emanated from a fight rather than an unprovoked attack. This assumption pervaded the investigation and resulted in a failure to treat it as a racially motivated assault. Mr. and Mrs. Lawrence, the victim's parents, were deemed by the inquiry to have been treated with insensitivity and a lack of sympathy by the police service. Indeed, it was suggested by one witness to the inquiry that the victim's race determined the nature of the investigative response. Mr. Patton, a lawyer, noted that had the victim been white, "my submission history suggests that the police would have probably swamped the estate that night and they would remain there, probably for however long it took, to ensure that if the culprits were on that estate something would be done about the situation" (MacPherson, 1999). The MacPherson Inquiry contrasted racism, which it defined as "conduct or words or practices which advantage people because of their colour, culture or ethnic origin," with institutional racism, which it defined as the "collective failure of an organisation to provide an appropriate and professional service because of their colour, culture or ethnic origin." The inquiry argued that such racism could be "seen or detected in processes, attitudes, and behaviour which amount to discrimination through unwitting prejudice, ignorance, thoughtlessness, and racist stereotyping which disadvantage minority ethnic people" (MacPherson, 1999).

Even though the inquiry dismissed the notion that institutional racism was the sole cause of the failure in the investigative process, it constituted an issue that would continue to manifest itself "because of the failure of the organisation openly and adequately to recognise and address its existence and causes by policy, example and leadership." Furthermore, the inquiry argued that "[w]ithout recognition and action to eliminate such racism it can prevail as part of the ethos or culture of the organisation. It is a corrosive disease" (MacPherson, 1999). Although the commissioner of the Metropolitan Police, which had been responsible for investigating the Lawrence case, rejected the assertion that institutionalized racism was present in his force, a number of other senior officers accepted the assertion in relation to their own forces. Thus, for example, the chief constable of the Greater Manchester Police argued that "[w]e have a society that has got institutional racism. Greater Manchester Police, therefore, has institutional racism. Some of it is not the overt type; it's that which has been internalised by individuals" (MacPherson, 1999). Equally, the deputy chief constable of the West Yorkshire Police noted that "if institutional racism means unintentional prejudice, that such prejudice is subconscious, almost subliminal, then I totally accept the comment" (Burrell, 1998).

The Home Secretary, responding to the report, argued that "any long-established, white-dominated organisation is liable to have procedures, practices and a culture that tend to exclude or to disadvantage non-white people. The police service, in that respect, is little different from other parts of the criminal justice system—or from Government Departments" (U.K. Parliament, 1999). This view was echoed by the chief constable of Derbyshire, John Newing, who noted that institutional racism was "the racism which is inherent in wider society which shapes our attitudes and behaviour . . . [which] are then reinforced or reshaped by the culture of the organisation a person works for" (MacPherson, 1999).

Arguably, the core difficulty in establishing the concept of institutional racism within policing is that the initial investigation processes are undertaken by individual police officers and it is not easy to discern from their behavior whether it exists, and if so, where within their governing organization the source of that behavior (racist or otherwise) is located. In the Lawrence case, the MacPherson Inquiry noted that "there was a 'collective failure' of a group of officers to provide an appropriate and professional service" (MacPherson, 1999). However, those officers' failure to provide the requisite service may not necessarily have been repeated by a different set of officers sent to investigate the murder of Lawrence. As Lea has noted, the context in which those officers were deemed to have failed makes it difficult to "distinguish institutionalised from individual racism, or racism from incompetence" (Lea, 2000). The MacPherson Inquiry noted that one of the indications of institutionalized racism was the failure by the Metropolitan Police Service to categorize the Lawrence murder as racist in nature. However, the MacPherson Inquiry itself reported that 50 percent of the officers involved in the murder inquiry regarded the incident as a racially motivated attack.

A core theme throughout the debate regarding the presence of institutionalized racism, whether in a criminal justice context or other institutional context, is the fact that the racist actions that occur as a result may not have been intentional and/or based on a racist attitude. It has been and continues to be difficult to establish whether the racism manifested at an organizational level within systems is covert or overt, intentional or accidental. It is perhaps a somewhat redundant exercise because arguably, the greatest endeavor lies in ensuring that the organizational causes and the operational consequences of institutional racism are addressed and ameliorated.

Evidence that institutional racism in U.K. policing is far from being ameliorated can be found in the results of a study released by the London School of Economics and the Open Society Justice Initiative in 2012. The study found that Black people in England and Wales are nearly 30 times more likely to be stopped and searched than are White people, even in predominantly White areas. The exact figure is that Blacks were 29.7 times more likely to be stopped than Whites in 2011. This was up from a 2010 figure of 26.6 (Townsend, 2012).

Rob McCusker

References

Bowling, B., and C. Phillips. *Racism, Crime and Justice.* London: Longman, 2002.

Burrell, I. "Twelve Police Forces Admit Racism." *The Independent,* October 16, 1998. http://www.independent.co.uk/news/twelve-police-forces-admit-racism-1178449.html.

Carmichael, S., and C. Hamilton. *Black Power: The Politics of Liberation in America.* New York: Penguin Books, 1967.

Lea, J. "The MacPherson Report and the Question of Institutional Racism." *The Howard Journal* 39, no. 3 (August 2000): 219–33.

MacPherson, W. "The Inquiry into the Matters Arising from the Death of Stephen Lawrence." London, February 15, 1999.

Scarman, L. *The Scarman Report.* London: Home Office, 1981.

Singh, G. "The Concept and Context of Institutional Racism." In A. Marlow and B. Loveday, *After MacPherson: Policing after the Stephen Lawrence Inquiry,* 29–40. Dorset, UK: Russell House Publishing, 2000.

Townsend, M. "Stop and Search 'Racial Profiling' by Police on the Increase Claims Study." *The Guardian,* January 14, 2012.

U.K. Parliament. House of Commons Hansard Debates, February 24, 1999. Column 391. http://www.publications.parliament.uk/pa/cm199899/cmhansrd/vo990224/debtext/90224-21.htm.

Inter-Racial Offending

The fear of inter-racial offending—that is, crime in which the perpetrator and victim are from different racial groups—tends to be high, especially among Whites fearing that they will be victimized by offenders from racial or ethnic minority groups. However, annual official statistics confirm that while fear of inter-racial offending is high, actual inter-racial offending is extremely low (see Homicide, Intra-Racial Offending, and Sex Crimes and Race). All official data sources confirm that while various groups fear criminal victimization, rates of violent victimization are highest for Blacks, particularly those in the inner city. Data from the National Crime Victimization Survey (NCVS) and the FBI's *Uniform Crime Reports* (UCR) confirm that for personal crimes, such as homicide and assault, most victims and offenders are from the same racial group and most often even know each other. Victims and offenders are often acquaintances, intimate partners, or family members. Women, for example, are more likely to be killed by intimate partners than strangers within or outside their racial group, and Black women are at an elevated level of risk for such victimization. Continued patterns of racially segregated residential living minimize contact across racial lines and thereby hold rates of intra-racial, or within-group, offending in place.

Hate crimes are the one area where the normal pattern of intra-racial offending is broken. The objective of a hate crime is to show disapproval, hate, discontent, or distrust for an entire social group. Data from the National Incident-Based Reporting System (NIBRS) documents that hate crimes based on race represent the highest percentage of reported hate crimes (see Hate Crimes) and that a significantly greater percentage of Blacks than Whites are its victims. Victims of hate crime can fall within more than one targeted category. In 2009, the U.S. Department of Justice reported that of 7,775 single-bias hate crime incidents, approximately 49 percent were racially motivated, with the majority being motivated by anti-Black bias. A staggering 71.4 percent of 3,816 racially motivated incidents resulted from anti-Black bias, roughly 50 percent greater than incidents reported as motivated by anti-White bias.

Victims of hate crimes are typically strangers who visually represent a particular group and incidents typically involve multiple perpetrators. The 2009 UCR reported that 64.6 percent of hate crimes against individuals involved intimidation, assault, rape, and murder. President George W. Bush signed the initial legislation authorizing the collection of data that would facilitate an aggressive federal response to those who commit hate crimes. The Matthew Shepard and James Byrd, Jr. Hate Crimes Prevention Act, including criminal penalties as severe as death, was signed by President Barack Obama in 2009.

In contrast to hate crimes statistics and the actual level of nationally reported inter-racial offending, focus on Black disproportionality (see Disproportionality and Crime) in arrest and conviction for so-called "street crime" receives the bulk of media and academic attention. This in turn creates heightened fear of random victimization by young Black men on the theory that they are seeking illegitimate economic gain or are naturally violent, hyper-masculine and predatory. Despite the existence of other statistics, conservatives point to the marginal difference in the percentage of White on Black homicide and Black on White homicide, 86 versus 94 percent (see Homicide), and similar robbery statistics to justify their inter-racial offending fears.

Robert Bing and Ruby Bouie

See also: Disproportionality and Crime; Hate Crimes; Homicide; Intra-Racial Offending; Sex Crimes and Race

References

D'Alessio, S. J., and L. Stolzenberg. "Racial Animosity and Interracial Crime." *Criminology* 47, no. 1 (2009): 269–96.

King, R. D., K. R. Johnson, and K. McGeever. "Demography of the Legal Profession and Racial Disparities in Sentencing." *Law and Society Review* 44, no. 1 (2010): 1–32.

Mears, D. P., C. Mancini, and E. A. Stewart. "Whites' Concern about Crime: The Effects of Interracial Contact." *Journal of Research in Crime and Delinquency* 46, no. 4 (2009): 524–52.

Parker, K. F., and P. L. McCall. "Adding Another Piece to the Inequality-Homicide Puzzle." *Homicide Studies* 1, no. 1 (1997): 35–60.

Saucier, D. A., T. L. Brown, R. C. Mitchell, and A. J. Cawman. "Effects of Victims' Characteristics on Attitudes toward Hate Crimes." *Journal of Interpersonal Violence* 21, no. 7 (2006): 890–909.

Saucier, D. A., J. M. Hockett, and A. S. Wallenberg. "The Impact of Racial Slurs and Racism on the Perceptions and Punishment of Violent Crime." *Journal of Interpersonal Violence* 23, no. 5 (2008): 685–701.

Saucier, D. A., J. M. Hockett, D. C. Zanotti, and S. Heffel. "Effects of Racism on Perceptions and Punishment of Intra- and Interracial Crimes." *Journal of Interpersonal Violence* 25, no. 10 (2010): 1767–84.

Tremblay, M., and P. Tremblay. "Social Structure, Interaction Opportunities, and the Direction of Violent Offenses." *Journal of Research in Crime and Delinquency* 35, no. 3 (1998): 295–315.

U.S. Department of Justice, Bureau of Justice Statistics. *National Crime Victimization Survey, 2008.* Washington, DC: Government Printing Office, 2009.

U.S. Department of Justice, Federal Bureau of Investigation. *Hate Crime Statistics, 2009.* Washington, DC: Government Printing Office, 2010.

Intra-Racial Offending

Intra-racial offending is a reference to crimes committed within racial groups. For example, the term "Black on Black crime" is frequently used to describe offending where the victim and perpetrator are both African American. But incidents involving White victims and White perpetrators are almost never referred to as "White on White" crime (Russell, 1998; Muhammad, 2010), although this intra-racial pattern is also the norm.

Information about the extent of intra-racial offending is available through the Bureau of Justice Statistics (BJS), the statistical arm of the U.S. Department of Justice (DOJ). With regard to homicides, the data reveal that between 1976 and 2005, 86 percent of White victims were killed by Whites and 94 percent of Black victims were killed by Blacks. Stranger homicides are an exception to this general pattern and are more likely to involve inter-racial crimes, but stranger homicides make up a small portion of homicides overall (DOJ, 2006; 2009; 2011). Women in particular are likely to become victims of homicide at the hands of acquaintances or intimate partners. Given patterns of social segregation, this means that the offenders are likely to be of their same race. Intra-racial offending also holds as the norm with regard to both rape and assault. For rape, the data reveal that for both Blacks and Whites, the figure for intra-racial incidents is around 74 percent (DOJ, 2011; 2009).

Since most crime tends to be intra-racial, the focus on Black on Black crime can be politically charged (Bing, 1990; 2010). While on the one hand it can be seen as a means to focus attention on reducing the number of Black victims, on the other, it is seen as a means of drawing Black offenders into the criminal justice system, while similar White offenders and victims go unnoticed (Muhammad, 2010; Alexander, 2010). The term "Black on Black crime" can be traced back to publications by Headley (1983) and Pouissant (1983) and a book titled *Black on Black Crime* edited by P. Ray Kedia in 1994. Kedia's book was motivated by research from conservative scholars like former U.S. senator and Harvard University sociologist Daniel Patrick Moynihan, whose 1965 report *The Negro Family: The Case for National Attention,* also known as *The Moynihan Report,* presented the social circumstances of Blacks in a very negative light. The report was criticized for "blaming the victim" (Ryan, 1971) of economic oppression and family disruption for its divided and economically depressed state, especially its reliance on government welfare, which required that men not be present in the home in order for women and children to receive welfare benefits. Those single female-headed households ultimately came to be and continue to be blamed as a primary contributor to "Black on Black" criminality and violence (Sampson & Wilson, 1995).

The focus on Black on Black intra-racial offending to the exclusion of White on White intra-racial offending creates the impression that crime is exclusively a Black phenomenon (Russell, 1998; Muhammad, 2010). It can perpetuate the belief that Blacks commit more crime than their White counterparts or that being Black is tantamount to being violent (Russell-Brown, 2004). It obscures the fact that each year, nearly 70 percent of persons arrested nationally are White. If crime is seen as part of Black culture, the net effect might be to reserve treatment and noncustodial programs for arrestees who are non-Black. The phrase "Black on Black crime" may also have the effect of intensifying aggressive policing of everyone in minority neighborhoods, rather than encouraging the police to look for individual criminals in order to address disproportionately high rates of crime (Jones-Brown, 2007). Finally, there is also evidence that the one-sided focus (Black on Black exclusive of White on White) on intra-racial offending has made the color of one's skin a source of fear and suspicion for the general public (Eberhardt et al., 2004; Gabbidon, 2003).

Robert Bing

See also: Inter-Racial Offending

References

Alexander, Michelle. *The New Jim Crow: Mass Incarceration in the Age of Colorblindness.* New York: The New Press, 2010.

Bing, Robert L. *Race, Crime and the Media.* New York: McGraw-Hill, 2010.

Bing, Robert L. "Politicizing Black-on-Black Crime: A Critique of Terminological Preference." Reprinted in *Race and Crime: Perspectives,* edited by Robert L. Bing and Alejandro del Carmen, 35–9. Madison, WI: Coursewise Publishing, 1990.

Eberhardt, Jennifer, Valerie Purdie, Phillip Goff, and Paul Davies. "Seeing Black: Race, Crime and Visual Processing." *Journal of Personality and Social Psychology* 87, no. 6 (2004): 876–93.

Gabbidon, Shaun. "Racial Profiling by Store Clerks and Security Personnel in Retail Establishments: An Exploration of 'Shopping While Black.'" *Journal of Contemporary Criminal Justice* 19, no. 3 (2003): 345–64.

Headley, Bernard. "Black on Black Crime: The Myth and the Reality." *Crime and Social Justice* 20 (1983): 50–62.

Jones-Brown, Delores. "Forever the Symbolic Assailant: The More Things Change the More They Remain the Same." *Criminology and Public Policy* 6, no. 1 (2007): 103–22.

Kedia, P. Ray. *Black on Black Crime: Facing Facts—Challenging Fictions.* Bristol, IN: Wyndham Hall Press, 1994.

Muhammad, Khalil G. *The Condemnation of Blackness: Race, Crime and the Making of Modern Urban America.* Cambridge, MA: Harvard University Press, 2010.

Pouissant, Alvin. "Black on Black Homicide: A Psychological Perspective." *Victimology* 8, nos. 3, 4 (1983): 161–69.

Russell, Katheryn. *The Color of Crime.* New York: New York University Press, 1998.

Russell-Brown, Katheryn. *Underground Codes: Race, Crime and Related Fires.* New York: New York University Press, 2004.

Ryan, William. *Blaming the Victim.* New York: Random House, 1971.

Sampson, Robert, and William Julius Wilson. "Toward a Theory of Race, Crime and Urban Inequality." In *Crime and Inequality,* edited by Ruth Peterson and John Hagan, 37–54. Palo Alto, CA: Stanford University Press, 1995.

U.S. Department of Justice (DOJ). *Criminal Victimization in the United States, 2008 Statistical Tables.* Washington, DC: U.S. Government Printing Office, 2011.

U.S. Department of Justice (DOJ). *Crime in the United States.* Washington, DC: U.S. Government Printing Office, 2009.

U.S. Department of Justice (DOJ). *Criminal Justice Sourcebook.* Washington, DC: U.S. Government Printing Office, 2006.

J

Jackson, Jesse (1941–)

Jesse Jackson was born on October 8, 1941, in Greenville, South Carolina. His mother, Helen Burns, a 16-year-old single mother, named him Jesse Louis Burns. His biological father, Noah Robinson, was already married and took no part in Jackson's childhood. In 1943, when Jackson's mother married Charles Jackson, Jesse took the surname of his stepfather. Much of Jackson's early childhood was marked by poverty and hardship. His experience as an impoverished African American would later inspire Jackson to fight poverty and hunger across the United States.

Jackson attended Sterling High School in Greenville, where he excelled in basketball. Upon his graduation in 1959, he received the offer of a professional basketball contract, which he rejected so he could attend the University of Illinois on a football scholarship. A year later he transferred to the North Carolina Agriculture and Technical College (North Carolina A & T) in Greensboro to study sociology. It was at this school that Jackson first became involved with the Civil Rights Movement. During 1963, fighting for the desegregation of local restaurants and theatres, he organized a series of sit-ins and marches that led to mass arrests. After graduating from college, Jackson expressed a desire to become an ordained minister. Despite receiving a scholarship to attend the Chicago Theological Seminary to become a minister, he left the program midway to commit himself full time to the Civil Rights Movement.

In 1965, Jackson joined Martin Luther King, Jr., in the Southern Christian Leadership Conference (SCLC) to help push for expanded voting rights for Blacks. He also helped organize Operation Breadbasket, which aided Black businesses and pressured segregated White businesses to end discriminatory practices. Through the use of selective buying and boycotts, Operation Breadbasket encouraged more local dairies and supermarkets to hire African American workers. Jackson's leadership as national director was seen as key in its success. In 1968, Jackson was officially ordained as a Baptist minister.

After a failed run for mayor of Chicago in 1971, Jackson resigned from the SCLC and founded his own organization, People United to Save Humanity (PUSH). His organization expanded into more areas of social development for Blacks across the nation. He advocated for Black self-help through radio programs, campaigns, and awards. PUSH helped to encourage many businesses to hire more Black workers and to buy from Black suppliers. During the 1970s, Jackson led several marches, such as the "March for Jobs" in 1975.

By the 1980s, Jackson had become one of the best-known civil rights activists and had gathered a large following. As a spokesman for the African American community, Jackson helped to influence voters, which contributed to the election of the first African American mayor of Chicago, Harold Washington. His growing interest and influence in politics led him to run for president of the United States. In 1984 he ran for the Democratic presidential nomination and won several primaries. He ran again for the nomination in 1988 and came in second to Michael Dukakis after gathering two million votes. Despite his failed election runs, Jackson helped to show the importance and power of African American voters. In response to the growing drug epidemic during the mid 1980s, Jackson called for a more efficient war on drugs, claiming that fighting the supply of drugs would be key in stopping drug abuse and violence in the African American community.

In the mid 1990s, Jackson returned to the leadership of PUSH, where he advocated for the hiring of more minority executives and the expansion of African American businesses. His efforts in the field of civil rights were officially recognized in 2000, when he was awarded the Presidential Medal of Freedom by President Clinton. Today, Jackson continues to campaign for the empowerment and equal rights of African Americans in addition to leading the fight against poverty. He still manages his organization, which is now named the Rainbow/Push Coalition.

Giovanni Circo

See also: Civil Rights Movement; Conyers, Jr., John; Racial Profiling; Sharpton, Jr., Alfred Charles; Southern Christian Leadership Conference (SCLS); Student Nonviolent Coordinating Committee (SNCC)

References

Bruns, R. *Jesse Jackson: A Biography.* Westport, CT: Greenwood Press, 2005.

Encyclopædia Britannica. "Jesse Jackson." 2011. http://www.britannica.com/EBchecked/topic/298824/Jesse-Jackson.

Frady, M. *Jesse: The Life and Pilgrimage of Jesse Jackson.* New York: Simon & Schuster Paperbacks, 1996.

Jackson, Jesse. "Keep Hope Alive." Democratic National Convention. Atlanta, Georgia, July 19, 1988.

Jefferson, The Honorable William Jennings (1947–)

William Jennings "Bill" Jefferson was born on March 14, 1947, in Lake Providence, a tiny hamlet located in northeastern Louisiana's East Carroll Parish. He was one of nine children. Although his family owned the land as opposed to following the predominant custom of sharecropping, he was still subjected to racism and exposed to racially motivated violence and the misuse of local law enforcement—efforts to instill fear in the Black community so that its members would accept an inferior status (Jefferson, 2007). This experience motivated him to get an education so that he could be of service and promote racial equality.

In 1969, Jefferson received his bachelor's degree from Southern University, a historically Black college located in Baton Rouge, Louisiana. Jefferson was outspoken and passionate in addressing social injustice. For example, he used legal arguments against a conservative Democratic governor, John McKeithen, to point out the lack of support for maintaining Southern University's physical and technological infrastructure and was able to successfully negotiate improvements, despite racial and economic turmoil in Baton Rouge at the time. Jefferson earned his JD from Harvard University in 1972 and his LLM in taxation from Georgetown University in 1996. He served as a commissioned officer in the U.S. Army with six years of reserve service, from 1969 to 1975, and he served as attorney and clerk of the court for the Eastern District of Louisiana from 1972 to 1973. His wife is Dr. Andrea Green Jefferson and they have five daughters, three of whom hold degrees from Harvard College and Harvard Law School, one from Boston University and Emerson College, and the youngest from Brown, Georgetown, and the School of Medicine at Tulane University (Jefferson, 2007).

According to his biography, much of Jefferson's passion for public service can be attributed to his desire for racial and economic equality, especially in the area of education. From 1973 to 1975, Jefferson served as a legislative assistant to conservative Democratic U.S. senator Bennett Johnson, Jr. (D-LA), seeking to learn the inner workings of the political process while developing education legislation. From 1979 to 1990, he served in the Louisiana State Senate (D-New Orleans). Twice he unsuccessfully ran for mayor of New Orleans, in 1982 and 1986. His service as chair of the Governmental Affairs Committee, the Finance Committee, and the Special Budget Stabilization Committee garnered him respect from diverse political constituencies, given his efforts to "rein in state spending and develop more accurate revenue projections" (*Congressional Quarterly,* 1994: 644).

In 1990, he won the U.S. congressional seat for Louisiana's second district, becoming the state's first Black U.S. representative since the end of Reconstruction. Jefferson was elected to this seat eight additional times, garnering more than 73 percent of the vote in nearly every successive run (Office of the Clerk, U.S.

House of Representatives, 2011). His seniority and influence grew after joining the Congressional Black Caucus and receiving appointments to the Education and Labor Committee and the Ways and Means Committee.

Starting in 2005, allegedly via a company owned by his wife and children, Jefferson was accused of engaging in schemes to funnel monetary inducements from *iGate,* an information technology company located in Louisville, Kentucky, into shell companies in West Africa. The accusations against him include that he promised *iGate* that he would influence the U.S. Army to procure its broadband networking technology, and that he encouraged the company to give him quid pro quo financial incentives in return for seeking to "influence high-ranking officials in Nigeria, Ghana, and Cameroon. He would meet with the personnel of the Export-Import Bank of the United States to facilitate potential financing for *iGate* business deals in those countries" (Department of Justice, 2009: 1).

On July 30, 2005, at the behest of the Federal Bureau of Investigation (FBI), Lori Mody, an *iGate* investor, donned video surveillance gear and carried a briefcase containing $100,000 in $100 bills to meet with Jefferson at the Ritz Carlton Hotel in Arlington, Virginia. Jefferson noted that $50,000 would need to be given to Nigerian vice president Atiku Abubakar "'as a motivating factor' to make sure they obtained contracts for *iGate*" (Lengel, 2006: 1). Several meetings between Mody and Jefferson were recorded. On August 3, 2005, FBI agents executed a search warrant at Jefferson's home, discovering approximately $90,000 in cash in the freezer, "in $10,000 increments wrapped in aluminum foil and stuffed inside frozen-food containers" (Lengel, 2006: 2). Further, serial numbers found on the currency in the freezer matched serial numbers of funds given by the FBI to their informant.

Although Jefferson maintained his innocence in the wake of these allegations as well as during the controversial raid on his office in the Rayburn House Office Building on May 20, 2006, a plea deal reached by former staff aide Brett M. Pfeffer provided further evidence of wrongdoing. Pfeffer "told federal prosecutors that 'Representative A,' whom he worked for from 1995 to 1998, insisted his wife should perform all the legal work for a $45 million deal that involved the sale of a Kentucky company's technology to Nigeria" (Radelat, 2006: 1). Sources noted that the raid on Jefferson's Washington, D.C., office was the first time the FBI subjected a sitting congressperson to such a search (Lengel, 2006).

In the midst of his legal battles, as the most senior seated Democrat, Jefferson lost his bid for a tenth term to a Republican candidate in December 2008. On August 5, 2009, he was found guilty of "soliciting bribes, depriving citizens of honest service, money laundering and using his office as a racketeering enterprise" (Tilove, 2009: 1). However, he was acquitted of obstructing justice, violating the Foreign Corrupt Practices Act, and seeking to bribe foreign government officials (Barakat, 2009). Although he was sentenced to 13 years of incarceration, the longest sentence ever imposed against a member of Congress on corruption charges, the former congressman remained free pending appeal. Oral arguments for his appeal were set for May 2011 (Alpert, 2011b). In December 2011, his request for a new trial began to seem more promising when a three-judge appellate panel expressed some reservations regarding the validity of 4 of the 11 counts for which Jefferson was convicted. At issue was whether the trial judge incorrectly instructed the jury regarding what constituted corruption as opposed to private business transactions outside the reach of bribery statutes for members of Congress (Alpert, 2011a).

In his 2008 book entitled *Daddy's Pelican*, Jefferson wrote that if one "is sincerely missed, at that moment a miracle can occur" (91). Despite the politician's hopes, in March 2012, a federal appeals court in Virginia affirmed Jefferson's conviction (Associated Press, 2012). Jefferson, who had been free on bond throughout the appeals process, reported to a low-security Texas prison in May 2012 to begin his 13-year sentence (Alpert, 2012).

Hank Brightman

See also: African Diaspora, Crime, and Justice; Conyers, Jr., John; Prisons; Sentencing Disparities

References

Alpert, B. 2012. "William Jefferson Reports to Texas Prison to Begin 13-Year Sentence." *The New Orleans Times-Picayune,* May 4, 2012.

Alpert, B. 2011a. "William Jefferson Has Chance to Shed 4 Guilty Counts, Experts Say." *The New Orleans Times-Picayune,* December 13, 2011.

Alpert, B. 2011b. "Virginia Court Sets Oral Arguments for William Jefferson's Appeal, in May." *The New Orleans Times-Picayune,* February 21, 2011.

Associated Press. "Virginia: Conviction Is Upheld." *The New York Times,* March 27, 2012. http://www.nytimes.com/2012/03/27/us/former-louisiana-congressmans-conviction-upheld.html?ref=williamjjefferson&_r=0.

Barakat, M. "William Jefferson, Former Congressman, Convicted in Freezer Cash Case." *The Huffington Post,* August 5, 2009. http://www.huffingtonpost.com/2009/08/05/william-jefferson-former-_n_252312.html.

Congressional Quarterly. Politics in America. Washington, DC: Congressional Quarterly Press, 1994.

Department of Justice. "Former Congressman William J. Jefferson Convicted of Bribery, Racketeering, Money Laundering, and Other Related Charges." Press Release, 2009. http://washingtondc.fbi.gov/dojpressrel/pressrel09/wfo080509.htm.

Jefferson, W. J. *Daddy's Pelican.* Tucson, AZ: Wheatmark, 2008.

Jefferson, W. J. *Dying Is the Easy Part.* Tucson, AZ: Wheatmark, 2007.

Lengel, A. "FBI Says Jefferson Was Filmed Taking Cash." *The Washington Post,* May 22, 2006. http://www.washingtonpost.com/wp-dyn/content/article/2006/05/21/AR2006052100167.html.

Office of the Clerk, U.S. House of Representatives. *Election Information,* 2011. http://
clerk.house.gov/member_info/electionInfo/index.html.

Radelat, A. "Former Congressional Aide Pleads Guilty to Bribery." *USA Today,* January
11, 2006. http://www.usatoday.com/news/washington/2006-01-11-exaideguilty_x.htm.

Tilove, J. "William Jefferson Sentenced to 13 Years in Prison." *The New Orleans Times-
Picayune,* November 13, 2009. http://www.nola.com/politics/index.ssf/2009/11/
william_jefferson_sentenced_ye.html.

Jena Six

"Jena Six" is the name given to a group of African American students who were
charged with attempted murder for their involvement in a racially charged incident
at their high school. Evidence that racial tension still exists around issues of criminal justice is apparent in the circumstances that surrounded the handling of the
school-related incident that took place in Jena, Louisiana, on December 4, 2006.
By most accounts, the events that drew national and international attention and
became the subject of congressional hearings occurred between August 2006 and
September 2007, when a group of Black students made the decision to sit under a
large oak tree at Jena High School—a tree that was reportedly a common hangout
for White students. Others have suggested that the series of events that have been
linked together in media accounts were, in fact, unrelated, but did serve to heighten
existing racial tensions in the town with a population of 3,000, and a high school
population that was roughly 10 percent Black and 90 percent White (City-data
.com, 2007; Simmons, 2007). While the facts that ultimately led to one of the
"largest civil rights demonstrations in years" (Gallacher, 2007; Newman, 2007) are
in conflict, for a while this small-town occurrence was the center stage of conversa-
tions about civil rights, human rights, and equal justice in America.

In today's society, one would think that it would be acceptable for Black
and White students to congregate in the same location. This apparently was not
the case in Jena. The day after the Black students sat under the tree, three
White students hung three hangman's nooses from it, reportedly in retaliation
for Black students having sat under what White students reportedly claimed
was "their" tree. Other sources have noted that the placement of the nooses was
a prank committed by members of a school club who did not realize the historical symbolism of hate and terror signified by their actions. After a series of
hearings and appeals, the White students, who reportedly had initially been
recommended for expulsion, received school suspensions for an offense that,
according to the district's U.S. Attorney, could easily have been classified as a
hate crime (Alberts, 2007).

The noose incident ignited immediate racial tension and sparked several violent events across the small town. Robert Bailey, Jr., a Black student, was attacked by a White male when he attempted to enter a high school party attended by mostly White students. The accounts of the attack are contested, including whether the attacker was a student and whether he used a beer bottle as a weapon during the attack. The attacker was charged with simple battery and placed on probation. A week later, Justin Barker, a White student, was attacked by Black students while eating lunch in the Jena High School cafeteria. The students, who were accused of punching and kicking Barker even after he was on the ground, said that they attacked Barker only after he provoked one of them by using a racial epithet, a claim that was later retracted. Barker was sent to the hospital where, according to reports and trial testimony, he was treated for substantial injuries. He was released the same day and attended a high school event later that night. (A serious fire that took place at the school on November 30, 2006, was ultimately determined not to be related to these racially charged events [CNN, 2007].)

For the attack on Justin Barker, the district attorney, J. Reed Walters, charged six Black students: Mychal Bell, 16; Robert Bailey, Jr., 17; Theo Shaw, 17; Bryant Purvis, 17; Carwin Jones, 18; and Jesse Ray Beard, 14, with second-degree attempted murder. And in contrast to the school suspensions given to the White offenders who displayed the nooses, the six Black juvenile offenders were expelled. The Black teens were arrested and charged as adults for felony offenses, including attempted murder and aggravated assault. To support the serious charges, the district attorney claimed that the tennis shoes worn by the Black students were deadly weapons. The seriousness of the charges filed against the Black students, in contrast to the lesser charges brought against the White students, angered many members of the Black community, who cited blatant racial discrimination as the only explanation for the severity of the treatment. Outside of Jena, civil rights advocates called the charges levied against the "Jena Six" "disproportionate" and noted that the case raised serious questions about how much race still plays a part in the workings of the legal system in the South (Alberts, 2007).

The stark differential treatment between Black and White students caught the attention of Rev. Al Sharpton, Rev. Jesse Jackson, and the NAACP civil rights organization. A call to action titled "The Message" was posted on the Internet. "The Message" outlined a series of steps that needed to be taken to address the racial injustices imposed by the legal system in Jena. Jena Six supporters grew to include the American Civil Liberties Union (ACLU) and thousands of individuals across the United States and some abroad. On September 20, 2007, the Revs. Sharpton and Jackson led thousands of protestors to Jena; they marched through the streets of the small town protesting the disparity in the justice system and showing their support for the Black defendants. The number of protestors who came to Jena is estimated to have been 15,000 to 20,000 (Whoriskey, 2007). Additional protests took place in different cities and on university campuses across the country (Alberts, 2007; Simmons, 2007). For the protesters, the incidents in Jena suggested that racism was prevalent in small towns, and that racial discrimination provided a viable explanation for the charging and sentencing disparities between the White and Black students in Jena (Kvansy et al., 2009).

The Jena Six became an illustration of how the Internet can be used as a tool of empowerment, as a mechanism to attract media attention, and as a means of creating and supporting social activism. The events in Jena happened in 2006. They were not reported nationally until 2007. Internet blog entries and comments helped bring the Jena Six case to the attention of the mainstream media (Kvansy et al., 2009). One reporter noted, "We still might not know what happened in Jena if the case hadn't been noticed by bloggers, who sounded the alarm" (Robinson, 2007).

The Chicago Tribune reported that the "Blackosphere," an informal group of Black cultural producers that has developed into a formidable grassroots organization, within a matter of a few weeks collected 220,000 petition signatures and more than $130,000 in donations for legal fees to support the Jena Six defense fund. The ColorOfChange, an Internet-based civil rights organization that was created in the wake of Hurricane Katrina, and which now has more than 400,000 members, also advocated on behalf of the Jena Six and served as the primary Web site for factual information, fundraising, organizing, and advocacy for them. The ColorOfChange online petition in support of the students received more than 320,860 signatures, which was 106 percent of the original goal of 300,000. One source commented that the "viral civil rights movement" was literally conjured out of the ether of cyberspace and spread via blogs, email, message boards, and talk radio (Kvansy et al., 2009). The Jena Six case has also been credited with creating a new generation of civil rights activists who learned about the events in Jena from Black political, entertainment, gossip, and hip-hop music blogs that featured the story, or from popular Black entertainers who turned the cause into a crusade.

After multiple court proceedings and the immense national protest movement, which essentially began over the Internet, the charges against the Jena Six were eventually reduced, including charges against Mychal Bell, who had initially been convicted of second-degree aggravated battery and conspiracy to commit battery. Bell's previous conviction by an all-White jury was overturned on the grounds that he should have been tried as a juvenile rather than as an adult because he was 16 at the time of the attack. Louisiana law permits adult prosecution starting at age 17. Bell pled guilty to simple battery in juvenile court and was sentenced to 18 months, incarceration in a juvenile facility. He was given credit for time served since his arrest. His initial bail had been set high because of his previous record for assaultive behavior. The remaining five pleaded no contest to charges of simple battery and were sentenced to one week's unsupervised probation, a $500 fine, court costs, and restitution.

Some members of the Jena Six have continued to be involved with the criminal justice system since their famous case and many residents of Jena and others have complained about the ways in which the factual details of the events were handled by the media (Kovach & Campo-Flores, 2007). It has been reported that the tree that was the impetus for the racial unrest has been cut down. The FBI has investigated a White supremacist organization's Web site that listed the names, addresses, and telephone numbers of Jena Six family members and suggested that they be lynched. The Jena Six movement and incident have been mentioned in songs by popular African American artists and are featured in a music video by John Mellencamp, a popular music artist who is White. Two members of the Jena Six, Carwin Jones and Bryant Purvis, were on air to present an award at the Black Entertainment Television (BET) Hip Hop Awards in Atlanta, Georgia, in October 2007. They thanked their families, friends, and the "Hip-Hop Nation" for supporting them through the resolution of their case.

Eric M. Heiple and Luise Pedroso-Kipler

See also: Civil Rights Movement; Hip-Hop Culture; Jackson, Jesse; Sharpton, Jr., Alfred Charles

References

Alberts, S. "U.S. Civil Rights Activists Rally for the 'Jena Six'; Nooses Hung from Tree; Black Students Charged with Beating White Teen." *National Post* (Canada), September 21, 2007, A11.

City-data.com. "Jena, Louisiana (LA) Detailed Profile." 2007.

CNN. "U.S. Attorney: 'Nooses, Beating at Jena High Not Related.'" September 19, 2007.

Gallacher, A. "Huge Rally in Small-Town Louisiana." *BBC News,* September 21, 2007.

Kovach, G. C., and A. Campo-Flores. "A Town in Turmoil: As the New School Year Approaches, Jena, La., Is Struggling to Move beyond the Racial Strife That Ripped It Apart and Left the Futures of Six Students in Disarray." *Newsweek,* August 20, 2007: 36.

Kvansy, L., F. Payton, and K. Hales. "Social Activism in the "Blackosphere": The Jena Six Case." In *Interpersonal Relations and Social Patterns in Communication Technologies: Discourse Norms, Language Structures and Cultural Variables,* edited by J. Parks and E. Abels, 277–91. Hershey, PA: IGI Global, 2009.

Newman, M. "Jena, La." *The New York Times,* September 24, 2007.

Robinson, H. A. "Standing Up to Jim Crow Justice in 2007." *The Bilerico Project,* August 14, 2007.

Simmons, C. "Jena 6: Protest at Justice Dept." *The Washington Post,* October 2, 2007.

Whoriskey, P. "Thousands Protest Blacks' Treatment; Six Students Who Were Prosecuted in Louisiana Town Garner Nationwide Support." *The Washington Post,* September 21, 2007, A1.

Jones, Jr., Prince Carmen (1975–2000)

Prince Carmen Jones, Jr., was a 25-year-old African American male who was fatally shot by a Prince George's County, Maryland, undercover police officer on September 1, 2000, in Fairfax County, Virginia.

Prince Jones, Jr., was born on March 30, 1975, in New Orleans, Louisiana, to Mable S. Jones and Prince Carmen Jones, Sr. After his parents' divorce, Prince and his younger sister Jennifer left rural Louisiana to live with their mother in Duncanville, Texas. Prince attended the Texas Academy of Mathematics and Science in Denton, and after graduation, moved to Washington, D.C., to attend Howard University.

In June 2000, a gun belonging to an officer of the Prince George's County, Maryland, Police Department was stolen from his unmarked car. The theft was linked to a driver of a black Jeep Cherokee with Maryland plates who had twice evaded county police by ramming their vehicles. According to reports, the Prince George's police learned that the rear-end damage to the Jeep had been repaired and the suspect had switched plates.

On Friday, September 1, 2000, at about 2:00 a.m., Prince Jones was driving a black Jeep Grand Cherokee with Pennsylvania plates registered to his mother. He was en route to Fairfax, Virginia, where Candace Jackson, his fiancée, and his daughter Nina Jones, age 10 months, resided. While driving, Prince was spotted by undercover narcotics police corporal Carlton B. Jones and supervisor Sergeant Alexandre Bailey, who were on surveillance in Washington, D.C., as part of an undercover narcotics operation for the Capitol Hill Police. Thirty-three-year-old Carlton B. Jones was a six-year veteran of the Prince George's County Police Department. The two were looking for a black Jeep Cherokee belonging to the suspect in the June gun theft—Darryl Lamont Gilchrest, a 250-pound, five-feet-six-inch Black male with dreadlocks.

The officers followed Prince Jones' Jeep after reportedly receiving a tip connected to the gun theft. The officers initially lost sight of the Jeep but later spotted it again in Hyattsville, Maryland, near a location reportedly known to be frequented by the suspect in the gun theft. Corporal Jones followed Prince Jones, who was six feet four inches tall, weighed 200 pounds, and wore a close-cropped haircut, for 15 miles, as he drove from Hyattsville, Maryland, across Washington, D.C., and into Fairfax County, Virginia. By his account, Corporal Jones had no intention of arresting the driver, only of following the Jeep in hopes of finding information. He did not notify other police departments as he went through their jurisdictions.

Sergeant Bailey, driving behind Corporal Jones in a separate unmarked Mitsubishi Montero, lost sight of Prince Jones' Jeep as the two officers trailed the Jeep into Virginia. Corporal Jones continued to follow Prince Jones into Fairfax County, Virginia, where Prince pulled into a driveway near the intersection of Beechwood Lane and Spring Terrace and parked. Corporal Jones then parked his Mitsubishi Montero SUV behind Prince Jones, blocking the driveway. Prince Jones then allegedly reversed his Jeep into the Mitsubishi, got out, and approached Corporal Jones. According to Corporal Jones, who is also African American, he then exited his vehicle, pulled his weapon, and identified himself as a police officer, but failed to present his badge. By the officer's account, Prince Jones then got back into the Jeep and rammed the driver's side of the SUV twice. Corporal Jones, claiming to fear for his life, emptied 16 bullets from his 9-mm Beretta pistol into the back window of the Jeep. Prince Jones, who was unarmed, was shot five times in the back and once in the forearm. It has been speculated that Prince Jones may have thought that he was being carjacked by the Black man in plainclothes and an unmarked SUV. Prince attempted to drive away, but crashed his Jeep three blocks from where he had been shot. Sergeant Bailey was not on the scene at this time. Prince died five hours later at the Anova Fairfax Hospital of internal bleeding.

The testimony of two nearby witnesses conflicted with Corporal Jones' story. Lettie Ballve testified that she had not seen anyone exit the Jeep after the Jeep and the Montero had been parked driver's side by driver's side for several minutes. From her husband Juan's account, when the shots were fired the Jeep was not in motion.

It was later determined that Prince Jones was shot in the back from a 45-degree downward angle. Corporal Jones was placed on paid leave and released his official version of the events 10 days after the shooting, as required by Maryland law. At that time, he claimed to have first spotted Prince's Jeep in an area "known for drug dealing." Prince Jones, Jr., had no police record. Virginia Commonwealth Attorney Robert F. Horan, Jr., opted not to charge Corporal Jones with a crime, stating that the corporal acted in self-defense.

This fatal confrontation caught the attention of activist Rev. Al Sharpton and then vice president (and presidential candidate) Al Gore. The incident also prompted student protests on Howard University's campus. Over a thousand students attended a memorial service held for Prince Jones on the college campus.

Corporal Carlton Jones had a history of using excessive force in his six years on the Prince George's County Police Department and had been a defendant in several lawsuits. In one case, John Robert Johnson of Landover, Maryland, filed a $3 million lawsuit against Corporal Jones for a 1997 beating that left him blind in one eye and with partial use of one hand. For that incident, the officer was suspended with pay.

Prince Jones' case and a growing number of shootings and accusations of excessive force prompted the U.S. Justice Department's Civil Rights Division and the Federal Bureau of Investigation to conduct investigations of the Prince George's County Police Department operations. At the time of Prince Jones' shooting, the county's police had shot 12 people, resulting in five fatalities, in 13 months. In addition to the five shooting fatalities, two other individuals also died while in police custody and excessive force complaints against the police were up 53 percent from previous years.

In July 2001, Acting Assistant Attorney General for Civil Rights William R. Yeomans announced that there was insufficient evidence to justify federal criminal charges against Corporal Jones. The Civil Rights Division continued to evaluate the incident as a part of its civil rights investigation into the practices of the Prince George's County Police Department. No criminal charges were filed after the Justice Department's investigation of Prince Jones' shooting.

In December 2001, Prince Jones' family filed a wrongful death suit in the Circuit Court for Prince George's County. The suit was filed against Corporal Jones, Sergeant Bailey, Prince George's County chief of police John S. Farrell, the Prince George's County Police Department, and Prince George's County, Maryland. They claimed that the shooting that resulted in the untimely death of Prince Jones, Jr., was an act of vengeance by an out-of-control undercover officer against an innocent man. The deceased, Prince Jones, was described as a student in his last year of studies at Howard University, with plans of joining the navy and later becoming a doctor or a diplomat. The lawsuit sought $145 million in punitive and compensatory damages.

In 2002, amid the lingering controversy from the Prince Jones shooting, county prosecutors announced they were dismissing multiple criminal cases in which Carlton Jones was a key witness. Serious doubts had been raised about the truthfulness of the story that the corporal provided regarding the facts of the shooting. His credibility was in serious doubt. Subsequently, Corporal Jones was assigned to the technical services division of the department. Sergeant Bailey retired from the police department and became a special agent with the Department of Homeland Security.

A civil jury found that Carlton Jones was negligent, used excessive force, and could not have reasonably believed his actions were lawful. However, they rejected a claim that the officer was liable for battery of Prince Jones and found that Prince Jones contributed to his death by his actions during the fatal encounter. On September 27, 2006, a Prince George's County jury awarded $3.7 million to Prince Jones's family for his wrongful death. The jury awarded $2.5 million in damages to Jones's daughter; $1 million to his mother; and $200,000 to his father. The jury award is one of the largest for a police misconduct lawsuit in Prince George's County history.

Nicole Branch

See also: Bell, Sean; Bumpurs, Eleanor; Civil Rights Movement; Diallo, Amadou; Mitchell, Margaret Laverne; Police Brutality; Racial Profiling; Sharpton, Jr., Alfred Charles; Young, Jr., Cornel

References

Castaneda, Ruben. "Civil Trial Is Underway for Pr. George's Officer: Student's Family Sues Over 2000 Killing." *Washington Post,* January 10, 2006. http://www.washingtonpost.com/wp-dyn/content/article/2006/01/09/AR2006010901764.html.

Castaneda, Ruben. "Officer Liable in Student's Killing: Pr. George's Jurors Award $3.7 Million." *Washington Post,* January 19, 2006. http://www.washingtonpost.com/wp-dyn/content/article/2006/01/19/AR2006011902346.html.

Coates, Ta-Nehisi. "Black and Blue: Why Does America's Richest Black Suburb Have Some of the Country's Most Brutal Cops?" *Washington Monthly,* June 2001. http://www.washingtonmonthly.com/features/2001/0106.coates.html.

Hewitt, Bill. "An Echo of Gunfire: A Black Man's Killing in the D.C. Suburbs Leads to Charges of Police Racial Profiling." *People,* May 14, 2001. http://www.people.com/people/archive/article/0,,20134412,00.html.

Jackman, Tom, and Jamie Stockwell. "Virginia Will Not Charge MD Officer." *Washington Post,* October 24, 2000. http://www.mapinc.org/drugnews/v00/n1600/a11.html.

Lang, Debbie. "Howard University Students Protest Police Murder: The Stolen Life of Prince Jones." *Revolutionary Worker,* October 1, 2000. http://revcom.us/a/v22/1070-79/1072/howard.htm.

Prince Carmen Jones, Sr., et al. v. Prince George's County, Maryland et al. Court of Appeals of Maryland. 2003. http://caselaw.findlaw.com/md-court-of-appeals/1198869.html.

U.S. Department of Justice. "Closing of the Prince Jones Case," press release, July 6, 2001. http://www.justice.gov/opa/pr/2001/July/310cr.htm.

Whitlock, Craig, and David Fallis. "A Deadly Case of Mistaken Identity." *Washington Post,* July 3, 2001.

Juries

The Sixth Amendment to the U.S. Constitution reads in part that "[i]n all criminal prosecutions, the accused shall enjoy the right to a speedy and public trial, by an impartial jury of the State and district wherein the crime shall have been committed." The applicability of the Sixth Amendment to the states was decided in the case of *Duncan v. Louisiana* (391 U.S. 145, 1968). In that case, Gary Duncan, an African American teenager, was charged with the simple assault of another youth who was White. The charge involved an alleged slap on the elbow. A judge denied

Duncan's request to have his case tried before a jury. Duncan was found guilty and sentenced to 60 days in jail and a $150 fine. In deciding whether Gary Duncan was entitled to a trial by jury, the U.S. Supreme Court noted that the tests that had been used to determine whether an amendment applied to the states (through the Fourteenth Amendment) included whether the right was one of the "fundamental principles of liberty and justice which lie at the base of all our civil and political institutions" (*Powell v. Alabama,* 287 U.S. 45, 1932, 67); is "basic in our system of jurisprudence" (*In re Oliver,* 333 U.S. 257, 1948, 273); or is "a fundamental right, essential to a fair trial" (*Gideon v. Wainwright,* 372 U.S. 335, 1963, 343–44). The Court decided that the right to a trial by an impartial jury met those tests and should therefore apply to the states. While the *Duncan* decision was important for all citizens, questions of who is eligible for jury service and how jury composition impacts a defendant's criminal trial have also been important issues throughout the history of the United States.

Prior to 1880, despite the passage of the Civil Rights Act of 1875—which made it a criminal offense to exclude people from jury service on account of their race—in some states, African Americans were barred from being eligible to sit on a jury. In 1880, the U.S. Supreme Court decided the case of *Strauder v. West Virginia* (100 U.S. 303). In that case, an African American man was on trial for murder. Under West Virginia state law, the only people who were authorized to serve as jurors were White men 21 years of age or older. The Supreme Court held that the state statute limiting jury service in this way violated the equal protection clause of the Fourteenth Amendment and was unenforceable because it was unconstitutional.

While it would seem that the *Strauder* case would resolve the issue of African Americans serving on juries, such was not the case. Even after the *Strauder* decision, prosecutors managed to exclude Black jurors through the use of challenges—the right of prosecutors and defense attorneys to remove individuals from jury service during a process called voir dire. During this process individuals can be excluded from juries either for cause or through the use of a peremptory challenge. Removal for cause is based on an assessment of a person's inability to render a fair and impartial decision. For example, if the juror is related to the defendant or is or has been the victim in a criminal case, he or she would be deemed biased and removed for cause. Peremptory challenges, on the other hand, are given to both the prosecution and the defense to remove potential jurors for other reasons, and those reasons do not have to be stated to the court. In practice, many African Americans were removed from potential jury service through the use of peremptory challenges, resulting in many all-White juries.

In 1985, this practice was challenged in the case of *Batson v. Kentucky* (476 U.S. 79). In that case, an African American man was charged with second-degree burglary and receipt of stolen goods. The prosecutor used peremptory challenges to strike all four African Americans from the pool of potential jurors, leaving only White jurors to be selected. The Supreme Court held that this practice violated the Sixth and Fourteenth Amendments and established the requirement that the prosecution must not use its peremptory strikes to eliminate a juror based on race. To enforce the requirement, prosecutors could be required to give race-neutral reasons for excluding jurors when using peremptory challenges.

Despite the decision in *Batson,* the use of race in jury selection was still being litigated in 2005 and 2008. In 2005, in the case of *Miller-El v. Dretke* (545 U.S. 231), the Court reversed a death sentence for a defendant in a case where the state had used peremptory strikes to remove 10 of the 11 jurors who were qualified to serve. Noting that the trial court is required to assess a *Batson* challenge based on all relevant information and facts presented by the defense, the Court highlighted the fact that 91 percent of the African Americans in the pool had been removed and that White jurors were not removed when their reasons were the same or similar to the reasons for removal of the African Americans. In the 2008 case of *Snyder v. Louisiana* (552 U.S. 472), an African American man was struck from the pool of potential jurors by the prosecution. The defense made a *Batson* challenge to the strike and the prosecutor stated that the young man looked anxious because he was a college senior and might miss his required student-teaching assignment.

In deciding that the prosecution's race-neutral reasons were implausible and that the conviction of the defendant should be reversed, it appeared that the Supreme Court was adamant about removing racial bias in the jury selection process. In another recent case, *Thayler v. Haynes* (559 U.S. 2010), the Court held that previous decisions did not establish a rule that a judge must witness the demeanor of a juror during voir dire when the peremptory strike of an African American is based on the demeanor of that individual. The effects of the *Thayler v. Haynes* case on the holdings in *Miller-El* and *Snyder* remain to be seen.

Another important issue regarding the racial composition of juries is in regard to felony disenfranchisement—the loss of the right to serve on a jury or vote because of a felony conviction. African Americans are disproportionately represented in state and federal prisons on felony charges and thereby disproportionately numbered among those ineligible for jury service because of criminal convictions. This factor alone significantly reduces the number of African Americans that will be included in jury pools. Existing research has estimated that one in three African American men are ineligible for jury service due to a felony conviction.

The benefits of a racially diverse jury have been examined over time. Historically, all-White juries have failed to convict White defendants of crimes committed against African Americans, no matter how compelling the evidence of guilt (see Evers, Medgar, and Till, Emmett). In 2006, Samuel Sommers conducted a well-designed study to assess whether benefits existed. He found that racially diverse jurors considered more information, made fewer factual mistakes, and spent more time considering the information when compared to their all-White counterparts. His research is particularly relevant considering that other research has suggested that all-White juries are significantly more conviction prone, especially when defendants are non-White, and they tend to assess harsher punishments against non-White defendants. Relatedly, research has shown that in general, jurors tend to convict African American defendants on lesser evidence than White defendants. Racially mixed juries may help counter this trend.

Increased diversity in the jury pool has not been without controversy. In 1991, the U.S. Supreme Court upheld the right of a White defendant to contest the prosecutor's use of peremptory challenges to remove African Americans from the jury pool in his criminal trial (*Powers v. Ohio,* 499 U.S. 400). In a 1995 *Yale Law Journal* article, former prosecutor and legal scholar Paul Butler encouraged Black jurors to engage in jury nullification—not convict an obviously guilty Black defendant—in protest of the overcriminalization of Blacks through drug law enforcement and other mechanisms of the criminal justice system. A study of the racial composition of different New York counties found that convictions were hard to secure in locations where the jury pool was predominately non-White and when the prosecution's case depended largely on the testimony of law enforcement officers. Such findings have fueled a continued debate over the role of race in jury decision-making, including suggestions that in order to insure fairness, it may be necessary to shield jurors from knowing the race of criminal defendants.

Patti Ross Salinas and Tana McCoy

See also: Davis, Angela Yvonne; Evers, Medgar; Shakur, Assata (aka Joanne Chesimard); Simpson, Orenthal James "O. J."; Till, Emmett

References

Batson v. Kentucky, 476 U.S. 79 (1985).

Butler, Paul. "Racially Biased Jury Nullification: Black Power in the Criminal Justice System." *Yale Law Journal* 105 (December 1995): 677–725.

Duncan v. Louisiana, 391 U.S. 145 (1968).

Equal Justice Initiative. "Illegal Racial Discrimination in Jury Selection: A Continuing Legacy." http://eji.org/eji/files/EJI%20Race%20and%20Jury%20Report.pdf.

Fukurai, Hiroshi, Edgar W. Butler, and Richard Krooth. *Race and the Jury: Racial Disenfranchisement and the Search for Justice.* New York: Plenum Press, 1993.

Fukurai, Hiroshi, and Richard Krooth. *Race in the Jury Box: Affirmative Action in Jury Selection.* New York: State University of New York Press, 2003.

Gideon v. Wainwright, 372 U.S. 335 (1963).

In re Oliver, 333 U.S. 257, 1948).

Levine, James P. "The Impact of Racial Demography on Jury Verdicts in Routine Adjudication." In *The System in Black and White: Exploring the Connections Between Race, Crime and Justice,* edited by Michael Markowitz and Delores Jones-Brown, 153–69. Westport, CT: Praeger, 2000.

Miller-El v. Dretke, 545 U.S. 231 (2005).

Powell v. Alabama, 287 U.S. 45 (1932).

Powers v. Ohio, 499 U.S. 400 (1991).

Snyder v. Louisiana, 552 U.S. 472 (2008).

Sommers, Samuel. "On Racial Diversity and Group Decision Making: Identifying Multiple Effects of Racial Composition on Jury Deliberations." *Journal of Personality and Social Psychology* 90 (2006): 597–612.

Strauder v. West Virginia, 100 U.S. 303 (1880).

Thayler v. Haynes, 559 U.S. (2010).

Wheelock, Darren. "Collateral Consequences and Racial Inequality: Felon Status Restrictions as a System of Disadvantage." *Journal of Contemporary Criminal Justice* 21, no. 1 (2005): 82–90.

K

King, Rodney Glen (1965–2012)

On the night of March 2, 1991, Rodney Glen King and two passengers were driving in the San Fernando Valley area of Los Angeles. At 12:30 a.m., two California Highway Patrol officers spotted King's car speeding. The officers pursued King, and the subsequent chase on the Foothill Freeway reached a speed of at least 117 miles per hour (*Koon v. U.S.,* 1996). According to King, he refused to pull over because he had been drinking earlier and a DUI would violate his parole for a robbery conviction (Cannon, 1999).

King exited the freeway and the high-speed (ranging from 55 to 80 miles per hour) chase continued through residential streets (Stevenson & Egan, 1991). Several police cars and a helicopter joined in the pursuit, and after approximately eight miles, officers cornered King's car. The first five LAPD officers there were Stacey Koon, Laurence Powell, Timothy Wind, Theodore Briseno, and Rolando Solano.

King and his passengers were ordered to get out of the car and lie face down on the ground, which King's passengers did. They were taken into custody without incident (Linder, 2001). King remained in the car, but when he eventually came out he acted strangely, laughing and waving to the police helicopter (Whitman, 1993). King then grabbed his buttocks and when he did reportedly Trooper Melanie Singer thought he was reaching for a gun (Cannon, 1999). She drew her gun and ordered King to lie on the ground, and King complied. Singer then approached King with her gun drawn in order to arrest him.

Sergeant Stacey Koon ordered Singer to holster her gun since there is a risk of a suspect gaining control of a police weapon if the police get too close (Cannon, 1999). Koon then ordered officers Briseno, Powell, Solano, and Wind to subdue and handcuff King. As the officers approached him, King rose and struck Officer Briseno in the chest. At this point Koon ordered the officers to fall back. Later the officers testified that they believed King was under the influence of PCP (Cannon, 1999).

Sergeant Koon, in response to King not following their commands to lie down, shot King with a Taser twice. The first Taser shot knocked King to the ground, but he stood back up and Koon fired the Taser again, knocking King back down.

With Taser wires hanging from his body, King rose to his feet again and at this time Koon ordered the officers to strike King with their batons. As he was being hit, King repeatedly tried to get back up. Koon ordered the officers to strike King's joints, including his elbows, knees, and ankles (Christopher Commission, 1991). After 56 such hits and six kicks, five or six officers placed King in handcuffs and cordcuffs and he was dragged on his stomach to the side of the road until an ambulance arrived (Christopher Commission, 1991).

Unknown to those involved, the police beating was videotaped by George Holliday from his apartment in Lake View, California. He contacted the LAPD about the videotape but was dismissed, so he took the tape to station KTLA (Christopher Commission, 1991). The footage became a media sensation and was shown around the world.[1]

King was taken to Pacifica Hospital immediately after his arrest. He had suffered "11 skull fractures, brain damage, kidney damage and emotional and physical trauma" (Christopher Commission, 1991: 8). Blood and urine samples showed that King was intoxicated under California law and traces of marijuana were found. There was no indication of PCP or any other drug in his system. At the hospital, nurses reported that the officers who accompanied King bragged and laughed about the number of times King had been hit (Christopher Commission, 1991).

The Los Angeles district attorney charged officers Koon, Powell, Briseno, and Wind with use of excessive force. The site of the trial was moved from Los Angeles to Simi Valley, California, in neighboring Ventura County, based on fears that the jury pool in Los Angeles had been contaminated by the media coverage of the incident. The Simi Valley jury (10 Whites, one Latino, and one Asian) acquitted three of the officers but could not agree about one of the charges for the fourth (Powell) (Linder, 2001). The Los Angeles mayor, Tom Bradley, said that the "system failed us," and Deputy District Attorney Terry White added that the verdicts "[send] out a message that whatever you saw on that tape was reasonable conduct" (Mydans, 1992: 1).

The acquittal of the officers sparked the Los Angeles Riots of 1992. The riots resulted in 53 deaths, 2,383 injuries, over 7,000 fires, and nearly $1 billion in financial losses. Order had to be restored by the police, the U.S. Army, the Marines, and the National Guard. There were smaller riots in Las Vegas, Nevada, and Atlanta, Georgia. On the third day of the riots, Rodney King appeared on television, and in an appeal for peace he famously said, "Can we all get along? Can we get along? Can we stop making it, making it horrible for the older people and the kids? . . . Please, we can get along here. . . . Let's try to work it out" (as quoted in Keyes, 2006: xii).

After the riots, the U.S. Department of Justice obtained an indictment against the four officers for the violation of King's federal civil rights and took them to trial. On March 9, 1993, King took the witness stand and described what the officers did to him (Mydans, 1993). The jury found officers Powell and Koon guilty and they were sentenced to 30 months in prison. Officers Wind and Briseno were acquitted of the charges. King was later awarded $3.8 million in a civil suit against the city of Los Angeles (BBC News, 2002).

Long after his infamous beating, King continued to have issues with drug and alcohol abuse and contact with the criminal justice system. In 2004, he was arrested for driving under the influence of PCP following a single-car auto accident. In 2005 and 2007 he was arrested on suspicion of domestic violence. In the 2007 incident he suffered non–life-threatening gunshot wounds. In 2010 he became engaged to Cynthia Kelley, who had served as juror number 5 in his civil case. His struggles with substance abuse landed him a role on the VH1 reality TV show *Celebrity Rehab with Dr. Drew* and were recorded in his 2012 memoir *The Riot Within: My Journey from Rebellion to Redemption* published by HarperCollins (CNN Wire Staff, 2012; *Biography Channel*, 2013). On June 17, 2012, Rodney King was found dead in his swimming pool in Rialto, California. A coroner's report indicates that there was a varied mixture of drugs and alcohol in his blood. He was 47 years old (Medina, 2012).

Philip Verrecchia

See also: Los Angeles Riots of 1992

Note

1. The video is under copyright. For authorization contact www.rodneykingvideo.com.ar.

References

BBC News. "Flashback: Rodney King and the LA Riots." July 10, 2002. http://news.bbc.co.uk/2/hi/americas/2119943.stm.

Biography Channel. Rodney King. 2013. http://www.biography.com/people/rodneyking-9542141.

Cannon, L. *Official Negligence: How Rodney King and the Riots Changed Los Angeles and the LAPD.* New York: Basic Books, 1999.

Christopher Commission. *The Rodney King Beating: Report of the Independent Commission on the Los Angeles Police Department,* 1991. http://www.parc.info/client_files/Special%20Reports/1%20-%20Chistopher%20Commision.pdf.

CNN Wire Staff. "A Timeline of Events in Rodney King's Life." *CNN,* June 17, 2012.

Keyes, R. *The Quote Verifier: Who Said What, Where and When.* New York: St. Martin's Press, 2006.

Koon v. U.S., 518 U.S. 81 (1996).

Linder, D. "The Rodney King Beating Trials." *Jurist* (December 2001). http://jurist.law .pitt.edu/trials24.htm.

Medina, Jennifer. "Rodney King Dies at 47; Police Beating Victim Who Asked 'Can We All Get Along?'" *The New York Times,* June 17, 2012.

Mydans, S. "Rodney King Testifies on Beating: "I Was Just Trying to Stay Alive." *The New York Times,* March 10, 1993. http://www.nytimes.com/1993/03/10/us/rodney-king-testifies-on-beating-i-was-just-trying-to-stay-alive.html?scp=15&sq=seth%20 mydans%20and%20rodney%20king&st=cse.

Mydans, S. "The Police Verdict; Los Angeles Policemen Acquitted in Taped Beating." *The New York Times,* April 30, 1992. http://www.nytimes.com/books/98/02/08/home/rod-ney-verdict.html?scp=1&sq=seth%20mydans%20and%20rodney%20king%20the%20 police%20verduct&st=cse.

Stevenson, R. W., and T. Egan. "Seven Minutes in Los Angeles: A Special Report: Videotaped Beating by Police Officers Puts Full Glare on Brutality Issue." *The New York Times,* March 18, 1991. http://query.nytimes.com/gst/fullpage.html?res=9D0CE5DE1 539F93BA25750C0A967958260&scp=1&sq=Seven%20Minutes%20in%20Los%20 Angeles&st=cse.

Whitman, D. "The Untold Story of the L.A. Riot." *U.S. News and World Report,* May 23, 1993. http://www.usnews.com/usnews/news/articles/930531/archive_015229.htm.

L

Lee, Anthony Dwain/Dwayne (1961–2000)

Anthony Dwain/Dwayne Lee, 39, was fatally shot by Los Angeles police officer Tarriel Hopper, 29, on October 27, 2000. Officer Hopper and his partner, Officer Natalie Humphreys, were responding to two separate noise complaints about a Halloween costume party at 9701 Yoakum Drive in the Benedict Canyon area of Los Angeles. According to a report from the Los Angeles County Office of the District Attorney (Los Angeles DA, 2002), Mr. Lee and more than 200 others were attending the costume party at a location known as "The Castle." The officers arrived shortly after midnight and made contact with private security officers at the home. As the officers circulated through the party attempting to find the hosts, they came upon a window looking into a dimly lit room. Inside were three men whom officers reportedly believed were participating in a drug transaction. As a flashlight was shone into the room, the officers reported that Mr. Lee reached into his waistband and produced a semi-automatic pistol that he pointed at the officers through the window. This would turn out to be a .357 replica semi-automatic pistol that had been used as a movie set prop. As Mr. Lee pointed the prop at the officers, Officer Hopper fired nine rounds. Four of these hit Lee in the back, two fatally.

The district attorney's report goes on to note that a green pharmaceutical residue was found by police in Mr. Lee's hand after the shooting. According to the report, the substance was later identified by toxicology tests as methylenedioxymethamphetamine, commonly known as the illegal drug Ecstasy. An autopsy was performed and samples of Mr. Lee's blood, urine, and stomach contents were analyzed. According to the report, significant amounts of alcohol, benzoylecgonine, and cocaine were all detected in in Mr. Lee's stomach contents and postmortem blood.

Officer Hopper had been with the LAPD for three years prior to the shooting. He was placed on paid leave pending an investigation. According to news reports at the time of the shooting, Mr. Lee had grown up in Sacramento, California, and dealt drugs before leaving the gang lifestyle behind to pursue an acting career. He had played supporting roles on television shows including *ER* and *NYPD Blue,* and in the 1997 Jim Carrey movie *Liar, Liar* (Kohn, 2003; Meyer et al., 2000).

Witnesses at the party challenged police reports of the events, criticizing the police for failing to identify themselves before firing on Mr. Lee. Civilian accounts of the incident make no mention of a meeting with private security and indicate that Officer Hopper entered the backyard of the home reportedly in search of the homeowner and observed Mr. Lee through a bedroom window. They confirm that though Mr. Lee was with others, Officer Hopper fired multiple times. There was no indication that Officer Hopper thought the other individuals with Lee were armed. There may have been additional confusion given that several of the party guests were reportedly dressed as police officers. Mr. Lee had drawn the replica firearm numerous times during the evening, joking with other guests about the replica weapon. Interviews with community members identified concerns about the willingness to shoot without clear identification as police. Some said that given the circumstances of the Halloween party, clearer communication should have been used with the partygoers about the presence of actual police officers (Kohn, 2003; Meyer et al., 2000).

Five of the rounds fired that night did not strike Mr. Lee but rather hit the wall behind him. The trajectory of these shots and the ones that did hit Mr. Lee were analyzed and found to be the result of his turning to his left as Officer Hopper fired the shots. Independent testing found that Officer Hopper may have been able to fire the nine shots in about two seconds. This could have resulted in the firing pattern found at the crime scene. Other theories are that Mr. Lee's back was turned the entire duration of the shooting. The resulting investigation by the Los Angeles County District Attorney's Office found the shooting justifiable and lawful given the presence and display of the prop firearm. Officer Hopper was identified as acting to preserve his own life, not knowing the displayed firearm was a replica (Los Angeles DA, 2002; Kohn, 2003).

Under California law, police officers are justified in using deadly force in self-defense or in the defense of others if it reasonably appears that the person claiming the right of self-defense or the defense of another actually and reasonably believed he or she was in imminent danger of great bodily injury or death (*People v. Williams* 75 Cal.App.3d 731, 1977). Similarly, under California law, the reasonableness of Officer Hopper's actions must be judged from the perspective of a reasonable officer on the scene. Given the necessity of a split-second judgment when faced with what he believed to be a real firearm, his response might be seen as justifiable self-defense. Mr. Lee's family and many in the community disagreed with the analysis (Los Angeles DA, 2002; Kohn, 2003).

Noted attorney Johnny Cochran filed a wrongful death suit against the Los Angeles Police Department for $100 million on behalf of Lee's sister,

Tina Lee-Vogt. An out-of-court settlement awarded $225,000 to Ms. Lee-Vogt. Lee was also survived by his former wife, Serena Scholl, who did not participate in the civil suit.

Nicole Hendrix

See also: Bumpurs, Eleanor; Cochran, Jr., Johnnie L.; Jones, Jr., Prince; Police Brutality; Racial Profiling

References

County of Los Angeles, Office of the District Attorney (Los Angeles DA). (2002). *Report on the Death of Anthony Dwayne Lee.* http://da.lacounty.gov/pdf/leeois.pdf.

Kohn, David. "Investigators: An Unexpected Turn, Real Life CSI at Work in Los Angeles." *48 Hours: CBS News,* July 25, 2003. http://www.cbsnews.com/stories/2002/10/23/48hours/main526691.shtml.

Meyer, Josh, Sue Fox, and Kurt Streeter. "Police Release Details of Party Shooting." *Los Angeles Times,* October 31, 2000. http://articles.latimes.com/2000/oct/31/news/mn-44638.

People v. Williams, 75 Cal.App.3d 731 (1977).

Legal Representation

The right to legal representation is the right of a person charged with a crime to have the assistance of a lawyer for his or her defense. The right is commonly known as the right to counsel, or the right to the assistance of counsel. The 1963 U.S. Supreme Court decision in *Gideon v. Wainwright* is perhaps the most well known right-to-counsel case. It became the topic of a classic best-selling book, *Gideon's Trumpet* by Anthony Lewis. The book tells the story of how a poor, simple man petitioned the U.S. Supreme Court, requesting that he be appointed a lawyer free of charge because he was too poor to afford one. Clarence Earl Gideon was a 51-year-old White man who had been in and out of prison most of his life.

March 2013 marked 50 years since the landmark decision declaring that all states must provide legal representation to indigent (poor) defendants in felony cases. Many cases before and after the *Gideon* decision involved African American defendants who were poor, undereducated, and afraid when they were hauled into court or held for questioning by police officers. For many, the assistance of counsel was the only thing that prevented them from being unduly subjected to long prison sentences or facing the penalty of death (Cole, 1999; Smith, 1993; *Palko v. Connecticut,* 1937).

The U.S. Supreme Court's decision in *Powell v. Alabama* in 1932 was the first to impose an obligation on the states to appoint free counsel for indigent defendants. Under the concept of federalism, the Sixth Amendment's guarantee that "[i]n all criminal prosecutions, the accused shall enjoy the right . . . to have the Assistance of Counsel for his defense" did not apply to the states, and the wording of the amendment did not include an explicit promise of free lawyers for defendants who could not afford one. Even with the enactment of the Fourteenth Amendment in 1868, mandating that "[n]o State shall . . . deprive any person of life, liberty, or property, without due process of law; nor deny to any person within its jurisdiction the equal protection of the laws," years of continuous litigation have ensued to make the guarantee of due process and equal protection a reality for defendants facing criminal trials in individual states.

In *Powell,* nine illiterate young African American males were accused of raping two White women during a train trip through Tennessee and Alabama (see Scottsboro Cases). In Alabama at that time, the crime of rape carried the possibility of being sentenced to death upon conviction, and it was at the discretion of the jury to impose the sentence.

The trial judge appointed "all of the members of the bar" to represent the defendants at arraignment only, and split the cases into three separate trials. One-day trials occurred about six days after arraignment. All defendants, including a juvenile, were convicted and sentenced to death. Their appeals ultimately reached the Supreme Court, which reversed their convictions, holding that even though the trial judge had, albeit only in a meaningless "expansive gesture," appointed counsel for the defendants, no lawyer appeared who adequately represented those accused.

In reaching its conclusion, the Court opined that the due process clause of the Fourteenth Amendment requires the appointment of counsel for state court defendants facing the possible imposition of the death penalty. The Court's 7 to 2 opinion underscored the importance of not only the presence of counsel but the effectiveness of counsel to the satisfaction of due process. Per the Court's decision:

> In light of the facts . . . the ignorance and illiteracy of the defendants, their youth, the circumstances of public hostility, the imprisonment and the close surveillance of the defendants by the military forces, the fact that their friends and families were all in other states and communication with them necessarily difficult, and, above all, that they stood in deadly peril of their lives—we think the failure of the trial court to give them reasonable time and opportunity to secure counsel was a clear denial of due process.

Though in the case of *Johnson v. Zerbst* (1938), the Supreme Court would later require the appointment of counsel in all federal cases where defendants were indigent, *Powell v. Alabama* was the first case in which the Court overturned a state criminal conviction because the trial court failed to appoint counsel and did not provide an opportunity for the defendants to secure their own private attorneys.

The *Powell* Court thus set forth the *ideal* that the presence of adequate counsel is a due process requirement for defendants in state capital punishment cases. But it also recognized that the physical presence of an attorney in court did not mean that the attorney was an effective advocate.

The Court did not definitively address the adequacy of legal representation until 1984 in the case of *Strickland v. Washington,* another capital case involving an African American man, this time one who was charged with three capital murder counts. Like Clarence Earl Gideon, David Washington faced trial in the state of Florida. According to the majority ruling in the case, in deciding if an appointed attorney was a defendant's effective representative, a court must answer two questions. The first is, did the attorney commit an error during the representation? If the answer is no, then the analysis stops; the attorney was effective. If the answer is yes, the analysis moves to the second question, which asks whether the error was prejudicial.

Counsel's error is prejudicial when it changes the outcome of the trial. For example, if the police stop a person's vehicle and find drugs inside after conducting an unconstitutional search, it is up to the defendant's attorney to contest the legality of the search. If the attorney does not file a motion to suppress the evidence and the evidence is admitted at trial, and the evidence is central to the jury's determination of guilt, then the attorney's error—his failure to zealously guard against the introduction of illegally obtained evidence—contributed to the guilty verdict, for without the evidence, the defendant should have been acquitted. That defendant is then entitled to a new trial with a different attorney.

The rules regarding the effective assistance of counsel established by *Strickland* have been criticized as insufficient and as placing too great a burden of proof on the defendant to establish his attorney's inadequacy. Justice Thurgood Marshall raises these concerns in his dissenting opinion (see also Rhodes, 1992). In addition to the effectiveness of appointed counsel, issues have been raised regarding when the right to counsel officially begins. The criminal justice system has many stages. At which stage is a defendant considered to be facing charges? After the litigation of many cases involving the right to counsel, the U.S. Supreme Court has ruled that a defendant is entitled to the presence of counsel at all "critical stages" of the system. Essentially, critical stages include custodial interrogation and any stage at or after arraignment when a defendant has become the focus of criminal allegations (see, for example, *Miranda v. Arizona* and *Escobedo v. Illinois*).

Though the right to the assistance of adequate counsel for a person's defense was initially granted in death penalty cases at the state and federal level, today state and federal defendants have the right to the assistance of counsel when facing any charge for which a sentence of incarceration may be imposed (see *Argersinger v. Hamlin*). Stated another way, a person cannot receive a sentence of confinement unless he or she is first represented by adequate counsel, unless he or she waives that right. In such cases, if a defendant is indigent, the court must appoint an attorney. Courts have devised various procedures for determining the financial status of defendants who request assistance.

The cases that have led to the provision of free lawyers for defendants who are unable to hire their own have most often involved racial and ethnic minorities (Cole, 1999). But 50 years after the *Gideon* decision, and 80 years after *Powell*, states are beginning to complain that they do not have the funds to maintain their public defender, legal aid, and other appointed counsel systems. Unless alternate sources of funding can be garnered, given their numbers among those who live at or below the poverty level and their current overrepresentation among those who are in contact with the criminal justice system, it is African Americans and other racial and ethnic minorities who will bear the brunt of the shortage of lawyers for the poor.

Michael Thompson with Delores Jones-Brown

See also: False Confessions; Inequality Theory; Innocence Project; Racial Stereotyping and Wrongful Convictions; Scottsboro Cases; Wrongful Convictions

References

Argersinger v. Hamlin, 407 U.S. 25 (1972).

Cole, David. *No Equal Justice: Race and Class in the American Criminal Justice System.* New York: Norton, 1999.

Escobedo v. Illinois, 378 U.S. 478 (1964).

Gideon v. Wainwright, 372 U.S. 335 (1963).

Johnson v. Zerbst, 304 U.S. 458 (1938).

Miranda v. Arizona, 384 U.S. 436 (1966).

Palko v. Connecticut, 302 U.S. 319 (1937).

Powell v. Alabama, 287 U.S. 45 (1932).

Rhodes, Jr., R. "*Strickland v. Washington:* Safeguard of the Capital Defendant's Right to Effective Assistance of Counsel?" *Boston College Third World Law Journal* 12, no. 1 (1992): 121–55.

Smith, J. Clay. *Emancipation: The Making of the Black Lawyer, 1844–1944.* Philadelphia: University of Pennsylvania Press, 1993.

Strickland v. Washington, 466 U.S. 668 (1984).

Legal Socialization and Race

The criminal justice system is one of the most important institutions in American society. It is designed to regulate relations between states and its citizens, and, less formally, between private parties. More specifically, the system performs the twin functions of prescribing and proscribing behavior based on a utility calculus designed to yield the greatest happiness for the greatest number. At its nucleus, one finds the seeds of utilitarianism and social contractarian theory. Like many other institutions of its kind, the power and authority of the criminal justice system to bind its subordinates rests upon the principle of voluntariness. In other words, the legitimacy of the criminal justice system to rule over and bind the citizens of the state depends largely upon the justness of its laws. In the 1970s, in the aftermath of the civil disobedience and racial violence of the 1950s and 1960s, social psychologist June Tapp developed the concept of legal socialization to examine several factors and ways whereby objectives set by formal laws can be challenged or, at worst, ignored.

How or when does an individual learn about or become engaged in the science of government? Individuals learn about the vital relationship between society and its laws through a process called "legal socialization" (Piquero et al., 2005). For example, from childhood through early adolescence, a person's attitudes and respect for the law are shaped largely through the lenses of those within his or her immediate surroundings. Such surroundings may include, but are not limited to, the nuclear and extended family, church, school, and so on. These social institutions provide a theoretical as well as a practical understanding about the interconnectedness among race, law, and society.

"Law is a body of rules prescribed and enforced by government for the regulation and protection of society" (Scheb & Scheb, 2008: 3). However, law as a written text does not guarantee automatic compliance. In order for laws to be honored and respected, they must be perceived as just by those whom they bind: citizens of the state. This test can be measured in a number of different ways. Here I will examine two ways in which this is accomplished: substantively and procedurally. First, challenges based on the substantive provision of a law question the validity of the law as law. For example, say New York State passed a law prohibiting women from owning cars without providing any compelling reason for its policy. Based on the face of this law, anyone can justifiably challenge the substantive provision of that law and rightfully argue that such a law should be abolished. In so doing, the challenger is in fact arguing that the law is morally unacceptable.

Second, laws can also be challenged on procedural grounds. As an illustration, imagine New York State enacts a law guaranteeing persons charged with murder the right to counsel. This law is valid; it recognizes that suspected criminals are entitled to the basic fundamental right of legal representation. Now, suppose Mr. X, a citizen of the state of New York, is arrested by a police officer of the same state on the charge of murder and is denied the right to an attorney. Under the given circumstances, Mr. X can justifiably argue that the police officer violated a legally protected right by denying him the right to seek legal counsel. In that vein, Mr. X is arguing that a procedural violation has occurred.

In addition, obedience, more precisely obedience to law, is absolutely vital and essential for sustaining the legitimacy of the criminal justice system. This concept attracted much jurisprudential discussion throughout the late eighteenth and nineteenth centuries, most notably among social contractarian and positivist philosophers. Positivists believe that people obey laws because the opposite will result in punishment, thus denying the implicit link between law and justice as a possible motivating factor (Templeman, 2000: 71). In contrast, social contractarian theorists maintain that obedience to the law is based on the mutual terms of promise and rewards. While the position advocated by positivists contains a grain of truth, the fact is, obedience backed only by fear is inadequate to maintain an orderly and cohesive society. To illustrate this point, let us say that Mrs. X has shown an impeccable respect for the law against murder throughout her life because she fears going to jail (the punishment). Further, suppose that Mrs. X's hometown recently suffered from a major earthquake, which resulted in many deaths and much destruction to property, leaving only one grocery store standing. After going a full day without food, Mrs. X broke into the only grocery store available in her town and stole a few bags of chips. She was immediately followed by the store owner, who demanded that she either pay for the chips or leave the store empty-handed. Stricken with sheer hunger and unable to pay for the items, Mrs. X reached over the counter of the cash register where she noticed a knife in plain view, grabbed the knife, and stabbed and killed the store owner. She also regained possession of the chips, and exited the store along with a few more stolen goods. Not surprisingly, since fear was the sole impetus for compliance, Mrs. X will definitely opt for the defense of necessity as a shield against punishment. On a more important note, because Mrs. X has never recognized the prohibition against murder as morally just or socially right, under the challenging circumstances, said law became a mere nuisance undeserving of compliance.

On the other hand, social contractarian theories hold that people obey laws because they both appreciate and value the policies secured therein (Templeman, 2000: 42). This explanation is conditional upon the sub-principles of commitment and obligation. In other words, people are more likely to appreciate and support the social benefits secured by laws when such laws create in them a *prima facie* sense of commitment and obligation, akin to the concept of ownership. For instance, if a piece of legislation is viewed as a repressive tool or as a device to institutionalize racism and/or all other types of abhorrent and discriminatory practices, then those to whom such policy appears to be undemocratic or discriminatory may challenge the law or ignore it, and ultimately run the risk of facing prosecution. U.S. landmark cases dealing with slavery issues both before and after the Civil War provide powerful evidence of this sort. Likewise, a piece of legislation may receive widespread support among voters and still come under attack, not because the law ceases to be good law but because the law is arbitrarily enforced, resulting in a denial of equal protection. Examples of this sort are commonly found in disputes involving racial or neighborhood profiling.

Furthermore, discriminatory practices in the execution and interpretation of a just law not only weaken the authority of the criminal justice system but also plant the seeds of legal cynicism. For one thing, such practices carry within them the seed of destruction for anyone falsely convicted of a felonious crime, even after such an individual has been exonerated. Legal exoneration is the term used when individuals falsely convicted of a crime are later acquitted on the basis of newly discovered exculpatory evidence. Legal exoneration, while it establishes a cause for celebration, by itself is insufficient to both address and redress the harms and the injuries suffered by exonerated prisoners. In fact, studies have shown that exonerated inmates face monumental challenges as they seek reentry into a free society. Among the challenges are: a) difficulties in rebuilding family relationships; b) irrevocable societal and individual stigmatization; and c) emotional and psychological damages as a result of wrongful confinement (Roberts & Stanton, 2007: para. 7).

In sum, the authority of the criminal justice system to exercise control over the citizens of the state/country depends upon various variables. Such variables include, but are not limited to, fairness in practice and in policy.

Manouska Saint Gilles

See also: American Law and African Americans; Black Panther Party; Brown, H. Rap (aka Jamil Abdullah Al-Amin); Carmichael, Stokely; Civil Rights Movement; Davis, Angela Yvonne; Mapp, Dollree; Racial Profiling; Shakur, Assata (aka Joanne Chesimard); Slavery; Southern Christian Leadership Conference (SCLC); Student Nonviolent Coordinating Committee (SNCC)

References

Piquero, A. R., J. Fagan, E. P. Mulvey, L. Steinberg, and C. Odgers. "Developmental Trajectories of Legal Socialization among Serious Adolescent Offenders." *The Journal of Criminal Law & Criminology* 96, no. 1 (2005): 267–98.

Roberts, J., and E. Stanton. "A Long Road Back after Exoneration, and Justice Is Slow to Make Amends." *The New York Times,* November 25, 2007. http://www.nytimes.com/2007/11/25/us/25dna.html.

Scheb, J. M., and J. M. Scheb II. *Criminal Law & Procedure.* 6th ed. Belmont, CA: Thomson/Wadsworth, 2008.

Templeman, S. W. *Jurisprudence: The Philosophy of Law.* London: Old Bailey Press, 2000.

Los Angeles Riots of 1992

The Los Angeles Riots of 1992 (also known in the media as the "Rodney King Uprising") serve as a prime example of American collective violence, termed by historians as one of the deadliest and most hate-filled American confrontations since the Civil War. The events that began on Wednesday, April 29, 1992, and concluded the following Sunday were preceded by the state trial acquittal of three Los Angeles Police Department (LAPD) officers and one sergeant who had been accused of utilizing excessive force against a Black motorist, Rodney King. This suburban jury decision ignited a long-brewing rage among African Americans from South Central Los Angeles. However, the court decision was really only one deposit in a

Fires burn in South Central Los Angeles, set off in the riots which ensued after Los Angeles police officers were acquitted of beating Rodney King on April 30, 1992. (Peter Turnley/Corbis)

grievance bank full of civil unrest within Los Angeles. In order to fully understand and appreciate the effects of the Los Angeles Riots and the broader impact on African Americans and the justice system, one must first review the poor economic, social, and organizational conditions of Los Angeles that made it ripe for such an occurrence.

Underlying Causes

The beating of African American motorist Rodney King and the subsequent acquittal of the officers charged with using excessive force against him are often cited as the causes of the Los Angeles Riots of 1992. While it is true that these events certainly contributed to the riots, they are not the sole explanation. The city of Los Angeles had a long and rocky history of economic instability and racial tensions between ethnic groups, as well as a history of corruption, brutality, racism, and inefficiency within the LAPD. These trends, some dating back to the late nineteenth century, all served as predictive factors to the violent uprising.

Economic Instability

The state of California suffered a major economic recession as the Cold War drew to a close. This recession created massive layoffs and unemployment, with an estimated 140,000 aerospace jobs lost between 1988 and 1993. The shutdown of General Motors due to foreign competition took a heavy toll on blue-collar African Americans, who were unable to gain employment in other automobile industries that sought employees in research, design, and sales (Medoff & Sklar, 1994). This essentially led to the economic demise of the South Central area. By 1990, the only positions in demand for the citizens of South Central were in textiles and apparel manufacturing. The median annual salary declined 250 percent, instigating a decrease in consumer spending and a dramatic cut in government revenues from sales and income taxes. Housing and the real estate market also suffered the effects of this recession. Housing prices fell far below their listed values as Californians desperately tried to vacate their communities in search of better employment and housing prospects elsewhere. The passage of Proposition 13, which fixed property taxes on homes at a low level, also had grave consequences. As promising and beneficial as the proposition appeared for homeowners, it essentially stripped local governments of fiscal authority and entrusted it to the state, a prime example being state distribution of revenues to support schools. The collapse of prestigious aerospace jobs and prime real estate created a dramatic reduction in state revenues, thereby leading to local government funding cuts for services, namely medical trauma centers and police emergency communication equipment (both of which would be greatly needed during the impending riot).

Racial Tensions

The racial quarrels that instigated the Los Angeles Riots had a long-standing presence in California since its admission to the union in 1850. The gold rush, which brought a heavy influx of gold-seeking Whites, Blacks, and Mexicans to California, was noted as a period of intense Mexican guerrilla warfare as the practice of lynching Mexicans became an outdoor sport in Southern California. Economic competition between races further provoked racial animosities, particularly in the 1980s, when many downtown L.A. businesses fired Black blue-collar workers and replaced them with illegal Latino immigrants (Davis, 1992a; 1992b) who would be earning half the wages paid to their Black predecessors. Another source of strain between races resulted from friction created between Korean-owned family businesses and the Black residents they served in South Central. In addition to treating Black customers poorly, these businesses also refused to hire Blacks from the South Central area (Davis, 1992a; 1992b). The 1991 shooting of Black teenager Latasha Harlins by Korean store owner Soon Ja Du further exacerbated these tensions. Following a heated argument over an alleged shoplifting incident, Harlins was shot in the back of the head by Du. Facing a maximum sentence of 11 years in prison for involuntary manslaughter, Du's sentence was suspended and she was instead placed on probation. This decision enraged the Black community of South Central and would serve as a catalyst for targeting Korean shops and markets during the riot the following year.

The LAPD

Once known as the citadel of police professionalism, the LAPD was the final ingredient that primed the city of Los Angeles for the upcoming riot. Despite efforts of reform and progressivist visions, the LAPD had a reputation as a police force where elements of corruption, racism, brutality, and inefficiency ran rampant. These elements took a foothold as early as the turn of the twentieth century, when it was revealed that Chief Louis Oaks was involved in illegal gambling and bootlegging, and was also a member of the Ku Klux Klan. During the reign of Chief William Parker in the 1950s and 1960s, police corruption had decreased while police brutality and racism were on the rise, particularly against Mexican Americans. Brutality and aggressive policing caused further social unrest when Chief Daryl Gates took over the department in 1978, as evidenced by fatal shootings and choke hold deaths in which the victims were almost exclusively Black. The videotaped beating of

Rodney King on March 3, 1991, would become the most controversial of the LAPD's violent encounters with citizens.

Rodney King Trial

On March 2, 1991, Rodney King was speeding on Interstate 210 with two passengers in his car. At the time of the incident, King's blood alcohol level was estimated at 0.19. It is reported that in an interview, King admitted that he attempted to evade authorities because driving under the influence of alcohol would result in revocation of his parole for a crime for which he had previously been convicted. For a while, King evaded authorities in a high-speed chase. Eventually, as King exited the highway, LAPD squad cars with five officers surrounded him. The officers were Laurence Powell, Timothy Wind, Theodore Briseno, Rolando Salano, and Sergeant Stacy Koon. Also present at the scene was a female California highway patrol officer, Melanie Singer, who took no part in the beating. Upon exiting the car, officers reported that they noticed King's strange and erratic behavior, and concluded that he was under the influence of phencylidine (PCP). When King allegedly lunged at one officer, a Taser was fired into King's back. The officers reported that the taser failed to subdue him, and two officers (Powell and Wind) administered heavy blows with batons to King's head as well as his wrists, ankles, and other joints under the orders of Sergeant Koon. The events of this beating were captured on amateur videotape, which would soon reach the airways of Los Angeles, and eventually the rest of the country (CNN Wire Staff, 2012).

The Los Angeles district attorney charged three officers (Powell, Wind, and Briseno) and Sergeant Koon with use of excessive force. Attorneys for the defense filed for a change of venue, claiming the defendants could not receive a fair trial in Los Angeles given the extensive media coverage and potential bias of the jury. The trial was subsequently moved to Simi Valley, a wealthy Los Angeles suburb in Ventura County, where on April 29, 1992, a predominantly White jury acquitted the three officers and were unable to reach a verdict on the fourth. A later federal retrial of the four officers found Officer Powell and Sergeant Koon guilty of civil rights violations, while officers Briseno and Wind were again acquitted. Powell and Koon were each sentenced to 30-month prison sentences. After months of legal maneuvers to avoid incarceration, Koon and Powell began serving their sentences at the Federal Correctional Institution in Dublin, California, in October 1993.

Despite the not guilty verdict, King was awarded $3.8 million in compensatory damages by the U.S. District Court in a civil suit against the LAPD (CNN Wire Staff, 2012). After the incident, much of King's life involved visits to jail and rehabilitation centers resulting from his excessive drug and alcohol abuse. On June 17,

2012, King was found dead in his swimming pool at the home he shared with his fiancée. He was 47 years old (Medina, 2012).

The Riots

On April 29, 1992, news of the officers' acquittal in state criminal court for the beating of Rodney King quickly reached the streets of South Central, where the reaction was explosive and racially charged. News helicopters transmitted powerful images of innocent citizens being dragged from their cars and savagely beaten with bricks and concrete slabs, most of them non–African American. The beating of a White truck driver named Reginald Denney received particular media attention. Like the grainy video of King being beaten, video images showed Denney being dragged from his truck by young Black males who were later caught, tried, and acquitted (Pierce, 2000). While reactions to the Los Angeles Riots tended to be divided along racial lines, Denney issued a statement acknowledging that he understood the reasons for the violent reaction and essentially forgiving his attackers. Similarly, during the course of the riots, Rodney King was shown on mass media issuing his now famous statement: "Can't we all [just] get along?"

In addition to the personal attacks, there was devastating property damage. Among others, Korean-owned shops and businesses became targets of widespread looting and arson, particularly in the Koreatown District of Los Angeles. Pierce reports that:

> Unlike earlier civil unrest, property damage extended beyond the black community in Los Angeles. While south-central Los Angeles was the hardest hit, Beverly Hills was also affected. Schools were closed, mail service was discontinued, final examinations at area colleges and universities were canceled and federal troops were requested by city officials. (2000: 89)

Reaction to the acquittals in the King beating case was not limited to the Los Angeles area. Disturbances were also reported in Madison, Wisconsin; Las Vegas; Atlanta; San Francisco; Minneapolis; Seattle; and Eugene, Oregon. Nonviolent demonstrations were held in Baton Rouge, Louisiana; Kansas City, Missouri; Newark, New Jersey, and other cities, demonstrating the profound sense of betrayal that the African American community felt toward the American justice system (Hunt, 1996).

The Los Angeles Riots officially drew to a close on Monday, May 4, 1992, after federal troops from Fort Ord and Camp Pendleton were enlisted to suppress the mobs and restore order. Final estimates of the riots' outcome vary. One source notes that over the five-day span, 54 people were killed, another 2,000 injured, and over 800 buildings were set ablaze. In total, estimates of the property damages exceeded 900 million dollars—the greatest of any riot in U.S. history (Hunt, 1996).

It has been suggested that the duration and intensity of these riots were products of the lack of any meaningful preparation on behalf of the LAPD and the broader Los Angeles community, and that this ill-preparedness stemmed from lack of communication between the LAPD and the mayor prior to the onset of the riot, along with a lack of coordination between local, state, and federal government agencies for cooperation, mutual aid, and protection during a local emergency (Cannon, 1997).

Over 100 years of tumultuous history, tension, and collective behaviors had laid the foundation for the brutal riots. The naiveté of citizens about the economic crisis in Los Angeles combined with the social strains between races and with the LAPD created a perfect storm of elements that primed the city of Los Angeles for widespread collective brutality.

Jeremy Braithwaite

See also: Civil Rights Movement; Inequality Theory; Institutional Racism; King, Rodney; Juries; Louima, Abner; Police Brutality; Socioeconomic Factors; Structural Racism and Violence; Theories of Race and Crime

References

Cannon, L. *Official Negligence: How Rodney King and the Riots Changed Los Angeles and the LAPD.* New York: Random House, 1997.

CNN Wire Staff. "A Timeline of Events in Rodney King's Life." *CNN,* June 17, 2012.

Davis, M. 1992a. "In L.A., Burning All Illusions." *The Nation,* June 1, 1992.

Davis, M. 1992b. "The L.A. Inferno." *Socialist Review,* January–March, 1992.

Hunt, D. M. *Screening the Los Angeles "Riots": Race, Seeing and Resistance.* New York: Cambridge University Press, 1996.

Medina, Jennifer. "Rodney King Dies at 47; Police Beating Victim Who Asked 'Can We All Get Along?'" *The New York Times,* June 17, 2012.

Medoff, Peter, and Holly Sklar. *Streets of Hope: The Fall and Rise of an Urban Neighborhood.* Cambridge, MA: South End Press, 1994.

Pierce, B. "The King-Denney Tapes: Their Analysis and Implications for Police Use of Force." In *The System in Black and White: Exploring the Connections between Race, Crime and Justice,* edited by M. Markowitz and D. Jones-Brown, 85–91. Westport, CT: Praeger, 2000.

Louima, Abner (1966–)

On August 9, 1997, Abner Louima went to Club Rendez-vous in New York City with friends and family to see the Haitian band Phantom. At 4:00 a.m. when the club closed, the patrons were ushered into the street. Outside the club, a fight broke out between two female patrons. When police were called to the scene, the altercation escalated. Louima, a 30-year-old legal immigrant from Haiti who worked as a security guard and had been in the country since 1991, was cuffed and arrested for allegedly assaulting an officer during the melee. Officers transported Louima from the Flatbush Avenue club to the 70th Precinct in Brooklyn, during which Louima repeatedly protested his arrest. Louima told his lawyer that the officers became furious with his claims of innocence and stopped the patrol car twice to beat him on the way to the precinct. He reported being beaten with fists, nightsticks, and police radios while handcuffed. In a lengthy and confusing set of judicial proceedings that included multiple trials and appeals, Officers Charles Schwarz, Thomas Weise, and Thomas Bruder, who are White, were later acquitted of charges related to beating Louima during the ride to the station house, but convicted of conspiring to cover up an attack that Louima suffered at the hands of Officer Justin Volpe, who is also White, once they arrived at the police station.

On the night of the incident, once they arrived at Brooklyn's 70th Precinct, officers led Louima into the men's restroom. Louima told investigators that one officer held him down in a bathroom stall while now ex-officer Justin Volpe jammed a broken broomstick handle into Louima's rectum and then into his mouth, breaking multiple teeth, while shouting racial slurs. Volpe only admits to shoving the stick into Louima's face but not to causing the damage to his teeth. Louima was carried into a holding cell after the violent assault and locked inside. Other inmates began to complain shortly afterward that Louima was bleeding profusely, after which an ambulance was called. Louima was taken to Coney Island Hospital, where he underwent surgery to repair a puncture to his small intestine and injuries to his bladder.

The case became a national symbol of police brutality. The sadistic and sexual nature of the attack made it particularly newsworthy, along with the contrasting racial identities of the officers and the victim. The media has used the word "torture" to describe the attack. At the federal trial, where the officers were charged with conspiracy to deprive the victim of his civil rights, depriving him of his civil rights, obstruction of justice, and conspiracy to obstruct justice, a controversy emerged in testimony over the identification of the officers involved in the assault and the identification of the officer who held Louima down in the bathroom. Though Louima himself could not make a positive identification of all of the officers involved, midway through the federal trial, by then former officer Justin Volpe retracted his not guilty plea and admitted to brutalizing Louima. Volpe admitted that he had attacked Louima because he mistakenly believed that Louima had punched him during the brawl outside Club Rendez-vous and that he wanted to "break him down." For his role in the incident, Justin Volpe received 30 years in prison and was ordered to pay $277,495 in restitution to Louima, along with a $525 fine.

Although the facts remain in controversy, at the initial trial there was evidence that in an effort to protect Officer Schwarz, Volpe, Weise, Bruder, and Schwarz all initially claimed that only Officer Weise was in the restroom with Louima and Volpe. Louima maintained that the officer who drove the patrol car also held him down in the bathroom stall but he was unable to positively identify the officer. Police records identify Schwarz as the driver, and he was later convicted of holding Louima down during the attack and sentenced to 15 years in prison. That conviction was subsequently reversed on appeal, with the federal appellate court determining that Schwarz had been denied a fair trial. In a *60 Minutes* interview, Volpe identified Thomas Weise as the person who held Louima down in the stationhouse bathroom, not Charles Schwarz.

Officers Weise and Bruder and Sgt. Michael Bellomo were charged with conspiracy to cover up the beating and perjury regarding which officer held down Louima in the stall. Records indicate that nearly 50 telephone calls were made between Officers Schwarz, Weise, and Bruder, in which it is alleged that they conspired to cover up Schwarz's role in the attack. Calls were also made to members of the Patrolman's Benevolent Association (PBA), where union representatives were also alleged to have been involved in the cover-up. At the time of the attack on Louima, Mayor Rudolph W. Giuliani was commonly known for rising to the defense of police officers under suspicion. In this case, Giuliani demanded a thorough investigation of the beating and assault. Giuliani and the New York Police Department initially tried to claim the investigation of Louima's case as the rightful and swift examination of the corruption of a few cops. However, other accounts report that the investigation was launched only after an emergency room nurse at Coney Island Hospital contacted the media about Louima's injuries. It has been argued that the subsequent front-page media accounts are what actually prompted the inquiry into the assault on Louima. On August 29, 1997, the case prompted a protest march on city hall and the 70th Precinct stationhouse. The march, called "A Day of Outrage against Police Brutality and Harassment," is estimated to have included nearly 7,000 demonstrators.

The case attracted the attention of top lawyers such as Johnnie L. Cochran, Jr., who later joined Louima's legal defense team. In July 2001, Louima settled his civil case for $8.75 million dollars. The city of New York would pay $7.125 million and the PBA would pay $1.625 million of the settlement, the largest police brutality settlement in the city's history. Louima stated he would like to use some of the settlement to start an organization to help other victims of police brutality, and has, in fact, participated in anti–police brutality protests with Rev. Al Sharpton, most notably the 2006 shooting of Sean Bell by NYPD officers in Queens, New York. Sharpton's National Action Network has honored Louima for his dedication to helping other victims of police brutality.

Although on March 9, 2000, Thomas Wiese, Thomas Bruder, and Charles Schwarz were convicted of conspiring to obstruct a federal investigation into the assault on Louima, a federal appeals court reversed those convictions in February 2002. The court held that there was insufficient evidence to sustain the convictions. Sgt. Michael Bellomo was found not guilty of conspiring to cover up the beating of Louima and another person who had been present at the initial scene. After two more hung juries, Schwarz was retried in 2002 but opted to plead guilty to a charge of perjury regarding his role in the attack. He has never admitted that he was the officer who held Louima down in the bathroom and the prosecution was unable to prove that to a jury. Following his guilty plea, Schwarz was sentenced to five years in prison. Part of the plea agreement included that he would not be able to publicly proclaim his innocence. In 2006, he made a request for leniency and early release from prison. It was rejected. Justin Volpe also requested a reduction in his sentence and early release from prison. Thus far his requests have also been denied. He is currently scheduled for release from a federal correctional facility in Florida in 2025.

Abner Louima and his wife and three children lived in the Miami, Florida, area as of 2007. Louima has established a nonprofit foundation in Haiti, is helping to build several hospitals in Haiti, and is helping to pay tuition for children in the neighborhood where he grew up.

Valerie Stackman

See also: African Diaspora, Crime, and Justice; Bell, Sean; Cochran, Jr., Johnnie L.; Jackson, Jesse; Police Brutality; Sharpton, Jr., Alfred Charles

References

CNN Justice Online. "$8.75 Settlement over N.Y. Police Brutality Case." July 12, 2001. http://articles.cnn.com/2001-07-12/justice/louima.settlement_1_police-brutality-abner-louima-brooklyn-s-70th-precinct?_s=PM:LAW.

CNN Justice Online. "Abner Louima Testifies at Retrial of Ex-Officer." June 25, 2002. http://articles.cnn.com/2002-06-25/justice/police.beating.trial_1_ronald-fischetti-brooklyn-nightclub-police-station-bathroom?_s=PM:LAW.

CNN Justice Online. "Louima Police Conspiracy Trial Nears End." March 30, 2000. http://articles.cnn.com/2000-02-29/us/police.torture_1_ronald-fischetti-thomas-wiese-thomas-bruder?_s=PM:US.

Feuer, Alan. "Three Are Guilty of Cover-Up Plot in Louima Attack." *The New York Times,* March 7, 2000. http://www.nytimes.com/2000/03/07/nyregion/three-are-guilty-of-cover-up-plot-in-louima-attack.html.

Fried, Joseph P., and Blaine Harden. "The Louima Case: The Overview; Officer Is Guilty in Torture of Louima." *The New York Times,* June 9, 1999. http://www.nytimes.com/1999/06/09/nyregion/the-louima-case-the-overview-officer-is-guilty-in-torture-of-louima.html.

Glaberson, William. "News Analysis; Case Closed, Not Resolved." *The New York Times,* September 23, 2002. http://www.nytimes.com/2002/09/23/nyregion/news-analysis-case-closed-not-resolved.html.

Greene, Leonard, and Stephanie Cohen. "Louima's Haunted High Life 10 Years Later." *New York Post,* July 30, 2007. http://www.nypost.com/p/news/regional/item_sSpajgfkdpK9VK45n8JtuN.

Kicieniewski, David. "Injured Man Says Brooklyn Officers Tortured Him in Custody." *The New York Times,* August 13, 1997. http://topics.nytimes.com/top/reference/timestopics/people/l/abner_louima/index.html.

Lynching

Lynching is a form of punishment for presumed criminal offenses that is often carried out by mobs or vigilantes by hanging or burning the victim in public. For almost 30 years after World War II, no major academic work focused on lynching. The interest in the topic resurfaced in the 1980s when scholars such as Jacquelyn

A White crowd gathers to witness the killing of Tom Shipp and Abe Smith, two Black victims of lynch law in Indiana in 1930. (Getty Images)

Dowd Hall, Trudier Harris, and Joel Williamson reopened the topic as its own field of study. This paved the way for others to stimulate the social memory of lynching and create a social consciousness of the violent and racist U.S. past (see Till, Emmett).

Public interest in the topic was intensified by a collection of photographs and postcards depicting scenes from lynchings that was released in 2000, edited by James Allen, Hilton Als, Congressman John Lewis, and Leon Litwack. The photos from the book that was titled *Without Sanctuary: Lynching Photography in America* became a traveling exhibit that toured the country. In 2005, the U.S. Senate passed a resolution that apologized to victims, survivors, and their descendants for not passing anti-lynching legislation in a timely manner (Wood & Donaldson, 2008) (see Wells-Barnett, Ida B).

Despite these efforts, many Americans have no clear understanding of what constitutes lynching because many find it hard to understand if lynching occurred due to racism, deterrence, revenge, a need for racial empowerment, or economic hardship. Raper (1933), in his study of lynchings that occurred in 1930, concluded that lynchings were an angry response to economic competition between White and Black laborers. Others offered a "subculture of violence theory" as an explanation, stating that White supremacists exerted absolute power over Blacks in the region through the public spectacle of lynching (Clarke, 1998). According to Wiegman (1993), the atrocities committed against African American men, especially increased use of castration as a preferred method of mutilation, were used to demonstrate White masculine supremacy over Black men. No matter what explanations are proffered for such atrocities, lynching studies have provided insights into the United States' violent racial history (Wiegman, 1993).

By some accounts, prior to the U.S. Civil War (1861–1865) and the emancipation of slaves in 1863, lynching was primarily a frontier phenomenon where there was a need for swift retribution. By those accounts, until 1868, the majority of lynching victims were White men accused of murder and of stealing livestock (Clarke, 1998). By other accounts, though slaves were protected by their owners as a valuable commodity similar to their livestock, lynchings were frequently used a means of making examples out of slaves who dared defy the slave system.

A shift in lynching targets to free Blacks occurred in 1868 when a group of Ku Klux Klan members killed at least 281 Black males and left countless other men, women, and children tortured and sexually mutilated. Over the next three years, more Blacks were murdered by the Klan (Clarke, 1998). Other mobs who were involved in lynching were known as "White clappers," "night riders," or "regulators." These groups targeted unruly Whites, Blacks who threatened insurrection, Black tenant farmers who might pose economic competition, and people who reported moonshiners to authorities. Many of these lynchings were carried out in secrecy and often with the support of local law officers (Garland, 2005).

Lynchings that involved torture and public spectacle were primarily a Southern phenomenon. But a 2013 book, *Lynchings beyond Dixie,* edited by John Jay College history professor Michael Pfeifer, documents the significant number of lynchings that took place in the North. Post–Civil War Southern lynchings became more public after the removal of federal troops and the restoration of states' rights in 1877, which showed the power—and White supremacist element—of the Southern wing of the Democratic Party (Trelease, 1971).

Because lynching was not a punishable offense in the South, it continued unchecked. Reports show that between 1880 and 1940, approximately 90 percent of lynchings occurred in former slave states, and about 90 percent of those lynchings were committed by White mobs against Black men (Wood & Donaldson, 2008), and sometimes against Black women (Brundage, 1993; Browne-Marshall, 2007). White men charged with serious crimes were rarely lynched in public, with the exception of Leo Frank, who was lynched by a small crowd in 1915 (Dray, 2002).

Although there were public lynchings of many Black men, the savage killings of Henry Smith in Paris, Texas, in 1893, and Sam Hose in Newnan, Georgia, in 1899, were covered in national newspapers and the photographs of the killings were circulated widely. Hose's ears, fingers, and genitals were severed. The skin from his face was removed and he was burned alive. The savage and public nature of these killings served as models for future lynchings of Black men (Hale, 1996).

Whites believed that young Black men were a threat because they had begun to challenge the racial status quo and resisted unfair treatment (Clarke, 1998). However, the newspaper accounts at the time reported that most Black men were lynched because of sexual crimes, especially against White women (Frederickson, 1971). In the South, lynchings peaked in the 1890s, and dropped off slowly until 1910 and more rapidly in the 1920s.

Unlike other states, Florida showed an upsurge in the number of lynchings in the 1930s and 1940s, making Florida the worst state in the nation at that time (Jean, 2005). Of the 292 victims whose race was documented, an overwhelming majority (94%) were Black. Of these men, 32 percent were charged with murder and 21 percent were charged with sexual crimes; other charges included insulting White girls or women, entering a White girl or woman's bedroom, or theft of property (Jean, 2005). Entire Black communities in Rosewood, Florida, and Tulsa, Oklahoma, were terrorized and destroyed by White lynch mobs based on claims of sexual assault against individual White women, but the likelier motive has emerged as jealousy over the economic prosperity of Black residents.

There were about 4,000 documented cases of lynching incidents between 1882 and 1940. Common headlines reporting lynching included "Brute's Heinous

---

Scenes from a Lynching, as Reported by *The New York Herald,* June 9, 1903

The crowd in the jail broke into Wyatt's cell. He fought fiercely for his life, but a blow from a sledge hammer felled him. A rope was tied around his neck. He was dragged out into the corridor, down the stairs and into the jail yard, then into Spring Street, up to Main Street and to the center of the square.

A man riding a white horse led the way to an electric light pole in the square. The end of the rope was thrown over it, and the body was drawn up above the heads of the crowd, who cheered and waved hats. Men on the pole kicked Wyatt in the face. The swaying form was stabbed repeatedly. Mutilations followed.

Kerosene was bought and poured over the body and it was set on fire, while the crowd cheered. The rope burned through and the body fell. More kerosene was poured on the body as the flames slowly consumed it.

Source: Ginzburg, Ralph. *One Hundred Years of Lynchings.* Baltimore: The Black Classic Press, 1988.

Crime," "Burned at the Stake," and "Hung and Horribly Mangled" (Jean, 2005). Lynchings were understood at that time as collective punishment and a preferred (by Whites) alternative to more formal justice (Garland, 2005). Not all lynchings, however, were supported by the people in the community. For instance, when six men were lynched at the same time in Lake City in 1911 on charges of murdering a sawmill man, a local newspaper expressed its disapproval, stating that the actions were not lynch law but "lynch lawlessness."

Between the period 1859 to 1962, one source puts the estimated number of African Americans lynched in the United States at roughly 5,000 (Ginzburg, 1988). While one source has claimed that there were no recorded incidents of public lynchings in the second half of the twentieth century (Garland, 2005), the dragging death of James Byrd by three male White Supremacists in Jasper, Texas, in 1998 was considered a lynching and led to the enactment of a federal hate crimes statute in his name in 2009.

Sesha Kethineni with Delores Jones-Brown

See also: Byrd, Jr., James; Civil Rights Movement; Hate Crimes; Slavery; Structural Racism and Violence; Till, Emmett; Wells-Barnett, Ida B.; White, Walter Francis

References

Allen, A., H. Als, J. Lewis, and L. Litwack. *Without Sanctuary: Lynching Photography in America.* Santa Fe, NM: Twin Palms Publishers, 2000.

Browne-Marshall, G. *Race, Law and American Society: 1607 to Present.* New York: Routledge, 2007.

Brundage, W. F. *Lynching in the New South: Georgia and Virginia, 1890–1930.* Urbana: University of Illinois Press, 1993.

Clarke, J. W. "Without Fear or Shame: Lynching, Capital Punishment and the Subculture of Violence in the American South." *British Journal of Political Sciences* 28, no. 2 (1998): 269–89.

Dray, P. *In the Hands of Persons Unknown: The Lynching of Black America.* New York: Random House, 2002.

Frederickson, G. M. *The Black Image in the White Mind: The Debate on Afro-American Character and Destiny, 1817–1914.* New York: Harper & Row, 1971.

Garland, D. "Penal Excess and Surplus Meaning: Public Torture Lynchings in Twentieth-Century America." *Law & Society Review* 39, no. 4 (2005): 793–834.

Ginzburg, R. *One Hundred Years of Lynchings.* Baltimore: The Black Classic Press, 1988.

Hale, G. E. "Deadly Amusements: Spectacle Lynchings and Southern Whiteness, 1890–1940." *Contributions in American History* 169 (1996): 63–78.

Jean, S. "'Warranted' Lynchings: Narratives of Mob Violence in White Southern Newspapers, 1880–1940." *American Nineteenth Century History* 6, no. 3 (2005): 351–72.

Pfeifer, M. J. *Lynchings beyond Dixie: American Mob Violence outside the South.* Champaign: University of Illinois Press, 2013.

Raper, A. F. *The Tragedy of Lynching.* Chapel Hill: University of North Carolina Press, 1933.

Trelease, A. W. *White Terror: The Ku Klux Klan Conspiracy and Southern Reconstruction.* New York: Harper & Row, 1971.

Wiegman, R. "The Anatomy of Lynching." *Journal of the History of Sexuality* 3, no. 3 (1993): 445–67.

Wood, A. L., and S. V. Donaldson. "Lynching Legacy in American Culture." *Mississippi Quarterly* (Winter–Spring 2008): 5–25.

M

Malcolm X (aka El-Hajj Malik El-Shabazz) (1925–1965)

Civil rights activist Malcolm X was highly revered by many. However, his outspokenness, commanding personality, and controversial views also earned him fear within the White community. He overcame numerous adversities in childhood and his young adult life prior to becoming the leader he was at the time of his assassination. His struggles helped mold him into an individual who would command international attention and fight for Black Nationalism.

Malcolm X was born Malcolm Little in Omaha, Nebraska, on May 19, 1925, to Earl and Louisa Little. Malcolm was the seventh child among eight siblings. Louisa Norton Little was a homemaker and Earl Little was an outspoken Baptist minister and avid supporter of Black Nationalist leader Marcus Garvey. It is reported that Earl had great dreams for this seventh son, who was to take the name of Earl's father, John. However, when word spread that Malcolm was born "White," like his grandmother, John prohibited the use of his name being passed on to this "albino" (Perry, 1991). Malcolm endured constant harassment because of his light skin, but was favored by his father to the dismay of his siblings. His mother encouraged him to go outside so that the sun could "darken his skin" (Perry, 1991). Later in life, his skin and hair color would earn him the nickname "Red."

Early in Malcolm's life, Earl Little's civil rights activism prompted death threats to himself and his family. The main threats came from a White supremacist organization called the Black Legion, forcing the family to relocate twice before Malcolm's fourth birthday. In 1929, they moved from Omaha, Nebraska, to Lansing, Michigan; there, their home was burned to the ground, and two years later, in 1931, Earl's mutilated body was found lying across the town's trolley tracks. Police ruled that both incidents were accidental, but the surviving Littles were certain that members of the Black Legion were responsible. In 1939, Malcolm's mother, who never fully recovered from the shock and grief of her husband's death, was found to be

Black Muslim leader Malcolm X holds up a paper for the crowd to see during a Black Muslim rally in New York City on August 6, 1963. (Associated Press)

mentally ill by the courts and was civilly committed to a mental hospital. With his father already dead, his mother's institutionalization led to the break-up of the family (Perry, 1991). Malcolm's initial stay in a group foster home was followed by a period of living with his older half-sister, Ella, in Boston, Massachusetts.

Despite the childhood trauma he suffered, Malcolm began exhibiting the traits of a leader. He would defend the underdogs and excelled academically, becoming class president in the eighth grade (Perry, 1991). He began having aspirations of becoming a lawyer. He shared this ambition with one of his teachers, who told him that he should look for an alternate career because his vision of becoming a lawyer was not a "realistic goal for a nigger" (Simon, 2005). He consequently lost interest in academics, dropped out of school at the age of 15, spent some time working odd jobs in Boston, and eventually traveled to Harlem, New York, where he began committing petty crimes. By 1942, he was "coordinating various narcotics, prostitution and gambling rings" (Malcolm X Official Web Site, n.d.). He also developed a drug addiction and was participating in burglaries. His fast life caught up with him and in 1946, he was arrested and sentenced to 10 years in prison (Simon, 2005).

He used his time in prison to further his education and to successfully complete drug rehabilitation. During this time he also studied the teachings of the Nation of Islam (NOI) leader Elijah Muhammad and made the decision to join the organization and convert to the Islamic faith. By the time he was paroled in 1952, he had changed his name from Malcolm Little to Malcolm X, signifying his acceptance of NOI teachings that the surnames of African Americans were those of slave owners and needed to be shed in order to cut ties with their enslaved past (Simon, 2005).

After his release from prison, Malcolm X became a minister and leading spokesperson within the Nation of Islam (Simon, 2005). In 1958, he married Betty Shabazz (born Betty Dean Sanders), a fellow NOI member, and they had six children. The teachings of the NOI were controversial. They included the idea that White society actively worked to suppress the political, economic, and social progress of African Americans. The NOI advocated for Black empowerment and separation from White America. Many saw this stance as an expression of hatred against Whites. In 1959, Malcolm X was invited to participate in a week-long discussion with television journalist Mike Wallace titled *The Hate That Hate Produced.*

The broadcast aired in five parts during the week of July 13 through 17 and was co-produced by African American journalist Louis Lomax. Lomax, who is credited with being the first African American television journalist, brought the topic to Wallace's attention. By many accounts, Malcolm X did an effective job of explaining the fundamentals of the NOI as a response to the historic and contemporary injustices experienced by African Americans in the United States. Following the television interview, Malcolm X emerged as one of NOIs most important and influential leaders. He founded temples in Detroit, Boston, New York, and Connecticut, and in 1960 he established a national newspaper, *Muhammad Speaks.*

In 1963, Malcolm X discovered that his mentor, NOI leader Elijah Muhammad, was involved in multiple extramarital affairs. Such conduct was strictly forbidden within the religion (Malcolm X Official Web Site, n.d.). The discovery resulted in his break from the NOI in 1964 and the founding of his own religious organization, the Muslim Mosque, Inc. (Simon, 2005). According to an interview with A. B. Spellman on March 19, 1964, Malcolm described the Muslim Mosque, Inc., as having its religious base in the Islamic religion, with its political philosophy rooted in Black Nationalism. He urged young African Americans to educate themselves politically, to think for themselves, and to regain control of their communities (Rabaka, 2002). He also advocated for the right to use violence in self-defense, which resulted in many viewing him as a supporter of violence. On multiple occasions he disputed this, saying that he

Dr. Betty Shabazz was born Betty Sanders on May 28, 1934, to Shelman Sandlin and Ollie Mae. Her parents were unwed at the time. She was raised by her mother in Detroit, Michigan, but was later adopted informally by Helen and Lorenzo Malloy in 1944 or 1945. Betty would consider the Malloys her parents for the remainder of her life. After graduating from high school, Betty enrolled at the Tuskegee Institute in Alabama, where she studied elementary education. Unsatisfied with her time there, she later transferred to Brooklyn State College School of Nursing, where she earned her undergraduate degree in nursing in 1956. During her time in New York City, Betty began attending lectures given by the Nation of Islam. It was then, in 1955, that she met Malcolm X, and she joined the Nation of Islam several months later in 1956. Her parents were against this spiritual change, as Betty had been raised Methodist as a child. Still, she remained devout in her conversion, taking on more definitive roles within the Nation of Islam. During this time, Malcolm did not court her, but they spent time together in group settings. He eventually proposed to her through a phone call, asking her, "Are you ready to make that move?" in January 1958. They married two days later. Betty bore six daughters with Malcolm during the seven years that they were married. Due to revelations of Elijah Muhammad's (the leader of the Nation of Islam) marital infidelities and fraudulent practices, Malcolm and Betty left the Nation of Islam in 1964. In February 1965, Betty and her daughters witnessed the death of Malcolm in Manhattan's Audubon Ballroom. One month after the assassination, Betty made her own pilgrimage to Mecca. With the help of committee-raised funds, Betty and her daughters settled into a new home in Mount Vernon, New York. While raising six daughters as a single mother, Betty enrolled in Jersey City State College to finish her bachelor's degree in education. Upon completing her bachelor's degree, she re-enrolled to complete a master's degree in health administration. Immediately after completing her master's degree, Betty enrolled at the University of Massachusetts–Amherst to complete an EdD with a specialty in higher education administration and curriculum development. She earned her EdD three years later, in 1975. In 1976, Betty became the associate professor of health sciences with a concentration in nursing at Medgar Evers College in New York City. She was later promoted to Director of Institutional Advancement. She held this position until her death. Throughout the remainder of her life, Dr. Betty Shabazz remained active as a volunteer and public speaker. Speaking on topics such as health education, civil rights, and her late husband, she became a legendary icon in her own right. In June 1997, at age 63, Dr. Betty Shabazz died of injuries sustained from a fire set in her home by her grandson, Malcolm Shabazz (Rickford, 2003).

promoted and encouraged nonviolence; however, if someone became violent, he supported the use of violence in self-defense (Spellman, 2005).

Also in 1964, Malcolm went on a pilgrimage to Mecca, Saudi Arabia. The trip proved life altering. Malcolm issued a statement that he met "blonde-haired, blued-eyed men I could call my brothers." He returned to the United States with a new outlook on integration. At this time, instead of just preaching to African Americans, he had a message for all races. Malcolm X was committed to ending discrimination and to "bring[ing] into being human liberation by any means necessary" (Rabaka, 2002: 160). Following the trip to Mecca, Malcolm X also adopted the name El-Hajj Malik El-Shabazz. According to one interpretation, in Arabic, the name El-Hajj means "the pilgrim." Malik means "king" and Shabazz means "mighty people."

By 1965, rumors emerged that Malcolm X had been marked for assassination. There were reports of repeated attempts on his life, including a planned car bombing. He began to travel with bodyguards. His home in East Elmhurst, New York, was firebombed on February 14, 1965, but he and his family were unharmed. Seven days later, on February 21, 1965, Malcolm X was shot 15 times at close range by three men while he was delivering a speech on the stage of the Audubon Ballroom in Manhattan, New York. He was 39 years old at the time of his death. Later that year, Betty gave birth to their twin daughters ("Malcolm X," 2012a; 2012b).

Though he had been known by many titles and had filled many roles, Malcolm X's legacy as a civil rights leader was cemented in the posthumous 1965 publication by Alex Haley, *The Autobiography of Malcolm X*. It recast him as one of the greatest political and spiritual leaders of the twentieth century. The life and death of Malcolm X has been the subject of numerous documentaries, books and movies, including *Malcolm X*, released by director Spike Lee in 1992, with the role of Malcolm X played by popular actor Denzel Washington. The film received much acclaim and is credited with having renewed interest in his life, his work, and his legacy.

Nearly 50 years later, the circumstances of Malcolm X's death continue to be the topic of question and controversy. Though NOI members Talmadge Hayer, Norman 3X Butler, and Thomas 15X Johnson were each convicted of first-degree murder for the shooting in 1966, a book released in 2011 calls those convictions into question. *Malcolm X: A Life of Reinvention* was authored by Columbia University history professor Manning Marable. Marable founded the African American Studies Department at Columbia and the book is described as his life's work (NPR, 2011). Professor Marable died days before the book was released. The 592-page Pulitzer Prize–winning book contains contested information about the life of Malcolm X before he became a Muslim leader and civil rights icon. (The Shabazz family has objected to some content.) The book also alleges that at least one of the actual killers of Malcolm X was never prosecuted. In the book, Marable, who began studying Malcolm X in 1969, five years after the assassination, names

Malcolm Lateef Shabazz was the son of Qubilah Shabazz, the second daughter of Malcolm X and Dr. Betty Shabazz. On June 1, 1997, when he was 12 years old, Malcolm Shabazz obtained gasoline and deliberately set fire to his grandmother's apartment (Zimring, 1998). Betty Shabazz had taken her grandson in to live with her several months earlier while his mother underwent drug and alcohol treatment as part of a negotiated plea on criminal charges (see Nation of Islam). There are reports that prior to moving in with his grandmother, the relationship between Malcolm and his mother had grown increasingly violent. It is also reported that upon seeing her apartment on fire, Betty Shabazz believed that Malcolm was in danger amid the fire and, in an attempt to save her grandson, became engulfed in the flames herself.

Betty Shabazz suffered burns over 80 percent of her body, and remained in intensive care for three weeks at Jacobi Medical Center in the Bronx, New York. She underwent five skin grafts but died from her injuries three weeks later on June 23, 1997.

Malcolm was charged with second-degree manslaughter. It is reported that during the trial, the defense claimed that Malcolm had never intended to harm his grandmother. He only intended to scare her into sending him back to San Antonio to live with his mother. Malcolm eventually pled guilty to second-degree manslaughter and arson, and was sentenced to 18 months' detention in a home for emotionally troubled children. He was released four years later in 2001 (Rickford, 2003).

After his release, Malcolm was arrested again in 2002 for attempted robbery. He was accused of following a man home and stealing $100 from him. Malcolm pled guilty to the charge, and was sentenced to three-and-a-half years' confinement. He was released from prison in 2006 (Wilson, 2003). In 2006, Malcolm was arrested for punching a glass window, and was later charged with reckless endangerment, assault, and criminal mischief (*The New York Times*, 2006). Vowing to turn his life around, in 2011 Malcolm Shabazz became a student at John Jay College of Criminal Justice, City University of New York (John Jay College of Criminal Justice, 2011).

After reportedly beginning a life of activism that spanned the globe, Malcolm Shabazz was beaten to death in Mexico City, Mexico, in May 2013 in an apparent robbery attempt. Reports that his death was preceded by a February 2013 arrest by the FBI when he was en route to Iran for a conference on Hollywoodism and the troubled history of the relationship between his family and authorities have caused some to question the public accounts of his death.

Malikah Shabazz

In July 2011, at the age of 46, Malikah Shabazz, the youngest of Malcolm X's six daughters, was sentenced to five years' probation for the crime of identity theft. New York prosecutors say that she opened credit cards in the name of a 70-year-old woman whose husband had been one of her father's bodyguards. The bodyguard had been present during the assassination of Malcolm X in 1965. Shabazz pled guilty to the charge that she made $55,000 in illegal purchases with the credit cards she opened. A condition of her probation was that she would make full restitution. Shabazz incurred at least one violation of her probation and was held without bail in December 2011. The violation appears to have been related to changing residence without permission. She was arrested in North Carolina and extradited back to New York. Sources indicate that prior to her arrest for the violation, she had also lived in Vermont. During that time, officials thought that she was still in New York.

five alleged conspirators. Only one, Talmadge Hayer, served time in prison; he was released in 2010. Hayer had been caught at the scene and later confessed to his involvement. The other two men who were convicted for the killing maintained their innocence and were paroled in the 1980s. In a court affidavit, Hayer confirmed the innocence of both Butler and Johnson and named four accomplices who have never been tried. In the book, Marable alleges that the man who fired the first and deadliest shot is Newark, New Jersey, resident Al-Mustafa Shabazz, once known as William Bradley, and that Shabazz is still alive, though currently in his seventies. According to Marable, one conspirator has died. The book does not provide definitive information about the other two.

Shannon O'Brien with Delores Jones-Brown

See also: Black Panther Party; Civil Rights Movement; Nation of Islam

References

Haley, Alex. *The Autobiography of Malcolm X: As Told to Alex Haley.* New York: Grove Press, 1965.

John Jay College of Criminal Justice. *In the News.* July 2011.

"Malcolm X." 2012a. *Biography.com,* 2012. http://www.biography.com/people/malcolm -x-9396195.

"Malcolm X." 2012b. *Biography,* 2012. http://www.africawithin.com/malcolmx/estateof malcolmx.

Malcolm X Official Web Site. N.d. http://www.malcolmx.com/index.html.

Marable, M. *Malcolm X: A Life of Reinvention.* New York: Viking Press, 2011.

The New York Times. "New York: Yonkers: Malcolm X's Grandson Arrested." August 4, 2006.

NPR. "Manning Marable's 'Reinvention' of Malcolm X." April 5, 2011. http://www.npr.org/2011/04/05/135144230/manning-marables-reinvention-of-malcolm-x.

Perry, B. *Malcolm.* New York: Station Hill Press, 1991.

Rabaka, R. "Malcolm X and/as Critical Theory: Philosophy, Radical Politics, and the African American Search for Social Justice." *Journal of Black Studies* 33 (2002): 145–65.

Rickford, R. *Betty Shabazz: A Remarkable Story of Survival and Faith before and after Malcolm X.* Naperville, IL: Sourcebooks, 2003.

Simon, J. "Malcolm X—His Legacy—1. The Achievement of Malcolm X." *Monthly Review—An Independent Socialist Magazine* 56, no. 9 (2005): 25–31.

Spellman, A. "Malcolm X—His Legacy—2. Interview with Malcolm X." *Monthly Review—An Independent Socialist Magazine* 56, no. 9 (2005): 31–42.

Wilson, M. "For Malcolm X's Grandson, a Clouded Path." *The New York Times,* September 6, 2003.

Zimring, Franklin E. "Adolescent Homicide in Juvenile and Criminal Courts, the Hardest of the Hard Cases." *Virginia Journal of Social Policy and the Law* 6 (1998): 437–469.

Mapp, Dollree

In 1961, in the case of *Mapp v. Ohio,* the U.S. Supreme Court mandated the exclusion of evidence in state criminal cases when the police act improperly while gathering it. The defendant in the case was an African American female, Dollree Mapp, whose conviction for possession of obscene materials was overturned on the grounds that her home had been illegally searched and that items were illegally seized. Members of the Cleveland Police Department entered Mapp's home on May 23, 1957, claiming they were searching for a man on charges unrelated to pornography. The officers failed to produce a valid search warrant and opened several personal items belonging to Mapp, including dressers, chest of drawers, suitcases, and a trunk in Mapp's basement. While they failed to find the person they were looking for, they arrested Mapp based on the materials found during the extensive search. In a 6 to 3 decision, the Supreme Court overturned her conviction.

Nine years after her conviction was overturned in this landmark decision, Mapp again found herself in trouble with the law. In 1970, she was convicted of having heroin and stolen property in her home in Queens, New York, where she had moved after leaving Ohio. The police had a warrant this time. One source notes that her house was raided and she was found in possession of 50,000 envelopes of heroin and stolen property valued at more than $100,000. Another source places the combined value of drugs and stolen property seized at $250,000.

On April 23, 1971, she was convicted of felonious possession of dangerous drugs and was sentenced to a prison term of 20 years to life. During the trial and subsequent appeals, Mapp unsuccessfully argued against the legality of the search warrant and claimed that the charges were a vendetta against her because of her famous case. After serving nearly 10 years in a New York women's prison, on December 31, 1980, New York governor Hugh Carey commuted her minimum sentence, making Mapp eligible for parole the next day.

Before becoming a famous criminal defendant, Dollree Mapp was known in the boxing world. She was the ex-wife of former top-ranked boxer Jimmy Bivins and had filed a $750,000 civil suit against another champion boxer, Archie Moore, in 1956. In the suit, Mapp claimed that Moore physically assaulted her and broke a promise to marry her. One source notes that it was the now-famous boxing promoter Don King who led the Cleveland police to suspect criminal activity at Mapp's Ohio home in 1957.

Delores Jones-Brown

See also: American Law and African Americans; Legal Representation; Police Brutality

References

Inciardi, J. *Criminal Justice.* 4th ed. New York: Harcourt Brace Jovanovich Publishers, 1993.

Mapp v. Ohio, 367 U.S. 643 (1961).

"Who Was Dollree Mapp?" http://guidewhois.com/2010/12/who-was-dollree-mapp/.

Martin, Trayvon (1995–2012)

On February 26, 2012, at approximately 7:00 p.m., 17-year-old Trayvon Martin was shot and killed by George Zimmerman in Sanford, Florida. The shooting took place in the Retreat at Twin Lakes, a gated community, where Martin was visiting with his father.

The encounter with Zimmerman occurred while Martin was returning from a convenience store in the area. According to media accounts, at the time of the incident, Martin was unarmed, wearing a hooded sweatshirt, and carrying candy and a can of iced tea. Zimmerman, who has been described as a neighborhood watch volunteer, called 911 to report that Martin was in the area.

During the call, Zimmerman describes Martin as suspicious and makes reference to recent break-ins. He also makes a statement that he thinks Martin may be on drugs. At one point during the call he describes Martin as "just standing there," at another he says he is "looking at the houses."

During the recorded 911 call there is a point at which Zimmerman indicates that Martin is staring at him and then he says Martin ran away. When Zimmerman indicates that he is following Martin, the police dispatcher says, "We don't need you to do that." Zimmerman comments, "They always get away." There is also a point in the recording where Zimmerman makes a statement that is not clearly audible. Some have suggested that during that portion of the tape Zimmerman calls Martin a "coon," a racially derogatory term historically used in reference to African Americans. Once during the call, the police dispatcher asked Zimmerman to describe Martin's racial identity. More than once Zimmerman described Martin as Black (*Orlando Sentinel.com*, 2012).

On February 26, 2012, while walking home from a convenience store in Sanford, Florida, unarmed African American teenager, Trayvon Martin, was shot and killed by self-proclaimed neighborhood watch captain, George Zimmerman. Zimmerman's subsequent acquittal ignited months of debate about private racial profiling and the quality of American justice for African American victims. (Getty Images)

The details of what occurred after the 911 call are disputed. Sometime after the call there was a confrontation between 28-year-old George Zimmerman and the teenager that ended with Martin being shot in the chest at close range. Zimmerman claims that the shooting was in self-defense and that he sustained a broken nose and injuries to the back of his head during the encounter. Medical records from Zimmerman's family doctor confirm the injuries (CNN.com, 2013). Media coverage contains police statements that Zimmerman was not badly injured and did not seek medical treatment until the day after the shooting (see, for example, NBCNews.com). A key piece of evidence in the case is another 911 call in which someone is heard calling out for help immediately before the gunshot. In pretrial hearings, experts offered conflicting testimony about the identity of the person behind the voice.

The Trayvon Martin shooting sparked national controversy, much of it centered around race. Immediately following the shooting, Zimmerman was questioned by police and released. The Sanford Police Department said that they released Zimmerman because his claim of self-defense was supported by Florida's Stand-Your-Ground law, passed in 2005. The statute allows individuals to use deadly force in response to perceived threats of serious violence without first attempting to safely retreat. The results in several previous cases involving the defense were hotly contested, particularly in inter-racial encounters (Campo-Flores et al., 2012). According to one source, an Urban Institute study has found that in 34 percent of cases involving Black victims and White shooters, the shootings have been deemed justified. The same is true in only 3 percent of cases where the victim is White and the shooter is Black (Milner, 2013).

The shooting occurred on February 26. Zimmerman was not formally arrested until weeks later. Prior to his arrest, Trayvon Martin's parents posted a petition on Change.org calling for police action. Sources indicate that Tracy Martin, Trayvon's father, became aware of his son's death only after he filed a missing persons report with the Sanford police when his son did not return home the evening of the shooting. Tracy Martin reportedly identified the body of his son through police photos (CNN.com, 2013). At that point, George Zimmerman had already been released from custody.

By March 22, 2012, the petition calling for Zimmerman's arrest had garnered more than 1.3 million signatures (CNN.com, 2013). In a television interview, Benjamin Crump, the attorney for Martin's mother, Sybrina Fulton, indicated that the petition ultimately garnered more than 2 million electronic signatures before Zimmerman was arrested (*The View*, 2013). Amid the controversy over how the department handled the case, Sanford police chief William Lee temporarily stepped down and was later officially fired. Zimmerman's father, Robert Zimmerman, who reportedly is a retired judge, came forward to defend his son from claims of racism by noting that George's mother is Hispanic and that George grew up in a multicultural household (CNN.com, 2013).

Despite these claims, the Trayvon Martin shooting seemed to galvanize the nation into largely racialized camps. Many have debated whether Martin was approached, stopped, and seen as suspicious because he was young, male, and African American (Campo-Flores et al., 2012). Across the country, protestors wore hooded sweatshirts to support Martin's parents' request that Zimmerman be arrested for the death of their son. A gathering in Sanford, Florida, drew more than 30,000 people and a town hall meeting included noteworthy civil rights advocates Jesse Jackson and Rev. Al Sharpton. The U.S. Department of Justice also launched an investigation into the facts and circumstances surrounding the case (NBC News, 2012).

A member of the House of Representatives, Congressman Bobby Rush (D-IL), stirred controversy when, while giving a speech about Trayvon Martin, he addressed House members wearing a hooded sweatshirt, commonly called a "hoodie"

From Trayvon Martin to Jordan Davis

The death of Trayvon Martin is not the only Florida case that came under public scrutiny due to possible racial motivation. In November 2012, nine months after the Trayvon Martin case, Michael Dunn was arrested and charged with murder and attempted murder for shooting and killing unarmed 17-year-old Jordan Davis in Jacksonville, Florida. The shooting took place at a gas station where 46-year-old Dunn had stopped with his girlfriend after leaving his son's wedding reception. Dunn, who is White, approached Davis, who was African American, as he sat in a vehicle with friends. According to Dunn, he approached the youth and asked them to lower the volume of their music but felt threatened when they refused to do so. Dunn claims the youth flashed a shotgun at him before he began firing his gun at the SUV eight or nine times, killing Davis, who was seated in the back seat. No guns were recovered from the vehicle where Davis had been seated.

Dunn left the scene after the shooting, but was traced to his Satellite, Florida, home through his license plate number, which was recorded by an eyewitness. Davis' parents fear that Dunn will attempt to invoke the controversial "Stand-Your-Ground" law. Many drew comparisons between the death of Trayvon Martin and Jordan Davis. Both involved the deaths of unarmed African American teenage boys. Both called the "Stand-Your-Ground" law into question. Both raised questions about possible racial profiling and the prevalence of gun violence in America.

Stand-Your-Ground laws, also called Shoot First laws, have been found to increase the number of homicides in the states where they have been adopted. One study found the annual increase to be 500 to 700 more homicides. The debate and scrutiny over Stand-Your-Ground laws and how they have played out racially has been associated with the resistance against laws that allow police officers to stop and search private individuals, some would say without reason, under stop-and-frisk policies.

Claiming self-defense, Dunn pleaded not guilty to charges of first-degree murder and attempted murder. He was convicted of three counts of attempted second-degree murder and one count of firing into an occupied vehicle. He faces a sentence of up to 60 years' imprisonment on those charges. The jury could not reach a verdict on the first-degree murder charge for the death of Jordan Davis. That count has been set for retrial

Fabiel Jean-Philippe

by teens. During his speech, Rush removed his suit jacket, donned a hoodie and sunglasses, and subsequently called for an end to racial profiling. The congressman also issued the following statement: "Just because someone wears a hoodie does not make them a hoodlum." Soon after pulling the hood over his head, Rush was declared to be out of order, and was ushered away from the podium. Rush later stated that through his action, he wanted to deliver a message to the younger generation to "stand their ground, stand up and don't stand down." In addition to Rush, President Obama also commented on the matter, stating, "If I had a son, he would look like Trayvon Martin" (Goldberg, 2012).

In March 2012, a "Million Hoodie March" was held in New York City's Union Square to protest the fact that Zimmerman was not immediately charged for Martin's slaying. Hundreds of people, including Martin's parents, donned hooded sweatshirts and marched the streets of Manhattan, demanding legal justice for Martin and calling for an end to racial profiling (CBS News, 2012a; 2012b). A similar march took place in Los Angeles. Amid the mounting pressure for his arrest, George Zimmerman went into hiding. The New Black Panther Party is said to have offered a $10,000 reward for his "capture" (Branch, 2012).

Sanford homicide detective Christopher Serino made an initial recommendation that Zimmerman be charged with manslaughter. As media attention mounted around the case, it was turned over to the Florida state attorney, Norm Wolfinger. A week later, the governor of Florida announced that he was appointing a special prosecutor, Angela Corey, to handle the case. Following her investigation, on April 11, 2012, six weeks after the killing, a decision was made to charge George Zimmerman with second-degree murder (CNN.com, 2013; Campo-Flores et al., 2012). After being formally charged, George Zimmerman turned himself into authorities, but for a while was held in an undisclosed location, claiming fear for his personal safety. His not-guilty plea was submitted to the court in writing by his new attorney, Mark O'Mara. His original attorney, Hal Uhrig, resigned from the case during the time that Zimmerman was in hiding (CNN.com, 2013).

After his indictment, Zimmerman's case took many unusual turns. He set up a Web site to raise money for his defense, which later led to his bail being revoked and his wife being charged with perjury for failing to properly disclose the couple's financial information. Zimmerman's bail was reinstated, but its status remained tenuous. His attorney filed and then withdrew a pretrial motion regarding the "Stand-Your-Ground" defense. The attorney also released negative information about Trayvon Martin, some of which he later admitted was "misleading." A judge ruled the remaining information inadmissible in the criminal trial that began on June 24, 2013, and ended in an acquittal of Zimmerman on July 13. The jury was composed of six women, five Whites and one Latina. The state of Florida allows fewer than 12 jurors in non-capital cases.

Although Zimmerman is a private individual, his role as neighborhood watch captain, as well as the police handling of his case, prompted intense debate and scrutiny about race and law enforcement. The jury verdict prompted new protests

Officer Fired for Using Trayvon Martin Targets

A White police sergeant and firearms trainer for the Port Canaveral, Florida, Police Department was fired for having shooting targets resembling an outline of Trayvon Martin. The target is a faceless dark outline of a hooded person holding Skittles and a can of iced tea, the items possessed by Trayvon Martin when he was approached by George Zimmerman. Sergeant Ron King brought these targets to a shooting range and asked other officers and a civilian if they wanted one. Such targets had been offered on the Internet as a novelty for over a year. In defense of his actions, King went on YouTube stating that he intended the targets to be an effective training tool for "no shoot" simulations. According to King, he bought the targets because the two items, iced tea and Skittles, were nonthreatening and therefore could be used to train officers when not to shoot. The bull's eye over the center chest of the target made the claim less credible.

King issued an apology to the family, stating, "I assure you that the use of those targets that are in question is to prevent a tragedy from taking place." The Martin family attorney has responded that "[u]sing a dead child's image as target practice is reprehensible," and that "[s]uch a deliberate and depraved indifference to this grieving family is unacceptable."

King had been a member of the Port Canaveral Police Department for two years at the time of the incident and had previously been with the Melbourne, Florida, Police Department for 22 years.

around the country and conflicting claims regarding the fairness of the American justice system. Despite the state court acquittal, the U.S. Department of Justice was called on to prosecute Zimmerman for engaging in a hate crime and violating Trayvon Martin's civil rights. In November 2013, U.S. Attorney General Eric Holder issued a statement that a decision regarding such charges was close, but some Department of Justice officials have stated that a successful conviction of Zimmerman is unlikely (Horwitz, 2013). The homeowners' association at Twin Lakes settled a civil suit with Trayvon Martin's family. A foundation to assist teens was established in his name.

After his acquittal George Zimmerman continued to get into trouble with the law. He was stopped for multiple speeding violations and domestic violence involving a gun, but currently remains a free man.

Fabiel Jean-Philippe with Delores Jones-Brown

See also: Black Panther Party; Hate Crimes; Jackson, Jesse; Juries; Racial Profiling; Sharpton, Jr., Alfred Charles

References

Branch, John. "Florida Man Pleads Not Guilty in Slaying of Teen in Loud Music Dispute." CNN, December 18, 2012.

Campo-Flores, A., C. McWhirter, and T. Martin. "Murder Charge in Shooting." *The Wall Street Journal,* April 12, 2012.

CBS News. 2012a. "Million Hoodie March Held in NYC in Memory of Trayvon Martin." March 22, 2012.

CBS News. 2012b. "Thousands March in Protest to Florida Hearing on Trayvon Martin Slaying." March 26, 2012.

CNN.com. "Trayvon Martin Shooting Fast Facts." June 5, 2013.

Goldberg, David Theo. "When Race Disappears." *Comparative American Studies* 10, no. 2–3 (August 2012): 116–27.

Gray, Melissa. "Fired Florida Officer Defends Use of 'Trayvon Martin' Targets." CNN, April 15, 2013.

Horwitz, S. "Holder: Justice Dept. Will Soon Announce Decision on Zimmerman Civil Rights Charges," *The Washington Post,* November 19, 2013.

Milner, Denise. "Jordan Davis: A Parent's Worst Nightmare." *Jet,* January 14, 2013.

NBC News. "Justice Department, FBI to Probe Shooting Death of Florida Teen Trayvon Martin." March 19, 2012. http://usnews.nbcnews.com/_news/2012/03/19/10766858-justice-department-fbi-to-probe-shooting-death-of-florida-teen-trayvon-martin.

New York Daily News. "Shooting in Florida over Loud Music Compared to Trayvon Martin Case." November 30, 2012.

Orlando Sentinel.com. "George Zimmerman 911 Call Reporting Trayvon Martin." March 27, 2012.

The View. Season 16, Episode 177, June 7, 2013. http://www.tvguide.com/tvshows/the-view-2013/episode-177-season-16/the-view/192276.

Mitchell, Margaret Laverne (1945–1999)

Margaret Laverne Mitchell, a widowed homeless Black college graduate, was shot to death by Hispanic Los Angeles police officer Edward Larrigan on May 21, 1999, after she allegedly waved a screwdriver at him on a populated street. The incident was preceded by the officer's attempt to ascertain whether the mentally unstable woman was in possession of a stolen shopping cart. Reports indicate that prior to becoming homeless, Mitchell had had a career as a bank teller, but had developed mental health problems upon the death of her husband.

The facts around the shooting are contested. Larrigan claims that he was in fear for his life while on bicycle patrol when the 102-pound, 54-year-old woman supposedly "lunged" at him, an assertion that has been contradicted by some witnesses. Although he and his partner, Kathy Clark, were equipped with pepper spray, Larrigan opted to use his gun after a bystander tried to intervene in the confrontation between Ms. Mitchell and the police. Larrigan's decision to use his gun has been questioned in part because he acknowledged the fact that Ms. Mitchell's initial response to being questioned about the ownership of the shopping cart was to walk away from the officers. Forensic reports, which could have helped determine the distance from which Officer Larrigan fired his weapon, omit vital details that would have assisted in the investigation. In addition, when a request for an independent pathologist examination was made, the parts of Ms. Mitchell's corpse containing the bullet's entry and exit wounds had been removed, rendering it harder for her family to look further into the matter.

On August 7, 2001, District Attorney Steve Cooley's office chose not to file criminal charges against Officer Larrigan, whose use of lethal force was considered justified. In contradiction to the district attorney's ruling, a civilian oversight commission voted 3 to 2 that the shooting amounted to excessive use of force. In 2003, the police department's three-member panel on professional standards overturned the civilian commission's decision. Consequently, Officer Larrigan was not professionally disciplined for the shooting in any way. Although the death of Margaret Mitchell did not result in criminal charges or disciplinary action by the police department, Ms. Mitchell's son, Richard, was awarded a civil settlement of $975,000 by the Los Angeles City Council. The death of Margaret Mitchell led to changes in how the police department handles civilians who exhibit signs of mental illness.

Rhodine Moreau

See also: Bell, Sean; Bumpurs, Eleanor; Dorismond, Patrick; Institutional Racism; Mapp, Dollree; Police Brutality; Zongo, Ousmane

References

Edds, Kimberly. "District Attorney's Office Rejects Demand It Reopen Mitchell Probe, Says Report Was Thorough." *Metropolitan News-Enterprise,* August 10, 2001. http://www.metnews.com/articles/mitc0810.htm.

Fremon, Celeste. "Small and Deadly Threat: Tiny Margaret Mitchell and Her Screwdriver." *L.A. Weekly,* June 19, 2003. http://www.laweekly.com/2003-06-26/news/small-and-deadly-threat/.

Gorman, Anna. "Officer Won't Face Trial in Fatal Shooting." *Los Angeles Times,* August 8, 2001. http://articles.latimes.com/2001/aug/08/local/me-31676.

"Panel Clears Officer in Killing of Woman." *The New York Times,* June 18, 2003. http://www.nytimes.com/2003/06/18/us/panel-clears-officer-in-killing-of-woman.html.

Staff & Wire Service Reports. "Cooley's Office Declines to Charge Officer in Mitchell Shooting." *Metropolitan News-Enterprise*, August 8, 2001. http://www.metnews.com/articles/mitc0808.htm.

"Statement by Chief Parks on Margaret Mitchell Incident." Los Angeles Police Department News Release. November 23, 1999. http://www.lapdonline.org/november_1999/news_view/28520.

N

Nation of Islam

The Nation of Islam (NOI), often referred to as The Nation for short, was the first movement of African American Muslims in America to gain large-scale public attention. Founded on July 4, 1930, in Detroit, Michigan, by Wallace Fard Muhammad (alternately Fard Muhammad) and originally called Allah's Temple of Islam, within one year of its founding the organization is reported to have recruited nearly 25,000 followers. The NOI emerged toward the tail end of a period of heightened Black Nationalism in the United States—a Black Nationalism that was rooted not only in shared physical appearance, but in a sense of shared culture and the promotion of high self-esteem, self-determination, and racial solidarity. The Black Nationalism of the NOI was defined by its opposition to integration into European or American culture.

The NOI's founder was often referred to as Master Fard Muhammad by its members. When Wallace Fard Muhammad appeared in Detroit in July 1930, he claimed to be from the holy city of Mecca. He taught what he called "the original" religion of the Black man to inner-city residents of Detroit. His teachings included the idea that White people were "blue-eyed devils" not to be trusted, and that Black people were the original, and superior, people of the earth. Black people living in America were all considered to be members of the lost, and now found, ancient Tribe of Shabazz.

Among the recruits was an unemployed autoworker named Robert Poole, also known as Elijah Poole. Poole became one of Fard Muhammad's most devoted and trusted lieutenants, dutifully spreading the teachings of the organization, which earned him the title of Supreme Minister. Like other Muslims, the NOI believes that that is no other God but Allah. The organization also teaches that intermarriage or race mixing should be prohibited. This is point 10 of the official platform, "What the Muslims Want," published in 1965.

For many years, Betty Shabazz harbored resentment toward the Nation of Islam, and Louis Farrakhan in particular, for what she felt was their role in the assassination of her husband, Malcolm X. In January 1995, Qubilah Shabazz, the second daughter of Malcolm X and Betty Shabazz, was charged with trying to hire an assassin to kill Louis Farrakhan in retaliation for the murder of her father. Farrakhan surprised the Shabazz family when he defended Qubilah, saying he did not think she was guilty and that he hoped she would not be convicted. That May, Betty Shabazz and Farrakhan shook hands on the stage of the Apollo Theatre during a public event intended to raise money for Qubilah's legal defense. Some heralded the evening as a reconciliation between the two, but others thought Shabazz was doing whatever she had to in order to protect her daughter. Nearly $250,000 was raised that evening. In the aftermath, Shabazz maintained a cool relationship with Farrakhan, although she agreed to speak at his Million Man March in October 1995. Qubilah accepted a plea agreement with respect to the charges, in which she maintained her innocence but accepted responsibility for her actions. Under the terms of the agreement, she was required to undergo psychological counseling and treatment for drug and alcohol abuse for a two-year period in order to avoid a prison sentence. For the duration of her treatment, Qubilah's 10-year-old son Malcolm, was sent to live with his grandmother, Betty Shabazz, at her apartment in Yonkers, New York. This arrangement would later lead to the death of Betty Shabazz (see Malcolm X).

At the suggestion of Fard, Elijah Poole changed his name to Elijah Karriem for a period of time. After about three years, Wallace Fard Muhammad disappeared and was never heard from again. Members of the NOI, sometimes referred to as Black Muslims, believe that it was Allah (God) that appeared in the form of Wallace Fard Muhammad. After the disappearance, Poole assumed leadership of the organization and became known as the Honorable Elijah Muhammad, believed by NOI members to be the last of Allah's messengers. He moved the organization's headquarters from Detroit to Chicago and was often referred to as the "Messenger of Allah." Elijah Muhammad led the Nation of Islam the rest of his life until his death in 1975.

Fard and Poole laid the groundwork for what the group was to become in the 1950s and 1960s. From the start, the NOI was tightly organized, a fact most clearly seen in its creation of the elite "Fruit of Islam," a group envisioned by Fard as a paramilitary wing to defend the NOI against police attacks. In the 1940s, "Messenger" Elijah Muhammad also began constructing what would later be considered the Nation's "Empire," purchasing the group's first bit of Michigan farmland in 1945 and founding businesses and educational ventures in several states that a decade later were valued in the millions.

The NOI's concept of justice was grounded in economic independence. The NOI preached a message of Black liberation and economic empowerment. Its message that Black people should separate from White society was due in part to the belief that no Black person could achieve justice, freedom, or equality in a society dominated by those who were inherently evil and who engaged in blatant racism and the debasement of people of African descent. Justice could only be achieved by complete separation of the races. This necessitated economic independence and Muhammad encouraged his followers to create their own businesses and to do business with their own people. The NOI publishes its own paper, called *The Final Call.*

The NOI's real boom came during the 1950s, when the advent of the Civil Rights Movement, and the violent reactions it provoked, converged to make the NOI's depiction of the "white devil" pertinent to a much larger sector of Black America. New members, including Malcolm X and heavyweight champion Muhammad Ali (Cassius Clay before joining the NOI), added visibility to the group and contributed directly to a meteoric membership increase.

The mid 1960s saw a second membership surge for the NOI as a new and more militant generation of Black leaders began focusing on the residual racial problems of the North. As urban riots rocked the nation, the NOI's message that Black elevation could only come through a radical separation from the structures of White oppression continued to resonate for many. Consequently, one of the most famous members of the Nation of Islam was Malcolm X. During the 1950s and 1960s, Malcolm X spread the teachings of Elijah Muhammad and served as a national spokesman for NOI. His popularity greatly aided in creating awareness of the NOI. His experience of a jailhouse conversion is also well known among many beyond the NOI membership (see Malcolm X [aka El-Hajj Malik El-Shabazz]). Appointed to the prestigious leadership of Harlem's Temple No. 7 in New York City just two years after his 1952 release from prison, Malcolm X was wildly popular and his years as a prominent member of NOI (1952–1964) saw membership skyrocket from around 400 to between 100,000 and 300,000. But the NOI's language changed and its advocacy of self-defense in place of nonviolence alienated it from mainstream civil rights groups. In 1964, Malcolm X left the NOI led by Elijah Muhammad and formed his own subdivision or sect.

It has been noted that efforts at prison reform did not begin with the conversion of Malcolm X. The history of the connection between the Nation of Islam and the criminal justice system dates back to the 1930s with the founding of the organization and the incarceration of early Muslims. Efforts toward rejuvenation and the promotion of a sense of self-worth and positive racial identity were part of the Nation of Islam since its inception and efforts on the part of Black Muslims to bring about a moral and spiritual rejuvenation among Black inmates have been ongoing since that time. The NOI strove not only to provide for justice and liberation to nonincarcerated people of African descent, but indirectly encouraged the subversion of an unjust system through the rehabilitative power of Islam. According to the organization's Web site, prison converts to Islam were in a position to acquire the moral strength and development of character that could help them live independent lives once released. It notes further that for many impoverished converts, their connection to the NOI represented one of the few chances to be integrated into a positive network while in prison and that once these individuals were released from prison they were able to take additional advantage of the communal rewards of membership through their integration into new networks. In the current age of mass incarceration, such networks are equally important as in the overtly racialized past.

Membership in the NOI has carried benefits both inside and outside of correctional facilities. Historically, membership has served as a means of protection. In the brotherhood of the NOI, members protect one another. The culture of prison has helped foster the creation of strong bonds among members of the NOI. Membership can be a means of survival. Additionally, members of the NOI are able to celebrate certain holidays exclusive to the NOI. Litigation over the rights of Black Muslims in prison has helped to expand the religious rights of all inmates (see *Cooper v. Pate*, 378 U.S. 546 [1964]), though prison officials and some civil rights organizations see NOI as a hate group, gang, or disciplinary problem in correctional facilities.

The majority of inmates who have converted to Islam have been men. Some scholars believe that the comparatively low number of female conversions in prison is due to an aversion to the patriarchal nature of Islamic teachings. The privileges and opportunities available to women who practice Christianity, the dominant faith among most African Americans, far outweigh those available through the practice of Islam. Other scholars have suggested that the cultural environment in female prisons differs significantly from that of male facilities and that female inmates do not feel the need to join the NOI for protection. At the beginning of the twenty-first century, there were an estimated 30,000 annual prison conversions to Islam reported, only a fraction of which were women. The vast majority of inmates who convert to Islam in the contemporary period become Sunni Muslims, considered more orthodox and adherent to the traditional Muslim practices and beliefs.

Following Malcolm X's 1964 split from his erstwhile mentor, Elijah Muhammad, a rising star in the NOI was appointed to replace him at Temple No. 7. Louis Farrakhan had been working as a cabaret singer until he met Malcolm X and joined NOI in 1955. Ascending rapidly through the ranks, he proved to be a superb speaker and organizer and became the national spokesman in 1967. He faced a firestorm after Malcolm X's 1965 assassination, for which many blamed the NOI. Talmadge Hayer, an NOI member, was arrested on the scene. Eyewitnesses identified two more suspects, Norman 3X Butler and Thomas 15X Johnson, also members of the NOI. All three were charged in the case. At first

Hayer denied involvement, but during the trial he confessed to having fired shots at Malcolm X. Hayer testified that Butler and Johnson were not present and were not involved in the assassination, but he declined to name the men who had joined him in the shooting. All three men were convicted. Butler, now known as Muhammad Abdul Aziz, was paroled in 1985. He became the head of the Nation of Islam's Harlem mosque in New York in 1998.

After the death of Elijah Muhammad in 1975, the leadership of the organization fell to one of his sons, Wallace Muhammad. Wallace began to take the organization toward a more orthodox practice of Islam. Farrakhan initially remained faithful to Wallace Deen Muhammad (later Imam Warithuddin Muhammad), but the younger Muhammad's dismantling of the NOI's material empire and his attempts to bring NOI into the fold of mainstream Islam ultimately alienated Farrakhan. In 1977, Farrakhan rejected the younger Muhammad and declared the creation of a "resurrected" NOI based on the original ideology of Elijah Muhammad. From 1978 onwards Louis Farrakhan has led the NOI. The NOI has maintained its role in prison reform and has also attempted to play a role in the reduction of urban violence. In the mid 1980s, the NOI started a new prison reform program based on the teachings of Elijah Muhammad. The purpose of this program is to teach inmates knowledge of self and their divine identity. These inmates follow the Nation of Islam's dietary standards, excluding all pork, and members are encouraged to avoid other meat and fish as well. These inmates are expected to read the required texts of the NOI, the Qur'an, and the Bible. Converts are encouraged to observe NOI religious holidays such as Savior's Day and the Holy Day of Atonement/Reconciliation. In 1995, during his "Million Man March" in Washington, D.C., Farrakhan gave eight steps for atonement: pointing out the wrong deed, personally admitting the wrong, confessing the wrong, repentance, atonement, forgiveness, reconciliation and restoration, and perfect union with Allah.

During the 1990s, the Fruit of Islam served as paid private security for public housing projects in Baltimore, Washington, D.C., Philadelphia, Chicago, and Los Angeles. Their efforts showed a noteworthy measure of success in Washington, D.C. However, the government contracts were eventually cancelled amid controversy over unpaid taxes, allegations about organizational recruitment and identity, and alleged use of overly aggressive tactics.

Despite the NOI's long history of activism, the Anti-Defamation League and the Southern Poverty Law Center (2012) list the organization as a hate group. It has also been criticized as being antigay and sexist.

Brian Coleman and Rebecca Hill

See also: Civil Rights Movement; Malcolm X (aka El-Hajj Malik El-Shabazz); Prisons

References

Clear, Todd R., and Melvina T. Sumter. "Prisoners, Prison, and Religion." *Journal of Offender Rehabilitation* 35 (2002): 125–56.

Cooper v. Pate, 378 U.S. 546 (1964).

Dix-Richardson, Felecia, and Billy R. Close. "Intersections of Race, Religion, and Inmate Culture: The Historical Development of Islam in American Corrections." *Journal of Offender Rehabilitation* 35 (2002): 87–107.

Gardell, Mattias. *In the Name of Elijah Muhammad: Louis Farrakhan and the Nation of Islam*. Durham, NC: Duke University Press, 1996.

Kusha, Hamid Reza. *Islam in American Prisons: Black Muslims' Challenge to American Penology*. Burlington, VT: Ashgate, 2009.

Lincoln, Charles Eric. *The Black Muslims in America*. Boston, MA: Beacon Press, 1960.

Malcolm X. 2012. *Biography.com*. http://www.biography.com/people/malcolm-x-9396195.

Mamiya, Lawrence. "From Black Muslim to Bilalian: The Evolution of a Movement." *Journal for the Scientific Study of Religion* 21 (1982): 138–52.

Nation of Islam. 2012. http://noi.org/about_beliefs_and_wants.shtml.

Nation of Islam. 2012. http://en.wikipedia.org/wiki/Nation_of_Islam.

NPR. "Manning Marable's 'Reinvention' of Malcolm X." April 5, 2011. http://www.npr.org/2011/04/05/135144230/manning-marables-reinvention-of-malcolm-x.

Robinson, Dean E. *Black Nationalism in American Politics and Thought*. Cambridge, UK: Cambridge University Press, 2001.

Southern Poverty Law Center. Nation of Islam, 2012. http://www.splcenter.org/get-informed/intelligence-files/groups/nation-of-islam.

O

100 Blacks in Law Enforcement Who Care

100 Blacks in Law Enforcement Who Care (100 Blacks), which has also been known as One Hundred Black Men in Law Enforcement Who Care, was founded in New York City in 1995 through the stewardship of Vernon C. Wells, Noel Leader, and Joel Ottley. Eric Adams has also been identified as a co-founder of 100 Blacks (see Adams, The Honorable Eric L.). The organization was formed because, as police officers, the three felt encumbered when they attempted to address the racism and abuse that they observed among the tactics being used by the New York City Police Department (NYPD) and within the criminal justice system generally.

Membership in the newly formed organization quickly grew to 100 sworn and unsworn law enforcement personnel as well as members of the public interested in proposing solutions for addressing racially discriminatory and abusive police tactics. The organization currently consists of a core of more than 100 concerned African American men and women from a variety of law enforcement professions; it has a seven-point mission that, according to its Web site, stems from a "shared sense of community, cultural and professional pride" and the "desire to 'give back' in some meaningful way." One of the tenets of its mission is to act as a "vanguard for justice on behalf of those who traditionally have no voice in society." In fulfillment of its goal to "give back," the Web site reports that within the first year of its formation, the membership collected and distributed $10,000 in grants to needy individuals and organizations across New York City.

While the 100 Blacks mission prioritizes advocating on behalf of others, the group also claims victory for having successfully challenged and broken through the "Blue Wall of Silence," an unwritten rule that discourages law enforcement officers from criticizing, disagreeing with, questioning, or reporting the misconduct of other officers. Supporting evidence for this claim can be found in the fact that co-founder and former NYPD captain Eric Adams has testified on behalf of plaintiffs in a significant federal lawsuit against the department, *Floyd et al v. City of New York*. The lawsuit alleges that the NYPD engages in the illegal stop-and-frisk of Black and Latino pedestrians.

The 100 Blacks organization has become involved with the investigation and criminal prosecution of multiple cases where members of the NYPD have been accused of serious misconduct. The case of Haitian immigrant Abner Louima was one of the first. In 1997, Louima accused police officers of the 70th Precinct of assaulting and sodomizing him with a broomstick handle while he was being held at the police station (see Louima, Abner); 100 Blacks demanded that the chief of police and then governor George Pataki conduct a proper and in-depth investigation into the charges. The organization also took a stand in the infamous and controversial shootings of Amadou Diallo in 1999 and Sean Bell in 2006 (see Diallo, Amadou, and Bell, Sean). The Louima case resulted in criminal convictions and imprisonment for two officers. The Diallo and Bell cases resulted in civil settlements only.

In 2009, 100 Blacks demanded that then governor David Patterson probe further into the cop-on-cop shooting death of Black off-duty officer Omar Edwards. In this case, 100 Blacks brought pressure by threatening to withhold campaign support in future elections. Their efforts led in part to the forming of a task force to study the issue of officer-on-officer shootings, so-called "friendly fire." The task force issued a report that found that since the mid 1990s, Black officers had been most at risk of becoming the victims of such incidents, and offered some recommendations for reducing that risk.

Members of 100 Blacks have expressed their commitment to seek solutions to racism and sexism in law enforcement. The organization believes that the best individuals to carry forward this mission are those in law enforcement. One of the organization's missions is to serve as a model for individuals and other professions. The group believes that no matter the professional obligation, individuals should stand up and speak out against abuse and exploitation. In law enforcement, this has meant that 100 Blacks must face and fight against racial profiling, harassment, and police brutality.

In addition to its advocacy, 100 Blacks gives back to the community. The organization is committed to education and the financial support of individuals in need. One of 100 Blacks' major points in its mission is uplift through education. It provides education by offering workshops on gang prevention and gang awareness. Members teach citizens how to prepare for and how to conduct themselves during court appearances. They also provide disaster training and helpful hints for how to behave if stopped by the police on the street or if the police come to your door.

The organization has been successful in achieving its financial commitment to economically empower people of color by pooling its resources. It has provided

New Jersey Turnpike Shooting (1998): Troopers Admit Racial Profiling

On April 23, 1998, two White New Jersey State troopers, John Hogan and James Kenna, stopped a van carrying four young men. They were passengers Danny Reyes, age 20, a Latino, and African Americans Keshon L. Moore, age 22, and Leroy Grant, age 23. The driver, Rayshawn Brown, age 20, was also African American. The troopers said they stopped the vehicle for speeding. They also said that as they approached, the vehicle began to travel in reverse. The troopers fired 11 shots into the van, seriously injuring two of the men. The four men insisted they were not speeding and that the van began moving in reverse by accident. 100 Blacks was one of the first organizations to express concern. The group traveled to New Jersey and took up observation posts where they were able to see who was being pulled over. In addition, they drove the highway and noted how often they themselves were stopped. One officer, a state police sergeant, wrote that he had been stopped 40 times by state troopers while off duty. The shooting and the efforts of 100 Blacks shed light on New Jersey's racial profiling problem. The troopers involved in the shooting were eventually fired.

Although the New Jersey troopers were criminally charged with aggravated assault and attempted murder, they struck a deal with the prosecutor to have serious charges dropped. In order to receive the plea agreement, the officers had to admit wrongdoing. Hogan and Kenna admitted to falsifying documents to cover up their actions and admitted their actions were racially motivated. There was some evidence suggesting that their superiors had supported their race-based stops in the past. Despite their admissions, their punishment was only a $280 fine and no probation. In 2002, Hogan and Kenna were denied pension benefits from the state. The New Jersey turnpike incident led to 150 criminal cases being dropped because a Superior Court judge found that New Jersey state troopers singled out defendants by race. A federal oversight panel was instituted to review state police behavior. The case also led to the commissioning and publication of a 1,000-page report on racial profiling by law enforcement in the state of New Jersey (Farmer & Zoubek, 1999).

financial support to the community by using a portion of its yearly membership fees to provide grants to local organizations to support community-based functions such as baseball teams and afterschool programs. In its first 12 years, it reports having disseminated $1,000 a month in grants and distributed funds to needy organizations all over New York City.

The organization has extended the reach and availability of law enforcement personnel by creating an open forum on community television where members of 100 Blacks are available live to answer questions on their *Community Cop* show.

The group has also distributed pamphlets about racial profiling on community streets. It has not limited its fight for racial justice to New York City. The organization has reached out to other communities, including those in neighboring states like New Jersey, where it has helped to negotiate racially charged incidents involving police and minorities.

The organization continues to fight against racism and racial profiling. Nationally, it has taken its concerns to Washington, D.C. The group met with officials at the Department of Justice to discuss solving the problem of racial profiling.

The group's public presence has not gone without repercussions. Many of the officers involved in 100 Blacks have suffered career setbacks because of their vocal stance. Many involved in the organization have been reassigned to different areas and passed over for promotions and several have become the subjects of unsuccessful investigations. The role that 100 Blacks has taken on requires great resilience and courage.

Teresa Francis

See also: Adams, The Honorable Eric L.; Bell, Sean; Conyers, Jr., Congressman John; Diallo, Amadou; Louima, Abner; Police Brutality; Racial Profiling

References

100 Blacks in Law Enforcement Who Care. www.100blacksinlawenforcement.com.

Baker, Al. "3 Detectives Are Indicted in 50-Shot Killing in Queens." *The New York Times,* March 17, 2007.

Bode, Nicole, and Corky Siemaszko. "Sean Bell Scene Probe Intentionally Botched, Says Black Police Group." *Daily News,* March 29, 2008.

Chen, David M., and Al Baker. "New York to Pay $7 Million for Sean Bell Shooting." *The New York Times,* July 27, 2010.

Cooper, Michael. "Officers in Bronx Fire 41 Shots and an Unarmed Man Is Killed." *The New York Times,* February 5, 1999.

Einhorn, Erin. "Group Wants Cuomo to Investigate NYPD for Racial Profiling after Stop-and-Frisk Numbers Soar." *Daily News,* February 21, 2010.

Farmer, John, Jr., and Paul Zoubek. *Final Report of the State Police Review Team.* Trenton, NJ: Office of the Attorney General, 1999.

Floyd et al. v. City of New York et al., 08 Civ. 1034 (SAS) (August 12, 2013).

Fritsch, Jane. "The Diallo Verdict: The Overview; 4 Officers in Diallo Shooting Are Acquitted of All Charges." *The New York Times,* February 26, 2010.

Jones, Richard Lezin. "New Jersey Prosecutors Cite Racial Profiling in Dismissal of 86 of Criminal Cases." *The New York Times,* April 20, 2002.

Joseph, Fred P., and Blaine Harden. "The Louima Case: The Overview; Officer Is Guilty in Torture of Louima." *The New York Times,* June 9, 1999.

Kocieniewski, David. "On Politics; Troopers Are off the Hook, but the State Is Still Mired." *The New York Times,* July 20, 2002.

Lueck, Thomas. "216 Held in Protests of Police Acquittals." *The New York Times,* May 8, 2008.

McFadden, Robert. "Police Kill Man after a Queens Bachelor Party." *The New York Times,* November 26, 2006.

Mfuni, Tanangachi. "Police Racial Profiling Angers Brooklyn Activists." *New York Amsterdam News,* October 19, 2006.

"New Jersey: Trenton Troopers Denied Pensions." *The New York Times,* June 27, 2002.

Ramirez, Anthony. "Officer in Louima Case Returns to State to Finish." *The New York Times,* February 4, 2007.

Samuels, Tanyanika, and Will Cruz. "With Campaign Support Pending, Black Officers Push Gov. Paterson Paterson Probe Cop-on-Cop Slay." *Daily News,* August 14, 2009.

Organized Crime

For many people, the term "organized crime" may conjure up images of the Italian mafia, Chinese triads, Mexican gangs, and Colombian cartels. After all, these are perhaps some of the more common—and dangerous—varieties of organized crime, which have infiltrated popular culture through the production of numerous Hollywood films, television series, news documentaries, and true crime novels. One ethnic group, African Americans, which can include Jamaicans, Nigerians, Haitians, West Indians, and others, have become more associated with instances of urban crime and violence and thus noted by Martens (1990) as "an ignored phenomenon" in organized crime. On the other hand, in his textbook *Organized Crime,* Howard Abadinsky (1997: 283) explains how "Black opportunity in organized crime has roughly paralleled opportunity in the wider legitimate community" to show how this group has embraced a rich history in the United States for engaging in this type of offending. Through limited scholarship, the dedicated efforts of a handful of researchers have helped provide a more complete picture of the history, activities, and structures of African American organized crime syndicates and the dilemmas, challenges, and dangers they pose to American society.

The emergence of African American organized crime stretches back to the latter nineteenth and early twentieth centuries. However, well before this time, beginning around the sixteenth century, millions of Blacks began to arrive in North America by slave ship. Those who survived the long and precarious voyage from Africa were sold into slavery up until January 1863, when Abraham Lincoln signed the Emancipation Proclamation, which immediately freed a majority of the country's slave population, and in December 1865, when legalized slavery was prohibited through passage of the Thirteenth Amendment to the Constitution. Shortly thereafter, the United States began to experience an influx of immigration from the Caribbean region, which, according to U.S. census information, added to the nearly nine million Blacks already living in the country by 1900—doubling the number compared to 1850 (U.S. Department of Commerce, 1975). Like other newly arrived ethnic groups, many Black immigrants settled in major metropolitan areas in the eastern half of the country. Eventually, this led to high concentrations of Blacks in some cities, for example, Harlem in New York, and Philadelphia and Washington, D.C.

By the latter nineteenth century, the formation of dense and tightly woven Black communities helped lay the groundwork for African American organized crime to flourish. By the 1930s, serious illegitimate opportunities arose. During World War I and the Prohibition era, African Americans were known to regularly engage in organized activities such as bootlegging and illegal gambling, taking advantage of the socioeconomic and legal conditions created by these events (Schatzberg, 1994; Griffin, 2003c). In the decades that followed, the advantages, freedoms and opportunities awarded by improved civil rights and acceptance in American society helped facilitate the growth of Black organized crime (Schatzberg, 1994; Griffin, 2003c). By the 1970s, large-scale drug trafficking operations involving heroin, cocaine, and marijuana, and in the 1980s, crack cocaine, became regular foci of Black organized crime activities. Accordingly, major organized syndicates such as the Young Boys Inc. in Michigan were reportedly generating a million dollars per month in drug sales revenue. In the 1990s, larger groups—the Gangster Disciplines in Chicago and the Black Mafia in Philadelphia—were reportedly reaping ten times that amount of monthly profit and attracting the eye of federal agencies (Griffin 2003a; 2003b).

According to Griffin (2003a: 290), "[T]here may be numerous reasons for the lack of African American organized crime research . . . namely, the government's absolute preoccupation with Sicilian/Italian-American organized crime." The limited available scholarly literature has also focused on relatively few cities in the United States, for example, New York (Ianni, 1974; Schatzberg, 1993; Schatzberg, 1994; Schatzberg & Kelly, 1997), Philadelphia (Griffin, 2003a; 2003b; 2005), and more recently, Chicago, in which Lombardo (2002) provides a historic overview of the problem from 1890 to 1960. In his article, Lombardo describes how African American organized crime powerfully flourished independently of other ethnic groups and even played a significant role in the activities of the city's Italian mafia, known as the Chicago Outfit. Chicago saw the first Blacks arrive during the mid nineteenth century as escapees from the Civil War. This was followed by a second wave of 50,000, between 1916 and 1920, in response to industrialists recruiting in the South to fill the need for labor caused by World War I. Over time, a large Black population grew in Chicago's South Side, which became known as the "Black Belt," and had the highest urban Black population in the United States after New York's Harlem. By the 1920s, the Black population in Chicago numbered more than 300,000, with many holding jobs such as teachers, politicians, doctors, and police officers. In addition, Blacks, like the other ethnic groups, began to engage in organized crime (Lombardo, 2002; Schatzberg & Kelly, 1997; Griffin, 2003c).

Gambling and vice syndicates were hallmarks of African American organized crime in Chicago. As Lombardo notes, this city's first known vice lord—John "Mushmouth" Johnson—moved from St. Louis to Chicago in 1895 and initially worked as a hotel waiter and then in a downtown gambling hall before opening his own saloon and gambling house in 1890. He was followed by another Black vice lord named Frotenac, who operated in Chicago's red-light district in 1906. Over time, Johnson became known as the "Negro Gambling King of Chicago," although he never gambled. He attributed his success to the regular donations he made to city politicians to "ensure immunity for his gambling operations" (2002: 37). In 1916, a "colored voters club" was organized by Oscar De Priest to demand campaign contributions from local gamblers. These contributions would be used to support upcoming elections and to pay bribes to candidates for protecting Black gambling clubs—an example of vice and corruption among Chicago's politicians.

During the 1920s, Prohibition fueled the creation of numerous Black nightclubs. With their jazz music, prostitution, bootlegging, gambling, and commercialized vice, these nightclubs appealed to all ethnic groups. Some were run by Daniel McKee Jackson, a Black college graduate who moved to Chicago from Pittsburgh in 1892 and became known as the most powerful vice king the city had ever known. Elections were also "swung" by major gamblers such as Dan Jackson in order to bring in mayors like William Hale Thompson, who tolerated and protected the city's Black gambling operations until 1931, when Anton Cemark was elected to "clean up" the crime plaguing the city, especially that stemming from Black organized crime. A major gambling game called "policy" dominated Black organized crime in Chicago until the 1980s, when Illinois began to create legitimate lotteries coupled with greater action by police, which in turn helped eradicate Black organized crime (Lombardo, 2002).

While New York is another city known for African American organized crime, Philadelphia has embraced an even richer history. With a historically high population of Blacks, this city had organized crime similar to that of New York's Italian mafia. Simply known as the "Black Mafia," this form of African American organized crime began to emerge during the late 1960s and was originally started by Samuel Christian, among others, who turned small craps games and illegal drug sales, and later prostitution, into a large-scale operation shielded by legitimate nonprofit organizations established in Black sections of the city. Like the Italian Mafia, the Black Mafia developed a highly structured hierarchy in order to instill discipline among members. This crime syndicate regularly used tactics of

Table 1 Major African American Organized Crime Syndicates

Name	Location(s)	Established	Leader(s)	Activities
Black Mafia	Philadelphia	1968	Samuel Christian	Prostitution; extortion; extreme violence and intimidation
Country Boys, then merged with several other drug rings to form a new syndicate, the Council	New York City	1960s	Frank Lucas and brothers Vernon, Lee, Lee Van, Larry, and Ezell; Leroy "Nicky" Barnes/"Mr. Untouchable," Guy Fisher, Wallace Rice,	Drug trafficking; extreme violence
Jamaican posses: Shower, Spangler, Dunkirk Boys, Tel Aviv, and Waterhouse posses	New York City, expanded to Philadelphia, Baltimore, and Washington, D.C.	Early 1980s	Delroy "Uzi" Edwards Affiliated with leaders of Jamaican political parties—Jamaican Labor Party and the People's National Party	Controlled crack trade in Brooklyn; extreme violence
Padmore group and others of West Indian origin	New Jersey	1980s	Padmore brothers, Wayne and Wade	Cocaine trafficking; extreme violence; money laundering
Black Mafia Family	Detroit	1980s	Flenory brothers, Demetrius and Terry	Drug trafficking; money laundering; extreme violence and intimidation
Chambers Brothers Organization	Detroit	1980s	Four Chambers brothers, Larry, Billy Joe, Willie Lee, and Otis	Operated 200 crack houses employing 500 staff
El Rukns/ Black P. Stone Nation	Chicago's South Side	1965	Jeff Fort and son Watkeeta "The Prince" Valenzuela	Extortion; dealing of crack and powder cocaine
Young Boys Inc.	Detroit, and later in Boston	Mid 1970s	Dwayne David	Drug dealing of heroin, and later crack

Name	Location(s)	Established	Leader(s)	Activities
Gangster Disciples	Based in Chicago; sales operations in Wisconsin, Indiana, Missouri, Oklahoma, and Georgia	1969	Larry Hoover, "King" David Barksdale	Drug dealing and trafficking of cocaine and heroin; extortion of money from other drug dealers for sales rights
Black Disciples	Chicago	1960s	David Barksdale	Extreme violence; drug trafficking; extortion
Crips	Los Angeles and other cities in California, primarily concentrated in Western U.S.	Late 1960s	Raymond Washington, Stanley Williams	Extreme violence and intimidation; dealing of crack; identity theft
Junior Black Mafia	Philadelphia, including Camden, NJ, and Burlington Countie	Mid 1980s	Aaron Jones	Extreme violence and intimidation; money laundering; crack and powder cocaine distribution

Data compiled by the author.

intimidation and extortion in order to maintain power and control in neighborhoods and to keep their illegitimate activities from being reported to the police. Successful intimidation made it difficult for law enforcement agencies to attempt to conduct investigations or take action against the group.

The Black Mafia's strategies forced many legitimate businesses to leave the city and reestablish themselves in areas free of Black organized crime. At one point, Angelo Bruno, of Philadelphia's (Italian) crime family, attempted to stop drug-dealing operations between his city and New York's Gambino crime family, but changed his mind and agreed to continue such dealings as long as the Black Mafia provided both families with a portion of its drug proceeds.

Religion symbolized strength and was a strong feature of the Black Mafia. Many of its members were followers of the Nation of Islam. The group greatly expanded after two vicious crimes—the 1971 robbery of a furniture store by eight members resulting in the beating of 13 employees and two deaths; and the 1973 Washington, D.C., murders of two adults and five children by seven members. Other expansion tactics included the murder of witnesses, political power provided through connections with African American attorneys, and the preoccupation of police with the Italian mafia problem.

Michael Puniskis

See also: African Diaspora, Crime, and Justice; Gangs; Nation of Islam, Slavery; Socioeconomic Factors; Structural Racism and Violence

References

Abadinsky, H. *Organized Crime.* 4th ed. Chicago: Nelson-Hall Publishers, 1997.

Griffin, S. P. *Black Brothers, Inc.: The Violent Rise and Fall of Philadelphia's Black Mafia.* Wrea Green, UK: Milo Books, 2005.

Griffin, S. P. 2003a. *Philadelphia's Black Mafia: A Social and Political History.* Dordrecht, Netherlands: Kluwer Academic Publishers, 2003.

Griffin, S. P. 2003b. "Philadelphia's 'Black Mafia': Assessing and Advancing Current Interpretations." *Crime, Law and Social Change* 39, no. 3 (2003): 263–83.

Griffin, S. P. 2003c. "'Emerging' Organized Crime Hypotheses in Criminology Textbooks: The Case of African-American Organized Crime." *Journal of Criminal Justice Education* 14, no. 2 (2003): 287–301.

Ianni, F.A.J. *Black Mafia: Ethnic Succession in Organized Crime.* New York: Simon & Schuster, 1974.

Lombardo, R. M. "The Black Mafia: African-American Organized Crime in Chicago 1890–1960." *Crime, Law & Social Change* 38, no. 1 (2002): 33–65.

Martens, F. T. "African American Organized Crime: An Ignored Phenomenon." *Federal Probation* 54, no. 1 (1990): 43–50.

Schatzberg, R. "African American Organized Crime." In *The Handbook of Organized Crime in the United States,* edited by R. J. Kelly and K. L. Chin, 189–212. Westport, CT: Greenwood Press, 1994.

Schatzberg, R. *Black Organized Crime in Harlem: 1920–1930.* New York: Garland Press, 1993.

Schatzberg, R., and R. J. Kelly. *African American Organized Crime: A Social History.* Rutgers, NJ: Rutgers University Press, 1997.

U.S. Department of Commerce. *Historical Statistics of the United States: Colonial Times to 1970.* Washington, DC: Bureau of Census, 1975.

P

Petit Apartheid

The twenty-first century bears witness to disproportionate African American Part One and Part Two FBI Crime Index rates, criminal victimization rates, and detention and prison incarceration rates for African Americans, a continuation of patterns noted during the twentieth century. Few, if any, reputed criminologists dispute Black disproportionality in criminal offending, victimization, pretrial detention, and post-conviction incarceration. What is disputed is the extent of the disproportionality and the reasons for it. Daniel E. Georges-Abeyie, a criminologist, social-political geographer, and forensic psychologist, introduced the theory of petit apartheid in the U.S. criminal and juvenile justice systems in *Racism, Empiricism and Criminal Justice* (Georges-Abeyie, 1990a; 1990b), as a means of explaining and understanding this disproportionality.

Georges-Abeyie noted that although overt race- and ethnic-based laws, or what he terms grand apartheid, have been successfully challenged and eliminated by court rulings, legislation, and executive order, de facto racially biased practices continue to plague the U.S. criminal and juvenile justice systems (Georges-Abeyie, 2001). The theory of petit apartheid was introduced to describe and analyze the de facto discriminatory discretionary acts engaged in by law enforcement officers, correctional officers, officers of the court, jurors, defense attorneys, probation officers, corrections officers, correctional officials, parole officers, and other justice system personnel and the ways in which this discretionary decisionmaking works to the advantage or disadvantage of individuals interfacing with the U.S. criminal justice system and are based on one's personal characteristics, group identity, spatial characteristics, and criminal justice agents' responses to these factors (Georges-Abeyie 1990a; 1990b).

The theory was also introduced to challenge William Wilbanks' *The Myth of a Racist Criminal Justice System* (1987), which alleged that the U.S. criminal justice system did not negatively disadvantage Blacks; it also postulated that if advantage or disadvantage occurred, the U.S. criminal justice system informally advantaged Blacks while disadvantaging Whites. Wilbanks' assertions were based in part on the analysis of sentencing patterns and outcomes for various intra-racial and inter-racial offenses, including sentencing for so-called "Black-on-Black" crimes, which, according to the available evidence, tended to result in more lenient sentencing. Georges-Abeyie refuted Wilbanks' thesis, in part by noting the White devaluation of Black life, as evidenced by the severe sentencing of Blacks who victimize Whites, and the lenient sentencing of Whites who victimize Blacks (Georges-Abeyie 1990a; 1990b).

The concept of petit apartheid has since been utilized by various criminal justice agencies, including in academy and postacademy training and certification programs, to sensitize employees to the outcomes of conscious, unconscious, subconscious, nonconscious, and preconscious motivations and biases; and as a tool for screening potential employees. Petit apartheid has also been discussed and analyzed in academic settings—on college campuses and at meetings of academic and practitioner associations (Georges-Abeyie, 2006a). The theory is the center of discussion in several scholarly publications, with Dragan Milovanovic and Katheryn K. Russell's edited volume *Petit Apartheid in the U.S. Criminal Justice System: The Dark Figure of Racism* (2001) and Georges-Abeyie's "Race, Ethnicity, and Social Distance Severity" (2006b) being the most notable explorations of the concept.

The theory of petit apartheid is the legacy of the following three realities.

- *De jure* racism, i.e., grand apartheid, the Black Codes and Jim Crow Laws; statutory racism, which is currently unconstitutional in the United States due to the Supreme Court decision in *Brown v. the Board of Education of Topeka, Kansas,* 347 U.S. 483 (1954) (excluding laws that result in covert identity based advantaging and disadvantaging, such as drug laws, sentence enhancement for weapons offenses, such as concealed weapons, weapons preferences, recidivism, etc.).
- *De facto* racism, i.e., customary racism based upon the acting out of role-sets, morals, and related norms.
- Social distance, i.e., the degree of closeness or remoteness one desires in interaction with members of a particular group, including one's own; also the type, duration, frequency, and level of desired or acceptable/tolerable intimacy.

Beverly D. Frazier and Daniel Georges-Abeyie

Over time, the theory of petit apartheid has been refined to address not only individuals interfacing with the U.S. criminal and juvenile justice systems, but also individuals interfacing with all systems where the exercise of discretion can mutate into discrimination.

The most recent version of the theory of petit apartheid includes a numerical scale that predicts when *positive social distance—prejudice—is likely to advantage an individual* interfacing with the criminal or juvenile justice system and when *negative social distance—also prejudice—is likely to disadvantage* an individual interfacing with those systems. The 27 items in the scale can be found, in some variant, in virtually all nation-states and all sociocultural interaction (Georges-Abeyie, 2006b). The theory of petit apartheid can also be used to explain when interfacing with these systems is likely to neither advantage nor disadvantage an individual. The current theory explains how social distance beliefs, and prejudice transmutes discretion into positive or negative de facto discriminatory actions and racism. It acknowledges that biased discretionary decisionmaking in the justice systems is alive and well and that it continues to manifest in both subtle and overt ways, including but not limited to:

1. formal processing of some criminal suspects and the informal warning of others;
2. psychiatric remands for some criminal defendants by courts and the harsh sentencing of others;
3. jury instructions by judges, which virtually assure conviction in some cases and not guilty verdicts in others;
4. the qualifying by states attorneys of some murder cases for the death penalty and the exemption of the death penalty for others;
5. the qualifying by states attorneys of some suspects for potential enhanced sentences, if convicted, and the nonqualifying of others;
6. jury nullification of evidence in some cases and the fixation on questionable evidence in others;
7. the granting of probation by courts and parole by corrections or parole agencies in some cases while denying probation and parole in other cases, due to the rigid reliance on salient factor scores;
8. bizarrely extended or bizarrely brief sentence recommendations by juries;
9. differential job assignments and security and custody ratings in correctional, jail, and detention settings;
10. traffic stops and the subsequent search of some motor vehicles apparently due to the personal identity characteristics of the driver and/or passengers;
11. defense strategies; and
12. culture-based legislation that negatively impacts—and covertly criminalizes—the norms of some personal identity groups, such as ethnic, nationality, religious, and racial groups more than others, thereby directly covertly reintroducing grand apartheid.

In brief, the theory of petit apartheid posits that the key to understanding the transmutation of discretion into positive or negative discrimination in criminal or juvenile justice systems is to understand the reality of actual outcome, not alleged intent.

The theory of petit apartheid is indebted to a broad spectrum of social sciences for its development. They include the geographic/spatial, social-ecological, sociological, social anthropological, criminological, criminal justice, social-psychological, and psychoanalytic theories. Most specifically, its formulation draws from conflict theory, critical theory, labeling theory, structural-functionalism, cognitive dissonance theory, Freudian and neo-Freudian theory, and geographical and social-ecological theories, such as the Chicago School of Sociology and Spatial Analysis/Geography and forensic psychologist Robert Hare's *Psychopathy Checklist—Revised* (Hare, 2003).

Conflict, critical, and labeling theories as old as those noted in William Whyte's social anthropological classic *Street Corner Society* (Whyte, 1943) were cognizant of the formal processing of some juvenile delinquents and the informal warning of others. Structural-functionalism notes that behavioral norms remain long after the original reason for their origin. Thus, should one desire to permanently change a specific individual's mores, beliefs, or cognitions, one must first get the specific individual to opt into desired behavior. Cognitive dissonance theory notes that one has to get persons to choose the desired behaviors because of perceived benefits, not coercion. Only then can the desired behaviors be rationalized and result in permanent change in cognition.

Freudian theory and neo-Freudian theory both acknowledge motivation on five levels of consciousness: the conscious, preconscious, unconscious, nonconscious and subconscious. The conscious is self-evident. The preconscious is that which can readily be brought to consciousness by psychoanalysis and therapeutic psychopharmacological intervention. The subconscious stubbornly resists conscious comprehension even after protracted psychoanalysis and long-term comprehensive therapeutic psychopharmacological intervention. The unconscious is cognitive activity—or "thoughts" outside of awareness; and the nonconscious refers to body processes initiated and controlled by the mind that we do not attend to (Stafani & Schrier, 2002).

Hare's *Psychopathy Checklist—Revised* (Hare, 2003) notes that trained observers can score behavior without weighting the multiple salient factors, yet identify individuals with a severe personality disorder: psychopathy. Social-ecological and geographic/spatial theory, including geographic information systems (GIS) applications (like crime mapping programs), note the relationship between site and situation information and formal charging and criminal justice processing, or the lack thereof.

The theory of petit apartheid acknowledges that there are many opportunities within the criminal justice system or juvenile justice system for discretion to transmute into positive or negative discrimination, including but not limited to the following (Georges-Abeyie, 2006b: 106; Bohm & Haley, 1997):

- Entry into the criminal justice system or juvenile justice system
- Prosecution and pretrial services
- Adjudication
- Sentencing and corrections
- Parole

Thus decisions may vary based on the location where an incident occurs (e.g., in an area labeled "high crime" versus "low crime"; urban versus suburban); or whether a defendant or victim is a racial or ethnic "minority" or White; or the observer's beliefs about either the location, offender, or victim. For example, whether an incident occurs in a "safe" neighborhood, was allegedly committed by a "repeat" offender, or happened to a "deserving" or "undeserving" victim, or some combination of all three. The theory of petit apartheid acknowledges that certain discretionary discriminatory acts may be conscious and overtly discriminatory on the part of the actor, while others are not. Nonetheless, petit apartheid keys on outcome, not intent.

According to the theory of petit apartheid, the transmutation of discretion into discrimination can result in a positive or a negative decision; e.g., to not formally process the suspect or defendant, or to formally process the suspect or defendant—or even to see an individual as a suspect or not. Such discretionary decisions dictate what charge or charges the accused will be subjected to and the terms that will be offered during any plea arrangements, and ultimately sentencing severity/outcome.

The issue in terms of social distance and petit apartheid within the U.S. criminal or juvenile justice system is the extent to which non-crime-related social, psychological, cultural, spatial, biological (including racial), gender, and sex-related factors result in the decision to formally process, or to not process, a suspect or defendant. The connection between social distance and petit apartheid is that such decisions are often based on differences or similarities in the social position of the decisionmaker and that of the suspect or defendant. If a decision is made to process the individual, petit apartheid is implicated in the severity of the processing or penalty options selected (e.g., criminal trial versus conditional discharge; life imprisonment versus the death penalty). Social distance and resultant petit apartheid also impact the quality and type of response to noncriminal requests for service and assistance.

The theory of petit apartheid contends that the mind is a biometric computer, which instantaneously notes social, psychological, cultural, spatial, and biological similarities and differences on a conscious, preconscious, unconscious, nonconscious, and subconscious level, resulting in positive and negative social distance, which in turn results in conscious, preconscious, unconscious, nonconscious, and subconscious acts of advantaging and disadvantaging behavior.

In brief, the theory of petit apartheid posits that the 27-factor Georges-Abeyie Social Distance Petit Apartheid Severity Scale (G-ASDPASS) can predict when social distance transmutes into de facto discretionary positive and negative discrimination. The G-ASDPASS can be utilized in all components of the criminal and juvenile justice systems, including but not limited to the selection (including hiring and dismissal) and subsequent training of criminal justice officials, juvenile justice officials, defense attorneys, officers of the court, probation officers, and correctional officers—in other words, anywhere discretionary decisions are made. It can also be used in the identification of likely or actual positive and negative discrimination toward identity group characteristics and individual identity characteristics, and their attempted remediation. The Georges-Abeyie Social Distance Petit Apartheid Severity Scale is, in part, discussed in "Race, Ethnicity, and Social Distance Severity" (Georges-Abeyie, 2006b).

It is important to note that the theory of petit apartheid does not treat Black populations or their propensity for offending as monolithic. Georges-Abeyie has posited a theory of social cultural resistance to explain why adult crime and juvenile delinquency rates may be higher among antebellum Africans of the Western hemisphere diaspora in comparison to Western hemisphere postbellum Africans and persons of European and Asian descent (Georges-Abeyie, 2009). He suggests that the descendants of persons of African descent, once enslaved in the Western hemisphere—antebellum Africans (Parrillo, 2000)—commit FBI Index crimes, especially Part One crimes and drug-related crimes, at a higher rate than other groups due to the legacy of macro-level resistance (slave rebellions and sabotage) and micro-level resistance (the conscious, preconscious, and unconscious rejection of European role-sets, and subsequent elevated rates of crime commission and criminal victimization) in the manner noted by cognitive dissonance theory, conflict theory, critical theory, labeling theory, social structure theory, and psychopathy, as noted by Robert Hare and various other forensic psychological and psychiatric theories.

The theory of petit apartheid suggests that such nuances are not considered when Blacks come into contact with various social institutions in the United States including, but not limited to, the criminal and juvenile justice systems. Instead, under the theory, one's Black racial identity, regardless of its ancestral or national origin, is likely to impact discretionary decisionmaking in a negative way. For

Current research by Georges-Abeyie on petit apartheid has identified 27 specific conscious, unconscious, and preconscious socio-cultural-spatial-biological salient factors that can be scaled that predict social distance and subsequent petit apartheid discriminatory actions (Georges-Abeyie, 2006b: 103–17), as follows:

- Racial delineation
- Ethnic delineation
- Phenotypic difference and similarity in terms of phrenology
- Phenotypic difference and similarity in terms of physiognomy
- Phenotypic difference and similarity in terms of skin color
- Phenotypic difference and similarity in terms of the amount and physical characteristics of facial hair and body hair
- Hair style and hair color
- Body/facial adornment, such as tattoos and body/facial piercing
- Phenotypic difference and similarity in terms of somatotype
- Facial expression
- Difference in attire, including jewelry, ethnic identifiers, neatness, and slovenliness
- Linguistic characteristics
- Body language
- Gaze
- Body odor
- Actual and perceived age
- Physical indicators of perceived intelligence, such as Down syndrome
- Scarification
- Actual or apparent sex
- Perceived or actual sexual orientation difference, or similarity to the respondent/observer
- Gender difference or gender similarity to the respondent/observer
- Site of the incident
- Situational factors existent between where the incident occurred; where the offender resides relative to the site location; and whether the observer/respondent resides in, at, or near the site of the incident
- Site difference (whether the site of the incident or residence of the observer/subject has characteristic[s] different from the site of residence of the respondent)
- Actual or apparent religion of the subject
- Actual or apparent income/wealth of the subject
- Grunt (nonword sound) and nod response to spoken and nonspoken verbal and nonverbal cues

those exposed to the criminal justice system, this means that they are more likely than their White counterparts to be disadvantaged—e.g., have more police contact, endure formal processing even for minor offenses, be prosecuted more rigorously, receive less favorable plea offers, be convicted, receive harsher sentences, and serve those sentences under more restrictive conditions, including high security incarceration.

Daniel Georges-Abeyie

See also: African Diaspora, Crime, and Justice; Black Panther Party; Civil Rights Movement; Disproportionality and Crime; Inequality and Crime; Institutional Racism; Slavery; Structural Racism and Violence; Theories of Race and Crime

References

Bohm, R. M., and K. N. Haley. *Introduction to Criminal Justice.* New York: Glencoe/McGraw Hill, 1997.

Georges-Abeyie, D. E. "Black Racial Monolith." In *Encyclopedia of Race and Crime,* Vol. 1, edited by H. T. Greene and S. L. Gabbidon, 62–5. Thousand Oaks, CA: Sage, 2009.

Georges-Abeyie, D. E. 2006a. "Toward the Development of a Social Distance Severity Scale for the Processing of Juvenile Justice System Offenders and Adult Criminal Justice System Offenders: The Phenomenological Reality of Race, Ethnicity, Social Ecology, and Social Distance—The Georges-Abeyie Petit Apartheid Social Distance Severity Scale." Paper presented at the meeting of the National Association of Blacks in Criminal Justice, July 2006.

Georges-Abeyie, D. E. 2006b. "Race, Ethnicity, and Social Distance Severity." *The Western Journal of Black Studies* 30, no. 2 (2006): 103–17.

Georges-Abeyie, D. E. "Petit Apartheid in Criminal Justice: "The More 'Things' Change, the More 'Things' Remain the Same." In *Petit Apartheid in the U.S. Criminal Justice System: The Dark Figure of Racism,* edited by D. Milovanovic and K. K. Russell, ix–xiv. Durham, NC: Carolina Academic Press, 2001.

Georges-Abeyie, D. E. 1990a. "The Myth of a Racist Criminal Justice System." In *Racism, Empiricism and Criminal Justice,* edited by B. D. MacLean and D. Milovanovic, 11–14. Vancouver, BC: The Collective Press, 1990.

Georges-Abeyie, D. E. 1990b. "Criminal Justice Processing of Non-White Minorities." *In Racism, Empiricism and Criminal Justice,* edited by B. D. MacLean and D. Milovanovic, 25–34. Vancouver, BC: The Collective Press, 1990.

Hare, R. D. *The Hare Psychopathy Checklist—Revised.* 2nd ed. Toronto: Multi-Health Systems, 2003.

MacLean, B. D., and D. Milovanovic. *Racism, Empiricism and Criminal Justice.* Vancouver, BC: The Collective Press, 1990.

Milovanovic, D., and K. K. Russell, eds. *Petit Apartheid in the U.S. Criminal Justice System: The Dark Figure of Racism.* Durham, NC: Carolina Academic Press, 2001.

Parrillo, V. N. *Strangers to These Shores: Race and Ethnic Relations in the United States.* Boston: Allyn and Bacon, 2000.

Stefani, J. C., and K. Schrier. *Psychology.* New York: SparkCharts, Division of Barnes & Noble, 2002.

Whyte, W. F. *Street Corner Society: The Social Structure of an Italian Slum.* Chicago: University of Chicago Press, 1943.

Wilbanks, W. *The Myth of a Racist Criminal Justice System.* Monterey, CA: Brooks/Cole Publishing Company, 1987.

Police Brutality

In an Amnesty International (AI) report released in 1999, police brutality was identified as a topic of "growing national concern" (Amnesty International, 1999: 1). Amnesty International is one of the world's leading human rights watchdogs. Police brutality and the excessive use of force was one of the central themes of its campaign on human rights violations in the United States, launched in October 1998.

John Lewis of the Student Nonviolent Coordinating Committee (currently a U.S. congressman) is clubbed to the ground by an Alabama state trooper during the first Selma voting rights march on March 7, 1965. State and local police attacked the silent, orderly protesters at the Edmund Pettus Bridge. (AP/Wide World Photos)

In *USA: Race, Rights and Police Brutality,* AI examined police shootings, dangerous restraint procedures, the use of pepper spray and Tasers, misuse of police dogs, and police use of force against individuals who are mentally ill or homeless. While only a minority of law enforcement officers in the United States were found to have engaged in deliberate and wanton brutality, AI found that little was being done to monitor or check persistent abusers or to ensure that police tactics in certain common situations would be conducted in a way to minimize rather than increase the risk of unnecessary force and injury. It also found systematic abuses in some jurisdictions or police precincts, and that those systematic abuses typically disproportionately occurred against racial and ethnic minorities, particularly those of Black racial identity.

These abuses included misconduct other than overt physical injury, for example false arrest, harassment, and the use of profanity, racial slurs, and verbal insults. This broader conception of police brutality, encompassing verbal, emotional, psychological, and physical violence, is consistent with the work of criminologist Albert Reiss. In some observational studies, researchers have included the fact that minority males are disproportionately subjected to field interrogations and are more likely to be frisked or searched once they are stopped, as an additional form of police abuse (Holmes & Smith, 2008).

One policing scholar, the late James Fyfe, suggested that a useful way to distinguish police brutality from other forms of excessive or unnecessary force is based on intent. Under this distinction, use of excessive force may result from officers' misjudgment of a situation and the risks involved, while brutality involves willful and wrongful use of force by officers who knowingly exceed the boundaries of their power. This focus on intentionality or lack thereof has been an area of considerable disagreement as to the prevalence of police brutality and the proper means of measuring and defining it, or disciplining officers for it.

The impact of police brutality, however measured or defined, is captured in this quote from the former attorney general, Janet Reno, from April 1999:

> The issue is national in scope and reaches people all across the country. For too many people, especially in minority communities, the trust that is so essential to effective policing does not exist because residents believe that police have used excessive force, that law enforcement is too aggressive, that law enforcement is biased, disrespectful, and unfair. (Amnesty International, 1999: 1)

Although in general, evidence shows that police use of force is an infrequent occurrence, and researchers have found that nonphysical brutality happens more frequently than physical assaults (Garner et al., 2002), most evidence points to African Americans and others of Black racial identity as disproportionately the victims of such force. In addition, a consistent number of high-profile use-of-force incidents, especially lethal force, have gained national and international attention (see Bell, Sean; Diallo, Amadou; Dorismond, Patrick; Grant, Oscar; Jones, Jr., Prince Carmen; King, Rodney Glen; Lee, Anthony Dwain/Dwayne; Louima, Abner; Mitchell, Margaret Laverne; Russ, Robert; Young, Jr., Cornel; Zongo, Ousmane), supporting the notion that Blacks are overwhelmingly the victims of police brutality.

In one such case in 2001, unarmed 19-year-old Timothy Thomas was fatally shot during a foot pursuit involving several officers. The Thomas incident was the fifteenth fatal shooting of an African American by the Cincinnati police in five years. The shooting of Thomas, who turned out to be wanted on a motor vehicle violation, sparked a 1960s-style riot marked by violence, looting, and vandalism. The subsequent acquittal of the officer who shot Thomas in the back and who initially gave a false account of the shooting led to additional community unrest.

The number of such shootings continues to mount against Black victims, even though in 1985, the U.S. Supreme Court issued a ruling that was intended to limit the use of police deadly force against non-felony suspects and suspects for whom there was no clear evidence of immediate danger to the officer or the public. The ruling in *Tennessee v. Garner,* a case involving the shooting of an unarmed Black teen by a Memphis police officer on suspicion of having committed a burglary, led to an initial drop in police shootings, particularly of civilians who were unarmed. The initial impact of the *Garner* decision seems to have dissipated over time. In a comprehensive review of literature, Jerome Skolnick and James Fyfe report that in general, African Americans are more than six times as likely as Whites to be shot by police, and in large cities, African Americans are killed by police at least three times more often than Whites. As confirmed by the Amnesty International report, Black victims also die at the hands of the police via choke holds, beatings, pepper spray, taser use, and other excessive or improper use of force. Officers are rarely convicted of crimes or departmentally disciplined for such incidents, contributing to feelings of injustice and mistrust of the system among members of the Black community, both native and foreign born.

Reasons for the overrepresentation of racial minorities as victims of brutality are hotly debated. Popular beliefs among White civilians and police administrators are that the police exert greater coercion over some groups because they have to respond to the dangers posed by the members of the group as a legitimate means of protecting themselves and the society. Police brutality, according to this point of view, is unavoidable due to the dangerous, unpredictable nature of policing, requiring officers to make split-second decisions to control the worst citizens in the society.

People who hold this view also tend to believe that police brutality largely consists of isolated and aberrant acts by individual officers or small groups of officers. A theory that represents this view is the "rotten apple" thesis, arguing that police brutality is confined to a few officers who have individual problematic traits, such as a violence-prone personality and overt racial prejudice. Under the rotten apple thesis, a few officers are the source of abuse and bring in the majority of citizen complaints. According to the International Association of Chiefs of Police (IACP), during the past two decades, the development of community policing programs, civilian review programs, enhanced training strategies, and early warning systems have improved police response and reduced police misconduct including brutality. The IACP believes that incidents of police brutality are rare events that the media overemphasize, creating an exaggerated impression of its magnitude and prevalence. Reports such as that issued by Amnesty International and government reports on racial profiling (see Racial Profiling) suggest that the IACP may be underestimating the problem and overestimating the extent to which the two decades of policing innovations have addressed it.

The research of several scholars confirms that issues of racial inequality, stereotypes, and conflicting ideas about social control contribute to police brutality against minority citizens. This line of explanation derives from the conflict theory of law that views law and the criminal justice system as instruments for powerful groups to control the subordinate groups as a means to maximize their own interests. Similarly, under the recently developed racial threat theory, when minorities are seen as posing threats to the existing social order, they are subject to intensified control by local police. Both conflict theory and racial threat theory suggest that police brutality may be more systemic than individually based within policing agencies.

There are two general approaches to controlling and preventing police brutality. Internal control mechanisms include efforts from police departments themselves, such as strong internal leadership, close oversight and guidance from immediate supervisors, clear written policies and rules, fair reward-punish systems, proper use of early warning systems, effective internal investigations of incidents and officers, high standards for police recruitment, and diversity among police personnel. External controls include the courts, citizens' review boards, and news media. The effects of external control are to a certain degree contingent upon the functioning and effectiveness of internal control mechanisms. Most researchers endorse a mixed approach of controlling police misconduct that blends both internal and external mechanisms. It is noted that until recently, civil liability has proved much easier to obtain against offending officers than criminal charges. Because most civil awards are not paid by the officers themselves, it has been suggested that they have little possibility of deterring police misconduct and brutality. In the absence of frequent criminal sanctions and that are sufficiently punitive (see Grant, Oscar, and Zongo, Ousmane), the strength of internal mechanisms for controlling the occurrence of police brutality is questionable.

Bonnie Wu and Delores Jones-Brown

See also: Institutional Racism; Racial Profiling; Structural Racism and Violence; Theories of Race and Crime

References

Amnesty International. *USA: Race, Rights and Police Brutality*, AI Index: 51/147/99. New York: Amnesty International, 1999.

Burns, Ronald, and Charles Crawford. *Policing and Violence*. Upper Saddle River, NJ: Prentice Hall, 2002.

Collins, Allyson. *Shielded from Justice: Police Brutality and Accountability in the United States*. New York, NY: Human Rights Watch, 1988.

Fitzgerald, Sheila, ed. *Police Brutality: Opposing Viewpoints*. Farmington Hills, MI: Greenhaven Press, 2006.

Garner, Joel, Christopher Maxwell, and Cedrick Heraux. "Characteristics Associated with the Prevalence and Severity of Force Used by the Police." *Justice Quarterly* 19 (December 2002): 705–46.

Geller, William, and Hans Toch, eds. *Police Violence: Understanding and Controlling Police Abuse of Force*. New Haven, CT: Yale University Press, 1996.

Geoffrey, Alpert, and Roger Dunham. *Understanding Police Use of Force: Officers, Suspects, and Reciprocity*. New York: Cambridge University Press, 2004.

Herbert, Steve. "Police Subculture Reconsidered." *Criminology* 36 (1998): 343–69.

Holmes, Malcolm, and Bradley Smith. *Race and Police Brutality: Roots of an Urban Dilemma*. Albany: State University of New York Press, 2008.

Human Rights Watch. "Human Rights Watch World Report 2003." http://www.hrw.org/wr2k3/.

International Association of Chiefs of Police (IACP). FY 2011–2016 Strategic Plan, August 2010. http://www.theiacp.org/portals/0/pdfs/IACPStrategicPlan.pdf.

Johnson, Marilynn. *Street Justice: A History of Police Violence in New York City*. Boston: Beacon, 2003.

Juarez, Juan. *Brotherhood of Corruption: A Cop Breaks the Silence on Police Abuse, Brutality, and Racial Profiling*. Chicago, IL: Chicago Review, 2004.

Koon, Stacey, and Robert Deitz. *Presumed Guilty: The Tragedy of the Rodney King Affair*. Washington, DC: Regnery Gateway, 1992.

Langan, Patrick, et al. *Contacts between Police and the Public: Findings from the 1999 National Survey*. Washington, DC: U.S. Department of Justice.

Lawrence, Regina. *The Politics of Force: Media and the Construction of Police Brutality*. Los Angeles: University of California Press, 2000.

Lersch, Kim, and Tom Mieczkowski. "Violent Police Behavior: Past, Present, and Future Research Directions." *Aggression and Violent Behavior* 10 (July–August 2005): 552–68.

Manning, Peter. "Violence and the Police Role." *Annals of the American Academy of Political and Social Science* 452 (1980): 135–44.

McArdle, Andrea, and Tanya Erzen, eds. *Zero Tolerance: Quality of Life and the New Police Brutality in New York City*. New York: New York University Press, 2001.

Nelson, Jill, ed. *Police Brutality*. New York: W.W. Norton & Company, 2000.

Pollock, Joycelyn. "Ethics and Law Enforcement." In *Critical Issues in Policing*, edited by R. Dunham and G. Alpert, 280–303. Long Grove, IL: Waveland Press, 2005.

Roleff, Tamara. *Police Brutality*. San Diego: Greenhaven Press, 1999.

Ross, Jeffrey. *Making News of Police Violence: A Comparative Study of Toronto and New York City.* Westport, CT: Praeger, 2000.

Skolnick, Jerome, and Fyfe, James. *Above the Law: Police and the Excessive Use of Force.* New York: The Free Press, 1993.

Tennessee v. Garner, 471 U.S. 1 (1985).

Walker, Samuel. *The New World of Police Accountability.* Thousand Oaks, CA: Sage Publication, 2005.

Websdale, Neil. *Policing the Poor: From Slave Plantation to Public Housing.* Boston: Northeastern University Press, 2001.

Weisburd, David, et al. *Police Attitudes toward Abuse of Authority: Findings from a National Study.* Washington, DC: U.S. Department of Justice, 2000.

Weitzer, Ronald, and Steven Tuch. *Race and Policing in America: Conflict and Reform.* New York: Cambridge University Press, 2006.

Williams, Kristian. *Our Enemies in Blue: Police and Power in America.* Brooklyn: Soft Skull Press, 2004.

Price, Craig (1974–)

Craig Price has been described as a troubled Black teenager and the youngest serial killer in the United States. On July 27, 1987, when he was just 13 years old, Price broke into a house in his neighborhood of Warwick, Rhode Island. High on marijuana at the time of the break-in, Price removed a knife from a kitchen drawer and used it to stab 27-year-old Rebecca Spencer to death (*The Worchester Telegram and Gazette,* 1989). Spencer, a White mother of one, was stabbed 58 times. Her murder went unsolved for two years (Bell, n.d.).

On September 1, 1989, when Price was 15 years old, he broke into another house in his neighborhood. This time he killed 39-year-old Joan Heaton and her two daughters, Melissa, 8, and Jennifer, 10. Like the Spencer murder, the killings are alleged to have occurred while Price was high on marijuana, this time combined with LSD. Again, Price used knives retrieved from the kitchen to stab his victims, who again were White. Each victim was stabbed multiple times. Evidence at the scene indicated that in addition to stabbing Joan Heaton, Price strangled and bludgeoned her. One source indicates that her daughter Jennifer was stabbed as many as 62 times and that the younger daughter, Melissa, had her skull crushed in addition to being stabbed (*The Boston Globe,* 1994). It was reported that Melissa's stabbing was so brutal that the blade of the knife broke off in her neck. Prior to the killings, Price had been in trouble for minor offenses and had a criminal record for petty theft. After the killings, he was dubbed the "Warwick Slasher" by the media. He has spent the last 22 years trying to gain his release from confinement for these crimes that he committed as a juvenile.

Craig Price sits in Providence Family Court during a hearing on September 22, 2004, in Providence, Rhode Island. A judge denied the Warwick teenage killer's bid to have his prison sentence reduced. Price is serving 29 years for the murders of Joan Heaton and her daughters, Melissa and Jennifer, who were his neighbors in Warwick. He also confessed to a separate 1987 murder in that city. (Associated Press)

One source notes that "nothing in Price's background explained his rage" (O'Neill, 2007b). By all accounts, he had been raised in a stable home with two parents who worked to provide a comfortable life for him and his siblings. However, there are some indications that a sense of racial isolation and teasing about his size (he is described as being 5 feet 10 inches tall and 240 pounds) may have contributed to his emotional instability. When Price was questioned by the police, he confessed to the four killings and is even said to have bragged about killing Rebecca Spencer. He was arrested just prior to his sixteenth birthday. At the time of his arrest, Rhode Island law did not allow juveniles under the age of 16 to be tried as adults and, under the same law, they could not be confined by the state past their twenty-first birthdays. If Price had been an adult when he committed his crimes, he could have been sentenced to life in prison without the possibility of parole. As a juvenile offender, he was sentenced to five years' confinement at the Rhode Island Training School's Youth Correctional Center. The sentence also included a mandate that he undergo intense psychological examination and therapy.

The extent to which race played a role in the subsequent handling of Craig Price's case may never be known or admitted, or whether what some have described as the "crusade" to keep him confined is simply a matter of perceived justice. O'Neill (2007b) noted that in the Price case, "the legal system would bend the laws it was sworn to uphold, because, it 'was simply the right thing to do.'" Within a month of Price's arrest, the state legislature passed a law allowing juveniles to be tried in adult court for serious crimes. On two previous occasions, attempts to pass such a provision had failed. The new law would allow teen murderers to be prosecuted as adults, and, when appropriate, receive life sentences (*The Milford Daily News,* 2011). Because the law was passed in 1990, it could not be applied retroactively to Price, who had committed his crimes in 1987 and 1989. This meant the state would have no choice but to release him on his twenty-first birthday.

In 1993, when Craig Price was about a year and a half from being released from the juvenile facility, an article about him was published in a local paper. The article described how, during his confinement, Price had developed a reputation for good behavior, and had earned a GED and started taking college classes (Marcis, 1993). Despite the serious nature of his charges, Price had also been assigned a light security job at the facility. His release, which was scheduled for October 11, 1994, was imminent and seemed inevitable. But members of the Heaton family and the lead homicide investigator on the case, Kevin Collins, were outraged that Price would receive such a light punishment for the four murders. They banded together and formed a group known as Citizens Opposed to the Release of Craig Price (CORP). This group, along with Assistant Attorney General Jeffrey Pine, had been instrumental in getting the 1990 legislation passed.

Fearing that Price would be released on his twenty-first birthday, CORP launched a national media campaign. The purpose of the campaign was to heighten public awareness across the United States of Price's impending release. The group organized rallies, launched fundraisers, and gave interviews on local and national radio and television shows. CORP also hired pilots to fly banners in major cities across the country that read, "Killer Craig Price. Moving to Your City? Beware." One such banner led to a meeting with President Clinton, after which the president made public statements calling for states to make juvenile criminal records accessible to the public and urging that juveniles with violent histories be prevented from purchasing firearms (Smolowe, 1994).

Along with CORP, Assistant Attorney General Jeffery Pine voiced frustration over the legal dilemma that the Price case represented. He was quoted as saying, "There is something fundamentally wrong with a system that allowed someone who killed four people to simply go free at 21" (O'Neill, 2007a). In 1992, Pine was elected attorney general, and he made it his mission to make sure Price would remain behind bars. Pine pushed for legislation that would allow judges to consider an offender's criminal record in deciding whether he or she should be committed to a psychiatric facility at the expiration of a criminal sentence. In 1993, he introduced a controversial bill giving the Office of the Attorney General the power to civilly commit a mentally ill offender to a mental institution if he poses a danger to society. The bill was controversial because it singled out the mentally ill and those with psychological problems for special handling by the Attorney General's Office, when previously such power had been primarily under the control of the judiciary. The bill specifically targeted Craig Price, to prevent him from being released at the end of his juvenile sentence. Despite the controversy, the "Craig Price Bill" was passed the same year it was introduced (O'Neill, 2007a; *The Providence Journal,* 2004; Lang, 2000).

Along with introducing the bill, Pine took the extraordinary step of consulting with Federal Bureau of Investigation serial killer expert Greg McCrary. In a detailed report, McCrary described Price as a "human predator" who expressed no remorse for the killings or empathy (*The Erie Times News,* 2007). The report went on to state that there was a high probability that Price would kill again if released. In contrast to his reputation for good behavior while in the juvenile facility (Marcis, 1993), McCrary's report on Price was consistent with the reports of state psychologists, who also concluded that he posed a substantial risk of violent reoffending.

McCrary's report, coupled with those of the state psychologists, helped to bolster Pine's position that judges should be allowed to consider an offender's past criminal record in determining whether he or she should be committed to a psychiatric facility after completing his assigned criminal term. Once the legislation passed, judges in Rhode Island were allowed to commit prisoners to psychiatric facilities when the judges believed such prisoners posed a substantial risk of violence upon release (*The Providence Journal,* 2004; Lang, 2000).

Although intense psychological examination and therapy were ordered as part of his original sentence, once the civil commitment statute passed, on the advice of his lawyers, Price withdrew from treatment. His lawyers recognized that the evaluation results might be used as a means to place him in a psychiatric facility for confinement past his twenty-first birthday. As Price approached his scheduled release date of October 11, 1994, a series of events transpired that resulted in substantial extensions of the time he would have to spend in custody. First, on June 8, 1994, he was indicted for one count of simple assault and extortion for threatening to injure a corrections officer at the training school. A $500,000 bail was set for those offenses and the trial was set for the fall of 1994, the same time period during which he was due to be released. On June 27, 1994, while awaiting trial on the criminal charges, he was found guilty of civil contempt for failing to comply with the portion of his juvenile sentence that mandated psychological evaluation and treatment. An extra year of incarceration was added to his original sentence. Now an adult, he was ordered to serve the extra year at the Adult Correctional Institute in Cranston. In order to reduce that sentence, Price had to submit to the psychological evaluations that his attorneys had previously advised him to discontinue (*The Providence Journal,* 2004; Lang, 2000).

Although Price resumed the psychological evaluations and treatment, the simple assault and extortion charges were still pending. He was tried for those charges on October 3, 1994. He was convicted of assault and extortion for making verbal threats to "snuff" corrections officer Mark Petrella and for being in possession of cigarettes and a lighter. In December, past his original release date, he was given a 15-year sentence (8 years suspended) for the simple (verbal) assault and a felony extortion charge (*The Milford Daily News,* 2011).

Another year was added to Price's sentence in 1996 after he was accused of biting a correction officer's finger during a "brawl" inside the institution. A judge found Price guilty of violating his probation (from the suspended sentence) even though he was still incarcerated (*The New Hampshire Union Leader,* 1998). Accounts vary, but in 1995 or 1997, he was found guilty of criminal contempt for defying a court order to undergo a psychiatric evaluation and treatment. These charges were based on an accusation that he lied about the facts related to the murders during the psychiatric evaluation and treatment sessions. Price admitted the charges. And, according to court records, he received a 25-year sentence, with 10 years to be served, followed by 15 years of probation contingent on not getting into additional trouble and not refusing continued treatment (*The Milford Daily News,* 2011). This sentence was in addition to the others he was already serving. In October 1998 he received an additional seven-year sentence for assaulting a corrections officer. Similar charges were filed against him again, for which he received four-year sentences in February 1999 and October 2001. The incidents primarily involved verbal threats or minor injuries to the officers (*The Providence Journal,* 2004; Lang, 2000).

In 2004, Price was transferred from Rhode Island to the Florida Department of Corrections. Although his move has been described as part of a routine interstate transfer, it was Price who made the request. In that same year, he also filed an appeal, arguing that his 25-year sentence for criminal contempt violated the double jeopardy clause because he had already been found guilty of civil contempt. He made additional claims that his conviction was as a result of inadequate legal representation and that the sentence amounted to cruel and unusual punishment. That appeal was denied in 2005.

Undaunted, Price filed a subsequent appeal with the Rhode Island Supreme Court. He maintains that he has paid his debt to society and that his continued confinement is due in part to racism. Prosecutors argue that the criminal contempt charge is valid due to Price's failure to undergo the court-ordered psychiatric evaluations and treatment. Price, who filed his own handwritten request for post-conviction relief, also asked to return to Rhode Island to represent himself during the proceedings (WPRI, 2011c). Those requests were denied. Susan Iannitelli, the court-appointed attorney representing Price, argued that Price had refused psychiatric testing on the advice of his lawyers at the time. Price again asked the court to throw out the contempt sentence because it was "unduly harsh and unconstitutional" (WPRI, 2011a).

The Rhode Island Supreme Court heard Craig Price's case in November 2011. It rendered a decision denying his appeal at the beginning of December (WPRI, 2011b; Krause, 2011). The court rejected his double jeopardy argument, noting that the Fifth Amendment "does not preclude a criminal penalty after a civil penalty has been imposed for the same act." It also rejected the claim on procedural grounds. Patrick Young, a special assistant to the current Rhode Island attorney general, Peter Kilmartin, and lead prosecutor on the case, praised the court for its decision, noting that Price had "thumbed his nose at the Family Court" during almost all of his juvenile sentence (WPRI, 2011a).

During the appeals process, Florida corrections administrators would not allow Price to be interviewed by the media because of what they deemed "serious security concerns" (*The Bucks County Courier Times,* 2007). Price continues to insist that the outcomes in his case have a lot to do with race. He raised the issue of race after his 1994 conviction on the extortion charge. He is quoted as noting that "[t]he media has once again done a good job of creating a monster. Not just a boogeyman, but a black boogeyman" (O'Neill, 2007b). Price's current projected release date is in February 2022.

Kimberly Dodson

References

Bell, R. "Craig Price: Confessions of a Teenage Serial Killer." TruTV.com, n.d. http://www .trutv.com/library/crime/serial_killers/predators.

The Boston Globe. "Prison Violations Land R.I. Killer Price in Isolation Unit." October 14, 1994.

The Bucks County Courier Times. "Officials Cooperate to Keep Juvenile Murderer behind Bars." December 15, 2007.

The Erie Times News. "Killer Tests Rhode Island System." December 16, 2007.

Krause, N. "Murderer Craig Price Appeal Denied." December 2, 2011. http://www.fox-providence.com/dpps/news/local_news/region.

Lang, D. *A Call for Justice: A New England Town's Fight to Keep a Stone Cold Killer in Jail.* New York: Avon Books, 2000.

Marcis, G. "Craig Price Is a 'Peer Counselor.'" *The Providence Journal,* May 11, 1993.

The Milford Daily News. "R.I. Objects to Appeal from Notorious Killer." February 11, 2011.

The New Hampshire Union Leader. "R.I. Killer Craig Price in Prison Trouble Again." May 13, 1998.

O'Neill, H. 2007a. "Kid Killer Target of New Juvenile Justice Law: Officials Work Together to Keep Young Murderer behind Bars Well into Adulthood." *Long Beach Press-Telegram,* December 16, 2007, A1, A5.

O'Neill, H. 2007b. "Price Case Still Felt in Juvenile Justice System." *USA Today,* December 15, 2007.

The Providence Journal. "A Chronology of How R.I. Kept Craig Price in Prison." March 2004.

Smolowe, J. "Not in My Backyard!: Citizens Rally to Keep Paroled Murderers and Sex Offenders from Settling in Their Communities." *Time Magazine,* September 5, 1994.

The Worchester Telegram and Gazette. "R.I. Teenager in Four Murders." September 22, 1989.

WPRI. 2011a. "Craig Price's Appeal Rejected by RI Supreme Court." December 2, 2011. http://www.630wpro.com/article.asp?id=2346363&spid+37719.

WPRI. 2011b. "Craig Price Appeal to Be Heard on Wed." November 1, 2011. http://www.wpri.com/dpp/news/local_news/providence/.

WPRI. 2011c. "Notorious Killer Wants to Return to RI." February 10, 2011. http://www.wpri.com/dpp/news/local_news/notorious-rhode-island.

Prisoner Reentry and African Americans

More than 2.3 million Americans are incarcerated in prisons and jails across the nation, while another 5 million are either on parole or probation. African Americans, while comprising only 12 percent of the U.S. population, disproportionately represent 41 percent and 47 percent of its jail and prison populations, respectively (Sabol et al., 2007). A striking 60 percent of prison and jail populations at the end of 2004 were ethnic or racial minority, while 60 percent of state and federal prisoners were African American or Hispanic (Harrison & Beck, 2005), of which only 11 percent were serving time for violent offenses (Sentencing Project, 2006). After sharp, unprecedented increases in the 1980s and 1990s, the incarceration rate has recently grown at a slower pace and more recently began to show a modest 2.5 percent decrease (Glaze, 2010). However, over the same period, prison release increased by the about the same percentage (2.2%), thereby slightly increasing the rate of those returning from prisons and jails back to their communities.

In 2009, it is estimated that over 650,000 individuals were released from state and federal prisons throughout the nation, a fourfold increase over the past three decades. Increasing numbers of African American ex-offenders (about 97% of those incarcerated)—more now than at any other time in our history—are leaving prisons across the country to return to their families and communities.

In addition, because of the U.S. Supreme Court recent ruling in *Plata v. Schwarzenegger* (2011), which demanded a reduction in California inmate population, it stands that other states will see similar lawsuits as the one filed on behalf of plaintiffs seeking relief from inhumane prison overcrowding. This in combination with increasing state and municipal budget constraints and some repealing of draconian drug laws, more ex-offenders are expected to be released over the next few years, making prisoner reentry a most urgent social concern, especially among African Americans.

In many cases, however, African Americans are less prepared for their return to society and less connected to community-based social support structures than their predecessors were 10 to 20 years ago. Similar to previous years, many prisoners are released with only a bus ticket and a small amount of money. In addition to this lack of economic or financial capital, most prisoners also have limited human capital, such as education and employment skills. Due to decreased funding, society's changed ideology of prison, and the skyrocketing number of individuals behind bars, fewer higher education and other programs to prepare inmates for life outside prison walls are offered in comparison to years past.

Upon their release, many African American ex-offenders must face the immediate challenges of obtaining food, clothing, housing, and health care, which are often made available by service providers within the community. Their lack of sufficient human, social, economic, and spiritual capital puts many at a disadvantage as they attempt to manage the most basic ingredients for successful reintegration—reconnecting with their families and accessing needed substance abuse and health care treatment. Longer-term reintegration needs of returning prisoners range from finding and maintaining employment to accessing other needed community services. Previous reports indicate most ex-offenders will be rearrested within three years, and many will be returned to prison for new crimes or parole violations (Sabol et al., 2007). This cycle of incarceration and reentry into society carries the potential for profound adverse consequences for African American ex-offenders, their families, and communities, and translates into thousands of new victimizations each year and more than $74 billion in annual correction expenditures (Sabol et al., 2007).

A closer examination of the full scope of African Americans and prisoner reentry first requires a working definition of prisoner reentry, including the stages of the reentry process, to better understand how is it used in the body of literature and public discourse on the topic.

Prisoner Reentry Defined

"Prisoner reentry" is a broad term used to refer to the transition of ex-offenders from prison to their communities (U.S. DOJ, n.d.) or the process of leaving prison or jail and returning to society (Solomon et al., 2005). This includes prisoners who are either released when their maximum court-ordered sentence has been served or who have not completed their maximum court-ordered sentence and have been granted release on the condition of a period of community supervision (parolees) (U.S. DOJ, n.d.). It applies to individuals released from prisons, jails, federal institutions, juvenile facilities, or even pretrial detention. Although both adults and juveniles experience reentry, their experiences are significantly different. We limit our discussion of prisoner reentry here to adult reintegration.

Reentry entails planning for inmates' transition to free living, including how they spend their time during confinement, the process by which they are released, and how they are supervised after they are released (Petersilia, 2003). Although reentry in its most basic incarnation denotes a process, there is a notion of success that is implied in its meaning. Reentry or reintegration is treated as "the concept of rejoining and becoming a productive member of society" (Taxman, 2004: 2), implying that reentry includes all activities and programming conducted to prepare ex-offenders to return safely to the community and to live as law-abiding citizens. Likewise, the U.S. Department of Justice posited that reentry entails the "use of programs targeted at promoting the effective reintegration of offenders back to communities upon release from prison and jail" (U.S. DOJ, n.d.). In this context, then, reentry can be viewed as the pro-social integration of ex-offenders into the community.

"Pro-social" suggests behavior in accordance with the law, as opposed to anti-social, which can be described as "behavior in violation of the law" or deviance (Gottfredson & Hirschi, 1990). One might argue that what is now referred to as "reentry programming"—such as parole or probation—previously fell under the title of community supervision. Explicit inclusion of pro-social community actors, however, such as family members, block group presidents, community watch group organizers, community development corporation leaders, clergy persons, and others, separates reentry programs from community supervision programs. Increasingly, reentry programming, planning, and policy are being addressed on many fronts, including from a community institutional capacity perspective. An overview of the many and complex issues surrounding the topic will help explain why this is so. First, however, at this juncture it is necessary to provide a profile of the prison and reentry populations.

Stages of Reentry

It is becoming increasingly clear that reentry is a multistep process and every step is highly dependent upon the success of another. Recent studies provide an understanding of the life demands on ex-offenders (Cnaan, et al., 2008). While the classic community supervision model's primary focus is on recidivism (i.e., rearrest, reconviction, and/or reincarceration), alternate reentry models do not consider preventing recidivism as their sole objective. Rather, these models look at ways in which to provide programming and social supportive services that will assist ex-offenders in overcoming reentry challenges, such as reconnecting to families, finding housing and employment, improving education, training and vocational skills

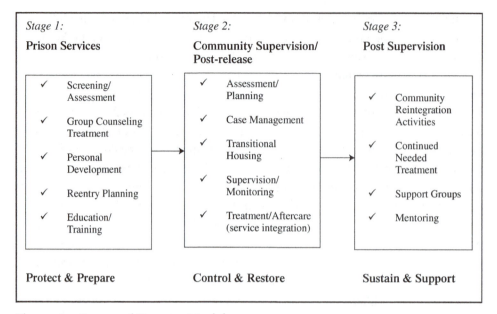

Figure 1 Stages of Reentry Model

and "staying clean"—that is, overcoming substance abuse and building a positive, pro-social network. A slightly modified reentry model outlining the stages of reentry was created by the National Institutes of Justice to assess the federally funded Serious and Violent Offender Reentry Initiative (SVORI) (see Figure 1) (Lattimore et al., 2004).

Phase I—Protect and Prepare: Institution-Based Programs
These programs are designed to prepare inmates to reenter society. Services provided include education, mental health and substance abuse treatment, job training, mentoring, and full diagnostic and risk assessment.

Phase II—Control and Restore: Community-Based Transition Programs
In this phase, inmates or ex-offenders work prior to, and immediately following, their release from correctional institutions. It also includes those on community supervision, such as parole. Services provided in this phase can include education, monitoring, mentoring, life skills training, assessment, job skills development, and mental health and substance abuse treatment.

Phase III—Sustain and Support
Community-based long-term support programs match ex-offenders with appropriate social service agencies and community-based organizations. This phase of reentry does not consist of any formal supervision or mandated reentry programming or

planning. It is simply what is made available to those who are in need and want continued support in their personal process of pro-social reintegration.

Statement of the Reentry Problem for African Americans

Prison Population Growth, Racial Disparity, and the Criminal Justice System

Since the mid 1970s, there has been a shift in American criminal justice policies that affect the three primary areas of the criminal justice system: law enforcement, the judicial system, and correction. The effect of these shifts can be seen in the monumental growth in the number of individuals in state and federal prisons most of which (nearly 60%) are disproportionately African American (Harrison & Beck, 2005). Harrison and Beck (2005) estimated that nearly 8.4 percent of Black males and 2.5 percent of Hispanic males between 25 and 29 were in prison at the end of 2004, compared to about 1 percent of White males in the same age group: "[T]he black/white differential in incarceration is a ratio of more than seven to one. Likewise, during the same period, black females were more than twice as likely than white females to be in prison. African Americans, therefore, have a seven times greater chance of being incarcerated that do whites" (Mauer, 2006: 139). More than 20 percent of Black males will experience a prison term before reaching the age of 35, compared to fewer than 3 percent of White males (Petersilia, 2003). Further, about 33 percent of parole entrants are White, 47 percent are Black, and 16 percent are Hispanic. Hence, while Blacks and Hispanics are only 20 to 22 percent of the U.S. population, about two-thirds of all returning prisoners are racial or ethnic minorities, compared with less than one-third in the general population (Petersilia, 2003).

Remarkable growth in the African Americans in the U.S. prison population can also be attributed to the sentencing reform movement of the 1980s, which produced the following: truth-in-sentencing to ensure offenders serve full sentences without possibility of parole; mandatory penalties to ensure designated prison terms for crimes; Three Strikes laws to keep persistent offenders in for life; and an increasing dependence on physical isolation of criminals (Blumstein & Beck, 1999). Further, under the Sentencing Reform Act of 1984 (SRA) and subsequent U.S. Congress–mandated federal sentencing guidelines and federal mandatory minimum statues, some argue that Blacks and Hispanics have experienced "massive unfairness and extreme bias" (Petersilia, 2000: 20). Mandatory minimum sentences forced judges to give fixed prison terms to those convicted of specific crimes, most often offenses for drug-related crimes. Such sentencing requires much steeper penalties for small amounts of inexpensive street drugs—amounts most often dealt with by poor African Americans and Hispanics—than for the large amounts of more expensive recreational drugs most often associated with the White middle class. In addition, the fact that the mandatory provisions now in effect in at least 16 states have not extended to white-collar crime provides persuasive evidence of class bias. These provisions demand a three-time felony offender—regardless of severity of crime—to be sentenced to long-term prison terms. A brief overview of the statistics gives a picture of the striking racial disparities in incarceration rates, as well as the development of the *prison industry* or the dramatic proliferation of prisons and those imprisoned. The results of the provisions are larger cohorts of young minority male ex-offenders as well as higher proportions of young minority males who serve longer sentences due to their histories of drug abuse and drug dealing, who are disproportionately African American.

Sentencing reform has not only impacted the numbers of African Americans who are incarcerated; it also impacts how and when they are released. At the same time the sentencing policies were experiencing significant changes, states also were making fundamental changes in parole, an institution considered to be "one of the cornerstones of the American criminal justice system" (Travis & Lawrence, 2002: 1). Travis and Lawrence (2002) asserted that the power over the release process has shifted from the executive branch (e.g., parole boards) to the legislative branch, as is indicated in the move toward a number of indeterminate sentencing models. As a result, while 80 percent of those who leave prison are placed on parole, nearly 75 percent will never see a parole board. Thus many may never be required to have postrelease monitoring or a discharge plan, which ensures housing, employment prospects, and the social support of family and friends (Travis & Lawrence, 2002). Travis and Lawrence asserted, "[F]or some large numbers of exiting prisoners, we have lost the link between pre-release preparation and post-release supervision, a link that the classic parole model was intended to create" (2002: 24). The research community, however, has not answered conclusively the question of whether or not parole supervision reduces crime.

Lastly, a shift in political ideology during the same period greatly influenced the correctional model used in both prisons and jails. For from its Quaker beginnings in 1790 with the construction of the first penitentiary, rehabilitation was replaced as the core mission of corrections with programs designed to deter and incapacitate. Fewer states offered continued treatment that would support pro-social reintegration, and among those that did, many were retained primarily as a means of keeping inmates manageable rather than methods to reduce recidivism. Legislators looked more favorably on programs that could generate goods and services that states needed than on education and work programs that might reform inmates. Logan voiced the sentiment of the changing ideology toward corrections when he wrote, "[I]t is the duty of prisons to govern fairly and well within their own walls. It is not their duty to reform, rehabilitate, or reintegrate offenders into society" (1993: 13). A confluence of disparate harsh criminal justice legislation harnessed masses of African Americans; kept them incarcerated longer periods of time; offered fewer if any forms of rehabilitation or reentry support pre- or postrelease; and left communities bereft of mothers, fathers, sons, and daughters, creating a phenomenon that would assure that two of every three would end up back in prison or jail within three years of release, making spending time in prison or jail in some communities normal, and weakening even more many African American urban communities.

Reentry and the Urban African American Community

In its early stages, research demonstrates that those returning from prison and jail are likely to return to the same neighborhood in which they resided prior to incarceration (Shah, 2006). Research shows that African American communities with the highest count of returning ex-offenders are the same or at least overlap with those with the highest density or ratio of ex-offenders to adult population (Frazier, 2007). For example, in Philadelphia, with one exception, all of the neighborhoods with the highest numbers of returnees are in the top twenty-fifth percentile of the ratio of ex-offenders to adult population. These statistics tell us that these neighborhoods receive a disproportionate—by count and by number of adult population—number of those ex-offenders returning from federal prison and county jails.

In addition, the neighborhoods are essentially in a concentrated area of the city. Unfortunately, this is the case in many urban contexts with high African American populations like Detroit, Washington, D.C., Los Angeles, and Brooklyn. In these mostly Black and Hispanic neighborhoods, from 50 percent to 80 percent of the households are less than two times the poverty threshold, well above the city average of 41 percent in other parts of urban cities. In comparison, the neighborhoods with the lowest proportion of ex-offenders have poverty rates as low as 3.45 percent, at 200 percent below the poverty level. In other words, the majority of the families in all of these neighborhoods live in poverty (Frazier, 2007). In terms of education, most of these neighborhoods are slightly above the city average of 32.14 percent of the population whose highest level of educational attainment is a high school diploma. Finally, the violent crime rate in these neighborhoods, in proportion to the total population, is among the highest in the city. It stands that the impact of racial disparity, poverty, and crime in communities can be harmful to their ability to address community problems such as reentry. Limited financial resources and other resources make it difficult for families to support those returning from prison and jail.

Indeed, these neighborhoods are among the most distressed in the country and disproportionately have higher levels of poverty, lower high school completion rates, higher visible crime and high unemployment, and high levels of economic disinvestment, making reentry even more of a daunting challenge. The effect of structural factors that have facilitated the massive numbers of incarceration, the conditions for poor reentry preparedness, and resulting consequences are devastating to the African American ex-offender. In addition to laws and the public ideology toward prisoner rehabilitation, which have resulted in more correctional facilities and less prerelease reentry programming and postrelease supervision, most African American ex-offenders must also face the disadvantaging effects of urbanism, such as spatial mismatch, economic disinvestment, and racism (see Wilson, 1987; 1991), complicating the challenge of meeting their reentry needs and overcoming obstacles.

Reentry Needs and Obstacles

While there is little systemic effort, community organizations and institutions, as well as family and friends, address what research overwhelmingly has found to be the ex-offenders' most urgent needs and significant challenges: employment and economic/financial capital, substance abuse rehabilitation, physical and mental health, family support, social capital, and housing.

Employment and Economic/Financial Capital

Despite the fact that African American ex-offenders' experiences in the workforce after release can play a significant role in their reentry transition and may influence recidivism outcomes, fewer inmates are receiving prison-based job and vocational training now than in the past. Fewer still have access to transitional programs that help connect them to jobs in the community. Prior research shows that a majority of offenders were employed prior to incarceration and presumably want to find legal and stable employment following their release (Visher et al., 2004). Two-thirds of state prisoners reportedly held a job just prior to their incarceration as did slightly more than one-half in finding and maintaining a legitimate job after release. Employment is critical, as it can reduce the chances of re-offending following release from prison, and the higher the wages, the less likely ex-offenders will return to crime.

Many African American ex-offenders, however, experience even greater difficulties finding jobs after their release. They often enter prison with poor educational backgrounds and little work experience. During the time they spend in prison, inmates often lose work skills and forfeit the opportunity to gain work experience (Western et al., 2001).

In addition, long periods of incarceration may weaken social contacts that lead to legal employment opportunities upon release (Western et al., 2001). While the period of incarceration could be viewed as an opportunity to build skills and prepare for placement at a future job, few prisoners participate in such programming, and the evaluation literature provides mixed or negative support for the effectiveness of in-prison, job-training programs. After release, the stigma of their ex-offender status, compounded by discriminatory employment practices, makes the job search even more difficult (Mauer, 2006: 199). Pager (2003) found that Whites with a felony conviction were called back for job interviews at the same rate as Blacks with comparable credentials and no criminal record. Further, a survey of 3,000 employers in four major metropolitan areas revealed that two-thirds would not knowingly hire an ex-offender (Holzer, 2000). There are also legal barriers that make finding employment difficult. About six states permanently bar ex-offenders from holding any public employment (Bushway, 2000). Most states impose restrictions to licensing such trades as barbering and asbestos removal, which have no discernible control objective (Mauer, 2006). States also prohibit the hiring of ex-offenders in certain fields such as law, education, real estate, nursing, and medicine.

Substance Abuse

The substance use history and behaviors of an ex-offender can have important implications for his or her reentry experience, posing an additional hurdle to the already significant challenge to successful reentry. The link between substance use and criminal activity has been well documented (Lynch & Sabol, 2001). In a Bureau of Justice Statistics national survey (1997), three-fourths of state prisoners reported that they were under the influence of drugs or alcohol at the time they committed the offense that led to their imprisonment. Nevertheless, only about a third (36%) received treatment while incarcerated, despite research that shows treatment reduces drug use and criminal activity (Harrison, 2001).

In addition, many crimes are motivated by the need for money to purchase drugs (Yacoubian et al., 2002). Prior research suggests that a large proportion of released prisoners are at risk of re-offending due to both drug-induced behavior and the commission of economically motivated crimes linked to their drug use (Belenko, 2006). Furthermore, those who use illegal drugs risk arrest when they purchase and use those drugs. Substance use problems not only increase the chance of re-offending, but they may also hinder the returning prisoner's ability to complete job requirements and reestablish relations with family.

Physical and Mental Health

Prisoners nationwide suffer from mental disorders and chronic and infectious disease at rates greater than those among the general population (Williams, 2007; Visher et al., 2004). For example, in 1999, the overall rate of confirmed AIDS cases among the nation's prison population was five times higher than in the general U.S. population—0.60 percent versus 0.12 percent (Maruschak & Beck, 2001).

Rates of mental health disorders such as schizophrenia/psychosis, major depression, bipolar disorder, and post-traumatic stress disorder are estimated to be at least twice as high among prisoners than among the general population (Ditton, 1999). Prisoners also report a range of other physical and mental health problems, including learning or speech disabilities and hearing or vision problems (see Mallik-Kane & Visher, 2008; Maruschak, 2008; and Maruschak & Beck, 2001). While in prison, inmates may have access to preventive, standard, and emergency mental health services, but the chances that treatment will continue after release are often slim. Furthermore, Visher and colleagues (2004) asserted that accessing and paying for necessary prescription or over-the-counter drugs can be difficult for many released prisoners. Thus, mental and physical health issues present yet another reentry challenge for some released inmates, one that could significantly affect the ease of transition to life on the outside (see Baillargeon et al., 2010).

Family Support

Research suggests that both family history and current family relationships, which are aspects of social capital, can facilitate or inhibit a released prisoner's propensity to re-offend (Visher et al., 2004). Previous research has also tied a history of family emotional and physical abuse to increased risk of criminal activity (e.g., Sampson & Laub, 1993). Substance abuse is another risk factor associated with family dysfunction (Beck, 2000). Research also provides strong support for the idea that families that provide emotional and economic support for released prisoners contribute to the social control of such ex-offenders, helping to reduce the risk of re-offending (Sampson & Laub, 1993). Furthermore, some research suggests that prisoners who have meaningful contact with their families while imprisoned have more positive postprison adjustment experiences than those who do not (Hairston, 1998).

Contrary to the relatively extensive research findings on the role of family factors on criminal behavior described above, the effects of family relationships on postprison adjustment and on postrelease reintegration into the family and the larger community have not been well documented. Visher and colleagues concluded that "the role of family in the reentry process is perhaps more complex than previously understood, and poses important questions about the extent to which family histories, relationships, support, and expectations affect the experiences of released prisoners as they attempt to surmount the challenges of reentry" (2004: 103). While there has been research on the effects of in-prison contact on recidivism, in general it is not known how family relationships and support facilitate the reentry process (Visher et al., 2004). It also is not clear whether a difference in prisoners' expectations versus actual experiences pertaining to the quality and frequency of contact with family members has an effect on the reentry process. However, Visher et al. argue that "[t]he support of family members is likely to be an important component of the reintegration process of recently released prisoners" (2004: 104). Family can play a critical role in providing social capital, which can mean both tangible and intangible support.

Housing

Upon reentering the community, housing also is likely to present a substantial challenge to returning prisoners (Roman & Travis, 2004). One explanation for the difficulty in finding housing is that since prisoners may be cut off from their families due to their prior criminal involvement, relationships can become strained with family members and partners, causing household disruption (Richie, 2001). Another explanation is that many prisoners' families had to move to new housing that does not contain space for the newly released ex-offender. The housing problem for ex-offenders is compounded by a number of issues: the scarcity of community-based facilities, such as halfway houses or community reentry centers; formal and informal regulations and prejudices of federally subsidized and administered housing; and limited financial resources to secure housing in the private market.

Research has shown that ex-offenders have an increased risk of ending up in shelters or on the streets once they reenter society (Langan & Levin, 2002). Roman and Travis reported that "about a tenth of the population coming into prisons have recently been homeless, and at least the same percent of those who leave prisons end up homeless, for at least a while" (Roman & Travis, 2004: iv). Those with histories of mental illness and drug abuse are even more likely to be homeless (Rossman et al., 1999). Furthermore, research by Nelson, Dees, and Allen (1999) showed that those with temporary housing fared worse than those who had secured housing. When comparing those who reported living in temporary shelters upon release to those who were not, those in temporary housing abounded from parole supervision more often and had more difficulty resisting drugs and finding employment than those who reported they were not in a shelter. Furthermore, even if housing is secured upon reentry, ex-offenders may experience higher levels of residential mobility (e.g., frequent moves) than average citizens.

Both the needs of and obstacles facing the ex-offender are great. As shown, African Americans returning from prisons and jails need housing, mental/behavioral health, alcohol/substance abuse treatment, education, employment/training, and faith-based/spiritual and advocacy/legal services. These needs are not easy to meet, as ex-offenders face mountains of obstacles—from stigma to legal barriers to a deficit of capital (human, economic, social, and spiritual). African American ex-offenders must struggle to stay clean, reunite with their families, and lead productive lives.

The Future of Prisoner Reentry

There has been some progress on repealing some of the harsh drug laws that perpetuated the mass numbers of those incarcerated over the past few decades, as well as legislation to address the overall ineffectiveness and disparity in the criminal justice system (including the Fairness in Cocaine Sentencing Act, the Fairness Sentencing Act, the Second Chance Act of 2007, and the National Criminal Justice Commission Act of 2011). In addition, there are new practices and planning at the correctional level that is also gaining ground (see Carter et al., 2007). Lastly, the federal government also set up a reentry initiative in the U.S. Department of Justice Planning, and there are nonprofit organizations such as policy and advocacy groups that also work to support systemic change that will improve the process of reentry for millions of Americans (including the Reentry Policy Council, the Sentencing Commission, and the Sentencing Project).

Beverly D. Frazier

See also: Community-Based Crime and Reentry Theory; Faith-Based Prisoner Reentry

References

Baillargeon, J., S. K. Hoge, and J. V. Penn. "Addressing the Challenge of Community Reentry among Released Inmates with Serious Mental Illness." *American Journal of Community Psychology* 46, no. 1 (2010): 361–75. doi:10.1007/s10464-010-9345-6.

Beck, A. J. *Prisoners in 1999.* Washington, DC: U.S. Department of Justice, Bureau of Justice Statistics, 2000.

Belenko, S. "Assessing Released Inmates for Substance-Abuse-Related Service Needs." *Crime and Delinquency* 52, no. 1 (2006): 94–113. doi:10.1177/0011128705281755.

Blumstein, A., and A. J. Beck (1999). "Population Growth in U.S. Prisons, 1980–1996." In *Prisons,* vol. 26, edited by M. Tonry and J. Petersilia, 17–62. Chicago: University of Chicago Press.

Bushway, S. "The Stigma of Criminal History Record in the Labor Market." In *Building Violence: How America's Rush to Incarcerate Creates More Violence,* edited by J. P. May, 187–203. Thousand Oaks, CA: Sage, 2000.

Carter, M. M., S. Gibel, R. Giguere, and R. Stroker. *Increasing Public Safety through Successful Reentry: Evidence-Based and Emerging Practices in Corrections.* Silver Spring, MD: Center for Effective Public Policy, 2007.

Cnaan, R. A., J. Draine, B. Frazier, and J. W. Sinha. "Ex-Prisoners' Reentry: An Emerging Frontier and a Social Work Challenge." *Journal of Policy Practice* 7, no. 2–3 (2008): 178–98. doi:10.1080/15588740801938035.

Ditton, P. M. *Mental Health and Treatment of Inmates and Probationers.* Washington, DC: U.S. Department of Justice, Bureau of Justice Statistics, 1999.

Frazier, B. D. "Assessing Philadelphia's Community Capacity for Prisoner Reentry." PhD diss. University of Pennsylvania, Philadelphia, PA, 2007.

Glaze, L. E. *Correctional Populations in the United States, 2009* (NCJ 231681), 2010. http://bjs.ojp.usdoj.gov/index.cfm?ty=pbdetail &iid=2316.

Glaze, L. E., and L. M. Maruschak. *Parents in Prison and Their Minor Children* (NCJ 222984), 2010. http://bjs.ojp.usdoj.gov/index.cfm?ty =pbdetail &iid=823.

Gottfredson, M. R., and T. Hirschi. *A General Theory of Crime.* Palo Alto, CA: Stanford University Press, 1990.

Hairston, C. F. "The Forgotten Parent: Understanding the Forces That Influence Incarcerated Fathers' Relationships with Their Children." *Child Welfare* 77 (1998): 617–38.

Harrison, L. D. "The Revolving Prison Door for Drug-Involved Offenders: Challenges and Opportunities." *Crime and Delinquency* 47 (2001): 462–85.

Harrison, P. M., and A. J. Beck. *Prisoners in 2004.* Bureau of Justice Statistics Bulletin (NCJ 210677), October. Washington, DC: U.S. Department of Justice, 2005.

Holzer, H. J. *Employer Attitudes towards Hiring Ex-Offenders.* Washington, DC: The Urban Institute Press, 2000.

Langan, P., and L. Levin. *Recidivism of Prisoners Released in 1994.* Washington, DC: U.S. Department of Justice, Bureau of Justice Statistics, 2002.

Lattimore, P. K., S. Brumbaugh, C. Visher, C. Winterfield, M. Salas, and J. Zweig. *National Portrait of SVORI: Serious and Violent Reentry Initiative.* Washington, DC: The Urban Institute Press, 2004.

Logan, C. "Criminal Justice Performance Measures for Prisons." In *Performance Measure for the Criminal Justice System,* edited by J. J. Dilulio, Jr., 19–60. Washington, DC: U.S. Department of Justice, Bureau of Justice Statistics, 1993.

Lynch, J. P., and W. Sabol. *Prisoners Reentry in Perspective.* Washington, DC: The Urban Institute Press, 2001.

Mallik-Kane, K., and C. A. Visher. "Health and Prisoner Reentry: How Physical, Mental and Substance Abuse Conditions Shape the Process of Reintegration." The Urban Institute, 2008. http://www.urban.org/url.cfm?ID=411617.

Maruschak, L. M. *Medical Problems of Prisoners* (NCJ 221740). Washington, DC: U.S. Department of Justice, Bureau of Justice Statistics, 2008. http://bjs.ojp.usdoj.gov/index .cfm?ty=pbdetail&iid=1097.

Maruschak, L. M., and A. J. Beck. *Medical Problems of Inmates, 1997*. Washington, DC: U.S. Department of Justice, Bureau of Justice Statistics, 2001.

Mauer, M. *The Race to Incarcerate*. New York: The New Press, 2006.

Nelson, M., P. Dees, and C. Allen. *The First Month Out: Post-Incarceration Experiences in New York*. New York: The Vera Institute, 1999.

Pager, D. "The Mark of a Criminal Record." *American Journal of Sociology* 108, no. 5 (2003): 937–75. http://www.princeton.edu/~pager/pager_ajs.pdf.

Petersilia, J. *When Prisoners Come Home: Parole and Prisoner Reentry*. Cary, NC: Oxford University Press, 2003.

Petersilia, J. "When Prisoners Return to the Community: Political, Economic, and Social Consequences (Research in Brief)." *Sentencing and Corrections: Issues for the 21st Century,* November. Washington, DC: U.S. Department of Justice, National Institute of Justice, 2000.

Richie, B. E. "Challenges Incarcerated Women Face as They Return to Their Communities: Findings from Life History Interviews." *Crime & Delinquency* 36 (2001): 441–79.

Roman, C., and J. Travis. *Taking Stock: Housing, Homelessness, and Prisoner Reentry*. Washington, DC: The Urban Institute Press, 2004.

Rossman, S., C. G. Roman, J. Buck, and E. Morley. *Impact of the Opportunity to Succeed (OPTS) Aftercare Program for Substance Abusers*. Washington, DC: The Urban Institute Press, 1999.

Sabol, W. J., H. Couture, and P. M. Harrison. "Prisoners in 2006." *Bureau of Justice Statistics Bulletin,* December 2007. Washington, DC: U.S. Department of Justice.

Sampson, R. J., and J. H. Laub. *Crime in the Making: Pathways and Turning Points through Life*. Cambridge, MA: Harvard University Press, 1993.

Sentencing Project, The. *New Incarceration Figures: Thirty-Three Consecutive Years of Growth*. Washington, DC: The Sentencing Project, 2006. http://www.sentencingproject.org/pdfs/1044.pdf.

Shah, R. "Where Did They Come From? Where Did They Go?: Recycling and Characteristics of Ex-Offender Neighborhoods." Paper presented at the meeting of the American Society of Criminology, Los Angeles, CA, 2006.

Solomon, A., M. Waul, A. Van Ness, and J. Travis, eds. *Outside the Walls: A National Snapshot of Community-Based Prisoner Reentry Programs*. Washington, DC: The Urban Institute Press, 2005.

Taxman, F. *Brick Walls Facing Reentering Offenders*. Paper presented at the Reentry Roundtable, Prisoner Reentry and Community Policing: Strategies for Enhancing Public Safety, Washington, DC, May 12–13, 2004.

Travis, J., and S. Lawrence. *Beyond the Prison Gates: The State of Parole in America*. Washington, DC: The Urban Institute Press, 2002.

U.S. Department of Justice, Office of Justice Programs (U.S. DOJ). "Learn about Reentry." Washington, DC: U.S. Department of Justice, n.d. http://www.ojp.usdoj.gov/reentry/learn.html.

Visher, C., V. Kachnnowski, N. LaVigne, and J. Travis. *Baltimore Prisoners' Experiences Returning Home*. Washington, DC: The Urban Institute Press, 2004.

Western, B., J. Kling, and D. Weiman. "The Labor Market Consequences of Incarceration." *Crime & Delinquency* 47 (2001): 410–27.

Williams, N. H. "Prison Health and the Health of the Public: Ties That Bind." *Journal of Correctional Health Care* 13, no. 2 (2007): 80–92. doi:10.1177/1078345807301143.

Wilson, W. J. *The Truly Disadvantaged.* Chicago: University of Chicago Press, 1987.

Wilson, W. J. "Studying Inner-City Social Dislocations: The Challenge of Public Agenda Research." *American Sociological Review* 56 (1991): 1–14.

Yacoubian, G., M. Hsu, and E. D. Wish. *Estimating the Need for Substance Abuse Treatment in Maryland: An Update of Reuter et al. (1998).* College Park, MD: Center for Substance Abuse Research, 2002.

Web Sites

Reentry Policy Council: http://reentrypolicy.org/

Sentencing Commission: http://www.ussc.gov/

Sentencing Project: http://www.sentencingproject.org/Default.aspx

Urban Institute: http://www.urban.org/center/jpc/index.cfm

Prisoner Reentry Models: A Focus on Arkansas

The reentry of prisoners into society is the process of incarcerated individuals being released from the prison environment and their transition into the outside world to coexist with the mainstream population they existed in prior to being incarcerated. The importance of what is commonly referred to simply as either "prisoner reentry" or "community reentry" is that the success of the inmate in society upon release largely has to do with his or her understanding of and respect for making decisions that will reduce returning to prison (Seiter & Kadela, 2003). From a policy perspective, rehabilitative programs like reentry are important because they have been shown to help reduce recidivism among those released from prison, which in turn reduces incarceration costs paid through state budgets (Jacobson, 2005).

Empowering former inmates to exist in "free" society requires resources gained while incarcerated (Bellotti, 2005) supplemented by others that are provided upon release (Petersilia, 2001). In some prison systems, narrowly focused reentry programs exist that typically provide a one- or two-pronged approach to providing education, training, and/or services to the incarcerated with the intent of improving their chances of not returning (Rhine et al., 2006). Some examples of this narrow focus include providing motivational inspiration or education on how to obtain housing. Essentially, these narrower reentry programs are useful in that they concentrate the efforts of interested parties on the outside in ways that address the concrete needs of essentially all inmates who will eventually be released from confinement—the majority of inmates (Beck et al., 1993). These narrow, definitive foci produce measurable outcomes on the outside (for example, a place to live or legal employment) and allow programs to provide comprehensive reentry efforts to numerous prison facilities (Travis et al., 2003).

On the other side of this continuum, some reentry programs are more broadly focused, and provide multiple modules of curriculum in which instructors use seminars to provide one- to two-hour blocks of information covering multiple topics over the course of the program.

Essentially, over roughly an 8- to 12-week period, seminars using guest speakers considered specialists in their respective areas, and who provide a detailed synopsis about a particular area as well as present specific tools that inmates can use to apply the information within their lives (Bellotti, 2005). An example of this exists in Arkansas, where the two official reentry programs recognized by the State Department of Correction use the vice president of a local bank to explain financial literacy, and to instruct inmates regarding how to improve their financial situations in ways that make their transition back into society more favorable. Such a presenter is one of a slate of presenters covering personal topics such as choices, consequences, conflict resolution, journaling, organizing one's life, resume building, housing, and the criminal justice system. Such broader-focused reentry programs tend to use the same slate of presenters for each new class of inmates/students in order to provide uniformity and greater overall value (as assessed by the inmates) in relation to the overall rehabilitation programs offered by correctional institutions.

Importantly, reentry programs often function based on a relationship between those on the outside who provide needed services and inmate leadership councils, which are groups within prisons comprised typically of representatives of each section/barrack of that institution (Bouffard & Bergeron, 2006; 2007). It is important to note that by having this collaboration, inmate leadership councils demonstrate their belief in reentry value by using their budgets (comprised of fundraising projects) to help support reentry program participation, often in the form of snacks, school supplies, or even graduation certificates (Anonymous, 2008). The leadership council program members who work closely in these collaborations are often referred to as "mentors" by those in the reentry program and typically refresh their mentor numbers by looking to recruit reentry inmates/students who demonstrate significant growth during the program.

In terms of the future of reentry, support for them largely relies on two factors: advocacy by those associated with these programs, and the public view(s) on rehabilitation at any given time (Fehr, 2009). One important dimension with respect to this future will be the level of official support from departments of correction, which can help ensure that those incarcerated receive reentry support on both the inside and on the outside of confinement, with the aim being to reduce recidivism (*Arkansas 2020,* 2007).

The mass incarceration of African Americans over successive generations (Alexander, 2010) has meant the confinement and release of hundreds of thousands of individuals who return to communities that are underresourced and socioeconomically challenged. Rather than adopt a single one-size-fits-all approach, the state of Arkansas and other jurisdictions utilize both narrowly focused and broad-based reentry programs in their efforts to break the existing cycle of confinement, release, and reincarceration. The fact that these programs provide both essential life-skills training and address important socio-emotional cognitive issues increases the likelihood of their success. Those that use peer mentors increase the likelihood that these programs may be culturally competent, less isolating, and less likely to perpetuate discriminatory thinking and practices that can inhibit reentry success.

David Montague

See also: Community-Based Crime and Reentry Theory; Correctional System and African Americans; Faith-Based Prisoner Reentry; Healing Communities; Institutional Racism; Prisoner Reentry and African Americans; Prisons; Socioeconomic Factors

References

Alexander, M. *The New Jim Crow: Mass Incarceration in the Age of Colorblindness.* New York: The New Press, 2010.

Anonymous. "Statement of a Member-Mentor of the Inmate Leadership Council." *Community Reentry Board of Directors Meeting.* Pine Bluff Prison Unit, Pine Bluff, AR, April 7, 2008.

Arkansas 2020: The Changing Demographics and Challenges Facing Arkansas' State Government in 2020. Produced in 2006 for Senator Shane Broadway and the 85th General Assembly of the State of Arkansas. Faculty Coordinators: Ty Borders, PhD; David R. Montague, PhD; Gregory Russell, PhD, JD; Joe Schriver, PhD, LCSW; David Underwood, PhD; Ashvin Vibhakar, PhD. Other major contributors: Gregory Hamilton, PhD; Terre McLendon; Vaughan Wingfield; Martha Phillips, PhD, MPH, MBA; Willa Sanders, MPA, January 2007.

Beck, A., Gilliard, D., Greenfield, L., Harlow, C., Hester, T., Jankowski, L., Snell, T., Stephan, J., and Morton, D. *Survey of State Prison Inmates, 1991.* Washington, DC: U.S. Department of Justice, 1993.

Bellotti, M. "Life Skills Project." *Journal of Correctional Education* (June 2005): 115–23.

Bouffard, J. A., and L. E. Bergeron. "Reentry Works." *Journal of Offender Rehabilitation* 44, no. 2 (2007): 1–29.

Bouffard, J., and L. E. Bergeron. "Reentry Works: The Implementation and Effectiveness of a Serious and Violent Offender Reentry Initiative." *Journal of Offender Rehabilitation* 44, no. 2 (2006): 1–29.

Fehr, L. M. "Reentry Matters." *Corrections Today* (2009): 8, 13.

Jacobson, Michael. *Downsizing Prisons: How to Reduce Crime and End Mass Incarceration.* New York: New York University Press, 2005.

Petersilia, J. "When Prisoners Return to the Community: Political, Economic and Social Consequences." *Corrections Management Quarterly* 5, no. 3 (2001): 1–10.

Rhine, E., T. L. Mawhorr, and E. C. Parks. "Implementation: The Bane of Effective Correctional Programs." *Ohio Department of Rehabilitation and Corrections* 5, no. 2 (2006): 347–58.

Seiter, R., and K. R. Kadela. "Prisoner Reentry: What Works, What Does Not and What Is Promising." *Crime and Delinquency* 49, no. 3 (2003): 360–88.

Travis, J., E. M. Cincotta, and A. L. Solomon. *Families Left Behind: The Hidden Costs of Incarceration and Reentry.* A research project by the Urban Institute Justice Policy Center, October 2003.

Prisons

Prisons are simply defined as places of confinement where individuals are subjected to nearly total control (Jewkes & Johnston, 2006). The prison population is a figure that receives public attention. The estimated prison population in 2010 was approximately 1.4 million and it has consistently been at or near 2 million for 40 years (Pew, 2010). Black males are overrepresented in the prison population and are more likely than their White counterparts to be confined in high security settings (e.g., maximum security facilities or solitary confinement) (Foster, 2006). Prior research suggests that racial identity and socioeconomic status contribute to the likelihood of imprisonment (Christianson, 1998). The long-term relationship between poverty and criminality ties Blacks to American prisons. Currently, approximately half of the prison population in the United States is Black, although Blacks make up less than 13 percent of the general population.

American Prisons

The Simsbury Prison in Simsbury, Connecticut, was one of the earliest state prisons in America (Foster, 2006). However, the Walnut Street Jail is considered the first true American correctional institution. The Walnut Street facility was established in 1790 in Philadelphia, Pennsylvania. Walnut Street adopted some of the concepts of the charter of William Penn (1682) (Allen et al., 2007). William Penn, leader of the Quakers, introduced the idea of more humanitarian treatment for offenders in America, Italy, and England (Allen et al., 2007). Some of these humanitarian concepts were that all prisoners are bailable; those wrongfully imprisoned could recover double damages; prisons were free of fees for food; and lands and goods of felons were to be liable for confiscation in order to provide double restitution for injured parties (Foster, 2006). However, the application of humane treatment was not afforded to the underclass.

Penal goals began to emerge out of the Walnut Street Jail, such as punishment, reform, education, medical models of corrections, and reintegration. Nevertheless, scandals at the Walnut Street Jail drove the construction of radical new prisons. These included the Western State Penitentiary in Pittsburgh, which was based on a cellular design and isolation (Allen et al., 2007), followed by the Eastern State Penitentiary, which became the model of the "square" prison; its very first admitted inmate was African American. There was also New York's Auburn Prison. The Auburn system had an "inside" cell design and small size cells for sleeping only; a new style of discipline, the "congregate system," and solitary confinement for punishment; congregations that worked in shops during the day; separation of prisoners into small cells at night; silence at all times; and lockstep marching (Allen et al., 2007). Another new prison was Wethersford Prison in Connecticut. Comparatively, prisons were judged by production records and escapes, not their ability to rehabilitate. By the same token, discipline was an ongoing challenge.

Postslavery Prisons

Ex-slaves and their descendants began to become overrepresented in prison populations as the idea of a need for inmate reform emerged. The Reformatory Era, from 1870 to 1910, came after the cellular prison system, founded on international changes given the Maconochie and Crofton plans of Australia, a European prison colony whose original inhabitants were Black. In the United States, the first reformatory was built in 1876 in Elmira, New York. Elmira was a hybrid of the Auburn and the Pennsylvania systems, with reform at the forefront of its stated goals. The reform included modern physical attributes such as:

1. modern sanitary appliances;
2. prison uniforms;
3. a diet to promote vigor;
4. a gymnasium with baths and sport fields;
5. training facilities;
6. trade instruction based upon needs and capacities of individuals;

7. regimental military organizations (bands, etc.);
8. schools from kindergarten to college subjects;
9. a library;
10. weekly prison newspapers;
11. entertainment;
12. religious opportunities; and
13. emotional occasions. (Allen et al., 2007)

Reformatories became known for two significant features: indeterminate sentences and a "marks" grading system for early release (Foster, 2006). The reform movement also planted the seeds of education, vocational training, and rehabilitation for prisons. Currently the prison system in Elmira, and upstate New York generally, is the main employer for local Whites, while the inmates are primarily from seven neighborhoods in New York City, neighborhoods whose residents are predominantly Black and Latino.

From 1870 to 1900, Blacks became disproportionately represented among the prison population, seemingly overnight, according to some. The political climate of the time changed prisons again. Prisons replaced slavery as a social institution (Muhammad, 2010). In the post–Civil War era in the North and West, prisons were built based on the Auburn model. Improvements to the original design were limited to plumbing/running water, abandonment of the silent system, and the use of indeterminate sentencing. In the post–Civil War South, prisons had been wiped out by war (Allen et al., 2007). States tried to compensate by "leasing out" prisoners or by taking in contracts, thus establishing another group of slaves, the convict lessees, the only form of involuntary servitude still permitted under the U.S. Constitution after the war (Foster, 2006). Southern agrarian economies exploited cheap/free labor (Allen et al., 2007). Many prisoners had previously been plantation workers with little influence or resources. Southern prison farms were an outgrowth of the convict lease system (Foster, 2006). This was not a civilized time for treatment of Southern prisoners, specifically Blacks.

With the twentieth century, industrialized prisons emerged. By the end of Reconstruction, only 15 percent of prison populations were not Black in most Southern states (Carleton, 1971). The industrial prisons were based upon the extension of early "factory workshops" (Allen et al., 2007). The prison industries exploited free labor. Prison industries had to adhere to organized labor guidelines under two federal acts that lowered profits. The Hawes-Cooper Act required that prison products be subject to the laws of any state to which they were shipped. The Ashurst-Summers Act of 1935 stopped the interstate shipment of goods by requiring labeling of the prison-produced items and forbidding their interstate shipment in some cases. The social context of 1935 to 1960, during the "Great" Depression and approaching the Civil Rights Movement, caused prisons to lack the ability to provide meaningful work to prisoners. White incarceration rates decreased slightly while Black incarceration rates increased steadily (Hentig, 1973).

Only some transitions and new prison treatments that began after the 1960s remain in place today. By the mid twentieth century, the urban poor began to make up the bulk of the prison population, and Blacks were the face of the urban poor. The "War on Drugs" from 1980 to 1990 brought more Blacks into prison than Whites (Foster, 2006). Blacks and Hispanics are brought into prison for drug and violent crimes at a higher rate than Whites. The U.S. Bureau of Prisons (federal BOP) gradually emerged as the leader in corrections (Allen et al., 2007). The federal BOP introduced new concepts to prisons, such as diagnosis and classification, use of professionals such as psychiatrists and psychologists, more humane treatment, better living conditions, and a professional approach to corrections (Allen et al., 2007). However, it was the U.S. Supreme Court that became the primary agent for change within prisons. Inmates, through direct means—riots, peaceful demands of inmate councils, unions, ombudsmen, and correctional staff lawsuits—have been influential in internal prison reform (Allen et al., 2007).

Doshie Piper

See also: Correctional System and African Americans; Prisoner Reentry and African Americans; War on Drugs; Zebratown

References

Allen, H. E., C. E. Simonsen, and E. J. Latessa. *Corrections in America: An Introduction.* Upper Saddle River, NJ: Pearson Prentice Hall, 2007.

Carleton, M. T. *Politics and Punishment: The History of the Louisiana State Penal System.* Baton Rouge: Louisiana State University, 1971.

Christianson, S. *With Liberty for Some: 500 Years of Imprisonment in America.* Boston: Northeastern University, 1998.

Foster, B. *Corrections: The Fundamentals.* Upper Saddle River, NJ: Pearson Prentice Hall, 2006.

Hentig, H. *Punishment: Its Origin, Purpose and Psychology.* Montclair, NJ: Patterson Smith, 1973.

Jewkes, Y., and H. Johnston. *Prison Readings: A Critical Introduction to Prisons and Imprisonment.* Cullompton, UK: Willan, 2006.

Muhammad, K. G. *The Condemnation of Blackness: Race, Crime and the Making of Modern Urban America.* Cambridge, MA: Harvard University Press, 2010.

Pew Center on the States. *Prison Count 2010: State Population Declines for the First Time in 38 Years.* Washington, DC: Pew Center on the States, 2010. http://www.pewcenter onthestates.org/report_detail.aspx?id=57653.

Public Housing

The first major federal program providing subsidized housing was created in 1937 and reactivated in 1949. The primary focus of the legislation was the creation of jobs and stimulation of the construction industry, not the provision of affordable housing. Housing was an important collateral outcome. The original beneficiaries of the program were largely White working- and middle-class families who had faced economic hardship during the Depression, including widespread foreclosures on their home mortgages (Massey & Denton, 1993).

By 1995, the Department of Housing and Urban Development (HUD) reported that 48 percent of public housing was occupied by non-Hispanic Blacks, compared to 39 percent of non-Hispanic Whites (HUD, 1995). Years earlier, many Whites had escaped public housing through another federal program, the Federal Housing Administration or FHA loan program, which liberally granted low interest mortgages to Whites while "redlining" and denying similar loans to Blacks. As a result of racial restrictions on where they could live, racial restrictions on legitimate employment, and limited opportunities to receive mortgages, for low-income Black families, public housing became a residential mainstay, especially for those in the urban neighborhoods of the North (Massey & Denton, 1993; Hirsch, 1983).

The construction of government subsidized housing had been expanded under President Theodore Roosevelt's New Deal legislation at the same time that the practice of discriminatorily denying mortgage loans to Blacks meant that construction improvements did not occur in Black neighborhoods. As Whites moved out of public housing, low-income Blacks were given more access to it. Even among Blacks who had begun to command higher salaries, public housing became a preferable place to live when compared to racially segregated private slums (National Commission on Fair Housing and Equal Opportunity, 2008). The 1949 Housing Act required the demolition of slums, which caused the displacement and relocation of many poor Blacks into public housing. The mass migration of Blacks from the South to Northern cities between 1940 and 1970 also contributed significantly to the number of urban Black poor who needed to be housed (National Commission on Fair Housing and Equal Opportunity, 2008; Hirsch, 1983).

A substantial number of public housing developments were constructed as part of the Public Works Administration (PWA), whose workers also built other government buildings. The residential buildings came to be called "housing projects," later shortened to simply "the projects." Many of the buildings were built as high-rise apartment complexes capable of housing hundreds of people. As the residential population of the housing projects began to change, so too did the level of care and maintenance provided by the government to the buildings and grounds. Blacks began to form tenant councils in an effort to contest the changing conditions and attempt to force the government to address the fact that the once relatively comfortable public housing projects were falling into disrepair (Massey & Denton, 1993; National Commission on Fair Housing and Equal Opportunity, 2008).

The primary decline was during the 1950s and 1960s. Requests for better upkeep were largely met with government unresponsiveness and with the residents themselves being blamed for the poor conditions. During the 1970s and 1980s, amid declining opportunities for employment in the inner city and fewer obstacles in the private housing market, middle-class Blacks began to move away from public housing, as had their White counterparts. The effects of these shifts were devastating. The Chicago researcher and sociologist William Julius Wilson has noted that the concentration of Blacks in inner cities fostered the social ills of high unemployment, teen pregnancy, drug and alcohol abuse, high dropout rates, drug trafficking, broken families, and delinquency (Wilson, 1987, 2008; National Commission on Fair Housing and Equal Opportunity, 2008). Coupled with welfare policies that excluded males from living in households with women and children who were receiving benefits (Williams, 2004), public housing has been described as a primary part of the marginalization of Blacks from mainstream America and a significant contributor to inner-city Blacks' involvement in the criminal justice system (Wilson, 2008, 1987; Sampson & Wilson, 1995).

Public housing communities have had higher rates of violence than similar non-public housing. Public housing residents have been twice as likely as others to be victims of gun violence, and nearly one person was killed daily in the 1990s by gunfire in the United States' 100 largest public housing communities (HUD, 2000). High rates of domestic violence and the assault and harassment of females are also reported as prevalent in public housing complexes. Some attribute this to a harsh existence with substantial financial stress particularly experienced by the men (Renzetti, 2009; Williams, 2004) (see Inequality Theory). It is reported that domestic violence incidents among public housing residents appeared to worsen during the height of the crack cocaine epidemic in the 1980s (Dekeseredy et al., 2003, citing Bourgois & Dunlap, 1993; Maher, 1997; Miller, 1995) (see War on Drugs).

In 1980, President Ronald Reagan cut the funding for social programs in public housing substantially. According to Wilson (2008), the result for many Blacks left behind in public housing was gangs, drug trafficking, homelessness, failing schools, stressed families, and high rates of AIDS (Wilson, 2008). Estimates for the year 2000 place the number of people living in public housing at 2.6 million, a million of whom were children and over 300,000 of whom were senior citizens. In the absence of substantial social programming, crime-fighting efforts in public housing have relied heavily on law enforcement and security measures. But striking an appropriate balance between controlling crime and respecting the civil rights of public housing residents has proved difficult.

In 1988, the government attempted to utilize the Nation of Islam (NOI), an African American religious-based organization (see Nation of Islam), as a quasi-private security firm to patrol and staff public housing complexes in tough urban areas like Baltimore, Washington, D.C., Philadelphia, Chicago, and Los Angeles. The organization was reportedly awarded at least $20 million in government contracts for its security work in public housing during the 1990s and had notable success in reducing crime within the public housing projects of Washington, D.C. Complaints that the patrol officers were sometimes overly aggressive in some of the remaining cities or used the security detail as a means of recruiting new members led to the contracts not being renewed. Despite its success in Washington, D.C., NOI faced opposition by some members of Congress and the Anti-Defamation League, among others (Southern Poverty Law Center, 2012; Nation of Islam, n.d.).

Under President Clinton, in the 1990s there was some improvement in public housing life. In more recent times, the Housing Choice Voucher Program ("Section 8") has grown in popularity. This has been an effort to counter the negative effects of concentrated poverty of the traditional public housing high-rises by allowing poor families who are receiving a government rent subsidy to live in an apartment or privately owned home of their choice. Crime in public housing has also been tackled in recent decades by environmental design, moving away from high-rises to buildings with fewer floors where residents might feel a greater sense of responsibility for the property's upkeep.

In 1992, the HOPE VI program, an urban revitalization effort, began in response to recommendations by the Commission on Severely Distressed Public Housing. The program invested billions into public housing demolition and revitalization and the application procedure for public housing encouraged a mix of persons with varied incomes. Initial results indicate that diversity in these communities increased and crime levels decreased (Turner et al., 2008). However, African Americans remain the group with the highest rates of concentrated poverty in the United States (Wilson, 2008).

To combat public housing crime, the U.S. Department of Housing and Urban Development (HUD) has the authority to craft leases prohibiting the possession of a gun. The Housing Opportunity Program Extension Act of 1996 requires careful screening of housing applicants and the eviction of persons who engage in criminality including illicit drug activity. HUD also introduced a number of programs such as Operation Safe Home Initiative, a partnership with law enforcement to confiscate guns; the Grassroots Youth Intervention Demonstration to reduce juvenile drugs, gangs, and delinquency; and the Youth Violence Prevention Program, which discourages youth violence (HUD, 2000). Illinois enacted a Safe School Zone law with enhanced penalties for specific weapons violations within 1,000 feet of public housing.

HUD v. Rucker Impact

Department of Housing and Urban Development v. Rucker was a 2002 case that ruled that public housing authorities have the right to evict tenants and their household members and guests if they are involved in illegal drug activity. The Court went on to rule that such decisions are permissible even if the tenant has no knowledge or control over the criminal activity. Four plaintiffs were tried, with the case of one, Pearlie Rucker, resulting in a subsequent eviction. Rucker was 63 years old at the time, and had lived in the complex for nearly 20 years. The case was brought against Rucker after housing authorities had attempted to evict her upon finding Rucker's daughter in possession of cocaine several blocks away from the apartment. Despite the fact that Rucker was unaware of her daughter's criminal activity, the Court ruled against her, arguing that such evictions were not unconstitutional, as housing authorities were permitted to take whatever steps necessary in order to provide a safe, crime-free environment for law-abiding tenants (Fleming, 2005).

Though the decision was well intended, with hopes that it would decrease drug-related crimes in urban neighborhoods, the breadth of literature in reaction to this decision and its impact has been overwhelmingly negative. The broad scope of this decision has created an increased possibility of innocent tenants, who are considerably vulnerable to becoming associated with illegal activity in their high-crime neighborhoods, facing eviction from their homes. Prior to the ruling, district and state courts had struggled with the issue of whether knowledge of a tenant's third-party criminal activity was required in order to evict the tenant, with some courts ruling that knowledge was required. However, with the Supreme Court ruling in *HUD v. Rucker,* tenants who possessed no knowledge of the third party's actions were at risk of homelessness (Castle, 2003). Though it is apparent that the Court's hope in this ruling was that tenants would keep a watchful eye over their household members and guests so as not to violate the safety of law-abiding tenants, the ruling nonetheless places many innocent tenants in danger of sudden homelessness (Saghir, 2003).

On March 26, 2002, in the case of *HUD v. Rucker,* the U.S. Supreme Court ruled that public housing authorities are permitted to evict tenants when they, their household members, or their guests are involved in illegal drug activity. The Court agreed with the Washington Legal Foundation (WLF), which filed a brief in support of the housing authorities that such evictions are permissible even if the tenant has no knowledge of, or control over, the criminal activity. WLF argued that housing authorities should be permitted to take strong steps to rid public housing of the criminal element, or law-abiding tenants will continue to be denied a safe living environment (WLF, 2002). But the situation is not so simple. Each of the public housing residents challenging the federal eviction law in *HUD v. Rucker* were senior citizens who had lived in their apartments for many years and were not themselves involved with any illegal conduct. In one instance, the tenant was a disabled senior who was being evicted based on the behavior of a person who did not live at the apartment but had been hired to act as his caregiver.

Similarly, the organization Human Rights Watch has issued a report titled "No Second Chance: People with Criminal Records Denied Access to Public Housing." The 101-page report questions the humanity and soundness of a law that prevents people who need it most from getting affordable housing. The report features a quote from P. C., a 41-year-old African American mother who was denied public housing because of an arrest that did not result in a conviction and that had occurred four years prior to her application.

In New York City, residents who live in buildings run by the New York City Housing Authority (NYCHA) have filed a federal lawsuit against the city and the police department, claiming that their Fourth and Fourteenth Amendment rights are violated by aggressive stop-and-frisk procedures that harass innocent members of the public housing community, while the police claim that such stops are necessary to keep residents safe. In an unprecedented move, a supervising district attorney in the Bronx has refused to accept future trespassing complaints from police officers who patrol in that borough's NYCHA housing unless the officer is willing to submit to an in-person interview to verify the validity of the charge. The trial in *Davis et al. v. the City of New York* was set for October 2013, but has not yet occurred.

Dezarai Frank and Camille Gibson with Delores Jones-Brown

See also: Correctional System and African Americans; Inequality Theory; Institutional Racism; Nation of Islam; Slavery; War on Drugs

References

Bourgois, P., and E. Dunlap. "Exorcising Sex-for-Crack: An Ethnographic Perspective from Harlem." In *Crack Pipe as Pimp: An Ethnographic Investigation of Sex-for-Crack Exchanges,* edited by M. S. Ratner, 97–132. New York: Lexington Books, 1993.

Castle, Caroline. "You Call That a Strike? A Post-Rucker Examination of Eviction from Public Housing Due to Drug-Related Criminal Activity of a Third Party." *Georgia Law Review* 37 (2002–2003): 1435–70.

Davis et al. v. City of New York 10 Civ. 0699 (SDNY) (pending).

Dekeseredy, W. S., S. Alvi, M. D. Schwartz, and E. A. Tomaszewski. *Under Seige: Poverty and Crime in a Public Housing Community.* Lanham, MD: Lexington Books, 2003.

Fleming, Anne C. "Protecting the Innocent: The Future of Mentally Disabled Tenants in Federally Subsidized Housing after *HUD v. Rucker.*" *Harvard Civil Rights-Civil Liberties Law Review* 40 (2005): 197–222.

Hirsch, Arnold R. *Making the Second Ghetto: Race and Housing in Chicago, 1940–1960.* Chicago: University of Chicago Press, 1983.

HUD v. Rucker, 535 U.S. 125 (2002).

Maher, L. *Sexed Work: Gender, Race and Resistance in a Brooklyn Drug Market.* London: Oxford University Press, 1997.

Massey, Douglas S., and Nancy A. Denton. *American Apartheid, Segregation and the Making of the Underclass.* Cambridge, MA: Harvard University Press, 1993.

Miller, J. "Gender and Power on the Streets: Street Prostitution in the Era of Crack Cocaine." *Journal of Contemporary Ethnography* 23, no. 4 (1995): 427–52.

Nation of Islam. "Nation of Islam in America: A Nation of Beauty & Peace." Chicago: Nation of Islam, n.d. http://www.noi.org/noi-history/.

National Commission on Fair Housing and Equal Opportunity. "The Future of Fair Housing: Report of the National Commission on Fair Housing and Equal Opportunity. How We Got Here: The Historical Roots of Housing Segregation." Washington, DC: National Fair Housing Alliance, December 2008. http://www.civilrights.org/publications/reports/fairhousing/historical.html.

Renzetti, C. M. *In Brief: Economic Stress and Domestic Violence.* Harrisburg, PA: National Resource Center on Domestic Violence, 2009. http://new.vawnet.org/Assoc_Files_VAWnet/AR_EconomicStress.pdf.

Saghir, Peter. "Home Is Where the No-Fault Conviction Is: The Impact of the Drug War on Families in Public Housing." *Journal of Law and Policy* 12 (2003): 369–419.

Sampson, R. J., and W. J. Wilson. "Toward a Theory of Race, Crime, and Urban Inequality." In *Crime and Inequality,* edited by J. Hagan and R. Peterson, 37–56. Palo Alto, CA: Stanford University Press, 1995.

Southern Poverty Law Center. "Nation of Islam, 2012." http://www.splcenter.org/get-informed/intelligence-files/groups/nation-of-islam.

Turner, M. A., S. J. Popkin, and L. A. Rawlings. *Public Housing and the Legacy of Segregation.* Baltimore: Urban Institute Press, 2008.

U.S. Department of Housing and Urban Development (HUD). *In the Crossfire: The Impact of Gun Violence on Public Housing Communities.* Washington, DC: U.S. Department of Housing and Urban Development, 2000.

U.S. Department of Housing and Urban Development (HUD). *Family Data on Subsidized Housing.* Washington, DC: U.S. Department of Housing and Urban Development, 1995.

Washington Legal Foundation (WLF). *HUD vs. Rucker: Case Date: March 26, 2002; Project Name: Health Care Project.* Washington, DC: Washington Legal Foundation, 2002.

Williams, R. Y. *The Politics of Public Housing: Black Women's Struggles against Urban Inequality.* New York: Oxford University Press, 2004.

Wilson, W. J. "The Political and Economic Forces Shaping Concentrated Poverty." *Political Science Quarterly* 123 (2008): 555–71.

Wilson, W. J. *The Truly Disadvantaged: The Inner City, the Underclass and Public Policy.* Chicago: University of Chicago Press, 1987.

R

Racial Hoaxes and Media Representations

A hoax is an attempt to deceive or to cheat. A *racial hoax* is an attempt to deceive by using race as pretext for that deception (Russell, 1998). Two well-known racial hoax cases involved Charles Stuart (in 1989), a White lawyer from the suburbs of Boston who implicated a "black man" as the killer of his pregnant wife in October 1989, and Susan Smith (in 1994), a White woman from South Carolina who accused a "black man" of carjacking her vehicle with her two young sons in it and subsequently murdering them. In both cases the accusers were later found to be the killer.

While in most cases private individuals perpetrate racial hoaxes, the media is the most dominant contributor to racial hoaxes. Within American society, the media is a constant perpetuator of racial hoaxes, particularly those that portray African American males as the most likely offenders. Most news stories that deal with a negative situation involve a "black male," whether they are old or young, as a suspect (Robinson, 2000). This coverage is largely based on stereotypical views of minority individuals. These stereotypical views are often informed by economic class and historical portrayals of minorities (Eberhardt et al., 2004). Economically, minorities and women currently make up the majority of the lowest 20 percent of income earners, and thus are often at the mercy of the criminal justice system (Barak et al., 2010). Those individuals with larger incomes are often viewed by the media as "less dangerous" than those individuals with smaller incomes. As minorities often have smaller incomes, African American males are usually viewed as more dangerous and are quickly pointed to as the main suspects of crime (Robinson, 2000; Sampson & Wilson, 1995).

The perpetuation of racial hoaxes by the media is also dependent upon historical constructions of African Americans (Muhammad, 2010). Within America, minorities have often been used as scapegoats, and their status and role in society have been devalued as a result of White supremacy (Barak et al., 2010). Throughout history, there has existed the "demonization" of young African American men

(Russell, 1998), especially in regards to sexual assault (see Scottsboro Cases and Sex Crimes and Race). These views, which were largely developed after slavery, hold that African American men are animals and unable to control their urges, which lead them to prey upon others, especially White women. In past cases, such as the Scottsboro Boys (1931), the Martinsville Seven (1951), and more recently the Central Park Jogger case (1989), the media has held firmly to views of African American men as violent predators, and as such, has played a pivotal role in perpetuating racial hoaxes. Within all of these cases, the suspected offenders were African American men, who were depicted as violent and uncontrollable. In each case, it would later be discovered that these depictions were unfounded.

This media coverage perpetuates the view of young Black males as typical criminal offenders. Evidence suggests that such stereotypes, when supported by media images, are readily embraced by "White" America to rationalize and legitimize their fears associated with young Black males (Robinson, 2000; Reiman & Leighton, 2010). Racial hoaxes are the worst kind of coverage for young Black males because the very stereotype the real offender is hoping to take advantage of is the same stereotype people use to justify their racialized image of the "average criminal." Throughout American history, race has been a driving force for those in power to subject social subordinates to hardship; racial hoaxes are among the most recent mechanisms to be publicly recognized (Russell, 1998).

Many ethnic men will argue that society and the media characterize their racial group as troublesome. These men, particularly African Americans, believe that the media portrays them negatively. It is commonly assumed that White men are less likely to commit a crime because the media disproportionately depicts racial or ethnic minority men in crime incidents, especially incidents involving violent crime (Robinson, 2000). According to Walker, Spohn, and DeLone, "the majority of racial hoax cases were perpetrated by a white person charging an African American person, with a smaller number of African Americans charging whites in racial hoaxes" (2007: 63). Certain opinions and thoughts about racial status have been with American society for a very long time (Jones-Brown, 2007). The struggles that African American men had to endure in the past to gain respect and equality also affects the hoaxes that they face in today's society. From the beginning of slavery, African Americans in general were considered lesser and were not looked upon as good men in particular. It may be argued that the negative images imposed upon Black men during the slave period still play a role in society's view of the group today. Some posit that as the social majority, it is only natural for the White media and White people in general to put more blame on the minorities. According to Gabbidon and Greene, "some of these [crime] statistics probably reflect a bias against all of the minority races but especially against the Negro" (2009: 18) (see also Hacker, 1992; Jones-Brown, 2007).

While many African Americans complain about negative media images, others argue that the negative images are deserved based on their disproportionate offending. Walker, Spohn, and DeLone point out that "in 2003 the incarceration rate for African American males in state and federal prisons was 7.3 times the rate for whites" (2007: 1). The reporting of statistics like these suggests that the men themselves, through their criminal behavior, are at least partly responsible for creating these statistics and their negative reputation. Such a belief ignores the role of bias within the criminal justice system among those of different backgrounds who commit similar offenses (see Fair Sentencing Act of 2010), and the ways in which media construction of crime can create false impressions. For example, while the number of White arrests in any given year substantially outnumber the number of Black arrests (see Disproportionality and Crime), upon conviction, Blacks are substantially more likely to receive sentences of incarceration (Jones-Brown, 2000). Robinson (2000) points out that during time periods when homicides remained unchanged, news coverage of homicide increased by 721 percent, creating a false impression that homicide was on the rise. Other sources have noted that Black males are overrepresented as perpetrators in media coverage of homicide (and other violent crime), when annually the raw number of Whites and Blacks arrested for homicide are very close. In 2010, for example, nationally, the numbers were 4,000 Whites arrested for homicide versus 4,149 Blacks arrested (BJS, 2011). Rather than focus on these small differences in raw numbers, Americans are encouraged to compare these raw numbers to the proportion of the general population that each group represents. As only 13 percent of the population, Blacks can be made to appear more dangerous in comparison to their White counterparts, who make up nearly 80 percent of the population. It is these proportional comparisons that allow some commentators to suggest that Blacks, and Black males in particular, bring their bad reputations on themselves.

There have been racial hoaxes where non-Whites have implicated Whites as the perpetrator of a horrendous crime, thereby inciting racial tensions and increasing racial polarization. Tawana Brawley in New York (1987) and Crystal Gail Mangum, who is infamous for the Duke lacrosse players' rape case in North Carolina (2006), are two cases that tested the boundaries of racial hoaxes (Kosse, 2007). In both instances the African American "victims" were subsequently found to have made up their stories, falsely identifying White males as the perpetrators.

Anyone who watches any type of media, whether news, films, sitcoms, and so on, will observe that members of ethnic and visible minority groups are represented with stereotypes in mind. The portrayals of minorities, for example, are often stereotypical and demeaning, allowing stereotypical views of one or some of a group to apply to everyone: "Stereotypes build on the dynamics of categorizing people, but they have the property of being fixed and largely negative generalizations about a group of people" (Barak et al., 2010: 100). These stereotypes can perpetuate themselves through multiple sources, whether media outlets, friends, family members, coworkers, and/or personal experiences with individual members of the groups, and through media portrayals can become the mainstream view of how a particular racial group behaves.

The tendency toward racial/ethnic stereotyping is particularly problematic in a historically multicultural country such as the United States. The media plays a major role in creating and sustaining perceptions of different racial groups, and in particular with negative news coverage when discussing them (Robinson, 2000). These stereotypes become the basis for determining what is newsworthy, and hence the types of stories that will receive coverage. For example, since there is a stigma attached to African Americans that relates them to violence, drugs, gang affiliation, and crime, the media then uses these stereotypes in deciding what they will show viewers. In this way, the media not only gives into the stereotypes of many racial hoaxes, but also continually reinforces the stereotypes by emphasizing one story over another and by creating an environment that reinforces racial stigmas. The relationship between media portrayals and racial hoaxes is a key factor in making these false accusations believable.

For a more in-depth understanding of the impact of racial hoaxes, read the transcript or listen to the interview of Katheryn Russell-Brown discussing the topic on National Public Radio (NPR), or view *Ethnic Notions,* Marlon Riggs' Emmy Award–winning documentary (1987) that takes viewers on a disturbing voyage through American history, tracing the deep-rooted stereotypes that have fueled anti-Black prejudice. Through these images one can begin to understand the evolution of racial consciousness in America.

Francis M. Williams

See also: Critical Race Theory; Eyewitness Misidentification; False Confessions; Lynching; Racial Profiling; Racial Stereotyping and Wrongful Convictions; Sex Crimes and Race; Structural Racism and Violence; Wrongful Convictions

References

Alexander, M. *The New Jim Crow: Mass Incarceration in the Age of Colorblindness.* New York: The New Press, 2010.

Barak, G., P. Leighton, and J. Flavin. *Class, Race, Gender, and Crime: The Social Realities of Justice in America.* 3rd ed. Lanham, MD: Rowman & Littlefield, 2010.

Bureau of Justice Statistics (BJS). *Sourcebook of Criminal Justice Statistics Online,* 2011.

Eberhardt, J., P. Goff, V. Purdie, and G. Davies. "Seeing Black: Race, Crime and Visual Processing." *Journal of Personality and Social Psychology* 87, no. 6 (2004): 876–93.

Gabbidon, S. L., and H. T. Greene. *Race and Crime.* 2nd ed. Thousand Oaks, CA: Sage, 2009.

Hacker, A. *Two Nations, Black and White, Separate, Hostile, Unequal.* New York: Ballantine Books, 1992.

Jones-Brown, D. "Forever the Symbolic Assailant: The More Things Change the More They Remain the Same." *Criminology and Public Policy* 6, no. 1 (2007): 103–21.

Jones-Brown, D. *Race, Crime and Punishment.* Philadelphia: Chelsea House, 2000.

Kosse, S. H. "Race, Riches & Reporters: Do Race and Class Impact Media Rape Narratives? An Analysis of the Duke Lacrosse Case." *Southern Illinois University Law Journal* 31 (2007): 243–79.

Martin, M. "Racial Hoaxes: Black Men and Imaginary Crimes" [Audio podcast]. *NPR News: Tell Me More.* June 8, 2009. www.npr.org/template/story/story.php?storyId=105096024.

Muhammad, K. G. *The Condemnation of Blackness: Race, Crime and the Making of Modern Urban America.* Cambridge, MA: Harvard University Press, 2010.

Reiman, J., and P. Leighton. *The Rich Get Richer and the Poor Get Prison: Ideology, Class, and Criminal Justice.* 9th ed. Boston: Allyn & Bacon, 2010.

Riggs, M., director. *Ethnic Notions,* documentary film. California Newsreel, 1987.

Robinson, M. "The Construction and Reinforcement of Myths of Race and Crime." *Journal of Contemporary Criminal Justice* 16, no. 2 (2000): 133–56.

Russell, K. *The Color of Crime: Racial Hoaxes, White Fear, Black Protectionism, Police Harassment, and Other Macroaggressions.* New York: New York University Press, 1998.

Sampson, R., and W. J. Wilson. "Toward a Theory of Race, Crime and Urban Inequality." In *Crime and Inequality,* edited by J. Hagan and R. Peterson, 37–54. Palo Alto, CA: Stanford University Press, 1995.

Walker, S., C. Spohn, and M. DeLone. *The Color of Justice; Race, Ethnicity, and Crime in America.* 4th ed. Belmont, CA: Thomson/Wadsworth, 2007.

Racial Profiling

Racial profiling occurs when law enforcement officials exercise their discretion to seize and/or search someone based on his or her race. Discretion is the power to make a choice. The equal protection clause of the Fourteenth Amendment to the U.S. Constitution prohibits government officials from making choices that treat individuals from one group differently than individuals from other groups. In other words, with few exceptions, discretion is proper only when it is exercised in a race-neutral way.

The legal standards allowing the police to search or seize individuals are contained in the words of the Fourth Amendment to the Constitution. The amendment states:

> The right of the people to be secure in their persons, houses, papers, and effects, against unreasonable searches and seizures, shall not be violated, and no Warrants shall issue, but upon probable cause, supported by Oath or affirmation, and particularly describing the place to be searched, and the persons or things to be seized.

The last phrase in the Fourth Amendment, often referred to as the "particularity requirement," is violated when police officers use race as a basis for searching or seizing an individual because of a generalized belief about the criminal propensities of the racial (or ethnic) group to which that person belongs.

The racial profiling policy utilized by the New York City Police Department (NYPD), one of the world's largest local law enforcement agencies, prohibits the use of "race, color, ethnicity or national origin as *the* determinative factor for initiating police action." Like many such written policies, the definition leaves wide latitude for officers to use race or the other personal characteristics listed in the policy as a determinative factor in deciding whether or not to stop and investigate a pedestrian or motorist for potential involvement in crime.

In fact, while being praised for its role in maintaining record low levels of crime in a city of more than 8 million people, the NYPD has simultaneously been criticized for illegally infringing on the privacy and liberty rights of millions of racial and ethnic minorities. Commissioned reports, departmental statistics, and multiple lawsuits revealed huge racial disparities in who was stopped, questioned, and sometimes frisked or searched as part of discretionary police procedures. Nearly 90 percent of the stops involved Blacks or Latinos, and nearly 90 percent of the stops did not result in detection of crime (see *Floyd v. City of New York; Ligon et al. v. City of New York*).

The frequency with which racial and ethnic minorities were stopped when no crime was discovered led to a groundswell of complaints that the police were unconstitutionally using race or ethnicity to decide who was suspicious and criminal. Such complaints have existed for nearly as long as there have been formal police agencies, and statistics consistently confirm that Blacks receive a disproportionate share of police attention, whether they are involved in criminal activity or not.

There has been a great deal of academic and political debate as to whether the racial disproportionality in police contact is indicative of intentional racial bias and discrimination on the part of the police or simply reflects differential offending by different racial groups. In New York City, for example, while Blacks made up 23 percent of the general population, they made up more than 50 percent of those who were stopped for suspicion of crime. This is contrasted with Whites, who made up 33 percent of the city's population but roughly 9 percent of those who were stopped. It has been claimed that the racial disproportion in stopping Blacks is justified based on statistics related to violent crimes, but no charges were filed in roughly 88 percent of the stops and there was a high dismissal rate for legal insufficiency among the charges that were filed (NYSOAG, 2013).

Claims that the racial disparity in stops was due to suspect descriptions given by victims—that is, that the majority of all suspects were described as male and Black or Latino—were confronted with statistical evidence that police officers said they were using a description in only 15 to 16 percent of stops. This meant that roughly 85 percent of the time the officers were acting on their own discretion in deciding who looked suspicious. Claims that the racial disproportion in stops could be explained by Blacks' involvement in violent crimes were confronted with statistical evidence that the number of Blacks stopped was 15 times greater than the number of Black suspects for a combination of six violent crimes (robbery, felony assault, gun possession, shootings, rape, and homicide).

In response to claims that these statistics were indicative of racial profiling, the department pointed out that its officers are the most diverse in the country, suggesting that minority officers cannot engage in racial profiling. But social psychological research has confirmed that racial biases exist at the unconscious level as well as the conscious and that Blacks are frequently associated with crime in the minds of people in general. This stereotyped belief about Blacks as criminals sometimes results in the racial profiling of Whites when they associate with Blacks. For example, Whites who are observed by police in urban predominantly Black poor neighborhoods are presumed to be there to buy drugs. Criminal stereotypes affect other racial and ethnic groups as well, with Black, Latino, and Asian youth, for example, all being suspected of being prone to gang membership.

The criminal stereotyping of Blacks can be traced back to the introduction of African slavery (see Slavery) and postemancipation fearmongering (see Lynching, Institutional Racism, and Structural Racism and Violence). But after many years of denial by law enforcement agencies, racial profiling in the United States garnered the most attention during the 1990s. In a lawsuit against the Maryland State Police brought by an African American lawyer, a 1992 internal memorandum was found stating in reference to drug crimes that "[t]he dealers and couriers are predominantly black males and black females." There was no evidence supporting the claim, but statistics revealed that Blacks were being stopped and their vehicles searched at a rate that was four times that of Whites, with only an 11 percent difference in finding something illegal in the cars of Blacks as opposed to the cars of Whites (*Wilkins v. Maryland State Police, et al.*). In 1999, the highest-ranking official in the New Jersey State Police made the following statement, reported in *The Newark Star Ledger*: "Today with this drug problem, the drug problem is cocaine or marijuana. It is most likely a minority group that's involved with that." He later resigned.

These statements by high-ranking police officials coupled with high-profile police shootings (see Diallo, Amadou, and the box titled "New Jersey Turnpike Shooting (1998): Troopers Admit Racial Profiling" in 100 Blacks in Law Enforcement Who Care) led to concentrated efforts to investigate and respond to complaints of racial profiling by federal, state, and local police. Racial disparities in arrests for drug crimes also raised questions about the fairness of policing, even among the guilty (see War on Drugs). Both the New York and New Jersey attorney generals published reports noting that there was substantial evidence of racial profiling, especially against Blacks. Cities large and small were successfully sued for racial profiling, mostly related to vehicle stops. Law professor David Harris wrote about the phenomenon of "driving while Black" (DWB), and in an unprecedented decision, *State v. Soto,* a New Jersey Superior Court judge dismissed many drug cases that stemmed from highway stops of African American and Latino motorists after determining that the drivers had been the victims of racial profiling. Even Black and Latino police personnel sued, both for having been instructed to engage in racial profiling and for being discriminated against within the department. Ultimately, New Jersey became the first state to make racial profiling by law enforcement officers a felony offense. Nationally, similar racial profiling claims were raised in the states of California, Colorado, Florida, Illinois, Michigan, Indiana, Maryland, Massachusetts, Pennsylvania, Oklahoma, Ohio, Rhode Island, and Texas.

At the federal level, Janet Reno, the attorney general under President Bill Clinton, vowed to address issues of police racial bias and brutality in 1999. Congressman John Conyers (see Conyers, Jr., John) introduced legislation requiring that policing agencies collect statistics regarding the racial identities of motorists and officers involved in traffic stops and the disposition of stop cases. By 2009, only four states (North Dakota, Mississippi, Vermont, and Hawaii) plus Puerto Rico were reported to not be collecting these data in some form.

On February 27, 2001, President George W. Bush commented to Congress, "Racial profiling is wrong and we will end it in America." However, the terrorist attacks of September 11 of that same year seemed to slow the movement for ending racial profiling, as many Middle Eastern and South Asian individuals began to be rounded up and detained indefinitely on suspicion of being connected to terrorist cells. The USA Patriot Act was rushed through Congress, giving the government wide latitude in determining who could be suspected of being a terrorist and how such people could be treated. By 2009, less than half of all states (22) were reported to have adopted a law prohibiting the racial profiling of either motorists or pedestrians, and some of the existing laws were being reconsidered.

Even though NYPD statistics indicate that overwhelmingly the Blacks who are stopped under its stop-and-frisk policy are not guilty of crimes, in 2013, then New York City mayor Michael Bloomberg and then police commissioner Raymond Kelly made many media statements indicating that "Blacks are under-stopped" because the percentage of stops that involve Blacks is not equal to the percentage of criminal suspects who are reported as Black. This reporting of group statistics instead of individual numbers can be seen as classic racial profiling. For example, in 2012, Blacks as a group were identified as 66 percent of violent crime suspects and 54.8 percent of stops, hence the claim of being under-stopped (see Disproportionality and Crime). Counting each suspect as an individual, the number of individual stops in which a Black person was suspected of a crime exceeds the number of violent crime incidents in which a Black person was suspected of a crime by nearly 270,000. In the same year, only just over 50,000 White individuals were stopped.

According to some legal scholars, even if they are not overtly racist, police officers may have a difficult time deciding whether their consideration of race in "initiating police action" is legal or illegal; or, if overtly racist, they may find it easier to act on that racism, because of several U.S. Supreme Court decisions. First, in his dissenting opinion in *Terry v. Ohio,* the landmark decision that created the national authority for police to conduct searches and seizures based on "reasonable suspicion," a lower legal standard than the probable cause stated in the Fourth Amendment, Justice William O. Douglas warned that the ruling would allow the police to make decisions that could be influenced by the personal biases of individual officers. In *Whren v. U.S.,* a 1996 case where the suspects claimed that they were racially profiled, the Court has been accused of allowing the police to search for drugs or other contraband by making traffic stops. These so-called pretext stops had previously been ruled unconstitutional by lower appellate courts. In *Illinois v. Wardlow,* the Court ruled that the police could use the fact that the defendant ran when the police came into his neighborhood as evidence of his involvement in crime. In a series of cases, the Court has also ruled that one's presence in a high-crime or high-drug area and/or appearing racially "out of place" may be valid reasons to make a stop (see *California v. Hodari,* 1991; *U.S. v. Broadie,* 2006). By accepting police references to various neighborhoods as "high crime" or "high drug" as a basis for suspicion to make a stop, rulings by the federal courts indirectly suggest that innocent Blacks who live in these economically distressed areas have a reduced level of constitutional protection.

Though heralded for their crime reduction accomplishments for 10 years, in February and August 2013 a federal judge, Shira Scheindlin, ruled that the stop-and-frisk practices of the NYPD amounted to unconstitutional racial profiling in that they targeted innocent Blacks and Latinos, especially males, for police action. Following the decision, over the objection of the mayor and police commissioner, the New York City Council voted to pass two new laws—one to appoint an inspector general to oversee the practices of the police department and one that allows civilians to sue the police department if they believe they have been unfairly and illegally targeted. Prior to the ruling, many cities had considered adopting similar stop-and-frisk practices to address their crime problems. Though the ruling was appealed and faces future legal challenges, it reinforced the notion that the constitutional rights of African Americans and other identifiable groups cannot be taken away, even in the interest of public safety, and that by law, policing agencies have an obligation to exercise their discretionary powers in ways that are consistent with human rights and constitutional standards of equal protection and Fourth Amendment law.

Delores Jones-Brown with Michael Thompson

See also: Adams, The Honorable Eric L.; American Law and African Americans; Black Panther Party; Civil Rights Movement; Conyers, Jr., John; Disproportionality and Crime; Institutional Racism; Lynching; Slavery; Structural Racism and Violence; War on Drugs

References

Alschuler, A. W. "Racial Profiling and the Constitution." *University of Chicago Legal Forum* (2002): 163–269.

Ashar, S. "Immigration Enforcement and Subordination: The Consequences of Racial Profiling after September 11." *Connecticut Law Review* 34 (2002): 1185–1200. http://ssrn.com/abstract=925719.

California v. Hodari, 499 U.S. 621 (1991).

Eberhardt, J., V. Purdie, P. Goff, and P. Davies. "Seeing Black: Race, Crime and Visual Processing." *Journal of Personality and Social Psychology* 87 (2004): 876–93.

Fagan, J., and G. Davies. "Street Stops and Broken Windows: *Terry,* Race and Disorder in New York City." *Fordham Urban Law Journal* 28 (2002): 457–504.

Farmer, J., Jr., and P. Zoubek. *Final Report of the State Police Review Team.* Trenton, NJ: Office of the Attorney General, 1999.

Floyd v. City of New York, 08 Civ. 01034 (SDNY)(2013).

Gabbidon, S., and H. Taylor Greene. *Race and Crime.* Thousand Oaks, CA: Sage, 2005.

Glover, K. *Racial Profiling: Research, Racism, and Resistance.* Lanham, MD: Rowman and Littlefield, 2009.

Harris, D. A. *Driving while Black: Racial Profiling on Our Nation's Highways.* American Civil Liberties Union Special Report, 1999. http://www.aclu.org/racialjustice/racialprofiling/15912pub19990607.html.

Illinois v. Wardlow, 528 U.S. 119 (2000).

Jones-Brown, D. "Forever the Symbolic Assailant: The More Things Change, the More They Remain the Same." *Criminology and Public Policy* 6 (2007): 103–22.

Jones-Brown, D. "Debunking the Myth of Officer Friendly: How Male African Americans Experience Community Policing." *Journal of Contemporary Criminal Justice* 16 (2000): 209–29.

Jones-Brown, D., and B. Maule. "Racially Biased Policing: A Review of the Judicial and Legislative Literature." In *Race, Ethnicity and Policing: New and Essential Readings,* edited by S. Rice and M. White, 140–73. New York: New York University Press, 2010.

Jones-Brown, D., B. Stoudt, B. Johnston, and K. Moran. *Stop and Frisk Policing Practices in New York City (Revised).* New York: Center on Race, Crime and Justice, John Jay College, 2013. www.stopandfriskinfo.org.

Ligon et al. v. City of New York 12 Civ. 2274 (SDNY)(2013).

New York State Office of the Attorney General (NYSOAG). "A Report on the Arrests Arising from the New York City Police Department's Stop-and-Frisk Practices." Albany, NY: Civil Rights Bureau, November 2013.

New York State Office of the Attorney General (NYSOAG). *New York State Attorney General's Report: The New York City Police Department's Stop and Frisk Practices: A Report to the People of the State of New York from the Office of the Attorney General.* Albany, NY: Civil Rights Bureau, December 1, 1999. http://www.ag.ny.gov/bureaus/civil _rights/pdfs/stp_frsk.pdf.

Ridgeway, G. *Analysis of Racial Disparities in the New York Police Department's Stop, Question, and Frisk Practices.* Santa Monica, CA: RAND Corporation, 2007.

State v. Soto, 324 N.J. Super 66 (1996).

Terry v. Ohio, 392 U.S. 1 (1968).

U.S. v. Broadie, 452 F.3rd 875 (2006).

Whren v. United States, 517 U.S. 806 (1996).

Wilkins v. Maryland State Police et al. Civil Action No. CCB-93-468 (1993).

Racial Stereotyping and Wrongful Convictions

Wrongful conviction is closely associated with racial stereotypes and discrimination, eyewitness misidentification, and other criminal justice system problems such as investigative and prosecutorial errors and misconduct. The Innocence Project, a nonprofit legal clinic that works to overturn wrongful convictions, found that approximately 60 percent of the cases it handles involve African Americans. While it is impossible to know for certain how many incarcerated individuals are wrongly convicted, based on the results from a variety of studies, the Innocence Project has estimated that between 2.3 and 5 percent of the nation's 2.3 million incarcerated persons are innocent, which amounts to well over 40,000 people. National statistics indicate that African Americans have borne the brunt of the high incarceration rate in the United States (Pager, 2007; Mauer, 1990). This is especially true of young African American men with little education (Western & Pettit, 2010). Undereducated defendants are overrepresented among the wrongly convicted. The overrepresentation of African Americans within the prison system reinforces perceptions of them as criminal and dangerous (Eberhardt et al., 2004; 2006).

Current research has found that African Americans are rated by others as the racial group most prone to violence (Pager, 2007; Quillian & Pager, 2010), and that stereotypes influence people's perceptions about the level of crime within neighborhoods. Specifically, neighborhoods with higher numbers of young African American men are frequently perceived as having higher levels of crime (Quillian

& Pager, 2001). Taslitz goes so far as to state that not only are African American suspects more likely to be considered guilty of specific crimes, there is also a general perception that "black character is paradigmatically criminal and deceptive" (2009: 1092). Such racial stereotypes have been found to factor into police decisions to arrest suspects; prosecutors' decisions to charge defendants; jurors' decisions to convict; probation officers' sentencing recommendations; and judges' decisions about sentence type and length (Western & Pettit, 2010).

While some bias is overt, unconscious racial bias plays an important role in wrongful convictions. Racial stereotypes are unconscious processes that can translate into a lack of awareness and intention on the part of the person experiencing them (Graham & Lowery, 2004; Taslitz, 2006). Taslitz (2009) offers five effects that raise the risk of wrongful conviction for African Americans:

1. the "selection effect," also known as racial profiling, refers to police attention tending to be drawn to African American suspects over White suspects;
2. the "blinders effect," or "tunnel vision," refers to police focusing in on African American suspects to the point they do not see other evidence or consider alternative crime theories or suspects;
3. the "ratchet effect" refers to the increased focus on African American suspects by fostering a belief in "black criminality," resulting in increases in crime by African Americans that exacerbate racial stereotypes;
4. the "procedural justice effect" addresses the fact that harsh treatment of African Americans translates into lack of African American trust in police and can reduce needed cooperation between police and the community. More African American crime brings more arrests and a system that reinforces itself. The lack of acceptance of police legitimacy reduces the effectiveness of policing when public safety officials are not monitored in their behavior towards specific populations; and
5. the "bystander effect" refers to the effects of racial profiling, where a rise in crime means that more African Americans are arrested, and where law-abiding citizens are left in poor and disorganized surroundings at greater risk of victimization (see Harrell, 2007; O'Flaherty & Sethi, 2010).

The net effect of these various risks is that more African Americans enter the criminal justice system, which increases the likelihood of wrongful convictions.

Eyewitness misidentification is the most common reason for wrongful conviction (Gross et al., 2005; Warden, 2001). Research shows that people of the same racial group are more likely to remember faces within their racial group than faces of individuals from other racial groups. Interestingly, reduction in facial recognition can be more tied to facial features than to actual skin color (Bar-Haim et al., 2009). In their review of wrongful convictions in the United States from 1989 through 2003, Gross and colleagues (2005) found that in 64 percent of cases at least one person misidentified the defendant. The rate of misidentification of at

Earl Washington, Jr.

An official declaration of innocence was a hard-won battle for Earl Washington, Jr. Convicted of rape and murder, Earl Washington was incarcerated for 17 years in Virginia, with nine of those years spent on death row (Burke, 2006; Glod, 2007). Washington, a mentally retarded African American farm worker with an IQ of 69, was found guilty of raping and murdering a 19-year-old mother of two in her apartment in 1982. The conviction was based upon a coerced confession.

Gross et al. (2005) found that 15 percent of defendants falsely confess to crimes. The majority of false confessions are due to intense police interrogation practices that emphasize obtaining a conviction of a specific suspect rather than seeking the truth. The belief that a suspect is guilty precludes police investigators from looking objectively at the evidence and seeking alternative suspects and theories. In Washington's case, a federal jury ruled that a police investigator fabricated some of the testimony in order to achieve a conviction (Glod, 2007; Gould, 2008). Considered by those who knew him well as easily led and anxious to please, Washington confessed to the murder with statements that were clearly false. He said the victim was White when she was African American; that he kicked in the door to her apartment when no damage to the door was found; and that he stabbed her 2 to 3 times, when in fact she had been stabbed 38 times (Justice Project, n.d.). It was through DNA testing that Washington's innocence was proven, and he was exonerated in 2001. In the Washington case, the following questions have been asked: What was the contribution of race? Did the stereotype of the Black male rapist come into play? What was the contribution of mental retardation? Did each factor come together to increase the opportunity for wrongful conviction? (See also False Confessions.)

least one witness was almost 90 percent for rape cases and 50 percent for homicides. Gross et al. (2005) explain that the large difference in cases of misidentification rests upon police investigations. In a rape case where there is no murder, the actual victim may be able to identify the perpetrator. A murder often leaves no eyewitness and compels police to work at obtaining other kinds of evidence on their own where racial biases about "most likely suspects" may come into play.

By some accounts, beginning in the 1980s specifically, the war on drugs contributed heavily to the high rate of African American incarceration (Roberts, 2004). African American drug arrests increased from 25 percent of drug arrests in 1980 to 37 percent of drug arrests in 1995 (Mauer, 1999). Importantly, drug arrests have to do with selective law enforcement and have been associated with the type of drug, especially crack cocaine (Free, 2004). It has long been a scourge of the criminal justice system that longer sentences have been given to those using crack cocaine, thought to be used mostly by racial minorities living in poverty (Mauer, 1990). Research by the Federal Sentencing Commission has exposed this belief to be a myth. Nonetheless, police stereotypes about crack cocaine use have focused enforcement efforts on minority, poor urban neighborhoods. Pressures on police to make arrests have increased their use of informants. These combinations have resulted in wrongful convictions and unnecessary deaths. For example, both the Philadelphia and Los Angeles Police Departments have been investigated for corruption in the form of planting drugs on civilians in minority, poor urban areas, and innocent elderly civilians have been killed during inaccurate drug raids in New York, Atlanta, and other locations.

Racial discrimination and wrongful conviction are also a reality in death penalty cases. A key research finding in such cases has been that it is the race of the victim that is more important than the race of the perpetrator in determining whether the death penalty is sought in murder cases. In their classic study of death sentences, Baldus, Pulaski, and Woodworth (the Baldus Study, published in 1983) found defendants accused of killing White victims were 4.3 times more likely to receive a death sentence than defendants who killed African American victims. Overall, African Americans were 1.7 times more likely to be given a death sentence than White defendants. The Baldus Study findings were submitted to the U.S. Supreme Court in the case of *McClesky v. Kemp* (1987) in defense of Warren McClesky, an African American who was convicted of killing a White police officer in Georgia. Although the Court accepted the study's finding of a racially disparate impact in Georgia's application of the death penalty, it ruled that McClesky had not proven racial discrimination in his specific case. McClesky was executed in 1991. Just over 6 percent of wrongful conviction cases handled by the Innocence Project have involved inmates who were sentenced to death.

Gross et al. (2005) found that of 66 percent of the defendants who were exonerated for the crime of rape, 13 percent were Hispanic and 55 percent were African American. For Earl Washington, Jr. (see box), it appears that the prosecution was looking for the confession and did not focus on surrounding circumstances that may have shown that Washington was innocent (Burke, 2006). Even in light of powerful evidence, prosecutors may deny that a wrongful conviction has occurred because it is too difficult to acknowledge they may have been participants in a critical miscarriage of justice based in part on their own racial and other biases (Burke, 2006).

It does not seem realistic that wrongful conviction will be eliminated from the criminal justice system (Rattner, 1988), but it may be possible to reduce the amount of racial disparity in its occurrence. It has been suggested that overall, discrimination, eyewitness misidentification, coerced confessions, and other risks of wrongful conviction are much more likely to result from systemic factors such as police priorities and sentencing policies rather than individual bias in specific cases (Mauer, 1999; Roberts, 2004). However, unconscious racial bias is part of a system of institutionalized racism that is often difficult to recognize or expose (see Eberhardt et al., 2006). Wrongful convictions that involve racial stereotyping may be reduced by use of updated DNA evidence, thorough and ethical police investigation, and prosecutorial integrity. However, these procedures must be employed early in the investigative process if the harmful effects of criminal justice processing on innocent civilians are to be effectively avoided.

Sylvia Mignon

See also: Death Penalty; DNA Testing; Eyewitness Misidentification; False Confessions; Innocence Project; War on Drugs; Wrongful Convictions

References

Baldus, D. C., C. Pulaski, and G. Woodworth. "Comparative Review of Death Sentences: An Empirical Study of the Georgia Experience." *The Journal of Criminal Law and Criminology* 74, no. 3 (1983): 661–753.

Bar-Haim, Y., T. Saidel, and G. Yovel. "The Role of Skin Colour in Face Recognition." *Perception* 38 (2009): 145–248.

Burke, A. S. "Improving Prosecutorial Decision Making: Some Lessons of Cognitive Science." *William and Mary Law Review* 47, no. 5 (2006): 1587–1633.

Eberhardt, J., P. Davies, V. Purdie-Vaughns, and S. L. Johnson. "Looking Deathworthy: Perceived Stereotypicality of Black Defendants Predicts Capital-Sentencing Outcomes." *Psychological Science* 17, no. 5 (2006): 383–86.

Eberhardt, J., V. Purdie, P. Goff, and P. Davies. "Seeing Black: Race, Crime, and Visual Processing." *Journal of Personality and Social Psychology* 87, no. 6 (2004): 876–93.

Free, M. D., ed. *Racial Issues in Criminal Justice: The Case of African Americans.* New York: Criminal Justice Press, 2004.

Graham, S., and B. S. Lowery. "Priming Unconscious Racial Stereotypes about Adolescent Offenders." *Law and Human Behavior* 28, no. 5 (2004): 483–504.

Gross, S. R., K. Jacoby, D. J. Matheson, N. Montgomery, and S. Patil. "Exoneration in the United States 1989 through 2003." *The Journal of Criminal Law and Criminology* 95, no. 2 (2005): 523–60.

Harrell, E. *Black Victims of Violent Crime.* Special Report. NCJ214258, August. Washington, DC: US Department of Justice, Bureau of Justice Statistics, 2007.

Mauer, M. *The Crisis of the Young African American Male and the Criminal Justice System.* Prepared for the U.S. Commission on Civil Rights, April 15–16, 1999. Washington, DC: The Sentencing Project, 1999.

Mauer, M. *Young Black Men and the Criminal Justice System: A Growing National Problem.* Washington, DC: The Sentencing Project, 1990.

McClesky v. Kemp. 481 U.S. 279 (1987), 107 S. Ct 1756, 95 L. Ed. 262 (1987).

O'Flaherty, B., and R. Sethi. "Homicide in Black and White." *Journal of Urban Economics* 68 (2010): 215–30.

Pager, D. *Marked: Race, Crime and Finding Work in an Era of Mass Incarceration.* Chicago: University of Chicago Press, 2007.

Quillian, L., and D. Pager. "Black Neighbors, Higher Crime? The Role of Racial Stereotypes in Evaluations of Neighborhood Crime." *American Journal of Sociology* 107, no. 3 (2001): 717–67.

Rattner, A. "Convicted but Innocent: Wrongful Conviction and the Criminal Justice System." *Law and Human Behavior* 12, no. 3 (1988): 283–93.

Roberts, D. E. "The Social and Moral Cost of Mass Incarceration in African American Communities." *Stanford Law Review* 56, no. 5 (2004): 1271–1305.

Taslitz, A. E. "Wrongly Accused Redux: How Race Contributes to Convicting the Innocent; The Informants Example." *Southwestern University Law Review* 37 (2009): 1091–1148.

Taslitz, A. E. "Wrongly Accused: Is Race a Factor in Convicting the Innocent?" *Ohio State Journal of Criminal Law* 4 (2006): 121–33.

Warden, R. "How Mistaken and Perjured Eyewitness Identification Testimony Put 86 Innocent Americans on Death Row." Remarks at Andrews University, Berrien Springs, Michigan, May 2, 2001. http://www.deathpenaltyinfo.org/StudyCWC2001.pdf.

Western, B., and B. Pettit. "Incarceration & Social Inequality." *Daedalus* 139, no. 3 (2010): 8–19.

Robeson, Paul (1898–1976)

A civil rights pioneer and perhaps the truest Renaissance man of the Harlem Renaissance, Paul Robeson holds the added distinction of accumulating one of the largest FBI files of any of the entertainers caught up in the McCarthyist "Red Scare" of the 1950s (Duberman, 1989: 563). A vocal proponent of international socialism and a vigorous campaigner for African American equality, Robeson kept the attention of a number of intelligence organizations (including the CIA and Britain's MI5 and MI6) throughout his life by combining international activism with his world travels as a singer and actor—travels that included numerous visits to the Soviet Union.

Robeson was born in 1898 in Princeton, New Jersey, and was one of the first African American students to attend Rutgers University. There he excelled in both academics and athletics, becoming the valedictorian of his class and a first-team All-American football player. While subsequently studying law at New York's Columbia University Law School, Robeson began acting and singing to fund his studies. His successes as a performer—and the entrenched racism he encountered when he began his career as a lawyer—led him to abandon law and dedicate himself to a career as a performer.

Paul Robeson, star college athlete, Rhodes scholar, international performer, and among one of the first Blacks to attend Rutgers University. A native of Princeton, New Jersey, his anti-segregationist political views led to him being labeled a communist and blackballed from many circles. This image appeared on the 37-cent United States postage stamp in 2004. (Associated Press)

Robeson achieved fame as a singer and actor throughout the 1920s, starring in both the stage and film versions of Eugene O'Neill's *The Emperor Jones,* as well as musicals such as *Showboat.* His career led him to live and travel extensively in Europe, and gave him broad exposure to elite society and the intellectual currents of his day. Robeson followed many American expatriates in embracing socialism, in which he saw the greatest potential for African Americans to achieve equal rights, as well as social and economic justice.

The FBI began its lifelong surveillance of Robeson—as with many intellectuals and entertainers—in response to his involvement with causes supporting the Republican side in the Spanish Civil War (FBI, 1941: 4). After the loss of Spain to Franco's Fascists, Robeson continued speaking out against Nazism and Fascism throughout World War II, advocating direct military aid to the Soviet Union well before the U.S. entry into the conflict.

After the war's close, Robeson's politics grew more radical, even as anti-Communist fervor in the United States began to build. In a widely reported statement at the 1949 Paris Peace Conference, Robeson "stated that it was 'unthinkable that American Negroes would go to war [against the Soviet Union] on behalf of those who have oppressed us for generations'" (Baldwin, 2002: 205). Reaction to the perceived anti-American content of Robeson's statement led to the infamous Peekskill (New York) riots on August 27 and September 4, 1949, where violent protesters attacked attendees at concerts where Robeson was scheduled to perform. Also present was famed Black actor, performer, and activist Harry Belafonte.

Because of his outspoken views on African Americans' civil rights and social-ism, Robeson's passport was revoked from 1950 until 1958. When called before the House Committee on Un-American Activities in 1956, Robeson took the Fifth when asked if he was a member of the Communist Party. He ended his testimony with a direct attack on the committee: "[Y]ou are the nonpatriots, and you are the un-Americans, and you ought to be ashamed of yourselves" (House Committee on Un-American Activities, 1956).

Robeson's health declined steeply after a suicide attempt in Moscow in 1961, an incident that his son, Paul Robeson, Jr., has claimed was brought on by his in-tentional poisoning with LSD by a CIA agent under the MK-Ultra program, a covert illegal human experimentation project run by the CIA's Office of Scientific Intelligence (Robeson, 1999). Following the incident, Robeson remained in many respects a shell of his former self until his death in 1976.

Daniel Stageman

References

Baldwin, K. A. *Beyond the Color Line and the Iron Curtain: Reading Encounters between Black and Red.* Chapel Hill, NC: Duke University Press, 2002.

Duberman, M. B. *Paul Robeson: A Biography.* New York: Ballantine, 1989.

Federal Bureau of Investigation (FBI). *FBIHQ File 100-12304 Section 1: Paul Robeson, Sr.* February 17, 1941. http://foia.fbi.gov/robeson/robes1a.pdf.

House Committee on Un-American Activities, U.S. Congress. "Investigation of the Unauthorized Use of US Passports." 84th Congress, Part 3, June 12, 1956.

Robeson, P., Jr. "The Paul Robeson Files." *The Nation,* December 20, 1999.

Rockefeller Drug Laws: Policy Review

The war on drugs has caused enormous debate in the United States' criminal justice system for decades. Beginning in the 1960s through today, America's drug problem became a national topic of concern for the public and policymakers. In 1971, President Nixon initiated the "War on Drugs," and since then U.S. drug policies have been shaped by harsh drug laws and harsh treatment of those in-volved with drug offenses (Kohler-Hausmann, 2010). Perhaps one of the most important and noteworthy pieces of legislation in the war on drugs was the Rockefeller Drug Laws.

Initially, New York governor Nelson Rockefeller tried to tackle the issue of drugs by creating the Narcotic Addiction and Control Commission and Metha-done Maintenance programs. At the time, these programs proved to be unsuccessful and costly, causing the public and right-wing politicians to put the pressure on Rockefeller to come up with a different solution to the drug problem in New York (Gray, 2009). Rockefeller then reversed his position that rehabilitation was preferable to punishment and addressed the legislature, declaring that programs to cure the drug problem in the state of New York were not effective. In his address, he stated that harsh, punitive measures were necessary because "[t]he hard drug pusher destroys lives just as surely as and far more cruelly than a cold-blooded killer. He threatens our society as a whole" (Kohler-Hausmann, 2010: 71). He asked that drug dealers' prison sentences be more harsh than sentences for murderers, rapists, and kidnappers:

> I, therefore, will ask for legislation making the penalty for all illegal trafficking in hard drugs a life sentence in prison. To close all avenues for escaping the full force of this sentence, the law would forbid acceptance of a plea to a lesser charge, forbid probation, forbid parole and forbid suspension of sentence. (Kohler-Hausmann, 2010: 71)

In response, the Rockefeller Drug Laws were passed in 1973, and from that point on America's treatment of those involved with selling or using drugs took a completely different turn (Gray, 2009). According to Kohler-Hausmann, this was the beginning of politicians framing addicts and drug dealers as people separate from society, and wanting to "protect" society from them: "In terms of the dominant medical metaphor of addiction, pusher/addicts moved from being considered diseased to being cast as the disease" (Kohler-Hausmann, 74).

This law included three main provisions. The first was mandatory minimum sentences for heroin dealers, the second was restrictions on plea bargaining for heroin dealers, and the third was mandatory prison sentences for repeat offenders (Walker, 2011). People who sold or possessed two ounces or less of heroin had to serve mandatory prison sentences, and could potentially receive sentences of life in prison. Although this law was intended to stop high-level drug traffickers, it often targeted low-level drug dealers (Walker, 2011).

As would be expected, these laws had a huge impact on the criminal justice system of New York. From the years 1974 to 2002, New York State's prison population increased by nearly 500 percent, from about 14,400 to 70,700 inmates, and those prisoners were serving significantly more time than they would have before the change in the law. This was the highest rate of incarceration in the state's history (Drucker, 2002). As a result of the strict sentencing, the percentage of offenders demanding trials went from 6 to 15 percent, costing the courts more money and time. The new law had no apparent effect on the level of drug use in New York (Walker, 2011).

In 2009, it was reported that 21 percent of all state prisoners were in prison under these laws, costing an estimated $525 million dollars per year. Two-thirds of these prisoners had no prior incarcerations, and 80 percent had never been convicted of a felony. Although African Americans are disproportionately represented in the criminal justice system in general, the numbers are even more shocking with regard to the Rockefeller Drug Laws. About 90 percent of those incarcerated under this law were African Americans (Walker, 2011). Perhaps most significantly, the Rockefeller Drug Laws unleashed a wave of similar punitive drug laws. Many states followed the example of New York and began to adopt legislation that demanded harsher prison sentences for drug offenders (Walker, 2011).

Although there is a common stereotype that African Americans disproportionately use drugs, there is no empirical evidence to support this assumption. According to Drucker (2002), there is no evidence that drug use/dealing is more prevalent in African American communities. There is some evidence suggesting that overdose incidences are higher for African Americans than for Whites; however, these figures are not nearly enough to explain the gaps in the drug-related incarceration rates for African Americans as compared to Whites. Evidence suggests that one collateral consequence of the enforcement of the drug laws is that many people in the minority community feel that an injustice is being done to them through governmental policies, and they have lost their trust in government and in law enforcement agencies in particular (Drucker, 2002). The overrepresentation of African Americans in prison under these laws has had damaging effects on the overall purpose of the law and undermines relationships between African Americans and the police and has contributed to an unwillingness to cooperate with the justice system (Drucker, 2002).

The effects of the Rockefeller Drug Laws were devastating to a large number of offenders, and as mentioned before, these laws seemed to have very little impact in deterring drug use. Activists increasingly criticized the drug laws and claimed that they were too harsh and that nonviolent offenders were being treated the same as violent kingpins. Celebrities such as music mogul Russell Simmons and actors Susan Sarandon and Tim Robbins spoke out about this issue and were very active in trying to get legislation passed to reform the law (Gray, 2009). In 2004, New York governor George Pataki signed the Drug Law Reform Act, which eliminated life sentences for some drug crimes and reduced the length of other drug sentences. This reform also allows offenders who were previously convicted to apply for lighter sentencing (Gray, 2009). However, certain mandatory sentences remain in place (Peters, 2009).

After decades of criticism and activism to try and change the Rockefeller Drug laws, a movement that came to be known as "drop the Rock," the laws were thoroughly reformed on October 7, 2009. Mandatory sentences were eliminated for first-time offenders who were convicted of possession or sales of class B, C, D, and E drugs. Also, mandatory sentences for second-time offenders of class C, D, and E drugs were eliminated. However, incarceration is still mandatory for second-time drug offenders of class B drugs if the defendant has been convicted or has a pending violent felony on his/her record in the last decade. There are also still mandatory prison sentences for class A-I and class A-II drug felonies (Walker, 2011).

These revisions allowed some form of resentencing for about 1,500 people who were incarcerated at that time. A noteworthy aspect of this reform is that drug treatments as an alternative to incarceration expanded greatly, and $71 million was added to the budget for drug treatment (Walker, 2011). These revisions also allowed judges to send nonviolent/first-time drug offenders (not class A) to treatment instead of prison. The offenders would still plead guilty, but be given a chance to complete treatment. If they did not successfully complete treatment, they would go back before a judge who would have the option of sentencing the offender to prison. It costs about $45,000 per year to house an inmate in a correctional facility, which appears to have little deterrent power regarding drug use/distribution. Drug treatment options cost far less (Peters, 2009). Gabriel Sayegh, from the Drug Policy Alliance, a group that works to eliminate certain drug sentencing laws, stated that as a result of the reforms, "New York could actually become a national leader; we're going in a public health direction here. We're making that turn, and that's what's significant" (Peters, 2009).

Sara Attarchi

References

Drucker, E. "Population Impact of Mass Incarceration under New York's Rockefeller Drug Laws: An Analysis of Years of Life Lost." *Journal of Urban Health: Bulletin of the New York Academy of Medicine* 79, no. 3 (September 2002): 1–10.

Gray, M. "New York's Rockefeller Drug Laws." *Time,* April 2, 2009. http://www.time.com/time/nation/article/0,8599,1888864,00.html.

Kohler-Hausmann, J. "New York's Rockefeller Drug Laws and the Making of a Punitive State." *Journal of Social History* 44, no. 1 (Fall 2010): 71–95.

N.Y. Penal Law Sections 221.01-220.40; 220.22; 220.33; 220.44 (1969) (Revised 2004 & 2009).

Peters, J. W. "Albany Reaches Deal to Repeal '70s Drug Laws." *The New York Times,* March 25, 2009. http://www.nytimes.com/2009/03/26/nyregion/26rockefeller.html?_r=1.

Walker, S. *Sense and Nonsense.* 7th ed. Belmont, CA: Wadsworth/Cengage Learning, 2011.

Ross, Ricky "Freeway" (1960–)

Ricky "Freeway" Ross was one of Los Angeles' largest crack cocaine dealers in the early 1980s. There are two stories regarding the origin of his nickname. One suggests that the name came from Ross' ownership of several motels along the Los Angeles–area Harbor Freeway. The other points to the fact that there was a freeway near his childhood home. Born in 1960 in Troup, Texas, Ricky Ross' father was an oil tank cleaner who left the family when Ricky was three years old. He and his mother moved to Los Angeles while he was still a child. There he was befriended by adult males who encouraged his love of tennis. He became a good tennis player at Dorsey High School and played on the tennis team at Long Beach University (LBU). His time at LBU was short, for although he was a high school graduate, he was illiterate. Ross reports being surprised to discover that college professors would not simply give him passing grades, a practice that he had come to expect from his time in high school. His involvement with selling cocaine began when he attended auto repair classes at L.A. Trade Tech Junior College. Sources identify Fraser Brown as the person who introduced Ross to the illicit drug trade. Brown has been described as an upholstery instructor at the junior college and a "college friend" who introduced Ross to cocaine dealing as a means of part-time employment.

Ross' notoriety as a drug dealer stemmed from the fact that he eventually obtained his supply of cocaine from Oscar Danilo Blandón, a Nicaraguan drug trafficker with ties to the Contras, a rebel group in Nicaragua trying to overthrow the Sandinista-led government, reportedly with the help of the U.S. Congress and the Central Intelligence Agency (CIA). The Sandinistas were a socialist political party named after Augusto Cesar Sandino, who led the resistance to the U.S. occupation of Nicaragua during the 1930s. Blandón provided mass quantities of powder cocaine to Ross at low prices, which allowed him to undercut his competition in the United States.

In a controversial 1996 series called "Dark Alliance," Gary Webb, a reporter for *The San Jose Mercury News,* exposed the connection between the CIA and Ross' drug dealing. The series broadly hinted that the CIA was using money gleaned from Ross' cocaine sales to buy weapons for the Contras. Webb alleged that the funds Blandón and Norwin Menenses, another Nicaraguan living in the San Francisco Bay Area, made through cocaine sales were funneled to the Nicaraguan Democratic Force (FDN), a subset of the Contras that, according to Webb, was funded and supported by the CIA. According to Webb's reports, these illegal monies were needed to finance the organization after the U.S. Congress enacted a series of laws collectively known as the Boland Amendment (1982–1984). The Boland Amendment prohibited U.S. funding of efforts designed to aid the clandestine overthrow of the Nicaraguan government. In fact, in addition to passing the Boland Amendment, several members of the congressional Black Caucus joined other plaintiffs in *Sanchez-Espinoza v. Reagan,* a suit filed to stop U.S. support of military and other action aimed at unseating Nicaragua's socialist party.

With Blandón as his direct supplier, Ross' cocaine sales flourished and were greatly enhanced by the introduction of crack to the Los Angeles market. His powder cocaine customers had traditionally been middle- to upper-class Whites, but with crack he was able to sell to a new customer base: lower-income African Americans. Members of the Bloods and Crips street gangs were reportedly part of his distribution network. Ross' direct connection to his distribution source facilitated a continued lowering of prices to the consumer. Ross became such a successful drug dealer that the Freeway Ricky Task Force was created within the Los Angeles Police Department (LAPD) as a means to undermine and capture him. According to *The Oakland Tribune,* "In the course of his rise, prosecutors estimate that Ross exported several tons of cocaine to New York, Ohio, Pennsylvania and elsewhere, and made more than $600 million" (2011). At the height of his operation, Ross is reported as selling up to $3 million worth of cocaine per day and purchasing roughly 455 kilograms of cocaine per week.

His reputation was legendary in the Los Angeles community. Although Ross had ready access to large amounts of cocaine, he vowed to be a drug-free seller. He employed numerous people and contributed to community building projects. Much like New York City's Frank Lucas, whose life is depicted in the 2007 film *American Gangster,* and the legendary White organized crime figures of the past, despite his involvement with criminal enterprises, Ross was very much involved in philanthropy and community-building endeavors. His drug "empire" is reported to have involved thousands of employees across the cities of Los Angeles, St. Louis, New Orleans, Kansas City, Cleveland, Baltimore, and Seattle, and to have stretched across various states, including Texas, Oklahoma, Indiana, and both North and South Carolina.

Law enforcement investigations of Ross began in 1985 and eventually came to involve local, county, and federal authorities across different states. There were many failed prosecutions before Ross spent four years in jail following a drug arrest in 1989. At one point he was released from custody because of a successful motion to suppress inadmissible evidence; in addition, a controversial arrest of Ross by the LAPD while he was working at a construction site led to an investigation by the U.S. Department of Justice. During the arrest, Ross was chased by the police, shot at, and severely beaten when captured. This initiated a federal investigation into potential abuses engaged in by the LAPD in its efforts to dismantle his drug network. Ross was a key government witness in a subsequent corruption trial against law enforcement officers.

In the late 1980s, Ricky Ross moved to Cincinnati with his girlfriend and made efforts to live a law-abiding life as a house builder. But after some time in Cincinnati, he began to sell drugs again and eventually left Ohio and moved back to Los Angeles. Although he once vowed not to become re-involved in drug trafficking, in

1995 Ross says he reluctantly met with Oscar Danilo Blandón again to discuss one last drug deal. According to Ross, Blandón was insistent about the meeting and stated that he needed Ross's help. When Ross relented and met with Blandón, Drug Enforcement Agents (DEA) were waiting to arrest him. Blandón became the government's key witness against Ross and also subsequently became a paid employee of the DEA.

Ross, who is often referred to as a drug "kingpin," was convicted and sentenced to life in prison in 1996, but on appeal, the sentence was reduced to 20 years based on a legal technicality related to California's Three Strikes law. His sentence was reduced further because Ross was a model prisoner. He is reportedly the first federal inmate to create a social networking Web site while serving time at a Federal Bureau of Prisons facility in Texarkana, Texas. In 2009, he was moved to a halfway house in California and released from custody that same year.

Since his release, Ross has conducted numerous interviews and has had book and movie deals. The notoriety of his case, namely that his supplier had CIA and DEA connections while distributing cocaine in the Los Angeles area, led to two congressional investigations, one of which confirmed the CIA's knowledge of his cocaine distributions—a finding that was not well known since Gary Webb's journalism was vehemently criticized in the press. An investigation by the CIA's Office of Inspector General revealed that "the CIA responded inconsistently to allegations or information that . . . other individuals providing support to the Contra program were involved in drug trafficking." For many, the Ricky Ross story is a symbol of the willful negligence or intentional corruption of the CIA and other federal agencies in allowing cocaine into the economically disadvantaged communities of the United States.

James Michael Botts

See also: Conyers, Jr., John; Education; Gangs; Three Strikes Legislation

References

Cockburn, A., and J. St. Clair. *Whiteout: The CIA, Drugs and the Press.* London: Verso, 1998.

Gerstel, D., and A. Segal. "Conference Report: Human Rights in American Courts." *American University International Law Review* 1, no. 1 (1986): 137–66.

Hitz, Frederick P. "Obscuring Propriety: The CIA and Drugs." *International Journal of Intelligence and Counterintelligence* 12, no. 4 (Winter 1999): 448–62.

The Oakland Tribune. "The Return of "Freeway" Ricky Ross, the Man behind a Crack Empire." April 18, 2011. http://www.insidebayarea.com/topstories/ci_17113312.

PBS. "The CIA's Supposed Link to Crack Cocaine." November 18, 1996. http://www.pbs.org/newshour/bb/race_relations/july-dec96/cia_11-18.html.

Ross, R. *Freewayenterprise.com,* n.d.

Sanchez-Espinoza v. Reagan, 568 F. Supp. 596 (D.D.C. 1983) affirmed 770 F.2d 202 (D.C. Cir. 1985).

Schou, N. *Kill the Messenger: How the CIA's Crack-Cocaine Controversy Destroyed Journalist Gary Webb.* New York: Nation Books, 2006.

U.S. Inspector General. *Central Intelligence Agency.* April 26, 2007. https://www.cia.gov/library/reports/general-reports-1/cocaine/contra-story/intro.html.

Webb, G. *Dark Alliance.* New York: Seven Stories Press, 1999.

Russ, Robert (1977–1999)

Robert Russ was 22 years old when he was shot and killed by a Chicago police officer following a traffic stop in the early morning hours of June 5, 1999. Russ was set to graduate from Northwestern University, where he had played football, later that month. He and his girlfriend were expecting their first child. Russ' death came just hours after Chicago police shot another unarmed motorist, 26-year-old computer analyst LaTanya Haggerty, whose cellular phone was mistaken for a weapon (Revolutionary Worker, 1999a). Both Russ and Haggerty were African American, as were the officers who fired the fatal shots in each case.

Police accounts of the incident that led to Russ' death vary from accounts offered later in expert and eyewitness testimony. According to police, the shooting was justified. In their version of events, an officer saw Russ driving erratically while he was en route to his mother's suburban Chicago home. When an officer approached his vehicle at a red light and knocked on one of the car's darkly tinted windows, Russ drove off, inciting a chase. Through the course of the chase, Russ' car allegedly rammed a police vehicle multiple times. The chase concluded when Russ lost control of his car. At that point, officers approached the vehicle and demanded that Russ put his hands in sight. Police say Russ was unresponsive to that command, leading officer Van Watts IV to break the driver's side rear window and to point his gun inside the vehicle at Russ. Reports say Russ then turned to grab the gun with both hands and in the process of trying to grab the gun from the officer, the gun accidentally discharged, killing Russ (Revolutionary Worker, 1999a).

Those who gave testimony in a subsequent wrongful death lawsuit gave a different account of the facts. Two eyewitnesses testified that they saw no struggle between Watts and Russ. A ballistics expert also testified that Russ could not have had his hands on the gun when it was fired, estimating that his hands were likely one to three inches from the firearm. A second gun expert determined that it was unlikely that the firearm in question would discharge accidentally. A police-training expert likewise concluded that the officers acted inappropriately in breaking the window and pointing the gun inside the vehicle (Revolutionary Worker, 1999a).

After the incident, there were also contrasting accounts of Russ' character. The local media seemed apt to portray Russ as violent, emphasizing an incident that had occurred months earlier where Russ pleaded guilty to battery of a police officer (Revolutionary Worker, 1999b). In contrast, those who knew Russ, his parents in particular, described him as sensible. They doubted that he would have tried to grab a gun from an officer's hands. One media source suggested that a more plausible explanation might be that the officers acted out of misplaced fear. That is, the officers may have been more fearful of the two Blacks, Russ and Haggerty, because a Black suspect had shot and killed a police officer a few months earlier.

Many city officials dismissed claims of racism and police brutality in the wake of the Russ and Haggerty shootings. Chicago Mayor Richard M. Daley was among them. Rather than reprimanding the officers involved, he called for a ban on tinted windows (Janega & Washburn, 1999) and mandatory jail time for those who refuse to comply with police commands (Revolutionary Worker, 1999b). Chicago Police Superintendant Terry Hilliard had a less antagonistic response. He reacted by launching a review of the department's traffic stop, pursuit, and deadly force policies (Greenfield, 1999). He also proposed putting video cameras in police cars to resolve conflicting stories and to restore public confidence in the police (Greenfield, 1999).

The Russ and Haggerty shootings, coupled with the unwillingness of officials to admit police wrongdoing, inspired a great deal of public protest. Local residents mobilized. They gathered outside of city hall, delivered a public letter to Mayor Daley, and emphasized the racial implications of the cases in letters they sent to local news outlets (Revolutionary Worker, 1999b). Activists with national profiles such as the Rev. Al Sharpton also spoke out on Russ' behalf.

In the end, the officers who participated in the Russ shooting and the chase that preceded it received minimal punishments. Watts, who fired the fatal shot, was suspended from the force for 15 days. Another officer was issued a one-day suspension for joining the pursuit without authorization and a third was reprimanded for failing to report Russ' tinted windows to the dispatcher. In October 2003, the jury in the wrongful death suit ruled that the city was 80 percent responsible for Russ' death and ordered the city of Chicago to pay $9.6 million dollars to the heir of Russ' estate (Mendell, 2003; Revolutionary Worker, 2003), his son, who was born shortly after the shooting. Jurors who were interviewed after they rendered the verdict stated that they did not believe the police officers' version of the story. The family of LaTanya Haggerty, represented by acclaimed African American attorney Johnnie Cochran, had received an $18 million dollar settlement against the city in 2001 (Digital Journal Staff, 2001). The Haggerty case was atypical in that both the victim and the shooting officer were female.

Taken together, the Russ and Haggerty cases raised important questions about police brutality, racial profiling, and public confidence in the police. After Russ' death, many began to question the militaristic style of policing that had become commonplace among officers in Chicago and elsewhere. Others levied claims about racial profiling. In the eyes of many, the fact that the officers who fired the shots in both cases were Black did not rule out the possibility of racial profiling; instead, it demonstrated the extent to which racial profiling was pervasive in the Chicago police force, even among officers of African descent (Revolutionary Worker, 1999b). Finally, because two young African Americans with bright futures were shot and killed in incidents involving minor traffic offenses (Haggerty was a passenger), public trust in the police—especially among African Americans, who have historically been distrustful of law enforcement—eroded even more (Revolutionary Worker, 1999b).

Jamie Longazel

References

Digital Journal Staff. "Chicago Judge Oks $18M Settlement." *Digital Journal,* May 9, 2001. http:www.digitaljournal.com/article/32613.

Greenfield, J. "Police Chief Unveils Reforms Aimed at Training, Accountability." *Chicago Tribune,* September 28, 1999.

Janega, J., and G. Washburn. "Daley Links 1 Death to Car's Tinted Windows." *Chicago Tribune,* June 10, 1999.

Mendell, D. "$9.6 Million Russ Case Award." *Chicago Tribune,* October 18, 2003.

Revolutionary Worker. "City Begins Defense in Robert Russ Trial." *Chicago Tribune,* September 26, 2003.

Revolutionary Worker. 1999a. "Outrage in Chicago: Police Murder 2 for DWB, #1011." June 20, 1999. http://reor.org/a/v21/1010-019/1011/chicdwb.htm.

Revolutionary Worker. 1999b. "Cops, Blacks and Mutual Distrust." *Chicago Tribune,* June 9, 1999.

S

Scottsboro Cases

In the midst of the "Great" Depression, a freight train rolled through Tennessee into Alabama that would forever change the route of American criminal procedure. During that time, many youths and young adults rode the freights, looking for work at stops along the way. On March 25, 1931, a fight broke out on one of these freight trains and the African American youths on board threw all but one young White male off that train. Those who were thrown off complained to a stationmaster, who radioed ahead to the next stop, near Scottsboro, Alabama. When the train entered the station near Scottsboro, nine African American young men, two White women wearing men's overalls, and a White male were taken off the train by the authorities. Their ages are not certain, but according to available records, they were Charlie Weems, 20; Clarence Norris, 19; Haywood Patterson, 19; Andrew Wright, 19; Willie Roberson, 17; Ozie Powell, 16; Olen Montgomery, 15; Eugene Williams, 14; Leroy (Roy) Wright, 13; Victoria Price, 24; Ruby Bates, 17; and Orville Gilley (age unknown). Victoria Price and Ruby Bates accused the African Americans of raping them, a capital offense in Alabama. Two medical doctors examined the young women within two hours of the alleged rapes. Inactive sperm was present, indicating that intercourse had not taken place recently. The "Scottsboro Boys," as the nine came to be called, aged 13 to 20, eight illiterate, one nearly blind, and one limping from venereal diseases, were taken into the sheriff's custody and the National Guard was called in to protect them from the lynch mob that quickly gathered (Carter, 2007).

The trials commenced in April, 12 days after the arrests, and were held in Scottsboro, population 3,500, the seat of Jackson County. Judge A. E. Hawkins presided over the trials of all nine of the accused, for a total of four trials in four days. Judge Hawkins appointed two lawyers, Stephen Roddy and Milo Moody, to "defend" the nine. Roddy was a Chattanooga, Tennessee, real estate lawyer, a chronic alcoholic, and completely unprepared. Moody was a senile 70-year-old who had not tried a case in decades. The defense's cross-examination was either

Fearing a mob lynching, Alabama governor B.M. Miller called the National Guard to the Scottsboro jail to protect the young Black men who were accused of raping two White women on March 20, 1931, in Scottsboro, Alabama. From left to right, the accused are: Clarence Norris, Olen Montgomery, Andy Wright, Willie Roberson, Ozie Powell, Eugene Williams, Charlie Weems, Roy Wright, and Haywood Patterson. (Bettmann/Corbis)

perfunctory or nonexistent. The eight oldest defendants were all found guilty and sentenced to death in the electric chair. A mistrial was declared in the case of Roy Wright because although he was only 13 years old, most of the jurors wanted to sentence him to death, even though the prosecutor asked for life in prison. In March 1932, the Alabama Supreme Court also reversed the conviction of Eugene Williams because he was under age 16 at the time of his arrest, but voted 6 to 1 to affirm the other seven convictions. Justice Thomas Knight, Sr., wrote a majority opinion. His son, Attorney General Thomas Knight, Jr., argued the state's case and was a relentless prosecutor in the cases, even while he later served as lieutenant governor (Carter, 2007; Linder, n.d.; Linder, 1998).

On November 7, 1932, the U.S. Supreme Court reversed all seven convictions in *Powell v. Alabama*, 287 U.S. 45, 53 S. Ct. 55. Justice Sutherland wrote for seven justices in stating that the lack of individual counsel for illiterate defendants in a capital case violated the due process of law under the Fourteenth Amendment to the Constitution. Although Justices Butler and McReynolds dissented, the decision in

Powell v. Alabama meant that going forward, in any case where a state seeks the death penalty against defendants who cannot afford to hire their own attorneys, each individual who has been accused is entitled to his or her own court-appointed lawyer.

The International Labor Defense (ILD), an auxiliary of the Communist Party, offered its services to secure legal representation for the Scottsboro defendants for the retrials. They hired Samuel Leibowitz, a 39-year-old Jewish trial lawyer from New York City. In 78 murder trials, Leibowitz had secured 77 acquittals and one hung jury, earning him praise as "the next Clarence Darrow." Ironically, the National Association for the Advancement of Colored People's Legal Defense Fund tried to engage Darrow to represent the original nine, but negotiations with ILD had broken down. Haywood Patterson's second trial was moved to Decatur in Morgan County, and set for March 1933, before Judge Edwin Horton, Jr., a 55-year-old Southern gentleman-farmer with a year of medical training before studying law (Carter, 2007; Linder, n.d.; Linder, 1998).

In a pretrial motion, Leibowitz argued "that Blacks had been illegally excluded from the grand jury" (Geis & Bienen, 1998: 59) and the petit jury, in violation of the U.S. Constitution. Judge Horton denied the motions, but the issues were preserved for appeal. The defense case was strong. Dr. R. R. Bridges, a gynecologist, testified regarding the inactive state of the sperm in the semen found in Victoria Price's cervix and regarding the fact that she lacked injuries that she would have sustained from chert, a fine quartz gravel in the boxcar that would have produced skin abrasions or cuts had she been forcibly raped while riding on the train. In private, the second examining doctor told Judge Horton that the women had not been raped, and they had laughed in response to his questioning whether they might have been. It is reported that given the racially volatile nature of the case, in order to save his local practice, the judge excused this doctor from testifying (Carter, 2007; Linder, n.d.; Linder, 1998).

During the 1933 retrial, Leslie Carter, an acquaintance of Ruby Bates, testified that he had intercourse with her on the night of March 24, 1931, and that he saw Jack Tiller do the same with Victoria Price. Carter also stated that Price made up the rape story to avoid arrest for vagrancy or a Mann Act violation (crossing state lines for immoral purposes, i.e., prostitution). On the stand, Ruby Bates recanted all of her 1931 testimony, but during the trial she was wearing fancy clothes and admitted to living in New York, subsidized by the Communist Party. The jury once again found Patterson guilty and once again sentenced him to death. In a stunning turn of events that June, Judge Horton set aside the guilty verdict and ordered a new trial, explaining that "the evidence greatly preponderates in the favor of the defendant" and the medical evidence showed there was no group rape (Geis & Bienen, 1998: 62). This was a brave gesture on the part of a Southern judge and one that did not win him many local supporters. In fact, in 1934, when he sought re-election as circuit judge, he was defeated in a runoff election, after having served for 12 years. He credited that defeat for his long life. He died in March of 1973 at the age of 95 (Carter, 2007).

The third set of trials was in November 1934 before Judge William Callahan, 70, a racist, pro-prosecution jurist. Roy Wright and Eugene Williams were transferred to juvenile court and stayed. Haywood Patterson was put on trial a third time, found guilty, and again sentenced to death. Clarence Norris was on trial a second time, represented by Samuel Leibowitz, with Attorney General Thomas Knight, Jr., prosecuting. Orville Gilley testified that he was held at knifepoint while Price was raped. It was discovered that Knight sent weekly checks to Gilley's mother and "occasional spending money to Gilley," perhaps in exchange for his favorable testimony. Norris was again found guilty and sentenced to death. In July 1934, the Alabama Supreme Court in *Norris v. State* rejected evidence that grand and petit jury commissioners in two counties excluded African Americans on account of race, even though one had never served on a jury in at least 24 years. Under an Alabama statute, jury service required "integrity, good character, and sound judgment," and the commissioners claimed not to know any African Americans who qualified. On April 1, 1935, the U.S. Supreme Court unanimously reversed Norris' conviction and ordered Alabama to reverse Patterson's (*Norris v. Alabama,* 294 U.S. 587, 55 S. Ct. 579; *Patterson v. Alabama,* 294 U.S. 600, 55 S. Ct. 575). Leibowitz represented Norris and he showed the U.S. Supreme Court justices how officials had forged African American names on the jury rolls after the trials. Chief Justice Charles Evans Hughes authored both opinions of the Court, in which it found systematic exclusion of African Americans from grand and petit juries, in violation of the defendant's rights under the Fourteenth Amendment's equal protection clause (Carter, 2007; Linder, n.d.; Linder, 1998).

The Scottsboro Defense Committee, a coalition of five nonprofit activist and religious groups, raised money for the fourth trial of Haywood Patterson. The 14-person grand jury included one African American, but only 10 people (two-thirds) were needed to vote for indictment. Now, Lieutenant Governor Thomas Knight, Jr., appointed himself as special prosecutor, and the lead defense attorney was a local Southerner, Clarence Watts. During this trial, Samuel Leibowitz kept a low profile in court. By some accounts, Judge Callahan hassled the defense and let Knight make outrageously inflammatory remarks. The jury again found Patterson guilty and sentenced him to 75 years in prison. This sentence was the first time in state history that a "Black Male on White Female" rape was not punished by death. In December 1936, Knight and Leibowitz met secretly in New York to discuss a compromise, and one was apparently worked out, but Knight died in May 1937 before it could be implemented. On June 14, 1937, the Alabama Supreme Court upheld the conviction and sentence; on October 25, the U.S. Supreme Court denied review (Carter, 2007; Linder, n.d.; Linder, 1998).

The fifth set of trials continued in Decatur in July 1937. Clarence Norris, at his third trial, was found guilty and sentenced to death. The governor later reduced this sentence to life in prison. The local attorney Clarence Watts dropped out of defending the Scottsboro cases. At Andrew Wright's second trial, Leibowitz returned as lead counsel. Wright was found guilty, with the state asking for and receiving a 99-year sentence. At Charlie Weems' second trial, he was found guilty, with the state asking for and receiving a 75-year sentence (Carter, 2007; Linder, n.d.; Linder, 1998). Ozie Powell stabbed a deputy sheriff during a transport, and in return he was shot in the head, causing brain damage. He pled guilty to assault on the deputy, who recovered, and Powell received a 20-year sentence. On July 24, 1937, the prosecutor dismissed charges against Willie Roberson, Olen Montgomery, and the two defendants who had been juveniles at the time of the alleged rapes, Eugene Williams and Leroy Wright (Carter, 2007; Kinshasa, 1997).

Charlie Weems was paroled in November 1943. Clarence Norris and Andrew Wright were paroled in January 1944. Ozie Powell was paroled in June 1946. Powell died in Atlanta in 1975. Patterson escaped from a prison farm in July 1948, drowning the pursuit dogs. The FBI captured him in Detroit, but the Michigan governor refused to extradite him. Patterson co-wrote the book *Scottsboro Boy* (with Earl Conrad, 1950). In 1951, he was sent to prison for manslaughter for a stabbing that occurred during a barroom brawl. He died of cancer on August 24, 1952, at the age of 39. Roy Wright joined the merchant marines, but subsequently ended his life in a domestic violence murder-suicide. Montgomery became a heavy-drinking drifter who was in and out of legal troubles. He died in Alabama in 1974. While on parole, Norris and Wright fled north, then voluntarily returned to Alabama. Norris was back in prison from October 1944 to September 29, 1946, and Wright was back in prison from October 1946 to June 9, 1950. Wright was accused of rape again and found not guilty. Though Clarence Norris continued to have trouble with the law, in October 1976, Governor George Wallace, once known for his strong segregationist beliefs, awarded Norris a full pardon for the 1931 rapes. The pardon became effective on November 29, 1976. Norris went on to co-author the book *The Last of the Scottsboro Boys* (with Sybil Washington, 1979); he was the subject of the book *The Man from Scottsboro* (1997), and was the group's last survivor at his death in 1989 at age 76.

Ruby Bates died in Yakima, Washington, on October 27, 1976. Victoria Price died in Lincoln City, Tennessee, in 1983. They both sued the National Broadcasting Company (NBC) over the broadcast of the made-for-television movie *Judge Horton & the Scottsboro Boys*. Bates died while her appeal was pending, and NBC settled with Price after the U.S. Supreme Court accepted her case for review on the issue of whether she was still a "public figure." The Court of Appeals for the Sixth Circuit had previously affirmed a decision by the U.S. District Court, which had ruled in favor of the television network. Price used the settlement money to buy a house.

One source has dubbed the Scottsboro incident "an American Tragedy" and "the case that sparked the civil rights movement" (Anker & Goodman, 2005). Though more that 80 years have passed since the first Scottsboro trials, the justice system's handling of those nine vulnerable young African American men continues to be seen as a symbol of how unjust the American criminal justice system can be toward the poor and the undereducated, and to racial and ethnic minorities. It is generally accepted that the alleged rapes did not occur, but it is noted that while Ruby Bates recanted her 1931 testimony during the 1933 retrial of Haywood Patterson, Bates allegedly told a writer in 1964 that she had been raped but had changed her testimony for personal reasons (Geis & Bienen, 1998). The fact that a lynch mob was quick to gather upon hearing the allegation that Black men had raped two White women was evidence of the strength of the "rape myth" as a means of inciting racial violence. It has been suggested by Kinshasa (1997) that the struggle that took place on the train in 1931 is reflective of the struggle that poor Blacks and Whites continue to experience in their quest for some measure of power today, and that the struggle for justice that the Scottsboro defendants and their lawyers and supporters engaged in for more than 40 years is also reflective of the current struggles for justice that African Americans continue to face.

Nigel Cohen

See also: Civil Rights Movement; Davis, Angela Yvonne; Legal Representation; Lynching; Sex Crimes and Race; Wells-Barnett, Ida B.

References

Anker, Daniel, and Barak Goodman. *American Experience—Scottsboro: An American Tragedy.* PBS Home Video, 2005.

Carter, Dan T. *Scottsboro: A Tragedy of the American South.* Rev. ed. Baton Rouge, LA: Louisiana State University Press, 2007.

Geis, Gilbert, and Leigh B. Bienen. *Crimes of the Century.* Boston: Northeastern University Press, 1998.

Kinshasa, Kwando M. *The Man from Scottsboro: Clarence Norris and the Infamous 1931 Alabama Rape Trial, in His Own Words.* Jefferson, NC: McFarland & Company, 1997.

Linder, Douglas O. "The Trials of 'The Scottsboro Boys.'" 1998. http://law2.umkc.edu/faculty/projects/FTrials/scottsboro/SB_acct.html.

Linder, Douglas O. "Without Fear or Favor: Judge James Edwin Horton and the Trial of the 'Scottsboro Boys.'" N.d. http://law2.umkc.edu/faculty/projects/FTrials/trialheroes/essayhorton.html.

Norris, Clarence, and Sybil Washington. *The Last of the Scottsboro Boys.* New York: G.P. Putnam & Sons, 1979.

Norris v. Alabama, 294 U.S. 587, 55 S. Ct. 579 (1935).

Patterson, Haywood, and Earl Conrad. *Scottsboro Boy.* Garden City, NY: Doubleday, 1950.

Patterson v. Alabama, 294 U.S. 600, 55 S. Ct. 575 (1935).

Powell v. Alabama, 287 U.S. 45, 53 S. Ct. 55 (1932).

Sentencing Disparities

African Americans have endured a long period of racial inequalities at all levels of society. A long line of social science research has confirmed that such inequalities for African Americans are particularly acute within the criminal justice system (CJS). While racial disparities are evident across virtually all components of the system, sentencing disparities play a key role in understanding the overrepresentation of African Americans among those who experience CJS processing, and especially among those who experience incarceration.

Theoretical Perspectives

There is a common perception that African Americans tend to be incarcerated at higher rates than any other racial group because they are more criminal (see Eberhardt et al., 2004). While this belief is common, it is refuted by research that demonstrates that there are a myriad of factors that influence the likelihood of African Americans being convicted and receiving harsher punishment than Whites or Hispanics, even when members of each group are accused of engaging in similar behavior (Miller, 1996). Members of the court play an integral role in the sentencing phase of the CJS. Research findings have shown that court decisionmakers hold stereotypical views that shape the types of sentences African Americans receive. Matthew Crow and Julie Kunselman (2009) employ the focal concerns theoretical perspective as a basis for explaining the sentences received by offenders. Crow and Kunselman note:

> The perspective posits that because sentencing authorities have limited time and information with which to make their decisions, they rely on a perceptual short-hand or patterned response to assess these focal concerns. The patterned responses are influenced by legal considerations (such as the offense and offender's prior record) but also by non-legal considerations (such as stereotypical assessments that associate race, ethnicity, and gender with perceptions of dangerousness and culpability). (2009: 197)

This theoretical perspective suggests that one's perception of the risk associated with an individual's race influences the exercise of discretion by court decisionmakers, including judges, prosecutors, and those preparing presentence reports. Similar to the focal concerns theory, Brennan and Spohn (2008) note that "judges and prosecutors . . . rely on stereotypes of minorities as more dangerous, more threatening, and more likely to recidivate to help them achieve [perceived] rational outcomes in the face of limited information" (2008: 374). The sometimes extreme variations in sentencing severity handed down to Blacks as opposed to Whites for similar conduct and comparable criminal records suggests that something other than legal variables are sometimes at work in decisions being made about what constitutes an appropriate sentence for one defendant versus another. The term "extra-legal" has been developed to describe these other factors that influence the sentencing decisions of court personnel and a substantial body of research has documented the role of extra-legal factors in producing racial disparities in sentencing outcomes.

The Illinois Perspective

Drug offending is one area in which racial disparities in sentences have consistently been apparent. Researchers Arthur Lurigio and Pamela Loose (2008) present the findings of a disproportionate minority confinement group in relation to racial disparities in drug offender incarcerations in Illinois. The research revealed that the "number of African Americans admitted to Illinois prisons for drug offenses far outweighs that of Whites and Hispanics" (Lurigio & Loose, 2008: 228). They proposed that outdoor drug sales might account for this racial disparity. It was posited that African Americans have a higher risk of being arrested and imprisoned for drug offenses because their drug sales are conducted in an open environment, thus making them more vulnerable to the police (Lurigio & Loose, 2008: 234). While this proposal had a common sense ring of truth, Olson reported "persons of color (mostly African Americans) were three times more likely than Whites to be sentenced to prison for *any* drug law violation" (2001, cited in Lurigio & Loose, 2008: 236) and comparable research from Seattle, Washington (Beckett et al., 2006), found that when Whites were engaged in the outdoor sale of drugs, police tended to ignore them in favor of arresting their Black counterparts.

Mandatory Minimum Sentences

Laws and the manner in which they are enacted have often been viewed as targeting minorities. During the late seventies and throughout the eighties and into the early nineties, lawmakers began passing sentencing statutes that imposed mandatory minimum prison terms as a means of getting tough on crime and criminals. Mandatory minimum statutes became a common means of dealing with gun possession and repeat violent offending (see Three Strikes Legislation). But racially disparate sentencing patterns have emerged in many of the states where such sentencing schemes exist.

Mandatory minimum penalties under the federal sentencing system have also been affected. For example, Mauer specifically notes that "mandatory minimum penalties . . . serve to exacerbate racial disparities within the criminal justice system" (2010: 7). Sentencing disparities are most evident as one examines the application of mandatory minimum penalties for crack cocaine and powdered cocaine offenses. The table below illustrates the number of federal drug defendants in each racial/ethnic group for 2009. The data vividly illustrate the racial disparity, as a substantially greater percentage of Blacks face sentencing for crack cocaine offenses (79%) in comparison to Hispanics (10.3%) and Whites (9.8%) (U.S. Sentencing Commission, 2009b: 39). This is true despite the fact that a 1995 study by the U.S. Sentencing Commission found that Whites comprise greater than 50 percent of crack users (52%) and Blacks represent 38 percent.

Since 1986, federal statutes have authorized more severe sentences for drug offenders who possess smaller amounts of crack cocaine than those who possess larger amounts of powder cocaine. This distinction becomes important given that a study by the U.S Sentencing Commission notes "that 64.4 percent of drug offenders were convicted under statutes carrying a mandatory minimum penalty . . . [t]he highest percentages of offenders receiving a mandatory minimum penalty were crack cocaine offenders (80.3%)" (2009a: 40). With Blacks being 79 percent of offenders who are processed for the possession of crack cocaine, this means that an overwhelming majority of drug offenders receiving mandatory periods of imprisonment without parole eligibility are Black. These statistics are reflective of the impact of the 100:1 ratio, which was enacted as a part of the 1986 legislation and was used under the federal sentencing guidelines as a means of imposing mandatory minimum sentences for cocaine-related offenses. In 1996, U.S. District Court Judge Clyde S. Cahill in Missouri refused to give a 10-year mandatory sentence to a young African American convicted of trafficking crack cocaine. He stated that the federal law was discriminatory. He used the terms "subtle racism" to describe the fact that no Whites had been charged by federal prosecutors in his district with trafficking crack cocaine. His sentencing decision was overturned on appeal.

Table 1   Race of Drug Defendants, 2009

	White N	%	Black N	%	Hispanic N	%
Type of Drug						
Crack Cocaine	558	9.8	4,476	79.0	584	10.3
Powder Cocaine	1,031	17.1	1,684	28.0	3,202	53.2

Source: U.S. Sentencing Commission, *2009 Sourcebook of Federal Statistics.*

Sentencing for drug offenses have produced racially disparate impacts beyond Illinois and the federal system. In the first five years following the passage of the Omnibus Anti-Drug Abuse Act of 1986, African Americans came to account for more than 80 percent of the increase in state and federal prison inmates. In state facilities, during the course of the five years, Blacks incarcerated for drug offenses increased by 465.5 percent compared to a 110.6 percent increase for whites. In the state of Minnesota for the period 1988 to 1994, the per capita increase in felony drug sentences for Blacks versus that for whites was 1,096 percent compared to 71 percent (Jones-Brown, 2000). Such sentencing disparities led analysts to refer to the "War on Drugs" campaign as that of a "War on African Americans." Supporting evidence could be found in the fact that where states, such as Georgia, imposed "Three Strikes" legislation to address drug offenses, those strikes were disproportionately enforced against African Americans. In fact, Georgia imposed a tough two-strikes law, which mandated a life imprisonment sentence for a second drug offense. In 1995, the statute had been used against only 1 percent of White defendants facing a second drug conviction and against more than 16 percent of eligible Black defendants. This resulted in 98.4 percent of all inmates serving life sentences in the state under this statute being African American (Jones-Brown, 2000).

In 2010, the enactment of the federal Fair Sentencing Act sought to reduce sentencing disparities based on the distinction between crack and powder cocaine by reducing the existing 100:1 ratio to a ratio of 18:1. This required individuals to be in possession of 28 grams of crack cocaine (instead of 5 grams) to trigger mandatory minimum penalties (Sentencing Project, 2010). Ironically, Minnesota lawmakers saw the wisdom in eliminating this distinction as early as 1992, after one of its judges, Pamela Alexander, had ruled (in 1990) that the sentencing disparities the law created were unconstitutional. With the 2010 federal legislative action, racial disparity within this area of drug sentencing is expected to decrease; however, statistics on other sentencing practices reveal a similar disparity.

Life without Parole

Beyond drug sentencing, African Americans are overrepresented as one examines the number of individuals sentenced to life without parole (LWOP). According to Nellis, "Blacks comprise 56.4 percent of the LWOP population; . . . in some states, the proportion of Blacks serving LWOP sentences is as high as 73.3 percent, as is the case in Louisiana" (2010: 28). A similar pattern was found when LWOP sentencing was examined at the federal level. Nellis noted that "[i]n the federal system, 877 (71.3%) of the 1,230 LWOP prisoners are African American" (2010: 28). The offenders who received this sentence were representative of a variety of offense types. Individuals convicted of murder were more likely to receive this sentence; however, some states use

LWOP sentences for other serious offenses such as robbery and kidnapping (Nellis, 2010). This disparity contributes to the aging population of America's prison system, a factor that keeps more African Americans behind bars, thus sustaining the notion of the criminal justice system as an unfair race-based system. Racial disparity is also found in prosecutors' decisions to seek the death penalty and the decision of judges and juries to impose it. This is particularly true in cases where Black defendants are accused of killing White victims (see Death Penalty).

Juvenile Justice

Juvenile justice is also an area in which the issue of race plays a role in sentencing. Jordan and Freiburger (2010) examined the role of race and ethnicity in the sentencing outcomes for juveniles sentenced in adult court. It was found that "Black youth are more likely to be sentenced to both prison and jail (rather than probation), as compared to White youth" (195). Variations in sentencing based on region were also found as "Black youths were less likely to receive probation in the Northeast than in the South" (Jordan & Freiburger, 2010: 196). A substantial body of evidence notes that Black youth are more likely to be waived or transferred to adult court for crimes committed as a juvenile than are their White counterparts and are less likely to be sentenced to treatment alternatives as opposed to secure juvenile correctional facilities for their juvenile crimes, including drug use.

As previously noted, a myriad of factors influence the sentencing practices of judges. Consequently, the sentence a defendant receives may be based on extra-legal factors. Beyond overt or implicit racial stereotypes, extra-legal variables may also include factors such as employment history, length of residence, and family ties, all of which may appear to be race neutral, but in reality are all factors that are impacted by historical and contemporary racial discrimination that often leave African American defendants at a serious disadvantage. For example, research by Pager (2003) has found that a White male with a criminal record has a greater likelihood of being hired for a job than a Black male without one. For defendants accused of less serious or nonviolent crimes, employment or the promise of employment is a significant factor when it comes to being considered for release on probation or other forms of community supervision as opposed to serving time in jail (Miller, 1996). Research also suggests that African American defendants are less likely to receive noncustodial sentences of fines, restitution, or community service than are their White counterparts (Gilbert, 2000) (see Alternative Sentencing). Since these sentencing alternatives may be based upon a defendant's ability to pay, economic disadvantage may make such alternatives inaccessible to those who live in an urban environment, are from a minority group, and are less economically advantaged.

La-Shawn Stewart

See also: Alternative Sentencing; Correctional System and African Americans; Death Penalty; Fair Sentencing Act of 2010; Federal Death Penalty Abolition Act of 2009 (S. 650); Federal Sentencing Disparity; Socioeconomic Factors; Three Strikes Legislation; War on Drugs

References

Beckett, K., K. Nyrop, and L. Pfingst. "Race, Drugs, and Policing: Understanding Disparities in Drug Delivery Arrests." *Criminology* 44, no. 1 (2006): 105–38.

Brennan, P., and C. Spohn. "Race/Ethnicity and Sentencing Outcomes among Drug Offenders in North Carolina." *Journal of Contemporary Criminal Justice* 24 (2008): 371–98.

Crow, M., and J. C. Kunselman. "Sentencing Female Drug Offenders: Reexamining Racial and Ethnic Disparities." *Women & Criminal Justice* 19, no. 3 (2009): 191–216.

Eberhardt, J., V. Purdie, P. Goff, and P. Davies. "Seeing Black: Race, Crime, and Visual Processing." *Journal of Personality and Social Psychology* 87, no. 6 (2004): 876–93.

Gilbert, E. "The Significance of Race in the Use of Restitution." In *The System in Black and White: Exploring the Connections between Race, Crime and Punishment,* edited by M. Markowitz and D. Jones, 199–212. Westport, CT: Praeger, 2000.

Jones-Brown, D. *Race, Crime and Punishment.* Philadelphia: Chelsea House, 2000.

Jordan, K. L., and T. L. Freiburger. "Examining the Impact of Race and Ethnicity on the Sentencing of Juveniles in Adult Court." *Criminal Justice Policy Review* 21, no. 2 (2010): 185–201.

Lurigio, A., and P. Loose. "The Disproportionate Incarceration of African Americans for Drug Offenses: The National and Illinois Perspective." *Journal of Ethnicity in Criminal Justice* 6, no. 3 (2008): 223–47.

Mauer, M. "Viewpoint: The Impact of Mandatory Minimum Sentences Penalties in Federal Sentencing." *Judicature* 94, no. 1 (2010): 6–8, 40. http://www.ajs.org/ajs/publications/ajs_j udicature.asp.

Miller, J. *Search and Destroy: African American Males in the Criminal Justice System.* New York: Cambridge University Press, 1996.

Nellis, A. "Throwing Away the Key: The Expansion of Life without Parole Sentences in the United States." *Federal Sentencing Reporter* 23, no. 1 (2010): 27–32.

Olson, D. E. *Racial Disparities in Drug Sentencing. Testimony Presented to the Illinois House Judiciary, Criminal Justice Committee.* Chicago, IL: Olive-Harvey College, 2001.

Pager, D. "The Mark of a Criminal Record." *American Journal of Sociology* 108, no. 5 (2003): 937–75.

The Sentencing Project. *Federal Crack Cocaine Sentencing,* 2010. http://www.sentencing-project.org/detail/publication.cfm?publication_id=153&id=120.

U.S. Sentencing Commission. 2009a. *U.S. Sentencing Commission 2009 Annual Report.* Washington, DC: U.S. Sentencing Commission, 2009. http://www.ussc.gov/Data_and _Statistics/Annual _Reports_and_Sourcebooks /2009/ Chap5_09.pdf.

U.S. Sentencing Commission. 2009b. *2009 Sourcebook of Federal Statistics.* Washington, DC:

U.S. Sentencing Commission, 2009. http://www.ussc.gov/Data_and_Statistics/Annual_Reports_and_Sourcebooks/2009/Table34.pdf.

U.S. Sentencing Commission. *Special Report to the Congress: Cocaine and Federal Sentencing Policy.* Washington, DC: U.S. Sentencing Commission, February 1995.

Sex Crimes and Race

There has been a binary model of race in the United States since its inception, and within this racial model there is also a binary gender hierarchy (Jewell, 1993). Patriarchal ideologies shape the ways in which "othered" or "subordinated" groups are often stigmatized to maintain group exclusion and oppression (i.e., the feminization of African American males or the masculinization of African American females) (Garfield, 2010; Jewell, 1993; Miller-Sommerville, 2004). Black women have been deemed Jezebels and therefore deserving of sexual violation, and the myth of Black male hypersexuality has interacted with the archetype of White female sexual purity (Jewell, 1993; Lindquist-Dorr, 2004), feeding a mythical belief that all Black men secretly desire to sexually "ravish" White women (Hamlin, 2001) (see Lynching and Ida B. Wells-Barnett). The preservation of White female chastity from Black men, along with the tacitly accepted abuse of Black women's bodies by both White and Black men, has served the process of racial and gender marginalization in the United States (Garfield, 2005; Jewell, 1993; Block, 2006). For both historical and contemporary reasons, the relationship between race and sex crimes is considered within these binary racial frameworks.

Contrary to popular myths about the prevalence of Black men raping White women, within the context of racial hierarchies and the criminalization of African Americans (particularly men), and the creation and enforcement (both formally and informally) of racially segregated environments, inter-racial rape becomes a difficult endeavor, and, if attempted or completed by Black men, the likelihood of "getting away with it" is slim. It is important to note that, under the same myth, rape is a feminized crime, which has excluded the possibility of male victims though available statistics document the occurrence of same-sex victimizations.

Since the 1980s, there have been headline-making cases that have shaped and reinforced the racialized myths regarding sexual violence in the American context (Hamlin, 2001), and serve as prime examples of their differential social and systemic treatment. The way we "read" these cases, like that of Tawana Brawley, a 15-year-old Black female who accused six White men of rape, a case that was branded the "Tawana Brawley Hoax," engages the sexualized myths of race (e.g., rape doesn't happen to Black women or girls). Similarly, the 1992 case of world heavyweight champion and African American boxer, Mike Tyson, a case referred to as "The Rape of Mike Tyson" (Lule, 1995), rather than the rape of his alleged victim, drew forth gendered discussions of sexual violence. Tyson was accused and convicted of raping an 18-year-old Miss Black America contestant, Desiree Washington. In both these cases, the alleged victims were African American.

By contrast, in 1989, while jogging alone in New York's Central Park, a 29-year-old White female, Trisha Meili, was attacked, raped, and left for dead. On the same evening, a group of more than 30 Black teenage boys were reportedly in the park, engaged in what became known as "wildin'," or attacking strangers at random. They immediately became suspects in the attack, which became infamously known as the "Central Park Jogger" case. Five of the boys were convicted of rape in 1990. In 2002 the judgments against the five were vacated when convicted rapist Matias Reyes, already serving a life sentence for other crimes, confessed, and DNA evidence linked him alone to the rape. The fact that the unidentified DNA sample existed at the time of the initial investigation had not stopped law enforcement officials from moving forward with the prosecution and conviction of the Black and Latino youths. Public debates about sex crime cases like these engage racialized and gendered myths about sex crimes and race. The debates are shaped by sexualized constructions of race and racialized constructions of sex, raising questions about how to extricate ourselves from the harmful social consequences of these constructions (Hamlin, 2001).

Data show that racialized myths of sexual violence can be shattered using official statistics. Statistics from sources such as the National Crime Victimization Survey (NCVS) reveal facts that are in stark contrast to the prevailing beliefs about the prevalence of inter-racial sex crimes, and their victims and perpetrators. For example, according to NCVS data from 2007, White men are dramatically more likely to experience sexual victimization compared to Black men, thus dispelling the notion that White women are the only ones susceptible to sexualized "stranger danger" (Table 1). Additionally, *intra*-racial sexual violence is more likely to occur, contrasting the myth of the inter-racial rape of White women by Black men (Table 2).

Details included in Table 3 help to shatter the myth of the animalistic pack or "wild" Black male gang-rape scenario, showing that nearly half of all White victimizations are committed by groups of White-only perpetrators, and that over three-fourths of Black victims are gang raped by persons perceived to be from their own racial group (Bureau of Justice Statistics, 2008). Consistent with common beliefs, women are substantially more likely to be victims of rape/sexual assault (attempted or completed) than are men (Table 4). But it is noted that the lack of data for Black male sexual victimization may be due to Black males' unwillingness to report such incidents when they occur.

Controlling for the substantial difference in the size of the Black and White female populations, Tables 5 and 6 include figures that show a greater rate of sexual victimization per 1,000 White women and girls over age 12 than for their Black

Table 1 Percent of Sexual Victimizations Involving Strangers, by Gender and Race of Victims (2007)[a]

	Percent of Victimizations Involving Strangers
Gender and Race[b]	Rape/ Sexual Assault[c]
Both Genders	%
White only	52
Black only	57.8*
Male	
White only	57.4*
Black only	0*
Female	
White only	44.9
Black only	57.8*

[a]Bureau of Justice Statistics (2008). Criminal Victimization in the United States, 2007 Statistical Tables *National Crime Victimization Survey*. U.S. Department of Justice, Office of Justice Programs: Washington, D.C. (Table 30).

[b]Excludes data on persons of "other" races and persons indicating two or more races.

[c]Includes verbal threats of rape and threats of sexual assault.

*Estimate is based on about 10 or fewer sample cases.

Table 2 Percent Distribution of Single-Offender Victimizations, Based on Race of Victims, by Type of Crime and Perceived Race of Offender (2007)[a]

Type of Crime & Race[b] of Victim	# of Single-Offender Victimizations	% of Single-Offender Victimizations by Perceived Race of Offender		
		Total %	White	Black
Rape/Sexual Assault[c]				
White Only	185,430	100	75.5	7.6*
Black Only	12,780*	100*	0*	100*

[a]Bureau of Justice Statistics (2008). Criminal Victimization in the United States, 2007 Statistical Tables *National Crime Victimization Survey*. U.S. Department of Justice, Office of Justice Programs: Washington, D.C. (Table 42). Detail may not add to total shown because of rounding.

[b]Excludes data on persons of "other" races and persons indicating two or more races.

[c]Includes verbal threats of rape and threats of sexual assault.

*Estimate is based on about 10 or fewer sample cases.

Table 3 Percent Distribution of Multiple-Offender Victimizations by Type of Crime, Race of Victims, and Perceived Race of Offenders (2007)[a]

| | | Percent of Multiple-Offender Victimizations | | | | | |
| | | | Perceived Race of Offenders | | | | |
Crime Type & Victim Race[b]	# of Multiple-Offender Victimizations	Total	All White	All Black	All Other	Mixed Races	Not Known and Not Available
Crimes of Violence[c]							
White Only	66,940	100%	45.8%	25.5%	4.9%	11.5%	12.4%
Black Only	159,610	100%	6.6%*	75.1%	2.6%*	10.2%*	5.6%*

[a]Bureau of Justice Statistics (2008). Criminal Victimization in the United States, 2007 Statistical Tables *National Crime Victimization Survey*. U.S. Department of Justice, Office of Justice Programs: Washington, D.C. (Table 48). Detail may not add to total shown because of rounding.

[b]Excludes data on persons of "other" races and persons indicating two or more races.

[c]Includes data on rape and sexual assault, not shown separately.

*Estimate is based on about 10 or fewer sample cases.

Table 4 Number of Victimizations and Victimization Rates for Persons Age 12 and Over, by Type of Crime and Gender of Victims (2007)[a]

| | Rate per 1,000 Persons Age 12 and Over | | | | | |
| | Both Genders | | Male | | Female | |
Type of Crime	Number	Rate	Number*	Rate*	Number	Rate
Rape/Sexual Assault	248,280	1.0	11,300	0.1	236,980	1.8
Rape/Attempted Rape	140,620	0.6	8,400	0.1	132,220	1.0
Rape	69,850	0.3	3,120	0.0	66,730	0.5
Attempted Rape[b]	70,770	0.3	5,280	0.0	65,490	0.5
Sexual Assault[c]	107,660	0.4	2,900	0.0	104,760	.8
Population Age 12 and Over	250,344,870	...	122,122,700	...	128,222,170	...

[a]Bureau of Justice Statistics (2008). Criminal Victimization in the United States, 2007 Statistical Tables *National Crime Victimization Survey*. U.S. Department of Justice, Office of Justice Programs: Washington, D.C. (Table 2). Detail may not add to total shown because of rounding.

[b]Includes verbal threats of rape.

[c]Includes threats.

*Estimate is based on about 10 or fewer sample cases.

...Not applicable.

Table 5 Number of Victimizations and Victimization Rates for Persons Age 12+, by Type of Crime and Race of Victims (2007)[a]

| | Rate per 1,000 Persons Age 12 and Over | | | |
| | White Only | | Black Only | |
Type of Crime	Number	Rate	Number*	Rate*
Rape/Sexual Assault	198,890	1.0	15,670	0.5
Rape/Attempted Rape	109,420	0.5	12,900	0.4
Rape	49,350	0.4	6,730	0.2
Attempted Rape[b]	60,070	0.3	6,170	0.2
Sexual Assault[c]	89,480	0.4	2,780	0.1
Population Age 12 +	203,470,370	...	30,385,460	...

[a]Bureau of Justice Statistics (2008). Criminal Victimization in the United States, 2007 Statistical Tables *National Crime Victimization Survey*. U.S. Department of Justice, Office of Justice Programs: Washington, D.C. (Table 5). Detail may not add to total shown because of rounding.
[b]Includes verbal threats of rape.
[c]Includes threats.
* Estimate is based on about 10 or fewer sample cases.
...Not applicable.

counterparts. Research suggests that these differences may be accounted for in part by racial differentials in victims' willingness to report such crimes and authorities' willingness to believe that such victimization has taken place (Irving, 2008). Overall, these official data can be used to dispel at least two prevailing myths about sex crimes and race—the prevalence of raging Black male sexual aggression targeting White women only and suggestions that Black women are sexually provocative and are therefore unlikely to experience sexual interactions as rape.

Brenda Vollman

See also: Dating Violence; Death Penalty; Domestic Violence and African American Females; False Confessions; Francois, Kendall; Inter-Racial Offending; Intra-Racial Offending; Lynching; Price, Craig; Racial Hoaxes and Media Representations; Racial Stereotyping and Wrongful Convictions; Shakur, Tupac Amaru

References

Block, Sharon. *Rape and Sexual Power in Early America.* Chapel Hill: The University of North Carolina Press, 2006.

Bureau of Justice Statistics. *Criminal Victimization in the United States, 2007 Statistical Tables, National Crime Victimization Survey.* U.S. Department of Justice, Office of Justice Programs: Washington DC, 2008.

Table 6 Number of Victimizations and Victimization Rates Age 12+, by Type of Crime and Gender and Race[a] of Victims (2007)[b]

Type of Crime	Rate per 1,000 Persons Age 12 and Over							
	Male				Female			
	White Only		Black Only		White Only		Black Only	
	Number	Rate	Number	Rate	Number	Rate	Number	Rate
Rape/Sexual Assault[c]	8,180*	0.1	0*	0.0*	190,720	1.8	15,670	0.9*
Population Age 12+	100,276,590	...	13,868,320	...	103,193,780	...	16,517,140	...

[a]Excludes data on persons of "other" races and persons indicating two or more races.
[b]Bureau of Justice Statistics (2008). Criminal Victimization in the United States, 2007 Statistical Tables *National Crime Victimization Survey.* U.S. Department of Justice, Office of Justice Programs: Washington, D.C. (Table 6).
[c]Includes verbal threats of rape and threats of sexual assault.
*Estimate is based on about 10 or fewer sample cases.
...Not applicable.

Garfield, G. *Through Our Eyes: African American Men's Experiences of Race, Gender and Violence.* Piscataway, NJ: Rutgers University Press, 2010.

Garfield, G. *Knowing What We Know: African American Women's Experience of Violence and Violation.* Piscataway, NJ: Rutgers University Press, 2005.

Hamlin, J. "List of Rape Myths." Sociology of Rape, University of Minnesota–Duluth, 2001. http://www.d.umn.edu/cla/faculty/jhamlin/3925/myths.html, last modified March 3, 2005.

Irving, T. "Decoding Black Women: Policing Practices and Rape Prosecution on the Streets of Philadelphia." *National Women's Studies Association Journal* 20, no. 2 (Summer 2008): 100–20.

Jewell, K. Sue. *From Mammy to Miss America and Beyond: Cultural Images and the Shaping of U.S. Social Policy.* New York: Routledge, 1993.

Lindquist-Dorr, Lisa. *White Women, Rape, and the Power of Race in Virginia, 1900–1960.* Chapel Hill: The University of North Carolina Press, 2004.

Lule, J. "The Rape of Mike Tyson: Race, the Press and Symbolic Types." *Critical Studies in Media Communication* 12, no. 2 (1995): 176–95.

Miller-Sommerville, Diane. *Rape and Race in the Nineteenth-Century South.* Chapel Hill: The University of North Carolina Press, 2004.

Shakur, Assata (aka Joanne Chesimard) (1947–)

Assata Shakur was born Joanne Byron on July 16, 1947, in Jamaica, New York. In 1967, she married fellow student activist Louis Chesimard. Though they divorced in 1970, she retained her ex-husband's last name. In May 2013, she became the first woman on the FBI's list of most wanted terrorists (Perkins, 2000; Porter, 2013). May 2 marked the fortieth anniversary of a confrontation between Shakur/Chesimard and the New Jersey State Police, during which she was wounded and a trooper, Werner Foerster, was fatally shot (Perkins, 2000). For more than 30 years Shakur/Chesimard has been a fugitive. Since 1984, she has been living in Cuba, a nation that has no extradition agreement with the United States (Perkins, 2000). On May 2, 2013, New Jersey State police superintendent colonel Joseph "Rick" Fuentes announced that the reward for information leading to the capture of Shakur/Chesimard had been raised to $2 million, double the $1 million offered in 2005. The Department of Justice is offering $1 million and the state police are providing the additional million through civil and criminal forfeiture funds (Cleaver, 2005; Porter, 2013).

Though born in New York, at age three, Shakur/Chesimard moved with her family to Wilmington, North Carolina (Perkins, 2000). The family returned to Queens when Shakur/Chesimard was a teenager (Scheffler, 2002). In 1970, Joanne

A poster with photographs of Joanne Chesimard, a fugitive for more than 30 years, is on display during a news conference giving updates on the search for Chesimard on May 2, 2013, in Newark, New Jersey. The reward for the capture and return of convicted murderer Chesimard, one of New Jersey's most notorious fugitives, was doubled to $2 million on the 40th anniversary of the violent confrontation that led to the slaying of a New Jersey state trooper. The FBI also announced it has made Chesimard, now living in Cuba as Assata Shakur, the first woman on its list of most wanted terrorists. (Associated Press)

Chesimard changed her name to Assata Shakur, with Assata meaning "she who struggles" and Shakur meaning "the thankful one" (Serrano, 2007). During the late 1960s, Shakur/Chesimard was a student activist at the Borough of Manhattan Community College (BMCC), protesting the lack of Black faculty and lack of a Black studies curriculum (Williams, 1993). Today, Shakur lives a conflicted life, with some describing her as a political activist, freedom fighter, and ex-political prisoner, while others see her as a "cop killer" and fugitive from justice (Porter, 2013).

During the Civil Rights era of the 1960s, Shakur was a part of the Black Panther Party and the Black Liberation Army (BLA), and an active participant in both the Black liberation and student rights movements (Perkins, 2000). By 1969, during a conservative era that included J. Edgar Hoover's directorship of the FBI, a mission was developed to disban all antigovernment, radical, and activist groups. Hoover described organizations such as the Black Panther Party as "the greatest threat to the internal security" of the United States. The Black Panther Party was also the FBI's COINTELPRO (COunter INTELligence PROgram) number-one targeted organization.

Between 1973 and 1977, Assata Shakur/Joanne Chesimard was accused of several crimes, including two armed robberies, the kidnapping of a Brooklyn heroin dealer, a failed ambush, and the attempted murder of two Queens police officers (Panache, 2011). Of these charges, three resulted in acquittals, one in a hung jury, and two in dismissals (Panache, 2011). Though she faced criminal charges and served periods of incarceration in both New York and New Jersey, the most well-known crimes of which Assata Shakur was accused were the shootings of her friend and comrade Zayd Shakur and New Jersey State Trooper Foerster (Perkins, 2000). Shakur was convicted of these charges by an all-White jury in 1977 and sentenced to life in prison plus 33 years to be spent at the Clinton Correctional Facility for Women. Two years after she began serving her sentence, Shakur/Chesimard escaped with the assistance of three armed members of the BLA. During a visit with her at the prison, the members pulled guns and took two guards hostage before escaping with Shakur/Chesimard in a prison van.

There are stark contrasts in the accounts given about the incident that led to the life sentence. According to defense witnesses, during the incident, Assata Shakur was badly beaten and shot twice while defenseless. It is reported that three medical experts—a neurologist, pathologist, and a surgeon—testified it was impossible to have shot the trooper and her friend based upon the location of her own wounds (Shakur, 1987; Lewis, 2000). One source contends that no evidence was ever found that Assata Shakur held the 9-mm weapon used in the shooting. The source also claims that there was no fingerprint evidence connecting Assata Shakur to the crime (Panache, 2011).

By contrast, the New Jersey State Police version of the incident is that during a traffic stop for a broken tail light, Shakur and two companions, one of them being Zayd Shakur, engaged in a gunfight with Trooper Foerster and his partner, James Harper. The agency also claims that during the incident, once both troopers where injured, Shakur/Chesimard took Foerster's gun and shot him twice in the head as he lay on the ground (Porter, 2013).

The shootings took place during a tumultuous time for race relations in the United States. Much of the turmoil centered around police use of force against African Americans and the response by groups such as the Black Panther Party and the BLA. In a press conference announcing the increased reward for the capture of Shakur/Chesimard, agent Aaron Ford of the FBI noted that the BLA was responsible for killing more than a dozen police officers during the 1970s and 1980s (Porter, 2013).

In contrast to the coldblooded assassination described by the state police, Shakur described being "shot once with my arms held up in the air and then once again from the back" (Shakur & Lewis, 2000: 1). In an interview she gave the following account of the events:

> After being almost fatally wounded, I managed to climb in the back seat of the car to get away from the shooting. Sundiata drove the car five miles down the road, carried me into a grassy area because he was afraid that the police would see the car parked on the side of the road and would start shooting at it again. It was there that I was captured, dragged out of the car, stomped and then left on the ground.

> Although I drifted in and out of consciousness, I remember clearly, both while I was lying on the ground and while I was in the ambulance, the state troopers repeatedly ask, "'Is she dead yet?'" (Shakur & Lewis, 2000: 1)

In her 1987 autobiography, she also recounts that once brought to the hospital, she was handcuffed and beaten further by police, and nearly blinded by one officer who repeatedly dug his nails into her eyes (Shakur, 1987: 8). At her trial, Shakur/Chesimard was represented by legendary trial attorney William Kunstler. The National Conference of Black Lawyers, the National Alliance Against Racist and Political Repression, and the United Church of Christ Commission for Racial Justice filed a petition with the United Nations on her behalf. The petition delineated the treatment of political prisoners in U.S. prisons, noting that they were often targeted for execution. Shakur/Chesimard contends that her escape from prison and departure from the United States is predicated upon her fear of harm from government entities, namely the FBI and the New Jersey and New York State police.

From Cuba, Shakur continues to speak out against what she describes as the harsh realities of race relations in New Jersey and the broader United States, specifically as they relate to the experiences of African American people. In December 1997, Assata Shakur made contact with Pope John Paul II when she learned that efforts were being made by the New Jersey State Police to involve him as a possible mediator in a plan to extradite her back to New Jersey from Cuba (Perkins, 2000). In media interviews Shakur continues to denounce the United States for police brutality and socioeconomic inequality based on race. The messages in such interviews have contributed to a characterization of her as anti-American and the government's labeling of her as a terrorist.

In acknowledging the 40-year anniversary of the incident between Shakur and Troopers Foerster and Harper, Colonel Fuentes expressed optimism that authorities might soon be able to bring Shakur/Chesimard to justice, citing the cases of several other fugitives who had recently been returned from Cuba. Assata Shakur is now in her mid sixties. When she arrived in Cuba she was in her mid thirties. While some see Cuba as harboring a fugitive, others say her presence there is a grant of political asylum under international and Cuban law. To some, Assata Shakur is a violent criminal; to others, she was persecuted as a political prisoner for fighting against an oppressive superstructure that fostered an environment of hostility and injustice toward African Americans during a conflict-filled period in the United States. Shakur has written an autobiography that depicts in detail the trials and tribulations she faced as a political prisoner, her life as an activist, and the government destruction of revolutionary groups fighting for equality (Perkins, 2000). According to a Web site in her name, she is known to many as a Black revolutionary who seeks justice for all.

Further information about Assata Shakur can be found at www.assatashakur.org.

Nishaun Battle and Delores Jones-Brown

See also: Black Panther Party; Carmichael, Stokely; Civil Rights Movement; Davis, Angela Yvonne; Prisons; Shakur, Tupac Amaru

References

Cleaver, Kathleen. "The Fugitive." *Essence Magazine,* 2005.

Lewis, Ida E. "Assata Shakur: Profiled and On the Run." *The New Crisis* 107, no. 6 (November/December 2000): 23–5.

Panache, Myra. "Assata Shakur." Panache Report, 2011. http://panachereport.com/channels/hip%20hop%20gallery/AssataShakur1.htm.

Perkins, Margo V. *Autobiography as Activism*: *Three Black Women of the Sixties.* Jackson, MS: University Press of Mississippi, 2000.

Porter, David. "Joanne Chesimard, Black Liberation Army Fugitive in Cuba, Added to FBI's Most Wanted Terrorists List." *The Huffington Post,* May 2, 2013. http://www.huffingtonpost.com/2013/05/02/joanne-chesmard-fbi-_n_3200053.html?view.

Scheffler, Judith. *Wall Tappings: An International Anthology of Women's Prison Writings, 2000 to the Present.* New York: Feminist Press at The City University of New York, 2002.

Serrano, Alina. "Assata Shakur: A Woman Warrior." *Socialism and Liberation Magazine* 4, no. 2 (February 1, 2007): 1–3. http://www2.pslweb.org/site/News2?page=NewsArticle&id=10667&news_iv_ctrl=1044.

Shakur, Assata. *Assata: An Autobiography.* London: Lawrence Hill Books, 1987.

Shakur, A., and I. E. Lewis. "Assata Shakur: Profiled and on the Run." *New Crisis* (November/December 2000): 1–4. http://www.assatashakur.org/profiled.htm.

Williams, Evelyn. *Inadmissible Evidence: The Story of the African-American Trial Lawyer Who Defended the Black Liberation Army.* London: Lawrence Hill Books, 1993.

Shakur, Tupac Amaru (1971–1996)

Tupac Amaru Shakur was born Lesane Parish Crooks on June 16, 1971, in New York City. His mother, Alice Williams, also known as Afeni Shakur (Davis), was pregnant with him while in jail awaiting trial on charges stemming from a 1969 arrest for activities associated with her membership in a group that came to be known as the "New York Panther 21" (Dyson, 2001). She successfully defended herself against charges of conspiracy and possession of weapons (Dyson, 2001). The Panther 21 were members of the New York Chapter of the Black Panther Party who were accused of conspiring to blow up the New York Botanical Gardens and

Known for his career as a "Gangsta" rapper, Tupac Shakur was fatally shot on September 7, 1996. His homicide has not been solved. (Time Life Pictures/Getty Images)

other locations. Their trial has been called "the longest political trial in New York's history." All 21 defendants were acquitted (Dyson, 2001). Williams gave birth to a son one month after being released from jail. Shortly after giving birth, Alice Williams changed her own name to Afeni Shakur, and gave her son the name Tupac Amaru Shakur, after a revolutionary Incan leader (Dyson, 2001). The name Tupac Amaru is Incan for "shining serpent" (Dyson, 2001).

It has been suggested that Afeni's years of deep involvement with the Black Panther movement and her battles with the criminal justice system influenced her son's worldview (Dyson, 2001). He was once quoted as saying, "I was cultivated in prison, my embryo was in prison" (Shakur, 1999). His stepfather, Mutulu Shakur, also known as Jeral Wayne Williams, was sentenced to 60 years in prison while Tupac was still young, and an aunt, Assata Shakur, also known as Joanne Chesimard, is currently wanted by the FBI for the murder of a New Jersey state trooper (Dyson, 2001) (see the entry on Assata Shakur). (Some sources refer to Assata Shakur as Tupac's godmother or the sister of his stepfather.) Reportedly, all of these things affected him deeply (Ardis, 2004; Shakur, 1999). As a young child, Tupac was surrounded by political activists from his mother's inner circle of friends and relatives (Dyson, 2001). At age 10, when asked what he wanted to be when he grew up, Tupac proudly declared, "A Revolutionary" (White, 1997). It is reported that the exposure and encouragement that Tupac received from his mother was instrumental in developing his acclaimed creative skills (Jenkins, 2006).

Tupac Shakur has been described as a musical genius, providing creative works through rap music, acting, and poetry. His lyrics focused on the ills of urban life—poverty, unemployment, teenage pregnancy, and crack addiction. Through his music he described his experiences with police brutality and life in a subculture of violence (Ardis, 2004). The conditions that Tupac confronted while growing up were in many ways similar to those experienced by other African American urban males, and in other ways they were not so typical (Jenkins, 2006). Growing up, he participated in a Harlem theatre group, and at age 16 he studied both ballet and acting. He began rapping while at the Baltimore School for the Arts (Dyson, 2001; Bastfield, 2002). Tupac's life changed drastically when his mother sent him and his siblings to Marin City, California (Dyson, 2001). Although she made the move to protect them, the vices of Marin City proved similar to other urban settings, and soon Tupac began selling crack. Tupac reportedly saw selling crack as a vital means of survival (Jenkins, 2006).

In California, he landed a spot with the musical group Digital Underground, but soon his talents outshined the talents of the other members of the group. Shortly after having joined the group, he released his first solo album, *2Pacalypse Now*. Three months after the release of the album, he made his big-screen debut in the movie *Juice*. Around the same time, Tupac filed a $10 million dollar lawsuit against the Oakland Police Department, alleging that he had been the victim of police brutality during an arrest for jaywalking. It is reported that he received $42,000 from the suit. Battles with the criminal justice system would become a constant in his life and would follow him until his death.

Less than a year after the release of his first album, a six-year-old boy was shot in the head and killed during an altercation in Marin City. Tupac was somehow implicated in the underlying dispute that resulted in the injury to the child. One month after the incident, Vice President Dan Quayle denounced Tupac's music as having "no place in our society" (Broder, 1992). However, scholars have suggested that the hip-hop industry's packaging of rap artists as dangerous Black criminals was a significant part of the attraction of rap music for suburban Whites and an expanding international audience (Riley, 2005).

Tupac continued to make music and movies, and to find trouble with the law. He was arrested four different times in 1993, primarily for assault charges. The last incident was the most serious; in November of that year Tupac, along with three of his friends, was accused of sexual abuse and sodomy of a young woman (Powell, 1997; Smith, 1997). The various arrests, legal problems, and personal "industry beefs" that Tupac endured were incorporated into his rap music and suggested to the listener that he had no general expectation of a positive outcome for his life (Riley, 2005). Tupac continued to record music during his sexual assault trial (Hoye & Ali, 2003). On November 30, 1994, he was shot five times during a robbery in a Times Square recording studio. He was there to meet with hip-hop artist and producer Puffy (Sean Combs) and fellow rapper Notorious B.I.G (Brooklyn native Christopher Wallace). Up until that time they were all considered friends, but after the shooting Tupac expressed his belief that the robbery had been a setup and that Puffy and B.I.G. had somehow been involved (Dyson, 2001). The "gangsta" mentality perpetuated by negative elements within hip-hop culture instigated cries for retaliation (Riley, 2005) that led to a dangerous and violent West Coast/East Coast rivalry in the rap music industry.

On February 14, 1995, Tupac was sent to New York's Rikers Island as part of his four-and-a-half-year prison sentence for sexual assault. *Me against the World,* the album he released while serving time for the conviction, reached number one on the Billboard charts. Sources indicate that Tupac Shakur is the first artist to have a number one hit while serving a felony sentence. After serving eight months in prison, Marion "Suge" Knight, Jr., the CEO of Death Row Records, posted a $1.4 million dollar bond for the release of Tupac (Powell, 1997; Smith 1997). Upon release, Tupac immediately returned to California and signed with the Death Row label and resumed recording music (Powell, 1997; Smith, 1997). Less than one year later, Tupac Amaru Shakur was dead. Tupac and Knight were in Las Vegas the night of September 7, 1996, attending a boxing event (Scott, 1997). They were involved in a brief altercation after the fight, and later that evening both rode in a black BMW that had been rented by Knight (Scott, 1997). They were stopped at a red light when a passenger in another car fired several bullets into the BMW, critically injuring Tupac (Scott, 1997). Knight escaped with minor injuries, but Tupac Shakur was pronounced dead six days later on September 13, 1996 (Scott, 1997). He was 25 years old.

As gifted as Tupac was, an examination of the trajectory of his life reveals that he had embraced some concepts and individuals that created conditions for him to become a victim of violence (Riley, 2005; Jenkins, 2006; Ardis, 2004; Fink, 2006; Gobi, 2005). (Notorious B.I.G. also died a violent death, on March 9, 1997.) There are several theories circulating as to who might be responsible for the death of Tupac Shakur. To date, no arrest has been made for his murder. He remains an icon among urban dwellers and consumers of rap music (Mills, 2008; Golus, 2007). Several movies featuring him were released after his death, causing some to question, as with Elvis Presley, whether he is really dead. He has become perhaps larger in death than he was in life, or at least as popular (Mills, 2008; Golus, 2007; Monjauze, 2008). In September 1996, his mother established the Tupac Amaru Shakur Foundation with funds from his posthumous albums. It is reported that he has been cited as one of the top-earning dead celebrities, with his estate estimated to have earned $15 million in 2008. The mission statement for the foundation notes that its purpose is "to provide training and support for students who aspire to enhance their creative talents."

Jennifer Trombley

See also: Black Panther Party; Hip-Hop Culture; Homicide; Jena Six; Police Brutality; Shakur, Assata (aka Joanne Chesimard); Youth Violence

References

Ardis, A. *Inside a Thug's Heart.* New York: Kensington Publishing Corp, 2004.

Bastfield, D. K. *Back in the Day: My Life and Times with Tupac Shakur.* Cambridge, MA: Da Capo Press, 2002.

Broder, J. "Quayle Calls for Pulling Rap Album Tied to Murder Case." *Los Angeles Times,* September 23, 1992. http://articles.latimes.com/1992-09-23/news/mn-1144_1_rap-album.

Dyson, M. E. *Holler If You Hear Me.* New York: Basic Civitas Books, 2001.

Fink, M. *The Last Days of Dead Celebrities.* New York: Miramax Books, 2006.

Gobi. *Thru My Eyes: Thoughts on Tupac Amaru Shakur, in Pictures and Words.* New York: Atria Books, 2005.

Golus, C. *Tupac Shakur.* Minneapolis: Lerner Publications Company, 2007.

Hoye, J., and K. Ali, eds. *Tupac: Resurrection 1971–1996.* New York: Atria Books, 2003.

Jenkins, T. S. "Mr. Nigger: The Challenge of Educating Black Males within American Society." *Journal of Black Studies* 37, no. 1 (September 2006): 127–55.

Mills, C. W. *Tupac Shakur.* New York: Chelsea House Publishers, 2008.

Monjauze, M., ed. *Tupac Remembered: Bearing Witness to a Life and Legacy.* San Francisco: Chronicle Books, 2008.

Powell, K. *This Thug's Life.* New York: Three Rivers Press, 1997.

Riley, A. "The Rebirth of Tragedy out of the Spirit of Hip Hop: A Cultural Sociology of Gangsta Rap Music." *Journal of Youth Studies* 8, no. 3 (September 2005): 297–311.

Scott, C. *The Killing of Tupac Shakur.* Las Vegas: Huntington Press, 1997.

Shakur, T. A. *The Rose That Grew from Concrete.* New York: MTV Books/Pocket Books, 1999.

Smith, D. "Introduction." In *The Vibe History of Hip Hop,* edited by A. Light, 15–19. New York: Three Rivers Press, 1997.

The Tupac Amaru Shakur Foundation, Atlanta, Georgia. http://www.tasf.org/the-foundation/about-tasf/.

White, A. *Rebel for the Hell of It: The Life of Tupac Shakur.* New York: Thunder's Mouth Press, 1997.

Tupac Shakur Discography

1991 - Digital Underground. *This Is an E.P. Release.* Tommy Boy Records.

1991 - *2Pacalypse Now.* Interscope Records.

1993 - *Strictly 4 My N.I.G.G.A.Z.* Interscope Records.

1993 - *Poetic Justice* (soundtrack). Epic Records.

1994 - *Above the Rim* (soundtrack). Death Row Records.

1994 - *Thug Life, Volume 1.* Interscope Records.

1995 - *Me against the World.* Interscope Records.

1995 - *One Million Strong: The Album.* Mergela Records.

1996 - *Makaveli—The Don Killuminati: The 7Day Theory.* Death Row Records.

1996 - *Greatest Hits.* Death Row/Amaru/Interscope Records.

1997 - *Gridlock'd* (soundtrack). Death Row Records.
1997 - *Gang Related* (soundtrack). Death Row Records.
1997 - *R U Still Down? (Remember Me)*. Amaru/Jive Records.
1998 - *Greatest Hits*. Amaru/Death Row/Interscope Records.
1999 - *2Pac & Outlawz—Still I Rise*. Interscope Records.
2000 - *The Rose That Grew from Concrete, Volume 1, an Interpretation of 2Pac's Poetry*. Amaru/Interscope Records.
2001 - *Until the End of Time*. Amaru/Death Row/Interscope Records.

Tupac Shakur Filmography

1992 - *Juice*. Paramount Home Video.
1993 - *Poetic Justice*. Columbia TriStar.
1994 - *Above the Rim*. New Line Home Video.
1997 - *Bullet*. New Line Home Video.
1997 - *Gridlock'd*. Gramercy Pictures.
1997 - *Gang Related*. Orion Pictures.
2003 - *Tupac: Resurrection*. Paramount Pictures.

Tupac Shakur Documentaries

1997 - *Tupac Shakur: Thug Immortal*
1997 - *Tupac Shakur: Words Never Die* (TV)
2001 - *Tupac Shakur: Before I Wake*
2001 - *Welcome to Deathrow*
2002 - *Tupac Shakur: Thug Angel; The Life of an Outlaw*
2002 - *Biggie & Tupac*
2002 - *Tha Westside*
2003 - *2Pac 4 Ever*
2003 - *Tupac: Resurrection*
2004 - *Tupac vs.*
2004 - *Tupac: The Hip Hop Genius* (TV)
2006 - *So Many Years, So Many Tears*
2007 - *Tupac: Assassination*
2009 - *Tupac: Assassination II: Reckoning*

Sharpton, Jr., Alfred Charles (1954–)

Civil rights activist, Christian pastor, and sometimes political candidate Alfred Charles Sharpton, Jr., best known as the Rev. Al Sharpton, was born October 3, 1954, in Brooklyn, New York. Biographer Jay Mallin (2007) revealed that Al Sharpton's mother was from Alabama and his father was from Florida. He began preaching at age four, and was an ordained Pentecostal minister by age 10. Reports note that as a youngster he toured with gospel great Mahalia Jackson and later in life served as tour manager for well-known music artist James Brown (Marcovitz, 2002; Mallin, 2007).

Growing up, Sharpton admired Adam Clayton Powell, Jr., a minister and politician, and the work of Marcus Garvey, a proponent of Black Nationalism and the founder of the Back to Africa Movement (Marcovitz, 2002). At age 10, he had the opportunity to travel to Jamaica, where he began a lengthy friendship with Garvey's widow. Although his father abandoned the family when Sharpton reached age nine, at this age, he also participated in the 1963 March on Washington, organized by Dr. Martin Luther King, Jr., emphasizing freedom and jobs for African Americans. Sharpton has noted that his father's departure sensitized him considerably to the victimization of females. His political candidacies, none of which have garnered him elected office, have included campaigns for the New York State Senate (1978), New York City mayor (1997), the U.S. Senate (1992, 1994), and the U.S. presidency (2004).

Sharpton has had a long and varied history of social activism, primarily focused on fighting against racial prejudice and injustice. In the late 1960s he was active with the Southern Christian Leadership Conference (SCLC). Subsequently, he was an organizer with Jesse Jackson's Operation Breadbasket, which sought to encourage diversity in the workplace, taking on large businesses such as A&P supermarkets. In 1971, at the age of 16, he began his own organization, the National Youth Movement (NYM), with the mission of fighting drugs and raising money to support impoverished inner-city youth.

In 1991, Al Sharpton founded the National Action Network, a civil rights organization in Harlem, from which he currently operates. The organization is involved in efforts to prevent police misconduct. Sharpton also hosts a radio show, "Keeping It Real." He has engaged in activism for justice in situations, including the Howard Beach incident, where White youths attacked three Black males in 1986, and the 1989 murder of Yusuf Hawkins, a 17-year-old African American who was killed by a White mob in Bensonhurst, Brooklyn (Mallin, 2007). Sharpton also protested police abuses such as the police sodomy and beating of Haitian immigrant Abner Louima in 1997; the police killing of Amadou Diallo, a West African immigrant whom New York City police officers shot at 41 times in 1999; and the fatal shooting of Patrick Dorismond, a Black male of Caribbean descent who was shot after a scuffle with an undercover officer who attempted to engage him in a drug deal. In May 2001, Sharpton was sentenced to serve 90 days in jail for trespassing on naval property in Vieques, Puerto Rico. Sharpton was part of a group protesting issues associated with U.S. Navy bombing exercises in Vieques. During his 86-day incarceration, he engaged in a hunger strike as an additional means of civil disobedience to contest the health threats and other problems associated with U.S. naval practices at the site. Sharpton also protested on behalf of former Enron employees. In a 2002 book, he reported that he was invited to do so by a few prominent African American pastors in Houston who had several church members who not only lost employment with the collapse of the former corporate giant, but all of their retirement funds as well. In spite of this explanation, he was criticized in the press for going to Houston to advance his presidential campaign.

A substantial amount of Sharpton's police reform and advocacy work has focused on the issue of racial profiling (Bumgarner, 2004). In 1998, he was involved in the "Jersey Four" case, which brought the question of racial profiling of African Americans by law enforcement agents to the national and international forefront. The case involved four basketball players from New York College, Keshon Moore, Danny Reyes, Rayshawn Brown, and Jarmaine Grant. On April 23, 1998, as the four were traveling on the New Jersey Turnpike, they were fired upon by two state troopers, John Hogan and James Kenna, under a contested set of facts that some have claimed primarily had to do with the fact that they were young Black and Latino males traveling on the highways of New Jersey.

The troopers claimed that they stopped the young men for speeding and that during the course of the stop the driver tried to back over one of the troopers with the van. The young men denied attacking the troopers with the vehicle and a subsequent investigation revealed that in order to thwart allegations of racial profiling, in official reports the two troopers had repeatedly lied about the racial identity of drivers they stopped. They also claimed that they were told to do so by multiple supervisors within the agency. The troopers apparently opened fire out of fear because the vehicle's occupants were minority males. Both pled guilty to charges of making false reports and official misconduct. They were dismissed from the New Jersey State Police and barred from any future employment as law enforcement officers in the state of New Jersey. Felony charges of attempted murder and aggravated assault were dismissed. While the shooting resulted in substantial monetary awards for each young man in the vehicle in settlement of their civil suits (the total is reported as $12.95 million), it also ended the men's rather promising athletic careers.

In 2007, one of Sharpton's most prominent causes was the police shooting of unarmed Sean Bell on November 25, 2006, the night before the young man's wedding. In this incident, four New York City police officers fired 50 bullets at Bell and his companions, who were also unarmed. One officer, who was White, fired 31 of the 50 bullets. Sharpton led multiple public protests of the police action after the shooting and following their acquittal in a bench trial. At various points, he also acted as advisor to the Bell family and Bell's fiancée Nicole Paultre Bell. The protests led to the arrest of Sharpton and other prominent figures in New York. The civil case resulted in monetary awards to the Bell family and his two passengers totaling more than $7 million, which have been used, in part, to open a recreation center in Sean Bell's name.

By fall 2007, Sharpton participated in the Jena Six protest against prosecutorial racial bias in Jena, Louisiana. The case involved an altercation between Black and White juveniles that resulted in one White classmate needing medical attention. His injuries did not prevent him from attending a dance that evening, but six Black juveniles were charged with a serious offense—attempted murder—while no White students were charged. After substantial media attention and a large protest that drew participants from across the nation, the serious charges against the Black youngsters were dismissed and they were released from custody.

However, it is for the 1987 Tawana Brawley case that "Rev. Al" is most known (Marcovitz, 2002). Tawana Brawley was a 15-year-old African American female who claimed that she had been abducted and brutally raped by six White men, including police officers. Brawley had reportedly been missing for four days and had been found unconscious with racial slurs written on her body amid feces and garbage. The case shocked many in the New York area, as Sharpton and attorneys C. Vernon Mason and Alton Maddox kept it in the media. However, the physical evidence and witness reports did not support Brawley's claims but instead suggested that she had staged the story. Sharpton was sued for libel, and along with former civil rights attorney C. Vernon Mason was ordered to pay $65,000 to Stephen Pagones, one of the accused and a former assistant district attorney in Duchess County, New York. Despite the adverse civil case outcome, Sharpton maintains his belief in Brawley's story.

In his book *Al on America* (2002), Sharpton addressed some facets of criminal justice directly. Regarding the war on drugs, he stated that instead of a focus on incarcerating low-level street dealers, the government should target individuals and countries connected with supplying the illicit drugs. He opposed New York's Rockefeller Drug Laws and mandatory sentences that lead to lengthy incarcerations for nonviolent offenders. Sharpton lamented that such efforts persist because incarceration is profitable. Effective justice reform, he wrote, requires laws based on what is right as opposed to economics; leaders who value people; judges who are sensitive about bigotry and bias; juries that reflect demographics; and trial by jury for public servants accused of crimes.

The Rev. Al Sharpton remains a civil rights activist, a church minister, a radio host, and since August 2011, an MSNBC television host and regular media commentator on matters of justice. He has also managed to obtain an occasional audience with members of the Obama administration regarding domestic race issues. It appears that he was successful in influencing that administration to reduce the crack cocaine sentencing disparity from 100:1 to 18:1 as part of the Fair Sentencing Act of 2010. Despite his advocacy for the rights of all people, many sources portray and perceive Al Sharpton as a racially divisive figure.

Camille Gibson

See also: Brown, James Joseph; Diallo, Amadou; Dorismond, Patrick; Fair Sentencing Act of 2010; Louima, Abner; Jena Six; Racial Profiling; Rockefeller Drug Laws: Policy Review; Southern Christian Leadership Conference (SCLC)

References

Bumgarner, J. B. *Profiling and Criminal Justice in America: A Reference Handbook.* Santa Barbara, CA: ABC-CLIO, 2004.

Mallin, J. *Al Sharpton: Community Activist.* New York: Franklin Watts, 2007.

Marcovitz, H. *Black Americans of Achievement: Al Sharpton.* Philadelphia: Chelsea House Publishers, 2002.

Sharpton, A., and K. Hunter. *Al on America.* New York: Kensington Publishing Corp, 2002.

Simpson, Orenthal James "O. J." (1947–)

Orenthal James Simpson, nicknamed O. J. and "The Juice," was born July 9, 1947, in San Francisco, California. He is a former American professional football player, spokesperson for commercial products and services, sports commentator, and actor, and current convicted felon. He is best known for three things: 1) becoming an American football hero; 2) the not guilty verdicts in his highly publicized and controversial 1995 trial for the murders of his former wife, Nicole Brown Simpson, and her friend Ronald Goldman; and 3) his 2008 trial in Las Vegas, Nevada, in which he was found guilty of multiple felonies related to the armed robbery of a memorabilia dealer. As a result of that trial, he is incarcerated in a Nevada prison, where he continues to serve a 33-year sentence for robbery and kidnapping (Associated Press, 2008).

Long before he became famous, O. J. Simpson was a juvenile delinquent. He lived part of his life in a housing project, ran with a gang, got arrested for theft, and spent some time in a youth detention facility, the San Francisco Youth Guidance Center. He credits African American baseball great Willie Mays, whom he met through a youth leader at the center, with inspiring him to change his life. Simpson has noted that seeing Mays accomplish what he did as an African American made him believe that he could do it too, despite his challenging childhood. His mother Eunice encouraged his involvement in sports.

During his college career at the University of Southern California, Simpson won the prestigious Heisman Trophy as well as the Walter Camp Award and the Maxwell Award. Simpson played professional football with the Buffalo Bills and the San Francisco 49ers, setting a NFL professional football record for rushing more than 2,000 yards during the 1973 season. He was inducted into the Pro Football Hall of Fame in 1985.

Simpson began his acting career before leaving professional football, acting in television mini-series and several motion pictures before creating his own company, Orenthal Productions, through which he produced films for the television market. He also became a spokesman for a number of commercial companies, endorsing products such as automobile rentals (Hertz Corporation), food, soft drinks, and boots.

O. J. Simpson was married and divorced twice. He first married his high school sweetheart and had three children. One of those children drowned as a toddler. Two children were born of Simpson's second marriage to Nicole Brown—first a girl, Sydney, and then a boy, Justin. The murder of Nicole Brown Simpson and her friend Ronald Goldman while the children, then ages 8 and 5, were sleeping inside the home is considered one of the 25 most infamous crimes in modern history (Schauer, 2009a).

On June 12, 1994, Nicole Brown Simpson and Ronald Goldman were found brutally slain outside her Brentwood, California, home (Schauer, 2009a). Suspicions quickly turned to O. J., as the marriage had been plagued by a history of domestic violence dating back to 1989. At one point, he was placed in handcuffs during questioning but later released due to insufficient evidence. Eventually, Simpson was formally charged with double murder. The accusation of Simpson quickly became a media circus. On June 17, he led the police on a low-speed highway chase while riding in a white Ford Bronco driven by his best friend and former football teammate Al Cowlings. Cowlings stated that Simpson was a backseat passenger and was holding a gun to his head, apparently contemplating suicide. Many interpreted this as an admission of guilt in the murders. The chase drew national and international media coverage and interrupted the broadcasting of the National Basketball Association (NBA) finals. After his arrest, a darkened photo of Simpson appeared on the cover of *Time Magazine*. When questioned about the distortion of Simpson's skin tone on the magazine cover, the publishers apologized. It was speculated that Simpson's skin was darkened to make him appear more "menacing," and consistent with racist stereotypes of the "dangerous" Black man.

During the trial, Simpson was represented by a group of lawyers who were dubbed "the Dream Team." The group included African American lead attorney Johnnie Cochran and other well-known attorneys such as Robert Shapiro (the original lead attorney), F. Lee Bailey, Alan Dershowitz, Robert Kardashian, Gerald Uelman, Carl Douglas, and Barry Scheck and Peter Neufeld (of the Innocence

Project). Defending against these serious charges was costly, estimated at between $3 million and $6 million. The trial, dubbed by some as "the trial of the century," lasted over nine months. It involved complicated DNA evidence, allegations of police misconduct and sloppiness, racial bias, tainted evidence, allegations of a drug-trafficking connection, and a crucial piece of evidence, a bloody glove, that did not fit Simpson (Toobin, 1996).

Some suggested that the trial received more media attention than perhaps it was due because of Simpson's celebrity status and because of the racial difference between the accused and the victims. Simpson was African American and both Nicole Brown Simpson and Ronald Goldman were White. Nicole Brown Simpson was also depicted as beautiful and blond, formerly married to Simpson who, according to police reports, had been brutal to her in the past—a classic image of beauty and the beast. Despite what some saw as overwhelming evidence of his guilt, on October 3, 1995, O. J. Simpson was found not guilty by the criminal trial jury, which was composed of nine Blacks, one Hispanic, and two Whites. The racial composition of the jury would become an issue in subsequent evaluations of the soundness of the jury decision. The decisions of the Japanese American judge, Lance Ito, who presided over the case, would also be called into question.

On the whole, the murder trial and its outcome caused great disagreement, contention, and debate across the United States. The verdict was one of the most anticipated and watched events in media history. Reports indicate that even the federal government shut down in order to pay attention to the outcome of this case. One source places the dollar value of lost productivity during the time that the verdict was being announced at $480 million. Opinions about whether Simpson was responsible for the Brown and Goldman murders were racially and politically polarized both during and immediately following the trial. In a chapter titled "Are We Still Talking about O. J.?" in her 1998 book *The Color of Crime,* legal scholar Katheryn Russell (later Russell-Brown) notes that, according to populations polled, 70 percent of Blacks believed that Simpson was not guilty, while 70 percent of Whites believed that he was guilty. More than 200 million opinions were included in the poll.

Legal experts strongly disagreed in their interpretations of the trial, its actors, and the evidence. On the one hand, Johnnie L. Cochran, Jr., who led the Simpson defense team, felt that the outcome of the Simpson murder trial was one major battle won against racial and civil injustice (Cochran & Rutten, 1996). On the other hand, Vincent T. Bugliosi, prosecutor of the infamous Manson family murder trial, felt that the Simpson murder trial was a travesty of justice and a media circus, and that through mediocre legal practice a murderer had been set free (1996).

Simpson's acquittal of the criminal charges did not preclude him from potential liability in civil court. In a subsequent civil trial, Simpson was found responsible for the wrongful death of and battery against Goldman and Brown and was ordered to pay $33.5 million in damages—$8.5 million to compensate the Goldman family and $25 million in punitive damages to be shared by both families (Ayres, 1997; Spence, 1997). Simpson has done little by his own volition to satisfy the judgment of the court. Because of his current imprisonment, it is unlikely that the full award will ever be paid.

In mid-November 2006, Fox News announced that Simpson had received a prepayment of an undisclosed amount toward the $3.5 million he was to receive for a proposed book, *If I Did It, Here's How It Happened* (Schauer, 2009b). Through the actions of several courts, the Goldmans were able to direct Simpson's income from publicity for the book toward satisfying the civil judgment. The Goldmans ultimately purchased the rights to the book from a bankruptcy court and began publishing the book under the title *If I Did It: Confessions of the Killer.* The proceeds from sales of the book were divided between the Ron Goldman Foundation for Justice and the Brown-Simpson children, who were allowed to remain in the custody of their father. They are both now in their twenties and living on their own.

On October 3, 2008, Orenthal James Simpson, along with his co-defendant Clarence Steward, was found guilty by the Clark County District Court of the armed robbery and kidnapping of a memorabilia dealer in a Las Vegas hotel room in 2007. The 12-count indictment accused Simpson of entering the hotel room with a group of men with guns and demanding various items from the dealer (Vercammen, 2009). Simpson's version of the story was that no guns were involved and that he confronted the dealer to get back valuable sports mementos that were stolen from him after the murder trial. In an October 2012 appeal of his case, Simpson alleges that his attorney, Yale Galanter, advised him that the retrieval of the items would be "okay" so long as there was no trespass or violence involved with the action. Galanter denies that claim. Simpson was sentenced to 33 years in prison, of which he must serve at least nine years before being eligible for parole (Associated Press, 2008). In October 2012, based on claims that his attorney was ineffective during the original trial, a Nevada judge agreed to reopen his case. After several additional hearings, Simpson's request for a new trial was denied in 2013. He remains confined at the Lovelock Correctional Center. His earliest parole date is 2017.

Although he is behind bars, Simpson's life continues to be filled with controversy. In 2011 there were claims that he was beaten unconscious by White inmates who were members of the Skinheads gang. There are also claims that, in 2012, he offered to sell the murder weapon (a knife) from the 1994 killings to a private collector for $5 million.

Edward J. Schauer with Delores Jones-Brown

See also: Cochran, Jr., Johnnie L.; Gangs

Professional Athletes and Crime

Despite their celebrity status and substantial salaries, like their noncelebrity counterparts, African American professional athletes have disproportionately been associated with incidents of crime and violence as both perpetrators and victims. In the case of some defendants, the argument has been made that if the individual was not a celebrity, the prosecution might not have been pursued.

Defendants

Plaxico Burress

Plaxico Burress, who at that time played for the NFL's New York Giants, was arrested and charged with criminal possession of a handgun in November 2008, after accidently shooting himself in the right thigh while in a Manhattan nightclub. Burress had the gun concealed in the waistband of his sweatpants, but as the gun began sliding down his leg, he reached for it and accidently pressed the trigger. Burress went to a local hospital and was treated and released. Police only learned of the incident after it was reported on TV. Burress surrendered to police two days later. New York City mayor Michael Bloomberg took the position that Burress should be prosecuted to the fullest extent. He was released by the Giants before that season ended.

After being indicted on two counts of criminal possession of a weapon in the second degree, Burress accepted a plea deal in August 2009. He was sentenced to two years' imprisonment, with an additional two years of supervised release. Burress served 20 months in prison before being released in June 2010. He returned to the NFL for the 2011 season at age 34, after signing with the New York Jets.

Michael Vick

While a member of the NFL's Atlanta Falcons in 2007, Michael Vick was charged by federal authorities with operating an unlawful interstate dogfighting ring. Vick was accused of financing the operation, directly participating in dogfighting and executions, and participating in gambling activities connected with dogfighting. In August 2007, Vick and three co-defendants agreed to separate plea deals. In plea documents, Vick pleaded guilty to conspiracy to travel in interstate commerce in the aid of unlawful activities and to sponsor a dog in an animal-fighting venture. He admitted to being involved in dogfighting in Maryland, Virginia, North Carolina, and South Carolina. He admitted to being the primary financer of the dogfighting operation, and to knowing that his colleagues killed dogs that did not perform well. Vick also admitted to participating in the killing of six to eight dogs by hanging or drowning.

Vick voluntarily began serving time in November 2007, getting time-served credit before his sentencing in December. He was sentenced to 23 months in prison and was assigned to the U.S. Penitentiary in Leavenworth, Kansas. He was released in May 2009, and after being reinstated to the NFL, Vick signed with the Philadelphia Eagles in August 2009.

Victims

Sean Taylor

Sean Taylor of the NFL's Washington Redskins died at age 24 in Miami on November 27, 2007, after being shot in his home by an intruder. According to Taylor's girlfriend, Jackie Garcia, they were awakened by loud noises coming from another part of the house. Taylor grabbed a machete that he kept in the bedroom for protection. However, the gunman entered the bedroom and fired two shots, one hitting Taylor and damaging the femoral artery in his leg. Taylor lost significant blood and died the next morning without regaining consciousness. The couple's 18-month-old daughter was in her crib during the home invasion, while Garcia hid under the sheets. Both escaped without physical harm. Three days after Taylor's murder, four suspects between the ages of 17 and 20 were arrested in connection with Taylor's death: Jason Mitchell, Eric Rivera, Charles Wardlow, and Venjah Hunte. They were charged with murder, home invasion with a firearm, and armed burglary. A fifth suspect, 16-year-old Timothy Brown, was also arrested in connection with Taylor's murder, but not until May 2008. Brown was charged with first-degree murder and armed burglary of an occupied dwelling. The trial for Taylor's murder was originally scheduled to begin in April 2008, but was postponed until June 2009. In May 2008, it was announced that the suspects would not face the death penalty if convicted because the suspected gunman, Rivera, was only 17 years old at the time of the shooting. Venjah Hunte then accepted a plea deal and was sentenced to 29 years in prison. He subsequently unsuccessfully petitioned the court to withdraw his guilty plea.

A trial date for the remaining defendants was postponed at least two additional times. On November 4, 2013, a jury found Rivera guilty of second-degree murder and armed burglary. On January 23, 2014, he was sentenced to 57 and a half years in prison. As of January 2014, Brown, Mitchell, and Wardlow were still awaiting trial.

Darrent Williams

Darrent Williams of the NBA's Denver Broncos was killed in a drive-by shooting during the early morning hours of New Year's Day, 2007. Williams was riding in the back seat of a limousine with two other passengers. He was 24 years old.

(Continued)

Williams had been attending a birthday party for Kenyon Martin of the Denver Nuggets at a downtown nightclub. According to the police report, there was an altercation at the party between members of the Crips street gang and several patrons, including Brandon Marshall, who also played for the Broncos.

The shooting occurred shortly after Williams left the club and was riding in the limousine. Another vehicle pulled up alongside the limousine and someone opened fire. According to the coroner, Williams was struck once in the neck and died almost instantly, falling into the lap of Broncos teammate Javon Walker.

Police impounded a vehicle registered to Brian Hicks, a 28-year-old Crips member. Hicks was already in prison awaiting trial for attempted murder and drug charges. Williams was questioned by police but never charged in Williams' murder.

In May 2008, *The Rocky Mountain News* published a story claiming that it had a signed confession letter by Crips member Willie D. Clark, in which he claimed he had murdered Williams. In October 2008, Clark was indicted for murder; he was found guilty in 2010 and sentenced to life in prison.

Clifton Brown

References

Associated Press. "O. J. Simpson Sentenced to Long Term." December 5, 2008. http://www.msnbc.msn.com/id/28067187/.

Ayres, B. D., Jr. "Jury Decides Simpson Must Pay $25 Million in Punitive Award." *The New York Times,* February 11, 1997.

Bugliosi, V. T. *Outrage: The Five Reasons Why O. J. Simpson Got Away with Murder.* New York: W.W. Norton, 1996.

Cochran, J. L., Jr., and T. Rutten. *Journey to Justice.* New York: One World/Ballantine Books, 1996.

Russell, K. *The Color of Crime: Racial Hoaxes, White Fear, Black Protectionism, Police Harassment and Other Macroaggressions.* New York: New York University Press, 1998.

Schauer, E. J. 2009a. "June 12, 1994: Nicole Brown Simpson and Ronald Goldman Are Found Murdered." In *Great Events from History: Modern Scandals,* edited by R. Carl L. Bankston III. Pasadena, CA: Salem Press, 2009.

Schauer, E. J. 2009b. "November 15–20, 2006: Fox News Abandons Plan to Publish O. J. Simpson Book." In *Great Events from History: Modern Scandals,* edited by R. Carl L. Bankston III. Pasadena, CA: Salem Press, 2009.

Spence, G. *O. J.: The Last Word.* New York: St. Martin's Press, 1997.

Toobin, J. *The Run of His Life: The People v. O. J. Simpson.* New York: Random House, 1996.

Vercammen, P. "O. J. Simpson Guilty of Armed Robbery, Kidnapping." CNN, October 4, 2009. http://www.cnn.com/2008/CRIME/10/04/ojsimpson.verdict/index.html.

Slavery

Slavery has served as a source of historical trauma that has impacted the African American population throughout much of the history of the United States. Even though the practice of African slavery ended over 100 years ago, there have been successive laws, policies, customs, and practices implemented that have kept African Americans from sharing an equal standard of life and liberty with White Americans (Alexander, 2010; Muhammad, 2010; Browne-Marshall, 2007; Jones-Brown, 2000a, 2000b; McIntyre, 1993). Indeed, many of the advances in civil rights gained by African Americans are the result of a fight from slave to freed person to a people of equality. That fight has included having to break unjust laws and enduring terrible punishments for doing so. The origins of many of the disparities that exist between the African American population and the White American population today lie in the early American practice of slavery and the laws and social norms created to sustain it.

What separates the African slave experience in the continental United States from that of other European cultures is the U.S. proclamation of an ideological and legal commitment to notions of liberty, freedom, and equality while simultaneously holding hundreds of thousands of Africans and their progeny captive for nearly two and a half centuries. The legislative enactment of formal laws to underpin this social institution, which directly contradicted the important and somewhat unique governmental ideological dictates concerning the inherent rights to freedom and equality, also separated the U.S. adoption of African slavery during the 1600s from the European adoption of such slavery during the 1400s. Though the British colonies would not become the United States of America until the late 1700s, from the beginning there was a sense that the "New World" was a place where many came seeking freedom, whether

The COMMITTEE confisting of, &c. to whom was referred a MOTION of Mr. King, for the Exclufion of involuntary Servitude in the States defcribed in the Refolve of Congrefs of the 23d Day of April, 1784, fubmit the following RESOLVE.

RESOLVED, That after the year 1800 of the Chriftian æra, there fhall be neither flavery nor involuntary fervitude in any of the States defcribed in the refolve of Congrefs of the 23d day of April, 1784, otherwife than in punifhment of crimes whereof the party fhall have been perfonally guilty, And that this regulation fhall be an article of compact, and remain a fundamental principle of the conftitutions between the thirteen original ftates, and each of the ftates defcribed in the faid refolve of Congrefs of the 23d day of April, 1784; any implication or conftruction of the faid refolve to the contrary notwithftanding. Provided always, that upon the efcape of any perfon into any of the ftates defcribed in the faid refolve of Congrefs of the 23d day of April, 1784, from whom labor or fervice is lawfully claimed in any one of the thirteen original ftates, fuch fugitive may be lawfully reclaimed and carried back to the perfon claiming his labor or fervice as aforefaid, this refolve notwithftanding.

Fugitive slave laws required everyone to participate in the return of runaway slaves or be subject to criminal prosecution and punishment. (Library of Congress)

religious, economic, or political, or simply as a means of avoiding the dungeon (Goomman, 2001).

Despite being viewed as a haven for those seeking freedom, in the early to mid 1600s, the first legally recognized African slaves in the United States began to appear (Frosch, 1997; Kolchin, 2003). Attempts had been made to enslave the indigenous populations (often referred to as American Indians or Native Americans), but such efforts proved difficult. Knowing the land well, Native Americans could successfully escape captivity but also suffered catastrophic population losses due to disease contracted from their captors. European indentured servants who served for a set period of time rather than for life could also run away and blend in with the other European immigrants who were not indentured or who had completed their terms. By contrast, having been kidnapped from their native lands, the enslaved Africans were faced with the fear of the unknown if they even thought about escaping. Though their immune systems proved more resilient to diseases to which Native Americans had fallen victim, their physical appearance made them highly visible amid the other immigrant and native populations (Behrendt et al., 1999).

Most historical sources recognize the introduction in 1619 of 20 African males and females to the colony at Jamestown, Virginia, as the beginning of African slavery in what would become the United States (Behrendt et al., 1999) and of African American informal social and formal legal subordination in the nascent nation (Browne-Marshall, 2007). Prior to 1619, like other immigrants, free Blacks had come to the continent seeking the benefits that the new emerging society offered. But from 1619 forward, the practice of Black slavery spread throughout the colonies and would be particularly common in the Southern colonies due to their agrarian economy, which was dependent upon large but cheap labor forces to maintain plantation operations (Behrendt et al., 1999). As with other parts of the Americas, the Southern colonies, later the U.S. South, became dependent upon this system to raise cash crops such as tobacco and cotton.

The enslavement of Africans also allowed for a social hierarchy that had been prevalent in Britain and other parts of Europe, a class or caste system where there was a clear distinction between masters and servants—royalty and serfs (Laguerre, 2002). In the nascent United States, these lines came to be drawn along racial lines rather than bloodlines, and applied to Blacks in ways that criminalized their behavior whether they were free or enslaved (see American Law and African Americans).

With the importation of African slaves, statutory Slave Codes and Black Codes began to be enacted by individual colonies—later states—that denied various rights that previously had been considered common. These codes prohibited Blacks from learning to read or write, owning property, carrying weapons, acting in self-defense, working in certain professions, gathering at each other's homes, participating as witnesses or jurors in criminal trials, entering into or breaking employment contracts, being on public streets after dark, being off the plantation without a pass, looking at or talking back to a White person, marrying or otherwise entering into civil contracts, traveling to or residing in certain states, harboring runaway slaves, helping slaves to escape, or escaping from enslavement (Browne-Marshall, 2007). The punishments for violating these restrictions were often brutal. They included whipping, torture, or amputation and death by being boiled or skinned alive, hanged, or decapitated (Adamson, 1983; Louisiana Public Broadcasting, 2010).

For free or enslaved Blacks, such punishments would also be used for common crimes such as theft. Free Blacks who could left the new nation and fled to Canada or elsewhere where their liberty might not be predetermined or assumed based on the color of their skin (McIntyre, 1993). For those who remained or who became emancipated, there were often "freedom suits" to confirm their free status. Such suits were necessary to overcome the legal presumption that Black skin tone meant slave status unless the person could prove otherwise, in court proceedings where Blacks were not permitted to testify or serve on the jury.

Although the American Revolution (1775–1783) resulted in the American colonies obtaining freedom from England, African slavery continued in the United States and was legally recognized in both the North and South. The Constitution ratified in 1787 included provisions that counted slaves as three-fifths of a human being (in article 1, section 2); imposed an obligation upon everyone to return runaway slaves (in article 4, section 2); and allowed the importation of slaves until 1808, 20 years beyond its ratification (in article 1, section 9). Under the same provision, the federal government was authorized to collect $10 per person in taxes on all slaves imported (Jones-Brown, 2000b).

Though slavery is often attributed solely to the South, the "fugitive slave" provision in article 4, section 2 of the Constitution makes clear that slaves who escaped to nonslave states were still the property of their owners, a proposition that was reaffirmed with the enactment of the Congressional Fugitive Slave Laws in 1790 and 1850 and the U.S. Supreme Court ruling in the case of *Dred Scott v. Sandford* in 1857. Slavery continued to be an important economic institution for Southern states. And, though most Northern states passed emancipation acts from the 1780s to the early 1800s, racial segregation became a mainstay of both Northern and Southern life. Criminal statutes and local police would be used to enforce racial segregation for years to come. By 1860, the U.S. Census recorded that approximately 8 percent of all U.S. families owned slaves, with a total of 3,950,528 slaves across the United States, of which only about one-third were owned by families in the South (Frosch, 1997).

The criminal statutes put in place to maintain the institution of slavery were the beginning of criminalizing Blackness in the United States that many argue has continued to today (Bell, 1987; McIntyre, 1993; Mann, 1993; Browne-Marshall, 2007; Alexander, 2010; Muhammad, 2010). Slave patrols became the precursors to modern American police forces (Williams & Murphy, 1990), with slave patrollers inflicting brutal punishments on those accused of being runaway slaves. Slave owners also committed atrocities against slaves as a means of punishing and controlling them. Masters could even kill slaves with legal impunity and often sexually victimized the females (Louisiana Public Broadcasting, 2010).

Though the Bill of Rights, the first 10 amendments, was added to the Constitution in 1791, virtually none of the substantive or procedural rights contained in it pertained to Blacks, and none pertained to slaves. The right of individual states to enact and maintain criminal and civil laws that restricted the freedoms of Blacks whether slave or free was upheld by the federal courts well into the 1950s. Race became the dividing line between who was protected by the Constitution and who was not, and for some behaviors, the dividing line between who was a criminal and who was not. In many states, those who were Black, regardless of their economic status, were not protected and were not at liberty to exercise many of the substantive rights outlined in the amendments. The "one drop rule" became the legal standard for determining who was Black and therefore subject to restriction—meaning that any degree of African ancestry made a person Black for legal purposes, regardless of appearance (Davis, 1994). This legal rule led in part to a phenomenon called "passing," in which fair-skinned Blacks, often the offspring of slave masters, lived their lives denying their African ancestry in order to have the freedoms afforded to Whites.

The practice of slavery was cruel and harsh, with slaves being given no rights to family or other considerations. In fact, the Southern system would commonly break up slave families as a means of controlling the population and keeping them docile. Indeed, most slaves lived in fear of being transported away from their family and/or friends. This psychological tactic of gaining compliance impacted the entire population and intensified the historical trauma that African Americans would carry with them for generations after the practice was ended. According to several current social scientific theories, family disruption continues to be a contributing factor to Black crime and criminal justice system contact (Louisiana Public Broadcasting, 2010).

The work of abolitionists and the 1860 election of President Abraham Lincoln are customarily credited with ending African slavery in the United States. Lincoln's Emancipation Proclamation, given in 1863, during the American Civil War, is often viewed as an official statement declaring all slaves in the United States (both North and South) to be free. Yet wording in the written document indicates that the Emancipation Proclamation was only designed to free the slaves in the rebel states, leaving slavery intact in those states that supported the Union. Historians have disagreed over the proper interpretation of the words of the Emancipation Proclamation, which are as follows:

That on the first day of January, in the year of our Lord one thousand eight hundred and sixty-three, *all persons held as slaves within any State or designated part of a State, the people whereof shall then be in rebellion against the United States, shall be then, thenceforward, and forever free*; and the Executive Government of the United States, including the military and naval authority thereof, will recognize and maintain the freedom of such persons, and will do no act or acts to repress such persons, or any of them, in any efforts they may make for their actual freedom. (Italics added)

While many popular presentations of Lincoln's role in the abolition of slavery depicts his involvement as a recognition of the moral rightness of that position, in an August 22, 1862, letter to the *New York Tribune* editor, Horace Greeley, Lincoln makes clear that his primary goal is to save the Union, not free the slaves. He writes:

If I could save the Union without freeing any slave I would do it, and if I could save it by freeing all slaves I would do it; and, if I could save it by freeing some and leaving others alone I would also do that. What I do about slavery, and the colored race, I do because I believe it helps to save the Union. . . .

It was the passage of the Thirteenth Amendment in 1865 that officially ended the legal practice of slavery in the United States. However, the amendment ends with wording that permits involuntary servitude for those who have been convicted of a crime. The growth in the Black prison population after the Civil War and the modern-day mass incarceration of Blacks has led to an ongoing debate as to whether, for African Americans, the prison system is a replacement for the plantation system.

Robert Hanser and Delores Jones-Brown

See also: American Law and African Americans; Correctional System and African Americans; Death Penalty; Institutional Racism; Police Brutality; Racial Profiling; Termination of Parental Rights

References

Adamson, C. R. "Punishment after Slavery: Southern State Penal Systems, 1865–1890." *Social Problems* 30, no. 5 (1983): 555–69.

Alexander, M. *The New Jim Crow: Mass Incarceration in the Age of Colorblindness.* New York: The New Press, 2010.

Behrendt, S. D., D. Eltis, and H. S. Klein. *The Transatlantic Slave Trade: A Database on CD-ROM.* New York: Cambridge University Press, 1999.

Bell, D. *And We Are Not Saved: The Elusive Quest for Racial Justice.* New York: Basic Books, 1987.

Browne-Marshall, G. *Race, Law, and American Society: 1607 to Present.* New York: Routledge, 2007.

Davis, F. J. *Who Is Black? One Nation's Definition.* University Park: Pennsylvania State University Press, 1994.

Frosch, M. Civil War Home Page. 1997. http://www.civil-war.net/pages/1860_census.html.

Goomman, J. E. *A Long and Uncertain Journey: The 27,000 Mile Voyage of Vasco Da Gama.* New York: Mikaya Press, 2001.

Jones-Brown, D. 2000a. *Race, Crime and Punishment.* Philadelphia: Chelsea House, 2000.

Jones-Brown, D. 2000b. "Race as a Legal Construct: The Implications for American Justice." In *The System in Black and White: Exploring the Connections between Race, Crime and Justice,* edited by M. Markowitz and D. Jones-Brown, 137–52. Westport, CT: Praeger, 2000.

Kolchin, P. *American Slavery: 1619–1877.* New York: Hill and Wang, 2003.

Laguerre, E. *The History of Haiti.* 2002. http://www.travelinghaiti.com/history_of_haiti/slave_rebellion.asp.

Lincoln, Abraham. "Letter to Horace Greeley." *New York Tribune,* August 22, 1862.

Lincoln, Abraham. "Emancipation Proclamation." January 1, 1863. http://www.nps.gov/ncro/anti/emancipation.html.

Louisiana Public Broadcasting. "Africans in America: 1831–1865." Baton Rouge, LA, 2010. http://www.pbs.org/wgbh/aia/part4/4narr1.html.

Mann, C. *Unequal Justice: A Question of Color.* Bloomington: Indiana University Press, 1993.

McIntyre, C. *Criminalizing a Race: Free Blacks during Slavery.* Queens, NY: Kayode, 1993.

Muhammad, K. G. *The Condemnation of Blackness: Race, Crime, and the Making of Modern Urban America.* Cambridge, MA: Harvard University Press, 2010.

Williams, H., and P. Murphy. *Evolving Strategy of the Police: A Minority View.* Washington, DC: National Institute of Justice, 1990.

Snitching, The Miseducation of

Whether it is termed tattletaling, ratting, whistleblowing or snitching, the code of silence centering on criminal activity goes back several generations. With its roots in the old Mafia code of omertà, the best way to protect turf and assets was through fear (Malone, 2008). This code is not a new order of business. Police departments endorse this behavior among themselves (Walker et al., 1996). The unwritten rule is that an officer cannot report on other officers. Many officers live by the "do not tell" clause or what they term the "blue wall of silence"; however, they are surprised when neighborhood citizens choose to do the same.

Unlike the old definition of snitching, the term has evolved from being a mere tattletale (what youth are called who are telling to get attention [COPS, 2009]), to a confidential informant (C.I.), a criminal who informs on a law-breaking counterpart in exchange for judicial leniency. According to street politics, snitching is what happens when "people can't handle their weight" (Wesley, 2005). Veteran gangsta rapper and actor Ice-T's assertion mirrors the definition of what many consider to be a snitch:

> A snitch is someone who commits a crime with a partner and gets caught. Instead of keeping his mouth shut and taking responsibility for his criminal activity, he cuts a deal with the police for lighter sentencing in exchange for ratting out his partner. The "Stop Snitching" code is one shared among those in the underworld and has nothing to do with someone who is uninvolved in being a witness to a crime. (Natapoff, 2009: 125)

However, this act of informing is mistakenly interchanged with the civic duty of crime reporting, which consists of witnesses telling what they saw to assist in the apprehension and prosecution of a perpetrator (McGee, 1962). Critics argue that popular culture has blurred the line between the two, making solving crimes in inner cities difficult and giving birth to the "stop snitching" mentality. Amber asserts, "These days, the distinction between snitches and crime reporters has become so blurred that the term snitch is being applied to anyone ranging from someone who's talking to police to save his own skin to the little old lady who wants to get the drug dealers off her corner" (2007: 107). The term "snitch" does not apply to common neighborhood residents, only to informants who often lie on the witness stand and accomplices who testify to keep themselves out of prison (Brown, 2007).

Snitches are despised because they are commonly known criminals who accept bribes from police, prosecutors, or correctional officers in exchange for sworn testimony against a defendant—whether the information is true or false (Brown, 2007; George, 2010). The street code does not apply to the majority of the community: "They aren't being snitches. They're being good citizens. They are bamboozled into believing they are snitching and are betraying their community" (Smith, 2008: 21). Residents are being held hostage with this bogus "stop snitching" credo that is indirectly granting lawbreakers a form of criminal amnesty (In the Margins, 2010).

The "code of silence," or what is widely labeled as the grassroots "stop snitching" phenomenon, deals with citizens' reluctance to speak with law enforcement officials when they have important information that could lead to solving a crime and putting an assailant behind bars (Malone, 2008). Many blame Baltimore's *Stop Snitching* producers and cast (see Stop Snitching Campaign) and the rap music industry for a marketing world that glorifies crime, violence, and anti-police sentiment for profit (Natapoff, 2009). Moreover, they blame rap for endorsing noncompliance with crime reporting. A survey created by the Police Executive Research Forum (PERF) found that 47 percent of respondents attributed the increase of the stop snitching movement to the recent sales of *Stop Snitching* t-shirts, DVDs, and compact discs (COPS, 2009). In 2004, a *Stop Snitching* DVD was produced as a wake-up call about how violent and corrupt Baltimore police had become in recent years and how important it is to take it back to "old-school" street values and "old-school" street rules of taking responsibility for your actions (Brown, 2007). The homemade *Stop Snitching* DVD, which mirrored the messages of hip-hop lyricists, garnered national attention and allegedly reinforced the "stop snitching" rhetoric that is heavy in inner cities throughout America (Natapoff, 2009). Apparel reinforcing this sentiment became popular among inner-city residents, especially among urban youth and hip-hop fans, after Cam'ron and the Diplomats wore it during a video shoot (Brown, 2007) (see Stop Snitching Campaign). While t-shirts, mottos, and popular music may fade away, the underlying problems of violence, fear, and noncooperation will likely remain a part of urban life (Natapoff, 2009).

It may appear that rap music and the *Stop Snitching* DVDs are the culprits that cause inner-city residents not to cooperate with the police, but the majority of the rap songs in question are taken out of context by rap's juvenile followers and uninformed antagonists. For those that are totally foreign to some of the topical themes of rap music, the lyrical content comes across as reprehensible because it delivers its messages in such a raw form. In addition, young listeners who focus exclusively on the beat and the chorus and ignore the substantive lyrics may overlook the overall message of the songs.

To a portion of these listeners, urban violence is seen as "normal" because it happens so often that impoverished residents, especially youth, are immune to it (Harris, 2010), and neighborhood conditions parallel the music. Since hip-hop was born out of inner-city poverty and despair, people adapt to the culture of poverty around them and react to it accordingly (McGee, 1962; Brown, 2005). "The families in poverty stricken areas are affected by the conflicting systems of values and the problems of survival and conformity with which it is confronted" (Shaw & McKay, 1942: 177). Instead of jeopardizing their personal safety and the safety of their loved ones, many residents who do not conform to the destructive "stop snitching" phenomenon still exercise their right to remain silent.

The callous relationship between police and many urban communities is not adding to the solution. When evidence is held constant, law-abiding minorities are more likely to be harassed by the police than their White counterparts (Tucker, 1995). Facts show that when police actually respond to inner-city residents' calls, minorities are arrested more often than Whites. Moreover, minority group members are found guilty more often and given harsher punishments than Whites when they have encounters with the justice system (Lindholm & Christianson, 1998;

Walker & Katz, 2008). National statistics show that the usual victims of brutality are people of color, the poor, and young people perceived by the police to be powerless (Powers, 1995). Known petty drug dealers have gotten beaten up by the police and sent on their way without their drugs being confiscated. The beating is seen as a form of "street" justice. In turn, a "code of silence" is enacted and reinforced not only by the victims, but onlookers, family members, and friends.

Ladel Lewis

See also: Shakur, Tupac Amaru; Stop Snitching Campaign

References

Amber, Jeannine. "The Streets Are Watching." *Essence* 37, no. 9 (2007): 106–12.

Brown, E. *Snitch: Informants, Cooperators & the Corruption of Justice.* New York: Public Affairs, 2007.

Brown, E. *Queens Reigns Supreme: Fat Cat, 50 Cent, and the Rise of the Hip-Hop Hustler.* New York: Anchor Books, 2005.

COPS. *The Stop Snitching Phenomenon: Breaking the Code of Silence.* Washington, DC: U.S. Department of Justice of Community Oriented Policing Services, 2009.

George, E. *A Woman Doing Life: Notes from a Prison for Women.* New York: Oxford University Press, 2010.

Harris, D. "'Merrill Hood' Had Most Felonious Assaults in 2009; Residents Say Crime Is Rampant." *The Flint News,* September 19, 2010. http://www.mlive.com/news/flint/index.ssf/2010/09/merrill_hood_had_most_feloniou.html.

In the Margins. "Willing Eyes & Ears Can Multiply Power of Police to Take Back Flint." *The Flint Journal,* October 8, 2010. http://www.mlive.com/opinion/flint/index.ssf/2010/10/in_the_margins_willing_eyes_an.html.

Lindholm, T., and S. Christianson. "Intergroup Biases and Eyewitness Testimony." *The Journal of Social Psychology* 138, no. 6 (1998): 710–23.

Malone, M. "Broadcasting & Cable." *New York* 138, no. 21 (May 2008): 10.

McGee, R. *Social Disorganization in America.* San Francisco: Chandler Publishing, 1962.

Natapoff, A. *Snitching.* New York: New York University Press, 2009.

Powers, M. D. *Policing the Police: Civilian Oversight Is Necessary to Prevent Police Brutality.* San Diego: Greenhaven Press, 1995.

Shaw, C. R., and H. D. McKay. *Juvenile Delinquency and Urban Areas: A Study of Rates of Delinquents in Relation to Differential Characteristics of Local Communities in American Cities.* Chicago: University of Chicago Press, 1942.

Smith, B. "Keeping a 'Snitch' from Being Scratched." *ABA Journal* 94, no. 12 (December 2008): 20–2.

Tucker, W. *Policing the Police: Inner-City Crime Is a Worse Problem Than Police Brutality.* San Diego: Greenhaven Press, 1995.

Walker, S., and C. Katz. *The Police in America: An Introduction.* 6th ed. Boston: McGraw Hill, 2008.

Walker, Samuel, Cassia Spohn, and Miriam DeLone. *The Color of Justice: Race, Ethnicity and Crime in America.* Belmont, CA: Wadsworth, 1996.

Wesley, J., writer, director, and producer. *Hoodz Stop Snitchin: The Code of the Streets.* Videotape, 2005.

Socioeconomic Factors

In everyday life, the activities, experiences, attitudes, lifestyles, and realities of individuals are socially and economically shaped by a combination of forces. Otherwise referred to as socioeconomic factors, these include education; wealth, income, and occupation; religion and culture; ethnicity, and place of residence, as well as age and gender. A combined measure of education, income, and occupation thus gives an indication of the socioeconomic status for an individual or family household in society relative to others. As such, these factors play a powerful role in helping to define neighborhoods, communities, and regions where families and individuals of similar socioeconomic statuses may concentrate residentially. Consequently, these factors may also play a significant role in exposure to a number of vulnerabilities and inequalities, such as poor health and disease, prejudice and discrimination, lack of opportunity, low education, poverty, and so forth—all of which may contribute to instances of crime and violence for adversely affected ethnic minority groups, such as African Americans.

Historically, African Americans have been empirically linked to poverty, which is perhaps the main socioeconomic factor affecting this group. In their 1999 article "The Likelihood of Poverty across the American Adult Life Span," Mark Rank and Thomas Hirschl summarized findings from data collected longitudinally over 25 years—1968 through 1992—from 4,800 households in the United States, for a total of over 18,000 individuals. When analyzing the data by race, they found startling results for African Americans—by age 25, 48.1 percent had experienced one year or more in poverty, with over two-thirds by age 50 and 91 percent by age 75, leading to a 9:10 ratio of African Americans who experienced poverty over a normal lifespan. Similarly, according to a 2003 U.S. Census report entitled "The Black Population in the United States," while more than half of African American families had annual incomes over $50,000 in 2001, in the same year, a disproportionate number of single-parented African American families led to the overrepresentation of Blacks as poor. Because a large number of African American families were supported by a single parent, this characteristic contributed most to the poverty rate for the group. The disproportionate number of female single-headed households in particular has been found to be the greatest contributor to the income gap between Black and White families, with the former earning 65 percent of the wages earned by the latter.

Education is another factor contributing to differences in income levels (and thus wealth and poverty) between African Americans and Whites. In his 1998 article "The Disproportionate Representation of African Americans in Special Education," James M. Patton (1998) explored the sociopolitical and historical factors leading to the overrepresentation of African Americans in special education programs in the United States. He notes,

> The current realities of the overrepresentation of African Americans in special education perpetuates . . . by allowing the general and special education enterprises to continue the creation of programmatic and classroom arrangements that jeopardize the life chances of large numbers of African American youth [whom are] being persistently diagnosed as disabled and placed in special education programs constitutes a problem—for many of these students are inappropriately placed. (25)

Such an overrepresentation may be a self-perpetuating cycle for many reasons. For example, in the 1997 chapter "The Social Consequences of Growing Up in a Poor Neighborhood," authors Christopher Jencks and Susan E. Mayer explore a number of effects of attending schools in poor areas. They included: the inability to attract and retain high-quality teachers, and dealing with behavioral, crime, and violence problems in school, which interferes with teachers' ability to teach and with students' ability to concentrate. These difficulties contributed to others, such as difficulties in securing funding because of poor student performance and low scores on standardized tests. Without adequate funding, schools are unable to provide essential services and extracurricular activities. Such schools suffer from high dropout rates, and are vulnerable to the formation of deviant subcultures within the schools, along with many other adverse factors.

Place of residence is another factor that influences African American involvement in crime. Historically, many African American communities in the United States have been concentrated in poverty-stricken areas, a fact that may give rise to or stem from other problems (McKinnon, 2003). Typically, such areas suffer socioeconomically because they lack opportunities for lawful employment, have low-performing schools, and have limited or overburdened social services for residents. Concurrently, residents may be psychosocially overcome by problems that interfere with their ability to hold steady employment, and thus rise from poverty. In turn, this may actually contribute to or produce a perpetuating cycle of violent crime, for example through youth turning to drug dealing for money and joining gangs for protection, as a means of survival. In their 1996 article, authors Lauren J. Krivo and Ruth D. Peterson explored the relationship between extremely disadvantaged neighborhoods and urban crime in Columbus, Ohio, and discovered marked differences between Black and White communities. They found Blacks to be at higher risk for criminal involvement due to a number of racial and structural inequalities.

Finally, the legacy of slave labor and the racial stereotypes associated with Black racial identity are perhaps the main factors affecting African Americans' socioeconomic well-being. Historically, Blacks have been legally restricted in terms of their labor force participation, first by slavery and then by Jim Crow legislation. While being legally kept out of various forms of employment, they were also stereotyped as lazy and incapable of performing certain employment tasks. For many, limited legitimate employment opportunities and various institutional biases contributed to multigenerational overrepresentation in the criminal justice system.

This overrepresentation has perpetuated negative stereotypes about their labor force capabilities and desires, both from outside and within the African American community. The institutional biases that have been detrimental to Black participation in the workforce and other indicators of economic participation and well-being (such as homeownership and residential stability) have included Blacks being unfairly targeted by police. In her 2004 article "The Social and Moral Costs of Mass Incarceration in African American Communities," Dorothy E. Roberts examines the reasons for the disproportionate imprisonment of Blacks and the harm this does to Black communities. For example, being imprisoned may disrupt social networks, such as the family, leading to high numbers of single-parented families that may be unable to deal with the economic hardship of living off of a single income. Low income earners and imprisoned residents are unable to contribute to community organizations and religious institutions that residents of other communities may rely on in times of need. Roberts continues to explain how this lack of prosocial community support may in turn weaken social control by distorting social norms in favor of readily available socioeconomically effective illegal opportunities—for example, those that provide immediate and continuous cash. This leads to a prevalence of "disorganized communities that cannot enforce social norms because it is too difficult to reach consensus on common values and on avenues for solving common problems" (1285).

Michael Puniskis

See also: American Law and African Americans; *Code of the Street*; Correctional System and African Americans; Disproportionality and Crime; Education; Early Intervention for African Americans; Inequality Theory; Racial Profiling; Theories of Race and Crime; *When Work Disappears: The World of the New Urban Poor*; Youth Violence

References

Jencks, C., and S. E. Mayer. "The Social Consequences of Growing Up in a Poor Neighborhood." In *Inner-City Poverty in the United States,* edited by L. E. Lynn and M. G. H. McGeary, 111–86. Washington, DC: National Academic Press, 1997.

Krivo, L. J., and R. D. Peterson. "Extremely Disadvantaged Neighborhoods and Urban Crime." *Social Forces* 75, no. 2 (1996): 619–48.

McKinnon, J. *The Black Population in the United States: March 2002*. U.S. Census Bureau, Current Population Reports, Series P20-541. Washington, DC, 2003. http://www .census.gov/prod/2003pubs/p20-541.pdf.

Patton, J. M. "The Disproportionate Representation of African-Americans in Special Education: Looking behind the Curtain for Understanding and Solutions." *Journal of Special Education* 32, no. 1 (1998): 25–31.

Rank, M. R., and T. A. Hirschl. "The Likelihood of Poverty across the American Adult Life Span." *Social Work* 44, no. 3 (1999): 201–16.

Roberts, D. E. "The Social and Moral Costs of Mass Incarceration in African American Communities." *Stanford Law Review* 56, no. 5 (2004): 1271–1305.

Southern Christian Leadership Conference (SCLC)

The modern Civil Rights Movement was born from the turbulent era of the 1950s and 1960s. During this time, African Americans across the country and especially in the South came together to demand fulfillment of their rights as full citizens of the United States. At the center of the movement were a set of individual activists, frequently led by the Rev. Dr. Martin Luther King, Jr. Born Michael King, Jr., and the son of a prominent Baptist minister, Michael King, Sr., Dr. King and his father changed their first names in honor of the German Protestant religious leader Martin Luther. The name became reflective of the profound religious and political leader that Dr. King, Jr., would become. Much of Dr. King's civil rights organizing would be led from the Ebenezer Baptist Church in Atlanta, Georgia, where he pastored, as had his father and maternal grandfather before him. Consistent with his religious background, his political organizing was conducted primarily through collaboration with other clergy and religious congregants.

In addition to Dr. King, Rosa Parks—often called "the mother of the Civil Rights Movement"—is noted for her courageous stance on a Montgomery, Alabama, bus. On December 1, 1955, Rosa Parks refused to give up her seat to a White male. The diminutive Black seamstress and field secretary to the local chapter of the NAACP was arrested, and the Montgomery Bus Boycott began. The boycott lasted 381 days, in part due to the organizing efforts of Dr. King and his Montgomery Improvement Association.

Recognizing a need for coordinated action, Dr. King called together clergymen from across the South in an attempt to provide such action. Sixty men, representing 10 Southern states, responded to the call, and on January 11, 1957, they formed the Southern Conference on Transportation and Nonviolent Integration. One month later, another

The Dehli Freedom Movement, also known as the Chicago Freedom Movement, represented the alliance of the Southern Christian Leadership Conference (SCLC) and the Coordinating Council of Community Organizations (CCCO). The movement included a large rally, marches, and demands to the city of Chicago. These specific demands covered a wide range of areas, including housing, education, transportation, job access, income, employment, health, wealth generation, crime and the criminal justice system, community development, and quality of life. The Chicago Freedom Movement was the most ambitious civil rights campaign in the North of the United States, and lasted from mid 1965 to early 1967. Demands related to criminal justice included:

- creation of a citizens' review board for grievances against police brutality and false arrests, and stops and seizures; and
- locked lobbies and increased police protection in Chicago's public housing.

conference was held with over 100 Black ministers in attendance. At this meeting, the group's name was changed to the Southern Christian Leadership Conference (SCLC). Dr. King was elected president. From this beginning, the history of SCLC is almost indistinguishable from the history of Dr. King himself. Both King and SCLC would be major contributors to the civil rights movement, particularly in the Deep South.

Religion and nonviolence played a primary role in the work of the SCLC. In choosing this approach, Dr. King was heavily influenced by the teachings of Mahatma Gandhi of India and other pacifists. He believed the cause of civil rights could be furthered through direct action, but without resorting to violent behavior. Throughout the civil rights era, SCLC maintained this stance. Meetings were organized along the same lines as religious services and the messages from the group were couched in Biblical terms.

Once the SCLC was organized, the organization produced a list of goals for its members and for the African American population of the South. Those goals included 1) gathering White support for the cause; 2) encouraging more Blacks to become involved in the movement to demand justice and equality; and 3) building a "Beloved Community" where everyone would be treated with love and respect.

SCLC members traveled throughout the South looking for injustices and ways to correct them. In the early years, it was difficult to gather the attention needed to make significant gains. Initially, SCLC members became involved in various small-scale boycotts, sit-ins, demonstrations, and other forms of nonviolent protest. These actions were controversial among both Blacks and Whites. There were some Black community leaders who believed that segregation should only be challenged through the courts. Direct action on the streets contradicted the judicial approach and was seen by some as unacceptably prone to stirring White hostility. Class divisions were also evident among Blacks seeking to change their civil rights status. Traditionally, many Black community leaders were ministers, teachers, and other professionals who advocated on behalf of themselves and the Black working poor. The working poor made up a majority of the Black population but were seen by some members of the professional groups as unsuitable to advocate for themselves.

The SCLC encouraged Blacks of all ages, genders, and socioeconomic statuses to work with the organization in its efforts to secure civil rights. Young people were particularly active in the direct action campaigns. However, some youth members of the Student Nonviolent Coordinating Committee (SNCC) and the Congress of Racial Equality who participated in sit-ins and Freedom Rides were critical of SCLC and Dr. King for being too passive in the quest for justice and equality. The appropriate role of religious leaders and churches was another area of disagreement between the SCLC and others who pushed for civil rights. While the SCLC believed that churches should be involved in political activism against social injustice, the prevailing ideology among many religious leaders, both Black and White, at the time was that instead of becoming involved with politics, the churches should primarily focus on doing charitable work and providing spiritual guidance to their congregations.

From 1961 to 1962, SCLC joined with SNCC to participate in nonviolent protests against segregation in Albany, Georgia. From some perspectives, the Albany Movement, as it was called, did not garner much national attention and few changes were made in Albany during this nonviolent campaign. Subsequent organizing in Birmingham, Alabama, however, would prove to be substantially more effective.

SCLC launched its memorable nonviolent campaign in Birmingham, Alabama, in 1963. The campaign focused on the desegregation of Birmingham's downtown businesses. Images of the nonviolent protests being met with police brutality at the direction of the infamous police chief Theophilus Eugene "Bull" Connor sent a chilling message to the world that he, like many other White Southerners, was not going to accept desegregation.

SCLC planned to use Connor's violent ways to benefit its cause. The organization began with sit-ins at segregated lunch counters. Connor's men arrested the protestors, but the sit-ins continued for several days. Sit-ins were followed by increasingly large marches on city hall. The first march included 50 Black individuals, all of whom were arrested and jailed. More marches followed with more arrests. Dr. King himself was arrested and subsequently wrote his famous "Letter from the Birmingham Jail." The Birmingham protests continued with over 1,000 Black children, some as young as six years old, engaging in demonstrations. Connor's men arrested many of these children while news cameras filmed the events.

The most dramatic moment came in May, when over 1,000 young people gathered at a local church after the arrests, singing hymns and showing support for the movement. Connor ordered his men to seal the church, trapping many of those gathered inside. Those who escaped were met with police batons, dogs, and fire hoses. News footage of the Birmingham police using such violent tactics against children and young people stunned the nation. After more than a week of protests countered by extreme police violence, the end finally came. SCLC won its largest victory. Lunch counters, public restrooms, drinking fountains, and department store dressing rooms in Birmingham were desegregated. In addition to being national and international news at the time, the violent action used by the police against the peaceful protesters has been memorialized in an award-winning 1992 documentary titled *Eyes on the Prize*.

After his arrest in April 1963, Dr. King wrote the "Letter from a Birmingham Jail" in response to a group of clergy who had criticized the Birmingham Campaign, writing that it was "directed and led in part by outsiders" and that the demonstrations were "unwise and untimely." The letter included the now famous statement that "[i]njustice anywhere is a threat to justice everywhere."

Desegregation remained a core issue for SCLC; however, other issues also emerged. Voting rights, poverty, and inequality in other forms received SCLC attention. Voter registration campaigns became a common activity throughout the South. The belief was that the power of the vote would move Blacks more quickly toward equality. Efforts at Black voter registration and Black citizens' attempts to vote were met with violent resistance by White law enforcement agents, elected officials, and private citizens.

On August 28, 1963, SCLC participated in the historic March on Washington. This march was a united effort from many of the civil rights groups of the day. Over 200,000 persons attended the march, demanding civil rights, jobs, and other freedoms for the Black community. Despite the large crowd, King's nonviolence policy held and there were no violent incidents reported. During this march, King addressed the crowd with his famous "I Have a Dream" speech.

SCLC was also involved in a voting rights campaign in Selma, Alabama, and a desegregation campaign in St. Augustine, Florida, and a similar campaign in Grenada, Mississippi. In many of these activities, SCLC acted in concert with other civil rights groups, including SNCC and CORE. SCLC's activities remained nonviolent despite a growing militancy movement among the Northern Black population. Led by Malcolm X, many Northern Blacks were frustrated with the lack of progress in their section of the nation. Southern Blacks seemed to be receiving all the attention and making all the strides. Malcolm X promoted equality "by any means necessary," including violence. King promoted a peacefully integrated society based on principles of religious faith and nonviolence. Both men would be assassinated for their stand on racial issues.

After the assassination of Dr. King on April 4, 1968, SCLC spent several years in disarray. Many of the other civil rights organizations also struggled during this time. Many of their major goals had been accomplished and a search was on for what remained to be accomplished.

Although many saw the civil rights era as finished with the passing of the Civil Rights Act of 1964 and the Voting Rights Act of 1965, SCLC remains active today in pursuit of equality and justice for the Black population. SCLC is currently divided into local chapters throughout the country, with an international component as well. Voter registration and education continues to be a mainstay of SCLC focus. New issues include conflict resolution and nonviolence training, economic empowerment, healthcare, and youth development. While issues surrounding the African American population are still prominent, the work of SCLC has been expanded to address civil rights concerns faced by all minorities in America, and basic human rights worldwide.

Since its beginning, SCLC has had seven presidents, four of whom were ordained ministers. Rev. Dr. Martin Luther King, Jr., served as the first president until his assassination in 1968. He was followed by Rev. Ralph Abernathy, who served from 1968 to 1977. Rev. Joseph Lowery served from 1977 to 1997, and was followed by Martin L. King III, who served until 2004. Rev. Fred Shuttlesworth was the fifth president, serving only 10 months in 2004, followed by Charles Steele, Jr., who served from November 2004 to 2008. Dr. Byron Clay was named interim head of the SCLC in February 2009.

Having been founded by ministers, religion remains a unifying force within the SCLC. The religious basis is nondenominational but provides emphasis on nonviolence, peace, and love. As reported on the organization's Web site, the ideas of Dr. King, influenced by his faith and the teachings of Gandhi, have endured. In 1957, writing in the newly formed Southern Christian Leadership Conference newsletter, Dr. King described the purpose and goal of the organization as follows: "The ultimate aim of SCLC is to foster and create the 'beloved community' in America where brotherhood is a reality. . . . SCLC works for integration. Our ultimate goal is genuine intergroup and interpersonal living—integration." In his last book, Dr. King declared: "Our loyalties must transcend our race, our tribe, our class, and our nation. . . ." His was a vision of a completely integrated society, a community of love and justice wherein brotherhood would be an actuality in all of social life. In his mind, such a community would be the ideal corporate expression of the Christian faith.

SCLC produces a magazine five times per year. In publication since 1971, the magazine provides a national forum for continuing civil rights issues. Articles focus on minority concerns, gains, and struggles. The magazine also serves as a recruitment tool where major corporations can advertise positions and recruit quality minority candidates.

The Poor People's Campaign addressed the issues of economic justice and housing for the poor in the United States. The campaign would help the poor by dramatizing their needs, uniting all races under the commonality of hardship and presenting a plan toward a solution. Under the "economic bill of rights," the Poor People's Campaign asked for the federal government to prioritize helping the poor with a $30 billion anti-poverty package that included a commitment to full employment, a guaranteed annual income measure, and more low-income housing. Before a planned march, Dr. Martin Luther King, Jr., was assassinated. The march was subsequently led by Revs. Jesse Jackson and Ralph Abernathy. Thousands gathered on the National Mall on May 12, 1968, and camped out for six weeks, during which time U.S. senator and presidential candidate Robert Kennedy was assassinated.

The Poor People's Campaign is considered a failure by some because in 1968, 25 million people, or roughly 13 percent of the population, were living below the poverty level, while census data for 2006 indicate that that figure had increased by more than 10 million to 36 million, which still represents about 13 percent of the population.

SCLC also hosts an annual convention. Local chapters come together to discuss the ongoing fight, strategize, share victories, and learn from each other. The organization still uses King's idea of the "Beloved Community" in its call for action: "Be part of the solution."

Lorie Rubenser

See also: Civil Rights Movement; Malcolm X (aka El-Hajj Malik El-Shabazz); Police Brutality; Student Nonviolent Coordinating Committee (SNCC)

References

Appiah, Kwame Anthony, and Henry Louis Gates, Jr., eds. *Africana: Civil Rights, an A–Z Reference of the Movement That Changed America*. Philadelphia: Running Press, 2004.

Biography.com. "Martin Luther King, Jr." 2012. http://www.biography.com/people/martin-luther-king-jr-9365086.

Carson, Clayborne. *The Autobiography of Martin Luther King, Jr.* New York: Warner Books, 2001.

Fairclough, Adam. *To Redeem the Soul of America: The Southern Christian Leadership Conference and Martin Luther King, Jr.* Athens: University of Georgia Press, 1987.

Garrow, David J. *Bearing the Cross: Martin Luther King, Jr. and the Southern Christian Leadership Conference.* New York: Harper Collins, 1986.

Hampton, Henry, director. *Eyes on the Prize: America's Civil Rights Movement 1954–1965.* PBS Online/WGBH, 1992.

King, Martin Luther, Jr. "Letter from a Birmingham Jail." Published as "The Negro Is Your Brother" in *The Atlantic* 212, no. 2 (August 1963): 78–88.

Lohr, Kathy. "Poor People's Campaign: A Dream Unfulfilled." NPR, June 19, 2008.

New Georgia Encyclopedia. www.georgiaencyclopedia.org.

Pediaview Open Source Encyclopedia, citing "Eyes on the Prize: America's Civil Rights Movement 1954–1985," PBS Online/WGBH.

SCLC Web Site. http://www.sclcnational.org.

Sitkoff, Harvard. *The Struggle for Black Equality: 1954-1992.* Revised Edition. New York: Hill and Wang, 1993.

Southern Christian Leadership Conference. http://www.historylearningsite.co.uk.

Stop Snitching Campaign

In recent years, a movement known as the Stop Snitching Campaign has emerged, capturing the attention of many teenagers, parents, teachers, police, and legislators (Carr et al., 2007). While the basic premise of not cooperating with police is an old one, certain features of the Stop Snitching Campaign have brought the "keep your mouth shut" attitude to the attention of mainstream society (Conan, 2006). A dominant feature of the campaign involves the 2004 release of an underground DVD entitled *Stop Snitching.* The video, filmed in West Baltimore, depicts drug dealers, guns, and strong anti-snitching messages, including threats of violence toward witnesses (Gregory, 2005; Kahn, 2007; Smith, 2008). The video, and effectively the movement, made national headlines owing in part to an appearance made by NBA star Carmelo Anthony. The DVD has circulated widely across the nation (Kahn, 2007; Natapoff, 2009), and a sequel, *Stop Snitching 2,* was released in 2007 (Fox News, 2007).

Popularity stemming from the campaign and DVD prompted the making of a variety of anti-snitching t-shirts (Natapoff, 2009). The most popular versions of the t-shirts glamorize the words "Stop Snitching" in large letters, within a stop sign, or the word "snitching" circled and crossed out in a thick red line (Natapoff, 2005; 2009). The shirts have been in high demand in major metropolitan areas including New York, Boston, Philadelphia, and Baltimore (Gregory, 2005; Kahn, 2007; Sanneh, 2005; Smith, 2008). The t-shirts garnered media attention after several high-profile events, including a courtroom uproar when assault victim Rayco Saunders, a former drug dealer turned professional boxer, sported one during the prosecution of his own attackers (Natapoff, 2009). Mayor Thomas M. Menino attempted to ban the selling of the shirts in retail stores in Boston (Natapoff, 2005; 2009), and was successful in convincing some store owners to stop selling them (Smalley, 2005).

Among those most affected by the Stop Snitching Campaign are inner-city community members, particularly youth (Natapoff 2005; 2009). Within these inner cities are an innumerable amount of disadvantaged neighborhoods largely characterized by a disproportionate population of minorities, particularly African Americans (Newman, 2000). Across the nation, talking to the police in such neighborhoods is considered "a mortal sin, a dishonorable act punishable by social banishment—or worse" (Kahn, 2007: 82). Many attribute the stop snitching attitude in poor minority neighborhoods to a greater problem—distrust of the police (see Carr et al., 2007; Natapoff, 2009; Tyler & Huo, 2002). A long-standing history of negative policing tactics in African American neighborhoods has contributed to this lack of trust (Kennedy, 1997).

The Black music industry, predominantly hip-hop and rap, has been charged with embracing and promoting the Stop Snitching Campaign through both lyrics and actions (Kahn, 2007; Sanneh, 2007; Schorn, 2007). The campaign's slogan, "Stop Snitching," was first made fashionable in 1999 by Boston rapper Tangg da Juice (Kahn, 2007). In 2007, rapper Cam'ron sat down with Anderson Cooper in a *60 Minutes* interview and discussed the relationship between the music industry and the Stop Snitching Campaign. When asked what he would do if he lived next door to a serial killer, Cam'ron stated that he "wouldn't call and tell anyone" and that he would "probably just move." Another well-known rap artist, Lil' Kim, refused to cooperate with authorities after allegedly witnessing a shooting incident (Natapoff, 2009; Schorn, 2007). According to CNN news, she was convicted of perjury and conspiring with a co-defendant to lie before a grand jury. To many urban supporters, this case represented honor and heroism, as Lil' Kim was evidently willing to do time in federal prison rather than "snitch" on peers.[1] Other hip-hop and rap artists including Eminem, Lil Wayne, and Jay-Z have expressed anti-snitching messages through their lyrics.

There is great debate over what the Stop Snitching Campaign represents and who it is directed toward (Natapoff, 2009). In other words, there is disagreement surrounding the underlying message of the campaign as well as the target audience. As Hodge (2008) points out, the Stop Snitching Movement is much more complicated than people think. Some view it as an antisocial message to not cooperate with or report crime to the police for any reason, while others contend that the campaign conveys a specific message to a specific audience, in which criminals need to stop snitching on other criminals (Natapoff, 2009). In some circles, terms such as "wet" snitching and "dry" snitching have been used to describe two main types of informing to the police. "Wet" snitching occurs when criminals report the crimes of other criminals to gain a benefit. "Dry" snitching occurs when ordinary civilian witnesses report crime or crime-related information to the police.

Advocates of the Stop Snitching Campaign see it as an instructive movement that specifically aims to prevent or minimize violence between individuals involved in criminal behavior. In this way, anti-snitching messages are considered warnings to and from criminals to avoid making statements that otherwise incite violence and distrust within communities (Fox News, 2007; Kahn, 2007; Natapoff, 2009). This position has been well documented and supported by Alexandra Natapoff, a prominent law professor at Loyola Law School and nationally recognized expert on criminal snitching. Natapoff argues that not only does snitching engender retaliatory violence and mistrust in communities, it also exacerbates some of the worst features of the American justice system, as police tend to overrely on criminal informants (Natapoff, 2009) to make their cases rather than their own independent efforts.

Further, supporters argue that this basic premise of the campaign has been misconstrued and blown out of proportion. For example, Rodney Bethea, producer of the controversial snitching DVD, vehemently argues that the point of the Stop Snitching Movement is not to encourage violence against typical witnesses such as an elderly woman who calls the police on drug dealers in her neighborhood (Kahn, 2007; Natapoff, 2009). Instead, he argues that in both the streets and the DVD, a snitch refers "to a person engaging and profiting from illegal activities; and when they get arrested, to save themselves, they tell on everyone else they know" (Natapoff, 2009: 125). Natapoff also notes that the war on drugs and heavy police presence in urban neighborhoods have placed tremendous pressure on young Black males to act as informants in order to avoid long prison sentences and other unwanted criminal justice system contact.

Conversely, critics of the Stop Snitching Movement, who typically include police, prosecutors, state legislators, city officials, and community members, see it as both procriminal and antisocial (Natapoff, 2005). To them, Stop Snitching promotes a culture of silence that impedes law enforcement from solving a significant amount of cases. Moreover, they argue that anti-snitching messages are consumed not only by active street offenders (see Rosenfeld et al., 2003), but also by law-abiding citizens, particularly youth (Gosselin, 2007; Delgado, 2008; Kahn, 2007; Sweeney, 2008). According to Brooklyn Law School assistant professor Lisa C. Smith, "[a] mentality has started to seep into the neighborhood where ordinary, upstanding people who would come forward because a crime occurred are now being told they are snitches." Kahn suggests that distinctions drawn "between the drug dealer who flips and the civilian who is just trying to get dealers off her stoop" (2007: 88) are futile considering the number of incidents that have resulted in the

Table 1 Offenses Known to Police and Percent Cleared by Arrest[a] by Offense and Population Group, 2010 (2010 estimated population)

| Population group | | | | Violent crime | | | | Property crime | | | |
	Total	Murder and non-negligent manslaughter	Forcible rape	Robbery	Aggravated assault	Total	Burglary	Larceny-theft	Motor vehicle theft	Arson[b]
Total all agencies										
14,565 agencies; population 271,571,110:										
Offenses known	1,080,242	12,760	73,934	315,115	678,433	8,064,964	1,936,341	5,466,667	661,956	50,567
Percent cleared by arrest	47.2%	64.8	40.3	28.2	56.4	18.3	12.4	21.1	11.8	19.0
Total cities										
10,457 cities; population 180,504,683:										
Offenses known	845,386	9,579	54,586	270,811	510,410	6,229,128	1,401,687	4,309,372	518,069	37,375
Percent cleared by arrest	45.3%	63.9	38.6	27.6	55.1	18.4	11.9	21.5	10.6	18.6
Group I										
71 cities, 250,000 and over; population 44,953,427:										
Offenses known	347,014	4,728	17,236	132,178	192,872	1,861,697	456,470	1,177,739	227,488	13,529
Percent cleared by arrest	39.9%	61.1	41.3	24.5	49.8	13.8	9.3	16.8	7.5	14.4
8 cities, 1,000,000 and over; population 14,654,178:										
Offenses known	106,371	1,348	5,026	44,472	55,525	550,627	128,862	349,516	72,249	3,890
Percent cleared by arrest	39.2%	69.3	44.1	24.6	49.7	13.1	7.6	16.6	5.7	13.0

520

24 cities, 500,000 to 999,999; population 16,465,103:										
Offenses known	135,800	1,794	6,440	48,538	79,028	736,004	179,520	469,207	87,277	4,942
Percent cleared by arrest	39.5%	56.7	40.6	23.6	48.8	12.8	8.9	15.3	7.7	14.4
39 cities, 250,000 to 499,999; population 13,834,146:										
Offenses known	104,843	1,586	5,770	39,168	58,319	575,066	148,088	359,016	67,962	4,697
Percent cleared by arrest	41.0%	59.0	39.8	25.3	51.1	15.7	11.2	18.9	9.0	15.6
Group II										
196 cities, 100,000 to 249,999; population 29,191,226:										
Offenses known	151,801	1,683	9,505	49,851	90,762	1,115,390	263,754	751,059	100,577	6,254
Percent cleared by arrest	44.3%	62.5	36.6	27.6	54.0	17.6	11.0	20.9	10.0	16.6
Group III										
451 cities, 50,000 to 99,999; population 30,903,160:										
Offenses known	122,519	1,219	8,595	37,337	75,368	997,549	219,527	700,032	77,990	5,908
Percent cleared by arrest	47.6%	67.8	37.1	30.1	57.2	20.0	12.6	23.4	11.2	19.2
Group IV										
766 cities, 25,000 to 49,999; population 26,508,712:										
Offenses known	84,032	836	6,996	23,350	52,850	797,465	167,143	584,108	46,214	4,114
Percent cleared by arrest	49.9%	66.4	34.9	32.0	59.5	21.3	12.8	24.3	13.7	22.4

(*Continued*)

Table 1 *Continued*

Population group	Violent crime					Property crime				
	Total	Murder and non-negligent manslaughter	Forcible rape	Robbery	Aggravated assault	Total	Burglary	Larceny-theft	Motor vehicle theft	Arson[b]
Group V										
1,685 cities, 10,000 to 24,999; population 26,752,794:										
Offenses known	77,050	685	6,592	17,796	51,977	777,824	162,578	576,615	38,631	3,784
Percent cleared by arrest	53.9%	72.3	38.3	36.0	61.8	23.0	15.0	25.6	17.6	25.1
Group VI										
7,288 cities under 10,000; population 22,195,364:										
Offenses known	62,970	428	5,662	10,299	46,581	679,203	132,215	519,819	27,169	3,786
Percent cleared by arrest	56.5%	70.8	40.9	35.1	63.0	21.7	16.5	22.9	22.8	24.7
Metropolitan counties										
1,761 agencies; population 65,773,804:										
Offenses known	185,397	2,337	13,815	40,210	129,035	1,426,858	390,869	918,318	117,671	9,817
Percent cleared by arrest	52.1%	64.7	44.7	30.7	59.3	17.7	13.2	19.9	14.5	18.7
See notes at end of table.										
Nonmetropolitan counties										
2,347 agencies; population 25,292,623:										
Offenses known	49,459	844	5,533	4,094	38,988	408,978	143,785	238,977	26,216	3,375
Percent cleared by arrest	61.1%	75.0	46.3	43.6	64.8	18.2	15.4	19.3	23.2	24.3

Suburban areas[c]
7,746 agencies; population 119,065,296:

Offenses known	320,825	3,509	24,740	74,711	217,865	2,864,008	673,000	1,993,229	197,779	16,926
Percent cleared by arrest	52.6%	65.5	41.7	32.0	60.6	19.6	13.7	22.0	14.8	20.9

Note: These data were compiled by the Federal Bureau of Investigation through the Uniform Crime Reporting (UCR) Program. On a monthly basis, law enforcement agencies report the number of offenses that become known to them in the following crime categories: murder and nonnegligent manslaughter, forcible rape, robbery, aggravated assault, burglary, larceny-theft, motor vehicle theft, and arson. Arrest statistics are compiled as part of this monthly data collection effort. Participating law enforcement agencies are instructed to count one arrest each time a person is taken into custody, notified, or cited for criminal infractions other than traffic violations. Annual arrest figures do not measure the number of individuals taken into custody because one person may be arrested several times during the year for the same type of offense or for different offenses. A juvenile is counted as a person arrested when he/she commits an act that would be a criminal offense if committed by an adult.

An offense is "cleared by arrest" or solved for crime reporting purposes when at least one person is: (1) arrested; (2) charged with the commission of the offense; and (3) turned over to the court for prosecution. An offense is also counted as cleared by arrest if certain "exceptional" conditions pertain, including: suicide of the offender; deathbed confession; offender killed by police or citizen; confession by offender already in custody; extradition denied; victim refuses to cooperate in prosecution; warrant is outstanding for felon but prior to arrest the offender dies of natural causes or as a result of an accident, or is killed in the commission of another offense; or, handling of a juvenile offender either orally or by written notice to parents in instances involving minor offenses where no referral to juvenile court is customarily made.

This table presents data from all law enforcement agencies submitting complete reports for at least 6 months in 2010 (Source, Table 25, Data Declaration). Beginning with publication of the 2003 data, the "rural" county designation was changed to "nonmetropolitan" county. Population figures are estimates calculated from U.S. Census Bureau data. For definitions of offenses, city and suburban areas, and nonmetropolitan counties, see Appendix 3.

[a]Includes offenses cleared by exceptional means.

[b]The number of agency reports used in arson clearance rates is less than those used in compiling other offense clearance rates because arson is reported to the FBI separately from other offenses.

[c]Includes law enforcement agencies in cities with less than 50,000 inhabitants and county law enforcement agencies that are within a Metropolitan Statistical Area; excludes all metropolitan agencies associated with a principal city. The agencies associated with suburban areas also will appear in other groups within this table.

Source: U.S. Department of Justice, Federal Bureau of Investigation, Crime in the United States, 2010, Table 25 [Online]. Available: http://www.fbi.gov/about-us/cjis/ucr/crime-in-the-u.s.-2010/tables/10tbl25.xls [Nov. 7, 2011]. Table adapted by SOURCEBOOK staff.

Table 2 Offenses Known to Police and Percent Cleared by Arrest[a]
by Type of Offense, United States, 1971–2010

	Violent crime[b]		Property crime[c]	
	Offenses known to police	Percent cleared by arrest	Offenses known to police	Percent cleared by arrest
1971	473,126	46.5%	3,126,936	15.7%
1972	506,938	48.8	3,189,111	16.1
1973	685,982	45.2	5,726,784	18.3
1974	750,341	45.2	6,475,738	18.5
1975	797,688	44.7	7,400,925	18.5
1976	791,409	45.5	7,855,894	18.0
1977	773,328	45.8	7,233,807	18.3
1978	830,565	45.5	7,601,079	18.1
1979	914,576	43.7	8,228,506	17.1
1980	1,242,511	43.6	11,240,527	16.5
1981	1,275,135	42.9	11,440,759	16.9
1982	1,195,533	45.4	10,737,211	17.3
1983	1,166,888	46.5	10,236,253	17.7
1984	1,172,616	47.4	9,948,802	17.9
1985	1,240,134	47.6	10,522,406	17.8
1986	1,445,965	46.3	11,288,440	17.5
1987	1,354,012	47.4	11,148,256	17.7
1988	1,355,693	45.7	10,703,955	17.5
1989	1,364,705	45.8	10,759,757	18.0
1990	1,700,303	45.6	11,767,925	18.1
1991	1,682,487	44.7	11,651,612	17.8
1992	1,854,630	44.6	11,789,664	17.7
1993	1,772,279	44.2	11,091,352	17.4
1994	1,720,302	45.3	10,865,925	17.7
1995	1,531,703	45.4	10,327,426	17.6
1996	1,293,408	47.4	9,125,896	18.1
1997	1,343,642	48.3	9,584,841	17.9
1998	1,178,388	49.1	8,405,350	17.4
1999	1,164,380	50.0	8,495,347	17.5
2000	1,131,923	47.5	8,235,013	16.7
2001	1,024,134	46.2	7,860,198	16.2
2002	1,184,453	46.8	8,937,268	16.5
2003	1,126,180	46.5	8,728,536	16.4
2004	1,152,733	46.3	8,925,398	16.5
2005	1,197,089	45.5	8,935,714	16.3
2006	1,240,985	44.3	8,851,465	15.8

	Violent crime[b]		Property crime[c]	
	Offenses known to police	**Percent cleared by arrest**	**Offenses known to police**	**Percent cleared by arrest**
2007	1,227,330	44.5	8,716,315	16.5
2008	1,204,655	45.1	8,628,538	17.4
2009	1,142,108	47.1	8,229,516	18.6
2010	1,080,242	47.2	8,064,964	18.3

Note: These data were compiled by the Federal Bureau of Investigation through the Uniform Crime Reporting (UCR) Program. On a monthly basis, law enforcement agencies report the number of offenses that become known to them in the following crime categories: murder and nonnegligent manslaughter, forcible rape, robbery, aggravated assault, burglary, larceny-theft, motor vehicle theft, and arson. Arrest statistics are compiled as part of this monthly data collection effort. Participating law enforcement agencies are instructed to count one arrest each time a person is taken into custody, notified, or cited for criminal infractions other than traffic violations. Annual arrest figures do not measure the number of individuals taken into custody because one person may be arrested several times during the year for the same type of offense or for different offenses. A juvenile is counted as a person arrested when he/she commits an act that would be a criminal offense if committed by an adult.

An offense is "cleared by arrest" or solved for crime reporting purposes when at least one person is: (1) arrested; (2) charged with the commission of the offense; and (3) turned over to the court for prosecution. An offense is also counted as cleared by arrest if certain "exceptional" conditions pertain, including suicide of the offender; double murder; deathbed confession; offender killed by police or citizen; confession by offender already in custody; extradition denied; victim refuses to cooperate in prosecution; warrant is outstanding for felon but prior to arrest the offender dies of natural causes or as a result of an accident, or is killed in the commission of another offense; or, handling of a juvenile offender either orally or by written notice to parents in instances involving minor offenses where no referral to juvenile court is customarily made.

The number of agencies reporting and the populations represented vary from year to year. Due to National Incident-Based Reporting System conversion efforts beginning in 1991 as well as other reporting problems, complete arrest data were not available for a small number of jurisdictions for certain years. See Appendix 3 for a list of jurisdictions omitted. This table presents data from all law enforcement agencies submitting complete reports for 12 months or fewer in 1971-80 and at least 6 months in 1981-2010. For definitions of offenses, see Appendix 3.

[a]Includes offenses cleared by exceptional means.

[b]Violent crimes are offenses of murder and nonnegligent manslaughter, forcible rape, robbery, and aggravated assault.

[c]Property crimes are offenses of burglary, larceny-theft, and motor vehicle theft. Data are not included for the property crime of arson.

Source: U.S. Department of Justice, Federal Bureau of Investigation, Crime in the United States, 1971, p. 104; 1972, p. 107; 1973, p. 109; 1974, p. 166; 1975, p. 166; 1976, p. 162; 1977, p. 162; 1978, p. 177; 1979, p. 179; 1980, p. 182; 1981, p. 153; 1982, p. 158; 1983, p. 161; 1984, p. 154; 1985, p. 156; 1986, p. 156; 1987, p. 155; 1988, p. 159; 1989, p. 163; 1990, p. 165; 1991, p. 204; 1992, p. 208; 1993, p. 208; 1994, p. 208; 1995, p. 199; 1996, p. 205; 1997, p. 213; 1998, p. 201; 1999, p. 203; 2000, p. 207; 2001, p. 222; 2002, p. 223; 2003, p. 257; 2004, p. 266 (Washington, DC: USGPO); 2005, Table 25 [Online]. Available: http://www2.fbi.gov/05cius/ data/table_25.html [Oct. 12, 2006]; 2006, Table 25 [Online]. Available:http://www2.fbi.gov/ucr/cius2006/ data/table_25.html [Oct. 27, 2007]; 2007, Table 25 [Online]. Available:http://www2.fbi.gov/ucr/cius2007/data/ table_25.html [Jan. 15, 2009]; 2008, Table 25 [Online]. Available: http://www2.fbi.gov/ucr/cius2008/data/ table_25.html [Jan. 21, 2010]; 2009, Table 25 [Online]. Available: http://www2.fbi.gov/ucr/cius2009/data/ table_25.html [Nov. 12, 2010]; 2010, Table 25 [Online]. Available: http://www.fbi.gov/about-us/cjis/ucr/crime-in-the-u.s/2010/crime-in-the-u.s.-2010/tables/10tbl25.xls [Nov. 11, 2011]. Table constructed by SOURCEBOOK staff.

Table 3   Percent of Offenses Known to Police That Were Cleared by Arrest[a] by Extent of Urbanization and Type of Offense, 1972–2010

	Cities		Suburban[b]		Rural (nonmetropolitan) counties	
	Violent crime[c]	Property crime[d]	Violent crime[c]	Property crime[d]	Violent crime[c]	Property crime[d]
1972	48.8%	16.1%	50.3%	14.0%	70.2%	20.1%
1973	45.2	18.3	51.2	17.0	69.5	19.3
1974	45.2	18.5	50.0	17.3	69.7	19.7
1975	44.7	18.5	50.0	17.6	70.1	19.4
1976	45.5	18.0	51.3	16.9	69.5	18.7
1977	45.8	18.3	50.9	16.9	69.2	18.8
1978	45.5	18.1	49.9	17.0	67.9	18.4
1979	43.7	17.1	49.3	16.6	67.0	18.8
1980	41.7	16.6	48.4	16.2	64.9	16.7
1981	40.9	17.0	48.7	17.0	63.8	17.0
1982	43.5	17.3	50.9	17.8	66.4	18.1
1983	44.5	17.7	52.3	18.4	66.9	18.0
1984	45.5	18.0	53.8	18.8	65.7	18.1
1985	45.7	17.9	53.2	18.2	67.0	18.4
1986	44.6	17.5	51.7	18.3	63.9	17.7
1987	46.0	17.9	51.3	18.4	61.8	17.6
1988	44.2	17.7	51.7	18.4	63.5	17.8
1989	44.4	18.2	51.3	18.7	61.7	18.2
1990	43.9	18.3	51.7	18.7	61.3	18.1
1991	42.9	18.1	51.2	18.6	63.0	18.6
1992	43.1	18.0	51.1	18.6	60.7	18.4
1993	42.5	17.6	51.0	18.3	60.7	18.3
1994	43.5	17.8	52.5	18.5	60.9	18.7
1995	43.5	17.7	52.7	18.6	60.9	18.6
1996	45.9	18.3	53.7	19.1	62.3	19.8
1997	46.2	17.9	54.5	18.9	62.2	19.2
1998	47.7	17.5	54.5	18.4	60.2	18.7
1999	48.3	17.6	54.4	18.4	61.4	18.4
2000	45.4	16.8	53.8	17.9	61.3	18.7
2001	44.0	16.2	53.5	17.2	62.0	18.1
2002	44.5	16.4	53.4	17.8	61.4	18.3

	Cities		Suburban[b]		Rural (nonmetropolitan) counties	
	Violent crime[c]	Property crime[d]	Violent crime[c]	Property crime[d]	Violent crime[c]	Property crime[d]
2003	44.7	16.3	51.4	17.4	59.9	17.8
2004	43.7	16.4	53.3	17.9	60.6	17.8
2005	42.9	16.2	52.9	17.4	61.6	18.0
2006	42.0	15.7	50.9	16.8	59.3	16.8
2007	42.5	16.6	50.6	17.6	57.4	17.1
2008	43.1	17.6	51.1	18.6	57.7	17.9
2009	45.1	18.7	52.8	19.9	60.3	18.3
2010	45.3	18.4	52.6	19.6	61.1	18.2

Note: These data were compiled by the Federal Bureau of Investigation through the Uniform Crime Reporting (UCR) Program. On a monthly basis, law enforcement agencies report the number of offenses that become known to them in the following crime categories: murder and nonnegligent manslaughter, forcible rape, robbery, aggravated assault, burglary, larceny-theft, motor vehicle theft, and arson. Arrest statistics are compiled as part of this monthly data collection effort. Participating law enforcement agencies are instructed to count one arrest each time a person is taken into custody, notified, or cited for criminal infractions other than traffic violations. Annual arrest figures do not measure the number of individuals taken into custody because one person may be arrested several times during the year for the same type of offense or for different offenses. A juvenile is counted as a person arrested when he/she commits an act that would be a criminal offense if committed by an adult.

An offense is "cleared by arrest" or solved for crime reporting purposes when at least one person is: (1) arrested; (2) charged with the commission of the offense; and (3) turned over to the court for prosecution. An offense is also counted as cleared by arrest if certain "exceptional" conditions pertain, including suicide of the offender; double murder; deathbed confession; offender killed by police or citizen; confession by offender already in custody; extradition denied; victim refuses to cooperate in prosecution; warrant is outstanding for felon but prior to arrest the offender dies of natural causes or as a result of an accident, or is killed in the commission of another offense; or, handling of a juvenile offender either orally or by written notice to parents in instances involving minor offenses where no referral to juvenile court is customarily made.

The number of agencies reporting and the populations represented vary from year to year. Due to National IncidentBased Reporting System conversion efforts beginning in 1991 as well as other reporting problems, complete arrest data were not available for a small number of jurisdictions for certain years. See Appendix 3 for a list of jurisdictions omitted. Beginning with publication of the 2003 data, the "rural" county designation was changed to "nonmetropolitan" county. For definitions of offenses, city and suburban areas, and nonmetropolitan counties, see Appendix 3.

[a]Includes offenses cleared by exceptional means.

[b]Includes law enforcement agencies in cities with less than 50,000 inhabitants and county law enforcement agencies that are within a Metropolitan Statistical Area; excludes all metropolitan agencies associated with a principal city. The agencies associated with suburban areas also will appear in other groups within this table.

(Continued)

[c]Violent crimes are offenses of murder and nonnegligent manslaughter, forcible rape, robbery, and aggravated assault.

[d]Property crimes are offenses of burglary, larceny-theft, and motor vehicle theft. Data are not included for the property crime of arson.

Source: U.S. Department of Justice, Federal Bureau of Investigation, Crime in the United States, 1972, pp. 107, 108; 1973, pp. 109, 110; 1974, pp. 166, 167; 1975, pp. 166, 167; 1976, pp. 162, 163; 1977, pp. 162, 163; 1978, pp. 177, 178; 1979, pp. 179, 180; 1980, pp. 182, 183; 1981, pp. 153, 154; 1982, pp. 158, 159; 1983, pp. 161, 162; 1984, pp. 154, 155; 1985, pp. 156, 157; 1986, pp. 156, 157; 1987, pp. 155, 156; 1988, pp. 159, 160; 1989, pp. 163, 164; 1990, pp. 165, 166; 1991, pp. 204, 205; 1992, pp. 208, 209; 1993, pp. 208, 209; 1994, pp. 208, 209; 1995, pp. 199, 200; 1996, pp. 205, 206; 1997, pp. 213, 214; 1998, pp. 201, 202; 1999, pp. 203, 204; 2000, pp. 207, 208; 2001, pp. 222, 223; 2002, pp. 223, 224; 2003, pp. 257, 258; 2004, pp. 266, 267 (Washington, DC: USGPO); 2005, Table 25 [Online]. Available: http://www2.fbi.gov/ucr/05cius/data/table_25.html [Oct. 12, 2006]; 2006, Table 25 [Online]. Available: http://www2.fbi.gov/ucr/cius2006/data/table_25.html [Oct. 25, 2007]; 2007, Table 25 [Online]. Available: http://www2.fbi.gov/ucr/cius2007/data/table_25.html [Jan. 15, 2009]; 2008, Table 25 [Online]. Available: http://www2.fbi.gov/ucr/cius2008/data/table_25.html [Jan. 21, 2010]; 2009, Table 25 [Online]. Available: http://www2.fbi.gov/ucr/cius2009/data/table_25.html [Nov. 12, 2010]; 2010, Table 25 [Online]. Available: http://www.fbi.gov/ about-us/cjis/ucr/ crime-in-the-u.s/2010/crime-in-the-u.s.-2010/tables/10tbl25.xls [Nov. 11, 2011]. Table constructed by SOURCEBOOK staff.

intimidation or death of those who inform. Therefore, regardless of original intention, the Stop Snitching Campaign is highly criticized and opposed for its perceived threat to ordinary citizens who call the police (Natapoff, 2005).

Efforts have been made to challenge the Stop Snitching Campaign. For example, in 2008, Rev. Al Sharpton joined forces in promoting his own campaign: "It's Not Snitching, It's Saving a Life." These encouraging words were painted over an anti-snitching mural in Harlem by Sharpton himself and a number of community members and activists (Warren, 2008). Sharpton is one of many activists who have spoken out about the Stop Snitching phenomenon in the New York area. The Baltimore Police Department released its own DVD entitled *Keep Talkin'* in an effort to mitigate the effects of the Stop Snitching Campaign and encourage witnesses to come forward (Kahn, 2007). In addition, rejoinders to the campaign have been aired on television, including the CNN special with Anderson Cooper and Cam'ron as well as the Fox News series called *Step Up and Speak Out.* Notwithstanding, the Stop Snitching Campaign is a controversial issue that continues to thrive in society as clearance rates, the amount of crime that results in an arrest, are low and witness intimidation is high.

Tarra Jackson

See also: Correctional System and African Americans; Federal Sentencing Disparity; Gangs; Hip-Hop Culture; Homicide, Intra-Racial Offending; Prisons; Shakur, Assata; Shakur, Tupac Amaru; Sharpton, Jr., Alfred Charles; Snitching, The Miseducation of; Youth Violence

Note

1. See related blog: http://nyourwill.blogspot.com/2006/07/is-lil-kim-role-model.html.

References

Carr, P. J., L. Napolitano, and J. Keating, J. "We Never Call the Cops and Here Is Why: A Qualitative Examination of Legal Cynicism in Three Philadelphia Neighborhoods." *Criminology* 45 (2007): 445–78.

Conan, N. "Examining the Causes of Witness Intimidation." *Talk of the Nation, National Public Radio,* May 1, 2006.

Delgado, R. "Law Enforcement in Subordinated Communities: Innovation and Response." *Michigan Law Review* 106 (2008): 1193–1212.

Fox News. "'Stop Snitching' Sequel Video Disturbs Baltimore Officials." December 21, 2007. http://www.foxnews.com/story/0,2933,317753,00.html.

Gregory, K. "A Snitch in Time." *Philadelphia Weekly,* July 20, 2005. http://www.philadelphiaweekly.com/view.php?id=9974.

Gosselin, T. "The Stop Snitching Campaign." *Associated Content,* May 24, 2007. http://www.associatedcontent.com/article/253959/the_stop_snitching_campaign.html.

Hodge, D. "See No Evil." *Las Vegas Sun,* June 26, 2008. http://www.lasvegassun.com/news/2008/jun/26/see-no-evil/.

Kahn, J. "The Story of a Snitch." *The Atlantic* 299 (April 2007): 80–92.

Kennedy, R. *Race, Crime, and the Law.* New York: Pantheon Books, 1997.

Natapoff, A. *Snitching: Criminal Informants and the Erosion of American Justice.* New York: New York University Press, 2009.

Natapoff, A. "Bait and Snitch. *Slate Magazine,* December 12, 2005. http://www.slate.com/id/2132092.

Newman, K. *No Shame in My Game: The Working Poor in the Inner City.* New York: Vintage, 2000.

Rosenfeld, R., B. A. Jacobs, and R. Wright. "Snitching and the Code of the Street." *The British Journal of Criminology* 43 (2003): 291–309.

Sanneh, K. "Don't Blame Hip-Hop." *The New York Times,* April 25, 2007.

Sanneh, K. "Cracking the Code in Hip-Hop." *The New York Times,* October 13, 2005.

Schorn, D. "Stop Snitchin'." *CBS News,* August 12, 2007. http://www.cbsnews.com/stories/2007/04/19/60minutes/main2704565.shtml.

Smalley, S. "Snitching T-Shirts Come off the Shelves." *The Boston Globe,* December 5, 2005. http://www.boston.com/news/local/massachusetts/articles/2005/12/05/snitching_t_shirts_come_off_the_shelves/.

Smith, B. L. "Keeping a 'Snitch' from Being Scratched." *ABA Journal* (December 2008). http://abajournal.com/magazine/keeping_a_snitch_from_being_scratched/.

Sweeney, A. "Police Blame 'No Snitching' for Unsolved Murders." *The Chicago Sun-Times,* January 22, 2008.

Tyler, T. R., and Y. J. Huo. *Trust in the Law: Encouraging Public Cooperation with the Police and Courts.* New York: Russell Sage Foundation, 2002.

Warren, M. R. "City Room; Whitewashing a Cartoon Rat's Message on Snitching." *The New York Times,* July 18, 2008. http://query.nytimes.com/gst/fullpage.html?res=9D00E 6D61739F93BA25754C0A96E9C8B63.

Streetwise Project

"Streetwise—Language, Culture and Police Work in New York" was conceived, developed, and originally delivered by the New York State Regional Community Policing Institute. Regional Community Policing Institutes (RCPIs) were established by the Office of Community Oriented Policing Services (COPS), U.S. Department of Justice, in 1997.

The RCPI network was designed to provide training to law enforcement professionals and the citizens they serve in region-specific community policing issues in all 50 states and the five U.S. territories. RCPIs sought to achieve a level of practice that would become the standard for dealing with issues of public trust and personnel accountability.

Partner organizations of the New York State (NYS) RCPI included educational institutions, law enforcement agencies, and community organizations. The educational institutions were John Jay College of Criminal Justice, New York City (NYC) as the host agency and the Police Institute at Rutgers University in Newark, New Jersey. The law enforcement agencies included the New York City Police Department (NYPD), NYS Division of Criminal Justice Services, and the Department of Public Safety, White Plains, New York. The community organizations included Citizens for NYC; Neighborhood Watch of Jamestown, New York; Community Action Organization; United Neighborhoods of Buffalo, New York; North American Family Institute headquartered in White Plains, New York; and Berkshire Farm Center and Services for Youth in Albany, New York. In 2009, when RCPI funding was no longer available from the U.S. Department of Justice, the NYS RCPI was restructured as a center of excellence within the John Jay College of Criminal Justice as the Community Policing Leadership Institute (CPLI).

The African/Caribbean American Experience and the Haitian Experience modules for the training were influenced in part by two infamous violent interactions involving members of the NYPD. In August 1997, Abner Louima, a Haitian immigrant, was arrested and sodomized with a broomstick in the station house restroom of Brooklyn's 70th Precinct. The case became a national symbol of police brutality and fostered perceptions that New York City police officers were harassing or abusing young Black men as part of a citywide crackdown on crime. The police officer who assaulted him was arrested, tried, convicted, and sentenced to 30 years in prison. In February 1999, Amadou Diallo, an immigrant from Guinea, West Africa, was fatally shot as a result of the mistaken belief that he was armed with a gun. The four New York City police officers involved in the shooting were arrested, tried, and found not guilty. The verdict of this racially charged case led to antipolice demonstrations and arrests, and the eventual disbanding of the department's Street Crime Unit, to which the officers belonged.

The Streetwise course provided participants with basic linguistic skills and cultural knowledge about one of seven groups of people: African/Caribbean American; Chinese; Haitian; Hispanic; Russian; South Asian; and Lesbian, Gay, Bisexual, and Transgender communities. The training used testimonies of mentor officers, role play, case studies, problem-solving exercises, media presentations, and interactive language instruction to graphically demonstrate the impact of language and culture on day-to-day police/community interactions.

Each Streetwise training session began with a video presentation from the NYPD police commissioner endorsing the training. This was followed by a presentation by a high-ranking police commander and, where appropriate, comments by the host of the training location.

Multiple facilities were utilized to deliver the material. Subject matter information consisted of lessons dealing with ethics and integrity, cultural aspects of perception, attitude, myths and stereotypes, communication skills, and problem solving. The language portion of the classroom training was supported by supplemental information, including "say the word" language cards and audio recordings.

When appropriate, community trainers joined with police department instructors in designing the curriculum. As part of the curriculum development process, 16 focus groups were held—8 in relevant communities and 8 in designated precincts. Between October 23 and November 17, 2000, over 2,300 police officers from the March and October 2000 NYPD Police Academy classes received Streetwise training in one of the seven diversity curricula.

Subsequently, the NYPD received a Cultural Awareness and Diversity Training Program grant through the Bureau of Justice Assistance (BJA) to expand the department's cultural awareness training. BJA cited NYPD's already-established Streetwise training program as the reason for awarding the grant. The grant was used to expand Streetwise into a comprehensive, ongoing in-service training program.

For many years, the U.S. Commission on Civil Rights has been at the forefront of reviewing police practices in the United States. Through its influential 1981 report *Who Is Guarding the Guardians?* and numerous subsequent reports, the commission made important recommendations to improve the quality of police protection while ensuring the protection of civil rights for all Americans. The commission consistently endeavored to underscore these connected goals (U.S. Commission on Civil Rights, 2000). In November 2000, under the leadership of chairperson Mary Frances Berry, the commission issued *Revisiting Who Is Guarding the Guardians? A Report on Police Practices and Civil Rights in America.* Included in the report were references to testimony before the commission's June 16, 2000, national police practices and civil rights briefing, which spoke positively about the potential value and impact of Streetwise.

The Streetwise Project was followed by the NYPD Leadership Program, a credit-bearing academic program designed to enhance police leadership in a multiracial and multicultural city. The 12-credit undergraduate or graduate program is offered tuition free to sworn NYPD officers and is hosted by John Jay College of Criminal Justice at the City University of New York (CUNY). Funding for the program is provided by New York State and New York City government. The program is more than a decade old and is credited by many of its students with having changed the way that they think about and interact with racial and ethnic minorities in the communities that they serve.

Robert Louden

See also: African Diaspora, Crime, and Justice; Diallo, Amadou; Louima, Abner; 100 Blacks in Law Enforcement Who Care; Police Brutality; Racial Profiling

References

Office of Community Oriented Policing Services (COPS) Web Site. U.S. Department of Justice. http://www.cops.usdoj.gov/.

United States Commission on Civil Rights. *Who Is Guarding the Guardians?* Washington, DC: U.S. Department of Justice, 1981.

United States Commission on Civil Rights. *Revisiting Who Is Guarding the Guardians? A Report on Police Practices and Civil Rights in America.* Washington, DC: U.S. Department of Justice, 2000.

Structural Racism and Violence

The term structural racism implies that, within the very fabric of the institutions and social arrangements of American society, there are both overt and covert forms of racism that exist in both official and informal relationships between different racial groups. In particular, this term points toward a system where one racial group holds the majority of political, economic, and social power and uses this power in a discriminatory fashion against another group (Lawrence & Keleher, 2004). This type of racism tends to be pervasive and exists within and among public and private organizations, agencies, institutions, and services in society (Lawrence & Keleher, 2004).

Evidence suggests that in the United States, one impact of structural racism on the African American population is that it affects rates of violence committed both against and by members of that group. As a by-product of structural racism, violence experienced by African Americans is high compared to other groups and tends to be intra-racial in nature—that is, involving an African American perpetrator and an African American victim. The contention is that structural racism has had an insidious and debilitating undercurrent that has impacted the African American psyche so that, in its most covert and malevolent sense, African Americans now victimize themselves, perpetuating levels of harm that were originally set in motion by out-group social rule makers, i.e., Whites, who initially used violence and victimization as a means of controlling Blacks under a brutal caste system of chattel slavery (Crenshaw, 1995; PBS, 2008).

Marginalization of African Americans

As Kubisch (2006) notes, the term "structural racism" has been increasingly used in the past few years as a means of describing racial dynamics that are observed in the twenty-first century. The study of structural racism has both academic and practical components. In the academic realm, this concept has tended to focus on race as a social and political concept that works to perpetuate the advantages that White Americans typically have had in U.S. society while also identifying the challenges presented to people of color. Studies associated with this topic tend to identify, analyze, and explain how racial outcome gaps continue in areas of society that impact opportunities related to income, education, employment, housing, health, criminal justice responses, and political power (Kubisch, 2006; Crenshaw, 1995).

Within the practical realm of public policy and legislation, issues tend to focus on civil rights and social and/or economic justice. Kubisch has noted that for those who work in the social services and other similar areas, there has been an increased interest in "improving outcomes for the poor and disenfranchised that are caused by interracial dynamics and racism, and are re-evaluating the extent to which these dynamics are being factored into anti-poverty strategies" (2006: 2). This is important because it is the economic disparity between Whites and African Americans that tends to perpetuate other forms of discrimination within American society. In making this point, consider that nearly 100 years after emancipation from chattel slavery, one-fourth of all African Americans fall below the poverty line and continue to live in poverty in the United States (Mauk & Oakland, 2005: 239), and more than half of all African American children live in poverty (Jennings, 1997).

The cause of this long-term poverty may be difficult to precisely unravel, but it is evident that prejudiced views of African Americans still persist in today's society and may contribute significantly to the restricted opportunities that many African Americans face. Research by Brown (2005: 41) shows that while most White Americans indicate that they have good intentions toward African Americans, they still have negative views of African Americans. Indeed, 34 percent of participants interviewed felt that most African Americans were lazy (Brown, 2005: 41). In addition, this same research found that 52 percent of White American participants believed that most African Americans were aggressive and violent. Research findings similar to these demonstrate that even among White people who do not view themselves as biased or prejudiced, there are informal, perhaps even unintentional, real biases and negative stereotypes that serve to reinforce the marginalization of African Americans. As Riphagen states, "this continuing stigmatization of an entire race based on stereotypes of group attributes highly impairs African-Americans to develop their talents and makes it extremely difficult to be successful in the eyes of mainstream white Americans" (2008: 3).

Historical Victimization

Though it is common knowledge that in America's past, African Americans were abducted, kidnapped, imprisoned, brought across the Atlantic under ghastly conditions, systematically separated from loved ones and those who were familiar to them, and enslaved and brutalized via atrocious and relentless acts of violence, little effort has been made to systematically understand how this government-sanctioned treatment has impacted the psyche and cultural development of the African American community (PBS, 2008). The widespread, intentional, and total disintegration of the original African community once brought to the United States caused family and generational ties to be lost forever. Further, throughout American history, the one-down position of African Americans has been taken as the norm. Even early American presidents, considered by many as the founders and champions of democracy and freedom, were guilty of having owned African American slaves (Marable, 2002).

After more than two centuries of government sanctioned human bondage, it took the Civil Rights Movement of the 1960s to address the continuing legal and social inequalities that continued to be enforced against African Americans after the abolition of slavery. The hard-fought gains of the Civil Rights Movement did not result in substantial efforts for wealth redistribution along racial lines, nor did they substantially help to provide cultural reorientation addressing race and racism (Winant, 2004: 21). Rather, racial injustices were simply seen as an outcome of the prejudiced attitudes of a few individuals to be addressed on a case-by-case basis. They were not seen as macro-level or structural problems that created and reinforced inequality and its negative outcomes. This micro-level, short-sighted analysis left the gate open for persons to carry on racially driven agendas, but on a covert rather than an overt basis. While official laws and written civil rights were overtly established in the United States, very little stopped covert practices of inequality that, while seeming to diminish slowly over time, have taken an immeasurable toll on the African American population (Winant, 2007).

Impact of Structural Racism, Crime, Violence, and Criminal Justice

The impact of structural racism on the African American community has been profound and has poisoned many African American communities that are plagued with higher rates of violence and victimization (Middlemass, 2006). Oliver (2003) notes that there is a high rate of homicide and nonfatal violence that is committed against African American men. Further, this violence tends to be intra-racial and, proportionally speaking, more African Americans are victims of violent crime than any other racial group in the United States. According to the Bureau of Justice Statistics, in 2009, the rate of violent victimization against African Americans was 27 per 1,000, whereas the rate for Whites was 16 per 1,000, followed by an even lower rate for other races: 10 out of 1,000. Further, African Americans were victims of rape/sexual assault, robbery, and aggravated assault at rates that were higher than those for Whites (BJS, 2009).

When considering the higher rates of victimization that are experienced by African Americans, on the one hand, coupled with the higher rates of violent crime that are committed by African Americans (most often against other African Americans), Oliver (2003) provides a possible explanation for this observation. He contends that structural pressures (i.e., institutional and cultural racism and restructured economic conditions) serve as independent variables, whereas dysfunctional cultural adaptations (i.e., a lack of a coherent cultural identity and dysfunctional definitions of manhood) serve as mediating variables that aggravate the conditions, behaviors, and rationalizations that lead to violent victimization among African Americans (2003).

Oliver (2003) proposes that there are two specific dysfunctional adaptations that contribute to the high rates of violent offending and victimization that are common among African American men. They include the lack of a cogent cultural identity and the adoption of dysfunctional definitions of manhood. These counter-productive behaviors are theorized as having been produced through generations of aversive macro-level group victimizations such as racial segregation, unprovoked violent acts against African American people, blocked access to educational and/or vocational opportunities, inadequate access to adequate housing and homeowner-ship opportunities, and the cumulative effects of intergenerational institutional racism. These contemporary victimizations have further reinforced the macro-level historical trauma within the African American community and have been the basis of violent adaptations in reaction to the debilitating effects of structural racism upon those communities.

Robert Hanser

See also: Black Panther Party; Carmichael, Stokely; Civil Rights Movement; *Code of the Street*; Homicide; Inequality Theory; Institutional Racism; Inter-Racial Offending; Intra-Racial Offending; Racial Stereotyping and Wrongful Convictions; Slavery; Theories of Race and Crime; *When Work Disappears: The World of the New Urban Poor*; Wolfgang, Marvin; Youth Violence

References

Brown, R. H. *Culture, Capitalism and Democracy in the New America.* New Haven, CT: Yale University Press, 2005.

Bureau of Justice Statistics (BJS). *Victim Characteristics: Violent Crime Victims.* Washington, DC: Bureau of Justice Statistics, 2009. http://bjs.ojp.usdoj.gov/index.cfm?ty=tp&tid=92.

Crenshaw, K., et al. *Critical Race Theory: The Key Writings That Formed the Movement.* New York: The New Press, 1995.

Jennings, J. *Race and Politics: New Challenges and Responses for Black Activism.* London: Verso, 1997.

Kubisch, A. C. "Structural Racism." *Poverty & Race* 15, no. 6 (2006): 1–7.

Lawrence, K., and T. Keleher. *Structural Racism.* Queenstown, MA: Aspen Institute for Community Change, 2004.

Marable, M. "The Political and Theoretical Contexts of the Changing Racial Terrain." *Souls* 4, no. 3 (2002): 1–16.

Mauk, D., and J. Oakland. *American Civilization: An Introduction.* London: Routledge, 2005.

Middlemass, K. M. "America at the Crossroads." *Souls* 8, no. 2 (2006): 1–6.

Oliver, M. L., and T. M. Shapiro. *Black Wealth/White Wealth: A New Perspective on Racial Inequality.* London: Routledge, 1995.

Oliver, W. "The Structural-Cultural Perspective: A Theory of Black Male Violence." In *Violent Crime: Assessing Race and Ethnic Differences,* edited by D. F. Hawkins, 280–302. Nyack, NY: Cambridge University Press, 2003.

Public Broadcasting Service (PBS). "Africans in America: Conditions of Antebellum Slavery." Arlington, VA: PBS, 2008. http://www.pbs.org/wgbh/aia/part4/4p2956.html.

Riphagen, L. "Marginalization of African-Americans in the Social Sphere of United States Society." *Interdisciplinary Journal of International Studies* 5, no. 1 (2008): 1–26.

Winant, H. *New Politics of Race: Globalism, Difference, Justice.* Minneapolis: University of Minnesota Press, 2007.

Student Nonviolent Coordinating Committee (SNCC)

Every movement for social change has at its core individuals or organizational units that function as catalysts for increased political momentum. In the early 1960s, the Student Nonviolent Coordinating Committee (SNCC) became such an organization as it galvanized the energies of young people while the energies and enthusiasm of earlier protests waned (Carson, 1981). On February 1, 1960, a group of Black college students from North Carolina A&T University refused to leave a Woolworth's lunch counter in Greensboro, North Carolina, where they had been denied service. This sparked a wave of other sit-ins in college towns across the South. The Student Nonviolent Coordinating Committee, or SNCC (pronounced "snick"), was created on the campus of Shaw University in Raleigh, North Carolina, two months later to coordinate these sit-ins and support their leaders, and to publicize these activities. Over the next decade, civil rights activism moved beyond lunch counter sit-ins. In this violently changing political climate, the SNCC struggled to define its purpose as it fought White oppression.

Ella Baker enlisted youth in an assertive direct action strategy against racism. Formerly of the Southern Christian Leadership Conference (SCLC) and a Shaw University alumna, Baker made it clear that while nonviolence as a strategic approach to changing American racism had its benefits, the goals of the Civil Rights Movement needed updating (Carson, 1981). Baker's statement implied that all philosophical limitations on how and when racism would be challenged must be reviewed, if not revised. More importantly, she argued that a pragmatic analysis of racism and institutionalized naked criminality in America dictates that civil rights activists and organizations must confront and challenge racism through enhanced strategic and tactical use of direct action. Key to this new civil rights paradigm was a social movement structured for "the development of people who are interested not in being leaders as much as in developing leadership among other people" (Baker, 1960: 4, as cited in Lerner, 1973: 352; Carson, 1981: 20).

However, not all civil rights proponents agreed with the concept of "direct action." Reverend C. T. Vivian, a key activist and minister within the movement and one who valued the benefits of direct action, recalled a discussion he had in 1960 with Thurgood Marshall, the lead attorney in the 1954 *Brown v. Board of Education of Topeka, Kansas,* decision. Vivian stated that Thurgood Marshall came to Nashville and was in a backroom talking around the table about ways of confronting racism, when he pointed his finger at me and said, "You're a dangerous man." When Vivian asked Marshall why he took such an attitude, Marshall stated he saw no action outside the courtroom. He did not understand direct action. As far as he was concerned, the existing racial issues were all going to be settled in the courtroom (C. T. Vivian, interview by Clayborne Carson, December 7, 1978, Philadelphia).

One year later, on May 4, 1961, SNCC, in conjunction with the Congress of Racial Equality (CORE), organized what would be called "Freedom Rides" (Meier & Rudwick, 1973). Primarily organized by James Farmer of CORE as a series of bus trips through the South to test the U.S. Justice Department's effectiveness and willingness after seven years of the *Brown* desegregation decision, "Freedom Rides" sought to protect the rights of African Americans to use terminal facilities on a nonsegregated basis. The first Freedom Riders left Washington, D.C., in two buses and came into direct conflict with racist mobs in Rock Hill, South Carolina, when SNCC organizer John Lewis, one of the seven Black riders, attempted to use a "White" waiting room at the Greyhound terminal (Kinshasa, 2006). Beaten brutally by a White mob in full view of local police, Lewis and the inter-racial group of Freedom Riders were able to extract themselves from the mob, reboard their buses, and proceeded further South, eventually arriving in Anniston, Alabama. However, when they arrived,

> [a] mob attacked one of the two buses, breaking windows and slashing tires before the police arrived. When the bus continued its journey, white men in cars followed and forced the bus to stop outside of Anniston. The pursuers then hurled a smoke bomb inside, and the Freedom Riders fled the vehicle into the hands of the waiting group of angry whites. As the bus burst into flames, the mob beat up the riders before police again arrived belatedly. . . . The Freedom Riders regrouped and continued on to Birmingham where they expected further trouble since they heard rumors that a white mob would be waiting for them. A large crowd of whites were present when their bus entered the Birmingham terminal, and local police were conspicuously absent for a fifteen minute period while a group of white men assaulted the Freedom Riders as they emerged from the bus. . . . After this incident, no bus driver could be found to take the riders to Montgomery. (Peck, 1962: 98–99; as cited in Carson, 1981: 34)

After learning about the attack, and much to the chagrin of SNCC, James Farmer, the director of CORE, decided to abandon the rides (Morris, 1986).

However, in the spirit enunciated by Ella Baker, Diana Nash, a field organizer and leader for SNCC in Nashville, Tennessee, expressed determination to continue the rides. Revealing in this regard is a telephone conversation between Nash and Rev. Fred Shuttlesworth, whose organization, the Alabama Christian Movement for Human Rights, rescued the Freedom Riders in Birmingham after they were attacked:

> Reverend Shuttlesworth asked, "Young lady, do you know that the Freedom Riders were almost killed here?" Diane said, "Yes, and that is exactly why the Ride must not be stopped." Shuttlesworth agreed and assisted Nash in working out the details for continuing the Ride. They devised secret codes because Eugene "Bull" Connor (Birmingham Police Chief) had Shuttlesworth's phones tapped. Shuttlesworth, in a language understood by the Southern black community but not Connor, told Nash to send the speckled chickens (integrated group), who included pullets (women) and roosters (men), on to Birmingham, and the Ride would continue. (Morris, 1986: 232)

The historian Howard Zinn noted that this new synergy within the movement, as projected by youthful SNCC activists, immediately drew the attention of the federal government. Realizing that a heightened level of confrontation between White racists and SNCC civil rights activists was likely to occur, federal marshals were quickly sent into Birmingham to keep White mobs at bay. However,

> [a]t seven-thirty in the morning on Wednesday, May 24th, with National Guardsmen lining both sides of the street near the bus terminal, twelve Freedom Riders (eleven Negro, one white), accompanied by six Guardsman and sixteen newspapermen, left Montgomery for Jackson (Mississippi). Before leaving, they tasted victory by eating in the "white" cafeteria at the Trailways terminal. On the road, a convoy of three airplanes, two helicopters, and seven patrol cars accompanied the bus while, inside, James Lawson held a workshop on non-violence. (Zinn, 1965: 40–61; Morris, 1986: 233)

The attraction that SNCC field activists brought with them when interacting with countless thousands of Southern African Americans throughout this period was dramatic and effective. When asked what effect SNCC had on her decision to attempt registering to vote in Mississippi, sharecropper and eventual founder of the Mississippi Freedom Democratic Party (MFDP) Fannie Lou Hamer stated,

> Nobody ever came out into the country and talked to real farmers and things because this is the next thing this country has done: it divided us into classes. And if you hadn't arrived at a certain level, you wasn't treated no better by blacks than you was by the whites. And it was these kids who broke a lot of that down. They treated us like we were special and we loved 'em. . . . We didn't feel uneasy about our language might not be right or something. We just felt we could talk to 'em. (Kinshasa, 2006: 127)

SNCC members viewed gaining the right to vote as a significant move toward racial equality in the South. If Blacks had the power of the vote, SNCC felt they would have influence over many important aspects of Southern politics. SNCC organized the Freedom Ballot in the fall of 1963 in the state of Mississippi, which set the stage for the Mississippi Summer Project, organized primarily by Bob Moses. SNCC worked hard in the winter and spring of 1963–1964 preparing for the project, which was an urgent call to action for students in Mississippi to challenge and overcome the White racism in the state of Mississippi. But during the summer of 1964, three SNCC workers were murdered: Andrew Goodman, James Chaney, and Michael Schwerner.

SNCC will historically be remembered for its successful dramatic voter registration efforts in Southern states such as Georgia, Mississippi, Tennessee, and North Carolina. But it was in Lowndes County, Alabama, where its support for the development of the Lowndes County Freedom Organization (LCFO), and the eventual spawning of the term "Black Power" by one of the SNCC organizers, according to some sources by Willie Ricks (who was interviewed by Clayborne Carson on May 10, 1976, at Sanford; see Carson, 1981) that was critical to the movement's attractiveness (Carson, 1981). Black Power was the guiding philosophy of SNCC in its later years. It began to develop and take hold sometime after 1964, and came to prominence in 1966, when Stokely Carmichael became head of the organization.

SNCC formally came out against the Vietnam War in the beginning of 1966 as a result of pressure from Northern supporters and from members working on the Southern projects. Many people feel that SNCC opened the door for the second-wave feminist movement in the United States, as it first established many of the principles later used by this generation of feminists.

Out of SNCC came some of today's Black leaders, such as Congressman John Lewis and former NAACP chairman Julian Bond. Together with hundreds of students, they left a lasting impact on American history.

Kwando M. Kinshasa

See also: Civil Rights Movement; Southern Christian Leadership Conference (SCLC)

References

Baker, Ella. "Bigger Than a Hamburger." *Southern Patriot* (May 1960): 4.

Carson, Clayborne. *In Struggle: SNCC and the Black Awakening of the 1960's.* Cambridge, MA: Harvard University Press, 1981.

Kinshasa, Kwando. *African American Chronology: Chronologies of the American Mosaic.* Westport, CT: Greenwood Press, 2006.

Lerner, Gerda. *Black Women in White America: A Documentary History.* New York: Vintage Books, 1973.

Meier, August, and E. Rudwick. *A Study in the Civil Rights Movement 1942–1968.* New York: Oxford University Press, 1973.

Morris, A. D. *The Origins of the Civil Rights Movement: Black Communities Organizing for Change.* New York: Free Press, 1986.

Peck, James. *Freedom Ride.* New York: Grove Press, 1962.

Vivian, C. T. Interview by Clayborne Carson, December 7, 1978, Philadelphia, Pennsylvania.

Zinn, Howard. *The New Abolitionist.* Boston: Beacon Press, 1965.

T

Termination of Parental Rights

A little-known consequence of the mass incarceration of African Americans is that imprisonment can lead to the loss of their children, first to the foster care system and then to permanent adoption by strangers. A New York State statute and similar laws in other states allow child welfare agencies to institute court proceedings to terminate the parental rights of incarcerated fathers and mothers who are sentenced to confinement for as little as 15 months. This collateral consequence of African American contact with the criminal justice system has received far less attention than the loss of voting rights, but the risk of such loss for incarcerated parents is substantially higher than one might expect.

The termination of parental rights is, in effect, the permanent legal severing of ties between parent and child. African American parents and their children can be exposed to this risk based on any of the following factors, for which their group is at high risk:

- Severe or chronic abuse or neglect
- Abuse or neglect of other children in the household
- Long-term mental illness or deficiency of the parent(s)
- Failure to support or maintain contact with child
- Involuntary termination of the rights of the parent to another child
                    (Child Welfare Information Gateway [CWIG], 2010)

Each of these factors are correlated with others that bring African Americans into contact with child welfare and criminal justice procedures, based primarily on characteristics related to their socioeconomic status. These very factors may contribute to a court determination that parent(s) are unfit and that severing the parent-child relationship is in the child's best interest (Child Welfare Information Gateway [CWIG], 2010). The court can make a final decision to permanently separate parents from their biological children without regard for the wishes and efforts of either the parent or the child.

For generations, African Americans lived without the protective services that existed to assist needy White children and their parents. The creation of child welfare policies and agencies and their application to Black families has both helped and hurt the life chances of parent and child. Research has confirmed that children exposed to the foster care system are substantially more likely to also become a part of the juvenile justice system, and that parents, especially mothers, who are separated from their children during incarceration are more likely to be depressed and have more difficulties with their institutional adjustment. Poor institutional adjustment may in turn result in disciplinary infractions, leading to longer confinement before release. This longer confinement may increase the likelihood of parental rights termination for lack of contact, and the exhibition of signs of mental health instability may be deemed a reason to institute a termination petition with the courts.

Cultural differences in the use of corporal punishment can both bring Black parents into contact with the justice system; and, lead to the termination of parental rights because of that contact. Public policy that inextricably links child protection and adoption policies have been criticized for failing to respect diversity in childrearing practices and family formation, and has been accused of essentially being a pretext to standardize the family unit and mainstream White parenting practices while promoting legal adoption as the best means of uniformly serving the best interest of all children exposed to the five circumstances identified previously, especially lack of contact due to long-term parental incarceration.

For African Americans who have historically relied on extended family and fictive kin to help with childrearing during challenging economic and other circumstances, the imposition of formal mechanisms such as the dictates of judges, medical professionals, and social workers, though intended for the child's best interest, is reminiscent of government control under slave laws. The permanent loss of one's child, even in the absence of any affirmative physical abuse, by virtue of correctional confinement becomes eerily similar to the parental loss suffered by African slaves and their progeny, regardless of the good intentions envisioned by the practice.

African American children make up 15 percent of the child population, yet they represent 45 percent of the child welfare system. The overrepresentation of African Americans in the child welfare system is not explained by behavioral differences, since available data reveal no difference in the occurrence of child abuse and neglect among the races. Research has revealed that African Americans are more likely than Whites to be reported for maltreatment by hospitals for similar injuries to their children; to be evaluated and reported for pediatric fractures and blamed for child abuse; to face greater chances that allegations will be perceived as substantiated; and to be placed in foster care. These findings suggest that whether Black parents, especially mothers, are facing allegations of abuse and neglect or charges unrelated to child care, they face an elevated risk for termination of their parental rights by virtue of being overrepresented as criminal defendants sentenced to terms of imprisonment.

Alice Thomas

See also: Alternative Sentencing; American Law and African Americans; Correctional System and African Americans; Sentencing Disparities; Slavery; Socioeconomic Factors

References

Azar, Sandra T., and Corina L. Benjet. "A Cognitive Perspective on Ethnicity, Race, and Termination of Parental Rights." *Law and Human Behavior* 18, no. 3 (1994): 249–68.

Billingsley, A., and J. Giovannoni. *Children of the Storm: Black Children and American Child Welfare.* New York: Harcourt Brace Jovanovich, 1972.

Child Welfare Information Gateway (CWIG). *Grounds for Involuntary Termination of Parental Rights,* 2010. www.childwelfare.gov/systemwide/law_policies/statutes/groundtermin.cfm.

Costin, Lela B., Howard Jacob Karger, and David Stoesz. *The Politics of Child Abuse in America.* New York: Oxford University Press, 1996.

Downs, S. W., L. B. Costin, and E. J. McFadden. *Child Welfare and Family Services.* New York: Longman, 1996.

Goodman, C., M. Potts, E. M. Pasztor, and D. Scorzo. "Grandmothers as Kinship Caregivers: Private Arrangements Compared to Public Child Welfare Oversight." *Children and Youth Services Review* 26 (2004): 287–305.

Jimenez, Jillian. "The History of Child Protection in the African American Community: Implications for Current Child Welfare Policies." *Children and Youth Services Review* 28 (2006): 888–905.

Lane, Wendy G., D. M. Rubin, R. Monteith, and C. W. Christian. "Racial Differences in the Evaluation of Pediatric Fractures for Physical Abuse." *Journal of American Medical Association* 288, no. 13 (2002): 1603–9.

Muhammad, G. *The Condemnation of Blackness: Race, Crime and the Making of Modern Urban America.* Cambridge, MA: Harvard University Press, 2010.

Trattner, Walter I. *Crusade for Children: A History of the National Child Labor Committee and Child Labor Reform in America.* Chicago: University of Chicago Press, 1970.

Theories of Race and Crime

Theories of race are among the oldest theories utilized by criminology. As criminology emerged as a distinct field of social science, race was one of the earliest variables used to predict criminal or deviant conduct. For a time, biological theories of crime (see Eugenics) proliferated the field until flaws in the methods of study were exposed along with the racial, ethnic, and class biases of the researchers (Butler, 2010; Barak, 2010; Burke, 2005). In Europe, certain White ethnics, such as the Irish, Italians, and Germans, were considered the dangerous or criminal classes. In the United States, though initially focused on White ethnics and the Native American population, theories of race and crime, particularly Blackness and crime, were developed to justify African slavery and the social exclusion of Blacks following emancipation (see Slavery and Civil Rights Movement) (McIntyre, 1993; Mann, 1993; Owens & Bell, 1977).

Theories of crime may be categorized into three general types:

Individual-level theories focus on factors internal to the person. Variables such as age, gender, education, personality type, and race are used to predict criminality.

Social structural theories consider the relationship between the individual and society, such as theories based on geography and social forces that encourage goal-oriented crime (like theft or other property crime).

Symbolic interactionist theories consider the way the individual is affected by social forces, as well as the opportunities for crime the individual regularly experiences (Burke, 2005).

A close look at any of these theoretical frameworks reveals that while they may attempt to establish a causal connection between race and crime, they more accurately measure the impact of racism and its impact on social structure and the consequent impact of social structures on the socially oppressed (Butler, 2010; Barak, 2010).

Within *individual-level theories,* two theories have had the biggest impact on the intersection of race and crime: trait theories and social control theories.

Trait theories consider the social, economic, and/or demographic elements of the individual to be the best predictors of criminal or deviant conduct. This theory considers race a primary predictor of criminality, recognizing that other individual-level factors may be associated with race, making any assessment of the pure impact of race difficult to ascertain. Years of such attempts (see Eugenics) have proved them to be invalid. However, some researchers and laymen continue to associate race with crime because many racial minorities under the control of the justice system are substance-abusing males who are poorly educated, score poorly on standardized intelligence tests, lack vocational skills, and live in the most criminogenic areas. This makes it difficult to statistically separate these elements into those that are most predictive of crime, making trait theories of little use in controlling crime. They are viewed as tautological—predicting who will be criminal by looking at those who are already criminals (Einstadter & Henry, 2006).

Social control theories are similar to trait theories. They take into account the background of the individual and consider crime the result of the interaction between the individual's background and the social conditions present at the time of the crime. These theories consider factors other than personal traits when predicting crime, which distinguishes control theory from other individual-based theories. An example of this is Travis Hirschi's social bond theory (1969). By formulating social bond theory, Hirschi broke away from prior theoretical perspectives that relied on race as a primary indicator of criminality, postulating that crime is the result of a weak social bond to the rules and norms of the society. The theory posited that four elements are necessary to bond a person to the society: commitment to a socially acceptable goal, as evidenced by the investment of time in the pursuit of that goal; involvement in socially responsible and conventional activities; attachment to conventional others, especially adults; and belief, which is the certainty that the outcomes promised by society for behaving in a conventional manner will, in fact, materialize. This more complex theory could help explain why some impoverished inner-city minority residents became involved in crime or avoided it. It could also be used to explain why working-class Whites, the primary subjects in Hirshi's studies, also became involved with the criminal justice system. However, social bond theory still focused on crime as mainly an individually based choice. As such, race traits continued to be assumed by some to account for any apparent lack of social control (Einstadter & Henry, 2006).

Social structural theories focused on the impact of the physical or normative environment on the behaviors of those within that environment. These theories downplayed the role of race in the prediction of crime, and instead looked at the impact of social setting on the individual, and predicted behavior on the basis of environmental influences regardless of the race of the individual in question.

Of the theories that fit within this group, there are three that exemplify this theoretical category: the social-ecological model, social disorganization theory, and strain theory.

The social-ecological model represented the application of an earlier theory of urban development to the study of crime. This school of thought, developed at the University of Chicago, utilized the concept of "concentric zones" to explain crime patterns. Researchers discovered that there was a specific area of the city that seemed to have the greatest problem with crime, and this crime pattern was stable and unrelated to the ethnic population that inhabited the area. This was important in that the occupants of the criminogenic area changed over time, but crime remained, indicating that race was not the cause of crime, but rather the norms of the area were driving crime. The Chicago School theorists believed that the area between the factories and the low-income housing was an area constantly in "transition" and lacked any sense of supervision, making it an easy place to commit crimes because the chances of being apprehended were minimal. Again, it did not rely on race, but rather on the social and economic instability of residents in these transitional areas, due in part to the absence of socially stabilizing structures such as good schools, religious institutions, legitimate jobs, and pro-social recreational opportunities. History shows that the ethnicity and race of the residents of these areas were constantly changing, which did not allow for community cohesion, efficacy, or trust. This made individual victimization easier and arguably more acceptable (Einstadter & Henry, 2006).

Social disorganization theory maintained that the heterogeneity and transitional nature of the population in these areas, coupled with the lack of stabilizing social structures, allowed these locations to remain home to stable pockets of criminal activity. The racialization of American society allowed some groups to escape these areas through better employment and alternate residential arrangements while Blacks and other visible minorities, who were restricted from certain jobs and residential communities by formal and informal race restrictive covenants, became the primary occupants. Over time, their proliferation in such locations where crime was high was interpreted as and contributed to a belief that their race was somehow directly associated with the criminality in the area (Einstadter & Henry, 2006).

The final social structural theory of race and crime is strain theory, which is based on a relatively simple premise: people desire certain things, and if they are not able to achieve those things through legitimate means, they will be forced to either abandon the goal or establish a less legitimate method of attaining those desired goals. Media influences encourage society to attain material or lifestyle goals. If the path to these goals is blocked, this theory argues that one may adapt to this "strain" by either abandoning the goal or finding an illegitimate method to achieve it. Again, this crime explanation, as developed by Emile Durkheim and refined by Robert Merton, was not rooted in race or ethnicity, but rather in differential access to legitimate means of social achievement and the creation of a state of strain by being subjected to this blockage. Under the theory, individuals placed in a similar state of strain will react similarly, regardless of race or ethnicity. Following the logic of Merton's strain theory, the disproportionate number of crimes committed by racial and ethnic minorities is an indicator of strain caused by blocked opportunities, and the removal of barriers and the creation of legitimate opportunity is seen as the primary mechanism for reducing crime (Lilly et al., 2011; Einstadter & Henry, 2006).

Under general strain theory, developed by Robert Agnew, strain is not simply present through the lack of opportunity to legitimately achieve material goals. It is also present when individuals are under stress from crime, violence, and the inability to experience personal respect, autonomy, and dignity. Agnew has suggested that general strain theory has particular salience for African American populations, given their ancestral experience of slavery and lengthy history of discrimination after emancipation, which concentrates their numbers in highly stressed urban environments and constrains opportunities for respect and social autonomy even outside those environments (Lilly et al., 2011).

The symbolic interactionism theoretical perspective focuses on the "micro" level interactions between individuals and their physical and social environments. Symbolic interactionism insists that actions must be interpreted within the environment where they occur, and the environment may be partially responsible for those actions.

One of the most noteworthy symbolic interactionist theories is the rational choice/routine activity theory, which claims that all societies have an unlimited supply of potential offenders; the specific elements present at the time the potentially criminal situation is presented is what limits offending. Most potential offenders are exposed to a great number of potentially criminogenic situations every day as part of their routine activities, but they do not offend because the environment works to control them. According to rational choice/routine activity theory there are three elements necessary to control crime: the presence (or absence) of a guardian whose role is to protect the target; the presence of a suitable or desirable target; and the presence of a motivated offender. If an unsupervised and desirable target is placed in the context of a motivated offender, this theory predicts that criminal conduct is virtually guaranteed, irrespective of the race or ethnicity of the potential offender. In social settings where guardians are largely absent due to any number of forces (the need to work outside the home, incarceration, physical or emotional disability), opportunities for crime are greater and knowledge of such absence, coupled with other factors, may serve as a motivation for crime. The lengthy history of blocked legitimate opportunities for those of African ancestry may contribute to motivation to achieve material and emotional goals through methods that are formally or informally viewed by larger society as illegitimate (Einstadter & Henry, 2006).

Labeling theory also fits under this heading because of the location of the individual in the social context of others who have beliefs regarding the individual's activities, and their subsequent label. Labeling theory is similar to earlier theories in that it did not rely on race, but rather first on the reaction of the group to the actions of the individual, and later to the individual's actions as function of the label attached to him or her by the group. This theory posits that the label may be both undeserved and counterproductive, in that the label may lead to deviance or crime, although the initial label of deviant was undeserved. This is especially important to the discussion of race and crime due to the visible nature of race, and the social expectation of criminality as a function of race. According to labeling theory, some criminals are simply behaving in accordance with a label placed upon them by society, and that labels applied improperly may nonetheless produce later criminal conduct.

Social reaction theory argues that the social reaction to crime and the perception of threat may be in some ways much more important than the reality of the threat, and this perception may result in increasing rather than decreasing crime. The most central theory within this perspective is conflict theory.

Conflict theory argues that actions are not crimes until a group decides to criminalize them through formal law, thereby creating crime from a noncriminal action. Conflict theorists argue that those who decide what will and will not be crime are motivated by selfish interests, and are not wholly concerned with the safety or well-being of society. These persons may in fact criminalize certain behavior to further a political agenda, to control an underclass, or simply to make money. Conflict theorists believe that laws may be created by the entire group, and these laws will reflect "consensus" or agreement regarding acceptable behavior. Laws, however, that are created by the powerful to further their interests are not examples of consensus, but rather represent conflict between the controlling and the controlled classes.

Conflict theory is a popular tool to examine race and crime. Many conflict theorists believe that certain laws were created to control the minority underclass and to possibly stabilize the underclass's position at the bottom of the social order. Drug laws that criminalize the drugs of choice of the minority underclass are examples of this type theory (Gabbidon, 2010).

Overall, efforts to connect criminal behavior directly to biological racial identities have largely been discredited but continue to periodically resurface. See, for example, the life history theory by J. Philippe Rushton, a professor at Western Ontario University (1999), and *The Bell Curve* by Herrnstein and Murray (1994). The first uses gene-based evolutionary theory to link racial differences in crime patterns to migrations out of Africa (Gabbidon & Greene, 2005). The second attempts to link Black imprisonment rates to lower IQ scores than those attained by Whites. One the most controversial attempts to connect race and crime came in 2001, when John Donohue and Steven Levitt attempted to link national crime declines to the abortion of Black babies after the 1973 *Roe v. Wade* U.S. Supreme Court decision, claiming that the criminality of such persons would have been "more likely" (2001). On closer examination, such theories cannot be divorced from the differential social experiences that are, in part, a function of social construction and reactions to racial identities, which over time have served to either benefit or burden individuals and groups who are racially different (Gabbidon, 2010; Gabbidon & Greene, 2005).

The colonial model, with its roots in the writings of the psychiatrist and activist Frantz Fanon and subsequent work by Blauner (1969; 1972), Staples (1975), and Tatum (1994), and which leans heavily on the teachings of the intellectuals from the Black power movement (Gabbidon & Greene, 2005), involves one of the strongest attempts to explain this connection between racial identity and crime for African Americans. The theory suggests that crime and delinquency and the desire to protest stems from the African American experience of existing within a caste system that is based on racism, controlled by a White dominant power structure, and is alienating and culturally conflicting. It points out that police and policing are essential to maintaining the subordinate status of Blacks, in part to contain the cultural clashes and to support the dominant status of Whites. The tensions that naturally flow from this state of subordination and conflict produce resistant behavior that can be both destructive and facilitative and both internally and externally helpful or harmful (Butler, 2010; Gabbidon, 2010).

Matthew Leone with Delores Jones-Brown

See also: American Law and African Americans; Black Panther Party; Carmichael, Stokely; Civil Rights Movement; Correctional System and African Americans; Inequality Theory; Institutional Racism; Malcolm X (aka El-Hajj Malik El-Shabazz); Slavery; Structural Racism and Violence; War on Drugs

References

Barak, G. *Class, Race, Gender, and Crime: The Social Realities of Justice in America.* 3rd ed. Lanham, MD: Rowman & Littlefield, 2010.

Blauner, R. *Racial Oppression in America.* New York: Harper and Row, 1972.

Blauner, R. "Internal Colonialism and Ghetto Revolt." *Social Problems* 16 (1969): 393–408.

Burke, R. H. *An Introduction to Criminological Theory.* 2nd ed. Portland, OR: Willan, 2005.

Butler, P. "One Hundred Years of Race and Crime." *Journal of Criminal Law & Criminology* 100, no. 3 (2010): 1043–60.

Cullen, F. T., and R. Agnew. *Criminological Theory Past to Present: Essential Readings.* 3rd ed. Los Angeles, CA: Roxbury, 2006.

Donohue, J., and S. Levitt. "The Impact of Legalized Abortion on Crime." *The Quarterly Journal of Economics* CXVI (2001): 379–420.

Einstadter, W. J., and S. Henry. *Criminological Theory: An Analysis of Its Underlying Assumptions.* 2nd ed. Lanham, MD: Rowman & Littlefield, 2006.

Gabbidon, S. L. *Criminological Perspectives on Race and Crime.* 2nd ed. Hoboken, NJ: Taylor & Francis, 2010.

Gabbidon, S., and H. T. Greene. *Race and Crime.* Thousand Oaks, CA: Sage, 2005.

Herrnstein, R., and C. Murray. *The Bell Curve: Intelligence and Class Structure in American Life.* New York: The Free Press, 1994.

Hirschi, T. *Causes of Delinquency.* Berkeley: University of California Press, 1969.

Lilly, J. R., F. T. Cullen, and R. A. Ball. *Criminological Theory: Context and Consequences.* 5th ed. Thousand Oaks, CA: Sage Publications, 2011.

Mann, C. *Unequal Justice: A Question of Color.* Bloomington: Indiana University Press, 1993.

McIntyre, C. *Criminalizing a Race: Free Blacks during Slavery.* Queens, NY: Kayode, 1993.

Owens, C. E., and J. Bell. *Blacks and Criminal Justice.* Lexington, KY: D.C. Heath, 1977.

Rushton, J. P. *Race, Evolution, and Behavior.* Special abridged ed. New Brunswick, NJ: Transaction, 1999.

Staples, R. "White Racism, Black Crime, and American Justice: An Application of the Colonial Model to Explain Crime and Race." *Phylon* 36 (1975): 14–22.

Tatum, B. L. "The Colonial Model as a Theoretical Explanation of Crime and Delinquency." In *African American Perspectives on Crime Causation, Criminal Justice Administration and Prevention,* edited by A. T. Sulton, 33–52. Englewood, CO: Sulton Books, 1994.

Three Strikes Legislation

Three Strikes and You're Out ("Three Strikes") laws mandate long sentences for certain habitual offenders, usually 25 years to life in prison for third-time violent offenders. Since 1993, Three Strikes has been implemented for federal offenses and in at least 25 states.[1]

Although they share a common name, Three Strikes laws are quite diverse. The number of offenses that trigger the Three Strikes mechanism, the types of crimes counted as strikes, and the sentences mandated upon conviction vary widely. Most states have relatively narrow laws and have not sentenced many prisoners under Three Strikes. The laws of most states limit strikes-eligible offenses to a small number of violent felonies, and require three violations to trigger a mandatory sentence such as life without parole, or 25 years to life. In some states, the law can be triggered by more or fewer than three strikes (Clark et al., 1997).

The broadest and most widely used Three Strikes law was implemented in California in 1994 and not modified until 2013. Offenses eligible to count as strikes in California include 21 "violent" felonies and 25 "serious" felonies, with some overlap between the two categories. If an offender already has one strike and then commits *any* of the state's approximately 500 felonies, the sentence is automatically doubled. With two strikes, any additional felony conviction sends the offender to prison for 25 years to life. The law requires a state prison sentence in all Three Strikes cases, restricts "good time" credits to 20 percent, and prohibits plea bargaining. As of October 2005, over 87,500 individuals had been sentenced under the second- and third-strike provisions of California's Three Strikes law, including over 7,500 offenders who received a sentence of 25 years to life in prison for a third strike (Legislative Analyst's Office, 2005). In comparison, no other state has sentenced more than 400 offenders under a Three Strikes law (Chen, 2008a). However, in order to reform the harsh nature of the Three Strikes legislation, California

Despite Racial Disparities and Excessive Punishments, U.S. Supreme Court Supports Three Strikes

Lockyear v. Andrade, 538 U.S. 63 (2003)

For stealing about $150 worth of videotapes, Leandro Andrade was found guilty of two felony counts of petty theft. With previous felony convictions on his record, he was sentenced to two consecutive terms of 25 years to life under California's Three Strikes law. Andrade appealed his case all the way to the U.S. Supreme Court, based on an argument that the sentence was in violation of the Constitution's protection against cruel and unusual punishment under the Eighth Amendment. In a 5 to 4 decision decided on March 5, 2003, the court upheld his sentence, stating that the previously imposed sentence was not grossly disproportionate to the offenses he committed.

Ewing v. California, 538 U.S. 11 (2003)

On March 5, 2003, the Supreme Court also upheld the 25-years-to-life sentence of Gary Ewing, who while on parole stole three golf clubs valued at $399 each. Ewing had been given the harsh sentence for the relatively minor crime due to the fact that he had previously been convicted of four felonies. In another 5 to 4 decision, the Court decided that Ewing's claim that his sentence was highly disproportionate to the offense with which he was charged was unfounded. His sentence was affirmed.

In both the *Lockyear* and *Ewing* cases, under California law, the thefts could have been treated as misdemeanors, which would have allowed Andrade and Ewing to avoid Three Strikes sentencing. Legal scholars have questioned whether the prosecutorial and judicial discretion exercised in these cases may have been influenced by the race and class status of the defendants. Andrade was an admitted heroin addict since 1977. Ewing was a long-time drug addict who was dying of AIDS at the time of his sentencing.

According to a report by the Policy Institute in Washington, D.C., during the first three years after the law took effect, African Americans were imprisoned under California's Three Strikes law at a rate 13 times that of Whites.

voters passed Proposition 36 in November 2012 (effective in 2013). According to this law, with two strikes, an offender would be sentenced to 25 years to life if and only if the offender commits an additional felony of a serious or violent nature (previously, the law had stated that any felony would induce a long-term sentence). With this reformative law, the state of California is estimated to save up to $90 million a year, and approximately 3,000 inmates serving life sentences would be eligible to petition for a reduced sentence (Sankin, 2012).

African American men, who constitute only about 3 percent of California's population, represent approximately 44 percent of third-strikers among California prison inmates (U.S. Census Bureau, 2006; California Department of Corrections and Rehabilitation, 2008). Some of the racial disparities in Three Strikes sentencing are explained by differences between Blacks and Whites in factors such as offenses committed, prior record, and parole status; however, after these "legally relevant" factors are taken into account, Blacks remain significantly more likely than Whites to receive third-strike sentences (Chen, 2008b).

Uneven application of prosecutorial or judicial discretion may be responsible for some of the Black/White disparity in Three Strikes sentences. A prosecuting attorney may file a motion to dismiss one or more prior convictions that would otherwise count as strikes, thus sparing a defendant the mandatory third-strike sentence of 25 years to life in prison if convicted (Legislative Analyst's Office, 2005). Discretion may also be exercised by prosecutors or judges to charge multiple counts, including strikes, from a single incident, or to charge certain offenses known as "wobblers" as either felonies (which trigger Three Strikes) or misdemeanors (which carry a maximum sentence of one year in jail) (Legislative Analyst's Office, 2005; Ricciardulli, 2002). The gap between Blacks and Whites in Third Strikes sentences is greater for "wobblers" than for offenses that are unequivocally charged as felonies, suggesting that discretion in "wobbler" charging may be exercised to the detriment of African American defendants (Chen, 2008b).

Studies of the crime-reduction effects of Three Strikes laws have produced mixed results. Ramirez and Crano (2003) detect few immediate impacts of Three Strikes on crime in California, some deterrence and incapacitation effects over time for violent and premeditated offenses and for "minor" crimes not targeted by Three Strikes, and no impacts on drug offenses. Worrall (2004) finds "virtually no deterrent or incapacitative effects on serious crime." Kovandzic, Sloan, and Vieratis (2002; 2004) find significant declines in crime trends for some offenses in some states in the aftermath of Three Strikes' adoption, but they also find significant increases in roughly the same number of states, suggesting either that the findings were either random statistical artifacts or that the law has both positive and negative impacts that cancel each other out on the whole. The only exception to this finding is for rates of homicide, for which more significant *increases* than declines are found (Kovandzic et al., 2004). The finding supports the hypothesis that criminals who face a Three Strikes sentence may have an increased incentive to kill potential witnesses.

The law's limited proven crime-reduction effects combined with high costs led some critics to call for reform of the law. In 2005, California's Three Strikes policy cost approximately $500 million per year to implement, with expenses expected to

---

Three Strikes Laws in Other Places

In 1994, the state of Georgia enacted a tough "two strikes" law that imposed a life sentence for a second drug offense. By 1995, the state had invoked the law against only 1 percent of White defendants facing a second drug conviction, but against more than 16 percent of eligible Black defendants. The result: by 2000, 98.4 percent of those serving life sentences in Georgia under its two strikes provision were Black.

---

escalate dramatically in the long run (Legislative Analyst's Office, 2005). The increased rate of incarceration associated with the law also imposed human and social costs for sentenced individuals, their families, and their communities (for discussion see, e.g., Mauer and Chesney-Lind, 2002; Travis, 2002; Travis and Waul, 2003). Those social costs were borne disproportionately by African American men. The full impact of the Proposition 36 changes remain to be seen but, another cost of Three Strikes laws may be that they seriously damage the perception of fairness and legitimacy in the criminal sentencing process, particularly among African Americans.

Elsa Chen

Note

1. States with Three Strikes laws are Alaska, Arkansas, California, Colorado, Connecticut, Florida, Georgia, Indiana, Kansas, Louisiana, Maryland, Montana, Nevada, New Jersey, New Mexico, North Carolina, North Dakota, Pennsylvania, South Carolina, Tennessee, Utah, Vermont, Virginia, Washington, and Wisconsin. Source for all states except Alaska: National Conference of State Legislatures, "Three Strikes" Legislation Update, December 1997. Alaska law information obtained via personal communication with Ms. Teri Carnes, Senior Staff Associate, Alaska Judicial Council, September 22, 2006.

References

California Department of Corrections and Rehabilitation. Second and Third Striker Felons in the Adult Institution Population, December 31, 2007. Sacramento, CA: California Department of Corrections and Rehabilitation, Offender Information Services Branch, Estimates and Statistical Analysis Section, Data Analysis Unit, 2008.

Chen, E. Y. 2008a. "Impacts of 'Three Strikes and You're Out' on Crime Trends in California and throughout the United States." *Journal of Contemporary Criminal Justice* 24, no. 4 (2008): 345–70.

Chen, E. Y. 2008b. "The Liberation Hypothesis and Racial and Ethnic Disparities in the Application of California's Three Strikes Law." *Journal of Ethnicity in Criminal Justice* 6, no. 2 (2008): 83–102.

Clark, J., J. Austin, et al. "'Three Strikes and You're Out': A Review of State Legislation." Washington, DC: National Institute of Justice, 1997.

Kovandzic, T. V., J. J. Sloan, and L. M. Vieratis. "'Striking Out' as Crime Reduction Policy: The Impact of 'Three Strikes' Laws on Crime Rates in U.S. Cities." *Justice Quarterly* 21, no. 2 (2004): 207–39.

Kovandzic, T. V., J. J. Sloan, and L. M. Vieratis. "Unintended Consequences of Politically Popular Sentencing Policy: The Homicide Promoting Effects of 'Three Strikes' in U.S. Cities (1980–1999)." *Criminology and Public Policy* 1, no. 3 (2002): 399–424.

Legislative Analyst's Office. "A Primer: Three Strikes: The Impact after More Than a Decade." Sacramento, CA: Legislative Analyst's Office, 2005.

Mauer, M., and M. Chesney-Lind, eds. *Invisible Punishment: The Collateral Consequences of Mass Imprisonment.* New York: The New Press, 2002.

Ramirez, J. R., and W. D. Crano. "Deterrence and Incapacitation: An Interrupted Time-Series Analysis of California's Three-Strikes Law." *Journal of Applied Social Psychology* 33, no. 1 (2003): 110–45.

Ricciarduli, A. "The Broken Safety Valve: Judicial Discretion's Failure to Ameliorate Punishment under California's Three Strikes Law." *Duquesne Law Review* 41, no. 1 (Fall 2002): 36.

Sankin, A. "California Prop 36, Measure Reforming State's Three Strikes Law, Approved by Wide Majority of Voters." *Huffington Post,* November 12, 2012. http://www.huffingtonpost.com/2012/11/07/california-prop-36_n_2089179.html.

Travis, J. "Invisible Punishment: An Instrument of Social Exclusion." In *Invisible Punishment: The Collateral Consequences of Mass Imprisonment,* edited by M. Mauer and M. Chesney-Lind, 15–36. New York: The New Press, 2002.

Travis, J., and M. Waul, eds. *Prisoners Once Removed.* Washington, DC: Urban Institute Press, 2003.

U.S. Census Bureau. "Table 3: Annual Estimates of the Population by Sex, Race, and Hispanic or Latino Origin for California: April 1, 2000 to July 1, 2006 (SC-EST2006-03-06)."

Worrall, J. L. "The Effect of Three-Strikes Legislation on Serious Crime in California." *Journal of Criminal Justice* 32, no. 4 (2004): 283–96.

Till, Emmett (1941–1955)

On August 20, 1955, two Black youths, 14-year-old Emmett Till and his 17-year-old cousin Curtis Jones, boarded a train in Chicago and headed south to visit relatives in Money, Mississippi. The train arrived in Money on August 21, 1955. On August 24, Emmett and Curtis went into town to buy some candy at Bryant's Grocery and Meat Market. Outside the store they met up with some local youths and started swapping stories. One of the locals dared Emmett to speak to Carolyn Bryant, the White woman who ran the store. Emmett went inside, bought some candy, and by varying accounts said "Bye, baby" or whistled at her as he left.

At about 2:30 a.m. on August 28, Carolyn Bryant's husband Roy Bryant and his half brother, J. W. Milam, abducted Emmett Till at gunpoint from the home of his great uncle, Moses Wright. His body was found later at the bottom of the Tallahatchie River with a 75-pound cotton gin fan tied around his neck with barbed wire. The boy had been stripped naked and beaten, one eye had been gouged out, and he had been shot through the head with a 45-caliber handgun. Emmett's mutilated body could be identified only by a ring on his finger—a ring that had belonged to his father, given to him by his mother Mamie.

Bryant and Milam were arrested and charged with kidnapping and murder. Initially they admitted abducting Emmett but denied killing him. The two men went on trial in a segregated courthouse in Summer, Mississippi, on September 19, 1955. Emmett's 64-year-old great uncle, Moses Wright, identified the two defendants as the men who had abducted his nephew. After his testimony, he and other Blacks who testified against Bryant and Milam had to be hurried out of the state for their safety.

Defense attorney John C. Whitten told the all-White jurors, "Your fathers will turn over in their graves if [Milam and Bryant are found guilty] and I'm sure that every last Anglo-Saxon one of you has the courage to free these men." On September 23, the jury deliberated for a little over an hour and returned not guilty verdicts for both. One juror later remarked that they would have been done even quicker had they not stopped to drink a soda.

The badly disfigured body of Emmett Till had been received back in Chicago by his mother, Mamie Till, on September 2. She collapsed at the sight of the casket containing her only son. In a 2003 documentary about the killing, Mrs. Till, later Mamie Till Mobley, says she made a decision to hold an open casket funeral, despite the fact that Emmett's face was unrecognizable, because she wanted the world to see what racism had done to her son. She described Emmett as a beautiful boy before he was attacked. A picture of him when he was alive was held alongside the open casket containing the mutilated body.

Many have described the killing of Emmett Till and the acquittal of his killers as a catalyst for the American Civil Rights Movement. It was preceded by the deaths of two Black men in Mississippi, Reverend George Lee and Lamar Smith, who were killed because of their efforts to vote. Emmett Till's death followed the U.S. Supreme Court's decision outlawing segregated public schooling by little over a year, and was followed by the arrest of NAACP field secretary Rosa Parks in Montgomery, Alabama, 100 days later.

Just two weeks before the 2003 premiere of *The Murder of Emmett Till*, a PBS documentary chronicling the events of Emmett Till's death, his mother Mamie Till Mobley died of heart failure at age 81. The photograph of Till's horribly disfigured face made international news and still haunts American race relations and notions of justice. J. W. Milam died in Mississippi in 1980. Roy Bryant died there in 1990. Despite later confessions, neither was ever brought to justice for the killing of 14-year-old Emmett Till.

Delores Jones-Brown

See also: Civil Rights Movement; Southern Christian Leadership Conference (SCLC)

References

Jones-Brown, D. *Race, Crime and Punishment.* Philadelphia: Chelsea House Publishers, 2000.

Nelson, S., director and producer. *American Experience: The Murder of Emmett Till.* Boston: Firelight Media, 2003.

War on Drugs

The U.S. war on drugs, a term that implies the use of force to combat drug use and abuse, has been fought on a number of fronts over the course of 40 years, earnestly funded by both Democratic and Republican administrations alike. Its arsenal of weapons includes heightened law enforcement response to drug use, mandatory minimum sentences for drug users and traffickers, and more extensive use of incarceration as a response. The war has had significant and profound implications for both foreign and domestic U.S. policy, and involves a web of governmental agencies, from the Department of Defense to Housing and Urban Development. Finally, the war on drugs has made very distinct, cumulative, and punitive impacts on African Americans in this country and in the Afro-Caribbean.

Historical Background of the War on Drugs

Although there have been various policies designed to deal with drugs in the United States even before the Harrison Act of 1914 (Walker, 2011), the official start of the war on drugs began in the 1970s under the Nixon administration, when Nixon was informed that many Vietnam soldiers were arriving back from foreign duty stoned on marijuana or heroin from Southeast Asia (Wallace-Wells, 2007). He convened a panel to study the problem and make policy recommendations to handle it, but the suggestions put forth by the panel—including decriminalization of marijuana and buying up the world's supply of heroin—didn't fit with Nixon's "law and order" platform. Though there is evidence that he initially saw treatment as the appropriate solution, he made a final decision to approach the problem as one that primarily needed a law enforcement response. From that point forward, America's approach to illegal drug use and abuse has been one of force, a *hawkish* approach that embodies the imagery of war (Reuter, quoted in Walker, 2011).

In 1973, the first National Drug Control Strategy was published by the U.S. government (Robinson & Scherlen, 2007). That same year, the Drug Enforcement Administration (DEA) was established, making it the central agency responsible for enforcing federal law around drug trafficking. By 1978, federal laws incorporated asset forfeiture as a major weapon in the war on drugs, allowing federal agents to seize any property or assets used by drug dealers as part of their business or gained through profits from drug sales.

President Ronald Reagan first used the term "War on Drugs" in 1982, before the crack epidemic (Alexander, 2010). Just a few years later, crack arrived in American cities and brought with it an alarming spike in violence, particularly among young urban minorities. In response, the war on drugs accelerated and became decidedly more punitive. There was an important shift in public sentiment, where the drug user became seen as more of a criminal fiend than a pitiable victim, and distinctions between user and dealer began to blur. The U.S. Congress responded to the crisis by passing the Anti-Drug Abuse Acts of 1986 and 1988, marking a watershed in the war on drugs. Interestingly, the 1986 act was passed in the wake of NBA star Len Bias' cocaine overdose, when the mood in the country had reached fever pitch about the harms of drug use. Congress produced this expansive legislation in just a few weeks' time (Bikel, 1999). The 1988 act established the Office of National Drug Control Policy (ONDCP), which both expanded the role of the federal government in drug crimes and created a centralized agency that was supposed to spearhead and coordinate the war on drugs nationally. The acts, amended in 1990, brought about a variety of responses to drug crimes, including lengthening sentences for convicted drug dealers; establishing and strengthening school zone laws, which enhanced penalties for drug crimes committed within a specified reach of schools; curtailing or excluding drug offenders from federal housing assistance; and increased reporting to Congress about progress on the war on drugs (Robinson & Scherlen, 2007). Many states followed suit, enacting mandatory minimums and enhanced penalties. In 1998, the Higher Education Act was amended to exclude convicted drug offenders from receiving financial aid. While the war on drugs can be viewed as one piece of the broader "get tough" movement, it should be noted that no similar exclusions have been established for alcohol or even violent offenders, making the penalties for drug use and trafficking particularly punitive (Robinson & Scherlen, 2007).

Somewhat peculiarly, in the 1990s the federal war on drugs began to focus on marijuana, despite diverging goals among the states. Because marijuana was believed to be a "gateway drug" to harder drugs (like heroin and cocaine), federal policy shifted to try to stop more serious drug use by targeting marijuana use. At the same time, more than 11 states passed medical marijuana laws or decriminalized small amounts of marijuana. During this time, the federal government began to enforce marijuana laws in earnest, even to the extent of targeting dying patients trying to relieve pain who were in compliance with state law (Wallace-Wells, 2007).

At the same time, the government launched a media campaign to attempt to dissuade youth from becoming involved in drugs. Unfortunately, the result of this campaign has been at best negligible and at worst, counterproductive. According to a study done by Hornik and his colleagues (2008), children who were exposed to the media campaign during the early 1990s demonstrated either no difference or a slightly higher probability of trying marijuana. Other efforts, including the Drug Abuse Resistance and Education (DARE) program, became wildly popular (and were funded with hundreds of millions of dollars) through the 1980s and 1990s, also with equally dismal empirical results in deterring drug use by youth (Greenwood, 2006).

While the war on drugs has crept into the goals of numerous government agencies, its effect on the court system, prisons, and jails in this country has been nothing short of profound. In 1970, the Uniform Crime Reports indicated that there were just under 400,000 drug abuse arrests among adults in the United States. By 2004, this figure had soared to over 1.6 million. Not surprisingly, there has been a similar astronomical increase in the incarceration rates. In 1980, there were less than 25,000 people in state correctional populations for drug-related crimes. By 2005, this number multiplied tenfold to 250,000. By 2009, more than half of all federal prisoners were sentenced for drug offenses (Walker, 2011).

Furthermore, not only are more people arrested and incarcerated; the trend is that people are serving much more time behind bars than before as well. The start of these sentencing changes began with the Rockefeller Drug Laws of New York, passed in 1973. These laws created mandatory sentences for various types of drug dealers and they were quickly modeled around the country over the next two decades. Diverging from the usual indeterminate sentences, which allowed for flexibility in the length of sentence pending an offender's correctional progress or growth, these laws focused instead on severe and certain punishment. Overall, the focus on correctional processing became less about rehabilitation and more about punishment.

In addition to domestic policy changes in the 1980s and 1990s, foreign policy also shifted with drug war goals during this time. In 1989, the United States pursued "Operation Just Cause" in Panama, a military (invasion) effort that captured leader Manuel Noriega and brought him to trial for drug trafficking charges in the United States. Military operations in Peru, Bolivia, and Colombia were also pursued. Crop destruction and interdiction have been major goals in the drug war, particularly in the 1990s. The impact and efficacy of these policies is discussed in the next section.

The Obama administration has taken a slightly different tact than earlier administrations, explicitly rejecting the "war on drugs" terminology, and demoting the (previously dubbed) "drug czar" position out of the presidential cabinet. This strategic move suggests that the administration does not believe the drug war is as important as has been considered by previous federal administrations. President Obama also signed into law the Fair Sentencing Act of 2010, which reduced the disparities in sentencing between crack and powder cocaine for offenders (see Fair Sentencing Act of 2010). Similarly, with fiscal budget crunches in every state, state legislatures are currently looking for ways to save money, and many recently have targeted mandatory sentences modification or repeal, including New York's Rockefeller Laws (National Conference of State Legislators, 2010). It remains to be seen whether these changes mark a new period—perhaps even the beginning of the end—in America's war on drugs or whether these reforms will tinker at the margins of this massive governmental effort.

Despite these changes instituted by the Obama administration, the drug war continues to be fueled by a host of governmental agencies, including the Department of Defense (which tracks drug trafficking internationally), the Department of Education (which invests in prevention efforts), the National Institute of Drug Abuse (treatment and prevention research), Customs and Border Protection (interdiction and intelligence), Immigration and Customs Enforcement (investigation and interdiction), the U.S. Coast Guard (interdiction), the Bureau of Prisons (incarcerating convicted drug offenders), the Office of Justice Programs (treatment and state and local aid), and of course the Office of National Drug Control Policy (Robinson & Scherlen, 2007). Estimates of the cost of the war to date vary from between $500 billion (Wallace-Wells, 2007) to $1 trillion (NewsOne, 2010).

Has It Worked?

Perhaps the most significant questions about the drug war involve whether or not it actually reduced drug use and abuse in America, and what the unintended consequences of the policy were. Simply, did it work, and at what cost?

If one of the goals of the drug war is to reduce use of drugs in this country, and to reduce the potency of drugs available on the street, then White House Drug Policy data may be enlightening (http://www.whitehousedrugpolicy.gov). The average purity of cocaine has steadily increased between 1981 and 2007, moving from about 40 percent purity to 64 percent purity (for purchases of 2 grams or less). Heroin has followed a similar pattern. Further, the relative costs of cocaine, heroin, and methamphetamines have declined significantly over the last three decades. Finally, death rates from drug-induced causes tripled between 1980 and 2007. In summary, the harder drugs on America's streets seem to be cheaper and stronger, and to be causing more deaths, than before the drug war started.

Perhaps one of the reasons for the lack of progress lies in the drug war tactics, which have been heavily "supply-side" focused, trying to destroy or contain foreign production. As such, a significant piece of the war on drugs has been fought on foreign soil. Interdiction efforts (which try to destroy or intercept drug production or traffic) have had mixed results. For instance, "Plan Colombia," a focal point for the U.S. foreign policy related to the drug war, was heralded as a success not only in reducing the Colombian production and exportation of cocaine, but also in strengthening the Colombian government (Walker, 2011: 313). However, it did not necessarily translate into significantly less cocaine being available on the open market. Specifically, although the interdiction efforts were able to cut, by more than half, the supply of cocaine coming from Colombia, Peru and Bolivia filled in much of the vacuum by increasing their production.

Heroin provides a second example of this displacement effect. While the U.S. government was successful in reducing the flow of heroin from South and Central America, Afghanistan then became the leading producer and exporter of heroin. In fact, despite significant governmental attempts to curtail supply, global heroin production has increased fairly steadily from 1987 through to 2009, ballooning from 2,200 metric tons to nearly 7,800 metric tons (UNODC, 2010).

On the streets in America, a similar phenomenon can be found. Policy analyst Sam Walker calls this "the replacement effect" (2011: 314). When one street-level drug dealer is arrested, another quickly steps in, rendering the efforts to clean the streets often ineffective.

While intuitively, interdiction efforts hold some appeal (that is, that reducing the supply should reduce drug abuse overall), the instability of many foreign countries makes interdiction very risky at best. Although efforts may decrease supply in one area, like squeezing a balloon, this usually results in more production somewhere else. As Ben Wallace-Wells reported in his piece "How America Lost the War on Drugs" (2007), the role of corruption in government often undermines any operations designed to reduce supply on foreign soil. Because of this, the RAND Corporation, a social policy think tank, has advised, "increased drug interdiction efforts are not likely to greatly affect the availability of cocaine in the United States" (Walker, 2011: 314).

Finally, any analysis of the war on drugs interdiction efforts would be remiss without considering the role of Mexico, America's southern neighbor. Over the last 20 years and in great part due to the role of drug cartels, parts of Mexico have lapsed into chaos, with the government basically incapable of maintaining order (Caputo, 2009). In particular, in the province of Juarez, just over the New Mexico border, officials recorded nearly 3,000 murders in 2010, making it perhaps one of the most violent places on earth (Caputo, 2009; Associated Press, 2010). Because of the cartel control, the free press has virtually evaporated. UNODC officials estimate that nearly 90 percent of the cocaine in America enters via Mexico. It is also the leading source of methamphetamines and marijuana (Walker, 2011). That said, Mexico is just one of several countries whose economies are based primarily on narco-trafficking, where without illicit drugs the governments would likely collapse into (sometimes further) failed states.

Rather than tackling the supply side of drug use, RAND has suggested that shifting demand could have more significant impact in reducing the drug problem in the United States. Specifically, they suggest that targeting the group of hardcore drug users (who use prolifically) for treatment could have the potential to reduce demand and thereby cut into drug-related crimes.

Differential Impact on African Americans

As Robinson and Scherlen (2007) note, the war on drugs has historically been less about the drugs themselves than about who was using them. Interestingly, they chronicle how both cocaine and opium were used in the United States without regulation or criminalization, and claim that trade and ethnocentrism played a major role in the criminalization of certain drugs. More recently, critics have pointed out that drug usage was actually declining when the drug war was officially declared (Alexander, 2010), yet panic over "crack fiends" and urban violence fueled the implementation of harsh penalties for both high-ranking drug traffickers and casual users alike.

While ardent drug abuse enforcers might argue that African Americans are disproportionately involved in drugs and so drug arrest rates simply reflect these differences, multiple studies have demonstrated that Black and White youth use and sell drugs at remarkably similar rates (Alexander, 2010). Western notes:

> High rates of homicide among black men fully explain the parallel high rates of imprisonment for murder. However, for less serious offenses, race differences in incarceration are not well explained by high crime rates. Black men are much more likely than whites to be arrested for a drug offense, and to go to prison if arrested, even though they are no more likely to use drugs than whites. (2006: 50)

Indeed, there are a growing number of critics of the criminal justice system who question whether the mass incarceration of African Americans (fueled in part by the war on drugs) may be "the new Jim Crow" (Alexander, 2010). With the revelation that some inner-city blocks were "million dollar blocks"—meaning that it cost the government upwards of a million dollars to incarcerate residents from these small areas, many critics question whether incarceration, and not welfare or health care, has become the "principle instrument of our social policy" for many inner city residents (Loury, quoted in Alexander, 2010).

Nowhere is the disparity between Black and White sentencing more stark than in the (now repealed) 100:1 crack/powder cocaine sentencing disparities. Until its repeal in 2010, the federal penalties for possession of 5 grams of crack triggered a five-year minimum mandatory prison sentence, while it took 100 times this amount of powder cocaine (500) to trigger the same sentence. Given that crack and powder cocaine are virtually the same chemical substance, the 100:1 ratio seemed wildly disproportionate. While crack markets did bring significant violence to cities in the 1980s and 1990s, others point out that the major difference between the two substances largely centers around who was using the different substances. It was thought that crack cocaine was predominantly consumed by poor urban African Americans, and that powder cocaine was more frequently used by middle- or upper-class Whites. A U.S. Sentencing Commission study would reveal the inaccuracy of the beliefs about crack use, but Blacks continued to be the group most often prosecuted for crack cocaine offenses.

Another point of racial disparity in the drug war has involved the response to illegal use of prescription drugs. While the war on drugs has largely been fought against communities of color, often in urban environments, enforcement of laws against illegal prescription drug abuse has not been a focus of the war to date. This is particularly relevant because some estimates suggest that prescription drug abuse is both more popular than cocaine, heroin, and methamphetamines combined, and is responsible for many more deaths; for example, in Florida, prescription drugs kill nearly five times as many people as other illegal drugs (CNN, 2010). Like the differences between crack and powder cocaine users, the rates of illegal prescription drug abuse also vary by race, ethnicity, and social class. In particular, efforts to stop trafficking of illegal prescription drugs could not be more different than those for street drugs, with "pill doctors" who extensively prescribe controlled narcotics (out of proportion to their peers) often unimpeded by traditional law enforcement. Acknowledging the impact of such drug abuse, White House point-person Gil Kerlikowske noted that prescription drug abuse has become the country's fastest-growing drug problem (Davenport, 2011). In fact, according to a federal study in 2006, opium analgesics have become more popular among teenagers than marijuana (Davenport, 2011). Between 1999 and 2005, unintentional death from prescription drug overdoses skyrocketed, second only to automobile accidents (Davenport, 2011).

In addition to these differences in enforcement, there is also concern that racial disparities may influence prosecution patterns of drug offenses (see Stop Snitching Campaign). Although the minimum mandatory sentences enacted in the 1980s and 1990s were meant in part to reduce the discretion of justice officials, there is some evidence that discretion wasn't eliminated—it was simply moved from the judge to the prosecutor, and race may continue to influence decisionmakers, perhaps in subtle, less obvious ways than in earlier generations.

Because of these disparities—the lack of obvious interest in going after prescription drug "pill mills," combined with drug law enforcement and prosecution that targets urban communities that are often primarily African American, many minorities have come to feel that the war on drugs is, in effect, a war on them.

Bruce Western and Becky Petit discuss the racial implications of the drug war and mass incarceration in general. In their analysis, they note the impact on African Americans at the lower end of social wealth:

> Most of the growth in incarceration rates is concentrated at the very bottom, among young men with very low levels of education. In 1980, around 10% of young African American men who dropped out of high school were in prison or jail. By 2008, this incarceration rate had climbed to 37%, an astonishing level of institutionalization given that the average incarceration rate in the general population was 0.76 of 1 percent. (2010: 10)

Considering that incarceration severely limits employment opportunities for offenders and families, the cumulative effect of having so many African Americans behind bars is enormous. The National Criminal Justice Commission stated that the number of African Americans behind bars in this country has reached the level of "social catastrophe" (Walker, 2011: 311).

That said, it is also important to consider the "collateral consequences" of having so many African Americans behind bars. One is that the percentage of African American children who have a parent behind bars increased dramatically between 1980 and 2008, significantly more than changes for White or Latino children. The rate for African Americans is more than double the rate for White or Latino children, at nearly 12 percent (Western & Petit, 2010). The effects of this scale of incarceration, then, will likely be cumulative, since parental incarceration is related to a host of negative consequences for children, including a heightened risk of living in poverty and becoming involved in the criminal justice system themselves.

Conclusion

The United States has some of the harshest drug laws in the world, alongside some of the highest rates of cocaine and marijuana use, and substantial racial disparities in enforcement of its drug war. These facts have, and will continue to have, important implications for the African American community in particular. Critics, and even some agents involved directly in the drug war (like the group Law Enforcement Against Prohibition) have begun to question the deterrent value of such harsh drug laws since rates of use and abuse continue to soar.

War on Drugs: H.R. 3245

The Fairness in Cocaine Sentencing Act of 2009 (H.R. 3245) was proposed to "amend the Controlled Substances Act and the Controlled Substances Import and Export Act regarding penalties for cocaine offenses, and for other purposes." It was first introduced on July 29, 2009, but had been in the making since 1996. The legislation was in response to findings by a U.S. Sentencing Commission study that exposed tremendous sentencing disparity for defendants convicted of crimes involving small amounts of crack cocaine, referred to as "cocaine base," and those in possession of substantially larger amounts of cocaine powder. Based on laws enacted in 1986, the "100 to 1 ratio," as the discrepancy came to be called, placed defendants possessing 5 grams of crack cocaine in the position to receive a mandatory prison sentence equal to that of those possessing 500 grams of cocaine powder. The 1986 legislation required proof of the intent to distribute "cocaine base" before the mandatory prison sentences would occur, but a 1988 amendment allowed the 100 to 1 difference to apply to a defendant even if he or she possessed the drug for his or her personal use. After its study, the Sentencing Commission found the significant sentencing differences to be unjustified by the small differences between the two forms of cocaine. Congress rejected the commission's proposals to change the law from 1995 to 2010. Over time, the crack versus powder cocaine laws put thousands of people behind bars. Nearly 85 percent (84.7%) of federal crack cases were brought against African Americans and the number of drug offenders in prisons and jails increased 1,100 percent from levels recorded in 1980 (to 493,800 compared to an estimated 41,100). Additionally, national statistics reveal that nearly 6 in 10 persons in state prison for a drug offense have no history of violence or high-level drug selling activity, and that, largely due to racially disparate sentencing laws such as the 100 to 1 crack versus powder cocaine disparity, African Americans serve almost as much time in federal prison for a drug offense (58.7 months) as Whites do for a violent offense (61.7 months).

Though two-thirds of crack cocaine users in the United States are White or Hispanic, Blacks were disproportionately subject to the penalties associated with both types of cocaine, through disproportionate arrests, federal prosecution, and sentencing.

The Sentencing Commission quickly determined that since crack and powder cocaine are derivatives of the same substance, there was no reason to define the law and the applicable punishments differently. The blatant racial disparity in those being prosecuted and imprisoned for federal crack offenses prompted the Sentencing Commission to press for change in the law despite an active and ongoing government sponsored "war on drugs." However, the provisions of H.R. 3245, which called for the repeal of "provisions of the Controlled Substances Act that provide different criminal penalties for the manufacturing, distributing, or dispensing of cocaine and cocaine base (i.e., crack cocaine), including the mandatory minimum five-year prison sentence for simple possession of cocaine base," and also called for repeal of the "provisions of the Controlled Substances Import and Export Act that provide different criminal penalties for the importing and exporting of cocaine and cocaine base" (Official Congressional Summary located at http://www.opencongress.org/bill/111 -h3245/show), did not become law until August 2010, when the Fair Sentencing Act of 2010 was signed by President Barack Obama—nearly 25 years after the differential sentencing was put into effect.

Anastasia Teper

Mass incarceration, fueled in great part by the war on drugs, has had the effect of heavily burdening families, communities, and state and federal budgets. In many communities, education funding has declined in order to increase or sustain funding for prisons. Moreover, the expenditures don't seem to work at reducing drug crimes or any other crimes for that matter. The Bureau of Justice statistics indicate that nearly two-thirds of most prisoners will be re-arrested for another crime within three years of release. These dismal figures suggest that incarceration doesn't rehabilitate many offenders.

After 40 years, many have come to question the value of the "war" metaphor in this particular social problem, and whether some other approach instead of force might be more successful in reducing drug use and abuse. The question of how *else* to deal with drug use remains. In the past 10 years, Portugal has decriminalized all drugs (even heroin and cocaine), moving resources from law enforcement to treatment, with some success in reducing disease and increasing the number of people seeking drug treatment (Hatton & Medoza, 2010). Other countries, like Canada, have attempted different "harm reduction" initiatives to respond to drug abuse. Although these countries are different from the United States in many respects, some policy analysts are carefully watching the results of these efforts (Hatton & Mendoza, 2010). For now, though, in the United States the emphasis remains on policing as the first response, as scholar Peter Moskos notes, "Drugs became a police problem as many problems do: Nobody else wanted to deal with it. Society's buck stops with the police" (2008: 159). Still, many question whether justice is effectively being served. The unintended consequences of this war of force may have been to alienate many African

Americans—particularly those who are poor and uneducated—from believing in the legitimacy of the law.

Jennifer Balboni

See also: Fair Sentencing Act of 2010; Federal Sentencing Disparity; Gangs; Institutional Racism; Legal Socialization and Race; Prisoner Reentry and African Americans; Sentencing Disparities

References

Alexander, Michelle. *The New Jim Crow: Mass Incarceration in the Age of Color Blindness.* New York: The New Press, 2010.

Associated Press. "Cuidad Juarez Drug War Death Toll Hits 3,000." December 15, 2010. http://www.cbsnews.com/stories/2010/12/15/world/main7151506.shtml.

Bikel, Ofra, producer. *Snitch.* WGBH Educational Foundation, 1999.

Brown, Campbell. "Prescription Drug Abuse." CNN, February 11, 2010. http://www.gatehouseacademy.com/blog/2010/02/11/shocking-video-on-cnn-pain-clinics-in-florida/.

Caputo, Philip. "The Fall of Mexico." *Atlantic,* December 2009.

Davenport, Christian. "Doctors Who Prescribe Oft-Abused Drugs Face Scrutiny." *The Washington Post,* January 1, 2011.

Fairness in Cocaine Sentencing Act of 2009 (H.R. 3245). 111th Congress, 2009–2010.

Greenwood, Peter. *Changing Lives: Delinquency Prevention as Crime-Control Policy.* Chicago: University of Chicago Press, 2006.

Hatton, Barry, and Martha Mendoza. "Portugal's Drug Policy Pays Off; US Eyes Lessons." *The Washington Post,* December 27, 2010.

Hornik, Robert, Lela Jacobsohn, Robert Orwin, Andrea Piesse, and Graham Kalton. "Effects of National Youth Anti-Drug Media Campaign on Youth." *American Journal of Public Health* 98, no. 12 (2008): 2229–36.

Moskos, Peter. *Cop in the Hood.* Princeton, NJ: Princeton University Press, 2009.

National Conference of State Legislatures. *Significant State Sentencing and Corrections Legislation in 2009.* Posted October 5, 2010. http://www.ncsl.org/research/civil-and-criminal-justice/significant-state-sentencing-and-corrections-legis.aspx.

NewsOne. "Despite Spending 1 Trillion Dollars, the Drug War Has Failed." Posted by Associated Press, May 13, 2010. http://newsone.com/nation/associated-press/despite-spending-1-trillion-the-war-on-drugs-has-failed/.

Office of National Drug Policy Control. "White House Drug Policy." Washington, DC. http://www.whitehousedrugpolicy.gov/publications/policy/ndcs10/ndcs10_data_supl/ds_list_of_tables.pdf.

Robinson, Matthew, and Renee Scherlen. "Lies, Damned Lies and Drug War Statistics." Albany: State University of New York Press, 2007.

United Nations Office on Drugs and Crime (UNODC). *World Drug Report.* New York, NY: United Nations, 2010. http://www.unodc.org/documents/wdr/WDR_2010/World_Drug_Report_2010_lo-res.pdf.

U.S. Sentencing Commission. "Special Report to the Congress: Cocaine and Federal Sentencing Policy," February 1995. http://www.ussc.gov/Legislative_and_Public_Affairs/Congressional_Testimony_and_Reports/Drug_Topics/199502_RtC_Cocaine_Sentencing_Policy/index.cfm.

Walker, Sam. *Sense and Nonsense about Crime, Drugs and Communities.* Belmont, CA: Wadsworth, 2011.

Wallace-Wells, Ben. "How America Lost the War on Drugs." *Rolling Stone,* December 13, 2007.

Western, Bruce. *Punishment and Inequality in America.* New York: Russell Sage Foundation, 2006.

Western, Bruce, and Becky Petit. "Incarceration and Social Inequality." *Daedalus* 139, no. 3 (Summer 2010): 8–19.

Wells-Barnett, Ida B. (1862–1931)

Ida B. Wells (later Wells-Barnett) was born on July 16, 1862, in Holly Springs, Mississippi, and died on March 25, 1931, in Chicago, Illinois. She grew up during the time when the political gains of Reconstruction were being lost and the evils of segregation, disenfranchisement, and lynching launched themselves upon the American scene to keep African Americans in their place. Born of parents who were slaves at the time of her birth, Wells became a schoolteacher, journalist, author, activist and protester, researcher and investigator, suffragist, and probation officer. She is best known for her anti-lynching journalism, though some of her other achievements included the support of social reforms for women and for youth.

In the 1870s, Wells' parents and infant brother died in a yellow fever epidemic that overtook Memphis, Tennessee, and cut the

Portrait of journalist and civil rights activist Ida B. Wells-Barnett, in 1891. (Library of Congress)

city's population by 75,000. Despite being orphaned and having to raise her siblings, Ida B. Wells attended the Freedmen's School of Shaw University (later Rust College), under the leadership of the Methodist Episcopal Church, in Holly Springs. Though she did not graduate, her subsequent achievements and pioneering activism prompted the institution to later award her an honorary degree. Ida B. Wells spent the early part of her career as a schoolteacher but favored journalism. Teaching brought her valuable social connections among the African American elite of Memphis and made her more aware of racism and politics, topics that would later become the primary focus of her life's work.

Writing under the pen name of "Iola," Wells eventually published in several Memphis-area media outlets, including the *Evening Star* of the Memphis Lyceum and *Living Way,* a weekly of the African American Baptist Church. In 1885, Paul Taylor, pastor of the Beale Street Church, offered Ms. Wells the editorship of the *Memphis Free Speech and Headlight.* Wells agreed to take the job if she would be an equal partner with Taylor and business manager J. L. Fleming, and if she would be allowed to continue teaching and writing columns for other papers. Her terms were accepted and Ida B. Wells became "the . . . only black woman of record to become editor in chief and part owner of a major city newspaper" (Giddings, 2008: 155).

Her coverage of the 1892 lynching of Thomas Moss, Calvin McDowell, and Lee Stewart in Memphis eventually brought Ida B. Wells national and international fame as an investigative journalist, protester, writer, and speaker against lynching and as a researcher who revealed the true reason(s) underlying the murders. Wells was away when the lynching and funerals took place, but the Moss family were her good friends and she was godmother to their daughter. Her unflinching editorial about the atrocities led to her being "exiled" from Memphis and to the loss of her newspaper, the offices of which were destroyed while she was out of town, because of what she wrote. Her partner and co-owner of the paper, J. L. Fleming, had to flee the city, as a lynch mob was looking for him because they thought that he wrote the editorial.

Wells' editorial exposed the myth that rape was the main cause of lynching because White Southerners wanted to protect their women. She analyzed White and Black newspaper accounts and uncovered interesting facts, such as that two-thirds of the lynch cases did not charge the defendant with rape, that there was often considerable doubt when an accused was charged with rape, and that sometimes a Black male was charged with rape for simply looking at a White woman "in the wrong way." She also reported that there were instances in which a sexual act was consensual and the rape claim was used by the White female sexual partner as a defense against the ostracism she would face from the White community when the relationship became known. On the other hand, rape was never an issue when the sexual act took place between a White male and a Black female, whether the sexual act was consensual or nonconsensual.

Beyond allegations of the rape of White women, Wells documented that Blacks were lynched for "offenses" such as failing to pay debts, not appearing sufficiently respectful of Whites, being drunk in public, and, as with her friend Thomas Moss, competing with Whites economically. Moss had been the owner of a grocery store that was seen as competitive with a White-owned store across the street. Wells was in Natchez, Mississippi, when the Memphis store was attacked. When a group of Whites attacked the store, three White men were injured by gunfire. Moss, McDowell, and Steward were arrested for shooting the White men. Without trial or conviction, they were taken from their cells by a White mob and killed.

In her writings, Wells identified lynching as racial terrorism that was designed to force the ex-slaves to give up political enfranchisement and to accept segregation as inferior people in all aspects of life. Lynching was used to bolster White supremacy and the protection of White women under the "cult of true womanhood" (Welter, 1966). Thus true reasons for lynching were hidden under that "cult" and liberals in the North and South accepted the myth. During the decade of the 1890s, lynching increased to an average of more than two per week. In one editorial Wells had the courage to write, "If Southern White men are not careful, they will overreach themselves and public sentiment will have a reaction; a conclusion will then be reached which will be very damaging to the moral reputation of their women" (Wells-Barnett, 1969: 61).

In her newspaper *The Free Speech,* Ida B. Wells also supported the emigration of Black people to the Oklahoma territory and encouraged them to "stick to the course" even when White merchants began complaining about the ensuing economic impact. The Black people of Memphis were motivated by the purported last words of Thomas Moss, one of the lynching victims: "[T]ell my people to go West—there is no justice for them here." It is reported that at least 6,000 Blacks actually left the Memphis area, and others boycotted White-owned businesses.

Instead of going West, Wells went to Chicago. There she married Ferdinand Barnett, a prominent Chicago lawyer and publisher of the *Chicago Conservator.* Barnett was also assistant state attorney for Illinois from 1896 to 1911. Now Ida B. Wells-Barnett, she wrote articles for the *Chicago Conservator,* became its editor, and later bought it. Undaunted by her experience in Memphis, Chicago became Wells-Barnett's new base for her activities to expose and address racism. In Chicago, she wrote about the 1908 Springfield, Illinois, race riot, which resulted from a thwarted lynching attempt and ultimately led to the founding of the NAACP. In 1910, with help from the *Chicago Daily News* owner Victor Lawson, she officially established the Negro Fellowship League (NFL) Reading Room and Social Club. Along with Frederick Douglass and others, including her husband, she wrote and widely distributed a pamphlet to protest the exclusion of African Americans from the planning and primary exhibit at the 1893 World's Fair. The document, entitled *"Reason Why the Colored American Is Not in the World's Columbian Exposition,"* included an introduction and chapter on "Class Legislation and the Convict Lease System" by Frederick Douglass, a chapter on "Lynch Law" by Wells-Barnett, a chapter on "The Progress of the Afro-American since Emancipation," and a final chapter summarizing the efforts of Black people to get representation at the Chicago World's Fair written by Ferdinand Barnett. The document was reportedly distributed to more than 20,000 people at the fair alone. Others were provided with copies of the document by making a request to Wells-Barnett at the newspaper.

Wells-Barnett established the NFL Reading Room and Social Center as a shelter from the places of vice on State Street that young African American males frequented on arrival from the South (soon finding themselves with criminal records). In contrast to the vice dens, the NFL provided reading and writing materials, cultural programs, holiday celebrations, employment sources, and inexpensive lodging. Establishment of the NFL reflected Wells-Barnett's personal emphasis on Black self-help and represented one of her primary efforts to cut down on Black crime. She noted to others who complained about Black involvement in crime that the YMCA, YWCA, and the settlement houses did not welcome African Americans. Thus, in the absence of the NFL, many of the young people had few options besides hanging on the streets and going into the saloons and gambling houses for entertainment and into buffet rooms for lodging. Her work with the NFL led to her characterization as a probation officer.

Some of Wells-Barnett's work through the NFL was quite controversial. In 1910, she became involved in helping Steve Green, a Southern Black landless, uneducated tenant farmer who paid to work someone else's land in Arkansas. When the landlord doubled the money for the rent, Green left and went to work for someone else. The former landlord became angry and shot and wounded Green. Green fired back in self-defense and the White former landlord was killed. After the shooting, fearing that he might be lynched, Green fled to Chicago but was betrayed and extradited back to Arkansas. Joel Spingarn, noted Jewish university professor, soldier, and civil rights activist, donated funds to the Green case when he found out that the newly formed NAACP and the NFL were seeking to block Green's extradition (Ross, 1972). Wells-Barnett succeeded in getting a writ of habeas corpus and reward money for any sheriff along the Arkansas route who would return Green to Chicago. One sheriff responded to the offer of a $100 reward and returned Green to Chicago. With assistance, Wells-Barnett eventually helped Steve Green escape to Canada to avoid being lynched and further legal action (McMurry, 1998).

Ida B. Wells-Barnett's anti-lynching work also gained attention outside the United States. In 1893, Catherine Impey, an English Quaker, and Isabelle Mayo, a novelist, who was against racism and interested in pacifism, invited Ida B. Wells to come to England to speak about lynching, including statistics about it and underlying causes. The newspapers publicized the speeches and the tour provided international attention to the crime of lynching. Once again, Wells-Barnett's speeches gave rise to controversy when she noted that statements made by Frances Willard, president of the Women's Christian Temperance Union (WCTU), a 200,000-member women's organization in the United States, were erroneous and "seemed to condone lynching and to accept the usual charge of black bestiality." Wells-Barnett interpreted several comments made by Willard in support of alcohol prohibition and White women's voting rights as legitimizing the rape myth as the cause of lynching—a position against which Wells-Barnett was adamantly opposed, given all of the contrary evidence that she had accumulated. Wells-Barnett's criticism of Willard led to her being attacked in prominent U.S. newspapers, including *The New York Times*. For a time, Wells-Barnett's anti-lynching message was also kept out of British papers with the assistance of one of Willard's influential friends. Despite Willard's efforts, the British Anti-Lynching Committee was formed and counted high-ranking British religious and political leaders among its members.

Wells-Barnett visited Great Britain again in 1894 and was asked by a Chicago-based paper, *The Daily Inter-Ocean,* to write for the newspaper while she was there. Though considered conservative and republican, *The Daily Inter-Ocean* is reported as being the only paper in the United States that persistently denounced lynching. Wells-Barnett's writings on lynchings for that Chicago paper while traveling abroad led to her being credited as the first Black woman to be a paid correspondent to a "mainstream" White newspaper.

Seemingly tireless in her organizing efforts, Wells-Barnett is credited with having established the Alpha Suffrage Club in 1913, chairing the Chicago Equal Rights League in 1915, and founding and/or participating in the National American Women's Suffrage Association, Ida B. Wells Club, National Afro-American Council, and Universal Negro Improvement Association. She was also the first woman officer of the National Colored Press Association.

By the time of her death in 1931 at age 68, Wells-Barnett and other sources had documented thousands of reported lynchings that took place in the United States. One source puts the figure at 4,742 between 1882 and 1968 (Marus, 2005). There is little doubt that many more went unreported. In addition to her numerous newspaper publications, Wells-Barnett published several lengthy research reports or exposés on lynching that were later released as books. *Southern Horrors: Lynch Law in All Its Phases* and *The Red Record* are perhaps the most well known. The 100-page writing *The Red Record: Tabulated Statistics and Alleged Causes of*

Lynchings in the United States describes lynchings and Black struggles in the United States both pre- and postemancipation. In it, Wells-Barnett lists 14 pages of statistics on lynchings that occurred between 1892 and 1895. She also includes graphic details of lynchings done in the South, though lynchings were not confined to the South (see Lynching). In addition, she emphasizes the public spectacle of lynching, as evidenced by photographs that include the smiling faces of White children present at lynching events.

Despite the tireless work and arduous documentation of Wells-Barnett and others, the federal government refused to pass an anti-lynching law, claiming that it would intrude on states' rights. The law would have prohibited the practice and imposed federal punishment for anyone who engaged in it. Over the years, the legislation was approved by the House of Representatives three times but defeated by those in the Senate, despite the fact that seven U.S. presidents, from William Henry Harrison (1841) to Harry Truman (1945–1953), also requested such a law (Stolberg, 2005). In June 2005, the U.S. Senate passed a resolution that issued an official apology for refusing to pass the requested anti-lynching legislation for over 100 years. It is worth noting that the resolution was supported by only 80 out of 100 senators.

Seventy-one years prior to Rosa Parks becoming the mother of the American Civil Rights Movement by refusing to give up her seat on a Montgomery, Alabama, bus, Ida B. Wells made history by refusing to give up her seat on a train (Duster, 1970: xvi–xvii, 18–20). Her successful lawsuit against the Chesapeake, Ohio, and Southwestern Railroad (1884) was subsequently overturned by the Tennessee Supreme Court (1887) (Duster, 1970: xvi–xvii, 18–20). As a final tribute to her contributions to law and justice in the United States, a picture of Ida B. Wells-Barnett was featured on a U.S. postal stamp in 1990.

Marvie Brooks with Delores Jones-Brown

References

Chesapeake, Ohio & Southwestern Railroad Company v. Wells, 85 Tenn. 613; 4 S.W 5 (1887).

Duster, Alfreda M., ed. *Crusade for Justice: The Autobiography of Ida B. Wells.* Chicago: University of Chicago Press, 1970.

Giddings, Paula J. *Ida: A Sword among Lions: Ida B. Wells and the Campaign against Lynching.* New York: HarperCollins, 2008.

Marus, Robert. "Senate Apologizes for Failure to Pass Anti-Lynching Law." *Associated Baptist Press,* June 14, 2005. http://www.abpnews.com.

McMurry, Linda O. *To Keep the Waters Troubled: The Life of Ida B. Wells.* New York: Oxford University Press, 1998.

Ross, Barbara Joyce. *J. E. Spingarn and the Rise of the NAACP, 1911–1939.* New York: Atheneum, 1972.

Stolberg, Sheryl Gay. "Senate Issues Apology over Failure on Lynching Law." *The New York Times,* June 14, 2005.

Wells, Ida B., et al. *The Reason Why the Colored American Is Not in the World's Columbian Exposition.* From the reprint of the 1893 edition, edited by Robert W. Rydell. Urbana, IL: University of Illinois Press, 1999.

Wells-Barnett, Ida B. *On Lynchings: Southern Horrors, A Red Record, Mob Rule in New Orleans.* New York: Arno Press and *The New York Times,* 1969.

Welter, Barbara. "The Cult of True Womanhood: 1820–1860." *American Quarterly* 18, no. 2, pt. 1 (Summer 1996): 151–74.

When Work Disappears: The World of the New Urban Poor

When Work Disappears: The World of the New Urban Poor (Wilson, 1996) by William Julius Wilson, the Lewis P. and Linda L. Geyser University Professor at Harvard University, explores how the absence of legitimate work has contributed to many of the problems in inner-city ghetto neighborhoods including crime, family dissolution, social disorganization, and welfare dependency. According to Wilson, this joblessness can be explained in part by changes in the global economy and national patterns of economic structural dislocation that have adversely affected low-wage workers. Job disappearance, combined with racial isolation and concentrated poverty, produces constraints at the community and societal level. Wilson dismisses explanations for poverty that stress individual and group attitudes, habits, styles, and values as the reasons for different economic and social outcomes, arguing instead that deleterious aspects of the environment, rather than personal shortcomings of individuals and families, have led to economic distress. He concludes by calling for better social policies to address the processes in the global economy that have contributed to inequality.

When Work Disappears extends the arguments first laid out in Wilson's 1987 book *The Truly Disadvantaged: The Inner City, the Underclass, and Public Policy.* Those arguments included 1) that several social initiatives aimed at stemming poverty for African Americans and other members of society did not work; 2) that there has been a major economic shift on a national and global level that has sent a sizable amount of industrial and low-skilled jobs overseas and has placed an emphasis on choosing "ideal" job candidates; 3) that the current plight of record unemployment rates among African American men, African American youth, and single female-headed households led by African American women are the direct result of decades of overt racism that can be found in several sectors of today's society; and 4) that joblessness rates are the result of multiple forms of isolation, including economic and labor market isolation, housing isolation, and educational and training isolation.

In the book, Wilson also points to "the warehousing" of African American men, women, and youth in the criminal justice system and the lack of funding for extensive ex-offender programs, which could reduce recidivism, as significant contributors to African Americans' potential or actual isolation from the work force. He also identifies the disappearance of low-skilled and low-paying industrial jobs, a staple of African American employment in the past, as one of the primary mechanisms that has directly facilitated African Americans' economic isolation in various sectors of society. He also addresses the "flight" of working-class and middle-class African Americans away from certain residential areas. Wilson takes note that the African Americans who took advantage of training programs and college as a way out of public housing and other challenges of urban life by escaping to the fringes of the city limits or the suburbs deprived African Americans growing up in public housing and other challenged urban environments of positive, assertive, educated, and economically successful role models. Wilson concludes that, for African Americans, this "multifaceted societal isolation" contributes to low self-esteem, cycles of generational poverty, and involvement in the criminal justice system (Greenstein, 1987).

When Work Disappears draws on social psychological research using survey and ethnographic data collected in the Urban Poverty and Family Life Study (UPFLS), a comprehensive research project explicitly designed to test Wilson's ideas about the relationship between neighborhood structure and individual behavior. The book is divided into two parts: Part I, "The New Urban Poverty" (containing chapters 1–5), and Part II, "The Social Policy Challenge" (containing chapters 6–8). Part I presents an analysis of his data on poor inner-city communities. Part II engages policy debates.

When Work Disappears is less about *why* work disappears than the effects of the disappearance of steady jobs in a community. Pointing to social structural factors, cultural factors, and social psychological variables, Wilson examines the significance of limited employment opportunities in poor neighborhoods and finds that high rates of unemployment create social disorganization and problems, including crime. According to Wilson's analysis, to a certain extent, one should expect a significant level of crime and/or illicit drug usage among those who reside in "isolated" ghettos under challenged urban conditions. Furthermore, according to this same analysis, what indirectly facilitates involvement in criminal activity are the feelings of hopelessness, low self-esteem, anger, resentment, and anxiety engendered by such conditions. If a considerable amount of the population in these "isolated" ghettos and challenged communities view their opportunities as limited and fixed, then engaging in criminal activity is seen as a means for survival. In the absence of meaningful sociostructural change, the mindset is passed on to the next generation of residents (Ford, 2009).

Avi Brisman

See also: Inequality Theory; Institutional Racism; Socioeconomic Factors; Structural Racism and Violence; Theories of Race and Crime

References

Ford, R. T. "Why the Poor Stay Poor." *The New York Times,* March 8, 2009. http://www.nytimes.com/2009/03/08/books/review/Ford-t.html?ref=williamjuliuswilson.

Greenstein, R. "The Prisoners of the Economy." *The New York Times,* October 25, 1987. http://www.nytimes.com/books/98/12/06/.../wilson-disadvantaged.html.

Wilson, William Julius. *The Truly Disadvantaged: The Inner City, the Underclass, and Public Policy.* Chicago: University of Chicago Press, 1987.

Wilson, William Julius. *When Work Disappears: The World of the New Urban Poor.* New York: Vintage Books, 1996.

White, Walter Francis (1893–1955)

Walter Francis White was born July 1, 1893, in Atlanta, Georgia, and died in New York City on March 21, 1955. White's career achievements were many and varied. He served as executive secretary of the National Association for the Advancement of Colored People (NAACP) from 1931 to 1955 (Johnson, 1933; White, 1948; Dyja, 2008). In 1941, White and A. Philip Randolph persuaded President Franklin Roosevelt to sign Executive Order #8802, which would stop racial discriminatory employment practices in the defense industries and establish the Fair Employment Practices Committee (White, 1948; Janken, 2003; Dyja, 2008). He published a book titled *A Rising Wind: A Report of Negro Soldiers in the European Theatre of War* (1945), based on his work as a foreign correspondent during World War II. The book exposed the discrimination African American soldiers faced and resulted in President Harry Truman desegregating the armed forces in 1948.

In 1935, along with the NAACP headquarters, its various branches, and other interest groups, White organized a successful publicity campaign to block President Hoover's nomination of Judge John J. Parker, a North Carolina Republican, to the U.S. Supreme Court because of a statement he made in an interview indicating that he did not approve of Black people having the right to vote (Johnson, 1933; White, 1948; Janken, 2003; Dyja, 2008). He went with W. E. B. Du Bois as a delegate to the NAACP's 1921 Second Pan-African Congress in London, Paris, and

Portrait of Walter Francis White, executive secretary of the National Association for the Advancement of Colored People, in 1942. (Library of Congress)

Brussels. He also served as one of three NAACP advisors to the U.S. delegation to the 1945 conference that founded the United Nations.

White wrote numerous books and articles. His book *Rope and Faggot* was an investigation of lynching that contained statistics on the crime by state, region, and race, and a discussion of its causes, and listed the myths underlying the motives for lynching (1929a). In his autobiography, *A Man Called White* (1948), he explained that while he was White in appearance, he was "a Negro" because five of his ancestors for three generations were Black, although White himself was fair-skinned, blonde-haired, and blue-eyed. During his life, he also served as a columnist for *The New York Herald Tribune* and *The Chicago Defender* and as a reporter for *The Chicago Daily News.*

White's efforts to end racial discrimination in employment, especially the lucrative employment of the defense industry, helped to expand socioeconomic opportunities for African Americans, allowing some to escape poverty and living conditions likely to contribute to crime and criminal victimization (White, 1948; Janken, 2003; Dyja, 2008). He was an extraordinary investigative reporter. As he performed his duties for different media outlets, he exposed the horrors of lynchings (White, 1918; "The Lynching Industry," 1920; White, 1929b; Guzman & Hughes, 1947; Meyers, 2006), the chaos of the Chicago Race Riot of 1919, and the exploitation occasioned by the sharecropping system, and the vagaries of the convict lease system (Dyja, 2008; Janken, 2003; Johnson, 1933; White, 1948).

Marvie Brooks

See also: Civil Rights Movement; Lynching; Prisons; Wells-Barnett, Ida B.

References

Dyja, T. *Walter White: The Dilemma of Black Identity in America.* Chicago: Ivan R. Dee, 2008.

Guzman, J. P., and W. H. Hughes. "Lynching—Crime." In *Negro Year Book: A Review of Events Affecting Negro Life, 1945–1946,* 302–11. Tuskegee, AL: Negro Year Book, 1947.

Janken, K. R. *White: The Biography of Walter White: Mr. N.A.A.C.P.* New York: The New Press, 2003.

Johnson, J. W. *Along This Way: The Autobiography of James Weldon Johnson.* New York: Viking Press, 1933.

"The Lynching Industry." *The Crisis 19,* no. 4 (February 1920): 183.

Meyers, C. C. "'Killing Them by the Wholesale': A Lynching Rampage in South Georgia." *Georgia Historical Quarterly* 90, no. 2 (2006): 214–35.

White, W. F. *A Man Called White: The Autobiography of Walter White.* New York: Viking, 1948.

White, W. F. *A Rising Wind: A Report of Negro Soldiers in the European Theatre of War.* Garden City, NY: Doubleday, Doran and Company, 1945.

White, W. F. 1929a. *Rope and Faggot: A Biography of Judge Lynch.* New York: Knopf, 1929.

White, W. F. 1929b. "I Investigate Lynchings." *American Mercury* (January 1929): 1–8. National Humanities Center Resource Toolbox. The Making of African American Identity; Vol. 111, 1917–68. http://nationalhumanitiescenter.org/pds/maai3/segregation/text2/investigatelynchings.pdf.

White, W. F. "The Work of a Mob." *The Crisis* 16, no. 5 (September 1918): 221–3.

Williams, Wayne (1958–)

On February 27, 1982, Wayne Williams was found guilty of the murders of Nathaniel Cater, 28, and Jimmy Ray Payne, 21. Williams was sentenced to consecutive life sentences. The two murders that Williams was convicted of committing are not the reason Wayne Williams will be remembered. Williams has been linked to the infamous Atlanta Child Murders, which occurred from July 21, 1979, to May 22, 1981. Although he continues to maintain his innocence, he is known as one of the most famous serial killers in U.S. history. His capture, trial, and conviction caused a media frenzy. Williams and his supporters believe he was a scapegoat and convicted on circumstantial evidence (Baldwin, 1985). He believes that one day the actual killer will be caught and he will be set free (CNN, 2010). Whether one believes he is the killer or not, the horrific tale has been told in fiction and nonfiction around the world (Baldwin, 1985; Bambara, 2003). The case continues

to draw attention and investigation 30 years later. A prosecutor in the case, Jack Mallard, published a book in 2009 and CNN aired a documentary on the case as recently as June 2010. Despite numerous appeals, Wayne Williams has been incarcerated since June 21, 1981, when he was first arrested on the charges for which he was convicted.

The Atlanta Child Murders

On July 28, 1979, two bodies, distorted by exposure, were found in the woods. After several days and a review of missing children reports, family members identified the bodies as Edward H. Smith, 14, and Alfred James Evans, 13. It was the beginning of a spate of murders that haunted Atlanta's Black community (Bardsley & Bell, n.d.; Mallard, 2009).

In the space of two years, over two dozen bodies of Black male children and young adults turned up in the woods and rivers of Georgia. The victims came from poor neighborhoods; several lived in Dixie Hills, where

Wayne B. Williams was found guilty in the murder of two Atlanta youths on February 27, 1982. In his first public comments since his 1982 conviction in the slaying of Nathaniel Cater and Jimmy Ray Payne, Williams said he has been "wrongly accused and connected with a series of heinous crimes." (Associated Press)

Williams was born (on May 27, 1958) and raised. In order to make money, youngsters would do odd jobs for family members and friends. Many would disappear while on errands. For example, Jeffery Mathis, age 10, went to the store to buy cigarettes for his mother and never returned (Bardsley & Bell, n.d.).

Jeffery's mother, Camille Belle, joined forces with two other mothers representing murdered or missing children (Willie Mae Mathis and Venus Taylor). They formed the Mother's Committee to Stop Children's Murders (STOP). The committee met with city officials and private sector representatives when the death count reached six and the number of missing children was at four. They were told by officials that there was no serial killer stalking Atlanta and that they were overreacting. Bell and the committee believed they were ignored because their children were Black, poor, and Southern (Headley, 1998). It would be a year before the city would take action. On July 17, 1980, Police Commissioner Lee Brown announced the formation of the Missing and Murdered Children's Task Force (Bardsley & Bell, n.d.; Headley, 1998).

An Unlikely Suspect

Wayne Bertram Williams was not a likely suspect. His parents, Homer and Faye Williams, were schoolteachers. Williams graduated from Frederick Douglass High School with honors and attended Georgia State University for one year before dropping out. Community members suspected a White person. Many also suspected that the killer would be big and scary. But others thought that the victims would not have easily been abducted by a White person in the predominantly Black areas where they disappeared. Wayne Williams was African American, short, chubby, and wore glasses at the time of his arrest. He did not appear to be the monster for which the city task force was searching. He was 23 years old and lived with his parents in a middle-class community (Associated Press, 1982a).

His Capture

For months, residents of Atlanta lived in fear of the next disappearance. On May 21, 1981, as part of the ongoing investigation, Atlanta patrolman Carl Holden and rookie police officers Bob Campbell and Freddie Jacobs were staked out at the Chattahoochee River and James Jackson Parkway Bridge in Atlanta. Around 3:00 a.m., Campbell said he heard a sudden splash and noted ripples in the water. He later said he saw the lights of a vehicle. He used his radio to ask if Officer Jacobs, who was posted on the other side of the river, had seen a vehicle. The vehicle slowly crossed the bridge and pulled into a liquor store parking lot and turned around and came back across the bridge. The team stopped the car and found Williams inside. When he exited the vehicle, one of his first comments was, "I know it's about those boys, isn't it." A flashlight, gloves, and nylon cord were seen in the back of his vehicle. After talking to him, the team let him go. The items in his car were never found or put into evidence. Two days later, the body of Nathaniel Carter was found in the river 1.2 miles downstream from the point where Williams was stopped on the bridge (Bardsley & Bell, n.d.; Mallard, 2009).

After two interrogations of Williams and a search of his home where police seized samples of his carpet, blankets, and dog hair, Wayne Williams was arrested and charged with the murder. The last victim, Jimmy Ray Payne, was pulled from the river on June 21, 1981. The grand jury charged Williams with Payne's death because they determined that the body might have been thrown into the river from the same area where they believed Carter's body was thrown in and where Williams was questioned. District Attorney Lewis Slaton connected Wayne Williams to Carter through a witness who saw the men holding hands on the night of Carter's disappearance (Bardsley & Bell, n.d.; Mallard, 2009).

Wayne Williams was convicted of the two murders primarily on fibers found on the bodies and in the hair of the victims. His unique green carpet is one of the fibers found along with hair similar to his dog, a German Shepherd named Sheba. Williams' supporters believe that because there were no fingerprints to connect him to the murders, it is possible he is not the killer (Associated Press, 1982b; Associated Press, 1982a; CNN, 2010; Weber, 2007).

In 2007, at the request of Williams' lawyers, a superior court judge ordered the testing of hairs and other evidence in the nearly 30-year-old case. While then District Attorney Paul Howard insisted that the results show that the dog hairs belonged to Williams' dog, the lab that conducted the tests reported the results as "fairly significant" but could not say conclusively that the hairs belonged to Sheba. The lab noted that the DNA sequence found in the samples occurs in about 1 in 100 dogs, based on the more than 1,200 dogs in their DNA database (Weber, 2007). Although the Fulton County task force has closed the case on the other 22 murders and has declared Williams responsible for those deaths, he has never been tried and convicted for them and it seems that some questions still remain.

The victims in the Atlanta Child Murders include Edward H. Smith, 14; Alfred James Evans, 13; Milton Harvey, 14; Yusef Bell, 9; Angel Lanier, 12; Jeffery Mathis, 10; Eric Antonio Middlebrooks, 14; Christopher Richardson, 11; La Tonya Wilson, 7; Aaron Wyche, 10; Anthony Carter, 9; Earl Lee Terrell, 11; Clifford Jones, 13; Darron Glass, 10; Charles Stephens, 12; Aaron Jackson, 9; Patrick Rogers, 16; Lubie Geter, 14; Terry Lorenzo Pue, 15; Patrick Baltazar, 11; Curtis Walker, 13; Joseph Jo-Jo Bell, 15; Timothy Hill, 13; Eddie Duncan, 21; Michael McIntosh, 23; Larry Rogers, 20; John Porter, 28; Jimmy Ray Payne, 21; William Barrett, 17, and Nathaniel Carter, 28 (Associated Press, 1982c; Bardsley & Bell, n.d.).

Teresa Francis

See also: Homicide; Wrongful Conviction

References

Associated Press. 1982a. "Evidence Allegedly Links Williams to 26 Deaths." *The Palm Beach Post,* March 1, 1982.

Associated Press. 1982b. "It's Up to the Jury Now in Atlanta Slaying Case." *Pittsburgh Press,* February 27, 1982.

Associated Press. 1982c. "Williams Compared to Hitler." *Daily Times,* February 27, 1982.

Baldwin, James. *Evidence of Things Not Seen.* New York: Henry Holt and Company, 1985.

Bambara, Toni Cade. *Those Bones Are Not My Child.* New York: Vintage Books, 2003.

Bardsley, Marilyn, and Rachel Bell. *The Atlanta Child Murders.* TruTV, n.d. http://www.trutv.com/library/crime/serial_killers/predators/williams/2.html.

CNN. "Special Coverage: The Atlanta Child Murders, Documentary with Soledad O'Brien." June 10, 2010. http://www.cnn.com/SPECIALS/2010/atlanta.child.murders/.

Headley, Bernard. *The Atlanta Youth Murders and the Politics of Race.* Carbondale: Southern Illinois University Press, 1998.

Mallard, Jack. *The Atlanta Child Murders: The Night Stalker.* Self-published, 2009.

Weber, Harry. "DA, Defense Spar over Meaning of New DNA Test on Dog Hairs in Atlanta Child Murder Case." *Associated Press,* June 26, 2007.

Wolfgang, Marvin (1924–1998)

Marvin Wolfgang was a major influence within the field of criminal justice during the time when it was emerging as a separate discipline from its roots as a subset of sociology. It was the timing of these circumstances, coupled with Wolfgang's privileged education at the University of Pennsylvania and the ensuing Civil Rights Movement, that ensured him his position of prominence in criminology and criminal justice.

Born on November 14, 1924, in Millersburg, Pennsylvania, in a rural Dutch community, Wolfgang first attended Pennsylvania State University, being the first in his family to attend college. Service in the U.S. Army during World War II interrupted his education. However, this experience introduced him to Italy, where his research endeavors and interests took him during his professional career. Once released from the army, Wolfgang continued his college education at Dickerson College in Carlisle, Pennsylvania, graduating with a bachelor of arts degree in 1948. He then pursued his studies at the University of Pennsylvania, earning a master of arts degree in 1950 and continuing on for a PhD under the tutelage of Thorsten Sellin, one of the leading criminologists at the time. Wolfgang received his PhD in 1955 and married Lenora Poden, a member of the faculty at Lehigh University, in 1957.

Wolfgang remained at the University of Pennsylvania for his entire career, which spanned 45 years, benefiting greatly from his affiliation with Thorsten Sellin. One of these benefits was serving from 1972 until 1998 as president of the American Academy of Political and Social Sciences where Sellin was the long-term editor of the academy's journal, *The Annals*; he served in this capacity from September 1929 until July 1968. Wolfgang went on to direct the Sellin Criminology Center for Studies in Criminology and Criminal Law from 1962 until his death in 1998. He also served a term as president of the American Society of Criminology and was the recipient of numerous awards.

Eventually, both Marvin Wolfgang's fame and shame centered around his doctoral dissertation research, conducted under Sellin's supervision. His secondary (ex post facto) analysis of Philadelphia's homicide data from January 1, 1948, until December 31, 1952 (published by the University of Pennsylvania Press in 1958), propelled Wolfgang onto the national scene and to prominence within the fast-growing field of criminal justice. *Patterns in Criminal Homicide,* a book based on the 588 homicide cases presented in his dissertation, made it into all the major criminal justice textbooks of the time, overshadowing other competent research including that of his mentor, Thorsten Sellin (1938), as well as the works of Frank Tannenbaum (1924), John Dollard (1949), Eleanor and Sheldon Glueck (1950), Robert E. Park (1950), Stuart Palmer (1960), Kenneth Clark (1965), Richard Quinney (1973), and Franklin Frazier (1957), to mention a few. His research based on police data and the biases within these data, coupled with the unraveling of social discontent (the Civil Rights Movement, anti–Vietnam War demonstrations), made Wolfgang a leader of the emerging conservative "law and order" movement that inadvertently demonized Blacks and other minorities, including protesting students.

Essentially, Wolfgang's homicide study (1958), along with Menachem Amir's rape study (1967), became classics within criminal justice, serving as unchallenged models of society's most serious forms of violence. Both studies came out of the criminology program at the University of Pennsylvania and involved secondary analysis of Philadelphia police data. From his data set, Wolfgang found that 621 offenders killed 588 victims, and that 26 percent of these cases (150) involved victim precipitation; he thus concluded that homicides in general are characterized by: 1) "Negro" victims; 2) "Negro" offenders; and 3) male victims primarily. Amir's data for the calendar years 1958 and 1960 concluded that Blacks are over-represented in rape statistics, both as victims and as offenders, and that extremely violent rapes usually involve Black men and White women.

Both these studies have been widely cited in criminal justice, criminology, deviance, and social problems texts, among others, with attention usually limited to their summary conclusions, and with little attention paid to the methodology or other limitations; for example, these studies were portrayed as being representative of the United States in general though the data are from limited geographic areas. A consequence of the wide dissemination of these rather unsophisticated studies that use race as a variable in explaining crime has been the creation of a general misconception about race and crime in the minds of college and university students, especially in majority-White schools, across the nation and beyond. The misconception also extends into the general public and may also be found among criminal justice personnel. Hence, Blacks are commonly associated with criminal violence such as murder and rape contributing to the rapid emergence of racial profiling. Moreover, Wolfgang's continued focus on a Black subculture of violence, a notion based on these oversimplified profiles, contributed greatly to a general fear of Blacks by Whites within American society, influencing passage of the Omnibus Crime Control and Safe Streets Act (PL 90-351) in 1968 and subsequently to the overrepresentation of Blacks in U.S. prisons and on death row (French, 1987).

The limitations of Wolfgang's dissertation data and subsequent research is that they did not attempt to control for intervening factors such as racism and prejudice within the Philadelphia Police Department at that time, or the biases of J. Edgar Hoover, as director of the FBI, who collected, compiled, and disseminated local Index Crime data in his annual Uniform Crime Report (Ginzburg, 1962). It is now common knowledge that the Uniform Crime Report data were biased and unreliable prior to 1958 and that Frank Rizzo, the chief of police of Philadelphia and later the city's mayor, engaged in and supported racialized policing practices. Ironically, Marvin Wolfgang, who strongly associated himself with the Italian school of criminology, replicated the Lombroso bias—that is, using a selective, biased data set to draw inferences about the general population.

In 1967, Wolfgang and his Italian colleague, Franco Ferracuti, put forth their work on the subculture of violence, again using Black Americans as an example of this phenomenon. This "Black subculture of violence" thesis and his homicide cohort study are the work for which Wolfgang became best known. Absent from the work was any mention of the surge of violence precipitated by law enforcement and the military (National Guard), mainly toward nonviolent protests by African Americans. Wolfgang's work remained unchallenged until the Department of Justice initiated and funded the Education Project in Criminal Justice in 1977 at the State University of New York–Albany (SUNY–A). This program was intended to develop a minority criminal justice curriculum to be used in college and university programs. Toward this end, 20 college instructors representing minority faculty from across the country were to be tutored by a select group of "major professors" from leading criminal justice programs. The major block of college instructors (16) who came to learn from the program represented the country's historically Black colleges and universities (HBCUs), while the professors represented the

SUNY–A faculty and other associates led by Marvin Wolfgang. There was a disconnect between the mostly White professors and the mostly minority college instructors that led one of the latter to describe the former as "condescending and arrogant," and led to a revolt among the minority participants.

Particularly contentious was the notion that Wolfgang and the other White professors were there to teach "the minority perspective." The program's outcome assessment stated that "the patronizing elitism of the Major Professors and their associates obviated the two-way communication necessary for a project like this to succeed. The program evaluators, the National Council of Black Lawyers, concurred with this assessment" (Wailes & Bell, 1987: 88). This project gave notice to the White-dominant, basically conservative criminal justice educators, practitioners, and organizations (the American Society of Criminology, the Academy of Criminal Justice Sciences) that the Wolfgang model was not a viable one and that it would continue to be challenged. As methods of research became more sophisticated and the pool of criminology and criminal justice researchers and legal scholars became more diverse, the early findings and interpretations of Marvin Wolfgang's research came under intense scrutiny and severe criticism. The research and its reporting were attributed with creating and perpetuating stereotypes about race and crime that helped feed unwarranted racial disproportionality in criminal justice policy and practice.

After an academic career that spanned more than four decades, Marvin Wolfgang died in 1998. Despite his early prominence in the field, one member of the 1977 Education Project in Criminal Justice, which was funded by the U.S. Department of Justice, notes that Wolfgang died without publicly acknowledging his work's negative impact on minority justice in the United States.

Laurence French

See also: Eugenics; Homicide; Inequality Theory; Institutional Racism; Sex Crimes and Race; Structural Racism and Violence; Theories of Race and Crime

References

Amir, M. "Forcible Rape." *Federal Probation* XXI (March 1967): 51–8.

Clark, K. B. *Dark Ghetto: Dilemmas of Social Power.* New York: Harper & Row, 1965.

Dollard, J. *Caste and Class in a Southern Town.* Garden City, NY: Doubleday, 1949.

Frazier, F. *Black Bourgeoisies.* New York: The Free Press, 1957.

French, L. A., special issue editor. *Minority Justice—Quarterly Journal of Ideology* 11 (1987): 1–135.

Ginzburg, R. *100 Years of Lynchings: The Shocking Record behind Today's Black Militancy.* New York: Lancer Books, 1962.

Glueck, S., and E. Glueck. *Unraveling Juvenile Delinquency.* New York: The Commonwealth Fund, 1950.

Palmer, S. H. *The Psychology of Murder.* New York: Thomas Y. Crowell, 1960.

Park, R. E. *Race and Culture.* New York: The Free Press, 1950.

Quinney, R. *Critique of Legal Order.* Boston: Little, Brown, 1973.

Sellin, T. *Conflict and Crime.* New York: Social Science Research Council, 1938.

Tannenbaum, F. *Darker Phases of the South.* New York: G.P. Putnam's Sons, 1924.

Wailes, S. N., and J. Bell. "Critique of Criminal Justice Minority Education." *Minority Justice—Quarterly Journal of Ideology* 11 (1987): 85–93.

Wolfgang, M. *Patterns in Criminal Homicide.* Philadelphia: University of Pennsylvania Press, 1958.

Wolfgang, M., and F. Ferracuti. *The Subculture of Violence.* London: Tavistock, 1967.

Wrongful Convictions

Wrongful convictions often involve multiple causes. The Innocence Project, a non-profit legal clinic closely affiliated with the Benjamin N. Cardozo School of Law, has found that the leading cause of wrongful convictions is eyewitness misidentification, a factor in 75 percent of cases. Of those cases, 40 percent involve cross-racial identifications. Other major causes of wrongful convictions are unvalidated or improper forensic science, a contributing factor in 50 percent of cases; false confessions or incriminating statements, a factor in 25 percent of cases; and the use of informants or snitches, a factor in 19 percent of cases. Other contributing factors to wrongful convictions are government misconduct, including police or prosecutorial misconduct and "bad lawyering" or "ineffective assistance of counsel."

Recommended reforms to the criminal justice system to prevent wrongful convictions address all of these areas and include changes in eyewitness identification procedures, changes in interview and interrogation processes, access to DNA testing, evidence preservation, forensic oversight, innocence commissions, and exoneree compensation.

Despite the fact that it has been well established for over 100 years that problems exist with regard to the reliability of eyewitness identification, law enforcement continues to use traditional methods of securing such evidence. The Innocence Project notes that relatively simple changes can be made that have been demonstrated to dramatically improve the reliability of eyewitness identification and decrease the 75 percent of wrongful convictions in which mistaken eyewitness identification was a factor. These system improvements include blind administration of photo arrays and live line-ups in which the officer or detective administering the line-up does not know who the suspect is; the requirements that "fillers," non-suspects participating in the photo array or live line-up, resemble the description of the suspect; that the victim or witness be instructed that the suspect may or may not be included in the line-up; that immediately following the line-up, victims or witnesses give a statement regarding their level of confidence in the identification; and that whenever possible, the line-up procedures be recorded.

Recommendations to improve forensic oversight to reduce the 50 percent of wrongful convictions due to unvalidated forensic techniques or improper forensic science include structural and procedural changes. The Innocence Project recommends the creation of a national forensic science agency to support research, assess the validity and reliability of forensic techniques, and develop and enforce quality assurance, accreditation, and certification standards for public and private laboratories. It also recommends enforcement of existing standards for those crime laboratories that receive federal funding, and the creation of state oversight commissions or advisory boards to secure adequate resources for forensic investigation.

To reduce the 25 percent of wrongful convictions due to false confessions or incriminating statements, the Innocence Project recommends the recording of all custodial interrogations in their entirety. Approximately 500 jurisdictions record interrogations at the present time. Several states mandate recording of interrogations by statute or judicial interpretation of state constitutions. Many police departments and sheriff's agencies have proactively implemented the process through policies and procedures and consider it good law enforcement.

Reforms to reduce unreliable informant or snitch testimony as a contributing factor in wrongful convictions focus on reducing the impact of their statements on jurors. To better assess the reliability of their testimony, jurors need to be aware of incentives provided to informants and jailhouse snitches. These incentives often take the form of cash, release from prison, or avoiding incarceration. The Innocence Project notes that given the powerful impact of informant/snitch testimony on jurors, additional steps to reduce the impact of unreliable testimony are necessary.

While many wrongful convictions are not intentional and instead are the result of mistakes by law enforcement, prosecutors, courts, and witnesses, others involve purposeful misconduct. Law enforcement misconduct may include impermissively suggestive identification procedures, coercing false confessions, lying or intentionally misleading jurors, and failing to turn over exculpatory evidence to prosecutors. Prosecutorial misconduct may include withholding exculpatory evidence from defense attorneys, deliberately mishandling or destroying evidence, pressuring defense witnesses not to testify, relying on fraudulent forensic experts, and making misleading arguments. The Innocence Project recommends the creation of broad-based criminal justice reform or innocence commissions to investigate the circumstances that lead to wrongful convictions and make recommendations to improve the system. At least 10 states have criminal justice reform commissions.

In order to ensure justice for the wrongfully convicted, it is necessary to preserve biological evidence and provide access to DNA testing. This is typically achieved by statute. The Innocence Project has proposed model federal and state legislation on these and other issues. Justice also requires that exonerees receive compensation for the injustices they suffered as a result of their wrongful convictions. Tragically, about half of all exonerees have not been compensated for their wrongful incarceration. The Innocence Project recommends that states pay a fixed sum for each year of incarceration plus provide health, education, job training, and related reentry benefits, plus necessary legal services.

The true extent of wrongful convictions is unknown. The Innocence Project estimates that between 2.3 percent and 5 percent of all prisoners are innocent based upon a variety of studies and points out that even if the number is only 1 percent, more than 20,000 men and women are wrongfully incarcerated. Exonerations to date tend to involve convictions for serious offenses involving lengthy periods of imprisonment, on average 13 years. It is unclear how many innocents are convicted of lesser offenses, which receive far less investigative and judicial resources from the criminal justice system.

The work of attorneys Barry Scheck and Peter Neufeld and the Innocence Project provides significant insight into the causes of wrongful convictions, workable solutions to reduce wrongful convictions, and the injustices that result from wrongful convictions. *After Innocence,* an award-winning film by Jessica Sanders and Marc Simon released in 2005, vividly depicts the severe challenges faced by exonerees in the aftermath of their release. The fact that 60 percent of those exonerated to date are African American, despite the fact that African Americans comprise approximately 12 percent of the U.S. population, provides substantial evidence of the relationship between race and involvement in the criminal justice system, even while innocent, and the need for systemic improvements.

Michael M. Berlin

See also: DNA Testing; Eyewitness Misidentification; False Confessions; Innocence Project; Racial Stereotyping and Wrongful Convictions

References

Christianson, Scott. *Innocent: Inside Wrongful Conviction Cases.* New York: New York University Press, 2004.

Dwyer, Jim. 2000. *Actual Innocence: Five Days to Execution and Other Dispatches from the Wrongfully Convicted.* New York: Doubleday.

The Innocence Network Web Site. www.innocencenetwork.org.

The Innocence Project Web Site. www.innocenceproject.org.

Simon, Taryn. *The Innocents/Photographs and Interviews.* New York: Umbrage, 2003.

Young, Jr., Cornel (1971–2000)

Cornel Young, Jr., was a 29-year-old police officer with the Providence Police Department in Rhode Island. He had served three years with the department when he was killed by fellow police officers in an apparent case of mistaken identity. On the night of January 28, 2000, Officer Young was off duty and eating at Fidas Restaurant when two female patrons began to argue. The argument escalated into a physical confrontation between the women outside the restaurant. A male friend of one of the women, Aldrin Diaz, drew a gun. Officer Young saw Diaz with the gun and went outside to confront him. In the meantime, two officers, Carlos Saraiva and Michael Solitro III, were dispatched at 1:43 a.m. to a call of a disturbance of "two girls fighting" at Fidas Restaurant. The officers were familiar with Fidas because it was a frequent trouble spot on Valley Street in Providence (*The Lowell Sun,* 2009). Accounts of what transpired after Saraiva and Solitro arrived on the scene are contested. An opinion of the U.S. Court of Appeals, First Circuit, summarizes the uncontested facts as follows:

> [T]wo on-duty Providence, Rhode Island, police officers, . . . while responding to a call, shot and killed an off-duty Providence police officer . . . who was attempting to respond to the same incident under a city policy . . . that required him to act despite being off-duty and out of uniform. The two officers, who are white, apparently mistook Cornel, an African-American, for a threat. (*Young v. City of Providence et al.,* Nos. 04-1374, 04-1390, 04-1418, April 11, 2005)

At the time of the Cornel Young, Jr., shooting, Providence police were required to carry guns while off duty and intervene when they saw an immediate threat to life or property. In other words, at the time he was shot, Officer Young was following the standard operating procedures of his department. Both Solitro and Saraiva claimed that they repeatedly ordered Young to drop his weapon, but that he refused to comply. They both claimed that they only shot Young after he pointed the gun in their direction.

Testimony in a subsequent civil trial indicated that when the two officers arrived on the scene, they saw a man outside of the restaurant running toward a Chevrolet Camaro. That man was Aldrin Diaz. Diaz got into the vehicle and began pointing a gun out of the window. According to at least one version of the trial testimony, Officer Solitro then said "gun" to Saraiva and no other words were exchanged between them until after Young had been shot. Both officers exited the patrol car and drew their guns. Saraiva took cover behind some poles while Solitro took cover behind the patrol car. According to the trial testimony, both officers yelled commands at Diaz to drop the gun and get out of the car. Diaz had dropped the gun and was starting to get out of the car by the time the officers saw Cornel Young.

Rhode Island policeman Cornel Young, Jr., was shot and killed on January 28, 2000, by two fellow officers responding to an emergency call at a Providence restaurant where, according to police, he was mistaken for a suspect. Young was off-duty and in civilian clothes at the time of the shooting. (Associated Press)

Diaz testified that he saw Cornel Young walk out of the restaurant holding his gun and heard him scream "freeze." He also testified that he thought that Young was a police officer by the tone of his voice and his body language, and by the way he held the gun. By the time Young came onto the scene, Solitro had left his position of cover and walked into the open, directly in front of the Camaro, while Saraiva remained behind the poles. Dr. James Fyfe, a distinguished professor at John Jay College of Criminal Justice, former deputy commissioner of training for the NYPD and an expert on police tactics, especially police use of force, testified that leaving cover was "inconsistent with accepted police practices" because it made Solitro more vulnerable and increased the likelihood that Saraiva would have to use deadly force to protect him.

According to Diaz, Young's gun was angled downward when the other two officers began to shoot. Apparently not recognizing Young as a fellow police officer, they fired at him six times. Young was shot once in the head and twice in the chest. According to their testimony, Saraiva fired first and Solitro fired immediately thereafter. Solitro fired the shot that hit Young in the head. Once Young was down, they discovered they had shot a fellow officer. The entire episode lasted three minutes from the time that the police arrived on the scene to the time that the ambulance was called (Jones-Brown, 2001). Officers Solitro and Saraiva were cleared of any criminal charges related to the shooting. Both the local grand jury and the U.S. Attorney General's Office failed to indict them. The incident immediately raised questions about racism. Young was Black and the two officers, Carlos Saraiva and Michael Solitro III, were Latino and White, respectively. Young was the son of the highest-ranking African American officer in the Providence Police Department, Major Cornel Young, Sr. At the time of the shooting, Solitro had only been on the job eight days, while Saraiva was a three-year veteran of the department and had been in the same police academy class with Cornel Young, Jr.

A community group, Direct Action for Rights and Equality (DARE), made claims that Saraiva and Solitro had been involved in racially motivated acts in the past (Malinowski et al., 2000). These allegations led leaders in Providence's minority community to call for an independent investigation of Young's shooting— one that would be conducted outside of the police department. A police report filed in 1989 indicated that, as a civilian, Solitro had had an altercation with an off-duty Providence police officer, Gregorio Small, who was Black. The report stated that Solitro pushed Small, then threatened him, and finally punched him in the head. Solitro pleaded "no contest" to simple assault. In 1990, his record was expunged, and therefore did not impede his hiring by the police department.

Like Solitro, Saraiva also was involved in an incident that some viewed as questionable. At 2:00 a.m. on September 18, 1999, Saraiva was working his shift alone. Providence bars had closed, and Saraiva was trying to disperse the crowd outside the 30–30 Club on Westminster Street. There was a physical confrontation between Saraiva and a man in the crowd, Rafael Nunez. When the fight was over, Saraiva had suffered injuries to his face, and Nunez, who was unarmed, had been shot twice in the legs by Saraiva (Malinowski et al., 2000). The U.S. Attorney General's Office cleared Saraiva of any wrongdoing.

Although the case did not result in criminal charges, Leisa E. Young, the mother of Cornel Young, Jr., filed a $20 million federal civil rights lawsuit against the City of Providence, the Providence chief of police, the two officers, and various police department supervisors for the death of her son (*Young v. City of Providence*, 2005). The suit accused the officers of using excessive force, and thereby violating Cornel Young, Jr.'s, constitutional and civil rights. It accused the department and its various supervisors of failing to properly train all three officers regarding off-duty/on-duty interactions under the always armed/always on-duty policy. It also accused the department of making bad hiring and disciplinary decisions regarding Saraiva and Solitro given their previous violent incidents with minority men. New York lawyers Barry C. Scheck and Nick Brustin, of the (Johnnie) Cochran, Neufeld, and Scheck firm, were the lead attorneys in the Young civil case along with Rhode Island attorney Robert Mann.

The civil trial had many twists and turns. At one point, U.S. District Court judge Mary Lisi removed the two out-of-state attorneys, Scheck and Brustin, and threatened them with sanctions. A bifurcated trial was ordered. During the first stage of that trial, Solitro but not Saraiva was found liable for violating Cornel Young's civil rights. Leisa Young claimed the police department failed to adequately train Solitro to recognize off-duty or plainclothes officers, although it was also unclear why Officer Saraiva did not recognize Young, since they had been together for weeks in the same police academy class.

At some point, a strategic decision was made to dismiss the case against the two individual officers and to focus on the hiring, training, and disciplinary issues against the police department and its trainers. Leisa Young eventually lost the lawsuit because the Providence Police Department was able to document officer training on the "off-duty" issues. It included decisionmaking training that included "shoot/don't shoot" scenarios. It also included training on an interactive firearms simulator where officers would have to give verbal commands, make decisions regarding cover, and in some cases make the ultimate decision of whether to shoot or not. An appellate court also eventually affirmed that there was insufficient evidence to prove that the department had acted with deliberate indifference by hiring or retaining Saraiva or Solitro given the previous incidents of confrontations with minority males.

While both police officers escaped criminal and civil liability for the death of Cornel Young, Jr., a decision was made to begin a prosecution against Aldrin Diaz, the original suspect with a gun. Although he dropped his weapon when ordered to by the police, Diaz was charged with murder under a felony murder statute which states that anyone committing a crime during which a person is killed is responsible for the person's death. The underlying felony in Diaz's case was assault with a deadly weapon—brandishing a gun during the fight outside the restaurant. After some protests and letters to the judge, the felony-murder charge was eventually dropped, though he was still sentenced to prison for 20 years because of a violation of his probation on previous escape and larceny of a motor vehicle charges. It is believed that his tough sentence may be due in part to the feelings of then Providence police chief Urbano Prignano, Jr., who was named in the civil suit. According to him, "It is important to point out that the responsibility for this tragic incident lies with the suspect, Aldrin Diaz, who introduced the use of a firearm into this disturbance." Others see Diaz as a scapegoat in an incident of police misconduct, racial profiling, or extremely poor judgment.

Several positive things came out of this policing tragedy. Officer Young was posthumously promoted to sergeant, and in 2001 the Providence Police Department eliminated its policy of requiring off-duty police officers to carry firearms. Several law enforcement agencies across the United States also did away with their policies requiring off-duty police officers to be armed (Suprynowicz, 2005).

Leisa Young and Cornel Young, Sr., established the Cornel Young, Jr., Scholarship Fund at the Community College of Rhode Island's (CCRI) Providence campus. Leisa Young is an adjunct professor and coordinator of counseling and advising at CCRI. The fund provides a scholarship to a deserving graduating senior from a Providence public high school (Milkovits, 2001). As an enduring testament to his memory, the Sergeant Cornel Young, Jr., Elementary School is located at 674 Prairie Avenue in Providence.

Kimberly Dodson

See also: Bell, Sean; Bumpurs, Eleanor; Diallo, Amadou: Dorismond, Patrick; Grant, Oscar; Jones, Jr., Prince; Lee, Anthony Dwain/Dwayne; Russ, Robert; Young, Jr., Cornel; Zongo, Ousmane

References

Jones-Brown, D. "Fatal Profiles: Too Many 'Tragic Mistakes,' Not Enough Justice." *New Jersey Lawyer Magazine* (February 2001): 48–53.

The Lowell Sun. "It's a Tragedy to Do Nothing." December 18, 2009.

Malinowski, Z., J. D. Rockoff, and M. Stanton. "Rookie Patrolman Struggles with Reality of Shooting Brother Officer." *The Providence Journal,* February 13, 2000. http://www.projo.com/cgi-bin/include.pl/news/young/archive/cy0213a.htm.

Milkovits, A. "Slain Officer's Haunted Parents Try to Move On." *The Providence Journal,* February 4, 2001.

Suprynowicz, V. "If a Black Man Is Armed, Is He a Criminal?" *Las Vegas Review-Journal,* December 4, 2005.

Young v. City of Providence, 396 F. Supp. 2D 125 (D.R.I. 2005).

Youth Violence

Much attention has been given to youth violence in the United States. During the 1990s, one college professor, John DiUllio of the University of Pennsylvania, predicted the coming of the "super-predators," a cohort of ruthless, unloved young urban criminals, who would engage in unthinkable acts of violence without blinking an eye. The reign of the "super-predators" never materialized. Instead, since roughly the mid 1990s, like adult crime, nationally, youth crime has substantially declined.

Juvenile violent offenders were responsible for 13 percent of violent crimes cleared by arrest in 2006 (Snyder, 2008). Over half of the arrests for these crimes were African American juvenile offenders, though they represented only 17 percent of the total juvenile population (Snyder, 2008). African American youths were arrested five times more often than White juveniles in 2006 (Snyder, 2008). Overall, male juveniles are more likely to commit acts of violence than females, with African American youth significantly more likely to report committing an assault than White or Hispanic youth (Bureau of Labor Statistics, 2002).

Rates of all youth violence, as measured by arrests, are generally lower than in previous years; however, male juvenile violent crime arrests declined by as much as 22 percent between 1997 and 2006, as compared to a 12 percent decline for females. In fact, female juveniles accounted for 29 percent of the juvenile arrests for violent crime in 2006 (Snyder, 2008). Statistics reveal that most juvenile offenders do not continue to commit crimes as adults. The National Longitudinal Survey of Youth found that most youth that had reported committing an assault in adolescence reported committing no such offenses in early adulthood. A consistent line of research documents that most adolescents who commit crimes will likely stop by middle age (Hirschi & Gottfredson, 1983).

Juvenile offenders were responsible for 8 percent of all U.S. murders in 2002, acting alone in 52 percent of them, with one or more other juveniles in 9 percent, and with one or more adults in 39 percent. In 2002, the numbers of African American and White juvenile murderers were approximately equivalent. More than three-fourths (76 percent) of the murder victims of African American juveniles are also African American, though these offenders are more likely than White murder offenders (26 percent compared with 10 percent) to commit inter-racial murder (Snyder & Sickmund, 2008).

Like rates for murder, arrests of juveniles for aggravated assault decreased between 1997 and 2006, though more for males than for females (24 percent versus 10 percent). In fact, during this time frame, female arrests for simple assault rose 19 percent, compared to a 4 percent decline for males (Snyder, 2008). The Centers for Disease Control and Prevention's Youth Risk Behavior Survey found that in 2003, 33 percent of high school students reported being in at least one physical fight in the past year, though this was a decrease from 1993, when 43 percent of high school students reported that they had been in a physical fight. Reports of fights were more common among males than females and among African American or Hispanic students than White students (Dinkes et al., 2009).

Table 1   Black Youth Violent Crime, 2010

The Majority of Serious Black Youth Violence in the United States Occurs in Cities		
Offense	Total Arrests under Age 18	Arrests in Cities
Homicide	439	365
Forcible Rape	787	654
Robbery	14,046	12,389
Agg. Assault	14,482	11,876

Source: Sourcebook of Criminal Justice Statistics Online, http:www.albany.edu/sourcebook/pdf/t4122010.pdf.

Assaults are not uncommon in or around schools. African American and Hispanic students were more likely to report fighting at school, though for all youth, a spike in rates of juvenile violence occurred immediately after school hours (from 3:00 to 4:00 p.m.) on school days. In 2003, 5 percent of high school students missed at least one school day in the prior month due to fear of violence at or around school. African American students were more than twice as likely and Hispanics were three times as likely as White students to miss school due to feeling unsafe (CDC, 2004).

In 2006, juvenile offenders were arrested for 18 percent of general sex offenses and 15 percent of all forcible rapes (Snyder, 2008). The proportion of juveniles responsible for sexual assaults increases as the age of the victim decreases; one-third of sexual assaults of female victims under the age of 14 in 2002 were committed by offenders under the age of 18 (Lauritsen, 2003; Loeber et al., 2001). Ikomi et al. (2009) found that while White juveniles are more likely to commit aggravated sexual assaults as compared with African American and Hispanic youth, African American juveniles were more likely to be referred for indecency with children involving sexual exposure.

Much research has found either a direct or indirect relationship between poverty and delinquency. Some have correlated low income in childhood with teenage violence and violent offense convictions in adulthood (Farrington, 1989), while others (Sampson, 1987) found a link between poverty and disruption of the family, a factor that influences juvenile violent crime for both Black and White youth. According to the U.S. Census Bureau, in 2002, 17 percent of juveniles were living in poverty, compared with 11 percent of those aged 18 to 64, and 10 percent of those over 64. Low income is disproportionately experienced by African American juveniles, almost one-third of whom live in poverty.

Several research studies have also linked family structure to juvenile violence. One study (McCurley & Snyder, 2007) found that youth aged 12 to 17 living with both biological parents reported fewer problem behaviors, including assault.

Seventeen-year-old youth living with both biological parents were substantially less likely to report ever being in a gang (Egley & Majors, 2006). According to the Survey of Income and Program Participation (SIPP), while 69 percent of children in the United States live with married parents, the proportions are racially unequal. Compared with 82 percent of Asian, 77 percent of White non-Hispanic, 64 percent of Hispanic, and 56 percent of American Indian children, only 35 percent of African American children live with two married parents. Children in two-parent families are also far less likely to live in poverty than children living with either parent or neither parent. In 1996, 52 percent of African American children lived with only their mothers; 38 percent of children living in single-parent households headed by a woman were in poverty. Furthermore, African American children were three times as likely as White children and twice as likely as Hispanic children to live with only their mothers (Fields, 2003).

Family may also play a role in youth violence through the modeling of violent behavior. Juveniles with friends or family members in gangs were three times more likely to report committing one or more acts of vandalism, major theft, serious assault, carrying a handgun, selling drugs, using drugs, or running away from home (Egley & Majors, 2006).

Further risk factors for youth violence are dropping out of school and youth unemployment (Snyder & Sickmund, 2008). In 2002, the unemployment rate for non-Hispanic White juveniles between the ages of 15 and 17 was 18 percent; African American juveniles had a 40 percent unemployment rate, and Hispanic juveniles had a rate of 24 percent (Bureau of Labor Statistics, 2002). The status dropout rate (the percentage of people aged 16 to 24 who are not high school graduates, students, or equivalency certificate holders) in 2000 differed substantially by race. Hispanics had the highest dropout rate at 27.8 percent, followed by African Americans at 13.1 percent, White non-Hispanics at 6.9 percent, and Asians at 3.8 percent (Kaufman et al., 2001). Juveniles who were both unemployed and no longer in school have a greater risk of drug use or selling, gang membership, committing theft or serious assault, and carrying a gun (Snyder & Sickmund, 2008).

Gang membership is also correlated with violent behavior; in one Denver study, gang members made up 14 percent of the high-risk youth sample but committed 80 percent of the serious and violent crimes. A Rochester study found similar results; while gang members were 30 percent of the sample, they committed 69 percent of the violent crimes. Even when compared with other juvenile delinquents (even those who associate with non-gang-affiliated delinquent peers), gang members are routinely found to be more criminally active (Snyder & Sickmund, 2008). According to the National Youth Gang Surveys, Hispanic youth made up 49 percent of gang members in 2004, while African American youth accounted for 37 percent, White youth 8 percent, and Asian youth 5 percent.

More than half of the Rochester sample of gang members said that they had followed friends into gangs. Nineteen percent cited protection as a major factor and 15 percent reported joining a gang for fun or excitement. Early use of marijuana, neighborhood conditions associated with readily available marijuana, and learning disabilities were associated with youth who joined gangs in a Seattle longitudinal study (Hill et al., 2001). Risk factors for long-term gang membership included early violence and acting out, and childhood association with antisocial peers.

Use of drugs has also been linked with violent behavior. According to the 2006 National Survey on Drug Use and Health Report, Youth Violence and Illicit Drug Use, juveniles aged 12 to 17 who had used at least one illegal drug in the previous 12 months were nearly twice as likely to have participated in violent behavior compared with non-drug users. The more illicit drugs that were used in the past year, the greater the likelihood was of violent behavior.

Justice system responses to youth behavior may also play a role in juvenile violence. An OJJDP report found that transfers of youth to adult court increased recidivism, most often in violent offenders, possibly acting as an antecedent to persistent, long-term criminal careers (Redding, 2008; Sherman et al., 1997). A long line of research has documented that African American youth are disproportionately transferred to adult court and stand at a greater risk of such transfer than do their White counterparts.

Nicole Hanson with Delores Jones-Brown

See also: Gangs; Hip-Hop Culture; Homicide; Sex Crimes and Race

References

Bureau of Labor Statistics, U.S. Department of Labor. *National Longitudinal Survey of Youth 1997 Cohort, 1997–2001 (Rounds 1–5)* [machine-readable data file]. Chicago, IL: National Opinion Research Center, University of Chicago (producer); Columbus, OH: Center for Human Resource Research, Ohio State University (distributor), 2002.

Centers for Disease Control and Prevention (CDC). "Youth Risk Behavior Surveillance—United States, 2003." *Morbidity and Mortality Weekly Report* 53(SS–2), 2004.

Dinkes, R., J. Kemp, and K. Baum. *Indicators of School Crime and Safety: 2008* (NCES 2009–022/ NCJ 226343). National Center for Education Statistics, Institute of Education Sciences, U.S. Department of Education, and Bureau of Justice Statistics, Office of Justice Programs, U.S. Department of Justice. Washington, DC, 2009.

Egley, A., and A. Majors. *Highlights of the 2004 National Youth Gang Survey. OJJDP Fact Sheet (#01).* Washington, DC: U.S. Department of Justice, Office of Justice Programs, Office of Juvenile Justice and Delinquency Prevention, 2006.

Farrington, D. "Early Predictors of Adolescent Violence and Adult Violence." *Violence and Victims* 4 (1989).

Fields, J. "Children's Living Arrangements and Characteristics: March 2002." *Current Population Reports*, P20–547. Washington, DC: U.S. Census Bureau, 2003.

Fields, J. "Living Arrangements of Children: Fall 1996." *Current Population Reports*, P70–74. Washington, DC: U.S. Census Bureau, 2001.

Hill, K., C. Lui, and J. Hawkins. "Early Precursors of Gang Membership: A Study of Seattle Youth." *OJJDP Juvenile Justice Bulletin*. Washington, DC: U.S. Department of Justice, Office of Justice Programs, Office of Juvenile Justice and Delinquency Prevention, 2001.

Hirschi, Travis, and Michael Gottfredson. "Age and the Explanation of Crime." *American Journal of Sociology* 89 (1983): 552–84.

Ikomi, Philip A., H. Elaine Rodney, and Tana McCoy. "Male Juveniles with Sexual Behavior Problems: Are There Differences among Racial Groups?" *Journal of Child Sexual Abuse* 18, no. 2 (2009): 154–73.

Kaufman, P., M. Alt, and C. Chapman. *Dropout Rates in the United States: 2000*. Washington, DC: National Center for Education Statistics, 2001.

Lauritsen, J. "How Families and Communities Influence Youth Victimization." *OJJDP Juvenile Justice Bulletin*. Washington, DC: U.S. Department of Justice, Office of Justice Programs, Office of Juvenile Justice and Delinquency Prevention, 2003.

Loeber, R., L. Kalb, and D. Huizinga. "Juvenile Delinquency and Serious Injury Victimization." *OJJDP Juvenile Justice Bulletin*. Washington, DC: U.S. Department of Justice, Office of Justice Programs, Office of Juvenile Justice and Delinquency Prevention, 2001.

McCurley, C., and H. Snyder. "Risk, Protection, and Family Structure." *OJJDP Juvenile Justice Bulletin*. Washington, DC: U.S. Department of Justice, Office of Justice Programs, Office of Juvenile Justice and Delinquency Prevention, 2007.

Redding, R. "Juvenile Transfer Laws: An Effective Deterrent to Delinquency?" *OJJDP Juvenile Justice Bulletin*, Washington, D.C.: U.S. Department of Justice, Office of Justice Programs, Office of Juvenile Justice and Delinquency Prevention, 2008.

Sampson, R. J. "Urban Black Violence: The Effect of Male Joblessness and Family Disruption." *American Journal of Sociology* 93, no. 2 (September 1987): 348–82.

Sherman, L., D. Gottfredson, D. MacKenzie, J. Eck, P. Reuter, and S. Bushway. *Preventing Crime: What Works, What Doesn't, What's Promising. Report to the U.S. Congress*. Washington, DC: U.S. Department of Justice, 1997.

Snyder, H. N. *Juvenile Arrests 2006*. Washington, DC: U.S. Department of Justice, Office of Justice Programs, Office of Juvenile Justice and Delinquency Prevention, 2008.

Snyder, Howard N., and Melissa Sickmund. *Juvenile Offenders and Victims: 2006 National Report*. Washington, DC: U.S. Department of Justice, Office of Justice Programs, Office of Juvenile Justice and Delinquency Prevention, 2006.

Z

Zebratown

"Zebratown" is the name that some locals have given to a section of the east side of Elmira, New York, where the inhabitants are primarily inter-racial families made up of local White females and their children, and African American males who previously resided in New York City, and who choose to remain in semi-rural Elmira once they are released from state prison. Elmira Correctional Facility, also known as "The Hill," overlooks downtown and has been a fixture in the city since 1876, when it opened as the first reformatory in the United States.

The term also appears in the title of a book authored by John Jay College professor Greg Donaldson in which he chronicles the formation and experiences of one of these couples. *Zebratown: The True Story of a Black Ex-Con and a White Single Mother in Smalltown America* (Scribner, 2010) follows the lives of Kevin Davis, a former Elmira inmate, originally from the Brownsville section of Brooklyn, and his live-in girlfriend Karen, who is the mother of one daughter. Eight years in the making, the book is an in-depth account that follows an African American felon's attempt to find a new life for himself with a White woman in a small-town neighborhood, where—as the book's title implies—such relationships are common.

Davis has survived on the streets and in prison with a sharp intellect and a rigid code of practical morality and physical fitness, while yearning to make a better life for himself. The book follows Davis as he relocates from Brooklyn to Elmira and tries to put a life of crime behind him and reinvent himself as a working man, husband, and father.

Relationships between White women and Black men have long been an inflammatory issue in American culture. Even years after the 2008 presidential election, when society was expected to have moved to a "postracial" perspective, people still have a lot to say about inter-racial relationships. *Zebratown* takes the reader into the heart of one such relationship and offers the paradoxical truth that while race is rarely not an issue in such unions, in the end, what transpires between a couple is intensely individual.

While there are not yet census figures to support the popular belief among Elmira residents that former inmates from New York City have chosen to stay in the area and that they are sometimes joined by relatives and friends, there is visible confirmation that some number of formerly incarcerated Black men have fathered children with local White women.

Economic decline in this, the so-called "Rustbelt," has had an effect on demographic changes and, although Elmira does not present the safety challenges of living in an urban center like New York City, wholesale factory closings have made it difficult for Kevin and others like him to find legal employment. Successfully reentering society is an ongoing problem for former inmates no matter where they live. Kevin Davis confronts not only his criminal record and his poor formal education but also the cruelties of the postindustrial economy. His story is a rare source of information about the personal struggles behind prisoner reentry in the first decade of the twenty-first century.

In *Zebratown,* Donaldson explores a largely hidden world. Month by month, Donaldson follows Kevin's and Karen's attempt to make a home together. Because his is a factual story, Kevin Davis is repeatedly stymied not only by economic and social factors, but also by the ways he views the world. Even in Elmira, the dangerous lures of the streets remain for him and he is not always successful at avoiding them. In the view of his new neighbors, Kevin is the embodiment of hip-hop gangsterism—a heavily muscled, feared thug who has beaten a murder rap.

The change in demographics has led some Elmira residents to believe that the urban newcomers are responsible for recent reported spikes in crime. The idea that recent African American transplants are responsible for the spike in crime overlooks the fact that Elmira has been home to a significant African American population since the days when the city was a stop on the Underground Railroad in the years leading up to the Civil War. Elmira's favorite son is football player Ernie Davis, "The Elmira Express," who was the first African American to win the Heisman Trophy in 1961 for his exploits as a running back for Syracuse University.

In writing *Zebratown,* in addition to spending long periods of time with Kevin and Karen, Donaldson used prison diaries, letters, and lengthy first-person accounts. He interviewed policemen, judges, family members, and others in Kevin and Karen's orbit, providing a panoramic account of their lives. *Kirkus Reviews* called *Zebratown* "grim, poignant and illuminating."

Greg Donaldson

Reference

Donaldson, Greg. *Zebratown: The True Story of a Black Ex-Con and a White Single Mother in Smalltown America.* New York: Scribner's, 2010.

Zongo, Ousmane (1960–2003)

Ousmane Zongo was an unarmed immigrant art restorer who was shot and killed by plain-clothed New York City police officer Bryan A. Conroy during a raid on the third floor of Chelsea Mini-Storage Warehouse on May 22, 2003. His case represents one of the rare occasions on which a sworn police officer has been convicted for the death of a civilian during the course of his police work.

In the incident with Officer Conroy and Ousmane Zongo, the New York City Police Department (NYPD), investigating a CD and DVD counterfeiting operation, had targeted the Manhattan location to arrest two suspects for piracy. Zongo, a 43-year-old native of the West African nation of Burkina Faso, repaired art and musical instruments at the storage facility. He was not connected to any of its illegal activities, as the NYPD later admitted. Officer Conroy, who was White and in his mid-twenties, was guarding a cache of counterfeit compact discs alone when Mr. Zongo emerged from a dark corridor to turn on a light. This led to a brief chase that ended when Zongo ran into a dead end, and where Conroy shot him four times, twice in the back. Prosecutors contended that Morre-speaking Zongo, who could not understand English well, ran from the undercover police officer because he was frightened and confused when Conroy, disguised in a postal worker's uniform, pulled out his gun. At the time of the shooting, Conroy had been on the police force for two and a half years.

Conroy was tried twice for the shooting. The first case was declared a mistrial, when two members of the jury refused to vote to convict. The jurors who were in favor of conviction questioned Conroy's claim that Zongo, a married father of two, had twice attempted to take his service weapon, especially in light of contradictory forensic evidence. After an appeals court refused to move the second trial out of New York City, Conroy's lawyer asked that the trial be held without a jury. In October 2005, New York supreme justice Robert H. Straus convicted Conroy of criminally negligent homicide and later sentenced him to five years of probation and 500 hours of community service. Conroy unsuccessfully appealed his conviction and sentence and was fired from the police department.

In delivering his verdict, Justice Straus criticized the NYPD's insufficient training and sloppy supervision of the shooter and the disorganized manner in which the raid was conducted. He cited the fact that the officers involved did not know how to find their way around the building (which had a staircase that was inaccessible on Conroy's floor and some nonfunctioning elevators). He also noted that the officers on the scene were not quick to offer the victim assistance when they did reach him. He also criticized Conroy's attempt to paint his unarmed victim as a savage who illogically lunged at and struggled with him for his revolver.

This rare conviction was preceded by another in 1998, in which officer Francis X. Livoti (with 11 abuse-of-force complaints in his decade and a half with the NYPD) was found guilty of taking the life of asthmatic civilian Anthony Ramon Baez, whom he reportedly put in a choke hold, a practice that had been banned by the NYPD. In New York State court, Livoti was indicted by a grand jury for second-degree manslaughter but was acquitted in a bench trial by Judge Gerald Sheindlin. He was subsequently indicted by a federal grand jury and was found guilty of violating Anthony Baez's civil rights and was sentenced to seven and a half years in federal prison. Livoti was released from prison in 2005 and began making a living as a wedding singer.

Ousmane Zongo's widow, Salimata Sanfo, and their two young children still reside in Burkina Faso, where he was buried. After two years of litigation, they were awarded a $3 million settlement in a civil suit against the city of New York.

Rhodine Moreau

See also: Bell, Sean; Diallo, Amadou; Grant, Oscar; Jones, Jr., Prince; Lee, Anthony Dwain/Dwayne; Racial Profiling; Russ, Robert; Young, Jr., Cornel

References

Boyd, Herb. "African Craftsman Slain by Police." *New York Amsterdam News,* June 4, 2003.

Brick, Michael, and Nicholas Confessore. "Suit Is Settled in 2003 Killing of Immigrant." *The New York Times,* July 21, 2006.

Brick, Michael, and Nicholas Confessore. "$3 Million Settlement Killing of Immigrant in 2003 Police Raid." *The New York Times,* July 21, 2006.

Gendar, Alison, and Barbara Ross. "No Jail For Zongo-Kill Cop." *New York Daily News,* December 10, 2005.

Hartocollis, Anemona. "Former Officer Gets Probation in Homicide." *The New York Times,* December 10, 2005.

Hartocollis, Anemona. "Officer Guilty of Negligence in '03 Killing." *The New York Times,* October 22, 2005.

Hays, Elizabeth." City Awards Zongo's Kin $3m in Slay." *New York Daily News,* July 21, 2006.

Jacobs, Andrew. "Judge to Retry Police Officer in '03 Killing of Immigrant." *The New York Times,* September 13, 2005.

Levitt, Leonard. "Ray Kelly: No Wind of Change." *NYPD Confidential*, June 2, 2008
. http://NYPDconfidential.com/columns/2008/080602.html.

The People of the State of New York, Respondent, v. Bryan Conroy, Appellant. 52 A.D.3d
320 (2008) 858 N.Y.S.2d 606.

Ross, Barbara, and Corky Siemaszko. "Cop Guilty in Slay of Zongo, but Beats Manslaughter
Rap in Immigrant's '03 Shooting." *New York Daily News,* October 22, 2005.

Santos, Fernanda. "Retrial Begins for Officer in Killing." *The New York Times,* September
27, 2005.

Contributors

Sara Attarchi
Curry College

Jennifer Balboni
Curry College

Nishaun Battle
Howard University

Allana Beddoe
John Jay College of Criminal Justice

Walter Berbrick
U.S. Naval War College

Michael M. Berlin
Coppin State University

Robert Bing
University of Texas–Arlington

Carol F. Black
Newberry College

Stephanie Boddie
Independent Scholar

James Michael Botts
Arkansas State University

Ruby Bouie
Independent Scholar

Jessica Melain Boyd
John Jay College of Criminal Justice

Jeremy Braithwaite
University of California, Irvine

Nicole Branch
Howard University

Hank Brightman
U.S. Naval War College

Avi Brisman
Emory University

Clifton Brown
Independent Scholar

Cherise Bruce
John Jay College of Criminal Justice

Robert C. Butler
Lane College

Elsa Chen
Santa Clara University

Giovanni Circo
Illinois State University

Rochelle Cobbs
Mississippi Valley State University

Nigel Cohen
Independent Scholar

Brian Coleman
Rutgers University

Angela West Crews
Marshall University

Gordon Crews
Marshall University

Marika Dawkins
Prairie View A&M University

John DeCarlo
John Jay College of Criminal Justice

Ashley Derome
Curry College

Kimberly Dodson
Western Illinois University

Greg Donaldson
John Jay College of Criminal Justice

Peter Donna
John Jay College of Criminal Justice

O. Oko Elechi
Prairie View A&M University

Beth Ellefson
University of Cincinnati

Traqina Q. Emeka
University of Houston

Cory Feldman
John Jay College of Criminal Justice

Teresa Francis
Central Washington University

Dezarai Frank
Prairie View A&M University

Robert Franklin
Morehouse College

Andrew Franz
University of Pittsburg

Laurence French
University of New Hampshire

Daniel Georges-Abeyie
Texas Southern University

Camille Gibson
Prairie View A&M University

Lior Gideon
John Jay College of Criminal Justice

Katherine Grady
Illinois State University

Mia Green
Bridgewater State University

Anne Gregory
John Jay College of Criminal Justice

Johnnie Griffin
Jackson State University

Robert Hanser
University of Louisiana–Monroe

Nicole Hanson
John Jay College of Criminal Justice

Eric M. Heiple
Southern Illinois University

Nicole Hendrix
Radford University

Zelma W. Henriques
John Jay College of Criminal Justice

Rebecca Hill
John Jay College of Criminal Justice

Richard Hough
University of West Florida

Tarra Jackson
John Jay College of Criminal Justice

Fabiel Jean-Philippe
University of Pennsylvania

Casey Jordan
Western Connecticut State University

Sesha Kethineni
Illinois State University

Kwando M. Kinshasa
John Jay College of Criminal Justice

Jennifer Lanterman
University of South Florida

Matthew Leone
University of Nevada

Ladel Lewis
Western Michigan University

Jamie Longazel
University of Dayton

Robert Louden
Georgian Court University

Marc Balcells Magrans
John Jay College of Criminal Justice

Tana McCoy
Roosevelt University

Rob McCusker
University of Teesside

Sylvia Mignon
University of Massachusetts–Boston

David Montague
University of Arkansas–Little Rock

Rhodine Moreau
New York State Insurance Fund

Roz Myers
John Jay College of Criminal Justice

Jamie Newsome
University of Cincinnati

Lorie A. L. Nicholas
John Jay College of Criminal Justice

Shannon O'Brien
University of Houston

Joseph Pascarella
St. Johns College

Luise Pedroso-Kipler
John Jay College of Criminal Justice

Everette Penn
University of Houston

Natalie Petit
Curry College

Doshie Piper
Prairie View A&M University

Michael Puniskis
Middlesex University

John David Reitzel
Virginia Commonwealth University

Frank Anthony Rodriguez
Prairie View A&M University

Lorie Rubenser
Sul Ross State University

Manouska Saint Gilles
John Jay College of Criminal Justice

Patti Ross Salinas
Missouri State University

Edward J. Schauer
Prairie View A&M University

Daniel Scott
University of California–Irvine

Beau Shine
University of Cincinnati

Valerie Stackman
University of Pikeville

Daniel Stageman
John Jay College of Criminal Justice

La-Shawn Stewart
Slippery Rock University of Pennsylvania

John Stogner
University of Florida

Tracy Tamborra
University of New Haven

Anastasia Teper
Good Shepherd Services

Alice Thomas
Howard University

Michael Thompson
University of Sioux Falls

Jennifer Trombley
Prairie View A&M University

Harold Dean Trulear
Independent Scholar

Deidre Tyler
Salt Lake City Community College

Mathew Vairamon
Texas Southern University

Philip Verrecchia
York College of Pennsylvania

Brenda Vollman
Loyola University

Benjamin Wilbur
John Jay College of Criminal Justice

Francis M. Williams
Plymouth State University

Bonnie Wu
Wayne State University

Angela Yarbrough
John Jay College of Criminal Justice

Ashley York-Kurtz
John Jay College of Criminal Justice

Marvin Zalman
Wayne State University

Index

Note: Page numbers in **bold** indicate main entries in the encyclopedia.

About the Editors

DELORES JONES-BROWN, JD, PhD, is a professor in the Department of Law, Police Science and Criminal Justice Administration at John Jay College of Criminal Justice, City University of New York. She is the founding director of the Center on Race, Crime and Justice and author of *Race, Crime and Punishment,* which won a New York Public Library award in 2001.

BEVERLY D. FRAZIER, PhD, is an assistant professor in the Department of Law, Police Science and Criminal Justice Administration at John Jay College of Criminal Justice, City University of New York. Her research interests include prisoner reentry and faith-based initiatives in criminal justice administration.

MARVIE BROOKS, MA, is retired from the City University of New York library system after 50 years of service. Her most recent research explores the rise of African American women within the ranks of criminal justice agencies.

- In an *RLC* series network, the angular frequency that yields a maximum capacitor voltage is given by

$$\omega_{mC} = \sqrt{\frac{1}{LC} - \frac{1}{2}\left(\frac{R}{L}\right)^2}$$

and the maximum capacitor voltage will be

$$\frac{V_C}{V} = \frac{Q_{so}}{\sqrt{1 - \frac{1}{4}(1/Q_{so})^2}}$$

- In *RLC* parallel and series networks with quality factor Q_o, the bandwidth between the two half-power frequencies

$$\omega_2 = \omega_o\left[\sqrt{1 + \left(\frac{1}{2Q_o}\right)^2} + \frac{1}{2Q_o}\right] \quad \text{and} \quad \omega_1 = \omega_o\left[\sqrt{1 + \left(\frac{1}{2Q_o}\right)^2} - \frac{1}{2Q_o}\right]$$

is

$$\beta = \omega_2 - \omega_1$$

- The bandwidth is related to the quality factor and the resonance frequency

$$\beta = \frac{\omega_o}{Q_o} \quad \text{and} \quad Q_o = \frac{\omega_o}{\beta}$$

- The resonance angular frequency is the geometric mean between the two half-power frequencies:

$$\omega_o = \sqrt{\omega_1 \omega_2}$$

Additional Readings

Blackwell, W.A., and L.L. Grigsby. *Introductory Network Theory*. Boston: PWS Engineering, 1985, pp. 366–372.

Bobrow, L.S. *Elementary Linear Circuit Analysis*. 2d ed. New York: Holt, Rinehart and Winston, 1987, pp. 27–40, 160–172, 456–471.

Del Toro, V. *Engineering Circuits*. Englewood Cliffs, N.J.: Prentice Hall, 1987, pp. 224–233.

Dorf, R.C. *Introduction to Electric Circuits*. New York: Wiley, 1989, pp. 469–476.

Hayt, W.H., Jr., and J.E. Kemmerly. *Engineering Circuit Analysis*. 4th ed. New York: McGraw-Hill, 1986, pp. 374–398.

Irwin, J.D. *Basic Engineering Circuit Analysis*. 3rd ed. New York: Macmillan, 1989, pp. 616–637.

Johnson, D.E., J.L. Hilburn, and J.R. Johnson. *Basic Electric Circuit Analyis*. 4th ed Englewood Cliffs, N.J.: Prentice-Hall; 1989, pp. 489–494.

Karni, S. *Applied Circuit Analysis*. New York: Wiley, 1988, pp. 306–318.

Madhu, S. *Linear Circuit Analysis*. Englewood Cliffs, N.J.: Prentice-Hall, 1988, pp. 528–565.

Nilsson, J.W. *Electric Circuits*. 3d ed. Reading, Mass: Addison-Wesley, 1990, pp. 493–526.

Paul, C.R. *Analysis of Linear Circuits*. New York: McGraw-Hill, 1989, pp. 369–379.

PROBLEMS   CHAPTER 13

Section 13.3

13.1 Find the resonance frequency for the network of Fig. P13.1.

Figure P13.1

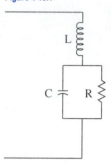

13.2 Find the resonance frequency for the network of Fig. P13.2.

Figure P13.2

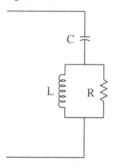

13.3 Find the resonance frequency for the network of Fig. P13.3.

Figure P13.3

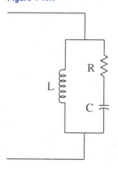

13.4 In Fig. P13.1, if $L = 2$ mH and $C = 10$ nF, what value of R will produce a resonance angular frequency of $\omega_o = 200{,}000$ rad/s?

13.5 What value of L in the tank circuit of Fig. P13.1 will produce a resonance frequency of 1239 rad/s if $C = 7.5 \ \mu$F and $R = 15 \ \Omega$?

13.6 For the phasor domain network in Fig. P13.4, what impedance should be placed across terminals a–b to cause the network to be in resonance?

Figure P13.4

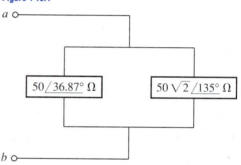

13.7 For the phasor domain network in Fig. P13.5, what impedance should be placed across terminals a–b to cause the network to be in resonance?

Figure P13.5

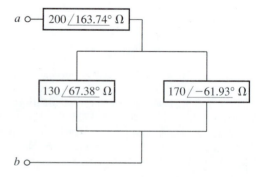

13.8 For the phasor domain network in Fig. P13.6, what impedance should be placed across terminals a–b to cause the network to be in resonance?

Figure P13.6

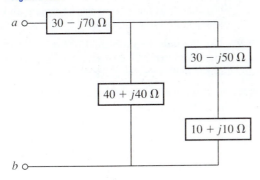

$a \circ$ — $30 - j70 \ \Omega$

$30 - j50 \ \Omega$

$40 + j40 \ \Omega$

$10 + j10 \ \Omega$

$b \circ$

13.9 A 120-V, 100-Hz source supplies a series network consisting of a capacitor with reactance $X_C = 2 \ \Omega$, a 2-Ω resistor, and a coil with $X_L = 2.5 \ \Omega$. Find the input impedance, the current drawn, the voltage across the coil, and the adjustment in frequency that is necessary to cause the network to be in resonance.

Section 13.5

13.10 A 120 V source supplies a series network and is in resonance at 8 MHz. It contains a coil of 50 μH and a 10-Ω resistor. Find the value of the capacitor, the voltage across the capacitor, the impedance of the network, and the impedance of the network when $f = 8.02$ MHz.

13.11 In a parallel resonance network with $L = 150$ mH and $Q_{po} = 100$, the resonance frequency is 1 MHz. Find R, C, and Z at resonance and the impedance if Q_{po} is changed to 80 by the addition of more resistance.

13.12 If Q_{po} of a parallel network is to be 2, find the values of R, L, and C to make the network impedance $Z = 4000 + j0 \ \Omega$ at a frequency of 1.6 MHz.

13.13 A signal generator provides a constant current of 20 mA at all frequencies to a parallel RLC network where $C = 25$ nF and the network resonates at $\omega_o = 2$ Mrad/s. If $Q_{po} = 8$, find R, L, the frequency at which the inductor current is a maximum, and the value of this maximum inductor current.

13.14 In a series RLC network with $R = 100 \ \Omega$, the current drawn by the network from a 120-V source achieves its maximum value at $\omega_o = 4000$ rad/s. Under this circumstance, $V_C = 1920$ V. Find ω_o, Q_{so}, L, and C.

13.15 In a series RLC network, the Q of the coil is 40 at $\omega = 5000$ rad/s. When the capacitance in the network is set at 1 μF, the network is observed

to draw maximum power from a 60-V variable-frequency source at an angular frequency of 2500 rad/s. Find L, the resistance associated with L, and assuming that the capacitor is lossless, the additional lumped resistance in the network.

13.16 An RLC parallel network is driven by a current source and draws maximum power of 800 mW when $\omega = 20,000$ rad/s and the magnitude of the current through the inductor is 1.6 A. If $R = 80 \ \Omega$, find ω_o, Q_{po}, L, C, the magnitude of the current source, the frequency at which maximum inductor current occurs, and the magnitude of this maximum inductor current.

Section 13.6

13.17 A coil is used with a 500-pF capacitor to form a series network that is resonant at 500,000 Hz. If the power supplied by an ideal generator (no internal impedance) at 490,000 Hz is half that supplied at the resonance frequency, what are the values of R, L, Q_{so} and β?

13.18 A coil of 100 μH is in series with a capacitor and resistor with $R = 10 \ \Omega$. The network is resonant at 250 Mrad/s and is connected to a generator with zero impedance. The generator delivers 10 V at the resonance frequency. Find the voltage across the capacitor, the value of C, the network bandwidth, and the upper and lower half-power frequencies.

13.19 A coil with a resistance of 2 Ω and an inductance of 80 mH is connected in series with a capacitor of 80 pF a resistor of 8 Ω and a signal generator that provides 120 V at all frequencies. What are ω_o, Q_{so}, β, V_C/V at resonance, the maximum value of V_o, and the frequency where this maximum value occurs?

13.20 The bandwidth of a series resonant network is 100 rad/s, and the resonance frequency is 80,000 rad/s. If the network resistance is 20 Ω, find L, C, and the upper and lower half-power frequencies.

13.21 A 20-nF capacitor is connected in series with a coil of 1 mH and a resistor of 4 Ω. What are the resonance frequency, the bandwidth, and the upper and lower half-power frequencies?

13.22 Using an inductor with $L = 0.25$ mH and a Q of 100 at a frequency of 250,000 rad/s, design an RLC series network to have a bandwidth of 8000 rad/s with a resonance frequency of 400,000 rad/s.

13.23 A voltage generator provides power to an RLC series network, and a power of 2.56 W is measured by a wattmeter. One-half of maximum power is measured at angular frequencies of 96,000 and 104,000 rad/s. If the magnitude of the voltage source at all frequencies is 16 V, find ω_o, R, L, C, and the network quality factor, Q_{so}.

13.24 An RLC parallel network contains an inductor that has a value $L = 0.625$ mH and has a Q of 100 at a frequency $\omega_o = 500{,}000$ rad/s. What are the values of R and C, what are the half-power frequencies, what is the bandwidth, and what voltage appears across the network if the current source has a magnitude of 50 mA?

13.25 In the parallel RLC network shown in Fig. P13.7, the voltmeter (designated by V) reads a maximum of 50 V at an angular frequency of 800,000 rad/s. At this frequency, the wattmeter (designated by W) reads 2 W; and the ammeter (designated by A) reads 1.25 A. Find ω_o, R, L, C, Q_o, β, the two half-power frequencies, and the magnitude of the current source.

13.26 Use the data in Problem 13.18 to evaluate the impedance at the resonance frequency and the lower half-power frequency.

13.27 Use the data in Problem 13.19 to evaluate the impedance at the resonance frequency and the upper half-power frequency.

13.28 Use the data in Problem 13.20 to evaluate the impedance at the resonance frequency and the lower half-power frequency.

13.29 Use the data in Problem 13.21 to evaluate the impedance at the resonance frequency and the upper half-power frequency.

13.30 Use the data in Problem 13.24 to evaluate the impedance at the resonance frequency and the lower half-power frequency.

13.31 Use the data in Problem 13.25 to evaluate the impedance at the resonance frequency and the lower half-power frequency.

Figure P13.7

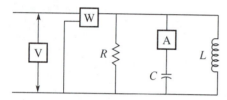

MUTUAL INDUCTANCE AND TRANSFORMERS

14

OBJECTIVES

The objectives of this chapter are to:

- Introduce the subject of mutual inductance and describe mutual coupling.

- Show how the physical orientation of the coils is handled in a network diagram by means of *the dot convention*.

- Provide a derivation of the *coefficient of coupling*, and show how mesh analysis may be conducted when mutual inductance is present.

- Discuss the transformer, the turns ratio, and the relationship between *primary* and *secondary* voltages and currents.

- Consider three transformer models, show how their equivalent networks are constructed, and provide relationships for the evaluation of their performance.

- Develop relationships for impedance transformation.

INTRODUCTION

SECTION 14.1

In Section 1.3, it was observed that a magnetic field can be produced by the flow of charge or a current. If a time-varying current flows through a coil of inductance L_1, the time-varying magnetic flux induces a voltage in accordance with Faraday's law (Section 1.8). If a portion of the time-varying flux produced in the inductor L_1 also links the turns of another coil of inductance L_2, a voltage will be induced across the terminals of L_2. When two or more coils are linked by a common or *mutual magnetic field*, a condition known as *mutual inductance* exists, and the network is referred to as a *magnetically coupled network*.

Transformers are electric devices that exploit this phenomenon. They may be used in a variety of applications. Perhaps the most important application is in the adjustment of the amplitude of sinusoidal voltages and currents. This has a tremendous advantage in the transmission of electric power. Transformers are also frequently employed in electronic circuits. This chapter introduces the subject of mutual inductance, explores some of the theory concerning the modeling and analysis of transformers, and concludes with a discussion of impedance transformation.

SECTION 14.2   **MUTUAL INDUCTANCE**

It can be observed that a changing magnetic field produced by a nonsteady current can induce a voltage across a coil. These observations lead to the concept of magnetic flux linkages,

$$\lambda = n\phi \tag{1.14}$$

and because in a linear inductive element, the flux is directly proportional to the current flow, so is the number of flux linkages:

$$\lambda = Li$$

Here, the proportionality constant L is the inductance. Faraday's law relates the generation of induced voltage with the rate of change of flux linkages,

$$v = \frac{d\lambda}{dt} \tag{1.38}$$

and with $\lambda = Li$, the elemental equation for the inductor is obtained:

$$v = L\frac{di}{dt} \tag{1.24}$$

If two inductors or coils are in proximity, the flux linkages created by the changing flow of current in one may induce a voltage in the other. For example, in Fig. 14.1, there is a component of voltage v_1 due to the current i_1,

$$v_{11} = L_1\frac{di_1}{dt}$$

and because of the flux linkages set up by the current i_2, there will be an additional component of voltage in coil 1:

$$v_{12} = M_{12}\frac{di_2}{dt}$$

Because the network elements are linear, superposition indicates that the total voltage across coil 1 will be

$$v_1 = v_{11} + v_{12} = L_1\frac{di_1}{dt} \pm M_{12}\frac{di_2}{dt} \tag{14.1}$$

where the plus or minus depends upon the physical coil orientations. An identical thought process will yield an expression for the voltage across coil 2:

$$v_2 = v_{22} + v_{21} = L_2\frac{di_2}{dt} \pm M_{21}\frac{di_1}{dt} \tag{14.2}$$

The parameters M_{12} and M_{21} are known as *mutual inductances* and they bear the units of inductance, or henrys. In the following subsections, it will be shown that $M_{12} = M_{21} = M$, and the choice of the plus or minus sign will be considered.

14.2.1 Mutual Coupling

Refer again to Fig. 14.1, and imagine that the two coils are oriented such that a plus sign may be used for the mutual terms in eqs. (14.1) and (14.2). Let a current i_1 begin to flow in coil 1 from a zero value at $t = 0$, and let it reach a value I_1 at $t = t_1$. If $i_2 = 0$ over this interval, then eq. (1.35) dealing with the energy stored in an inductor,

$$w = \frac{1}{2} L(i_1^2 - i_o^2) \tag{1.35}$$

can be applied with $i_o = 0$ and $i_1 = I_1$ to give

$$w_1 = \frac{1}{2} L_1 I_1^2$$

Here, there is no contribution to the energy stored in coil 1 by the current in coil 2, and there is no energy stored in coil 2 because $i_2 = 0$.

Now if i_1 is held at I_1 and i_2 is allowed to increase from its zero value at $t = t_1$ to a value $i_2 = I_2$ at $t = t_2$, then over the interval from t_1 to t_2, coil 2 will store energy

$$w_2 = \frac{1}{2} L_2 I_2^2$$

But coil 2 also delivers energy to coil 1 during the interval from t_1 to t_2,

$$w_{12} = \int_{t_1}^{t_2} v_{12} i_1 \, dz = \int_{t_1}^{t_2} M_{12} \frac{di_2}{dz} i_1 \, dz = \int_0^{I_2} M_{12} i_1 \, di_2$$

However, $i_1 = I_1$ over the interval and M_{12} is a constant, so that

$$w_{12} = M_{12} I_1 I_2$$

Two inductors (coils) in close proximity

FIGURE 14.1

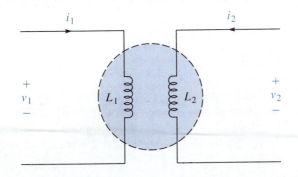

and the total energy stored in the two coils over the entire interval from $t = 0$ to $t = t_2$ will be

$$w_a = w_1 + w_2 + w_{12} = \frac{1}{2} L_1 I_1^2 + \frac{1}{2} L_2 I_2^2 + M_{12} I_1 I_2 \qquad (14.3)$$

If the foregoing procedure is repeated in reverse by first holding i_1 equal to zero and bringing i_2 from 0 to I_2 during the interval from $t = 0$ to $t = t_1$ and then bringing i_1 from 0 to I_1 during the interval from $t = t_1$ to $t = t_2$, the result will be

$$w_b = w_1 + w_2 + w_{21} = \frac{1}{2} L_1 I_1^2 + \frac{1}{2} L_2 I_2^2 + M_{21} I_1 I_2 \qquad (14.4)$$

Clearly, in any pair of situations where a particular network is involved and where initial and final conditions are identical for each situation, conservation of energy dictates that the energy stored must be the same for each situation. Thus, $w_a = w_b$, and eqs. (14.3) and (14.4) may be equated. When this is done, it is observed that

$$M_{12} = M_{21}$$

14.2.2 Coil Orientation and the Dot Convention

The use of a plus or a minus sign in eq. (14.1) or (14.2) depends on the orientation of the coils. This orientation is indicated in a network by a pair of dots or some other demarcating convention such as squares or triangles in the network diagram. The placement of the dots is associated with the direction of the magnetic flux, which may be ascertained by using the *right-hand rule*.

> **Right-Hand-Rule**: If the fingers of the right hand are placed around a wire so that the thumb points to the direction of the current flow, the fingers will be pointing to the direction of the magnetic field produced by the current in the wire.

Figure 14.2a shows a pair of coils wound on a magnetic core, with the current i_1 entering coil 1 at the top. In accordance with the right-hand rule, the flux produced by coil 1 is in the upward direction. Observe that coil 2 possesses the same orientation as coil 1; and if the current i_2 enters the top of coil 2, the right-hand rule indicates that the flux will also be in the upward direction.

If the fluxes produced by the two coils are aiding, a plus sign is used before the mutual terms in eqs. (14.1) and (14.2). A minus sign is required when the fluxes are opposing. Observe in Figs. 14.2b and 14.2c that the placement of the dots is in accordance with the coil orientation and the direction of the current, which implies the aiding flux directions.

The rules for the placement of the dots are as follows:

1. Assume that M will be positive.
2. Place a dot at the point where i_1 enters coil 1.
3. Determine the direction of the flux produced in coil 1 due to current i_1.
4. Consider coil 2 and the direction of the current i_2. If i_2 provides a flux in the same direction as the flux due to i_1 a dot is placed on coil 2 where i_2 enters. If the flux in coil 2 opposes the flux due to i_1, a dot is placed on coil 2 where i_2 leaves.

(a) Two coils wound on a magnetic core and (b) and (c) illustrations of coil
orientation, current flow, and the dot convention

FIGURE 14.2

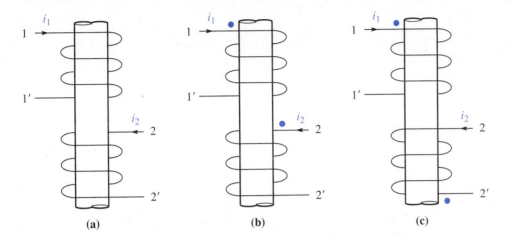

(a) (b) (c)

■ EXAMPLE 14.1

The current flows through L_1, L_2, and L_3 in the series network in Fig. 14.3.
What is the value of v?

Solution The solution requires some elaborate bookkeeping. First, due
to the inductances themselves,

$$v_1 = (L_1 + L_2 + L_3)\frac{di}{dt} = (4 + 9 + 4)\frac{di}{dt} = 17\frac{di}{dt}$$

Here, the L's are also referred to as the *self-inductance* terms.
Next, for the mutual inductance terms, begin with coil 1 and note that
because of the dots between coils 1 and 2,

$$v_2 = -6\frac{di}{dt}$$

A series network composed of three coils

FIGURE 14.3

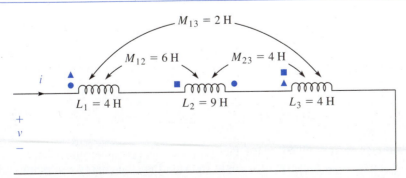

and the triangles between coils 1 and 3 indicate that

$$v_3 = 2\frac{di}{dt}$$

Coils 1 and 3 have an effect on coil 2. The dots between coils 1 and 2 show that

$$v_4 = -6\frac{di}{dt}$$

and the squares between coils 2 and 3 give

$$v_5 = 4\frac{di}{dt}$$

Finally, note that coil 3 is influenced by coils 1 and 2. For coils 1 and 3, look at the triangles and write

$$v_6 = 2\frac{di}{dt}$$

Then, for the squares on coils 2 and 3, obtain

$$v_7 = 4\frac{di}{dt}$$

The result is the sum of all of the foregoing:

$$v = \sum_{k=1}^{7} v_k = (17 - 6 + 2 - 6 + 4 + 2 + 4)\frac{di}{dt} = 17\frac{di}{dt}$$

The cancellation of all of the mutual terms is a coincidence. If, for example $M_{12} = 5\,\text{H}$ then

$$v = \sum_{h=1}^{7} v_k = (17 - 5 + 2 - 5 + 4 + 2 + 4)\frac{di}{dt} = 19\frac{di}{dt}$$ ∎

14.2.3 The Maximum Value of *M* and the Coefficient of Coupling

Equations (14.3) and (14.4) represent the energy storage in two coupled coils over a time interval $0 < t < t_2$ where neither coil contained any energy at $t = 0$. Either of these equations yields the energy storage in *both* coils, and clearly, this energy must be positive. If the coils are oriented so that the fluxes oppose, then both eqs. (14.3) and (14.4) become

$$w = \frac{1}{2}L_1I_1^2 + \frac{1}{2}L_2I_2^2 - MI_1I_2 \tag{14.5}$$

where advantage is now taken of the fact that $M = M_{12} = M_{21}$ and where this is the only case where the mathematics might indicate that the energy can possibly be negative. Algebraic adjustment of eq. (14.5) will yield

$$w = \frac{1}{2}(\sqrt{L_1}I_2 - \sqrt{L_2}I_2)^2 + \sqrt{L_1L_2}I_1I_2 - MI_1I_2$$

and here, the first term must always be positive but could be as small as zero. In this event, to prohibit w from being negative

$$(\sqrt{L_1L_2} - M)I_1I_2 \geq 0$$

and

$$\sqrt{L_1L_2} \geq M \qquad \text{or} \qquad M \leq \sqrt{L_1L_2}$$

which says that M must always be equal to or less than the geometric mean of L_1 and L_2. Thus, the upper limit on M is $\sqrt{L_1L_2}$, and to account for values of $M < \sqrt{L_1L_2}$, the coefficient of coupling is defined as

$$k \equiv \frac{M}{\sqrt{L_1L_2}} \qquad\qquad (14.6a)$$

so that

$$M = k\sqrt{L_1L_2} \qquad\qquad (14.6b)$$

Observe that in the case of tight coupling, the value of M may exceed the value of either L_1 or L_2 but not both. For example, if $k = 0.8$, $L_1 = 4$ H, and $L_2 = 9$ H, then

$$M = 0.8\sqrt{(4)(9)} = 0.8\sqrt{36} = 4.8 \text{ H}$$

However, if $k = 0.6$, then $M = 3.6$ H, which is a value less than either L_1 or L_2.

EXERCISE 14.1

In Fig. 14.4, the coefficient of coupling between coils 1 and 2 is $k_{12} = 0.64$. Between coils 1 and 3, the value is $k_{13} = 0.80$, and between coils 2 and 3, the value is $k_{23} = 0.72$. Find $v = f(i)$.

Answer $v = 2.438\, di/dt$.

A combination of three coils in series (Exercise 14.1)

FIGURE 14.4

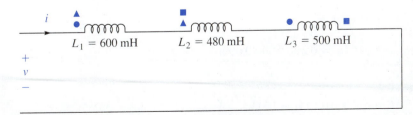

$L_1 = 600$ mH $L_2 = 480$ mH $L_3 = 500$ mH

FIGURE 14.5   A network used to demonstrate the procedure for mesh analysis in the presence
of mutual elements: (a) with the network elements and (b) in the phasor domain

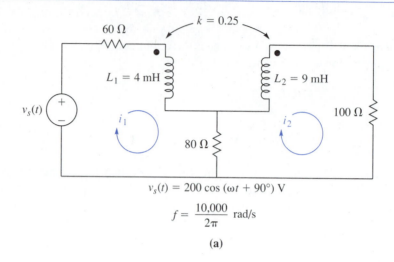

$$v_s(t) = 200 \cos (\omega t + 90°) \text{ V}$$

$$f = \frac{10,000}{2\pi} \text{ rad/s}$$

(a)

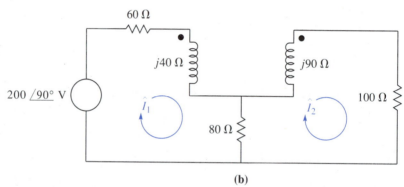

(b)

14.2.4 Mesh Analysis in the Presence of Mutual Inductance

The network of Fig. 14.5a will be used to demonstrate how a mesh analysis is
conducted when mutual inductance is present.

■ **EXAMPLE 14.2**

Find the two mesh currents $\hat{I}_1$ and $\hat{I}_2$ in the network of Fig. 14.5a.

Solution   The first step is to note that the frequency, $f = 10,000/2\pi$,
yields a value of $\omega = 2\pi f = 2\pi(10,000/2\pi) = 10,000$ rad/s, and to calculate

$$X_{L_1} = 10,000(0.004) = 40 \ \Omega \qquad X_{L_2} = 10,000(0.009) = 90 \ \Omega$$

And by eq. (14.6b),

$$M = k\sqrt{L_1 L_2} = 0.25\sqrt{0.004(0.009)} = 1.5 \text{ mH}$$

so that

$$\omega M = 10,000(0.0015) = 15 \ \Omega$$

The phasor domain network can be developed with these values, and the mesh currents, in phasor form, will be $\hat{I}_1$ and $\hat{I}_2$. The phasor domain network is shown in Fig. 14.5b.

Caution is required in the writing of the mesh equations when mutual inductance is present. For mesh 1, KVL provides

$$60\hat{I}_1 + j40\hat{I}_1 + 80(\hat{I}_1 - \hat{I}_2) - j15\hat{I}_2 = 200\underline{/90°}$$

where the $-j15\hat{I}_2$ term is due to the effect of the 9-mH coil on mesh 1, with the minus sign due to the dot orientation. For mesh 2, the effect of the 4-mH coil is also $-j15\hat{I}_2$, and here, too, the minus sign is due to the orientation of the dots. Thus, the second mesh equation is

$$j90\hat{I}_2 + 100\hat{I}_2 + 80(\hat{I}_2 - \hat{I}_1) - j15\hat{I}_1 = 0$$

The two mesh equations can be rearranged and simplified,

$$(140 + j40)\hat{I}_1 - (80 + j15)\hat{I}_2 = 200\underline{/90°}$$
$$-(80 + j15)\hat{I}_1 + (180 + j90)\hat{I}_2 = 0$$

and put into matrix form,

$$\begin{bmatrix} (140 + j40) & -(80 + j15) \\ -(80 + j15) & (180 + j90) \end{bmatrix} \begin{bmatrix} \hat{I}_1 \\ \hat{I}_2 \end{bmatrix} = \begin{bmatrix} 200\underline{/90°} \\ 0 \end{bmatrix}$$

Here, the symmetry in the coefficient matrix may be noted, but it must be understood that because of the mutual inductance, symmetry, in general, will not always be observed.

Neither Cramer's rule nor matrix inversion is needed to find the values of $\hat{I}_1$ and $\hat{I}_2$. Notice from the second mesh equation that

$$(80 + j15)\hat{I}_1 = (180 + j90)\hat{I}_2$$

or

$$(81.39\underline{/10.62°})\hat{I}_2 = (201.25\underline{/26.57°})\hat{I}_2$$

Thus, $\hat{I}_1$ can be represented in terms of $\hat{I}_2$:

$$\hat{I}_1 = (2.47\underline{/15.95°})\hat{I}_2$$

When this value of $\hat{I}_1$ is put into the first mesh equation, the result is

$$(140 + j40)(2.47\underline{/15.95°})\hat{I}_2 - (80 + j15)\hat{I}_2 = 200\underline{/90°}$$
$$(145.60\underline{/15.95°})(2.47\underline{/15.95°})\hat{I}_2 - (80 + j15)\hat{I}_2 = 200\underline{/90°}$$
$$(360\underline{/31.90°})\hat{I}_2 - (80 + j15)\hat{I}_2 = 200\underline{/90°}$$
$$[(305.66 + j190.19) - (80 + j15)]\hat{I}_2 = 200\underline{/90°}$$
$$(225.66 + j175.19)\hat{I}_2 = 200\underline{/90°}$$
$$(285.68\underline{/37.82°})\hat{I}_2 = 200\underline{/90°}$$

$$\hat{I}_2 = 0.70\underline{/52.18°} = 0.43 + j0.55 \text{ A}$$

FIGURE 14.6   Network (Exercise 14.2)

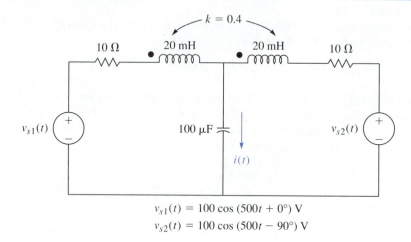

$$v_{s1}(t) = 100 \cos (500t + 0°) \text{ V}$$
$$v_{s2}(t) = 100 \cos (500t - 90°) \text{ V}$$

Then,

$$\hat{I}_1 = (2.47\underline{/15.95°})\hat{I}_2 = (2.47\underline{/15.95°})(0.70\underline{/52.18°})$$
$$= 1.73\underline{/68.12°} = 0.65 + j1.61 \text{ A}$$ ∎

EXERCISE 14.2

Find the current $i(t)$ in Fig. 14.6.

Answer $i(t) = 4.00 \cos(500t + 118.61°)$ amperes.

14.2.5 Node Analysis in the Presence of Mutual Inductance

A mutual inductance, $j\omega M$, is an impedance in ohms. Because of the way it provides a link between coils, it does not possess a simple admittance. The reader is cautioned against attempting nodal analysis when mutual inductance is present. While node analysis can be conducted, an exposition of how it is done is somewhat beyond the scope of this book.

SECTION 14.3   **TRANSFORMERS**

A transformer is an electric component consisting of two or more multiturn coils placed in close proximity, usually, on a core of magnetic material. The placement of the coils causes the magnetic field of one coil to link with the other coil, with an efficient transfer of electric energy by magnetic induction from one to the other.

The coils are often called windings, and one of them may be connected to the source of ac power. This winding is then called the *primary winding*, or merely the *primary*. The other winding, called the *secondary winding*, or *secondary*, may be connected to a load. It is possible to have a third winding, which is referred to as the *tertiary winding*, or *tertiary*.

Almost all transformers employ a *core* of magnetic material to provide a flux path between the windings. The magnetic core may take on a variety of shapes and may consist of magnetic materials ranging from silicon sheet steel to solid iron. Magnetic materials are characterized by a high permeability μ, a property that was discussed in Section 1.3.4. It is related to the permeability of free space,

$$\mu_o = 4\pi \times 10^7 \quad \text{(henrys per meter)}$$

by the relative permeability

$$\mu_r = \frac{\mu}{\mu_o} \tag{1.13}$$

The flux ϕ is related to the magnetic flux density B by the cross-sectional area of the flux path,

$$\phi = BA$$

and the magnetic flux density derives from the magnetic field strength H via the permeability,

$$B = \mu H$$

where H is established by the current flowing in a wire in accordance with the *Biot-Savart law*:

$$dH = \frac{i \sin \theta \, dl}{4\pi r^2} \tag{1.11}$$

Observe that H depends only on the current flow and the distance from the conductor and not on the material. However, the flux ϕ (via the magnetic flux density B) is influenced substantially by the permeability μ.

THE TURNS RATIO

SECTION 14.4

Two coils are shown in Fig. 14.7. One of them, the primary winding having n_1 turns, is connected to an ac voltage source. The voltage source provides a current that induces a magnetic flux, which is related to the voltage by Faraday's law:

$$v_1 = \frac{d\lambda}{dt} = n_1 \frac{d\phi}{dt}$$

A simple transformer with coils having negligible resistance and a core of very high permeability

FIGURE 14.7

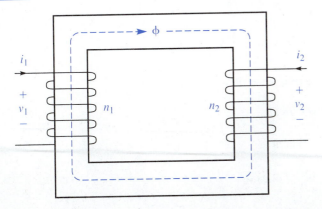

If the permeability of the core material is presumed to be very large ($\mu \to \infty$), all of the flux produced by the primary winding will link the secondary winding having n_2 turns. A voltage across the secondary will be produced:

$$v_2 = n_2 \frac{d\phi}{dt}$$

A simple division then yields

$$\frac{v_1}{v_2} = \frac{n_1}{n_2} = a \tag{14.7}$$

where a is defined as the *turns ratio*.

The ability to change the amplitude of a sinusoidal voltage is the primary attribute of the transformer. The magnitude of the turns ratio a dictates a voltage *step-up* ($a < 1$) or a voltage *step-down* ($a > 1$) from the primary to the secondary winding.

If the transformer is considered as a device, or indeed a simple system, with negligible losses (the ideal transformer will be considered in Section 14.6), the energy supplied to the primary must equal the energy leaving the secondary. Because power is the rate of transformation of energy, when there are no losses,

$$v_1 i_1 = v_2 i_2$$

so that

$$\frac{i_1}{i_2} = \frac{v_2}{v_1} = \frac{n_2}{n_1} = \frac{1}{a} \tag{14.8}$$

and this shows that a voltage step-up results in a current step-down, and a voltage step-down results in a current step-up. This is very useful in the transmission of power.

■ **EXAMPLE 14.3**

Consider a single-phase synchronous generator rated at 24 KVA and with a line-to-line terminal voltage of 120 V. It is to deliver power to a transmission line that is 100 km long and that possesses a line resistance of 0.0078 Ω/km. Investigate the power transmission capabilities of the line.

Solution   For an apparent power of $S = 24{,}000$ VA and a sending-end voltage of 120 V, the line is required to carry

$$I = \frac{S}{V} = \frac{24{,}000}{120} = 200 \text{ A}$$

The 100-km line has a resistance of

$$R = 100(0.0078) = 0.78 \ \Omega$$

and the line losses are therefore

$$P = I^2 R = (200)^2(0.78) = 31{,}200 \text{ W}$$

The losses of 31.2 KW exceed the power-carrying requirement of 24 KVA. It is therefore concluded that it is impossible for this particular line to carry 24 KVA with a sending-end voltage of 120 V.

However, the voltage at the sending end may be stepped up. Assume that a transformer with a turns ratio of $a = \frac{1}{10}$ is available. Then, at the output of the transformer,

$$V_2 = \frac{V_1}{a} = 10(120) = 1200 \text{ V}$$

so that

$$I = \frac{24{,}000}{1200} = 20 \text{ A}$$

Now, the losses are

$$P = I^2 R = (20)^2 (0.78) = 312 \text{ W}$$

which is tolerable.

If a transformer with a turns ratio of $a = \frac{1}{20}$ were used, the sending-end voltage would be 2400 V, the current would be 10 A, and the line loss would be only 78 W. It may be concluded that the use of a transformer in power transmission applications can dramatically reduce transmission losses. ∎

THE LINEAR TRANSFORMER

A transformer whose flux is proportional to the currents in its windings is called a linear transformer. The windings possess both resistance and inductance and are mutually coupled by the magnetic core. The linear transformer with a load on its secondary is shown in Fig. 14.8, where the currents $\hat{I}_1$ and $\hat{I}_2$ may be considered as mesh currents. With due cognizance of the orientation of the coils, as indicated by the dots (Section 14.2.2), two mesh equations may be written:

$$(R_1 + j\omega L_1)\hat{I}_1 \qquad -j\omega M\hat{I}_2 = \hat{V}_1$$
$$-j\omega M\hat{I}_1 + (R_2 + j\omega L_2 + Z_o)\hat{I}_2 = 0$$

The linear transformer

FIGURE 14.8

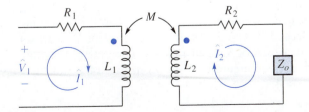

If primary and secondary impedances are defined as

$$Z_p = R_1 + j\omega L_1 \tag{14.9a}$$

$$Z_s = R_2 + j\omega L_2 + Z_o \tag{14.9b}$$

the mesh equations become

$$Z_p \hat{I}_1 - j\omega M \hat{I}_2 = \hat{V}_1 \tag{14.10a}$$

$$-j\omega M \hat{I}_1 + Z_s \hat{I}_2 = 0 \tag{14.10b}$$

These may be used to show that the secondary current $\hat{I}_2$ can be expressed in terms of the primary current $\hat{I}_1$:

$$\hat{I}_2 = \frac{j\omega M}{Z_s} \hat{I}_1 \tag{14.11}$$

When eq. (14.11) is put into eq. (14.10a), the result is

$$\hat{V}_1 = Z_p \hat{I}_1 - j\omega M \left(\frac{j\omega M}{Z_s}\right) \hat{I}_1 = \left(Z_p + \frac{\omega^2 M^2}{Z_s}\right) \hat{I}_1$$

which yields the value of the input impedance to the primary,

$$Z_{in} = \frac{\hat{V}_1}{\hat{I}_1} = Z_p + \frac{\omega^2 M^2}{Z_s} = Z_p + Z_r \tag{14.12}$$

where Z_r can be designated as the *reflected impedance*,

$$Z_r = \frac{\omega^2 M^2}{Z_s} \tag{14.13}$$

This important relationship shows how the secondary impedance is reflected into the primary circuit, and it may be observed that when the coefficient of coupling $k = 0$, so that $M = 0$, $Z_{in} = Z_p$, as it should.

The form of eqs. (14.10) indicates that an equivalent network may be constructed as shown in Fig. 14.9a. The reader may wish to verify that a mesh analysis of this network will yield eqs. (14.10). However, the use of this network becomes awkward when the network is tightly coupled (k is very close to unity). In this case, as Section 14.2.3 clearly shows, the value of M can exceed the value of *either* L_1 or L_2, and *either* $L_1 - M$ or $L_2 - M$ may become negative. This would mean that the network was not physically realizable unless additional reactive elements were used. Although this arrangement would still allow a mathematical analysis of the network, the presence of the additional reactive elements would pose a problem when the performance at a different frequency was desired. Because of this, the equivalent network of Fig. 14.9b is frequently employed. It can be verified that the same mesh equations will derive from either of the network configurations shown in Fig. 14.9, and Fig. 14.9b reduces to Fig. 14.9a when $a = 1$.

FIGURE 14.9

(a) An equivalent circuit for the linear transformer of Fig. 14.8 and (b) an improvement made possible through the use of the turns ratio a

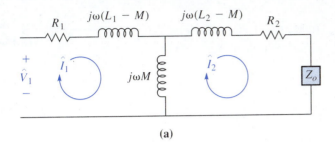

(a)

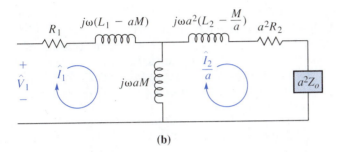

(b)

If the load impedance is put into rectangular form,

$$Z_o = R_o + jX_o \tag{14.14}$$

where X_o may be positive or negative, depending on whether the load is inductive or capacitive, expressions may be written for Z_s and Z_{in} in rectangular form. Consider, first, the secondary impedance given by eq. (14.9b), and use eq. (14.14):

$$Z_s = (R_2 + R_o) + j(\omega L_2 + X_o) \tag{14.15}$$

Equation (14.15) can be used to adjust the reflected impedance of eq. (14.13):

$$Z_r = \frac{\omega^2 M^2}{Z_s} = \frac{\omega^2 M^2}{(R_2 + R_o) + j(\omega L_2 + X_o)} \cdot \frac{(R_2 + R_o) - j(\omega L_2 + X_o)}{(R_2 + R_o) - j(\omega L_2 + X_o)}$$

$$= \frac{\omega^2 M^2 [(R_2 + R_o) - j(\omega L_2 + X_o)]}{(R_2 + R_o)^2 + (\omega L_2 + X_o)^2}$$

or

$$Z_r = \frac{(\omega M)^2 Z_s^*}{|Z_s|^2} \tag{14.16}$$

where $|Z_s|$ is the magnitude of Z_s and where it is observed that the complex conjugate of Z_s is reflected to the primary by the multiplier $(\omega M)^2/|Z_s|$.

Use of this in Z_{in} given by eq. (14.12) yields

$$Z_{in} = Z_p + Z_r = R_1 + j\omega L_1 + \frac{(\omega M)^2 [(R_2 + R_o) - j(\omega L_2 + X_o)]}{(R_2 + R_o)^2 + (\omega L_2 + X_o)^2}$$

or

$$Z_{\text{in}} = R_{\text{in}} + jX_{\text{in}} \qquad\qquad (14.17)$$

where

$$R_{\text{in}} = R_1 + \frac{(\omega M)^2 (R_2 + R_o)}{(R_2 + R_o)^2 + (\omega L_2 + X_o)^2} \qquad\qquad (14.18a)$$

and

$$X_{\text{in}} = \omega L_1 - \frac{(\omega M)^2 (\omega L_2 + X_o)}{(R_2 + R_o)^2 + (\omega L_2 + X_o)^2} \qquad\qquad (14.18b)$$

■ EXAMPLE 14.4

Consider the linear transformer shown in Fig. 14.10a, and observe that it is being driven by a 400-V source having an internal resistance of 200 Ω operating at 500 rad/s. The load connected to the secondary consists of a 1200-Ω resistance in series with a 1.25-μF capacitor. The coefficient of coupling between L_1 and L_2 is $k = 0.9$. It is desired to find Z_p, Z_s, Z_r, Z_{in}, $\hat{I}_1$, $\hat{I}_2$, the voltage at the input to the transformer, the voltage across the load, and the power drawn by the load.

FIGURE 14.10   (a) A linear transformer for Example 14.4 and (b) its phasor domain representation

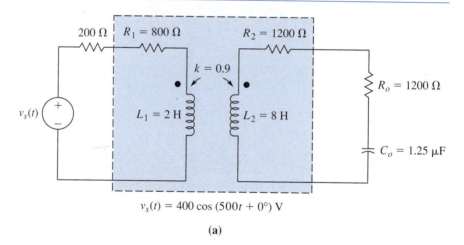

$$v_s(t) = 400 \cos (500t + 0°) \text{ V}$$

(a)

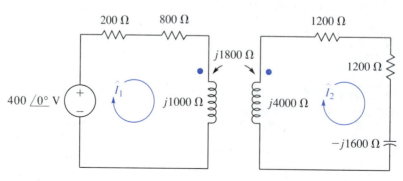

(b)

Solution The phasor domain network is shown in Fig. 14.10b. It is based on $\omega = 500$ rad/s, in which

$$X_{L_1} = \omega L_1 = 500(2) = 1000 \ \Omega \qquad X_{L_2} = \omega L_2 = 500(8) = 4000 \ \Omega$$

$$X_o = \frac{1}{\omega C} = \frac{1}{500(1.25 \times 10^{-6})} = 1600 \ \Omega$$

$$M = k\sqrt{L_1 L_2} = 0.90\sqrt{2(8)} = 3.6 \ \text{H} \qquad \omega M = 500(3.6) = 1800 \ \Omega$$

By eq. (14.9a),

$$Z_p = R_1 + j\omega L_1 = 800 + j1000 = 1280.62 \underline{/51.34°} \ \Omega$$

By eq. (14.15),

$$Z_s = (R_2 + R_o) + j(\omega L_2 - X_o) = (1200 + 1200) + j(4000 - 1600)$$
$$= 2400 + j2400 = 2400\sqrt{2}\underline{/45°} \ \Omega$$

By eq. (14.16),

$$Z_r = \frac{(\omega M)^2 Z_s^*}{|Z_s|^2} = \frac{(1800)^2(2400\sqrt{2}\underline{/-45°})}{(2400\sqrt{2})^2}$$
$$= 675\sqrt{2}\underline{/-45°} = 675 - j675 \ \Omega$$

Using $Z_{\text{in}} = Z_p + Z_r$ yields

$$Z_{\text{in}} = 800 + j1000 + (675 - j675) = 1475 + j325 = 1510.38\underline{/12.43°} \ \Omega$$

The value of the current drawn, $\hat{I}_1$, can be determined from

$$\hat{I}_1 = \frac{\hat{V}_s}{R_s + Z_{\text{in}}} = \frac{400\underline{/0°}}{200 + (1475 + j325)} = \frac{400\underline{/0°}}{1675 + j325}$$
$$= \frac{400\underline{/0°}}{1706.24\underline{/10.98°}}$$

or

$$\hat{I}_1 = 0.234\underline{/-10.98°} \ \text{A}$$

Now, by eq. (14.11),

$$\hat{I}_2 = \frac{j\omega M}{Z_s}\hat{I}_1 = \frac{j1800}{2400\sqrt{2}\underline{/45°}} \ 0.234\underline{/-10.98°}$$
$$= \frac{1800\underline{/90°}}{2400\sqrt{2}\underline{/45°}} \ 0.234\underline{/-10.98°} = 0.124\underline{/34.02°} \ \text{A}$$

The voltage across the load is $\hat{V}_o = Z_o\hat{I}_2$, or

$$\hat{V}_o = (1200 - j1600)(0.124\underline{/34.02°}) = (2000\underline{/-53.13°})(0.124\underline{/34.42°})$$
$$= 248.66\underline{/-19.11°} \ \text{V}$$

FIGURE 14.11
A linear transformer (Exercise 14.3)

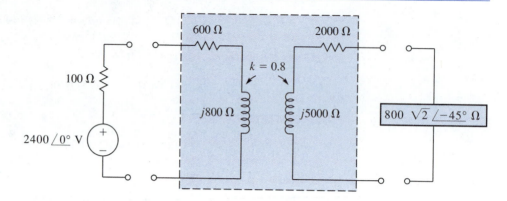

The power drawn by the load is

$$P_{Ro} = I_2^2 R_o = (0.124)^2(1200) = 18.45 \text{ W}$$

EXERCISE 14.3

A load of $800\sqrt{2}\,\underline{/-45°}\ \Omega$ is connected to the transformer shown in the phasor domain in Fig. 14.11. If a 2400-V source with an internal resistance of 100 Ω is connected to the primary, what power is transferred to the load?

Answer   418.2 W.

SECTION 14.6

THE IDEAL TRANSFORMER

Because actual transformers consist of coils containing a large number of turns wound on a core of high permeability, attention will now be focused on what is termed the *ideal transformer*. The modeling of a transformer as an ideal transformer, shown in the phasor domain in Fig. 14.12a involves making three assumptions:

1. The core material possesses extremely high permeability. It may therefore be assumed that there is no flux leakage. All of the flux links both coils and, the coefficient of coupling is taken as unity ($k = 1$).
2. The large number of turns in each coil tends to make the inductance very high. Thus, it is assumed that $L_1 \to \infty$ and $L_2 \to \infty$, although the ratio L_1/L_2 remains finite.
3. The ideal transformer is assumed to be lossless. Both coils and the core are assumed to contain no resistance and therefore dissipate no energy.

The foregoing conditions lead to the simple voltage and current ratios of eqs. (14.7) and (14.8):

$$\frac{v_1}{v_2} = \frac{n_1}{n_2} = a \tag{14.7}$$

FIGURE 14.12

(a) The ideal transformer and (b) the ideal transformer with a load Z_o connected across the terminals of its secondary

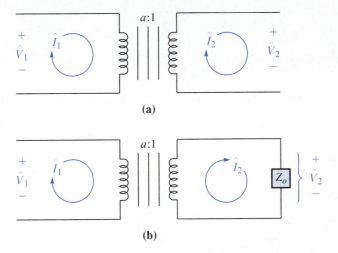

(a)

(b)

$$\frac{i_1}{i_2} = \frac{n_2}{n_1} = \frac{1}{a} \tag{14.8}$$

where a is the turns ratio.

If a load Z_o is connected across the secondary terminals, as indicated in Fig. 14.12b, $\hat{V}_2$ appears across the load and $\hat{I}_2$ flows into the load. Thus,

$$Z_o = \frac{\hat{V}_2}{\hat{I}_2}$$

and use of eqs. (14.7) and (14.8) shows that

$$Z_o = \frac{\hat{V}_1/a}{a\hat{I}_1} = \frac{1}{a^2} \cdot \frac{\hat{V}_1}{\hat{I}_1}$$

or in terms of the primary voltage and current,

$$Z'_o = \frac{\hat{V}_1}{\hat{I}_1} = a^2 Z_o$$

where the prime is intended to show that the load in the secondary has been reflected into the primary.

A little more insight can be gained by examining the input impedance of the ideal transformer in terms of the load impedance. Consider eqs. (14.17) and (14.18a):

$$Z_{in} = R_{in} + jX_{in} \tag{14.17}$$

$$R_{in} = R_1 + \frac{(\omega M)^2(R_2 + R_o)}{(R_2 + R_o)^2 + (\omega L_2 + X_o)^2} \tag{14.18a}$$

The ideal transformer requires coils 1 and 2 to be lossless, so that $R_1 = R_2 = 0$. Moreover, because $k = 1$, $(\omega M)^2 = (\omega L_1)(\omega L_2)$, and eq. (14.18a) reduces to

$$R_{in} = \frac{(\omega L_1)(\omega L_2)R_o}{(\omega L_2)^2\left[(R_o/\omega L_2)^2 + (1 + X_o/\omega L_2)^2\right]}$$

$$= \frac{R_o\omega L_1}{\omega L_2} \cdot \frac{1}{(R_o/\omega L_2)^2 + (1 + X_o/\omega L_2)^2}$$

The ideal transformer also requires that $L_2 \to \infty$ and that the ratio L_1/L_2 be finite, so that

$$R_{in} = \frac{L_1}{L_2} R_o$$

The ratio L_1/L_2 can be expressed in terms of the turns ratio $a = n_1/n_2$. Because

$$\lambda = n\phi \tag{1.14}$$

and because λ is also related to the current flow,

$$\lambda = Li$$

then,

$$L = \frac{n\phi}{i}$$

In the configuration of Fig. 14.12b, all of the flux links both coils. Thus, $\phi_1 = \phi_2 = \phi$, and

$$\phi = \frac{L_1 i_1}{n_1} = \frac{L_2 i_2}{n_2}$$

so that

$$\frac{L_1}{L_2} = \frac{n_1}{n_2}\left(\frac{i_2}{i_1}\right) = a(a) = a^2 \tag{14.19}$$

With this,

$$R_{in} = a^2 R_o \tag{14.20}$$

A similar expression can be obtained for X_{in}. Obtaining the eventual result requires a little more algebraic manipulation. Begin with eq. (14.18b):

$$X_{in} = \omega L_1 - \frac{(\omega M)^2(\omega L_2 + X_o)}{(R_2 + R_o)^2 + (\omega L_2 + X_o)^2}$$

Here, too, with $R_2 = 0$ and with $k = 1$, so that $(\omega M)^2 = (\omega L_1)(\omega L_2)$,

$$X_{in} = \omega L_1\left[1 - \frac{(\omega L_2)(\omega L_2 + X_o)}{R_o^2 + (\omega L_2 + X_o)^2}\right]$$

The bracketed term may be put over a common denominator. With

$$(\omega L_2 + X_o)^2 = (\omega L_2)^2 + 2\omega L_2 X_o + X_o^2$$

then,

$$X_{\text{in}} = \omega L_1 \left[\frac{R_o^2 + (\omega L_2)^2 + 2\omega L_2 X_o + X_o^2 - (\omega L_2)^2 - \omega L_2 X_o}{R_o^2 + (\omega L_2 + X_o)^2} \right]$$

$$= \omega L_1 \frac{R_o^2 + \omega L_2 X_o + X_o^2}{R_o^2 + (\omega L_2 + X_o)^2}$$

If ωL_2 is factored from both the numerator and denominator, then

$$X_{\text{in}} = \frac{(\omega L_1)(\omega L_2)}{(\omega L_2)^2} \left\{ \frac{[(R_o^2 + X_o^2)/\omega L_2] + X_o}{[R_o^2/(\omega L_2)^2] + [1 + (X_o/\omega L_2)]^2} \right\}$$

With $L_2 \to \infty$, as required by the ideal-transformer assumption, and with $L_1/L_2 = a^2$, as indicated by eq. (14.12),

$$X_{\text{in}} = \frac{L_1}{L_2} X_o$$

or

$$X_{\text{in}} = a^2 X_o \tag{14.21}$$

Equations (14.20) and (14.21) are important because they confirm that the load impedance can be transferred or reflected into the transformer primary by merely multiplying the resistive and reactive components by the square of the turns ratio. This can be demonstrated in an enhancement of Example 14.3, as shown in Example 14.5.

■ EXAMPLE 14.5

The single-phase generator of Example 14.3 (24 kVA, 120 V) is to supply a load of $2.4 + j1.8 \ \Omega$ through a 100-km line having a resistance of 0.0078 Ω/km and an inductive reactance of 0.0104 Ω/km. The system of generator, line, and load is shown in Fig. 14.13a. Two transformers are available, and the performance of each can be assumed as approaching the performance of an ideal transformer. One transformer has a turns ratio of $1:10$ ($a = \frac{1}{10}$) and can be used as a step-up transformer at the sending end of the line. The other possesses a turns ratio of $10:1$ ($a = 10$) and can be used as a step-down transformer at the receiving end of the line. What is the voltage at the load?

Solution The configuration with the generator, both transformers, the transmission line, and the load is shown in Fig. 14.13b. The line resistance is

$$R_{\text{line}} = 100(0.0078) = 0.78 \ \Omega$$

and its reactance is

$$X_{\text{line}} = 100(0.0104) = 1.04 \ \Omega$$

The line impedance is therefore

$$Z_{\text{line}} = 0.78 + j1.04 = 1.30\underline{/53.13°} \ \Omega$$

FIGURE 14.13   (a) A power transmission system consisting of a generator, a transmission line, and
                        a load and (b) the same system with ideal transformers placed at the sending and
                        receiving ends of the line

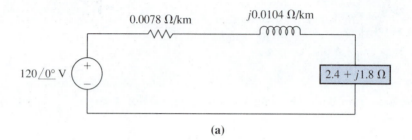

(a)

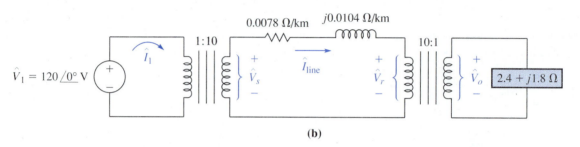

(b)

Figure 14.14a shows the system with the receiving-end transformer removed and the load reflected into the line via $Z'_o = a^2 Z_o$, or

$$Z'_o = (10)^2(2.4 + j1.8) = 240 + j180 \ \Omega$$

This is to be added to the transmission line impedance to obtain the impedance at the output or secondary of the ideal transformer at the sending end
of the line:

$$Z_s = Z_{line} + Z'_o = 0.78 + j1.04 + (240 + j180) = 240.78 + j181.04 \ \Omega$$

Another reflection to the input or primary side of the sending-end transformer (Fig. 14.14b) provides the impedance seen by the generator:

$$Z_{in} = a^2 Z_s = \left(\frac{1}{10}\right)^2 (240.78 + j181.04) = 2.4078 + j1.8104$$

$$= 3.0125 \underline{/36.94°} \ \Omega$$

The current that leaves the generator will be

$$\hat{I}_1 = \frac{\hat{V}_1}{Z_{in}} = \frac{120\underline{/0°}}{3.0125\underline{/36.94°}} = 39.83\underline{/-36.94°} \ \text{A}$$

and the current in the line may be determined from eq. (14.8):

$$\hat{I}_{line} = a\hat{I}_1 = \left(\frac{1}{10}\right)(39.83\underline{/-36.94°} = 3.98\underline{/-36.94°} \ \text{A}$$

FIGURE 14.14

The power transmission system of Example 14.5 showing the removal of the ideal transformers at the (a) load and (b) sending ends

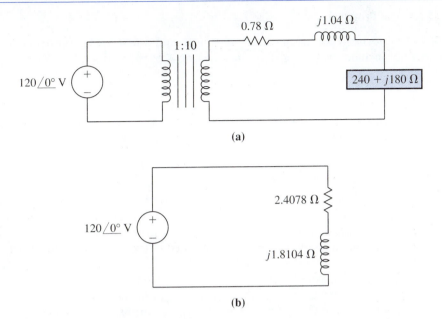

(a)

(b)

The voltage at the sending end of the line must be in accordance with eq. (14.7):

$$\hat{V}_s = \frac{\hat{V}_g}{a} = \frac{120\underline{/0^\circ}}{\frac{1}{10}} = 1200\underline{/0^\circ}\ \text{V}$$

The impedance of the line is $Z_{\text{line}} = 1.30\underline{/53.13^\circ}\ \Omega$, so that the voltage drop along the line is $I_{\text{line}}Z_{\text{line}}$, or

$$\Delta\hat{V}_{\text{line}} = (3.98\underline{/-36.94^\circ})(1.30\underline{/53.13^\circ}) = 5.18\underline{/16.19^\circ} = 4.97 + j1.44\ \text{V}$$

The voltage at the receiving end of the line is

$$\hat{V}_r = \hat{V}_s - \Delta\hat{V}_{\text{line}} = 1200 + j0 - (4.97 + j1.44) = 1195.03 - j1.44$$
$$= 1195.03\underline{/-0.07^\circ}\ \text{V}$$

The voltage across the load is obtained by using eq. (14.7):

$$\hat{V}_o = \frac{\hat{V}_r}{a} = \frac{1195.03\underline{/-0.07^\circ}}{10} = 119.50\underline{/-0.07^\circ}\ \text{V}$$

It can be noted in passing that the line losses are only

$$P_{\text{line}} = (I_{\text{line}})^2 R_{\text{line}} = (3.98)^2(0.78) = 12.36\ \text{W}$$

but the line, because of this particular load, is transmitting only

$$|S| = \hat{V}_s I_{\text{line}} = 1200(3.98) = 4776\ \text{VA}$$

14.7.1 The Proposal

Real transformers are neither linear nor ideal, and a first-order approximation that does not include stray capacitance is based on a consideration of the following facts:

1. The mutual flux linking the primary and secondary coils exists primarily in the magnetic core. Any flux that does not link the coils is called leakage flux, and this leakage flux exists almost exclusively in the air surrounding the magnetic core.

2. Because the coils are fabricated from real-world materials and consist of many turns of wire that may be very thin, it is reasonable to assume that they will possess some resistance that will give rise to I^2R losses.

3. Equation (14.2) indicates that the primary current will be zero if the secondary is open-circuited so that a secondary current may not flow. But it can be observed that if a voltage source is connected to the primary terminals, with the secondary terminals open-circuited, a current will flow in the primary. This current, however small, is proposed to have two components:

   a. One component is a magnetizing current i_ϕ, which is assumed to generate the flux in the magnetic core via its passage through an inductor with a proposed inductance L_ϕ.

   b. The second component is a core loss current i_c, which is assumed to account for losses in the magnetic core[1] via its passage through a proposed core resistance R_c.

With these observations, the first step in the construction of the network model of what will come to be called *the real transformer* is to add resistance and inductance to the primary and secondary windings of the ideal transformer, as indicated in Fig. 14.15a. Then, the core resistor R_c and the magnetizing reactance $X_\phi = \omega L_\phi$ are placed across the primary of the ideal transformer, as shown in Fig. 14.15b. Note that the added inductances do not link magnetically, either with each other or with the windings of the transformer. The reasoning for the placement of the components in this manner is not difficult to follow.

The I^2R losses in the primary and secondary are due to the primary and secondary currents. Thus, R_1 and R_2 must be placed so that the primary and secondary currents pass through them. The placement of the inductors L_1 and L_2 in series with R_1 and R_2 is due to the same reason. The leakage fluxes, primarily in the air surrounding the magnetic core, must be proportional to the primary and secondary currents and must produce voltages across them, which lead the current producing them by 90°.

The magnetizing inductance, which carries i_ϕ and which is indicated by its reactance X_ϕ in Fig. 14.15b, is placed across the primary side of the ideal transformer so that the small current i_ϕ can flow when a voltage is applied to the primary with the

---

[1] The losses are the *hysteresis* and *eddy current* losses. A discussion of the physical phenomena leading to these losses is not germane here.

FIGURE 14.15

Steps in the establishment of a real-world transformer network model: (a) the addition of R and L to primary and secondary coils and (b) the addition of the magnetizing and core loss components across the primary of the ideal transformer

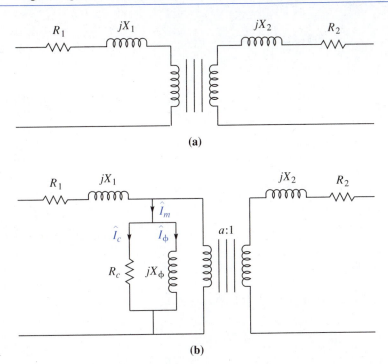

secondary terminals open-circuited. The core loss current i_c must also be present, but it cannot be influenced by the magnetizing current i_ϕ. It flows through R_c, which is placed in parallel with L_ϕ. The two currents are not necessarily related except by the KCL relationship $i_m = i_c + i_\phi$.

This arrangement, shown in Fig. 14.15b, can be adjusted by removing the ideal transformer entirely. The resulting phasor domain network is shown in Fig. 14.16a. But observe carefully that in Fig. 14.16a, the secondary quantities have been reflected into the primary, so that

$$R'_2 = a^2 R_2 \tag{14.22a}$$

$$X'_2 = a^2 X_2 \tag{14.22b}$$

This is now a primary-side equivalent, and R_c and X_ϕ have been replaced with $R_{c,p}$ and $X_{\phi,p}$. Note also that because of this, the secondary current is specified as $\hat{I}_s/a$, and the voltage across the secondary terminals is $a\hat{V}_s$. Finally, observe that KCL must not be violated in two places:

$$\hat{I}_m = \hat{I}_c + \hat{I}_\phi \tag{14.23a}$$

$$\hat{I}_p = \hat{I}_m + \frac{\hat{I}_s}{a} \tag{14.23b}$$

Phasor domain networks for transformer with ideal transformer removed, (a)
primary equivalent and (b) secondary equivalent

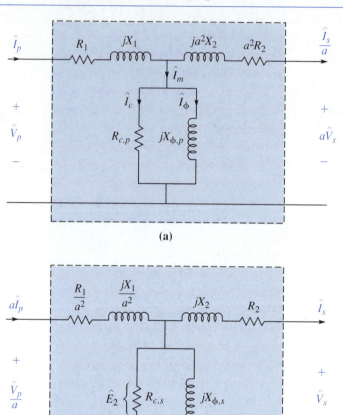

(a)

(b)

The phasor domain secondary equivalent network is shown in Fig. 14.16b. Here

$$R''_1 = \frac{R_1}{a^2} \tag{14.24a}$$

$$X''_1 = \frac{X_1}{a^2} \tag{14.24b}$$

and because this is a secondary equivalent, R_c and X_ϕ are replaced with

$$R_{c,s} = \frac{R_c}{a^2} \tag{14.24c}$$

and

$$X_{\phi,s} = \frac{X_\phi}{a^2} \tag{14.24d}$$

In this case, the primary voltage is specified as $\hat{V}_p/a$ and the primary current is $a\hat{I}_p$.

The network elements for both of the models in Fig. 14.16 are obtained from dc measurements and open and short circuit tests. A discussion of these measurements and tests is beyond the scope of this book.

14.7.2 A Note on Nomenclature

It is best to discuss the nomenclature that will be used in the balance of this section at this point.

1. Primary and secondary voltage and current phasors will always be designated in the customary way (phasors bear hats, and phasor magnitudes are indicated with a capital letter and with any necessary subscript) but with the additional subscripts p for primary and s for secondary.
2. Resistance and reactance values that appear in the primary will bear the subscript 1, and those that appear in the secondary will bear the subscript 2.
3. When secondary quantities are reflected to the primary, they will carry a prime, as in $R'_2 = a^2 R_2$. When primary quantities are reflected to the secondary, they will carry a double prime, as in $R''_1 = R_1/a^2$.
4. When equivalents are formed, they will bear a subscript e followed by a p or an s, to indicate whether they are a primary or a secondary equivalent.
5. The values of R_c and X_ϕ may carry no subscript in the general case, but when they are placed in the primary or secondary equivalent networks, they must bear the subscripts p or s.

14.7.3 Simplifications of the Real Transformer Network Model

The network models of Fig. 14.16 can be simplified by using equivalent values of the coil resistances and reactances. Figure 14.17 shows the simplified primary- and secondary-side equivalents. The use of these simplified network models is justified because the magnitudes of the core resistance and magnetizing reactance make the current drain $\hat{I}_m$ negligible. The primary equivalent with terminal quantities $\hat{V}_p$, $\hat{I}_p$, $a\hat{V}_s$, and $\hat{I}_s/a$ in Fig. 14.17a has been constructed by using

$$R_{eq,p} = R_1 + R'_2 = R_1 + a^2 R_2 \tag{14.25a}$$

$$X_{eq,p} = X_1 + X'_2 = X_1 + a^2 X_2 \tag{14.25b}$$

In Fig. 14.17b, the terminal quantities are seen to be $\hat{V}_p/a$, $a\hat{I}_p$, $\hat{V}_s$, and $\hat{I}_s$. The network elements are

$$R_{eq,s} = R''_1 + R_2 = \frac{R_1}{a^2} + R_2 \tag{14.26a}$$

$$X_{eq,s} = X''_1 + X_2 = \frac{X_1}{a^2} + X_2 \tag{14.26b}$$

$$R_{c,s} = \frac{R_c}{a^2} \tag{14.27a}$$

$$X_{\phi,s} = \frac{X_\phi}{a^2} \tag{14.27b}$$

FIGURE 14.17   Simplified transformer models: (a) primary side and (b) secondary side

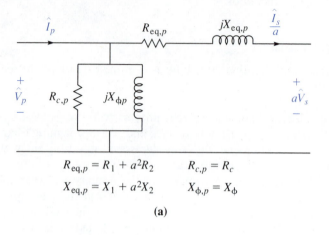

$$R_{eq,p} = R_1 + a^2 R_2 \qquad R_{c,p} = R_c$$
$$X_{eq,p} = X_1 + a^2 X_2 \qquad X_{\phi,p} = X_\phi$$

(a)

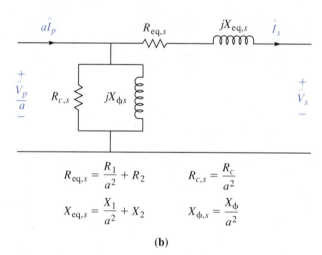

$$R_{eq,s} = \frac{R_1}{a^2} + R_2 \qquad R_{c,s} = \frac{R_c}{a^2}$$

$$X_{eq,s} = \frac{X_1}{a^2} + X_2 \qquad X_{\phi,s} = \frac{X_\phi}{a^2}$$

(b)

■ **EXAMPLE 14.6**

Consider the transformer of Fig. 14.18 and provide the elements of the simplified, secondary equivalent circuit of Fig. 14.17b.

Solution   With $R_1 = 0.112\ \Omega$, $X_1 = 1.22\ \Omega$, and $a = 4$, eqs. (14.26) indicate that

$$R_1'' = \frac{R_1}{a^2} = \frac{0.112}{16} = 0.0070\ \Omega$$

$$X_1'' = \frac{X_1}{a^2} = \frac{1.22}{16} = 0.076\ \Omega$$

These would make

$$R_{eq,s} = R_1'' + R_2 = 0.007 + 0.021 = 0.028\ \Omega$$
$$X_{eq,s} = X_1'' + X_2 = 0.076 + 0.076 = 0.152\ \Omega$$

FIGURE 14.18

Primary equivalent for the transformer in Example 14.6.

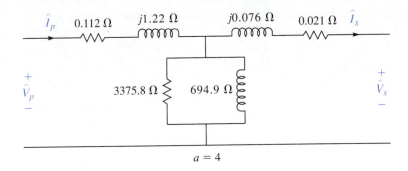

$$a = 4$$

Then, from eqs. (14.27),

$$R_{c,s} = \frac{R_c}{a^2} = \frac{3375.8}{16} = 211.0\ \Omega \qquad X_{\phi,s} = \frac{X_\phi}{a^2} = \frac{694.9}{16} = 43.43\ \Omega \qquad \blacksquare$$

EXERCISE 14.4

Use Fig. 14.19 to show a simplified transformer model in the form of Fig. 14.17b.

Answer See Fig. 14.20.

FIGURE 14.19

Network (Exercise 14.4)

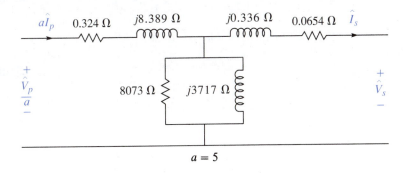

$$a = 5$$

FIGURE 14.20

Solution (Exercise 14.4)

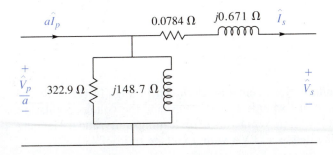

14.7.4 Voltage Regulation and Efficiency

The performance of a transformer may be assessed by a parameter known as the *voltage regulation* and by its *efficiency*. The voltage regulation compares the transformer output voltage at no load and full load and is usually expressed as a percentage:

$$VR = 100\left(\frac{V_{s,nl} - V_s}{V_s}\right)$$

where V_s is the secondary voltage at full load. Because at no load

$$V_s = \frac{V_p}{a}$$

The voltage regulation can be written as

$$VR = 100\left[\frac{(V_p/a) - V_s}{V_s}\right] \tag{14.28}$$

where

$$\frac{\hat{V}_p}{a} = \hat{V}_s + \hat{I}_s Z_s \tag{14.29}$$

Another measure of comparison is through the efficiency expressed in percent and defined by

$$\eta = 100\left(\frac{P_{out}}{P_{out} + P_{lost}}\right) = 100\left(\frac{V_s I_s \cos\theta}{V_s I_s \cos\theta + P_{cu} + P_{core}}\right) \tag{14.30}$$

where either model of Fig. 14.17 can be employed to give

$$P_{cu} = I_s^2 R_{eq,s} \tag{14.31a}$$

or

$$P_{cu} = \left(\frac{I_s}{a}\right)^2 R_{eq,p} \tag{14.31b}$$

and

$$P_{core} = \frac{(V_p/a)^2}{R_{c,s}} \tag{14.32a}$$

or

$$P_{core} = \frac{V_p^2}{R_{c,p}} \tag{14.32b}$$

■ **EXAMPLE 14.7**

Consider the secondary equivalent model shown in Fig. 14.17b with the parameters developed in Example 14.6 to determine the voltage regulation and efficiency at loads with power factors of 0.8 leading, unity, and 0.8 lagging if the transformer is rated at 12 kVA with a voltage ratio of 480/120.

FIGURE 14.21

Simplified model of a transformer for Example 14.7

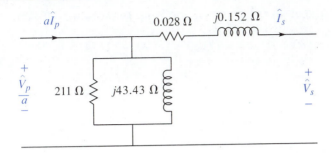

Solution   The phasor domain network model is shown in Fig. 14.21. For all cases,

$$Z_{eq,s} = R_{eq,s} + jX_{eq,s} = 0.028 + j0.152 = 0.155\underline{/79.56°}\ \Omega$$

And with rated kVA to the load, the magnitude of the load current will always be

$$I_s = \frac{VA}{V_s} = \frac{12{,}000}{120} = 100\ \text{A}$$

For all cases, the voltage reference will be

$$\hat{V}_s = 120\underline{/0°}\ \text{V}$$

For PF = 0.8 lagging, so that $\theta = -36.87°$,

$$\frac{\hat{V}_p}{a} = \hat{V}_s + \hat{I}_s Z_{eq,s} = 120\underline{/0°} + (100\underline{/-36.87°})(0.155\underline{/79.56°})$$

$$= 120\underline{/0°} + 15.46\underline{/42.69°} = 120 + j0 + (11.36 + j10.48)$$

$$= 131.36 + j10.48 = 131.78\underline{/4.56°}\ \text{V}$$

By eq. (14.28),

$$VR = 100\left(\frac{131.78 - 120}{120}\right) = 9.82\%$$

The copper losses are

$$P_{cu} = (I_s)^2 R_{eq,s} = (100)^2(0.028) = 280\ \text{W}$$

The core losses are

$$P_{core} = \frac{(V_p/a)^2}{R_{c,s}} = \frac{(131.78)^2}{211.0} = 82.3\ \text{W}$$

Then, by eq. (14.30), with $P_{out} = V_s I_s \cos\theta = 12{,}000(0.8) = 9600$ W,

$$\eta = 100\left(\frac{9600}{9600 + 280 + 82.3}\right) = 100\left(\frac{9600}{9962}\right) = 96.36\%$$

For unity power factor, where $\theta = 0°$,

$$\frac{\hat{V}_p}{a} = 120\underline{/0°} + (100\underline{/0°})(0.155\underline{/79.56°}) = 120\underline{/0°} + 15.46\underline{/79.56°}$$

$$= 120 + j0 + (2.80 + j15.20) = 122.80 + j15.20 = 123.74\underline{/7.06°}\ \text{V}$$

Then,

$$\text{VR} = 100\left(\frac{123.74 - 120}{120}\right) = 3.12\%$$

and with $P_{\text{out}} = 12{,}000$ W,

$$\eta = 100\left(\frac{12{,}000}{12{,}000 + 280 + 82.3}\right) = 97.07\%$$

For PF = 0.8 leading, with $\theta = 36.87°$,

$$\frac{\hat{V}_p}{a} = 120\underline{/0°} + (100\underline{/36.87°})(0.155\underline{/79.56°}) = 120\underline{/0°} + 15.46\underline{/116.43°}$$

$$= 120 + j0 + (-6.88 + j13.84) = 113.12 + j13.84 = 113.96\underline{/6.98°}\ \text{V}$$

Here,

$$\text{VR} = \left(\frac{113.96 - 120}{120}\right) = -5.03\%$$

and again, with $P_{\text{out}} = 9600$ W at rated secondary current, the efficiency will be the same as that for the case of PF = 0.8 leading:

$$\eta = 96.36\%$$ ■

EXERCISE 14.5

With the transformer in Exercise 14.4 providing power to a 0.925-lagging-power-factor load, use the simplified model of Exercise 14.4 to predict its voltage regulation and efficiency if it is rated at 30 kVA with voltage ratio 1200/240.

Answer　VR = 20.99% and η = 94.94%.

SECTION 14.8　　**IMPEDANCE TRANSFORMATION**

In Sections 4.6 and 11.6, it was demonstrated that maximum power can be transferred from a source to a load when certain conditions pertaining to impedance matching are met. However, in practice, because of the necessity of fixing the load impedance at a prescribed or specified value, it may not be possible to achieve such a match. In such cases, the use of additional reactive elements can yield the sought-after maximization.

Two el sections used to match the load resistance R_o at terminals 2–2′ to the resistance of the source at terminals 1–1′

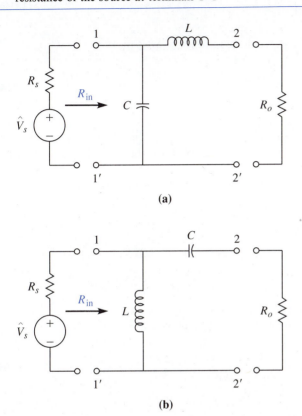

(a)

(b)

In Fig. 14.22a, a capacitor and an inductor have been put into an *el section* (so named because of the resemblance to the letter L and called an *el* to avoid confusion with the inductance parameter) between the source resistance R_s and a load resistance R. The combination of R, L, and C to the right of terminals 1–1′ will possess a real input resistance R_{in} at the resonance frequency ω_o. The objective is to achieve a match with $R_{in} = R_s$ so that maximum power is transferred to R.

The network to the right of terminals 1–1′ in Fig. 14.22a is identical to the one shown in Fig. 13.4a, which applied to Example 13.1 in Section 13.3. There it was shown that

$$\omega_o = \sqrt{\frac{1}{LC} - \left(\frac{R_o}{L}\right)^2} \qquad R_o < \sqrt{\frac{L}{C}} \tag{14.33}$$

Let the quality factor of this network be defined as

$$Q_o = \frac{\omega_o L}{R_o}$$

and with this put into eq. (14.33),

$$\omega_o^2 = \frac{1}{LC} - \frac{R_o^2}{L^2} = \frac{1}{LC} - \frac{\omega_o^2}{Q_o^2}$$

or

$$\omega_o = \sqrt{\frac{1}{LC}\left(\frac{Q_o^2}{Q_o^2 + 1}\right)} \tag{14.34}$$

results. If Q_o is high ($Q_o > 10$), ω_o is clearly approximated by

$$\omega_o \approx \frac{1}{\sqrt{LC}} \tag{14.35}$$

which is the undamped resonance frequency of the RLC parallel network and RLC series network. This infers that when $Q_o = \omega_o L/R > 10$, the input impedance of the network in Fig. 14.22a is real.

The impedance looking into terminals 1–1' with the load resistor R_o connected across terminals 2–2' is

$$\begin{aligned}
Z_{\text{in}} &= \frac{-jX_C(R_o + jX_L)}{R_o + j(X_L - X_C)} = \frac{X_L X_C - jR_o X_C}{R + j(X_L - X_C)} \cdot \frac{R_o - j(X_L - X_C)}{R_o - j(X_L - X_C)} \\
&= \frac{R_o X_L X_C - R_o X_C(X_L - X_C)}{R_o^2 + (X_L - X_C)^2} - j\frac{R_o^2 X_C + X_L X_C(X_L - X_C)}{R_o^2 + (X_L - X_C)^2}
\end{aligned}$$

And when $Q_o > 10$, $X_L \approx X_C$, so that Z_{in} can be considered real:

$$Z_{\text{in}} = R_{\text{in}} = \frac{R_o X_L X_C}{R_o^2} = \frac{X_L X_C}{R_o} = \frac{L}{R_o C} \tag{14.36}$$

The value of L,

$$L = R_{\text{in}} C R_o$$

may be inserted into the square of eq. (14.33):

$$\omega_o^2 = \frac{1}{LC} - \frac{R_o^2}{L^2} = \frac{1}{R_{\text{in}} R_o C^2} - \frac{1}{R_{\text{in}}^2 C^2}$$

This leads to the value of C:

$$C = \frac{1}{\omega_o}\sqrt{\frac{1}{R_{\text{in}} R_o} - \frac{1}{R_{\text{in}}^2}}$$

or

$$C = \frac{1}{\omega_o R_{\text{in}}}\sqrt{\frac{R_{\text{in}}}{R_o} - 1} \tag{14.37}$$

Here, it is observed that R_{in} is restricted to values that are greater than R_o. With this value of C, the value of L will be

$$L = \frac{R_o}{\omega_o}\sqrt{\frac{R_{\text{in}}}{R_o} - 1} \tag{14.38}$$

If $R_{in} < R_o$, the inductor and capacitor are interchanged, as shown in Fig. 14.22b. Here, too, a resonant frequency will exist for the combination of elements to the right of terminals 1–1'. A similar procedure will show that when $R_o > R_{in} = R_s$,

$$C = \frac{1}{\omega_o R_o} \sqrt{\frac{R_o}{R_{in}} - 1} \tag{14.39}$$

$$L = \frac{R_{in}}{\omega_o} \sqrt{\frac{R_o}{R_{in}} - 1} \tag{14.40}$$

■ **EXAMPLE 14.8**

Design an el section to match an 8-Ω load to a generator with a voltage of $v_s = 51 \cos(10{,}000t + 30°)$ volts and that possesses an internal impedance of 976 Ω. Then, calculate the power drawn both before and after the insertion of the el section.

Solution   Here, R_{in} is to be equal to R_s:

$$R_{in} = R_s = 976 \ \Omega$$

And in this case, where $R_o = 8 \ \Omega$, $R_{in} > R$, and eqs. (14.37) and (14.38) can be employed with $\omega_o = 10{,}000$ rad/s to find C and L. With $R_o = 8 \ \Omega$, eq. (14.37) gives

$$C = \frac{1}{\omega_o R_{in}} \sqrt{\frac{R_{in}}{R} - 1} = \frac{1}{10{,}000(976)} \sqrt{\frac{976}{8} - 1}$$
$$= 1.0246 \times 10^{-7} \sqrt{121} = 1.127 \ \mu F$$

Then, from eq. (14.38),

$$L = \frac{R_o}{\omega_o} \sqrt{\frac{R_{in}}{R_o} - 1} = \frac{8}{10{,}000} \sqrt{121} = 8.8 \ mH$$

Observe that

$$Q_o = \frac{\omega_o L}{R_o} = \frac{10{,}000(0.0088)}{8} = 11$$

which is greater than 10 and which permits the foregoing approximation. Without the el section, the magnitude of the load current is

$$I = \frac{V}{R_s + R_o} = \frac{51}{976 + 8} = 0.0518 \ A$$

And the power drawn by the load is

$$P = I^2 R_o = (0.0518)^2(8) = 0.0215 \ W$$

With the el section inserted, R_s is matched to R_{in} ($R_s = R_{in} = 976\ \Omega$):

$$I = \frac{V}{2R_s} = \frac{51}{2(976)} = 0.0261\ \text{A}$$

$$P = I^2 R_s = (0.0261)^2(976) = 0.6662\ \text{W}$$ ∎

EXERCISE 14.6

Select values of L and C for an el section to match a 160-Ω load to a generator operating at 60 Hz with an internal impedance of 32 Ω.

Answer $C = 33.16\ \mu\text{F}$ and $L = 169.8\ \text{mH}$.

SECTION 14.9   THE USE OF A REACTIVE TEE SECTION

Consider the network shown in Fig. 14.23 in which a tee network has been placed between a voltage source having impedance Z_s and a load having impedance Z_o. Suppose that it is desired to make the input impedance of the tee section to the right of the terminals 1–1' equal to the impedance of the source and the impedance of the tee looking backward into terminals 2–2' equal to the impedance of the load. Under these conditions,

$$Z_{in,1} = Z_s \qquad \text{and} \qquad Z_{in,2} = Z_o$$

Here, $Z_{in,1}$ and $Z_{in,2}$ are called the *image impedances* of Z_s and Z_o, respectively. The values of $Z_{in,1}$ and $Z_{in,2}$ are

$$Z_{in,1} = Z_s = Z_1 + \frac{(Z_2 + Z_o)Z_3}{Z_o + Z_2 + Z_3}$$

and with $\hat{V}_s$ replaced with a short circuit,

$$Z_{in,2} = Z_o = Z_2 + \frac{(Z_1 + Z_s)Z_3}{Z_1 + Z_3 + Z_s}$$

FIGURE 14.23   A network with a tee section inserted between a load Z_o and a source having an internal impedance Z_s

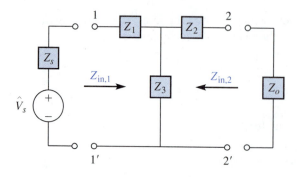

These may be adjusted algebraically to yield the pair of equations

$$Z_s(Z_2 + Z_3) + Z_o Z_s - Z_o(Z_1 + Z_3) = Z_1 Z_2 + Z_1 Z_3 + Z_2 Z_3$$

$$Z_o(Z_1 + Z_3) + Z_o Z_s - Z_s(Z_2 + Z_3) = Z_1 Z_2 + Z_1 Z_3 + Z_2 Z_3$$

which, when solved for Z_o and Z_s, yield

$$Z_{in,1} = Z_s = \sqrt{\frac{(Z_1 + Z_3)(Z_1 Z_2 + Z_1 Z_3 + Z_2 Z_3)}{Z_2 + Z_3}} \qquad (14.41)$$

$$Z_{in,2} = Z_o = \sqrt{\frac{(Z_2 + Z_3)(Z_1 Z_2 + Z_1 Z_3 + Z_2 Z_3)}{Z_1 + Z_3}} \qquad (14.42)$$

Now, consider just the tee network. If the terminals 2–2′ are shorted,

$$Z_{in,1sc} = Z_1 + \frac{Z_2 Z_3}{Z_2 + Z_3} = \frac{Z_1 Z_2 + Z_1 Z_3 + Z_2 Z_3}{Z_2 + Z_3}$$

and if terminals 1–1′ are shorted,

$$Z_{in,2sc} = Z_2 + \frac{Z_1 Z_3}{Z_1 + Z_3} = \frac{Z_1 Z_2 + Z_1 Z_3 + Z_2 Z_3}{Z_1 + Z_3}$$

With the terminals open-circuited,

$$Z_{in,1oc} = Z_1 + Z_3 \qquad \text{and} \qquad Z_{in,2oc} = Z_2 + Z_3$$

Use of these in eqs. (14.41) and (14.42) provide

$$Z_{in,1} = \sqrt{Z_{in,1sc} Z_{in,1oc}} \qquad (14.43)$$

$$Z_{in,2} = \sqrt{Z_{in,2sc} Z_{in,2oc}} \qquad (14.44)$$

which shows that the input impedance of the tee network can be obtained from open- and short-circuit calculations or measurements.

If all Z's are purely reactive, then Z_1, Z_2, and Z_3 become X_1, X_2, and X_3. In the event that Z_s is resistive, it becomes R_s; and if the load is resistive, Z_o becomes R_o. This situation is indicated in Fig. 14.24, where it is desired that the input impedance looking into terminals 1–1′ match R_s. Under these circumstances,

$$Z_{in,1} = R_s = jX_1 + \frac{jX_3(R_o + jX_2)}{R_o + j(X_2 + X_3)}$$

Algebraic adjustment yields

$$R_o R_s + jR_s(X_2 + X_3) = -(X_1 X_2 + X_1 X_3 + X_2 X_3) + jR_o(X_1 + X_3)$$

Then, the real and imaginary parts may be equated to give

$$R_o R_s = -X_1 X_2 - X_1 X_3 - X_2 X_3 \qquad (14.45)$$

$$X_1 + X_3 = \frac{R_s}{R_o}(X_2 + X_3) \qquad (14.46)$$

FIGURE 14.24   A reactive tee network placed between a source with a resistive internal impedance
                     and a resistive load

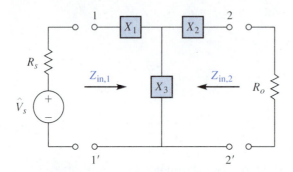

Equation (14.45) indicates that because R_o and R_s are real, at least one of X_1, X_2, or X_3 must be negative. This equation may also be rewritten as

$$R_o R_s = -(X_1 + X_3)(X_2 + X_3) + X_3^2 \qquad (14.47)$$

and then combined with eq. (14.46) to provide values of X_1 and X_2 in terms of X_3:

$$X_1 = \pm \sqrt{\frac{R_s}{R_o}(X_3^2 - R_o R_s)} - X_3 \qquad (14.48a)$$

$$X_2 = \pm \sqrt{\frac{R_o}{R_s}(X_3^2 - R_o R_s)} - X_3 \qquad (14.48b)$$

where the plus or minus signs can be used at the designers' discretion to give inductive or capacitive reactances, as required.

If X_3 is chosen such that

$$X_3 = \sqrt{R_o R_s} \qquad (14.49)$$

then the absolute value of all of the reactances in the tee will be equal, with the sign of X_3 opposite to the signs of X_1 and X_2. This condition is called *critical coupling*. If $X_3 < \sqrt{R_o R_s}$, then X_1 and X_2 will be imaginary, and a match between R_s and $Z_{in,1}$ will be impossible. This condition is known as *insufficient coupling*.

SECTION 14.10   SPICE EXAMPLE

Reading: In addition to reading Sections C.1 through C.8, which were recommended for reading in previous chapters, the reader should read and understand Section C.9 before proceding to the SPICE example that follows.

EXAMPLE S14.1

This example is a confirmation of Example 14.2, which requires that two mesh currents in the network shown in Fig. 14.5 (repeated here as Fig. S14.1) be determined. The network made ready for analysis with PSPICE is shown in Fig. S14.2, the input file is reproduced in Fig. S14.3, and pertinent extracts from the output file are presented in Fig. S14.4.

Figure S14.1   Network for the mutual inductance example

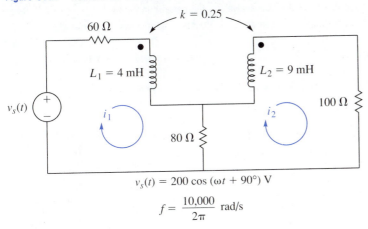

$$v_s(t) = 200 \cos (\omega t + 90°) \text{ V}$$

$$f = \frac{10,000}{2\pi} \text{ rad/s}$$

Figure S14.2   The network of Fig. S14.1 ready for PSPICE analysis

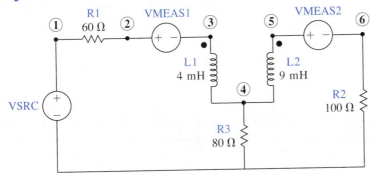

Figure S14.3   Input PSPICE file for analysis of the network of Fig. S14.1

```
SPICE EXAMPLE - CHAPTER 14 - NUMBER 1 - MUTUAL INDUCTANCE PROBLEM
******************************************************************
*FIRST, THE DATA FOR FIVE NETWORK ELEMENTS AND THE VOLTAGE SOURCE
VSRC      1       0       AC        200       90
R1        1       2       60
L1        3       4       .004
L2        5       4       .009
R2        6       0       100
R3        4       0       80
******************************************************************
*TO HANDLE THE COUPLING BETWEEN L1 AND L2 USE
K12       L1      L2      .25
******************************************************************
*TO MEASURE THE MESH CURRENTS, I1 AND I2, USE
VMEAS1    2       3       DC        0
VMEAS2    5       6       DC        0
******************************************************************
*HERE ARE THE CONTROL STATEMENTS
.AC       LIN     1       1591.55        1591.55
.PRINT    AC      IR(VMEAS1)    II(VMEAS1)    IR(VMEAS2)    II(VMEAS2)
.END
```

(continues)

Example S14.1 (continued)
Figure S14.4   Pertinent output for the PSPICE analysis of the network in Fig. S14.1
```
SPICE EXAMPLE - CHAPTER 14 - NUMBER 1 - MUTUAL INDUCTANCE PROBLEM


****       AC ANALYSIS                         TEMPERATURE =    27.000 DEG C


***************************************************************************


FREQ           IR(VMEAS1)   II(VMEAS1)   IR(VMEAS2)   II(VMEAS2)


 1.592E+03     6.450E-01    1.606E+00    4.293E-01    5.530E-01


            JOB CONCLUDED
```

CHAPTER 14

SUMMARY

- The primary and secondary voltages and currents in a transformer are related by the turns ratio:

$$\frac{i_1}{i_2} = \frac{v_2}{v_1} = \frac{n_2}{n_1} = \frac{1}{a}$$

- A linear transformer is a transformer whose flux is proportional to the currents in its windings. It will have a primary impedance

$$Z_p = R_1 + j\omega L_1$$

a secondary impedance

$$Z_s = R_2 + j\omega L_2 + Z_o$$

where Z_o is the load impedance, and an input impedance

$$Z_{\text{in}} = Z_p + Z_r$$

where the reflected impedance is

$$Z_r = \frac{(\omega M)^2}{Z_s}$$

The input impedance possesses a resistive term

$$R_{\text{in}} = R_1 + \frac{(\omega M)^2 (R_2 + R_o)}{(R_2 + R_o)^2 + (\omega L_2 + X_o)^2}$$

and a reactive term

$$X_{\text{in}} = \omega L_1 - \frac{(\omega M)^2 (\omega L_2 + X_o)}{(R_2 + R_o)^2 + (\omega L_2 + X_o)^2}$$

- An ideal transformer is assumed to be lossless and has no flux leakage; and the inductances of both coils are assumed to be infinite. For a load $Z_o = R_o + jX_o$, the input impedance components are

$$R_{in} = \frac{L_1}{L_2} R_o = a^2 R_o$$

$$X_{in} = \frac{L_1}{L_2} X_o = a^2 X_o$$

and this shows that the load impedance can be reflected into the primary via a multiplication by the square of the turns ratio.

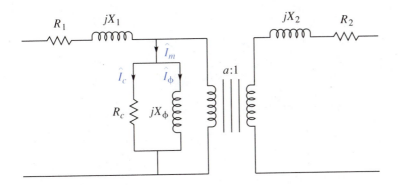

- In the transformer model shown here, the network elements are obtained from a dc measurement to obtain R_1 and from open- and short-circuit tests.

- The voltage regulation is

$$VR = 100\left(\frac{V_{s,nl} - V_s}{V_s}\right)$$

- The efficiency is

$$\eta = 100\left(\frac{P_{out}}{P_{out} + P_{lost}}\right) = 100\left(\frac{V_s I_s \cos\theta}{V_s I_s \cos\theta + P_{cu} + P_{core}}\right)$$

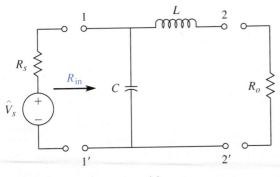

(a)

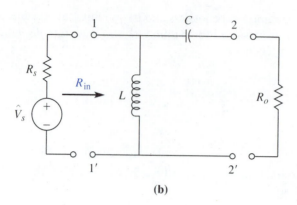

(b)

▪ Impedances may be transformed through the use of an el section. If $R_{in} > R_o$, the configuration of part (a) in the figure shown here is used, with

$$C = \frac{1}{\omega_o R_{in}} \sqrt{\frac{R_{in}}{R_o} - 1} \qquad L = \frac{R_o}{\omega_o} \sqrt{\frac{R_{in}}{R_o} - 1}$$

If $R_{in} < R_o$, the configuration of part (b) is used, with

$$C = \frac{1}{\omega_o R_o} \sqrt{\frac{R_o}{R_{in}} - 1} \qquad L = \frac{R_{in}}{\omega_o} \sqrt{\frac{R_o}{R_{in}} - 1}$$

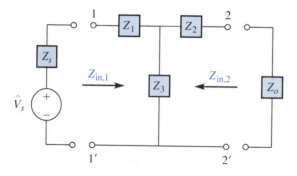

▪ A reactive tee section can also be used, with

$$Z_{in,1} = \sqrt{Z_{in,1sc} Z_{in,1oc}} \qquad Z_{in,2} = \sqrt{Z_{in,2sc} Z_{in,2oc}}$$

If all Z's are purely reactive, select a value of X_3 and make

$$X_1 = \pm \sqrt{\frac{R_s}{R_o}(X_3^2 - R_o R_s) - X_3} \qquad X_2 = \pm \sqrt{\frac{R_o}{R_s}(X_3^2 - R_o R_s) - X_3}$$

Additional Readings

Blackwell, W.A., and L.L. Grigsby. *Introductory Network Theory*. Boston: PWS Engineering, 1985, pp. 412–435.

Bobrow, L.S. *Elementary Linear Circuit Analysis*. 2d ed. New York: Holt, Rinehart and Winston, 1987, pp. 552–570.

Del Toro, V. *Engineering Circuits*. Englewood Cliffs, N.J.: Prentice-Hall, 1987, p. 498.

Dorf, R.C. *Introduction to Electric Circuits.* New York Wiley, 1989, pp. 400–409.

Hayt, W.H. Jr., and J.E. Kemmerly. *Engineering Circuit Analysis.* 4th ed. New York: McGraw-Hill, 1986, pp. 428–450.

Irwin, J.D. *Basic Engineering Circuit Analysis.* 3rd ed. New York: Macmillan, 1989, pp. 542–584.

Johnson, D.E., J.L. Hilburn, and J.R. Johnson. *Basic Electric Circuit Analysis.* 4th ed. Englewood Cliffs, N.J.: Prentice-Hall; 1989, pp. 516–543.

Karni, S. *Applied Circuit Analysis.* New York: Wiley, 1988, pp. 166–170, 351–370.

Madhu, S. *Linear Circuit Analysis.* Englewood Cliffs, N.J.: Prentice-Hall, 1988, pp. 485–504.

Nilsson, J.W. *Electric Circuits.* 3rd ed. Reading, Mass.: Addison-Wesley, 1990, pp. 447—483.

Paul, C.R. *Analysis of Linear Circuits.* New York: McGraw-Hill, 1989, pp. 210–226.

CHAPTER 14   **PROBLEMS**

Section 14.2

14.1   Two coils are connected in series so that the equivalent inductance is measured as L_{sa}. When the terminals of one of the coils are reversed and then reconnected, the equivalent inductance is measured as L_{so}. What is the mutual inductance of the two-coil arrangement in terms of L_{sa} and L_{so}?

14.2   What is the equivalent inductance of the network in Fig. P14.1 if $k_{12} = 0.8$, $k_{13} = 0.6$, and $k_{23} = 0.5$?

Figure P14.1

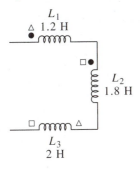

L_1
△ 1.2 H

L_2
1.8 H

L_3
2 H

14.3   What is the equivalent inductance of the network in Fig. P14.2 if $k_{12} = 0.92$, $k_{13} = 0.86$, $k_{14} = 0.72$, $k_{23} = 0.66$, $k_{24} = 0.875$, and $k_{34} = 0.782$?

Figure P14.2

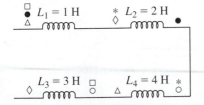

$L_1 = 1$ H   * $L_2 = 2$ H

$L_3 = 3$ H $L_4 = 4$ H *

14.4   In the network of Fig. P14.3, $L_1 = 9$ mH, $L_2 = 4$ mH, and $k = 0.75$. If i_1 and $i_2 = 24 \sin 500t$ amperes find v_1 and v_2.

Figure P14.3

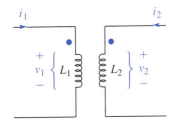

i_1 i_2

v_1 { L_1 L_2 } v_2

14.5   For the conditions outlined in Problem 14.4, what is the maximum amount of energy that can be stored in the coils?

Figure P14.4

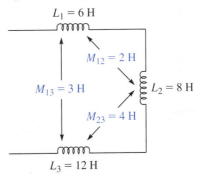

$L_1 = 6$ H

$M_{12} = 2$ H

$M_{13} = 3$ H $L_2 = 8$ H

$M_{23} = 4$ H

$L_3 = 12$ H

14.6   If the equivalent inductance for the network shown in Fig. P14.4 is $L_{eq} = 8$ H, assign the necessary polarity markings and determine the three coefficients of coupling.

14.7   Use mesh analysis to find the current through
the 125-μF capacitor in Fig. P14.5.

Figure P14.5

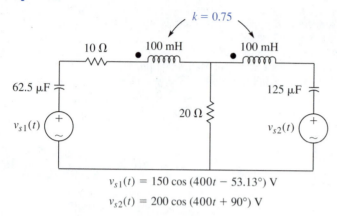

$$v_{s1}(t) = 150 \cos{(400t - 53.13°)} \text{ V}$$
$$v_{s2}(t) = 200 \cos{(400t + 90°)} \text{ V}$$

14.8   Use mesh analysis to find the current through
the 16-μF capacitor in Fig. P14.6.

Figure P14.6

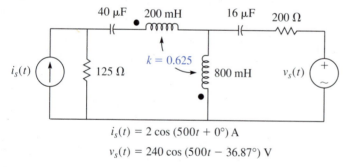

$$i_s(t) = 2 \cos{(500t + 0°)} \text{ A}$$
$$v_s(t) = 240 \cos{(500t - 36.87°)} \text{ V}$$

14.9   Use mesh analysis to find the current through
the 125 μF capacitor in Fig. P14.7.

Figure P14.7

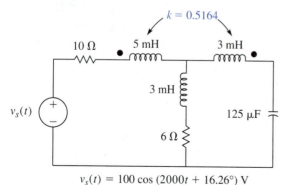

$$v_s(t) = 100 \cos{(2000t + 16.26°)} \text{ V}$$

14.10   Use mesh analysis to find the voltage across the
40-Ω resistor in Fig. P14.8.

Figure P14.8

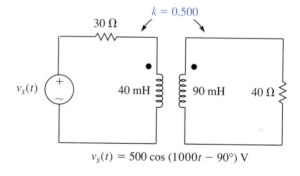

$$v_s(t) = 500 \cos{(1000t - 90°)} \text{ V}$$

Section 14.4

14.11 The primary side of a transformer with 750 turns in the primary and 150 turns in the secondary is connected to a 120-V line. Determine the turns ratio and the secondary voltage.

14.12 Consider a transformer containing 60 primary turns and 750 secondary turns. When the transformer is connected to a 240-V line, a current of 48 A flows into the primary. What are the values of the secondary voltage and the secondary current?

14.13 A power transformer is rated at 20 kVA with a nameplate showing the rated primary-to-secondary turns ratio as 480 V/120 V. What are the nominal currents for the primary and secondary?

14.14 What turns ratio is required for a transformer with a primary voltage of 135 V and a secondary voltage of 9 V?

14.15 What voltage applied to a transformer with turns ratio 5:1 ($a = 5$) will cause a current $i_s(t) = 20 \cos 377t$ to flow in the secondary?

Section 14.5

Problems 14.16 through 14.19 are based on the linear transformer configuration shown in Fig. P14.10. In all cases, find Z_p, Z_s, Z_r, Z_{in}, $\hat{I}_1$, $\hat{I}_2$, the voltage at the input of the transformer, the voltage across the load, and the power drawn by the load.

Figure P14.9

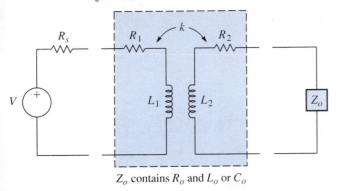

Z_o contains R_o and L_o or C_o

14.16 $V = 240$ V, $R_1 = 650$ Ω, $R_2 = 300$ Ω, $R_o = 1000$ Ω, $R_s = 100$ Ω, $L_1 = 1$ H, $L_2 = 4$ H, $C_o = 1$ μF, $k = 0.85$, $\omega = 1000$ rad/s.

14.17 $V = 300$ V, $R_1 = 120$ Ω, $R_2 = 400$ Ω, $R_o = 600$ Ω, $R_s = 120$ Ω, $L_1 = 0.8$ H, $L_2 = 1.8$ H, $L_o = 0.7$ H, $k = 0.92$, $\omega = 400$ rad/s.

14.18 $V = 1200$ V, $R_1 = 200$ Ω, $R_2 = 750$ Ω, $R_o = 750$ Ω, $R_s = 300$ Ω, $L_1 = 4.8$ H, $L_2 = 4.8$ H, $C_o = 10$ μF, $k = 0.80$, $\omega = 250$ rad/s.

14.19 $V = 480$ V, $R_1 = 560$ Ω, $R_2 = 800$ Ω, $R_o = 700$ Ω, $R_s = 240$ Ω, $L_1 = 1.6$ H, $L_2 = 0.4$ H, $L_o = 0.2$ H, $k = 0.75$, $\omega = 2000$ rad/s.

14.20 A voltage source with a maximum amplitude of 60 V has an internal impedance of $Z_s = 12 + j14$ Ω. It provides power at an angular frequency of 800 rad/s, and it is attached to the primary terminals of a linear transformer having $R_1 = 18$ Ω, $L_1 = 75$ mH, $R_2 = 420$ Ω, $L_2 = 2.75$ H, and $M = 240$ mH. Find k, Z_r, Z_{in}, and the power transferred to the primary terminals of the transformer.

Section 14.6

14.21 For the ideal transformer arrangement in Fig. P14.10, prove that $n_1 i_1 - n_2 i_2 - n_3 i_3 = 0$ where n_1, n_2 and n_3 are the turns on coils 1, 2, and 3 respectively.

Figure P14.10

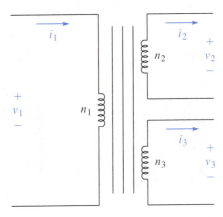

14.22 What turns ratio is needed in an ideal audio output transformer to transfer maximum power from a 4000-Ω amplifier to a 16-Ω speaker?

14.23 In the network of Fig. P14.11, what turns ratio, a, is required to make the 4 Ω resistor dissipate 225 W.

Figure P14.11

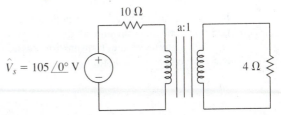

14.24 In Fig. P14.12, the 8-Ω load is to receive three times as much power as the 16 Ω load. If the source impedance is 480 Ω, determine the turns ratios, a_1 and a_2.

Figure P14.12

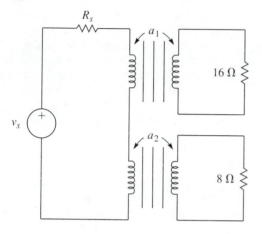

14.25 In the ideal transformer arrangement shown in the phasor domain in Fig. P.14.13, what power is dissipated by the 30 Ω resistor?

Figure P14.13

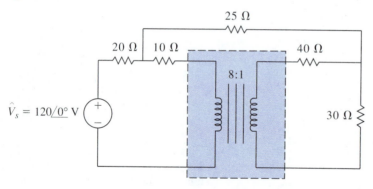

14.26 A generator with an output voltage of 10 kV supplies power to a load of $625\sqrt{2}/45°$ Ω through a rather long transmission line having a total impedance of $60/53.13°$ Ω.

   a. Determine the transmission losses of the system and the voltage at the load.

   b. If two ideal transformers are installed at the generator end ($a = \frac{1}{12}$) and at the load end ($a = 12$), determine the transmission losses and the voltage at the load.

Section 14.7

14.27 The secondary of a transformer with a turns ratio of $a = 0.25$ has a secondary voltage of $v_s(t) = 480 \cos 400t$ volts and delivers a current to a lagging load of $i_s(t) = 5 \cos(400t - 45°)$ amperes. If the impedances of a simplified primary model of the transformer are $R_{eq} = 0.0523$ Ω, $R_c = 83.2$ Ω, $X_{eq} = 0.2263$ Ω, and $X_m = 21.3$ Ω, determine the voltage regulation and the efficiency.

14.28 A 12-kVA, 2400/240-V transformer has the following resistances and reactances referred to its primary side:

$R_1 = 4.44$ Ω	$R_2 = 0.0412$ Ω	$R_c = 48.3$ kΩ
$X_1 = 5.48$ Ω	$X_2 = 0.0593$ Ω	$X_c = 4.37$ kΩ

Draw the equivalent network of this transformer referred to the secondary side in the form of Fig. 14.16b. If the transformer supplies a 0.855 lagging load, determine its voltage regulation and its efficiency.

14.29 Repeat problem 14.28 using the secondary equivalent model of Fig. 14.17b.

14.30 Repeat problem 14.28 for a unity power factor load.

14.31 Repeat problem 14.29 for a unity power factor load.

14.32 Repeat problem 14.28 for a 0.832 leading load.

14.33 Repeat problem 14.29 for a 0.832 leading load.

Section 14.8

14.34 Design an el section network to couple a generator having a peak amplitude of 2.5 V and 1000 Ω internal resistance to a 100-Ω load to transfer maximum power at a frequency of 500,000 Hz.

14.35 Design an el section network to couple a generator having a peak amplitude of 2.5 V and 1000 Ω internal resistance to a 10,000-Ω load to transfer maximum power at a frequency of 500,000 Hz.

14.36 Design an el section network to couple a generator having a peak amplitude of 12.5V and $400 + j400 \, \Omega$ internal impedance to a 7500-Ω load to transfer maximum power at a frequency of 500,000 Hz. What current and power are delivered to the load?

14.37 Design an el section network to couple a generator having a peak amplitude of 12.5 V and $400 + j400 \, \Omega$ internal impedance to a $(100 + j75)$-Ω load to transfer maximum power at a frequency of 500,000 Hz. What current and power are delivered to the load?

Section 14.8

14.38 Design a reactive tee section to match an 8000-Ω generator to a 200-Ω load for critical coupling at a frequency of 2 MHz.

14.39 Design a reactive section with $X_1 = 0$ to match an 8000-Ω generator to a 200-Ω load for critical coupling at a frequency of 2 MHz.

14.40 Design a reactive tee section to match an 8000-Ω generator to a 200-Ω load for critical coupling at a frequency of 2 MHz. On hand are just one variable inductor and several variable capacitors.

LAPLACE TRANSFORM AND CONVOLUTION

IV

THE LAPLACE TRANSFORMATION

15

OBJECTIVES

The objectives of this chapter are to:

- Provide the definition for the Laplace transform.

- Derive the Laplace transforms for the basic operations of the sum of two time functions, the multiplication of a time function by a constant, differentiation, and integration.

- Derive the Laplace transforms of the exponentially damped function and a function translated in time.

- Derive and illustrate several methods for obtaining the inverse Laplace transform.

- Present additional useful concepts involving the initial and final values of the time function and the use of the complex frequency s (the Laplace transform variable) as a differential and integration operator.

INTRODUCTION

Two numbers may be multiplied by first taking their logarithms, then adding the logarithms, and finally, obtaining the product by taking the inverse logarithm. This is an example of a transformation that converts the process of multiplication to one of addition. It is a well-recognized and common procedure that involves the following steps:

- A transformation to a logarithmic domain
- The performance of the operation of addition
- The use of an inverse transformation to obtain the product

In this book, the differential equations of network theory involve time as the independent variable, and the differential equation is said to be in the *time domain*. The Laplace transformation and its use in a prescribed procedure takes a linear differential equation with constant coefficients in the time domain and transforms it, as

FIGURE 15.1   Two methods for solution of a problem in the time domain. Transformation to the
s-domain allows the use of algebraic techniques.

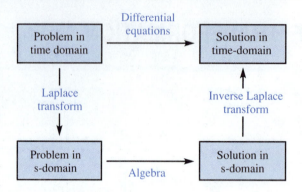

in Fig. 15.1, as follows:

1.   Transforms the differential equation into the complex frequency, or s *domain*,
     where the dependent variable is the complex frequency $s = \sigma + j\omega$.
2.   Permits the use of algebraic methods to obtain the Laplace transform of the
     solution.
3.   Allows the solution in the time domain to be recovered by an inverse trans-
     formation.

   This procedure has several advantages. The first, and most obvious, advantage
is that all work is done within an algebraic framework. The second is the ease with
which the common exponential and transcendental functions can be represented by
simple algebraic functions in the s-domain. The third advantage is that the transform
method incorporates initial or boundary conditions into the solution procedure. This
eliminates much of the tedium involved in the evaluation of the arbitrary constants
of integration. The fourth advantage is the ability to work with integro-differential
equations without a transformation of variable, and the fifth advantage is the effective
use of step and impulse forcing functions (discussed in Chapter 5) whose responses
are so important in *transfer function analysis* (considered in Chapter 19) and *superposition methods* (discussed in Chapter 17).

SECTION 15.2   THE DEFINITION OF THE LAPLACE TRANSFORM

The Laplace transformation, or Laplace transform, of a function $f(t)$ is defined as

$$\mathscr{L}[f(t)] = F(s) = \int_{0^-}^{\infty} f(t)e^{-st}\,dt \tag{15.1}$$

where, in general, s is a complex number $\sigma + j\omega$ and where the lower limit of the
integral is taken as 0^- in order to accommodate the unit impulse function.
   In eq. (15.1), the independent variable is t and the dependent variable is $f(t)$. The
choice of variables is arbitrary, of course; x and $f(x)$ can also be employed, with the
result

$$\mathscr{L}[f(x)] = F(s) = \int_{0^-}^{\infty} f(x)e^{-sx}\,dx$$

If the integral in eq. (15.1) is written as

$$F(s) = \lim_{T \to \infty} \int_{0^-}^{T} f(t)e^{-st}\,dt \qquad (15.2)$$

then it is seen that the Laplace transform will exist as long as the limit given by eq. (15.2) exists. When this limit exists, then eq. (15.1) is said to converge, and the Laplace transform exists and has meaning. If the limit of the integral does not exist, the Laplace transform does not exist. The reader is assured, however, that the Laplace transform does exist for most of the time functions dealt with in this book.

In eqs. (15.1) and (15.2), it should be noted that functions in the time domain are indicated by a lowercase letter $[f(t), g(t), \ldots]$, and their corresponding Laplace transforms are designated by the corresponding uppercase letter $[F(s), G(s), \ldots]$.

The inverse Laplace transformation

$$f(t) = \mathscr{L}^{-1}[F(s)] \qquad (15.3)$$

recovers $f(t)$ from $F(s)$.

SOME BASIC OPERATIONS   SECTION 15.3

In Sections 15.3.1 and 15.3.2, it is shown that because integration is a linear operator, the Laplace transform is also a linear operator. Sections 15.3.3 and 15.3.4 then deal with derivatives.

15.3.1 The Laplace Transform of the Sum of Two Functions

Let

$$\mathscr{L}[f(t)] = F(s) \qquad \text{and} \qquad \mathscr{L}[g(t)] = G(s)$$

Then,

$$\mathscr{L}[f(t) + g(t)] = \int_{0^-}^{\infty} [f(t) + g(t)]e^{-st}\,dt = \int_{0^-}^{\infty} f(t)e^{-st}\,dt + \int_{0^-}^{\infty} g(t)e^{-st}\,dt$$

Thus, the Laplace transform of the sum of two functions is the sum of the individual transforms of the functions:

$$\mathscr{L}[f(t) + g(t)] = F(s) + G(s) \qquad (15.4)$$

The reader is cautioned that this result *does not* imply that it can be extended to the product of two functions. That is, the Laplace transform of the product of two time functions is *not* the product of their transforms

$$\mathscr{L}[f(t) \cdot g(t)] \neq F(s) \cdot G(s)$$

but it does extend to any finite sum.

15.3.2 The Laplace Transform of a Constant Times a Function

Let

$$\mathcal{L}[f(t)] = F(s)$$

Then,

$$\mathcal{L}[Cf(t)] = \int_{0^-}^{\infty} Cf(t)e^{-st}\,dt = C\int_{0^-}^{\infty} f(t)e^{-st}\,dt$$

or

$$\mathcal{L}[Cf(t)] = CF(s) \tag{15.5}$$

The Laplace transform of a constant times a function is equal to the constant times the Laplace transform of the function.

Sections 15.3.1 and 15.3.2 demonstrate that the Laplace transform is a linear operator:

$$\mathcal{L}\left[\sum_{k=1}^{k=\infty} C_k f_k(t)\right] = \sum_{k=1}^{k=\infty} C_k F_k(s) \tag{15.6}$$

15.3.3 The Laplace Transform of the Derivative of a Function

Let

$$\mathcal{L}[f(t)] = F(s)$$

Then, assuming that $f(t)$ possesses a derivative,

$$\mathcal{L}\left[\frac{d}{dt}f(t)\right] = \int_{0^-}^{\infty} \left[\frac{d}{dt}f(t)\right]e^{-st}\,dt$$

An integration by parts with

$$u = e^{-st} \qquad\qquad dv = \frac{d}{dt}f(t)\,dt$$

$$du = -se^{-st}\,dt \qquad v = f(t)$$

in

$$\int_{0^-}^{\infty} u\,dv = uv\Big|_{0^-}^{\infty} - \int_{0^-}^{\infty} v\,du$$

gives

$$\mathcal{L}\left[\frac{d}{dt}f(t)\right] = f(t)e^{-st}\Big|_{0^-}^{\infty} + s\int_{0^-}^{\infty} f(t)e^{-st}\,dt$$

or

$$\mathcal{L}\left[\frac{d}{dt}f(t)\right] = sF(s) - f(0^-) \tag{15.7}$$

15.3.4 The Laplace Transform of the Second Derivative of a Function

Again, let

$$\mathscr{L}[f(t)] = F(s)$$

By eq. (15.7),

$$\mathscr{L}[f'(t)] = sF(s) - f(0^-)$$

Thus,

$$\mathscr{L}[f''(t)] = s\mathscr{L}[f'(t) - f'(0^-)] = s[sF(s) - f(0^-)] - f'(0^-)$$

and hence,

$$\mathscr{L}[f''(t)] = s^2 F(s) - sf(0^-) - f'(0^-) \tag{15.8}$$

These results may be extended by mathematical induction to the Laplace transform of the nth derivative:

$$\mathscr{L}[f^n(t)] = s^n F(s) - s^{n-1}f(0^-) - s^{n-2}f'(0^-) - \cdots - f^{n-1}(0^-) \tag{15.9}$$

15.3.5 The Laplace Transform of the Integral of a Function

With

$$\mathscr{L}[f(t)] = F(s)$$

the Laplace transform of the integral with the upper limit t replaced by T and where $-\infty \leq a \leq 0^-$ will be

$$\mathscr{L}\left[\int_a^T f(t)\,dt\right] = \int_{0^-}^\infty \left[\int_a^t f(z)\,dz\right] e^{-st}\,dt$$

An application of integration by parts with

$$u = \int_a^t f(z)\,dz \qquad dv = e^{-st}\,dt$$

$$du = f(t)\,dt \qquad v = -\frac{1}{s}e^{-st}$$

gives

$$\mathscr{L}\left[\int_a^T f(t)\,dt\right] = -\frac{1}{s}e^{-st}\int_a^t f(z)\,dz\bigg|_{0^-}^\infty + \frac{1}{s}\int_{0^-}^\infty f(t)e^{-st}\,dt$$

or with the limits substituted,

$$\mathscr{L}\left[\int_a^T f(t)\,dt\right] = \frac{1}{s}F(s) + \frac{1}{s}\int_a^{0^-} f(t)\,dt \tag{15.10}$$

The integral $\int_a^{0^-} f(t)\,dt$ is often called the accumulation from $t = a$ to $t = 0^-$ and is represented as the value of a quantity at $t = 0^-$:

$$\int_a^{0^-} f(t)\,dt = \int f(t)\,dt\Big|_{t=0^-}$$

The accumulation represents the value of the integral at $t = 0^-$. For example, the charge that has accumulated on the plates of a capacitor during the time interval between some time $t = a$ and $t = 0^-$ is the value at $t = 0^-$

$$q(0^-) = \int_a^{0^-} i\,dt = \int i\,dt\Big|_{t=0^-}$$

The flux set up around an inductor during the time interval $a < t < 0^-$ is the value $\phi(0^-)$ which derives from Faraday's law

$$\phi(0^-) = \int_a^{0^-} v\,dt = \int v\,dt\Big|_{t=0^-}$$

Both of these permit the evaluation of initial voltages across capacitors

$$v_C(0^-) = \frac{q(0^-)}{C} = \frac{1}{C}\int i\,dt\Big|_{t=0^-}$$

and initial currents through inductors

$$i_L(0^-) = \frac{\phi(0^-)}{L} = \frac{1}{L}\int v\,dt\Big|_{t=0^-}$$

SECTION 15.4   TWO MORE FUNDAMENTAL OPERATIONS

For the Laplace transform of $f(t)$,

$$\mathscr{L}[f(t)] = F(s)$$

the effect of an extra exponential factor both in the time domain,

$$e^{-at}f(t)$$

and in the transform or s domain,

$$e^{-as}F(s)$$

is to shift the argument in the respective domains. The first of these is important because it greatly reduces the size of a table of Laplace transform pairs, and the second is important because it permits time delays to be handled conveniently.

15.4.1 The Laplace Transform of an Exponentially Damped Function

By definition,

$$\mathscr{L}[e^{-at}f(t)] = \int_{0^-}^\infty [e^{-at}f(t)]e^{-st}\,dt = \int_{0^-}^\infty f(t)e^{-(s+a)t}\,dt$$

and hence,

$$\mathcal{L}[e^{-at}f(t)] = F(s + a) \tag{15.11}$$

where $(s + a)$ has taken the place of s.

15.4.2 The Shifting Theorem

In the analysis of dynamic systems, it is not uncommon to encounter variables that are zero from time $t = 0$ to some time $t = a$. It is often desirable to find the Laplace transform of the function $f(t - a)u(t - a)$, where $u(t - a)$ guarantees that the function $f(t)$, translated to the right by a time units to become $f(t - a)$, vanishes for all $t < a$. If

$$\mathcal{L}[f(t)] = F(s)$$

then

$$\mathcal{L}[f(t - a)u(t - a)] = \int_{0^-}^{\infty} [f(t - a)u(t - a)]e^{-st}\,dt$$

The integrand is zero for $t < a$. One may therefore write, noting a change in the lower limit of integration,

$$\mathcal{L}[f(t - a)u(t - a)] = \int_{a}^{\infty} [f(t - a)u(t - a)]e^{-st}\,dt$$

Let a new variable τ, selected so that $u(\tau)$ is equal to zero for values of $\tau < 0$, be defined by

$$\tau \equiv t - a$$

so that

$$t = \tau + a \qquad \text{and} \qquad d\tau = dt$$

When $t = a$, $\tau = 0$, and

$$\mathcal{L}[f(t - a)u(t - a)] = \mathcal{L}[f(\tau)u(\tau)] = \int_{0^-}^{\infty} [f(\tau)u(\tau)]e^{-s(\tau + a)}\,d\tau$$

or because $u(\tau) = 0$ for values of $\tau < 0$,

$$\mathcal{L}[f(t - a)u(t - a)] = e^{-as}\int_{0^-}^{\infty} f(\tau)e^{-s\tau}\,d\tau$$

This means that

$$\mathcal{L}[f(t - a)u(t - a)] = e^{-as}\mathcal{L}[f(t)]; \qquad a > 0$$

because an integration does not depend on what the variable of integration is called. The result is the well-known and often used shifting theorem:

$$\mathcal{L}[f(t - a)u(t - a)] = e^{-as}\mathcal{L}[f(t)] \tag{15.12}$$

TABLE 15.1   A short table of function–Laplace transform pairs

$f(t)$	$F(s)$	$f(t)$	$F(s)$
$u(t)$	$\dfrac{1}{s}$	$e^{-at}\cos \omega t$	$\dfrac{s+a}{(s+a)^2+\omega^2}$
$r(t)=t$	$\dfrac{1}{s^2}$	$t\sin \omega t$	$\dfrac{2\omega s}{(s^2+\omega^2)^2}$
C	$\dfrac{C}{s}$	$t\cos \omega t$	$\dfrac{s^2-\omega^2}{s^2+\omega^2}$
e^{-at}	$\dfrac{1}{s+a}$	te^{-at}	$\dfrac{1}{(s+a)^2}$
$\sin \omega t$	$\dfrac{\omega}{s^2+\omega^2}$	t^2	$\dfrac{2}{s^3}$
$\cos \omega t$	$\dfrac{s}{s^2+\omega^2}$	t^3	$\dfrac{3!}{s^4}$
$\delta(t)$	1	$t^n, n=1, 2, 3, \ldots$	$\dfrac{n!}{s^{n+1}}$
$e^{-at}\sin \omega t$	$\dfrac{\omega}{(s+a)^2+\omega^2}$	$t^n, n \neq -1, -2, -3, \ldots$	$\dfrac{\Gamma(n+1)}{s^{n+1}}$

SECTION 15.5   A SHORT TABLE OF LAPLACE TRANSFORM PAIRS—PART I

Table 15.1 is a table of *function* ↔ *Laplace transform* pairs. Here, the symbol ↔ means "can go either way." Table 15.1 is developed in this chapter by a systematic procedure, taking each entry in turn.

15.5.1 A Constant

If $f(t) = C$, then

$$\mathscr{L}[C] = \int_{0^-}^{\infty} (C)e^{-st}\, dt = -\frac{C}{s}\, e^{-st}\Big|_{0^-}^{\infty} = 0 - \left(-\frac{C}{s}\right)$$

or

$$\mathscr{L}[C] = \frac{C}{s} \qquad\qquad\qquad (15.13)$$

15.5.2 The Unit Step Function

One can make the immediate observation that in the definition of the unit step function,

$$u(t) = \begin{cases} 0, & t < 0 \\ 1, & t > 0 \end{cases}$$

the lower limit effectively coincides with the lower limit of the defining integral for the Laplace transform. Hence,

$$\mathscr{L}[u(t)] = \int_{0-}^{\infty} (1)e^{-st}\, dt = -\frac{1}{s}e^{-st}\Big|_{0-}^{\infty} = 0 - \left(-\frac{1}{s}\right)$$

or

$$\mathscr{L}[u(t)] = \frac{1}{s} \tag{15.14}$$

15.5.3 The Unit Ramp Function

By the same argument, the Laplace transform of the unit ramp function, defined as

$$r(t) = \begin{cases} 0, & t < 0 \\ t, & t > 0 \end{cases}$$

can be determined from

$$\mathscr{L}[r(t)] = \int_{0-}^{\infty} te^{-st}\, dt$$

using an integration by parts with

$$u = t \qquad dv = e^{-st}\, dt$$

$$du = dt \qquad v = -\frac{1}{s}e^{-st}$$

Then,

$$\mathscr{L}[r(t)] = -\frac{1}{s}te^{-st}\Big|_{0-}^{\infty} - \int_{0-}^{\infty} -\frac{1}{s}e^{-st}\, dt = -(0 - 0) - \frac{1}{s^2}e^{-st}\Big|_{0-}^{\infty}$$

or

$$\mathscr{L}[r(t)] = \frac{1}{s^2} \tag{15.15}$$

15.5.4 The Exponential Function e^{-at}

In this case, $f(t) = e^{-at}$, and

$$\mathscr{L}[e^{-at}] = \int_{0-}^{\infty} (e^{-at})e^{-st}\, dt = -\frac{1}{s+a}e^{-(s+a)t}\Big|_{0-}^{\infty} = 0 - \left(-\frac{1}{s+a}\right)$$

or

$$\mathscr{L}[e^{-st}] = \frac{1}{s+a} \tag{15.16}$$

15.5.5 The Laplace Transform of sin ωt and cos ωt

One of the Euler equations,

$$e^{j\omega t} = \cos \omega t + j \sin \omega t$$

can be applied to the previous result. The Laplace transform of the sum of two functions shows that

$$\mathscr{L}[e^{j\omega t}] = \mathscr{L}[\cos \omega t] + j\mathscr{L}[\sin \omega t]$$

Moreover,

$$\mathscr{L}[e^{j\omega t}] = \int_{0^-}^{\infty} (e^{j\omega t})e^{-st}\, dt = \int_{0^-}^{\infty} e^{-(s-j\omega)t}\, dt = \left(\frac{-1}{s-j\omega}\right)e^{-(s-j\omega)t}\Big|_{0^-}^{\infty}$$

$$= 0 - \left(\frac{-1}{s-j\omega}\right) = \frac{1}{s-j\omega} = \left(\frac{1}{s-j\omega}\right)\left(\frac{s+j\omega}{s+j\omega}\right) = \frac{s+j\omega}{s^2+\omega^2}$$

Therefore,

$$\mathscr{L}[e^{j\omega t}] = \frac{s}{s^2+\omega^2} + j\frac{\omega}{s^2+\omega^2}$$

Recall that two complex numbers are equal if and only if their real and imaginary parts are equal.[1] Hence,

$$\mathscr{L}[\sin \omega t] = \frac{\omega}{s^2+\omega^2} \tag{15.17}$$

$$\mathscr{L}[\cos \omega t] = \frac{s}{s^2+\omega^2} \tag{15.18}$$

SECTION 15.6   **TWO ADDITIONAL ASPECTS**

The determination of Laplace transforms of derivatives and integrals of functions in the time domain has been considered in Section 15.3, and repeated use of these will be quite evident in what will follow. The use of derivatives and integrals of the Laplace transforms themselves is sometimes convenient, and these are the two additional aspects that are treated in this section.

The differentiation with respect to s in the transform domain is equivalent to the multiplication of the function in the time domain by $-t$:

$$\mathscr{L}[tf(t)] = -\frac{dF(s)}{ds}$$

This may be seen when one considers the fundamental definition

$$F(s) = \int_{0^-}^{\infty} [f(t)]e^{-st}\, dt$$

---

[1] See Appendix A.

and differentiates once with respect to s to obtain

$$\frac{d}{ds} F(s) = -\int_{0-}^{\infty} tf(t)e^{-st} dt = -\mathscr{L}[tf(t)]$$

This can be extended to n differentiations. For example,

$$\frac{d^2}{ds^2} F(s) = \int_{0-}^{\infty} t^2 f(t)e^{-st} dt = \mathscr{L}[t^2 f(t)]$$

and mathematical induction leads to the general result

$$\mathscr{L}[t^n f(t)] = (-1)^n \frac{d^n F(s)}{ds} \tag{15.19}$$

The integration with respect to s in the transform domain is equivalent to a division by t in the time domain. Suppose that the fundamental definition

$$\mathscr{L}[f(t)] = \int_{0-}^{\infty} f(t)e^{-st} dt$$

is integrated from s to ∞ with respect to s. Then,

$$\int_{s}^{\infty} F(s)\, ds = \int_{s}^{\infty} \int_{0-}^{\infty} [f(t)e^{-zt}\, dt]\, dz$$

Let the order of integration be reversed. Thus,

$$\int_{s}^{\infty} F(s)\, ds = \int_{0-}^{\infty} \int_{s}^{\infty} [f(t)e^{-zt}\, dz]\, dt$$

or because t is independent of z,

$$\int_{s}^{\infty} F(s)\, ds = \int_{0-}^{\infty} \left[-\frac{f(t)}{t} e^{-zt} \right]_{s}^{\infty} dt = \int_{0-}^{\infty} \frac{f(t)}{t} e^{-st} dt$$

or

$$\int_{s}^{\infty} F(s)\, ds = \mathscr{L}\left[\frac{f(t)}{t} \right] \tag{15.20}$$

Both eqs. (15.19) and (15.20) are useful in obtaining inverses.

A SHORT TABLE OF LAPLACE TRANSFORM PAIRS—PART II   SECTION 15.7

Equations (15.19) and (15.20) make it very easy to determine the Laplace transforms of functions that are multiplied and divided by t.

15.7.1 The Functions $t \sin \omega t$ and $t \cos \omega t$

Perhaps the easiest way to find the Laplace transform of $f(t) = t \sin \omega t$ and $t \cos \omega t$ is via eq. (15.19). Take $f(t) = t \sin \omega t$:

$$\mathscr{L}[t \sin \omega t] = -\frac{d}{ds} \mathscr{L}[\sin \omega t] = -\frac{d}{ds} \frac{\omega}{s^2 + \omega^2}$$

or

$$\mathscr{L}[t \sin \omega t] = \frac{2\omega s}{(s^2 + \omega^2)^2} \qquad (15.21)$$

For $f(t) = t \cos \omega t$, a similar procedure provides

$$\mathscr{L}[t \cos \omega t] = \frac{s^2 - \omega^2}{(s^2 + \omega^2)^2} \qquad (15.22)$$

15.7.2 The Laplace Transform of t^2

There is a choice here between the use of the fundamental definition of eq. (15.1) or eq. (15.19). In the use of eq. (15.19), it is observed that

$$\mathscr{L}[t^2] = \mathscr{L}[t \cdot t] = -\frac{d}{ds}\left(\frac{1}{s^2}\right)$$

or

$$\mathscr{L}[t^2] = \frac{2}{s^3} = \frac{2!}{s^3} \qquad (15.23)$$

15.7.3 The Laplace Transform of t^n

First, obtain

$$\mathscr{L}[t^3] = \mathscr{L}[t \cdot t^2] = -\frac{d}{ds}\left(\frac{2}{s^3}\right) = \frac{6}{s^4} = \frac{3!}{s^4}$$

and then by mathematical induction, observe that[2]

$$\mathscr{L}[t^n] = \frac{n!}{s^{n+1}} \qquad (15.24)$$

15.7.4 The Laplace Transform of Exponentially Damped Functions

The Laplace transform of any exponentially damped function can be found by first taking the Laplace transform of the function itself and then applying eq. (15.11). For example,

$$\mathscr{L}[t^2 e^{-at}] = \frac{2}{(s + a)^3}$$

$$\mathscr{L}[e^{-at} \cos \omega t] = \frac{s + a}{(s + a)^2 + \omega^2}$$

$$\mathscr{L}[te^{-at} \sin \omega t] = \frac{2\omega(s + a)}{[(s + a)^2 + \omega^2]^2}$$

---

[2] Equation (15.24) only holds for cases where n is a positive integer. Any other value of n, except for the cases where n is a negative integer, requires the use of the gamma function, which is the generalization of the factorial. Here, $\mathscr{L}[t^n] = \Gamma(n + 1)/s^{n+1}$ $(n \neq 0, -1, -2, -3 \ldots)$.

15.7.5 The Laplace Transform of the Unit Impulse Function

The unit impulse function, defined in Chapter 5, can also be defined in terms of a rectangular pulse. Such a pulse of duration x and height or strength $1/x$ is shown in Fig. 15.2. The pulse may be represented in terms of a step function and a delayed step function:

$$f(t) = \frac{1}{x}\left[u(t) - u(t - x)\right]$$

The unit impulse has been observed to be a function that possesses unbounded strength and infinitesimal duration. It may therefore be defined in terms of the pulse as

$$\delta(t) = \lim_{x \to 0} \frac{1}{x}\left[u(t) - u(t - x)\right] \qquad (x > 0) \tag{15.25}$$

This definition and the shifting theorem of eq. (15.12) may be employed to obtain the Laplace transform of the unit impulse. With eq. (15.12)

$$\mathscr{L}[\delta(t)] = \lim_{x \to 0} \frac{1}{x}\left(\frac{1}{s} - \frac{e^{-xs}}{s}\right) = \lim_{x \to 0} \frac{1}{xs}(1 - e^{-xs})$$

But a Maclaurin series expansion can be written for e^{-xs}, so that

$$\mathscr{L}[\delta(t)] = \lim_{x \to 0} \frac{1}{xs}\left\{1 - \left[1 - xs + \frac{(xs)^2}{2!} - \frac{(xs)^3}{3!} + \cdots\right]\right\}$$

$$= \lim_{x \to 0}\left[1 - \frac{xs}{2!} + \frac{(xs)^2}{3!} - \frac{(xs)^3}{4!} + \cdots\right]$$

A pulse of height $1/x$ and duration x, which can be considered to represent the unit impulse in the limit as $x \to 0$

FIGURE 15.2

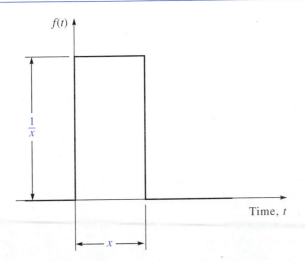

When the limit is taken, it is observed that

$$\mathscr{L}[\delta(t)] = 1 \tag{15.26}$$

SECTION 15.8   PROCEDURAL EXAMPLE

It is well at this point to demonstrate the procedure used to solve a linear differential equation with constant coefficients by the Laplace transform method. Let the differential equation to be solved be somewhat formidable

$$\frac{dy}{dt} + 4y = 8 + 16t + 2e^{-4t}$$

where the initial condition is $y(0^-) = 2$.

It has been shown in Section 15.3.1 that the Laplace transform of the sum of a group of functions is the sum of the individual Laplace transforms. The equation can therefore be transformed term by term:

$$\mathscr{L}\left[\frac{dy}{dt}\right] + \mathscr{L}[4y] = \mathscr{L}[8] + \mathscr{L}[16t] + \mathscr{L}[2e^{-4t}]$$

In addition, Section 15.3.2 shows that the Laplace transform of a constant times a function is equal to the constant times the Laplace transform of the function. Thus,

$$\mathscr{L}\left[\frac{dy}{dt}\right] + 4\mathscr{L}[y] = \mathscr{L}[8] + 16\mathscr{L}[t] + 2\mathscr{L}[e^{-4t}]$$

Next, as usual, set

$$\mathscr{L}[y(t)] = Y(s)$$

and remember the expression for the Laplace transform of the derivative (which automatically incorporates the initial condition):

$$\mathscr{L}\left[\frac{dy}{dt}\right] = sY(s) - y(0^-)$$

Then, with the help of Table 15.1 and the fact that $y(0^-) = 2$, one obtains

$$sY(s) - 2 + 4Y(s) = \frac{8}{s} + \frac{16}{s^2} + \frac{2}{s+4}$$

or

$$(s+4)Y(s) = 2 + \frac{8}{s} + \frac{16}{s^2} + \frac{2}{s+4}$$

Now, it just a matter of algebra to solve for $Y(s)$. First,

$$(s+4)Y(s) = \frac{2s^2(s+4) + 8s(s+4) + 16(s+4) + 2s^2}{s^2(s+4)}$$

and then

$$Y(s) = \frac{2s^3 + 18s^2 + 48s + 64}{s^2(s + 4)^2} \qquad (15.27)$$

The Laplace transform of the dependent variable has been found. The next step is to recover the time domain function $y(t)$ from the s or Laplace transform domain. The background for this recovery is provided in Section 5.9. First, however, make two observations.

The first observation concerns the use of the Laplace transform as a linear transformation. If the differential equation

$$\frac{dy}{dt} + 4y = 8 + 16t + 2e^{-4t}$$

is multiplied, term by term, by e^{-st}

$$\frac{dy}{dt} e^{-st} + 4ye^{-st} = 8e^{-st} + 16te^{-st} + 2e^{-4t}e^{-st}$$

Then, a term-by-term integration between the limits 0^- and ∞ can be effected:

$$\int_{0^-}^{\infty} \frac{dy}{dt} e^{-st} dt + \int_{0^-}^{\infty} 4ye^{-st} dt = \int_{0^-}^{\infty} 8e^{-st} dt + \int_{0^-}^{\infty} 16te^{-st} dt + \int_{0^-}^{\infty} 2e^{-4t}e^{-st} dt$$

This is a term-by-term listing of the Laplace transform for the given differential equation,

$$\mathcal{L}\left[\frac{dy}{dt}\right] + \mathcal{L}[4y] = \mathcal{L}[8] + \mathcal{L}[16t] + \mathcal{L}[2e^{-4t}]$$

and demonstrates the use of the Laplace transform as a linear operator. It also indicates that the Laplace transform of the sum of a group of functions that each possess a Laplace transform is equal to the sum of the individual transforms. Moreover, the use of the Laplace transform satisfies the homogeneity and superposition conditions for linearity discussed in Chapters 1 and 6.

The second observation pertains to the form of the Laplace transform of the dependent variable. As an alternative to finding a least common denominator, the case being considered,

$$(s + 4)Y(s) = 2 + \frac{8}{s} + \frac{16}{s^2} + \frac{2}{s + 4}$$

can be written as the sum of four Laplace transforms:

$$Y(s) = Y_1(s) + Y_2(s) + Y_3(s) + Y_4(s)$$

or

$$Y(s) = \frac{2}{s + 4} + \frac{8}{s(s + 4)} + \frac{16}{s^2(s + 4)} + \frac{2}{(s + 4)^2} \qquad (15.28)$$

The reader will be able to draw a conclusion regarding the labor involved in working with either of eqs. (15.27) or (15.28) when both of these forms are considered in an example in Section 15.9.3.

THE INVERSE LAPLACE TRANSFORMATION

15.9.1 Introduction

Taking the inverse Laplace transform is a process that recovers the function in the time domain $f(t)$ from the Laplace transform in the algebraic s domain, $F(s)$. As is customary, one designates this operation by

$$\mathcal{L}^{-1}[F(s)] \equiv f(t) \tag{15.29}$$

Certain operations on the Laplace transform suggest a procedure that will isolate each part of the response into relatively simple forms so that Table 15.1 may be used in reverse.

Recall eqs. (15.4) and (15.5):

$$\mathcal{L}[f(t) + g(t)] = F(s) + G(s) \tag{15.4}$$

$$\mathcal{L}[Cf(t)] = CF(s) \tag{15.5}$$

Using these, one observes that

$$\mathcal{L}^{-1}[F(s) + G(s)] = \mathcal{L}^{-1}[F(s)] + \mathcal{L}^{-1}[G(s)] = f(t) + g(t) \tag{15.30}$$

$$\mathcal{L}^{-1}[CF(s)] = C\mathcal{L}^{-1}[F(s)] = Cf(t) \tag{15.31}$$

The task at hand is to take the Laplace transform, regardless of its form, and decompose it into a sum of simple terms. The inverse transform can then be obtained from each term in accordance with eqs. (15.30) and (15.31). The task always begins with an investigation of the denominator of the Laplace transform.

In the pages that follow, reference will be made to a general Laplace transform,

$$F(s) = \frac{P(s)}{Q(s)}$$

where $P(s)$ and $Q(s)$ are polynomials in the transform variable s and where the degree of $Q(s)$ is always equal to or greater than the degree of $P(s)$.

If $P(s)$ has a degree equal to or greater than $Q(s)$, then one must proceed with caution, because the inverse will contain impulses. Notice that a long division of something like

$$F(s) = \frac{P(s)}{Q(s)} = \frac{s^2 + 3s + 2}{s^2 + 2s + 1}$$

contains an impulse, because

$$\mathcal{L}^{-1}\left[\frac{s^2 + 3s + 2}{s^2 + 2s + 1}\right] = \mathcal{L}^{-1}\left[1 + \frac{s + 1}{s^2 + 2s + 1}\right]$$

and

$$\mathscr{L}^{-1}[1] = \delta(t)$$

Thus, the presence of the impulse is confirmed.

The inverse is obtained by employing a rather standard process from elementary calculus, where it was referred to as *partial fractions*. The procedure, which will now be repeated carefully in some detail, depends on the form of $Q(s)$. There are three possibilities for the form:

1. $Q(s)$ is separable into distinct, nonrepeating linear factors.
2. $Q(s)$ contains repeated linear factors.
3. $Q(s)$ contains quadratic factors.

15.9.2 Q(s) Contains Distinct, Nonrepeating Linear Factors

Consider the form of $F(s)$,

$$F(s) = \frac{P(s)}{Q(s)} = \frac{(s + a_1)(s + a_2)(s + a_3) \cdots (s + a_n)}{(s + b_1)(s + b_2)(s + b_3) \cdots (s + b_m)}$$

where $m > n$ and where $b_1 \neq b_2 \neq b_3 \neq \cdots \neq b_m$. In this case, $F(s)$ may be written as a partial-fraction expansion,

$$F(s) = \frac{K_1}{s + b_1} + \frac{K_2}{s + b_2} + \frac{K_3}{s + b_3} + \cdots + \frac{K_m}{s + b_m}$$

and the task is to find the values of K_i, $i = 1, 2, 3, \ldots, m$.

Consider K_1. Its value can be determined by multiplying all terms by $(s + b_1)$. This yields

$$F(s) = \frac{(s + a_1)(s + a_2) \cdots (s + a_n)(s + b_1)}{(s + b_1)(s + b_2) \cdots (s + b_m)}$$

$$= K_1 \frac{s + b_1}{s + b_1} + K_2 \frac{s + b_1}{s + b_2} + \cdots + K_m \frac{s + b_1}{s + b_m}$$

If all of the common $(s + b_1)$ terms are canceled, the result is

$$\frac{(s + a_1)(s + a_2) \cdots (s + a_n)}{(s + b_2)(s + b_3) \cdots (s + b_m)} = K_1 + K_2 \frac{s + b_1}{s + b_2} + \cdots + K_m \frac{s + b_1}{s + b_m}$$

Then, K_1 can be isolated,

$$K_1 = \frac{(s + a_1)(s + a_2) \cdots (s + a_n)}{(s + b_2) \cdots (s + b_m)} - K_2 \frac{s + b_1}{s + b_2} - \cdots - K_m \frac{s + b_1}{s + b_m}$$

and then obtained by letting $s = -b_1$. In this event, $K_2, K_3, \ldots, K_m$ vanish, because they are annihilated by the associated factor $s + b_1$. Thus,

$$K_1 = \frac{(s + a_1)(s + a_2) \cdots (s + a_n)}{(s + b_2) \cdots (s + b_m)} \bigg|_{s = -b_1}$$

To find K_2, follow the same procedure:

$$K_2 = \frac{(s + a_1)(s + a_2) \cdots (s + a_n)}{(s + b_1)(s + b_3) \cdots (s + b_m)}\bigg|_{s = -b_2}$$

Then, via mathematical induction, obtain the relationship

$$K_i = \frac{P(s)}{Q(s)}(s + b_i)\bigg|_{s = -b_i} \qquad (i = 1, 2, 3, \ldots, m) \qquad (15.32)$$

If $Q(s)$ can be factored and there are no repeating factors and $F(s)$ is a proper rational function, the partial-fraction expansion is obtained quite easily. Two examples now follow. In the first $Q(s)$ is a quadratic and in the second, $Q(s)$ is a cubic.

■ **EXAMPLE 15.1**

The Laplace transform of $f(t)$ is given by

$$F(s) = \frac{s + 2}{s^2 + 5s + 4}$$

Find $f(t)$.

Solution   Here $P(s) = s + 2$ and

$$Q(s) = s^2 + 5s + 4 \qquad \cdot$$

the degree of $Q(s)$ is greater than the degree of $P(s)$. The factors of $Q(s)$ are obtained from $Q(s) = 0$

$$s^2 + 5s + 4 = (s + 1)(s + 4) = 0$$

which shows that the roots of $Q(s)$ are $s_1 = -1$ and $s_2 = -4$. Thus

$$F(s) = \frac{s + 2}{(s + 1)(s + 4)} = \frac{K_1}{s + 1} + \frac{K_2}{s + 4}$$

Using eq. (15.32) twice gives

$$K_1 = \frac{s + 2}{s + 4}\bigg|_{s = -1} = \frac{1}{3}$$

$$K_2 = \frac{s + 2}{s + 1}\bigg|_{s = -4} = \frac{-2}{-3} = \frac{2}{3}$$

Thus

$$F(s) = \frac{1}{3}\left[\frac{1}{s + 1} + \frac{2}{s + 4}\right]$$

and reference to Table 15.1 shows that

$$f(t) = \frac{1}{3}(e^{-t} + 2e^{-4t})$$

■

■ **EXAMPLE 15.2**

The Laplace transform of $f(t)$ is given by

$$F(s) = \frac{1}{s^3 + 12s^2 + 47s + 60}$$

Find $f(t)$.

Solution   Here, $P(s) = 1$ and

$$Q(s) = s^3 + 12s^2 + 47s + 60$$

The degree of $Q(s)$ is greater than the degree of $P(s)$. The factors of $Q(s)$ are obtained from $Q(s) = 0$,

$$s^3 + 12s^2 + 47s + 60 = 0$$

and the reader may verify that the roots are $s_1 = -3$, $s_2 = -4$, and $s_3 = -5$. Thus,

$$F(s) = \frac{1}{(s+3)(s+4)(s+5)} = \frac{K_1}{s+3} + \frac{K_2}{s+4} + \frac{K_3}{s+5}$$

Equation (15.32) is employed three times:

$$K_1 = \frac{1(s+3)}{(s+3)(s+4)(s+5)}\bigg|_{s=-3} = \frac{1}{(1)(2)} = \frac{1}{2}$$

$$K_2 = \frac{1(s+4)}{(s+3)(s+4)(s+5)}\bigg|_{s=-4} = \frac{1}{(-1)(1)} = -1$$

$$K_3 = \frac{1(s+5)}{(s+3)(s+4)(s+5)}\bigg|_{s=-5} = \frac{1}{(-2)(-1)} = \frac{1}{2}$$

Thus,

$$F(s) = \frac{1}{2}\left(\frac{1}{s+3} + \frac{1}{s+5}\right) - \frac{1}{s+4}$$

and reference to Table 15.1 shows that

$$f(t) = \frac{1}{2}(e^{-3t} + e^{-5t}) - e^{-4t} = \frac{1}{2}(e^{-3t} - 2e^{-4t} + e^{-5t})$$

Note that the real difficulty is in finding the roots of $Q(s)$. The advent of the hand calculator has, of course, alleviated this difficulty.   ■

EXERCISE 15.1

Find $f(t)$ if

$$F(s) = \frac{4(s+4)}{s^3 + 6s^2 + 11s + 6}$$

Answer $f(t) = 6e^{-t} - 8e^{-2t} + 2e^{-3t}$.

15.9.3 Q(s) Contains Some Repeating Linear Factors

There are two methods that can be used to find the inverse transform when $Q(s)$ contains repeated linear factors. The first method is based on what are called *residues*, and the second is nothing more than a method of algebra.

The Residue Approach   Suppose in

$$F(s) = \frac{P(s)}{Q(s)}$$

$Q(s)$ contains a factor $(s+b)$, which is repeated r times. Then,

$$F(s) = \frac{P(s)}{(s+b_1)(s+b_2)\cdots(s+b)^r \cdots (s+b_{m-r})}$$

The repeated factors $(s+b)$ lead to r terms in the partial-fraction expansion, which can be written as

$$F(s) = \frac{P(s)}{Q(s)} = \frac{p(s)}{(s+b)^r}$$

$$= \frac{C_1}{s+b} + \frac{C_2}{(s+b)^2} + \cdots + \frac{C_{r-1}}{(s+b)^{r-1}} + \frac{C_r}{(s+b)^r} + G(s) \qquad (15.33)$$

where $G(s)$ contains all of the partial-fraction terms that are not due to the repeated factors, and where

$$p(s) = \frac{P(s)}{Q(s)} (s+b)^r$$

The task is to determine all of the C's, and the first step is to multiply both sides of eq. (15.33) by $(s+b)^r$ to obtain

$$p(s) = C_1(s+b)^{r-1} + C_2(s+b)^{r-2} + C_3(s+b)^{r-3} + \cdots$$
$$+ C_{r-1}(s+b) + C_r + (s+b)^r G(s)$$

If $s = -b$, then

$$C_r = p(s)\Big|_{s=-b}$$

Next, obtain the derivative of $p(s)$. Here, use is made of the prime to indicate a differentiation:

$$p'(s) = C_1(r-1)(s+b)^{r-2} + C_2(r-2)(s+b)^{r-3} + \cdots$$
$$+ C_{r-1} + r(s+b)^{r-1}G(s) + (s+b)^r G'(s)$$

and again, let $s = -b$. Then,

$$C_{r-1} = p'(s)\Big|_{s=-b}$$

Another differentiation gives

$$p''(s) = C_1(r-1)(r-2)(s+b)^{r-3} + C_2(r-2)(r-3)(s+b)^{r-4} + \cdots$$
$$+ 2C_{r-2} + r(r-1)(s+b)^{r-2}G(s) + 2r(s+b)^{r-1}G'(s) + (s+b)^r G''(s)$$

so that

$$C_{r-2} = \frac{p''(s)}{2!}\Big|_{s=-b}$$

It can be verified that a continuation of this process provides

$$C_{r-3} = \frac{p'''(s)}{3!}\Big|_{s=-b}$$

and mathematical induction provides a general relationship:

$$C_{r-i} = \frac{p^i(s)}{i!} \qquad i = 0, 1, 2, 3, \ldots, (r-1) \tag{15.34}$$

One can anticipate doing a fair amount of work if r is a moderately large integer, like 5 or 6. Furthermore, if $p(s)$ is somewhat ungainly, the repeated differentiations may be difficult to handle. The actual differentiation technique is, of course, at the discretion of the analyst.

■ **EXAMPLE 15.3**

Find $f(t)$ if

$$F(s) = \frac{s+2}{(s+1)^3(s+3)}$$

Solution The partial-fraction expansion with $r = 3$ is

$$F(s) = \frac{P(s)}{Q(s)} = \frac{s+2}{(s+1)^3(s+3)} = \frac{C_1}{s+1} + \frac{C_2}{(s+1)^2} + \frac{C_3}{(s+1)^3} + \frac{K_1}{s+3}$$

Note that the highest-numbered C coefficient is associated with the highest power of the factor $s+1$.

Constant K_1 is found quickly by employing eq. (15.32):

$$K_1 = \frac{(s+2)(s+3)}{(s+1)^3(s+3)}\bigg|_{s=-3} = \frac{s+2}{(s+1)^3}\bigg|_{s=-3} = \frac{-1}{(-2)^3} = \frac{1}{8}$$

The value of $p(s)$ will be

$$p(s) = \frac{P(s)}{Q(s)}(s+1)^3 = \frac{s+2}{s+3}$$

and with this value of $p(s)$, C_1, C_2, and C_3 may be found from an application of eq. (15.34).

For $i = 0$, so that $r = 3$,

$$C_3 = p(s)\bigg|_{s=-1} = \frac{1}{2}$$

For $i = 1$ and $r = 2$,

$$p'(s) = \frac{(s+3) - (s+2)}{(s+3)^2} = \frac{1}{(s+3)^2}$$

Then,

$$p'(s)\bigg|_{s=-1} = \frac{1}{(2)^2} = \frac{1}{4} \qquad \text{and} \qquad C_2 = \frac{p'(s)}{1!}\bigg|_{s=-1} = \frac{1}{4}$$

Finally, for $i = 2$ and $r = 1$,

$$p''(s) = -\frac{2}{(s+3)^3} \qquad \text{and} \qquad C_1 = \frac{p''(s)}{2!}\bigg|_{s=-1} = -\frac{1}{2}\frac{2}{(2)^3} = -\frac{1}{8}$$

The result is

$$F(s) = -\frac{\frac{1}{8}}{s+1} + \frac{\frac{1}{4}}{(s+1)^2} + \frac{\frac{1}{2}}{(s+1)^3} + \frac{\frac{1}{8}}{s+3}$$

But before Table 15.1 can be used, the third term must be represented as

$$\frac{1}{4} \cdot \frac{2}{(s+1)^3}$$

Then, use of the damping property of eq. (15.11) in applying Table 15.1 shows that

$$f(t) = -\frac{1}{8}e^{-t} + \frac{1}{4}te^{-t} + \frac{1}{4}t^2e^{-t} + \frac{1}{8}e^{-3t}$$

A Method of Algebra   After $F(s)$ is set up in a partial-fraction expansion, the coefficients may be evaluated by an algebraic method. This method has advantages over the residue method when r is large, although it may require the solution of as many as r linear algebraic equations in r unknowns. The procedure is identical to the point where $F(s)$ is separated into factors and work begins on the determination of the constants. Example 15.4 is presented to illustrate this method and to afford a means of comparison between the two methods.

■ **EXAMPLE 15.4**

Use the function given in Example 15.3,

$$F(s) = \frac{s + 2}{(s + 1)^3(s + 3)}$$

and find $f(t)$ by an algebraic method.

Solution   The partial-fraction expansion is as before:

$$F(s) = \frac{s + 2}{(s + 1)^3(s + 3)} = \frac{C_1}{s + 1} + \frac{C_2}{(s + 1)^2} + \frac{C_3}{(s + 1)^3} + \frac{K_1}{s + 3}$$

The first step is to put everything over a least common denominator:

$$
\begin{aligned}
F(s) &= \frac{s + 2}{(s + 1)^3(s + 3)} \\
&= \frac{C_1(s^3 + 5s^2 + 7s + 3) + C_2(s^2 + 4s + 3) + C_3(s + 3) + K_1(s^3 + 3s^2 + 3s + 1)}{(s + 1)^3(s + 3)} \\
&= \frac{(C_1 + K_1)s^3 + (5C_1 + C_2 + 3K_1)s^2 + (7C_1 + 4C_2 + C_3 + 3K_1)s + (3C_1 + 3C_2 + 3C_3 + K_1)}{(s + 1)^3(s + 3)}
\end{aligned}
$$

Four simultaneous, linear algebraic equations with the constants as variables can be formed by equating the coefficients of each power of s on the right with the coefficients of $P(s) = s + 2$ on the left:

$$
\begin{aligned}
\text{for } s^4\text{:} \quad & 0 = C_1 && + K_1 \\
\text{for } s^3\text{:} \quad & 0 = 5C_1 + C_2 && + 3K_1 \\
\text{for } s^2\text{:} \quad & 1 = 7C_1 + 4C_2 + C_3 + 3K_1 \\
\text{for } s^1\text{:} \quad & 2 = 3C_1 + 3C_2 + 3C_3 + K_1
\end{aligned}
$$

Much labor will be saved if K_1 is first found in the customary manner, using eq. (15.32). From a procedure used in Example 15.3,

$$K_1 = \frac{1}{8}$$

Then, from the first equation with this value of K_1:

$$C_1 = -K_1 = -\frac{1}{8}$$

Next, use the second equation with the additional information that $C_1 = -\frac{1}{8}$:

$$C_2 = -5C_1 - 3K_1 = -5\left(-\frac{1}{8}\right) - 3\left(\frac{1}{8}\right) = \frac{1}{4}$$

Finally, obtain C_3 from the third equation, using the additional value of $C_2 = \frac{1}{4}$:

$$C_3 = 1 - 7C_1 - 4C_2 - 3K_1 = 1 - 7\left(-\frac{1}{8}\right) - 4\left(\frac{1}{4}\right) - 3\left(\frac{1}{8}\right)$$

$$= 1 + \frac{7}{8} - 1 - \frac{3}{8} = \frac{1}{2}$$

The partial-fraction expansion looks like this:

$$F(s) = -\frac{\frac{1}{8}}{s+1} + \frac{\frac{1}{4}}{(s+1)^2} + \frac{\frac{1}{2}}{(s+1)^3} + \frac{\frac{1}{8}}{s+3}$$

and reference to Table 15.1, again with an assist from the damping property of eq. (15.11), shows that the function in the time domain is

$$f(t) = -\frac{1}{8}e^{-t} + \frac{1}{4}te^{-t} + \frac{1}{4}t^2e^{-t} + \frac{1}{8}e^{-3t}$$

which is the same result as the one obtained in Example 15.3 by residues. ■

EXERCISE 15.2

Find $f(t)$ if

$$F(s) = 2\left(\frac{s^2 + 2s + 6}{s^3 + 3s^2}\right)$$

Answer $f(t) = 4t + 2e^{-3t}$.

■ **EXAMPLE 15.5**

The intent of this example is to enable the reader to make a comparison of the labor involved in finding the inverse Laplace transform from the two alternative forms of $F(s)$:

$$Y(s) = \frac{2s^3 + 18s^2 + 48s + 64}{s^2(s+4)^2} \tag{15.27}$$

$$Y(s) = \frac{2}{s+4} + \frac{8}{s(s+4)} + \frac{16}{s^2(s+4)} + \frac{2}{(s+4)^2} \tag{15.28}$$

Solution First, for eq. (15.27),

$$Y(s) = \frac{2s^3 + 18s^2 + 48s + 64}{s^2(s+4)^2} = \frac{C_1}{s} + \frac{C_2}{s^2} + \frac{D_1}{s+4} + \frac{D_2}{(s+4)^2}$$

Let

$$p_C(s) = \frac{2s^3 + 18s^2 + 48s + 64}{(s+4)^2} \quad \text{and} \quad p_D(s) = \frac{2s^3 + 18s^2 + 48s + 64}{s^2}$$

so that

$$p_C'(s) = \frac{(s+4)^2(6s^2 + 36s + 48) - 2(2s^3 + 18s^2 + 48s + 64)(s+4)}{(s+4)^4}$$

$$p_D'(s) = \frac{s^2(6s^2 + 36s + 48) - (2s^3 + 18s^2 + 48s + 64)2s}{s^4}$$

Then, eq. (15.34) gives

$$C_2 = \frac{p_C(0)}{0!} = \frac{64}{16} = 4$$

$$C_1 = \frac{p_C'(0)}{1!} = \frac{16(48) - 2(64)(4)}{256} = \frac{256}{256} = 1$$

$$D_2 = \frac{p_D(-4)}{0!} = \frac{2(-64) + 18(16) + 48(-4) + 64}{16} = \frac{32}{16} = 2$$

$$D_1 = \frac{p_D'(-4)}{1!}$$

$$= \frac{16[6(16) + 36(-4) + 48] - [2(-64) + 18(16) + 48(-4) + 64](2)(-4)}{256}$$

$$= \frac{256}{256} = 1$$

Thus,

$$Y(s) = \frac{1}{s} + \frac{4}{s^2} + \frac{1}{s+4} + \frac{2}{(s+4)^2}$$

$$y(t) = 1 + 4t + e^{-4t} + 2te^{-4t}$$

Equation (15.28) is the sum of four Laplace transforms:

$$Y(s) = Y_1(s) + Y_2(s) + Y_3(s) + Y_4(s)$$

which will yield inverses in the time domain such that

$$y(t) = y_1(t) + y_2(t) + y_3(t) + y_4(t)$$

Observe that

$$Y_1(s) = \frac{2}{s+4} \quad \text{and} \quad Y_4(s) = \frac{2}{(s+4)^2}$$

so that

$$y_1(t) = 2e^{-4t} \qquad \text{and} \qquad y_4(t) = 2te^{-4t}$$

A little work on $Y_2(s)$ and $Y_3(s)$ will provide the sought-after result:

$$Y_2(s) = \frac{8}{s(s+4)} = \frac{K_1}{s} + \frac{K_2}{s+4}$$

so that by eq. (15.32)

$$K_1 = \left.\frac{8}{s+4}\right|_{s=0} = \frac{8}{4} = 2 \qquad \text{and} \qquad K_2 = \left.\frac{8}{s}\right|_{s=-4} = \frac{8}{-4} = -2$$

Then,

$$Y_2(s) = \frac{2}{s} - \frac{2}{s+4} \qquad \text{and} \qquad y_2(t) = 2 - 2e^{-4t}$$

Finally,

$$Y_3(s) = \frac{16}{s^2(s+4)} = \frac{C_1}{s} + \frac{C_2}{s^2} + \frac{K_1}{s+4}$$

with

$$p(s) = \frac{16}{s+4} \qquad \text{and} \qquad p'(s) = -\frac{16}{(s+4)^2}$$

One obtains C_1, C_2, and K_1 by eqs. (15.32) and (15.34):

$$C_2 = \frac{p(0)}{0!} = \frac{16}{4} = 4 \qquad C_1 = \frac{p'(0)}{1!} = \frac{-16}{16} = -1$$

$$K_1 = \left.\frac{16}{s^2}\right|_{s=-4} = \frac{16}{16} = 1$$

Thus,

$$Y_3(s) = -\frac{1}{s} + \frac{4}{s^2} + \frac{1}{s+4} \qquad \text{and} \qquad y_3(t) = -1 + 4t + e^{-4t}$$

When $y_1(t)$ through $y_4(t)$ are added, the result is $y(t)$:

$$y(t) = (2e^{-4t}) + (2 - 2e^{-4t}) + (-1 + 4t + e^{-4t}) + (2te^{-4t})$$
$$= 1 + 4t + e^{-4t} + 2te^{-4t}$$

Observe that in this particular case, the decomposition of the Laplace transform into four simpler Laplace transforms leads to less work in obtaining the inverse. Of course, either method must provide the identical result. ■

15.9.4 Q(s) Contains Quadratic Factors

A quadratic equation such as

$$as^2 + bs + c = 0$$

has roots

$$s_1, s_2 = \frac{-b \pm \sqrt{b^2 - 4ac}}{2a}$$

When a quadratic factor appears in $Q(s)$, one begins by looking at the discriminant of the quadratic factor. If $b^2 - 4ac > 0$, then there are two real distinct roots, and the procedure of Section 15.9.2 may be used. If $b^2 - 4ac = 0$, there are two equal roots, and either the residue method or the algebraic approach in Section 15.9.3 may be used. However, if $b^2 - 4ac < 0$, neither of the foregoing pertain, and a method of algebra must be employed in conjunction with the partial-fraction expansion.

Completing the Square   There are many procedures for the solution of a quadratic equation. One of them is by the *quadratic formula*. Another is by a method known as *completing the square*, which is the method used to derive the quadratic formula. This is best illustrated by an example; the example that follows will show how a method of algebra must be employed in conjunction with the partial-fraction expansion.

■ **EXAMPLE 15.6**
  Find $f(t)$ if

$$F(s) = \frac{3s - 1}{s^2 + 2s + 5}$$

Solution   First, observe in $Q(s) = s^2 + 2s + 5$ that

$$b^2 - 4ac = (2)^2 - 4(1)(5) = 4 - 20 = -16$$

and that this negative value indicates that $Q(s)$ will possess complex conjugate roots.

Now, complete the square in $Q(s)$:

$$s^2 + 2s + 5 = s^2 + 2s + 1 + 4 = (s + 1)^2 + 4$$

This makes

$$F(s) = \frac{3s - 1}{(s + 1)^2 + 4}$$

Let the numerator be adjusted so that an $(s + 1)$ factor is obtained:

$$F(s) = \frac{3s - 1}{(s + 1)^2 + 4} = \frac{3s + 3 - 1 - 3}{(s + 1)^2 + 4}$$

$$= \frac{3(s + 1) - 4}{(s + 1)^2 + 4} = 3\frac{s + 1}{(s + 1)^2 + 4} - \frac{4}{2} \cdot \frac{2}{(s + 1)^2 + 4}$$

Table 15.1 shows that

$$\mathcal{L}^{-1}\left[\frac{s}{s^2 + 4}\right] = \cos 2t \quad \text{and} \quad \mathcal{L}^{-1}\left[\frac{2}{s^2 + 4}\right] = \sin 2t$$

The $(s + 1)$ term merely suggests the presence of a damping term e^{-t}, so that

$$f(t) = 3e^{-t}\cos 2t - 2e^{-t}\sin 2t$$

The Partial-Fraction Expansion   The partial-fraction expansion for a single quadratic factor

$$s^2 + \frac{b}{a}s + \frac{c}{a}$$

is

$$F(s) = \frac{As + B}{s^2 + (b/a)s + (c/a)}$$

and the task is to evaluate A and B. If the factor appears r times, then

$$F(s) = \frac{A_1 s + B_1}{s^2 + (b/a)s + (c/a)} + \frac{A_2 s + B_2}{[s^2 + (b/a)s + (c/a)]^2} + \cdots$$
$$+ \frac{A_r s + B_r}{[s^2 + (b/a)s + (c/a)]^r}$$

The method of algebra must be employed to evaluate all of the A's and B's, and then one proceeds to complete the square to recover the time function $f(t)$.

■   **EXAMPLE 15.7**

Find $f(t)$ if

$$F(s) = \frac{s^2 + 4s + 1}{(s^2 + 2s + 5)(s^2 + 6s + 10)}$$

Solution   Expand into partial fractions:

$$F(s) = \frac{s^2 + 4s + 1}{(s^2 + 2s + 5)(s^2 + 6s + 10)} = \frac{A_1 s + B_1}{s^2 + 2s + 5} + \frac{A_2 s + B_2}{s^2 + 6s + 10}$$

Now, find a least common denominator:

$$F(s) = \frac{s^2 + 4s + 1}{(s^2 + 2s + 5)(s^2 + 6s + 10)}$$
$$= \frac{(A_1 s + B_1)(s^2 + 6s + 10) + (A_2 s + B_2)(s^2 + 2s + 5)}{(s^2 + 2s + 5)(s^2 + 6s + 10)}$$

Note that because the coefficients of the numerator terms are to be equated, further consideration of the denominator in this part of the procedure is unnecessary.

Expand the numerator of the right-hand term, and then equate the coefficients of like terms of s. This procedure is summarized in the following list:

$$\text{for } s^3: \quad 0 = \quad A_1 + A_2$$

$$\text{for } s^2: \quad 1 = \quad 6A_1 + 2A_2 \quad + B_1 \quad + B_2$$

$$\text{for } s^1: \quad 4 = 10A_1 + 5A_2 \quad + 6B_1 + 2B_2$$

$$\text{for } s^0: \quad 1 = \quad\quad\quad\quad\quad\quad 10B_1 + 5B_2$$

Note from the foregoing that

$$A_1 = -A_2 \quad \text{and} \quad B_2 = \frac{1}{5} - 2B_1$$

These may be substituted into the second and third equations to obtain

$$4A_1 - B_1 = \frac{4}{5} \quad \text{and} \quad 5A_1 + 2B_1 = \frac{18}{5}$$

From all of this, the reader may verify that

$$A_1 = \frac{2}{5} \quad A_2 = -\frac{2}{5} \quad B_1 = \frac{4}{5} \quad B_2 = -\frac{7}{5}$$

With these values, $F(s)$ becomes

$$F(s) = \frac{1}{5}\left(\frac{2s + 4}{s^2 + 2s + 5} - \frac{2s + 7}{s^2 + 6s + 10}\right)$$

and the inverse can be obtained by completing the squares:

$$F(s) = \frac{1}{5}\left(\frac{2s + 4}{s^2 + 2s + 1 - 1 + 5} - \frac{2s + 7}{s^2 + 6s + 9 - 9 + 10}\right)$$

$$= \frac{1}{5}\left[\frac{2s + 4}{(s + 1)^2 + 4} - \frac{2s + 7}{(s + 3)^2 + 1}\right]$$

$$= \frac{2}{5}\left[\frac{s + 2}{(s + 1)^2 + 4}\right] - \frac{2}{5}\left[\frac{s + \frac{7}{2}}{(s + 3)^2 + 1}\right]$$

$$= \frac{2}{5}\left[\frac{s + 1}{(s + 1)^2 + 4} + \frac{1}{(s + 1)^2 + 4}\right]$$

$$\quad - \frac{2}{5}\left[\frac{s + 3}{(s + 3)^2 + 1} + \frac{\frac{1}{2}}{(s + 3)^2 + 1}\right]$$

$$= \frac{2}{5}\left[\frac{s + 1}{(s + 1)^2 + 4}\right] + \frac{1}{5}\left[\frac{2}{(s + 1)^2 + 4}\right]$$

$$\quad - \frac{2}{5}\left[\frac{s + 3}{(s + 3)^2 + 1}\right] - \frac{1}{5}\left[\frac{1}{(s + 3)^2 + 1}\right]$$

The inverse may now be found by referring to Table 15.1:

$$f(t) = \frac{1}{5}\left[e^{-t}(2\cos 2t + \sin 2t) - e^{-3t}(2\cos t + \sin t)\right]$$

EXERCISE 15.3

Find $f(t)$ if

$$F(s) = \frac{6s^2 + 63s + 102}{s^3 + 12s^2 + 57s + 100}$$

Answer $f(t) = e^{-4t}(12 \cos 3t + 5 \sin 3t) - 6e^{-4t}$.

Method   It has been observed that a Laplace transform such as

$$F(s) = \frac{4s + 25}{s^2 + 16s + 25}$$

can be adjusted by a process known as completing the square to yield an inverse expressed as a damped combination of a sine and a cosine:

$$f(t) = e^{-4t}(4 \cos 3t + 3 \sin 3t)$$

It is sometimes desirable to express $f(t)$ in what is referred to as the *amplitude–phase angle form*:

$$f(t) = Ce^{-\alpha t} \cos(\omega_d t + \phi) \qquad \text{or} \qquad f(t) = Ce^{-\alpha t} \sin(\omega_d t + \theta)$$

To find the Laplace transforms of these functions, first consider just

$$\cos(\omega_d t + \phi)$$

and use the trigonometric identity

$$\cos(A + B) = \cos A \cos B - \sin A \sin B$$

to write

$$C \cos(\omega_d + \phi) = C(\cos \phi \cos \omega_d t - \sin \phi \sin \omega_d t)$$

and its Laplace transform,

$$\mathcal{L}[C \cos(\omega_d t + \phi)] = C\left(\frac{s \cos \phi - \omega_d \sin \phi}{s^2 + \omega_d^2}\right)$$

The Laplace transform with the damping factor $e^{-\alpha t}$ then derives from a simple shift of argument from s to $s + \alpha$:

$$\mathcal{L}[Ce^{-\alpha t} \cos(\omega_d t + \phi)] = C\left[\frac{(s + \alpha) \cos \phi - \omega_d \sin \phi}{(s + \alpha)^2 + \omega_d^2}\right] \qquad \text{(15.35)}$$

The Laplace transform of

$$f(t) = Ce^{-\alpha t} \sin(\omega_d t + \theta)$$

is obtained in an identical procedure and is

$$\mathscr{L}[Ce^{-\alpha t}\sin(\omega_d + \theta)] = C\left[\frac{(s + \alpha)\sin\theta + \omega_d\cos\theta}{(s + \alpha)^2 + \omega_d^2}\right] \tag{15.36}$$

Now, consider $F(s)$ as a quotient of two polynomials in s,

$$F(s) = \frac{P(s)}{Q(s)}$$

For a single quadratic factor $s^2 + 2\alpha s + \omega_n^2$, let

$$q(s) = \frac{Q(s)}{s^2 + 2\alpha s + \omega_n^2}$$

so that

$$F(s) = \frac{P(s)}{(s^2 + 2\alpha s + \omega_n^2)q(s)}$$

or

$$F(s) = \frac{P(s)}{(s + \alpha - j\omega_d)(s + \alpha + j\omega_d)q(s)}$$

where $\omega_d = +(\omega_n^2 - \alpha^2)^{1/2}$.

The partial-fraction expansion of $F(s)$ is

$$F(s) = \frac{P(s)}{(s + \alpha - j\omega_d)(s + \alpha + j\omega_d)q(s)} = \frac{K}{s + \alpha - j\omega_d} + \frac{K^*}{s + \alpha + j\omega_d}$$

where K^* is the complex conjugate of K.

The inverse transformation is obtained by using eq. (15.32). Only K need be found, because $|K^*| = |K|$:

$$K = (s + \alpha - j\omega_d)F(s)\Big|_{s = -\alpha + j\omega_d}$$

or

$$K = \frac{P(s)}{(s + \alpha + j\omega_d)q(s)}\Bigg|_{s = -\alpha + j\omega_d} = |K|e^{j\phi} \tag{15.37}$$

The portion of $F(s)$ due to the quadratic factor can be written as

$$F(s) = \frac{|K|e^{j\phi}}{s + \alpha - j\omega_d} + \frac{|K|e^{-j\phi}}{s + \alpha + j\omega_d}$$

Then, $f(t)$ becomes

$$f(t) = \mathscr{L}^{-1}[F(s)] = |K|e^{j\phi}e^{-(\alpha - j\omega_d)t} + |K|e^{-j\phi}e^{-(\alpha + j\omega_d)t}$$
$$= |K|e^{-\alpha t}(e^{j(\omega_d t + \phi)} + e^{-j(\omega_d t + \phi)}) = 2|K|e^{-\alpha t}\cos(\omega_d t + \phi)$$

■ **EXAMPLE 15.8**

Find $f(t)$ in amplitude–phase angle form for

$$F(s) = \frac{1}{8}\left(\frac{s}{s^2 + 6s^2 + 25}\right)$$

Solution   Note that

$$s^2 + 6s + 25 = (s + 3 - j4)(s + 3 + j4)$$

and write

$$F(s) = \frac{1}{8}\left(\frac{s}{s^2 + 6s + 25}\right) = \frac{K}{s + 3 - j4} + \frac{K^*}{s + 3 + j4}$$

Then, use eq. (15.32) to obtain

$$K = \frac{1}{8}\left[\frac{s(s + 3 - j4)}{(s + 3 - j4)(s + 3 + j4)}\right]_{s = -3 + j4} = \frac{1}{8} \cdot \frac{s}{s + 3 + j4}\bigg|_{s = -3 + j4}$$

$$= \frac{1}{8}\left(\frac{-3 + j4}{j8}\right) = \frac{1}{8}\left(\frac{1}{2} + j\frac{3}{8}\right) = \frac{5}{64} e^{j36.87°}$$

Then,

$$f(t) = 2|K|e^{-\alpha t}\cos(\omega_d t + \phi) = \frac{5}{32} e^{-3t}\cos(4t + 36.87°)$$ ■

EXERCISE 15.4
___

Find $f(t)$ in the cosine amplitude–phase angle form if

$$F(s) = \frac{6s - 20}{s^2 + 4s + 20}$$

Answer $f(t) = 10e^{-2t}\cos(4t + 53.13°).$

SECTION 15.10   **FIVE ADDITIONAL CONCEPTS**

15.10.1 The Initial-Value Theorem

Recall the definition of the Laplace transform of the derivative of $f(t)$,

$$\mathcal{L}[f'(t)] = \int_{0^-}^{\infty} [f'(t)]e^{-st}\,dt = sF(s) - f(0^-) \tag{15.7}$$

and assume that both $f(t)$ and $f'(t)$ are transformable in order to consider two separate cases. First, assume that $f(t)$ is continuous so that

$$f(0^+) = f(0^-)$$

FIGURE 15.3

A function with a discontinuity at $t = 0$

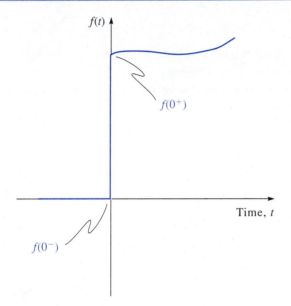

If s is allowed to approach infinity,

$$\lim_{s \to \infty} \int_{0^-}^{\infty} f'(t)e^{-st} \, dt = \lim_{s \to \infty} sF(s) - \lim_{s \to \infty} f(0^-) = \lim_{s \to \infty} sF(s) - f(0^+)$$

With

$$\lim_{s \to \infty} \int_{0^-}^{\infty} f'(t)e^{-st} \, dt = \int_{0^-}^{\infty} f'(t) \left(\lim_{s \to \infty} e^{-st} \right) dt = 0$$

it is seen that

$$f(0^+) = \lim_{s \to \infty} sF(s) \tag{15.38}$$

Equation (15.38) is called the initial-value theorem.

Consider Fig. 15.3, and observe the discontinuity. Here, $f(0^+)$ is clearly defined, $f(0^-) = 0$, and

$$f(0^+) \neq f(0^-)$$

If $f(t)$ is written as $f(t)u(t)$, where $u(t)$ is the unit step function, then

$$\frac{d}{dt} \left[f(t)u(t) \right] = f(0^+)\delta(t) + f'(t)u(t)$$

$$\int_{0^-}^{\infty} f(0^+)\delta(t)e^{-st} \, dt + \int_{0^-}^{\infty} f'(t)u(t)e^{-st} \, dt = sF(s) - f(0^-)$$

The impulse acts between $0^- < t < 0^+$, so that the limits of the first integral may be adjusted. Moreover, the exponential during this interval is equal to unity. With $f(0^-) = 0$,

$$f(0^+) \int_{0^-}^{0^+} \delta(t)\,dt + \int_{0^-}^{\infty} f'(t)e^{-st}\,dt = sF(s)$$

The integral on the left is precisely the definition of the unit impulse function as given by eq. (5.8b), and it is equal to unity. Hence,

$$f(0^+) + \int_{0^-}^{\infty} f'(t)e^{-st}\,dt = sF(s)$$

Now, when the limit is taken,

$$\lim_{s \to \infty} f(0^+) + \lim_{s \to \infty} \int_{0^-}^{\infty} f'(t)e^{-st}\,dt = \lim_{s \to \infty} sF(s)$$

and it is observed that

$$f(0^+) = \lim_{s \to \infty} sF(s) \tag{15.38}$$

The initial-value theorem of eq. (15.58) always provides the initial value at $t = 0^+$, even though the defining integral for the Laplace transformation has 0^- as its lower limit.

15.10.2 The Final-Value Theorem

If $\lim_{t \to \infty} f(t)$ exists, then an adjustment of eq. (15.7) can be considered with $s \to 0$:

$$\lim_{s \to 0} sF(s) - f(0^-) = \lim_{s \to 0} \int_{0^-}^{\infty} f'(t)e^{-st}\,dt$$

$$\lim_{s \to 0} sF(s) = f(0^-) + \lim_{s \to 0} \int_{0^-}^{\infty} f'(t)e^{-st}\,dt \tag{15.39}$$

Because

$$\lim_{s \to 0} e^{-st} = 1$$

eq. (15.39) becomes

$$\lim_{s \to 0} sF(s) = f(0^-) + \int_{0^-}^{\infty} f'(t)\,dt = f(0^-) + f(t)\Big|_{0^-}^{\infty} = f(0^-) + f(\infty) - f(0^-)$$

The final-value theorem is therefore

$$f(\infty) = \lim_{s \to 0} sF(s) \tag{15.40}$$

EXERCISE 15.5

Find $f(0^+)$ and $f(\infty)$ if

$$F(s) = \frac{s+8}{s^2 + 2s}$$

Answer $f(0^+) = 1$ and $f(\infty) = 4$.

15.10.3 The Use of s as a Differential Operator

If $f(t)$ is continuous at $t = 0$ in the time domain so that $f(0^+) = f(0^-)$, then multiplication by s in the transform domain is equivalent to a differentiation in the time domain.

Let

$$F(s) = \mathcal{L}[f(t)] \qquad G(s) = \mathcal{L}[g(t)]$$

and propose that

$$F(s) = sG(s)$$

so that by eq. (15.7)

$$\mathcal{L}[g'(t)] = sG(s) - g(0^-)$$

But by the initial-value theorem of eq. (15.38),

$$g(0^+) = \lim_{s \to \infty} sG(s)$$

so that with $g(0^-) = g(0^+)$

$$\mathcal{L}[g'(t)] = sG(s) - \lim_{s \to \infty} sG(s) = sG(s) - \lim_{s \to \infty} s \int_{0^-}^{\infty} g(t)e^{-st}\, dt$$

Notice here that the presence of e^{-st} causes the integral to vanish as $s \to \infty$, so that

$$\lim_{s \to \infty} sG(s) = 0$$

This leaves

$$\mathcal{L}[g'(t)] = sG(s) = \mathcal{L}[f(t)]$$

and

$$f(t) = \frac{dg(t)}{dt} = \frac{d}{dt}\mathcal{L}^{-1}[G(s)] \qquad\qquad (15.41)$$

The use of s as a differential operator is very useful for recovering functions in the time domain.

■ **EXAMPLE 15.9**

Determine $f(t)$ if

$$F(s) = \frac{4s}{(s + 1)^3}$$

and then confirm the result by using a partial-fraction expansion.

Solution   Suppress the s in the numerator of $F(s)$, and consider

$$G(s) = \frac{4}{(s + 1)^3}$$

This has an inverse [use the damping property of eq. (15.11) and Table 15.1]

$$g(t) = 2t^2 e^{-t}$$

Now, invoke eq. (15.41) and expeditiously obtain

$$f(t) = \frac{d}{dt} 2t^2 e^{-t} = 4te^{-t} - 2t^2 e^{-t}$$

By a partial-fraction expansion,

$$F(s) = \frac{4s}{(s + 1)^3} = \frac{C_1}{s + 1} + \frac{C_2}{(s + 1)^2} + \frac{C_3}{(s + 1)^3}$$

Here,

$$p(s) = 4s \qquad p'(s) = 4 \qquad p''(s) = 0$$

By eq. (15.34),

$$C_3 = \left.\frac{p(s)}{0!}\right|_{s=-1} = \left.\frac{4s}{0!}\right|_{s=-1} = \frac{-4}{1} = -4$$

$$C_2 = \left.\frac{p'(s)}{1!}\right|_{s=-1} = \frac{4}{1} = 4 \qquad C_1 = \left.\frac{p''(s)}{2!}\right|_{s=-1} = \frac{0}{2!} = 0$$

Thus,

$$F(s) = \frac{4}{(s + 1)^2} - \frac{4}{(s + 1)^3} = \frac{4}{(s + 1)^2} - 2\frac{2}{(s + 1)^3}$$

$$f(t) = 4te^{-t} - 2t^2 e^{-t}$$

■

EXERCISE 15.6

Find $f(t)$ if

$$F(s) = \frac{8s}{(s+2)^2}$$

Answer $f(t) = 8e^{-2t} - 16te^{-2t}$.

15.10.4 The Use of 1/s as an Integration Operator

Again, let

$$F(s) = \mathscr{L}[f(t)] \qquad \text{and} \qquad G(s) = \mathscr{L}[g(t)]$$

This time, propose that

$$F(s) = \frac{G(s)}{s}$$

so that by eq. (15.10),

$$\mathscr{L}\left[\int_a^t g(t)\,dt\right] = \frac{1}{s}\,\mathscr{L}[g(t)] + \frac{1}{s}\int_a^{0^-} g(t)\,dt$$

If $a = 0$,

$$\mathscr{L}\left[\int_a^t g(t)\,dt\right] = \frac{1}{s}\,\mathscr{L}[g(t)] = \frac{G(s)}{s} \qquad\qquad (15.42)$$

■ **EXAMPLE 15.10**

Find $f(t)$ if

$$F(s) = \frac{4}{s(s+2)}$$

and verify the result by a partial-fraction expansion.

Solution Suppress the $1/s$ in $F(s)$, and let

$$G(s) = \frac{4}{s+2}$$

so that from memory or from Table 15.1,

$$g(t) = 4e^{-2t}$$

Now, use eq. (15.42):

$$f(t) = \int_0^t 4e^{-2z}\,dz = -2e^{-2z}\Big|_0^t = -2(e^{-2t} - 1) = 2(1 - e^{-2t})$$

The partial-fraction expansion is

$$F(s) = \frac{4}{s(s+2)} = \frac{K_1}{s} + \frac{K_2}{s+2}$$

By eq. (15.32),

$$K_1 = \frac{4}{s+2}\bigg|_{s=0} = \frac{4}{2} = 2 \qquad K_2 = \frac{4}{s}\bigg|_{s=-2} = \frac{4}{-2} = -2$$

so that

$$F(s) = \frac{2}{s} - \frac{2}{s+2} \qquad \text{and} \qquad f(t) = 2(1 - e^{-2t})$$

■

EXERCISE 15.7

Find $f(t)$ if

$$F(s) = \frac{12}{s^2(s+1)}$$

Answer $f(t) = 12t + 12(e^{-t} - 1)$.

15.10.5 The Scaling Property

Consider the scaled time variable αt, where $\alpha > 0$. Then,

$$\mathscr{L}[f(\alpha t)] = \int_{0-}^{\infty} f(\alpha t)e^{-st}\, dt$$

Let $z = \alpha t$, so that

$$dz = \alpha\, dt$$

Then,

$$\mathscr{L}[f(\alpha t)] = \int_{0-}^{\infty} f(z)e^{-s(z/\alpha)}\, \frac{dz}{\alpha}$$

or

$$\mathscr{L}[f(\alpha t)] = \frac{1}{\alpha} F\!\left(\frac{s}{\alpha}\right) \tag{15.43}$$

CHAPTER 15

SUMMARY

▪ The definition of the Laplace transform of the function $f(t)$ is

$$\mathscr{L}[f(t)] = F(s) = \int_{0-}^{\infty} f(t)e^{-st}\, dt$$

▪ There are eight fundamental operations.

—The Laplace transform of the sum of two functions is

$$\mathcal{L}[f(t) + g(t)] = F(s) + G(s)$$

—The Laplace transform of a constant times a function is

$$\mathcal{L}[Cf(t)] = CF(s)$$

—The Laplace transform of the first derivative is

$$\mathcal{L}\left[\frac{d}{dt} f(t)\right] = sF(s) - f(0^-)$$

—The Laplace transform of the second derivative is

$$\mathcal{L}[f''(t)] = s^2 F(s) - sf(0^-) - f'(0^-)$$

—The Laplace transform of the nth derivative is

$$\mathcal{L}[f^n(t)] = s^n F(s) - s^{n-1} f(0^-) - s^{n-2} f'(0^-) - \cdots - f^{n-1}(0^-)$$

—The Laplace transform of the integral is

$$\mathcal{L}\left[\int_a^T f(t)dt\right] = \frac{1}{s} F(s) + \frac{1}{s} \int_a^{0^-} f(t)\, dt$$

where the integral $\int_a^{0^-} f(t)\, dt$ is called the accumulation from $t = a$ to $t = 0^-$.

—The Laplace transform of the exponentially damped function is

$$\mathcal{L}[e^{-a}f(t)] = F(s + a)$$

—The shifting theorem states that

$$\mathcal{L}[f(t - a)u(t - a)] = e^{-as}f(t); \qquad a > 0$$

▪ Table 15.1 is a table of Laplace transform pairs.

▪ Several additional aspects related to Laplace transforms must be considered.

—Differentiation with respect to s in the s domain is equivalent to multiplication by $-t$ in the time domain:

$$\mathcal{L}[t^n f(t)] = (-1)^n F^n(s)$$

—Integration with respect to s in the s domain is equivalent to dividing by t in the time domain:

$$\int_s^\infty F(s)\, ds = \mathcal{L}\left[\frac{f(t)}{t}\right]$$

—The initial-value theorem states that

$$f(0^+) = \lim_{s \to \infty} sF(s)$$

—The final-value theorem states that

$$f(\infty) = \lim_{s \to \infty} sF(s)$$

—Multiplication by s in the s domain is equivalent to differentiation with respect to t in the time domain:

$$f(t) = \frac{dg(t)}{dt} = \frac{d}{dt} \mathcal{L}^{-1}[sG(s)]$$

—Division by s in the s domain is equivalent to integration in the time domain:

$$\frac{1}{s} \mathcal{L}\left[\int g(t)\, dt \right] = \frac{G(s)}{s}$$

▪ Time functions are obtained from their Laplace transforms by an inverse transformation that employs a partial-fraction expansion. In general,

$$F(s) = \frac{P(s)}{Q(s)}$$

where $P(s)$ and $Q(s)$ are polynomials in s with the degree of $Q(s)$ greater than the degree of $P(s)$.

—If $Q(s)$ contains nonrepeated linear factors of the form $(s + b_i)$, then the partial-fraction expansion is

$$F(s) = \frac{K_1}{s + b_1} + \frac{K_2}{s + b_2} + \frac{K_3}{s + b_3} + \cdots + \frac{K_m}{s + b_m}$$

and the constants K_i are obtained from

$$K_i = \frac{P(s)}{Q(s)} (s + b_i) \Big|_{s = -b_i} \qquad i = 1, 2, 3, \ldots, m$$

—If $Q(s)$ contains a factor $(s + b)$ that is repeated r times, the partial-fraction expansion is

$$F(s) = \frac{P(s)}{Q(s)} = \frac{C_1}{s + b} + \frac{C_2}{(s + b)^2} + \cdots + \frac{C_{r-1}}{(s + b)^{r-1}} + \frac{C_r}{(s + b)^r}$$

All of the C's are determined from

$$C_{r-i} = \frac{p^i(s)}{i!} \Big|_{s = -b} \qquad i = 0, 1, 2, 3, \ldots, (r - 1)$$

where

$$p(s) = \frac{P(s)}{Q(s)}(s + b)^r$$

—If $Q(s)$ contains quadratic factors of the form $s^2 + 2\alpha_i s + \omega_{ni}^2$, the partial-fraction expansion is

$$F(s) = \frac{P(s)}{Q(s)} = \frac{A_1 s + B_1}{s^2 + 2\alpha_1 s + \omega_{n1}^2} + \frac{A_2 s + B_2}{s^2 + 2\alpha_2 s + \omega_{n2}^2} + \cdots$$

where the constants A_i and B_i are found by using an algebraic method described in Section 15.9.4. The actual time function is obtained after the factors $s^2 + 2\alpha_i s + \omega_{ni}^2$ are adjusted by completing the square:

$$s^2 + 2\alpha_i s + \omega_{ni}^2 = (s + \alpha_i)^2 + \omega_{di}^2$$

where $\omega_{di} = \sqrt{\omega_{ni}^2 - \alpha^2}$.

Additional Readings

Blackwell, W.A., and L.L. Grigsby. *Introductory Network Theory*. Boston: PWS Engineering, 1985, pp. 25–40, 55–72, 106, 443–476.

Bobrow, L.S. *Elementary Linear Circuit Analysis*. 2d ed. New York: Holt, Rinehart and Winston, 1987, pp. 496–517.

Del Toro, V. *Engineering Circuits*. Englewood Cliffs, N.J.: Prentice-Hall, 1987, pp. 346–368.

Dorf, R.C. *Introduction to Electric Circuits*. New York: Wiley, 1989, pp. 506–522.

Hayt, W.H., Jr., and J.E. Kemmerly. *Engineering Circuit Analysis*. 4th ed. New York: McGraw-Hill, 1986, pp. 567–591.

Irwin, J.D. *Basic Engineering Circuit Analysis*. 3d ed. New York: Macmillan, 1989, pp. 728–752, 756–758.

Johnson, D.E., J.L. Hilburn, and J.R. Johnson, *Basic Electric Circuit Analysis*. 4th ed. Englewood Cliffs, N.J.: Prentice-Hall, 1989, pp. 590–610.

Karni, S. *Applied Circuit Analysis*. New York: Wiley, 1988, pp. 428–450.

Madhu, S. *Linear Circuit Analysis*. Englewood Cliffs, N.J.: Prentice-Hall, 1988, pp. 734–744, 748–759, 768.

Nilsson, J.W. *Electric Circuits*. 3d ed. Reading, Mass: Addison-Wesley, 1990, pp. 546–572.

Paul, C.R. *Analysis of Linear Circuits*. New York: McGraw-Hill, 1989, pp. 605–628.

CHAPTER 15   PROBLEMS

Section 15.5

In Problems 15.1 through 15.9, $f(t)$ is given and $F(s)$ is to be found.

15.1 $f(t) = 6t + 8$

15.2 $f(t) = t^2 + 2t + 4$

15.3 $f(t) = 8 + 6e^{-2t}$

15.4 $f(t) = 16 \cos^2 4t$

15.5 $f(t) = 12(t^2 + 1) - 16e^{-2t}$

15.6 $f(t) = 8t + 16 + 4 \cos 3t$

15.7 $f(t) = 12 \sin 4t + 16 \cos 4t$

15.8 $f(t) = 16e^{-2t} + 24e^{-5t} - 32$

15.9 $f(t) = 24t + 12e^{-4t}$

15.10   Find $\mathcal{L}[\cosh at]$ if

$$\cosh at = \frac{1}{2}(e^{at} + e^{-at})$$

15.11   Find $\mathcal{L}[\sinh at]$ if

$$\sinh at = \frac{1}{2}(e^{at} - e^{-at})$$

15.12   If $f(t) = 6 \cosh 2t - 8 \sinh 3t$, find $F(s)$.

Section 15.6

In Problems 15.13 through 15.20, $f(t)$ is given and $F(s)$ is to be found.

15.13 $f(t) = 4e^{-2t} \cosh 3t$

15.14 $f(t) = 8e^{-t} \sinh 2t - 12$

15.15 $f(t) = 12e^{-2t} \cos 4t + 16e^{-2t} \sin 4t$

15.16 $f(t) = 3t^2 e^{-2t} + te^{-3t}$

15.17 $f(t) = 8(t - 2)e^{-2(t-2)}u(t - 2)$

15.18 $f(t) = [16e^{-2(t-1)} \cos 4(t - 1)]u(t - 1)$

15.19 $f(t) = 4(t - 1)^2 e^{-3(t-1)}u(t - 1) - 8$
$\qquad\qquad + 2e^{-4(t-2)}u(t - 2)$

15.20 $f(t) = 2e^{-3t}(\sinh 2t + \cosh 2t) + 4(t - 2)u(t - 2)$

Section 15.7

In Problems 15.21 through 15.27, $f(t)$ is given and $F(s)$ is to be found.

15.21 $f(t) = 4t \cos 2t - 2e^{-3t}$

15.22 $f(t) = 8te^{-2t} \sin 2t$

15.23 $f(t) = 2te^{-4t} \cos 3t$

15.24 $f(t) = 12 + 3t^2 e^{-4t}$

15.25 $f(t) = 6te^{-2t} \cosh 3t$

15.26 $f(t) = 6\delta(t) + 4t + 12$

15.27 $f(t) = 5e^{-2t} + 3e^{-3t} \sin 8t$

Section 15.8

In Problems 15.29 through 15.35, $y(t)$ is the dependent variable and its Laplace transform is sought.

15.28 $\dfrac{d^2y}{dt^2} + 12\dfrac{dy}{dt} + 36y = 12 + 6t^2$
with $y(0) = 4$, $y'(0) = 2$

15.29 $\dfrac{d^2y}{dt^2} + 64y = 0$ with $y(0) = 4$, $y'(0) = 0$

15.30 $\dfrac{d^2y}{dt^2} + 4\dfrac{dy}{dt} + 80y = 6 \cos 4t + 12$
with $y(0) = 0$, $y'(0) = 8$

15.31 $\dfrac{d^2y}{dt^2} + 7\dfrac{dy}{dt} + 12y = 6t + 4$
with $y(0) = 2$, $y'(0) = 36$

15.32 $\dfrac{d^2y}{dt^2} + 6\dfrac{dy}{dt} + 109y = 10e^{-2t} \sin 6t$
with $y(0) = 4$, $y'(0) = 8$

15.33 $\dfrac{d^2y}{dt^2} + 320\dfrac{dy}{dt} + 19{,}200y = 48e^{-12t} + 32$
with $y(0) = 24$, $y'(0) = 16$

15.34 $\dfrac{d^2y}{dt^2} + 64\dfrac{dy}{dt} + 100y = t + 18 \sin 6t$
with $y(0) = 0$, $y'(0) = 12$

15.35 $\dfrac{d^2y}{dt^2} + 8\dfrac{dy}{dt} + 12y = 4t^2 + 6t + 12$ with
$y(0) = 4$, $y'(0) = -8$

Section 15.9

In Problems 15.36 through 15.47, the Laplace transform $F(s)$ is given and the time domain function $f(t)$ is to be found.

15.36 $F(s) = \dfrac{48(s + 3)}{s(s^2 + 8s + 12)}$

15.37 $F(s) = \dfrac{36(s^2 + 6s + 8)}{s(s^3 + 9s^2 + 23s + 15)}$

15.38 $F(s) = \dfrac{18(s^2 + 3s + 2)}{s(s^2 + 16s + 100)}$

15.39 $F(s) = \dfrac{96(s + 8)}{s(s + 4)^2}$

15.40 $F(s) = \dfrac{40(s + 2)}{s^2(s^2 + 16s + 25)}$

15.41 $F(s) = \dfrac{16(s - 3)}{s^3 + 7s^2 + 14s + 8}$

15.42 $F(s) = \dfrac{80(s^2 + 5s + 6)}{s^2(s^2 + 8s + 16)}$

15.43 $F(s) = \dfrac{20s^2 + 80s + 60}{s^3(s + 2)}$

15.44 $F(s) = \dfrac{24(s^3 + 3s^2 + 7s + 5)}{(s^2 + 4s + 5)(s^2 + 4s + 29)}$

15.45 $F(s) = \dfrac{24(s^3 + 6s^2 + 11s + 6)}{(s^2 + 4s + 5)(s^2 + 16s + 25)}$

15.46 $F(s) = \dfrac{20s(s^2 + 12s + 15)}{s^4 + 3s^3 + 18s^2 + 48s + 32}$

15.47 $F(s) = \dfrac{4800(s^2 + 1200s + 3.6 \times 10^6)}{s(s^2 + 5000s + 6 \times 10^6)}$

Section 15.10

In Problems 15.48 through 15.59, find $f(0^+)$ and $f(\infty)$ for the $F(s)$ indicated.

15.48 $F(s)$ in Problem 15.36

15.49 $F(s)$ in Problem 15.37

15.50 $F(s)$ in Problem 15.38

15.51 $F(s)$ in Problem 15.39

15.52 $F(s)$ in Problem 15.40

15.53 $F(s)$ in Problem 15.41

15.54 $F(s)$ in Problem 15.42

15.55 $F(s)$ in Problem 15.43

15.56 $F(s)$ in Problem 15.44

15.57 $F(s)$ in Problem 15.45

15.58 $F(s)$ in Problem 15.46

15.59 $F(s)$ in Problem 15.47

16

APPLICATIONS OF THE LAPLACE TRANSFORMATION

OBJECTIVES

The objectives of this chapter are to:

- Formulate the differential equations and present their solutions obtained via the Laplace transform for first- and second-order networks with excitation by initial energy storage and step, ramp, sinusoidal, and impulse forcing functions.

- Show how the Laplace transform is used to expeditiously handle the voltage and current responses in more advanced networks.

- Consider the Laplace transform of pulses and show how the Laplace transform can provide solutions to the differential equations for networks with pulsed forcing functions.

SECTION 16.1   INTRODUCTION

The value and utility of the Laplace transformation and its use in solving the first- and second-order differential equations of network theory can be amply demonstrated by repeating several of the examples in Chapters 6 (first-order networks) and 7 (higher-order networks).

Three conditions must be met for the use of the Laplace transform:

1. Initial conditions must be known or determined.
2. All terms in the differential equation that is subjected to scrutiny must possess a Laplace transform.
3. The inverse transform must be easily obtained.

SECTION 16.2   APPLICATIONS TO FIRST-ORDER NETWORKS

In Chapter 6, several examples were presented in order to consider the response of first-order networks to various forcing functions. Many of these examples will be presented in this section, with the Laplace transform used to obtain the total response.

16.2.1 Excitation by Initial Energy Storage

■ **EXAMPLE 16.1**

In the network of Fig. 6.7, repeated here as Fig. 16.1, the switch closes at $t = 0$ with the capacitor charged to V_o. Find the current as a function of time.

Solution   An application of KVL provides the integro-differential equation:

$$Ri + \frac{1}{C} \int_{-\infty}^{t} i\,dz = 0; \qquad t > 0$$

With $\mathscr{L}[i(t)] = I(s)$, a term-by-term transformation with eq. (15.10) yields

$$RI(s) + \frac{1}{C} \cdot \left[\frac{I(s)}{s} + \frac{1}{s} \int_{a}^{0^-} i\,dt \right] = 0$$

Observe that there is no need to differentiate to remove the integral in the governing integro-differential equation, and there is no need to formulate the problem on a charge ($q = \int i\,dt$) or capacitor voltage ($i = C\,dv/dt$) basis. Here, because of the assumed direction of current flow,

$$\int_{a}^{0^-} i\,dt = \int i\,dt \Big|_{t=0^-} = -q(0^-) = -CV_o$$

$$RI(s) + \frac{I(s)}{Cs} - \frac{V_o}{s} = 0 \qquad \text{or} \qquad \frac{RCs + 1}{Cs} I(s) = \frac{V_o}{s}$$

$$I(s) = \frac{V_o/R}{s + (1/RC)}$$

Reference to Table 15.1 indicates that

$$i(t) = \frac{V_o}{R} e^{-t/RC} \text{ amperes}$$

An *RC* series network that is excited when the switch closes at $t = 0$ by the energy stored in the capacitor

FIGURE 16.1

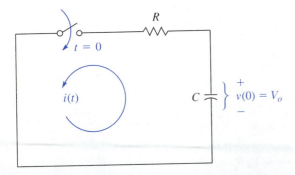

FIGURE 16.2   Network (Exercise 16.1)

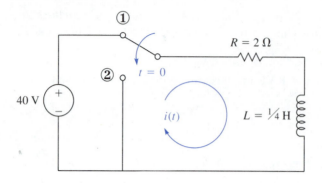

and this confirms the result obtained in Example 6.3 in Section 6.9. Observe that the initial current,

$$i(0^+) = \frac{V_o}{R}$$

could have been predicted by the initial-value theorem, eq. (15.38):

$$i(0^+) = \lim_{s \to \infty} sI(s) = \lim_{s \to \infty} \frac{sV_o/R}{s + (1/RC)} = \frac{V_o}{R}$$

■

EXERCISE 16.1

In the network of Fig. 16.2, the switch moves instantaneously from position 1 to position 2 at $t = 0$. Find $i(t)$.

Answer $i(t) = 20e^{-8t}$ amperes.

16.2.2 Excitation by a Constant (Step) Input

■ **EXAMPLE 16.2**

In the network of Fig. 6.9, repeated here as Fig. 16.3, the switch, which has been in position 1 for a considerably long period of time, is suddenly and instantaneously moved to position 2. What is the current after $t = 0$?

Solution   Here, too, KVL is applied to obtain the differential equation,

$$L\frac{di}{dt} + Ri = V_s; \qquad t > 0$$

and it is to be noted that because of the continuity of stored energy principle, at $t = 0^-$, $i(0^-) = v_{s1}/R = V_o/R$. With $\mathscr{L}[i(t)] = I(s)$, a term-by-term

FIGURE 16.3

An *RL* first-order network in which the switch moves instantaneously from position 1 to position 2 at $t = 0$

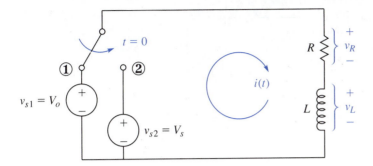

transformation with eq. (15.7) yields

$$L[sI(s) - i(0^-)] + RI(s) = \frac{V_s}{s}$$

and with $i(0^-) = V_o/R$, a little algebra provides

$$(Ls + R)I(s) = \frac{V_s}{s} + \frac{LV_o}{R}$$

Then, with further simplification, $I(s)$ can be isolated:

$$I(s) = \frac{(LV_o s/R) + V_s}{Ls[s + (R/L)]}$$

The initial-value theorem of eq. (15.38) can be employed as a confidence builder:

$$\lim_{s \to \infty} sI(s) = \lim_{s \to \infty} \frac{s[(LV_o s/R) + V_s]}{Ls[s + (R/L)]}$$

or

$$\lim_{s \to \infty} \frac{(LV_o/R) + (V_s/s)}{L[1 + (R/Ls)]} = \frac{V_o}{R}$$

This result checks the initial condition, and one can proceed with confidence. Thus,

$$I(s) = \frac{1}{L} \cdot \frac{(LV_o/R)(s) + V_s}{s[s + (R/L)]} = \frac{K_1}{s} + \frac{K_2}{s + (R/L)}$$

and K_1 and K_2 are found by using eq. (15.32):

$$K_i = \frac{P(s)}{Q(s)} (s + b_i) \Big|_{s = -b_i} \qquad (i = 1, 2, 3, \ldots, m) \qquad \textbf{(15.32)}$$

FIGURE 16.4   Network (Exercise 16.2)

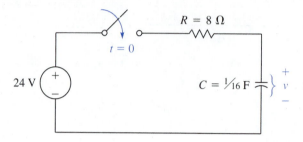

Thus,

$$K_1 = \frac{1}{L} \cdot \frac{(LV_o s/R) + V_s}{s + (R/L)}\bigg|_{s=0} = \frac{V_s}{R}$$

$$K_2 = \frac{1}{L} \cdot \frac{(LV_o s/R) + V_s}{s}\bigg|_{s=-R/L} = \frac{V_o - V_s}{R}$$

The value of $I(s)$ is

$$I(s) = \frac{V_s/R}{s} + \frac{(V_o - V_s)/R}{s + (R/L)}$$

and with reference to Table 15.1, if desired,

$$i(t) = \frac{V_o - V_s}{R} e^{-(R/L)t} + \frac{V_s}{R}$$

which is identical to the result obtained in Example 6.4 in Section 6.10.1. ■

EXERCISE 16.2

In Fig. 16.4, the switch closes at $t = 0$ when the voltage across the capacitor is 4 V. Determine $v(t)$.

Answer $v = 24 - 20e^{-2t}$ volts.

16.2.3 Excitation by a Ramp Input

■ **EXAMPLE 16.3**

In the network shown in Fig. 6.11, repeated here as Fig. 16.5, a current ramp is applied when the switch closes instantaneously at $t = 0$. If at the time of switching, the capacitor voltage is V_o, find the voltage across the parallel combination as a function of time.

Solution   This time KCL is employed, and the differential equation is

$$C\frac{dv}{dt} + \frac{1}{R}v = Kt; \qquad t > 0$$

An RC parallel network that is driven by a current ramp

FIGURE 16.5

Before the switch closes instantaneously at $t = 0$, a voltage V_o exists across the capacitor terminals.

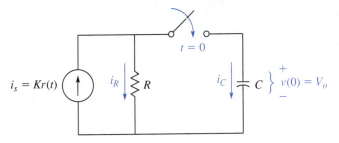

With

$$\mathscr{L}[v(t)] = V(s)$$

it may be transformed term by term:

$$C[sV(s) - v(0^-)] + \frac{1}{R} V(s) = \frac{K}{s^2}$$

With $v(0^-) = V_o$, a little algebra provides

$$V(s) = \frac{1}{C} \cdot \frac{K + CV_o s^2}{s^2[s + (1/RC)]}$$

A verification of this comes from an application of the initial-value theorem, where the aim is to show that $v(0^+) = V_o$:

$$v(0^+) = \lim_{s \to \infty} sV(s) = \lim_{s \to \infty} s\left(\frac{1}{C}\right)\left[\frac{K + CV_o s^2}{s^2(s + 1/RC)}\right]$$

$$= \lim_{s \to \infty} \frac{1}{C}\left(\frac{K/s^2 + CV_o}{1 + 1/RCs}\right) = \frac{1}{C}(CV_o) = V_o$$

The partial-fraction expansion is

$$V(s) = \frac{1}{C} \cdot \frac{K + CV_o s^2}{s^2(s + 1/RC)} = \frac{C_1}{s} + \frac{C_2}{s^2} + \frac{K_1}{s + 1/RC}$$

and K_1 can be found immediately by applying eq. (15.32):

$$K_1 = \frac{1}{C} \cdot \frac{K + CV_o s^2}{s^2}\bigg|_{s = -1/RC} = R^2 CK + V_o$$

To find C_1 and C_2, set

$$p(s) = \frac{1}{C} \cdot \frac{K + CV_o s^2}{s + 1/RC}$$

so that

$$p'(s) = \frac{1}{C}\left[\frac{(s + 1/RC)(2CV_o s) - (K + CV_o s^2)}{(s + 1/RC)^2}\right]$$

Then, by applying eq. (15.34), one obtains

$$C_2 = \frac{p(s)}{0!}\bigg|_{s=0} = \frac{1}{C}\left(\frac{K}{1/RC}\right) = RK$$

$$C_1 = \frac{p'(s)}{1!}\bigg|_{s=0} = \frac{1}{C}\left[\frac{-K}{(1/RC)^2}\right] = -R^2CK$$

Thus,

$$V(s) = -\frac{R^2CK}{s} + \frac{RK}{s^2} + \frac{R^2CK + V_o}{s + 1/RC}$$

and by taking the inverse transform (Table 15.1), one obtains

$$v(t) = (R^2CK + V_o)e^{-t/RC} - R^2CK + RKt$$

A little rearrangement then gives

$$v(t) = V_o e^{-t/RC} + RKt - R^2CK(1 - e^{-t/RC}) \text{ volts}$$

which is an alternative to the form obtained in Example 6.5 in Section 6.10.2. ■

EXERCISE 16.3

In Fig. 16.6, the switch moves from position 1 to position 2 instantaneously at $t = 0$. Find the total current response.

Answer $i = \frac{97}{16}e^{-8t} + \frac{1}{2}t - \frac{1}{16}$ amperes.

FIGURE 16.6   Network (Exercise 16.3)

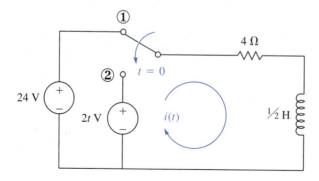

An RC series network that is excited at $t = 0$ by a sinusoidal voltage

FIGURE 16.7

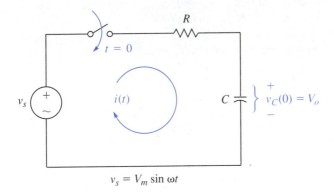

$$v_s = V_m \sin \omega t$$

16.2.4 Excitation by a Sinusoidal Input

■ EXAMPLE 16.4

In Fig. 6.14, which is repeated here as Fig. 16.7, the switch closes at $t = 0$. The initial voltage across the capacitor is V_o. Find the current as a function of time.

Solution The differential equation derives from an application of KVL:

$$Ri + \frac{1}{C} \int_{-\infty}^{t} i \, dz = V_m \sin \omega t; \quad t > 0$$

With

$$\mathscr{L}[i(t)] = I(s)$$

a term-by-term-transformation with the help of eq. (15.10) gives

$$RI(s) + \frac{1}{Cs}\left[I(s) + \int i \, dt \Big|_{t=0^-}\right] = \frac{V_m \omega}{s^2 + \omega^2}$$

where the integral within the brackets represents the initial charge on the capacitor:

$$\int i \, dt \Big|_{t=0^-} = q(0^-) = Cv(0^-) = CV_o$$

Thus, $(1/Cs)(CV_o) = V_o/s$, and

$$\left(R + \frac{1}{Cs}\right)I(s) = \frac{V_m \omega}{s^2 + \omega^2} - \frac{V_o}{s}$$

After some algebra, $I(s)$ can be isolated into two transform components:

$$I(s) = I_{zi}(s) + I_{zs}(s) = -\frac{V_o/R}{s + 1/RC} + \frac{(\omega V_m/R)s}{(s + 1/RC)(s^2 + \omega^2)}$$

where the subscripts are intended to show that these are the transforms of the zero-input and zero-state current responses. Moreover, there is no need to include $I_{zl}(s)$ in any algebraic procedure to recover $i(t)$, because at this point, the inverse transform of $I_{zl}(s)$ is known.

The transform of $I_{zs}(s)$ must be subjected to a partial-fraction expansion, with the evaluation of the constants performed by a method of algebra:

$$I_{zs}(s) = \frac{(\omega V_m/R)s}{(s + 1/RC)(s^2 + \omega^2)} = \frac{K_1}{s + 1/RC} + \frac{As + B}{s^2 + \omega^2}$$

In working with only the numerators, one finds that

$$\frac{\omega V_m}{R} s = K_1(s^2 + \omega^2) + (As + B)\left(s + \frac{1}{RC}\right)$$

$$= (K_1 + A)s^2 + \left(\frac{A}{RC} + B\right)s + \left(\omega^2 K_1 + \frac{B}{RC}\right)$$

so that a term-by-term comparison provides a set of three simultaneous algebraic equations in three unknowns:

$$K_1 + A = 0$$

$$\frac{1}{RC} A + B = \frac{\omega V_m}{R}$$

$$\omega^2 K_1 + \frac{1}{RC} B = 0$$

However, by eq. (15.32),

$$K_1 = \frac{\omega V_m/R}{s^2 + \omega^2} s \Big|_{s = -1/RC} = -\frac{(\omega V_m/R)(1/RC)}{(1/RC)^2 + \omega^2} = -\frac{(\omega RC)(V_m/R)}{1 + (\omega RC)^2}$$

This leads directly to A and B

$$A = -K_1 = \frac{(\omega RC)(V_m/R)}{1 + (\omega RC)^2} \qquad B = -\omega^2 RCK_1 = \frac{(\omega RC)^2(V_m/R)\omega}{1 + (\omega RC)^2}$$

Thus,

$$I_{zs}(s) = \frac{(\omega RC)(V_m/R)}{1 + (\omega RC)^2}\left[-\frac{1}{s + 1/RC} + \frac{s}{s^2 + \omega^2} + \frac{(\omega RC)\omega}{s^2 + \omega^2}\right]$$

and, if necessary, with the help of Table 15.1,

$$i_{zs}(t) = \frac{(\omega RC)(V_m/R)}{1 + (\omega RC)^2}\left[-e^{-t/RC} + \cos \omega t + (\omega RC) \sin \omega t\right]$$

The inverse transform of

$$I_{zl}(s) = -\frac{V_o/R}{s + 1/RC}$$

Network (Exercise 16.4)

FIGURE 16.8

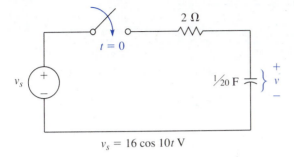

$v_s = 16 \cos 10t$ V

is

$$i_{ZI}t = -\frac{V_o}{R} e^{-t/RC}$$

The total current response is

$$i(t) = \frac{(\omega RC)(V_m/R)}{1 + (\omega RC)^2} \left[-e^{-t/RC} + \cos \omega t + (\omega RC) \sin \omega t \right] - \frac{V_o}{R} e^{-t/RC}$$

$$= \frac{\omega C V_m}{1 + (\omega RC)^2} \left[(\omega RC) \sin \omega t + \cos \omega t \right]$$

$$- \frac{1}{R} \left[V_o + \frac{(\omega RC) V_m}{1 + (\omega RC)^2} \right] e^{-t/RC} \text{ amperes}$$

which is a confirmation of the result obtained in Example 6.6 in Section 6.10.3. ∎

EXERCISE 16.4

In Fig. 16.8, the switch closes instantaneously at $t = 0$ when the voltage across the capacitor terminals is $v(0) = 12$ V. Find the total voltage response.

Answer $v = 4e^{-10t} + 8 \cos 10t + 8 \sin 10t$ volts.

16.2.5 Excitation by an Impulse

■ **EXAMPLE 16.5**

The RL series network in Fig. 16.9 (a repeat of Fig. 6.16) is subjected to an impulse of voltage of strength 10 V at $t = 0$ when no current is flowing in the network. The impulse, as shown in Section 6.10.4, leaves a current of magnitude $i(0^+) = 1/L$ amperes in its wake at $t = 0^+$. What is the current for all $t > 0^+$?

Solution   An application of KVL provides

$$L\frac{di}{dt} + Ri = 0; \qquad t > 0$$

FIGURE 16.9   An *RL* series network excited by a unit voltage impulse

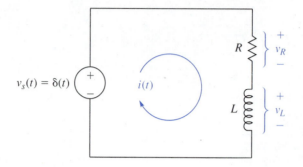

With

$$\mathscr{L}[i(t)] = I(s)$$

and $i(0^+) = 1/L$, a term-by-term transformation gives

$$L[sI(s) - 1/L] + RI(s) = 0$$

After a modest amount of algebra, $I(s)$ is determined simply as

$$I(s) = \frac{1/L}{s + R/L}$$

so that

$$i(t) = \frac{1}{L}\,e^{-(R/L)t}\ \text{amperes}$$

which confirms the result in Example 6.7 in Section 6.10.4.   ■

EXERCISE 16.5

In Fig. 16.10, the current impulse strikes when the voltage across the parallel combination of the resistor and capacitor $v(0) = 0$ V. Find the voltage as a function of time after $t = 0$.

Answer $v = 40e^{-4t}$ volts.

FIGURE 16.10   Network (Exercise 16.5)

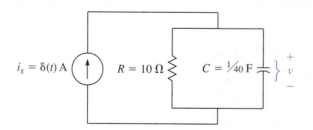

APPLICATIONS TO HIGHER-ORDER NETWORKS

SECTION 16.3

16.3.1 Excitation by Initial Energy Storage

■ **EXAMPLE 16.6**

In the *RLC* parallel network shown in Fig. 7.1, repeated here as Fig. 16.11, the switch closes instantaneously at $t = 0$ when V_o exists across the capacitor terminals and no current is flowing through the inductor. Because the current through the inductor may not change instantaneously, $i(0^+) = i(0^-)$, and this can be related to the accumulated flux $\int_a^{0^-} v\,dt = 0$. Find the voltage across the parallel combination as a function of time.

Solution   An application of KVL provides the integro-differential equation. With $C = \frac{1}{3}$ F, $R = \frac{3}{4}\,\Omega$, $L = 1$ H, and $V_o \sim 2V$

$$\frac{1}{3}\frac{dv}{dt} + \frac{4}{3}v + \int_{-\infty}^{t} v\,dz = 0; \qquad t > 0$$

and it may again be noted that the Laplace transform method is easily applied to an integro-differential equation. There is no need to work in terms of the flux merely to avoid the integral.
   With

$$\mathscr{L}[v(t)] = V(s) \qquad v(0^-) = V_o = 2 \text{ V} \qquad \int_a^{0^-} v\,dt = 0$$

a term-by-term transformation yields

$$\frac{1}{3}[sV(s) - 2] + \frac{4}{3}V(s) + \left(\frac{V(s)}{s} + \frac{0}{s}\right) = 0$$

$$\left(s + 4 + \frac{3}{s}\right)V(s) = 2$$

Then,

$$V(s) = \frac{2s}{s^2 + 4s + 3}$$

An *RLC* parallel network that is excited when the switch closes at $t = 0$ by the energy stored in the capacitor

FIGURE 16.11

Here, $C = \frac{1}{3}$ F, $R = \frac{3}{4}\,\Omega$, and $L = 1$ H. At $t = 0$, the initial voltage across the capacitor is $V_o = 2$ V, and no current is flowing through the inductor.

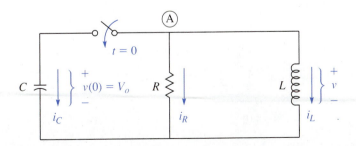

The initial-value theorem of eq. (15.38) shows that

$$v(0^+) = \lim_{s \to \infty} sV(s) = \lim_{s \to \infty} \frac{2s^2}{s^2 + 4s + 3} = \lim_{s \to \infty} \frac{2}{1 + 4/s + 3/s^2} = 2 \text{ V}$$

which is consistent with the given initial condition.

The denominator of $V(s)$ can be factored to

$$s^2 + 4s + 3 = (s + 1)(s + 3)$$

so that the partial-fraction expansion will involve nonrepeated linear factors:

$$V(s) = \frac{2s}{(s + 1)(s + 3)} = \frac{K_1}{s + 1} + \frac{K_2}{s + 3}$$

Now, eq. (15.32) will apply:

$$K_1 = \left.\frac{2s}{s + 3}\right|_{s = -1} = \frac{-2}{2} = -1 \qquad K_2 = \left.\frac{2s}{s + 1}\right|_{s = -3} = \frac{-6}{-2} = 3$$

This makes

$$V(s) = \frac{3}{s + 3} - \frac{1}{s + 1}$$

and with or without the help of Table 15.1,

$$v(t) = 3e^{-3t} - e^{-t} \text{ volts}$$

which confirms the result in Example 7.1 in Section 7.3 for this overdamped case.   ■

EXERCISE 16.6

In Fig. 16.12, the switch closes instantaneously at $t = 0$ with 10 V across the capacitor terminals and no current flowing through the inductor. Find $i(t)$.

Answer $i(t) = 8te^{-40t}$ amperes.

FIGURE 16.12   A second-order undriven network (Exercise 16.6)

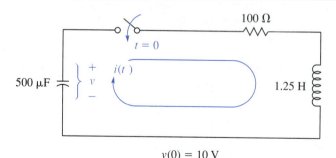

$v(0) = 10 \text{ V}$

FIGURE 16.13

An *RLC* series network driven by a constant voltage after the switch closes instantaneously $t = 0$

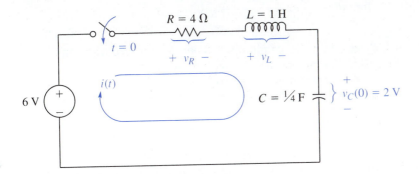

16.3.2 Excitation by a Constant (Step) Input

■ **EXAMPLE 16.7**

In the network of Fig. 7.4, repeated here as Fig. 16.13, the switch closes instantaneously at $t = 0$ when the capacitor has a voltage of 2 V across its terminals and no current flows in the inductor. What is the current as a function of time?

Solution   Here, too, KVL is applied to obtain the differential equation. With

$$\mathcal{L}[i(t)] = I(s)$$

and $L = 1$ H, $R = 4\ \Omega$, $C = \frac{1}{4}$ F, and $v_{\text{in}} = 6$ V,

$$\frac{di}{dt} + 4i + 4\int_{-\infty}^{t} i\,dt = 6; \qquad t > 0$$

which must be solved using the initial conditions:

$$i(0^-) = 0 \qquad q(0^-) = \int i\,dt\bigg|_{t=0^-} = Cv_C(0^-) = \left(\frac{1}{4}\right)(2) = \frac{1}{2}$$

A term-by-term transformation yields

$$[sI(s) - 0] + 4I(s) + 4\left[\frac{I(s)}{s} + \frac{\frac{1}{2}}{s}\right] = \frac{6}{s}$$

and algebraic manipulation gives

$$\left(s + 4 + \frac{4}{s}\right)I(s) = \frac{6}{s} - \frac{2}{s} = \frac{4}{s}$$

Then, with further simplification, $I(s)$ can be isolated:

$$I(s) = \frac{4}{s^2 + 4s + 4} = \frac{4}{(s+2)^2}$$

The initial-value theorem of eq. (15.38) can be employed as a confidence builder:

$$i(0^+) = \lim_{s \to \infty} sI(s) = \lim_{s \to \infty} \frac{4s}{s^2 + 4s + 4} = 0$$

This result checks the initial condition, and one can proceed with confidence.

The fact that $I(s)$ contains a single term means that the inverse transform can be found directly without resort to the labor required by the partial-fraction expansion. Use of Table 15.1 shows that

$$i(t) = 4te^{-4t} \text{ amperes}$$

and this confirms the result in Example 7.2 in Section 7.4.1.

It is worth the trouble to show that the partial-fraction expansion gives the same result. Here,

$$I(s) = \frac{4}{(s + 2)^2} = \frac{C_1}{s + 2} + \frac{C_2}{(s + 2)^2}$$

and the constants C_1 and C_2 are found by using eq. (15.34), which applies to r repetitions of the factor $s + b$:

$$C_{r-i} = \left. \frac{p'(s)}{i!} \right|_{s=-b} \qquad i = 0, 1, 2, 3, \ldots, (r - 1) \qquad\qquad \textbf{(15.34)}$$

First, use

$$p(s) = 4 \qquad \text{and} \qquad p'(s) = 0$$

By eq. (15.34),

$$C_2 = \left. \frac{p(s)}{0!} \right|_{s=-2} = \frac{4}{1} = 4 \qquad \text{and} \qquad C_1 = \frac{p'(s)}{1!} = \frac{0}{1} = 0$$

The value of $I(s)$ is

$$I(s) = \frac{4}{(s + 2)^2}$$

and the result is the same:

$$i(t) = 4te^{-2t} \text{ amperes}$$ ■

EXERCISE 16.7

In the network shown in Fig. 16.14, the switch closes instantaneously when the voltage across the capacitor terminals is $v(0^+) = 8$ V and there is no current flow in the inductor. What is the total response for $v(t)$?

Answer $v(t) = 12 - \dfrac{1}{5} e^{-8t}(20 \cos 20t + 8 \sin 20t)$ volts.

FIGURE 16.14

A second-order network excited by a voltage step (Exercise 16.7)

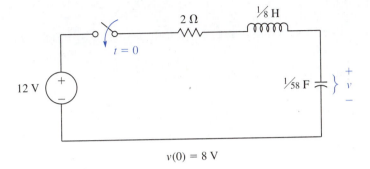

$v(0) = 8$ V

16.3.3 Excitation by a Ramp Input

■ **EXAMPLE 16.8**

The network shown in Fig. 7.7, repeated here as Fig. 16.15, has a current ramp $i_s(t) = t$ amperes applied to it at $t = 0$, when there is no voltage across the capacitor, and there is no current through the inductor. What is the voltage across the parallel combination?

Solution This time, KCL is employed with $R = 1\ \Omega$, $L = \frac{1}{2}$ H, $C = \frac{1}{4}$ F, and $i_s = r(t) = t$ amperes to show that the governing differential equation is

$$\frac{1}{4}\frac{dv}{dt} + \frac{1}{1}v + 2\int_{-\infty}^{t} v\,dz = t; \qquad t > 0$$

and this is to be solved under the condition that

$$v(0^-) = 0$$

Because there is no current flowing in the network at $t = 0$, there is no magnetic flux in the network at $t = 0$. Thus,

$$\phi(0^+) = \int v\,dt\Big|_{t=0^-} = 0$$

FIGURE 16.15

An RLC parallel network that is driven by a current ramp

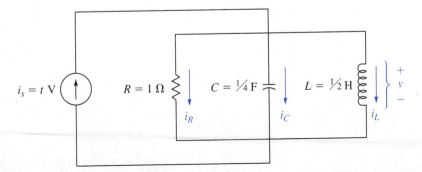

With

$$\mathscr{L}[v(t)] = V(s)$$

the governing differential equation may be transformed term-by-term:

$$\frac{1}{4}[sV(s) - v(0^+)] + V(s) + \frac{2}{s}\left[V(s) + \int v\,dt\,\Big|_{t=0^-}\right] = \frac{1}{s^2}$$

With the initial conditions inserted, this becomes

$$\frac{1}{4}sV(s) + V(s) + \frac{2V(s)}{s} = \frac{1}{s^2}$$

and after some algebra,

$$\left(\frac{s^2 + 4s + 8}{s.}\right)V(s) = \frac{4}{s^2}$$

which leads to

$$V(s) = \frac{4}{s(s^2 + 4s + 8)}$$

Observe that $s^2 + 4s + 8$ is a quadratic factor that when set equal to zero, yields complex conjugate roots. This leads to an underdamped response, and the determination of the constants in the partial-fraction expansion must be in accordance with the procedures set forth in Section 15.9.4.

However, one first obtains the verification that comes from an application of the initial-value theorem of eq. (15.38), where the aim is to show that $v(0^+) = 0$:

$$v(0^+) = \lim_{s \to \infty} sV(s) = \lim_{s \to \infty} \frac{4}{s^2 + 4s + 8} = 0$$

which is required.

The partial-fraction expansion is

$$V(s) = \frac{4}{s(s^2 + 4s + 8)} = \frac{K_1}{s} + \frac{As + B}{s^2 + 4s + 8}$$

and K_1 can be found immediately by applying eq. (15.32):

$$K_1 = \frac{4}{s^2 + 4s + 8}\Big|_{s=0} = \frac{4}{8} = \frac{1}{2}$$

To find A and B, find a least common denominator,

$$\frac{4}{s(s^2 + 4s + 8)} = \frac{K_1(s^2 + 4s + 8) + (As + B)s}{s(s^2 + 4s + 8)}$$

and work with the numerators, where, to preserve the equality, the coefficients of like powers of s must match on either side of the equation. Three equations in three unknowns are obtained:

$$K_1 + A = 0$$
$$4K_1 + B = 0$$
$$8K_1 = 4$$

This confirms that

$$K_1 = \frac{1}{2} \qquad A = -K_1 = -\frac{1}{2} \qquad B = -4K_1 = -4\left(\frac{1}{2}\right) = -2$$

Hence,

$$V(s) = \frac{1}{2}\left(\frac{1}{s} - \frac{s+4}{s^2 + 4s + 8}\right)$$

Now, by completing the square, one obtains

$$V(s) = \frac{1}{2}\left(\frac{1}{s} - \frac{s+4}{s^2 + 4s + 4 + 4}\right) = \frac{1}{2}\left[\frac{1}{s} - \frac{s+4}{(s+2)^2 + 4}\right]$$
$$= \frac{1}{2}\left[\frac{1}{s} - \frac{s+2}{(s+2)^2 + 4} - \frac{2}{(s+2)^2 + 4}\right]$$

Finally, with the help of Table 15.1, $v(t)$ may be found:

$$v(t) = \frac{1}{2}\left[1 - e^{-2t}(\cos 2t + \sin 2t)\right] \text{ volts}$$

and this confirms the result in Example 7.2 in Section 7.4.2. ■

EXERCISE 16.8

In the network shown in Fig. 16.16, the switch closes instantaneously when the voltage across the capacitor terminals is $v(0) = 4$ V. What is the total response for $v(t)$?

Answer $v(t) = \frac{1}{5}(40t - 18 + 150e^{-4t} - 112e^{-5t})$ volts.

A second-order network excited by a voltage ramp (Exercise 16.8)

FIGURE 16.16

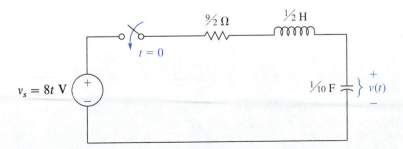

16.3.4 Excitation by a Sinusoidal Input

■ **EXAMPLE 16.9**

Suppose that in the network shown in Fig. 16.15, a sinusoidal current $i_{in} = 2 \sin 4t$ is applied at $t = 0$. What is the voltage response if $v_c(0^-) = 0$ and $i_L(0^-) = 0$? These are the same initial conditions used for the case of ramp excitation in the previous section.

Solution   The differential equation derives from an application of KCL:

$$\frac{1}{4}\frac{dv}{dt} + v + 2 \int_{-\infty}^{t} v\, dz = 2 \sin 4t; \qquad t > 0$$

or

$$\frac{dv}{dt} + 4v + 8 \int_{-\infty}^{t} v\, dz = 8 \sin 4t$$

With

$$\mathscr{L}[v(t)] = V(s) \qquad v(0^-) = 0 \qquad \int v\, dt \Big|_{t=0^-} = 0$$

a term-by-term-transformation provides

$$sV(s) + 4V(s) + 8\frac{V(s)}{s} = \frac{32}{s^2 + 16}$$

or after algebraic adjustment,

$$V(s) = \frac{32s}{(s^2 + 4s + 8)(s^2 + 16)}$$

Two quadratic factors are observed in the denominator of $V(s)$. One of them derives from the network itself, which is known to yield an underdamped natural response. The other derives from the sinusoidal forcing function.

The initial-value theorem of eq. (15.38) can be used to show that

$$v(0^+) = \lim_{s \to \infty} sV(s) = \lim_{s \to \infty} \frac{32s^2}{(s^2 + 4s + 8)(s^2 + 16)}$$

$$= \lim_{s \to \infty} \frac{s^2}{s^4}\left[\frac{32}{(1 + 4/s + 8/s^2)(1 + 16/s^2)}\right] = 0$$

which is required.

The partial-fraction expansion can be written as

$$V(s) = \frac{32s}{(s^2 + 4s + 8)(s^2 + 16)} = \frac{A_1 s + B_1}{s^2 + 4s + 8} + \frac{A_2 s + B_2}{s^2 + 16}$$

and the method of algebra discussed in Section 15.9.4 is to be employed to determine the constants A_1, B_1, A_2, and B_2.

Put the right-hand side over a common denominator:

$$\frac{32s}{(s^2 + 4s + 8)(s^2 + 16)} = \frac{(A_1s + B_1)(s^2 + 16) + (A_2s + B_2)(s^2 + 4s + 8)}{(s^2 + 4s + 8)(s^2 + 16)}$$

In working with the numerators only, one finds an equality

$$32s = (A_1s + B_1)(s^2 + 16) + (A_2s + B_2)(s^2 + 4s + 8)$$
$$= (A_1 + A_2)s^3 + (4A_2 + B_1 + B_2)s^2 + (16A_1 + 8A_2 + 4B_2)s$$
$$+ (16B_1 + 8B_2)$$

In order for this equality to be preserved, the coefficients of like powers of s must match. Thus, a term-by-term comparison produces a set of four simultaneous algebraic equations in four unknowns:

$$A_1 + A_2 \qquad\qquad B = 0$$
$$4A_2 + B_1 + B_2 = 0$$
$$16A_1 + 8A_2 \qquad + 4B_2 = 32$$
$$16B_1 + 8B_2 = 0$$

The reader may verify that the solution to this set of equations is

$$A_1 = \frac{4}{5} \qquad B_1 = -\frac{16}{5} \qquad A_2 = -\frac{4}{5} \qquad B_2 = \frac{32}{5}$$

With these values, $V(s)$ can be written as

$$V(s) = \frac{1}{5}\left(\frac{4s - 16}{s^2 + 4s + 8} - \frac{4s - 32}{s^2 + 16}\right)$$

Now, if the square is completed and other appropriate adjustments are made, one obtains

$$V(s) = \frac{1}{5}\left(\frac{4s - 16}{s^2 + 4s + 4 + 4} - \frac{4s}{s^2 + 16} + 8\frac{4}{s^2 + 16}\right)$$
$$= \frac{1}{5}\left[\frac{4s - 16}{(s + 2)^2 + 4} - \frac{4s}{s^2 + 16} + 8\frac{4}{s^2 + 16}\right]$$
$$= \frac{1}{5}\left[\frac{4(s + 2)}{(s + 2)^2 + 4} - \frac{24}{(s + 2)^2 + 4} - \frac{4s}{s^2 + 16} + 8\frac{4}{s^2 + 16}\right]$$
$$= \frac{1}{5}\left[\frac{4(s + 2)}{(s + 2)^2 + 4} - 12\frac{2}{(s + 2)^2 + 4} - \frac{4s}{s^2 + 16} + 8\frac{4}{s^2 + 16}\right]$$

The last step is to obtain $v(t)$, possibly with the help of Table 15.1:

$$v(t) = \frac{1}{5}\left[e^{-2t}(4\cos 2t - 12\sin 2t) - 4\cos 4t + 8\sin 4t\right]$$

and this confirms the result in Example 7.5 in Section 7.4.3.

■

FIGURE 16.17   A second-order network excited by a voltage sinusoid (Exercise 16.9)

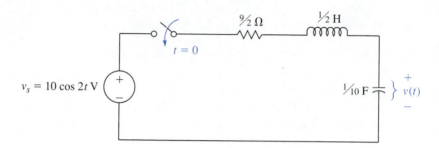

EXERCISE 16.9

In the network shown in Fig. 16.17, the switch closes instantaneously when the voltage across the capacitor terminals is $v(0) = 4$ V. What is the total response for $v(t)$?

Answer $v(t) = \dfrac{1}{29} (536e^{-5t} - 580e^{-4t} + 160 \cos 2t + 360 \sin 2t)$ volts.

16.3.5 Excitation by an Impulse

■ **EXAMPLE 16.10**

A voltage $v_{\text{in}} = 10\delta(t)$ is impressed upon the *RLC* series network in Fig. 7.10 (repeated here as Fig. 16.18) at $t = 0$. At $t = 0^-$, the capacitor is uncharged and no current is flowing in the network. However, the impulse, as shown in Section 7.4.4, leaves a current of $i(0^+) = 10$ A in its wake at $t = 0^+$. Find the current for all $t > 0^+$.

Solution   An application of KVL provides

$$\frac{di}{dt} + 5i + 6 \int_{-\infty}^{t} i\,dt = 0; \qquad t > 0$$

FIGURE 16.18   A *RLC* series network excited by a voltage impulse at $t = 0$. Here $v_s(t) = 10\delta t$ volts

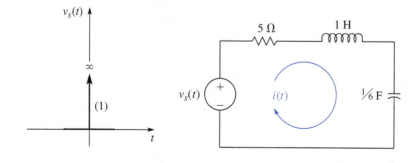

because at $t = 0^+$, the impulse is no longer present. With

$$\mathscr{L}[i(t)] = I(s) \qquad i(0^+) = 10 \qquad \int_a^{0^-} i\,dt = \int i\,dt\Big|_{t=0^-} = q(0^+) = 0$$

a term-by-term transformation provides

$$sI(s) - 10 + 5I(s) + \frac{6I(s)}{s} = 0$$

The current $I(s)$ is found quite simply from

$$\frac{s^2 + 5s + 6}{s} I(s) = 10 \qquad \text{or} \qquad I(s) = \frac{10s}{s^2 + 5s + 6}$$

The initial-value theorem of eq. (15.38) shows that

$$\lim_{s\to\infty} sI(s) = \lim_{s\to\infty} \frac{10s^2}{s^2 + 5s + 6} = \lim_{s\to\infty} \frac{10}{1 + 5/s + 6/s^2} = 10 \text{ A}$$

which is required.

The denominator of $I(s)$ can be factored, and the partial-fraction expansion is

$$I(s) = \frac{10s}{(s+2)(s+3)} = \frac{K_1}{s+2} + \frac{K_2}{s+3}$$

The constants K_1 and K_2 are evaluated by using eq. (15.32):

$$K_1 = \frac{10s}{s+3}\Big|_{s=-2} = \frac{-20}{1} = -20 \qquad K_2 = \frac{10s}{s+2}\Big|_{s=-3} = \frac{-30}{-1} = 30$$

Thus,

$$I(s) = \frac{30}{s+3} - \frac{20}{s+2}$$

and the time function is

$$i(t) = 30e^{-3t} - 20e^{-2t} \text{ amperes}$$

which confirms the result in Example 7.6 in Section 7.4.4. ■

EXERCISE 16.10

In the network shown in Fig. 16.19, the voltage impulse strikes at $t = 0$. Find $i(t)$.

Answer $i(t) = 10e^{-3t} - 30te^{-3t}$.

FIGURE 16.19

FIGURE 16.19   A second-order network excited by a voltage impulse (Exercise 16.10)

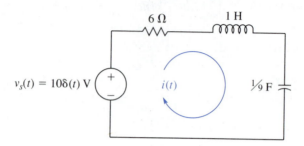

The solution of the differential equations of network theory is economically and expeditiously handled through the use of the Laplace transformation. Sections 16.2 and 16.3 have demonstrated this, and a one-for-one comparison with the identical equations and their *classical* solutions presented in Chapters 6 and 7 supports this argument.

SECTION 16.4   **SIMULTANEOUS DIFFERENTIAL EQUATIONS**

The Laplace transform is very useful in the solution of simultaneous differential equations. This will now be demonstrated by repeating Example 7.9, which involved the network shown in Fig. 7.15, repeated here as Fig. 16.20.

■ **EXAMPLE 16.11**

In Fig. 16.20, the switch closes instantaneously at $t = 0$ when there is no current flow in the inductor and no voltage across the capacitor. Find the two mesh currents i_1 and i_2.

Solution   Application of KVL to each mesh in Fig. 16.20 yields the pair of mesh equations which apply after $t = 0$,

$$\frac{di_1}{dt} + 400i_1 - 400i_2 = 100$$

$$-400i_1 + 1000i_2 + 40,000 \int_{-\infty}^{t} i_2 \, dz = 0$$

FIGURE 16.20   A more advanced network with two loops or meshes

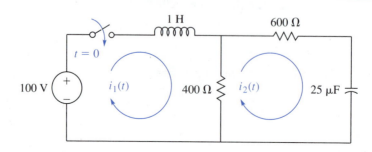

one of which is differential and one of which is integro-differential. These equations may be transformed term-by-term, with

$$\mathscr{L}[i_1(t)] = I_1(s) \quad \text{and} \quad \mathscr{L}[i_2(t)] = I_2(s)$$

and with

$$i_1(0^-) = i_2(0^-) = 0 \quad \text{and} \quad \int_a^{0^-} i_2 \, dt = 0$$

to obtain

$$sI_1(s) + 400I_1(s) - 400I_2(s) = \frac{100}{s}$$

$$-400I_1(s) + 1000I_2(s) + 40{,}000 \frac{I_2(s)}{s} = 0$$

After a little algebra to put the coefficient of $I_2(s)$ in the second equation over a common denominator, these may be put into matrix form:

$$\begin{bmatrix} (s + 400) & -400 \\ -400 & \dfrac{1000s + 40{,}000}{s} \end{bmatrix} \begin{bmatrix} I_1(s) \\ I_2(s) \end{bmatrix} = \begin{bmatrix} \dfrac{100}{s} \\ 0 \end{bmatrix} \tag{16.1}$$

The isolation of $I_1(s)$ and $I_2(s)$ can be accomplished by using a matrix inversion. In either case, the determinant of the coefficient matrix in eq. (16.1) must be evaluated. Use the symbol Δ to represent this determinant:

$$\Delta = \begin{vmatrix} (s + 400) & -400 \\ -400 & \dfrac{1000s + 40{,}000}{s} \end{vmatrix}$$

$$= (s + 400)\left(\frac{1000s + 40{,}000}{s} \right) - 160{,}000$$

$$= \frac{1000}{s}[(s + 400)(s + 40) - 160s] = \frac{1000}{s}(s^2 + 280s + 16{,}000)$$

Notice that the term within the parentheses can be factored, so that

$$\Delta = \frac{1000}{s}(s + 80)(s + 200)$$

The solution now continues via the matrix inversion process:

$$\begin{bmatrix} I_1(s) \\ I_2(s) \end{bmatrix} = \frac{1}{\Delta} \begin{bmatrix} \dfrac{1000s + 40{,}000}{s} & 400 \\ 400 & (s + 400) \end{bmatrix} \begin{bmatrix} \dfrac{100}{s} \\ 0 \end{bmatrix}$$

$$= \begin{bmatrix} \dfrac{(100/s^2)(1000s + 40{,}000)}{(1000/s)(s + 80)(s + 200)} \\ \dfrac{40{,}000/s}{(1000/s)(s + 80)(s + 400)} \end{bmatrix}$$

Then,

$$I_1(s) = \frac{100s + 4000}{s(s + 80)(s + 200)}$$ (16.2)

$$I_2(s) = \frac{40}{(s + 80)(s + 200)}$$ (16.3)

The time domain functions may now be reclaimed with some confidence, because when each of eqs. (16.2) and (16.3) are multiplied by s, one obtains the limits

$$\lim_{s \to \infty} sI_1(s) = 0 \qquad \text{and} \qquad \lim_{s \to \infty} sI_2(s) = 0$$

as required by the initial-value theorem of eq. (15.38).
The partial-fraction expansion for eq. (16.2) is

$$I_1(s) = \frac{100s + 4000}{s(s + 80)(s + 200)} = \frac{K_1}{s} + \frac{K_2}{s + 80} + \frac{K_3}{s + 200}$$

and use of eq. (15.32) gives

$$K_1 = \frac{100s + 4000}{(s + 80)(s + 200)}\bigg|_{s=0} = \frac{4000}{(80)(200)} = \frac{1}{4}$$

$$K_2 = \frac{100s + 4000}{s(s + 200)}\bigg|_{s=-80} = \frac{-4000}{(-80)(120)} = \frac{-4000}{-9600} = \frac{5}{12}$$

$$K_3 = \frac{100s + 4000}{s(s + 80)}\bigg|_{s=-200} = \frac{-16,000}{(-200)(-120)} = \frac{-16,000}{24,000} = -\frac{2}{3}$$

Thus,

$$I_1(s) = \frac{\frac{1}{4}}{s} + \frac{\frac{5}{12}}{s + 80} - \frac{\frac{2}{3}}{s + 200}$$

$$i_1(t) = \frac{1}{4} + \frac{5}{12} e^{-80t} - \frac{2}{3} e^{-200t} \text{ amperes}$$

which confirms one of the results in Example 7.9 in Section 7.6.
For $I_2(s)$ and $i_2(t)$, use eq. (16.3) and again employ eq. (15.32):

$$I_2(s) = \frac{40}{(s + 80)(s + 200)} = \frac{K_1}{s + 80} + \frac{K_2}{s + 200}$$

so that

$$K_1 = \frac{40}{s + 200}\bigg|_{s=-80} = \frac{40}{120} = \frac{1}{3}$$

$$K_2 = \frac{40}{s + 80}\bigg|_{s=-200} = \frac{40}{-120} = -\frac{1}{3}$$

Hence,

$$I_2(s) = \frac{1}{3}\left(\frac{1}{s + 80} - \frac{1}{s + 200}\right)$$

$$i_2(t) = \frac{1}{3}(e^{-80t} - e^{-200t}) \text{ amperes}$$

which confirms the other result in Example 7.9 in Section 7.6.   ■

PULSED INPUT FUNCTIONS
SECTION 16.5

Figure 16.21 shows a single rectangular pulse of unity amplitude or strength and duration a. This pulse is composed of two step functions $u(t)$ and $u(t - a)$, and as shown in Chapter 5, the pulse can be represented by

$$g(t) = u(t) - u(t - a)$$

Here, $g(t)$ is used to indicate a *gate* or *filter function*, because when any other function is multiplied by $g(t)$, it is obliterated completely at any point outside the interval $0 < t < a$.

In accordance with the shifting theorem, eq. (15.12), the Laplace transform of $g(t)$ is

$$\mathscr{L}[g(t)] = \mathscr{L}[u(t) - u(t - a)] = \frac{1 - e^{-as}}{s} \tag{16.4}$$

The Laplace transform method permits the analysis of systems with pulsed inputs in an expeditious manner, because the analysis does not depend on a decomposition into two solutions, one for which the pulse is present and one for which the pulse has been removed. However, it may be convenient to write the solution in the transform domain as a difference of two solutions.

A rectangular pulse of unity amplitude or strength and duration of a time units
FIGURE 16.21

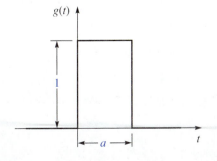

An *RL* series network driven by a pulsed input applied at $t = 0$

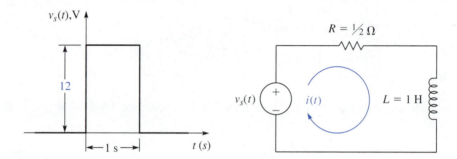

■ EXAMPLE 16.12

In Fig. 16.22, the inductor carries no current when the 12-V pulse of duration 1 s is suddenly and instantaneously applied at $t = 0$. The current at $t = 3$ s is to be found.

Solution   The pulse is written as

$$g(t) = 12[u(t) - u(t - 1)]$$

because the pulse width is 1 s. KVL may be employed to obtain the differential equation:

$$L\frac{di}{dt} + Ri = 12[u(t) - u(t - 1)]$$

and with $L = 1$ H and $R = \frac{1}{2}$ Ω,

$$\frac{di}{dt} + \frac{1}{2}i = 12[u(t) - u(t - 1)]$$

With $\mathscr{L}[i(t)] = I(s)$, this first-order differential equation can be transformed term-by-term, using the shifting theorem, to obtain

$$[sI(s) - i(0^-)] + \frac{1}{2}I(s) = \frac{12(1 - e^{-s})}{s}$$

and with $i(0^-) = 0$, algebraic manipulation gives

$$I(s) = \frac{12(1 - e^{-s})}{s(s + \frac{1}{2})}$$

which can be expressed in terms of two Laplace transforms:

$$I_a(s) = \frac{12}{s(s + \frac{1}{2})} \tag{16.5a}$$

$$I_b(s) = \frac{12}{s(s + \frac{1}{2})}e^{-s} \tag{16.5b}$$

Observe that the intent in eq. (16.5*b*) is to show that the algebraic entity

$$\frac{12}{s(s + \frac{1}{2})}$$

is equal to eq. (16.5*a*) and that e^{-s} may be treated as a multiplier. This indicates that the response $i(t)$ will be treated as the difference of two responses:

$$i(t) = i_a(t) - i_b(t)$$

where

$$i_a(t) = \mathscr{L}^{-1}[I_a(s)] \qquad \text{and} \qquad i_b(t) = \mathscr{L}^{-1}[I_b(s)]$$

The partial-fraction expansion for $I_a(s)$ is

$$I_a(s) = \frac{12}{s(s + \frac{1}{2})} = \frac{K_1}{s} + \frac{K_2}{s + \frac{1}{2}}$$

and the values of K_1 and K_2 are obtained from eq. (15.32):

$$K_1 = \frac{12}{s + \frac{1}{2}}\bigg|_{s=0} = \frac{12}{\frac{1}{2}} = 24 \qquad K_2 = \frac{12}{s}\bigg|_{s=-1/2} = \frac{12}{-\frac{1}{2}} = -24$$

Hence,

$$I_a(s) = 24\left(\frac{1}{s} - \frac{1}{s + \frac{1}{2}}\right)$$

and

$$i_a(t) = 24(1 - e^{-(1/2)t}) \text{ amperes} \tag{16.6}$$

where it may be noted that the time constant is $T = 2$ s.

The inverse of $I_b(s)$ would be equal to eq. (16.6) if the factor e^{-s} were not present. The presence of this factor requires that eq. (16.6) be translated to the right and have a value of zero for times less than $t = 1$ s. Thus,

$$i_b(t) = 24(1 - e^{-(1/2)(t-1)})u(t - 1) \tag{16.7}$$

Observe that the $t - 1$ factor in the exponent is the time translation to the right and that the presence of the $u(t - 1)$ guarantees that $i_b(t) = 0$ to the left of $t = 1$ s.

The current as a function of time is the difference of eqs. (16.6) and (16.7):

$$i(t) = i_a(t) - i_b(t) = 24(1 - e^{-(1/2)t}) - 24(1 - e^{-(1/2)(t-1)})u(t - 1) \text{ amperes}$$

At $t = 3$ s,

$$i(t = 3) = 18.645 - 15.171 = 3.474 \text{ A}$$

CHAPTER 16

SUMMARY   The entire chapter has been devoted to examples of the Laplace transform method for the solution of the differential equations of network theory.

Additional Readings

Blackwell, W.A., and L.L. Grigsby. *Introductory Network Theory*. Boston: PWS Engineering, 1985, pp. 541–580.

Bobrow, L.S. *Elementary Linear Circuit Analysis*. 2d ed. New York: Holt, Rinehart and Winston, 1987, pp. 518–528.

Del Toro, V. *Engineering Circuits*. Englewood Cliffs, N.J.: Prentice-Hall, 1987, pp. 388–418.

Dorf, R.C. *Introduction to Electric Circuits*. New York: Wiley, 1989, pp. 506–522.

Hayt, W.H., Jr., and J.E. Kemmerly. *Engineering Circuit Analysis*. 4th ed. New York: McGraw-Hill, 1986, pp. 595–599.

Irwin, J.D. *Basic Engineering Circuit Analysis*. 3d ed. New York: Macmillan, 1989, pp. 759–762, 766–801.

Johnson, D.E., J.L. Hilburn, and J.R. Johnson. *Basic Electric Circuit Analysis*. 4th ed. Englewood Cliffs, N.J.: Prentice-Hall, 1989, pp. 611–620.

Karni, S. *Applied Circuit Analysis*. New York: Wiley, 1988, pp. 456–465.

Madhu, S. *Linear Circuit Analysis*. Englewood Cliffs, N.J.: Prentice-Hall, 1988, pp. 745–748, 759–768.

Nilsson, J.W. *Electric Circuits*. 3d ed. Reading, Mass.: Addison-Wesley, 1990, pp. 578–595.

Paul, C.R. *Analysis of Linear Circuits*. New York: McGraw-Hill, 1989, pp. 628–647.

PROBLEMS   CHAPTER 16

Section 16.2

 All problems (16.1–16.37) can be handled by SPICE.

16.1   In the network of Fig. P16.1, the switch opens instantaneously at $t = 0$. Find the current response for all $t \geq 0$.

16.2   In the network of Fig. P16.2, the switch opens instantaneously at $t = 0$. Find the voltage response for all $t \geq 0$.

Figure P16.1

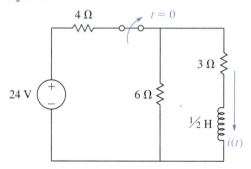

Figure P16.2

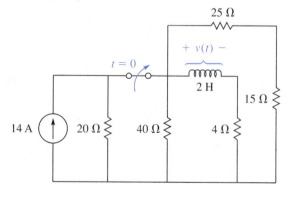

16.3 In the network of Fig. P16.3, the switch opens instantaneously at $t = 0$. Find the voltage response for all $t \geq 0$.

Figure P16.3

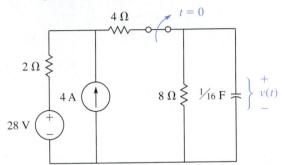

16.4 In the network of Fig. P16.4, the switch opens instantaneously at $t = 0$. Find the voltage response for all $t \geq 0$.

Section 16.3

Figure P16.4

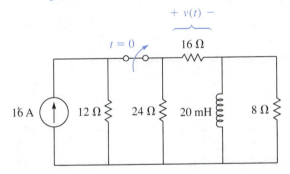

16.5 In the network of Fig. P16.5, the switch closes instantaneously at $t = 0$. Find the current response for $t \geq 0$.

Figure P16.5

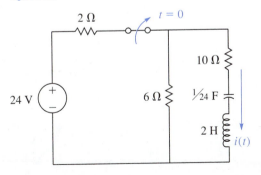

16.6 In the network of Fig. P16.6, the switch moves from position 1 to position 2 instantaneously at $t = 0$. Find the voltage response for $t \geq 0$.

Figure P16.6

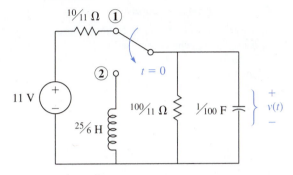

16.7 In the network of Fig. P16.7, the switch opens instantaneously at $t = 0$. Find the current response for $t \geq 0$.

Figure P16.7

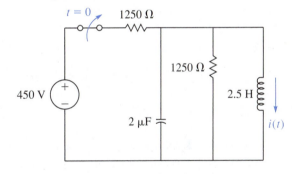

Problems 16.8 through 16.12 are based upon Fig. P16.8, where the current designated by i_s is applied to the network at $t = 0$. In all cases, $i(t)$ is to be found for the specified forcing function i_s.

Figure P16.8

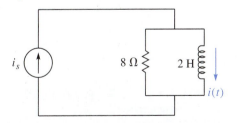

16.8 $i_s = 4$ amperes

16.9 $i_s = 4t + 12$ amperes

16.10 $i_s = 10 + 16 \sin 2t$ amperes

16.11 $i_s = 24 + 8e^{-4t}$ amperes

16.12 $i_s = 24t + 18e^{-t}$ amperes

Problems 16.13 through 16.17 are based upon Fig. P16.9, where the switch closes instantaneously at $t = 0$. In all cases, $v(t)$ is to be found for the specified forcing function v_s.

Figure P16.9

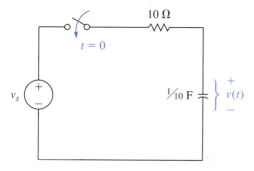

16.13 $v_s = 12 + 6e^{-2t} - 8e^{-3t}$ volts

16.14 $v_s = 16t + 4e^{-t}$ volts

16.15 $v_s = 8t^2$ V

16.16 $v_s = 12e^{-2t} + 4 \cos 2t$ volts

16.17 $v_s = 12t^2 + 64$ amperes

Problems 16.18 through 16.22 are based upon Fig. P16.10, where the current designated by i_s is applied to the network at $t = 0$. In all cases, $v(t)$ is to be found for the specified element values, initial voltage, $v(0^-)$, and forcing function i_s.

Figure P16.10

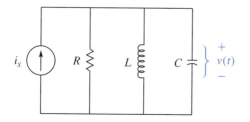

16.18 $R = \frac{4}{5}\,\Omega$, $L = \frac{1}{3}$ H, $C = \frac{1}{8}$ F, $v(0^-) = 16$ V, and $i_s = 6t + 4$ amperes

16.19 $R = \frac{5}{8}\,\Omega$, $L = \frac{1}{5}$ H, $C = \frac{1}{5}$ F, $v(0^-) = 12$ V, and $i_s = 8t + 12 \cos 4t$ amperes

16.20 $R = 3\,\Omega$, $L = 1$ H, $C = \frac{1}{36}$ F, $v(0^-) = 10$ V, and $i_s = 6e^{-4t} - 4$ amperes

16.21 $R = 1\,\Omega$, $L = \frac{4}{5}$ H, $C = \frac{1}{4}$ F, $v(0^-) = 8$ V, and $i_s = 12t^2$ amperes

16.22 $R = \frac{2}{3}\,\Omega$, $L = \frac{1}{4}$ H, $C = \frac{1}{8}$ F, $v(0^-) = 6$ V, and $i_s = 20 + 4 \sin 4t$ amperes

Problems 16.23 through 16.27 are based upon Fig. P16.11, where the switch closes instantaneously at $t = 0$. In all cases, $i(t)$ is to be found for the specified forcing function v_s.

Figure P16.11

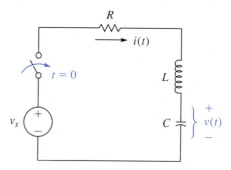

16.23 $R = 2\,\Omega$, $L = 1$ H, $C = \frac{1}{5}$ F, $v(0^-) = 2$ V, and $v_s = 16 - 12 \cos 2t$ volts

16.24 $R = 2\,\Omega$, $L = \frac{1}{2}$ H, $C = \frac{1}{2}$ F, $v(0^-) = 4$ V, and $v_s = 12t + 4e^{-2t}$ volts

16.25 $R = 7\,\Omega$, $L = 1$ H, $C = \frac{1}{12}$ F, $v(0^-) = 6$ V, and $v_s = 8 + 6e^{-2t} + 8e^{-6t}$ volts

16.26 $R = 4\,\Omega$, $L = 1$ H, $C = \frac{1}{13}$ F, $v(0^-) = 8$ V, and $v_s = 3e^{-4t} + 6 \cos 2t$ volts

16.27 $R = \frac{5}{2}\,\Omega$, $L = \frac{1}{2}$ H, $C = \frac{1}{3}$ F, $v(0^-) = 10$ V, and $v_2 = 6te^{-2t} + 12$ volts

16.28 In the network of Fig. P16.12, the switch moves instantaneously from position 1 to position 2 at $t = 0$. Find $v(t)$ for $t \geq 0$.

Figure P16.12

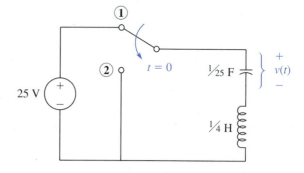

16.29 In the network of Fig. P16.13, the switch opens instantaneously at $t = 0$. Find $v(t)$ for $t \geq 0$.

Figure P16.13

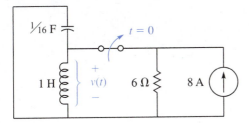

Section 16.4

16.30 In the network of Fig. P16.14, the switch moves from position 1 to position 2 instantaneously at $t = 0$. Find $v(t)$ for $t \geq 0$.

Figure P16.14

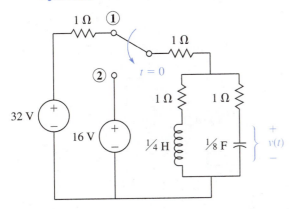

16.31 In the network of Fig. P16.15, the current source is applied to the network instantaneously at $t = 0$. Find $v(t)$ for $t \geq 0$.

Figure P16.15

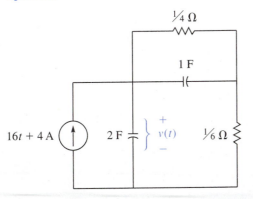

16.32 In the network of Fig. P16.16, the switch moves from position 1 to position 2 instantaneously at $t = 0$. Find $i(t)$ for $t \geq 0$.

Figure P16.16

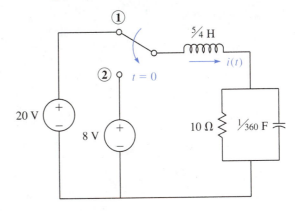

16.33 In the network of Fig. P16.17, the switch moves from position 1 to position 2 instantaneously at $t = 0$. Find $i(t)$ for $t \geq 0$.

Figure P16.17

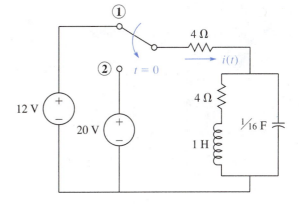

16.34   In the network of Fig. P16.18, the switch moves from position 1 to position 2 instantaneously at $t = 0$. Find $v(t)$ for $t \geq 0$.

Figure P16.18

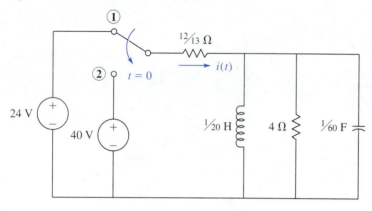

Section 16.5

Problems 16.35 through 16.38 are based upon Fig. P16.10 where the current i_s is applied to the network at $t = 0$. In all cases, $R = 2\,\Omega$, $L = \frac{2}{5}$ H, $C = \frac{1}{20}$ F, $v(0^-) = 2$ V, and $v(t)$ is to be found. The forcing function i_s is specified in each problem.

16.35   The pulse shown in Fig. P16.19

Figure P16.19

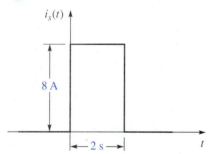

16.36   The pulse shown in Fig. P16.20

Figure P16.20

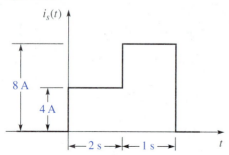

16.37   The pulse shown in Fig. P16.21

Figure P16.21

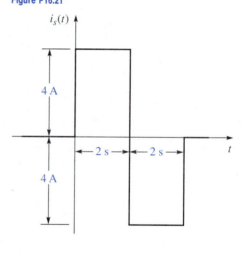

CONVOLUTION

OBJECTIVES

The objectives of this chapter are to:

- State and prove the convolution theorem and define the convolution or *faltung* integral.

- Show how the convolution integral is related to the product of two Laplace transforms.

- Demonstrate the usefulness of the convolution integral in obtaining the inverse Laplace transform.

- Provide the condition for the approximation of impulses by pulses.

- Consider analytical convolution and Borel's theorem.

- Consider the superposition or Duhamel integrals.

- Provide a procedure for graphical convolution.

INTRODUCTION

There are many ways of solving the differential equations of network theory. Methods discussed in previous chapters include the classical approach (Chapters 6 and 7) and the Laplace transform Method (Chapters 15 and 16). This chapter considers convolution and superposition methods to determine the response of a linear network. If the response to a single impulse can be determined, then because any arbitrary input function can be represented as a train of impulses, superposition methods can be applied to determine the response to the arbitrary input. The *convolution* or *Faltung integral*, considered in this chapter, is requisite to the superposition approach. It is also extremely useful in the determination of the inverse Laplace transformation.

SECTION 17.2   ## THE CONVOLUTION INTEGRAL

In Section 15.3.1, it was shown that if

$$\mathscr{L}[f_1(t)] = F_1(s) \qquad \text{and} \qquad \mathscr{L}[f_2(t)] = F_2(s)$$

the Laplace transform of the sum of the time domain functions is equal to the sum of the Laplace transforms:

$$\mathscr{L}[f_1(t) + f_2(t)] = F_1(s) + F_2(s)$$

It was also pointed out that the same idea does not apply to the product of two time domain functions; that is,

$$\mathscr{L}[f_1(t)f_2(t)] \neq F_1(s)F_2(s)$$

Consider the product $F_1(s)F_2(s)$. The inverse transform of this product,

$$\mathscr{L}^{-1}[F_1(s)F_2(s)]$$

can be obtained through an application of the *convolution theorem*, which is considered in detail in this section.
  If

$$\mathscr{L}[f_1(t)] = F_1(s) \qquad \text{and} \qquad \mathscr{L}[f_2(t)] = F_2(s)$$

both exist, then

$$\mathscr{L}^{-1}[F_1(s)F_2(s)] = \int_0^t f_1(t - \tau)f_2(\tau)\,d\tau = \int_0^t f_1(\tau)f_2(t - \tau)\,d\tau \qquad (17.1)$$

In order to prove this, consider the definition

$$\mathscr{L}\left[\int_0^t f_1(t - \tau)f_2(\tau)\,d\tau\right] = \int_0^\infty \left[\int_0^t f_1(t - \tau)f_2(\tau)\,d\tau\right]e^{-st}\,dt$$

The limits of the integral within the brackets can be changed from $0 \to t$ to $\tau \to \infty$ if the delayed unit step,

$$u(t - \tau) = \begin{cases} 0, & t < \tau \\ 1, & t > \tau \end{cases} \qquad (17.2)$$

is introduced. Then,

$$\int_0^\infty \left[\int_0^t f_1(t - \tau)f_2(\tau)\,d\tau\right]e^{-st}\,dt = \int_0^\infty \left[\int_\tau^\infty f_1(t - \tau)f_2(\tau)u(t - \tau)\,d\tau\right]e^{-st}\,dt$$

  The order of the integration may be interchanged because the Laplace transforms of both $f_1(t)$ and $f_2(t)$ are assumed to exist. Thus,

$$F_1(s)F_2(s) = \int_0^\infty f_2(\tau)\left[\int_\tau^\infty f_1(t - \tau)u(t - \tau)e^{-st}\,dt\right]d\tau \qquad (17.3)$$

and it is to be noted that all functions of t are contained in the inner integral of eq. (17.3). Moreover, because of the presence of the delayed unit step, $u(t - \tau)$, the lower limit of integration within the brackets is at $t = \tau$ and not at $t = 0$.

In the inner integral, let $\phi = t - \tau$ so that $dt = d\phi$. When $t = \tau$, $\phi = 0$; and hence,

$$F_1(s)F_2(s) = \int_0^\infty f_2(\tau)\left[\int_0^\infty f_1(\phi)e^{-s(\phi+\tau)}\,d\phi\right]d\tau$$

$$= \int_0^\infty f_2(\tau)\left[\int_0^\infty f_1(\phi)e^{-s\phi}e^{-s\tau}\,d\phi\right]d\tau$$

Then when the $e^{-s\tau}$ term is removed from the inner integral, the result is

$$F_1(s)F_2(s) = \left[\int_0^\infty f_2(\tau)e^{-s\tau}\,d\tau\right]\left[\int_0^\infty f_1(\phi)e^{-s\phi}\,d\phi\right] \tag{17.4}$$

Either of the integrals in eq. (17.1),

$$\int_0^t f_1(t-\tau)f_2(\tau)\,d\tau \tag{17.5a}$$

or

$$\int_0^t f_1(\tau)f_2(t-\tau)\,d\tau \tag{17.5b}$$

is called the *convolution* or *Faltung integral* and represents the convolution of the functions $f_1(t)$ and $f_2(t)$. They are often written in abbreviated form, using an asterisk to designate the operation of convolution:

$$\int_0^t f_1(\tau)f_2(t-\tau)\,d\tau = f_1(t) * f_2(t) \tag{17.6}$$

The operation of convolution is associative,

$$f_1(t) * f_2(t) = f_2(t) * f_1(t) \tag{17.7a}$$

and commutative,

$$f_1(t) * [f_2(t) * f_3(t)] = [f_1(t) * f_2(t)] * f_3(t) \tag{17.7b}$$

The convolution integral is extremely useful in obtaining the inverse Laplace transform when the transform is moderately complicated.

■ **EXAMPLE 17.1**

Find $f(t)$ if

$$F(s) = \frac{1}{(s^2 + 4s + 8)^2}$$

Solution Write $F(s)$ as

$$F(s) = \frac{1}{[(s+2)^2 + 4]^2}$$

and use the shifting theorem of Section 15.4.2,

$$f(t) = e^{-2t}\mathscr{L}^{-1}\left[\frac{1}{(s^2 + 4)^2}\right]$$

Then let

$$F_1(s) = F_2(s) = \frac{1}{s^2 + 4}$$

so that

$$f_1(t) = f_2(t) = \frac{1}{2} \sin 2t$$

By the convolution theorem,

$$\mathscr{L}^{-1}\left[\frac{1}{(s^2 + 4)^2}\right] = \frac{1}{4} \int_0^t \sin 2(t - \tau) \sin 2\tau \, d\tau$$

Note the trigonometric identity,

$$\sin A \sin B = \frac{1}{2} \left[\cos(A - B) - \cos(A + B)\right]$$

and let $A = 2\tau$ and $B = 2(t - \tau)$. Then,

$$\frac{1}{4} \int_0^t \sin 2(t - \tau) \sin 2\tau \, d\tau = \frac{1}{8} \int_0^t \left[\cos(4\tau - 2t) - \cos 2t\right] d\tau$$

$$= \frac{1}{8} \left[\frac{\sin(4\tau - 2t)}{4} - \tau \cos 2t\right]_0^t$$

$$= \frac{1}{8} \left[\frac{\sin 2t - \sin(-2t)}{4} - t \cos 2t\right]$$

But $-\sin(-2t) = \sin 2t$, and thus,

$$\mathscr{L}^{-1}\left[\frac{1}{(s^2 + 4)^2}\right] = \frac{1}{16} (\sin 2t - 2t \cos 2t)$$

and $f(t)$ is

$$f(t) = \mathscr{L}^{-1}\left[\frac{1}{(s^2 + 4s + 8)^2}\right] = \frac{1}{16} e^{-2t}(\sin 2t - 2t \cos 2t)$$

EXERCISE 17.1

Use convolution to find $f(t)$ if

$$F(s) = \frac{1}{(s + 1)(s + 2)}$$

Answer

$$f(t) = e^{-t} - e^{-2t}$$

FIGURE 17.1

(a) A simple RL series network with a voltage source consisting of (b) a unit impulse and (c) a rectangular pulse of unit area

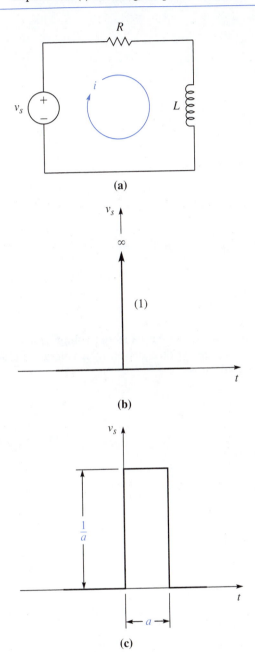

(a)

(b)

(c)

THE APPROXIMATION OF IMPULSES BY PULSES

A simple RL series network is shown in Fig. 17.1a. If the network is excited by the unit impulse voltage,

$$\int_{0^-}^{0^+} \delta(t)\,dt = 1$$

as indicated in Fig. 17.1b, the differential equation for the current response, obtained from a consideration of KVL, is

$$\frac{di}{dt} + \frac{R}{L} i = \frac{\delta(t)}{L}; \qquad t > 0$$

A term-by-term transformation gives

$$sI(s) - i(0^-) + \frac{R}{L} I(s) = \frac{1}{L}$$

and because $i(0^-) = 0$,

$$\left(s + \frac{R}{L}\right) I(s) = \frac{1}{L} \qquad \text{or} \qquad I(s) = \frac{1/L}{s + R/L}$$

In the time domain,

$$i(t) = \frac{1}{L} e^{-Rt/L} = \frac{1}{L} e^{-t/T} \tag{17.8}$$

where T is the time constant, $T = L/R$.

Figure 17.1c shows a voltage pulse with the same area as the voltage impulse in Fig. 17.1b. During the period $0 \leq t \leq a$, the network is driven by a voltage of magnitude $1/a$. This time the differential equation is

$$\frac{di}{dt} + \frac{R}{L} i = \frac{1/a}{L}; \qquad t > 0$$

and after transformation, again with $i(0^-) = 0$,

$$\left(s + \frac{R}{L}\right) I(s) = \frac{1/aL}{s} \qquad \text{or} \qquad I(s) = \frac{1/aL}{s(s + R/L)}$$

A partial-fraction expansion gives

$$\frac{1/aL}{s(s + R/L)} = \frac{K_1}{s} + \frac{K_2}{s + R/L}$$

and K_1 and K_2 are obtained by using eq. (15.32):

$$K_1 = \frac{1}{aL(s + R/L)}\bigg|_{s=0} = \frac{1}{aR} \qquad K_2 = \frac{1}{aLs}\bigg|_{s=-R/L} = -\frac{1}{aR}$$

Thus,

$$I(s) = \frac{1}{aR}\left(\frac{1}{s} - \frac{1}{s + R/L}\right)$$

and

$$i(t) = \frac{1}{aR}(1 - e^{-t/T}) \tag{17.9}$$

At $t = a$, the voltage is removed and the current begins its decay to zero. The current is at its peak value at $t = a$,

$$i(t = a) = \frac{1}{aR}(1 - e^{-a/T})$$

The exponential may be written as a Maclaurin series, so that the term in parentheses becomes

$$i(t = a) = \frac{1}{aR}\left[1 - \left(1 - \frac{a}{T} + \frac{a^2}{2T^2} - \frac{a^3}{6T^3} + \cdots\right)\right]$$
$$= \frac{1}{aR}\left(\frac{a}{T} - \frac{a^2}{2T^2} + \frac{a^3}{6T^3} - \cdots\right)$$

or because the time constant of the RL network is $T = L/R$,

$$i(t = a) = \frac{1}{L}\left(1 - \frac{a}{2T} + \frac{a^2}{6T^2} - \cdots\right)$$

If a is small with respect to T, all higher-order terms above $a/2T$ can be neglected, and

$$i(t = a) = \frac{1}{L}\left(1 - \frac{a}{2T}\right) \tag{17.10}$$

Similar reasoning can be applied to the impulse response current given by eq. (17.8) to show that

$$i(t = a) = \frac{1}{L}\left(1 - \frac{a}{T} + \frac{a^2}{2T^2} - \frac{a^3}{6T^3} + \cdots\right)$$

and with $a \ll T$,

$$i(t = a) = \frac{1}{L}\left(1 - \frac{a}{T}\right) \tag{17.11}$$

The impulse and pulse responses are plotted together in Fig. 17.2. Note that the pulse response is below the impulse response at $t = a$ by an amount

$$\epsilon = \left|\frac{1}{L}\left(1 - \frac{a}{T}\right) - \frac{1}{L}\left(1 - \frac{a}{2T}\right)\right| = \frac{a}{2LT}$$

and that after $t = a$, the two curves fall in a similar manner. If the pulse duration a approaches zero in the limit ($a \to 0$), then the two curves will be identical.

FIGURE 17.2

The current response of an RL series network to a pulsed and impulse voltage input

Note the difference between the two responses at $t = a$.

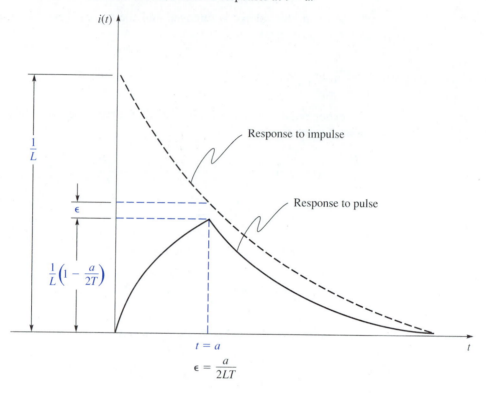

$$\epsilon = \frac{a}{2LT}$$

It can be concluded that the pulse response is equivalent to the impulse response as long as the pulse duration is short relative to the network time constant. This reasoning can be extended to higher-order networks containing pulsed inputs by insisting that the pulse duration be very short relative to the dominant network time constant.

SECTION 17.4   ANALYTIC CONVOLUTION AND BOREL'S THEOREM

Consider the arbitrary signal $e(t)$ shown in Fig. 17.3. If the time axis is divided into arbitrary increments of duration $\Delta\tau$, the signal can be approximated by a train of pulses. If the signal is an input signal to a system or network, the approximation may be represented by

$$e(t) \approx e_1(t) + e_2(t) + e_3(t) + \cdots + e_k(t) + \cdots$$

where e is intended to stand for "excitation." For n such pulses,

$$e(t) \approx \sum_n e_k(t)$$

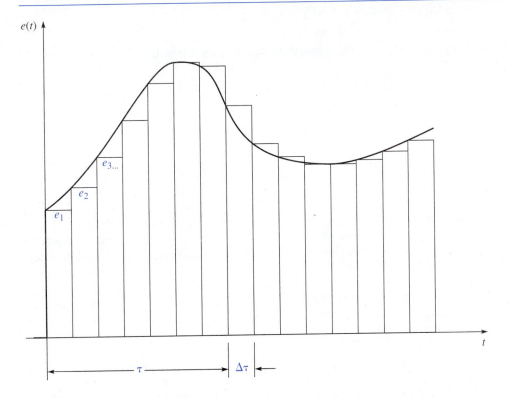

where

$$e_k(t) = \begin{cases} e(t), & \tau_k - \Delta\tau \le t \le \tau_k \\ 0, & t < \tau_k - \Delta\tau, \, t > \tau_k \end{cases}$$

If $r_k(t)$ is the response of a linear, time-invariant network to the input signal $e_k(t)$, the principle of superposition may be employed to give

$$r(t) \approx r_1(t) + r_2(t) + r_3(t) + \cdots + r_k(t) + \cdots$$

or

$$r(t) \approx \sum_n r_k(t)$$

If $\Delta\tau \to 0$, each of the pulses shown in Fig. 17.3 is approximated by an impulse of the same area. Thus, the kth pulse may be approximated by

$$e_k(t) \approx e(\tau_k) \Delta\tau \, \delta(t - \tau_k)$$

If $h(t)$ is designated as the response to the unit impulse $\delta(t)$, then for a time-invariant network, the kth input, $\delta(t - \tau_k)$, produces the response $h(t - \tau_k)$. For $\Delta\tau$ sufficiently small, the kth-response component becomes

$$r_k(t) \approx e(\tau_k) \Delta\tau \, h(t - \tau_k)$$

By superposition, the response from 0 to t is

$$r(t) \approx \sum_{k=1} e(\tau_k)h(t - \tau_k)\,\Delta\tau$$

In the limit as $\Delta\tau \to 0$, the summation becomes an integral,

$$r(t) = \sum_{n} e(\tau_k)h(t - \tau_k)\,\Delta\tau \to \int_0^t e(\tau)h(t - \tau)\,d\tau$$

and the response is

$$r(t) = \int_0^t e(\tau)h(t - \tau)\,d\tau = \int_0^t h(\tau)e(t - \tau)\,d\tau \qquad (17.12)$$

Equation (17.12) shows that the zero-state response of a linear, time-invariant network to an arbitrary input signal may be found from a convolution of the unit impulse response of the network and the input signal. This statement is frequently referred to as *Borel's theorem*; and although it was obtained by employing superposition, it is rarely referred to as a *superposition integral*, a terminology usually associated with the *Duhamel integral* treated in the next section.

Equation (17.12) can be obtained in a more straightforward manner by merely applying the convolution theorem, given here as eq. (17.1). The linear, time-invariant network has an input-output relationship in the s domain given by

$$R(s) = H(s)E(s) \qquad (17.13)$$

where $H(s)$, the zero-state response to the unit impulse, is the *transfer function* relating the input $E(s)$ and the output $R(s)$.

The product on the right-hand side suggests the use of the convolution theorem of eq. (17.1):

$$r(t) = \mathscr{L}^{-1}[R(s)] = \mathscr{L}^{-1}[H(s)E(s)]$$

$$r(t) = \int_0^t h(t - \tau)e(\tau)\,d\tau = \int_0^t h(\tau)e(t - \tau)\,d\tau \qquad (17.14)$$

■ **EXAMPLE 17.2**

Use convolution to determine the current in the *RLC* network of Fig. 17.4 if the input voltage is $e(t) = 2e^{-3t}$ volts.

Solution   Consider eq. (17.13),

$$R(s) = H(s)E(s)$$

with the current response $I(s) = R(s)$, and observe that when $E(s)$ is the unit impulse, $E(s) = 1$. Thus, the s domain response to the unit impulse is the transfer function between $I(s) = H(s)$ and the input $E(s) = 1$. This is the admittance, $Y(s) = 1/Z(s)$; and the impedance $Z(s)$ is

$$Z(s) = Ls + R + \frac{1}{Cs} = \frac{LCs^2 + RCs + 1}{Cs} = \frac{L}{s}\left(s^2 + \frac{R}{L}s + \frac{1}{LC}\right)$$

RLC series network for Example 17.2

FIGURE 17.4

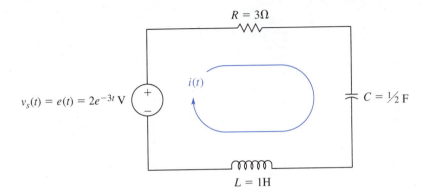

$R = 3\Omega$

$i(t)$

$v_s(t) = e(t) = 2e^{-3t}$ V

$C = \frac{1}{2}$ F

$L = 1$H

With element values inserted ($L = 1$ H, $R = 3$ Ω, and $C = \frac{1}{2}$ F),

$$Z(s) = \frac{s^2 + 3s + 2}{s}$$

and this makes

$$H(s) = Y(s) = \frac{1}{Z(s)} = \frac{s}{s^2 + 3s + 2}$$

The time domain response $h(t)$ may be obtained from a partial-fraction expansion:

$$\frac{s}{s^2 + 3s + 2} = \frac{s}{(s + 1)(s + 2)} = \frac{K_1}{s + 1} + \frac{K_2}{s + 2}$$

$$K_1 = \frac{s}{s + 2}\bigg|_{s = -1} = \frac{-1}{1} = -1 \qquad K_2 = \frac{s}{s + 1}\bigg|_{s = -2} = \frac{-2}{-1} = 2$$

Thus,

$$H(s) = \frac{-1}{s + 1} + \frac{2}{s + 2}$$

and the impulse response is

$$h(t) = -e^{-t} + 2e^{-2t} \text{ amperes}$$

If $e(t) = 2e^{-3t}$ volts, then by eq. (17.14),

$$i(t) = r(t) = \int_0^t (2e^{-2\tau} - e^{-\tau})2e^{-3(t-\tau)} \, d\tau = 4e^{-3t} \int_0^t e^\tau \, d\tau - 2e^{-3t} \int_0^t e^{2\tau} \, d\tau$$

$$= 4e^{-3t}(e^t - 1) - e^{-3t}(e^{2t} - 1) = 4e^{-2t} - 4e^{-3t} - e^{-t} + e^{-3t}$$

$$= -e^{-t} + 4e^{-2t} - 3e^{-3t} \text{ amperes}$$

The reader may wish to check this result by the direct Laplace transform approach.

FIGURE 17.5   Network (Exercise 17.2)

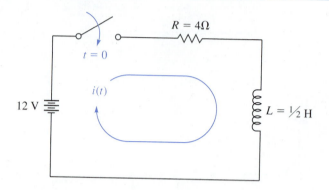

EXERCISE 17.2

In Fig. 17.5, the switch closes at $t = 0$. Use convolution to find $i(t)$.

Answer $i(t) = \dfrac{1}{2}(1 - e^{-8t})$ amperes.

SECTION 17.5   THE SUPERPOSITION OR DUHAMEL INTEGRALS

The zero-state response of a linear, time-invariant network is also completely characterized by its response to a unit step function. If in

$$R(s) = H(s)E(s) \tag{17.13}$$

$e(t)$ is the unit step function,

$$e(t) = u(t)$$

then,

$$R(s) = \frac{1}{s}H(s)$$

or

$$R(s) = \frac{H(s)}{s} = A(s) \tag{17.15}$$

where $A(s)$ is sometimes called the *indicial admittance*. The transform of the unit impulse can be written as

$$H(s) = sA(s)$$

and with this in eq. (17.13), one obtains

$$R(s) = sA(s)E(s) \tag{17.16}$$

which is the s domain expression for the output in terms of the indicial admittance and any arbitrary input function.

The form of eq. (17.16) suggests an application of the convolution theorem. From eq. (17.1), it is seen that

$$\mathscr{L}[r(t)] = s\mathscr{L}\left[\int_0^t a(t - \tau)e(\tau)\,d\tau\right] = s\mathscr{L}\left[\int_0^t a(\tau)e(t - \tau)\,d\tau\right]$$

where the factor s indicates a differentiation in the time domain.[1] Thus, by eq. (15.41),

$$r(t) = \frac{d}{dt}\left[\int_0^t a(t - \tau)e(\tau)\,d\tau\right] = \frac{d}{dt}\left[\int_0^t a(\tau)e(t - \tau)\,d\tau\right]$$

When the differentiation is performed (the primes indicate derivatives),

$$r(t) = \int_0^t a'(t - \tau)e(\tau)\,d\tau + a(0)e(t) \tag{17.17}$$

or

$$r(t) = \int_0^t a(t - \tau)e'(\tau)\,d\tau + a(t)e(0) \tag{17.18}$$

is obtained. These are the *Duhamel* or *superposition integrals*, which can be used to express the response of a network to an arbitrary input in terms of the response to a unit step.

■ EXAMPLE 17.3

Use the Duhamel integral to determine the current response of the network in Fig. 17.4 when the voltage $2e^{-3t}$ volts is applied at $t = 0$.

Solution   The s domain function $H(s)$ was found in Example 17.2:

$$H(s) = \frac{s}{s^2 + 3s + 2}$$

The indicial admittance is therefore

$$A(s) = \frac{H(s)}{s} = \frac{1}{s^2 + 3s + 2}$$

---

[1] See Section 15.10.3.

and $a(t)$ is easily found:

$$A(s) = \frac{1}{s^2 + 3s + 2} = \frac{1}{(s + 1)(s + 2)} = \frac{K_1}{s + 1} + \frac{K_2}{s + 2}$$

$$K_1 = \frac{1}{s + 2}\Big|_{s = -1} = \frac{1}{1} = 1 \quad \text{and} \quad K_2 = \frac{1}{s + 1}\Big|_{s = -2} = \frac{1}{-1} = -1$$

$$A(s) = \frac{1}{s + 1} - \frac{1}{s + 2} \quad \text{and} \quad a(t) = e^{-t} - e^{-2t}$$

Then,

$$a'(t) = 2e^{-2t} - e^{-t} \quad \text{and} \quad a(0) = 1 - 1 = 0$$

With

$$e(t) = 2e^{-3t}$$

eq. (17.17) gives

$$r(t) = i(t) = \int_0^t (2e^{-2(t-\tau)} - e^{-(t-\tau)})2e^{-3\tau}\, d\tau + 0$$

$$= 4e^{-2t} \int_0^t e^{-\tau}\, d\tau - 2e^{-t} \int_0^t e^{-2\tau}\, d\tau$$

$$= -4e^{-2t}(e^{-t} - 1) + e^{-t}(e^{-2t} - 1)$$

$$= -4e^{-3t} + 4e^{-2t} + e^{-3t} - e^{-t}$$

$$= -e^{-t} + 4e^{-2t} - 3e^{-3t} \text{ amperes}$$

This result is the same as the result obtained by using Borel's theorem in Example 17.2.   ∎

EXERCISE 17.3

Verify the result of Exercise 18.2 by Duhamel's integral.

Answer $i(t) = 3(1 - e^{-8t})$ amperes.

SECTION 17.6   GRAPHICAL CONVOLUTION

The German word *faltung* means "folding." In order to see why the convolution integral is called the Faltung integral, consider Fig. 17.6. The unit ramp $r(\tau)$ and the unit step $u(\tau)$ are shown, respectively, in Figs. 17.6a and 17.6b. If τ is replaced by $-\tau$ in the unit step, the result, $u(-\tau)$, will be as shown in Fig. 17.6c. Observe the folding or convolution about the vertical or $u(\tau)$ axis.

Next, consider $u(t - \tau)$. This implies a shift of $u(-\tau)$, and this shift will be t units in the *positive* τ direction, as indicated in Fig. 17.6d. Either representation of eqs. (17.5) can be used to represent the convolution, because it is only a matter of nomenclature to select $f_1(t - \tau)$ or $f_2(t - \tau)$ as $u(t - \tau)$. The convolution integral requires the multi-

FIGURE 17.6

(a) The unit ramp function $r(\tau)$, (b) the unit step $u(\tau)$, (c) the folding of $u(\tau)$ to make $u(-\tau)$, (d) the shift of $u(t-\tau)$ to the right by t units, and (e) the product $r(\tau)u(t-\tau)$

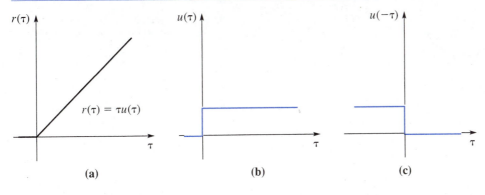

(a)   (b)   (c)

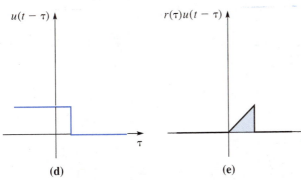

(d)   (e)

plication of $r(t)$ and $u(t-\tau)$, and this is shown in Fig. 17.6e, with subsequent evaluation of the area under the product between 0 and t.

The example that follows has been completely contrived but will show how this procedure works.

■ **EXAMPLE 17.4**

The unit impulse response of a particular network is shown in Fig. 17.7a, and the response of the network to the pulsed input, shown in Fig. 17.7b, is desired. Perform a graphical convolution, and plot the result.

Solution   With τ used as the time variable, $e(\tau)$ may be folded so that at $t=0$ (no shift to the right), $e(\tau)$ and $h(\tau)$ will be as shown in Fig. 17.7c. At $t=0$, the product $e(-\tau)$ and $h(\tau)$ is equal to zero, so that the response is $r(t)=0$.

At $t=\frac{1}{2}$ s, the picture is as shown in Fig. 17.7d. The shaded area is the value of

$$r\left(t=\frac{1}{2}\right) = \int_0^{1/2} h(\tau)e(t-\tau)\,d\tau = \frac{1}{2}\cdot\frac{1}{2}(1) = \frac{1}{4}$$

Similar calculations may be performed as the pulse is *slid* along the τ axis, and these are shown in Figs. 17.7d through 17.7k. The area computations are indicated in each figure, and the result of all of the area computations is shown in Fig. 17.8, which gives $r(t)$.

■

FIGURE 17.7   (a) The unit impulse response of a network, (b) the input to the network, and
(c) through (k) the graphical convolution process

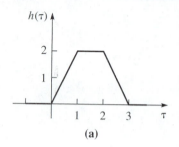
(a)

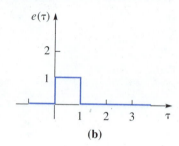
(b)

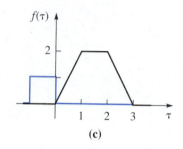
(c)

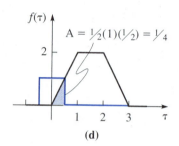
(d)

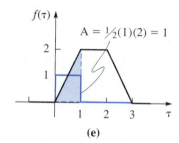
(e)

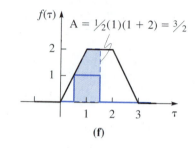
(f)

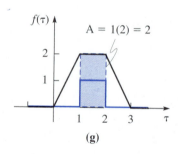
(g)

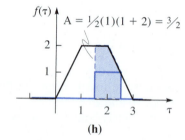
(h)

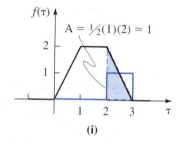
(i)

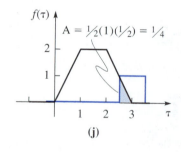
(j)

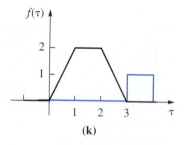
(k)

EXERCISE 17.4

The unit impulse response of a particular network is shown in Fig. 17.9a,
and the response of the network to the pulsed input, shown in Fig. 17.9b, is
desired. Perform a graphical convolution, and plot the result.

Answer   See Fig. 17.10.

FIGURE 17.8

The output of the network having the impulse response shown in Fig. 17.7a when excited by the pulse shown in Fig. 17.7b

This output was obtained by a graphical convolution.

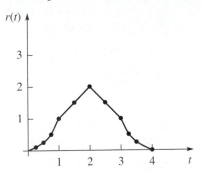

FIGURE 17.9

(a) The impulse response of a particular network and (b) the input to the network (Exercise 18.4)

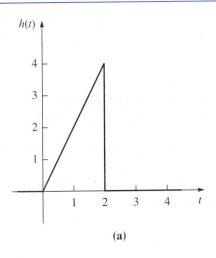

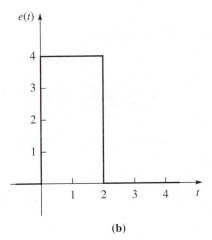

(a)

(b)

FIGURE 17.10

The output or response of the network (Exercise 17.4)

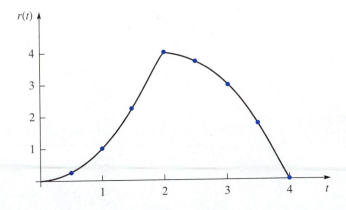

CHAPTER 17

SUMMARY

- The convolution integral relates the Laplace transforms of two time functions:

$$\mathscr{L}^{-1}[F_1(s)F_2(s)] = \int_0^t f_1(t-\tau)f_2(\tau)\,d\tau = \int_0^t f_1(\tau)f_2(t-\tau)\,d\tau$$

- The convolution integral (often referred to as the faltung integral) is useful for obtaining the inverse transform when the form of the Laplace transform is moderately complicated.

- Pulses and impulses with the same area are equivalent in first-order networks when the pulse duration is short relative to the network time constant.

- Analytic convolution in the time domain may be accomplished by using Borel's theorem:

$$r(t) = \int_0^t e(\tau)h(t-\tau)\,d\tau = \int_0^t h(\tau)e(t-\tau)\,d\tau$$

where $e(t)$ is the actual forcing function and $h(t)$ is the response of the network to the unit impulse.

- The superposition or Duhamel integrals,

$$r(t) = \int_0^t a'(t-\tau)e(\tau)\,d\tau + a(0)e(t) = \int_0^t a(t-\tau)e'(\tau)\,d\tau + a(t)e(0)$$

are also employed by using what is sometimes called the indicial admittance

$$A(s) = \frac{H(s)}{s}$$

Additional Readings

Blackwell, W.A., and L.L. Grigsby. *Introductory Network Theory*. Boston: PWS Engineering, 1985, pp. 476–480.

Bobrow, L.S. *Elementary Linear Circuit Analysis*. 2d ed. New York: Holt, Rinehart and Winston, 1987, pp. 536–543.

Dorf, R.C. *Introduction to Electric Circuits*. New York: Wiley, 1989, pp. 534, 535.

Hayt, W.H., Jr., and J.E. Kemmerly. *Engineering Circuit Analysis*. 4th ed. New York: McGraw-Hill, 1986, pp. 547, 548, 579–580.

Irwin, J.D. *Basic Engineering Circuit Analysis*. 3d ed. New York: Macmillan, 1989, pp. 753–756.

Johnson, D.E., J.L. Hilburn, and J.R. Johnson. *Basic Electric Circuit Analysis*. 4th ed. Englewood Cliffs, N.J.: Prentice-Hall, 1989, pp. 597–600.

Karni, S. *Applied Circuit Analysis*. New York: Wiley, 1988, pp. 503–518.

Madhu, S. *Linear Circuit Analysis*. Englewood Cliffs, N.J.: Prentice-Hall, 1988, pp. 708–717, 769.

Nilsson, J.W. *Electric Circuits*. 3d ed. Reading, Mass.: Addison-Wesley, 1990, pp. 625–635.

Paul, C.R. *Analysis of Linear Circuits*. New York: McGraw-Hill, 1989, pp. 575–586.

CHAPTER 17 **PROBLEMS**

Section 17.2

17.1 Use convolution to find $f(t)$ if $F(s)$ is

$$F(s) = \frac{2}{(s + 2)(s^2 + 4)}$$

17.2 Use convolution to find $f(t)$ if $F(s)$ is

$$F(s) = \frac{1}{s^2(s + 25)}$$

17.3 Use convolution to find $f(t)$ if $F(s)$ is

$$F(s) = \frac{3}{(s^2 + 2s + 10)^2}$$

17.4 Use convolution to find $f(t)$ if $F(s)$ is

$$F(s) = \frac{1}{(s^2 + 2s + 5)^2}$$

17.5 Use convolution to find $f(t)$ if $F(s)$ is

$$F(s) = \frac{18}{s^2 + 7s + 12}$$

17.6 Use convolution to find $f(t)$ if $F(s)$ is

$$F(s) = \frac{16}{s(s^2 + 4)}$$

17.7 Use convolution to find $f(t)$ if $F(s)$ is

$$F(s) = \frac{2}{(s + 2)(s + 4)}$$

17.8 Use convolution to find $f(t)$ if $F(s)$ is

$$F(s) = \frac{2}{(s + 1)(s^2 + 4)}$$

17.9 Use the convolution integral to find $t * e^{at} u(t)$.

17.10 Use the convolution integral to find $\sin t * \sin t\, u(t)$.

17.11 Use the convolution integral to find $\cos t * \cos t\, u(t)$.

17.12 Use the convolution integral to find $\sin t * \cos t\, u(t)$.

17.13 Use the convolution integral to find $e^{at} * e^{bt} u(t)$ $(a \neq b)$.

17.14 Use the convolution integral to find $(e^{-2t} - e^{-3t}) * e^{-4t} u(t)$.

17.15 Use the convolution integral to find $t * \cos t\, u(t)$.

17.16 Use the convolution integral to find $t * \sin t\, u(t)$.

Section 17.4

17.17 Use Borel's theorem to find $v(t)$ in Fig. P17.1.

 Figure P17.1

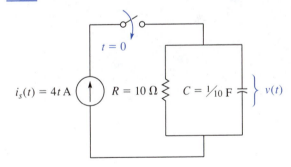

$i_s(t) = 4t$ A, $R = 10\ \Omega$, $C = \frac{1}{10}$ F, $v(t)$

17.18 Use Borel's theorem to find $v(t)$ in Fig. P17.2.

 Figure P17.2

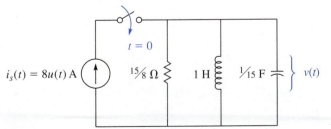

$i_s(t) = 8u(t)$ A, $\frac{15}{8}\ \Omega$, 1 H, $\frac{1}{15}$ F, $v(t)$

17.19   Use Borel's theorem to find $i(t)$ in Fig. P17.3.

   Figure P17.3

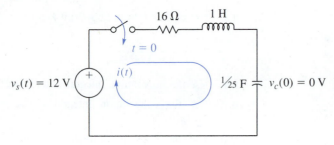

17.20   Use Borel's theorem to find $i(t)$ in Fig. P17.4.

   Figure P17.4

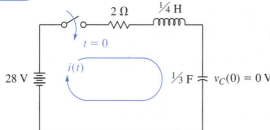

17.21   Use Borel's theorem to find $i(t)$ in Fig. P17.5.

   Figure P17.5

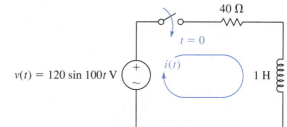

17.22   Use Borel's theorem to find $v(t)$ in Fig. P17.6.

   Figure P17.6

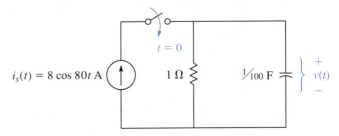

Section 17.5

17.23   Use Duhamel's integral to find $v(t)$ in Fig. P17.1.

17.24   Use Duhamel's integral to find $v(t)$ in Fig. P17.2.

17.25   Use Duhamel's integral to find $i(t)$ in Fig. P17.3.

17.26   Use Duhamel's integral to find $i(t)$ in Fig. P17.4.

17.27   Use Duhamel's integral to find $i(t)$ in Fig. P17.5.

17.28   Use Duhamel's integral to find $v(t)$ in Fig. P17.6.

Section 17.6

17.29   Figure P17.7a shows the response to the unit impulse of a particular network. Perform a graphical convolution and plot the result when the network is subjected to the excitation shown in Fig. P17.7b.

Figure P17.7

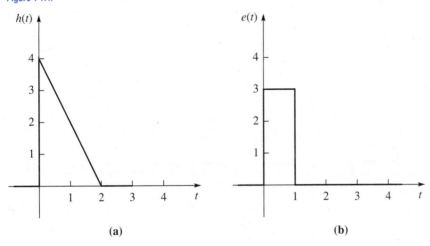

(a)   (b)

17.30   Figure P17.8a shows the response to the unit impulse of a particular network. Perform a graphical convolution and plot the result when the network is subjected to the excitation shown in Fig. P17.8b.

Figure P17.8

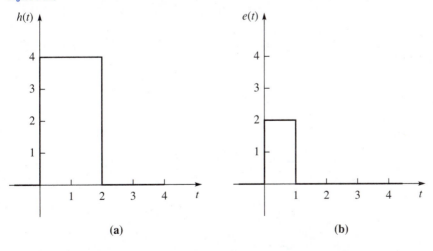

(a)   (b)

17.31 Figure P17.9a shows the response to the unit impulse of a particular network. Perform a graphical convolution and plot the result when the network is subjected to the excitation shown in Fig. P17.9b.

Figure P17.9

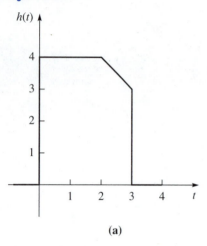

(a)

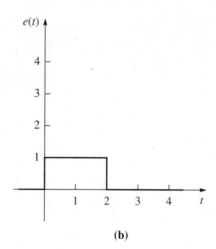

(b)

17.32 Figure P17.10a shows the response to the unit impulse of a particular network. Perform a graphical convolution and plot the result when the network is subjected to the excitation shown in Fig. P17.10b.

Figure P17.10

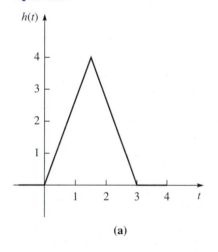

(a)

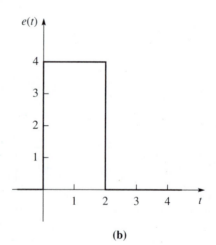

(b)

17.33 Figure P17.11a shows the response to the unit impulse of a particular network. Perform a graphical convolution and plot the result when the network is subjected to the excitation shown in Fig. P17.11b.

Figure P17.11

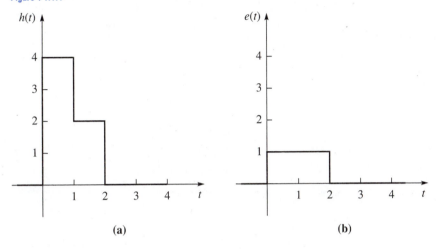

(a)   (b)

17.34 Figure P17.12a shows the response to the unit impulse of a particular network. Perform a graphical convolution and plot the result when the network is subjected to the excitation shown in Fig. P17.12b.

Figure P17.12

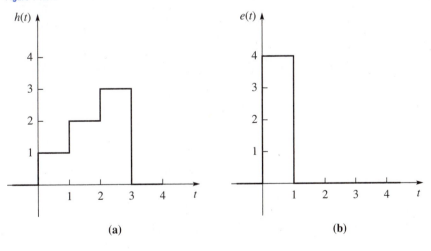

(a)   (b)

TWO-PORT NETWORKS AND TRANSFER FUNCTIONS

V

18

TWO-PORT NETWORKS

OBJECTIVES

The objectives of this chapter are to:

- Review the concept of the two-port network and define the six sets of two-port parameters.

- Indicate how each two-port parameter can be determined by calculation or measurement.

- Show how conversions between two-port parameters are made.

- Consider two-port networks with controlled sources.

- Show the two-port representation for single network elements.

- Provide algorithms for the combinations of two-port networks, and give examples of how these algorithms are employed.

INTRODUCTION   SECTION 18.1

In the one-terminal pair or one-port network shown in Fig. 18.1a, there are two variables of interest, the voltage across the terminals and the current that flows into the network. For an expeditious development of the theory of two-port networks, which will be undertaken in this chapter, these will be designated as V or I. Here, both V and I may represent constant or dc values, time-varying values such as $v(t)$ and $i(t)$, voltage or current phasors $\hat{V}$ and $\hat{I}$, or even voltages and currents in the transform domain, $V(s)$ and $I(s)$. When it is necessary to make any distinction, the general values of V and I will be adjusted accordingly.

It is often necessary to insert a device with a pair of input and a pair of output terminals into a system, and as will be seen in Chapter 19, a knowledge of the transfer function of such a network, called a two-port network, is of considerable importance. The study of two-port networks, such as the one shown in Figure 18.1b, is necessary because of the impact that the two-port network makes in the study of electrical and electronic systems. Indeed, devices such as transformers and electronic

FIGURE 18.1   (a) A one-terminal pair or one-port network and (b) a two-terminal pair or
                       two-port network

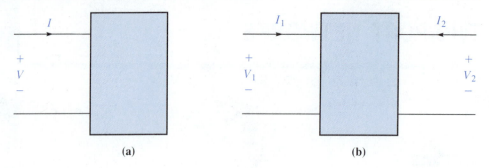

amplifiers may be modeled as two-port networks. When two-ports are used, interest is focused on the external variables of voltage and current at the individual ports, with little interest in what is happening in the interior of the network.

There are certain restrictions that pertain to the use of two-port networks. The current that enters the port must leave the port, no connections may be made to the network other than at the external ports; no energy may be stored in the network; and although dependent sources are allowed, there may be no independent voltage or current sources within the network.

SECTION 18.2   TWO-PORTS AND TWO-PORT PARAMETERS

The law of combination for the number of combinations of n items taken r at a time, shows that for the one-port, where there are two variables V and I taken two at a time ($n = 2$ and $r = 2$), there will be just one combination. This combination is the input or driving-point impedance, written here in the s domain,

$$Z(s) = \frac{V(s)}{I(s)}$$

Its reciprocal, the input or driving-point admittance, may also be used, but the admittance may be considered as providing a permutation and not another combination.

For the two-terminal pair or two-port network shown in Fig. 18.1b, there are four variables of interest, V_1, I_1, V_2, and I_2. Two of these variables may be chosen as independent, and the two not chosen as independent variables then become the dependent variables. If **D** is a 2×1 column vector of dependent variables and **W** is a 2×1 column vector of independent variables, then

D = LW   (18.1)

where **L** is a 2×2 square matrix that represents a linear transformation from **W** to **D**.

Because two variables may be selected for the vector **W**, the law of combination shows that for $n = 4$ and $r = 2$, there are six possible combinations for **L**. Thus, **L** may take six different forms, and these forms are shown, along with the selections for **W** and the enforced selections for **D**, in Table 18.1. The linear transformation matrix **L** is identified as a two-port parameter matrix, and the elements of **L** are

Two-port parameters

If **W** Is	Then **D** Is	And **L** Becomes	So That	And **L** Is Called the
$\begin{bmatrix} V_1 \\ V_2 \end{bmatrix}$	$\begin{bmatrix} I_1 \\ I_2 \end{bmatrix}$	$\mathbf{Z} = \begin{bmatrix} z_{11} & z_{12} \\ z_{21} & z_{22} \end{bmatrix}$	$\begin{bmatrix} V_1 \\ V_2 \end{bmatrix} = \mathbf{Z} \begin{bmatrix} I_1 \\ I_2 \end{bmatrix}$	Impedance parameter matrix
$\begin{bmatrix} I_1 \\ I_2 \end{bmatrix}$	$\begin{bmatrix} V_1 \\ V_2 \end{bmatrix}$	$\mathbf{Y} = \begin{bmatrix} y_{11} & y_{12} \\ y_{21} & y_{22} \end{bmatrix}$	$\begin{bmatrix} I_1 \\ I_2 \end{bmatrix} = \mathbf{Y} \begin{bmatrix} V_1 \\ V_2 \end{bmatrix}$	Admittance parameter matrix
$\begin{bmatrix} V_1 \\ I_1 \end{bmatrix}$	$\begin{bmatrix} V_2 \\ -I_2 \end{bmatrix}$	$\mathbf{T} = \begin{bmatrix} A & B \\ C & D \end{bmatrix}$	$\begin{bmatrix} V_1 \\ I_1 \end{bmatrix} = \mathbf{T} \begin{bmatrix} V_2 \\ -I_2 \end{bmatrix}$	Transmission parameter matrix
$\begin{bmatrix} V_2 \\ I_2 \end{bmatrix}$	$\begin{bmatrix} V_1 \\ -I_1 \end{bmatrix}$	$\mathbf{T}' = \begin{bmatrix} A' & B' \\ C' & D' \end{bmatrix}$	$\begin{bmatrix} V_2 \\ I_2 \end{bmatrix} = \mathbf{T}' \begin{bmatrix} V_1 \\ -I_1 \end{bmatrix}$	Inverse transmission parameter matrix
$\begin{bmatrix} V_1 \\ I_2 \end{bmatrix}$	$\begin{bmatrix} I_1 \\ V_2 \end{bmatrix}$	$\mathbf{H} = \begin{bmatrix} h_{11} & h_{12} \\ h_{21} & h_{22} \end{bmatrix}$	$\begin{bmatrix} V_1 \\ I_2 \end{bmatrix} = \mathbf{H} \begin{bmatrix} I_1 \\ V_2 \end{bmatrix}$	Hybrid parameter matrix
$\begin{bmatrix} I_1 \\ V_2 \end{bmatrix}$	$\begin{bmatrix} V_1 \\ I_2 \end{bmatrix}$	$\mathbf{G} = \begin{bmatrix} g_{11} & g_{12} \\ g_{21} & g_{22} \end{bmatrix}$	$\begin{bmatrix} I_1 \\ V_2 \end{bmatrix} = \mathbf{G} \begin{bmatrix} V_1 \\ I_2 \end{bmatrix}$	Inverse hybrid parameter matrix

called the two-port parameters. Each of the six forms of **L** is provided with a special name, as indicated in Table 18.1.

By convention, and as indicated in Fig. 18.1b, the current at port 2 enters the network. It is customary in the power industry, where the transmission and inverse transmission parameters are often employed, to consider the current I_2 as leaving the network. This explains the sign reversal in the definition of the transmission and inverse transmission parameter matrices in Table 18.1. So that the theory is kept general, the minus sign must be associated with the currents I_1 and I_2 and must not appear in the elements of the **T** and **T'** matrices. These matrices are, of course, not confined to use in the power industry, and as will be seen shortly, they have an enormous impact on the analysis and application of two-port networks.

Although it is customary to show the input to a network at the left and the output at the right, the two-port network requires no such consideration. Either port may be considered as the input, and when the input port is selected, the other becomes the output port. However, it is important to note that the voltages at both ports are positive with respect to the upper terminals, and except for the transmission and inverse transmission representations, the current flows into the network at the upper terminal of both ports.

Before the discussion proceeds to a detailed consideration of each of the two-port parameter matrices, two points concerning eq. (18.1) should be made. Consider the admittance parameter representation in Table 18.1,

$$\begin{bmatrix} I_1 \\ I_2 \end{bmatrix} = \mathbf{Y} \begin{bmatrix} V_1 \\ V_2 \end{bmatrix} = \begin{bmatrix} y_{11} & y_{12} \\ y_{21} & y_{22} \end{bmatrix} \begin{bmatrix} V_1 \\ V_2 \end{bmatrix} \tag{18.2}$$

and observe from an expanded form of this that

$$I_1 = y_{11} V_1 + y_{12} V_2 \tag{18.3a}$$

$$I_2 = y_{21} V_1 + y_{22} V_2 \tag{18.3b}$$

It is seen from eqs. (18.3) that conditions of voltage at the two pairs of terminals of the two-port device induce currents to flow into the terminals and that the values of the two currents may be obtained from a superposition of the individual effects of the two voltages.

SECTION 18.3   IMPEDANCE AND ADMITTANCE PARAMETERS

18.3.1 The Impedance Parameters

The impedance parameter matrix, which provides a linear transformation from both currents to both voltages, is the matrix $\mathbf{Z}$ in

$$\begin{bmatrix} V_1 \\ V_2 \end{bmatrix} = \mathbf{Z}\begin{bmatrix} I_1 \\ I_2 \end{bmatrix} = \begin{bmatrix} z_{11} & z_{12} \\ z_{21} & z_{22} \end{bmatrix}\begin{bmatrix} I_1 \\ I_2 \end{bmatrix} \tag{18.4}$$

This matrix equation may be expanded to show that

$$V_1 = z_{11}I_1 + z_{12}I_2 \tag{18.5a}$$

$$V_2 = z_{21}I_1 + z_{22}I_2 \tag{18.5b}$$

and the elements of $\mathbf{Z}$ may be obtained from measurement or from calculations via

$$z_{11} = \left.\frac{V_1}{I_1}\right|_{I_2 = 0} \tag{18.6a}$$

$$z_{12} = \left.\frac{V_1}{I_2}\right|_{I_1 = 0} \tag{18.6b}$$

$$z_{21} = \left.\frac{V_2}{I_1}\right|_{I_2 = 0} \tag{18.6c}$$

$$z_{22} = \left.\frac{V_2}{I_2}\right|_{I_1 = 0} \tag{18.6d}$$

All of the z parameters have the dimensions of ohms (Ω). Because all of the z parameters can be obtained from measurements or calculations involving a zero-current value, they are frequently referred to as the *open-circuit impedance* parameters.

■ EXAMPLE 18.1

Determine the impedance parameters for the s domain network in Fig. 18.2a.

Solution   The impedance parameters z_{11} and z_{22} are obtained immediately by noting that although they are not necessarily driving-point impedances under the open-circuit conditions proposed here, they are the driving-point impedances looking into Fig. 18.2b from left and right respectively. Thus,

$$z_{11} = \left.\frac{V_1(s)}{I_1(s)}\right|_{I_2(s) = 0} = 4 + \frac{1}{s} = \frac{4s + 1}{s} \text{ ohms}$$

$$z_{22} = \left.\frac{V_2(s)}{I_2(s)}\right|_{I_1(s) = 0} = 2s + \frac{1}{s} = \frac{2s^2 + 1}{s} \text{ ohms}$$

(a) A tee network in the s domain and (b) the same network showing the two-port
voltages and currents in the s domain

FIGURE 18.2

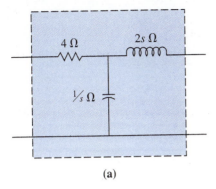

(a)

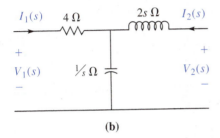

(b)

In Fig. 18.2b, if $I_2(s)$ is applied and $I_1(s) = 0$, then $V_1(s)$ appears as the open circuit voltage and is the voltage across the capacitor:

$$V_1(s) = \frac{1}{s} I_2(s) \quad \text{and} \quad z_{12} = \left.\frac{V_1(s)}{I_2(s)}\right|_{I_1(s)=0} = \frac{1}{s} \text{ ohms}$$

In similar fashion, with $I_1(s)$ applied and $I_2(s) = 0$, $V_2(s)$ also appears across the capacitor:

$$V_2(s) = \frac{1}{s} I_1(s) \quad \text{and} \quad z_{21} = \left.\frac{V_2(s)}{I_1(s)}\right|_{I_2(s)=0} = \frac{1}{s} \text{ ohms}$$

Thus,

$$\mathbf{Z} = \begin{bmatrix} \dfrac{4s + 1}{s} & \dfrac{1}{s} \\ \dfrac{1}{s} & \dfrac{2s^2 + 1}{s} \end{bmatrix}$$

and it is noted (for future reference) that

$$z_{12} = z_{21} = \frac{1}{s} \text{ ohms}$$

FIGURE 18.3   Tee network (Exercise 18.1)

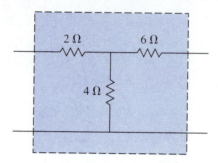

EXERCISE 18.1

Determine the impedance parameters for the tee network shown in Fig. 18.3.

Answer

$$\mathbf{Z} = \begin{bmatrix} 6 & 4 \\ 4 & 10 \end{bmatrix}$$

18.3.2 The Admittance Parameters

The admittance parameter matrix, which provides a linear transformation between voltages and currents, is the matrix $\mathbf{Y}$ in

$$\begin{bmatrix} I_1 \\ I_2 \end{bmatrix} = \mathbf{Y} \begin{bmatrix} V_1 \\ V_2 \end{bmatrix} = \begin{bmatrix} y_{11} & y_{12} \\ y_{21} & y_{22} \end{bmatrix} \begin{bmatrix} V_1 \\ V_2 \end{bmatrix} \tag{18.7}$$

This may be written as

$$I_1 = y_{11}V_1 + y_{12}V_2 \tag{18.8a}$$

$$I_2 = y_{21}V_1 + y_{22}V_2 \tag{18.8b}$$

The elements of $\mathbf{Y}$ may be obtained by measurements or by calculation from

$$y_{11} = \left. \frac{I_1}{V_1} \right|_{V_2=0} \tag{18.9a}$$

$$y_{12} = \left. \frac{I_1}{V_2} \right|_{V_1=0} \tag{18.9b}$$

$$y_{21} = \left. \frac{I_2}{V_1} \right|_{V_2=0} \tag{18.9c}$$

$$y_{22} = \left. \frac{I_2}{V_2} \right|_{V_1=0} \tag{18.9d}$$

Because the admittance parameters are calculated under zero-voltage conditions, they are often referred to as *short-circuit admittance* parameters; and as admittances should, they all bear the units mhos ($\mho$).

■ EXAMPLE 18.2

Determine the admittance parameters for the two-port network of Example 18.1 (Fig. 18.2a, repeated here as Fig. 18.4a).

Solution The elements of the two-port are provided in the s domain. Figure 18.4b shows the voltages and currents in the s domain, and this figure may be used to compute y_{11} and y_{21} because for these, $V_2(s) = 0$. The input or driving-point admittance will relate $I_1(s)$ and $V_1(s)$ in accordance with eq. (18.9a) and will be y_{11}. First,

$$I_1(s) = \frac{\frac{1}{4}(s + 1/2s)}{\frac{1}{4} + s + 1/2s} V_1(s) = \frac{2s^2 + 1}{8s^2 + 2s + 4} V_1(s)$$

(a) A two-port in the form of a tee network in the s domain, (b) the two-port with the right-hand terminals shorted so that $V_2(s) = 0$, and (c) the two-port with the left-hand terminals shorted so that $V_1(s) = 0$

FIGURE 18.4

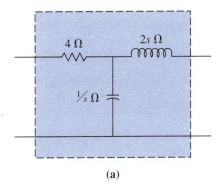

(a)

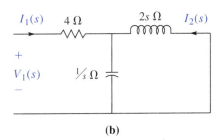

(b)

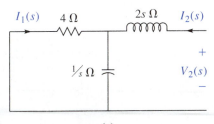

(c)

and then,

$$y_{11} = \frac{I_1(s)}{V_1(s)}\Bigg|_{V_2=0} = \frac{2s^2 + 1}{8s^2 + 2s + 4} \text{ mhos}$$

For y_{21}, obtain $I_2(s)$ by a current division, using Fig. 18.4b,

$$I_1(s) = y_{11}V_1(s)$$

and with careful attention to the direction of $I_2(s)$,

$$I_2(s) = \left(\frac{-1/s}{1/s + 2s}\right)y_{11}V_1(s) = -\left(\frac{1/s}{1/s + 2s}\right)\left(\frac{2s^2 + 1}{8s^2 + 2s + 4}\right)V_1(s)$$

$$= -\frac{1}{2s^2 + 1} \cdot \frac{2s^2 + 1}{8s^2 + 2s + 4} V_1(s)$$

Thus,

$$y_{21} = \frac{I_2(s)}{V_1(s)}\Bigg|_{V_2(s)=0} = -\frac{1}{8s^2 + 2s + 4} \text{ mhos}$$

Figure 18.4c can be used to find y_{12} and y_{22} in exactly the same manner. Here, with $V_2(s) = 0$, y_{22} will be the input or driving-point admittance at port 2 and the reader may verify that

$$y_{22} = \frac{I_2(s)}{V_2(s)}\Bigg|_{V_1(s)=0} = \frac{4s + 1}{8s^2 + 2s + 4} \text{ mhos}$$

and

$$y_{12} = \frac{I_1(s)}{V_2(s)}\Bigg|_{V_1(s)=0} = -\frac{1}{8s^2 + 2s + 4z} \text{ mhos}$$

Thus,

$$Y = \begin{bmatrix} \dfrac{2s^2 + 1}{8s^2 + 2s + 4} & -\dfrac{1}{8s^2 + 2s + 4} \\[3mm] -\dfrac{1}{8s^2 + 2s + 4} & \dfrac{4s + 1}{8s^2 + 2s + 4} \end{bmatrix}$$

and it may be noted (for future reference) that $y_{12} = y_{21}$.   ■

EXERCISE 18.2

Determine the admittance parameters for the tee network shown in Fig. 18.5.

Answer

$$Y = \begin{bmatrix} \frac{5}{22} & -\frac{1}{11} \\[2mm] -\frac{1}{11} & \frac{3}{22} \end{bmatrix}$$

FIGURE 18.5

Tee network (Exercise 18.2)

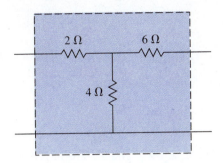

18.3.3 A Useful Relationship between Z and Y

The impedance parameter matrix is the inverse of the admittance parameter matrix. Take eq. (18.7),

$$\begin{bmatrix} I_1 \\ I_2 \end{bmatrix} = \mathbf{Y} \begin{bmatrix} V_1 \\ V_2 \end{bmatrix}$$

and put it into eq. (18.4):

$$\begin{bmatrix} V_1 \\ V_2 \end{bmatrix} = \mathbf{Z} \begin{bmatrix} I_1 \\ I_2 \end{bmatrix} = \mathbf{ZY} \begin{bmatrix} V_1 \\ V_2 \end{bmatrix}$$

The only way that this identity can occur is if $\mathbf{ZY} = \mathbf{YZ} = \mathbf{I}$, or $\mathbf{Z} = \mathbf{Y}^{-1}$, or $\mathbf{Y} = \mathbf{Z}^{-1}$. Of course, neither $\mathbf{Z}$ nor $\mathbf{Y}$ can be singular.[1] The reader may wish to verify that for the two-port in Figs. 18.2a and 18.4a,

$$\mathbf{Z} = \begin{bmatrix} \dfrac{4s + 1}{s} & \dfrac{1}{s} \\ \dfrac{1}{s} & \dfrac{2s^2 + 1}{s} \end{bmatrix}$$

which was evaluated in Section 18.3.1, yields $\mathbf{Y}$ as determined in Section 18.3.2:

$$\mathbf{Y} = \begin{bmatrix} \dfrac{2s^2 + 1}{8s^2 + 2s + 4} & -\dfrac{1}{8s^2 + 2s + 4} \\ -\dfrac{1}{8s^2 + 2s + 4} & \dfrac{4s + 1}{8s^2 + 2s + 4} \end{bmatrix}$$

18.3.4 Writing Z Directly from a Tee Network

If a two-port can be reduced to a tee network (or is already in the form of a tee network), the z parameters may be written directly from a consideration of the elements of the tee network. Figure 18.6 shows a general two-port in the form of a tee

[1] A singular matrix is a matrix that does not possess an inverse.

FIGURE 18.6   A tee network of impedances displayed as a two-port

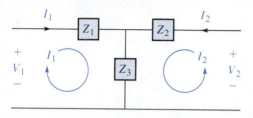

network, with two mesh currents indicated. Here, Z_1, Z_2, and Z_3 are impedances, and their order corresponds to the order of the resistances displayed in Fig. 2.27 (Section 2.11).

A mesh analysis will yield two equations in the unknown mesh currents I_1 and I_2:

$$V_1 = (Z_1 + Z_3)I_1 + Z_3 I_2 \tag{18.10a}$$
$$V_2 = Z_3 I_1 + (Z_2 + Z_3)I_2 \tag{18.10b}$$

When these are compared with eqs. (18.5),

$$V_1 = z_{11}I_1 + z_{12}I_2 \tag{18.5a}$$
$$V_2 = z_{21}I_1 + z_{22}I_2 \tag{18.5b}$$

it is observed that if both are to be true representations, the equivalences

$$z_{11} = Z_1 + Z_3 \tag{18.11a}$$
$$z_{12} = z_{21} = Z_3 \tag{18.11b}$$
$$z_{22} = Z_2 + Z_3 \tag{18.11c}$$

and

$$Z_1 = z_{11} - z_{12} = z_{11} - z_{21} \tag{18.12a}$$
$$Z_2 = z_{22} - z_{12} = z_{22} - z_{21} \tag{18.12b}$$
$$Z_3 = z_{12} = z_{21} \tag{18.12c}$$

must exist. The example that follows shows how easy it is to develop the z parameters from an inspection of the tee network.

■   EXAMPLE 18.3
Determine the impedance parameters for the network shown in Fig. 18.2a.

Solution   Here,

$$Z_1 = 4\,\Omega \qquad Z_2 = 2s \text{ ohms} \qquad Z_3 = \frac{1}{s} \text{ ohms}$$

FIGURE 18.7

Tee network for the z parameter matrix (Exercise 18.3)

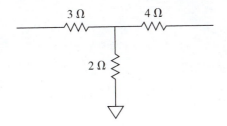

Then by eqs. (18.11),

$$z_{11} = Z_1 + Z_3 = 4 + \frac{1}{s} = \frac{4s + 1}{s} \text{ ohms}$$

$$z_{12} = z_{21} = Z_3 = \frac{1}{s} \text{ ohms}$$

$$z_{22} = Z_2 + Z_3 = 2s + \frac{1}{s} = \frac{2s^2 + 1}{s} \text{ ohms}$$

This makes

$$\mathbf{Z} = \begin{bmatrix} \dfrac{4s + 1}{s} & \dfrac{1}{s} \\ \dfrac{1}{s} & \dfrac{2s^2 + 1}{s} \end{bmatrix}$$

which was obtained in Section 18.3.1.   ■

EXERCISE 18.3

For the z parameter matrix

$$\mathbf{Z} = \begin{bmatrix} 5 & 2 \\ 2 & 6 \end{bmatrix}$$

draw an equivalent tee network.

Answer   See Fig. 18.7.

18.3.5 Writing Y Directly from a Pi Network

In this section, the procedure of Section 18.3.4 will be followed with respect to the pi network shown with admittances Y_{12}, Y_{23}, and Y_{31} and two nodes in Fig. 18.8. Here, the order of the Y's corresponds to the order of the R's (or G's) in Fig. 2.27.

FIGURE 18.8   A pi network of admittances shown as a two-port

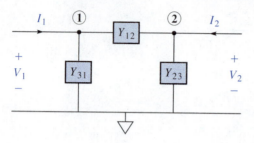

A pair of node equations is easily formed. For the nodes in Fig. 18.8,

$$I_1 = (Y_{12} + Y_{31})V_1 - Y_{12}V_2 \qquad \textbf{(18.13a)}$$

$$I_2 = -Y_{12}V_1 + (Y_{12} + Y_{23})V_2 \qquad \textbf{(18.13b)}$$

and these can be compared, term by term, with the y parameter representation of eqs. (18.8):

$$I_1 = y_{11}V_1 + y_{12}V_2 \qquad \textbf{(18.8a)}$$

$$I_2 = y_{21}V_1 + y_{22}V_2 \qquad \textbf{(18.8b)}$$

The equivalence can only occur if

$$y_{11} = Y_{12} + Y_{31} \qquad \textbf{(18.14a)}$$

$$y_{12} = y_{21} = -Y_{12} \qquad \textbf{(18.14b)}$$

$$y_{22} = Y_{12} + Y_{23} \qquad \textbf{(18.14c)}$$

or

$$Y_{12} = -y_{12} = -y_{21} \qquad \textbf{(18.15a)}$$

$$Y_{23} = y_{22} + y_{12} = y_{22} + y_{21} \qquad \textbf{(18.15b)}$$

$$Y_{31} = y_{11} + y_{12} = y_{11} + y_{21} \qquad \textbf{(18.15c)}$$

■   **EXAMPLE 18.4**

For the network shown in Fig. 18.4a, find the y parameters.

Solution   So that eqs. (18.14) can be used, a pi network is required. Use of the summary contained in Fig. 2.27 with the more general Y's and Z's in place of the G's and R's yields

$$Y_1 = \frac{1}{4} \qquad Y_2 = \frac{1}{2s} \qquad Y_3 = s$$

$$\sum Y = Y_1 + Y_2 + Y_3 = \frac{1}{4} + \frac{1}{2s} + s = \frac{8s^2 + 2s + 4}{8s}$$

Then,

$$Y_{12} = \frac{Y_1 Y_2}{\Sigma\, Y} = \frac{1}{4}\left(\frac{1}{2s}\right)\left(\frac{8s}{8s^2 + 2s + 4}\right) == \frac{1}{8s^2 + 2s + 4}$$

$$Y_{23} = \frac{Y_2 Y_3}{\Sigma\, Y} = \left(\frac{1}{2s}\right)(s)\left(\frac{8s}{8s^2 + 2s + 4}\right) = \frac{4s}{8s^2 + 2s + 4}$$

$$Y_{31} = \frac{Y_1 Y_3}{\Sigma\, Y} = \left(\frac{1}{4}\right)(s)\left(\frac{8s}{8s^2 + 2s + 4}\right) = \frac{2s^2}{8s^2 + 2s + 4}$$

From eqs. (18.14),

$$y_{11} = Y_{12} + Y_{31} = \frac{2s^2 + 1}{8s^2 + 2s + 4}$$

$$y_{12} = y_{21} = -Y_{12} = -\frac{1}{8s^2 + 2s + 4}$$

$$y_{22} = Y_{12} + Y_{23} = \frac{4s + 1}{8s^2 + 2s + 4}$$

The result is

$$\mathbf{Y} = \begin{bmatrix} \dfrac{2s^2 + 12}{8s^2 + 2s + 4} & -\dfrac{1}{8s^2 + 2s + 4} \\[2mm] -\dfrac{1}{8s^2 + 2s + 4} & \dfrac{4s + 1}{8s^2 + 2s + 4} \end{bmatrix}$$

EXERCISE 18.4

Determine the admittance parameters for the pi network shown in Fig. 18.9.

Answer

$$\mathbf{Y} = \begin{bmatrix} \frac{1}{6} + j\frac{1}{8} & -\frac{1}{6} \\[2mm] -\frac{1}{6} & \frac{1}{6} - j\frac{1}{6} \end{bmatrix}$$

Pi network (Exercise 18.4)

FIGURE 18.9

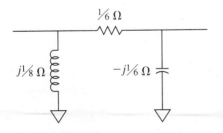

$\frac{1}{6}\,\Omega$

$j\frac{1}{8}\,\Omega$ $-j\frac{1}{6}\,\Omega$

TABLE 18.2	An efficient method for tee-pi or pi-tee transformations

From Tee to Pi	*From Pi to Tee*
Use eqs. (18.11) to form $\mathbf{Z}$ from Z_1, Z_2, and Z_3	Use eqs. (18.14) to form $\mathbf{Y}$ from Y_{12}, Y_{23}, and Y_{31}
Obtain $\mathbf{Y} = \mathbf{Z}^{-1}$	Obtain $\mathbf{Z} = \mathbf{Y}^{-1}$
Use eqs. (18.15) to determine Y_{12}, Y_{23}, and Y_{31} from $\mathbf{Y}$	Use eqs. (18.12) to determine Z_1, Z_2, and Z_3 from $\mathbf{Z}$
Take reciprocals to find Z_{12}, Z_{23}, and Z_{31} if necessary	Take reciprocals to find Y_1, Y_2, and Y_3 if necessary

18.3.6 An Efficient Method for Tee-Pi (Pi-Tee) Transformations

Because it is so easy to compute the inverse of a 2×2 matrix by swapping the elements on the principal diagonal, changing the sign of the off-diagonal elements, and then dividing all elements by the determinant of the matrix, an efficient method for the tee-pi (or pi-tee) transformation that exploits this may be proposed. The method is summarized in Table 18.2.

SECTION 18.4   THE TRANSMISSION AND INVERSE TRANSMISSION PARAMETERS

18.4.1 The Transmission Parameters

The transmission parameter matrix provides a linear transformation between conditions of voltage and current at port 2 to conditions of voltage and current at port 1.[2] Thus, with reference to Fig. 18.1b and in accordance with Table 18.1 with I_2 leaving the two-port,

$$\begin{bmatrix} V_1 \\ I_1 \end{bmatrix} = \mathbf{T} \begin{bmatrix} V_2 \\ -I_2 \end{bmatrix} = \begin{bmatrix} A & B \\ C & D \end{bmatrix} \begin{bmatrix} V_2 \\ -I_2 \end{bmatrix} \tag{18.16}$$

In expanded form, the foregoing transformation may be written as

$$V_1 = AV_2 - BI_2 \tag{18.17a}$$

$$I_1 = CV_2 - DI_2 \tag{18.17b}$$

The individual transmission parameters may be obtained from measurements o calculation via

$$A = \frac{V_1}{V_2}\bigg|_{I_2 = 0} \tag{18.18a}$$

$$B = -\frac{V_1}{I_2}\bigg|_{V_2 = 0} \quad \text{ohms} \tag{18.18b}$$

---

[2] The transmission parameters and inverse transmission parameters tend to relate *outputs* to *inputs* and, strictly speaking, represent a *transfer function*. Transfer functions will be considered in detail in Chapter 19.

$$C = \frac{I_1}{V_2}\bigg|_{I_2=0} \text{ mhos} \qquad \text{(18.18c)}$$

$$D = -\frac{I_1}{I_2}\bigg|_{V_2=0} \qquad \text{(18.18d)}$$

Observe that B and C bear the units of ohms and mhos, respectively, and that A and D are dimensionless and they are called voltage and current transfer ratios respectively.

■ **EXAMPLE 18.5**

For the two-port in Fig. 18.2a, repeated here as Fig. 18.10a, determine the transmission parameters.

Solution   The parameters A and C are determined with $I_2(s) = 0$, and Fig. 18.10b shows the two-port with port 2 open-circuited. This two-port may

(a) A two-port in the form of a tee network in the s domain, (b) the two-port with the right-hand terminals opened so that $I_2(s) = 0$, and (c) the two-port with the right-hand terminals shorted so that $V_2(s) = 0$

FIGURE 18.10

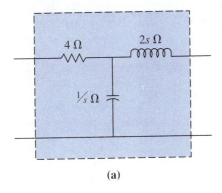

(a)

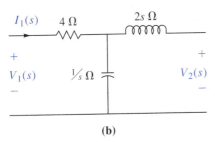

(b)

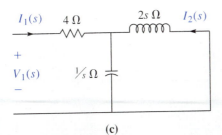

(c)

be assumed to be driven by $V_1(s)$, and it is noted that $V_2(s)$ appears across the capacitor. Thus, by a voltage division,

$$\left.\frac{V_2(s)}{V_1(s)}\right|_{I_2(s)=0} = \frac{1/s}{4 + 1/s} = \frac{1}{4s + 1}$$

or

$$A = \left.\frac{V_1(s)}{V_2(s)}\right|_{I_2(s)=0} = 4s + 1$$

and because $V_2(s) = (1/s)I_1(s)$,

$$\left.\frac{V_2(s)}{I_1(s)}\right|_{I_2(s)=0} = \left.\frac{(1/s)I_1(s)}{I_1(s)}\right|_{I_2(s)=0} = \frac{1}{s}$$

or

$$C = \left.\frac{I_1(s)}{V_2(s)}\right|_{I_2(s)=0} = s \text{ mhos}$$

The parameters B and D are obtained from considerations involving a short circuit at port 2, and this ramification is indicated in Fig. 18.10c. Observe that the direction of $I_2(s)$ is consistent with the model that defines the two-port parameters. With $V_1(s)$ acting as the source, current division provides

$$I_2(s) = -\frac{1/s}{2s + 1/s} I_1(s) = -\frac{1}{2s^2 + 1} I_1(s)$$

so that

$$D = -\left.\frac{I_1(s)}{I_2(s)}\right|_{V_2(s)=0} = 2s^2 + 1$$

Then by Ohm's law

$$\begin{aligned}V_1(s) &= 4I_1(s) - 2sI_2(s) \\ &= -4(2s^2 + 1)I_2(s) - 2sI_2(s) \\ &= -(8s^2 + 2s + 4)I_2(s)\end{aligned}$$

Hence,

$$B = -\left.\frac{V_1(s)}{I_2(s)}\right|_{V_2(s)=0} = 8s^2 + 2s + 4 \text{ ohms}$$

The result is

$$\mathbf{T} = \begin{bmatrix} 4s + 1 & 8s^2 + 2s + 4 \\ s & 2s^2 + 1 \end{bmatrix}$$

Tee network (Exercise 18.5)

FIGURE 18.11

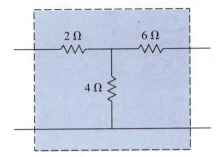

EXERCISE 18.5

Determine the transmission parameters for the tee network shown in Fig. 18.11.

Answer

$$\mathbf{T} = \begin{bmatrix} \frac{3}{2} & 11 \\ \frac{1}{4} & \frac{5}{2} \end{bmatrix}$$

18.4.2 The Inverse Transmission Parameters

The inverse transmission parameter matrix[3] $\mathbf{T}'$ provides a linear transformation between voltage and current at port 1 to voltage and current at port 2. It is based on the current leaving port 2, and Table 18.1 shows that it is defined by

$$\begin{bmatrix} V_2 \\ I_2 \end{bmatrix} = \mathbf{T}' \begin{bmatrix} V_1 \\ -I_1 \end{bmatrix} = \begin{bmatrix} A' & B' \\ C' & D' \end{bmatrix} \begin{bmatrix} V_1 \\ -I_1 \end{bmatrix} \tag{18.19}$$

In expanded form,

$$V_2 = A'V_1 - B'I_1 \tag{18.20a}$$

$$I_2 = C'V_1 - D'I_1 \tag{18.20b}$$

The inverse transmission parameters may also be determined by measurement or by calculation:

$$A' = \frac{V_2}{V_1}\bigg|_{I_1 = 0} \tag{18.21a}$$

$$B' = -\frac{V_2}{I_1}\bigg|_{V_1 = 0} \text{ ohms} \tag{18.21b}$$

$$C' = \frac{I_2}{V_1}\bigg|_{I_1 = 0} \text{ mhos} \tag{18.21c}$$

$$D' = -\frac{I_2}{I_1}\bigg|_{V_1 = 0} \tag{18.21d}$$

---

[3] Contrary to the implication in the name, the inverse transmission parameter matrix is *not* the inverse of the transmission parameter matrix.

Notice that B' and C' bear the units of ohms and mhos, respectively, and that A' and C' are dimensionless. Again, it is important to note that **T'** is not the inverse of **T**.

■ **EXAMPLE 18.6**

For the two-port network shown in Fig. 18.2a, repeated here as Fig. 18.12a, determine the inverse transmission parameters.

Solution   Figure 18.12b may be used to find A' and C', which are based on $I_1(s) = 0$ (an open circuit at port 1). By voltage division,

$$A' = \frac{V_2(s)}{V_1(s)}\bigg|_{I_1(s)=0} = \frac{2s + 1/s}{1/s} = 2s^2 + 1$$

FIGURE 18.12   (a) A two-port in the form of a tee network in the s domain, (b) the two-port with the left-hand terminals opened so that $I_1(s) = 0$, and (c) the two-port with the left-hand terminals shorted so that $V_1(s) = 0$

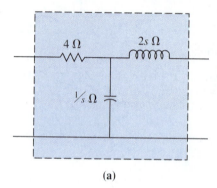

(a)

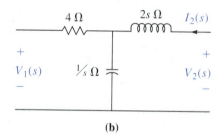

(b)

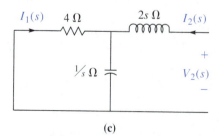

(c)

and because $V_1(s) = (1/s)I_2(s)$,

$$C' = \frac{I_2(s)}{V_1(s)}\bigg|_{I_1(s)=0} = \frac{I_2(s)}{(1/s)I_2(s)} = s$$

The parameters B' and D' may be obtained from Fig. 18.12c with port 1 shorted as required by the condition $V_1(s) = 0$ and where the *standard* direction of $I_1(s)$ is indicated. By a current division

$$I_1(s) = -\frac{1/s}{4 + 1/s} I_2(s) = -\frac{1}{4s + 1} I_2(s)$$

so that

$$D = -\frac{I_2(s)}{I_1(s)}\bigg|_{V_1(s)=0} = 4s + 1$$

Then by Ohm's law

$$\begin{aligned} V_2(s) &= -4I_1(s) + 2sI_2(s) \\ &= -4I_1(s) - 2s(4s + 1)I_1(s) \\ &= -(8s^2 + 2s + 4)I_1(s) \end{aligned}$$

and

$$B' = -\frac{V_2(s)}{I_1(s)}\bigg|_{V_1(s)=0} = 8s^2 + 2s + 4$$

This makes

$$\mathbf{T'} = \begin{bmatrix} 2s^2 + 1 & 8s^2 + 2s + 4 \\ s & 4s + 1 \end{bmatrix}$$

which is not the inverse of $\mathbf{T}$,

$$\mathbf{T} = \begin{bmatrix} 4s + 1 & 8s^2 + 2s + 4 \\ s & 2s^2 + 1 \end{bmatrix}$$

determined in Example 18.5. However, it can be noted (for future reference) that the determinants of both the $\mathbf{T}$ and $\mathbf{T'}$ matrices are equal to unity:

$$(4s + 1)(2s^2 + 1) - s(8s^2 + 2s + 4) = 1$$

But as a consequence of the sign reversal of the independent-variable currents, the off-diagonal elements in $\mathbf{T}$ are not the negative of those in $\mathbf{T'}$. ■

EXERCISE 18.6

Determine the inverse transmission parameters for the tee network shown in Fig. 18.13.

FIGURE 18.13   Tee network (Exercise 18.6)

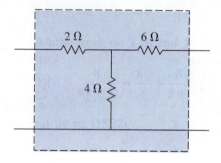

Answer

$$T' = \begin{bmatrix} \frac{5}{2} & 11 \\ \frac{1}{4} & \frac{3}{2} \end{bmatrix}$$

SECTION 18.5   **THE HYBRID AND INVERSE HYBRID PARAMETERS**

18.5.1 The Hybrid Parameters

The hybrid parameters, which are very useful in the analysis of electronic circuits containing transistors, are a mixed set, because they provide a linear transformation between I_1 and V_2 as independent variables and V_1 and I_2 (in this *cross order*) as dependent variables,

$$\begin{bmatrix} V_1 \\ I_2 \end{bmatrix} = \mathbf{H} \begin{bmatrix} I_1 \\ V_2 \end{bmatrix} = \begin{bmatrix} h_{11} & h_{12} \\ h_{21} & h_{22} \end{bmatrix} \begin{bmatrix} I_1 \\ V_2 \end{bmatrix} \tag{18.22}$$

or

$$V_1 = h_{11}I_1 + h_{12}V_2 \tag{18.23a}$$

$$I_2 = h_{21}I_1 + h_{22}V_2 \tag{18.23b}$$

As in the other cases, the values for the individual h parameters can be obtained from measurements or from calculations under short- and open-circuit conditions:

$$h_{11} = \frac{V_1}{I_1}\bigg|_{V_2=0} \quad \text{ohms} \tag{18.24a}$$

$$h_{12} = \frac{V_1}{V_2}\bigg|_{I_1=0} \tag{18.24b}$$

$$h_{21} = \frac{I_2}{I_1}\bigg|_{V_2=0} \tag{18.24c}$$

$$h_{22} = \frac{I_2}{V_2}\bigg|_{I_1=0} \quad \text{mhos} \tag{18.24d}$$

In the foregoing, it is observed that h_{11} has the dimensions of ohms and h_{22} has the dimensions of mhos. The parameters h_{12} and h_{21} are dimensionless.

(a) A two-port in the form of a tee in the s domain, (b) the two-port with the right-hand terminals shorted to make $V_2(s) = 0$, and (c) the two-port with the left-hand terminals open-circuited to make $I_1(s) = 0$

FIGURE 18.14

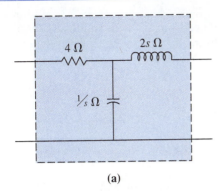

(a)

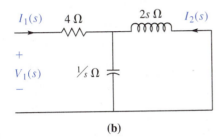

(b)

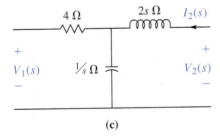

(c)

■ **EXAMPLE 18.7**

Determine the h parameters for the network in Fig. 18.2a, shown here as Fig. 18.14a.

Solution Figure 18.14b contains a short circuit at port 2, and it may be used to determine h_{11} and h_{21}. The input impedance of the network is equal to h_{11}:

$$h_{11} = \frac{V_1(s)}{I_1(s)}\bigg|_{V_2(s)=0} = 4 + \frac{2s(1/s)}{2s + 1/s} = 4 + \frac{2s}{2s^2 + 1} = \frac{8s^2 + 2s + 4}{2s^2 + 1}$$

The value of $I_2(s)$ can be obtained from a current division:

$$I_2(s) = -\frac{1/s}{2s + 1/s} I_1(s) = -\frac{1}{2s^2 + 1} I_1(s)$$

so that

$$h_{21} = \frac{I_2(s)}{I_1(s)}\bigg|_{V_2(s)=0} = -\frac{1}{2s^2 + 1}$$

The other two parameters are determined from an open-circuit condition at port 1 so that $I_1(s) = 0$. This is shown in Fig. 18.14c. Here, by a voltage division,

$$V_1(s) = \frac{1/s}{2s + 1/s} V_2(s) = \frac{1}{2s^2 + 1} V_2(s)$$

$$h_{12} = \frac{V_1(s)}{V_2(s)}\bigg|_{I_1(s)=0} = \frac{1}{2s^2 + 1}$$

The value of h_{22} is the value of the input admittance at port 2 in Fig. 18.14c:

$$h_{22} = \frac{I_2(s)}{V_2(s)}\bigg|_{I_1(s)=0} = \frac{s}{2s^2 + 1}$$

The complete representation is

$$\mathbf{H} = \begin{bmatrix} \dfrac{8s^2 + 2s + 4}{2s^2 + 1} & \dfrac{1}{2s^2 + 1} \\[2ex] -\dfrac{1}{2s^2 + 1} & \dfrac{s}{2s^2 + 1} \end{bmatrix}$$

and it is noted (for future reference) that $h_{12} = -h_{21}$.   ∎

EXERCISE 18.7

Determine the hybrid parameters for the tee network shown in Fig. 18.15.

Answer

$$\mathbf{H} = \begin{bmatrix} \frac{22}{5} & \frac{2}{5} \\[1ex] -\frac{2}{5} & \frac{1}{10} \end{bmatrix}$$

FIGURE 18.15   Tee network (Exercise 18.7)

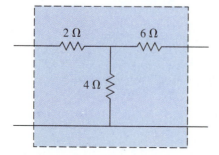

18.5.2 The Inverse Hybrid Parameters

The inverse hybrid or g parameters are also a mixed set, and the linear transformation is between the independent variables V_1 and I_2 and the dependent variables I_1 and V_2. Here, too, the *crossing* may be observed. Table 18.1 shows that

$$\begin{bmatrix} I_1 \\ V_2 \end{bmatrix} = G\begin{bmatrix} V_1 \\ I_2 \end{bmatrix} = \begin{bmatrix} g_{11} & g_{12} \\ g_{21} & g_{22} \end{bmatrix}\begin{bmatrix} V_1 \\ I_2 \end{bmatrix} \qquad (18.25)$$

and it is seen that

$$I_1 = g_{11}V_1 + g_{12}I_2 \qquad (18.26a)$$

$$V_2 = g_{21}V_1 + g_{22}I_2 \qquad (18.26b)$$

Here, the values of the g parameters can be obtained from

$$g_{11} = \left.\frac{I_1}{V_1}\right|_{I_2=0} \text{mhos} \qquad (18.27a)$$

$$g_{12} = \left.\frac{I_1}{I_2}\right|_{V_1=0} \qquad (18.27b)$$

$$g_{21} = \left.\frac{V_2}{V_1}\right|_{I_2=0} \qquad (18.27c)$$

$$g_{22} = \left.\frac{V_2}{I_2}\right|_{V_1=0} \text{ohms} \qquad (18.27d)$$

Note that g_{11} is an admittance (mhos) and g_{22} is an impedance (ohms). The parameters g_{12} and g_{21} have no units and represent transfer ratios.

■ EXAMPLE 18.8

Obtain the g parameters for the network shown in Fig. 18.2a, repeated here as Fig. 18.16a.

Solution If Fig. 18.16a is redrawn with an open circuit at port 2 so that $I_2(s) = 0$, as in Fig. 18.16b, then g_{11} and g_{21} are easily determined. The input admittance is g_{11}:

$$g_{11} = \left.\frac{I_1(s)}{V_1(s)}\right|_{I_2(s)=0} = \frac{\frac{1}{4}s}{\frac{1}{4} + s} = \frac{s}{4s + 1}$$

and by voltage division,

$$g_{21} = \left.\frac{V_2(s)}{V_1(s)}\right|_{I_2(s)=0} = \frac{1/s}{4 + 1/s} = \frac{1}{4s + 1}$$

The parameters g_{12} and g_{22} are determined from the condition of a short-circuited port 1, as indicated in Fig. 18.16c. A current division for $I_1(s)$ in terms of $I_2(s)$ gives

$$I_1(s) = \frac{-1/s}{4 + 1/s}I_2(s) = -\frac{1}{4s + 1}I_2(s)$$

FIGURE 18.16

(a) A two-port in the form of a tee in the s domain, (b) the two-port with the right-hand terminals open-circuited so that $I_2(s) = 0$, and (c) the two-port with the left-hand terminals short-circuited so that $V_1(s) = 0$

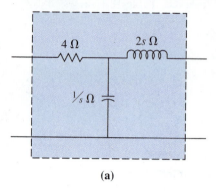

(a)

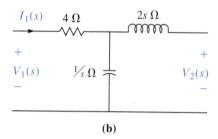

(b)

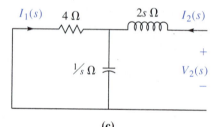

(c)

or

$$g_{12} = \left.\frac{I_1(s)}{I_2(s)}\right|_{V_1(s)=0} = -\frac{1}{4s+1}$$

The input impedance at port 2 is the value of g_{22}:

$$g_{22} = \left.\frac{V_2(s)}{I_2(s)}\right|_{V_1(s)=0} = 2s + \frac{4(1/s)}{4+1/s} = 2s + \frac{4}{4s+1} = \frac{8s^2 + 2s + 4}{4s+1}$$

This makes

$$\mathbf{G} = \begin{bmatrix} \dfrac{s}{4s+1} & -\dfrac{1}{4s+1} \\[3mm] \dfrac{1}{4s+1} & \dfrac{8s^2 + 2s + 4}{4s+1} \end{bmatrix}$$

and it is noted (for future reference) that $g_{12} = -g_{21}$.

FIGURE 18.17

Tee network (Exercise 18.8)

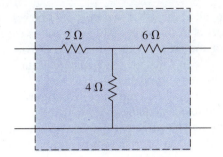

EXERCISE 18.8

Determine the inverse hybrid parameters for the tee network shown in Fig. 18.17.

Answer

$$\mathbf{G} = \begin{bmatrix} \frac{1}{6} & -\frac{2}{3} \\ \frac{2}{3} & \frac{22}{3} \end{bmatrix}$$

18.5.3 A Useful Relationship Between H and G

The inverse hybrid parameter matrix, as the name implies, is the inverse of the hybrid parameter matrix. Take eq. (18.25),

$$\begin{bmatrix} I_1 \\ V_2 \end{bmatrix} = \mathbf{G} \begin{bmatrix} V_1 \\ I_2 \end{bmatrix}$$

and put it into eq. (18.22) to obtain

$$\begin{bmatrix} V_1 \\ I_2 \end{bmatrix} = \mathbf{H} \begin{bmatrix} I_1 \\ V_2 \end{bmatrix} = \mathbf{HG} \begin{bmatrix} V_1 \\ I_2 \end{bmatrix}$$

This requires that $\mathbf{H} = \mathbf{G}^{-1}$ (or $\mathbf{G} = \mathbf{H}^{-1}$), and, of course, neither $\mathbf{H}$ nor $\mathbf{G}$ can be singular. Because of this, the reader can verify that $\mathbf{H}$ developed in Example 18.7,

$$\mathbf{H} = \begin{bmatrix} \dfrac{8s^2 + 2s + 4}{2s^2 + 1} & \dfrac{1}{2s^2 + 1} \\ -\dfrac{1}{2s^2 + 1} & \dfrac{s}{2s^2 + 1} \end{bmatrix}$$

is the inverse of $\mathbf{G}$ developed in Example 18.8,

$$\mathbf{G} = \begin{bmatrix} \dfrac{s}{4s + 1} & -\dfrac{1}{4s + 1} \\ \dfrac{1}{4s + 1} & \dfrac{8s^2 + 2s + 4}{4s + 1} \end{bmatrix}$$

SECTION 18.6   RELATIONSHIPS BETWEEN THE PARAMETERS

If any set of two-port parameters is known, all of the other two-port parameters may be determined. For example, if the two-port is in the form of a tee, then it is easy to determine the elements of the z-parameter matrix from the procedure provided in Section 18.3.4. It is extremely useful to be able to calculate the elements of the other five two-port parameter matrices directly from the elements of $\mathbf{Z}$.

Table 18.3 provides the relationships that may be used in converting from one set of parameters to any of the others. This table is actually a 6×6 array; in its use, the desired set of parameters is located along the principal diagonal of the array. Then, one moves across the row to locate the given or *from* representation, and the relationships for the conversions are thereby located.

For example, suppose that the z parameters are available. Then, the T parameters can be developed from the box in the third row and the first column of Table 18.3. Row 3 derives from the fact that the T parameters are sought. Column 1 comes from the fact that the z parameters are available.

The relationships for the actual conversion are easy to derive, but no useful purpose will be served by presenting all of them here. The entire process can be demonstrated by considering the conversion from $\mathbf{T}$ to $\mathbf{Z}$ and begins with the listing of eqs. (18.5) and (18.17) in sequence, with the letters a through d as designators:

$$V_1 = z_{11}I_1 + z_{12}I_2 \tag{a}$$

$$V_2 = z_{21}I_1 + z_{22}I_2 \tag{b}$$

$$V_1 = AV_2 - BI_2 \tag{c}$$

$$I_1 = CV_2 - DI_2 \tag{d}$$

Equation (d) may be solved for V_2,

$$V_2 = \frac{1}{C}I_1 + \frac{D}{C}I_2 \tag{e}$$

and the coefficients of I_1 and I_2 in eqs. (b) and (e) may be compared. The comparison shows that

$$z_{21} = \frac{1}{C} \quad \text{and} \quad z_{22} = \frac{D}{C}$$

With eq. (e) put into eq. (c),

$$V_1 = A\left(\frac{1}{C}I_1 + \frac{D}{C}I_2\right) - BI_2$$

or

$$V_1 = \frac{A}{C}I_1 + \left(\frac{AD}{C} - B\right)I_2 \tag{f}$$

A comparison of eqs. (a) and (f) will yield z_{11} and z_{12} in terms of A, B, C, and D. First, however, observe that

$$\frac{AD}{C} - B = \frac{AD - BC}{C} = \frac{\det \mathbf{T}}{C}$$

Conversion of two-port parameters

TABLE 18.3

	Z	Y	T	T'	H	G
Z	$\begin{matrix} z_{11} & z_{12} \\ z_{21} & z_{22} \end{matrix}$	$\begin{matrix} \dfrac{y_{22}}{\Delta_Y} & -\dfrac{y_{12}}{\Delta_Y} \\[2mm] -\dfrac{y_{21}}{\Delta_Y} & \dfrac{y_{11}}{\Delta_Y} \end{matrix}$	$\begin{matrix} \dfrac{A}{C} & \dfrac{\Delta_T}{C} \\[2mm] \dfrac{1}{C} & \dfrac{D}{C} \end{matrix}$	$\begin{matrix} \dfrac{D'}{C'} & \dfrac{1}{C'} \\[2mm] \dfrac{\Delta_{T'}}{C'} & \dfrac{A'}{C'} \end{matrix}$	$\begin{matrix} \dfrac{\Delta_H}{h_{22}} & \dfrac{h_{12}}{h_{22}} \\[2mm] -\dfrac{h_{21}}{h_{22}} & \dfrac{1}{h_{22}} \end{matrix}$	$\begin{matrix} \dfrac{1}{g_{11}} & -\dfrac{g_{12}}{g_{11}} \\[2mm] \dfrac{g_{21}}{g_{11}} & \dfrac{\Delta_G}{g_{11}} \end{matrix}$
Y	$\begin{matrix} \dfrac{z_{22}}{\Delta_Z} & -\dfrac{z_{12}}{\Delta_Z} \\[2mm] -\dfrac{z_{21}}{\Delta_Z} & \dfrac{z_{11}}{\Delta_Z} \end{matrix}$	$\begin{matrix} y_{11} & y_{12} \\ y_{21} & y_{22} \end{matrix}$	$\begin{matrix} \dfrac{D}{B} & -\dfrac{\Delta_T}{B} \\[2mm] -\dfrac{1}{B} & \dfrac{A}{B} \end{matrix}$	$\begin{matrix} \dfrac{A'}{B'} & -\dfrac{1}{B'} \\[2mm] -\dfrac{\Delta_{T'}}{B'} & \dfrac{D'}{B'} \end{matrix}$	$\begin{matrix} \dfrac{1}{h_{11}} & -\dfrac{h_{12}}{h_{11}} \\[2mm] \dfrac{h_{21}}{h_{11}} & \dfrac{\Delta_H}{h_{11}} \end{matrix}$	$\begin{matrix} \dfrac{\Delta_G}{g_{22}} & \dfrac{g_{12}}{g_{22}} \\[2mm] -\dfrac{g_{21}}{g_{22}} & \dfrac{1}{g_{22}} \end{matrix}$
T	$\begin{matrix} \dfrac{z_{11}}{z_{21}} & \dfrac{\Delta_Z}{z_{21}} \\[2mm] \dfrac{1}{z_{21}} & \dfrac{z_{22}}{z_{21}} \end{matrix}$	$\begin{matrix} -\dfrac{y_{22}}{y_{21}} & -\dfrac{1}{y_{21}} \\[2mm] -\dfrac{\Delta_Y}{y_{21}} & -\dfrac{y_{11}}{y_{21}} \end{matrix}$	$\begin{matrix} A & B \\ C & D \end{matrix}$	$\begin{matrix} \dfrac{D'}{\Delta_{T'}} & \dfrac{B'}{\Delta_{T'}} \\[2mm] \dfrac{C'}{\Delta_{T'}} & \dfrac{A'}{\Delta_{T'}} \end{matrix}$	$\begin{matrix} -\dfrac{\Delta_H}{h_{21}} & -\dfrac{h_{11}}{h_{21}} \\[2mm] -\dfrac{h_{22}}{h_{21}} & -\dfrac{1}{h_{21}} \end{matrix}$	$\begin{matrix} \dfrac{1}{g_{21}} & \dfrac{g_{22}}{g_{21}} \\[2mm] \dfrac{g_{11}}{g_{21}} & \dfrac{\Delta_G}{g_{21}} \end{matrix}$
T'	$\begin{matrix} \dfrac{z_{22}}{z_{12}} & \dfrac{\Delta_Z}{z_{12}} \\[2mm] \dfrac{1}{z_{12}} & \dfrac{z_{11}}{z_{12}} \end{matrix}$	$\begin{matrix} -\dfrac{y_{11}}{y_{12}} & -\dfrac{1}{y_{12}} \\[2mm] -\dfrac{\Delta_Y}{y_{12}} & -\dfrac{y_{22}}{y_{12}} \end{matrix}$	$\begin{matrix} \dfrac{D}{\Delta_T} & \dfrac{B}{\Delta_T} \\[2mm] \dfrac{C}{\Delta_T} & \dfrac{A}{\Delta_T} \end{matrix}$	$\begin{matrix} A' & B' \\ C' & D' \end{matrix}$	$\begin{matrix} \dfrac{1}{h_{12}} & \dfrac{h_{11}}{h_{12}} \\[2mm] \dfrac{h_{22}}{h_{12}} & \dfrac{\Delta_H}{h_{12}} \end{matrix}$	$\begin{matrix} -\dfrac{\Delta_G}{g_{12}} & -\dfrac{g_{22}}{g_{12}} \\[2mm] -\dfrac{g_{11}}{g_{12}} & -\dfrac{1}{g_{12}} \end{matrix}$
H	$\begin{matrix} \dfrac{\Delta_Z}{z_{22}} & \dfrac{z_{12}}{z_{22}} \\[2mm] -\dfrac{z_{21}}{z_{22}} & \dfrac{1}{z_{22}} \end{matrix}$	$\begin{matrix} \dfrac{1}{y_{11}} & -\dfrac{y_{12}}{y_{11}} \\[2mm] \dfrac{y_{21}}{y_{11}} & \dfrac{\Delta_Y}{y_{11}} \end{matrix}$	$\begin{matrix} \dfrac{B}{D} & \dfrac{\Delta_T}{D} \\[2mm] -\dfrac{1}{D} & \dfrac{C}{D} \end{matrix}$	$\begin{matrix} \dfrac{B'}{A'} & \dfrac{1}{A'} \\[2mm] \dfrac{\Delta_{T'}}{A'} & \dfrac{C'}{A'} \end{matrix}$	$\begin{matrix} h_{11} & h_{12} \\ h_{21} & h_{22} \end{matrix}$	$\begin{matrix} \dfrac{g_{22}}{\Delta_G} & -\dfrac{g_{12}}{\Delta_G} \\[2mm] -\dfrac{g_{21}}{\Delta_G} & \dfrac{g_{11}}{\Delta_G} \end{matrix}$
G	$\begin{matrix} \dfrac{1}{z_{11}} & -\dfrac{z_{12}}{z_{11}} \\[2mm] \dfrac{z_{21}}{z_{11}} & \dfrac{\Delta_Z}{z_{11}} \end{matrix}$	$\begin{matrix} -\dfrac{\Delta_Y}{y_{22}} & \dfrac{y_{12}}{y_{22}} \\[2mm] -\dfrac{y_{21}}{y_{22}} & \dfrac{1}{y_{22}} \end{matrix}$	$\begin{matrix} \dfrac{C}{A} & -\dfrac{\Delta_T}{A} \\[2mm] \dfrac{1}{A} & \dfrac{B}{A} \end{matrix}$	$\begin{matrix} \dfrac{C'}{D'} & -\dfrac{1}{D'} \\[2mm] \dfrac{\Delta_{T'}}{D'} & \dfrac{B'}{D'} \end{matrix}$	$\begin{matrix} \dfrac{h_{22}}{\Delta_H} & -\dfrac{h_{12}}{\Delta_H} \\[2mm] -\dfrac{h_{21}}{\Delta_H} & \dfrac{h_{11}}{\Delta_H} \end{matrix}$	$\begin{matrix} g_{11} & g_{12} \\ g_{21} & g_{22} \end{matrix}$

$$\Delta_Z = \det Z = z_{11}z_{22} - z_{12}z_{21}$$

$$\Delta_Y = \det Y = y_{11}y_{22} - y_{12}y_{21}$$

$$\Delta_T = \det T = AD - BC$$

$$\Delta_{T'} = \det T' = A'D' - B'C'$$

$$\Delta_H = \det H = h_{11}h_{22} - h_{12}h_{21}$$

$$\Delta_G = \det G = g_{11}g_{22} - g_{12}g_{21}$$

so that eq. (*e*) becomes

$$V_1 = \frac{A}{C} I_1 + \left(\frac{\det \mathbf{T}}{C}\right) I_2 \qquad\qquad (g)$$

Now, the term-by-term comparison between eqs. (*a*) and (*g*) can be made to show that

$$z_{11} = \frac{A}{C} \quad \text{and} \quad z_{12} = \frac{\det \mathbf{T}}{C}$$

The reader may wish to use Table 18.3 to verify that the *z* parameters for the tee network of Fig. 18.2 obtained in Example 18.1 will yield all of the other parameterizations obtained in Examples 18.2, 18.5, 18.6, 18.7, and 18.8.

SECTION 18.7   RECIPROCITY AND SYMMETRY

Two important considerations are those of reciprocity and symmetry, which will be discussed in this section. Suppose a two-port network contains only resistors, inductors, and capacitors (passive elements). This is a reciprocal two-port if an ideal voltage source at one port is interchanged with an ammeter used to measure the current at the other port and yields the same ammeter reading. A symmetrical two-port is a reciprocal two-port in which the two ports may be interchanged without changing the values of the terminal voltages and currents.

Figure 18.18a shows an ideal voltage source $V_{1a} = V$ at port 1 that produces a current I_{2a} through the short circuit at port 2. In Fig. 18.18b, the ideal voltage $V_{2b} = V$

FIGURE 18.18   (a) A two-port network with the right-hand terminals short-circuited and (b) a two-port network with the left-hand terminals short-circuited

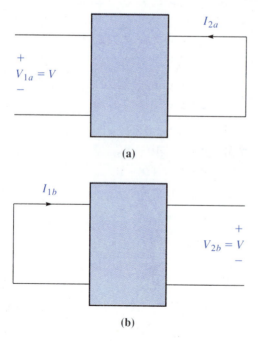

is placed across port 2 and a current I_{1b} flows through port 1. If $I_{2a} = I_{1b}$ when $V_{1a} = V_{2b} = V$, the two ports are said to be it *reciprocal*.

The conditions for reciprocity can be derived by using the admittance parameter matrix and then using the parameter conversions displayed in Table 18.3. For Fig. 18.18a, with $V_{1a} = V$ and $V_{2a} = 0$,

$$\begin{bmatrix} I_{1a} \\ I_{2a} \end{bmatrix} = \mathbf{Y} \begin{bmatrix} V \\ 0 \end{bmatrix} = \begin{bmatrix} y_{11} & y_{12} \\ y_{21} & y_{22} \end{bmatrix} \begin{bmatrix} V \\ 0 \end{bmatrix} \qquad \text{and} \qquad I_{2a} = y_{21} V$$

For Fig. 18.18b with $V_{2b} = V$ and $V_{1b} = 0$,

$$\begin{bmatrix} I_{1b} \\ I_{2b} \end{bmatrix} = \mathbf{Y} \begin{bmatrix} 0 \\ V \end{bmatrix} = \begin{bmatrix} y_{11} & y_{12} \\ y_{21} & y_{22} \end{bmatrix} \begin{bmatrix} 0 \\ V \end{bmatrix} \qquad \text{and} \qquad I_{1b} = y_{12} V$$

If for these identical values of V, $I_{1b} = I_{2a}$, then

$$y_{12} = y_{21} \tag{18.28a}$$

is the necessary and sufficient condition for two-port reciprocity.

Reference to Table 18.3 shows that if $y_{12} = y_{21}$, then

$$z_{12} = z_{21} \tag{18.28b}$$

$$\det \mathbf{T} = AD - BC = 1 \tag{18.28c}$$

$$\det \mathbf{T}' = A'D' - B'C' = 1 \tag{18.28d}$$

$$h_{12} = -h_{21} \tag{18.28e}$$

$$g_{12} = -g_{21} \tag{18.28f}$$

are also conditions for two-port reciprocity.

Now, in Fig. 18.19, if the two-port network is reciprocal and if $V_1 = V_2$ and $I_1 = I_2$, the two-port is symmetrical. The conditions required for symmetry may be obtained by considering one particular parametrization and then using Table 18.3 to determine the others. The z parameter representation with $V_1 = V_2 = V$ and $I_1 = I_2 = I$ is

$$\begin{bmatrix} V \\ V \end{bmatrix} = \mathbf{Z} \begin{bmatrix} I \\ I \end{bmatrix} = \begin{bmatrix} z_{11} & z_{12} \\ z_{21} & z_{22} \end{bmatrix} \begin{bmatrix} I \\ I \end{bmatrix}$$

A two-port network assumed to be reciprocal that is used to develop the conditions for two-port symmetry

FIGURE 18.19

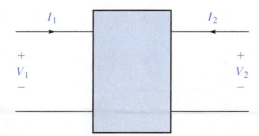

or

$$V = (z_{11} + z_{12})I \qquad \text{and} \qquad V = (z_{21} + z_{22})I$$

This indicates that

$$z_{11} + z_{12} = z_{21} + z_{22}$$

However, the two-port is reciprocal,

$$z_{12} = z_{21} \tag{18.28b}$$

which means that

$$z_{11} = z_{22} \tag{18.29a}$$

is the necessary and sufficient condition for a symmetrical two-port. The additional conditions for symmetry can be obtained via the conversions in Table 18.3:

$$y_{11} = y_{22} \tag{18.29b}$$

$$A = D \tag{18.29c}$$

$$A' = D' \tag{18.29d}$$

$$\det \mathbf{H} = h_{11}h_{22} - h_{12}h_{21} = 1 \tag{18.29e}$$

$$\det \mathbf{G} = g_{11}g_{22} - g_{12}g_{21} = 1 \tag{18.29f}$$

Equations (18.28) show that only three measurements or calculations are needed to determine any of the parameters for a reciprocal two-port network. If a reciprocal two-port is also symmetrical, only two measurements or calculations are required to determine the parameters.

SECTION 18.8   TWO-PORT NETWORKS WITH CONTROLLED SOURCES

The two-port networks that contain controlled sources will, in general, be neither reciprocal nor symmetrical.

■ EXAMPLE 18.9

The two-port network shown in Fig. 18.20a contains two controlled sources. Develop its z and h parametrizations.

Solution   The strategy is to develop the z parameters from a pair of mesh equations and then use Table 18.2 to obtain $\mathbf{H}$. Figure 18.20b with the ICIS transformed into an ICVS will be used. This transformation requires the recognition that $I_a = I_1 + I_2$. The mesh equations are

$$4I_1 + 2(I_1 + I_2) = V_1 + 8(I_1 + I_2)$$

$$3I_2 + 2(I_1 + I_2) = V_2 - 2V_2$$

or

$$-2I_1 - 6I_2 = \quad V_1$$

$$2I_1 + 5I_2 = -V_2$$

(a) A two-port containing a pair of controlled sources and (b) a two-mesh network ready for a mesh analysis, with the current source transformed

FIGURE 18.20

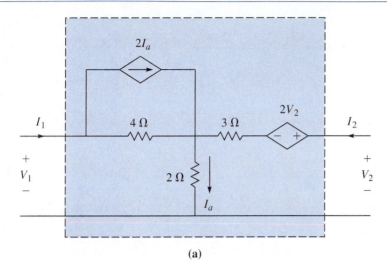

(a)

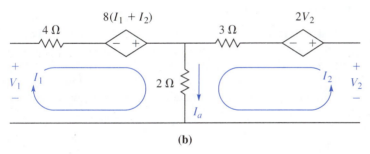

(b)

or

$$\begin{bmatrix} V_1 \\ V_2 \end{bmatrix} = \begin{bmatrix} -2 & -6 \\ -2 & -5 \end{bmatrix} \begin{bmatrix} I_1 \\ I_2 \end{bmatrix} = \mathbf{Z} \begin{bmatrix} I_1 \\ I_2 \end{bmatrix}$$

This indicates that

$$z_{11} = -2 \qquad z_{21} = -2 \qquad z_{12} = -6 \qquad z_{22} = -5$$

and det $\mathbf{Z} = -2$. The network is neither reciprocal nor symmetrical. The elements of $\mathbf{H}$ are found from Table 18.3:

$$h_{11} = \frac{\Delta_z}{z_{22}} = \frac{-2}{-5} = \frac{2}{5} \qquad\qquad h_{12} = \frac{z_{12}}{z_{22}} = \frac{-6}{-5} = \frac{6}{5}$$

$$h_{21} = -\frac{z_{21}}{z_{22}} = -\frac{-2}{-5} = -\frac{2}{5} \qquad h_{22} = \frac{1}{z_{22}} = \frac{1}{-5} = -\frac{1}{5}$$

so that

$$\mathbf{H} = \begin{bmatrix} \frac{2}{5} & \frac{6}{5} \\ -\frac{2}{5} & -\frac{1}{5} \end{bmatrix}$$

FIGURE 18.21   Network (Exercise 19.9)

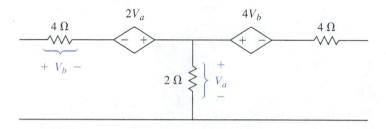

EXERCISE 18.9

Develop the T parameter representation for the network shown in Fig. 18.21.

Answer

$$\mathbf{T} = \begin{bmatrix} -\frac{1}{7} & \frac{8}{7} \\ -\frac{1}{14} & -\frac{3}{7} \end{bmatrix}$$

18.8.1 Application—Transistor Amplifier

A two-port, small-signal, low-frequency model of a Bipolar Junction Transistor in the common emitter configuration is shown in Fig. 18.22 and the presence of a voltage controlled voltage source and a current controlled current source may be noted. Because the two-port is composed of the h-parameters, it is commonly referred to as the h-parameter model and the h-parameters displayed in the figure can be used in eqs. (18.23)

$$V_1 = h_{11}I_1 + h_{12}V_2 \tag{18.23a}$$

$$I_2 = h_{21}I_1 + h_{22}V_2 \tag{18.23b}$$

The letters B, C, and E refer respectively to the base, emitter and collector of the device and it should be noted that it is a characteristic of the common emitter con-

FIGURE 18.22   Low-frequency, small-signal h-parameter model of Bipolar Junction Transistor connected in the common-emitter configuration

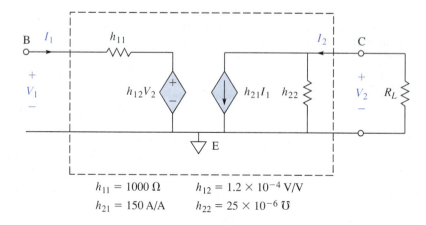

$$h_{11} = 1000\ \Omega \qquad h_{12} = 1.2 \times 10^{-4}\ \text{V/V}$$
$$h_{21} = 150\ \text{A/A} \qquad h_{22} = 25 \times 10^{-6}\ \mho$$

figuration to yield a negative collector voltage, $V_C = V_2$ when the current enters the base terminal. Typical values for the h-parameters are shown in Fig. 18.22.

Example 18.10 will illustrate some of the calculations that are routinely made for the h-parameter common emitter amplifier represented as the two port network in Fig. 18.22.

■ **EXAMPLE 18.10**

For the common emitter h-parameter model with the typical values and load resistor, $R_L = 2000\ \Omega$ shown in Fig. 18.22, determine the current gain, $A_I = I_2/I_1$, the voltage gain $A_V = V_2/V_1$, and the input resistance of the amplifier, R_i.

Solution The collector current is obtained from a current division. With the recognition that h_{22} is a conductance

$$I_2 = \left(\dfrac{\dfrac{1}{h_{22}}}{R_L + \dfrac{1}{h_{22}}} \right) h_{21} I_1 = \dfrac{h_{21} I_1}{1 + h_{22} R_L}$$

and with $h_{21} = 150\ \text{A/A}$, $h_{22} = 25 \times 10^{-6}\ \text{℧}$ and $R_L = 2000\ \Omega$

$$A_I = \dfrac{I_2}{I_1} = \dfrac{150}{1 + (25 \times 10^{-6})(2000)} = 143$$

If

$$R_p = \dfrac{\left(\dfrac{1}{h_{22}} \right) R_L}{\dfrac{1}{h_{22}} + R_L} = \dfrac{R_L}{1 + h_{22} R_L} = \dfrac{2000}{1 + (25 \times 10^{-6})(2000)} = 1905\ \Omega$$

then

$$V_2 = -h_{21} R_p I_1$$

At the input, KVL gives

$$V_1 = h_{11} I_1 + h_{12} V_2$$

so that

$$I_1 = \dfrac{V_1 - h_{12} V_2}{h_{11}}$$

Thus

$$V_2 = -h_{21} R_p \left(\dfrac{V_1 - h_{12} V_2}{h_{11}} \right) = \dfrac{h_{21} h_{12}}{h_{11}} R_p V_2 - \dfrac{h_{21}}{h_{11}} R_p V_1$$

$$\left(1 - \dfrac{h_{21} h_{12} R_p}{h_{11}} \right) V_2 = -\dfrac{h_{21}}{h_{11}} R_p V_1$$

and with some algebraic simplification

$$A_V = \frac{V_2}{V_1} = \frac{h_{21}R_p}{h_{21}h_{12}R_p - h_{11}}$$

With parameters from Fig. 18.22

$$A_V = \frac{150(1905)}{(1.2 \times 10^{-4})(150)(1905) - 1000} = -296$$

Finally

$$R_i = \frac{V_1}{I_1} = \frac{h_{11}I_1 + h_{12}V_2}{I_1}$$

and with

$$V_2 = -h_{21}R_pI_1$$

the input resistance is

$$R_i = h_{11} - h_{12}h_{21}R_p$$

and for this amplifier

$$R_i = 1000 - (1.2 \times 10^{-4})(150)(1905) = 966 \ \Omega \qquad \blacksquare$$

18.8.2 Application—Miller's Theorem

Figure 18.23a shows a two-port model of a transistor amplifier and it is observed that a feedback resistor connects nodes 1 and 2. Miller's theorem permits the replacement of the arrangement in Fig. 18.23a by the one in Fig. 18.23b as long as the voltage gain, $A_V = A = V_2/V_1$ is known.

Consider Fig. 18.23c and observe that

$$I_1 = Y(V_1 - V_2) = YV_1\left(1 - \frac{V_2}{V_1}\right)$$

or

$$I_1 = YV_1(1 - A)$$

If the two-port in Fig. 18.23d where

$$I_1 = Y_1V_1$$

is to be equivalent to the two-port in Fig. 18.23c, then

$$Y_1V_1 = YV_1(1 - A)$$

which shows that

$$Y_1 = (1 - A)Y$$

(a) Transconductance amplifier with feedback resistor, (b) the amplifier with
equivalent resistors at the input and output ends and (c) and (d) steps in the
development of Miller's theorem

FIGURE 18.23

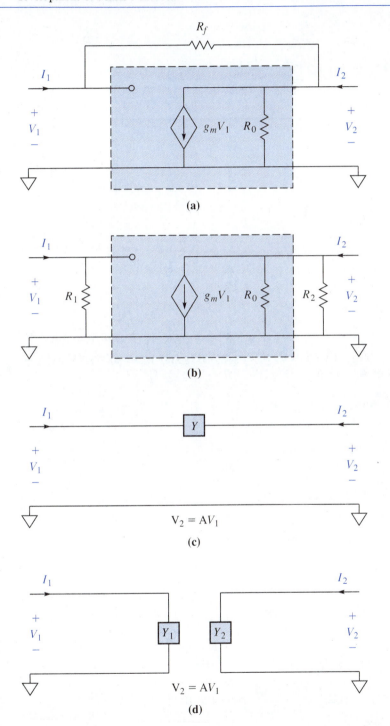

The same procedure is followed with regard to Y_2 in Fig. 18.23d where

$$I_2 = Y_2 V_2$$

In Fig. 18.23c,

$$I_2 = Y(V_2 - V_1) = YV_2\left(1 - \frac{V_1}{V_2}\right)$$

or

$$I_2 = YV_2\left(\frac{A - 1}{A}\right)$$

Then for the equivalence

$$Y_2 V_2 = YV_2\left(\frac{A - 1}{A}\right)$$

or

$$Y_2 = \left(\frac{A - 1}{A}\right)Y$$

■ **EXAMPLE 18.11**

In Fig. 18.23a, $g_m = 0.08$ A/V, $R_f = 800,000\ \Omega$ and $R_0 = 8000\ \Omega$. What are the values of R_1 and R_2 in Fig. 18.23b?

Solution   A node equation at port 2 in Fig. 18.23a gives the voltage amplification, A.

$$\frac{V_2 - V_1}{R_f} + g_m V_1 + \frac{V_2}{R_0} = 0$$

and a little algebra gives

$$A = \frac{V_2}{V_1} = \frac{R_0(1 - g_m R_f)}{R_0 + R_f}$$

With the given values

$$A = \frac{V_2}{V_1} = \frac{8000[1 - 0.08(800,000)]}{8000 + 800,000} = -633.7 \text{ V/V}$$

Then in Fig. 18.23b with $G = 1/R_f = 1/800,000$

$$G_1 = G(1 - A) = \frac{1 - (-633.7)}{800,000} = 7.94 \times 10^{-4}$$

or

$$R_1 = 1260.5\ \Omega$$

and

$$G_2 = G\left(\frac{A-1}{A}\right) = \frac{1}{800{,}000}\left(\frac{-634.7}{-633.7}\right) = 1.252 \times 10^{-6}$$

or

$$R_2 = 798{,}740\ \Omega$$

∎

TWO-PORT REPRESENTATIONS FOR SINGLE ELEMENTS   SECTION 18.9

Single elements in what are called the *series* arm of a ladder (Fig. 18.24a) and the *shunt* arm of a ladder (Fig. 18.24b) possess transmission parameter matrices. For the series arrangement, use may be made of eqs. (18.18). First,

$$A = \left.\frac{V_1}{V_2}\right|_{I_2=0} = 1$$

because if $I_2 = 0$, then $I_1 = 0$ and $V_1 = V_2$. Next,

$$B = -\left.\frac{V_1}{I_2}\right|_{V_2=0} = Z$$

because if $V_2 = 0$, port 2 is shorted, $I_1 = -I_2$, and B is merely the input impedance at port 1. Then,

$$C = \left.\frac{I_1}{V_2}\right|_{I_2=0} = 0$$

because if $I_2 = 0$, $I_1 = 0$. And finally,

$$D = -\left.\frac{I_1}{I_2}\right|_{V_2=0} = 1$$

because in this case, port 2 is shorted and $I_1 = -I_2$. Thus, for the series element,

$$T_{se} = \begin{bmatrix} 1 & Z \\ 0 & 1 \end{bmatrix} \tag{18.30}$$

Single elements represented as two-ports: (a) the series element and (b) the shunt element

FIGURE 18.24

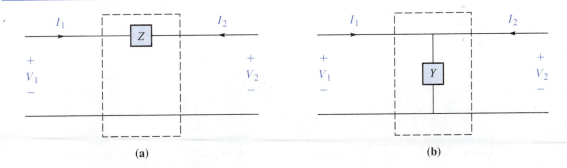

(a)   (b)

Equations (18.18) may also be used to determine the elements of the **T** matrix for the single shunt element displayed in Fig. 18.24b. First,

$$A = \left.\frac{V_1}{V_2}\right|_{I_2=0} = 1$$

because with $I_2 = 0$, $V_1 = V_2$. Then,

$$B = \left.-\frac{V_1}{I_2}\right|_{V_2=0} = 0$$

because with $V_2 = 0$ due to a short circuit at port 2, $V_1 = V_2 = 0$. Next,

$$C = \left.\frac{I_1}{V_2}\right|_{I_2=0} = Y$$

which is merely the input admittance at port 1 because $V_1 = V_2$. Finally,

$$D = \left.-\frac{I_1}{I_2}\right|_{V_2=0} = 1$$

because for this short-circuited condition at port 2, $I_1 = -I_2$.

The **T** matrix for the single shunt element is

$$\mathbf{T}_{sh} = \begin{bmatrix} 1 & 0 \\ Y & 1 \end{bmatrix} \tag{18.31}$$

SECTION 18.10   **ALGORITHMS FOR THE COMBINATIONS OF TWO-PORTS**

18.10.1 The Cascade Algorithm

Figure 18.25 shows n two ports connected in *cascade*. This configuration can be reduced to one that can be represented by an equivalent transmission parameter matrix. Consider the two ports 1 and 2 and write

$$\begin{bmatrix} V_{1,1} \\ I_{1,1} \end{bmatrix} = \begin{bmatrix} A_1 & B_1 \\ C_1 & D_1 \end{bmatrix} \begin{bmatrix} V_{2,1} \\ -I_{2,1} \end{bmatrix}$$

$$\begin{bmatrix} V_{1,2} \\ I_{1,2} \end{bmatrix} = \begin{bmatrix} A_2 & B_2 \\ C_2 & D_2 \end{bmatrix} \begin{bmatrix} V_{2,2} \\ -I_{2,2} \end{bmatrix}$$

FIGURE 18.25   A cascade arrangement of n two-port networks

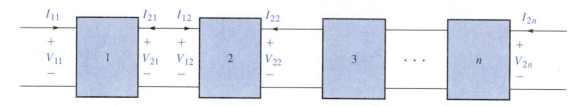

At the junction of two-ports 1 and 2, the voltages must match; and by KCL, $I_{1,2} = -I_{2,1}$. These compatability and continuity requirements can be represented by

$$\begin{bmatrix} V_{2,1} \\ -I_{2,1} \end{bmatrix} = \begin{bmatrix} V_{1,2} \\ I_{1,2} \end{bmatrix}$$

An exercise in matrix algebra will then yield

$$\begin{bmatrix} V_{1,1} \\ I_{1,1} \end{bmatrix} = \begin{bmatrix} A_1 & B_1 \\ C_1 & D_1 \end{bmatrix} \begin{bmatrix} V_{2,1} \\ -I_{2,1} \end{bmatrix} = \begin{bmatrix} A_1 & B_1 \\ C_1 & D_1 \end{bmatrix} \begin{bmatrix} V_{1,2} \\ I_{1,2} \end{bmatrix}$$

$$= \begin{bmatrix} A_1 & B_1 \\ C_1 & D_1 \end{bmatrix} \begin{bmatrix} A_2 & B_2 \\ C_2 & D_2 \end{bmatrix} \begin{bmatrix} V_{2,2} \\ -I_{2,2} \end{bmatrix}$$

and an equivalent **T** matrix can be formed:

$$\begin{bmatrix} A_{eq} & B_{eq} \\ C_{eq} & D_{eq} \end{bmatrix} = \begin{bmatrix} A_1 & B_1 \\ C_1 & D_1 \end{bmatrix} \begin{bmatrix} A_2 & B_2 \\ C_2 & D_2 \end{bmatrix}$$

This may be extended to n two-ports in cascade:

$$\begin{bmatrix} V_{1,1} \\ I_{1,1} \end{bmatrix} = \begin{bmatrix} A_{eq} & B_{eq} \\ C_{eq} & D_{eq} \end{bmatrix} \begin{bmatrix} V_{2,n} \\ -I_{2,n} \end{bmatrix} \tag{18.32}$$

where

$$\begin{bmatrix} A_{eq} & B_{eq} \\ C_{eq} & D_{eq} \end{bmatrix} = \begin{bmatrix} A_1 & B_1 \\ C_1 & D_1 \end{bmatrix} \begin{bmatrix} A_2 & B_2 \\ C_2 & D_2 \end{bmatrix} \begin{bmatrix} A_3 & B_3 \\ C_3 & D_3 \end{bmatrix} \cdots \begin{bmatrix} A_n & B_n \\ C_n & D_n \end{bmatrix} \tag{18.33}$$

Equations (18.32) and (18.33) describe the cascade algorithm.

The cascade algorithm is extremely useful in applications where ladder networks require reduction to a simple equivalent such as a tee or pi network or to a single input admittance or impedance. This will be demonstrated in the example that follows.

■ **EXAMPLE 18.12**

Figure 18.26a shows a ladder network consisting of six resistors. Reduce this ladder network to a single tee equivalent.

Solution   The cascade algorithm may be applied in two different ways, and each will lead to the same result.

Method One   The ladder may be considered to be composed of a tee and a pi network in cascade, as indicated in Fig. 18.26b. For the subnetwork consisting of the 3-, 4-, and 5-Ω resistors in the tee, eqs. (18.11) can be used to obtain

$$\mathbf{Z}_1 = \begin{bmatrix} (5+3) & 3 \\ 3 & (4+3) \end{bmatrix} = \begin{bmatrix} 8 & 3 \\ 3 & 7 \end{bmatrix}$$

FIGURE 18.26   (a) A resistive ladder network, (b) the ladder network shown as two two-ports in cascade, one a tee network and the other a pi network, and (c) the ladder network represented as a single two-port containing a tee network

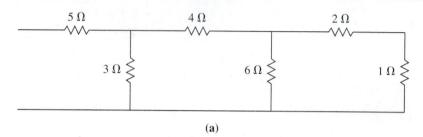

(a)

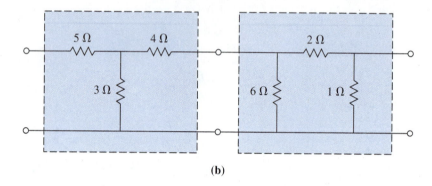

(b)

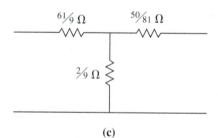

(c)

Here,

$$\det \mathbf{Z}_1 = \Delta_{Z_1} = 8(7) - 3(3) = 56 - 9 = 47$$

For the subnetwork consisting of the 1-, 2-, and 6-Ω resistors in the pi, eqs. (18.14) provide

$$\mathbf{Y}_2 = \begin{bmatrix} (\frac{1}{2} + \frac{1}{6}) & -\frac{1}{2} \\ -\frac{1}{2} & (\frac{1}{2} + 1) \end{bmatrix} = \begin{bmatrix} \frac{2}{3} & -\frac{1}{2} \\ -\frac{1}{2} & \frac{3}{2} \end{bmatrix}$$

and

$$\det \mathbf{Y}_2 = \Delta_{Y_2} = (\tfrac{2}{3})(\tfrac{3}{2}) - (-\tfrac{1}{2})(-\tfrac{1}{2}) = 1 - \tfrac{1}{4} = \tfrac{3}{4}$$

Each of these may be converted to a **T** matrix, using Table 18.3:

$$\mathbf{T}_1 = \begin{bmatrix} \frac{8}{3} & \frac{47}{3} \\ \frac{1}{3} & \frac{7}{3} \end{bmatrix} \quad \text{and} \quad \mathbf{T}_2 = \begin{bmatrix} 3 & 2 \\ \frac{3}{2} & \frac{4}{3} \end{bmatrix}$$

The cascade algorithm of eq. (18.32) can be used to form an equivalent **T** matrix:

$$\mathbf{T}_{eq} = \begin{bmatrix} A_{eq} & B_{eq} \\ C_{eq} & D_{eq} \end{bmatrix} = \begin{bmatrix} \frac{8}{3} & \frac{47}{3} \\ \frac{1}{3} & \frac{7}{3} \end{bmatrix} \begin{bmatrix} 3 & 2 \\ \frac{3}{2} & \frac{4}{3} \end{bmatrix} = \begin{bmatrix} \frac{63}{2} & \frac{236}{9} \\ \frac{9}{2} & \frac{34}{9} \end{bmatrix}$$

which has a determinant

$$\det \mathbf{T}_{eq} = \Delta_{T_{eq}} = \left(\frac{63}{2}\right)\left(\frac{34}{9}\right) - \left(\frac{9}{2}\right)\left(\frac{236}{9}\right) = \frac{2142}{18} - \frac{2124}{18} = \frac{18}{18} = 1$$

Table 18.3 can be used to reclaim an equivalent **Z**:

$$\mathbf{Z}_{eq} = \begin{bmatrix} 7 & \frac{2}{9} \\ \frac{2}{9} & \frac{68}{81} \end{bmatrix}$$

And an equivalent tee that represents the entire ladder can be formed by employing eqs. (18.12):

$$Z_1 = z_{11} - z_{12} = 7 - \frac{2}{9} = \frac{61}{9}\,\Omega$$

$$Z_2 = z_{22} - z_{12} = \frac{68}{81} - \frac{2}{9} = \frac{50}{81}\,\Omega$$

$$Z_3 = z_{12} = z_{21} = \frac{2}{9}\,\Omega$$

The equivalent tee is shown in Fig. 18.24c.

Method Two   The second method involves the representation of each resistor as either a single-series or single-shunt-element **T** matrix. The strategy is to combine the six **T** matrices to form a single **T** equivalent and then convert, via Table 18.3, to the **Z** representation.

Working from the left to the right (*Caution:* Lack of attention to the order of the matrix multiplications in the cascade is almost always a fatal error), one carefully writes the individual, single-parameter **T** matrices:

$$\mathbf{T}_{eq} = \begin{bmatrix} A_{eq} & B_{eq} \\ C_{eq} & D_{eq} \end{bmatrix}$$

$$= \begin{bmatrix} 1 & 5 \\ 0 & 1 \end{bmatrix} \begin{bmatrix} 1 & 0 \\ \frac{1}{3} & 1 \end{bmatrix} \begin{bmatrix} 1 & 4 \\ 0 & 1 \end{bmatrix} \begin{bmatrix} 1 & 0 \\ \frac{1}{6} & 1 \end{bmatrix} \begin{bmatrix} 1 & 2 \\ 0 & 1 \end{bmatrix} \begin{bmatrix} 1 & 0 \\ 1 & 1 \end{bmatrix}$$

$$= \begin{bmatrix} \frac{8}{3} & 5 \\ \frac{1}{3} & 1 \end{bmatrix} \begin{bmatrix} \frac{5}{3} & 4 \\ \frac{1}{6} & 1 \end{bmatrix} \begin{bmatrix} 3 & 2 \\ 1 & 1 \end{bmatrix} = \begin{bmatrix} \frac{95}{18} & \frac{47}{3} \\ \frac{13}{18} & \frac{7}{3} \end{bmatrix} \begin{bmatrix} 3 & 2 \\ 1 & 1 \end{bmatrix}$$

$$= \begin{bmatrix} \frac{63}{2} & \frac{236}{9} \\ \frac{9}{2} & \frac{34}{9} \end{bmatrix}$$

This matches **T**$_{eq}$ obtained previously, and from this point to the development of the equivalent tee, the two methods are identical. ∎

FIGURE 18.27   (a) Ladder network (Exercise 19.10) and (b) its equivalent tee network

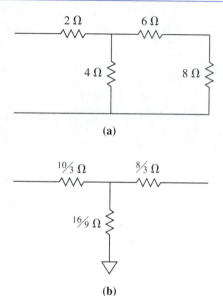

(a)

(b)

EXERCISE 18.10

Represent the ladder network shown in Fig. 18.27a as an equivalent tee network

Answer   See Fig. 18.27b.

18.10.2 The Series Algorithm

The n two-ports in Fig. 18.28 are said to be in series-series, and the difference between the cascade and series-series arrangement can be clearly observed. Here, KVL applies, and it is written in matrix form as

$$\begin{bmatrix} V_1 \\ V_2 \end{bmatrix} = \begin{bmatrix} V_{1,1} \\ V_{2,1} \end{bmatrix} + \begin{bmatrix} V_{1,2} \\ V_{2,2} \end{bmatrix} + \begin{bmatrix} V_{1,3} \\ V_{2,3} \end{bmatrix} + \cdots + \begin{bmatrix} V_{1,n} \\ V_{2,n} \end{bmatrix}$$

It is seen that

$$\begin{bmatrix} I_1 \\ I_2 \end{bmatrix} = \begin{bmatrix} I_{1,1} \\ I_{2,1} \end{bmatrix} = \begin{bmatrix} I_{1,2} \\ I_{2,2} \end{bmatrix} = \begin{bmatrix} I_{1,3} \\ I_{2,3} \end{bmatrix} = \cdots = \begin{bmatrix} I_{1,n} \\ I_{2,n} \end{bmatrix}$$

However, each vector $\mathbf{V}$ is related to its own $\mathbf{I}$ vector by the z parameter matrix $(\mathbf{V} = \mathbf{ZI})$, so that

$$\begin{bmatrix} V_1 \\ V_2 \end{bmatrix} = \mathbf{Z}_1 \begin{bmatrix} I_{1,1} \\ I_{2,1} \end{bmatrix} + \mathbf{Z}_2 \begin{bmatrix} I_{1,2} \\ I_{2,2} \end{bmatrix} + \mathbf{Z}_3 \begin{bmatrix} I_{1,3} \\ I_{2,3} \end{bmatrix} + \cdots + \mathbf{Z}_n \begin{bmatrix} I_{1,n} \\ I_{2,n} \end{bmatrix}$$

Because all of the I vectors are equal,

$$\begin{bmatrix} V_1 \\ V_2 \end{bmatrix} = (\mathbf{Z}_1 + \mathbf{Z}_2 + \mathbf{Z}_3 + \cdots + \mathbf{Z}_n) \begin{bmatrix} I_1 \\ I_2 \end{bmatrix}$$

n two-ports in series-series

FIGURE 18.28

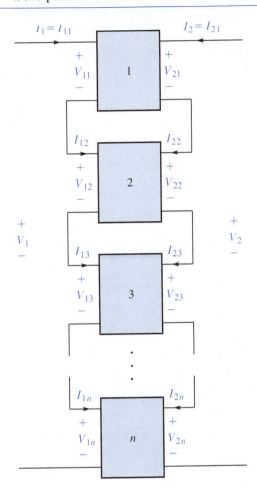

or

$$\begin{bmatrix} V_1 \\ V_2 \end{bmatrix} = \mathbf{Z}_{eq} \begin{bmatrix} I_1 \\ I_2 \end{bmatrix}$$

(18.34)

where

$$\mathbf{Z}_{eq} = \mathbf{Z}_1 + \mathbf{Z}_2 + \mathbf{Z}_3 + \cdots + \mathbf{Z}_n$$

(18.35)

Equations (18.34) and (18.35) describe the series algorithm, which says that *n* two-ports in series can be represented by an equivalent **Z** matrix that is the sum of the individual **Z** matrices.

■ **EXAMPLE 18.13**

Reduce the network shown in Fig. 18.29a to an equivalent pi network.

Solution Three subnetworks are shown in Fig. 18.29b. Subnetwork 1 is a balanced-pi network with 6-Ω elements and is in series with subnetwork 2, which is a single shunt element consisting of a 2-Ω resistor. Both of these

FIGURE 18.29   (a) A complex two-port network, (b) the two-port in the form of three
subnetworks, and (c) an equivalent pi network that represents the two-port in (a)

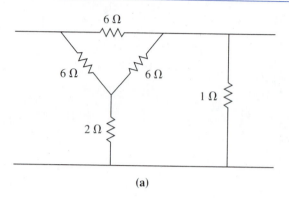

(a)

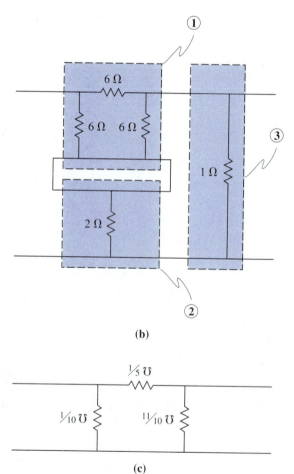

(b)

(c)

are in cascade with subnetwork 3, which is another single shunt element
consisting of a 1-Ω resistor.

Convert the balanced-pi network in subnetwork 1 to a balanced-tee network. The tee elements will be one-third the value of the value of the pi elements. Thus, a **Z** matrix can be formed for the pi, with $Z_1 = Z_2 = Z_3 = 2\ \Omega$,

and eqs. (18.11) give

$$\mathbf{Z}_1 = \begin{bmatrix} 4 & 2 \\ 2 & 4 \end{bmatrix}$$

The single shunt element in subnetwork 2 has a **T** representation,

$$\mathbf{T}_2 = \begin{bmatrix} 1 & 0 \\ \frac{1}{2} & 1 \end{bmatrix}$$

and Table 18.3 can be used to show that

$$\mathbf{Z}_2 = \begin{bmatrix} 2 & 2 \\ 2 & 2 \end{bmatrix}$$

Although this matrix is singular, it may still be used to form an equivalent **Z** for the series combination of subnetworks 1 and 2 via the series algorithm of eq. (18.35):

$$\mathbf{Z}_{eq} = \mathbf{Z}_1 + \mathbf{Z}_2 = \begin{bmatrix} 4 & 2 \\ 2 & 4 \end{bmatrix} + \begin{bmatrix} 2 & 2 \\ 2 & 2 \end{bmatrix} = \begin{bmatrix} 6 & 4 \\ 4 & 6 \end{bmatrix}$$

Observe that $\mathbf{Z}_{eq}$ is not singular, because $\det \mathbf{Z} = \Delta_Z = 6(6) - 4(4) = 36 - 16 = 20$.

Table 18.3 may be used to convert $\mathbf{Z}_{eq}$ to an equivalent **T** matrix for the combined effect of subnetworks 1 and 2:

$$\mathbf{T}_{1,2} = \begin{bmatrix} \frac{3}{2} & 5 \\ \frac{1}{4} & \frac{3}{2} \end{bmatrix}$$

The combination of subnetworks 1 and 2 is in cascade with the single 1-Ω shunt resistor in subnetwork 3, represented by

$$\mathbf{T}_3 = \begin{bmatrix} 1 & 0 \\ 1 & 1 \end{bmatrix}$$

The cascade algorithm of eq. (18.33) can be used to obtain $\mathbf{T}_{eq}$ for the entire configuration:

$$\mathbf{T}_{eq} = \begin{bmatrix} A & B \\ C & D \end{bmatrix}_{eq} = \begin{bmatrix} \frac{3}{2} & 5 \\ \frac{1}{4} & \frac{3}{2} \end{bmatrix} \begin{bmatrix} 1 & 0 \\ 1 & 1 \end{bmatrix} = \begin{bmatrix} \frac{13}{2} & 5 \\ \frac{7}{4} & \frac{3}{2} \end{bmatrix}$$

and it may be observed that $\det \mathbf{T}_{eq} = \Delta_{T_{eq}} = 1$.

The required equivalent pi network is obtained from the equivalent **Y** matrix transformed from $\mathbf{T}_{eq}$ via Table 18.3:

$$\mathbf{Y}_{eq} = \begin{bmatrix} \frac{3}{10} & -\frac{1}{5} \\ -\frac{1}{5} & \frac{13}{10} \end{bmatrix}$$

The elements of the equivalent pi network, shown in Fig. 18.29c, are found from eqs. (18.15):

$$Y_{12} = -y_{12} = -y_{21} = \frac{1}{5}$$

$$Y_{23} = y_{22} + y_{12} = \frac{13}{10} - \frac{1}{5} = \frac{11}{10}$$

$$Y_{31} = y_{11} + y_{12} = \frac{3}{10} - \frac{1}{5} = \frac{1}{10}$$

■

18.10.3 The Parallel Algorithm

A parallel-parallel combination of n two-ports is shown in Fig. 18.30. The voltages across each of the two-ports are identical at both ends:

$$\begin{bmatrix} V_1 \\ V_2 \end{bmatrix} = \begin{bmatrix} V_{1,1} \\ V_{2,1} \end{bmatrix} = \begin{bmatrix} V_{1,2} \\ V_{2,2} \end{bmatrix} = \begin{bmatrix} V_{1,3} \\ V_{2,3} \end{bmatrix} = \cdots = \begin{bmatrix} V_{1,n} \\ V_{2,n} \end{bmatrix}$$

FIGURE 18.30 n two-ports arranged in parallel-parallel

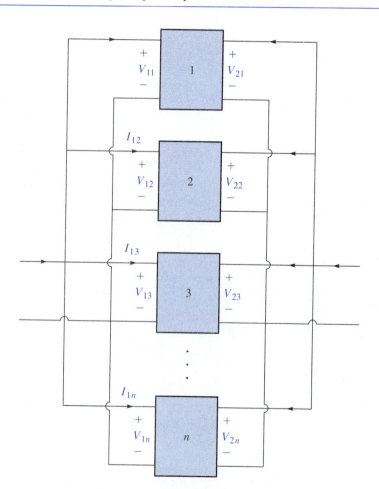

and the currents flowing into each two-port divide in accordance with KCL:

$$\begin{bmatrix} I_1 \\ I_2 \end{bmatrix} = \begin{bmatrix} I_{1,1} \\ I_{2,1} \end{bmatrix} + \begin{bmatrix} I_{1,2} \\ I_{2,2} \end{bmatrix} + \begin{bmatrix} I_{1,3} \\ I_{2,3} \end{bmatrix} + \cdots + \begin{bmatrix} I_{1,n} \\ I_{2,n} \end{bmatrix}$$

The relationship between **I** and **V** is the admittance parameter formulation **I** = **YV**. Thus,

$$\begin{bmatrix} I_1 \\ I_2 \end{bmatrix} = \mathbf{Y}_1 \begin{bmatrix} V_{1,1} \\ V_{2,1} \end{bmatrix} + \mathbf{Y}_2 \begin{bmatrix} V_{1,2} \\ V_{2,2} \end{bmatrix} + \mathbf{Y}_3 \begin{bmatrix} V_{1,3} \\ V_{2,3} \end{bmatrix} + \cdots + \mathbf{Y}_n \begin{bmatrix} V_{1,n} \\ V_{2,n} \end{bmatrix}$$

and because all of the **V** vectors are equal,

$$\begin{bmatrix} I_1 \\ I_2 \end{bmatrix} = (\mathbf{Y}_1 + \mathbf{Y}_2 + \mathbf{Y}_3 + \cdots + \mathbf{Y}_n) \begin{bmatrix} V_1 \\ V_2 \end{bmatrix}$$

or

$$\begin{bmatrix} I_1 \\ I_2 \end{bmatrix} = \mathbf{Y}_{eq} \begin{bmatrix} V_1 \\ V_2 \end{bmatrix} \tag{18.36}$$

where

$$\mathbf{Y}_{eq} = \mathbf{Y}_1 + \mathbf{Y}_2 + \mathbf{Y}_3 + \cdots + \mathbf{Y}_n \tag{18.37}$$

The parallel algorithm described by eqs. (18.36) and (18.37) says that an equivalent admittance parameter matrix for n two-ports in parallel can be formed from a summation of the individual admittance parameter matrices.

■ **EXAMPLE 18.14**

Obtain the equivalent h-parameter matrix for the network shown in Fig. 18.31a.

Solution The network shown in Fig. 18.31a contains three subnetworks as shown in Fig. 18.31b. Subnetwork 1 is a single-series element and subnetwork 2 is a single-shunt element. Subnetwork 3 is a pi network. The strategy here is to proceed through the following steps:

1. Form $\mathbf{T}_1$ and $\mathbf{T}_2$
2. Use the cascade algorithm to obtain an equivalent **T** for subnetworks 1 and 2. Call this $\mathbf{T}_{12}$
3. From $\mathbf{T}_{12}$ obtain $\mathbf{Y}_{12}$ (Table 18.3)
4. Form $\mathbf{Y}_3$
5. Form $\mathbf{Y}_{eq}$ by adding $\mathbf{Y}_{12}$ and $\mathbf{Y}_3$ in accordance with the parallel algorithm
6. Use Table 18.3 to convert from $\mathbf{Y}_{eq}$ to $\mathbf{H}_{eq}$. The computations now follow.

▪ From eqs. (18.30) and (18.31) for subnetworks 1 and 2

$$\mathbf{T}_1 = \begin{bmatrix} 1 & 4 \\ 0 & 1 \end{bmatrix} \quad \text{and} \quad \mathbf{T}_2 = \begin{bmatrix} 1 & 0 \\ 2 & 1 \end{bmatrix}$$

FIGURE 18.31   (a) A rather complicated network and (b) its representation as three two-ports

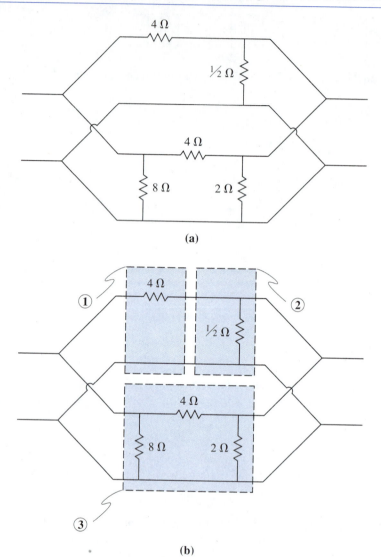

(a)

(b)

- By the cascade algorithm

$$\mathbf{T}_{12} = \begin{bmatrix} 1 & 4 \\ 0 & 1 \end{bmatrix}\begin{bmatrix} 1 & 0 \\ 2 & 1 \end{bmatrix} = \begin{bmatrix} 9 & 4 \\ 2 & 1 \end{bmatrix}$$

- From Table 18.3 with det $T_{12} = 9 - 8 = 1$

$$\mathbf{Y}_{12} = \begin{bmatrix} \frac{1}{4} & -\frac{1}{4} \\ -\frac{1}{4} & \frac{9}{4} \end{bmatrix}$$

- From eqs. (18.4) for subnetwork 3

$$\mathbf{Y}_3 = \begin{bmatrix} (\frac{1}{4} + \frac{1}{8}) & -\frac{1}{4} \\ -\frac{1}{4} & (\frac{1}{4} + \frac{1}{2}) \end{bmatrix} = \begin{bmatrix} \frac{3}{8} & -\frac{1}{4} \\ -\frac{1}{4} & \frac{3}{4} \end{bmatrix}$$

- By the parallel algorithm of eqs. (18.36) and (18.37)

$$\mathbf{Y}_{eq} = \mathbf{Y}_{12} + \mathbf{Y}_3 = \begin{bmatrix} \frac{1}{4} & -\frac{1}{4} \\ -\frac{1}{4} & \frac{9}{4} \end{bmatrix} + \begin{bmatrix} \frac{3}{8} & -\frac{1}{4} \\ -\frac{1}{4} & \frac{3}{4} \end{bmatrix}$$

$$\mathbf{Y}_{eq} = \begin{bmatrix} \frac{5}{8} & -\frac{1}{2} \\ -\frac{1}{2} & 3 \end{bmatrix}$$

- The h-parameter representation is found from Table 18.3. With det $\mathbf{Y}_{eq} = \frac{13}{8}$

$$\mathbf{H} = \begin{bmatrix} \frac{8}{5} & \frac{4}{5} \\ -\frac{4}{5} & \frac{13}{5} \end{bmatrix}$$

CHAPTER 18

SUMMARY

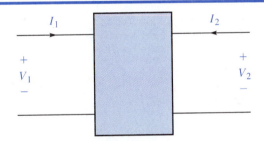

- Two-ports have the following representations and parameters.
  —The impedance parameters are

$$\begin{bmatrix} V_1 \\ V_2 \end{bmatrix} = \mathbf{Z} \begin{bmatrix} I_1 \\ I_2 \end{bmatrix} = \begin{bmatrix} z_{11} & z_{12} \\ z_{21} & z_{22} \end{bmatrix} \begin{bmatrix} I_1 \\ I_2 \end{bmatrix}$$

$$z_{11} = \frac{V_1}{I_1}\bigg|_{I_2=0} \qquad z_{12} = \frac{V_1}{I_2}\bigg|_{I_1=0} \qquad z_{21} = \frac{V_2}{I_1}\bigg|_{I_2=0} \qquad z_{22} = \frac{V_2}{I_2}\bigg|_{I_1=0}$$

  —The admittance parameters are

$$\begin{bmatrix} I_1 \\ I_2 \end{bmatrix} = \mathbf{Y} \begin{bmatrix} V_1 \\ V_2 \end{bmatrix} = \begin{bmatrix} y_{11} & y_{12} \\ y_{21} & y_{22} \end{bmatrix} \begin{bmatrix} V_1 \\ V_2 \end{bmatrix}$$

$$y_{11} = \frac{I_1}{V_1}\bigg|_{V_2=0} \qquad y_{12} = \frac{I_1}{V_2}\bigg|_{V_1=0} \qquad y_{21} = \frac{I_2}{V_1}\bigg|_{V_2=0} \qquad y_{22} = \frac{I_2}{V_2}\bigg|_{V_1=0}$$

  —The transmission parameters are

$$\begin{bmatrix} V_1 \\ I_1 \end{bmatrix} = \mathbf{T} \begin{bmatrix} V_2 \\ -I_2 \end{bmatrix} = \begin{bmatrix} A & B \\ C & D \end{bmatrix} \begin{bmatrix} V_2 \\ -I_2 \end{bmatrix}$$

$$A = \frac{V_1}{V_2}\bigg|_{I_2=0} \qquad B = -\frac{V_1}{I_2}\bigg|_{V_2=0} \qquad C = \frac{I_1}{V_2}\bigg|_{I_2=0} \qquad D = -\frac{I_1}{I_2}\bigg|_{V_2=0}$$

—The inverse transmission parameters are

$$\begin{bmatrix} V_2 \\ I_2 \end{bmatrix} = \mathbf{T}' \begin{bmatrix} V_1 \\ -I_1 \end{bmatrix} = \begin{bmatrix} A' & B' \\ C' & D' \end{bmatrix} \begin{bmatrix} V_1 \\ -I_1 \end{bmatrix}$$

$$A' = \frac{V_2}{V_1}\bigg|_{I_1 = 0} \qquad B' = -\frac{V_2}{I_1}\bigg|_{V_1 = 0} \qquad C' = \frac{I_2}{V_1}\bigg|_{I_1 = 0} \qquad D' = -\frac{I_2}{I_1}\bigg|_{V_1 = 0}$$

—The hybrid parameters are

$$\begin{bmatrix} V_1 \\ I_2 \end{bmatrix} = \mathbf{H} \begin{bmatrix} I_1 \\ V_2 \end{bmatrix} = \begin{bmatrix} h_{11} & h_{12} \\ h_{21} & h_{22} \end{bmatrix} \begin{bmatrix} I_1 \\ V_2 \end{bmatrix}$$

$$h_{11} = \frac{V_1}{I_1}\bigg|_{V_2 = 0} \qquad h_{12} = \frac{V_1}{V_2}\bigg|_{I_1 = 0} \qquad h_{21} = \frac{I_2}{I_1}\bigg|_{V_2 = 0} \qquad h_{22} = \frac{I_2}{V_2}\bigg|_{I_1 = 0}$$

—The inverse hybrid parameters are

$$\begin{bmatrix} I_1 \\ V_2 \end{bmatrix} = \mathbf{G} \begin{bmatrix} V_1 \\ I_2 \end{bmatrix} = \begin{bmatrix} g_{11} & g_{12} \\ g_{21} & g_{22} \end{bmatrix} \begin{bmatrix} V_1 \\ I_2 \end{bmatrix}$$

$$g_{11} = \frac{I_1}{V_1}\bigg|_{I_2 = 0} \qquad g_{12} = \frac{I_1}{I_2}\bigg|_{V_1 = 0} \qquad g_{21} = \frac{V_2}{V_1}\bigg|_{I_2 = 0} \qquad g_{22} = \frac{V_2}{I_2}\bigg|_{V_1 = 0}$$

▪ Three important relationships between the parameters are

$$\mathbf{Z} = \mathbf{Y}^{-1} \qquad \mathbf{G} = \mathbf{H}^{-1} \qquad \mathbf{T}' \neq \mathbf{T}$$

▪ The matrices **Z** and **Y** can be written directly from tee and pi networks:

$$Z_1 = z_{11} - z_{12} = z_{11} - z_{21} \qquad Z_2 = z_{22} - z_{12} = z_{22} - z_{21}$$
$$Z_3 = z_{12} = z_{21}$$

and

$$Y_{12} = -y_{12} = -y_{21} \qquad Y_{23} = y_{22} + y_{12} = y_{22} + y_{21}$$
$$Y_{31} = y_{11} + y_{12} = y_{11} + y_{21}$$

■ The fact that $\mathbf{Y} = \mathbf{Z}^{-1}$ allows for a very efficient method of executing a tee-pi or pi-tee transformation:

From Tee to Pi	*From Pi to Tee*
Use eqs. (18.11) to form $\mathbf{Z}$ from Z_1, Z_2, and Z_3	Use eqs. (18.14) to form $\mathbf{Y}$ from Y_{12}, Y_{23}, and Y_{31}
Obtain $\mathbf{Y} = \mathbf{Z}^{-1}$	Obtain $\mathbf{Z} = \mathbf{Y}^{-1}$
Use eqs. (18.15) to determine Y_{12}, Y_{23}, and Y_{31} from $\mathbf{Y}$	Use eqs. (18.12) to determine Z_1, Z_2, and Z_3 from $\mathbf{Z}$
Take reciprocals to find Z_{12}, Z_{23}, and Z_{31} if necessary	Take reciprocals to find Y_1, Y_2, and Y_3 if necessary

■ Conversions between the parameters are given in Table 18.3.

■ The conditions for reciprocity are

$$y_{12} = y_{21} \qquad z_{12} = z_{21} \qquad h_{12} = -h_{21} \qquad g_{12} = -g_{21}$$

$$\det \mathbf{T} = AD - BC = 1 \qquad \det \mathbf{T}' = A'D' - B'C' = 1$$

■ The conditions for symmetry are

$$z_{11} = z_{22} \qquad y_{11} = y_{22} \qquad A = D \qquad A' = D'$$

$$\det \mathbf{H} = h_{11}h_{22} - h_{12}h_{21} = 1 \qquad \det \mathbf{G} = g_{11}g_{22} - g_{21}g_{22} = 1$$

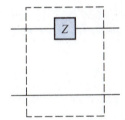 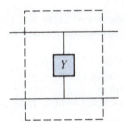

■ There are two two-port representations for single elements.

—The single series element is represented by

$$\mathbf{T}_{se} = \begin{bmatrix} 1 & Z \\ 0 & 1 \end{bmatrix}$$

—The single shunt element is represented by

$$\mathbf{T}_{sh} = \begin{bmatrix} 1 & 0 \\ Y & 1 \end{bmatrix}$$

■ Three algorithms describe the combination of two-ports.

—The cascade algorithm for n two-ports in cascade is

$$\begin{bmatrix} V_{1,1} \\ I_{1,1} \end{bmatrix} = \begin{bmatrix} A_{eq} & B_{eq} \\ C_{eq} & D_{eq} \end{bmatrix} \begin{bmatrix} V_{2,n} \\ -I_{2,n} \end{bmatrix}$$

where

$$\begin{bmatrix} A_{eq} & B_{eq} \\ C_{eq} & D_{eq} \end{bmatrix} = \begin{bmatrix} A_1 & B_1 \\ C_1 & D_1 \end{bmatrix} \begin{bmatrix} A_2 & B_2 \\ C_2 & D_2 \end{bmatrix} \begin{bmatrix} A_3 & B_3 \\ C_3 & D_3 \end{bmatrix} \cdots \begin{bmatrix} A_n & B_n \\ C_n & D_n \end{bmatrix}$$

—The series algorithm for n two-ports in series is

$$\begin{bmatrix} V_1 \\ V_2 \end{bmatrix} = \mathbf{Z}_{eq} \begin{bmatrix} I_1 \\ I_2 \end{bmatrix}$$

where

$$\mathbf{Z}_{eq} = \mathbf{Z}_1 + \mathbf{Z}_2 + \mathbf{Z}_3 + \cdots + \mathbf{Z}_n$$

—The parallel algorithm for n two-ports in parallel is

$$\begin{bmatrix} I_1 \\ I_2 \end{bmatrix} = \mathbf{Y}_{eq} \begin{bmatrix} V_1 \\ V_2 \end{bmatrix}$$

where

$$\mathbf{Y}_{eq} = \mathbf{Y}_1 + \mathbf{Y}_2 + \mathbf{Y}_3 + \cdots + \mathbf{Y}_n$$

Additional Readings

Blackwell, W.A., and L.L. Grigsby. *Introductory Network Theory*. Boston: PWS Engineering, 1985, pp. 193–217.

Bobrow, L.S. *Elementary Linear Circuit Analysis*. 2d ed. New York: Holt, Rinehart and Winston, 1987, pp. 571–588.

Del Toro, V. *Engineering Circuits*. Englewood Cliffs, N. J.: Prentice-Hall, 1987, pp. 479–504.

Hayt, W.H., Jr., and J.E. Kemmerly. *Engineering Circuit Analysis*. 4th ed. New York: McGraw-Hill, 1986, pp. 458–488.

Irwin, J.D. *Basic Engineering Circuit Analysis*. 3d ed. New York: Macmillan, 1989, pp. 683–721.

Johnson, D.E., J.L. Hilburn, and J. R. Johnson. *Basic Electric Circuit Analysis*. 4th ed. Englewood Cliffs, N.J.: Prentice-Hall, 1989, pp. 454–473.

Karni, S. *Applied Circuit Analysis*. New York: Wiley, 1988, pp. 127–143, 523–527.

Madhu, S. *Linear Circuit Analysis*. Englewood Cliffs, N.J.: Prentice-Hall, 1988, pp. 614–653.

Nilsson, J.W. *Electric Circuits*. 3d ed. Reading, Mass.: Addison-Wesley, 1990, pp. 756–779.

Paul, C.R. *Analysis of Linear Circuits*. New York: McGraw-Hill, 1989, pp. 715–753.

PROBLEMS   CHAPTER 18

Section 18.3

18.1 Find the impedance parameter matrix $\mathbf{Z}$ for the network shown in Fig. P18.1.

Figure P18.1

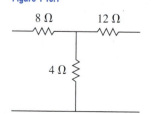

18.2 Find the impedance parameter matrix $\mathbf{Z}$ for the network shown in Fig. P18.2.

Figure P18.2

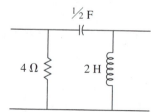

18.3 Find the impedance parameter matrix **Z** for the network shown in Fig. P18.3.

Figure P18.3

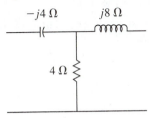

18.4 Find the impedance parameter matrix **Z** for the network shown in Fig. P18.4.

Figure P18.4

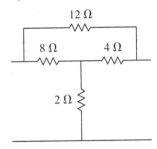

18.5 Find the impedance parameter matrix **Z** for the network shown in Fig. P18.5.

Figure P18.5

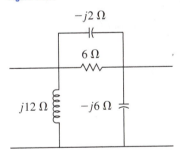

18.6 Find the impedance parameter matrix **Z** for the network shown in Fig. P18.6.

Figure P18.6

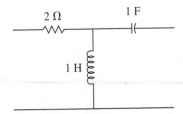

18.7 Find the admittance parameter matrix **Y** for the network shown in Fig. P18.1.

18.8 Find the admittance parameter matrix **Y** for the network shown in Fig. P18.2.

18.9 Find the admittance parameter matrix **Y** for the network shown in Fig. P18.3.

18.10 Find the admittance parameter matrix **Y** for the network shown in Fig. P18.4.

18.11 Find the admittance parameter matrix **Y** for the network shown in Fig. P18.5.

18.12 Find the admittance parameter matrix **Y** for the network shown in Fig. P18.6.

18.13 With regard to Fig. P18.1, show that the admittance parameter matrix **Y**, found in Problem 18.7 is the inverse of the impedance parameter matrix **Z** found in Problem 18.1.

18.14 With regard to Fig. P18.2, show that the admittance parameter matrix **Y** found in Problem 18.8 is the inverse of the impedance parameter matrix **Z** found in Problem 18.2.

18.15 With regard to Fig. P18.3, show that the admittance parameter matrix **Y** found in Problem 18.9 is the inverse of the impedance parameter matrix **Z** found in Problem 18.3.

18.16 With regard to Fig. P18.4, show that the admittance parameter matrix **Y** found in Problem 18.10 is the inverse of the impedance parameter matrix **Z** found in Problem 18.4.

18.17 With regard to Fig. P18.5, show that the admittance parameter matrix **Y** found in Problem 18.11, is the inverse of the impedance parameter matrix **Z** found in Problem 18.5.

18.18 With regard to Fig. P18.6, show that the admittance parameter matrix **Y** found in Problem 18.12 is the inverse of the impedance parameter matrix **Z** found in Problem 18.6.

18.19 Use the results of Problem 18.1 to convert Fig. P18.1 to a pi network.

18.20 Use the results of Problem 18.3 to convert Fig. P18.3 to a pi network.

18.21 Use the results of Problem 18.5 to convert Fig. P18.5 to a pi network.

18.22 Use the results of Problem 18.8 to convert Fig. P18.2 to a tee network.

18.23 Use the results of Problem 18.9 to convert Fig. P18.3 to a tee network.

18.24 Use the results of Problem 18.10 to convert Fig. P18.4 to a tee network.

18.25 Form a pi network from the matrix

$$\mathbf{Y} = \begin{bmatrix} \frac{3}{8} & -\frac{1}{8} \\ -\frac{1}{8} & \frac{1}{3} \end{bmatrix}$$

and then transform it into a tee network.

18.26 Form a pi network from the matrix

$$\mathbf{Y} = \begin{bmatrix} 1-j & -1 \\ -1 & 1+j \end{bmatrix}$$

and then transform it into a tee network.

18.27 Form a tee network from the matrix

$$\mathbf{Z} = \begin{bmatrix} 100 & 60 \\ 60 & 140 \end{bmatrix}$$

and then transform it into a pi network.

Section 18.4

18.28 Find the transmission parameter matrix $\mathbf{T}$ for the network shown in Fig. P18.1.

18.29 Find the transmission parameter matrix $\mathbf{T}$ for the network shown in Fig. P18.2.

18.30 Find the transmission parameter matrix $\mathbf{T}$ for the network shown in Fig. P18.3.

18.31 Find the transmission parameter matrix $\mathbf{T}$ for the network shown in Fig. P18.4.

18.32 Find the transmission parameter matrix $\mathbf{T}$ for the network shown in Fig. P18.5.

18.33 Find the transmission parameter matrix $\mathbf{T}$ for the network shown in Fig. P18.6.

18.34 Find the inverse transmission parameter matrix $\mathbf{T}'$ for the network shown in Fig. P18.1.

18.35 Find the inverse transmission parameter matrix $\mathbf{T}'$ for the network shown in Fig. P18.2.

18.36 Find the inverse transmission parameter matrix $\mathbf{T}'$ for the network shown in Fig. P18.3.

18.37 Find the inverse transmission parameter matrix $\mathbf{T}'$ for the network shown in Fig. P18.4.

18.38 Find the inverse transmission parameter matrix $\mathbf{T}'$ for the network shown in Fig. P18.5.

18.39 Find the inverse transmission parameter matrix $\mathbf{T}'$ for the network shown in Fig. P18.6.

Section 18.5

18.40 Find the hybrid parameter matrix $\mathbf{H}$ for the network shown in Fig. P18.1.

18.41 Find the hybrid parameter matrix $\mathbf{H}$ for the network shown in Fig. P18.2.

18.42 Find the hybrid parameter matrix $\mathbf{H}$ for the network shown in Fig. P18.3.

18.43 Find the hybrid parameter matrix $\mathbf{H}$ for the network shown in Fig. P18.4.

18.44 Find the hybrid parameter matrix $\mathbf{H}$ for the network shown in Fig. P18.5.

18.45 Find the hybrid parameter matrix $\mathbf{H}$ for the network shown in Fig. P18.6.

18.46 Find the inverse hybrid parameter matrix $\mathbf{G}$ for the network shown in Fig. P18.1.

18.47 Find the inverse hybrid parameter matrix $\mathbf{G}$ for the network shown in Fig. P18.2.

18.48 Find the inverse hybrid parameter matrix $\mathbf{G}$ for the network shown in Fig. P18.3.

18.49 Find the inverse hybrid parameter matrix $\mathbf{G}$ for the network shown in Fig. P18.4.

18.50 Find the inverse hybrid parameter matrix $\mathbf{G}$ for the network shown in Fig. P18.5.

18.51 Find the inverse hybrid parameter matrix $\mathbf{G}$ for the network shown in Fig. P18.6.

Section 18.6

18.52 Find $\mathbf{Y}$, $\mathbf{T}$, $\mathbf{T}'$, $\mathbf{H}$, and $\mathbf{G}$ if

$$\mathbf{Z} = \begin{bmatrix} 120 & 80 \\ 80 & 240 \end{bmatrix}$$

18.53 Find $\mathbf{Z}$, $\mathbf{T}$, $\mathbf{T}'$, $\mathbf{H}$, and $\mathbf{G}$ if

$$\mathbf{Y} = \begin{bmatrix} \left(\frac{1}{2} + j\frac{1}{2}\right) & -\frac{\sqrt{2}}{2} \\ -\frac{\sqrt{2}}{2} & \left(\frac{1}{2} + j\frac{1}{2}\right) \end{bmatrix}$$

18.54 Find $\mathbf{Z}$, $\mathbf{Y}$, $\mathbf{T}'$, $\mathbf{H}$, and $\mathbf{G}$ if

$$\mathbf{T} = \begin{bmatrix} 5 & 8 \\ 8 & 13 \end{bmatrix}$$

18.55 Find $\mathbf{Z}$, $\mathbf{Y}$, $\mathbf{T}$, $\mathbf{T}'$, and $\mathbf{G}$ if

$$\mathbf{H} = \begin{bmatrix} \dfrac{s^2 + s + 1}{s^2 + 1} & \dfrac{1}{s^2 + 1} \\ -\dfrac{1}{s^2 + 1} & \dfrac{s}{s^2 + 4} \end{bmatrix}$$

18.56 Find **Z**, **Y**, **T**, **T′**, and **H** if

$$\mathbf{G} = \begin{bmatrix} 22 & -\frac{2}{5} \\ \frac{2}{5} & \frac{1}{50} \end{bmatrix}$$

Section 18.6

18.57 Prove that the network in Fig. P18.1 is reciprocal and not symmetrical.

18.58 Prove that the network in Fig. P18.2 is reciprocal and not symmetrical.

18.59 Prove that the network in Fig. P18.3 is reciprocal and not symmetrical.

18.60 Prove that the network in Fig. P18.4 is reciprocal and not symmetrical.

Section 18.8

18.61 What is the z parameter representation for the network in Fig. P18.7?

Figure P18.7

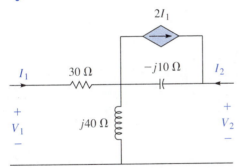

18.62 Show that the transistor model in Fig. P18.8 satisfies eqs. (18.23) which are in terms of the h-parameters.

Figure P18.8

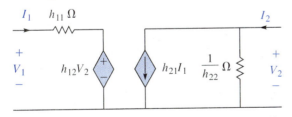

18.63 Represent the two-port network in Fig. P18.9 as a tee network, and determine whether the tee network is reciprocal.

Figure P18.9

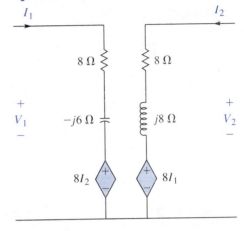

18.64 What is the y parameter representation for the network in Fig. P18.10?

Figure P18.10

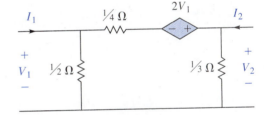

18.65 What are the z parameters for the op-amp configuration in Fig. P18.11?

Figure P18.11

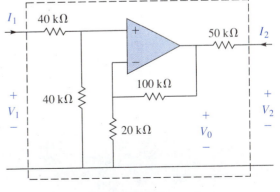

(b)

18.66 The two-port network in Fig. P18.12 represents a high-frequency equivalent for the bipolar junction transistor at $\omega = 4 \times 10^9$ rad/s. What is the z parameter representation for this equivalent?

Figure P18.12

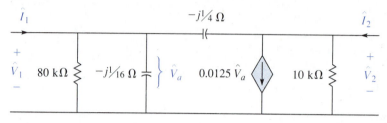

Section 18.10

18.67 Figure P18.13 shows two two-ports in parallel. What is the g parameter representation?

Figure P18.13

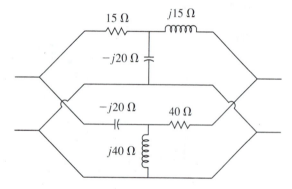

18.68 What is the $ABCD$ parameter representation for the network in Fig. P18.14?

Figure P18.14

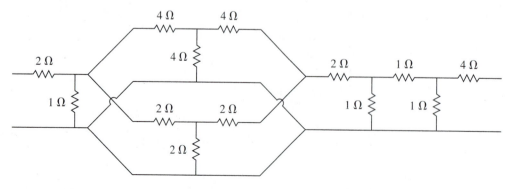

18.69 What value of R will make the input resistance
$R_{in} = R$ in the network in Fig. P18.15?

Figure P18.15

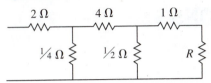

18.70 The arrangement of resistors shown in Fig.
P18.16 consists of a pair of cascaded tee networks
in parallel with another pair of cascaded tee networks. Find the y parameters.

Figure P18.16

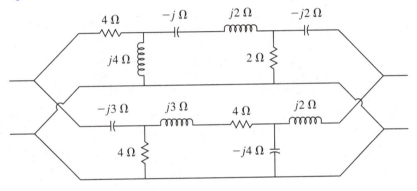

18.71 The arrangement of impedances shown in Fig.
P18.17 consists of a pair of cascaded tee networks
in parallel with another pair of cascaded tee networks. Find the y parameters.

Figure P18.17

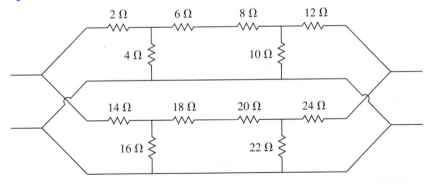

19

TRANSFER FUNCTIONS

OBJECTIVES

The objectives of this chapter are to:

- Introduce and become familiar with the concept of the transfer function.

- Show how the natural response of a network may be obtained from the network functions of impedance and admittance.

- Define the *poles* and *zeros* of the transfer function, examine the behavior of the transfer function at its poles and zeros, and show how the response of the system depends upon the s plane location of the poles and zeros.

- Consider the transfer functions that pertain to two-port networks, input impedance and admittance, voltage gain, current gain, and transfer admittance.

- Indicate the effect of terminating impedances on the voltage gain of two-port networks.

- Use passive filter structures to illustrate practical applications of transfer functions.

SECTION 19.1   **INTRODUCTION**

The concept of a linear system was considered as far back as Section 1.5 in Chapter 1. There it was proposed that if a system or network such as the one shown in Fig. 1.5 (repeated here as Fig. 19.1a) is excited by an input $e(t)$, an output $r(t)$ would be produced. Moreover, the system was (and is) considered to be linear if it satisfies certain conditions known as the *homogeneity* and *superposition* conditions. As the study progressed, these conditions for linearity were enhanced with the idea of certain types of linearity, and in Section 6.3.2, the notions of *zero-state linearity* and *zero-input linearity* were considered.

It also became apparent that outputs or responses in the s domain are algebraically related to inputs or excitations in the s domain. It appears logical, therefore, to propose a *transfer function* as the ratio of the Laplace transform of the output or response $R(s)$ to the Laplace transform of the input or excitation $E(s)$. Thus,

FIGURE 19.1

(a) A system in the time domain with excitation $e(t)$ and response $r(t)$ and
(b) the system in the s domain, where the system is characterized by the transfer
function $H(s)$

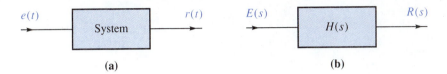

(a)   **(b)**

$H(s) = R(s)/E(s)$, or, as a *linear transformation* in the s domain between excitation and response,

$$R(s) = H(s)E(s) \tag{19.1}$$

Here, $H(s)$, which is shown in Fig. 19.1b, is called the *network function* or *transfer function* and $R(s)$ represents the zero-state response of the network due to the excitation $E(s)$.

THE NETWORK OR TRANSFER FUNCTION

SECTION 19.2

The transfer function plays an important role in the analysis and synthesis of physical systems, in general, and electric networks, in particular. In general, the transfer function will be represented as the quotient of two polynomials in s,

$$H(s) = \frac{P(s)}{Q(s)} = K \frac{b_m s^m + b_{m-1} s^{m-1} + b_{m-2} s^{m-2} + \cdots + b_1 s + b_0}{a_n s^n + a_{n-1} s^{n-1} + a_{n-2} s^{n-2} + \cdots + a_1 s + a_0} \tag{19.2}$$

where K is a constant. Notice that the polynomial $P(s)$ is of mth order and the polynomial $Q(s)$ is of nth order, and the elimination of particular output or response components for a particular excitation or input may place some restrictions on the values of m and n. For example, if impulses applied as input are not to be present in the output $r(t)$, then as discussed in section 15.9 it would be required that $m < n$.

Transfer functions, which are frequently referred to as *network functions*, can take many forms and can apply to a single pair of terminals, as in a one-port, or to two pairs of terminals, as in a two-port. In the former case, they represent the input impedance or admittance. For example, the s domain input impedance for the one-port in Fig. 19.2a is

$$Z(s) = L \frac{s^2 + (1/RC)s + 1/LC}{s + 1/RC} \text{ ohms}$$

and the input admittance is the reciprocal of $Z(s)$,

$$Y(s) = \frac{1}{L} \cdot \frac{s + 1/RC}{s^2 + (1/RC)s + 1/LC} \text{ ohms}$$

For two ports the transfer functions may represent voltage or current transfer ratios as well as driving-point impedances. For example in Fig. 19.2b, one may identify

FIGURE 19.2   (a) One-port and (b) two-port networks

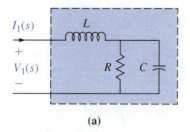
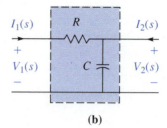

two driving-point impedances

$$Z_1(s) = \left.\frac{V_1(s)}{I_1(s)}\right|_{I_2(s)=0} = R\,\frac{s+1/RC}{s}\ \text{ohms} \quad \text{and} \quad Z_2(s) = \left.\frac{V_2(s)}{I_2(s)}\right|_{I_1(s)=0} = \frac{1}{Cs}\ \text{ohms}$$

The two driving-point admittances, are

$$Y_1(s) = \left.\frac{I_1(s)}{V_1(s)}\right|_{I_2(s)=0} = \frac{1}{R}\cdot\frac{s}{s+1/RC}\ \text{mhos} \quad \text{and} \quad Y_2(s) = \left.\frac{I_2(s)}{V_2(s)}\right|_{I_1(s)=0} = Cs\ \text{mhos}$$

and the two voltage transfer ratios or gains, which are truly transfer functions,

$$\alpha_{12}(s) = \left.\frac{V_2(s)}{V_1(s)}\right|_{I_2(s)=0} = \frac{1/RC}{s+1/RC} \quad \text{and} \quad \alpha_{21}(s) = \left.\frac{V_1(s)}{V_2(s)}\right|_{I_1(s)=0} = 1$$

The transfer function possesses considerable utility when one considers networks with multiple inputs in which the output is obtained, in a linear system, from a super-position of the effects of each input. Furthermore, the concept of the transfer function pertains to the input/output zero-state response characteristics of the linear system.

Now, once again, consider eq. (19.1), and observe that for a direct-current input, $s = 0$ and $H(s) = H$, a constant. In this case, there is no need to be in the s domain at all, and eq. (19.1) reduces to

$$r(t) = He(t)$$

But if the input to the system is sinusoidal, $s = j\omega$, and if the steady state response is desired, eq. (19.1) becomes

$$R(j\omega) = H(j\omega)E(j\omega)$$

In this case, $E(j\omega)$ and $R(j\omega)$ become the phasors $\hat{E}$ and $\hat{R}$, and the transfer function must be represented as a complex number,

$$H(j\omega) = |H(j\omega)|\,\underline{/\theta(j\omega)}$$

and if $\hat{E} = E\underline{/\alpha}$, then

$$\hat{R} = H\hat{E} = (|H|\underline{/\theta})E\underline{/\alpha} = R\underline{/\phi}$$

where $R = |H|E$ and where $\phi = \theta + \alpha$. Here, $|H(j\omega)|$ is called the magnitude or the *gain* of the transfer function, and $\theta(j\omega)$ is called the *phase* of the transfer function.

FIGURE 19.3

Simple RL network

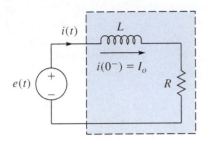

Observe that both of these are frequency-dependent; that is, they vary as the frequency varies.

It is a fact that the response of most physical systems to sinusoidal (harmonic) inputs will vary with the frequency of the forcing function. In some instances, this behavior is desirable and is often a design requirement. In other instances, this response is undesirable, although it must be accepted. Thus, the variation of the gain and phase of the system or network transfer function as a function of frequency becomes most important in many of the engineering disciplines, and the engineer must learn to predict the response of physical systems to harmonic inputs and to thoroughly understand why the output behavior is a function of frequency. An introduction to this subject is presented in Chapter 20.

In the simple RL network represented as a one-port, as shown in Fig. 19.3, suppose that $e(t)$, the excitation or forcing function, is a voltage $v(t)$, and that the current, $i(t) = r(t)$, is the desired response. The differential equation for the current response will be

$$L\frac{di}{dt} + Ri = v(t)$$

and the solution for the current will depend on the initial value of the current, $i(0^-) = I_0$. When the differential equation is transformed term by term, the result is

$$L[sI(s) - I_0] + RI(s) = V(s)$$

And after some algebra, $I(s)$ can be shown to be

$$I(s) = \frac{V(s)}{Ls + R} + \frac{LI_0}{Ls + R} \tag{19.3}$$

which shows that only one term is in the form of eq. (19.1), which relates the response transform $I(s)$ to the excitation transform $V(s)$. Here, $H(s)$ clearly represents an admittance

$$H(s) = Y(s) = \frac{1}{Ls + R}$$

Although this admittance does appear in the second term of eq. (19.3), this term does not fit the definition of eq. (19.1) because it does not contain the excitation or forcing function $V(s)$.

This simple example shows that the transfer function $H(s)$ is related to the response of the network corresponding to zero initial conditions. That is, $H(s)$ is the Laplace transform of the solution of the nonhomogeneous network differential equation with the initial conditions set equal to zero. Thus, $H(s)$ is derived from the network excitation. The example also demonstrates, however, that the transfer function, $H(s)$, is related to the source free or natural response associated with arbitrary initial conditions that have nothing to do with the characteristics of the network.

If the excitation or input is the unit impulse $\delta(t)$, then because

$$\mathscr{L}[\delta(t)] = 1$$

the output will be the zero-state response to the unit impulse $R(s) = H(s)$. In the time domain, this response is given by

$$h(t) = \mathscr{L}^{-1}[H(s)]$$

and because it is the time domain response to a unit impulse, $h(t)$ is called the *unit impulse response*.

SECTION 19.3   POLES AND ZEROS

In general, a network differential equation with $e(t)$ as the forcing function and $r(t)$ as the response can be written as

$$a_n \frac{d^n r}{dt^n} + a_{n-1} \frac{d^{n-1} r}{dt^{n-1}} + \cdots + a_1 \frac{dr}{dt} + a_0 r$$

$$= b_m \frac{d^m e}{dt^m} + b_{m-1} \frac{d^{m-1} e}{dt^{m-1}} + \cdots + b_1 \frac{de}{dt} + b_0 e \tag{19.4}$$

where the a's and b's are constants.

If $e(t) = E e^{st}$, the zero-state response $r(t)$ will have the same form. Hence, $r(t) = R e^{st}$; and after substitution of these into eq. (19.4), the result is

$$(a_n s^n + a_{n-1} s^{n-1} + \cdots + a_1 s + a_0) R e^{st}$$

$$= (b_m s^m + b_{m-1} s^{m-1} + \cdots + b_1 s + b_0) E e^{st}$$

After cancellation of the common e^{st} terms and a division, the result, with $K = R/E$, is

$$H(s) = \frac{P(s)}{Q(s)} = K \frac{b_m s^m + b_{m-1} s^{m-1} + \cdots + b_1 s + b_0}{a_n s^n + a_{n-1} s^{n-1} + \cdots + a_1 s + a_0} \tag{19.5}$$

If a_n and b_m are factored from eq. (19.5) and then incorporated into $K (K' = K b_m/a_n)$, $H(s)$ becomes

$$H(s) = \frac{P(s)}{Q(s)} = K' \frac{(s - s_{1z})(s - s_{2z})(s - s_{3z}) \cdots (s - s_{mz})}{(s - s_{1p})(s - s_{2p})(s - s_{3p}) \cdots (s - s_{np})} \tag{19.6}$$

Here, the roots of $P(s) = 0$ with subscript z are called the *zeros of the transfer function*, and the roots of $Q(s) = 0$ with subscript p are referred to as the *poles of the transfer function*. Once again, it is emphasized that the transfer function is the ratio of the Laplace transform of the *zero-state* response to the Laplace transform of the excitation.

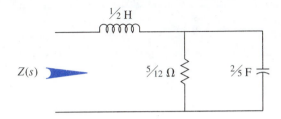

POLES AND ZEROS IN THE s-PLANE

SECTION 19.4

The driving-point impedance obtained for the network in Fig. 9.2 (repeated here as Fig. 19.4) for Example 9.1 in Section 9.3,

$$Z(s) = \frac{1}{2}\left(\frac{s^2 + 6s + 5}{s + 6}\right)$$

is a transfer function that relates the s domain input current $I(s)$, to the s domain output voltage $V(s)$ in the form of eq. (19.5) and it can be represented as combinations of factors, as in eq. (19.6),

$$H(s) = \frac{P(s)}{Q(s)} = K\frac{(s - s_{1z})(s - s_{2z})(s - s_{3z})\cdots(s - s_{mz})}{(s - s_{1p})(s - s_{2p})(s - s_{3p})\cdots(s - s_{np})} \qquad (19.6)$$

where $K = \frac{1}{2}$ and where $s_{1z}, s_{2z}, s_{3z}, \ldots, s_{mz}$ represent the roots of $P(s) = 0$. The subscript z suggests that these roots cause the transfer function to become zero, and this is why these roots are referred to as the *zeros* of the transfer function.

The roots of $Q(s) = 0$ are $s_{1p}, s_{2p}, s_{3p}, \ldots, s_{np}$ and are designated with the subscript p. It is these roots that cause $H(s)$ to become unbounded. This is why the roots of the denominator polynomial $Q(s)$ are called the *poles* of the transfer function.[1]

The pole-zero concept is an invaluable aid to the network analyst and carries with it many implications regarding natural and forced responses, stability, and the synthesis of networks. It is important to note that because $H(s)$ is the Laplace transform of the unit impulse response, the characteristic equation of the network is $Q(s) = 0$. The roots of the characteristic equation—namely, the poles of the transfer function—will determine the form of the response.

■ **EXAMPLE 19.1**

For the transfer function

$$Z(s) = \frac{1}{2}\left(\frac{s^2 + 6s + 5}{s + 6}\right)$$

find the poles and zeros, and plot them on the s plane.

Solution   In accordance with eq. (19.5)

$$P(s) = s^2 + 6s + 5$$

---

[1] The roots of $Q(s) = 0$ are often called the zeros of $Q(s)$ because they make $Q(s) = 0$. They are, however, the poles of the transfer function $H(s)$.

FIGURE 19.5

(a) The pole-zero diagram for the transfer function in Example 19.1 and (b) a plot of the magnitude of the transfer function for real values of s

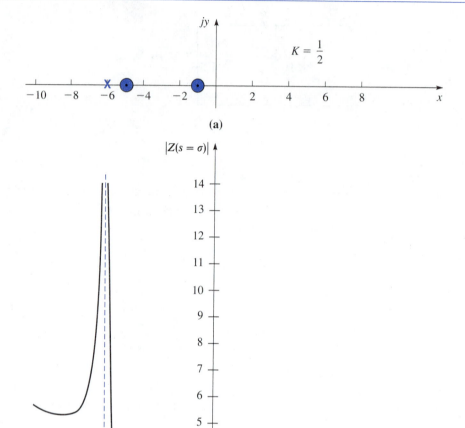

(a)

(b)

which has two roots, $s = -1$ and $s = -5$. These roots are the zeros of $H(s)$. The monomial

$$Q(s) = s + 6$$

has a single root, $s = -6$, which is a pole of $H(s)$. The s plane plot of the poles and zeros of $H(s)$ is called the pole-zero diagram and is shown in Fig. 19.5a, where it may be observed that poles are indicated by a large X and zeros are indicated by circles.

The magnitude of $H(s)$ as a function of $s = \sigma + j\omega$

FIGURE 19.6

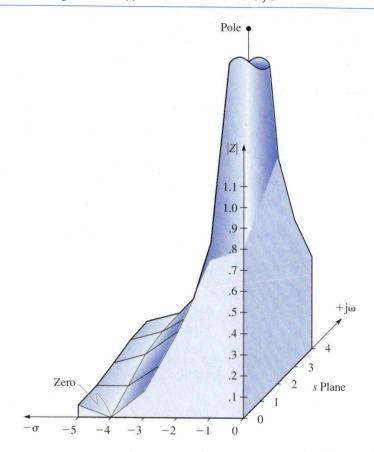

A plot of the magnitude of $Z(s)$ is presented for real values of s in Fig. 19.5b. Observe that the dashed line at $s = -6$ is an asymptote and that at $s = -6$, the magnitude of $Z(s)$, is unbounded. This figure and others like it for other transfer functions may have been the origin of the nomenclature *poles* and *zeros*.

Because the polynomial equations $Q(s) = 0$ and $P(s) = 0$, which derive from the polynomials $Q(s)$ and $P(s)$ in eq. (19.5), may possess complex conjugate roots of the form $s = \sigma \pm j\omega$, a plot of the magnitude of $H(s)$ will, in general, be a function of the real and imaginary parts of s. Such a plot, that for

$$H(s) = \frac{s+4}{s^2 + 2s + 5}$$

is shown in Fig. 19.6. Observe that the contour resembles a rubber sheet, which seems to tend to puncture due to the infinitely high poles propping it up at $s = -1 \pm j2$ and which appears to be tacked down at the single zero ($s = -4 + j0 = -4$). This idea is sometimes referred to as the *rubber-sheet analogy* and may also have had an impact on the *pole* and *zero* nomenclature.

EXERCISE 19.1

If the driving-point impedance of a network is

$$Z(s) = \frac{s^2 + 7s + 10}{s^2 + 4s + 3} \text{ ohms}$$

Find all of the poles and zeros.

Answer   Poles at $s = -1$ and $s = -3$; and zeros at $s = -2$ and $s = -5$.

SECTION 19.5   **TERMINATED TWO-PORTS AND THEIR TRANSFER FUNCTIONS**

The transfer function, as has been observed pertains to a linear system and is the ratio of the output or response function to the input or source function. The input, output, and transfer functions are usually specified in the s domain.

As indicated in a specific example in Section 19.2, there is a single transfer function for the one-port network. This is the input impedance

$$H(s) = Z(s) = \frac{V(s)}{I(s)}$$

where $V(s)$ is considered as the output function and $I(s)$ is considered as the input function. The transfer function $Z(s)$ has a reciprocal, the input admittance

$$Y(s) = \frac{1}{Z(s)} = \frac{I(s)}{V(s)}$$

and both of these functions are known as *driving-point immittances*. When dc networks are considered, $s = 0$, $Z = V/I$, and $Y = I/V$. For ac networks where $s = j\omega$, the driving-point impedance will possess a magnitude $|Z(j\omega)|$ and a phase $\theta(j\omega)$,

$$Z(j\omega) = |Z(j\omega)| \underline{/\theta(j\omega)} = \frac{\hat{V}}{\hat{I}}$$

where $\hat{V}$ and $\hat{I}$ are voltage and current phasors. Notice that neither $Z(j\omega)$ nor its reciprocal $Y(j\omega)$ are phasors.

Section 19.2 shows that two-port networks possess many more transfer functions. There is, of course, the input impedance at either port when no load $Z(s)$ is attached at the output port:

$$Z_{11}(s) = \frac{V_1(s)}{I_1(s)}\bigg|_{I_2(s) = 0} \quad \text{and} \quad Z_{22}(s) = \frac{V_2(s)}{I_2(s)}\bigg|_{I_1(s) = 0}$$

These have their reciprocals, which are the admittances at either port; in addition, there are several other possibilities.

The forward and backward voltage transfer ratios, which are often called the forward and backward voltage gains, are

$$\alpha_{12}(s) = \frac{V_2(s)}{V_1(s)}\bigg|_{I_2(s) = 0} \quad \text{and} \quad \alpha_{21}(s) = \frac{V_1(s)}{V_2(s)}\bigg|_{I_1(s) = 0}$$

A two-port network with a load $Z_0(s)$ at port 2

FIGURE 19.7

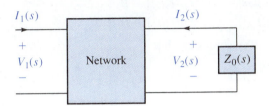

In addition, these are the forward and backward current gains are

$$\beta_{12}(s) = \frac{I_2(s)}{I_1(s)}\bigg|_{V_2(s)=0} \quad \text{and} \quad \beta_{21}(s) = \frac{I_1(s)}{I_2(s)}\bigg|_{V_1(s)=0}$$

19.5.1 The Effect of Terminating Impedance

The foregoing transfer functions for the two-port are interesting, but attention is usually focused on the transfer functions that are obtained when port 2 is loaded with an impedance $Z_0(s)$, as shown in Fig. 19.7. In this case, the four transfer functions of greatest interest are the input impedance (in ohms),

$$Z_{11}(s) = \frac{V_1(s)}{I_1(s)} \tag{19.7}$$

the forward voltage transfer or voltage gain,

$$\alpha_{12}(s) = \frac{V_2(s)}{V_1(s)} \tag{19.8}$$

the forward current transfer or current gain,

$$\beta_{12}(s) = \frac{I_2(s)}{I_1(s)} \tag{19.9}$$

and the output current–to–input voltage transfer (in mhos),

$$Y_{12}(s) = \frac{I_2(s)}{V_1(s)} \tag{19.10}$$

In Fig. 19.7, the subscript zero is used for the load so that capacitive loads as well as inductive loads can be considered.

Any set if parameters along with Table 18.3 may be employed to develop a set of relationships for these transfer functions. For the **T** matrix,

$$V_1(s) = AV_2(s) - BI_2(s) \tag{a}$$

$$I_1(s) = CV_2(s) - DI_2(s) \tag{b}$$

$$V_2(s) = -Z_0(s)I_2(s) \tag{c}$$

where the parameters themselves are functions of s. To obtain $Z_{11}(s)$, divide eq. (a) by eq. (b):

$$Z_{11}(s) = \frac{V_1(s)}{I_1(s)} = \frac{AV_2(s) - BI_2(s)}{CV_2(s) - DI_2(s)} = \frac{A[V_2(s)/I_2(s)] - B}{C[V_2(s)/I_2(s)] - D}$$

But $Z_0(s) = -V_2(s)/I_2(s)$, as indicated by eq. (c), so that

$$Z_{11}(s) = \frac{AZ_0(s) + B}{CZ_0(s) + D} \tag{19.11}$$

One may work with Table 18.3 to obtain $Z_{11}(s)$ in terms of all the other parameters. For example, $Z_{11}(s)$ may be determined in terms of the z parameters:

$$Z_{11}(s) = \frac{z_{11}Z_0(s) + z_{11}z_{22} - z_{12}z_{21}}{Z_0(s) + z_{22}} = \frac{z_{11}[Z_0(s) + z_{22}] - z_{12}z_{21}}{Z_0(s) + z_{22}}$$

or

$$Z_{11}(s) = z_{11} - \frac{z_{12}z_{21}}{Z_0(s) + z_{22}} \tag{19.12}$$

The algebra is laborious, and no useful purpose will be served if all of the details for the evaluation of the four important transfer functions in terms of the six two-port parameters are provided. Table 19.1 contains an organized summary.

TABLE 19.1   Transfer Function Summary

	$Z_{11}(s)$	$\alpha_{12}(s)$	$\beta_{12}(s)$	$Y_{12}(s)$
Z	$z_{11} - \dfrac{z_{12}z_{21}}{Z_0(s) + z_{22}}$	$\dfrac{z_{21}Z_0(s)}{z_{11}Z_0(s) + \Delta_Z}$	$-\dfrac{z_{21}}{Z_0(s) + z_{22}}$	$-\dfrac{z_{21}}{z_{11}Z_0(s) + \Delta_Z}$
Y	$\dfrac{1}{y_{11} - \dfrac{y_{12}y_{21}Z_0(s)}{y_{22}Z_0(s) + 1}}$	$-\dfrac{y_{21}Z_0(s)}{1 + y_{22}Z_0(s)}$	$\dfrac{y_{21}}{\Delta_Y Z_0(s) + y_{11}}$	$\dfrac{y_{21}}{1 + y_{22}Z_0(s)}$
T	$\dfrac{AZ_0(s) + B}{CZ_0(s) + D}$	$\dfrac{Z_0(s)}{AZ_0(s) + B}$	$-\dfrac{1}{CZ_0(s) + D}$	$-\dfrac{1}{AZ_0(s) + B}$
T'	$\dfrac{D'Z_0(s) + B'}{C'Z_0(s) + A'}$	$\dfrac{\Delta_{T'}Z_0(s)}{D'Z_0(s) + B'}$	$-\dfrac{\Delta_{T'}}{C'Z_0(s) + A'}$	$-\dfrac{\Delta_{T'}}{D'Z_0(s) + B'}$
H	$h_{11} - \dfrac{h_{12}h_{21}Z_0(s)}{1 + h_{22}Z_0(s)}$	$-\dfrac{h_{21}Z_0(s)}{\Delta_H Z_0(s) + h_{11}}$	$\dfrac{h_{21}}{h_{22}Z_0(s) + 1}$	$\dfrac{h_{21}}{\Delta_H Z_0(s) + h_{11}}$
G	$\dfrac{1}{g_{11} - \dfrac{g_{12}g_{21}}{Z_0(s) + g_{22}}}$	$\dfrac{g_{21}Z_0(s)}{Z_0(s) + g_{22}}$	$-\dfrac{g_{21}}{g_{11}Z_0(s) + \Delta_G}$	$-\dfrac{g_{21}}{Z_0(s) + g_{12}}$

$$\Delta_Z = z_{11}z_{22} - z_{12}z_{21} \qquad \Delta_{T'} = A'D' - B'C'$$
$$\Delta_Y = y_{11}y_{22} - y_{12}y_{21} \qquad \Delta_H = h_{11}h_{22} - h_{12}h_{21}$$
$$\Delta_T = AD - BC \qquad \Delta_G = g_{11}g_{22} - g_{12}g_{21}$$

■ **EXAMPLE 19.2**

For the two-port network and its load shown in Fig. 19.8a, with $\hat{V}_1 = 50\underline{/0°}$ and $f = 1000/2\pi$ Hz, determine the phasor domain quantities $\hat{I}_1$, $\hat{I}_2$, and $\hat{V}_2$.

Solution   With $f = 1000/2\pi$ Hz,

$$\omega = 2\pi f = 2\pi\left(\frac{1000}{2\pi}\right) = 1000 \text{ rad/s}$$

Then,

$$X_L = \omega L = 1000(0.004) = 4 \text{ Ω}$$

$$X_C = \frac{1}{\omega C} = \frac{1}{1000(500 \times 10^{-6})} = 2 \text{ Ω}$$

The impedance of the load is

$$Z(j\omega) = 2 + j(1000)(0.002) = 2 + j2 \text{ Ω}$$

and the phasor domain network is shown in Fig. 19.8b.

(a) A two-port with its load and (b) the two-port in the phasor domain

FIGURE 19.8

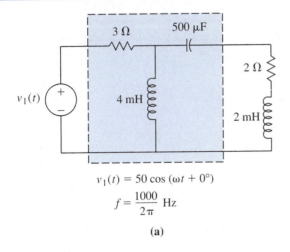

$$v_1(t) = 50 \cos (\omega t + 0°)$$

$$f = \frac{1000}{2\pi} \text{ Hz}$$

(a)

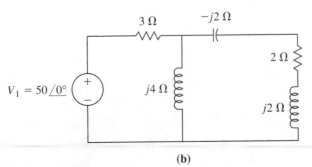

(b)

For the two-port containing the tee network, eqs. (18.11) show that

$$Z = \begin{bmatrix} 3 + j4 & j4 \\ j4 & j2 \end{bmatrix} = \begin{bmatrix} 5\underline{/53.13^\circ} & 4\underline{/90^\circ} \\ 4\underline{/90^\circ} & 2\underline{/90^\circ} \end{bmatrix}$$

The strategy is to determine $Z_{11}(j\omega)$ and then, because $\hat{V}_1$ is known, obtain $\hat{I}_1$ from

$$\hat{I}_1 = \frac{\hat{V}_1}{Z_{11}(j\omega)}$$

After the value of $\hat{I}_1$ has been obtained, the voltage transfer ratio can be used to find $\hat{V}_2$,

$$\hat{V}_2 = \alpha_{12}(j\omega)\hat{V}_1$$

The final step will be to determine $\hat{I}_2$ from

$$\hat{I}_2 = -\hat{V}_2/Z_0(j\omega)$$

From Table 19.1 with $Z_0(s) = Z_0(j\omega) = 2 + j2\ \Omega$,

$$Z_{11}(j\omega) = z_{11} - \frac{z_{12}z_{21}}{Z_0(j\omega) + z_{22}} = 3 + j4 - \frac{(j4)(j4)}{2 + j2 + j2}$$

$$= 3 + j4 - \frac{-16}{4.47\underline{/63.43^\circ}} = 3 + j4 + 3.58\underline{/-63.13^\circ}$$

$$= 3 + j4 + 1.60 - j3.20 = 4.60 + j0.8 = 4.67\underline{/9.87^\circ}\ \Omega$$

Then,

$$\hat{I}_1 = \frac{\hat{V}_1}{Z_{11}(j\omega)} = \frac{50\underline{/0^\circ}}{4.67\underline{/9.87^\circ}} = 10.71\underline{/-9.87^\circ}\ A$$

The voltage transfer ratio is obtained from Table 19.1, using the z parameters. First,

$$\det Z = \Delta_Z = (3 + j4)(j2) - (j4)(j4) = -8 + j6 + 16 = 8 + j6$$
$$= 10\underline{/36.87^\circ}$$

and then,

$$\alpha_{12}(j\omega) = \frac{z_{21}Z_0(j\omega)}{z_{11}Z_0(j\omega) + \Delta_Z} = \frac{j4(2 + j2)}{(3 + j4)(2 + j2) + 8 + j6}$$

$$= \frac{-8 + j8}{-2 + j14 + 8 + j6} = \frac{-8 + j8}{6 + j20} = \frac{8\sqrt{2}\underline{/135^\circ}}{20.88\underline{/73.30^\circ}}$$

$$= 0.54\underline{/61.70^\circ}$$

The voltage $\hat{V}_2$ is

$$\hat{V}_2 = \alpha_{12}(j\omega)\hat{V}_1 = (0.54\underline{/61.70°})(50\underline{/0°}) = 27.09\underline{/61.70°} \text{ V}$$

Finally, the current at port 2 will be

$$\hat{I}_2 = -\hat{V}_2/Z_0(j\omega) = -\frac{27.09\underline{/61.70°}}{2+j2} = -\frac{27.09\underline{/61.70°}}{2\sqrt{2}\underline{/45°}}$$
$$= 9.58\underline{/-163.30°} \text{ A} \qquad \blacksquare$$

19.5.2 The Effect of Generator Mismatch

The two-port in Fig. 19.9 has a terminating impedance, $Z_0(s)$, and is driven by a voltage generator with internal impedance $Z_g(s)$. The composite voltage gain between generator and load is given by

$$K_V(s) = \frac{V_0(s)}{V_g(s)} \qquad (19.13)$$

and unless, $V_g(s) = 0$, the composite voltage gain will not equal the voltage gain $\alpha_{12}(s)$. Notice that with $\alpha_{12}(s) = V_2(s)/V_1(s)$

$$K_V(s) = \frac{V_0(s)}{V_g(s)} = \frac{V_1(s)}{V_g(s)} \cdot \frac{V_2(s)}{V_1(s)} = \frac{V_1(s)}{V_g(s)}\alpha_{12}(s) \qquad (19.14)$$

and that $K_V(s)$ can be obtained from a modification of $\alpha_{12}(s)$ or from a cascade of $ABCD$-matrices.

Refer to Fig. 19.9 and form an equivalent $ABCD$-matrix for $Z_g(s)$ and the two port

$$\begin{bmatrix} V_g(s) \\ I_g(s) \end{bmatrix} = \begin{bmatrix} 1 & Z_g(s) \\ 0 & 1 \end{bmatrix}\begin{bmatrix} A & B \\ C & D \end{bmatrix}\begin{bmatrix} V_2(s) \\ -I_2(s) \end{bmatrix}$$
$$= \begin{bmatrix} A + CZ_g(s) & B + DZ_g(s) \\ C & D \end{bmatrix}\begin{bmatrix} V_2(s) \\ -I_2(s) \end{bmatrix}$$

Two-port network with a terminating impedance $Z_0(s)$ driven by generator with internal impedance $Z_g(s)$

FIGURE 19.9

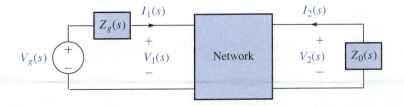

This may be written in expanded form

$$V_g(s) = [A + CZ_g(s)]V_2(s) - [B + DZ_g(s)]I_2(s)$$
$$I_g(s) = CV_2(s) - DI_2(s)$$

and with $I_2(s) = -V_2(s)/Z_0(s)$ in the first of these

$$V_g(s) = [A + CZ_g(s)]V_2(s) + \frac{B + DZ_g(s)}{Z_0(s)} V_2(s)$$

or

$$V_g(s) = \frac{[A + CZ_g(s)]Z_0(s) + B + DZ_g(s)}{Z_0(s)} V_2(s)$$

The composite gain in terms of the $ABCD$-parameters is

$$K_V(s) = \frac{V_2(s)}{V_g(s)} = \frac{Z_0(s)}{[A + CZ_g(s)]Z_0(s) + B + DZ_g(s)} \qquad (19.15a)$$

and in terms of the other parameters (using Table 18.3)

$$K_V(s) = \frac{z_{21}Z_0(s)}{[z_{11} + Z_g(s)][z_{22} + Z_0(s)] - z_{12}z_{21}} \qquad (19.15b)$$

$$K_V(s) = \frac{y_{21}Z_0(s)}{y_{12}y_{21}Z_g(s)Z_0(s) - [1 + y_{11}Z_g(s)][1 + y_{22}Z_0(s)]} \qquad (19.15c)$$

$$K_V(s) = \frac{\Delta_T \cdot Z_0(s)}{B' + A'Z_g(s) + D'Z_0(s) + C'Z_g(s)Z_0(s)} \qquad (19.15d)$$

$$K_V(s) = \frac{-h_{21}Z_0(s)}{[h_{11} + Z_g(s)][1 + h_{22}Z_0(s)] - h_{12}h_{21}Z_0(s)} \qquad (19.15e)$$

and

$$K_V(s) = \frac{g_{21}Z_0(s)}{[1 + g_{11}Z_g(s)][g_{22} + Z_0(s)] - g_{12}g_{21}Z_g(s)} \qquad (19.15f)$$

Notice that if $Z_g(s) = 0$, all of eqs. (19.15) reduce to the values given for $\alpha_{12}(s)$ in Table 19.1.

■ **EXAMPLE 19.3**

If the network in Example 19.2 is driven by a generator with $V_g = 50\underline{/0°}$ V and a generator impedance of $Z_g(s) = 1.00\underline{/-126.87°}$ ohms, what is the composite gain?

Solution   The network is specified in Example 19.2 in terms of its z-parameters

$$Z = \begin{bmatrix} 3 + j4 & j4 \\ j4 & j2 \end{bmatrix}$$

and the composite gain may be determined directly via eq. (19.15b) with $Z_g(s) = 1.00\underline{/-126.87°} = -0.6 - j0.8 \ \Omega$.

$$K_V(s) = \frac{z_{21}Z_0(s)}{[z_{11} + Z_g(s)][z_{22} + Z_0(s)] - z_{12}z_{21}}$$

$$= \frac{j4(2 + j2)}{[3 + j4 + (-0.60 - j0.80)][j2 + (2 + j2)] - (j4)(j4)}$$

$$= \frac{-8 + j8}{-8 + j16 + (16 + j0)} = \frac{-8 + j8}{8 + j16}$$

$$= \frac{11.31\underline{/135°}}{17.89\underline{/63.43°}} = 0.63\underline{/71.57°} \ \text{V/V}$$

■

PASSIVE FILTER STRUCTURES SECTION 19.6

A filter is a component or network that can be inserted between a voltage source with internal impedance $Z_g(s)$ and a load with impedance $Z_0(s)$ for the selective enhancement or specified degradation of a given class of input signals. Passive filters are usually synthesized as two-port networks containing RL, RC, or RLC combinations.

The ideal characteristics of the four common types of passive filters are shown in Fig. 19.10. Of course, it is not possible to realize networks that provide these ideal

Ideal characteristics of four types of filters: (a) low-pass, (b) high-pass, (c) band-pass, and (d) band-stop or band-elimination **FIGURE 19.10**

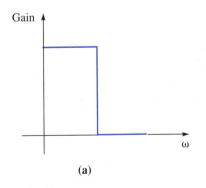

(a)

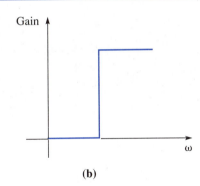

(b)

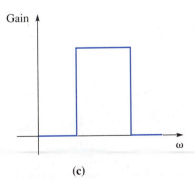

(c)

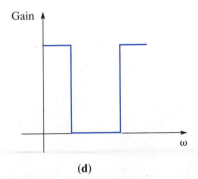

(d)

TABLE 19.2 Four passive filter structures with their s domain voltage gain $\alpha_{12}(s) = V_2(s)/V_1(s)$

Filter	$\alpha_{12}(s)$
Low-Pass (first order) 	$\alpha_{12}(s) = \dfrac{1/RC}{s + 1/RC}$
Low-Pass (second order) 	$\alpha_{12}(s) = \dfrac{1/LC}{s^2 + (R/L)s + 1/LC}$
High-Pass (first order) 	$\alpha_{12}(s) = \dfrac{s}{s + 1/RC}$
High-Pass (second order) 	$\alpha_{12}(s) = \dfrac{s^2}{s^2 + (R/L)s + 1/LC}$
Band-Pass 	$\alpha_{12} = \dfrac{s}{RC[s^2 + (1/RC)s + 1/LC]}$
Band-Stop 	$\alpha_{12} = \dfrac{s^2 + 1/LC}{s^2 + (1/RC)s + 1/LC}$

characteristics but, as the complexity of the network increases, the ideal may be approached.

Table 19.2 displays six filter networks with their s domain voltage gains, $\alpha_{12}(s) = V_2(s)/V_1(s)$. Notice that first and second order networks are shown for the low-pass and high-pass filters and that the band-pass and band-stop filters require at least a second order network.

The construction of Table 19.2 can be illustrated using the band-pass filter. The parallel resonant arrangement in Table 19.2 contains three single elements and with

$$Z_p(s) = \frac{Ls(1/Cs)}{Ls + 1/Cs} = \frac{Ls}{LCs^2 + 1}$$

a voltage division yields $\alpha_{12}(s)$

$$\alpha_{12}(s) = \frac{V_2(s)}{V_1(s)} = \frac{Z_p(s)}{R + Z_p(s)} = \frac{s}{RC[s^2 + (1/RC)s + 1/LC]}$$

This confirms the entry in Table 19.2.

Additional remarks pertaining to the performance of passive filters (and to active filters containing operational amplifiers) will be provided in the next chapter which deals with frequency response.

THE TOTAL RESPONSE FROM NETWORK IMMITTANCE

SECTION 19.7

Immittance is a term that derives from the combination of the *im* in *im*pedance and the *mittance* in ad*mittance*, and it relates, for a one-port, the input and output variables. From the general term *immittance*, the more specific terms *impedance* and *admittance* can be used, depending on whether the input forcing function is a current or a voltage.

19.7 The Natural Response

The transfer function relates an input function $E(s)$ with an output function $R(s)$, in accordance with eq. (19.1). And if $R(s) = V(s)$ and $E(s) = I(s)$, then the immittance $H(s)$ is an impedance $Z(s)$, $H(s) = Z(s) = 1/Y(s)$, and

$$V(s) = Z(s)I(s) = \frac{I(s)}{Y(s)}$$

A voltage $V(s)$ can be maintained as $I(s)$ decreases only if $Z(s)$ increases or $Y(s)$ decreases. Ideally, if $I(s)$ approaches zero, a prescribed value of $V(s)$ can only be maintained if $Z(s)$ becomes unbounded or $Y(s)$ approaches zero. This limiting case describes a natural response. The requirement that $Y(s)$ approaches zero, which can only occur at the zeros of $Y(s)$ or the poles of $Z(s)$, indicates that the open-circuit, natural-response voltage components are derived from the poles of the impedance function or the zeros of the admittance function.

The same reasoning can be applied to show that if the forcing function is a voltage, $H(s) = Y(s) = 1/Z(s)$, and the output response is the s domain current, so that

$$I(s) = Y(s)V(s) = \frac{V(s)}{Z(s)}$$

As the voltage decreases, the output current can be maintained at a prescribed value only if $Z(s)$ decreases. As $V(s)$ approaches zero, $Z(s)$ must also approach zero, and this can only occur at the zeros of $Z(s)$ [and the poles of $Y(s)$]. Hence, natural-response, short-circuit current components can be obtained, in the limiting case, as the input voltage approaches zero. This defines a natural response that can occur only at the zeros of the impedance function or the poles of the admittance function.

The foregoing establishes two significant facts:

1. Natural-response, short-circuit current components can be obtained from the zeros of the impedance function.
2. Natural-response, open-circuit voltage components can be obtained from the poles of the impedance function.

Because the admittance is the reciprocal of the impedance, two more facts emerge:

1. Natural-response, short-circuit current components can be obtained from the poles of the admittance function.
2. Natural-response, open-circuit voltage components can be obtained from the zeros of the admittance function.

■ **EXAMPLE 19.4**

The switch in Fig. 19.11 closes instantaneously at $t = 0$. What are the natural response components of the current i?

Solution The s domain impedance looking into the network is

$$Z(s) = \frac{1}{Cs} + \frac{RLs}{Ls + R} = R \left[\frac{s^2 + \dfrac{1}{RC} s + \dfrac{1}{LC}}{s \left(s + \dfrac{R}{L} \right)} \right] \Omega$$

FIGURE 19.11   A second-order network

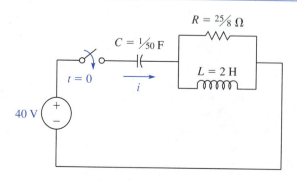

$R = {}^{25}\!/_{8}\ \Omega$

$C = {}^{1}\!/_{50}\ F$

$L = 2\ H$

$t = 0$

i

$40\ V$

and with $C = \frac{1}{50}$ F, $R = \frac{25}{8}$ Ω and $L = 2$ H so that $1/RC = 16$ and $1/LC = 25$

$$Z(s) = \frac{25}{8} \left[\frac{s^2 + 16s + 25}{s\left(s + \frac{25}{16}\right)} \right] \Omega$$

The zeros of $Z(s)$ are obtained from

$$s^2 + 16s + 25 = 0$$

and are

$$s_1, s_2 = -4 \pm j3$$

The natural response current components, obtained from the zeros of $Z(s)$ are assembled into the natural response

$$i_N(t) = e^{-4t}(I_1 \cos 3t + I_2 \sin 3t) \text{ A}$$

19.7.2 The Forced Response

The immittance concept leads to an expeditious evaluation of the forced response of a network if the forcing function is either constant (dc) or sinusoidal (ac) or, in fact, any $s_0 = \sigma_0 + j\omega_0$. Because the form of the forced response depends on the form of the forcing function, forced-response currents can be obtained by choosing the appropriate value of s and evaluating the forced-response current from

$$I(s) = \frac{V(s)}{Z(s)} = Y(s)V(s)$$

and forced-response voltages from

$$V(s) = \frac{I(s)}{Y(s)} = Z(s)I(s)$$

If the magnitude of the forcing function is constant (dc), then $s = 0$ and

$$i_F = \frac{V(s = 0)}{Z(s = 0)} = Y(s = 0)V(s = 0) \quad \text{and} \quad v_F = \frac{I(s = 0)}{Y(s = 0)} = Z(s = 0)I(s = 0)$$

If the forcing function is sinusoidal (ac), then $s = j\omega$ and

$$\hat{I}_F(j\omega) = \frac{\hat{V}(s = j\omega)}{Z(s = j\omega)} = Y(s = j\omega)\hat{V}(s = j\omega)$$

and

$$\hat{V}_F(j\omega) = \frac{\hat{I}(s = j\omega)}{Y(s = j\omega)} = Z(s = j\omega)\hat{I}(s = j\omega)$$

FIGURE 19.12   A second-order network

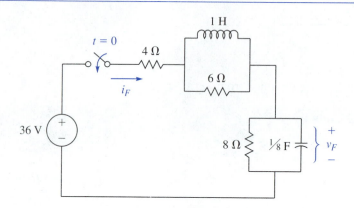

■ **EXAMPLE 19.5**

The switch in Fig. 19.12 closes instantaneously at $t = 0$. What is the forced-response current i_F and the forced-response voltage v_F?

Solution   Because $s = 0$, the strategy here is to determine i_F from

$$i_F = \frac{V(s = 0)}{Z(s = 0)}$$

and v_F from a voltage divider

$$v_F = \left[\frac{Z_{p2}(s = 0)}{Z(s = 0)} \right] V(s = 0)$$

Three impedances are needed:

$$Z_{p1}(s) = \frac{6s}{s + 6} \text{ ohms}$$

$$Z_{p2}(s) = \frac{8(8/s)}{8 + 8/s} = \frac{64}{8s + 8} = \frac{8}{s + 1} \text{ ohms}$$

$$Z(s) = 4 + Z_{p1}(s) + Z_{p2}(s) = 4 + \frac{6s}{s + 6} + \frac{8}{s + 1}$$

$$= \frac{4(s^2 + 7s + 6) + 6s(s + 1) + 8(s + 6)}{s^2 + 7s + 6} = \frac{10s^2 + 42s + 72}{s^2 + 7s + 6} \text{ ohms}$$

Then,

$$i_F = \frac{V(s = 0)}{Z(s = 0)} = \frac{36}{\frac{72}{6}} = 3 \text{ A}$$

$$v_F = \frac{Z_{p2}(s = 0)}{Z(s = 0)} V(s = 0) = \left(\frac{8}{\frac{72}{6}} \right)(36) = 24 \text{ V}$$

19.7.3 The Total Response

The total response can be obtained from the network immittance (see Section 19.7.1) if the forcing function is either constant in magnitude (dc) or sinusoidal (ac). The procedure is quite straightforward.

1. Write either the impedance function $Z(s)$ or the admittance function $Y(s)$.
2. Obtain the forced response, using the appropriate value of s and recalling the following:
   a. If the magnitude of the forcing function is constant (dc), then $s = 0$ and

$$i_F = \frac{V(s = 0)}{Z(s = 0)} = Y(s = 0)V(s = 0) \qquad v_F = \frac{I(s = 0)}{Y(s = 0)} = Z(s = 0)I(s = 0)$$

   b. If the forcing function is sinusoidal (ac), then $s = j\omega$ and

$$\hat{I}_F(j\omega) = \frac{\hat{V}(s = j\omega)}{Z(s = j\omega)} = Y(s = j\omega)\hat{V}(s = j\omega)$$

$$\hat{V}_F(j\omega) = \frac{\hat{I}(s = j\omega)}{Y(s = j\omega)} = Z(s = j\omega)\hat{I}(s = j\omega)$$

3. Identify the natural-response components by using the poles or zeros of impedance or admittance.
   a. Natural-response, short-circuit current components can be obtained from the zeros of the impedance function or the poles of the admittance function.
   b. Natural-response, open-circuit voltage components can be obtained from the poles of the impedance function or the zeros of the admittance function.
4. Evaluate all arbitrary constants.

■ **EXAMPLE 19.6**

Determine the current leaving the 18-V source in the network of Fig. 19.13a. The switch closes instantaneously at $t = 0$.

Solution   Figure 19.13 shows four impedances:

$$Z_1(s) = \frac{8(2s)}{2s + 8} = \frac{8s}{s + 4} \text{ ohms}$$

$$Z_2(s) = 4 + \frac{8s}{s + 4} = \frac{4s + 16 + 8s}{s + 4} = \frac{12s + 16}{s + 4} \text{ ohms}$$

$$Z_3(s) = \frac{12(12s + 16)/(s + 4)}{12 + (12s + 16)/(s + 4)} = \frac{144s + 192}{12s + 48 + 12s + 16}$$

$$= \frac{18s + 24}{3s + 8} \text{ ohms}$$

$$Z(s) = 6 + \frac{18s + 24}{3s + 8} = \frac{18s + 48 + 18s + 24}{3s + 8}$$

$$= \frac{36s + 72}{3s + 8} = 36\left(\frac{s + 2}{3s + 8}\right) \text{ ohms}$$

FIGURE 19.13   (a) A network for which the current leaving the source is to be found and (b) the network showing some of the impedances used in the evaluation of $Z(s)$

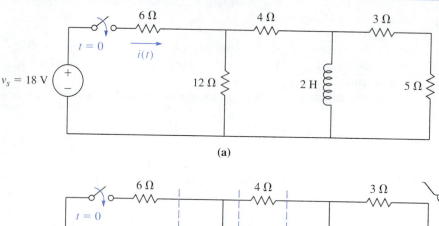

(a)

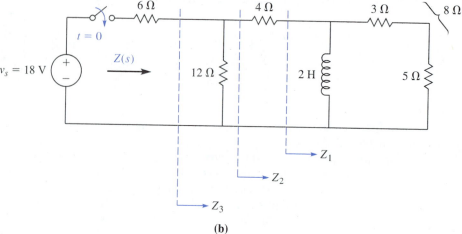

(b)

If $s = 0$,

$$Z(s = 0) = \frac{36(2)}{8} = 9 \, \Omega$$

and the forced-response current is

$$i_F = \frac{V(s = 0)}{Z(s = 0)} = \frac{18}{9} = 2 \, \text{A}$$

The natural-response current derives from the single zero of the impedance function, $s = -2$, and

$$i_N = Ie^{-2t} \text{ amperes}$$

The total response is

$$i(t) = i_N + i_F = Ie^{-2t} + 2 \text{ amperes}$$

The current at $t = 0$ is needed to evaluate the arbitrary constant I. Observe that at the instant the switch closes, the continuity of stored energy principle demands that no current can flow through the inductor. The inductor, therefore, behaves like an open circuit, so that the network is entirely resistive, with a resistance of

$$R_{in} = 6 + \frac{12(4 + 3 + 5)}{12 + 4 + 3 + 5} = 6 + \frac{144}{24} = 6 + 6 = 12 \, \Omega$$

presented to the 18-V source. Thus,

$$i(0) = \frac{v_s}{R_{in}} = \frac{18}{12} = \frac{3}{2} \, \text{A}$$

and

$$i(0) = I + 2 = \frac{3}{2} \quad \text{or} \quad I = -\frac{1}{2}$$

The total response is therefore

$$i(t) = i_F + i_N = 2 - \frac{3}{2} e^{-2t} \, \text{amperes}$$

The zero-input response is obtained from

$$i = Ie^{-2t}$$

with $i(0) = \frac{3}{2}$ A, so that

$$I = \frac{3}{2} \quad \text{and} \quad i_{ZI} = \frac{3}{2} e^{-2t} \, \text{amperes}$$

The zero-state response is obtained from the general solution for the total response,

$$i = Ie^{-2t} + 2$$

with $i(0) = 0$ A. In this case,

$$I = 0 - 2 = -2 \quad \text{and} \quad i = 2 - 2e^{-2t} \, \text{amperes}$$

Observe that

$$i = i_{ZI} + i_{ZS} = \frac{3}{2} e^{-2t} + 2 - 2e^{-2t} = 2 - \frac{1}{2} e^{-2t} \, \text{amperes}$$

as it should.

CHAPTER 19

SUMMARY

- The transfer function $H(s)$ in

$$R(s) = H(s)E(s)$$

where $R(s)$ is the Laplace transform of the response or output function and $E(s)$ is the Laplace transform of the input or excitation function, is an s domain transfer function when the input or excitation $e(t)$ is the unit impulse.

- Table 19.1 provides a summary of the transfer functions that are commonly employed when considering two-port networks. These transfer functions are the input impedance and admittance, the voltage gain, the current gain, and the transfer admittance.

- Terminating impedances can have a significant effect on the voltage gain of a two-port network.

- Component arrangements and voltage gains for low-pass, high-pass, band-pass, and band-stop passive filters are provided in Table 19.2.

- The natural response of a one-port network may be obtained from either the s domain driving point impedance or the s domain driving point admittance.

—Natural-response, short-circuit current components can be obtained from the zeros of the impedance function. Natural-response, open-circuit voltage components can be obtained from the poles of the impedance function.

—Natural-response, short-circuit current components can be obtained from the poles of the admittance function. Natural-response, open-circuit voltage components can be obtained from the zeros of the admittance function.

Additional Readings

Blackwell, W.A., and L.L. Grigsby. *Introductory Network Theory*. Boston: PWS Engineering, 1985, pp. 359–366, 480.

Bobrow, L.S. *Elementary Linear Circuit Analysis*. 2d ed. New York: Holt, Rinehart and Winston, 1987, pp. 441–456, 655, 656.

Del Toro, V. *Engineering Circuits*. Englewood Cliffs, N.J.: Prentice-Hall, 1987, pp. 353, 469–479, 514, 515, 517, 532, 533, 539, 561, 567, 570, 574, 576.

Dorf, R.C. *Introduction to Electric Circuits*. New York: Wiley, 1989, pp. 459–461, 480, 515, 528–533.

Hayt, W.H., Jr., and J.E. Kemmerly. *Engineering Circuit Analysis*. 4th ed. New York: McGraw-Hill, 1986, pp. 345–357, 592–594.

Irwin, J.D. *Basic Engineering Circuit Analysis*. 3d ed. New York: Macmillan, 1989, pp. 595–599.

Johnson, D.E., J.L. Hilburn, and J.R. Johnson. *Basic Electric Circuit Analysis*. 4th ed. Englewood Cliffs, N.J.: Prentice-Hall, 1989, pp. 444–448, 621–624.

Karni, S. *Applied Circuit Analysis*. New York: Wiley, 1988, pp. 124–127, 474, 475, 493–503, 533–541.

Madhu, S. *Linear Circuit Analysis*. Englewood Cliffs, N.J.: Prentice-Hall, 1988, pp. 139–144, 213—215, 426–436, 578–582.

Nilsson, J.W. *Electric Circuits*. 3d ed. Reading, Mass.: Addison-Wesley, 1990, pp. 616–625, 635–639.

Paul, C.R. *Analysis of Linear Circuits*. New York: McGraw-Hill, 1989, pp. 334–349, 364–369, 586–597.

Section 19.2

19.1 For the network in Fig. P19.1, determine the transfer function $Z_1(s) = V_1(s)/I_1(s)$.

Figure P19.1

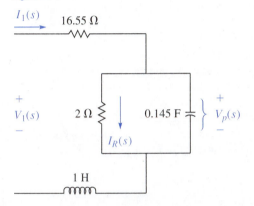

19.2 For the network in Fig. P19.1, determine the transfer function $\alpha_{1p} = V_p(s)/V_1(s)$.

19.3 For the network in Fig. P19.1, determine the transfer function $\beta_{1R}(s) = I_R(s)/I_1(s)$.

19.4 For the network in Fig. P19.2, determine the transfer function $Z_1(s) = V_1(s)/I_1(s)$.

Figure P19.2

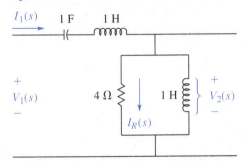

19.5 For the network in Fig. P19.2, determine the transfer function $\alpha_{12} = V_2(s)/V_1(s)$.

19.6 For the network in Fig. P19.2, determine the transfer function $\beta_{1R}(s) = I_R(s)/I_1(s)$.

Section 19.4

19.7 Determine all poles and zeros in the transfer function developed in Problem 19.1.

19.8 Determine all poles and zeros in the transfer function developed in Problem 19.2.

19.9 Determine all poles and zeros in the transfer function developed in Problem 19.3.

19.10 Determine all poles and zeros in the transfer function developed in Problem 19.4.

19.11 Determine all poles and zeros in the transfer function developed in Problem 19.5.

19.12 Determine all poles and zeros in the transfer function developed in Problem 19.6.

Section 19.5

19.13 Consider the network in Fig. P19.3 and determine the voltage gain $\alpha_{12} = V_2/V_1$ with and without the terminating 8 ohm resistor.

Figure P19.3

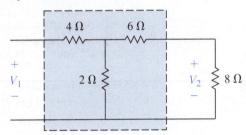

19.14 Consider the network in Fig. P19.4 and determine the voltage gain $\alpha_{12} = V_2/V_1$ with and without the terminating $-j200$ ohm capacitor.

Figure P19.4

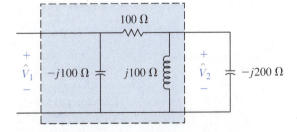

19.15 Consider the network in Fig. P19.5 and determine the voltage gain $\alpha_{12}(s) = V_2(s)/V_1(s)$ with and without the terminating 1 ohm resistor.

Figure P19.5

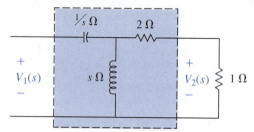

19.16 Consider the network in Fig. P19.6 and determine the voltage gain $\alpha_{12} = V_2/V_1$ with and without the terminating 2 ohm resistor.

Figure P19.6

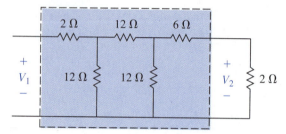

19.17 Suppose a generator with a 4 ohm internal impedance is used to drive the network in Fig. P19.3. Determine the composite voltage gain $K_V = V_2/V_g$.

19.18 Suppose a generator with a $j50$ ohm internal impedance is used to drive the network in Fig. P19.4. Determine the composite voltage gain $K_V = V_2/V_g$.

19.19 Suppose a generator with a 2 ohm internal impedance is used to drive the network in Fig. P19.5. Determine the composite voltage gain $K_V(s) = V_2(s)/V_g(s)$.

19.20 Suppose a generator with a 1 ohm internal impedance is used to drive the network in Fig. P19.6. Determine the composite voltage gain $K_V = V_2/V_1$.

Section 19.6

19.21 Consider the first-order low-pass filter structure shown in Table 19.2 and derive the expression for the voltage gain, $\alpha_{12}(s) = V_2(s)/V_1(s)$ that is shown.

19.22 Consider the second-order low-pass filter structure shown in Table 19.2 and derive the expression for the voltage gain, $\alpha_{12}(s) = V_2(s)/V_1(s)$ that is shown.

19.23 Consider the first-order high-pass filter structure shown in Table 19.2 and derive the expression for the voltage gain, $\alpha_{12}(s) = V_2(s)/V_1(s)$ that is shown.

19.24 Consider the second order high-pass filter structure shown in Table 19.2 and derive the expression for the voltage gain, $\alpha_{12}(s) = V_2(s)/V_1(s)$ that is shown.

19.25 Consider the band-stop filter structure shown in Table 19.2 and derive the expression for the voltage gain, $\alpha_{12}(s) = V_2(s)/V_1(s)$ that is shown.

Section 19.7

19.26 Find the natural-response components for the current i in Fig. P19.7.

Figure P19.7

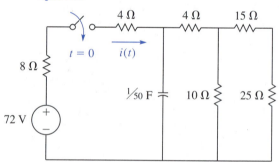

19.27 Find the natural-response components for the current i in Fig. P19.8.

Figure P19.8

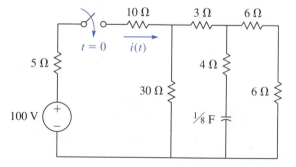

19.28 Find the natural-response components for the voltage v in Fig. P19.9.

Figure P19.9

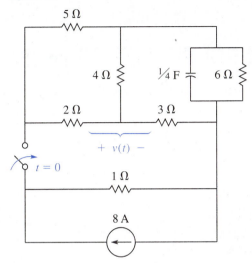

19.29 Find the natural-response components for the current i in Fig. P19.10.

Figure P19.10

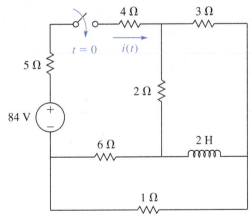

19.30 Find the natural-response components for the voltage v in Fig. P19.11.

Figure P19.11

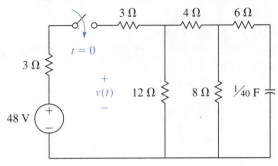

19.31 Find the natural-response components for the voltage v in Fig. P19.12.

Figure P19.12

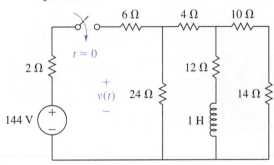

19.32 Find the natural-response components for the current i in Fig. P19.13.

Figure P19.13

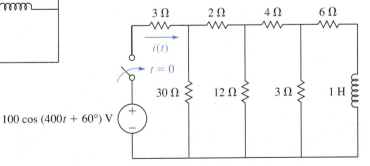

20

FREQUENCY RESPONSE AND FILTERS

OBJECTIVES

The objectives of this chapter are to:

- Describe what is meant by the gain and phase of the transfer function, and show how to express the gain of a transfer function in *decibels*.

- Show how to construct asymptotic gain and phase plots (*Bode plots*) of the transfer function, and show how to approximate the true curve.

- Consider frequency-selective networks called filters and then present design data for low-pass, high-pass, band-pass and band-elimination filters.

SECTION 20.1   **INTRODUCTION**

The response of most physical systems to sinusoidal (harmonic) inputs will vary with the frequency of the forcing function. In some instances, this behavior is desirable and is often a design requirement. In other instances, this response is undesirable, although it must be accepted. Thus, the variation of the gain and phase of the system or network transfer function as a function of frequency becomes very important in many of the engineering disciplines, and the engineer must learn to predict the response of physical systems to harmonic inputs and to thoroughly understand why the output behavior is a function of frequency.

SECTION 20.2   **THE GAIN AND PHASE OF THE TRANSFER FUNCTION**

Consider a network in which the points of signal input and output are clearly indicated, and suppose that it is desired to find the output or response $r(t)$ when the input or excitation is provided by a signal generator having a fixed amplitude at all frequencies,

$$e(t) = E_m \cos \omega t = \text{Re}(E_m e^{j\omega t})$$

where E_m is the amplitude and where the phase of the signal is arbitrarily taken as zero. Because the transfer function relates the zero-state response $r(t)$ to the input $e(t)$, and because the output must be in the same form as the input, the output can be given by

$$r(t) = R_m \cos(\omega t + \theta) = \text{Re}(R_m e^{j(\omega t + \theta)})$$

where the angle θ, the *phase angle* of the transfer function, accounts for the delay (or advance) of the output.

Under these circumstances, $s = j\omega$, and the transfer function given by eq. (19.5),

$$H(s) = \frac{P(s)}{Q(s)} = K \frac{b_m s^m + b_{m-1} s^{m-1} + \cdots + b_1 s + b_0}{a_n s^n + a_{n-1} s^{n-1} + \cdots + a_1 s + a_0} \tag{19.5}$$

can be written as

$$H(j\omega) = K \frac{b_m (j\omega)^m + b_{m-1}(j\omega)^{m-1} + \cdots + b_1(j\omega) + b_0}{a_n(j\omega)^n + a_{n-1}(j\omega)^{n-1} + \cdots + a_1(j\omega) + a_0} \tag{20.1}$$

or as a quotient of combinations of real and imaginary terms,

$$H(j\omega) = K \frac{B_R(\omega) + jB_I(\omega)}{A_R(\omega) + jA_I(\omega)} \tag{20.2}$$

The transfer function may also be written as

$$H(j\omega) = |H(j\omega)| e^{j\theta(j\omega)} \tag{20.3}$$

where the *magnitude* of $H(j\omega)$ is seen to depend on the frequency and is called the *gain* of the transfer function. The phase of $H(j\omega)$ also depends on the frequency and is

$$\theta(j\omega) = \underline{/H(j\omega)} \tag{20.4}$$

Under these circumstances, the input and output may be represented as phasors with magnitudes E_m and R_m, and the output will be equal to the input multiplied by the transfer function,

$$r(t) = \text{Re}\big[|H(j\omega)| e^{j\theta(j\omega)} \cdot E_m e^{j\omega t}\big] = \text{Re}\big[R_m e^{j[\omega t + \theta(j\omega)]}\big]$$

This shows that R_m, which is the magnitude of $r(t)$, is equal to the product of the magnitude of the forcing sinusoid and the magnitude of the transfer function evaluated at the driving frequency, ω

$$R_m = R_m |H(j\omega)|$$

and that the phase of $r(t)$ is due to the phase of the transfer function $\theta(j\omega)$ also evaluated at the driving frequency, ω.

Now, return to eqs. (20.2) to (20.4). Both the numerator and the denominator of eq. (20.2) may be written in polar form (in terms of a magnitude and an angle).

Equation (20.3) then becomes

$$H(j\omega) = |H(\omega)| \underline{/\theta(\omega)} = K \frac{\sqrt{[B_R(\omega)]^2 + [B_I(\omega)]^2} \underline{/\theta_B(\omega)}}{\sqrt{[A_R(\omega)]^2 + [A_I(\omega)]^2} \underline{/\theta_A(\omega)}} \qquad (20.5)$$

where

$$\theta_B(\omega) = \arctan \frac{B_I(\omega)}{B_R(\omega)} \qquad (20.6a)$$

$$\theta_A(\omega) = \arctan \frac{A_I(\omega)}{A_R(\omega)} \qquad (20.6b)$$

The magnitude can be written as

$$|H(\omega)| = K \sqrt{\frac{[B_R(\omega)]^2 + [B_I(\omega)]^2}{[A_R(\omega)]^2 + [A_I(\omega)]^2}} \qquad (20.7a)$$

and the phase as

$$\theta(\omega) = \theta_B(\omega) - \theta_A(\omega) = \arctan \frac{B_I(\omega)}{B_R(\omega)} - \arctan \frac{A_I(\omega)}{A_R(\omega)} \qquad (20.7b)$$

■ EXAMPLE 20.1

What are the magnitude and phase of the transfer function

$$H(s) = 2000 \frac{s^2 + 210s + 2000}{s^2 + 2100s + 200{,}000}$$

at an angular frequency of $\omega = 500$ rad/s?

Solution   With $s = j\omega$,

$$H(j\omega) = 2000 \frac{(j\omega)^2 + j210\omega + 2000}{(j\omega)^2 + j2100\omega + 200{,}000}$$

$$= 2000 \frac{2000 - \omega^2 + j210\omega}{200{,}000 - \omega^2 + j2100\omega}$$

Here,

$$B_R(\omega) = 2000 - \omega^2 \qquad A_R(\omega) = 200{,}000 - \omega^2$$

$$B_I(\omega) = 210\omega \qquad A_I(\omega) = 2100\omega$$

At $\omega = 500$ rad/s,

$$B_R = 2000 - (500)^2 = -248{,}000 \qquad A_R = 200{,}000 - (500)^2 = -50{,}000$$

$$B_I = 210(500) = 105{,}000 \qquad A_I = 2100(500) = 1{,}050{,}000$$

From eq. (20.7a),

$$|H(\omega = 500)| = 2000 \sqrt{\frac{(-248{,}000)^2 + (105{,}000)^2}{(-50{,}000)^2 + (1{,}050{,}000)^2}}$$

$$= 2000 \sqrt{\frac{7.253 \times 10^{10}}{1.105 \times 10^{12}}} = 2000(0.256) = 512.39$$

Then, from eq. (20.7b)

$$\theta(\omega = 500) = \arctan \frac{105{,}000}{-248{,}000} - \arctan \frac{1{,}050{,}000}{-50{,}000}$$

$$= 157.05° - 92.73° = 64.32° \qquad \blacksquare$$

EXERCISE 20.1

What are the gain and phase of the transfer function

$$H(s) = 12{,}000 \, \frac{s^2 + 1202s + 2400}{s^2 + 16{,}100s + 1.6 \times 10^6}$$

at an angular frequency of $\omega = 4000$ rad/s?

Answer $|H(\omega = 4000)| = 3037.63$ and $\theta(\omega = 4000) = 60.27°$.

THE GAIN IN DECIBELS   SECTION 20.3

Once again, consider eq. (20.1). The magnitude of $H(j\omega)$ may be written in terms of factors that have real and imaginary parts. One such representation of the magnitude might be

$$|H(j\omega)| = K \left| \frac{(b_{R1} + j\omega b_{I1})(b_{R2} + j\omega b_{I2}) \cdots (b_{Rm} + j\omega b_{Im})}{(a_{R1} + j\omega a_{I1})(a_{R2} + j\omega a_{I2}) \cdots (a_{Rn} + j\omega a_{In})} \right| \qquad (20.8)$$

and this shows that a calculation of the magnitude would involve a very laborious procedure for every ω of interest.

It would be much handier if the calculation of the magnitude involved a sum rather than a product. A simple approach to this is in the use of logarithms. Let it be clearly understood that in what follows

$$\log \equiv \log_{10} \qquad \text{and} \qquad \ln \equiv \log_e$$

Accordingly, define the gain in *decibels* (abbreviated dB) as

$$G(\omega) \equiv 20 \log |H(j\omega)| \qquad \text{(decibels)} \qquad (20.9)$$

If eq. (20.8) is rewritten by using the magnitude of each factor,

$$|H(j\omega)| = K \, \frac{|b_{R1} + j\omega b_{I1}| \, |b_{R2} + j\omega b_{I2}| \cdots |b_{Rm} + j\omega b_{Im}|}{|a_{R1} + j\omega a_{I1}| \, |a_{R2} + j\omega a_{I2}| \cdots |a_{Rn} + j\omega a_{In}|} \qquad (20.10)$$

then, by employing the logarithmic definition of the gain in decibels, one obtains

$$G(\omega) = 20 \log K + 20 \log|b_{R1} + j\omega b_{I1}| + 20 \log|b_{R2} + j\omega b_{I2}| + \cdots$$
$$+ 20 \log|b_{Rm} + j\omega b_{Im}| - 20 \log|a_{R1} + j\omega a_{I1}|$$
$$- 20 \log|a_{R2} + j\omega a_{I2}| - \cdots - 20 \log|a_{Rn} + j\omega a_{In}| \qquad (20.11)$$

Observe that the contribution due to K can be positive or negative depending on whether K is greater or less than unity.

Thus, if a transfer function is composed of factors,

$$H(j\omega) = K \frac{B_1(j\omega)B_2(j\omega)B_3(j\omega) \cdots B_m(j\omega)}{A_1(j\omega)A_2(j\omega)A_3(j\omega) \cdots A_n(j\omega)}$$

then the gain in decibels at a particular frequency can be written as

$$G = \pm G_K + G_{B1} + G_{B2} + G_{B3} + \cdots + G_{Bm} - G_{A1} - G_{A2} - G_{A3} - \cdots - G_{An}$$

where, in general, the ith gain G_i can be obtained from either

$$G_i = 20 \log|B_i(j\omega)| \qquad \text{or} \qquad G_i = 20 \log|A_i(j\omega)|$$

SECTION 20.4   GAIN AND PHASE PLOTS FOR LINEAR FACTORS

20.4.1 Gain and Phase Plots

Plots of gain and phase as a function of angular frequency ω are called *Bode plots* and bear the name of Hendrick Bode,[1] who formulated the technique at the Bell Telephone Laboratories in the 1930s. They are constructed on semilogarithmic paper.

Consider the simple transfer function

$$H(s) = K_o \frac{c_1 s + d_1}{c_2 s + d_2} = K \frac{1 + T_1 s}{1 + T_2 s}$$

where $T_1 = c_1/d_1$, $T_2 = c_2/d_2$, and $K = K_o d_1/d_2$. If s is replaced by $j\omega$, the result is

$$H(j\omega) = K \frac{1 + j\omega T_1}{1 + j\omega T_2}$$

The gain of this function in decibels will be

$$G(\omega) = 20 \log K + 20 \log|1 + j\omega T_1| - 20 \log|1 + j\omega T_2|$$

Take the factor $|1 + j\omega T_1|$ and plot the gain

$$G_1(\omega) = 20 \log|1 + j\omega T_1|$$

as a function of the angular frequency ω. At very low frequencies, where $1 \gg j\omega T_1$,

$$G_L(\omega) = 20 \log 1 = 0; \qquad j\omega T_1 \ll 1$$

---

[1] Pronounced *Bodah*, not *Boad* or *Bodie*.

which is a straight line along the 0-dB axis. At extremely high frequencies, where $j\omega T_1 \gg 1$,

$$G_H(\omega) = 20 \log \omega T_1 = 20 \log T_1 + 20 \log \omega; \qquad j\omega T_1 \gg 1$$

The $20 \log \omega$ term plots as an inclined straight line, which will have zero magnitude when

$$20 \log T_1 + 20 \log \omega = 0 \qquad \text{or when} \qquad \omega = \omega_o = \frac{1}{T_1}$$

The horizontal and inclined straight lines for both the numerator and the denominator factors are shown in Fig. 20.1. The angular frequency, ω_o, is called the break, cutoff, or corner frequency and will be defined in this section.

Consider $20 \log \omega$ and a tenfold increase in the frequency from ω to 10ω. The increase in decibels will be

$$G_\Delta = 20 \log 10\omega - 20 \log \omega = 20 \log \frac{10\omega}{\omega} = 20 \log 10 = 20 \text{ dB}$$

This shows that the slope of the inclined line is 20 dB per decade, where the term *decade* means a tenfold increase or decrease in frequency.

The increase or decrease in decibels for a twofold change in frequency is established in a similar manner:

$$G_\Delta = 20 \log 2\omega - 20 \log \omega = 20 \log 2 = 20(0.3010) = 6.0206 \approx 6 \text{ dB}$$

This shows that the slope is 6 dB per octave, where the term *octave* derives from the fact that musical notes with the same letter are separated by a 2:1 or $\frac{1}{2}$:1 ratio of frequencies and are also separated by eight notes.

The gains $G_{L1}(\omega)$ and $G_{H1}(\omega)$ are called the *low-* and *high-frequency asymptotes*, respectively. They are plotted in Fig. 20.1a. Notice that $G_L(\omega)$ and $G_H(\omega)$ intersect at a value of ω that is referred to as the *break* or *corner frequency*. Also, notice that the form of the factor, $G(\omega) = 20 \log|1 + j\omega T|$, will always put the low-frequency asymptote (not the entire transfer function) on the 0-dB axis.

Typical asymptotic-gain plots for single linear factors: (a) numerator factor and (b) denominator factor; note that both plots seem to "break" at $\omega = \omega_0$

FIGURE 20.1

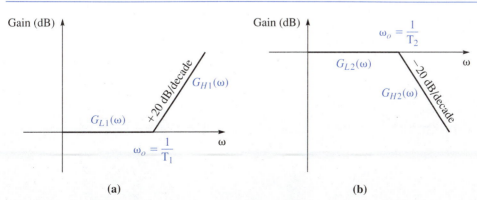

(a)   (b)

A similar story can be told for the denominator factor $20 \log|1 + j\omega T_2|$, and the result is indicated in Fig. 20.1b. Observe here that the high-frequency asymptote decreases at 20 dB per decade or 6 dB per octave.

At the break frequency, $G_{L2}(\omega) = G_{H2}(\omega)$, so that

$$0 = 20 \log \omega_o T_2$$

and the value of the break frequency, for both the numerator and the denominator factors, is

$$\omega_o = \frac{1}{T} \tag{20.12}$$

The total phase shift of the transfer function can also be obtained from an addition or subtraction of the contributions of the individual terms. This derives from the fact that complex numbers (in polar form), when multiplied or divided, require an addition or a subtraction of their angles. In the case of phase shift, it is fortunate that no use of logarithms is required.

Consider the linear factor $1 + sT$ and again substitute $j\omega$ for s. The factor will be written as $1 + j\omega T$, with magnitude

$$G(\omega) = \sqrt{1 + (\omega T)^2}$$

and a phase angle

$$\theta(\omega) = \arctan \frac{\omega T}{1} = \arctan \omega T$$

However, $\omega_o = 1/T$, so that

$$\theta(\omega) = \arctan \frac{\omega}{\omega_o} \tag{20.13}$$

which shows that the phase angle for the factor is a function only of ω and ω_o.

FIGURE 20.2   Asymptotic phase plots for single linear factors: (a) numerator factor and (b) denominator factor

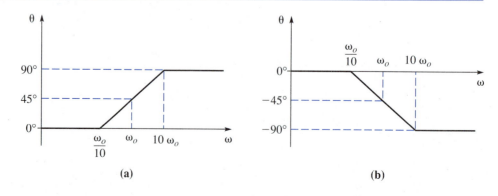

(a)   (b)

Observe that arctan $1 = 45°$, so that a single linear factor, at $\omega = \omega_o$, will possess a phase angle of $\pm 45°$, depending on whether it is in the numerator or denominator. Also, observe that arctan $\frac{1}{10} = 5.7°$ and that arctan $10 = 84.3°$, so that a reasonable approximation for the phase plot for the linear factor is to set $\theta = 0$ at $\omega/\omega_o = \frac{1}{10}$ and $\theta = \pm 90°$ at $\omega/\omega_o = 10$, depending upon whether the factor is in the numerator or denominator of the transfer function. Asymptotic phase plots for single linear factors are shown in Fig. 20.2.

20.4.2 Procedure for Gain Plots

A simple yet comprehensive procedure can be used to rapidly and accurately yield gain and phase plots. This procedure begins with an investigation of the transfer function

$$H(s) = \frac{P(s)}{Q(s)}$$

1. Obtain all factors of $P(s)$ and $Q(s)$ and put $H(s)$ in what can be referred to as standard form with all factors associated with a constant shown as

   $1 + sT$

   No adjustment need be made to factors not associated with a constant. These will contribute to the gain plot but will not contribute any break frequencies.
2. Identify all break frequencies

   $$\omega_o = \frac{1}{T}$$

   and list them. Be sure to categorize them as deriving from poles (denominator factors) or zeros (numerator factors).
3. Go back to $H(s)$, and in each of the terms $1 + sT$, let $s = 0$. Write the result as $H_L(s)$, which will be the transfer function of the overall low-frequency asymptote and which will indicate its slope. Then, select a low frequency (perhaps $1/10$ of the lowest break frequency) and evaluate $G_L(\omega) = 20 \log|H_L(\omega)|$ at this frequency. This will anchor the entire Bode plot at the low-frequency end.
4. Repeat step (3), but this time, ignore all of the 1's in each factor $1 + sT$. Write the result as $H_H(s)$, which will be the transfer function of the high-frequency asymptote and will provide its slope. This time, select a high frequency (say 10 times the highest break frequency) and evaluate $G_H(\omega) = 20 \log|H(\omega)|$ at this frequency. This will provide a point that can be used to check the final result.
5. Plot the asymptotic gain characteristic beginning with the low-frequency asymptote at the low-frequency end. Extend this low-frequency asymptote to higher frequency and begin the departure from it at the lowest break frequency. Continue by changing the slope at each break frequency. The curve can only change slope at a break frequency; permissible slopes are restricted, in the case of linear factors, to multiples of 20 dB per decade and multiples of s not associated with a constant are "built into" the low- and high-frequency asymptotes.

■   **EXAMPLE 20.2**

Construct the Bode asymptotic gain plot for the s domain transfer function

$$H(s) = 80 \frac{(s + 20)(2s + 80{,}000)}{(s + 2)(2s + 400)(4s + 16{,}000)}$$

Solution

1. Put the transfer function in the prescribed form:

$$H(s) = \frac{(80)(20)(80{,}000)}{(2)(400)(16{,}000)} \frac{(1 + 0.05s)(1 + 0.000025s)}{(1 + 0.5s)(1 + 0.005s)(1 + 0.00025s)}$$

$$= 10 \frac{(1 + 0.05s)(1 + 0.000025s)}{(1 + 0.5s)(1 + 0.005s)(1 + 0.00025s)}$$

2. The break frequencies are

zeroes: $\omega_o = \dfrac{1}{0.05} = 20$ rad/s

$\omega_o = \dfrac{1}{0.000025} = 40{,}000$ rad/s

poles: $\omega_o = \dfrac{1}{0.5} = 2$ rad/s

$\omega_o = \dfrac{1}{0.005} = 200$ rad/s

$\omega_o = \dfrac{1}{0.00025} = 4000$ rad/s

3. For the overall low-frequency asymptote of $H(s)$, let all $s = 0$,

$$H_L(s) = 10$$

and this is a horizontal straight line at magnitude

$$G_L = 20 \log 10 = 20(1) = 20 \text{ dB}$$

4. For the overall high-frequency asymptote of $H(s)$, reduce the 1's in each factor to 0, because at high frequency, $s = j\omega \gg 1$:

$$10 \frac{(0.05)(0.000025)s^2}{(0.5)(0.005)(0.00025)s^3} = \frac{20}{s}$$

The high-frequency asymptote is falling at 20 dB per decade because of the presence of the single s in the denominator. The highest break frequency is 40,000 rad/s, so that at a frequency of 400,000 rad/s,

$$|H_H(\omega = 400{,}000)| = G(400{,}000) = \frac{20}{400{,}000} = 0.00005$$

Bode asymptotic plot for the transfer function of Example 20.2

FIGURE 20.3

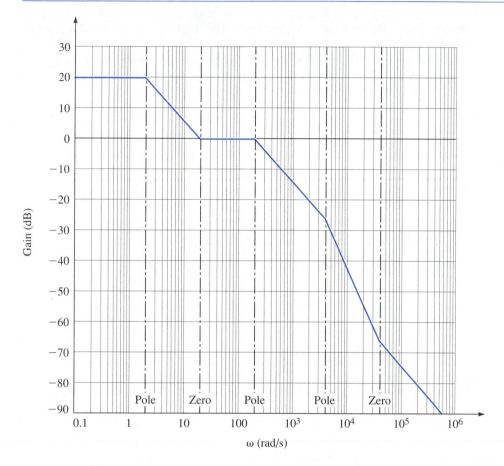

ω (rad/s)

and this gives a gain of

$$G_H = 20 \log 0.00005 = 20(-4.301) = -86.02 \approx -86 \text{ dB}$$

The high-frequency asymptote must fall at 20 dB per decade and must pass through -86 dB at $\omega = 400{,}000$ rad/s.

5. The Bode asymptotic gain plot is shown in Fig. 20.3, and the following commentary is offered to assist the reader. ■

20.4.3 Commentary on the Construction of the Bode Plot (Example 20.2)

Begin at the low-frequency asymptote, which has a magnitude of 20 dB. The plot departs from the low-frequency asymptote at the first breakpoint at $\omega = 2$ rad/s, breaking downward (denominator factor) at 20 dB per decade. The easiest way to carry on from $\omega = 2$ rad/s is to place a point at 14 dB and $\omega = 4$ rad/s (twice the frequency → 6 dB down). Connect these two points, and continue on the resulting downward-sloping line until the next breakpoint is reached.

The next breakpoint is at 20 rad/s and involves a numerator factor. The effect of this factor is to superpose a line rising at 20 dB per decade, and the net effect is to cancel the falling characteristic due to the factor that breaks at 2 rad/s. Thus, the overall characteristic will be horizontal above $\omega = 20$ rad/s and will remain that way until the next break frequency at $\omega = 200$ rad/s is reached.

Because the factor having 200 rad/s as its break frequency is a denominator factor, the overall plot will break downward at 20 dB per decade at $\omega = 200$ rad/s. As mentioned previously, the simplest way of obtaining the correct downward slope is to drop 6 dB and mark the point at 400 rad/s. The slanting line can then be inserted, and it will continue until the next break frequency, which occurs at 4000 rad/s.

Another downward contribution is required (another denominator factor) at $\omega = 4000$ rad/s. At $\omega = 8000$ rad/s, a point is inserted 12 dB below the point at $\omega = 4000$ rad/s. When these points are connected, the overall characteristic will be falling, as required by the two denominator factors that occur in sequence, at 40 dB per decade. This falling line continues until the final breakpoint of $\omega = 40,000$ rad/s is reached.

The numerator factor $(2s + 80,000)$ contributes a rising characteristic, which begins at the break frequency of $\omega_o = 40,000$ rad/s. The net effect is to raise the falling 40-dB-per-decade inclined line to one that falls at 20 dB per decade. Thus, at twice the frequency ($\omega = 80,000$ rad/s), a fictitious point is placed 6 (no longer 12) dB below the point at $\omega = 40,000$ rad/s. When these lines are connected, the extension gives the overall high-frequency asymptote.

The final step is to note, with gratification, that the high-frequency asymptote does indeed pass through -86 dB at $\omega = 400,000$ rad/s.

20.4.4 Procedure for Phase Plots

The key to the construction of the asymptotic phase plot is to recognize, in accordance with eq. (20.13), that at the break frequencies of linear factors, the phase contribution is 45°, −45° for poles and +45° for zeros. Moreover, Fig. 20.2 shows that at $\omega_o/10$, the contribution is 0° and at $10\omega_o$, the contribution is 90°, −90° for poles and +90° for zeros. The factor $s = j\omega$ contributes +90° if it is in the numerator of $H(s)$ and −90° if it is in the denominator.

Figure 20.4 shows the asymptotic phase plot for the transfer function

$$H(s) = 80 \, \frac{(s + 20)(2s + 80,000)}{(s + 2)(2s + 400)(4s + 16,000)}$$

Notice how the overall characteristic begins at the low frequency and how the slope changes as the contribution for each pole or zero begins to become significant.

20.4.5 Finding the True Curves of Gain and Phase

Much insight into the behavior of a system can be obtained from an inspection of the Bode plot. If one wishes to obtain the true gain curve, it may be sketched by considering points that are at 1/5, 1/2, 1, 2, and 5 times the break frequency. Consider the numerator factor

$$G(\omega) = 20 \log|1 + j\omega T|$$

and investigate the amplitude of this factor when

$$\omega = \eta\omega_o = \frac{\eta}{T}$$

as η takes on values of 1/5, 1/2, 1, 2, and 5. Thus,

$$\Delta G = G = 20 \log|1 + j\eta| \tag{20.14}$$

FIGURE 20.4

Asymptotic phase plot for the transfer function of Example 20.2

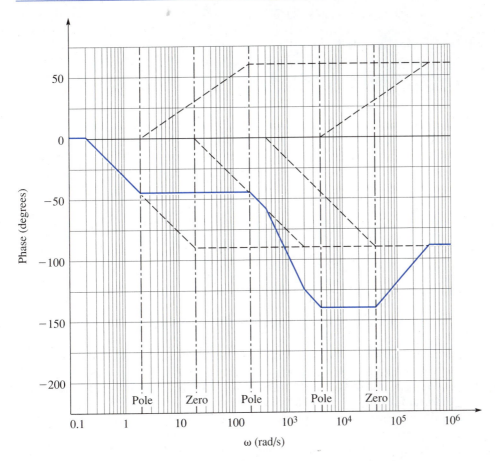

because the correction to the low-frequency asymptote, which is a horizontal straight line at 0 dB, will be the true value.

Thus, when $\eta = 1/5$,

$$\Delta G = 20 \log|1 + j0.2| = 20 \log 1.0198 = 0.1703 \text{ dB}$$

which is a correction of less than 0.2 dB. When $\eta = 1/2$,

$$\Delta G = 20 \log|1 + j0.5| = 20 \log 1.1180 = 20(0.0485) = 0.9691 \approx 1 \text{ dB}$$

And when $\eta = 1$,

$$\Delta G = 20 \log|1 + j1| = 20 \log \sqrt{2} = 20(0.1505) = 3.0103 \approx 3 \text{ dB}$$

Above ω_o, the true curve is represented by

$$20 \log|1 + j\omega T|$$

and the high-frequency asymptote for the individual factor is given by

$$20 \log \omega T$$

The difference is the correction

$$\Delta G = 20 \log|1 + j\omega T| - 20 \log \omega T$$

With $\eta = \omega/\omega_o$ and with $T = 1/\omega_o$, it is noted that

$$\Delta G = 20 \log|1 + j\eta| - 20 \log \eta \qquad\qquad (20.15)$$

Note that for $\eta = 1$,

$$\Delta G = 20 \log|1 + j| - 20 \log 1 = 20 \log \sqrt{2} - 0 = 20(0.1505) = 3.0103 \approx 3 \text{ dB}$$

and the two corrections (from the low-frequency and high-frequency sides) match. For $\omega = 2\omega_o$, $\eta = 2$ and

$$\Delta G = 20 \log|1 + j2| - 20 \log 2 = 20 \log 2.2361 - 20 \log 2$$
$$= 20(0.3495 - 0.3010) = 20(0.0485) = 0.9691 \approx 1 \text{ dB}$$

And for $\omega = 5\omega_o$, $\eta = 5$ and

$$\Delta G = 20 \log|1 + j5| - 20 \log 5 = 20 \log 5.0990 - 20 \log 5$$
$$= 20(0.7075 - 0.6990) = 20(0.0085) = 0.1703 \text{ dB}$$

Similar corrections exist for linear factors in the denominator; but because the high-frequency asymptotes for denominator factors slope downward, the corrections bear a minus sign. Table 20.1 gives the corrections to the asymptotic-gain and phase plots for linear factors ($n = 1$) and for repeated linear factors ($n = 2, 3$). Table 20.1 also includes the corrections for the phase angle developed at the end of Section 20.4.1.

With the information in Table 20.1, the true curves may be plotted or sketched. Figure 20.5a shows the true curve superimposed on the asymptotic-gain plot (Fig. 20.3) developed for the transfer function of Example 20.2. The phase characteristic is indicated in Fig. 20.5b.

TABLE 20.1 Corrections to the asymptotic gain and phase plots as a function of $\omega = \eta\omega_o$ for the numerator factor $(1 + s/\omega_o)^n$

η	Gain			Phase		
	$n = 1$	$n = 2$	$n = 3$	$n = 1$	$n = 2$	$n = 3$
0.10	0.04	0.09	0.13	5.7°	11.4°	17.1°
0.20	0.17	0.34	0.51	11.3°	22.6°	33.9°
0.25	0.26	0.53	0.79	14.0°	28.0°	42.0°
0.50	1.00	2.00	3.00	26.6°	53.2°	79.8°
1.00	3.00	6.00	9.00	45.0°	90.0°	135.0°
2.00	1.00	2.00	3.00	63.4°	126.8°	190.2°
4.00	0.26	0.53	0.79	76.0°	152.0°	228.0°
5.00	0.17	0.34	0.51	78.7°	157.4°	236.1°
10.00	0.04	0.09	0.13	84.3°	168.6°	252.9°

Note: For denominator factors, change the sign of the correction.

FIGURE 20.5

(a) The true gain curve for the transfer function of Example 20.2 and (b) the phase characteristic

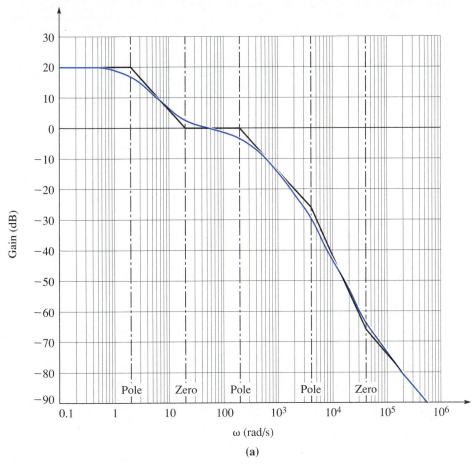

(a)

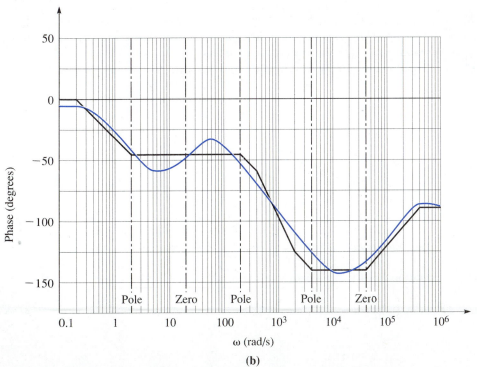

(b)

SECTION 20.5   GAIN AND PHASE PLOTS FOR REPEATED LINEAR FACTORS

Again, look at a rather simple transfer function,

$$H(s) = \frac{(1 + sT_1)(1 + sT_3)}{(1 + sT_2)^2}$$

Here, there is a repeated factor in the denominator. If s is replaced by $j\omega$, the repeated factor becomes $(1 + j\omega T_2)^2$, and special treatment is required because this factor occurs twice.

Thus, the contribution to the total gain by any repeated factor $1 + sT$ is obtained by replacing s with $j\omega$, so that

$$G(\omega) = 20 \log|1 + j\omega T|^2 = 40 \log|1 + j\omega T|$$

At low frequencies, where $1 \gg \omega T$,

$$G_L(\omega) = 40 \log 1 = 0$$

which shows that the repeated linear factor also has a low-frequency asymptote of 0 dB. At high frequencies, where $\omega T \gg 1$,

$$G_H(\omega) = 20 \log(\omega T)^2 = 40 \log \omega T = 40(\log \omega + \log T)$$

A tenfold increase in ω means that the increase in decibels will be

$$G_\Delta = 40(\log 10\omega + \log T) - 40(\log \omega + \log T) = 40(\log 10\omega - \log \omega)$$

$$= 40 \log \frac{10\omega}{\omega} = 40 \log 10 = 40 \text{ dB}$$

The factor that is repeated twice runs off at a slope of 40 dB per decade, and this is 12 dB per octave. This slope occurs regardless of whether the factor is in the numerator or denominator; the numerator factor has a high-frequency asymptote with a positive slope of 40 dB per decade, and the high-frequency asymptote of the denominator factor has a negative slope of the same value. Indeed, factors may be repeated more than twice, and under these circumstances, the slopes of the high-frequency asymptote are $20n$ decibels per decade or $6n$ decibels per octave, where n represents the number of times that the factor is repeated.

The phase for a repeated factor can be obtained from a consideration of eqs. (20.6). Suppose $H(s)$ consists of a simple repeated factor

$$H(s) = (1 + sT)^2$$

Then if $T = 1/\omega_o$ and $\eta = \omega/\omega_o$

$$H(s = j\omega) = (1 + j\omega/\omega_o)^2 = (1 + j\eta)^2 = (1 - \eta^2) + j2\eta$$

and in accordance with eqs. (20.6)

$$\theta = \arctan \frac{2\eta}{1 - \eta^2}$$

For $\eta \to 0$ and $\eta \to \infty$, $\theta = \arctan 0 = 0$ and for $\eta = 1$ where $\omega = \omega_o$, $\theta = 90°$. Thus θ is approximated by $0°$ at $\omega = \omega_o/10$ and $\pm 180°$ at $\omega = 10\omega_o$. This line of reasoning can be followed to show that if the linear factor is repeated three times, then $\theta = \pm 135°$ at $\omega = \omega_o$, and θ is approximated by $0°$ at $\omega = \omega_o/10$ and ± 270 at $\omega = 10\omega_o$. Of course, the sign of θ depends on whether the repeated factor is a multiple pole or a multiple zero and corrections from the asymptotic curve to the true curve can be obtained from Table 20.1.

■ **EXAMPLE 20.3**

Plot the asymptotic gain and phase as a function of angular frequency for the transfer function

$$H(s) = 36,000 \frac{s(4s + 1)}{(3s + 15)^2(s + 80)}$$

Solution

1. $H(s)$ must be put in standard form:

$$H(s) = \frac{36,000}{(15)^2(80)} \cdot \frac{s(1 + 4s)}{(1 + 0.2s)^2(1 + 0.0125s)} = 2 \frac{s(1 + 4s)}{(1 + 0.2s)^2(1 + 0.0125s)}$$

2. The break frequencies are

   zero: $\omega_o = \dfrac{1}{4}$ rad/s

   poles: $\omega_o = \dfrac{15}{3} = 5$ rad/s   (double pole)

   $\omega_o = 80$ rad/s

3. For the overall low-frequency asymptote of $H(s)$, set $s = 0$ in all factors of the form $(1 + sT)^n$. The single s factor in the numerator is not involved:

   $H_L(s) = 2s$

   At $\omega = 0.01$ rad/s,

   $$|H_L(\omega = 0.01)| = 2(0.01) = 0.02$$
   $$G_L(\omega = 0.01) = 20 \log(0.02) = 20(-1.6690) = -33.98 \approx -34 \text{ dB}$$

   The overall low-frequency asymptote is rising from -34 dB at $\omega = 0.01$ rad/s at a rate of 20 dB per decade because of the presence of the single s term in the numerator of $H_L(s)$.

4. For the overall high-frequency asymptote of $H(s)$, because it is assumed that $s = j\omega \gg 1$,

   $$H_H(s) = 2 \frac{s(4s)}{(0.2s)^2(0.0125s)} = \frac{16,000}{s}$$

FIGURE 20.6   Asymptotic-gain plot for the transfer function in Example 20.3

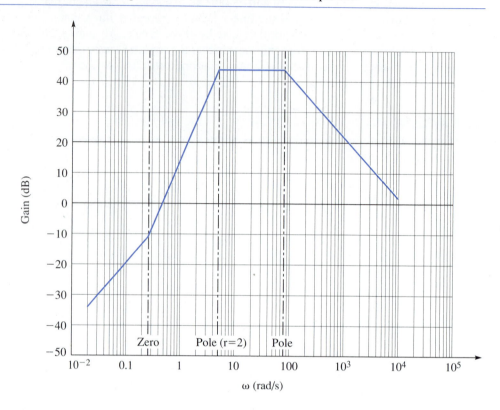

The presence of the single s in the denominator indicates that the overall high-frequency asymptote is falling at the rate of 20 dB per decade. At $\omega = 1000$ rad/s,

$$|H_H(\omega = 1000)| = \frac{16{,}000}{1000} = 16$$

$$G_H(\omega = 1000) = 20 \log 16 = 20(1.2041) = 24.08 \approx 24 \text{ dB}$$

5. The asymptotic-gain plot is shown in Fig. 20.6 and the phase plot is presented in Fig. 20.7. ■

SECTION 20.6   **GAIN AND PHASE PLOTS FOR QUADRATIC FACTORS**

A transfer function such as

$$H(s) = K \frac{s(s + 40)}{(2s + 8)^2(s^2 + 8s + 25)}$$

is seen to embrace all of the possible combinations of factors: a constant term K, a single s term, a linear factor, a repeated linear factor (where the factor is repeated

Plot of phase for the transfer function of Example 20.3

FIGURE 20.7

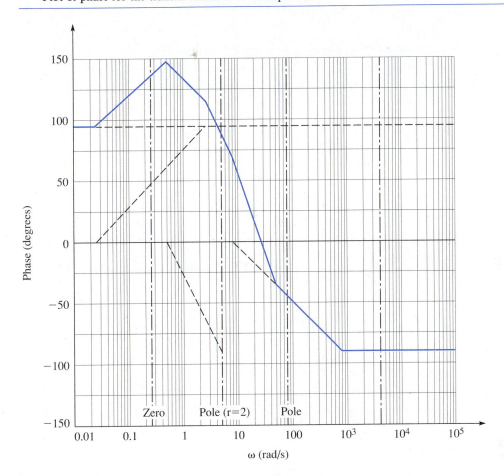

twice), and a quadratic factor. Observe that the quadratic factor possesses complex conjugate roots.

The quadratic factor of the form

$$as^2 + bs + c$$

may be expressed as

$$a(s^2 + 2\alpha s + \omega_o^2)$$

where

$$\alpha \equiv \frac{b}{2a} \qquad \text{and} \qquad \omega_o = \frac{c}{a}$$

Use of the damping factor

$$\zeta \equiv \frac{\alpha}{\omega_o}$$

permits the quadratic factor to be written as

$$s^2 + 2\zeta\omega_o s + \omega_o^2 \tag{20.16}$$

A quadratic factor in the denominator of a transfer function

$$\frac{1}{s^2 + 2\zeta\omega_o s + \omega_o^2}$$

contributes a gain to the overall transfer function when s is replaced by $j\omega$:

$$|H(j\omega)| = \frac{1}{|\omega_o^2 - \omega^2 + j2\zeta\omega_o\omega|} \quad \text{or} \quad |H(j\omega)| = \frac{1}{\sqrt{(\omega_o^2 - \omega^2)^2 + (2\zeta\omega_o\omega)^2}}$$

The ω_o^2 in the denominator may be factored to yield

$$|H(j\omega)| = \frac{1}{\sqrt{\omega_o^4[1 - (\omega/\omega_o)^2]^2 + \omega_o^4[2\zeta(\omega/\omega_o)]^2}}$$

And with

$$\eta \equiv \frac{\omega}{\omega_o}$$

one obtains

$$|H(j\omega)| = \frac{1}{\omega_o^2 \sqrt{(1 - \eta^2)^2 + (2\zeta\eta)^2}} \tag{20.17}$$

It may be noted that the gain is quite dependent on the value of the damping factor ζ. The contribution to the phase will be

$$\theta(\omega) = -\arctan\frac{2\zeta\eta}{1 - \eta^2} \tag{20.18}$$

The low- and high-frequency asymptotes are obtained by considering eq. (20.17) in light of very low and very high values of η. For η tending toward zero, eq. (20.17) gives with ω_o^2 as a modifier

$$|H_L(j\omega)| = 1$$

and in terms of decibels,

$$G_L(\omega) = 20 \log 1 = 0 \text{ dB}$$

If the square of the frequency, ω_o^2, is included as a modifier to the entire transfer function, eq. (20.17) may also be written without the ω_o^2. This will permit an examination of the effect of ω on $|H(j\omega)|$ and the gain contribution of the quadratic factor will then be

$$|H(j\omega)| = \frac{1}{\sqrt{1 - 2\eta^2 + \eta^4 + (2\zeta)^2\eta^2}}$$

and for η large, $\eta^4 \gg \eta^2$, so that

$$|H_H(j\omega)| = \frac{1}{\sqrt{\eta^4}} = \eta^{-2}$$

In terms of decibels,

$$G_H(\omega) = 20 \log \eta^{-2} = -40 \log \eta \text{ decibels}$$

which is an inclined line that falls at 40 dB per decade or 12 dB per octave as ω (or η) increases.

The break frequency occurs when the low- and high-frequency asymptotes intersect or when $G_L(\omega) = G_H(\omega)$:

$$20 \log 1 = -40 \log \eta$$

$$-\frac{1}{2} \log 1 = \log \eta$$

$$\log 1^{-1/2} = \log \eta$$

$$\log 1 = \log \eta$$

Or because $\eta = \omega/\omega_o$,

$$\omega = \omega_o$$

Figures 20.8 and 20.9 show plots of the actual gain and the actual phase shift, respectively, as function of frequency and the damping factor ζ. Observe that when ζ is small, close attention must be paid to the values of gain near the break frequency, because the departure of the true curve from the asymptotic plot can be drastic.

The corrections to the low- and high-frequency asymptotes of the denominator factor are computed by assuming that they can be established by the relationships

$$\Delta G = G(\omega) - G_L(\omega) = G(\omega)$$

because $G_L(\omega) = 0$ dB, and

$$\Delta G = G(\omega) - G_H(\omega)$$

where

$$G_H(\omega) = -40 \log \eta \text{ decibels}$$

Here, $G(\omega)$ derives from eq. (20.17) without the ω_o^2 and expressed in decibels:

$$\begin{aligned} G(\omega) &= 20 \log\left[\frac{1}{\sqrt{(1-\eta^2)^2 + (2\zeta\eta)^2}}\right] \\ &= 20 \log 1 - 20 \log\left[\sqrt{(1-\eta^2)^2 + (2\zeta\eta)^2}\right] \\ &= 0 - 10 \log\left[(1-\eta^2)^2 + (2\zeta\eta)^2\right] \end{aligned}$$

For values of $\eta < 1$,

$$\Delta G = G(\omega) = -10 \log[(1-\eta^2)^2 + (2\zeta\eta)^2] \qquad \textbf{(20.19)}$$

FIGURE 20.8

Gain in decibels as a function of $\eta = \omega/\omega_o$ and ζ for a quadratic denominator factor

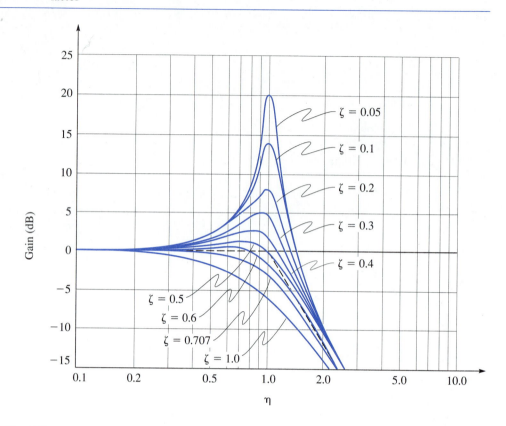

FIGURE 20.9

Phase in degrees as a function of $\eta = \omega/\omega_o$ and ζ for a quadratic denominator factor

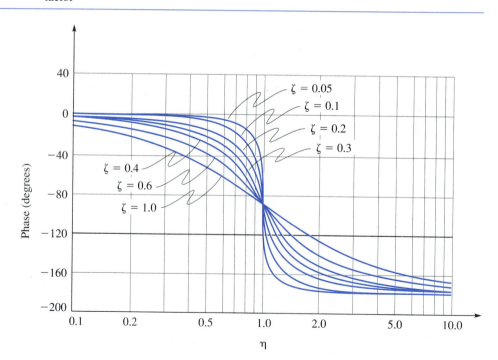

Note here that for extremely low values of ζ, this correction (and the true curve for the denominator factor) will be positive.

For $\eta = 1$,

$$\Delta G = -10 \log[(1 - \eta^2)^2 + (2\zeta\eta)^2] = -10 \log[(1 - 1)^2 + (2\zeta)^2]$$

or

$$\Delta G = -20 \log 2\zeta \qquad (20.20)$$

There will be no correction when $\zeta = 0.5$.

Finally, for $\eta > 1$, using $\Delta G = G(\omega) - G_H(\omega)$,

$$\Delta G = -10 \log[(1 - \eta^2)^2 + (2\zeta\eta)^2] - (-40 \log \eta)]$$

or

$$\Delta G = 40 \log \eta - 10 \log[(1 - \eta^2)^2 + (2\zeta\eta)^2] \qquad (20.21)$$

Again, it should be noted that for the lower values of ζ, this correction will be positive. Corrections to the low- and high-frequency asymptotes, computed from eqs. (20.19) through (20.21), are presented in Fig. 20.10.

Corrections to the asymptotic-gain–frequency plot for several values of the damping factor ζ and several values of η (denominator factor)

FIGURE 20.10

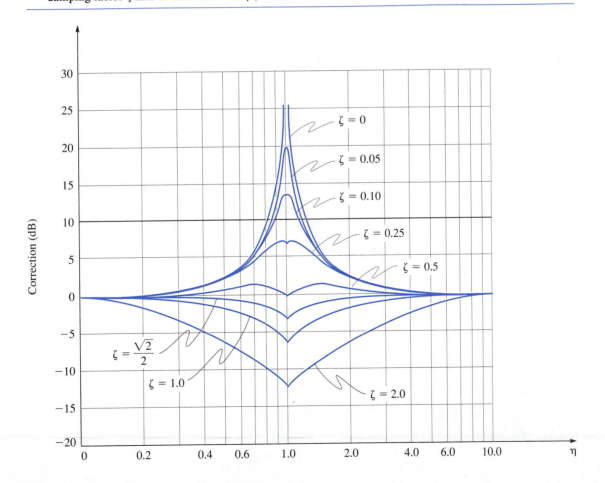

The contribution to the phase shift by a quadratic factor in the denominator, is computed from eq. (20.18).

■ **EXAMPLE 20.4**

Plot the asymptotic gain and phase shift as a function of frequency for the transfer function

$$H(s) = 10^6 \frac{(s + \frac{1}{2})(s + 10)^2}{s(s + 4000)(s^2 + 200s + 40{,}000)}$$

and determine the correction to the gain at $\omega = 180$ rad/s.

Solution

1. $H(s)$ must be put into standard form:

$$H(s) = 10^6 \frac{(0.5)(10)^2}{(4000)(40{,}000)} \frac{(1 + 2s)(1 + 0.1s)^2}{s(1 + 0.00025s)(1 + 0.005s + 0.000025s^2)}$$

$$= 0.3125 \frac{(1 + 2s)(1 + 0.1s)^2}{s(1 + 0.00025s)(1 + 0.005s + 0.000025s^2)}$$

2. The break frequencies are

zeros: $\omega_o = \dfrac{1}{2}$ rad/s

$\omega_o = \dfrac{1}{0.1} = 10$ rad/s   (double zero)

poles: $\omega_o = \dfrac{1}{\sqrt{0.000025}} = 200$ rad/s   ($\zeta = 0.5$)

$\omega_o = \dfrac{1}{0.00025} = 4000$ rad/s

3. The overall low-frequency asymptote of $H(s)$ is obtained by letting all $s = 0$ except for the single s in the denominator:

$$H_L(s) = \frac{0.3125}{s}$$

This indicates that the low-frequency asymptote falls off at 20 dB per decade. At the lowest frequency of interest (say 1/10 the lowest break frequency, or $\omega = 0.05$ rad/s),

$$|H_L(\omega = 0.05)| = \frac{0.3125}{0.05} = 6.25$$

$$G_L(\omega = 0.05) = 20 \log 6.25 = 20(0.7959) = 15.92 \approx 16 \text{ dB}$$

4. The overall high frequency asymptote of $H(s)$ is

$$H_H(s) = 0.3125 \frac{(2s)(0.1s)^2}{s(0.00025s)(0.000025s^2)} = \frac{10^6}{s}$$

This indicates that the high-frequency asymptote is falling at 20 dB per decade. With the highest frequency of interest taken as 10 times the highest break frequency, or $\omega = 40{,}000$ rad/s, it is seen that

$$|H_H(\omega = 40{,}000)| = \frac{10^6}{40{,}000} = 25$$

$$G_H(\omega = 40{,}000) = 20 \log 25 = 20(1.3979) = 27.96 \approx 28 \text{ dB}$$

The high-frequency asymptote falls off at 20 dB per decade and must pass through 27.96 dB at $\omega = 40{,}000$ rad/s.

5. The asymptotic-gain plot is shown in Fig. 20.11 and the phase shift is plotted in Fig. 20.12.

The correction to the asymptotic-gain plot at $\omega = 180$ rad/s is determined from Fig. 20.10 at $\eta = 180/200 = 0.90$ and $\zeta = 0.5$ or from eq. (20.19). Figure 20.10 shows a correction of about 0.6 dB, positive because the correction involves a denominator factor. This may be confirmed using eq. (20.19)

$$\Delta G = -10 \log[(1 - \eta^2)^2 + (2\zeta\eta)^2] = 0.73 \text{ dB}.$$

■

Asymptotic gain as a function of frequency for the transfer function of Example 20.4

FIGURE 20.11

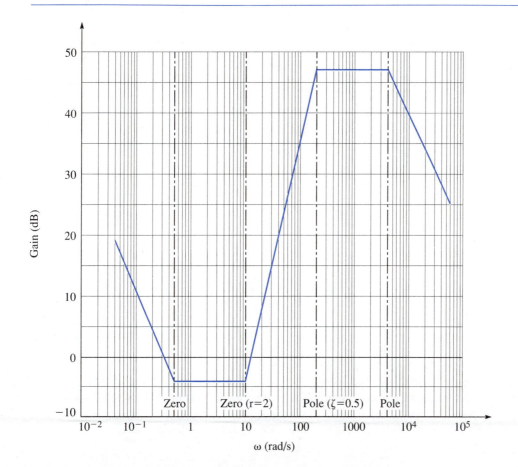

FIGURE 20.12   Phase shift as a function of frequency for the transfer function of Example 20.4

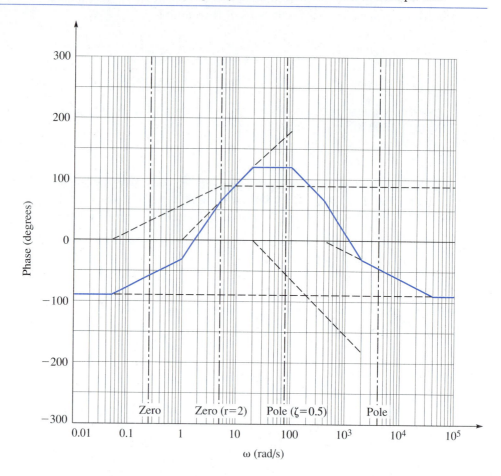

SECTION 20.7   FILTERS

As indicated in Section 19.6, a *filter* is a component or network used in an electrical or electronic system for the selective enhancement or the specified degradation of a given class of input signals. It is a network that possesses particular frequency response characteristics, and it is used in a variety of applications. These applications include the tuning of radio or TV receivers, the improvement of signal-to-noise ratios, and, in what is referred to as a phase shift network, the provision of a desired phase shift between input and output signals.

The networks in Table 19.2 show that *passive filters* can be synthesized as two-port networks containing RL, RC, or RLC combinations. They are generally inserted between a voltage source with internal resistance R_s and a load with impedance Z_o. These terminations always yield a passband voltage gain less than or equal to unity and have an effect on the performance of the filter. On the other hand, *active filters*, which contain operational amplifiers, might better be termed active filter amplifiers or filter amplifiers, because they have the feature of being able to provide a specified passband gain. Both active and passive filters are considered here.

Ideal characteristics of two types of filters: (a) low-pass and (b) high-pass

FIGURE 20.13

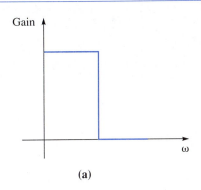

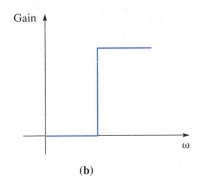

(a) (b)

THE DESIGN OF PASSIVE FILTERS

The ideal characteristics of the four common types of passive filters composed only of the network elements R, L, and C, are displayed in Fig. 19.10. The characteristics of the low- and high-pass filters are repeated here as Fig. 20.13. It should once again be emphasized that it is not possible to realize networks that provide these ideal characteristics; but as the complexity of the network increases, the ideal may be approached. This complexity involves the use of higher-order LC networks, usually in the form of a ladder network.

20.8.1 Low- and High-Pass Filters

Tables 20.2 and 20.3 summarize the pertinent characteristics and design data for the low- and high-pass filters shown in Table 19.2.

■ **EXAMPLE 20.5**

Design a first-order, low-pass filter and a $\zeta = \sqrt{2}/2$ second-order, low-pass filter to have a cutoff frequency of 15,916 Hz, using 100-pF capacitors, and plot the results.

Solution For both filters, the cutoff angular frequency is

$$\omega_o = 2\pi f = 2\pi(15{,}916) = 100{,}000 \text{ rad/s}$$

Table 20.2 shows that with the value of C given for the first-order filter,

$$R = \frac{1}{\omega_o C} = \frac{1}{(100{,}000)(100 \times 10^{-12})} = 100{,}000 \ \Omega$$

For the second-order filter, with C given

$$L = \frac{1}{\omega_o^2 C} = \frac{1}{(100{,}000)^2(100 \times 10^{-12})} = 1 \text{ H}$$

First order: Requires (1) horizontal LF asymptote, (2) falling HF asymptote

Structure

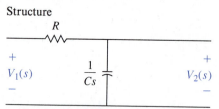

$$\alpha_{12}(s) = \frac{1/RC}{s + 1/RC}$$

Characteristics

1   A single pole and no zeros
2   HF asymptote falls at
    20 dB/decade

Bode asymptotic plot

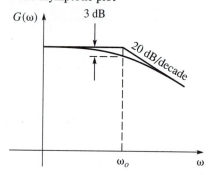

Break frequency

$$\omega_o = \frac{1}{RC}$$

Design equations (ω_o specified)

$$R = \frac{1}{\omega_o C} \qquad C = \frac{1}{\omega_o R}$$

Second order: Requires (1) horizontal LF asymptote, (2) falling HF asymptote

Structure

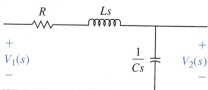

$$\alpha_{12}(s) = \frac{1/LC}{s^2 + (R/L)s + 1/LC}$$

Characteristics

1   A double pole and no zeros
2   HF asymptote falls at
    40 dB/decade
3   A single break frequency requires
    $\zeta < 1$
4   3 dB down at ω_o requires
    $\zeta = \sqrt{2}/2$

$$\zeta = \frac{R/2L}{1/\sqrt{LC}} = \frac{R}{2}\sqrt{\frac{C}{L}}$$

Break frequency

$$\omega_o = \frac{1}{\sqrt{LC}}$$

Bode asymptotic plot

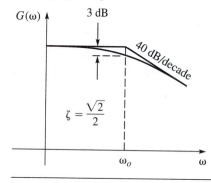

Design equations (ω_o specified and $\zeta = \sqrt{2}/2$)

    Given R   *Given L*   *Given C*

$$C = \frac{\sqrt{2}}{\omega_o R}, \quad L = \frac{1}{\omega_o^2 C} \qquad\qquad C = \frac{1}{\omega_o^2 L}, \quad R = \sqrt{2\frac{L}{C}} \qquad\qquad L = \frac{1}{\omega_o^2 C}, \quad R = \sqrt{2\frac{L}{C}}$$

First order: Requires (1) rising LF asymptote, (2) horizontal HF asymptote

Structure

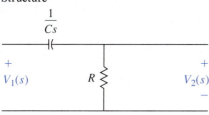

$$\alpha_{12}(s) = \frac{s}{s + 1/RC}$$

Characteristics
1 A single pole and a single zero
2 LF asymptote rises at
   20 dB/decade

Break frequency

$$\omega_o = \frac{1}{RC}$$

Bode asymptotic plot

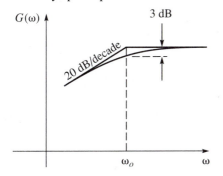

Design equations (ω_o specified)

$$R = \frac{1}{\omega_o C} \qquad C = \frac{1}{\omega_o R}$$

Second order: Requires (1) rising LF asymptote, (2) horizontal HF asymptote

Structure

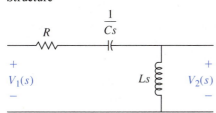

$$\alpha_{12}(s) = \frac{s^2}{s^2 + (R/L)s + 1/LC}$$

Characteristics
1 A double pole and a double zero
2 LF asymptote rises at
   40 dB/decade
3 A single break frequency requires
   $\zeta < 1$
4 3 dB down at ω_o requires
   $\zeta = \sqrt{2}/2$

$$\zeta = \frac{R/2L}{1/\sqrt{LC}} = \frac{R}{2}\sqrt{\frac{C}{L}}$$

Break frequency

$$\omega_o = \frac{1}{\sqrt{LC}}$$

Bode asymptotic plot

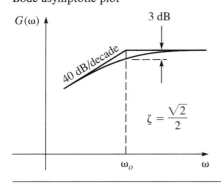

Design equations (ω_o specified and $\zeta = \sqrt{2}/2$)

Given R	Given L	Given C
$C = \dfrac{\sqrt{2}}{\omega_o R}, \quad L = \dfrac{1}{\omega_o^2 C}$	$C = \dfrac{1}{\omega_o^2 L}, \quad R = \sqrt{2\dfrac{L}{C}}$	$L = \dfrac{1}{\omega_o^2 C}, \quad R = \sqrt{2\dfrac{L}{C}}$

FIGURE 20.14   (a) Bode asymptotic plots and (b) true curves for a first-order, low-pass filter and a second-order, low-pass filter with $\zeta = \sqrt{2}/2$

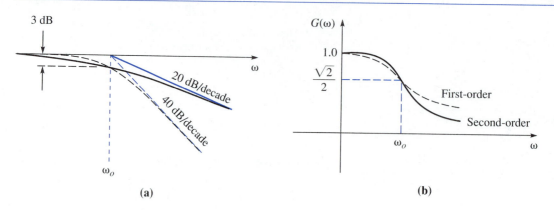

(a)   (b)

And

$$R = \sqrt{2\frac{L}{C}} = \sqrt{2\frac{1}{100 \times 10^{-12}}} = 141{,}421 \ \Omega$$

The comparison of the filter characteristics is shown in Fig. 20.14. ■

Higher order filters can yield sharper attenuations and are realizeable by adding more inductors and capacitors so that the filter resembles a ladder network. One such approximation will yield what is known as the *Butterworth response*.

EXERCISE 20.2

Design a first-order filter and a $\zeta = \sqrt{2}/2$ second-order, low-pass filter to have a cutoff frequency of 19,894 Hz, using 51.2-pF capacitors.

Answer   For a first-order filter, $R = 156{,}250 \ \Omega$; for a second-order filter, $R = 220{,}970 \ \Omega$ and $L = 1.25$ H.

■ EXAMPLE 20.6

Select values for the L's and C's in order to make the first- and second-order, high-pass filters ($\zeta = \sqrt{2}/2$) of Table 20.3 have the cutoff frequency of $\omega = 10{,}000$ rad/s. Let $R = 2000 \ \Omega$ in both networks.

Solution   From Table 20.3 with $R = 2 \ \Omega$, for the first-order filter,

$$C = \frac{1}{\omega_o R} = \frac{1}{(10{,}000)(2000)} = 50 \ \text{nF}$$

For the second-order filter with $\zeta = \sqrt{2}/2$ and $R = 2000 \ \Omega$, Table 20.3 shows that

$$C = \frac{\sqrt{2}}{\omega_o R} = \frac{\sqrt{2}}{(10{,}000)(2000)} = 70.71 \ \text{nF}$$

and

$$L = \frac{1}{\omega_o^2 C} = \frac{1}{(10,000)^2(70.71 \times 10^{-9})} = 0.141 \text{ H}$$

EXERCISE 20.3

Design a second-order, high-pass filter to have a cutoff frequency of 50,000 rad/s with $R = 10,000 \ \Omega$ and $\zeta = \sqrt{2}/2$.

Answer $L = 0.141$ H and $C = 2.83$ nF

20.8.2 Band-Pass and Band-Stop Filters

Tables 20.4 and 20.5 summarize the pertinent characteristics and design data for the band-pass and band-stop filters shown in Table 19.2.

Summary of pertinent characteristics and design data for band-pass filter   **TABLE 20.4**

Requires (1) horizontal LF asymptote, (2) falling HF asymptote, (3) two poles and one zero

Structure

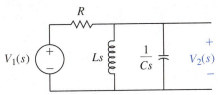

Bode asymptotic plot

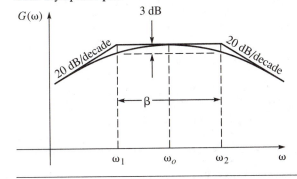

$$\alpha_{12}(s) = \frac{s}{RC[s^2 + (1/RC)s + 1/LC]}$$

Characteristics
1   Two poles and one zero
2   LF asymptote rises at
    20 dB/decade
3   HF asymptote falls at
    20 dB/decade
4   Half power frequencies at ω_1
    and ω_2

Bandwidth

$$\beta = \omega_2 - \omega_1 = \frac{1}{RC}$$

Center frequency

$$\omega_o = \frac{1}{\sqrt{LC}}$$

Design equations (β and ω_o specified)

Given R	Given L	Given C
$C = \dfrac{1}{R\beta}, \quad L = \dfrac{1}{\omega_o^2 C}$	$C = \dfrac{1}{\omega_o^2 L}, \quad R = \dfrac{1}{C\beta}$	$L = \dfrac{1}{\omega_o^2 C}, \quad R = \dfrac{1}{C\beta}$

TABLE 20.5   Summary of pertinent characteristics and design data for band-stop filter

Requires (1) four break frequencies: downward breaks at ω_a and ω_b, upward breaks at ω_1 and ω_2, (2) horizontal LF and HF asymptotes, (3) two poles and two zeros

Structure

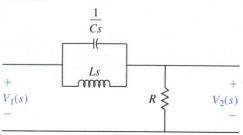

$$\alpha_{12}(s) = \frac{s^2 + 1/LC}{s^2 + (1/RC)s + 1/LC}$$

Characteristics
1   Two poles and two zeros
2   Horizontal LF and HF asymptotes
3   Half power frequencies at ω_1 and ω_2

Bode asymptotic plot

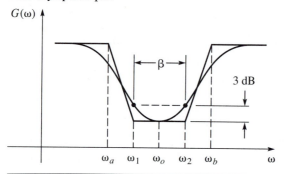

Bandwidth

$$\beta = \omega_2 - \omega_1 = \frac{1}{RC}$$

Center frequency

$$\omega_o = \frac{1}{\sqrt{LC}}$$

Design equations (β and ω_o specified)

Given R	Given L	Given C
$C = \dfrac{1}{R\beta}, \quad L = \dfrac{1}{\omega_o^2 C}$	$C = \dfrac{1}{\omega_o^2 L}, \quad R = \dfrac{1}{C\beta}$	$L = \dfrac{1}{\omega_o^2 C}, \quad R = \dfrac{1}{C\beta}$

■   **EXAMPLE 20.7**

Design a band-pass filter in the form of the structure in Table 20.4 with $R = 2000\ \Omega$ and a bandwidth of 400 rad/s at a center frequency of 10,000 rad/s.

Solution   From Table 20.4

$$C = \frac{1}{R\beta} = \frac{1}{(2000)(400)} = 1.25\ \mu F$$

and

$$L = \frac{1}{\omega_o^2 C} = \frac{1}{(10,000)^2 (1.25 \times 10^{-6})} = 8\ mH$$

EXERCISE 20.4

Select values of R and C for a band-pass filter with $L = 100$ mH, a center frequency of 20,000 Hz, and a bandwidth of 500 Hz.

Answer $C = 25$ nF and $R = 80,000\ \Omega$.

■ EXAMPLE 20.8

Design a band-stop filter with maximum attenuation at 2000 rad/s and with a bandwidth of rejection of $\beta = 100$ rad/s. An inductor of 0.5 H is available.

Solution   The value of the capacitor can be obtained immediately from the cutoff frequency. From Table 20.5

$$C = \frac{1}{\omega_o^2 L} = \frac{1}{(2000)^2(0.5)} = 0.5\ \mu F$$

Then, from the bandwidth specification,

$$R = \frac{1}{\beta C} = \frac{1}{(100)(5 \times 10^{-7})} = 20,000\ \Omega \qquad ■$$

EXERCISE 20.5

If $R = 4000\ \Omega$, select values of L and C for the band-stop filter structure in Table 20.5 to yield a center frequency of 12,500 rad/s and a bandwidth of 500 rad/s.

Answer $C = 0.5\ \mu F$ and $L = 12.8$ mH.

PASSIVE FILTERS AND TERMINATING IMPEDANCES

In most applications, the passive filter is installed in a network, as shown in Fig. 20.15, between a voltage source with an internal resistance R_s and a load Z_o or R_o. Notice that the transfer function, $H(s) = V_2(s)/V_1(s)$, applies only to the filter; and if the

An s domain filter network inserted between a voltage source with internal resistance R_s and a load R_o

FIGURE 20.15

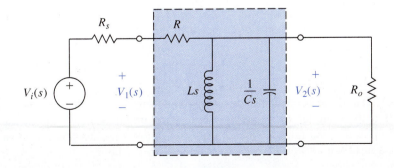

transfer function between $V_i(s)$ and $V_o(s)$ is of interest, it becomes the *composite gain*. For Fig. 20.15 with $V_o(s) = V_2(s)$,

$$H(s) = \frac{V_1(s)}{V_i(s)} \cdot \frac{V_o(s)}{V_1(s)} = \frac{V_o(s)}{V_i(s)}$$

In the band-pass filter arrangement of Fig. 20.15,

$$R_i = R_s + R \tag{20.22}$$

and observe that the admittance of the parallel portion of the network is

$$Y_p(s) = Cs + \frac{1}{R_o} + \frac{1}{Ls}$$
$$= C\left[\frac{s^2 + (1/R_oC)s + 1/LC}{s}\right]$$

which makes the impedance of this parallel entity

$$Z_p(s) = \frac{1}{C} \cdot \frac{s}{Cs^2 + (1/R_oC)s + 1/LC}$$

Voltage division will provide the composite gain. After some laborious algebra, the result is

$$H(s) = \frac{V_o(s)}{V_i(s)} = \frac{R_o}{R_i + R_o}\left[\frac{(R_i + R_o)/(R_iR_oC)(s)}{s^2 + (R_i + R_o)/(R_iR_oC)s + 1/LC}\right]$$

Here,

$$\omega_o = \frac{1}{\sqrt{LC}} \tag{20.23}$$

is the center frequency and the bandwidth is given by

$$\beta = \frac{R_i + R_o}{R_iR_oC} \tag{20.24}$$

with a scale factor defined by

$$\psi = \frac{R_o}{R_i + R_o} \tag{20.25}$$

and with these, the transfer function can be put into the form

$$\frac{V_o(s)}{V_i(s)} = \psi \frac{\beta s}{s^2 + \beta s + \omega_o^2} \tag{20.26}$$

so that eqs. (20.23) and (20.24) become the design equations.

Observe that the scale factor ψ can have a marked impact on the gain of the transfer function at any and all frequencies; thus, it behooves the designer, in most cases, to use a source with a low R_s and remove the R in the filter.

■ **EXAMPLE 20.9**

Design band-pass filters for a center frequency of 10,000 rad/s and a bandwidth of 400 rad/s.

a. With terminating resistances of $R_s = 100 \, \Omega$ and $R_o = 400 \, \Omega$ as in Fig. 20.15
b. With no load resistance but with $R = 100 \, \Omega$ as in Table 20.4.

Solution

a. With R_i determined from eq. (20.22) and with $R = 0$

$$R_i = R_s + R = 100 + 0 = 100 \, \Omega$$

then from eq. (20.24)

$$C = \frac{1}{\beta}\left(\frac{R_i + R_o}{R_i R_o}\right) = \frac{1}{400}\left[\frac{100 + 400}{(100)(400)}\right] = 31.25 \, \mu F$$

and from eq. (20.23)

$$L = \frac{1}{\omega_o^2 C} = \frac{1}{(10,000)^2(31.25 \times 10^{-6})} = 0.32 \, mH$$

b. From Table 20.4

$$C = \frac{1}{\beta R} = \frac{1}{(400)(100)} = 25 \, \mu F$$

and

$$L = \frac{1}{\omega_o^2 C} = \frac{1}{(10,000)^2(25 \times 10^{-6})} = 0.40 \, mH$$

■

EXERCISE 20.6

Select values of L and C for a band-pass filter with $R_o = 800 \, \Omega$ and $R_i = 4000 \, \Omega$. The filter is to have a center frequency of 20,000 Hz and a bandwidth of 500 Hz.

Answer $C = 3 \, \mu F$ and $L = 0.833 \, mH$.

MAGNITUDE AND FREQUENCY SCALING

SECTION 20.10

Magnitude and frequency scaling of the elements R, L, and C are useful techniques because scaled values of elements possessing magnitudes that are physically unrealizable permit simplified computations. In addition, scaled or normalized networks provide a common basis for the comparison of frequency-selective or tuned networks, and scaling is of considerable importance in the realm of network synthesis.

20.10.1 Magnitude Scaling

The elements R_1, L_1, and C_1 may be scaled in magnitude at a given frequency by selecting a positive real constant K_m, which may lie anywhere between zero and infinity. Multiplication of R and L by K_m and division of C by K_m will provide the scaled or normalized values R_2, L_2, and C_2:

$$R_2 = K_m R_1 \tag{20.27a}$$

$$L_2 = K_m L_1 \tag{20.27b}$$

$$C_2 = \frac{C_1}{K_m} \tag{20.27c}$$

20.10.2 Frequency Scaling

Frequency scaling is based on leaving the impedance of the network elements unchanged after the angular frequency is multiplied by a positive real constant K_f, which may be less than unity. Hence, if

$$\omega_2 = K_f \omega_1$$

then $Z_{R_1} = Z_{R_2}$, or

$$R_2 = R_1 \tag{20.28a}$$

because R does not depend on frequency. However, so that $X_{L_1} = X_{L_2}$,

$$L_2 = \frac{L_1}{K_f} \tag{20.28b}$$

and for $X_{C_1} = X_{C_2}$,

$$C_2 = \frac{C_1}{K_f} \tag{20.28c}$$

20.10.3 Magnitude and Frequency Scaling

If the network is to be scaled in both magnitude *and* frequency, then

$$R_2 = K_m R_1 \tag{20.29a}$$

$$L_2 = \frac{K_m}{K_f} L_1 \tag{20.29b}$$

$$C_2 = \frac{1}{K_m K_f} C_1 \tag{20.29c}$$

■ **EXAMPLE 20.10**

The network shown in Fig. 20.16a gives an input impedance of $2\sqrt{2}\underline{/-45°}$ at $\omega = 1$ rad/s. The value of C is unrealistic, and the value of ω is considered to be too low to be of practical importance. Determine the values of R_2, L_2, and C_2 if the impedance of the network is to be $200\sqrt{2}\underline{/-45°}$ at $\omega = 25{,}000$ rad/s.

(a) Network with unrealistic element and frequency values and (b) a scaled network

FIGURE 20.16

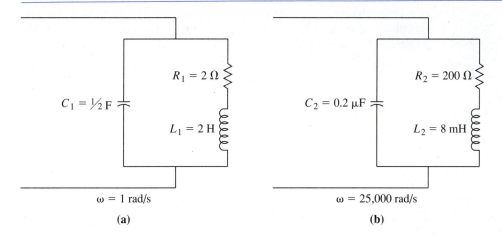

$\omega = 1$ rad/s

(a)

$\omega = 25{,}000$ rad/s

(b)

Solution   Here,

$$K_m = \frac{200\sqrt{2}}{2\sqrt{2}} = 100 \qquad K_f = \frac{25{,}000}{1} = 25{,}000$$

Then, by eqs. (20.29)

$$R_2 = K_m R_1 = 100(2) = 200\ \Omega$$

$$L_2 = \frac{K_m}{K_f} L_1 = \left(\frac{100}{25{,}000}\right)(2) = 8\ \text{mH}$$

$$C_2 = \frac{1}{K_m K_f} C_1 = \frac{1}{(100)(25{,}000)}\left(\frac{1}{2}\right) = 0.2\ \mu\text{F}$$

The result, shown in Fig. 20.16b, is easily verified. With

$$X_L = \omega L = 25{,}000(0.008) = 200\ \Omega$$

$$X_C = \frac{1}{\omega C} = \frac{1}{25{,}000(0.2 \times 10^{-6})} = 200\ \Omega$$

and $R = 200\ \Omega$,

$$Z = \frac{(200 + j200)(-j200)}{200 + j200 - j200} = \frac{40{,}000 - j40{,}000}{200} = 200 - j200$$

$$= 200\sqrt{2}\underline{/-45°}\ \Omega$$

■

EXERCISE 20.7

For the network shown in Fig. 20.17 which operates at 50 rad/s, select element values to make the driving-point impedance 80 times greater at a frequency of 20,000 rad/s.

Answer $R = 6400\ \Omega$, $L = 0.24$ H, and $C = 65.10$ nF.

FIGURE 20.17   A combination of three network elements (Exercise 20.7)

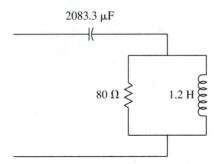

2083.3 μF

80 Ω   1.2 H

SECTION 20.11   ACTIVE FILTERS

Inductors used in filters in low-frequency (dc to 10,000 Hz) applications are bulky and unreliable and do not perform as ideal network elements. Moreover, they are impossible to manufacture as part of an integrated circuit, and in many cases, they are incompatible with present-day techniques for the assembly of electronic systems. The operational amplifier (or *op-amp*), discussed in detail in Chapter 8, provides the key to inductorless filter design. The use of the operational amplifier also leads to filter designs with gains that exceed unity.

Consider an operational amplifier connected in the inverting configuration, as indicated in Fig. 20.18. Recall that the operational amplifier is a high-gain device, and because of the high input impedance of the amplifier, negligible current flows into the negative terminal. Moreover, because of the high gain and because the positive terminal is connected to ground ($v_2 = 0$), a moderate voltage at the output causes a virtual ground at the inverting input and, while in the linear operating region

$$v_1 \approx v_2 \approx 0$$

The impedances $Z_i(s)$ and $Z_f(s)$ in Fig. 20.18 can contain any arrangement of resistors and capacitors. If *KCL* is applied at the negative terminal (remember that

FIGURE 20.18   An operational amplifier with input and feedback impedances connected in the inverting configuration

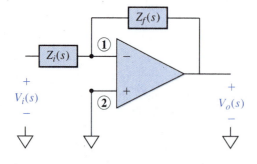

the current entering the amplifier is negligible), then

$$\frac{V_i(s)}{Z_i(s)} + \frac{V_o(s)}{Z_f(s)} = 0$$

This yields the transfer function

$$\alpha_{12}(s) = \frac{V_o(s)}{V_i(s)} = -\frac{Z_f(s)}{Z_i(s)} \tag{20.30}$$

and the form of $Z_i(s)$ and $Z_f(s)$ can be selected to provide the desired performance.

Tables 20.6 and 20.7 summarize the pertinent characteristics and design data for low- and high-pass op-amp filters (Table 20.6) and band-pass and band-stop op-amp filters (Table 20.7).

An example that illustrates the use of Table 20.6 follows.

■ **EXAMPLE 20.11**

Synthesize low- and high-pass filters with a cutoff frequency of 10,000 Hz and a midband gain of 32 dB, using resistors of at least 1000 Ω.

Solution   In both cases,

$$\omega_o = 10,000(2\pi) = 62,832 \text{ rad/s} \quad \text{and} \quad 20 \log K = 32 \text{ dB}$$

so that

$$\log K = \frac{32}{20} = 1.6 \quad \text{and} \quad K = 39.81$$

Table 20.6 shows that both the low- and high-pass gains are

$$K = \frac{R_f}{R_i}$$

If all $R \geq 1000 \ \Omega$, R_i may be selected for both cases as

$$R_i = 1000 \ \Omega$$

so that

$$R_f = 1000K = 1000(39.81) = 39.81 \text{ k}\Omega$$

For the low-pass filter,

$$C_f = \frac{1}{\omega_o R_f} = \frac{1}{62,832(39,810)} = 0.400 \text{ nF}$$

And for the high-pass filter,

$$C_i = \frac{1}{\omega_o R_i} = \frac{1}{62.832(1000)} = 15.92 \text{ nF}$$

■

TABLE 20.6

Summary of pertinent characteristics and design data for low pass and high pass op-amp filters

Structure

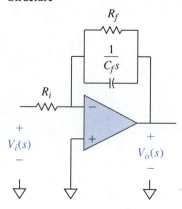

Bode asymptotic plot

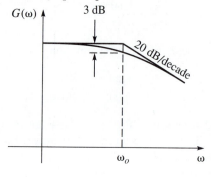

Low-Pass (see diagrams above)

$$\alpha_{12}(s) = -K \frac{\omega_o}{s + \omega_o}$$

Characteristics

1 A single pole and no zeros
2 HF asymptote falls at 20 dB/decade

Design equations

$$\omega_o = \frac{1}{R_f C_f}$$

$$K = \frac{R_f}{R_i}$$

High-Pass (see diagrams below)

$$\alpha_{12}(s) = -K \frac{s}{s + \omega_o}$$

Characteristics

1 A single pole and a single zero
2 LF asymptote rises at 20 dB/decade

Structure

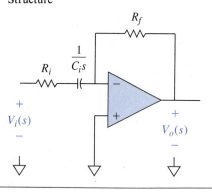

Bode asymptotic plot

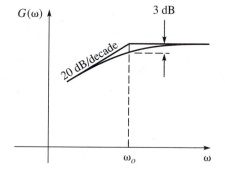

Design equations

$$\omega_o = \frac{1}{R_i C_i}$$

$$K = \frac{R_f}{R_i}$$

Summary of pertinent characteristics and design data for band-pass filter and band-stop op-amp filters

TABLE 20.7

Structure

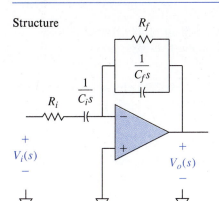

Bode asymptotic plot

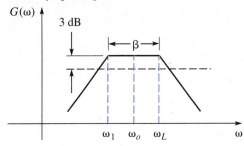

Band-Pass (see diagrams above)

$$\alpha_{12}(s) = -\frac{K_m \omega_2 s}{(s + \omega_1)(s + \omega_2)}$$

Characteristics
1 Two poles and one zero
2 LF asymptote rises at 20 dB/decade
3 HF asymptote falls at 20 dB/decade
4 Half power frequencies at ω_1 and ω_2

Design equations

$$K_m = \frac{R_f}{R_i} \qquad \omega_1 = \frac{1}{R_i C_i} \qquad \omega_2 = \frac{1}{R_f C_f}$$

Band-Stop (see diagrams below)

$$\alpha_{12}(s) = -K_m \frac{(s + \omega_1)(s + \omega_2)}{(s + \omega_a)(s + \omega_b)}$$

Characteristics
1 Two poles and two zeros
2 Horizontal LF and HF asymptotes
3 Half power frequencies at ω_1 and ω_2

Structure

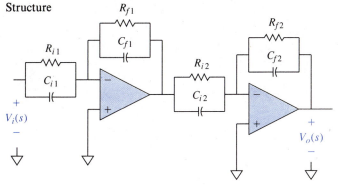

Bode asymptotic plot

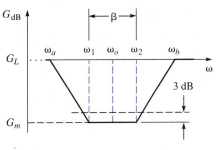

Design equations

$$\omega_a = K_m \omega_1 \qquad \omega_1 = \frac{1}{R_{i1} C_{i1}} \qquad \omega_2 = \frac{1}{R_{i2} C_{i2}}$$

$$\omega_b = \omega_2/K_m \qquad \omega_a = \frac{1}{R_{f1} C_{f1}} \qquad \omega_b = \frac{1}{R_{f2} C_{f2}}$$

$$\frac{R_{f1}}{R_{i1}} = \frac{R_{i2}}{R_{f2}}$$

EXERCISE 20.8

Synthesize low- and high-pass filters to have a gain of 48 dB with a cutoff frequency of 25,000 Hz. In both cases, the smallest resistor available has a resistance of 470 Ω.

Answer $R_i = 470\ \Omega$, $R_f = 118.1\ \text{k}\Omega$, low-pass $C_f = 53.92\ \text{pF}$, and high-pass $C_i = 13.55\ \text{nF}$.

The development of the design equations in Tables 20.6 and 20.7 is quite straightforward and will now be demonstrated for the case of the band-pass filter. Table 20.7 shows that the transfer function for the band-pass filter requires a pair of poles in the denominator and a zero in the numerator. The two half-power frequencies are ω_1 and ω_2. With the zero set at $s = 0$ in order to obtain as much attenuation at lower frequencies as possible, the transfer function will take the form

$$H(s) = \frac{Ks}{(s + \omega_1)(s + \omega_2)} \tag{20.31}$$

This transfer function can be realized by the op-amp network in Table 20.7 where

$$Z_i(s) = R_i + \frac{1}{C_i s} = \frac{R_i C_i s + 1}{C_i s}$$

$$Z_f(s) = \frac{R_f / C_f s}{R_f + 1/C_f s} = \frac{R_f}{R_f C_f s + 1}$$

which, in accordance with eq. (20.30), makes $\alpha_{12}(s)$

$$\alpha_{12}(s) = \frac{V_o(s)}{V_i(s)} = -\frac{Z_f(s)}{Z_i(s)} = -\frac{R_f / (R_f C_f s + 1)}{(R_i C_i s + 1)/C_i s} = -\frac{R_f C_i s}{(R_f C_f s + 1)(R_i C_i s + 1)}$$

or

$$\alpha_{12}(s) = -\frac{s/R_i C_f}{(s + 1/R_f C_f)(s + 1/R_i C_i)} \tag{20.32}$$

A comparison of eqs. (20.31) and (20.32) shows that the constant K must be selected to yield the specified midband gain. The magnitude of $\alpha_{12}(s)$ is obtained by letting $s = j\omega$ in eq. (20.31):

$$|\alpha_{12}(j\omega)| = \frac{jK\omega}{|\omega_1 + j\omega||\omega_2 + j\omega|}$$

In the center of the passband, $\omega > \omega_1$ and $\omega_2 > \omega$. Thus, $|\alpha_{12}(j\omega)|$ can be approximated by

$$|\alpha_{12}(j\omega)| = K_m \approx \frac{jK\omega}{j\omega(\omega_2)}$$

The midband gain is therefore

$$K_m = \frac{K}{\omega_2}$$

and the value of K can be obtained from the specified values of ω_2 and the midband gain requirement G_m in dB

$$G_m = 20 \log K_m$$

With this in eq. (20.31),

$$\alpha_{12}(s) = -\frac{K_m \omega_2 s}{(s + \omega_1)(s + \omega_2)} \tag{20.33}$$

When this is compared with eq. (20.32), it is seen that either

$$\omega_1 = \frac{1}{R_f C_f} \qquad \text{or} \qquad \omega_1 = \frac{1}{R_i C_i}$$

Let

$$\omega_1 = \frac{1}{R_i C_i}$$

so that

$$\omega_2 = \frac{1}{R_f C_f}$$

and by a comparison between eqs. (20.32) and (20.33),

$$K_m = \frac{R_f}{R_i}$$

Note that the band-pass RC active filter structure of Table 20.7 cannot be used to realize complex conjugate poles of $\alpha_{12}(s)$.

■ **EXAMPLE 20.12**

For the band-pass filter configuration in Table 20.7, select components with no resistor value below $100 \ \Omega$ to provide a passband between 50,000 and 100,000 rad/s with a midband gain of 66 dB.

Solution   Here

$$\log K_m = \frac{66}{20} = 3.3 \qquad \text{and} \qquad K_m = 1995$$

Then, with $R_i = 100 \ \Omega$, Table 20.7 gives

$$R_f = K_m R_i = 1995(100) = 199.5 \text{ k}\Omega$$

$$C_i = \frac{1}{R_i \omega_1} = \frac{1}{100(50,000)} = 0.2 \ \mu\text{F}$$

$$C_f = \frac{1}{R_f \omega_2} = \frac{1}{(199.5 \times 10^3)(100,000)} = 50.12 \text{ pF}$$

■

EXERCISE 20.9

Choose $R_i = 200 \, \Omega$ and design a band-pass filter to have a midband gain of 78 dB and half-power frequencies of 200,000 and 240,000 Hz.

Answer $R_f = 1.589 \, \text{M}\Omega$, $C_i = 3.98 \, \text{nF}$, and $C_f = 0.417 \, \text{pF}$.

■ **EXAMPLE 20.13**

For the band-elimination filter shown in Table 20.7b, select components with no resistor value below 200 Ω to provide a filter whose stopband lies between frequencies of 40 and 80 kHz with a midband rejection of -80 dB.

Solution   First,

$$\omega_1 = 2\pi(40{,}000) = 2.513 \times 10^5 \text{ rad/s}$$
$$\omega_2 = 2\pi(80{,}000) = 5.027 \times 10^5 \text{ rad/s}$$

Also,

$$20 \log K_m = -80$$
$$\log K_m = -4$$
$$K_m = \frac{1}{10{,}000}$$

Table 20.7 gives

$$\omega_a = K_m \omega_1 = \frac{1}{10{,}000}(2.513 \times 10^5) = 25.13 \text{ rad/s}$$

$$\omega_b = \frac{\omega_2}{K_m} = 10{,}000(5.027 \times 10^5) = 5.027 \times 10^9 \text{ rad/s}$$

Then, with

$$R_{i1} = R_{i2} = R_{f1} = R_{f2} = 200 \, \Omega$$

Table 20.7 gives

$$C_{i1} = \frac{1}{R_{i1}\omega_1} = \frac{1}{200(2.513 \times 10^5)} = 19.89 \text{ nF}$$

$$C_{i2} = \frac{1}{R_{i2}\omega_2} = \frac{1}{200(5.027 \times 10^5)} = 9.947 \text{ nF}$$

$$C_{f1} = \frac{1}{R_{f1}\omega_a} = \frac{1}{200(25.13)} = 198.9 \; \mu\text{F}$$

$$C_{f2} = \frac{1}{R_{f2}\omega_b} = \frac{1}{200(5.027 \times 10^9)} = 0.995 \text{ pF}$$

■

EXERCISE 20.10

Specify the components for a band-elimination filter with a midband gain of -66.02 dB and half-power frequencies of 100,000 and 120,000 Hz. Use 500-Ω resistors in the input impedances of both op-amp modules.

Answer $R_{f1} = R_{f2} = 500\ \Omega$, $C_{i1} = 3.18$ nF, $C_{i2} = 2.65$ nF, $C_{f1} = 6.37\ \mu$F, and $C_{f2} = 1.326$ pF.

SPICE EXAMPLES

SECTION 20.12

Reading: No additional reading of Appendix C is required for the understanding of the SPICE example that follows. Frequency response plots can be generated by requesting that the output be plotted in decibels. Use is made of the AC statement for a decade variation in the frequency.

EXAMPLE S20.1

The active band-pass filter of Table 20.7, repeated here as Fig. S20.1, is to be used with the results of Example 20.12 to show that when $R_i = 100\ \Omega$, $R_f = 199.5$ kΩ, $C_i = 0.2\ \mu$F, and $C_f = 50.12$ pF, the center frequency is $\omega_o = \sqrt{(50,000)(100,000)} = 79,711$ rad/s.

Figure S20.1   Active band-pass filter

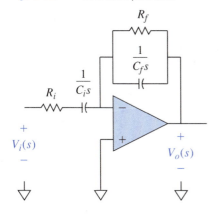

(continues)

Example S20.1 (Continued)

Figure S20.2 shows the network made ready for SPICE, Fig. S20.3 shows
the input file and pertinent output is displayed in Fig. S20.4.

Figure S20.2   The network of Fig. S20.1 ready for PSPICE analysis

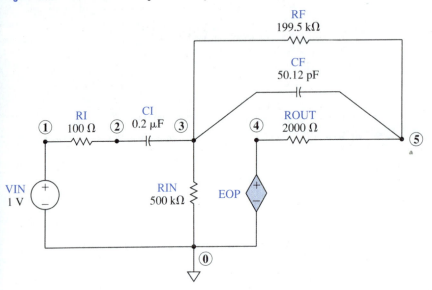

Figure S20.3   Input PSPICE file for analysis of the network of Fig. S20.1

```
OP-AMP ACTIVE BAND-PASS FILTER
************************************************
*FIRST, ENTER DATA FOR THE OP-AMP.
************************************************
RIN           3        0        500K
ROUT          4        5        2000
EOP           4        0        3        0        -1E-6
************************************************
*THEN ENTER THE BALANCE OF THE NETWORK.
************************************************
VIN           1        0        AC       1
RI            1        2        100
RF            3        5        199.5E3
CI            2        3        .2E-6
CF            3        5        50.12E-12
************************************************
*NOW ENTER THE CONTROL STATEMENTS.
************************************************
.AC           DEC      40       3183.1       31831
.PLOT         AC       VDB(5)
.END
```

Figure S20.4 Pertinent output for the PSPICE analysis of the network in Fig. S20.1

```
OP-AMP ACTIVE BAND-PASS FILTER

****      AC ANALYSIS                      TEMPERATURE =    27.000 DEG C

*************************************************************************

 FREQ          VDB(5)


(*)---------     5.6000E+01   5.8000E+01   6.0000E+01   6.2000E+01   6.4000E+01

 3.183E+03   5.722E+01 .        *      .            .            .            .
 3.372E+03   5.763E+01 .      *   .            .            .            .
 3.572E+03   5.803E+01 .        *            .            .            .
 3.783E+03   5.841E+01 .          .  *         .            .            .
 4.007E+03   5.879E+01 .          .     *      .            .            .
 4.245E+03   5.915E+01 .          .        *   .            .            .
 4.496E+03   5.950E+01 .          .          *  .            .            .
 4.763E+03   5.983E+01 .          .            *.            .            .
 5.045E+03   6.015E+01 .          .            . *          .            .
 5.344E+03   6.045E+01 .          .            .   *        .            .
 5.660E+03   6.074E+01 .          .            .      *     .            .
 5.996E+03   6.100E+01 .          .            .        *   .            .
 6.351E+03   6.125E+01 .          .            .          * .            .
 6.727E+03   6.148E+01 .          .            .           *.            .
 7.126E+03   6.168E+01 .          .            .            *            .
 7.548E+03   6.186E+01 .          .            .            .*           .
 7.996E+03   6.202E+01 .          .            .            . *          .
 8.469E+03   6.216E+01 .          .            .            .  *         .
 8.971E+03   6.227E+01 .          .            .            .   *        .
 9.503E+03   6.236E+01 .          .            .            .   *        .
 1.007E+04   6.242E+01 .          .            .            .    *       .
 1.066E+04   6.245E+01 .          .            .            .    *       .
 1.129E+04   6.247E+01 .          .            .            .    *       .
 1.196E+04   6.245E+01 .          .            .            .    *       .
 1.267E+04   6.241E+01 .          .            .            .    *       .
 1.342E+04   6.235E+01 .          .            .            .   *        .
 1.422E+04   6.226E+01 .          .            .            .   *        .
 1.506E+04   6.214E+01 .          .            .            .  *         .
 1.595E+04   6.200E+01 .          .            .            . *          .
 1.690E+04   6.184E+01 .          .            .            *            .
 1.790E+04   6.166E+01 .          .            .           *.            .
 1.896E+04   6.145E+01 .          .            .         *  .            .
 2.008E+04   6.122E+01 .          .            .       *    .            .
 2.127E+04   6.097E+01 .          .            .     *      .            .
 2.253E+04   6.070E+01 .          .            .   *        .            .
 2.387E+04   6.042E+01 .          .            . *          .            .
 2.528E+04   6.011E+01 .          .          *.            .            .
 2.678E+04   5.979E+01 .          .        *.            .            .
 2.837E+04   5.946E+01 .          .     *      .            .            .
 3.005E+04   5.911E+01 .          .  *         .            .            .
 3.183E+04   5.874E+01 .        *   .            .            .            .


           JOB CONCLUDED
```

- The gain and phase of a transfer function of the form

$$H(s) = \frac{P(s)}{Q(s)}$$

as a function of frequency may be obtained by letting $s = j\omega$ and by expressing the transfer function as

$$H(j\omega) = \frac{B_R(j\omega) + jB_I(j\omega)}{A_R(j\omega) + A_I(j\omega)}$$

Then, the gain and the phase at a particular value of ω will be

$$G(\omega) = \sqrt{\frac{B_R^2 + B_I^2}{A_R^2 + A_I^2}}$$

$$\theta(\omega) = \arctan\frac{B_I}{B_R} - \arctan\frac{A_I}{A_R}$$

- The gain in decibels, for a voltage transfer function, is given by

$$G_{dB} = 20\log\frac{V_2}{V_1}$$

For a current transfer function, it is

$$G_{dB} = 20\log\frac{I_2}{I_1}$$

For a power ratio or power transfer function, it is

$$G_{dB} = 10\log\frac{P_2}{P_1}$$

- For factors of the form $(s + a)^n$, whether or not $a = 0$, the Bode asymptotic-gain plot falls (denominator factor) or rises (numerator factor) at $6n$ decibels per octave or $20n$ decibels per decade.

- For factors of the form $(s + a)^n$, the phase plot falls (denominator factor) or rises (numerator factor) with the phase $\pm 45n°$ at $\omega = a$. The phase of factors s^n $(a = 0)$ is $+90n°$ for numerator factors and $-90n°$ for denominator factors.

- Gain and phase plots for the transfer function

$$H(s) = \frac{P(s)}{Q(s)}$$

are obtained via the following procedure.

—Obtain all factors of $P(s)$ and $Q(s)$ and put $H(s)$ in what can be referred to as standard form with all factors associated with a constant shown as

$$1 + sT$$

No adjustment needs to be made to factors not associated with a constant. These will contribute to the gain plot but will not contribute any break frequencies.

—Identify all break frequencies

$$\omega_o = \frac{1}{T}$$

and list them. (Be sure to categorize them as deriving from poles—denominator factors—or zeros—numerator factors.)

—Let $s = 0$ in all terms $(1 + sT)$ in $H(s)$. Write the result as $H_L(s)$ which will be the transfer function of the low-frequency asymptote and which will indicate its slope. Then select a low frequency (perhaps 1/10 of the lowest break frequency) and evaluate the gain in dB at this frequency. This will anchor the low frequency asymptote.

—Ignore all of the 1's in each factor $(1 + sT)$. Write the result as $H_H(s)$, which will be the transfer function of the high-frequency asymptote and which will provide its slope. Then select a high frequency (say 10 times the highest break frequency) and evaluate the gain in dB at this frequency. This will provide a point that can be used to check the final result.

—Plot the asymptotic gain characteristic beginning with the low-frequency asymptote at the low-frequency end. Extend this low-frequency asymptote to higher frequency and begin the departure from it at the lowest break frequency. Continue by changing the slope at each break frequency. The curve can only change slope at a break frequency, permissable slopes are restricted, in the case of linear factors, to multiples of 20 dB per decade and multiples of s not associated with a constant are "built into" the low- and high-frequency asymptotes.

▪ Corrections to the Bode asymptotic-gain and phase plots are a function of frequency if all factors are linear and are tabulated in Table 20.1.

▪ If quadratic factors are present, corrections to the Bode asymptotic-gain and phase plots are a function of both frequency and damping factor. Corrections to the gain plots are determined using eqs. (20.19), (20.20), and (20.21) or Fig. 20.10. The actual phase may be determined using eq. (20.18).

▪ Design equations for passive filters are contained in Section 20.8.

▪ The network elements R, L, and C may be scaled by defining magnitude and frequency scale factors:

$$K_m = \frac{|M|_2}{|M|_1} \qquad K_f = \frac{f_2}{f_1} = \frac{\omega_2}{\omega_1}$$

Then,

$$R_2 = K_m R_1 \qquad L_2 = \frac{K_m}{K_f} L_1 \qquad C_2 = \frac{1}{K_m K_f} C_1$$

▪ Design equations for active filters are contained in Section 20.11.

Additional Readings

Blackwell, W.A., and L.L. Grigsby. *Introductory Network Theory.* Boston: PWS Engineering, 1985, pp. 359–366, 480.

Bobrow, L.S. *Elementary Linear Circuit Analysis.* 2d ed. New York: Holt, Rinehart and Winston, 1987, pp. 441–456, 655, 656.

Budak, A. *Circuit Theory Fundamentals and Applications.* Englewood Cliffs, N.J.: Prentice-Hall, 1978, pp. 422–459.

Del Toro, V. *Engineering Circuits.* Englewood Cliffs, N.J.: Prentice-Hall, 1987, pp. 514–590.

Dorf, R.C. *Introduction to Electric Circuits.* New York: Wiley, 1989, pp. 461–468, 476–487.

Hayt, W.H., Jr., and J.E. Kemmerly. *Engineering Circuit Analysis.* 4th ed. New York: McGraw-Hill, 1986, pp. 273–276, 399–415.

Huelsman, L.P. and P.E. Allen. *Introduction to the Theory and Design of Active Filters.* New York: McGraw-Hill, 1980.

Irwin, J.D. *Basic Engineering Circuit Analysis.* 3d ed. New York: Macmillan, 1989, pp. 598–615, 637–671.

Johnson, D.E. *Introduction to Filter Theory.* Englewood Cliffs, N.J.: Prentice-Hall, 1976.

Johnson, D.E., J.L. Hilburn, and J.R. Johnson. *Basic Electric Circuit Analysis.* 4th ed. Englewood Cliffs, N.J.: Prentice-Hall, 1989, pp. 482–488, 497–504.

Karni, S. *Applied Circuit Analysis.* New York: Wiley, 1988, pp. 318–320, 541–558, 694–698.

Madhu, S. *Linear Circuit Analysis.* Englewood Cliffs, N.J.: Prentice-Hall, 1988, pp. 429, 582–598.

Nilsson, J.W. *Electric Circuits.* 3d ed. Reading, Mass.: Addison-Wesley, 1990, pp. 639–661.

Paul, C.R. *Analysis of Linear Circuits.* New York: McGraw-Hill, 1989, pp. 349–369, 379–389.

Van Valkenburg, M.E. and Kinariwala, B.K. *Linear Circuits.* Englewood Cliffs, N.J.: Prentice-Hall, 1982, pp. 380–395.

PROBLEMS   CHAPTER 20

Section 20.2

20.1   Find the gain and phase of the transfer function

$$H(s) = 640 \frac{s^2 + 2010s + 2000}{s^2 + 25,400s + 10^7}$$

at $\omega = 10,000$ rad/s.

20.2   Find the gain and phase of the transfer function

$$H(s) = 312.5 \frac{s^2 + 210s + 20,000}{s^3 + 20,800s^2 + 16.25 \times 10^6 s + 5 \times 10^9}$$

at $\omega = 8000$ rad/s.

20.3   Find the gain and phase of the transfer function

$$H(s) = 1500 \frac{s^3 + 1605s^2 + 648,000s + 3.2 \times 10^6}{s^3 + 800s^2 + 224,000s + 1.28 \times 10^7}$$

at $\omega = 200$ rad/s.

20.4   Find the gain and phase of the transfer function

$$H(s) = 24,500 \frac{s^3 + 88s^2 + 640,640s + 5.12 \times 10^6}{s^4 + 16,160s^3 + 6.65664 \times 10^7 s^2 + 1.03424 \times 10^{10} s + 4.096 \times 10^{11}}$$

at $\omega = 500$ rad/s.

20.5   Find the gain and phase of the transfer function

$$H(s) = 86.5 \frac{s^3 + 1020s^2 + 2000s}{s^4 + 16,164s^3 + 2.63104 \times 10^6 s^2 + 1.126656 \times 10^8 s + 4.096 \times 10^8}$$

at $\omega = 2500$ rad/s.

Section 20.3

Convert the following voltage gains V_2/V_1 into decibels.

20.6 $\dfrac{V_2}{V_1} = 120.4$

20.7 $\dfrac{V_2}{V_1} = 0.363$

20.8 $\dfrac{V_2}{V_1} = 18.45$

20.9 $\dfrac{V_2}{V_1} = 24,003$

20.10 $\dfrac{V_2}{V_1} = 1130.2$

Section 20.4

20.11   Construct asymptotic-gain and phase plots for the transfer function

$$H(s) = 2000 \frac{s^2 + 210s + 2000}{s^2 + 2100s + 200,000}$$

20.12 Construct asymptotic-gain and phase plots for the transfer function

$$H(s) = 320 \frac{s^2 + 16{,}004s + 64{,}000}{s^3 + 4080s^2 + 320{,}000s}$$

20.13 Construct asymptotic-gain and phase plots for the transfer function

$$H(s) = 16 \frac{s^2 + 268s + 4500}{s^2 + 4100s + 400{,}000}$$

20.14 Construct asymptotic-gain and phase plots for the transfer function

$$H(s) = 240 \frac{(3s + 12)(8s + 3200)}{(s + 80)(s + 5000)(s + 40{,}000)}$$

20.15 Construct asymptotic-gain and phase plots for the transfer function

$$H(s) = 8.4 \frac{s^3 + 6562s^2 + 1.03712 \times 10^6 s + 2.048 \times 10^6}{s^3 + 1256s^2 + 256{,}000s}$$

Section 20.5

20.16 Construct asymptotic-gain and phase plots for the transfer function

$$H(s) = 32 \frac{s^3 + 1605s^2 + 648{,}000s + 3.2 \times 10^6}{s^3 + 880s^2 + 224{,}000s + 1.28 \times 10^7}$$

20.17 Construct asymptotic-gain and phase plots for the transfer function

$$H(s) = 40 \frac{s^3 + 206s^2 + 11{,}200s + 60{,}000}{s^3 + 20{,}000s^2 + 10^8 s}$$

20.18 Construct asymptotic-gain and phase plots for the transfer function

$$H(s) = 2 \frac{s^3 + 1200s^2 + 360{,}000s}{s^3 + 24{,}040s^2 + 8.096 \times 10^7 s + 3.2 \times 10^9}$$

20.19 Construct asymptotic-gain and phase plots for the transfer function

$$H(s) = 6.4 \frac{s^3 + 5102s^2 + 5.102 \times 10^5 s + 10^6}{s^3 + 2400s^2 + 1.92 \times 10^6 s + 5.12 \times 10^8}$$

20.20 Construct asymptotic-gain and phase plots for the transfer function

$$H(s) = 840 \frac{\begin{array}{c} s^4 + 808s^3 + 166{,}416s^2 \\ + 1.2928 \times 10^6 s + 2.56 \times 10^6 \end{array}}{s^4 + 420s^3 + 48{,}000s^2 + 800{,}000s}$$

Section 20.6

20.21 Construct asymptotic-gain and phase plots for the transfer function

$$H(s) = 24{,}500 \frac{\begin{array}{c} s^3 + 88s^2 + 640{,}640s + 5.12 \times 10^6 \end{array}}{\begin{array}{c} s^4 + 16{,}160s^3 + 6.65664 \times 10^7 s^2 \\ + 1.03424 \times 10^{10} s + 4.096 \times 10^{11} \end{array}}$$

20.22 Construct asymptotic-gain and phase plots for the transfer function

$$H(s) = 24{,}500 \frac{s^3 + 120s^2 + 1.002 \times 10^6 s + 20 \times 10^6}{s^4 + 1080s^3 + 2.508 \times 10^7 s^2 + 2 \times 10^9 s}$$

20.23 Determine the angular frequency to within ± 5000 rad/s where the gain of the transfer function in Problem 20.22 is -81.43 dB.

20.24 Construct asymptotic-gain and phase plots for the transfer function

$$H(s) = 16.8 \frac{s^3 + 400s^2 + 160{,}000s}{s^3 + 405s^2 + 642{,}000s + 3.2 \times 10^6}$$

20.25 Determine the gain and phase shift for the transfer function in Problem 20.24 at $\omega = 2$ rad/s.

20.26 Construct asymptotic-gain and phase plots for the transfer function

$$H(s) = 34.5 \frac{\begin{array}{c} s^4 + 108s^3 + 1.000816 \times 10^6 s^2 \\ + 8.0016 \times 10^6 s + 16 \times 10^6 \end{array}}{s^4 + 300s^3 + 30{,}000s^2 + 10^6 s}$$

20.27 Determine the gain and phase shift for the transfer function in Problem 20.26 at $\omega = 95$ rad/s.

Section 20.8

20.28 Select R and C for a first-order, low-pass filter where $\omega_o = 4000$ Hz.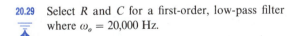

20.29 Select R and C for a first-order, low-pass filter where $\omega_o = 20{,}000$ Hz.

20.30 If $C = 62.5$ nF, select R and L for a second-order, low-pass filter where $\omega_o = 4000$ Hz and $\zeta = \sqrt{2}/2$.

20.31 If $C = 25$ nF, select R and L for a second-order, low-pass filter where $\omega_o = 4000$ Hz and $\zeta = \sqrt{2}/2$.

20.32 Select R and C for a first-order, high-pass filter where $\omega_o = 2500$ rad/s.

20.33 Select R and C for a first-order, high-pass filter where $\omega_o = 5000$ Hz.

20.34 If $L = 0.1$ H, select R and C for a second-order, high-pass filter where $\omega_o = 2500$ Hz and $\zeta = \sqrt{2}/2$.

20.35 If $L = 1$ H, select R and C for a second-order, high-pass filter where $\omega_o = 5000$ Hz and $\zeta = \sqrt{2}/2$.

20.36 Select components for a band-pass filter where the bandwidth is $\beta = 2000$ Hz and the cutoff frequency is $\omega_o = 20,000$ Hz. Let $R = 10$ kΩ.

20.37 Select components for a band-pass filter where the bandwidth is $\beta = 2500$ Hz and the cutoff frequency is $\omega_o = 40,000$ Hz. Let $R = 20$ kΩ.

20.38 Select components for a band-stop filter where the bandwidth is $\beta = 2000$ Hz and the cutoff frequency is $\omega_o = 20,000$ Hz. Let $R = 10$ kΩ.

20.39 Select components for a band-stop filter where the bandwidth is $\beta = 2500$ Hz and the cutoff frequency is $\omega_o = 40,000$ Hz. Let $R = 100$ kΩ.

20.40 Select components for a band-stop filter where the bandwidth is $\beta = 1000$ Hz and the cutoff frequency is $\omega_o = 50,000$ Hz. Let $R = 1$ kΩ.

Section 20.9

20.41 Select components for a band-pass filter in the form of Fig. 20.18 where $R_i = R_o$, $R_s = 500$ Ω, $R_o = 1200$ Ω, the bandwidth is $\beta = 1000$ Hz, and the cutoff frequency is $\omega_o = 50,000$ Hz.

20.42 Select components for a band-pass filter in the form of Fig. 20.18 where $R_i = R_o$, $R_s = 50$ Ω, $R_o = 250$ Ω, the bandwidth is $\beta = 800$ Hz, and the cutoff frequency is $\omega_o = 12,500$ Hz.

Section 20.10

20.43 Figure P20.1 shows a network with some unrealistic component values. The network operates at an angular frequency of $\omega = 2$ rad/s. Select components for network operation such that the

Figure P20.1

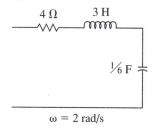

$$\omega = 2 \text{ rad/s}$$

input impedance is $500\underline{/36.87°}$ Ω at a frequency of $\omega = 40,000$ rad/s.

20.44 Figure P20.2 shows a network with some unrealistic component values. The network operates at an angular frequency of $\omega = 3$ rad/s. Select components for network operation such that the input impedance is $250\underline{/36.87°}$ Ω at a frequency of $\omega = 42,000$ rad/s.

Figure P20.2

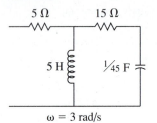

$$\omega = 3 \text{ rad/s}$$

20.45 Figure P20.3 shows a network with some unrealistic component values. The network operates at an angular frequency of $\omega = 4$ rad/s. Select components for network operation such that the input impedance is 400 Ω at a frequency of $\omega = 8000$ rad/s.

Figure P20.3

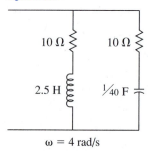

$$\omega = 4 \text{ rad/s}$$

20.46 Figure P20.4 shows a network with some unrealistic component values. The network operates at an angular frequency of $\omega = 2$ rad/s. Select components for network operation such that the input impedance is $500\underline{/-53.13°}$ Ω at a frequency of $\omega = 12,500$ rad/s.

Figure P20.4

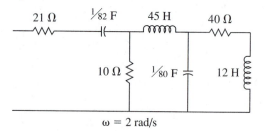

$$\omega = 2 \text{ rad/s}$$

Section 20.11

20.47 Select components for an active low-pass filter containing resistors of at least 1600 Ω to have a midband gain of 48.2 dB and a cutoff frequency of $\omega_o = 4000$ Hz.

20.48 Select components for an active low-pass filter containing resistors of at least 800 Ω to have a midband gain of 57.5 dB and a cutoff frequency of $\omega_o = 8000$ Hz.

20.49 Select components for an active high-pass filter containing resistors of at least 1600 Ω to have a midband gain of 48.2 dB and a cutoff frequency of $\omega_o = 4000$ Hz.

20.50 Select components for an active high-pass filter containing resistors of at least 800 Ω to have a midband gain of 57.5 dB and a cutoff frequency of $\omega_o = 8000$ Hz.

20.51 Select components for an active band-pass filter containing resistors of at least 100 Ω to have a midband gain of 48.2 dB and a passband between 392,000 and 408,000 Hz.

20.52 Select components for an active band-pass filter containing resistors of at least 200 Ω to have a midband gain of 57.5 dB and a passband between 22,500 Hz and 27,500 Hz.

20.53 Select components for an active band-stop filter containing resistors of at least 100 Ω to have a midband gain of -80 dB with a stopband between 48,000 and 64,000 Hz.

20.54 Select components for an active band-stop filter containing resistors of at least 200 Ω to have a midband gain of -92 dB with a stopband between 80,000 and 100,000 Hz.

FOURIER METHODS

VI

FOURIER ANALYSIS

OBJECTIVES

The objectives of this chapter are to:

- Present the necessary mathematical foundation for the Fourier series.

- Provide relationships for the determination of the Fourier coefficients.

- Show how the symmetry of the waveform can be exploited as a laborsaving mechanism in the determination of the Fourier coefficients.

- Discuss the errors involved in using the Fourier series.

- Consider the cosine–phase angle form and the exponential form of the Fourier series.

- Develop relationships for the effective value of a periodic waveform, and consider the periodic waveform and average power.

- Discuss the application of Fourier series to network analysis.

INTRODUCTION

SECTION 21.1

This book has considered the response of networks to several types of excitation or forcing functions. The zero-input, zero-state, natural, and forced responses to simple forcing functions such as steps, ramps, and impulses are considered in Chapters 6 and 7 and the Laplace transform method was developed and used in Chapter 15 and 16. In Chapter 17, it was shown how convolution is employed to provide solutions when even more complicated forcing functions are encountered.

However, when comparing the usefulness of different analytical methods, one is compelled to recognize the difficulty involved in the use of a particular technique. The Laplace transform, for example, loses much of its simplicity when it is used with a periodic forcing function. A complicated and laborious procedure arises because of the bookkeeping necessary to keep track of the various time delays. Moreover, most periodic functions are defined for all t ($-\infty < t < \infty$), and the Laplace transform is defined for functions that are zero until $t = 0$.

Because sinusoids are not difficult to generate and the steady-state response of networks to sinusoids is a straightforward analysis problem, it is fortunate that most periodic functions, which are everyday occurences in the laboratory and in communication, power distribution, and computer networks, can be expressed as a sum of sinusoidal components called a Fourier series. This chapter considers the Fourier series of a periodic function and the application of the Fourier series in the analysis of linear circuits.

SECTION 21.2 THE DIRICHLET CONDITIONS AND THE FOURIER SERIES

A function

$$f(t) = f(t \pm nT) \qquad (n = 1, 2, 3, \ldots) \tag{21.1}$$

is *periodic* if it repeats itself exactly every T seconds for $-\infty < t < \infty$. Here, T is known as the *period of $f(t)$*, and this can be related to the frequency f by

$$f = \frac{1}{T} \tag{21.2}$$

which is measured in *hertz* and which is related to the *fundamental angular frequency* or the *radian frequency* by

$$\omega_o = 2\pi f = \frac{2\pi}{T} \text{ rad/s} \tag{21.3}$$

The *Dirichlet conditions* are defined as follows:

1. The function $f(t)$ is single-valued.
2. The function $f(t)$ has, at most, a finite number of discontinuities in one period.
3. The function $f(t)$ has, at most, a finite number of maxima and minima in one period.
4. The integral over one period is finite:

$$\int_{t_o}^{t_o + T} f(t)\, dt < \infty$$

Any periodic function that satisfies these Dirichlet conditions can be written in the form of a *Fourier series*,

$$f(t) = \frac{a_0}{2} + a_1 \cos \omega_o t + a_2 \cos 2\omega_o t + \cdots + a_k \cos k\omega_o t + \cdots$$
$$+ b_1 \sin \omega_o t + b_2 \sin 2\omega_o t + \cdots + b_k \sin k\omega_o t + \cdots \tag{21.4}$$

In eq. (21.4), the $a_0/2$ term is the average value of $f(t)$ over one period, and the sine and cosine terms, which contain multiples of the *fundamental angular frequency* ω_o, are called the *harmonics*. The coefficients of the sine and cosine terms are called the *Fourier coefficients*.

If a sufficient number of harmonics are used, the Fourier series for the periodic function closely approximates the actual function. For example, the Fourier series for the periodic function illustrated in Fig. 21.1a can be shown to be

$$f(t) = \frac{4}{\pi} \left[\cos \omega_o t - \frac{1}{3} \cos 3\omega_o t + \frac{1}{5} \cos 5\omega_o t - \frac{1}{7} \cos 7\omega_o t + \cdots \right]$$

One half cycle of a square wave showing the approximations due to partial sums: (a) the square wave, (b) plot of $f(t) = (4/\pi)(\cos \omega_o t - \frac{1}{3} \cos 3\omega_o t)$, (c) plot of $f(t) = (4/\pi)(\cos \omega_o t - \frac{1}{3} \cos 3\omega_o t + \frac{1}{5} \cos 5\omega_o t)$, (d) plot of $f(t) = (4/\pi)(\cos \omega_o t - \frac{1}{3} \cos \omega_o t + \frac{1}{5} \cos 5\omega_o t - \frac{1}{7} \cos 7\omega_o t)$, and (e) plot of $f(t) = (4/\pi)(\cos \omega_o t - \frac{1}{3} \cos z\omega_o t + \frac{1}{5} \cos 5\omega_o t - \frac{1}{7} \cos 7\omega_o t + \frac{1}{9} \cos 9\omega_o t)$

FIGURE 21.1

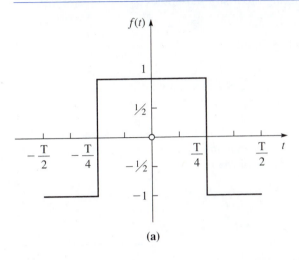

(a)

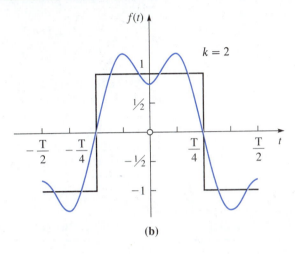

(b)

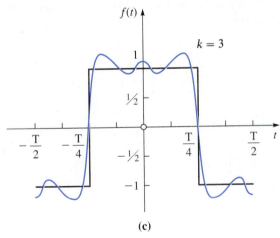

(c)

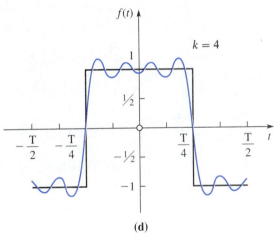

(d)

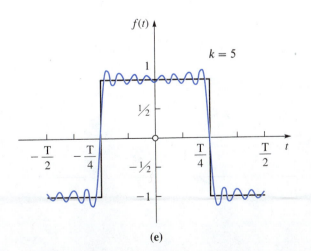

(e)

or

$$f(t) = \frac{4}{\pi} \sum_{k=1}^{\infty} \frac{(-1)^{(k+1)}}{(2k-1)} \cos(2k-1)\omega_o t$$

The partial sum formed by taking the first n harmonics is

$$S_n = \frac{4}{\pi} \sum_{k=1}^{n} \frac{(-1)^{(k+1)}}{(2k-1)} \cos(2k-1)\omega_o t$$

and Figs. 21.1b through 21.1d show how S_n begins to approximate $f(t)$ as k increases from 1 to 4. Figure 21.1e presents the sum for a larger value of k. Observe that as k increases, the approximation is improved everywhere except at the discontinuities at $t = -T/4$ and $t = T/4$. This is called the *Gibbs phenomenon* and is due to the fact the the periodic function $f(t)$ cannot converge uniformly at the discontinuities where the partial sums take on the mean value of the function $f(t)$.

SECTION 21.3   THE DETERMINATION OF THE FOURIER COEFFICIENTS

To determine the Fourier coefficients [the a_k's and b_k's in eq. (21.4)], one makes use of the *orthogonality* of the sine and the cosine and that for integer values of k,

$$\int_{t_o}^{t_o+T} \cos k\omega_o t \, dt = 0 \tag{21.5}$$

$$\int_{t_o}^{t_o+T} \sin k\omega_o t \, dt = 0 \tag{21.6}$$

Then, from the three trigonometric identities,

$$\sin A \cos B = \frac{1}{2}\left[\sin(A+B) + \sin(A-B)\right]$$

$$\cos A \cos B = \frac{1}{2}\left[\cos(A+B) + \cos(A-B)\right]$$

$$\sin A \sin B = \frac{1}{2}\left[\cos(A-B) - \cos(A+B)\right]$$

with $A = k\omega_o t$ and $B = m\omega_o t$, where k and m are integers, it can be shown that

$$\int_{t_o}^{t_o+T} \cos k\omega_o t \sin m\omega_o t \, dt = 0 \tag{21.7}$$

$$\int_{t_o}^{t_o+T} \sin k\omega_o t \sin m\omega_o t = \begin{cases} 0, & k \neq m \\ \dfrac{T}{2}, & k = m \neq 0 \end{cases} \tag{21.8}$$

$$\int_{t_o}^{t_o+T} \cos k\omega_o t \cos m\omega_o t \, dt = \begin{cases} 0, & k \neq m \\ \dfrac{T}{2}, & k = m \neq 0 \end{cases} \tag{21.9}$$

The a_k coefficients are determined by multiplying both sides of eq. (21.4) by $\cos m\omega_o t \, dt$ and then integrating over one period. The result just before integration is

$$\int_{t_o}^{t_o+T} f(t) \cos m\omega_o t \, dt = \int_{t_o}^{t_o+T} \frac{a_0}{2} \cos m\omega_o t \, dt$$

$$+ \sum_{k=1}^{\infty} \left[\int_{t_o}^{t_o+T} a_k \cos k\omega_o t \cos m\omega_o t \, dt + \int_{t_o}^{t_o+T} b_k \sin k\omega_o t \cos m\omega_o t \, dt \right]$$

Equations (21.5), (21.7), and (21.9) show that the coefficient a_k will be

$$a_k = \frac{2}{T} \int_{t_o}^{t_o+T} f(t) \cos k\omega_o t \, dt \qquad\qquad \textbf{(21.10\textit{a})}$$

or with $\omega_o = 2\pi/T$,

$$a_k = \frac{2}{T} \int_{t_o}^{t_o+T} f(t) \cos\left(\frac{2k\pi}{T} t\right) dt \qquad\qquad \textbf{(21.10\textit{b})}$$

If $k = 0$,

$$a_0 = \frac{2}{T} \int_{t_o}^{t_o+T} f(t) \, dt \qquad\qquad \textbf{(21.11)}$$

and it is observed that use of $a_0/2$ in eq. (21.4) permits the use of a uniform relationship for finding *all* of the a_k including a_0. Moreover, reference to eq. (5.18) in Section 5.7 shows that eq. (21.11) represents just twice the average value of $f(t)$ over one period.

The b coefficients are obtained in similar fashion, but this time, eq. (21.4) is multiplied by $\sin m\omega_o t \, dt$. The form just prior to the performance of the integration is

$$\int_{t_o}^{t_o+T} f(t) \sin m\omega_o t \, dt = \int_{t_o}^{t_o+T} \frac{a_0}{2} \sin m\omega_o t \, dt$$

$$+ \sum_{k=1}^{\infty} \left[\int_{t_o}^{t_o+T} a_k \cos k\omega_o t \sin m\omega_o t \, dt + \int_{t_o}^{t_o+T} b_k \sin k\omega_o t \sin m\omega_o t \, dt \right]$$

Use of eqs. (21.6), (21.7), and (21.8) shows that the coefficient b_k will be

$$b_k = \frac{2}{T} \int_{t_o}^{t_o+T} f(t) \sin k\omega_o t \, dt \qquad\qquad \textbf{(21.12\textit{a})}$$

or if $\omega_o = 2\pi/T$,

$$b_k = \frac{2}{T} \int_{t_o}^{t_o+T} f(t) \sin\left(\frac{2k\pi}{T} t\right) dt \qquad\qquad \textbf{(21.12\textit{b})}$$

■ **EXAMPLE 21.1**

Write a Fourier series for the square wave shown in Fig. 21.2a. Then, write a Fourier series when $\tau = T/2$ and $\tau = T/4$.

FIGURE 21.2   Square waves with different pulse durations: (a) arbitrary, (b) one-half period, and (c) one-quarter period

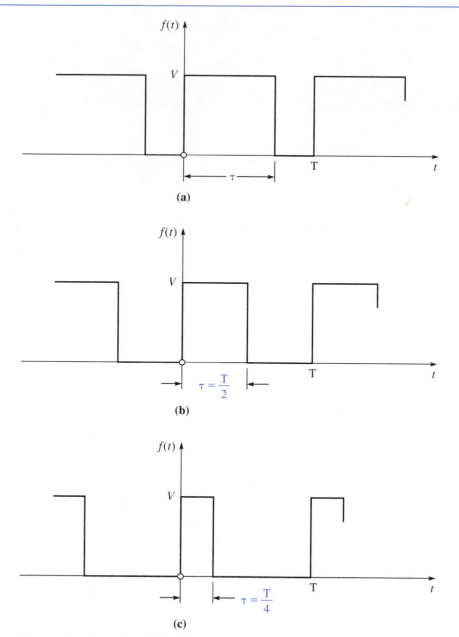

(a)

(b)

(c)

Solution   The function in Fig. 21.2a is represented by

$$f(t) = \begin{cases} V, & 0 < t < \tau \\ 0, & \tau < t < T \end{cases}$$

By eq. (21.11) with $t_o = 0$,

$$a_0 = \frac{2}{T} \int_0^T f(t)\,dt = \frac{2V}{T}\left(\int_0^\tau 1\,dt + \int_\tau^T 0\,dt\right) = \frac{2V}{T}\, t\Big|_0^\tau = 2V\left(\frac{\tau}{T}\right)$$

and

$$\frac{a_0}{2} = V\frac{\tau}{T}$$

Next, by eq. (21.10a), also with $t_o = 0$,

$$a_k = \frac{2}{T}\int_0^T f(t)\cos k\omega_o t\, dt = \frac{2V}{T}\left(\int_0^\tau 1\cos k\omega_o t\, dt + \int_\tau^T 0\cos k\omega_o t\, dt\right)$$

$$= \frac{2V}{T}\cdot\frac{1}{k\omega_o}\sin k\omega_o t\Big|_0^\tau$$

With $k\omega_o = 2k\pi/T$, a_k becomes

$$a_k = \frac{V}{k\pi}\sin\left(2k\pi\frac{\tau}{T}\right)$$

Finally, by eq. (21.12a) and again with $t_o = 0$,

$$b_k = \frac{2}{T}\int_0^T f(t)\sin k\omega_o t\, dt = \frac{2V}{T}\left(\int_0^\tau 1\sin k\omega_o t\, dt + \int_\tau^T 0\sin k\omega_o t\, dt\right)$$

$$= -\frac{2V}{T}\cdot\frac{1}{k\omega_o}\cos k\omega_o t\Big|_o^\tau$$

With $k\omega_o = 2k\pi/T$, b_k becomes

$$b_k = \frac{V}{k\pi}\left[1 - \cos\left(2k\pi\frac{\tau}{T}\right)\right]$$

The Fourier series for the waveform in Fig. 21.2a can then be written in the compact form

$$f(t) = V\frac{\tau}{T} + \frac{V}{\pi}\sum_{k=1}^\infty\frac{1}{k}\left[\sin 2k\pi\frac{\tau}{T}\cos k\omega_o t + \left(1 - \cos 2k\pi\frac{\tau}{T}\right)\sin k\omega_o t\right]$$

or in the expanded form of eq. (21.4),

$$f(t) = V\frac{\tau}{T} + \frac{V}{\pi}\left[\sin\left(2\pi\frac{\tau}{T}\right)\cos\omega_o t + \frac{1}{2}\sin\left(4\pi\frac{\tau}{T}\right)\cos 2\omega_o t\right.$$

$$+ \frac{1}{3}\sin\left(6\pi\frac{\tau}{T}\right)\cos 3\omega_o t + \frac{1}{4}\sin\left(8\pi\frac{\tau}{T}\right)\cos 4\omega_o t + \cdots\right]$$

$$+ \frac{V}{\pi}\left[\left(1 - \cos 2\pi\frac{\tau}{T}\right)\sin\omega_o t + \frac{1}{2}\left(1 - \cos 4\pi\frac{\tau}{T}\right)\sin 2\omega_o t\right.$$

$$+ \frac{1}{3}\left(1 - \cos 6\pi\frac{\tau}{T}\right)\sin 3\omega_o t$$

$$+ \frac{1}{4}\left(1 - \cos 8\pi\frac{\tau}{T}\right)\sin 4\omega_o t + \cdots\right]$$

This is the Fourier series for the periodic train of pulses whose pulse width τ is arbitrary.

Two specific values of τ deserve consideration. If $\tau = T/2$, the waveform is shown in Fig. 21.2b, and

$$f(t) = \frac{V}{2} + \frac{V}{\pi}\left(\sin \pi \cos \omega_o t + \frac{1}{2}\sin 2\pi \cos 2\omega_o t\right.$$

$$\left. + \frac{1}{3}\sin 3\pi \cos 3\omega_o t + \frac{1}{4}\sin 4\pi \cos 4\omega_o t + \cdots\right)$$

$$+ \frac{V}{\pi}\left[(1 - \cos \pi)\sin \omega_o t + \frac{1}{2}(1 - \cos 2\pi)\sin 2\omega_o t\right.$$

$$\left. + \frac{1}{3}(1 - \cos 3\pi)\sin 3\omega_o t + \frac{1}{4}(1 - \cos 4\pi)\sin 4\omega_o t + \cdots\right]$$

or

$$f(t) = \frac{V}{2} + \frac{2V}{\pi}\left(\sin \omega_o t + \frac{1}{3}\sin 3\omega_o t + \frac{1}{5}\sin 5\omega_o t + \cdots\right)$$

Note that when $\tau = T/2$, the Fourier series possesses an average term and only odd harmonics. It is not fair to say that the series contains only sine terms, because the average term derives from the coefficient a_0.

If $\tau = T/4$, then

$$f(t) = \frac{V}{4} + \frac{V}{\pi}\left(\sin \frac{\pi}{2} \cos \omega_o t + \frac{1}{2}\sin \pi \cos 2\omega_o t + \frac{1}{3}\sin \frac{3\pi}{2} \cos 3\omega_o t\right.$$

$$\left. + \frac{1}{4}\sin 2\pi \cos 4\omega_o t + \cdots\right) + \frac{V}{\pi}\left[\left(1 - \cos \frac{\pi}{2}\right)\sin \omega_o t\right.$$

$$+ \frac{1}{2}(1 - \cos \pi)\sin 2\omega_o t + \frac{1}{3}\left(1 - \cos \frac{3\pi}{2}\right)\sin 3\omega_o t$$

$$\left. + \frac{1}{4}(1 - \cos 2\pi)\sin 4\omega_o t + \cdots\right]$$

or

$$f(t) = \frac{V}{4} + \frac{V}{\pi}\left(\cos \omega_o t - \frac{1}{3}\cos 3\omega_o t + \frac{1}{5}\cos 5\omega_o t + \cdots\right)$$

$$+ \frac{V}{\pi}\left(\sin \omega_o t + \sin 2\omega_o t + \frac{1}{3}\sin 3\omega_o t + \frac{1}{5}\sin 5\omega_o t + \cdots\right)$$

Here, the Fourier series possesses an average value and both sine and cosine terms, and there are some even harmonics.

The form of the Fourier series for a particular waveform will depend on the location of the waveform with respect to the origin, as Exercise 21.1 will clearly show.

EXERCISE 21.1

The square wave shown in Fig. 21.3 is similar to the square wave shown in Fig. 21.2b with $\tau = T/2$. However, it has been shifted with respect to the origin. Write its Fourier series.

Square wave (Exercise 21.1)

FIGURE 21.3

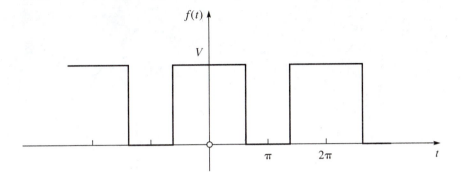

Answer

$$f(t) = \frac{V}{2} + \frac{2V}{\pi}\left(\cos \omega_o t - \frac{1}{3}\cos 3\omega_o t + \frac{1}{5}\cos 5\omega_o t - \frac{1}{7}\cos 7\omega_o t + \cdots\right)$$

SYMMETRY CONSIDERATIONS

Evaluation of the Fourier coefficients becomes a great deal simpler when certain types of symmetry are recognized. An *even function* is defined by

$$f(t) = f(-t) \tag{21.13}$$

and it is seen that cos ωt and the waveforms shown in Fig. 21.4 satisfy this definition. An *odd function* is defined by

$$f(t) = -f(-t) \tag{21.14}$$

The function sin ωt and many other functions such as those represented by the waveforms shown in Fig. 21.5 satisfy this definition. Notice that the average value of each of these waveforms is equal to zero, which means that the a_0 term vanishes.

21.4.1 Even-Function Symmetry

Consider the even function defined by eq. (21.13). If $t_o = -T/2$, the a_0 coefficient is obtained from eq. (21.11) as

$$a_0 = \frac{2}{T}\int_{-T/2}^{T/2} f(t)\,dt = \frac{2}{T}\left[\int_{-T/2}^{0} f(t)\,dt + \int_{0}^{T/2} f(t)\,dt\right]$$

Let $t = -x$, and observe that if the function is even

$$f(t) = f(-t) = f(x) \qquad dt = -dx$$

and $x = T/2$ when $t = -T/2$. Then,

$$a_0 = \frac{2}{T}\left[\int_{T/2}^{0} f(x)(-dx) + \int_{0}^{T/2} f(t)\,dt\right] = \frac{2}{T}\left[\int_{0}^{T/2} f(x)\,dx + \int_{0}^{T/2} f(t)\,dt\right]$$

FIGURE 21.4   Some examples of even periodic functions

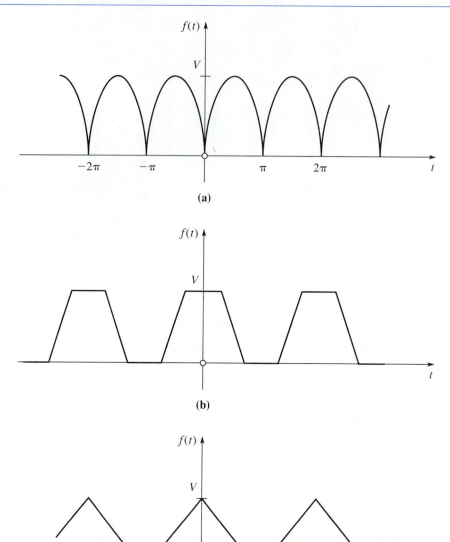

(a)

(b)

(c)

or because the two integrals within the brackets are identical,

$$a_0 = \frac{4}{T} \int_0^{T/2} f(t)\, dt$$

(21.15)

For all other a_k's, eq. (21.10a) is used with $t_o = -T/2$, so that $x = T/2$, and

$$a_k = \frac{2}{T}\left[\int_{-T/2}^{0} f(t)\cos k\omega_o t\, dt + \int_0^{T/2} f(t)\cos k\omega_o t\, dt\right]$$

$$= \frac{2}{T}\left[\int_{T/2}^{0} f(-x)\cos(-k\omega_0 x)(-dx) + \int_0^{T/2} f(t)\cos k\omega_o t\, dt\right]$$

Some examples of odd functions

FIGURE 21.5

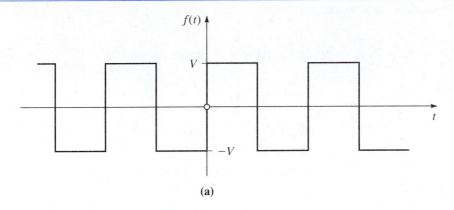

(a)

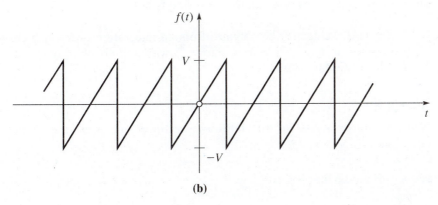

(b)

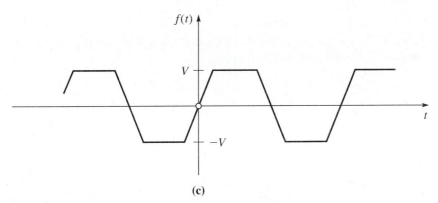

(c)

But $f(t) = f(-x)$, and the cosine function is even. With $\cos(-k\omega_o x) = \cos k\omega_o x$,

$$a_k = \frac{2}{T}\left[\int_{T/2}^{0} f(x) \cos k\omega_o x(-dx) + \int_{0}^{T/2} f(t) \cos k\omega_o t\, dt\right]$$

$$= \frac{2}{T}\left[\int_{0}^{T/2} f(x) \cos k\omega_o x\, dx + \int_{0}^{T/2} f(t) \cos k\omega_o t\, dt\right]$$

or

$$a_k = \frac{4}{T}\int_{0}^{T/2} f(t) \cos k\omega_o t\, dt \qquad\qquad\text{(21.16)}$$

The similar procedure for the b_k coefficients depends on the fact that the sine function is odd, $\sin k\omega_o t = -\sin(-k\omega_o t)$. With this in mind, observe that with $f(t)$ still an even function and $t_o = -T/2$, so that $x = T/2$, eq. (21.12a) gives

$$b_k = \frac{2}{T}\left[\int_{-T/2}^{0} f(t) \sin k\omega_o t\, dt + \int_{0}^{T/2} f(t) \sin k\omega_o t\, dt\right]$$

$$= \frac{2}{T}\left[\int_{T/2}^{0} f(-x) \sin(-k\omega_o x)(-dx) + \int_{0}^{T/2} f(t) \sin k\omega_o t\, dt\right]$$

$$= \frac{2}{T}\left[\int_{T/2}^{0} f(x) \sin k\omega_o x\, dx + \int_{0}^{T/2} f(t) \sin k\omega_o t\, dt\right]$$

$$= \frac{2}{T}\left[-\int_{0}^{T/2} f(x) \sin k\omega_o x\, dx + \int_{0}^{T/2} f(t) \sin k\omega_o t\, dt\right] = 0$$

Thus, for even functions, the following conditions hold:

1. The a_k coefficients may be obtained from an integration over a half period (say from t_o to $t_o + T/2$, or from 0 to $T/2$), with a doubling of the result.
2. The b_k coefficients vanish.

■ **EXAMPLE 21.2**

Write a Fourier series for the full-wave, rectified sine wave shown in Fig. 21.4a.

Solution   Here the function is

$$f(t) = V \sin t \qquad (0 < t < T)$$

where $T = \pi$, so that $\omega_o = 2\pi/T = 2\pi/\pi = 2$ rad/s. The function possesses even-function symmetry, and as a result,

$$a_k = \frac{4}{T}\int_{0}^{T/2} V \sin t \cos k\omega_o t\, dt = \frac{4V}{\pi}\int_{0}^{\pi/2} \sin t \cos 2kt\, dt$$

Use of

$$\sin A \cos B = \frac{1}{2}\left[\sin(A + B) + \sin(A - B)\right]$$

with $A = 1$ and $B = 2k$, gives

$$a_k = \frac{2V}{\pi}\left[\int_{0}^{\pi/2} \sin(1 + 2k)t\, dt + \int_{0}^{\pi/2} \sin(1 - 2k)t\, dt\right]$$

$$= -\frac{2V}{\pi}\left[\frac{\cos(1 + 2k)t}{1 + 2k}\bigg|_{0}^{\pi/2} + \frac{\cos(1 - 2k)t}{1 - 2k}\bigg|_{0}^{\pi/2}\right]$$

$$= -\frac{2V}{\pi}\left[\frac{\cos(1 + 2k)(\pi/2)}{1 + 2k} - \frac{1}{1 + 2k} + \frac{\cos(1 - 2k)(\pi/2)}{1 - 2k} - \frac{1}{1 - 2k}\right]$$

With k always an integer,

$$a_k = \frac{2V}{\pi}\left(\frac{1}{1+2k} + \frac{1}{1-2k}\right) = \frac{2V}{\pi}\left(\frac{1-2k+1+2k}{1-4k^2}\right) = \frac{4V}{(1-4k^2)\pi}$$

Observe that when $k = 0$, $a_0 = 4V/\pi = 1.272V$, and

$$\frac{a_0}{2} = 0.636V$$

The Fourier series for the rectified sine wave in Fig. 21.4a is written with $a_0/2$ as the average term:

$$\frac{2V}{\pi}\left(1 - \frac{2}{3}\cos 2t - \frac{2}{15}\cos 4t - \frac{2}{35}\cos 6t - \frac{2}{63}\cos 8t - \cdots\right) \qquad \blacksquare$$

EXERCISE 21.2

Exploit the fact that the square wave in Fig. 21.3 is an even function, and use eqs. (21.15) and (21.16) to show that the Fourier series for the square wave is the same as that obtained in Exercise 21.1.

Answer

$$f(t) = \frac{V}{2} + \frac{2V}{\pi}\left(\cos \omega_o t - \frac{1}{3}\cos 3\omega_o t + \frac{1}{5}\cos 5\omega_o t - \frac{1}{7}\cos 7\omega_o t + \cdots\right)$$

21.4.2 Odd-Function Symmetry

An odd function, as noted, is defined by

$$f(t) = -f(-t) \qquad \textbf{(21.14)}$$

The function $\sin \omega t$ and many other functions such as those represented by the waveforms shown in Fig. 21.5 satisfy this definition. Notice that the average value of each of these waveforms is equal to zero, which means that the a_0 term vanishes.

If $t_o = -T/2$, the a coefficients can be obtained from eq. (21.10a):

$$a_k = \frac{2}{T}\left[\int_{-T/2}^{0} f(t) \cos k\omega_o t\, dt + \int_{0}^{T/2} f(t) \cos k\omega_o t\, dt\right]$$

Again, let $t = -x$ so that $dt = -dx$, and observe that because $f(t)$ is odd,

$$f(t) = -f(-t) = -f(x)$$

When $t = -T/2$, $x = T/2$; and with these in the first integral within the brackets,

$$a_k = \frac{2}{T}\left[\int_{T/2}^{0} -f(x) \cos(-k\omega_o x)(-dx) + \int_{0}^{T/2} f(t) \cos k\omega_o t\, dt\right]$$

The cosine function is itself even, so that $\cos(-k\omega_o x) = \cos k\omega_o x$, and

$$a_k = \frac{2}{T}\left[\int_{T/2}^{0} f(x) \cos k\omega_o x \, dx + \int_{0}^{T/2} f(t) \cos k\omega_o t \, dt\right]$$
$$= \frac{2}{T}\left[-\int_{0}^{T/2} f(x) \cos k\omega_o x \, dx + \int_{0}^{T/2} f(t) \cos k\omega_o t \, dt\right] = 0$$

All a_k coefficients including a_0 are equal to zero. Thus, the odd function has a zero average value, and there are no cosine components in the Fourier series.

For the b_k coefficients, eq. (21.12a) is employed:

$$b_k = \frac{2}{T}\left[\int_{-T/2}^{0} f(t) \sin k\omega_o t \, dt + \int_{0}^{T/2} f(t) \sin k\omega_o t \, dt\right]$$

Again, let $t = -x$ in the first integral within the brackets, with the result

$$b_k = \frac{2}{T}\left[\int_{T/2}^{0} -f(x) \sin(-k\omega_o x)(-dx) + \int_{0}^{T/2} f(t) \sin k\omega_o t \, dt\right]$$

The sine function is odd, so that $\sin(-k\omega_o x) = -\sin k\omega_o x$, and

$$b_k = \frac{2}{T}\left[-\int_{T/2}^{0} f(x) \sin k\omega_o x \, dx + \int_{0}^{T/2} f(t) \sin k\omega_o t \, dt\right]$$
$$= \frac{2}{T}\left[\int_{0}^{T/2} f(x) \sin k\omega_o x \, dx + \int_{0}^{T/2} f(t) \sin k\omega_o t \, dt\right]$$

or

$$b_k = \frac{4}{T}\int_{0}^{T/2} f(t) \sin k\omega_o t \, dt \qquad\qquad (21.17)$$

Thus, for odd functions, the following conditions hold:

1. The b_k coefficients may be obtained from an integration over a half period (say from t_o to $t_o + T/2$, or from 0 to $T/2$), with a doubling of the result.
2. The a_k coefficients vanish.

■ **EXAMPLE 21.3**

Write a Fourier series for the triangular wave shown in Fig. 21.6a.

Solution   Here, the function is

$$f(t) = \frac{2V}{T}t \qquad \left(-\frac{T}{2} < t < \frac{T}{2}\right)$$

which is seen to be an odd function, because $f(t) = -f(-t)$. There will be no average term, and there will be no cosine terms. Thus, by eq. (21.17) with

Two triangular waves

FIGURE 21.6

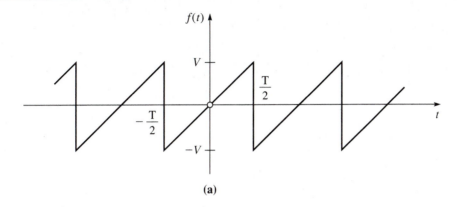

(a)

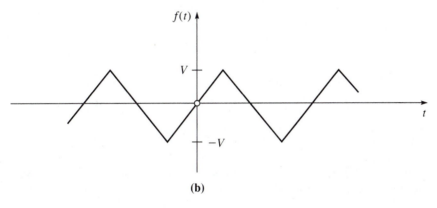

(b)

$\omega_o = 2\pi/T$,

$$b_k = \frac{4}{T}\int_0^{T/2} \frac{2V}{T} t \sin\left(\frac{2k\pi}{T} t\right) dt = \frac{8V}{T^2}\int_0^{T/2} t \sin\left(\frac{2k\pi}{T} t\right) dt$$

A table of integrals reveals that

$$b_k = \frac{8V}{T^2}\left(\frac{T}{2k\pi}\right)^2\left[\sin\left(\frac{2k\pi}{T} t\right) - \frac{2k\pi}{T} t \cos\left(\frac{2k\pi}{T} t\right)\right]_0^{T/2}$$

$$= \frac{2V}{(k\pi)^2}\left[\sin k\pi - 0 - (k\pi \cos k\pi - 0)\right]$$

and because $\sin k\pi = 0$ when k is an integer,

$$b_k = -\frac{2V}{k\pi}\cos k\pi$$

The Fourier series for the triangular wave in Fig. 21.6a is

$$f(t) = \frac{2V}{\pi}\left(\sin k\omega_o t - \frac{1}{2}\sin 2\omega_o t + \frac{1}{3}\sin 3\omega_o t - \frac{1}{4}\sin 4\omega_o t + \cdots\right)$$

FIGURE 21.7   Waveform (Exercise 22.3)

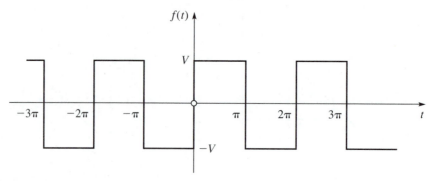

EXERCISE 21.3

The waveform in Fig. 21.7 represents an odd function. Write its Fourier series.

Answer

$$f(t) = \frac{4V}{\pi}\left(\sin \omega_o t + \frac{1}{3}\sin 3\omega_o t + \frac{1}{5}\sin 5\omega_o t + \frac{1}{7}\sin 7\omega_o t + \cdots\right)$$

21.4.3 A Decomposition of *f(t)* into Odd and Even Components

In general, any periodic function $f(t)$ with neither odd nor even symmetry can be decomposed into the sum of even and odd periodic functions. With the subscripts e and o to designate *even* and *odd*, respectively,

$$f(t) = f_e(t) + f_o(t) \tag{21.18}$$

The fact that $f_e(t)$ contains only cosine terms and $f_o(t)$ contains only sine terms can be exploited to simplify the computation of the Fourier coefficients. Notice, also, that because $f_e(t) = f_e(-t)$ and $f_o(t) = -f_o(-t)$,

$$f(-t) = f_e(-t) + f_o(-t) = f_e(t) - f_o(t)$$

which leads to

$$f_e(t) = \frac{1}{2}\left[f(t) + f(-t)\right] \quad \text{and} \quad f_o(t) = \frac{1}{2}\left[f(t) - f(-t)\right]$$

The periodic waveform in Fig. 21.8a is neither even nor odd, but it can be decomposed into even and odd components, as indicated respectively in Figs. 21.8b and 21.8c. Its Fourier series can be written quite expeditiously, as will be shown in Example 21.4.

■ EXAMPLE 21.4

The Fourier series for the waveform shown in Fig. 21.8a is known to be

$$f(t) = \frac{2V}{\pi}\left(1 + \frac{\pi}{2}\sin t - \frac{2}{3}\cos 2t - \frac{2}{15}\cos 4t - \frac{2}{35}\cos 6t - \cdots\right)$$

(a) The unsymmetrical half-wave rectifier, which can be decomposed into symmetrical waves that are (b) even and (c) odd

FIGURE 21.8

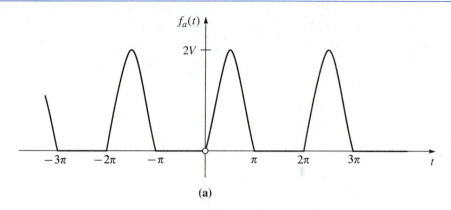

(a)

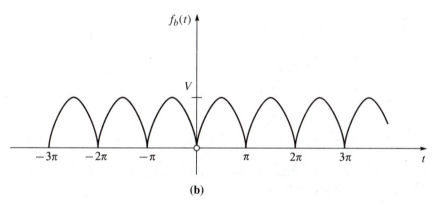

(b)

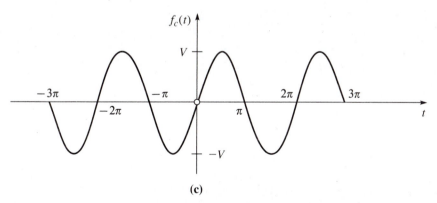

(c)

Write the Fourier series for each of the symmetrical waveforms in its decomposition into even and odd functions as shown in Figs. 21.8b and 21.8c, and show that their sum is equal to $f(t)$.

Solution   The waveform in Fig. 21.8a is not symmetrical, and its Fourier series should contain both sine and cosine terms. It can be represented by

$$f(t) = \begin{cases} 2V \sin t, & 0 < t < \pi \\ 0, & \pi < t < 2\pi \end{cases}$$

The waveform in Fig. 21.8b represents a function that is even,

$$f(t) = V \sin t \qquad (0 < t < \pi)$$

and the Fourier series for this function was developed in Example 21.2. Thus,

$$f_e(t) = \frac{2V}{\pi}\left(1 - \frac{2}{3}\cos 2t - \frac{2}{15}\cos 4t - \frac{2}{35}\cos 6t - \frac{2}{63}\cos 8t - \cdots\right)$$

Moreover, the sine wave in Fig. 21.8c needs no Fourier series because it is described completely by the function $f(t) = V \sin t$ for all t. Thus,

$$f_o(t) = V \sin t = \frac{2V}{\pi}\left(\frac{\pi}{2}\sin t\right)$$

And all that is left is the observation that

$$f(t) = f_e(t) + f_o(t)$$

■

21.4.4 Half-Wave Symmetry

A periodic function is said to possess *half-wave symmetry* if, for all t

$$f(t) = -f\left(t \pm \frac{T}{2}\right) \tag{21.19}$$

From this, it is seen that a shift of the function or waveform to the left or right by a half period with subsequent rotation about the horizontal axis (the time axis) will yield the original function.

Consider a form of eq. (21.10*b*)

$$a_k = \frac{2}{T}\int_{-T/2}^{T/2} f(t)\cos\frac{2k\pi}{T}t\,dt$$

and write it as the sum of two integrals

$$a_k = \frac{2}{T}\left[\int_{-T/2}^{0} f(t)\cos\frac{2k\pi}{T}t\,dt + \int_{0}^{T/2} f(t)\cos\frac{2k\pi}{T}t\,dt\right]$$

Let $y = t + T/2$ so that $dy = dt$. When $t = -T/2$, $y = 0$ and when $t = 0$, $y = T/2$. The first integral within the brackets becomes

$$\int_{-T/2}^{0} f(t)\cos\frac{2k\pi}{T}t\,dt = \int_{0}^{T/2} f\left(y - \frac{T}{2}\right)\cos\left(\frac{2k\pi}{T}y - k\pi\right)dy$$

and with

$$\cos\left(\frac{2k\pi}{T}t - k\pi\right) = \cos\frac{2k\pi}{T}t\cos k\pi + \sin\frac{2k\pi}{T}t\sin k\pi$$

and $f(y - T/2) = -f(y)$

$$\int_{-T/2}^{0} f(t) \cos \frac{2k\pi}{T} t \, dt = -\cos k\pi \int_{0}^{T/2} f(y) \cos \frac{2k\pi}{T} y \, dy$$

because, for integer values of k, $\sin k\pi = 0$.

Thus

$$a_k = \frac{2}{T}(1 - \cos k\pi) \int_{0}^{T/2} f(t) \cos \frac{2k\pi}{T} t \, dt$$

and

$$a_k = \begin{cases} \dfrac{4}{T} \displaystyle\int_{0}^{T/2} f(t) \cos k\omega_o t \, dt, & k = 1, 3, 5, 7, \ldots \\ 0, & k = 0, 2, 4, 6, \ldots \end{cases} \tag{21.20}$$

An identical development will show that

$$b_k = \begin{cases} \dfrac{4}{T} \displaystyle\int_{0}^{T/2} f(t) \sin k\omega_o t \, dt, & k = 1, 3, 5, 7, \ldots \\ 0, & k = 0, 2, 4, 6, \ldots \end{cases} \tag{21.21}$$

Equations (21.20) and (21.21) show that the Fourier series for waveforms possessing half-wave symmetry contain only odd harmonics.

21.4.5 Quarter-Wave Symmetry

If $f(t)$ possesses half-wave symmetry and, in addition, is either even or odd, $f(t)$ is said to possess *quarter-wave symmetry*. The waveforms displayed in Fig. 21.9 exhibit quarter-wave symmetry and show that to exploit the idea of quarter-wave symmetry, one must choose the $t = 0$ point judiciously in order to make the waveform odd or even.

For even quarter-wave symmetry, all even harmonics are zero, because quarter-wave symmetry implies half-wave symmetry. But only cosine terms are present. Equation (21.21) does not apply; and for even quarter-wave symmetry, it can be shown that

$$\begin{cases} a_k = 0, & k = 0, 2, 4, 6, \ldots \\ a_k = \dfrac{8}{T} \displaystyle\int_{0}^{T/4} f(t) \cos k\omega_o t \, dt, & k = 1, 3, 5, 7, \ldots \end{cases} \tag{21.22}$$

For odd quarter-wave symmetry, all even harmonics are zero, and only sine terms are present. Equation (21.20) does not apply; and for odd quarter-wave symmetry,

$$\begin{cases} b_k = 0, & k = 0, 2, 4, 6, \ldots \\ b_k = \dfrac{8}{T} \displaystyle\int_{0}^{T/4} f(t) \sin k\omega_o t \, dt, & k = 1, 3, 5, 7, \ldots \end{cases} \tag{21.23}$$

FIGURE 21.9   Waveforms that display quarter-wave symmetry: (a) even and (b) odd

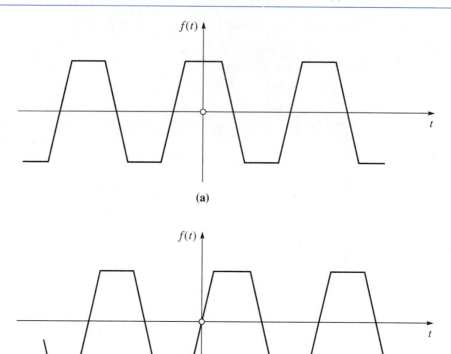

(a)

(b)

■ **EXAMPLE 21.5**

Write a Fourier series for the function described by the waveform in Fig. 21.10.

Solution   The waveform exhibits half-wave symmetry and is odd. It is anticipated that only odd sine terms will be present. It is described by the function

$$f(t) = \begin{cases} -V, & -\pi < t < 0 \\ V, & 0 < t < \pi \end{cases}$$

FIGURE 21.10   A periodic function

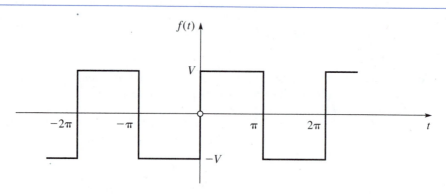

By inspection, $a_0 = 0$, so that there will be no average term. For the a_k coefficients, use eq. (21.10a):

$$a_k = \frac{2}{T} \int_{t_o}^{t_o + T} f(t) \cos k\omega_o t \, dt$$

With $T = 2\pi$, $\omega_o = 2\pi/T = 2\pi/2\pi = 1$ rad/s, and $t_o = -\pi$,

$$a_k = \frac{2}{2\pi} \left(\int_{-\pi}^{0} - V \cos kt \, dt + \int_{0}^{\pi} V \cos kt \, dt \right)$$

$$= \frac{V}{k\pi} \left(-\sin kt \Big|_{-\pi}^{0} + \sin kt \Big|_{0}^{\pi} \right) = \frac{V}{k\pi} [(-0 + \sin k\pi) + (\sin k\pi - 0)]$$

$$= 0$$

For the b_k coefficients, use eq. (21.12a):

$$b_k = \frac{2}{T} \int_{t_o}^{t_o + T} f(t) \sin k\omega_o t \, dt$$

Again, with $T = 2\pi$, $\omega_o = 1$ rad/s, and $t_o = -\pi$,

$$b_k = \frac{2}{2\pi} \left(\int_{-\pi}^{0} - V \sin kt \, dt + \int_{0}^{\pi} V \sin kt \, dt \right)$$

$$= \frac{V}{k\pi} \left(\cos kt \Big|_{-\pi}^{0} - \cos kt \Big|_{0}^{\pi} \right) = \frac{V}{k\pi} [(1 - \cos k\pi) - (\cos k\pi - 1)]$$

$$= \frac{2V}{k\pi} (1 - \cos k\pi) = \frac{4V}{k\pi} \qquad (k = 1, 3, 5, 7, \ldots)$$

The Fourier series for the function described by the waveform in Fig. 21.11 is

$$f(t) = \frac{4V}{\pi} \left(\sin \omega_o t + \frac{1}{3} \sin 3\omega_o t + \frac{1}{5} \sin 5\omega_o t + \frac{1}{7} \sin 7\omega_o t + \cdots \right]$$

∎

EXERCISE 21.4

Use eqs. (21.20) through (21.23) to show an alternative method of achieving the result of Example 21.5.

Answer

$$f(t) = \frac{4V}{\pi} \left(\sin \omega_o t + \frac{1}{3} \sin 3\omega_o t + \frac{1}{5} \sin 5\omega_o t + \frac{1}{7} \sin 7\omega_o t \cdots \right)$$

21.4.6 Functions That Yield Only Even Harmonics

Periodic functions of the form

$$f(t) = f\left(t \pm \frac{T}{2} \right)$$

TABLE 21.1   Summary of Fourier coefficient relationships ($t_o = 0$)

Symmetry Conditions	Characteristics	a_k	b_k
None	None	$\dfrac{2}{T}\displaystyle\int_0^T f(t)\cos k\omega_o t\,dt$	$\dfrac{2}{T}\displaystyle\int_0^T f(t)\sin k\omega_o t\,dt$
$f(t) = f(-t)$	Cosine terms only	$\dfrac{4}{T}\displaystyle\int_0^{T/2} f(t)\cos k\omega_o t\,dt$	0
$f(t) = -f(-t)$	Sine terms only	0	$\dfrac{4}{T}\displaystyle\int_0^{T/2} f(t)\sin k\omega_o t\,dt$
$f(t) = -f\left(t \pm \dfrac{T}{2}\right)$	Odd terms only	$\dfrac{4}{T}\displaystyle\int_0^{T/2} f(t)\cos k\omega_o t\,dt$	$\dfrac{4}{T}\displaystyle\int_0^{T/2} f(t)\sin k\omega_o t\,dt$
$f(t) = f\left(t \pm \dfrac{T}{2}\right)$	Even terms only	$\dfrac{4}{T}\displaystyle\int_0^{T/2} f(t)\cos k\omega_o t\,dt$	$\dfrac{4}{T}\displaystyle\int_0^{T/2} f(t)\sin k\omega_o t\,dt$

will possess a Fourier series that contains only even terms. Relationships for the evaluation of the coefficients in this case may be found in the summary chart in Table 21.1.

SECTION 21.5   **TRUNCATION AND MEAN SQUARE ERROR**

The Fourier series of a function $f(t)$ containing an infinite number of terms is written as

$$f(t) = \frac{a_0}{2} + \sum_{k=1}^{\infty} (a_k \cos k\omega_o t + b_k \sin k\omega_o t)$$

However, analyses that employ a Fourier series to represent a waveform involve a truncated Fourier series, where the number of terms is finite. If $2n + 1$ terms[1] are used to represent $f(t)$ in the interval $t_o < t < t_o + T$, then the function $f(t)$ will be represented by the finite sum

$$S_n(t) = \frac{a_0}{2} + \sum_{k=1}^{n} (a_k \cos k\omega_o t + b_k \sin k\omega_o t) \tag{21.24}$$

and the coefficients a_0, a_k, and b_k can be chosen to minimize the error

$$e_n(t) = f(t) - S_n(t) \tag{21.25}$$

that arises from the use of only $2n + 1$ terms.

There are many ways of specifying this error. One way is to use the mean square error, because interest is usually not focused on instantaneous positive or negative errors. Moreover, the mean square error is a function of the number of terms taken

---

[1] $n\,a_k$'s, $n\,b_k$'s, and one a_0.

in the approximation of S_n. The mean square error is

$$E_n = \frac{1}{T} \int_{t_o}^{t_o+T} e_n(t)^2 \, dt \qquad \textbf{(21.26)}$$

or

$$E_n = \frac{1}{T} \int_{t_o}^{t_o+T} [f(t) - S_n(t)]^2 \, dt \qquad \textbf{(21.27)}$$

where E_n is a function of the coefficients a_0, a_k, and b_k and is no longer a function of t.

If eq. (21.24) is put into eq. (21.27), the result is

$$E_n = \frac{1}{T} \int_{t_o}^{t_o+T} \left[f(t) - \frac{a_0}{2} - \sum_{k=1}^{n} (a_k \cos k\omega_o t + b_k \sin k\omega_o t) \right]^2 dt \qquad \textbf{(21.28)}$$

Now, consider E_n as a function of a_0, a_k, and b_k, and minimize E_n by using $2n + 1$ equations that are functions of the $2n + 1$ coefficients:

$$\frac{\partial E_n}{\partial a_0} = 0 \qquad \frac{\partial E_n}{\partial a_k} = 0 \qquad \frac{\partial E_n}{\partial b_k} = 0 \qquad (k = 1, 2, 3, 4, \ldots)$$

When the minimization procedure based on the foregoing is carried out, it is found that

$$a_0 = \frac{2}{T} \int_{t_o}^{t_o+T} f(t) \, dt \qquad \textbf{(21.11)}$$

$$a_k = \frac{2}{T} \int_{t_o}^{t_o+T} f(t) \cos k\omega_o t \, dt \qquad \textbf{(21.10a)}$$

$$b_k = \frac{2}{T} \int_{t_o}^{t_o+T} f(t) \sin k\omega_o t \, dt \qquad \textbf{(21.12a)}$$

These equations show that, based on a least mean square error criterion, the Fourier series represents the best possible trigonometric series approximation to $f(t)$.

THE AMPLITUDE–PHASE ANGLE FORMS   SECTION 21.6

Consider the Fourier series

$$f(t) = \frac{a_0}{2} + \sum_{k=1}^{\infty} (a_k \cos k\omega_o t + b_k \sin k\omega_o t)$$

Assume that $\sqrt{a_k^2 + b_k^2} \neq 0$ and multiply and divide the parenthetical term by $\sqrt{a_k^2 + b_k^2}$:

$$f(t) = \frac{a_0}{2} + \sum_{k=1}^{\infty} \sqrt{a_k^2 + b_k^2} \left(\frac{a_k}{\sqrt{a_k^2 + b_k^2}} \cos k\omega_o t + \frac{b_k}{\sqrt{a_k^2 + b_k^2}} \sin k\omega_o t \right)$$

FIGURE 21.11   Right triangle used to show the relationship between the Fourier coefficients
a_k, b_k, and c_k and the angle ϕ_k

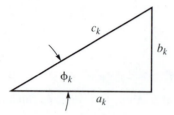

If a_k and b_k are, respectively, the base and height of a right triangle (see Fig. 21.11), then the hypotenuse will be

$$c_k = \sqrt{a_k^2 + b_k^2} \tag{21.29}$$

The cosine and sine of the angle ϕ_k will be

$$\cos \phi_k = \frac{a_k}{\sqrt{a_k^2 + b_k^2}} \tag{21.30}$$

$$\sin \phi_k = \frac{b_k}{\sqrt{a_k^2 + b_k^2}} \tag{21.31}$$

This, of course, makes

$$\phi_k = \arctan \frac{b_k}{a_k} \tag{21.32}$$

The Fourier series may therefore be written with $c_0 = a_0$ as

$$f(t) = \frac{c_0}{2} + \sum_{k=1}^{\infty} c_k(\cos \phi_k \cos k\omega_o t + \sin \phi_k \sin k\omega_o t)$$

The trigonometric identity

$$\cos(A - B) = \cos A \cos B + \sin A \sin B$$

with $A = k\omega_o t$ and $B = \phi_k$ can then be used to show that the *cosine–phase angle form* of the Fourier series is

$$f(t) = \frac{c_0}{2} + \sum_{k=1}^{\infty} c_k \cos(k\omega_o t - \phi_k) \tag{21.33a}$$

The coefficient c_k is called the *amplitude*, and the angle ϕ_k is called the *argument* or *phase angle*.

A similar development will yield the *sine–phase angle form*

$$f(t) = \frac{c_0}{2} + \sum_{k=1}^{\infty} c_k \sin(k\omega_o t + \theta_k) \tag{21.33b}$$

where $\theta_k = \pi/2 - \phi_k$. Both of eqs. (21.33) are referred to as the *amplitude–phase angle forms*.

■ **EXAMPLE 21.6**

A periodic voltage with fundamental frequency $\omega_o = 4$ rad/s is represented by the Fourier series

$$v(t) = 3.18 + 2.43 \cos 4t - 1.37 \cos 8t + 0.61 \cos 12t - 0.09 \cos 16t$$
$$+ 2.77 \sin 4t + 1.37 \sin 8t + 0.54 \sin 12t + 0.11 \sin 16t + \cdots \text{volts}$$

Put this Fourier series into the cosine–phase angle form of eq. (21.33).

Solution The average or dc term is $c_0/2 = 3.18$ V. The other harmonics will have amplitudes obtained from eq. (21.29):

$$c_4 = \sqrt{(2.43)^2 + (2.77)^2} = 3.68 \qquad c_{12} = \sqrt{(0.61)^2 + (0.54)^2} = 0.81$$
$$c_8 = \sqrt{(-1.37)^2 + (1.37)^2} = 1.94 \qquad c_{16} = \sqrt{(-0.09)^2 + (0.11)^2} = 0.14$$

The arguments or angles are obtained from eq. (21.32), with extreme care exercised in placing them in the correct quadrant:

$$\theta_4 = \arctan \frac{2.77}{2.43} = 48.74° \qquad \theta_{12} = \arctan \frac{0.54}{0.61} = 41.52°$$

$$\theta_8 = \arctan \frac{1.37}{-1.37} = 135.00° \qquad \theta_{16} = \arctan \frac{0.11}{-0.09} = 129.29°$$

The Fourier series in cosine–phase angle form is

$$v(t) = 3.18 + 3.68 \cos(4t + 48.74°) + 1.94 \cos(8t + 135.00°)$$
$$+ 0.81 \cos(12t + 41.52°) + 0.14 \cos(16t + 129.29°) + \cdots \text{volts} \qquad ■$$

EXERCISE 21.5

A periodic current with fundamental frequency $\omega_o = 3$ rad/s is represented by the Fourier series

$$i(t) = 432 + 281.5 \cos 3t - 117.6 \cos 6t + 88.3 \cos 9t + 14.6 \cos 12t$$
$$+ 3.1 \cos 15t - 212.4 \sin 3t + 79.7 \sin 6t - 47.2 \sin 9t$$
$$+ 13.9 \sin 12t - 4.5 \sin 15t + \cdots \text{milliamperes}$$

Put this Fourier series into the cosine–phase angle form of eq. (21.33).

Answer

$$i(t) = 432 + 352.6 \cos(3t - 37.04°) + 142.1 \cos(6t + 145.87°)$$
$$+ 100.1 \cos(9t - 28.13°) + 20.2 \cos(12t + 43.59°)$$
$$+ 5.5 \cos(15t - 55.44°) + \cdots \text{milliamperes}$$

SECTION 21.7 THE EXPONENTIAL FORM

Once again, consider the Fourier series

$$f(t) = \frac{a_0}{2} + \sum_{k=1}^{\infty} (a_k \cos k\omega_o t + b_k \sin k\omega_o t)$$

and observe that both the cosine and the sine functions can be expressed in terms of exponential functions (Appendix A):

$$\cos k\omega_o t = \frac{e^{jk\omega_o t} + e^{-jk\omega_o t}}{2} \qquad \text{and} \qquad \sin k\omega_o t = \frac{e^{jk\omega_o t} - e^{-jk\omega_o t}}{2j}$$

Thus, the Fourier series may also be written as

$$f(t) = \frac{a_0}{2} + \sum_{k=1}^{\infty} \left(a_k \frac{e^{jk\omega_o t} + e^{-jk\omega_o t}}{2} + b_k \frac{e^{jk\omega_o t} - e^{-jk\omega_o t}}{2j} \right)$$

or

$$f(t) = \frac{a_0}{2} + \sum_{k=1}^{\infty} \left(\frac{a_k - jb_k}{2} e^{jk\omega_o t} + \frac{a_k + jb_k}{2} e^{-jk\omega_o t} \right)$$

With

$$\alpha_0 = \frac{a_k}{2} \qquad\qquad\qquad (21.34a)$$

$$\alpha_k = \frac{1}{2}(a_k - jb_k) \qquad\qquad\qquad (21.34b)$$

$$\alpha_{-k} = \frac{1}{2}(a_k + jb_k) \qquad\qquad\qquad (21.34c)$$

the Fourier series can be written as

$$f(t) = \alpha_0 + \sum_{k=1}^{\infty} (\alpha_k e^{jk\omega_o t} + \alpha_{-k} e^{-jk\omega_o t})$$

If $-k$ is substituted for k in the second summation, then

$$\sum_{k=1}^{\infty} \alpha_{-k} e^{-jk\omega_o t} = \sum_{k=-\infty}^{-1} \alpha_k e^{jk\omega_o t}$$

and the Fourier series can be written as a single summation,

$$f(t) = \sum_{-\infty}^{\infty} \alpha_k e^{jk\omega_o t} \qquad\qquad\qquad (21.35)$$

where α_0 is included and where the α's are the Fourier coefficients evaluated by

$$\alpha_k = \frac{1}{T} \int_{t_o}^{t_o+T} f(t)e^{-jk\omega_o t}\, dt \tag{21.36}$$

The presence of negative values of k and the negative frequencies have no physical significance and are a result of the mathematical operations necessary to represent the sine and cosine functions as exponential functions.

■ **EXAMPLE 21.7**

Write a Fourier series in exponential form for the half-wave rectifier waveform shown in Fig. 21.12.

Solution   The function is described by

$$v(t) = \begin{cases} V \sin t, & 0 < t < \pi \\ 0, & \pi < t < 2\pi \end{cases}$$

and the period is $T = 2\pi$, which makes $\omega_o = 2\pi/T = 2\pi/2\pi = 1$ rad/s. Thus,

$$\alpha_k = \frac{1}{T} \int_{t_o}^{t_o+T} f(t)e^{-jk\omega_o t}\, dt = \frac{1}{2\pi}\left(\int_0^\pi Ve^{-jkt} \sin t\, dt + \int_\pi^{2\pi} 0\, dt \right)$$

Integration by parts gives

$$\alpha_k = -\frac{V}{2\pi}\left[\frac{e^{-jkt}}{1-k^2} (jk \sin t + \cos t) \right]_0^\pi$$

$$= -\frac{V}{2\pi}\left[\frac{e^{-jk\pi}}{1-k^2} (jk \sin \pi + \cos \pi) - \frac{1}{1-k^2}(0+1) \right]$$

$$= \frac{V(e^{-jk\pi}+1)}{2\pi(1-k^2)} = \left[\frac{V(\cos k\pi - j \sin k\pi + 1)}{2\pi(1-k^2)} \right]$$

If k is odd (except for $k = 1$),

$$\alpha_k = \frac{V(-1+1)}{2\pi(1-k^2)} = 0$$

Half-wave rectifier waveform

FIGURE 21.12

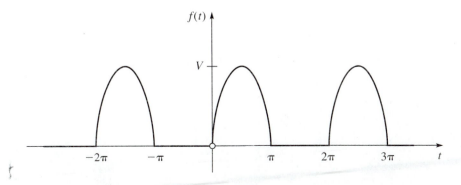

and if k is even,

$$\alpha_k = \frac{V}{\pi(1 - k^2)}$$

If $k = 1$, an indeterminate form results, and L'Hôpital's rule can be employed to show that

$$\alpha_1 = \frac{\partial/\partial k[V(\cos k\pi - j \sin k\pi + 1]}{\partial/\partial k[2\pi(1 - k^2)]} = \frac{-\pi V(\sin k\pi + j \cos k\pi)}{-4k\pi}$$

And now, with $k = 1$,

$$\alpha_1 = \frac{j\pi V}{-4\pi} = -\frac{jV}{4}$$

There is also an average term:

$$\alpha_0 = \frac{1}{2\pi} \int_0^\pi V \sin t \, dt = -\frac{V}{2\pi} \cos t \Big|_0^\pi = -\frac{V}{2\pi}(-1 - 1) = \frac{V}{\pi}$$

The series in exponential form is therefore

$$v(t) = \cdots - \frac{V}{35\pi} e^{-j6t} - \frac{V}{15\pi} e^{-j4t} - \frac{V}{3\pi} e^{-j2t} + j\frac{V}{4} e^{-jt}$$

$$+ \frac{V}{\pi} - j\frac{V}{4} e^{jt} - \frac{V}{3\pi} e^{j2t} - \frac{V}{15\pi} e^{j4t} - \frac{V}{35\pi} e^{j6t} + \cdots \qquad \blacksquare$$

EXERCISE 21.6

Write a Fourier series in exponential form for the square wave shown in Fig. 21.13.

Answer

$$i(t) = \cdots + j\frac{2I}{5\pi} e^{-j5t} + j\frac{2I}{3\pi} e^{-j3t} + j\frac{2I}{\pi} e^{-jt} - j\frac{2I}{\pi} e^{jt} - j\frac{2I}{3\pi} e^{j3t} - j\frac{2I}{5\pi} e^{j5t}$$

FIGURE 21.13   Square wave (Exercise 21.6)

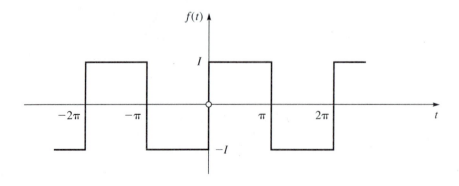

THE EFFECTIVE VALUE OF A PERIODIC FUNCTION

The cosine–phase angle form can be used to find the effective value of a periodic signal. Recall the definition of the effective value given in Section 5.7:

$$f_{\text{eff}} = \sqrt{\frac{1}{T} \int_0^T [f(t)]^2 \, dt} \tag{5.19}$$

If $f(t)$ is given by eq. (21.33), then working with the square yields

$$f_{\text{eff}}^2 = \frac{1}{T} \int_0^T \left[\frac{c_0}{2} + \sum_{k=1}^{\infty} c_k \cos(k\omega_o t - \phi_k) \right]^2 dt$$

When the term within the brackets is squared, the result, before the integration, is

$$\frac{c_0^2}{4} + c_0 \sum_{k=1}^{\infty} c_k \cos(k\omega_o t - \phi_k) + \sum_{k=1}^{\infty} c_k^2 \cos^2(k\omega_o t - \phi_k)$$

Here, it is noted, from an extension of eq. (21.5), that any term in the middle summation will vanish when integrated between the specified limits:

$$\int_0^T c_0 c_k \cos(k\omega_o t - \phi_k) \, dt = 0$$

This leaves

$$\frac{c_0^2}{4} + \sum_{k=1}^{\infty} c_k^2 \cos^2(k\omega_o t - \phi_k)$$

The second term here can be simplified through the use of the familiar trigonometric identity

$$\cos^2 A = \frac{1}{2} (1 + \cos 2A)$$

so that the effective value is determined from

$$f_{\text{eff}}^2 = \frac{1}{T} \int_0^T \left\{ \frac{c_0^2}{4} + \frac{1}{2} \sum_{k=1}^{\infty} c_k^2 [1 + \cos(2k\omega_o t - \phi_k)] \right\} dt$$

Another simplification occurs when it is recognized that

$$\int_0^T \cos(2k\omega_o t - \phi_k) \, dt = 0$$

Thus the effective value of a periodic function can be written in terms of the coefficients of its Fourier series expressed in the amplitude–phase angle form:

$$f_{\text{eff}}^2 = \frac{1}{T} \int_0^T \left(\frac{c_0^2}{4} + \frac{1}{2} \sum_{k=1}^{\infty} c_k^2 \right) dt = \frac{1}{T} \left[\frac{c_0^2}{4} t + \frac{1}{2} \sum_{k=1}^{\infty} c_k^2 t \right]_0^T$$

or

$$f_{\text{eff}} = \sqrt{\frac{c_0^2}{4} + \frac{1}{2} \sum_{k=1}^{\infty} c_k^2}$$ (21.37)

■ **EXAMPLE 21.8**

Determine the effective value of the periodic voltage given in Example 21.6,

$$v(t) = 3.18 + 2.43 \cos 4t - 1.37 \cos 8t + 0.61 \cos 12t - 0.09 \cos 16t$$
$$+ 2.77 \sin 4t + 1.37 \sin 8t + 0.54 \sin 12t + 0.11 \sin 16t + \cdots \text{volts}$$

Solution   With

$$\frac{c_0}{2} = 3.18 \qquad c_4 = 3.68 \qquad c_8 = 1.94 \qquad c_{12} = 0.81 \qquad c_{16} = 0.14$$

the effective value can be obtained from eq. (21.37),

$$v_{\text{eff}} = \sqrt{\frac{c_0^2}{4} + \frac{1}{2} \sum_{k=1}^{\infty} c_k^2}$$

Thus,

$$v_{\text{eff}} = \sqrt{(3.18)^2 + \frac{1}{2}[(3.68)^2 + (1.94)^2 + (0.81)^2 + (0.14)^2]}$$
$$= \sqrt{19.10} = 4.37 \text{ V}$$ ■

EXERCISE 21.7

Determine the effective value of the periodic current in Exercise 21.5,

$$i(t) = 432 + 281.5 \cos 3t - 117.6 \cos 6t + 88.3 \cos 9t + 14.6 \cos 12t$$
$$+ 3.1 \cos 15t - 212.4 \sin 3t + 79.7 \sin 6t - 47.2 \sin 9t$$
$$+ 13.9 \sin 12t - 4.5 \sin 15t + \cdots \text{milliamperes}$$

Answer   513.9 mA.

SECTION 21.9   **PERIODIC FUNCTIONS AND AVERAGE POWER**

If a periodic function is applied to the terminals of a linear network, it can be represented by a Fourier series in the amplitude–phase angle form,

$$v = V_o + \sum_{k=1}^{\infty} V_k \cos(k\omega_o t - \phi_k)$$

where V_o is the average or *dc* value and where the V_k's are peak or maximum amplitudes.

A current will flow into the network,

$$i = I_o + \sum_{k=1}^{\infty} I_k \cos(k\omega_o t - \psi_k)$$

where here, too, I_o is the average value and the I_k's are peak amplitudes.

The average power involves the product of v and i:

$$p_{av} = \frac{1}{T} \int_0^T vi\, dt$$

$$= \frac{1}{T} \int_0^T \left[V_o + \sum_{k=1}^{\infty} V_k \cos(k\omega_o t - \phi_k) \right]\left[I_o + \sum_{k=1}^{\infty} I_k \cos(k\omega_o t - \psi_k) \right] dt$$

The product of the bracketed quantities involves four types of terms. The first is merely the product $V_o I_o$ and

$$\frac{1}{T} \int_0^T V_o I_o\, dt = V_o I_o$$

Two other terms are of the form

$$V_o I_k \cos(k\omega_o t - \psi_k) \qquad \text{and} \qquad I_o V_k \cos(k\omega_o t - \phi_k)$$

By an extension of eq. (21.5), it is observed that both of these are annihilated by the integration process:

$$\frac{1}{T} \int_0^T V_o I_k \cos(k\omega_o t - \psi_k)\, dt = 0 \quad \text{and} \quad \frac{1}{T} \int_0^T I_o V_k \cos(k\omega_o t - \phi_k)\, dt = 0$$

The fourth type of term has the form

$$I_k V_k \cos(k\omega_o t - \phi_k) \cos(k\omega_o t - \psi_k)$$

which, by the trigonometric identity

$$\cos A \cos B = \frac{1}{2}[\cos(A + B) + \cos(A - B)]$$

can be written as

$$\frac{V_k I_k}{2}[\cos(2k\omega_o t - \phi_k - \psi_k) + \cos(\phi_k - \psi_k)]$$

With $\theta_k = \phi_k - \psi_k$, an extension of eq. (21.5) shows that

$$\frac{1}{T} \int_0^T \frac{V_k I_k}{2}[\cos(2k\omega_o t - \phi_k - \psi_k) + \cos\theta_k]\, dt = \frac{1}{T} \cdot \frac{V_k I_k}{2} \cos\theta_k t \Big|_{t_o}^{t_o + T}$$

$$= \frac{V_k I_k}{2} \cos\theta_k$$

All of the foregoing can be assembled into an expression for the average power,

$$p_{av} = V_o I_o + \frac{1}{2} \sum_{k=1}^{\infty} V_k I_k \cos \theta_k \qquad (21.38a)$$

where V_k and I_k are peak amplitudes and $\theta_k = \phi_k - \psi_k$. Observe that the effective or rms value of each sinusoidal component is related to the peak amplitude by the factor $\sqrt{2}/2$. Thus, an alternative form is

$$p_{av} = V_o I_o + \sum_{k=1}^{\infty} V_{k,rms} I_{k,rms} \cos \theta_k \qquad (21.38b)$$

■ **EXAMPLE 21.9**

Consider a network with an applied voltage represented by an average term and four harmonics of a Fourier series:

$$v = 100 + 50 \cos(400t + 15°) + 25 \cos(800t + 30°)$$
$$+ 10 \cos(1200t + 45°) + 4 \cos(1600t + 60°) \text{ volts}$$

The resulting current is

$$i = 4 + 2.24 \cos(400t - 12°) + 1.17 \cos(800t - 8°)$$
$$+ 0.93 \cos(1200t - 3°) + 0.61 \cos(1600t + 0°) \text{ amperes}$$

Assume all of the amplitudes are peak amplitudes, and find the effective values of both the voltage and the current and the average power delivered by the source.

Solution The effective values are found via eq. (21.37). For the voltage wave with $c_0 = 200$ V,

$$v_{eff} = \sqrt{\frac{1}{4}(200)^2 + \frac{1}{2}[(50)^2 + (25)^2 + (10)^2 + (4)^2]}$$
$$= \sqrt{11,620.50} = 107.80 \text{ V}$$

For the current with $c_0 = 8$ A,

$$i_{eff} = \sqrt{\frac{1}{4}(8)^2 + \frac{1}{2}[(2.24)^2 + (1.17)^2 + (0.93)^2 + (0.61)^2]}$$
$$= \sqrt{19.81} = 4.45 \text{ A}$$

The average power is obtained from eq. (21.38a), which assumes that all of the amplitudes are peak amplitudes:

$$p_{av} = V_o I_o + \frac{1}{2} \sum_{k=1}^{\infty} V_k I_k \cos \theta_k$$
$$= 100(4) + 50(2.24) \cos[15° - (-12°)] + 25(1.17) \cos[30° - (-8°)]$$
$$+ 10(0.93) \cos[45° - (-3°)] + 4(0.61) \cos 60°$$
$$= 400 + 99.79 + 23.05 + 6.22 + 1.22 = 530.28 \text{ W}$$

■

EXERCISE 21.8

Consider a network with an applied voltage represented by an average term and four harmonics of a Fourier series,

$$v = 82.5 + 37.3 \cos(377t + 17°) + 12.5 \cos(754t + 36.87°)$$
$$+ 1.3 \cos(1131t + 45°) + 0.4 \cos(1508t + 72°) \text{ volts}$$

The resulting current is

$$i = 4.61 + 2.04 \cos(377t - 12.5°) + 1.33 \cos(754t - 8°)$$
$$+ 0.73 \cos(1131t - 4.3°) + 0.29 \cos(1508t + 7.03°) \text{ amperes}$$

Assume all of the amplitudes are peak amplitudes, and find the effective values of both the voltage and the current and the average power delivered by the source.

Answer $v_{\text{eff}} = 87.1$ V, $i_{\text{eff}} = 4.95$ A, and $p_{\text{av}} = 459$ W.

APPLICATION TO NETWORK ANALYSIS

SECTION 21.10

When a periodic signal is applied as the forcing function or input to a linear network, the current or voltage response can be found by an application of superposition. The periodic forcing function is represented by its Fourier series, and the response to each component of the forcing function is established by the usual ac phasor methods. Then, all of the responses so determined are added to yield the total response.

■ EXAMPLE 21.10

Consider the network in Fig. 21.14a with the periodic input voltage as shown in Fig. 21.14b. Find the current entering the network.

Solution The input voltage is described by

$$v_s(t) = \begin{cases} -50\pi, & -0.0314 < t < -0.0157 \\ 50\pi, & -0.0157 < t < 0.0157 \\ -50\pi, & 0.0157 < t < 0.0314 \end{cases}$$

It is observed that the period is $T = 0.0628$ s, so that $\omega_o = 2\pi/T = 2\pi/0.0628 = 100$ rad/s. In addition, the function is an even function that possesses half-wave symmetry. There will be no average term, and the Fourier series representing the input function will contain only odd cosine terms. By eq. (21.22),

$$a_k = \frac{8}{T} \int_0^{T/4} f(t) \cos k\omega_o t \, dt = \frac{8}{0.0628} \int_0^{0.0157} 50\pi \cos 100kt \, dt$$

$$= \frac{20,000}{100k} \sin 100kt \Big|_0^{0.0157} = \frac{200}{k} \sin \frac{k\pi}{2}$$

FIGURE 21.14   (a) Simple RL network and its (b) voltage input function

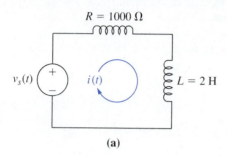

$R = 1000\ \Omega$

$v_s(t)$ $i(t)$ $L = 2\ \mathrm{H}$

(a)

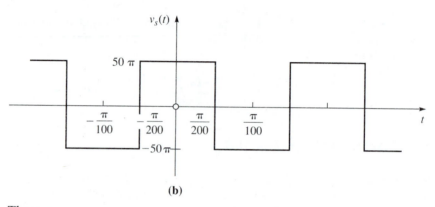

$v_s(t)$

$50\,\pi$

$-\dfrac{\pi}{100}$ $-\dfrac{\pi}{200}$ $\dfrac{\pi}{200}$ $\dfrac{\pi}{100}$ t

$-50\,\pi$

(b)

Thus,

$$v_s(t) = 200\left(\cos 100t - \frac{1}{3}\cos 300t + \frac{1}{5}\cos 500t - \frac{1}{7}\cos 700t + \cdots\right)\ \text{volts}$$

The network impedance for the simple RL network is a function of the angular frequency,

$$Z(j\omega) = 1000 + j2\omega$$

and in this case, with $\omega_o = 100$ rad/s,

$$Z(jk\omega_o) = 1000 + j200k$$

The current components are obtained in a straightforward manner. For $k = 1$, $k\omega_o = 100$ rad/s, and

$$\hat{V}_1 = 200\underline{/0^\circ} \qquad \text{and} \qquad Z = 1000 + j200 = 1019.80\underline{/11.31^\circ}$$

The current component is

$$\hat{I}_1 = \frac{\hat{V}_1}{Z_1} = \frac{200\underline{/0^\circ}}{1019.80\underline{/11.31^\circ}} = 0.196\underline{/-11.31^\circ}\ \text{A}$$

For $k = 3$, $k\omega_o = 300$ rad/s, and

$$\hat{V}_3 = 66.67\underline{/180^\circ} \qquad \text{and} \qquad Z_3 = 1000 + j600 = 1166.19\underline{/30.96^\circ}$$

The current component will be

$$\hat{I}_3 = \frac{\hat{V}_2}{Z_2} = \frac{66.67\underline{/180^\circ}}{1166.19\underline{/30.96^\circ}} = 0.057\underline{/149.04^\circ}\ A$$

For $k = 5$,

$$\hat{V}_5 = 40\underline{/0^\circ} \qquad Z_5 = 1000 + j1000 = 1000\sqrt{2}\underline{/45^\circ}$$

$$\hat{I}_5 = \frac{\hat{V}_5}{Z_5} = \frac{40\underline{/0^\circ}}{1000\sqrt{2}\underline{/45^\circ}} = 0.020\sqrt{2}\underline{/-45^\circ}\ A$$

For $k = 7$,

$$\hat{V}_7 = 28.57\underline{/180^\circ} \qquad Z_7 = 1000 + j1400 = 1720.47\underline{/54.46^\circ}$$

$$\hat{I}_7 = \frac{\hat{V}_7}{Z_7} = \frac{28.57\underline{/180^\circ}}{1720.47\underline{/54.46^\circ}} = 0.017\underline{/125.54^\circ}\ A$$

The first four terms of the steady-state current entering the network are

$$i(t) = 0.196\cos(100t - 11.31^\circ) + 0.057\cos(300t + 149.04^\circ)$$
$$+ 0.02\sqrt{2}\cos(500t - 45^\circ) + 0.017\cos(700t + 125.54^\circ) + \cdots \text{ amperes} \quad \blacksquare$$

CHAPTER 21

SUMMARY

- The Dirichlet conditions pertain to periodic functions.
  - The function $f(t)$ is single-valued.
  - The function $f(t)$ has, at most, a finite number of discontinuities in one period.
  - The function $f(t)$ has, at most, a finite number of maxima and minima in one period.
  - The integral over one period is finite:

$$\int_{t_o}^{t_o+T} dt < \infty$$

- The form of the Fourier series is

$$f(t) = \frac{a_0}{2} + a_1\cos\omega_o t + a_2\cos 2\omega_o t + \cdots + a_k\cos k\omega_o t + \cdots$$
$$+ b_1\sin\omega_o t + b_2\sin 2\omega_o t + \cdots + b_k\sin k\omega_o t + \cdots$$

- The Fourier coefficients are found from

$$a_0 = \frac{2}{T}\int_{t_o}^{t_o+T} f(t)\,dt \qquad a_k = \frac{2}{T}\int_{t_o}^{t_o+T} f(t)\cos k\omega_o t\,dt$$

$$b_k = \frac{2}{T}\int_{t_o}^{t_o+T} f(t)\sin k\omega_o t\,dt$$

■ A summary of Fourier series coefficient relationships when $t_o = 0$ is given in Table 21.1.

■ The cosine–phase angle form is

$$f(t) = \frac{c_0}{2} + \sum_{k=1}^{\infty} c_k \cos(k\omega_o t - \phi_k)$$

where

$$c_k = \sqrt{a_k^2 + b_k^2} \qquad \phi_k = \arctan \frac{b_k}{a_k}$$

■ The exponential form is

$$f(t) = \sum_{-\infty}^{\infty} \alpha_k e^{jk\omega_o t}$$

where

$$\alpha_k = \frac{1}{T} \int_{t_o}^{t_o + T} f(t) e^{-jk\omega_o t} \, dt$$

■ The effective value of a periodic function is

$$f_{\text{eff}} = \sqrt{\frac{c_0^2}{4} + \frac{1}{2} \sum_{k=1}^{\infty} c_k^2}$$

■ The average power is

$$p_{\text{av}} = V_o I_o + \sum_{k=1}^{\infty} V_{k,\text{rms}} I_{k,\text{rms}} \cos \theta_k$$

Additional Readings

Blackwell, W.A., and L.L. Grigsby. *Introductory Network Theory*. Boston: PWS Engineering, 1985, pp. 485–516.

Bobrow, L.S. *Elementary Linear Circuit Analysis*. 2d ed. New York: Holt, Rinehart and Winston, 1987, pp. 596–626.

Del Toro, V. *Engineering Circuits*. Englewood Cliffs, N.J.: Prentice-Hall, 1987, pp. 605–634.

Hayt, W.H., Jr., and J.E. Kemmerly. *Engineering Circuit Analysis*. 4th ed. New York: McGraw-Hill, 1986, pp. 501–523.

Irwin, J.D. *Basic Engineering Circuit Analysis*. 3d ed. New York: Macmillan, 1989, pp. 809–844.

Johnson, D.E., J.L. Hilburn, and J.R. Johnson. *Basic Electric Circuit Analysis*. 4th ed. Englewood Cliffs, N.J.: Prentice-Hall, 1989, pp. 551–571.

Karni, S. *Applied Circuit Analysis*. New York: Wiley, 1988, pp. 614–639.

Madhu, S. *Linear Circuit Analysis*. Englewood Cliffs, N.J.: Prentice-Hall, 1988, pp. 661–690.

Nilsson, J.W. *Electric Circuits*. 3d ed. Reading, Mass.: Addison-Wesley, 1990, pp. 668–707.

Paul, C.R. *Analysis of Linear Circuits*. New York: McGraw-Hill, 1989, pp. 654–689.

PROBLEMS CHAPTER 21

Section 21.3

21.1 Give the coefficients a_0, a_k, and b_k of the Fourier series for the periodic waveform shown in Fig. P21.1.

Figure P21.1

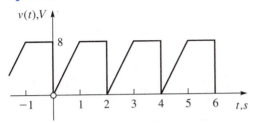

21.2 Give the coefficients a_0, a_k, and b_k of the Fourier series for the periodic waveform shown in Fig. P21.2.

Figure P21.2

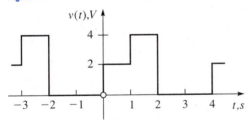

21.3 Give the coefficients a_0, a_k, and b_k of the Fourier series for the periodic waveform shown in Fig. P21.3.

Figure P21.3

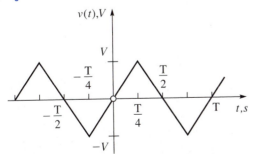

21.4 Give the coefficients a_0, a_k, and b_k of the Fourier series for the periodic waveform shown in Fig. P21.4.

Figure P21.4

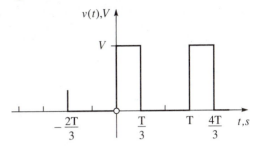

21.5 Give the coefficients a_0, a_k, and b_k of the Fourier series for the periodic waveform shown in Fig. P21.5.

Figure P21.5

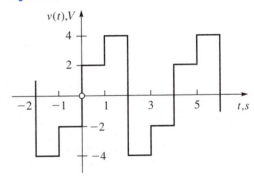

21.6 Give the coefficients a_0, a_k, and b_k of the Fourier series for the periodic waveform shown in Fig. P21.6.

Figure P21.6

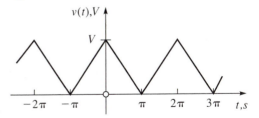

21.7 Give the coefficients a_0, a_k, and b_k of the Fourier series for the periodic waveform shown in Fig. P21.7.

Figure P21.7

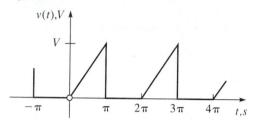

21.8 Give the coefficients a_0, a_k, and b_k of the Fourier series for the periodic waveform shown in Fig. P21.8.

Figure P21.8

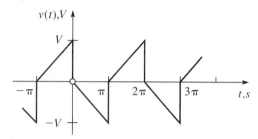

Section 21.4

21.9 Exploit any symmetry characteristics in the periodic waveform shown in Fig. P21.3 to save labor in writing the coefficients a_0, a_k, and b_k in the Fourier series.

21.10 Exploit any symmetry characteristics in the periodic waveform shown in Fig. P21.5 to save labor in writing the coefficients a_0, a_k, and b_k in the Fourier series.

21.11 Exploit any symmetry characteristics in the periodic waveform shown in Fig. P21.6 to save labor in writing the coefficients a_0, a_k, and b_k in the Fourier series.

21.12 Exploit any symmetry characteristics in the periodic waveform shown in Fig. P21.9 to save labor in writing the coefficients a_0, a_k, and b_k in the Fourier series.

Figure P21.9

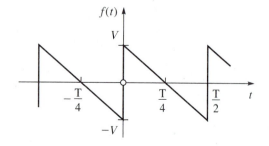

21.13 Exploit any symmetry characteristics in the periodic waveform shown in Fig. P21.10 to save labor in writing the coefficients a_0, a_k, and b_k in the Fourier series.

Figure P21.10

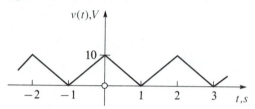

21.14 Exploit any symmetry characteristics in the periodic waveform shown in Fig. P21.11 to save labor in writing the coefficients a_0, a_k, and b_k in the Fourier series.

Figure P21.11

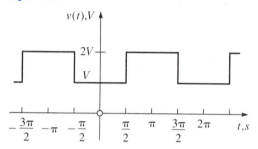

21.15 Exploit any symmetry characteristics in the periodic waveform shown in Fig. P21.12 to save labor in writing the coefficients a_0, a_k, and b_k in the Fourier series.

Figure P21.12

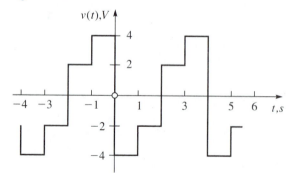

21.16 Exploit any symmetry characteristics in the periodic waveform shown in Fig. P21.13 to save labor in writing the coefficients a_0, a_k, and b_k in the Fourier series.

Figure P21.13

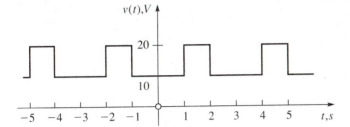

21.28 Write a Fourier series in exponential form for the periodic waveform shown in Fig. P21.4.

21.29 Write a Fourier series in exponential form for the periodic waveform shown in Fig. P21.5.

Section 21.6

21.17 Write a Fourier series in the cosine–phase angle form for the periodic waveform shown in Fig. P21.1.

21.18 Write a Fourier series in the cosine–phase angle form for the periodic waveform shown in Fig. P21.2.

21.19 Write a Fourier series in the cosine–phase angle form for the periodic waveform shown in Fig. P21.3.

21.20 Write a Fourier series in the cosine–phase angle form for the periodic waveform shown in Fig. P21.4.

21.21 Write a Fourier series in the cosine–phase angle form for the periodic waveform shown in Fig. P21.5.

21.22 Write a Fourier series in the cosine–phase angle form for the periodic waveform shown in Fig. P21.6.

21.23 Write a Fourier series in the cosine–phase angle form for the periodic waveform shown in Fig. P21.7.

21.24 Write a Fourier series in the cosine–phase angle form for the periodic waveform shown in Fig. P21.8.

Section 21.7

21.25 Write a Fourier series in exponential form for the periodic waveform shown in Fig. P21.1.

21.26 Write a Fourier series in exponential form for the periodic waveform shown in Fig. P21.2.

21.27 Write a Fourier series in exponential form for the periodic waveform shown in Fig. P21.3.

21.30 Write a Fourier series in exponential form for the periodic waveform shown in Fig. P21.6.

21.31 Write a Fourier series in exponential form for the periodic waveform shown in Fig. P21.7.

21.32 Write a Fourier series in exponential form for the periodic waveform shown in Fig. P21.8.

Section 21.8

21.33 Use the first five terms of the Fourier series developed in Problem 21.17 to establish the effective value of the waveform.

21.34 Use the first five terms of the Fourier series developed in Problem 21.18 to establish the effective value of the waveform.

21.35 Use the first five terms of the Fourier series developed in Problem 21.19 to establish the effective value of the waveform.

21.36 Use the first five terms of the Fourier series developed in Problem 21.20 to establish the effective value of the waveform.

21.37 Use the first five terms of the Fourier series developed in Problem 21.21 to establish the effective value of the waveform.

21.38 Use the first five terms of the Fourier series developed in Problem 21.22 to establish the effective value of the waveform.

21.39 Use the first five terms of the Fourier series developed in Problem 21.23 to establish the effective value of the waveform.

21.40 Use the first five terms of the Fourier series developed in Problem 21.24 to establish the effective value of the waveform.

Section 21.9

21.41 A voltage waveform that can be represented by the Fourier series

$$v(t) = 172.4 + 237.8 \cos 400t + 124.3 \cos 800t$$
$$+ 65.5 \cos 1200t + 29.6 \cos 1600t$$
$$+ 3.3 \cos 2000t + 0.47 \cos 2400t + \cdots$$
$$+ 322.1 \sin 400t - 177.3 \sin 800t$$
$$+ 94.1 \sin 1200t - 40.2 \sin 1600t$$
$$+ 4.7 \sin 2000t - 0.55 \sin 2400t$$
$$+ \cdots \text{ volts}$$

is applied to a network, and the following current flows into the network:

$$i(t) = 9.24 + 15.52 \cos 400t + 8.43 \cos 800t$$
$$+ 3.88 \cos 1200t + 1.06 \cos 1600t$$
$$+ 0.88 \cos 2000t + 0.17 \cos 2400t + \cdots$$
$$+ 22.71 \sin 400t + 11.63 \sin 800t$$
$$+ 8.46 \sin 1200t + 3.75 \sin 1600t$$
$$+ 1.27 \sin 2000t + 0.46 \sin 2400t$$
$$+ \cdots \text{ amperes}$$

Assume all amplitudes are peak amplitudes, and determine the average power delivered to the network.

21.42 A voltage waveform that can be represented by the Fourier series

$$v(t) = 292.3 + 428.6 \cos 500t - 297.3 \cos 1000t$$
$$+ 136.5 \cos 1500t - 89.4 \cos 2000t$$
$$+ 23.8 \cos 2500t - 6.47 \cos 3000t + \cdots$$
$$+ 332.5 \sin 500t - 233.4 \sin 1000t$$
$$+ 167.9 \sin 1500t - 63.4 \sin 2000t$$
$$+ 18.7 \sin 2500t - 3.55 \sin 3000t$$
$$+ \cdots \text{ volts}$$

is applied to a network, and the following current flows into the network:

$$i(t) = 7.13 + 11.13 \cos 500t + 7.18 \cos 1000t$$
$$+ 2.89 \cos 1500t + 1.15 \cos 2000t$$
$$+ 0.77 \cos 2500t + 0.39 \cos 3000t + \cdots$$
$$+ 13.66 \sin 500t - 11.65 \sin 1000t$$
$$+ 1.96 \sin 1500t + 1.44 \sin 2000t$$
$$- 1.16 \sin 2500t + 0.45 \sin 3000t$$
$$+ \cdots \text{ amperes}$$

Assume all amplitudes are peak amplitudes, and determine the average power delivered to the network.

21.43 A voltage waveform that can be represented by the Fourier series

$$v(t) = 120.1 + 177.3 \cos 200t + 104.1 \cos 400t$$
$$+ 57.8 \cos 600t + 19.6 \cos 800t$$
$$+ 4.3 \cos 1000t + 0.87 \cos 1200t + \cdots$$
$$+ 221.1 \sin 200t + 136.9 \sin 400t$$
$$+ 64.2 \sin 600t + 20.3 \sin 800t$$
$$+ 4.7 \sin 1000t + 0.94 \sin 1200t$$
$$+ \cdots \text{ volts}$$

is applied to a network, and the following current flows into the network:

$$i(t) = 6.14 + 9.52 \cos 200t + 4.43 \cos 400t$$
$$+ 1.69 \cos 600t + 1.03 \cos 800t$$
$$+ 0.78 \cos 1000t + 0.37 \cos 1200t + \cdots$$
$$+ 12.63 \sin 200t + 6.47 \sin 400t$$
$$+ 2.46 \sin 600t + 1.35 \sin 800t$$
$$+ 0.87 \sin 1000t + 0.45 \sin 1200t$$
$$+ \cdots \text{ amperes}$$

Assume all amplitudes are peak amplitudes, and determine the average power delivered to the network.

21.44 A voltage waveform that can be represented by the Fourier series

$$v(t) = 337.8 \cos 400t + 164.3 \cos 1200t$$
$$+ 85.5 \cos 2000t + 36.6 \cos 2800t$$
$$+ 4.3 \cos 3600t + 0.73 \cos 4400t + \cdots$$
$$+ 312.2 \sin 400t + 208.3 \sin 1200t$$
$$+ 113.1 \sin 2000t + 48.3 \sin 2800t$$
$$+ 5.2 \sin 3600t + 0.85 \sin 4400t$$
$$+ \cdots \text{ volts}$$

is applied to a network, and the following current flows into the network:

$$i(t) = 8.22 \cos 400t + 6.43 \cos 1200t$$
$$+ 2.79 \cos 2000t + 1.13 \cos 2800t$$
$$+ 0.79 \cos 3600t + 0.36 \cos 4400t + \cdots$$
$$+ 9.76 \sin 400t + 6.63 \sin 1200t$$
$$+ 3.41 \sin 2000t + 1.35 \sin 2800t$$
$$+ 0.84 \sin 3600t + 0.41 \sin 4400t$$
$$+ \cdots \text{ amperes}$$

Assume all amplitudes are peak amplitudes, and determine the average power delivered to the network.

Section 21.10

21.45 The voltage waveform shown in Fig. P21.14a is applied to the network shown in Fig. P21.14b. Write a Fourier series for the current waveform, and determine the average power delivered to the network.

Figure P21.14

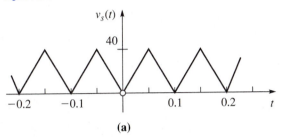

(a)

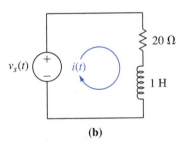

(b)

21.46 The voltage waveform shown in Fig. P21.15a is applied to the network shown in Fig. P21.15b. Write a Fourier series for the current waveform, and determine the average power delivered to the network.

Figure P21.15

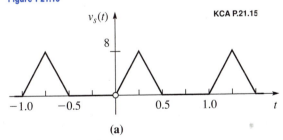

(a)

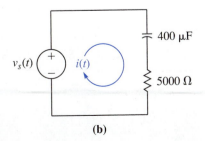

(b)

21.47 The voltage waveform shown in Fig. P21.16a is applied to the network shown in Fig. P21.16b. Write a Fourier series for the current waveform, and determine the average power delivered to the network.

Figure P21.16

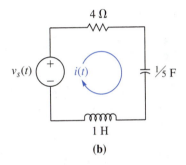

(a)

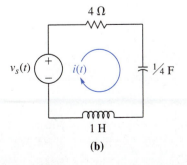

(b)

21.48 The voltage waveform shown in Fig. P21.17a is applied to the network shown in Fig. P21.17b. Write a Fourier series for the current waveform, and determine the average power delivered to the network.

Figure P21.17

21.49 The current waveform shown in Fig. P21.18a is applied to the network shown in Fig. P21.18b. Write a Fourier series for the voltage waveform, and determine the average power delivered to the network.

Figure P21.18

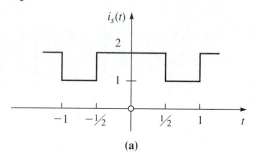

(a)

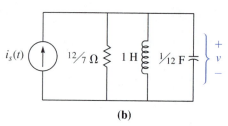

(b)

21.50 The current waveform shown in Fig. P21.19a is applied to the network shown in Fig. P21.19b. Write a Fourier series for the voltage waveform, and determine the average power delivered to the network.

Figure P21.19

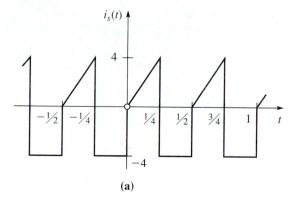

(a)

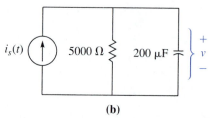

(b)

22

FOURIER METHODS

OBJECTIVES

The objectives of this chapter are to:

- Discuss the amplitude and phase spectra of a periodic signal.

- Introduce the Fourier integral and the Fourier transform.

- Describe some of the properties of the Fourier transform.

- Develop a set of Fourier transform pairs for some common functions.

- Show how the Fourier transform may be applied to network analysis.

- Develop the concept of energy spectral density using Parseval's theorem.

- Discuss the transition from Fourier transform to Laplace transform.

INTRODUCTION

SECTION 22.1

The discussion of Fourier series in the previous chapter has indicated that the frequency domain characteristics of amplitude and phase are useful in the analysis of systems that contain periodic inputs. Analysis by Fourier methods may also be extended to nonperiodic signals such as single pulses or a number (not an infinite number) of pulses. A discussion of frequency domain techniques applied to nonperiodic signals is the goal of this chapter.

AMPLITUDE AND PHASE SPECTRA

SECTION 22.2

The complex coefficient α_k, in the exponential form of the Fourier series, possesses both a magnitude and a phase angle:

$$\alpha_k = |\alpha_k| \underline{/\theta_k} \tag{22.1}$$

Both the magnitude and the phase may be plotted as a function of frequency in a graphical display known, respectively, as the *amplitude spectrum* and the *phase spectrum*. Because these spectra show components only at discrete frequencies, they are frequently referred to as *line spectra*.

■ **EXAMPLE 22.1**

A Fourier series for the square wave with $\tau = T/4$, shown in Fig. 22.1a, was determined in Example 21.1 to be

$$f(t) = \frac{V}{4} + \frac{V}{\pi}\left(\cos \omega_o t - \frac{1}{3}\cos 3\omega_o t + \frac{1}{5}\cos 5\omega_o t + \cdots\right)$$

$$+ \frac{V}{\pi}\left(\sin \omega_o t + \sin 2\omega_o t + \frac{1}{3}\sin 3\omega_o t + \frac{1}{5}\sin 5\omega_o t + \cdots\right)$$

Write an exponential Fourier series for this wave, and plot the amplitude and phase spectra.

Solution   The function in Fig. 22.1a is represented by

$$f(t) = \begin{cases} V, & 0 < t < \tau \\ 0, & \tau < t < T \end{cases}$$

With $t_o = 0$, eq. (21.36),

$$\alpha_k = \frac{1}{T}\int_{t_o}^{t_o+T} f(t)e^{-jk\omega_o t}\,dt \qquad\qquad\qquad\qquad\qquad \textbf{(21.36)}$$

is used to find the α_k's:

$$\alpha_k = \frac{1}{T}\int_{t_o}^{t_o+T} f(t)e^{-jk\omega_o t}\,dt = \frac{1}{T}\left[\int_0^\tau Ve^{-jk\omega_o t}\,dt + \int_\tau^T 0(e^{-jk\omega_o t})\,dt\right]$$

$$= \frac{V}{T}\cdot\frac{1}{-jk\omega_o}e^{-jk\omega_o t}\bigg|_0^\tau = \frac{V}{jk\omega_o T}(1 - e^{-jk\omega_o \tau})$$

If the numerator and denominator are multiplied by 2τ, then

$$\alpha_k = \frac{2V\tau}{j2k\omega_o\tau T}(1 - e^{-jk\omega_o\tau}) = \frac{V\tau}{T}\left(\frac{1 - e^{-jk\omega_o\tau}}{j2k\omega_o\tau/2}\right)$$

A further adjustment gives

$$\alpha_k = \frac{V\tau}{T}e^{-jk\omega_o\tau/2}\left(\frac{e^{jk\omega_o\tau/2} - e^{-jk\omega_o\tau/2}}{j2k\omega_o\tau/2}\right)$$

The parenthetical term is observed to in the form (Appendix A) of $\sin x/x$. Here, $x = k\omega_o\tau/2$, and hence,

$$\alpha_k = \frac{V\tau}{T}\left(\frac{\sin k\omega_o\tau/2}{k\omega_o\tau/2}\right)(e^{-jk\omega_o\tau/2})$$

(a) A square wave with a pulse duration of $T/4$ seconds, (b) its amplitude spectrum, and (c) its phase spectrum

FIGURE 22.1

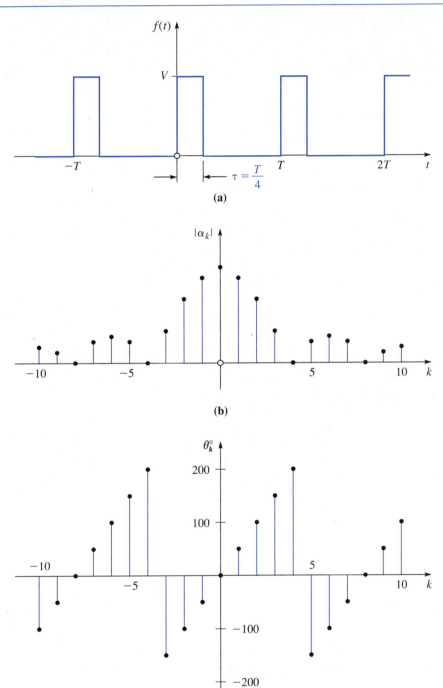

If $\tau = T/4$, then

$$\alpha_k = \frac{V}{4}\left(\frac{\sin k\omega_o T/8}{k\omega_o T/8}\right)(e^{-jk\omega_o T/8})$$

and with $\omega_o = 2\pi/T$,

$$\alpha_k = \frac{V}{4}\left(\frac{\sin k\pi/4}{k\pi/4}\right)(e^{-jk\pi/4}) = |\alpha_k|\underline{/\theta_k}$$

This is in the form of eq. (22.1), and this form leads to the amplitude and phase spectra that are plotted in Figs. 22.1b and 22.1c, respectively. They are plotted from computations contained in the following tabulation.

k	$\dfrac{k\pi}{4}$	$|\alpha_k|$	θ_k°	k	$\dfrac{k\pi}{4}$	$|\alpha_k|$	θ_k°
-10	$-\dfrac{5\pi}{2}$	$0.032V$	-90	1	$\dfrac{\pi}{4}$	$0.225V$	45
-9	$-\dfrac{9\pi}{4}$	$0.025V$	-45	2	$\dfrac{\pi}{2}$	$0.159V$	90
-8	-2π	0.000	0	3	$\dfrac{3\pi}{4}$	$0.075V$	135
-7	$-\dfrac{7\pi}{4}$	$0.032V$	45	4	π	0.000	180
-6	$-\dfrac{3\pi}{2}$	$0.053V$	90	5	$\dfrac{5\pi}{4}$	$0.045V$	-135
-5	$-\dfrac{5\pi}{4}$	$0.045V$	135	6	$\dfrac{3\pi}{2}$	$0.053V$	-90
-4	$-\pi$	0.000	180	7	$\dfrac{7\pi}{4}$	$0.032V$	-45
-3	$-\dfrac{3\pi}{4}$	$0.075V$	-135	8	2π	0.000	0
-2	$-\dfrac{\pi}{2}$	$0.159V$	-90	9	$\dfrac{9\pi}{4}$	$0.025V$	45
-1	$-\dfrac{\pi}{4}$	$0.225V$	-45	10	$\dfrac{5\pi}{2}$	$0.032V$	90
0	0	$0.250V$	0				

Notice that the absolute values of the amplitudes are plotted in Fig. 22.1b. Any negative amplitudes are handled appropriately in the phase spectrum. Also, notice that the amplitude at $k = 0$ cannot be obtained from the indeterminate form involving sin 0/0. In this case, L'Hôpital's rule was employed. ■

THE FOURIER INTEGRAL AND THE FOURIER TRANSFORM

It has been shown that a periodic function $f(t)$ that satisfies the Dirichlet conditions possesses a Fourier series that can be written in at least one of three forms. All three forms contain Fourier coefficients taken from among a_k, b_k, c_k, θ_k, and α_k. All of these coefficients are functions, not of time but of discrete multiples of the fundamental frequency ω_o. This indicates that the Fourier series of a periodic function can be thought of as a transformation from the time domain to the frequency domain. The advantages of working in the frequency domain are quite apparent, and the amplitude and phase spectra discussed in the previous section are definite aids to the understanding and use of superposition to find the response of a network subjected to a periodic input.

This transformation from the time to the frequency domain can also be accomplished even if the function in the time domain function is not periodic. The pulse shown in Fig. 22.2 occurs only once. But it can be represented by a periodic function of exactly the same shape that has an infinite period.

The periodic function $f(t)$ with period T ($\omega_o = 2\pi/T$) shown in Fig. 22.2 has an exponential series in the all-inclusive interval $-\infty < t < \infty$ given by eq. (21.35),

$$f(t) = \sum_{-\infty}^{\infty} \alpha_k e^{jk\omega_o t} \tag{21.35}$$

where the α's are the Fourier coefficients that are evaluated from eq. (21.36):

$$\alpha_k = \frac{1}{T} \int_{t_o}^{t_o + T} f(t) e^{-jk\omega_o t}\, dt \tag{21.36}$$

Use of the exponential form of the Fourier series permits the construction of an amplitude spectrum, which is actually a line spectrum plotted at the distinct harmonic frequencies $k\omega_o$. The spacing between the lines in the spectrum is the difference

A single pulse

FIGURE 22.2

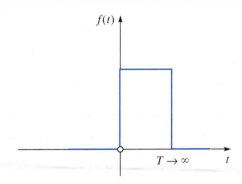

between two adjacent lines,

$$\Delta\omega_o = (k + 1)\omega_o - k\omega_o = \omega_o = \frac{2\pi}{T} \qquad (22.2)$$

As $T \to \infty$, the spacing between adjacent components of both the amplitude and the phase spectra narrows, and $k\omega_o$ becomes continuous:

$$\omega_o \to \Delta\omega \qquad (22.3a)$$

$$k\omega_o \to \omega \qquad (22.3b)$$

$$T \to \frac{2\pi}{\Delta\omega} \qquad (22.3c)$$

Consider eqs. (22.3) in eqs. (21.35) and (21.36) in the limit as $T \to \infty$ and with $t_o = -T/2$:

$$\lim_{T \to \infty} f(t) = \sum_{-\infty}^{\infty} \alpha_\omega e^{j\omega t} \qquad (22.4)$$

$$\alpha_\omega = \lim_{T \to \infty} \alpha_k = \frac{\Delta\omega}{2\pi} \int_{-T/2}^{T/2} f(t)e^{-j\omega t}\, dt \qquad (22.5)$$

When eq. (22.5) is put into eq. (22.4), the result is

$$f(t) = \frac{1}{2\pi} \left[\sum_{-\infty}^{\infty} \int_{-T/2}^{T/2} f(t)e^{-j\omega t}\, dt \right] e^{j\omega t}\, \Delta\omega$$

and as $T \to \infty$ and $\Delta\omega_o \to \omega_o$, the summation becomes an integral. Thus,

$$f(t) = \frac{1}{2\pi} \int_{-\infty}^{\infty} \left[\int_{-\infty}^{\infty} f(t)e^{-j\omega t}\, dt \right] e^{j\omega t}\, d\omega \qquad (22.6)$$

Equation (22.6) is called the *Fourier integral* of $f(t)$. The bracketed term within the integral, the *Fourier transform* of $f(t)$, can be defined for any ω as

$$\mathscr{F}[f(t)] = F(\omega) = \int_{-\infty}^{\infty} f(t)e^{-j\omega t}\, dt \qquad (22.7)$$

The Fourier integral can be defined by

$$f(t) = \mathscr{F}^{-1}[F(\omega)] = \frac{1}{2\pi} \int_{-\infty}^{\infty} F(\omega)e^{j\omega t}\, d\omega \qquad (22.8)$$

Equations (22.7) and (22.8) are often referred to as the *Fourier transform pair*, and it must be emphasized that the condition for the existence of the Fourier transform is

$$\int_{-\infty}^{\infty} |f(t)|\, dt < \infty$$

PROPERTIES OF THE FOURIER TRANSFORM

SECTION 22.4

The Fourier transform, like the Laplace transform, possesses many fundamental properties.

22.4.1 The Fourier Transform of a Constant Times a Function

If $\mathscr{F}[f(t)] = F(\omega)$, then

$$\mathscr{F}[Cf(t)] = \int_{-\infty}^{\infty} C[f(t)]e^{j\omega t}\,dt = C\int_{-\infty}^{\infty} [f(t)]e^{-j\omega t}\,dt$$

or

$$\mathscr{F}[Cf(t)] = C\mathscr{F}[f(t)] \qquad\qquad (22.9)$$

22.4.2 The Linearity Property

If

$$\mathscr{F}[f_1(t)] = F_1(\omega) = \int_{-\infty}^{\infty} [f_1(t)]e^{-j\omega t}\,dt$$

$$\mathscr{F}[f_2(t)] = F_2(\omega) = \int_{-\infty}^{\infty} [f_2(t)]e^{-j\omega t}\,dt$$

then

$$\mathscr{F}[f_1(t) \pm f_2(t)] = \int_{-\infty}^{\infty} [f_1(t) \pm f_2(t)]e^{-j\omega t}\,dt$$
$$= \int_{-\infty}^{\infty} f_1(t)e^{-j\omega t}\,dt \pm \int_{-\infty}^{\infty} f_2(t)e^{-j\omega t}\,dt$$

or

$$\mathscr{F}[f_1(t) \pm f_2(t)] = F_1(\omega) \pm F_2(\omega) \qquad\qquad (22.10)$$

Moreover, it is seen that

$$\mathscr{F}[C_1 f_1(t) \pm C_2 f_2(t)] = C_1 F_1(\omega) \pm C_2 F_2(\omega) \qquad\qquad (22.11)$$

22.4.3 The Fourier Transform of Derivatives

If $f(t) = \mathscr{F}^{-1}[F(\omega)]$, then

$$f(t) = \mathscr{F}^{-1}[F(\omega)] = \frac{1}{2\pi}\int_{-\infty}^{\infty} F(\omega)e^{j\omega t}\,d\omega$$

If this is differentiated with respect to t, the result is

$$\frac{df(t)}{dt} = \frac{j\omega}{2\pi}\int_{-\infty}^{\infty} F(\omega)e^{j\omega t}\,d\omega = j\omega\mathscr{F}^{-1}[F(\omega)]$$

When the Fourier transform is taken, one obtains

$$\mathcal{F}\left[\frac{df(t)}{dt}\right] = j\omega F(\omega) \tag{22.12}$$

and it can be noted that

$$\mathcal{F}\left[\frac{d^n f(t)}{dt^n}\right] = (j\omega)^n F(\omega) \tag{22.13}$$

22.4.4 The Fourier Transform of an Integral

With

$$f(t) = \frac{1}{2\pi}\int_{-\infty}^{\infty} F(\omega)e^{j\omega t}\,d\omega$$

an integration of both sides with respect to t gives

$$\int_{-\infty}^{t} f(t)\,dt = \frac{1}{2\pi}\int_{-\infty}^{\infty} F(\omega)\left(\int e^{j\omega t}\,dt\right)d\omega$$

If the integral in the parentheses is left without limits (an indefinite integral), then when the integration is performed, the result is

$$\int_{-\infty}^{t} f(t)\,dt = \frac{1}{2\pi}\int_{-\infty}^{\infty}\frac{F(\omega)}{j\omega}\,e^{j\omega t}\,d\omega$$

And when the Fourier transform of both sides is taken, one obtains

$$\mathcal{F}\left[\int_{-\infty}^{t} f(t)\,dt\right] = \frac{F(\omega)}{j\omega} + F(0)\delta(\omega) \tag{22.14}$$

where the additional impulse accounts for the discontinuity at $t = 0$.

22.4.5 Time Translation

To find $\mathcal{F}[f(t+\tau)]$, consider

$$\mathcal{F}[f(t)] = F(\omega)$$

and let $z = t + \tau$. Then $dz = dt$, $t = z - \tau$, and

$$\mathcal{F}[f(t+\tau)] = \int_{-\infty}^{\infty}[f(t+\tau)]e^{-j\omega t}\,dt = \int_{-\infty}^{\infty}[f(z)]e^{-j\omega(z-\tau)}\,dz$$
$$= \int_{-\infty}^{\infty}[f(z)]e^{-j\omega z}e^{j\omega\tau}\,dz$$

or

$$\mathcal{F}[f(t+\tau)] = e^{j\omega\tau}F(\omega) \tag{22.15}$$

22.4.6 Convolution in the Time Domain

Let

$$\mathcal{F}[f_1(t)] = F_1(\omega) = \int_{-\infty}^{\infty} [f_1(t)]e^{-j\omega t}\,dt$$

$$\mathcal{F}[f_2(t)] = F_2(\omega) = \int_{-\infty}^{\infty} [f_2(t)]e^{-j\omega t}\,dt$$

As shown in Chapter 17, the convolution of the two time domain functions $f_1(t)$ and $f_2(t)$ can take either of two equivalent forms given by

$$f_1(t) * f_2(t) = \int_{0}^{\infty} f_1(t-\tau)f_2(\tau)\,d\tau \qquad (17.5a)$$

$$f_1(t) * f_2(t) = \int_{0}^{\infty} f_1(\tau)f_2(t-\tau)\,d\tau \qquad (17.5b)$$

When $T \to \infty$, the limits in eqs. (17.5) become $-\infty$ and ∞, so that the convolution is represented by either

$$f_1(t) * f_2(t) = \int_{-\infty}^{\infty} f_1(t-\tau)f_2(\tau)\,d\tau \qquad (22.16a)$$

or

$$f_1(t) * f_2(t) = \int_{-\infty}^{\infty} f_1(\tau)f_2(t-\tau)\,d\tau \qquad (22.16b)$$

Take the Fourier transform of both sides of eq. (22.16b):

$$\mathcal{F}[f_1(t) * f_2(t)] = \mathcal{F}\left[\int_{-\infty}^{\infty} f_1(\tau)f_2(t-\tau)\,d\tau\right]$$
$$= \int_{-\infty}^{\infty} \left[\int_{-\infty}^{\infty} f_1(\tau)f_2(t-\tau)\,d\tau\right]e^{-j\omega t}\,dt$$

If the order of integration is reversed, one obtains

$$\mathcal{F}[f_1(t) * f_2(t)] = \int_{-\infty}^{\infty} f_1(\tau)\left[\int_{-\infty}^{\infty} f_2(t-\tau)e^{-j\omega t}\,dt\right]d\tau$$

The time translation property of eq. (22.15) can be used in the integral within the brackets:

$$\mathcal{F}[f_1(t) * f_2(t)] = \int_{-\infty}^{\infty} f_1(\tau)\left[e^{j\omega\tau}\int_{-\infty}^{\infty} f_2(t)e^{-j\omega t}\,dt\right]d\tau$$
$$= \left[\int_{-\infty}^{\infty} f_1(\tau)e^{j\omega\tau}\,d\tau\right]\left[\int_{-\infty}^{\infty} f_2(t)e^{-j\omega t}\,dt\right]$$

or

$$\mathcal{F}[f_1(t) * f_2(t)] = F_1(\omega)F_2(\omega) \qquad (22.17)$$

22.4.7 Convolution in the Frequency Domain

It can be shown, by the same arguments put forth in the preceding subsection, that multiplication in the frequency domain is equivalent to a convolution in the time domain:

$$\mathcal{F}^{-1}[F_1(\omega)F_2(\omega)] = f_1(t) * f_2(t) \qquad (22.18)$$

22.4.8 Time Scaling

If

$$\mathscr{F}[f(t)] = F(\omega) = \int_{-\infty}^{\infty} [f(t)]e^{-j\omega t}\, dt$$

then

$$\mathscr{F}[f(ct)] = \int_{-\infty}^{\infty} [f(ct)]e^{-j\omega t}\, dt$$

If $z = ct$, so that $dz = c\, dt$, then

$$\mathscr{F}[f(ct)] = \int_{-\infty}^{\infty} [f(z)]e^{-(j\omega/c)z} \frac{dz}{c}$$

A new frequency, ω/c, has appeared. This makes

$$\mathscr{F}[f(ct)] = \frac{1}{|c|} F\left(\frac{\omega}{c}\right) \tag{22.19}$$

Notice that if $c = -1$, then

$$\mathscr{F}[f(-t)] = F(-\omega) \tag{22.20}$$

22.4.9 Frequency Translation

It is observed that a multiplication of $f(t)$ by $e^{j\omega_a t}$ represents a frequency translation. Here,

$$\mathscr{F}[f(t)e^{j\omega_a t}] = \int_{-\infty}^{\infty} [f(t)e^{j\omega_a t}]e^{-j\omega t}\, dt = \int_{-\infty}^{\infty} [f(t)e^{j(\omega - \omega_a)t}]\, dt$$

or

$$\mathscr{F}[f(t)e^{j\omega_a t}] = F(\omega - \omega_a) \tag{22.21}$$

22.4.10 The Symmetry Property

If $\mathscr{F}^{-1}[F(\omega)] = f(t)$, then

$$2\pi f(t) = \int_{-\infty}^{\infty} F(\omega)e^{j\omega t}\, dt$$

If t is changed to $-t$, then

$$2\pi f(-t) = \int_{-\infty}^{\infty} F(\omega)e^{-j\omega t}\, dt$$

and if t and ω are interchanged, then

$$2\pi f(-\omega) = \mathscr{F}[F(t)] \tag{22.22}$$

Equation (22.22) is a statement of the symmetry property of the Fourier transform.

FOURIER TRANSFORMS OF SOME COMMON TIME FUNCTIONS

SECTION 22.5

In this section, the Fourier transforms of a few important time functions are developed. It is important to remember that the time functions extend over the interval $-\infty < t < \infty$.

22.5.1 The Fourier Transform of the Unit Impulse Function

If $f(t) = \delta(t)$, then

$$\mathscr{F}[f(t)] = \int_{-\infty}^{\infty} \delta(t)e^{-j\omega t}\,dt$$

By the sampling property of the impulse function,

$$\mathscr{F}[f(t)] = \int_{-\infty}^{\infty} \delta(t)e^{-j\omega t}\,dt = e^{-j\omega t}\Big|_{t=0} = 1$$

Thus,

$$\mathscr{F}[\delta(t)] = 1 \qquad\qquad (22.23)$$

Notice that

$$\delta(t) = \mathscr{F}^{-1}[1] = \frac{1}{2\pi}\int_{-\infty}^{\infty} 1e^{j\omega t}\,d\omega = \frac{1}{2\pi}\int_{-\infty}^{\infty} e^{j\omega t}\,d\omega$$

and in general, if $\omega = p$ and $t = q$,

$$\delta(q) = \frac{1}{2\pi}\int_{-\infty}^{\infty} e^{jpq}\,dp \qquad\qquad (22.24)$$

22.5.2 The Fourier Transform of a Constant

If $f(t) = V$, then

$$\mathscr{F}[f(t)] = \mathscr{F}[V] = \int_{-\infty}^{\infty} Ve^{-j\omega t}\,dt = 2\pi V\frac{1}{2\pi}\int_{-\infty}^{\infty} e^{j(-\omega)t}\,dt$$

Use of eq. (22.24) with $p = t$ and $q = -\omega$ shows that

$$\delta(-\omega) = \frac{1}{2\pi}\int_{-\infty}^{\infty} e^{j(-\omega)t}\,dt$$

Thus,

$$\mathscr{F}[V] = 2\pi V\delta(-\omega)$$

But $\delta(-\omega) = \delta(\omega)$, so that

$$\mathscr{F}[V] = 2\pi V\delta(\omega) \qquad\qquad (22.25)$$

This Fourier transform pair is shown in Fig. 22.3.

FIGURE 22.3   (a) The function $f(t) = V$ and (b) its Fourier transform

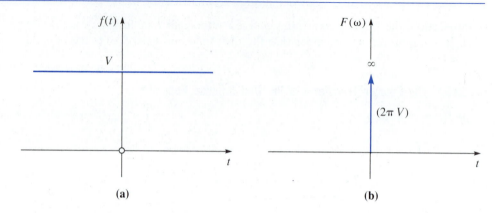

(a)   (b)

22.5.3 The Fourier Transform of the Unit Step Function

The unit steps $u(t)$ and $u(-t)$ are defined respectively by

$$u(t) = \begin{cases} 1, & t > 0 \\ 0, & t < 0 \end{cases} \quad \text{and} \quad u(-t) = \begin{cases} 0, & t > 0 \\ 1, & t < 0 \end{cases}$$

These definitions account for all time except $t = 0$. Thus,

$$u(t) + u(-t) = 1 \quad (t \neq 0)$$

and by the linearity property of eq. (22.10)

$$\mathscr{F}[u(t)] + \mathscr{F}[u(-t)] = \mathscr{F}[1] \quad \text{or} \quad F(\omega) + F(-\omega) = 2\pi\delta(\omega)$$

Assume now that

$$F(\omega) = A\delta(\omega) + \psi(\omega)$$

where A is a constant and $\psi(\omega)$ is a function of ω. Then,

$$F(\omega) + F(-\omega) = A\delta(\omega) + \psi(\omega) + A\delta(-\omega) + \psi(-\omega) = 2\pi\delta(\omega)$$

Because $\delta(\omega) = \delta(-\omega)$,

$$F(\omega) + F(-\omega) = 2A\delta(\omega) + \psi(\omega) + \psi(-\omega) = 2\pi\delta(\omega)$$

and it may be concluded that

$$\psi(\omega) = -\psi(-\omega)$$

which shows that $\psi(\omega)$ is an odd function of ω and that $A = \pi$.
    The derivative of the unit step is the unit impulse (Chapter 5),

$$\frac{du(t)}{dt} = \delta(t)$$

and this can be used to evaluate $\psi(\omega)$. By eq. (22.12),

$$\mathcal{F}\left[\frac{du(t)}{dt}\right] = j\omega\mathcal{F}[u(t)] = j\omega F(\omega) = j\omega[\pi\delta(\omega) + \psi(\omega)] = \mathcal{F}[\delta(t)] = 1$$

The sampling property of the unit impulse can be used to show that $\omega\delta(\omega) = 0$, so that

$$j\omega\psi(\omega) = 1 \qquad \text{or} \qquad \psi(\omega) = \frac{1}{j\omega}$$

The Fourier transform of the unit step is therefore

$$\mathcal{F}[u(t)] = \pi\delta(\omega) + \frac{1}{j\omega} \tag{22.26}$$

The unit step, its Fourier transform and its amplitude spectrum are shown in Fig. 22.4. Notice the impulse at $\omega = 0$ in Figs. 22.4b and 22.4c. The presence of such an impulse indicates that $u(t)$ does not satisfy the condition

$$\int_{-\infty}^{\infty} f(t)\,dt < \infty$$

(a) The unit step function, (b) its Fourier transform, and (c) its amplitude spectrum   FIGURE 22.4

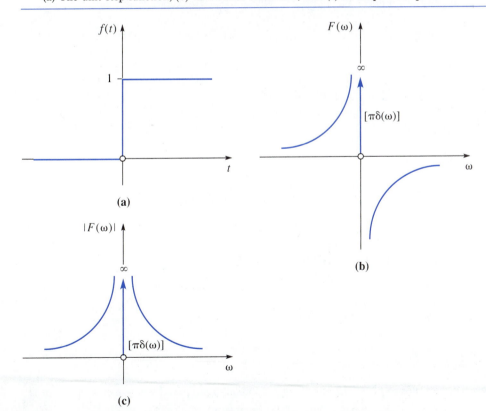

and that if $\omega F_1(\omega) = \omega F_2(\omega)$, it is not ensured that $F_1(\omega) = F_2(\omega)$, because an impulse may be present. However, it is correct to state that

$$F_1(\omega) = F_2(\omega) + A\delta(\omega)$$

where A is a constant that *may* take on the value $A = 0$.

22.5.4 The Fourier Transform of $e^{-at}u(t)$ $(a > 0)$

Because $a > 0$ and

$$\mathscr{F}[f(t)] = \mathscr{F}[e^{-at}u(t)] = \int_{-\infty}^{\infty} [e^{-at}u(t)]e^{-j\omega t}\, dt$$

and because $u(t) = 0$ for $t < 0$,

$$\mathscr{F}[e^{-at}u(t)] = \int_0^{\infty} e^{-at}e^{-j\omega t}\, dt = \int_0^{\infty} e^{-(a+j\omega)t}\, dt = -\frac{1}{a+j\omega}e^{-(a+j\omega)t}\bigg|_0^{\infty}$$

or

$$\mathscr{F}[e^{-at}u(t)] = \frac{1}{a+j\omega} \tag{22.27}$$

22.5.5 The Fourier Transform of $e^{j\omega_a t}$

Write the function as

$$f(t) = 1e^{j\omega_a t}$$

so that

$$\mathscr{F}[1e^{j\omega_a t}] = \int_{-\infty}^{\infty} [1e^{j\omega_a t}]e^{-j\omega t}\, dt$$

By eq. (22.25),

$$\mathscr{F}[1] = 2\pi\delta(\omega)$$

and then by the frequency translation property of eq. (22.21),

$$\mathscr{F}[e^{j\omega_a t}] = 2\pi\delta(\omega - \omega_a) \tag{22.28}$$

22.5.6 The Fourier Transform of $\cos \omega_a t$

The function can be represented in terms of exponentials (Appendix A):

$$\cos \omega_a t = \frac{1}{2}(e^{j\omega_a t} + e^{-j\omega_a t})$$

By eq. (22.28),

$$\mathscr{F}[\cos \omega_a t] = \frac{1}{2}[2\pi\delta(\omega - \omega_a) + 2\pi\delta(\omega + \omega_a)] = \pi[\delta(\omega - \omega_a) + \delta(\omega + \omega_a)]$$

$$\tag{22.29}$$

A similar development for $f(t) = \sin \omega_a t$ shows that

$$\mathscr{F}[\sin \omega_a t] = j\pi[\delta(\omega + \omega_a) - \delta(\omega - \omega_a)] \qquad \textbf{(22.30)}$$

A short table of Fourier transform pairs is shown in Table 22.1.

Summary of Fourier transforms properties and operations

TABLE 22.1

Properties	$f(t)$	$F(\omega)$
Constant times function	$Cf(t)$	$CF(\omega)$
Linearity property	$C_1 f_1(t) \pm C_2 f_2(t)$	$C_1 F_1(\omega) \pm C_2 f_2(\omega)$
Derivative	$\dfrac{d^n f(t)}{dt^n}$	$(j\omega)^n F(\omega)$
Integral	$\displaystyle\int_{-\infty}^{t} f(z)\,dz$	$\dfrac{F(\omega)}{j\omega} + F(0)\delta(\omega)$
Time translation	$f(t - \tau)$	$e^{-j\omega\tau}F(\omega)$
Frequency translation	$f(t)e^{j\omega_a t}$	$F(\omega - \omega_a)$
Time domain convolution	$f_1(t) * f_2(t)$	$F_1(\omega)F_2(\omega)$
Frequency domain convolution	$h(t)f(t)$	$\dfrac{1}{2\pi}\displaystyle\int_{-\infty}^{\infty} h(\omega - \tau)F(\tau)\,d\tau$
Time scaling	$f(ct)$	$\dfrac{1}{|c|}F\!\left(\dfrac{\omega}{c}\right)$
Symmetry	$f(t)$	$2\pi f(-\omega)$

	$f(t)$	$F(\omega)$
	$\delta(t)$	1
	C	$2\pi C\delta(\omega)$
	$u(t)$	$\dfrac{1}{j\omega} + \pi\delta(\omega)$
	$e^{-at}u(t); \ a \geq 0$	$\dfrac{1}{a + j\omega}$
	$e^{j\omega_a t}$	$2\pi\delta(\omega - \omega_a)$
	$\cos \omega_a t$	$\pi[\delta(\omega + \omega_a) + \delta(\omega - \omega_a)]$
	$\sin \omega_a t$	$j\pi[\delta(\omega + \omega_a) - \delta(\omega - \omega_a)]$
	$\operatorname{sgn}(t) = \dfrac{\sin t}{t}$	$\dfrac{2}{j\omega}$

SECTION 22.6   AN APPLICATION OF THE FOURIER TRANSFORM

If a linear, time-invariant system or network is subjected to a single excitation or input $e(t)$, which yields a single response or output $r(t)$, the process can be described by using the concept of the transfer function. If the system is in the zero state (no energy storage in capacitors and inductors), the transfer function (or the system function) is the impulse response $h(t)$; and a convolution of this with the input gives the zero-state output

$$r(t) = h(t) * e(t)$$

Equation (22.17) indicates that in the frequency domain, the input, output, and transfer function can be represented by their Fourier transforms and that the convolution in the time domain is equivalent to a simple multiplication in the frequency domain:

$$R(\omega) = H(\omega)E(\omega)$$

This is the basic idea in the analysis of networks using the Fourier transform.

■ EXAMPLE 22.2

The single voltage pulse shown in Fig. 22.5a is applied to the network in Fig. 22.5b at time $t = 0$. Find the output voltage.

Solution   The output voltage can be obtained by using voltage division. In the frequency domain,

$$V_o(\omega) = \left(\frac{R}{R + j\omega L} \right) V_i(\omega)$$

With $R = 4\ \Omega$ and $L = 1$ H,

$$V_o(\omega) = \left(\frac{4}{4 + j\omega} \right) V_i(\omega)$$

FIGURE 22.5   (a) Input voltage to (b) a simple RL network

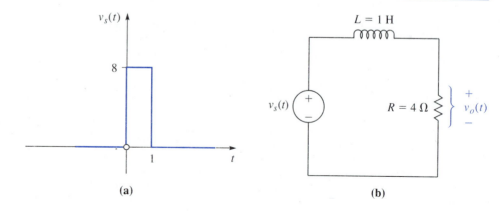

(a)   (b)

Here, the transfer function is

$$H(\omega) = \frac{4}{4 + j\omega}$$

and although the time domain impulse response is not required, it can be noted that

$$h(t) = \mathscr{F}^{-1}[H(\omega)] = 4e^{-4t}u(t)$$

The input voltage is described by the function

$$v_i(t) = 8u(t) - 8u(t - 1) \text{ volts}$$

and the Fourier transform of the input is (Table 22.1)

$$V_i(\omega) = 8\pi\delta(\omega) + \frac{8}{j\omega} - 8\pi\delta(\omega)e^{-j\omega} - \frac{8}{j\omega}e^{-j\omega}$$

The sampling property of the unit impulse shows that

$$\delta(\omega)e^{-j\omega} = \delta(\omega)$$

so that

$$V_i(\omega) = \frac{8}{j\omega}(1 - e^{-j\omega})$$

With these expressions for $H(\omega)$ and $V_i(\omega)$,

$$V_o(\omega) = H(\omega)V_i(\omega) = \left(\frac{4}{4 + j\omega}\right)\left[\frac{8}{j\omega}(1 - e^{-j\omega})\right] = \frac{32}{j\omega(4 + j\omega)}(1 - e^{-j\omega})$$

This indicates that the time domain output is composed of two terms:

$$v_o(t) = v(t) - v(t - 1)$$

where

$$v(t) = \mathscr{F}^{-1}\left[\frac{32}{j\omega(4 + j\omega)}\right]$$

A partial-fraction expansion may be applied:

$$\frac{32}{j\omega(4 + j\omega)} = \frac{K_1}{j\omega} + \frac{K_2}{4 + j\omega}$$

with

$$K_1 = \frac{32}{4 + j\omega}\bigg|_{j\omega = 0} = 8 \qquad K_2 = \frac{32}{j\omega}\bigg|_{j\omega = -4} = -8$$

$$V(\omega) = \frac{32}{j\omega(4 + j\omega)} = 8\left(\frac{1}{j\omega} - \frac{1}{4 + j\omega}\right)$$

Reference to Table 22.1 shows that

$$v(t) = 8(1 - e^{-4t})u(t)$$

and this can be adjusted for the time delay to yield the output

$$v_o(t) = 8(1 - e^{-4t})u(t) - 8(1 - e^{-4(t-1)})u(t - 1)$$ ■

SECTION 22.7   **PARSEVAL'S THEOREM**

Let the function $f(t)$ represent either the current through or the voltage across a 1-Ω resistor. Then, the instantaneous power can be represented by either $p = [f(t)]^2/1 = v^2/1$ or $p = [f(t)]^2 \cdot 1 = i^2 \cdot 1$. The total energy delivered to the 1-Ω resistor is represented by the integral

$$\omega = \int_{-\infty}^{\infty} p^2 \, dt = \int_{-\infty}^{\infty} [f(t)]^2 \, dt$$

Use of eq. (22.8),

$$f(t) = \mathscr{F}^{-1}[F(\omega)] = \frac{1}{2\pi} \int_{-\infty}^{\infty} F(\omega)e^{j\omega t} \, d\omega \tag{22.8}$$

for one of the $f(t)$'s under the integral yields

$$w = \int_{-\infty}^{\infty} f(t)\left[\frac{1}{2\pi} \int_{-\infty}^{\infty} F(\omega)e^{j\omega t} \, d\omega\right] dt$$

If the order of integration is interchanged,

$$w = \frac{1}{2\pi} \int_{-\infty}^{\infty} F(\omega)\left[\int_{-\infty}^{\infty} f(t)e^{j\omega t} \, dt\right] d\omega$$

Observe that because $e^{j\omega t} = [e^{-j\omega t}]^*$ and $f(t)$ is real, the integral within the brackets is the conjugate of $F(\omega)$. Thus,

$$w = \frac{1}{2\pi} \int_{-\infty}^{\infty} F(\omega)F^*(\omega) \, d\omega$$

or

$$w = \frac{1}{2\pi} \int_{-\infty}^{\infty} |F(\omega)|^2 \, d\omega \tag{22.31}$$

The integral in eq. (22.31) represents the area under the square of the amplitude spectrum of $f(t)$ over the interval $-\infty < \omega < \infty$. Thus, the total energy delivered is equal to the area under the square of the magnitude of the Fourier transform. This is a statement of what is known as *Parseval's theorem*, and the square of the magnitude of the Fourier transform, $|F(\omega)|^2$, is often referred to as *the energy spectral density*.

THE TRANSITION FROM FOURIER TO LAPLACE TRANSFORM

If interest is focused on functions of time that are equal to zero when $t < 0$, the Fourier transform pair of eqs. (22.7) and (22.8) become the *unilateral Fourier transform pair*:

$$\mathscr{F}[f(t)] = F(\omega) = \int_0^\infty f(t)e^{-j\omega t}\,dt \tag{22.32}$$

$$f(t) = \mathscr{F}^{-1}[F(\omega)] = \frac{1}{2\pi}\int_{-\infty}^\infty F(\omega)e^{j\omega t}\,d\omega \tag{22.33}$$

Although this pair of relationships is extremely useful, difficulties are still encountered in the determination of the Fourier transform of some functions. For example, the Fourier transform of the unit step,

$$u(t) = \begin{cases} 1, & t > 0 \\ 0, & t < 0 \end{cases}$$

in this case will be written as

$$F(\omega) = \int_0^\infty 1e^{-j\omega t}\,dt = -\frac{1}{j\omega}\,e^{-j\omega t}\Big|_0^\infty = \frac{j\sin\omega_o t - \cos\omega_o t}{j\omega}\Big|_0^\infty$$

But because $\cos\omega_o t$ and $\sin\omega_o t$ are both undefined as $t \to \infty$, $F(\omega)$ cannot be determined.

However, if $u(t)$ is defined as

$$e^{-at}u(t) = \begin{cases} e^{-at}, & t > 0, a > 0 \\ 0, & t < 0 \end{cases}$$

then the Fourier transform will be

$$F(\omega) = \mathscr{F}[e^{-at}] = \int_0^\infty e^{-at}e^{-j\omega t}\,dt = \int_0^\infty e^{-(a+j\omega)}\,dt = -\frac{1}{a+j\omega}\,e^{-(a+j\omega)}\Big|_0^\infty$$

The factor e^{-at} produces

$$F(\omega) = \frac{1}{a+j\omega}$$

and in the limit as $a \to \infty$, the Fourier transform of the unit step becomes

$$F(\omega) = \frac{1}{j\omega}$$

However, difficulties are still encountered in obtaining $u(t)$ from its Fourier transform, $F(\omega) = 1/j\omega$.

A slightly different approach employs a function defined as

$$\phi(t) = e^{-\sigma t} f(t) = \begin{cases} 1, & t > 0 \\ 0, & t < 0 \end{cases}$$

In this function, $f(t)$ is the function whose transform is required. Application of eqs. (22.32) and (22.33) then gives

$$F(\omega) = \mathscr{F}[\phi(t) = e^{-\sigma t} f(t)] = \int_0^\infty [e^{-\sigma t} f(t)] e^{-j\omega t}\, dt = \int_0^\infty f(t) e^{-(\sigma + j\omega)t}\, dt$$

and

$$\phi(t) = e^{-\sigma t} f(t) = \mathscr{F}^{-1}[F(\omega)] = \frac{1}{2\pi} \int_{-\infty}^\infty F(\omega) e^{j\omega t}\, d\omega \qquad (22.34)$$

If both sides of eq. (22.34) are multiplied by $e^{\sigma t}$, the result is

$$f(t) = \frac{e^{\sigma t}}{2\pi} \int_{-\infty}^\infty F(\omega) e^{j\omega t}\, d\omega$$

and because $e^{\sigma t}$ is a function only of t,

$$f(t) = \frac{1}{2\pi} \int_{-\infty}^\infty F(\omega) e^{j(\sigma + j\omega)t}\, d\omega$$

If a new variable is defined,

$$s \equiv \sigma + j\omega t$$

so that

$$ds = j\, d\omega$$

then with $s = \sigma + j\omega t = \sigma + j\infty$ when $\omega = \infty$ and $s = \sigma - j\omega t = \sigma - j\infty$ when $\omega = -\infty$,

$$f(t) = \frac{1}{2\pi j} \int_{\sigma - j\omega t}^{\sigma + j\omega t} F(\omega) e^{st}\, ds$$

And if $F(\omega)$ is written as $F(s)$,

$$f(t) = \frac{1}{2\pi j} \int_{\sigma - \omega t}^{\sigma + \omega t} F(s) e^{st}\, ds \qquad (22.35)$$

which is called the *complex inversion integral* and involves the reclamation of the time function from the Laplace transform,

$$F(s) = \mathscr{L}[f(t)] = \int_{-\infty}^\infty f(t) e^{-st}\, dt \qquad (22.36)$$

- Amplitude and phase spectra may be tabulated and plotted from the magnitude and phase angles of the coefficients in the exponential Fourier series.

- The Fourier transform possesses many useful properties, and network analysis may be conducted on the basis of

$$R(j\omega) = H(j\omega)E(j\omega)$$

where $R(j\omega)$ is the Fourier transform of the output function, $H(j\omega)$ is the Fourier transform of the zero-state input response of the network or system, and $E(j\omega)$ is the Fourier transform of the input or excitation function.

- The Fourier transform is obtained from $f(t)$ via

$$\mathscr{F}[f(t)] = \mathscr{F}(\omega) = \int_{-\infty}^{\infty} f(t)e^{-j\omega t}\, dt$$

and $f(t)$ can be obtained from the Fourier transform (the inverse Fourier transform) via

$$f(t) = \mathscr{F}^{-1}[F(\omega)] = \frac{1}{2\pi} \int_{-\infty}^{\infty} F(\omega)e^{j\omega t}\, d\omega$$

- Parseval's theorem states that

$$w = \frac{1}{2\pi} \int_{-\infty}^{\infty} |F(\omega)|^2\, d\omega$$

and shows that the total energy delivered to a system or network by an excitation function is equal to the area under the square of the magnitude of its Fourier transform.

Additional Readings

Blackwell, W.A., and L.L. Grigsby. *Introductory Network Theory*. Boston: PWS Engineering, 1985, pp. 517–531.

Bobrow, L.S. *Elementary Linear Circuit Analysis*. 2d ed. New York: Holt, Rinehart and Winston, 1987, pp. 633–663.

Del Toro, V. *Engineering Circuits*. Englewood Cliffs, N.J.: Prentice-Hall, 1987, pp. 635–641.

Hayt, W.H., Jr., and J.E. Kemmerly. *Engineering Circuit Analysis*. 4th ed. New York: McGraw-Hill, 1986, pp. 529–561.

Irwin, J.D. *Basic Engineering Circuit Analysis*. 3d ed. New York: Macmillan, 1989, pp. 844–860.

Johnson, D.E., J.L. Hilburn, and J.R. Johnson. *Basic Electric Circuit Analysis*. 4th ed. Englewood Cliffs, N.J.: Prentice-Hall, 1989, pp. 572–584.

Karni, S. *Applied Circuit Analysis*. New York: Wiley, 1988, pp. 643–665.

Madhu, S. *Linear Circuit Analysis*. Englewood Cliffs, N.J.: Prentice-Hall, 1988, pp. 690–707, 717–721.

Nilsson, J.W. *Electric Circuits*. 3d ed. Reading, Mass.: Addison-Wesley, 1990, pp. 718–748.

Paul, C.R. *Analysis of Linear Circuits*. New York: McGraw-Hill, 1989, pp. 689–707.

PROBLEMS   **CHAPTER 22**

Section 22.2

22.1 Plot the amplitude spectrum for the periodic waveform in Fig. P22.1.

Figure P22.1

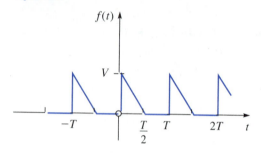

22.2 Plot the amplitude spectrum for the periodic waveform in Fig. P22.2.

Figure P22.2

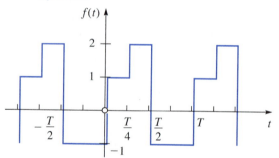

22.3 Plot the amplitude spectrum for the periodic waveform in Fig. P22.3.

Figure P22.3

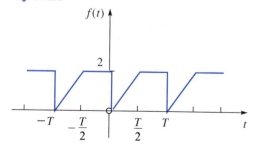

22.4 Plot the amplitude spectrum for the periodic waveform in Fig. P22.4.

Figure P22.4

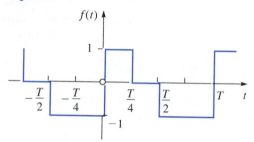

22.5 Plot the amplitude spectrum for the periodic waveform in Fig. P22.5.

Figure P22.5

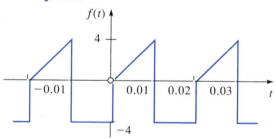

22.6 Plot the amplitude spectrum for the periodic waveform in Fig. P22.6.

Figure P22.6

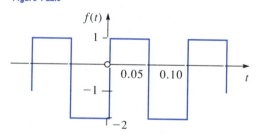

22.7 Plot the amplitude spectrum for the periodic waveform in Fig. P22.7.

Figure P22.7

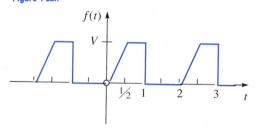

22.8 Plot the amplitude spectrum for the periodic waveform in Fig. P22.8.

Figure P22.8

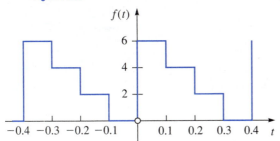

22.9 Plot the amplitude spectrum for the periodic waveform in Fig. P22.9.

Figure P22.9

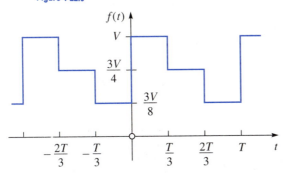

22.10 Plot the amplitude spectrum for the periodic waveform in Fig. P22.10.

Figure P22.10

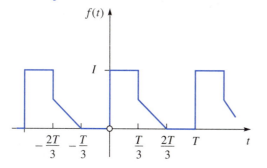

Section 22.5

22.11 What is the Fourier transform of the function shown in Fig. P22.11?

Figure P22.11

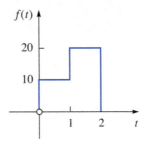

22.12 What is the Fourier transform of the function shown in Fig. P22.12?

Figure P22.12

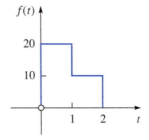

22.13 What is the Fourier transform of the function shown in Fig. P22.13?

Figure P22.13

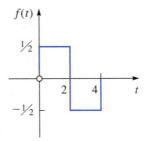

22.14 What is the Fourier transform of the function shown in Fig. P22.14?

Figure P22.14

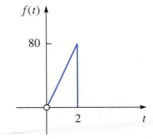

22.15   What is the Fourier transform of the function shown in Fig. P22.15?

Figure P22.15

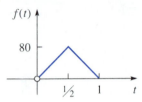

22.16   What is the Fourier transform of the function shown in Fig. P22.16?

Figure P22.16

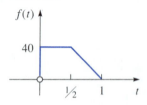

22.17   What is the Fourier transform of the function $f(t) = t \cos at$?

22.18   What is the Fourier transform of the function $f(t) = \delta(t - t_o)$?

22.19   What is the Fourier transform of the function $f(t) = 5e^{-4t}u(t)$?

22.20   What is the Fourier transform of the function $f(t) = e^{-at} \cos btu(t)$?

22.21   What is the Fourier transform of the function $f(t) = e^{-at} \sin btu(t)$?

22.22   What is the Fourier transform of the function $f(t) = t^2 e^{-at}$?

22.23   What is the Fourier transform of the function $f(t) = e^{-3t}u(-t)$?

22.24   What is the Fourier transform of the function $f(t) = u(t) - u(t - 5)$?

Section 22.6

22.25   The voltage input to the network shown in Fig. P22.17a is indicated in Fig. P22.17b. Find the voltage response $v_o(t)$.

Figure P22.17   2 Ω

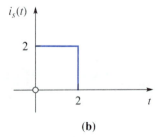

(a)

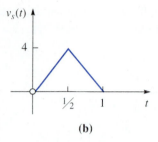

(b)

22.26   The voltage input to the network shown in Fig. P22.18a is indicated in Fig. P22.18b. Find the current response $i_o(t)$.

Figure P22.18

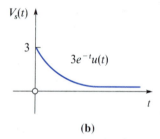

(a)

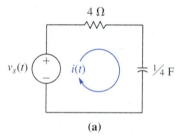

(b)

22.27   The current input to the network shown in Fig. P22.19a is indicated in Fig. P22.19b. Find the voltage response $v_o(t)$.

Figure P22.19

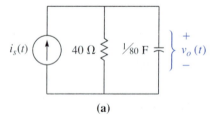

(a)

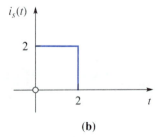

(b)

22.28 The current input to the network shown in Fig. P22.20a is indicated in Fig. P22.20b. Find the current response $i_o(t)$.

Figure P22.20

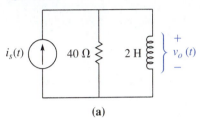

(a)

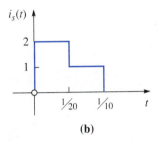

(b)

22.29 The voltage input to the network shown in Fig. P22.21a is indicated in Fig. P22.21b. Find the voltage response $v_o(t)$.

Figure P22.21

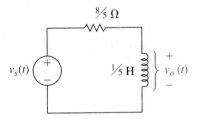

(a)

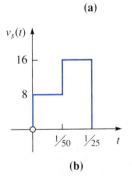

(b)

Section 22.7

22.30 Calculate the spectral energy density of the time function $f(t) = 2e^{-50t}u(t)$, and confirm the result by Parseval's theorem.

22.31 The current flowing through a 100-Ω resistor is $i(t) = 20e^{-4t}u(t)$ amperes. Determine the total energy dissipated and the percentage that is dissipated between 0 and 10 rad/s.

APPENDICES

VII

COMPLEX NUMBER ALGEBRA

INTRODUCTION

The equation $x^2 + 1 = 0$ has a pair of roots,

$$x_1, x_2 = \pm\sqrt{-1} = \pm j$$

where j (not i, which is reserved for current) is a purely imaginary number. The set of real numbers (like 2, ± 3.31, -13, 423.6) and the set of imaginary numbers are but subsets within the set of complex numbers. Thus, the complex number

$$c = a + jb$$

has a *real part*

$$a = \mathrm{Re}(c)$$

and an *imaginary part*

$$b = \mathrm{Im}(c)$$

and it may be noted that the imaginary part of a complex number is associated with the j but does not include the j.

With $j = \sqrt{-1}$, simple multiplication shows that

$$j^2 = -1$$
$$j^3 = j^2 \cdot j = -j$$
$$j^4 = j^2 \cdot j^2 = (-1)(-1) = 1$$
$$j^5 = j^4 \cdot j = j$$

This can be extended to show that

$$j^{n+4} = j^n \qquad \text{(A.1)}$$

SECTION A.2   POLAR AND RECTANGULAR FORMS

A complex number $c = a + jb$ can be represented in the complex plane as shown in Fig. A.1. This diagram showing the location of a complex number is often referred to as the *Argand diagram*, and it shows that the real part, a, is measured along the real axis (the abscissa) and that the imaginary part, b, is reckoned along the imaginary axis (the ordinate). The point P represents the complex number, and the number may also be written as $c = (a, b)$.

The complex number $c = a + jb$ may also be represented as the length or magnitude of a line segment, $|M|$, at an angle, θ, as indicated in Fig. A.1. Thus,

$$c = a + jb = |M|\underline{/\theta}$$

are equivalent representations for c. The form $a + jb$ is called the *rectangular form* of c. In the *polar form*, $c = |M|\underline{/\theta}$, $|M|$ is the *magnitude* and θ is called the *angle* or the *argument* of c.

Simple relationships exist for conversions from the rectangular to polar form and from the polar to rectangular form. These are deduced immediately from Fig. A.1 in conjuction with the Pythagorean theorem. For conversion from rectangular to polar form, the magnitude will be

$$|M| = \sqrt{a^2 + b^2} \tag{A.2a}$$

and with due cognizance paid to the proper quadrant, the angle will be

$$\theta = \arctan \frac{b}{a} \tag{A.2b}$$

The placement of θ in the proper quadrant depends on whether a and/or b are positive or negative. There are four possibilities:

a	b	Quadrant
+	+	I
−	+	II
−	−	III
+	−	IV

FIGURE A.1   The representation of the complex number $c = a + jb$ in the complex plane

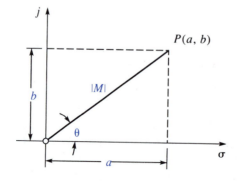

For conversion from polar to rectangular form,

$$a = |M| \cos \theta \tag{A.3a}$$

$$b = |M| \sin \theta \tag{A.3b}$$

It is noted that c can be written as

$$c = |M|(\cos \theta + j \sin \theta) \tag{A.4}$$

THE EULER RELATIONSHIPS   SECTION A.3

Consider eq. (A.4) with the magnitude $|M| = 1$,

$$c = \cos \theta + j \sin \theta \tag{A.5}$$

and perform a single differentiation with respect to θ:

$$\frac{dc}{d\theta} = -\sin \theta + j \cos \theta = j(\cos \theta + j \sin \theta) = jc$$

In this simple differential equation, the variables may be separated,

$$\frac{dc}{c} = j \, d\theta$$

and then solved by an integration,

$$\ln c = j\theta + K$$

where K is an arbitrary constant.

The magnitude of c is unity regardless of the value of the angle θ. Specifically, at $\theta = 0$,

$$c(\theta = 0) = 1 \quad \text{and} \quad \ln 1 = 0 = 0 + K$$

or $K = 0$. Thus,

$$\ln c = j\theta \quad \text{and} \quad c = e^{j\theta}$$

With c given by eq. (A.5),

$$e^{j\theta} = \cos \theta + j \sin \theta \tag{A.6a}$$

For an angle of $-\theta$, a similar development will yield

$$e^{-j\theta} = \cos \theta - j \sin \theta \tag{A.6b}$$

Equations (A.6) are the *Euler relationships*, which lead to the representations for $\cos \theta$ and $\sin \theta$,

$$\cos \theta = \frac{e^{j\theta} + e^{-j\theta}}{2} \tag{A.7a}$$

determined from the sum of eqs. (A.6), and

$$\sin \theta = \frac{e^{j\theta} - e^{-j\theta}}{2j} \tag{A.7b}$$

determined from the difference of eqs. (A.6).

The Euler relationships of eqs. (A.6) along with eq. (A.4) show that there is a third way of representing a complex number. This is the exponential form, $|M|e^{j\theta}$. Thus, the rectangular, polar, and exponential forms are all equivalent:

$$c = a + jb = |M|\underline{/\theta} = |M|e^{j\theta}$$

SECTION A.4   EQUALITY

Two complex numbers, $c_1 = a_1 + jb_1$ and $c_2 = a_2 + jb_2$, will be equal if, and only if, their real parts are equal and their imaginary parts are equal. Thus, for equality, $c_1 = c_2$ if and only if $a_1 = a_2$ and $b_1 = b_2$, or in polar and exponential form, $|M|_1 = |M|_2$ and $\theta_1 = \theta_2$.

SECTION A.5   ADDITION AND SUBTRACTION

Let the sum of two complex numbers, $c_1 = a_1 + jb_1$ and $c_2 = a_2 + jb_2$ be designated as $c_3 = a_3 + jb_3$. Then,

$$a_3 + jb_3 = (a_1 + jb_1) + (a_2 + jb_2)$$

can only be true if the law of equality presented in the previous section holds. Thus,

$$a_3 = a_1 + a_2 \qquad b_3 = b_1 + b_2$$
$$c_3 = c_1 + c_2 = a_3 + jb_3 = (a_1 + a_2) + j(b_1 + b_2)$$

The rule for addition is apparent: To form the sum of two complex numbers, add their real parts and their imaginary parts.

Because subtraction is the inverse of addition, the same line of reasoning leads to

$$c_4 = c_1 - c_2 = a_4 + jb_4 = (a_1 - a_2) + j(b_1 - b_2)$$

Note that both addition and subtraction are best handled with the complex numbers in rectangular form.

SECTION A.6   MULTIPLICATION

Consider $c_1 = |M|_1 e^{j\theta_1}$ and $c_2 = |M|_2 e^{j\theta_2}$. The product $c_5 = c_1 c_2$ will be

$$c_5 = c_1 c_2 = |M|_1 e^{j\theta_1} |M|_2 e^{j\theta_2} = |M|_1 |M|_2 e^{j(\theta_1 + \theta_2)}$$

or

$$c_5 = |M|_5 e^{j\theta_5} = |M|_5 \underline{/\theta_5}$$

where

$$|M|_5 = |M|_1 |M|_2 \qquad \theta_5 = \theta_1 + \theta_2$$

Multiplication may also be carried out with the complex numbers in rectangular form. Again, with $c_1 = a_1 + jb_1$ and $c_2 = a_2 + jb_2$,

$$c_5 = c_1 c_2 = (a_1 + jb_1)(a_2 + jb_2) = (a_1 a_2 - b_1 b_2) + j(a_1 b_2 + a_2 b_1)$$

This procedure seems to be somewhat more laborious than the procedure for multiplication with the complex numbers in polar form. The rule for the multiplication of complex numbers is: To form the product of two complex numbers, work in polar form, multiply the magnitudes, and add the angles. Be aware, however, that many hand-held calculators perform multiplication in rectangular form.

DIVISION

With $c_1 = |M|_1 e^{j\theta_1}$ and $c_2 = |M|_2 e^{j\theta_2}$, the quotient $c_6 = c_1/c_2$ will be

$$c_6 = \frac{c_1}{c_2} = \frac{|M|_1 e^{j\theta_1}}{|M|_2 e^{j\theta_2}} = \frac{|M|_1}{|M|_2} e^{(j\theta_1 - \theta_2)}$$

or

$$c_6 = |M|_6 e^{j\theta_6} = |M|_6 \underline{/\theta_6}$$

where

$$|M|_6 = \frac{|M|_1}{|M|_2} \qquad \theta_6 = \theta_1 - \theta_2$$

Division may also be carried out with the complex numbers in rectangular form. Again, with $c_1 = a_1 + jb_1$ and $c_2 = a_2 + jb_2$,

$$c_6 = \frac{c_1}{c_2} = \frac{a_1 + jb_1}{a_2 + jb_2} \cdot \frac{a_2 - jb_2}{a_2 - jb_2} = \frac{a_1 a_2 + b_1 b_2}{a_2^2 + b_2^2} + j\frac{a_2 b_1 - a_1 b_2}{a_2^2 + b_2^2}$$

Here

$$c_6 = a_6 + jb_6$$

where

$$a_6 = \frac{a_1 a_2 + b_1 b_2}{a_2^2 + b_2^2} \qquad b_6 = \frac{a_2 b_1 - a_1 b_2}{a_2^2 + b_2^2}$$

This indicates that hand calculations involving division should be performed with the complex numbers in polar form. The rule for division is: To form the quotient of two complex numbers, work in polar form, divide the magnitudes, and subtract the angles.

SECTION A.8   COMPLEX CONJUGATES

The complex conjugate of $c = a + jb = |M|\underline{/\theta}$ is

$$c^* = a - jb = |M|\underline{/-\theta}$$

with the superscript asterisk used to designate the complex conjugate. Notice that the complex number has the same magnitude as its conjugate.

The sum of a complex number and its conjugate is a real number:

$$c + c^* = (a + jb) + (a - jb) = 2a + j0 = 2a$$

And the difference between a complex number and its conjugate is a purely imaginary number:

$$c - c^* = (a + jb) - (a - jb) = 0 + j2b = j2b$$

The product of a complex number and its conjugate is the square of the magnitude:

$$cc^* = (|M|\underline{/\theta})(|M|\underline{/-\theta} = |M|^2\underline{/0} = |M|^2$$

And the quotient of a complex number and its conjugate is a complex number with a magnitude of unity and twice the argument of the complex number:

$$\frac{c}{c^*} = \frac{|M|\underline{/\theta}}{|M|\underline{/-\theta}} = 1\underline{/2\theta}$$

SECTION A.9   POWERS AND ROOTS

Powers of complex numbers are obtained by multiplication with the result

$$c^n = (|M|\underline{/\theta})^n = |M|^n\underline{/n\theta}$$

which recalls the *theorem of DeMoivre*:

$$[|M|(\cos\theta + j\sin\theta)]^n = |M|^n[\cos n\theta + j\sin n\theta] \tag{A.8}$$

The n roots of any complex number c may be found by means of DeMoivre's theorem. The number must be put into the form $c = |M|(\cos\theta + j\sin\theta)$. Recall that θ can be replaced by $\theta + 360k°$, and it is seen that the n roots of c, $r_1, r_2, r_3, \ldots, r_n$, will be

$$r_{k+1} = |M|^{1/n}\left[\cos\left(\frac{\theta + 360k}{n}\right) + \sin\left(\frac{\theta + 360k}{n}\right)\right] \quad (k = 0, 1, 2, \ldots, n - 1) \tag{A.9}$$

■ **EXAMPLE A.1**

Find the three roots of -64.

Solution   Begin by writing -64 as $64\underline{/180°}$. Here, $|M| = 64$ and $\theta = 180°$. Then, $|M|^{1/3} = (64)^{1/3} = 4$; and by eq. (A.9), first with $k = 0$,

$$r_1 = 4\left(\cos\frac{180}{3} + j\sin\frac{180}{3}\right) = 4(\cos 60° + j\sin 60°) = 4\left(\frac{1}{2} + j\frac{\sqrt{3}}{2}\right)$$
$$= 2 + j2\sqrt{3}$$

Then, with $k = 1$,

$$r_2 = 4\left[\cos\left(\frac{180 + 360}{3}\right) + j\sin\left(\frac{180 + 360}{3}\right)\right]$$
$$= 4(\cos 180° + j\sin 180°) = 4(-1 + j0) = -4 + j0 = -4$$

And with $k = 2$,

$$r_3 = 4\left[\cos\left(\frac{180 + 720}{3}\right) + j\sin\left(\frac{180 + 720}{3}\right)\right]$$
$$= 4(\cos 300° + j\sin 300°) = 4\left(\frac{1}{2} - j\frac{\sqrt{3}}{2}\right) = 2 - j2\sqrt{3}$$ ■

Additional Readings

Blackwell, W.A., and L.L. Grigsby. *Introductory Network Theory.* Boston: PWS Engineering, 1985, pp. 623–628.

Bobrow, L.S. *Elementary Linear Circuit Analysis.* 2d ed. New York: Holt, Rinehart and Winston, 1987, pp. 354–359.

Del Toro, V. *Engineering Circuits.* Englewood Cliffs, N.J.: Prentice-Hall, 1987, pp. 199–201.

Dorf, R.C. *Introduction to Electric Circuits.* New York, Wiley, 1989, pp. 581–585.

Hayt, W.H., Jr., and J.E. Kemmerly. *Engineering Circuit Analysis.* 4th ed. New York; McGraw-Hill, 1986, pp. 617–627.

Irwin, J.D. *Basic Engineering Circuit Analysis.* 3d ed. New York; Macmillan, 1989, pp. 361–363, 900–908.

Johnson, D.E., J.L. Hilburn, and J.R. Johnson. *Basic Electric Circuit Analysis.* 4th ed. Englewood Cliffs, N.J.: Prentice-Hall, 1989, pp. 638–645.

Karni, S. *Applied Circuit Analysis.* New York: Wiley, 1988, pp. 682–693.

Madhu, S. *Linear Circuit Analysis.* Englewood Cliffs, N.J.: Prentice-Hall, 1988, pp. 791–796.

Nilsson, J.W. *Electric Circuits.* 3d ed. Reading, Mass.: Addison-Wesley, 1990, pp. 807–813.

Paul, C.R. *Analysis of Linear Circuits.* New York: McGraw-Hill, 1989, pp. 248–256.

B MATRICES AND DETERMINANTS

INTRODUCTION

Before the advent of the digital computer, the hand-held calculator, and the desktop computer, one could talk about the solution of large-scale systems of linear algebraic equations. But few had ever attempted a solution of such a system, and those who had made the attempt were confronted with a most laborious and detailed computational procedure. Now, as a result of the technological revolution that began in the late 1940s and early 1950s, large systems of n algebraic equations in n unknowns (with n in the hundreds and even the thousands) can be formed expeditiously and solved efficiently by using the modern, high-speed, digital computer.

The formulation and solution of such equations relies on an ordered methodology that is matrix-oriented. This is why knowledge of the fundamental concepts in the theory of matrices is so important in the study of electric networks. This appendix seeks to provide a capsule review of this theory.

BASIC CONCEPTS

A system of n linear, algebraic equations in n unknowns $x_1, x_2, x_3, \ldots, x_n$ such as

$$a_{11}x_1 + a_{12}x_2 + a_{13}x_3 + \cdots + a_{1n}x_n = y_1$$

$$a_{21}x_1 + a_{22}x_2 + a_{23}x_3 + \cdots + a_{2n}x_n = y_2$$

$$a_{31}x_1 + a_{32}x_2 + a_{33}x_3 + \cdots + a_{3n}x_n = y_3$$

$$\cdots \qquad \cdots$$

$$a_{n1}x_1 + a_{n2}x_2 + a_{n3}x_3 + \cdots + a_{nn}x_n = y_n$$

can conveniently be represented by the matrix equation

$$\begin{bmatrix} a_{11} & a_{12} & a_{13} & \cdots & a_{1n} \\ a_{21} & a_{22} & a_{23} & \cdots & a_{2n} \\ a_{31} & a_{32} & a_{33} & \cdots & a_{3n} \\ & \cdots & \cdots & \cdots & \\ a_{n1} & a_{n2} & a_{n3} & \cdots & a_{nn} \end{bmatrix} \begin{bmatrix} x_1 \\ x_2 \\ x_3 \\ \cdots \\ x_n \end{bmatrix} = \begin{bmatrix} y_1 \\ y_2 \\ y_3 \\ \cdots \\ y_n \end{bmatrix}$$

or more simply by

$$\mathbf{AX} = \mathbf{Y}$$

where $\mathbf{A}$ is a *rectangular matrix* (in this case square) having elements a_{ij} and where $\mathbf{X}$ and $\mathbf{Y}$ are *column vectors* with elements x_i and y_i respectively. The foregoing representations imply that

$$\sum_{j=1}^{n} a_{ij}x_j = y_i \qquad i = 1, 2, 3, \ldots, n$$

The matrix $\mathbf{A}$ is called the *coefficient matrix*. If it is desired to associate the elements of $\mathbf{Y}$ with the coefficient matrix, $\mathbf{A}$, one may *augment* $\mathbf{A}$ and define an *augmented matrix*

$$\begin{bmatrix} a_{11} & a_{12} & a_{13} & \cdots & a_{1n} & y_1 \\ a_{21} & a_{22} & a_{23} & \cdots & a_{2n} & y_2 \\ a_{31} & a_{32} & a_{33} & \cdots & a_{3n} & y_3 \\ & \cdots & \cdots & \cdots & \cdots \\ a_{n1} & a_{n2} & a_{n3} & \cdots & a_{nn} & y_n \end{bmatrix}$$

which has n rows and $n + 1$ columns. This matrix may be written more simply as the augmented matrix

$$\mathbf{A}^a = [\mathbf{A}|\mathbf{Y}]$$

where the superscript means *augmented* and where the idea of a partitioned matrix[1] is apparent. For example, in the system of linear algebraic equations

$$\begin{aligned} 8x_1 - 3x_2 + 2x_3 &= 14 \\ -3x_1 + 7x_2 - x_3 &= -3 \\ x_1 - 6x_2 + 11x_3 &= 17 \end{aligned}$$

the matrix

$$\begin{bmatrix} 8 & -3 & 2 \\ -3 & 7 & -1 \\ 1 & -6 & 11 \end{bmatrix}$$

is called the coefficient matrix, $\mathbf{A}$, of the system

$$\mathbf{AX} = \mathbf{B}$$

and the matrix

$$\begin{bmatrix} 8 & -3 & 2 & 14 \\ -3 & 7 & -1 & -3 \\ 1 & -6 & 11 & 17 \end{bmatrix}$$

[1] Partitioned matrices are discussed in Section B.15.

which contains the constant terms, in addition to the elements of **A**, is called the augmented matrix of the system. Moreover, the unknowns and the constant terms form two column vectors **X** and **B**.

In the representation

$$\mathbf{AX} = \mathbf{B}$$

A is said to *premultiply* **X** (**A** is a *premultiplier*) and **X** is said to *postmultiply* **A** (**X** is a *postmultiplier*).

SECTION B.3   MATRIX AND VECTOR TERMINOLOGY

A matrix of order $m \times n$,

$$\begin{bmatrix} a_{11} & a_{12} & a_{13} & \cdots & a_{1n} \\ a_{21} & a_{22} & a_{23} & \cdots & a_{2n} \\ a_{31} & a_{32} & a_{33} & \cdots & a_{3n} \\ \cdots & \cdots & \cdots & \cdots & \cdots \\ a_{m1} & a_{m2} & a_{m3} & \cdots & a_{mn} \end{bmatrix}$$

is a rectangular ordered array of a total of mn entries arranged in m rows and n columns. The order of this matrix is $m \times n$, which is often written as (m, n).

If $m = n$, the matrix is square of order $n \times n$ (or of order n, or of nth order):

$$\begin{bmatrix} a_{11} & a_{12} & a_{13} & \cdots & a_{1n} \\ a_{21} & a_{22} & a_{23} & \cdots & a_{2n} \\ a_{31} & a_{32} & a_{33} & \cdots & a_{3n} \\ \cdots & \cdots & \cdots & \cdots & \cdots \\ a_{n1} & a_{n2} & a_{n3} & \cdots & a_{nn} \end{bmatrix}$$

In both the rectangular and square matrices, a_{ij} is called the ijth element of **A**. If the matrix is square and $i = j$, the element is said to define and be located on the *principal diagonal*. The elements $a_{n1}, a_{(n-1),2}, a_{(n-2),3}, \ldots, a_{1n}$ are located on and constitute the *secondary diagonal*.

All elements where $i \neq j$ are considered to be *off-diagonal*; they are *subdiagonal* if $i > j$ and *superdiagonal* if $i < j$. The sum of the elements on the principal diagonal of **A** is called the *trace* of **A**:

$$\mathrm{tr}(\mathbf{A}) = \sum_{k=1}^{n} a_{kk}$$

For example, the matrix

$$\mathbf{A} = \begin{bmatrix} 4 & 2 & 0 & 1 \\ -3 & 4 & 8 & 0 \\ -1 & -1 & 6 & 2 \\ -2 & 7 & 1 & 9 \end{bmatrix}$$

is square and is of fourth order (4×4). The elements 4, 4, 6, and 9 constitute the principal diagonal; and the elements -2, -1, 8, and 1 constitute the secondary diagonal. The element 8 is the a_{23} element, which lies at the intersection of the second row and third column. The trace of $\mathbf{A}$ is

$$\text{tr}(\mathbf{A}) = 4 + 4 + 6 + 9 = 23$$

A vector is a matrix containing a single row or a single column. If it is a $1 \times n$ matrix (a matrix of order $1 \times n$), it is a row vector:

$$\mathbf{V} = \begin{bmatrix} v_1 & v_2 & v_3 & \cdots & v_n \end{bmatrix}$$

If the vector is an $m \times 1$ vector (order $m \times 1$), it is a column vector:

$$\mathbf{V} = \begin{bmatrix} v_1 \\ v_2 \\ v_3 \\ \vdots \\ v_n \end{bmatrix}$$

This concept and the usual one regarding a vector have certain similarities. These similarities are the reason the elements of a vector are frequently called components. However, caution is necessary, because the usual three-dimensional space does not imply that m or n (for column or row vectors, respectively) is limited to an upper bound of 3.

SOME SPECIAL MATRICES

SECTION B.4

An $m \times n$ matrix such as the one displayed in the previous section is called a *null* matrix if every element in the matrix is identically equal to zero. For example, the 2×3 matrix

$$\begin{bmatrix} 0 & 0 & 0 \\ 0 & 0 & 0 \end{bmatrix}$$

is null.

The *transpose* of an $m \times n$ matrix is an $n \times m$ matrix with the rows and columns of the original matrix interchanged. For the 3×4 matrix

$$\mathbf{A} = \begin{bmatrix} 3 & 4 & -2 & 1 \\ 2 & 2 & 1 & 0 \\ 1 & -4 & -3 & 1 \end{bmatrix}$$

the transpose is the 4×3 matrix

$$\mathbf{A}^T = \begin{bmatrix} 3 & 2 & 1 \\ 4 & 2 & -4 \\ -2 & 1 & -3 \\ 1 & 0 & 1 \end{bmatrix}$$

Note the use of the superscript T to indicate the transpose, and observe that the transpose of the transpose is the original matrix:

$$[\mathbf{A}^T]^T = \mathbf{A}$$

The nth-order square matrix

$$\begin{bmatrix} a_{11} & a_{12} & a_{13} & \cdots & a_{1n} \\ a_{21} & a_{22} & a_{23} & \cdots & a_{2n} \\ a_{31} & a_{32} & a_{33} & \cdots & a_{3n} \\ \cdots & \cdots & \cdots & \cdots & \cdots \\ a_{n1} & a_{n2} & a_{n3} & \cdots & a_{nn} \end{bmatrix}$$

is said to be *diagonal* or a *diagonal matrix* if $a_{ij} = 0$ for all $i \neq j$:

$$\mathbf{A} = \begin{bmatrix} a_{11} & 0 & 0 & \cdots & 0 \\ 0 & a_{22} & 0 & \cdots & 0 \\ 0 & 0 & a_{33} & \cdots & 0 \\ \cdots & \cdots & \cdots & \cdots & \cdots \\ 0 & 0 & 0 & \cdots & a_{nn} \end{bmatrix}$$

If all a_{ij} are equal for all $i = j$—that is, $a_{ij} = \alpha$ for $i = j$ and $a_{ij} = 0$ for $i \neq j$—then the resulting matrix is said to be a *scalar matrix*, which is a diagonal matrix with all elements (principal diagonal elements) equal:

$$\mathbf{A} = \begin{bmatrix} \alpha & 0 & 0 & \cdots & 0 \\ 0 & \alpha & 0 & \cdots & 0 \\ 0 & 0 & \alpha & \cdots & 0 \\ \cdots & \cdots & \cdots & \cdots & \cdots \\ 0 & 0 & 0 & \cdots & \alpha \end{bmatrix}$$

If all α in the scalar matrix are equal to unity ($\alpha = 1$), the scalar matrix becomes the *identity matrix*:

$$\mathbf{I} = \begin{bmatrix} 1 & 0 & 0 & \cdots & 0 \\ 0 & 1 & 0 & \cdots & 0 \\ 0 & 0 & 1 & \cdots & 0 \\ \cdots & \cdots & \cdots & \cdots & \cdots \\ 0 & 0 & 0 & \cdots & 1 \end{bmatrix}$$

The identity matrix is often designated as $\mathbf{U}$ (for unity), because $\mathbf{I}$ is often used to designate a current vector.

SECTION B.5   MATRIX EQUALITY

A matrix $\mathbf{A} = [a_{ij}]_{m \times n}$ will be equal to a matrix $\mathbf{B} = [b_{ij}]_{m \times n}$ if and only if $a_{ij} = b_{ij}$ for all i and j. This means that two matrices will be equal if and only if they are of the same order and corresponding elements are equal.

MATRIX ADDITION AND SUBTRACTION

SECTION B.6

A matrix $\mathbf{A} = [a_{ij}]_{m \times n}$ may be added to a matrix $\mathbf{B} = [b_{ij}]_{m \times n}$ to form a matrix $\mathbf{C} = [c_{ij}]_{m \times n} = [a_{ij} + b_{ij}]_{m \times n}$. Observe that forming the sum of two matrices requires that the matrices be of the same order and that the elements of the sum are determined by adding the corresponding elements of the matrices forming the sum.

■ **EXAMPLE B.1**

Find $\mathbf{A} + \mathbf{B}$ and $\mathbf{A} + \mathbf{C}$ if

$$\mathbf{A} = \begin{bmatrix} 1 & 2 & 3 \\ 4 & 5 & 6 \end{bmatrix} \qquad \mathbf{B} = \begin{bmatrix} -1 & 0 & 4 \\ 3 & -2 & -4 \end{bmatrix} \qquad \mathbf{C} = \begin{bmatrix} 2 & 1 \\ 3 & -1 \end{bmatrix}$$

Solution

$$\mathbf{A} + \mathbf{B} = \begin{bmatrix} 1 & 2 & 3 \\ 4 & 5 & 6 \end{bmatrix} + \begin{bmatrix} -1 & 0 & 4 \\ 3 & -2 & -4 \end{bmatrix}$$

$$= \begin{bmatrix} (1-1) & (2+0) & (3+4) \\ (4+3) & (5-2) & (6-4) \end{bmatrix} = \begin{bmatrix} 0 & 2 & 7 \\ 7 & 3 & 2 \end{bmatrix}$$

The sum $\mathbf{A} + \mathbf{C}$ does not exist because the order of $\mathbf{C}$ does not equal the order of $\mathbf{A}$. ■

Matrix addition is both commutative and associative:

$$\mathbf{A} + \mathbf{B} = \mathbf{B} + \mathbf{A}$$

$$\mathbf{A} + (\mathbf{B} + \mathbf{C}) = (\mathbf{A} + \mathbf{B}) + \mathbf{C}$$

In addition, the sum $\mathbf{A} + \mathbf{C}$ is equal to the sum $\mathbf{B} + \mathbf{C}$ if and only if $\mathbf{A} = \mathbf{C}$. This is the cancellation law for addition.

The matrix $\mathbf{B} = [b_{ij}]_{m \times n}$ may be subtracted from the matrix $\mathbf{A} = [a_{ij}]_{m \times n}$ to form the matrix $\mathbf{D} = [d_{ij}]_{m \times n}$. This indicates that two matrices of the same order may be subtracted by forming the difference between the corresponding elements of the minuend and the subtrahend. Moreover, it is seen that

$$\mathbf{A} + \mathbf{B} = \mathbf{C} \qquad \text{and} \qquad \mathbf{A} = \mathbf{C} - \mathbf{B}$$

Finally, it may be observed that a square matrix possesses a unique decomposition into a sum of a subdiagonal, a diagonal, and a superdiagonal matrix. For example,

$$\mathbf{A} = \begin{bmatrix} 1 & 2 & 3 \\ 5 & 6 & 7 \\ 8 & 5 & 6 \end{bmatrix} = \begin{bmatrix} 0 & 0 & 0 \\ 5 & 0 & 0 \\ 8 & 5 & 0 \end{bmatrix} + \begin{bmatrix} 1 & 0 & 0 \\ 0 & 6 & 0 \\ 0 & 0 & 6 \end{bmatrix} + \begin{bmatrix} 0 & 2 & 3 \\ 0 & 0 & 7 \\ 0 & 0 & 0 \end{bmatrix}$$

MATRIX MULTIPLICATION

SECTION B.7

A matrix may be multiplied by a scalar or by another matrix. If $\mathbf{A} = [a_{ij}]$ and α is a scalar, then

$$\alpha \mathbf{A} = [\alpha a_{ij}]$$

This shows that multiplication by a scalar is commutative and involves the multiplication of every element of the matrix by the scalar. Moreover, note that

$$(\alpha + \beta)\mathbf{A} = \alpha\mathbf{A} + \beta\mathbf{A}$$

$$\alpha(\mathbf{A} + \mathbf{B}) = \alpha\mathbf{A} + \alpha\mathbf{B}$$

$$\alpha(\beta\mathbf{A}) = (\alpha\beta)\mathbf{A}$$

Observe that a scalar matrix is equal to the product of the scalar and the identity matrix. For example,

$$\begin{bmatrix} 3 & 0 & 0 \\ 0 & 3 & 0 \\ 0 & 0 & 3 \end{bmatrix} = 3\begin{bmatrix} 1 & 0 & 0 \\ 0 & 1 & 0 \\ 0 & 0 & 1 \end{bmatrix}$$

A modest effort must be expended to use the terminology *multiplication by a scalar* in order to avoid confusion with the process known as *scalar multiplication*.

The product of a row matrix of order $1 \times n$ and a column matrix of order $n \times 1$ forms a 1×1 matrix that has no important property that is not possessed by a scalar. This product is therefore called the *scalar* or *dot* product (some sources also use the terminology *inner product*). It is designated by the use of a dot placed between the two matrices in the product. That is, if $\mathbf{A}$ and $\mathbf{B}$ are column vectors, then

$$\mathbf{A} \cdot \mathbf{B} = [a_{ij}]_{1 \times n} \cdot [b_{ij}]_{n \times 1} = \mathbf{A}^T\mathbf{B} = \mathbf{B}^T\mathbf{A} = \gamma$$

where γ is a scalar obtained from

$$\gamma = \sum_{k=1}^{n} a_k b_k$$

If the scalar product of two vectors is uniquely equal to zero, then the vectors are said to be *orthogonal*.

■ **EXAMPLE B.2**

Find the dot product $\mathbf{A} \cdot \mathbf{B}$ if

$$\mathbf{A} = \begin{bmatrix} 1 \\ 2 \\ 3 \\ 4 \\ 2 \end{bmatrix} \qquad \mathbf{B} = \begin{bmatrix} 4 \\ -5 \\ -3 \\ -2 \\ 7 \end{bmatrix}$$

Solution

$$\mathbf{A} \cdot \mathbf{B} = 1(4) + 2(-5) + 3(-3) + 4(-2) + 2(7)$$
$$= 4 - 10 - 9 - 8 + 14 = -9$$ ■

In Section B.2, a set of linear, simultaneous algebraic equations was shown to be represented by the notation

$$\mathbf{AX} = \mathbf{Y}$$

where $\mathbf{A}$ is the $n \times n$ coefficient matrix and $\mathbf{A}$ and $\mathbf{X}$ are $n \times 1$ column vectors. Obtaining the original set of equations from a set where $n = 3$,

$$\begin{bmatrix} a_{11} & a_{12} & a_{13} \\ a_{21} & a_{22} & a_{23} \\ a_{31} & a_{32} & a_{33} \end{bmatrix} \begin{bmatrix} x_1 \\ x_2 \\ x_3 \end{bmatrix} = \begin{bmatrix} y_1 \\ y_2 \\ y_3 \end{bmatrix}$$

clearly suggests a row-by-column-element product and sum operation:

$$\begin{bmatrix} a_{11}x_1 + a_{12}x_2 + a_{13}x_3 = y_1 \\ a_{21}x_1 + a_{22}x_2 + a_{23}x_3 = y_2 \\ a_{31}x_1 + a_{32}x_2 + a_{33}x_3 = y_3 \end{bmatrix}$$

Observe that each element of y is obtained by multiplying the corresponding element of $\mathbf{A}$ by the elements of $\mathbf{X}$ and adding the results. Notice that the foregoing procedure will not be possible if the number of columns of $\mathbf{A}$ does not equal the number of rows of $\mathbf{X}$. In this event, there will not always be corresponding elements to multiply. Moreover, it should be noted that $\mathbf{Y}$ contains the same number of rows as both $\mathbf{A}$ and $\mathbf{X}$.

This suggests a general definition for the multiplication of two matrices. If $\mathbf{A}$ is $m \times n$ and $\mathbf{B}$ is $p \times q$, $\mathbf{AB} = \mathbf{C}$ will exist if $n = p$, in which case the matrix $\mathbf{C}$ will be $m \times q$ with elements given by

$$[c_{ij}]_{m \times q} = \sum_{k=1}^{n=p} a_{ik}b_{kj} \qquad \begin{cases} i = 1, 2, 3, \ldots, m \\ j = 1, 2, 3, \ldots, q \end{cases}$$

When $n = p$, the matrices $\mathbf{A}$ and $\mathbf{B}$ are said to be conformable for multiplication.

■ **EXAMPLE B.3**

Find $\mathbf{AB}$, $\mathbf{BA}$, and $\mathbf{AC}$ if

$$\mathbf{A} = \begin{bmatrix} 1 & 2 & 3 & 4 \\ -1 & 3 & -2 & 0 \end{bmatrix} \qquad \mathbf{B} = \mathbf{A}^T = \begin{bmatrix} 1 & -1 \\ 2 & 3 \\ 3 & -2 \\ 4 & 0 \end{bmatrix} \qquad \mathbf{C} \begin{bmatrix} 1 & 2 \\ 3 & 4 \end{bmatrix}$$

Solution The product $\mathbf{AB}$ exists because $\mathbf{A}$ is 2×4 and $\mathbf{B}$ is 4×2. The result $\mathbf{P}$ will be 2×2:

$$\mathbf{P} = \mathbf{AB} = \begin{bmatrix} 1 & 2 & 3 & 4 \\ -1 & 3 & -2 & 0 \end{bmatrix} \begin{bmatrix} 1 & -1 \\ 2 & 3 \\ 3 & -2 \\ 4 & 0 \end{bmatrix}$$

$$= \begin{bmatrix} (1 + 4 + 9 + 16) & (-1 + 6 - 6 + 0) \\ (-1 + 6 - 6 + 0) & (1 + 9 + 4 + 0) \end{bmatrix} = \begin{bmatrix} 30 & -1 \\ -1 & 14 \end{bmatrix}$$

The product **BA** also exists and will be 4×4:

$$\mathbf{BA} = \begin{bmatrix} 1 & -1 \\ 2 & 3 \\ 3 & -2 \\ 4 & 0 \end{bmatrix} \begin{bmatrix} 1 & 2 & 3 & 4 \\ -1 & 3 & -2 & 0 \end{bmatrix}$$

$$= \begin{bmatrix} (1+1) & (2-3) & (3+2) & (4+0) \\ (2-3) & (4+9) & (6-6) & (8+0) \\ (3+2) & (6-6) & (9+4) & (12+0) \\ (4+0) & (8+0) & (12+0) & (16+0) \end{bmatrix}$$

$$= \begin{bmatrix} 2 & -1 & 5 & 4 \\ -1 & 13 & 0 & 8 \\ 5 & 0 & 13 & 12 \\ 4 & 8 & 12 & 16 \end{bmatrix}$$

Notice that $\mathbf{AB} \neq \mathbf{BA}$, which shows that matrix multiplication, in general, is not commutative. Notice also that the product **AC** will not exist because **A** and **C** are not conformable for multiplication (**A** is 2×4 and **C** is 2×2). ∎

Although the commutative law does not hold, the multiplication of matrices is associative,

$$(\mathbf{AB})\mathbf{C} = \mathbf{A}(\mathbf{BC})$$

and matrix multiplication is distributive with respect to addition,

$$\mathbf{A}(\mathbf{B} + \mathbf{C}) = \mathbf{AB} + \mathbf{AC}$$

assuming that conformability exists for both addition and multiplication.

If the product **AB** is null—that is, $\mathbf{AB} = 0$—it cannot be concluded that either **A** or **B** is null. Furthermore, if $\mathbf{AB} = \mathbf{AC}$ or $\mathbf{CA} = \mathbf{BA}$, it cannot be concluded that $\mathbf{B} = \mathbf{C}$. This means that, in general, cancellation of matrices is not permissible.

The transpose of a product of matrices is equal to the product of the individual transposes taken in reverse order:

$$(\mathbf{AB})^T = \mathbf{B}^T \mathbf{A}^T$$

SECTION B.8   **MATRIX DIVISION AND MATRIX INVERSION**

Matrix division is not defined. Instead, use is made of a process called matrix inversion, which relies upon the existence of the identity matrix that is related to a square matrix **A** by

$$\mathbf{AI} = \mathbf{IA} = \mathbf{A}$$

Consider the identity for addition, 0, so that for all scalars α,

$$\alpha + 0 = 0 + \alpha = \alpha$$

and an identity element for multiplication, 1, so that

$$\alpha 1 = 1\alpha = \alpha$$

The scalar most certainly possesses a reciprocal or multiplicative inverse, $1/\alpha$, which, when multiplied by α, yields the identity element for scalar multiplication:

$$\frac{1}{\alpha} = (\alpha^{-1}\alpha) = 1$$

This reasoning may be extended to the $n \times n$ matrix $\mathbf{A}$ and the pair of identity matrices, the $n \times n$ identity matrix for multiplication $\mathbf{I}$ and the $n \times n$ identity matrix for addition $\mathbf{0}$ (a null matrix). Thus, as already noted,

$$\mathbf{AI} = \mathbf{IA} = \mathbf{A}$$

$$\mathbf{A} + \mathbf{0} = \mathbf{0} + \mathbf{A} = \mathbf{A}$$

If there is an $n \times n$ matrix $\mathbf{A}$ that pre- and postmultiplies $\mathbf{A}$ such that

$$\mathbf{A}^{-1}\mathbf{A} = \mathbf{AA}^{-1} = \mathbf{I}$$

then $\mathbf{A}^{-1}$ is an inverse of $\mathbf{A}$ with respect to matrix multiplication. The matrix $\mathbf{A}$ is said to be invertible or *nonsingular* if $\mathbf{A}^{-1}$ exists and singular if $\mathbf{A}^{-1}$ does not exist.

For example, the 3×3 matrix

$$\mathbf{A} = \begin{bmatrix} 3 & -2 & 0 \\ -2 & 4 & -1 \\ 0 & -1 & 6 \end{bmatrix}$$

can be shown to possess the inverse

$$\mathbf{A} = \begin{bmatrix} \frac{23}{45} & \frac{4}{15} & \frac{2}{45} \\ \frac{4}{15} & \frac{2}{5} & \frac{1}{15} \\ \frac{2}{45} & \frac{1}{15} & \frac{8}{45} \end{bmatrix}$$

A simple multiplication will produce the identity matrix:

$$\mathbf{AA}^{-1} = \begin{bmatrix} 3 & -2 & 0 \\ -2 & 4 & -1 \\ 0 & -1 & 6 \end{bmatrix} \begin{bmatrix} \frac{23}{45} & \frac{4}{15} & \frac{2}{45} \\ \frac{4}{15} & \frac{2}{5} & \frac{1}{15} \\ \frac{2}{45} & \frac{1}{15} & \frac{8}{45} \end{bmatrix} = \begin{bmatrix} 1 & 0 & 0 \\ 0 & 1 & 0 \\ 0 & 0 & 1 \end{bmatrix}$$

The reader may wish to verify that the identity is also produced if the product $\mathbf{A}^{-1}\mathbf{A}$ is taken.

The inverse of a product of matrices is equal to the product of the individual inverses taken in reverse order:

$$(\mathbf{AB})^{-1} = \mathbf{B}^{-1}\mathbf{A}^{-1}$$

B.9.1 Linear Independence

The coefficients in a set of linear, simultaneous algebraic equations can be represented as a set of row or column vectors. That is, in $\mathbf{AX} = \mathbf{B}$, the coefficient matrix $\mathbf{A}$ can be represented as an array of column vectors,

$$\mathbf{A} = [\mathbf{A}_1 \quad \mathbf{A}_2 \quad \mathbf{A}_3 \quad \cdots \quad \mathbf{A}_n]$$

or as an array of row vectors,

$$\mathbf{A} = \begin{bmatrix} \mathbf{A}_1 \\ \mathbf{A}_2 \\ \mathbf{A}_3 \\ \vdots \\ \mathbf{A}_n \end{bmatrix}$$

Observe that all of these vectors have the same order; for the row vectors, they are $1 \times n$; and for the column vectors, they are $n \times 1$. In either case, the set of vectors is said to be a *linearly dependent* set if in

$$\alpha_1 \mathbf{A}_1 + \alpha_2 \mathbf{A}_2 + \alpha_3 \mathbf{A}_3 + \cdots + \alpha_n \mathbf{A}_n = \mathbf{0} \tag{B.1}$$

there exists at least one value of the scalars α that is not identically equal to zero. If all α are equal to zero, the set of vectors is said to be *linearly independent*, and the vectors then constitute a *linearly independent set*. Observe that if a set of vectors is not linearly independent, it must be linearly dependent.

■ **EXAMPLE B.4**

Show that the row vectors in the matrix

$$\mathbf{A} = \begin{bmatrix} 3 & -2 & 0 \\ -2 & 4 & -1 \\ 0 & -1 & 6 \end{bmatrix}$$

are linearly independent.

Solution   The matrix may be represented as three row vectors:

$$\mathbf{A}_1 = [3 \quad -2 \quad 0]$$
$$\mathbf{A}_2 = [-2 \quad 4 \quad -1]$$
$$\mathbf{A}_3 = [0 \quad -1 \quad 6]$$

Equation (B.1) is used to determine whether these vectors constitute a linearly independent set:

$$\alpha_1[3 \quad -2 \quad 0] + \alpha_2[-2 \quad 4 \quad -1] + \alpha_3[0 \quad -1 \quad 6]$$
$$= [0 \quad 0 \quad 0]$$

Expansion leads to the set of three equations in three unknowns:

$$3\alpha_1 - 2\alpha_2 \qquad = 0$$
$$-2\alpha_1 + 4\alpha_2 \quad -\alpha_3 = 0$$
$$-\alpha_2 + 6\alpha_3 = 0$$

And it is noted that from the third of these, $\alpha_3 = \alpha_2/6$, and from the first, $\alpha_1 = 2\alpha_2/3$. With these in the second equation,

$$-2\left(\frac{2\alpha_2}{3}\right) + 4\alpha_2 - \frac{\alpha_2}{6} = 0$$

it is seen that

$$\alpha_1 = \alpha_2 = \alpha_3 = 0$$

and this means that the vectors form a linearly independent set. ∎

B.9.2 Linear Combinations

If the vectors $\mathbf{A}_1$, $\mathbf{A}_2$, $\mathbf{A}_3, \ldots, \mathbf{A}_n$ are linearly dependent, then at least one of them can be expressed as a linear combination of any or all of the others. This can be observed by letting the scalar α_k be nonzero in a rearrangement of eq. (B.1):

$$\mathbf{A}_k = \frac{\alpha_1}{\alpha_k}\mathbf{A}_1 - \frac{\alpha_2}{\alpha_k}\mathbf{A}_2 - \frac{\alpha_3}{\alpha_k}\mathbf{A}_3 - \cdots - \frac{\alpha_n}{\alpha_k}\mathbf{A}_n$$

which expresses $\mathbf{A}_k$ as a linear combination of all vectors that are associated with a nonzero value of α. Moreover, this indicates that if one vector in a set of vectors can be expressed as a linear combination of the others, the vectors are linearly dependent.

DETERMINANTS

SECTION B.10

B.10.1 Definitions and Terminology

A square matrix of order n (an $n \times n$ matrix),

$$\mathbf{A} = \begin{bmatrix} a_{11} & a_{12} & a_{13} & \cdots & a_{1n} \\ a_{21} & a_{22} & a_{23} & \cdots & a_{2n} \\ a_{31} & a_{32} & a_{33} & \cdots & a_{3n} \\ \cdots & \cdots & \cdots & \cdots & \cdots \\ a_{n1} & a_{n2} & a_{n3} & \cdots & a_{nn} \end{bmatrix}$$

possesses a uniquely defined scalar (a single number), which is designated as the determinant of $\mathbf{A}$ (or merely the determinant),

$$\det \mathbf{A} = |A|$$

where the order of the determinant is the same as the order of the matrix from which it derives. Observe that only square matrices possess determinants, that vertical lines and not brackets are used to designate determinants, and that the elements of the determinant are identical to the elements of the matrix:

$$
\det \mathbf{A} = \begin{vmatrix}
a_{11} & a_{12} & a_{13} & \cdots & a_{1n} \\
a_{21} & a_{22} & a_{23} & \cdots & a_{2n} \\
a_{31} & a_{32} & a_{33} & \cdots & a_{3n} \\
\cdots & \cdots & \cdots & \cdots & \cdots \\
a_{n1} & a_{n2} & a_{n3} & \cdots & a_{nn}
\end{vmatrix}
$$

A determinant of the first order consists of a single element α and has, therefore, the value $\det \mathbf{A} = a$. A determinant of the second order contains four elements in a 2×2 square array:

$$
\det \mathbf{A} = |A| = \begin{vmatrix}
a_{11} & a_{12} \\
a_{21} & a_{22}
\end{vmatrix}
$$

A determinant of the third order is described in similar fashion. It is a 3×3 square array containing nine elements:

$$
\det \mathbf{A} = |A| = \begin{vmatrix}
a_{11} & a_{12} & a_{13} \\
a_{21} & a_{22} & a_{23} \\
a_{31} & a_{32} & a_{33}
\end{vmatrix}
$$

One may deduce that a determinant of nth order consists of a square array of $n \times n$ elements a_{ij} and that the total number of elements in an nth-order determinant is n^2. Although this representation of the determinant appears to be purely abstract, the determinant can be proven to be a very rational function that can be evaluated in a number of ways. Moreover, the value of determinants in matrix inverses and in the solution of simultaneous, linear algebraic equations cannot be overemphasized.

B.10.2 Determinant Evaluation

Consider, for example, the following pair of simultaneous, linear algebraic equations that are assumed to be linearly independent:

$$a_{11}x_1 + a_{12}x_2 = b_1 \tag{B.2a}$$

$$a_{21}x_1 + a_{22}x_2 = b_2 \tag{B.2b}$$

Observe that they may also be written in the matrix form $\mathbf{AX} = \mathbf{B}$,

$$
\begin{bmatrix}
a_{11} & a_{12} \\
a_{21} & a_{22}
\end{bmatrix}
\begin{bmatrix}
x_1 \\
x_2
\end{bmatrix}
=
\begin{bmatrix}
b_1 \\
b_2
\end{bmatrix}
$$

In eqs. (B.2), the x's are the unknowns and the a's form the coefficient matrix $\mathbf{A}$. If $\det \mathbf{A} \neq 0$, the equations are said to be *linearly independent*, and one method of solving this second-order system is to multiply eq. (B.2a) by a_{22} and eq. (B.2b) by a_{12}:

$$a_{22}a_{11}x_1 + a_{22}a_{12}x_2 = a_{22}b_1$$

$$a_{12}a_{21}x_1 + a_{12}a_{22}x_2 = a_{12}b_2$$

A subtraction yields

$$(a_{22}a_{11} - a_{12}a_{21})x_1 = a_{22}b_1 - a_{12}b_2$$

And then, x_1 is obtained:

$$x_1 = \frac{a_{22}b_1 - a_{12}b_2}{a_{22}a_{11} - a_{12}a_{21}} \tag{B.3a}$$

A similar procedure yields x_2:

$$x_2 = \frac{a_{11}b_2 - a_{21}b_1}{a_{22}a_{11} - a_{12}a_{21}} \tag{B.3b}$$

Observe that the denominators of the equations that yield x_1 and x_2 can be represented by the determinant

$$\begin{vmatrix} a_{11} & a_{12} \\ a_{21} & a_{22} \end{vmatrix} = a_{22}a_{11} - a_{12}a_{21}$$

Also, the numerators of these equations can be represented by

$$\begin{vmatrix} b_1 & a_{12} \\ b_2 & a_{22} \end{vmatrix} = b_1 a_{22} - b_2 a_{21} \quad \text{and} \quad \begin{vmatrix} a_{11} & b_1 \\ a_{21} & b_2 \end{vmatrix} = a_{11}b_2 - a_{21}b_1$$

This must always hold unless the determinant in the denominators is equal to zero, which is ruled out because the discussion originally began with the statement that the two equations to be solved were linearly independent.

Thus, one may write the solutions for x_1 and x_2 in eqs. (B.2) as

$$x_1 = \frac{\begin{vmatrix} b_1 & a_{12} \\ b_2 & a_{22} \end{vmatrix}}{\begin{vmatrix} a_{11} & a_{12} \\ a_{21} & a_{22} \end{vmatrix}} \quad \text{and} \quad x_2 = \frac{\begin{vmatrix} a_{11} & b_1 \\ a_{21} & b_2 \end{vmatrix}}{\begin{vmatrix} a_{11} & a_{12} \\ a_{21} & a_{22} \end{vmatrix}}$$

and this is a demonstration of a method of solution of simultaneous, linear algebraic equations known as *Cramer's rule.*

The foregoing reasoning applies equally well to a set of n simultaneous algebraic equations. For a set of three equations in three unknowns,

$$a_{11}x_1 + a_{12}x_2 + a_{13}x_3 = b_1$$

$$a_{21}x_1 + a_{22}x_2 + a_{23}x_3 = b_2$$

$$a_{31}x_1 + a_{32}x_2 + a_{33}x_3 = b_3$$

which are assumed to be linearly independent and which may be written in matrix form as

$$\begin{bmatrix} a_{11} & a_{12} & a_{13} \\ a_{21} & a_{22} & a_{23} \\ a_{31} & a_{32} & a_{33} \end{bmatrix} \begin{bmatrix} x_1 \\ x_2 \\ x_3 \end{bmatrix} = \begin{bmatrix} b_1 \\ b_2 \\ b_3 \end{bmatrix}$$

it can be shown that x_1 can be evaluated from

$$\cdot x_1 = \frac{b_1 a_{22} a_{33} + b_3 a_{12} a_{23} + b_2 a_{13} a_{32} - b_3 a_{22} a_{13} - b_1 a_{32} a_{23} - b_2 a_{12} a_{33}}{a_{11} a_{22} a_{33} + a_{12} a_{23} a_{31} + a_{13} a_{21} a_{32} - a_{31} a_{22} a_{13} - a_{32} a_{23} a_{11} - a_{33} a_{21} a_{12}}$$

Both the numerator and the denominator can be rearranged by employing a litte algebra:

$$x_1 = \frac{b_1(a_{22} a_{33} - a_{32} a_{23}) - b_2(a_{12} a_{33} - a_{32} a_{13}) + b_3(a_{12} a_{23} - a_{22} a_{13})}{a_{11}(a_{22} a_{33} - a_{32} a_{23}) - a_{21}(a_{12} a_{33} - a_{13} a_{32}) + a_{31}(a_{12} a_{23} - a_{22} a_{13})} \quad \textbf{(B.4)}$$

An inspection of the terms within the parentheses shows that not only can the solution for x_1 be written (Cramer's rule) as the quotient of two determinants but also each of the determinants can be represented in terms of three second-order determinants:

$$x_1 = \frac{\begin{vmatrix} b_1 & a_{12} & a_{13} \\ b_2 & a_{22} & a_{23} \\ b_3 & a_{32} & a_{33} \end{vmatrix} = b_1 \begin{vmatrix} a_{22} & a_{23} \\ a_{32} & a_{33} \end{vmatrix} - b_2 \begin{vmatrix} a_{12} & a_{13} \\ a_{32} & a_{33} \end{vmatrix} + b_3 \begin{vmatrix} a_{12} & a_{13} \\ a_{22} & a_{23} \end{vmatrix}}{\begin{vmatrix} a_{11} & a_{12} & a_{13} \\ a_{21} & a_{22} & a_{23} \\ a_{31} & a_{32} & a_{33} \end{vmatrix} = a_{11} \begin{vmatrix} a_{22} & a_{23} \\ a_{32} & a_{33} \end{vmatrix} - a_{21} \begin{vmatrix} a_{12} & a_{13} \\ a_{32} & a_{33} \end{vmatrix} + a_{31} \begin{vmatrix} a_{12} & a_{13} \\ a_{22} & a_{23} \end{vmatrix}}$$

$$\textbf{(B.5)}$$

This expansion is known as the *Laplace expansion* or the *Laplace development*.[2]

The method of evaluating second- and third-order determinants is suggested in eqs. (B.3) and (B.4). The second-order determinant is evaluated as the remainder of the product resulting from the multiplication of the upper left and lower right elements (the principal-diagonal elements) minus the product of the lower left and the upper right elements (the secondary-diagonal elements). This procedure is demonstrated in Fig. B.1a.

The third-order determinant may be evaluated by taking the products and then the sums and differences of the elements shown in Fig. B.1b. This procedure may be assisted by rewriting the first two columns of the determinant and then proceeding as indicated in Fig. B.1c. It is important to note that for this purpose, the diagonals of the third-order determinant are continuous; that is, the last column is followed by the first column.

Caution is necessary: Fourth- and higher-order determinants may not be evaluated by following the procedures displayed in Fig. B.1. The Laplace expansion or *pivotal condensation* must be employed in these cases.

■ **EXAMPLE B.5**

Evaluate the determinants

$$|A| = \begin{vmatrix} 2 & 3 \\ 1 & 4 \end{vmatrix} \qquad |B| = \begin{vmatrix} 3 & 2 & 1 \\ 1 & 4 & 2 \\ 1 & 3 & 1 \end{vmatrix}$$

---

[2] To be discussed further in Section B.13.

(a) Procedure for evaluating a second-order determinant and (b) and (c) equivalent procedures for evaluating a third-order determinant

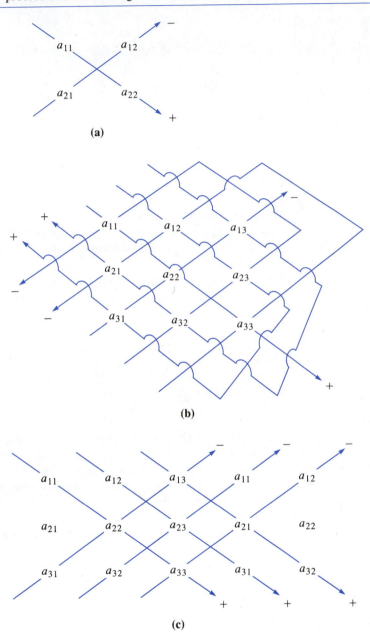

(a)

(b)

(c)

Solution   The second-order determinant is evaluated by the procedure indicated in Fig. B.1:

$$|A| = \begin{vmatrix} 2 & 3 \\ 1 & 4 \end{vmatrix} = 2(4) - 3(1) = 8 - 3 = 5$$

The third-order determinant is evaluated in accordance with Figs. B.1b or B.1c as

$$|B| = \begin{vmatrix} 3 & 2 & 1 \\ 1 & 4 & 2 \\ 1 & 3 & 1 \end{vmatrix}$$

$$= 3(4)(1) + 2(2)(1) + 1(1)(3) - 1(4)(1) - 3(2)(3) - 1(1)(2)$$

$$= 12 + 4 + 3 - 4 - 18 - 2 = -5$$

∎

B.10.3 Pivotal Condensation

The evaluation of a determinant by the Laplace expansion can be a long, tedious, and laborious procedure. Assuming that third-order determinants can be evaluated quickly, a fifth-order determinant containing no zero elements requires the evaluation of $5 \times 4 = 20$ third-order determinants. For a sixth-order determinant, this number becomes $6 \times 5 \times 4 = 120$.

Pivotal condensation is a much more efficient process. Take the determinant

$$\det A = \begin{vmatrix} a_{11} & a_{12} & a_{13} & \cdots & a_{1n} \\ a_{21} & a_{22} & a_{23} & \cdots & a_{2n} \\ a_{31} & a_{32} & a_{33} & \cdots & a_{3n} \\ \cdots & \cdots & \cdots & \cdots & \cdots \\ a_{n1} & a_{n2} & a_{n3} & \cdots & a_{nn} \end{vmatrix}$$

The element a_{11} is selected as the element in the *pivotal position*. It is called the *pivotal element*, or merely the *pivot*, in the following development. The objective is to find a determinant $|B|$ that is one order less than $|A|$ by operating on $|A|$ in such a manner as to produce a column of zeros in the column containing the pivot. If $a_{11} = 0$, a row or column interchange[3] can be performed to put a nonzero element in the pivotal position.

The condensation process that brings an nth-order determinant down to an $(n-1)$th-order determinant is continued until the order is reduced to three or two. Then, the evaluation can be accomplished by the methods provided in the previous subsection. The entire condensation procedure can be handled by the computationally efficient matrix relationship

$$|A| = \frac{1}{a_{11}^{n-2}} \det \left[a_{11} \begin{bmatrix} a_{22} & a_{23} & \cdots & a_{2n} \\ a_{32} & a_{33} & \cdots & a_{3n} \\ \cdots & \cdots & \cdots & \cdots \\ a_{n2} & a_{n3} & \cdots & a_{nn} \end{bmatrix} - \begin{bmatrix} a_{21} \\ a_{31} \\ \vdots \\ a_{n1} \end{bmatrix} \begin{bmatrix} a_{12} & a_{13} & \cdots & a_{1n} \end{bmatrix} \right]$$

$$\text{(B.6)}$$

[3] See Section B.10.4.

■ **EXAMPLE B.6**

Use pivotal condensation to evaluate the determinant

$$|A| = \begin{vmatrix} 2 & -1 & 1 & 1 & 2 \\ 0 & 2 & 3 & 2 & 1 \\ 0 & 1 & 2 & 1 & 2 \\ 0 & 1 & -1 & -1 & 3 \\ 0 & 2 & 1 & 1 & -2 \end{vmatrix}$$

Solution   By pivotal condensation,

$$|A| = \frac{1}{2^3} \det 2 \left[\begin{bmatrix} 2 & 3 & 2 & 1 \\ 1 & 2 & 1 & 2 \\ 1 & -1 & -1 & 3 \\ 2 & 1 & 1 & -2 \end{bmatrix} - \begin{bmatrix} 0 \\ 0 \\ 0 \\ 0 \end{bmatrix} \begin{bmatrix} -1 & 1 & 1 & 2 \end{bmatrix} \right]$$

$$= \frac{1}{8} \det \begin{bmatrix} 4 & 6 & 4 & 2 \\ 2 & 4 & 2 & 4 \\ 2 & -2 & -2 & 6 \\ 4 & 2 & 2 & -4 \end{bmatrix}$$

Then,

$$|A| = \frac{1}{8(4)^2} \det 4 \left[\begin{bmatrix} 4 & 2 & 4 \\ -2 & -2 & 6 \\ 2 & 2 & -4 \end{bmatrix} - \begin{bmatrix} 2 \\ 2 \\ 4 \end{bmatrix} \begin{bmatrix} 6 & 4 & 2 \end{bmatrix} \right]$$

$$= \frac{1}{128} \det \left[\begin{bmatrix} 16 & 8 & 16 \\ -8 & -8 & 24 \\ 8 & 8 & -16 \end{bmatrix} - \begin{bmatrix} 12 & 8 & 4 \\ 12 & 8 & 4 \\ 24 & 16 & 8 \end{bmatrix} \right]$$

$$= \frac{1}{128} \det \begin{bmatrix} 4 & 0 & 12 \\ -20 & -16 & 20 \\ -16 & -8 & -24 \end{bmatrix}$$

The third-order determinant is now evaluated as

$$|A| = \frac{1}{128}(1536 + 0 + 1920 - 3072 + 640 - 0) = \frac{1024}{128} = 8$$ ■

B.10.4 Additional Properties

Several rules pertaining to the simplification and manipulation of determinants will be presented in this subsection without formal proof.

1. Interchanging any row (or column) of a determinant with its immediately adjacent row (or column) changes the sign of the determinant.
2. The multiplication of any single row (column) of a determinant by a scalar constant is equivalent to the multiplication of the entire determinant by the

scalar. Observe that this differs from the multiplication of a matrix by a scalar; the multiplication of a matrix by a scalar results in the multiplication of every element of the matrix by the scalar.

3. If every element in an nth-order determinant is multiplied by the same scalar α, the value of the determinant is multiplied by α^n.

4. If any two rows (columns) of a determinant are identical, the value of the determinant is zero and the matrix from which the determinant derives is said to be *singular*.

5. If any row (or column) of a determinant contains nothing but zeros, the value of the determinant is zero.

6. If any two rows (columns) of a determinant are proportional, the determinant is equal to zero. In this case, the two rows (columns) are said to be *linearly dependent*.

7. If the elements of any row (column) of a determinant are added to or subtracted from the corresponding elements of another row (column), the value of the determinant is unchanged.

8. If the elements of any row (column) of a determinant are multiplied by a constant and then added to or subtracted from the corresponding elements of another row (column), the value of the determinant is unchanged.

9. The value of the determinant of a diagonal matrix is equal to the product of the terms on the diagonal.

10. The value of the determinant of a matrix is equal to the value of the determinant of the transpose of the matrix.

11. The determinant of the product of two matrices is equal to the product of the determinants of the two matrices.

12. If the determinant of the product of two square matrices is zero, then at least one of the matrices is singular; that is, the value of its determinant is equal to zero.

SECTION B.11   MINORS AND COFACTORS

Consider the nth-order determinant

$$\det \mathbf{A} = \begin{vmatrix} a_{11} & a_{12} & a_{13} & \cdots & a_{1n} \\ a_{21} & a_{22} & a_{23} & \cdots & a_{2n} \\ a_{31} & a_{32} & a_{33} & \cdots & a_{3n} \\ \cdots & \cdots & \cdots & \cdots & \cdots \\ a_{n1} & a_{n2} & a_{n3} & \cdots & a_{nn} \end{vmatrix} \tag{B.7}$$

which will be used for proposing two useful quantities.

The $(n-1)$th-*order minor* of an nth-order determinant $|A|$ is the determinant formed by deleting one row and one column from $|A|$. The minor, designated by $|M|_{ij}$, is the determinant formed by deleting the ith row and the jth column from $|A|$.

The *cofactor*, designated as A_{ij} (without vertical rules and with a double subscript), is the *signed* $(n-1)$th-order minor formed from the nth-order determinant. If the minor has been formed by deleting the ith row and the jth column from $|A|$, then

$$A_{ij} = (-1)^{i+j} M_{ij} \tag{B.8}$$

The checkerboard rule for finding the sign of a cofactor of an nth-order determinant: (a) for n odd and (b) for n even

$$
\begin{array}{ccccccc}
+ & - & + & - & + & \cdots & + \\
- & + & - & + & - & \cdots & - \\
+ & - & + & - & + & \cdots & + \\
- & + & - & + & - & \cdots & - \\
\cdots & \cdots & \cdots & \cdots & \cdots & \cdots & \cdots \\
+ & - & + & - & + & \cdots & +
\end{array}
\qquad
\begin{array}{ccccccc}
+ & - & + & - & + & \cdots & - \\
- & + & - & + & - & \cdots & + \\
+ & - & + & - & + & \cdots & - \\
- & + & - & + & - & \cdots & + \\
\cdots & \cdots & \cdots & \cdots & \cdots & \cdots & \cdots \\
- & + & - & + & - & \cdots & +
\end{array}
$$

$$\text{(a)} \qquad\qquad\qquad\qquad \text{(b)}$$

The sign of the cofactor can be determined from eq. (B.8) or from the *checkerboard rule* summarized in Fig. B.2.

■ **EXAMPLE B.7**

Consider the fourth-order determinant

$$
|A| = \det \begin{bmatrix}
1 & 3 & -1 & 2 \\
4 & 1 & 1 & 3 \\
3 & 1 & -2 & 1 \\
1 & 3 & 2 & 5
\end{bmatrix}
$$

What are the minor and the cofactor formed by deleting the third row and fourth column?

Solution

$$
|M|_{34} = \det \begin{bmatrix}
1 & 3 & -1 \\
4 & 1 & 1 \\
1 & 3 & 2
\end{bmatrix} = 2 + 3 - 12 + 1 - 3 - 24 = -33
$$

The cofactor is the *signed* minor. By the checkerboard rule of Fig. B.2 or by eq. (B.8),

$$A_{34} = (-1)^{3+4}(-33) = -(-33) = 33$$

■

THE COFACTOR MATRIX

A square nth-order matrix

$$
\mathbf{A} = \begin{bmatrix}
a_{11} & a_{12} & a_{13} & \cdots & a_{1n} \\
a_{21} & a_{22} & a_{23} & \cdots & a_{2n} \\
a_{31} & a_{32} & a_{33} & \cdots & a_{3n} \\
\cdots & \cdots & \cdots & \cdots & \cdots \\
a_{n1} & a_{n2} & a_{n3} & \cdots & a_{nn}
\end{bmatrix}
$$

possesses a cofactor matrix with elements indicated by capital letters with double subscripts:

$$\mathbf{A}^c = \begin{bmatrix} A_{11} & A_{12} & A_{13} & \cdots & A_{1n} \\ A_{21} & A_{22} & A_{23} & \cdots & A_{2n} \\ A_{31} & A_{32} & A_{33} & \cdots & A_{3n} \\ \cdots & \cdots & \cdots & \cdots & \cdots \\ A_{n1} & A_{n2} & A_{n3} & \cdots & A_{nn} \end{bmatrix}$$

■ **EXAMPLE B.8**

Determine the cofactor matrix for the third-order symmetrical matrix

$$\begin{bmatrix} 3 & -2 & 0 \\ -2 & 4 & -1 \\ 0 & -1 & 6 \end{bmatrix}$$

Solution   The nine cofactors with signs determined by eq. (B.8) or from the checkerboard rule in Fig. B.2 are formed from the possible second-order minors:

$$A_{11} = +|M|_{11} = \begin{vmatrix} 4 & -1 \\ -1 & 6 \end{vmatrix} = +(24 - 1) = 23$$

$$A_{12} = -|M|_{12} = -\begin{vmatrix} -2 & -1 \\ 0 & 6 \end{vmatrix} = -(-12) = 12$$

$$A_{13} = +|M|_{13} = \begin{vmatrix} -2 & 4 \\ 0 & -1 \end{vmatrix} = 2$$

$$A_{21} = -|M|_{21} = -\begin{vmatrix} -2 & 0 \\ -1 & 6 \end{vmatrix} = -(-12) = 12$$

$$A_{22} = +|M|_{22} = \begin{vmatrix} 3 & 0 \\ 0 & 6 \end{vmatrix} = 18$$

$$A_{23} = -|M|_{23} = -\begin{vmatrix} 3 & -2 \\ 0 & -1 \end{vmatrix} = -(-3) = 3$$

$$A_{31} = +|M|_{31} = \begin{vmatrix} -2 & 0 \\ 4 & -1 \end{vmatrix} = 2$$

$$A_{32} = -|M|_{32} = -\begin{vmatrix} 3 & 0 \\ -2 & -1 \end{vmatrix} = -(-3) = 3$$

$$A_{33} = +|M|_{33} = \begin{vmatrix} 3 & -2 \\ -2 & 4 \end{vmatrix} = +(12 - 4) = 8$$

Thus,

$$\mathbf{A}^c = \begin{bmatrix} 23 & 12 & 2 \\ 12 & 18 & 3 \\ 2 & 3 & 8 \end{bmatrix}$$

and this confirms that symmetrical matrices possess symmetrical cofactor matrices. ■

THE LAPLACE EXPANSION

In the denominator of eq. (B.5), the third-order determinant **A** was shown to be equal to some function of three second-order determinants:

$$\begin{vmatrix} a_{11} & a_{12} & a_{13} \\ a_{21} & a_{22} & a_{23} \\ a_{31} & a_{32} & a_{33} \end{vmatrix} = a_{11} \begin{vmatrix} a_{22} & a_{23} \\ a_{32} & a_{33} \end{vmatrix} - a_{21} \begin{vmatrix} a_{12} & a_{13} \\ a_{32} & a_{33} \end{vmatrix} + a_{31} \begin{vmatrix} a_{12} & a_{13} \\ a_{22} & a_{23} \end{vmatrix}$$

(B.9)

Notice that each of the second-order determinants is a second-order minor of **A**. This means that three cofactors exist, and hence, eq. (B.9) gives a rule for the evaluation of a third-order determinant that can be extended to an nth-order determinant. For the ith row,

$$|A| = \sum_{j=1}^{j=n} (-1)^{i+j} a_{ij} |M|_{ij}$$

or

$$|A| = \sum_{j=1}^{j=n} a_{ij} A_{ij}$$

(B.9a)

And for the jth column,

$$|A| = \sum_{i=1}^{i=n} (-1)^{i+j} a_{ij} |M|_{ij}$$

or

$$|A| = \sum_{i=1}^{i=n} a_{ij} A_{ij}$$

(B.9b)

Equations (B.9) describe a procedure known as the *Laplace development* or the *Laplace expansion*.

■ **EXAMPLE B.9**

Evaluate the determinant

$$|A| = \begin{vmatrix} 6 & 3 & 0 & 1 \\ 2 & 5 & 1 & -2 \\ 1 & 0 & -1 & 1 \\ 1 & 0 & 3 & 4 \end{vmatrix}$$

Solution   Expand by using the second column to reduce the labor (two zeros occur in this column):

$$|A| = -a_{12} |M|_{12} + a_{22} |M|_{22} = a_{12} A_{12} + a_{22} A_{22}$$

The cofactors derive from the appropriate minors, with their sign determined from eq. (B.8) or from the checkerboard rule illustrated in Fig. B.2:

$$A_{21} = -|M|_{21} = - \begin{vmatrix} 2 & 1 & -2 \\ 1 & -1 & 1 \\ 1 & 3 & 4 \end{vmatrix} = -(-8 + 1 - 6 - 2 - 6 - 4)$$

$$= -(1 - 26) = 25$$

$$A_{22} = +|M|_{22} = \begin{vmatrix} 6 & 0 & 1 \\ 1 & -1 & 1 \\ 1 & 3 & 4 \end{vmatrix} = (-24 + 0 + 3 + 1 - 18 - 0)$$

$$= 4 - 42 = -38$$

The value of the determinant is

$$|A| = a_{21}A_{21} + a_{22}A_{22} = 3(25) + 5(-38) = 75 - 190 = -115 \qquad \blacksquare$$

Observe that if the elements of a row or column of a determinant are multiplied by cofactors of the corresponding elements of a different row or column, the resulting sum of these products is zero:

$$\sum_{i=1}^{i=n} (-1)^{k+j} a_{kj} |M|_{kj} = 0 \qquad (i \neq k) \tag{B.10a}$$

$$\sum_{j=1}^{j=n} (-1)^{i+k} a_{ik} |M|_{ik} = 0 \qquad (j \neq k) \tag{B.10b}$$

SECTION B.14   MATRIX INVERSION

An nth-order set of simultaneous, linear algebraic equations in the n unknowns, $x_1, x_2, \ldots, x_n$, can conveniently be represented by the matrix equation

$$\mathbf{AX} = \mathbf{Y} \tag{B.11}$$

where $\mathbf{A}$, as indicated in Section B.2, is a square matrix of coefficients having elements a_{ij} and where $\mathbf{X}$ and $\mathbf{Y}$ are $n \times 1$ column vectors with elements x_i and y_i, respectively. Because division of matrices is not permitted, one method for the solution of matrix equations such as the one shown in eq. (B.11) is called matrix inversion.

If eq. (B.11) is premultiplied by an $n \times n$ square matrix $\mathbf{B}$, so that

$$\mathbf{BAX} = \mathbf{BY}$$

a solution for the unknowns $\mathbf{X}$ will evolve if the product $\mathbf{BA}$ is equal to the identity matrix $\mathbf{I}$:

$$\mathbf{BAX} = \mathbf{IX} = \mathbf{BY}$$

or

$$\mathbf{X} = \mathbf{BY} \tag{B.12}$$

If

$$BA = AB = I$$

the matrix **B** is said to be the inverse of **A**:

$$B = A^{-1} \tag{B.13a}$$

And, of course, the inverse of the inverse is the matrix itself:

$$A = B^{-1} \tag{B.13b}$$

or

$$(A)^{-1} = A$$

It may be recalled that, in general, matrix multiplication is not commutative. The multiplication of a matrix by its inverse is one specific case where matrix multiplication is commutative:

$$AA^{-1} = A^{-1}A = I$$

B.14.1 Properties of the Inverse

The inverse of a product of two matrices is the product of the inverses taken in reverse order. This is easily proved. Consider the product **AB** and postmultiply by $B^{-1}A^{-1}$. Because matrix multiplication is associative, this product can be taken with a rearrangement of the parentheses and then by a straightforward application of the definition of the matrix inverse:

$$AB(B^{-1}A^{-1}) = A(BB^{-1}A^{-1}) = AIA^{-1} = AA^{-1} = I$$

Moreover, the inverse of the transpose of a matrix is equal to the transpose of its inverse:

$$(A^T)^{-1} = (A^{-1})^T$$

Negative powers of a matrix are related to its inverse:

$$A^{-n} = (A^{-1})^n$$

And the determinant of the product of a matrix and its inverse must be equal to unity:

$$\det(AA^{-1}) = \det I = 1$$

If a matrix does not possess an inverse, it is said to be *singular*; but if a matrix does possess an inverse, the inverse is unique.

B.14.2 The Adjoint Matrix

The *adjoint matrix*, which is sometimes called the *adjugate matrix* and which, in this development, will be referred to merely as the *adjoint*, applies only to a square matrix and is the transpose of the cofactor matrix:

$$\text{adj } \mathbf{A} = \mathscr{A} = (\mathbf{A}^c)^T \tag{B.14}$$

Because symmetrical matrices possess symmetrical cofactor matrices, the adjoint of a symmetrical matrix is the cofactor matrix itself.

The matrix that is of nth order,

$$\mathbf{A} = \begin{bmatrix} a_{11} & a_{12} & a_{13} & \cdots & a_{1n} \\ a_{21} & a_{22} & a_{23} & \cdots & a_{2n} \\ a_{31} & a_{32} & a_{33} & \cdots & a_{3n} \\ \cdots & \cdots & \cdots & \cdots & \cdots \\ a_{n1} & a_{n2} & a_{n3} & \cdots & a_{nn} \end{bmatrix}$$

has been observed to possess a cofactor matrix

$$\mathbf{A}^c = \begin{bmatrix} A_{11} & A_{12} & A_{13} & \cdots & A_{1n} \\ A_{21} & A_{22} & A_{23} & \cdots & A_{2n} \\ A_{31} & A_{32} & A_{33} & \cdots & A_{3n} \\ \cdots & \cdots & \cdots & \cdots & \cdots \\ A_{n1} & A_{n2} & A_{n3} & \cdots & A_{nn} \end{bmatrix}$$

This cofactor matrix has an adjoint

$$\text{adj } \mathbf{A} = (\mathbf{A}^c)^T = \begin{bmatrix} A_{11} & A_{21} & A_{31} & \cdots & A_{n1} \\ A_{12} & A_{22} & A_{32} & \cdots & A_{n2} \\ A_{13} & A_{23} & A_{33} & \cdots & A_{n3} \\ \cdots & \cdots & \cdots & \cdots & \cdots \\ A_{1n} & A_{2n} & A_{3n} & \cdots & A_{nn} \end{bmatrix}$$

B.14.3 One Method for the Determination of the Inverse

Suppose an $n \times n$ matrix $\mathbf{A}$ is postmultiplied by its adjoint and that the product is designated as $\mathbf{P}$:

$$\mathbf{A}(\text{adj } \mathbf{A}) = \begin{bmatrix} a_{11} & a_{12} & a_{13} & \cdots & a_{1n} \\ a_{21} & a_{22} & a_{23} & \cdots & a_{2n} \\ a_{31} & a_{32} & a_{33} & \cdots & a_{3n} \\ \cdots & \cdots & \cdots & \cdots & \cdots \\ a_{n1} & a_{n2} & a_{n3} & \cdots & a_{nn} \end{bmatrix} \begin{bmatrix} A_{11} & A_{21} & A_{31} & \cdots & A_{n1} \\ A_{12} & A_{22} & A_{32} & \cdots & A_{n2} \\ A_{13} & A_{23} & A_{33} & \cdots & A_{n3} \\ \cdots & \cdots & \cdots & \cdots & \cdots \\ A_{1n} & A_{2n} & A_{3n} & \cdots & A_{nn} \end{bmatrix} = \mathbf{P}$$

The elements of $\mathbf{P}$ may be divided into two categories: those that lie upon its principal diagonal, of which p_{22} is typical, and those that do not. For the principal-diagonal element p_{22},

$$p_{22} = a_{21}A_{21} + a_{22}A_{22} + a_{23}A_{23} + \cdots + a_{2n}A_{2n}$$

and by eq. (B.9a),

$$p_{22} = |A|$$

For the off-diagonal element, of which p_{13} is typical,

$$p_{13} = a_{11}A_{31} + a_{12}A_{32} + a_{13}A_{33} + \cdots + a_{1n}A_{3n}$$

and by eq. (B.10a), it is seen that

$$p_{13} = 0$$

Thus, the product of **A** and its adjoint is

$$\mathbf{A}(\text{adj } \mathbf{A}) = \begin{bmatrix} |A| & 0 & 0 & \cdots & 0 \\ 0 & |A| & 0 & \cdots & 0 \\ 0 & 0 & |A| & \cdots & 0 \\ \cdots & \cdots & \cdots & \cdots & \cdots \\ 0 & 0 & 0 & \cdots & |A| \end{bmatrix} = (\det \mathbf{A})\mathbf{I}$$

If this is put into the form

$$\mathbf{A}\frac{\text{adj } \mathbf{A}}{\det \mathbf{A}} = \mathbf{I}$$

and compared with

$$\mathbf{A}\mathbf{A}^{-1} = \mathbf{I}$$

it becomes evident that the inverse of the matrix **A** is equal to its adjoint divided by its determinant:

$$\mathbf{A}^{-1} = \frac{\text{adj } \mathbf{A}}{\det \mathbf{A}} \tag{B.15}$$

Observe that if det **A** = 0, the inverse of **A** cannot exist and is therefore *singular*. Thus, the necessary condition for the matrix **A** to be singular is for det **A** = 0.

■ **EXAMPLE B.10**

Determine the inverse of the third-order symmetrical matrix

$$\mathbf{A} = \begin{bmatrix} 3 & -2 & 0 \\ -2 & 4 & -1 \\ 0 & -1 & 6 \end{bmatrix}$$

Solution   In Example B.8, it was shown that the given matrix possesses a cofactor matrix

$$\mathbf{A}^c = \begin{bmatrix} 23 & 12 & 2 \\ 12 & 18 & 3 \\ 2 & 3 & 8 \end{bmatrix}$$

and the reader may verify that the given matrix has a determinant det **A** = 45.

The given matrix is symmetrical, as is the cofactor matrix. The adjoint (the transpose of the cofactor matrix) is also symmetrical and is equal to the cofactor matrix. Thus, by eq. (B.15), the inverse is

$$\mathbf{A}^{-1} = \begin{bmatrix} \frac{23}{45} & \frac{4}{15} & \frac{2}{45} \\ \frac{4}{15} & \frac{2}{5} & \frac{1}{15} \\ \frac{2}{45} & \frac{1}{15} & \frac{8}{45} \end{bmatrix}$$

which is also observed to be symmetrical. ∎

It is important to note that symmetrical matrices possess symmetrical transposes, symmetrical cofactor matrices, symmetrical adjoints, and symmetrical inverses.

The evaluation of the inverse can always be concluded with a check on its validity. In the previous example,

$$\frac{1}{45} \begin{bmatrix} 3 & -2 & 0 \\ -2 & 4 & -1 \\ 0 & -1 & 6 \end{bmatrix} \begin{bmatrix} 23 & 12 & 2 \\ 12 & 18 & 3 \\ 2 & 3 & 8 \end{bmatrix} = \begin{bmatrix} 1 & 0 & 0 \\ 0 & 1 & 0 \\ 0 & 0 & 1 \end{bmatrix}$$

■ **EXAMPLE B.11**

Determine the inverse of the nonsymmetrical second-order matrix

$$\mathbf{A} = \begin{bmatrix} 4 & -1 \\ 1 & 6 \end{bmatrix}$$

Solution   The matrix has a determinant

$$\det \mathbf{A} = 24 + 1 = 25$$

a cofactor matrix

$$\mathbf{A}^c = \begin{bmatrix} 6 & -1 \\ 1 & 4 \end{bmatrix}$$

and an adjoint

$$\text{adj } \mathbf{A} = \begin{bmatrix} 6 & 1 \\ -1 & 4 \end{bmatrix}$$

Its inverse is

$$\mathbf{A}^{-1} = \frac{\text{adj } \mathbf{A}}{\det \mathbf{A}} = \begin{bmatrix} \frac{6}{25} & \frac{1}{25} \\ -\frac{1}{25} & \frac{4}{25} \end{bmatrix}$$

This result can be verified by the reader. ∎

It is observed from Example B.11 that the inverse of a second-order determinant is obtained by swapping the elements that lie on the principal diagonal, changing the sign of the off-diagonal elements, and then dividing all elements by the determinant.

THE PARTITIONING OF MATRICES

Computations with matrices of higher order can be assisted dramatically if the matrices involved are partitioned, that is, divided into a number of smaller rectangular blocks or submatrices. The partitioning is usually indicated by dashed partitioning lines, which must extend entirely through the matrix.

For example, the 3×4 matrix $\mathbf{M}$

$$\mathbf{M} = \begin{bmatrix} 1 & -1 & 0 & 2 \\ 0 & 2 & 3 & -1 \\ -1 & 2 & 0 & 4 \end{bmatrix}$$

can be partitioned into

$$\mathbf{M} = \left[\begin{array}{cc|cc} 1 & -1 & 0 & 2 \\ 0 & 2 & 3 & -1 \\ \hline -1 & 2 & 0 & 4 \end{array}\right] = \left[\begin{array}{c|c} \mathbf{A} & \mathbf{B} \\ \hline \mathbf{C} & \mathbf{D} \end{array}\right]$$

where the matrices $\mathbf{A}$, $\mathbf{B}$, $\mathbf{C}$, and $\mathbf{D}$ are given by

$$\mathbf{A} = \begin{bmatrix} 1 & -1 \\ 0 & 2 \end{bmatrix} \quad \mathbf{B} = \begin{bmatrix} 0 & 2 \\ 3 & -1 \end{bmatrix} \quad \mathbf{C} = [-1 \quad 2] \quad \mathbf{D} = [0 \quad 4]$$

The partitioning of $\mathbf{M}$

$$\mathbf{M} = \left[\begin{array}{cc|cc} 1 & -1 & 0 & 2 \\ 0 & 2 & 3 & -1 \\ -1 & 2 & 0 & 4 \end{array}\right] = [\mathbf{E} \mid \mathbf{F}]$$

and

$$\mathbf{M} = \left[\begin{array}{cccc} 1 & -1 & 0 & 2 \\ \hline 0 & 2 & 3 & -1 \\ \hline -1 & 2 & 0 & 4 \end{array}\right] = \begin{bmatrix} \mathbf{A} \\ \hline \mathbf{B} \\ \hline \mathbf{C} \end{bmatrix}$$

shows that the arrangement of the partitioned matrices is not unique.

B.15.1 Addition and Subtraction of Partitioned Matrices

Two matrices may be added or subtracted only if they are conformable for these operations; that is, they must be of the same order. When matrices are partitioned, there is an additional requirement for their addition and subtraction: The matrices must be identically partitioned; that is, the partitioned matrices must be of the same order.

B.15.2 Multiplication of Partitioned Matrices

Multiplication of partitioned matrices is accomplished by treating the submatrices derived from the partitioning as single elements. However, in the setup of these elements, careful attention must be paid to the conformability of these elements for their eventual multiplication.

Consider matrix M, which is $m \times n$ and which is partitioned into four submatrices A, B, C, and D:

$$M = \left[\begin{array}{c|c} A & B \\ \hline C & D \end{array}\right]$$

Also, consider matrix N, which is $p \times q$ and which is partitioned into four submatrices E, F, G, and H:

$$N = \left[\begin{array}{c|c} E & F \\ \hline G & H \end{array}\right]$$

As discussed in detail in Section B.7, if $n = p$, M and N are comformable for multiplication and the product $L = MN$ will be $m \times q$.

Now in M, if A is $j \times k$, then B will be $j \times (n - k)$, C will be $(m - j) \times k$, and D will be $(m - j) \times (n - k)$. The question then becomes: How should E, F, G, and H in N be arranged so that the product

$$MN = \left[\begin{array}{c|c} A & B \\ \hline C & D \end{array}\right]\left[\begin{array}{c|c} E & F \\ \hline G & H \end{array}\right] = \left[\begin{array}{c|c} (AE + BG) & (AF + BH) \\ \hline (CE + DG) & (CF + DH) \end{array}\right]$$

can be executed?

Let E be $r \times s$ so that F is $r \times (q - s)$, G is $(p - r) \times s$, and H is $(p - r) \times (q - s)$. If A, which is $j \times k$, is to premultiply E, then $r = k$; and the product AE, as well as the product BG, will be $j \times s$. Moreover, in the product BG, where B is $j \times (n - k)$ and G is $(p - r) \times s$, conformability dictates that $n - k = p - r$. This, of course, means that if $r = k$, then $p = n$, which is required if the product $L = MN$ is to be executed at all. Thus, the requirements are

$$p = n \quad \text{and} \quad r = k$$

B.15.3 The Transpose of a Partitioned Matrix

The transpose of a partitioned matrix such as

$$M = \begin{bmatrix} A & B \\ C & D \end{bmatrix}$$

is

$$M^T = \begin{bmatrix} A & C \\ B & D \end{bmatrix}$$

Additional Readings

Blackwell, W.A., and L.L. Grigsby. *Introductory Network Theory*. Boston: PWS Engineering, 1985, pp. 631–649.

Bobrow, L.S. *Elementary Linear Circuit Analysis*. 2d ed. New York: Holt, Rinehart and Winston, 1987, pp. 669–677.

Dorf, R.C. *Introduction to Electric Circuits*. New York: Wiley, 1989, pp. 575–579.

Hayt, W.H., Jr., and J.E. Kemmerly. *Engineering Circuit Analysis*. 4th ed. New York: McGraw-Hill, 1986, pp. 607–613.

Irwin, J.D. *Basic Engineering Circuit Analysis*. 3d ed. New York: Macmillan, 1989, pp. 870–878.

Johnson, D.E., J.L. Hilburn, and J.R. Johnson. *Basic Electric Circuit Analysis*. 4th ed. Englewood Cliffs, N.J.: Prentice-Hall, 1989, pp. 631–634.

Karni, S. *Applied Circuit Analysis*. New York: Wiley, 1988, pp. 669–680.

Madhu, S. *Linear Circuit Analysis*. Englewood Cliffs, N.J.: Prentice-Hall, 1988, pp. 785–790.

Nilsson, J.W. *Electric Circuits*. 3d ed. Reading, Mass.: Addison-Wesley, 1990, pp. 789–806.

Paul, C.R. *Analysis of Linear Circuits*. New York: McGraw-Hill, 1989, pp. 96–102.

C USING THE SPICE NETWORK ANALYZER PROGRAM

INTRODUCTION

PSPICE is a free-of-charge classroom version of the SPICE program, which is an acronym for Simulation Program with Integrated Circuit Emphasis. SPICE was developed at the University of California at Berkeley and is a program that simulates analog networks. Although it was originally developed for mainframe computers, several organizations have developed versions for use with desktop personal computers. PSPICE is produced by the Microsim Corporation of Irvine, California, and this classroom version comes in two diskettes.

SPICE, as used in conjunction with this text, will perform the following:

- DC analyses to provide all node-to-datum voltages, branch currents as specified by the analyst, branch voltages and currents, dc output/input characteristics, sensitivity analyses, and input and output resistances
- AC analyses with both magnitude and phase of quantities computed and with frequencies swept over a range of values; Bode plots may be generated
- Transient analyses in which voltage and current responses as a function of time may be tabulated and/or plotted for a variety of time-varying inputs

GETTING STARTED

The first step is to install the PSPICE diskettes in your computer, preferably in a hard disk. The following procedure assumes that the hard disk is drive C and the disks provided are placed in drive A. Computer screen interrogations are printed here in *italics*, and responses by the user are in **boldface**.

1. Be sure your DOS version is at least 3.0.
2. When you are in drive C, observe the prompt and create a directory called PSPICE.DIR as follows:

   C > **CD**
   C > **MD\PSPICE.DIR**

3. Using disk drive A, copy both diskettes containing all of the PSPICE files to the directory PSPICE.DIR as follows:

   C > **CD\PSPICE.DIR**
   C > **A:**
   A > **COPY *·* C:**

4. Whenever you wish to use PSPICE, go to the hard disk and get into the PSPICE.DIR directory:

C > PSPICE.DIR

5. Use a word processor such as WORDSTAR, EDLIN, or VEDIT to create the SPICE input file, which must bear the suffix .CIR.

PRELIMINARY GROUND RULES

SECTION C.3

Here are some preliminary ground rules:

1. All nodes must be numbered with positive integers but need not be in sequence. Numbers may be skipped. For example, 0, 1, 2, 3, 17, 18, 27, 32, 44, and 53 are permissible designators in a ten-node problem. Here, 0 is the ground or datum node and has been included in the node count.
2. The ground or datum node must always bear the numeral 0.
3. Every node must have two or more connections.
4. Each node must have a dc path to the ground or datum node.
5. Input format is of the free-form type, with all fields separated by one or more blanks, commas, left and right parentheses, or equal signs.
6. Number fields are entered in free-form format, either in integer (34, 41, −1832, −4) or floating-point (17.32, .707, −.866, −1200) format. Integer exponents or scale factors may also be used with integer and floating-point fields. A description of the scale factors will be found in Section C.4.2.
7. While it is a good idea to limit data lines to the width of the PC screen (80 spaces), continuations of data lines may be made by using a plus (+) sign as the first entry of the continued line.
8. Name fields must begin with a letter (A through Z) and should contain no more than eight elements, none of which may be a delimiter. For example, RTHEV and CBYPASS1 are permissible component names, but L1/HENRY is not.

THE SPICE INPUT FILE—SIMPLE DC ANALYSIS

SECTION C.4

The SPICE input file may bear any name but always bears the suffix .CIR. For example, input files such as PROB1.CIR, NYMETS.CIR, and SFNINERS.CIR consist of five types of statements:

- Title and comment statements
- Data statements
- Solution control statements
- Output specification statement
- END statement

C.4.1 Title and Comment Statements

The first line of any SPICE input file is always a title statement. It typically contains enough information to identify the problem being analyzed, and it will be printed as a heading for each section of output.

The comment statements are used to aid the programmer or analyst and will be ignored by the PSPICE program. They contain an asterisk (∗) as the leading term and are particularly useful if one comes back to an input file that has not been used for a long period of time.

A typical title statement might be

ANALYSIS OF OP-AMP CIRCUIT

and a comment statement might look like this:

∗NOTE: THIS IS SIMILAR TO THE CIRCUIT ON PRINT T-12345.

C.4.2 Data Statements

PSPICE performs a node-to-datum analysis, and the basic building block is the network branch. Although PSPICE contains the capability for handling electronic elements, only the ten elements shown in Table C.1 are considered here. Notice that in accordance with preliminary ground rule 8, only eight characters are used to identify (name) a network branch.

It was pointed out in preliminary ground rule 6 that numerical magnitudes could be specified by using integer exponents or scale factors. The exponential forms and the scale factors are displayed in Table C.2. Notice that, to avoid confusion, M specifies

TABLE C.1   Ten network elements

Type of element	Designator
Resistor	RXXXXXXX
Capacitor	CXXXXXXX
Inductor	LXXXXXXX
Mutual coupling	KXXXXXXX
Independent voltage source	VXXXXXXX
Independent current source	IXXXXXXX
Voltage-controlled voltage source	EXXXXXXX
Current-controlled current source	FXXXXXXX
Voltage-controlled current source	GXXXXXXX
Current-controlled voltage source	HXXXXXXX

TABLE C.2   Scale factors

Symbol	Value	Exponential form
F	10^{-15}	1E − 15
P	10^{-12}	1E − 12
N	10^{-9}	1E − 9
U	10^{-6}	1E − 6
M	10^{-3}	1E − 3
K	10^{3}	1E3
MEG	10^{6}	1E6
G	10^{9}	1E9
T	10^{12}	1E12

milli- (0.001) and MEG specifies *mega-* (10^6). Care must be exercised and continuous thought is necessary; 400 V, 400 RAD, 400 A, and 400 OHMS all mean 400, because V, RAD, A, and OHMS do not begin with any of the letters corresponding to the scale factors in Table C.2. Moreover, 4E3, 4 KOHMS, 4K, and 4000. all signify the numeral 4000.

Resistors, capacitors, and inductors are all specified in the following format:

ELEMENT   N1   N2   VALUE

where the ELEMENT can be RXXXXXXX, LXXXXXXX, or CXXXXXXX; N1 and N2 are node connections; and VALUE is the element value. The following list gives some examples.

RONE	3	4	10K
LPRIMARY	7	13	20M
CBYPASS	4	13	12U
R6	2	14	3560
C12	7	8	.00004
CAP3	4	9	2E − 6

Independent dc voltage and current sources are both specified in this format:

SOURCE   N1   N2   TYPE   VALUE

where SOURCE can be VXXXXXXX or IXXXXXXX, N1 and N2 indicate the node connections, TYPE is DC, and VALUE is the source magnitude. For an independent voltage source, N1 is at the positive terminal; and for an independent current source, the current proceeds through the source (the arrow is in the direction) from N1 to N2.

Because branch currents are not printed as output, an independent voltage source can be used as an ammeter. In this case, N1 and N2 are arranged to give the proper direction of the current, and VALUE is set equal to zero.

Voltage-controlled dependent sources are specified in the following format:

SOURCE   N1   N2   NC1   NC2   VALUE

where SOURCE can be EXXXXXXX or GXXXXXXX, N1 and N2 indicate the node connections, NC1 and NC2 are the controlling nodes, and VALUE is the voltage gain or the transconductance, as applicable.

Current-controlled dependent sources are specified in the following format:

SOURCE   N1   N2   VCONTROL   VALUE

where SOURCE can be FXXXXXXX or HXXXXXXX, N1 and N2 indicate the node connections, VCONTROL is the designator for a zero-valued voltage source used to measure the controlling current, and VALUE is the current gain or trans-resistance, as applicable. The following list gives some examples.

		N1	N2	NC1	NC2/VCONTROL	VALUE
1.	EDEP1	3	4	1	7	0.2
2.	FDEP2	7	13		VCONA	12.25
3.	GDEP3	4	13	2	6	0.04
4.	HDEP4	2	14		VCONB	8.375

In 1, EDEP1 is a voltage-controlled voltage source connected between nodes 3 and 4 (with the positive terminal at node 3) and controlled by v_{17} (with the positive terminal at node 1), in accordance with $v_{34} = 0.2v_{17}$. Here, the voltage gain is 0.2 V/V.

In 2, FDEP2 is a current-controlled current source connected between nodes 7 and 13 (with the current direction from node 7 to node 13) and controlled by a zero-valued voltage source used to measure the controlling current and designated as VCONA. Here, the current gain is 12.25 A/A.

In 3, GDEP3 is a voltage-controlled current source connected between nodes 4 and 13 (with the current direction from node 4 to node 13) and controlled by v_{26} (with the positive terminal at node 2), in accordance with $i = 0.04v_{26}$. Here, the transconductance is 0.04 A/V.

In 4, HDEP4 is a current-controlled voltage source connected between nodes 2 and 14 (with the positive terminal at node 2) and controlled by a zero-valued voltage source used to measure the controlling current and designated as VCONB. Here, the transresistance is 8.357 V/A.

C.4.3 Solution Control Statements

PSPICE has been programmed to provide three types of analysis: dc analysis, small-signal ac analysis, and transient analysis. Because PSPICE was orginally developed to analyze networks containing integrated circuits, the dc bias level is automatically determined prior to any specified analysis. Thus, for the simplest dc analysis, it is not necessary to provide a solution control statement such as .DC.

The .DC control statement permits the study of network performance over a range of independent input source variables. The format for the .DC statement is

.DC   SRCID1   BEG1   END1   INCR1   SRCID2   BEG2   END2   INCR2

Such a statement causes independent source SRCID2 to be swept over the range from BEG2 to END2 in steps of INCR2; and for each value for SRCID2, SCRC1 is incremented in steps of INCR1 from BEG1 to END1. The sweeping of two sources is not required, and the specification for the sweeping of only one source looks like this:

.DC   SRCID1   BEG1   END1   INCR1

The .DC control statement can generate a considerable amount of data and is most often used with a .PRINT or .PLOT statement. However, if the analyst requires a single set of branch voltages, the .DC control statement will take the form

.DC   SRCID1   BEG1   BEG1   1

Observe that it is necessary to identify a single source and set its magnitude in both the BEG1 and END1 fields. The value of the increment INCR1 is set equal to unity. The data statement for the source must then be adjusted to show 0 for the source magnitude. For example, suppose a source is shown as a data statement in input file SUPPOSE.CIR as

VIN   0   14   DC   24

In order to show the branch voltages v_{12}, v_{23} and v_{34} in the output file, one must change the source data statement to

VIN   0   14   DC   0

and the statement

.DC VIN 24 24 1

is added. A print statement (see Section C.4.4) is then used to show v_{12}, v_{23}, and v_{34}.

C.4.4 Output Specification Statements

PSPICE performs a nodal (node-to-datum) analysis and automatically provides all node-to-datum voltages and specified currents in the output file, with voltages always in volts and currents always in amperes. However, if branch voltages are desired, they may be obtained through the use of a .PRINT statement:

.PRINT TYPE OV1 OV2 OV3 $\cdots$ OV8

Here, TYPE refers to the type of analysis (dc, ac, or transient), and as many as eight printed output variables can be requested. Output variables in excess of eight can be requested through the use of multiple print statements, with no restriction on the number. For example,

.PRINT DC V(1,2) V(2,3) V(3,4)

requests that branch voltages v_{12}, v_{23}, and v_{34} between nodes 1 and 2, 2 and 3, and 3 and 4 be printed. The positive polarity is indicated by the first numeral. When the .PRINT statement is used in conjunction with the .DC control statement, branch voltages will appear in the output file.

Other output specification statements such as .PLOT and .PROBE are not required for elementary dc analyses. These will be discussed in subsequent sections.

C.4.5 The .END Statement

The .END statement is mandatory and is the last entry in the input file for all analyses.

C.4.6 Examples

Two examples will now be presented. The first network contains a single voltage source and the second has both a voltage and a current source.

■ **EXAMPLE C.1**

Find the currents through all of the resistors in the network shown in Fig. C.1.

Solution The network made ready for SPICE analysis is shown in Fig. C.2. Notice that the voltage sources labeled VMETER2, VMETER3 and VMETER4 are used to measure the currents through the 2-, 3- and 4-ohm resistors. No separate voltage source is needed to measure the current through the 1-ohm resistor because PSPICE lists the current flowing through voltage sources as output. However, the current through the voltage source will show a negative value because of the difference in the manner actual voltage sources and voltages sources used to measure current are specified.

FIGURE C.1   Network for SPICE Example C.1

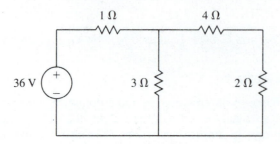

FIGURE C.2   Network for SPICE Example C.1 made ready for SPICE Analysis

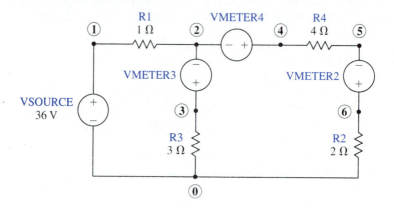

FIGURE C.3   Data statements for the network in Fig. C.2

```
SPICE EXAMPLE APPENDIX C NUMBER ONE
***********************************************
*LIST THE COMPONENTS FIRST
***********************************************
R1           1            2            1
R2           6            0            2
R3           3            0            3
R4           4            5            4
***********************************************
*THEN THE SINGLE VOLTAGE SOURCE
***********************************************
VSOURCE    1            0            DC          36
***********************************************
*ADDITIONAL VOLTAGE SOURCES ARE NEEDED TO
*MEASURE THE CURRENTS.
***********************************************
VMETER2    5            6            DC          0
VMETER3    2            3            DC          0
VMETER4    2            4            DC          0
***********************************************
*DO NOT FORGET THE .END STATEMENT
***********************************************
.END
```

Pertinent extracts from the SPICE output file for the network in Fig. C.2

FIGURE C.4

```
SPICE EXAMPLE APPENDIX C NUMBER ONE


****     SMALL SIGNAL BIAS SOLUTION       TEMPERATURE =    27.000 DEG C


***********************************************************************


 NODE    VOLTAGE       NODE    VOLTAGE     NODE    VOLTAGE     NODE    VOLTAGE


(    1)    36.0000   (     2)    24.0000   (    3)    24.0000   (     4)    24.0000

(    5)     8.0000   (     6)     8.0000



     VOLTAGE SOURCE CURRENTS
     NAME            CURRENT

     VSOURCE        -1.200E+01
     VMETER2         4.000E+00
     VMETER3         8.000E+00
     VMETER4         4.000E+00

     TOTAL POWER DISSIPATION   4.32E+02   WATTS


          JOB CONCLUDED
```

The input file is listed in Fig. C.3 and pertinent extracts from the output file are displayed in Fig. C.4. ∎

∎ **EXAMPLE C.2**

Find the current through the 12-ohm resistor in the network shown in Fig. C.5.

Solution   The network made ready for SPICE analysis is shown in Fig. C.6, and the output file is reproduced in Fig. C.7. Pertinent extracts from the output file are given in Fig. C.8. ∎

Network for SPICE Example C.2

FIGURE C.5

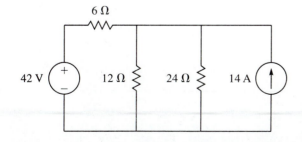

FIGURE C.6   Network for SPICE Example C.2 made ready for SPICE Analysis

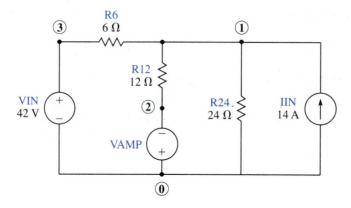

FIGURE C.7   Data statements for the network in Fig. C.6

```
SPICE EXAMPLE APPENDIX C NUMBER TWO
*********************************************
*HERE THERE ARE THREE COMPONENTS,
*********************************************
R6          3         1         6
R12         1         2         12
R24         1         0         24
*********************************************
*TWO SOURCES,
*********************************************
VIN         3         0         DC        42
IIN         0         1         DC        14
*********************************************
*ONE VOLTAGE SOURCE USED TO MEASURE CURRENT
*********************************************
VAMP        2         0         DC        0
*********************************************
*AND AN .END STATEMENT
*********************************************
.END
```

FIGURE C.8   Pertinent extracts from the SPICE output file for the network in Fig. C.6

```
SPICE EXAMPLE APPENDIX C NUMBER TWO


****      SMALL SIGNAL BIAS SOLUTION          TEMPERATURE =    27.000 DEG C


**********************************************************************************


NODE    VOLTAGE     NODE    VOLTAGE     NODE    VOLTAGE     NODE    VOLTAGE


(    1)    72.0000  (     2)     0.0000  (     3)    42.0000



        VOLTAGE SOURCE CURRENTS
        NAME            CURRENT

        VIN             5.000E+00
        VAMP            6.000E+00

            JOB CONCLUDED
```

Two additional examples of elementary dc analysis are presented in Section 2.12.

MODIFICATIONS FOR MORE ADVANCED DC ANALYSES   SECTION C.5

This section describes the control statements for more advanced dc analyses: the .SENS and the .TF statements.

C.5.1 The .SENS Control Statement

The .SENS control statement permits the determination of the dc small-signal sensitivity for all network parameters. This is useful in the prediction of the effects of loads at the output of networks. The .SENS control statement has this format:

    .SENS   OUTPUT(N1,N2)

where OUTPUT(N1,N2) is the output variable and N1 and N2 are the nodes across which the sensitivity is to be computed.

C.5.2 The .TF Control Statement

The .TF control statement has been cleverly designed to assist the analyst in the formulation of a Thévenin equivalent network. Its format is

    .TF   VAROUT   VARINP

With the .TF control statement, PSPICE computes the transfer function, the ratio of the output variable VAROUT to the input variable VARINP, the input resistance seen by the input source VARINP, and the output resistance at the location of VAROUT. Use of the .TF control statement will produce this output, and the .PRINT control statement is not necessary.

C.5.3 Output Specification Statements

The .PLOT statement takes the same form as the .PRINT statement, with an optional specification of high and low plot limits after any of the plot variables. The form is

    .PLOT   TYPE   OV1   OV2   ⋯   OV8⟨LIMHI   LIMLO⟩

When the optional high and low limits are not specified, SPICE will automatically determine the maximum and minimum values of all variables and scale the entire plot accordingly. Notice that here, too, the type of analysis (dc, ac, or transient) must be specified.

Multiple plot statements will yield additional plots, and the first output variable in each of these statements will be printed as well as plotted. This means that if it is desired to print all variables, the .PRINT statement must be used.

C.5.4 Examples

The two examples which now follow illustrate the use of PSPICE to obtain the Thévenin equivalent. The first is rather simple and the second contains a controlled source.

FIGURE C.9   Network for SPICE Example C.3

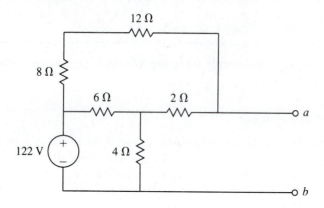

■ **EXAMPLE C.3**

What is the Thévenin equivalent with regard to terminals a–b in the network shown in Fig. C.9?

Solution   The network made ready for SPICE analysis is shown in Fig. C.10. A reproduction of the input file is provided in Fig. C.11 and pertinent extracts from the output file are displayed in Fig. C.12. Observe that the Thévenin equivalent voltage is V(3) which may be read directly. The Thévenin equivalent resistance is the output resistance at V(3) or 3.607 Ω.   ■

■ **EXAMPLE C.4**

What is the Thévenin equivalent resistance with regard to terminals a–b in the network shown in Fig. C.13?

Solution   The network made ready for SPICE analysis is shown in Fig. C.14. A reproduction of the input file is provided in Fig. C.15 and pertinent ex-

FIGURE C.10   Network for SPICE Example C.3 made ready for SPICE Analysis

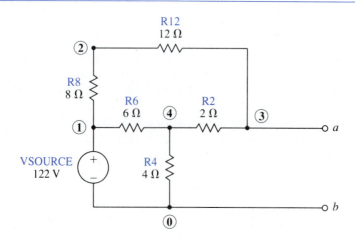

```
SPICE EXAMPLE APPENDIX C NUMBER THREE
*********************************************
*LIST THE COMPONENTS FIRST
*********************************************
R2        4        3        2
R4        4        0        4
R6        1        4        6
R8        1        2        8
R12       2        3        12
*********************************************
*THEN THE SINGLE VOLTAGE SOURCE
*********************************************
VSOURCE   1        0        DC       122
*********************************************
*A .TF STATEMENT IS NEEDED AND DO NOT FORGET
*THE .END STATEMENT
*********************************************
.TF       V(3)     VSOURCE
.END
```

tracts from the output file are displayed in Fig. C.16. The Thévenin equivalent resistance is the output resistance at V(4) or 10.31 Ω.

Two additional examples demonstrating the use of the modifications to the simple dc analyses are presented in Section 3.9. The first of these considers a sensitivity analysis.

```
SPICE EXAMPLE APPENDIX C NUMBER THREE

****     SMALL SIGNAL BIAS SOLUTION       TEMPERATURE =   27.000 DEG C


*************************************************************************


NODE   VOLTAGE     NODE   VOLTAGE     NODE   VOLTAGE     NODE   VOLTAGE

(   1)  122.0000  (   2)   98.0000  (   3)   62.0000  (   4)   56.0000


     VOLTAGE SOURCE CURRENTS
     NAME           CURRENT

     VSOURCE       -1.400E+01

     TOTAL POWER DISSIPATION   1.71E+03   WATTS

****     SMALL-SIGNAL CHARACTERISTICS

     V(3)/VSOURCE =   5.082E-01

     INPUT RESISTANCE AT VSOURCE =   8.714E+00

     OUTPUT RESISTANCE AT V(3) =   3.607E+00


        JOB CONCLUDED
```

FIGURE C.13   Network for SPICE Example C.4

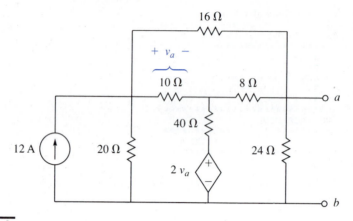

FIGURE C.14   Network for SPICE Example C.4 made ready for SPICE Analysis

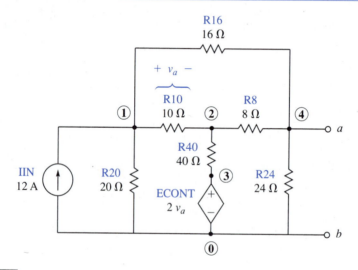

FIGURE C.15   Data statements for the network in Fig. C.14

```
SPICE EXAMPLE APPENDIX C NUMBER FOUR
*****************************************************
*LIST THE COMPONENTS FIRST
*****************************************************
R8          2          4          8
R10         1          2          10
R16         1          4          16
R20         1          0          20
R24         4          0          24
R40         2          3          40
*****************************************************
*THEN THE SINGLE CURRENT SOURCE
*****************************************************
IIN         0          1          DC          12
*****************************************************
*FINALLY, LIST THE VOLTAGE-CONTROLLED VOLTAGE SOURCE
*****************************************************
ECONT       3          0          1          2          2
*****************************************************
*A .TF STATEMENT IS NEEDED AND DO NOT FORGET
*THE .END STATEMENT
*****************************************************
.TF         V(4)       IIN
.END
```

Pertinent extracts from the SPICE output file for the network in Fig. C.14

FIGURE C.16

```
SPICE EXAMPLE APPENDIX C NUMBER FOUR


****     SMALL SIGNAL BIAS SOLUTION        TEMPERATURE =   27.000 DEG C


**************************************************************************


 NODE    VOLTAGE      NODE   VOLTAGE      NODE   VOLTAGE      NODE   VOLTAGE


 (   1)  134.8800  (    2)  107.1100  (    3)   55.5370  (    4)   95.2070



    VOLTAGE SOURCE CURRENTS
    NAME            CURRENT


    TOTAL POWER DISSIPATION    0.00E+00  WATTS




****     SMALL-SIGNAL CHARACTERISTICS

    V(4)/IIN =   7.934E+00

    INPUT RESISTANCE AT IIN =   1.124E+01

    OUTPUT RESISTANCE AT V(4) =   1.031E+01


        JOB CONCLUDED
```

TRANSIENT ANALYSES

SECTION C.6

C.6.1 The .TRAN Statement

The .TRAN statement takes the form

$$.TRAN \quad TSTEP \quad \langle TEND \quad TBEG \quad TMAX \quad UIC \rangle$$

Here, TSTEP is the print or plot interval, and TEND specifies the time at which the analysis concludes. Care should be exercised in the use of TEND because the SPICE default limit for the number of points to be printed or plotted is 201. Thus, a specification of TSTEP = 2 ms and TEND = 500 ms involves 251 output data points. This situation can, of course, be corrected.

The specification of TBEG is optional and provides the time at which printing or plotting begins. If TBEG is not indicated, printing or plotting will automatically commence at $t = 0$, where all transient analyses begin. The use of TBEG avoids unwanted printed or plotted output.

The optional TMAX entry is the maximum step size to be used by SPICE in performing the computations, and if TMAX does not appear, the default is to the

smaller of either TSTEP or (TEND − TBEG)/50. For example, if TMAX does not
appear and TSTEP = 10 ms, TBEG = 10 ms, and TEND = 400 ms, then because
(400 − 10)/50 = 7.8 ms, which is smaller than TSTEP = 10 ms, the program defaults
to a step size of 7.8 ms. Thus, if a maximum step size of 2 ms is required, it should
be included in the .TRAN statement.

The entry UIC means "use initial conditions," and its use, although optional, is
recommended. When it is used, the operating point is not computed before the transient analysis begins, and SPICE will use the initial conditions listed in each inductor
and capacitor specification. For example,

$$\text{.TRAN} \quad \text{1M} \quad \text{100M} \quad \text{UIC}$$

used in a transient analysis containing a single 20-mH inductor carrying an initial
current of 10 mA and a single 40-μF capacitor with an initial voltage of 8 V across
its terminals will require specifications of L and C as

$$\text{LTRANEX} \quad 1 \quad 3 \quad \text{20M} \quad \text{IC}=\text{10M}$$
$$\text{CTRANEX} \quad 4 \quad 7 \quad \text{40U} \quad \text{IC}=8$$

Here, care must be exercised to ensure the correct direction of initial current flow
and initial voltage polarity.

C.6.2 Time-Varying Source Functions

Transient analysis with SPICE is enhanced through the use of five time-varying
source functions. Four of them are shown in Fig. C.17. All time-varying source functions are used in conjunction with independent voltage or current source statements.

The Periodic Pulse (PULSE)   The periodic pulse, shown with its nomenclature in Fig.
C.17a, is specified by the input sequence

$$\text{PULSE (VL} \quad \text{VH} \quad \text{TD} \quad \text{TR} \quad \text{TF} \quad \text{WIDTH} \quad \text{TPER)}$$

where the nomenclature is defined as follows:

Symbol	Parameter	Default Value	Units
VL	Initial value	None	V or A
VH	Maximum value	None	V or A
TD	Delay time	0	s
TR	Rise time	TSTEP	s
TF	Fall time	TEND	s
WIDTH	Pulse width	TEND	s
TPER	Period	TSTEP	s

For example,

$$\text{VIN} \quad 10 \quad 11 \quad \text{PULSE(2} \quad 4 \quad 0 \quad \text{2M} \quad \text{2M} \quad \text{6M} \quad \text{10M)}$$

describes a trapezoidal voltage pulse between nodes 10 and 11 with a minimum value
of 2 V, a maximum value of 4 V, no delay time, a 2-ms rise time, a 2-ms fall time, a
6-ms pulse width, and a 10-ms period. The statement

$$\text{ISOURCE} \quad 3 \quad 7 \quad \text{PULSE(0} \quad \text{80M} \quad 0 \quad 0 \quad 0 \quad \text{6U} \quad \text{8U)}$$

Four time-varying source functions: (a) the periodic pulse (PULSE), (b) the exponential function (EXP), (c) the damped sinusoidal function (SIN) and (d) the piecewise linear function (PWL)

FIGURE C.17

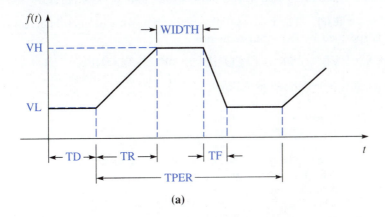

(a)

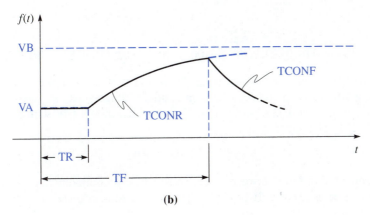

(b)

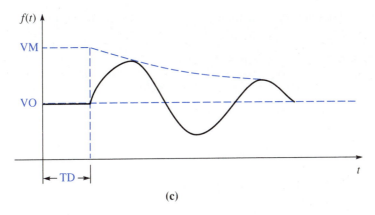

(c)

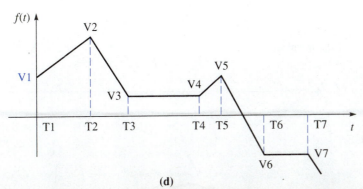

(d)

describes a rectangular current pulse between nodes 3 and 7 with a minimum value of 0 A, a maximum value of 80 mA, a 6-μs pulse width, and an 8-μs period.

The Exponential Function (EXP)   The exponential function, shown with its nomenclature in Fig. C.17b, is specified by the input sequence

$$\text{EXP(VA} \quad \text{VB} \quad \text{TR} \quad \text{TCONR} \quad \text{TF} \quad \text{TCONF)}$$

where the nomenclature is defined as follows:

Symbol	Parameter	Default Value	Units
VA	Initial value	None	V or A
VB	Maximum value	None	V or A
TR	Rise delay time	0	s
TCONR	Rise time constant	TSTEP	s
TF	Fall delay time	TD + TSTEP	s
TCONF	Fall time constant	TSTEP	s

For example,

$$\text{VIN} \quad 10 \quad 11 \quad \text{EXP(20} \quad 100 \quad 0 \quad .02 \quad .072 \quad .01625)$$

describes an exponential voltage between nodes 10 and 11 with a minimum value of 20 V and a maximum value of 100 V. The exponential voltage starts at $t = 0$ and rises with a time constant of 0.02 s until $t = 0.072$ s, at which time it falls with a time constant of 0.01625 s. The statement

$$\text{ISOURCE} \quad 3 \quad 7 \quad \text{EXP(0} \quad \text{20M} \quad .02 \quad .1 \quad .08 \quad .2)$$

describes an exponential current between nodes 3 and 7 with a minimum value of 0 V and a maximum value of 20 mA. It begins its rise with a time constant of 0.1 s at $t = 0.02$ s. It rises until $t = 0.08$ s, when it begins its fall with a time constant of 0.2 s.

The Damped Sinusoidal Function (SIN)   The damped sinusoid, which, in the time domain, is represented by

$$v(t) = V_o + V_m e^{-\alpha(t - T_d)} \sin[\omega_d(t - T_d) - \phi]$$

is shown with its nomenclature in Fig. C.17c. It is specified by the input sequence

$$\text{SIN(VO} \quad \text{VM} \quad \text{FREQ} \quad \text{TD} \quad \text{ALPHA} \quad \text{PHI)}$$

where the nomenclature is defined as follows:

Symbol	Parameter	Default Value	Units
VO	Initial value	None	V or A
VM	Undamped amplitude	None	V or A
FREQ	Frequency	1/TEND	Hz
TD	Delay time	0	s
ALPHA	Damping value	0	1/s
PHI	Phase	0	Degrees

For example,

$$\text{VIN} \quad 10 \quad 11 \quad \text{SIN(2} \quad 10 \quad 54 \quad \text{20M} \quad .04 \quad -36.87)$$

describes a damped sinusoidal voltage between nodes 10 and 11 of the form

$$v(t) = 2 + 10e^{-0.04(t-0.02)} \sin[339.29(t-0.02) - 36.87°]$$

Here, the damped angular frequency is $2\pi(54) = 339.29$ rad/s, and it is observed that frequencies must always be specified in hertz.

The Piecewise Linear Function (PWL)   The piecewise linear waveform, shown with its nomenclature in Fig. C.17d, is specified by the input sequence

PWL(T1   V1   T2   V2   T3   V3 $\cdots$ TN   VN)

where the nomenclature is defined as follows:

Symbol	Parameter	Default Value	Units
TN	Time at beginning of interval	None	s
VN	Value at beginning of interval	None	V or A

For example, the periodic trapezoidal pulse shown in Fig. C.18a is represented by the data statement

VIN   10   11   PULSE(0   4   0   2M   2M   6M   10M)

For a single, nonperiodic trapezoidal pulse, as shown in Fig. C.18b, the data statement would be

VIN   10   11   PWL(0   2   .002   4   8M   4   10M   2)

Trapezoidal pulses: (a) periodic and (b) nonperiodic

FIGURE C.18

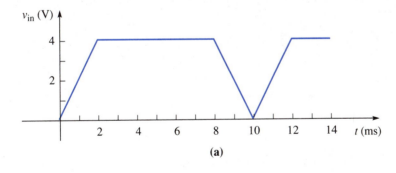

(a)

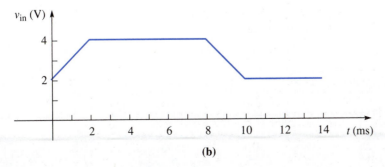

(b)

FIGURE C.19   Network for SPICE Example C.5

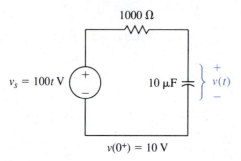

C.6.3 Examples

■ **EXAMPLE C.5**

The network in Fig. C.19 is excited by a voltage ramp at $t = 0$ when the voltage across the capacitor is 10 V. Plot $v(t)$ from $0 < t < 50$ ms.

Solution   The network made ready for SPICE analysis is shown in Fig. C.20. A reproduction of the input file is provided in Fig. C.21 and pertinent extracts from the output file are displayed in Fig. C.22. Notice that, after several time

FIGURE C.20   Network for SPICE Example C.5 made ready for SPICE Analysis

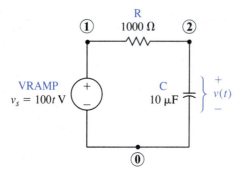

FIGURE C.21   Data statements for the network in Fig. C.20

```
SPICE EXAMPLE APPENDIX C NUMBER FIVE
******************************************************
*THERE ARE JUST TWO COMPONENTS,
******************************************************
R          1          2          1000
C          2          0          10E-6      IC=10
******************************************************
*AND ONE SOURCE, THE VOLTAGE RAMP,
******************************************************
VRAMP      1          0          PWL(0    0    .06    120)
******************************************************
*THE .TRAN, .PLOT AND .END STATEMENTS ARE REQUIRED.
******************************************************
.TRAN      2M         50M        UIC
.PLOT      TRAN       V(1)       V(2)
.END
```

Pertinent extracts from the SPICE output file for the network in Fig. C.20   **FIGURE C.22**

```
SPICE EXAMPLE APPENDIX C NUMBER FIVE

****     TRANSIENT ANALYSIS           TEMPERATURE =   27.000 DEG C


**********************************************************************

LEGEND:

*: V(1)
+: V(2)

 TIME         V(1)
 (*)--------    0.0000E+00   5.0000E+01   1.0000E+02   1.5000E+02   2.0000E+02
 (+)--------   -5.0000E+01   0.0000E+00   5.0000E+01   1.0000E+02   1.5000E+02

           - - - - - - - - - - - - - - - - - - - - - - - - - - - - - - - -
0.000E+00  0.000E+00  *             .    +        .           .           .
2.000E-03  4.000E+00  .*            .    +        .           .           .
4.000E-03  8.000E+00  .  *          .    +        .           .           .
6.000E-03  1.200E+01  .    *        .    +        .           .           .
8.000E-03  1.600E+01  .      *      .    +        .           .           .
1.000E-02  2.000E+01  .        *    .   +         .           .           .
1.200E-02  2.400E+01  .       *     .   +         .           .           .
1.400E-02  2.800E+01  .        *    .  +          .           .           .
1.600E-02  3.200E+01  .         *   .    +        .           .           .
1.800E-02  3.600E+01  .          *  .    +        .           .           .
2.000E-02  4.000E+01  .           * .   +         .           .           .
2.200E-02  4.400E+01  .          *  .    +        .           .           .
2.400E-02  4.800E+01  .           *.     +        .           .           .
2.600E-02  5.200E+01  .           .*      +       .           .           .
2.800E-02  5.600E+01  .           . *      +      .           .           .
3.000E-02  6.000E+01  .           .  *      + .    .           .           .
3.200E-02  6.400E+01  .           .   *      +.    .           .           .
3.400E-02  6.800E+01  .           .    *      +    .           .           .
3.600E-02  7.200E+01  .           .     *    .+    .           .           .
3.800E-02  7.600E+01  .           .      *    . +  .           .           .
4.000E-02  8.000E+01  .           .       *   .  + .           .           .
4.200E-02  8.400E+01  .           .        *  .    +           .           .
4.400E-02  8.800E+01  .           .         * .     +          .           .
4.600E-02  9.200E+01  .           .          *.      +         .           .
4.800E-02  9.600E+01  .           .          *.       +        .           .
5.000E-02  1.000E+02  .           .            *       +       .           .
           - - - - - - - - - - - - - - - - - - - - - - - - - - - - - - - -
```

constants, the capacitor voltage lags the input voltage ramp by one time constant (0.01 s).

A detail of the time period from $0 < t < 2$ ms is obtained using the input file in Fig. C.23 and is shown in Fig. C.24. ■

Data statements for the detailed output file for the network in Fig. C.20   **FIGURE C.23**

```
      SPICE EXAMPLE APPENDIX C NUMBER FIVE (FRONT END)
      ***************************************************
      *THERE ARE JUST TWO COMPONENTS,
      ***************************************************
      R         1        2        1000
      C         2        0        10E-6     IC=10
      ***************************************************
      *AND ONE SOURCE, THE VOLTAGE RAMP,
      ***************************************************
      VRAMP     1        0        PWL(0     0    .06     120)
      ***************************************************
      *THE .TRAN, .PLOT AND .END STATEMENTS ARE REQUIRED.
      ***************************************************
      .TRAN    .1M      2M        UIC
      .PLOT    TRAN     V(1)      V(2)
      .END
```

```
SPICE EXAMPLE APPENDIX C NUMBER FIVE (FRONT END)


****     TRANSIENT ANALYSIS                TEMPERATURE =   27.000 DEG C


*********************************************************************


LEGEND:

*: V(1)
+: V(2)

  TIME        V(1)
(*)--------     0.0000E+00   2.0000E+00   4.0000E+00   6.0000E+00   8.0000E+00
(+)--------     8.5000E+00   9.0000E+00   9.5000E+00   1.0000E+01   1.0500E+01

 0.000E+00    0.000E+00 * - - - - - - - . - - - - - . - - - - - - + - - - - - -
 1.000E-04    2.000E-01 .*          .          .          +  .
 2.000E-04    4.000E-01 .   *       .          .       +     .
 3.000E-04    6.000E-01 .      *    .          .    +        .
 4.000E-04    8.000E-01 .       *   .          . +           .
 5.000E-04    1.000E+00 .        *  .          .+            .
 6.000E-04    1.200E+00 .         * .       +. .             .
 7.000E-04    1.400E+00 .          *.      + .               .
 8.000E-04    1.600E+00 .          .*    +   .               .
 9.000E-04    1.800E+00 .          *.  +     .               .
 1.000E-03    2.000E+00 .          * +       .               .
 1.100E-03    2.200E+00 .         .*+        .               .
 1.200E-03    2.400E+00 .         + *        .               .
 1.300E-03    2.600E+00 .       +. .  *      .               .
 1.400E-03    2.800E+00 .     +    . .  *    .               .
 1.500E-03    3.000E+00 .    +     .      *  .               .
 1.600E-03    3.200E+00 .   +      .       * .               .
 1.700E-03    3.400E+00 .    +     .       * .               .
 1.800E-03    3.600E+00 .   +      .        *.               .
 1.900E-03    3.800E+00 . +        .        *.               .
 2.000E-03    4.000E+00 . +        .          *             .
                        - - - - - . - - - - - . - - - - - - . - - - - - -


JOB CONCLUDED
```

Additional examples that demonstrate the use of SPICE in transient analysis may be found in Sections 6.12 and 7.8.

SECTION C.7   THE OPERATIONAL AMPLIFIER

C.7.1 Modeling the Operational Amplifier

The operational amplifier of Fig. C.25a can be represented as a voltage-controlled voltage source; but as shown in Fig. C.25c (which also indicates the node identifiers), the gain A and the input resistance and output resistance RIN and ROUT must be specified. This takes three data statements, and for an ideal op-amp, A must be given a very high negative number, RIN a very high positive number, and ROUT a very

(a) An operational amplifier showing the identifiers for the data statement, (b) an example of an op-amp network, and (c) the network made ready for SPICE analysis

FIGURE C.25

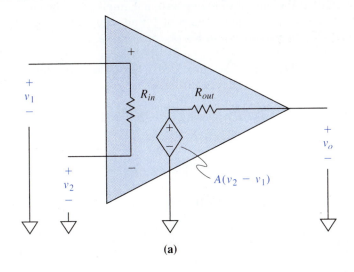

(a)

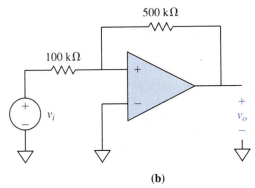

(b)

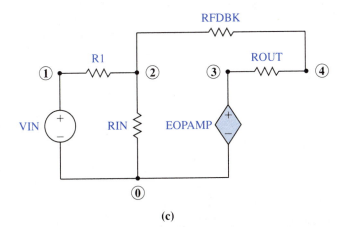

(c)

low positive number. For the identifiers in Fig. C.25c, the data statement for the voltage-controlled voltage source will take the form

EOPAMP   N1   N2   NPLUS   NMINUS   A

C.7.2 Example

■ EXAMPLE C.6

Determine the voltage at the output of the operational amplifier in the configuration of Fig. C.25b with an input voltage of 1 Volt using the network made ready for SPICE analysis shown in Fig. C.25c.

Solution   A reproduction of the input file is provided in Fig. C.26 and pertinent extracts from the output file are displayed in Fig. C.27.   ■

Additional examples of op-amp analysis using SPICE may be found in Section 10.10.

FIGURE C.26   Data statements for the network in Fig. C.25c (Example C.6)

```
SPICE EXAMPLE APPENDIX C NUMBER SIX
***************************************************
*FIRST THE OP-AMP ITSELF
***************************************************
RIN         2         0         1MEG
ROUT        3         4         50
EOPMAP      3         0         2         0         -1E6
***************************************************
*THEN THE BALANCE OF THE OP-AMP NETWORK
***************************************************
R1          1         2         100K
RFDBK       2         4         500K
VIN         1         0         DC        1
***************************************************
*DO NOT FORGET THE .END STATEMENT
***************************************************
.END
```

FIGURE C.27   Pertinent extracts from the SPICE output file for the network in Fig. C.25c

```
****      SMALL SIGNAL BIAS SOLUTION        TEMPERATURE =    27.000 DEG C


************************************************************************************


NODE    VOLTAGE     NODE    VOLTAGE     NODE    VOLTAGE     NODE    VOLTAGE

(    1)    1.0000  (    2) 5.000E-06  (    3)   -5.0005  (    4)   -5.0000


      VOLTAGE SOURCE CURRENTS
      NAME           CURRENT

      VIN           -1.000E-05

      TOTAL POWER DISSIPATION   1.00E-05  WATTS


          JOB CONCLUDED
```

AC ANALYSIS

AC analysis using SPICE requires the use of an .AC control statement, which can take any of three forms:

.AC	LIN	NPOINTS	FBEG	FEND
.AC	DEC	NDEC	FBEG	FEND
.AC	OCT	NOCT	FBEG	FEND

In all three cases, FBEG and FEND are the extremes of the frequency interval (the beginning and the end), and the frequencies must be specified in hertz. The designations LIN, DEC, and OCT are used to obtain linear, decade, and octave frequency variations. The number of points in the LIN variation is used to obtain the frequency increment, in accordance with

$$\Delta f = \frac{\text{FEND} - \text{FBEG}}{\text{NPOINTS} - 1}$$

In the DEC variation, NDEC is the number of points per decade, and the frequencies are determined from the relationship

$$f_k = (\text{FBEG})10^{k/\text{NDEC}}$$

A similar computational procedure applies to the OCT variation, where

$$f_k = (\text{FBEG})2^{k/\text{NOCT}}$$

An ac analysis at a single frequency requires the use of the .AC LIN control statement, with NPOINTS = 1 and FBEG = FEND = f, the frequency of interest. In this case, a .PRINT statement is also required to provide the proper output.

Both independent voltage and current sources require some additional considerations, because the sources must be specified with both magnitude and phase. An example is

VSOURCE1   4   0   AC   100 -36.87

to indicate a voltage source between node 4 and ground. The voltage source is of the form

$$v_s(t) = 100 \cos(377t - 36.87°)$$

But if one wishes to obtain the analysis at the single frequency of 60 Hz ($\omega = 377$ rad/s) without scanning, the statement

.AC   LIN   1   60   60

is also required.

For the independent current source between nodes 6 and 5,

$$i_s(t) = 8 \cos 2513t$$

two statements are needed. They are

INPUT3   6   5   AC   8   0

.AC   LIN   1   400   400

because with $f = 400$ Hz, the angular velocity will be $\omega = 2\pi(400) = 2513$ rad/s. Print statements take the form

.PRINT   AC   V1X(N1,N2) V2X(N1,N2) V3X(N1,N2) $\cdots$

where N1 and N2 are the nodes of interest and where the letters M, P, R, I, and DB to designate magnitude, phase, real part, imaginary part, and decibels, respectively, can be used in place of X. If N2 = 0 for the datum or ground node, it may be omitted.

Current values are obtained by using a voltage source as an ammeter and a print statement that looks like this:

.PRINT   AC   VM(6,2)   VP(6,2)   IR(VAMP)   II(VAMP)

This statement will print the magnitude and phase of the voltage in the branch or branches between nodes 6 and 2 and the real and imaginary parts of the currents flowing through the voltage source, VAMP.

■ **EXAMPLE C.7**

Express the current indicated i and the voltage indicated by v in Fig. C.28 in rectangular form.

Solution   The network made ready for SPICE analysis is shown in Fig. C.29. A reproduction of the input file is provided in Fig. C.30 and pertinent extracts from the output file are displayed in Fig. C.31. Notice that in order to provide a dc path to ground for node-6, a 100 megohm resistor is placed parallel with the capacitor between nodes-5 and -6. The effect of this very large resistor upon the network is negligible.   ■

FIGURE C.28   Network for SPICE Example C.7

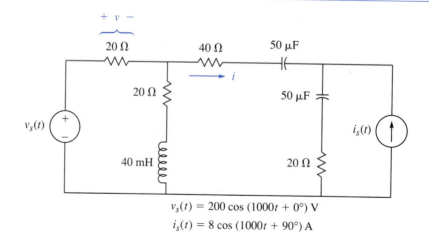

$v_s(t) = 200 \cos (1000t + 0°)$ V

$i_s(t) = 8 \cos (1000t + 90°)$ A

FIGURE C.29

Network for SPICE Example C.7 made ready for SPICE Analysis

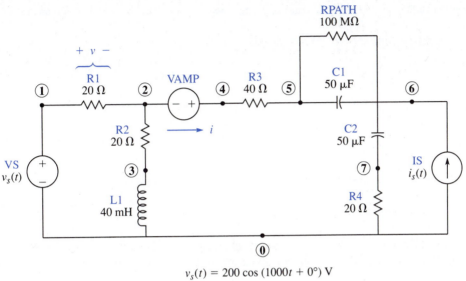

$$v_s(t) = 200 \cos (1000t + 0°) \text{ V}$$

$$i_s(t) = 8 \cos (1000t + 90°) \text{ A}$$

FIGURE C.30

Data statements for the network in Fig. C.29

```
SPICE EXAMPLE APPENDIX C NUMBER SEVEN
***********************************************
*LIST THE COMPONENTS FIRST
***********************************************
R1        1        2        20
R2        2        3        20
L1        3        0        40M
R3        4        5        40
C1        5        6        50UF
C2        6        7        50UF
R4        7        0        20
***********************************************
*NODE 6 DOES NOT HAVE A DC PATH TO GROUND.
*THIS PROBLEM IS SOLVED BY PUTTING A 100 MEG
*RESISTOR IN PARALLEL WITH C1.
***********************************************
RPATH     5        6        100E6
***********************************************
*HERE ARE THE VOLTAGE AND CURRENT SOURCES
***********************************************
VS        1        0        AC       200      0
IS        0        6        AC       8        90
***********************************************
*AN ADDITIONAL VOLTAGE SOURCE IS NEEDED TO
*MEASURE THE CURRENT IN THE 40 OHM RESISTOR.
***********************************************
VAMP      2        4        AC       0        0
***********************************************
*FINALLY, THE .AC, .PRINT AND .END STATEMENTS
***********************************************
.AC       LIN      1        159.15      159.15
.PRINT    AC  VR(1,2) VI(1,2) IR(VAMP) II(VAMP)
.END
```

FIGURE C.31
Pertinent extracts from the SPICE output file for the network in Fig. C.29

```
******* 10/01/   ******* Evaluation PSpice (January 19   ) ******* 03:03:13 ***

SPICE EXAMPLE APPENDIX C NUMBER SEVEN

****      AC ANALYSIS                              TEMPERATURE =    27.000 DEG C

************************************************************************

   FREQ        VR(1,2)      VI(1,2)       IR(VAMP)      II(VAMP)

  1.592E+02   6.307E+01  -6.657E+01    4.525E-01  -1.256E+00

       JOB CONCLUDED
```

Additional examples of ac analyses using SPICE may be found in Section 10.10. Examples of the frequency scan feature of SPICE are found in Sections 13.7 and 20.12.

SECTION C.9   MUTUAL INDUCTANCE

One of the types of network elements displayed in Table C.1 is a mutual coupling, which is called for by the designator KXXXXXXX. This designator can be used in a data statement of the form

KMUTUAL   LX   LY   COEFCOUP

where LX and LY are the designators of the two inductors to which the coupling applies and where COEFCOUP is the coefficient of coupling,

$$k = \frac{M}{\sqrt{L_x L_y}} \qquad (0 \le k \le 1)$$

Of course, the value of the coefficient of coupling is restricted as shown, and the orientation of the coils L_x and L_y is handled in the data statements for LX and LY. For example, assuming that all four nodes in Fig. C.32 have a dc path to ground, the mutual inductance between the pair of coils shown requires these three data statements:

```
LX       5       8      .2
LY      17      22      .8
KXY     LX      LY      .8
```

because

$$k = \frac{0.32}{\sqrt{(0.2)(0.8)}} = 0.8$$

Two mutually coupled inductors.

FIGURE C.32

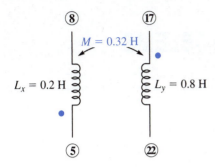

Notice how the orientation of the coils is handled by showing the node order, with the node bearing the dot listed first.

Examples of the use of SPICE in ac analysis with the presence of mutual elements may be found in Section 14.10.

BODE PLOTS

SECTION C.10

SPICE performs frequency response analysis by means of the scan feature in the .AC control statement. It does not specifically generate a Bode asymptotic plot. Examples of frequency response analysis are found in Sections 13.7 and 20.12.

Additional Readings

Bobrow, L.S. *Elementary Linear Circuit Analysis.* 2d ed. New York: Holt, Rinehart and Winston, 1987, pp. 678–695.

Irwin, J.D. *Basic Engineering Circuit Analysis.* 3d ed. New York: Macmillan, 1989, pp. 147–168.

Johnson, D.E., J.L. Hilburn, and J.R. Johnson. *Basic Electric Circuit Analyis.* 4th ed. Englewood Cliffs, NJ.: Prentice-Hall, 1989, pp. 646–656.

Madhu, S. *Linear Circuit Analysis.* Englewood Cliffs, N.J.: Prentice-Hall, 1988, pp. 797–809.

Nilsson, J.W. *Electric Circuits.* 3d ed. Reading, Mass.: Addison-Wesley, 1990, supplement (inside back cover).

Paul, C.R. *Analysis of Linear Circuits.* New York: McGraw-Hill, 1989, pp. 103–116.

Tuinenga, P.W. *SPICE A Guide to Circuit Simulation and Analysis Using PSPICE*, Englewood Cliffs, N.J.: Prentice-Hall, 1988.

D

ANSWERS TO
ODD NUMBERED PROBLEMS

Chapter 1

1.1 1.248×10^{21} electrons
1.3 32.04 A
1.5 5.44 mJ
1.7 400 J
1.9 704 V/m
1.11 17.90×10^6 J
1.13 both
1.15 neither
1.17 $8.11 \times 10^{-4}\ \Omega$
1.19 123.5 m
1.21 $-192 \sin 400t$ A
1.23 $q = 0.004 \cos 500t$ C $\qquad i = -2 \sin 500t$ A
$p = -100 \sin 1000t$ W $\qquad w = 0.00$ J

1.25 $v_L(t)$, V

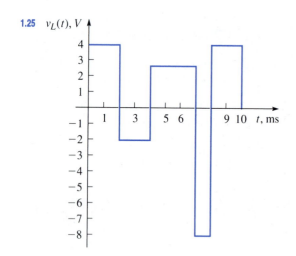

1.27 $p_R = 12.8$ W $\qquad p_C = 8.0$ W
$p_s = 20.8$ W $\qquad w_R = 34.13$ J
$w_C = 24$ J $\qquad w_s = 58.13$ J
1.29 15 A and 8 Ω
1.31 14 A
1.33 4.09 mJ
1.35 74.91 μJ removed
1.37 4 Ω

Chapter 2

2.1 $i_1 = -7$ A $\qquad i_2 = 6$ A $\qquad i_3 = -3$ A
2.3 $i_1 = 2$ A $\qquad i_2 = 0$ A
$i_3 = 2$ A $\qquad i_4 = -5$ A
2.5 $v_1 = 10$ V $\qquad v_2 = 20$ V $\qquad v_3 = 20$ V
$v_4 = 2$ V $\qquad v_5 = -2$ V $\qquad v_6 = 6$ V
$v_7 = 12$ V
2.7 $R_1 = 3\ \Omega$ $\qquad R_2 = 6\ \Omega$ $\qquad R_3 = 1\ \Omega$
2.9 $v_2 = 4$ V $\qquad v_3 = 6\ V$
2.11 21 Ω
2.13 48 Ω
2.15 6 Ω
2.17 120 Ω
2.19 (a) 2 H $\qquad$ (b) 4 H $\qquad$ (c) 3 mH
(d) 9.231 mH $\quad$ (e) 0.992 mH
2.21 $i_{12} = 6.25$ A
2.23 $v_4 = 24$ V

2.25

21 Ω

78 V

2.27 $i_3 = 18$ A $\qquad i_4 = 3$ A $\qquad v_{12} = 24$ V
$v_{14} = 14$ V
2.29 $i_9 = 9$ A $\qquad i_{40} = 1.8$ A $\qquad v_7 = 3.15$ V
2.31 $i_5 = 1.25$ A $\quad v_{20} = 100$ V $\quad p_{24} = 9.375$ W
2.33 $i_6 = 2$ A $\qquad i_8 = 9$ A $\qquad v_{12} = 36$ V
$p_{24} = 486$ W

2.35

$15/8\ \Omega$

$10/6\ \Omega$ $\qquad$ $10/6\ \Omega$

2.37 8.0003 Ω

Chapter 3

3.1 $b = 23$ $n = 14$ $\ell = 9$

3.3   Two loops which include branch-3 (node-to-node) are 3-4-8-7-3 and 3-4-9-8-7-3. Two paths from node-1 to node-4 in terms of branch numbers are 1-2-3 and 4-9-10-11-7.

3.5 $j_6 = 3.46$ A $v_3 = 8.56$ V

3.7 $j_8 = 0.457$ A $v_3 = 22.05$ V

3.9 $E = 48$ V

3.11
$$\begin{bmatrix} 14 & -4 & -2 & 0 & 0 \\ -4 & 16 & -6 & 0 & -5 \\ -2 & -6 & 12 & -4 & 0 \\ 0 & 0 & -4 & 20 & -16 \\ 0 & -5 & 0 & -16 & 33 \end{bmatrix} \begin{bmatrix} e_1 \\ e_2 \\ e_3 \\ e_4 \\ e_5 \end{bmatrix} = \begin{bmatrix} -6 \\ 6 \\ 14 \\ -11 \\ 8 \end{bmatrix}$$

3.13 $7\,\Omega$

3.15 $j_4 = 0.59$ A $v_4 = 2.36$ V

3.17 $E = 48$ V

3.19
$$\begin{bmatrix} 32 & -10 & -8 & -2 & 0 \\ -10 & 42 & 0 & -6 & -2 \\ -8 & 0 & 24 & -4 & 0 \\ -2 & -6 & -4 & 22 & -10 \\ 0 & -2 & 0 & -10 & 16 \end{bmatrix} \begin{bmatrix} i_1 \\ i_2 \\ i_3 \\ i_4 \\ i_5 \end{bmatrix} = \begin{bmatrix} 8 \\ -40 \\ 64 \\ 0 \\ 36 \end{bmatrix}$$

3.21 $b = 33$ $n = 13$ $\ell = 16$

3.23 $j_6 = 3.46$ A $v_3 = 8.58$ V

3.25 $j_{16} = 3.71$ A $v_8 = 47.50$ V

3.27 $i_a = -4.19$ A

3.29 $p = 1361$ W

Chapter 4

4.1 $i = 3.42$ A

4.3 $v = -\frac{24}{33}$ V

4.5 $i = 1.64$ A

4.7 $v_s = -468$ V

4.9 $i = 0.718$ A

4.11 $v_T = 57.78$ V $R_T = 600\,\Omega$

4.13 $R = 8\,\Omega$

4.15 $\mathbf{J} = \begin{bmatrix} -8 \\ \frac{8}{3} \\ \frac{16}{3} \\ \frac{16}{3} \end{bmatrix} A; \quad \mathbf{V} = \begin{bmatrix} 16 \\ 16 \\ \frac{32}{3} \\ \frac{16}{3} \end{bmatrix} V$

4.17 $\mathbf{J} = \begin{bmatrix} -0.12 \\ -0.12 \\ -0.24 \\ -0.36 \\ 0.18 \\ 0.18 \\ 0.18 \end{bmatrix} A; \quad \mathbf{V} = \begin{bmatrix} -48 \\ -24 \\ -72 \\ 288 \\ 216 \\ 144 \\ 72 \end{bmatrix} V$

4.19 $i = 1$ A

4.21 $v_{ab} = 24$ V

4.23 $R = 7.63\,\Omega$ $p = 12.71$ W

4.25 $p = 642.2$ W $R = 600\,\Omega$ $p = 2006.9$ W

Chapter 5

5.1 $v(t) = 2r(t) - 2r(t-3) - 3u(t-3) - r(t-5)$
$\quad\quad + r(t-9) - 8u(t-12) - 8u(t-16)$ V

5.3 $v(t) = r(t) - 2r(t-2) + r(t-6) + 2u(t-10)$
$\quad\quad + 2u(t-12) - r(t-12) + r(t-14)$ V

5.5 $v(t) = u(t) + u(t-2) + u(t-4) - u(t-6)$
$\quad\quad - u(t-8) - \frac{3}{2}u(t-10) + \frac{3}{2}r(t-12)$
$\quad\quad + 3u(t-12) + r(t-14) - r(t-16)$
$\quad\quad - 2u(t-16)$ V

5.7 $v(t)$, V

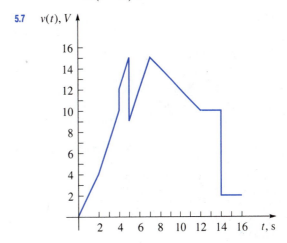

5.9

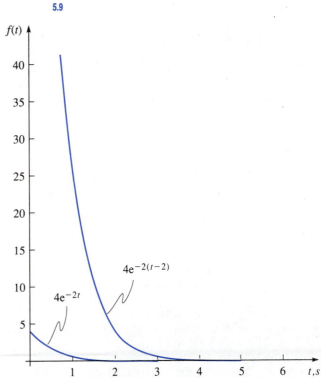

5.11

(a)   (b)

5.13 $q(t = 0)200 \ \mu C$ $T = 0.0025$ s
        $q(t = 0.625$ ms$) = 155.8 \ \mu C$
5.15 $i(t = 0) = 64.67$ mA $t = 265$ ms
5.17 $V = 120$ V $\omega = 160\pi$ rad/s
        $\phi = -1.973$ rad
5.19 $Q = 20 \ \mu C$ $\omega = 125\pi$ rad/s $\phi = \pi$ rad
5.21 $f = 66.65$ Hz $T = 15$ ms
5.23 $i_{av} = 0.8$ A $i_{eff} = 2.45$ A
5.24 $R = 7.63 \ \Omega$ $p = 12.71$ W
5.25 $i_{av} = -0.6$ A $i_{eff} = 1.91$ A

Chapter 6

6.1 $i_R(0^-) = \frac{4}{3}$ A $i_L(0^-) = \frac{4}{3}$ A
        $i_C(0^-) = 0$ A $v_C(0^-) = \frac{8}{3}$ V
        $v_L(0^-) = 0$ V $i_R(0^+) = \frac{4}{3}$ A
        $i_L(0^+) = \frac{4}{3}$ A $i_C(0^+) = 0$ A
        $v_C(0^-) = \frac{8}{3}$ V $v_L(0^+) = -32$ V
        $i'_L(0^+) = -32$ A/s

6.3 $i_{R1}(0^+) = 10$ A $i_L(0^+) = 10$ A
        $i_C(0^+) = 10$ A $i_{R2}(0^+) = 0$ A
        $v_L(0^+) = -80$ V $v_{R1}(0^+) = 40$ V
        $v_C(0^+) = 40$ V $i'_L(0^+) = -40$ A/s

6.5 $i_L(0^-) = 4$ A $v_L(0^-) = 0$ V
        $i_L(0^+) = 4$ A $v_L(0^+) = -6$ V
        $v_C(0^+) = 24$ V $i_R(0^-) = 4$ A
        $v_R(0^-) = 24$ V $i_R(0^+) = 4$ A
        $v_R(0^+) = 24$ V $i_C(0^-) = 0$ A
        $i_C(0^+) = 0$ A $v_C(0^+) = 24$ V
        $v_C(0^-) = 24$ V $i'_L(0^+) = -12$ A/s
        $v'_C(0^+) = 0$ V/s

6.7 $v_N = 11.91e^{-4t}$ V
        $v_F = \frac{3}{34} \cos 16t + \frac{6}{17} \sin 16t$ V
        $v_{ZI} = 12e^{-4t}$ V
        $v_{ZS} = -\frac{3}{34}e^{-4t} + \frac{3}{34} \cos 16t + \frac{6}{17} \sin 16t$ V

6.9 $i_N = 1.56e^{-8t}$ A
        $i_F = \frac{1}{8}t^2 + \frac{15}{32}t + \frac{113}{256}$ A
        $i_{ZI} = 2e^{-8t}$ A
        $i_{ZS} = -0.411e^{-8t} + \frac{1}{8}t^2 + \frac{15}{32}t + \frac{113}{256}$ A

6.11 $v_N = 14.32e^{-50t}$ V
        $v_F = 2.4e^{-40t} + 0.72$ V
        $v_{ZI} = 16e^{-50t}$ V
        $v_{ZS} = -3.12e^{-50t} + 2.4e^{-40t} + 0.72$ V
6.13 $v_N = 19.19e^{-24t}$ V
        $v_F = 0.84 \cos 10t + 2.02 \sin 10t + 0.75t$
                $+ 0.0312$ V
        $v_{ZI} = 20e^{-24t}$ V
        $v_{ZS} = -0.81e^{-24t} + 0.84 \cos 10t + 2.02 \sin 10t$
                $+ 0.75t + 0.0312$ V
6.15 $i_N = 0.189e^{-12t}$ A
        $i_F = 0.5t - 0.042 + 0.231 \cos 8t + 0.154 \sin 8t$ A
        $i_{ZI} = 0$ A
        $i_{ZS} = 0.189e^{-12t} + 0.5t - 0.042 + 0.231 \cos 8t$
                $+ 0.154 \sin 8t$ A
6.17 $v_N = -0.4e^{-200t}$ V
        $v_F = 20te^{-200t} + 0.4$ V
        $v_{ZI} = 0$ V
        $v_{ZS} = -0.4e^{-200t} + 20te^{-200t} + 0.4$ V
6.19 $i(t) = \frac{8}{3}e^{-18t}$ A
6.21 $v(t) = 18e^{-2t}$ V
6.23 $v(t) = 200e^{-1.01t}$ V
6.25 $i(t) = 8e^{-4t} + 8$ A
6.27 $i(t) = 13.167e^{-4t} - 10.67 \cos 2t + 21.33 \sin 2t$
                $+ 10t - 2.5$ A
6.29 $i(t) = -21.75e^{-4t} + 24e^{-t} + 24t^3 - 18t^2 + 9t$
                $- 2.5$ A
6.31 $v(t) = 1.8e^{-0.5t} - 0.2e^{-t} + 0.8t - 1.6$ V
6.33 $v(t) = 0.4 - 0.255e^{-0.5t} - 0.2e^{-2t}$
                $+ 0.0533 \cos 2t + 0.4133 \sin 2t$ V
6.35 $i_{1N}(t) = \frac{1}{3}e^{-(15/16)t}$ A
        $i_{2N}(t) = \frac{2}{3}e^{-(15/16)t}$ A
        $i_{1F}(t) = 0$ A
        $i_{2F}(t) = 0$ A
        $i_{1ZI}(t) = 0$ A
        $i_{2ZI}(t) = 0$ A
        $i_{1ZS}(t) = 12.5e^{-(15/16)t}$ A
        $i_{2ZS}(t) = 25e^{-(15/16)t}$ A
6.37 $t_1 = 56.8$ ms, $t_2 = 36.6$ ms, $t_3 = 11.1$ ms
6.39 $v_N = 30e^{-9t}$ V $v_F = 0$ V
        $v_{ZI} = 30e^{-9t}$ V $v_{ZS} = 0$ V
6.41 $v = 4.757(1 - e^{-0.595t})$ V
6.43 $v = 0.026(1 - e^{-1428.6t})$ V

Chapter 7

7.1   0.1 H
7.3   488.3 μF
7.5   125 Ω
7.7 $i = \frac{9}{4}(e^{-2t} - 6e^{-6t})$ A
7.9 $v = \frac{11}{5}(8e^{-8t} - 3e^{-3t})$ V
7.11 $v = -96te^{-8t}$ V
7.13 $v = 52e^{-6t} - 38e^{-4t}) + 2$ V
7.15 $v = \frac{1}{15}(2592e^{-4t} - 2055e^{-3t} - 387e^{-9t})$ V
7.17 $v = 42e^{-2t} - 36e^{-4t} - 48te^{-2t}$ V
7.19 $i = 6 - 8e^{-t} + 2e^{-2t} - 4te^{-2t}$ A

7.21 $i = \frac{1}{169}[416t - 128$
$+ e^{-2t}(128 \cos 3t + 504 \sin 3t)]$ A

7.23 $v = 25 \cos 10t$ V

Chapter 8

8.1

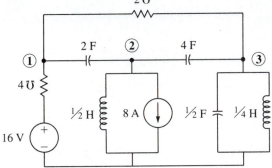

8.3

8.5

8.15 $v_o = (R_2/R_1)(v_{i2} - v_{i1})$ V

8.17 $v_o = 34.29$ V

8.19 $25\ k\Omega$

8.21 The problem statement contains the result.

8.23 -18 V

8.7 (a) $-5, 20\ k\Omega$ (b) $-2, 50\ k\Omega$
       (c) $-0.25, 40\ k\Omega$

8.9 $R_{in} = R_1 = 40\ k\Omega$

8.11 $v_3 = 3$ V

8.13 $C = 5\ \mu F$

8.25

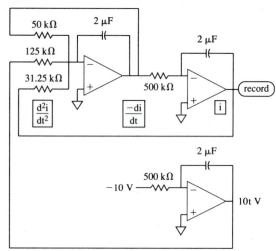

Chapter 9

9.1 $6 - j4$ $7.29\,\underline{/33.69°}$ $2.21e^{j33.69°}$

9.3 $100 - j105$ $145.00\,\underline{/-46.40°}$
    $145.00e^{-j46.40°}$

9.5 $-0.35 - j2.55$ $2.57\,\underline{/-97.82°}$ $2.57e^{-j97.82°}$

9.7 $0.59 + j0.97$ $1.13\,\underline{/58.74°}$ $1.13e^{j58.74°}$

9.9 $-44 - j104$ $112.92\,\underline{/-112.93°}$
    $112.92e^{-j112.93°}$

9.11 $Ae^{-3t}\cos(4t + \phi)$

9.13 Ae^{-2t}

9.15 $A\cos(6t + \phi)$

9.17 $20\ \Omega$

9.19 $80 - j60\ \Omega$

9.21 $150 - j80\ \Omega$

9.23 $F = 136,\ \phi = -118.07°$

9.25 $F = 182,\ \phi = 112.62°$

9.27 $A = -220,\ B = 165$

9.29 $A = -768,\ B = 224$

9.31 $A = -500\sqrt{2},\ B = 500\sqrt{2}$

9.33 $4\sqrt{2}\,\underline{/-135°},\ 4\sqrt{2}\,e^{-j135°},\ -4 - j4$

9.35 $1750\,\underline{/-163.74°},\ 1750e^{-j163.74°}$

9.37 $16.73\cos(377t + 155.27°)\text{A}$

Chapter 10

10.1 $\mathbf{J} = \begin{bmatrix} 8.00\,\underline{/-53.13°} \\ 11.31\,\underline{/171.87°} \\ 8.00\,\underline{/36.87°} \\ 8.00\,\underline{/36.87°} \end{bmatrix} A;$ $\mathbf{V} = \begin{bmatrix} 452.55\,\underline{/81.87°} \\ 452.55\,\underline{/81.87°} \\ 320.00\,\underline{/126.87°} \\ 320.00\,\underline{/36.87°} \end{bmatrix} V$

10.3 $\mathbf{J} = \begin{bmatrix} 8.00\,\underline{/-90°} \\ 13.33\,\underline{/143.13°} \\ 10.67\,\underline{/0°} \\ 10.67\,\underline{/0°} \\ 8.00\,\underline{/90°} \end{bmatrix} A;$ $\mathbf{V} = \begin{bmatrix} 376.86\,\underline{/26.92°} \\ 213.33\,\underline{/53.13°} \\ 128.04\,\underline{/0°} \\ 170.02\,\underline{/90°} \\ 464.00\,\underline{/180°} \end{bmatrix} V$

10.5 $\mathbf{J} = \begin{bmatrix} 358.58\,\underline{/-51.34°} \\ 28.00\sqrt{2}\,\underline{/45°} \\ 350.00\,\underline{/36.87°} \\ 70.00\,\underline{/90°} \\ 70.00\,\underline{/90°} \end{bmatrix} mA;$

$\mathbf{V} = \begin{bmatrix} 19.60\,\underline{/90°} \\ 8.40\sqrt{2}\,\underline{/45°} \\ 14.00\,\underline{/126.87°} \\ 8.40\,\underline{/180°} \\ 11.20\,\underline{/90°} \end{bmatrix} V$

10.7

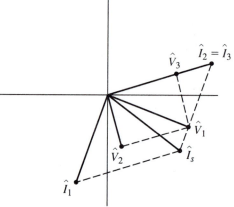

10.9

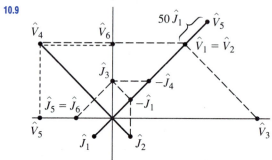

10.11 $\hat{J}_L = 8.00\,\underline{/36.87°}$ A $\hat{V}_C = 452.55\,\underline{/81.87°}$ V

10.13 $\hat{J}_L = 2.00\sqrt{2}\,\underline{/-45°}$ A $\hat{V}_C = 400.00\,\underline{/90°}$ V

10.15 $\hat{I} = 118.63\,\underline{/74.46°}$

10.17 $\hat{J}_L = 8.00\,\underline{/36.87°}$ A $\hat{V}_C = 452.55\,\underline{/81.87°}$ V

10.19 $\hat{J}_L = 2.00\sqrt{2}\,\underline{/-45°}$ A $\hat{V}_C = 400.00\,\underline{/90°}$ V

10.21 $\hat{I}_L = 350\,\underline{/-36.87°}$ mA $\hat{V}_R = 8.4\sqrt{2}\,\underline{/45°}$ V

10.23 $\hat{I} = 116.83\,\underline{/74.46°}$ mA

10.25 $\hat{I}_L = 8.00\,\underline{/36.87°}$ A $\hat{V}_C = 452.55\,\underline{/81.87°}$ V

10.27 $\hat{I}_L = 2\sqrt{2}\,\underline{/-45°}$ A $\hat{V}_C = 400\,\underline{/90°}$ V

10.29 $\hat{I} = 6.25\,\underline{/-157.21°}$ A

10.31 $\hat{V} = 9.79\,\underline{/55.83°}$ V

10.33 $\hat{V} = 1064.3\,\underline{/16.69°}$ V

10.35 $\hat{I} = 8.00\,\underline{/36.87°}$ A

10.37 $\hat{I} = 4\,\underline{/-180°}$ mA

10.39 $\hat{I} = 972.72\underline{/46.85°}$ A

10.41 $Z_{ab} = 24.46 - j0.31$ Ω

Chapter 11

11.1 $P = 103.7$ W $PF = 0.800$

11.3 $P = 321.1$ W $PF = 0.651$

11.5 $C = 20$ μF

11.7 $S = 1557.5\underline{/-1.61°}$ VA

11.9 $P = 187.1$ W

11.11 $j40$ Ω 16,402 VAR $j50$ Ω 58,004 VAR
$-j20$ Ω $-55,398$ VAR

11.13 $S = 5971.4\underline{/35.84°}$ VA

11.15 $S = 2688\sqrt{2}\underline{/45°}$ VA

11.17 $S = 2.159\underline{/-34.72°}$ mVA

11.19 $P = 2520$ W $Q = 2200$ VAR
$|S| = 3345.2$ VA $PF = 0.753$
capactive correction, 1244.2 VAR $C = 2.56$ μF

11.21 $L = 8.20$ H

11.23 $L = 6.37$ mH

11.25 $C = 15.39$ μF

11.27 $R = 25$ Ω

Chapter 12

12.1 $P = 2916$ W

12.3 $P = 2857.6$ W

12.5 $\hat{I}_b = -21 - j12.13$ A

12.7 $\hat{I}_1 = 12 + j9$ A $\hat{I}_2 = 3.93 + j9.20$ A
$\hat{I}_3 = 1.94 - j7.24$ A $\hat{I}_n = -17.87 + j10.95$ A

12.9 $v_{an} = 120.09\cos(377t + 0°)$ V
$v_{bn} = 120.09\cos(377t - 120°)$ V
$v_{cn} = 120.09\cos(377t + 120°)$ V
$v_{ab} = 208\cos(377t + 30°)$ V
$v_{bc} = 208\cos(377t - 90°)$ V
$v_{ca} = 208\cos(377t + 150°)$ V

12.11 $v_{ab} = 208\cos(377t + 0°)$ V
$v_{bc} = 208\cos(377t - 120°)$ V
$v_{ca} = 208\cos(377t + 120°)$ V

12.13 $v_{AN} = 254\cos(377t + 0°)$ V
$v_{BN} = 254\cos(377t - 120°)$ V
$v_{CN} = 254\cos(377t + 120°)$ V
$v_{AB} = 440\cos(377t + 30°)$ V
$v_{BC} = 440\cos(377t - 90°)$ V
$v_{CA} = 440\cos(377t + 150°)$ V
$i_{AN} = 10.16\cos(377t - 36.87°)$ A
$i_{BN} = 10.16\cos(377t - 156.87°)$ A
$i_{CN} = 10.16\cos(377t + 83.13°)$ A

12.15 $v_{AN} = 254\cos(377t + 0°)$ V
$v_{BN} = 254\cos(377t - 120°)$ V
$v_{CN} = 254\cos(377t + 120°)$ V
$v_{AB} = 440\cos(377t + 30°)$ V
$v_{BC} = 440\cos(377t - 90°)$ V
$v_{CA} = 440\cos(377t + 150°)$ V
$i_{AN} = 2.89\cos(377t + 0°)$ A
$i_{BN} = 10.16\cos(377t + 120°)$ A
$i_{CN} = 10.16\cos(377t - 120°)$ A

12.17 $P = 6193.5$ W

12.19 $P = 2202.2$ W

12.21 $P = 1536.4$ W

12.23 $P = 1105.9$ W

12.25 $P = 2592$ W

12.27 $P = 1536.4$ W

12.29 $P = 1105.9$ W

12.31 $P = 2592$ W

12.33 $P = 2768$ W

12.35 $P = 2190$ W

12.37 $P = 1083.9$ W

12.39 $P = 10919.3$ W

Chapter 13

13.1 $\omega_o = \sqrt{\dfrac{1}{LC} - \dfrac{1}{(RC)^2}}$

13.3 $\omega_o = \sqrt{\dfrac{1}{LC - (RC)^2}}$

13.5 1.655 mH

13.7 $-j108.35$ Ω

13.9 $Z_{IN} = 2 + j0.5$ Ω $|\hat{I}| = 58.21$ A
$|\hat{V}_C| = 145.52$ V   89.44 Hz

13.11 $R = 94.2$ $M\Omega$ $C = 0.169$ pF
$Z = 94.2$ $M\Omega$ new $Z = 75.4$ $M\Omega$

13.13 $R = 160$ Ω $L = 10$ μH
$f_{mL} = 317.1$ Hz $I_L = 160$ mA

13.15 $r = 20$ Ω $R' = 100$ Ω $L = 160$ mH

13.17 $R = 25.72$ Ω $L = 202.6$ μH
$Q_{so} = 24.75$ $\beta = 1.2695 \times 10^6$ rad/s

13.19 $\omega_o = 395,285$ rad/s $V_C/V = 3162.3$
$Q_{so} = 3162.3$ $\beta = 125$ rad/s
$\omega_{mC} = 395,285$ rad/s $V_C = 379,474$ V

13.21 $\omega_o = 223,607$ rad/s $\beta = 4000$ rad/s
$\omega_1 = 221,616$ rad/s $\omega_2 = 225,616$ rad/s

13.23 $\omega_o = 99,920$ rad/s $R = 100$ Ω
$Q_{so} = 12.49$ $L = 12.5$ mH
$C = 8.01$ nF

13.25 $\omega_o = 800,000$ rad/s $R = 1250$ Ω
$Q_{so} = 31.25$ $L = 50$ μH
$C = 31.35$ nF $\beta = 25,600$ rad/s
$\omega_1 = 787,302$ rad/s $\omega_2 = 812,902$ rad/s
$I_s = 40$ mA

13.27 $Z = 10\sqrt{2}\underline{/45°}$ Ω

13.29 $Z = R = 4$ Ω at ω_2, $Z = 4\sqrt{2}\underline{/\ 45°}$ Ω

13.31 $Z = R = 1250$ Ω at ω_1, $Z = 1250\underline{/-0.01°}$ Ω

Chapter 14

14.1 $M = \frac{1}{4}(L_{sa} - L_{so})$H

14.3 $L_{eq} = 14.63$ H

14.5 6.34 J

14.7 $\hat{I}_C = 5.33\underline{/-157.28°}$ A

14.9 $\hat{I}_C = 7.81\underline{/-22.40°}$ A

14.11 $a = 5$, $V_2 = 24$ V

14.13 $I_1 = 41.67$ A, $I_2 = 166.67$ A

14.15 $v_s(t) = 2500\cos 377t$ V

14.17 $Z_p = 120 + j320 \ \Omega$ $\qquad$ $Z_s = 1000 + j1000 \ \Omega$
$Z_r = 115.2 - j115.2 \ \Omega$ $\quad$ $Z_{in} = 235.2 + j204.8 \ \Omega$
$\hat{I}_1 = 0.962 \underline{/-41.05°}$ $\qquad$ $\hat{I}_2 = 0.326 \underline{/3.95°}$
$V_{in} = 300 \underline{/0°} \ V$ $\qquad\quad$ $V_o = 216.8 \underline{/28.97°}$
$P_o = 63.77 \ W$

14.19 $Z_p = 560 + j200 \ \Omega$
$Z_s = 1500 + j1200 \ \Omega$
$Z_r = 585.36 - j468.29 \ \Omega$
$Z_{in} = 1145.36 + j2731.71 \ \Omega$
$V_{in} = 480 \underline{/0°} \ V$
$V_o = 209.14 \underline{/\ 61.41°} \ V$
$\hat{I}_1 = 0.162 \underline{/-67.25°} \ A$
$\hat{I}_2 = 0.259 \underline{/28.97°} \ A$
$P_o = 46.96 \ W$

14.21 The problem requires a proof.

14.23 either $a = 2.50$ or $a = 1.00$

14.25 28.88 W

14.27 $VR = 3.30\%, \ \eta = 89.21\%$

14.29 $VR = 2.76\%, \ \eta = 96.79\%$

14.31 $VR = 4.71\%, \ \eta = 92.33\%$

14.33 $VR = 3.27\%, \ \eta = 94.17\%$

14.35 $C = 954.9 \ pF, \ L = 0.955 \ \mu H$

14.37 $C = 1.378 \ nF, \ L = 0.955 \ mH$

14.39 $C_1 = C_2 = 63.71 \ pF, \ L_3 = 3.26 \ mH$

Chapter 15

15.1 $F(s) = 2 \left[\dfrac{4s + 3}{s^2} \right]$

15.3 $F(s) = 2 \left[\dfrac{7s + 1}{s(s + 2)} \right]$

15.5 $F(s) = 4 \left[\dfrac{-s^3 + 6s^2 + 6s + 12}{s^3(s + 2)} \right]$

15.7 $F(s) = 16 \left[\dfrac{s + 3}{s^2 + 16} \right]$

15.9 $F(s) = 12 \left[\dfrac{s^2 + 2s + 8}{s^2(s + 4)} \right]$

15.11 $F(s) = \dfrac{a}{s^2 - a^2}$

15.13 $F(s) = 4 \left[\dfrac{s + 2}{s^2 + 4s - 12} \right]$

15.15 $F(s) = 4 \left[\dfrac{3s + 22}{s^2 + 4s + 20} \right]$

15.17 $F(s) = \dfrac{8e^{-2s}}{(s + 2)^2}$

15.19 $F(s) = \dfrac{2s(s+4)e^{-2s} - 8(s+3)^3(s+4) + 2s(s+3)^3 e^{-2s}}{s(s+4)(s+3)^3}$

15.21 $F(s) = \dfrac{-2s^4 + 8s^3 + 4s^2 - 28s - 80}{(s + 3)(s^2 + 4)^2}$

15.23 $F(s) = \dfrac{2s^2 + 32s + 14}{(s^2 + 8s + 25)^2}$

15.25 $F(s) = 6 \left[\dfrac{s^2 + 4s + 13}{s^2 + 4s - 5} \right]$

15.27 $F(s) = \dfrac{5s^2 + 54s + 389}{(s + 2)(s^2 + 6s + 73)}$

15.29 $Y(s) = \dfrac{4s}{s^2 + 64}$

15.31 $Y(s) = 2 \left[\dfrac{s^3 + 25s^2 + 2s + 3}{s^2(s + 3)(s + 4)} \right]$

15.33 $Y(s) = 8 \left[\dfrac{3s^3 + 998s^2 + 11{,}554s + 48}{s(s + 12)(s + 80)(s + 240)} \right]$

15.35 $Y(s) = 2 \left[\dfrac{2s^4 + 12s^3 + 6s^2 + 3s + 4}{s^3(s + 2)(s + 6)} \right]$

15.37 $f(t) = \frac{1}{10}[192 - 135e^{-t} - 30e^{-3t} - 27e^{-5t}]$

15.39 $f(t) = 48[1 - e^{-4t} - 2te^{-4t}]$

15.41 $f(t) = \frac{1}{3}[120e^{-2t} - 64e^{-t} - 56e^{-4t}]$

15.43 $f(t) = -\frac{5}{2} + 25t + 15t^2 + \frac{5}{2}e^{-2t}$

15.45 $f(t) = \frac{1}{5}[e^{-2t}(6 \cos t - 18 \sin t) + e^{-4t}(114 \cos 3t - 134 \sin 3t)]$

15.47 $f(t) = 2880 - 12{,}480e^{-2000t} + 14{,}400e^{-3000t}$

15.49 $f(0^+) = 0 \qquad f(\infty) = 19.20$

15.51 $f(0^+) = 0 \qquad f(\infty) = 48$

15.53 $f(0^+) = 0 \qquad f(\infty) = 0$

15.55 $f(0^+) = 0 \qquad f(\infty) = \infty$

15.57 $f(0^+) = 24 \qquad f(\infty) = 0$

15.59 $f(0^+) = 4800 \qquad f(\infty) = 2880$

Chapter 16

16.1 $i(t) = \frac{8}{3}e^{-18t} \ A$

16.3 $v(t) = \frac{144}{7}e^{-2t} \ V$

16.5 $i(t) = \frac{9}{2}[e^{-6t} - e^{-2t}] \ A$

16.7 $i(t) = e^{-200t}(0.36 \cos 400t + 0.82 \sin 400t) \ A$

16.9 $i(t) = 11 + 4t - 11e^{-4t} \ A$

16.11 $i(t) = 24 - 24e^{-4t} + 32te^{-4t} \ A$

16.13 $v(t) = 12 - 6e^{-4t} - 6e^{-2t} + 4e^{-3t} \ V$

16.15 $v(t) = 16 - 16t + 8t^2 - 12e^{-t} \ V$

16.17 $v(t) = 88 - 24t + 12t^2 - 84e^{-t} \ A$

16.19 $v(t) = 1.600 + 6.950 \cos 4t - 1.955 \sin 4t + e^{-4t}(3.450 \cos 3t - 4.794 \sin 3t) \ V$

16.21 $v(t) = \frac{1}{25}[480t - 384 + e^{-2t}(584 \cos t - 112 \sin t)] \ V$

16.23 $i(t) = \frac{1}{185}[e^{-t}(52 \cos 2t + 354 \sin 2t) - (52 \cos 4t + \frac{143}{2} \sin 4t)] \ A$

16.25 $i(t) = \frac{5}{2}e^{-3t} + \frac{23}{2}e^{-4t} - 6e^{-2t} - 8e^{-6t} \ A$

16.27 $i(t) = 8 - 8e^{-2t} + 12te^{-2t} - 6t^2e^{-2t} \ A$

16.29 $v(t) = -32 \sin 4t \ V$

16.31 $v(t) = \frac{1}{99}[660t - 484 + 486e^{-t} - 2e^{-12t}] \ V$

16.33 $i(t) = \frac{5}{2} + \cos 4t \ A$

16.35 $v(t) = e^{-5t}[32 \sin 5t + 2 \cos 5t]u(t) - 32e^{-5t} \sin 5(t - 2)u(t - 2) \ V$

16.37 $v(t) = e^{-5t}[\sin 5t + 2 \cos 5t]u(t) - 32e^{-5(t-2)} \sin 5(t - 2)u(t - 2) + 16e^{-5(t-4)} \sin 5(t - 4)u(t - 4)$

Chapter 17

17.1 $f(t) = \frac{1}{4}[\sin 2t - \cos 2t - e^{-2t}]u(t)$

17.3 $f(t) = \frac{1}{18}[\sin 3t - 3t \cos 3t]u(t)$

17.5 $f(t) = -18e^{-3t}(e^{-t} + 1)u(t)$

17.7 $f(t) = e^{-2t} - e^{-4t}]u(t)$

17.9 $f(t) = (e^{at}/a^2)u(t)$

17.11 $f(t) = \frac{1}{2}[\sin t + t \cos t]u(t)$

17.13 $f(t) = \dfrac{e^{bt} - e^{at}}{b - a}\, u(t)$

17.15 $f(t) = (1 - \cos t)u(t)$

17.17 $v(t) = 4000(e^{-t/100} - 1) + 40t$ V

17.19 $i(t) = 0.48e^{-4t}(3 \sin 3t - 4 \cos 3t) + 1$ A

17.21 $i(t) = 0.414 \sin 100t - 1.034 \cos 100t + 0.010e^{-40t}$ A

17.23 $v(t) = 4000(e^{-t/100} - 1) + 40t$ V

17.25 $i(t) = 0.48e^{-4t}(3 \sin 3t - 4 \cos 3t) + 1$ A

17.27 $i(t) = 0.414 \sin 100t - 1.034 \cos 100t + 0.010e^{-40t}$ A

17.29 $r(t)$

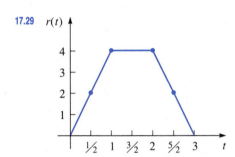

17.31 $r(t)$

17.33 $r(t)$

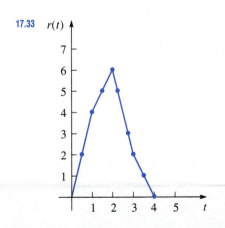

Chapter 18

18.1 $\mathbf{Z} = \begin{bmatrix} 12 & 4 \\ 4 & 16 \end{bmatrix}$

18.3 $\mathbf{Z} = \begin{bmatrix} 4 - j4 & 4 \\ 4 & 4 + j8 \end{bmatrix}$

18.5 $\mathbf{Z} = \begin{bmatrix} 4.80 - j21.60 & 2.40 - j16.80 \\ 2.40 - j16.80 & 1.20 - j14.40 \end{bmatrix}$

18.7 $\mathbf{Z} = \begin{bmatrix} \frac{1}{11} & -\frac{1}{44} \\ -\frac{1}{44} & \frac{3}{44} \end{bmatrix}$

18.9 $\mathbf{Y} = \begin{bmatrix} 0.20 + j0.15 & -0.10 + j0.05 \\ -0.10 + j0.05 & 0.05 - j0.15 \end{bmatrix}$

18.11 $\mathbf{Y} = \begin{bmatrix} \frac{1}{6} - j\frac{5}{12} & -\frac{1}{6} - j\frac{1}{2} \\ -\frac{1}{6} - j\frac{1}{2} & \frac{1}{6} + j\frac{2}{3} \end{bmatrix}$

18.13 See Problems 18.1 and 18.7

18.15 See Problems 18.3 and 18.9

18.17 See Problems 18.5 and 18.11

18.19 $Z_{12} = 44\ \Omega$ $\qquad Z_{23} = 22\ \Omega$ $\qquad Z_{31} = \frac{44}{3}\ \Omega$

18.21 $Z_{12} = 0.60 - j1.80\ \Omega$ $\qquad Z_{23} = -j6\ \Omega$
$Z_{31} = j12\ \Omega$

18.23 $Z_1 = -j4\ \Omega$ $\qquad Z_2 = j8\ \Omega$ $\qquad Z_3 = 4\ \Omega$

18.25 $Y_{12} = \frac{1}{8}\ \mho$ $\qquad Y_{23} = \frac{5}{24}\ \mho$ $\qquad Y_{31} = \frac{1}{4}\ \mho$

18.27 $Z_1 = 40\ \Omega$ $\qquad Z_2 = 80\ \Omega$ $\qquad Z_3 = 60\ \Omega$

18.29 $\mathbf{T} = \begin{bmatrix} \dfrac{s^2 + 1}{s^2} & \dfrac{2}{s} \\ \dfrac{s^2 + 2s + 1}{4s^2} & \dfrac{2s + 1}{2s} \end{bmatrix}$

18.31 $\mathbf{T} = \begin{bmatrix} \frac{11}{5} & \frac{42}{5} \\ \frac{3}{10} & \frac{8}{5} \end{bmatrix}$

18.33 $\mathbf{T} = \begin{bmatrix} \dfrac{s + 2}{s} & \dfrac{2s^2 + s + 2}{s^2 + 1} \\ \dfrac{1}{s} & \dfrac{s^2 + 1}{s^2} \end{bmatrix}$

18.35 $\mathbf{T'} = \begin{bmatrix} \dfrac{2s + 1}{2s} & \dfrac{2}{s} \\ \dfrac{s^2 + 2s + 1}{4s^2} & \dfrac{2s^2 + 2}{2s^2} \end{bmatrix}$

18.37 $\mathbf{T'} = \begin{bmatrix} \frac{8}{3} & \frac{42}{5} \\ \frac{1}{2} & \frac{11}{5} \end{bmatrix}$

18.39 $\mathbf{T'} = \begin{bmatrix} \dfrac{s^2 + 1}{s^2} & \dfrac{2s^2 + s + 2}{s^2} \\ \dfrac{1}{s} & \dfrac{s + 2}{s} \end{bmatrix}$

18.41 $\mathbf{H} = \begin{bmatrix} \dfrac{4}{2s + 1} & \dfrac{2s}{2s + 1} \\ -\dfrac{2s}{2s + 1} & \dfrac{s^2 + 2s + 1}{2s + 1} \end{bmatrix}$

18.43 $\mathbf{H} = \begin{bmatrix} \frac{21}{4} & -\frac{5}{8} \\ \frac{5}{8} & \frac{3}{16} \end{bmatrix}$

18.45 $\mathbf{H} = \begin{bmatrix} \dfrac{2s^2 + s + 2}{s^2 + 1} & -\dfrac{s^2}{s^2 + 1} \\ \dfrac{s^2}{s^2 + 1} & \dfrac{s}{s^2 + 1} \end{bmatrix}$

18.47 $\mathbf{G} = \begin{bmatrix} \dfrac{2s^2 + s + 2}{4(s^2 + 1)} & -\dfrac{s^2}{s^2 + 1} \\ \dfrac{s^2}{s^2 + 1} & \dfrac{2s}{s^2 + 1} \end{bmatrix}$

18.49 $\mathbf{G} = \begin{bmatrix} \frac{3}{22} & \frac{5}{11} \\ -\frac{5}{11} & \frac{42}{11} \end{bmatrix}$

18.51 $\mathbf{G} = \begin{bmatrix} \dfrac{1}{s + 2} & \dfrac{s}{s + 2} \\ -\dfrac{s}{s + 2} & \dfrac{2s^2 + s + 2}{s(s + 2)} \end{bmatrix}$

18.53 $\mathbf{Z} = \begin{bmatrix} -1 & \dfrac{\sqrt{2}}{2} + j\dfrac{\sqrt{2}}{2} \\ \dfrac{\sqrt{2}}{2} + j\dfrac{\sqrt{2}}{2} & -1 \end{bmatrix};$

$\mathbf{T} = \begin{bmatrix} -\left(\dfrac{\sqrt{2}}{2} + j\dfrac{\sqrt{2}}{2}\right) & \sqrt{2} \\ \dfrac{\sqrt{2}}{2} - j\dfrac{\sqrt{2}}{2} & -\left(\dfrac{\sqrt{2}}{2} + j\dfrac{\sqrt{2}}{2}\right) \end{bmatrix};$

$\mathbf{T}' = \begin{bmatrix} -\left(\dfrac{\sqrt{2}}{2} + j\dfrac{\sqrt{2}}{2}\right) & \sqrt{2} \\ \dfrac{\sqrt{2}}{2} - j\dfrac{\sqrt{2}}{2} & -\left(\dfrac{\sqrt{2}}{2} + j\dfrac{\sqrt{2}}{2}\right) \end{bmatrix};$

$\mathbf{H} = \begin{bmatrix} 1 - j & -\left(\dfrac{\sqrt{2}}{2} - j\dfrac{\sqrt{2}}{2}\right) \\ \dfrac{\sqrt{2}}{2} - j\dfrac{\sqrt{2}}{2} & 1 - j \end{bmatrix};$

$\mathbf{G} = \begin{bmatrix} 1 & -\left(\dfrac{\sqrt{2}}{2} - j\dfrac{\sqrt{2}}{2}\right) \\ \dfrac{\sqrt{2}}{2} - j\dfrac{\sqrt{2}}{2} & 1 - j \end{bmatrix}$

18.55 $\mathbf{Z} = \begin{bmatrix} \dfrac{s + 1}{s} & \dfrac{1}{s} \\ \dfrac{1}{s} & \dfrac{s^2 + 1}{s} \end{bmatrix};$

$\mathbf{Y} = \begin{bmatrix} \dfrac{s^2 + 1}{s^2 + s + 1} & -\dfrac{1}{s^2 + s + 1} \\ -\dfrac{1}{s^2 + s + 1} & \dfrac{s + 1}{s^2 + s + 1} \end{bmatrix}$

$\mathbf{T} = \begin{bmatrix} s + 1 & s^2 + s + 1 \\ s & s^2 + 1 \end{bmatrix};$

$\mathbf{T}' = \begin{bmatrix} -(s^2 + 1) & -(s^2 + s + 1) \\ -s & -(s + 1) \end{bmatrix}$

$\mathbf{G} = \begin{bmatrix} \dfrac{s}{s + 1} & -\dfrac{s}{s + 1} \\ \dfrac{s}{s + 1} & \dfrac{s^2 + s + 1}{s + 1} \end{bmatrix}$

18.57 $\mathbf{Z} = \begin{bmatrix} 12 & 4 \\ 4 & 16 \end{bmatrix}$

18.59 $\mathbf{Z} = \begin{bmatrix} 4 - j4 & 4 \\ 4 & 4 + j8 \end{bmatrix}$

18.61 $\mathbf{Z} = \begin{bmatrix} 30 + j40 & j40 \\ j60 & j30 \end{bmatrix}$

18.63 $\mathbf{Z} = \begin{bmatrix} 16 - j6 & 8 \\ 8 & 16 + j8 \end{bmatrix}$

18.65 $\mathbf{Z} = \begin{bmatrix} 1.25 \times 10^{-5} & 0 \\ 48{,}000 & 50{,}000 \end{bmatrix}$

18.67 $\mathbf{G} = \begin{bmatrix} 0.1543 - j0.0638 & -0.2610 - j2.5883 \\ 0.2610 + j2.5883 & 43.4307 + j30.2614 \end{bmatrix}$

18.69 $R = 2.44\ \Omega$

18.71 $\mathbf{Y} = \begin{bmatrix} \frac{1}{2} & -2 \\ -2 & \frac{3}{2} \end{bmatrix}$

Chapter 19

19.1 $Z_1(s) = \dfrac{s^2 + 3.48s + 63.97}{s + 1}$

19.3 $\beta_{1R}(s) = \dfrac{s}{s + 3.45}$

19.5 $\alpha_{12}(s) = \dfrac{s}{s^3 + 0.25s^2 + 2s + 0.25}$

19.7 $Z_1(s) = \dfrac{s^2 + 3.48s + 63.97}{s + 1}$

19.9   a pole at $s = 0$ and a zero at $s = -3.45$

19.11   poles at $s = -0.125$, $-0.062 \pm j1.41$ and a zero at $s = 0$.

19.13   without termination, $V_2/V_1 = \frac{1}{3}$; with termination $V_2/V_1 = \frac{4}{23}$

19.15   without termination, $\dfrac{V_2}{V_1} = \dfrac{s^2}{s^2 + 1}$;

with termination $\dfrac{V_2}{V_1} = \dfrac{s^2}{3s^2 + s + 3}$

19.17 $K_V = \frac{4}{39}$

19.19 $K_V = \dfrac{s^2}{5s^2 + 7s + 3}$

19.21   see Table 19.2

19.23   see Table 19.2

19.25   see Table 19.2

19.27 $i_n = Ie^{-25t/3}$ A

19.29 $i_n = Ie^{-1.34t}$ A

19.31 $v_n = Ve^{-16.8t}$ V

Chapter 20

20.1   242.25, 59.12°

20.3   4916.3, −0.91°

20.5 5.75×10^{-3}, 152.68°

20.7   −8.80 dB

20.9   87.61 dB

20.11

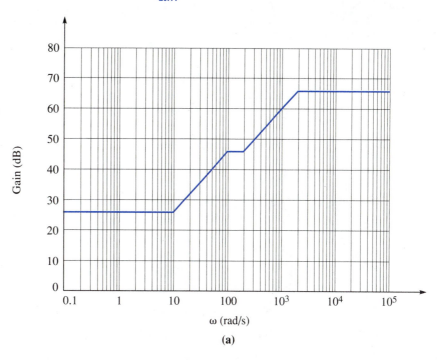

(a)

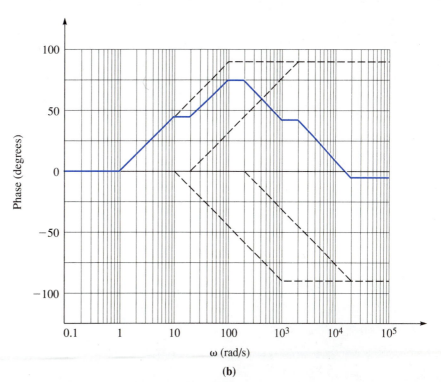

(b)

20.13

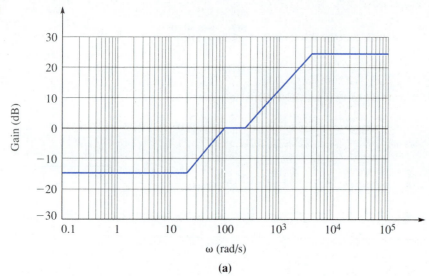

(a)

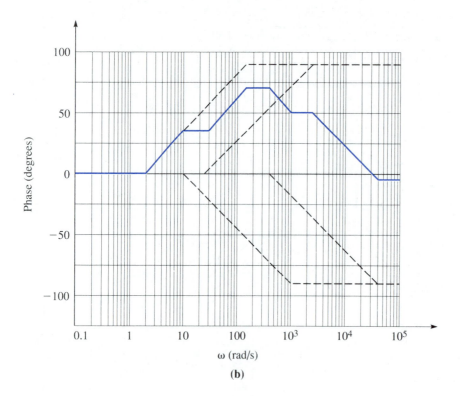

(b)

20.15

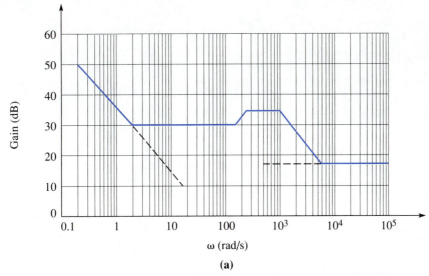

(a)

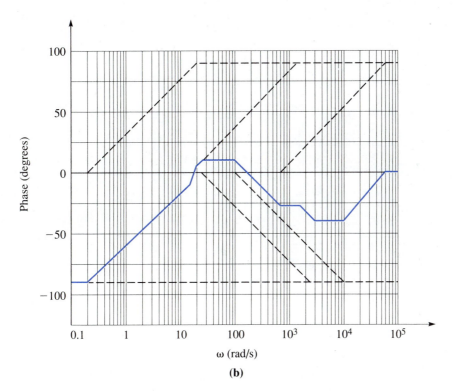

(b)

20.17

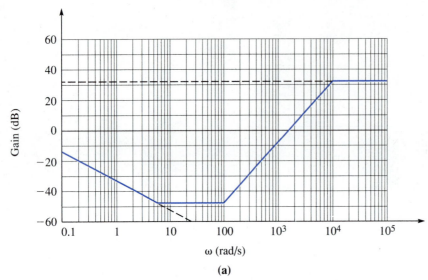

(a)

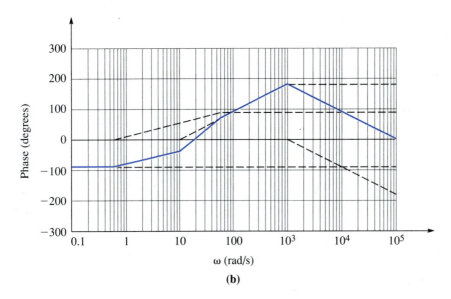

(b)

20.19

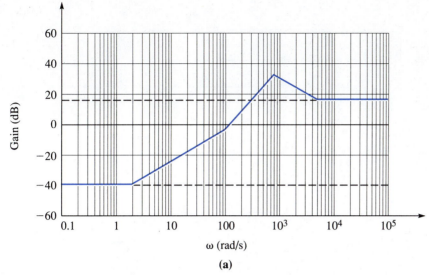

(a)

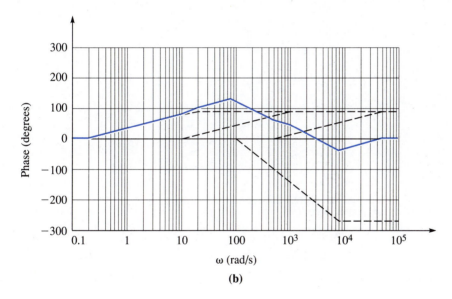

(b)

20.21

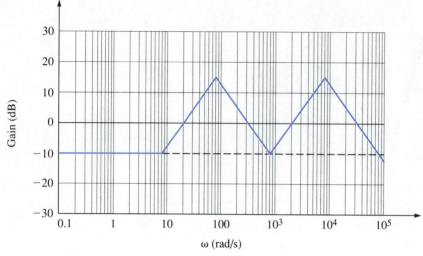

(a)

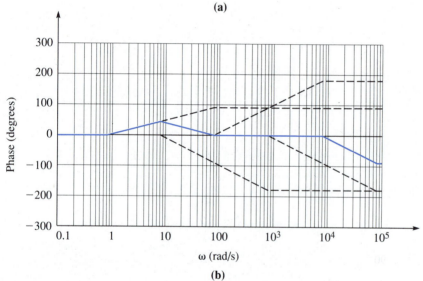

(b)

20.23 2.8885×10^8 rad/s

20.25   0.0928 or −20.65 dB, 68.41°

20.27   16.37 or 24.28 dB, 17.31°

20.29 $R = 1$ kΩ, $C = 50$ nF

20.31 $R = 2.23$ kΩ, $C = 25$ nF, $L = 100$ mH

20.33 $R = 5$ kΩ, $C = 40$ nF

20.35 $R = 7.07$ kΩ, $C = 40$ nF, $L = 1$ H

20.37 $R = 20$ kΩ, $C = 20$ nF, $L = 31.25$ mH

20.39 $R = 100$ kΩ, $C = 4$ nF, $L = 165.25$ mH

20.41 $R = 700$ Ω, $C = 1.67$ μF, $L = 0.24$ mH

20.43 $R = 400$ Ω, $C = 83.33$ nF, $L = 15$ mH

20.45 $R = 259.4$ Ω, $C = 481.9$ nF, $L = 324$ mH

Chapter 21

21.1 $\dfrac{a_0}{2} = 6$ $a_k = -\dfrac{16}{(k\pi)^2}$; $k = 1, 3, 5, 7, 9, 11, \ldots$

$b_k = \dfrac{8}{k\pi}$

21.3 $\dfrac{a_0}{2} = 0$

$a_k = 0$

$b_k = \begin{cases} \dfrac{8V}{(k\pi)^2}; & k = 1, 5, 9, 13, \ldots \\[2ex] -\dfrac{8V}{(k\pi)^2} & k = 3, 7, 11, 15 \ldots \end{cases}$

21.5 $\dfrac{a_0}{2} = 0$

$a_k = 0$

$b_k = \begin{cases} \dfrac{12}{k\pi}; & k = 1, 3, 5, 7, 9, 11, \ldots \\[2ex] -\dfrac{8}{k\pi}; & k = 2, 6, 10, 14, 18, \ldots \\[2ex] 0; & k = 4, 8, 12, 16, \ldots \end{cases}$

21.7 $\dfrac{a_0}{2} = \dfrac{V}{4}$ $a_k = -\dfrac{2V}{(k\pi)^2}$; $k = 1, 3, 5, 7, 9, \ldots$

$b_k = \begin{cases} \dfrac{V}{k\pi}; & k = 1, 3, 5, 7, 9, \ldots \\[2ex] -\dfrac{V}{(k\pi)} & k = 2, 4, 6, 8 \ldots \end{cases}$

21.9
$$\frac{a_0}{2} = 0$$
$$a_k = 0$$
$$b_k = \begin{cases} \dfrac{8V}{(k\pi)^2}; & k = 1, 5, 9, 13, \ldots \\[2ex] -\dfrac{8V}{(k\pi)^2} & k = 3, 7, 11, 15, \ldots \end{cases}$$

21.11
$$\frac{a_0}{2} = \frac{V}{2} \qquad a_k = \frac{4V}{(k\pi)^2}; \; k = 1, 3, 5, 7, 9, \ldots$$
$$b_k = 0$$

21.13
$$\frac{a_0}{2} = 5 \qquad a_k = \frac{40}{(k\pi)^2}; \; k = 1, 5, 9, 13, \ldots$$
$$b_k = 0$$

21.15
$$\frac{a_0}{2} = 0$$
$$a_k = 0 \qquad b_k = \begin{cases} -\dfrac{12}{k\pi}; & k = 1, 3, 5, 7, 9, 11, \ldots \\[1.5ex] -\dfrac{8}{k\pi}; & k = 2, 6, 10, 14, \ldots \\[1.5ex] 0; & k = 4, 8, 12, 16, \ldots \end{cases}$$

21.17
$$\begin{aligned} v(t) = {}& 6.000 + 3.018\cos(\pi t - 122.48°) \\ &+ 1.273\cos(2\pi t - 90.00°) \\ &+ 0.868\cos(3\pi t - 101.97°) \\ &+ 0.637\cos(4\pi t - 90.00°) \\ &+ 0.513\cos(5\pi t - 97.28°) \\ &+ 0.424\cos(6\pi t - 90.00°) \\ &+ 0.365\cos(7\pi t - 95.18°) + \cdots \, volts \end{aligned}$$

21.19
$$\begin{aligned} v(t) = \frac{8V}{\pi^2}\Big[& \cos(\omega_0 t + 90.00°) \\ & - \frac{1}{9}\cos(3\omega_0 t + 90.00°) \\ & + \frac{1}{25}\cos(5\omega_0 t + 90.00°) \\ & - \frac{1}{49}\cos(7\omega_0 t + 90.00°) + \cdots \Big] \, volts \end{aligned}$$

21.21
$$\begin{aligned} v(t) = \frac{1}{\pi}\Big[& 12\cos\left(\frac{\pi}{2}t + 90.00°\right) \\ & - 4\cos(\pi t - 90.00°) \\ & + 4\cos\left(\frac{3\pi}{2}t + 90.00°\right) \\ & + \frac{12}{5}\cos\left(\frac{5\pi}{2}t + 90.00°\right) \\ & - \frac{4}{3}\cos(3\pi t - 90.00°) \\ & + \frac{12}{7}\cos\left(\frac{7\pi}{2}t + 90.00°\right) + \cdots \Big] \, volts \end{aligned}$$

21.23
$$\begin{aligned} v(t) = {}& \frac{V}{4} + 0.3773V\cos(t + 122.48°) \\ &+ 0.1592V\cos(2t - 90.00°) \\ &+ 0.1085V\cos(3t + 101.97°) \\ &+ 0.0796V\cos(4t - 90.00°) \\ &+ 0.0642V\cos(5t + 97.28°) \\ &+ 0.0531V\cos(6t - 90.00°) \\ &+ 0.0455V\cos(7t + 95.18°) + \cdots \, volts \end{aligned}$$

21.25
$$\begin{aligned} v(t) = {}& (-0.0165 - j0.182)e^{-j7\omega_0 t} - j0.212e^{-j6\omega_0 t} \\ &+ (-0.0325 - j0.2545)c^{-j5\omega_0 t} \\ &- j0.3185e^{-j4\omega_0 t} \\ &+ (-0.0900 - j0.4245)e^{-j3\omega_0 t} \\ &- j0.6365e^{-j2\omega_0 t} \\ &+ (-0.8105 - j1.2730)e^{-j\omega_0 t} + 6.000 \\ &+ (-0.8105 - j1.2730)e^{j\omega_0 t} \\ &+ j0.6365e^{j2\omega_0 t} \\ &+ (-0.0900 + j0.4245)e^{j3\omega_0 t} \\ &+ j0.3185e^{j4\omega_0 t} \\ &+ (-0.0325 + j0.2545)e^{j5\omega_0 t} + j0.2120e^{j6\omega_0 t} \\ &+ (-0.0165 + 0.2545)e^{j7\omega_0 t} + \cdots \, volts \end{aligned}$$

21.27
$$\begin{aligned} v(t) = {}& -j\frac{4V}{49\pi^2}e^{-j7\omega_0 t} + j\frac{4V}{25\pi^2}e^{-j5\omega_0 t} \\ & -j\frac{4V}{9\pi^2}e^{-j3\omega_0 t} + j\frac{4V}{\pi^2}e^{-j\omega_0 t} - j\frac{4V}{\pi^2}e^{j\omega_0 t} \\ & +j\frac{4V}{9\pi^2}e^{j3\omega_0 t} - j\frac{4V}{25\pi^2}e^{j5\omega_0 t} \\ & +j\frac{4V}{49\pi^2}e^{j7\omega_0 t} + \cdots \, volts \end{aligned}$$

21.29
$$\begin{aligned} v(t) = {}& -j\frac{6V}{7\pi^2}e^{-j\tau\omega_0 t} + j\frac{4V}{25\pi^2}e^{-j5\omega_0 t} \\ & -j\frac{4V}{9\pi^2}e^{-j3\omega_0 t} + j\frac{4V}{\pi^2}e^{-j\omega_0 t} - j\frac{4V}{\pi^2}e^{j\omega_0 t} \\ & +j\frac{4V}{9\pi^2}e^{j3\omega_0 t} - j\frac{4V}{25\pi^2}e^{j5\omega_0 t} \\ & +j\frac{4V}{49\pi^2}e^{j7\omega_0 t} + \cdots \, volts \end{aligned}$$

21.31
$$\begin{aligned} v(t) = V\big[& (-0.00205 + j0.00275)e^{-j7\omega_0 t} \\ & - j0.02655e^{-j6\omega_0 t} \\ & + (-0.00405 - j0.03185)e^{-j5\omega_0 t} \\ & - j0.3198e^{-j4\omega_0 t} \\ & + (-0.01125 - j0.05305)e^{-j3\omega_0 t} \\ & - j0.0796e^{-j2\omega_0 t} \\ & + (-0.1013 - j0.15915)e^{-j\omega_0 t} \\ & + \frac{V}{4} + (-0.1013 + j0.15915)e^{j\omega_0 t} \\ & + j0.0796e^{j2\omega_0 t} \\ & + (-0.01125 - j0.05205)e^{j3\omega_0 t} \\ & + j0.0398e^{j4\omega_0 t} \\ & + (-0.00405 - j0.0318)e^{j5\omega_0 t} \\ & + j0.02655e^{j6\omega_0 t} \\ & + (-0.00205 - j0.02775)e^{j7\omega_0 t} \\ & + \cdots \big] \, volts \end{aligned}$$

21.33 $V_{eff} = 6.476 \; Volts$

21.35 $V_{eff} = 5.697V/\pi^2 \; Volts$

21.37 $V_{eff} = 12.65\pi \; Volts$

21.39 $V_{eff} = 0.5856 \; Volts$

21.41 $p_{av} = 7062.8 \; Watts$

21.43 $p_{av} = 3807 \; Watts$

21.45 $i(l) = 1.0000 + 0.1229 \cos(20\pi t + 107.65°)$
$+ 0.0143 \cos(60\pi t + 96.06°)$
$+ 0.0051 \cos(100\pi t + 93.64°)$
$+ 0.0026 \cos(140\pi t + 92.60°)$
$+ 0.0016 \cos(180\pi t + 92.01°)$
$+ \cdots Amperes$
$p_{av} = 19.85 \ Watts$

21.47 $i(t) = 0.353 \sin(8\pi t - 170.89°)$
$+ 0.0885 \sin(16\pi t - 175.44°)$
$+ 0.0394 \sin(24\pi t - 176.96°)$
$+ 0.0022 \sin(32\pi t - 177.92°)$
$+ 0.0142 \sin(40\pi t - 178.17°)$
$+ \cdots Amperes$
$p_{av} = -1.846 \ Watts$

21.49 $V(t) = 0.438 \sin(2\pi t - 58.01°)$
$+ 0.345 \sin(6\pi t - 21.02°)$
$+ 0.337 \sin(10\pi t - 12.71°)$
$+ 0.335 \sin(14\pi t - 9.10°)$
$+ 0.335 \sin(18\pi t - 7.08°) + \cdots Volts$
$p_{av} = 0.156 \ Watts$

Chapter 22

22.1

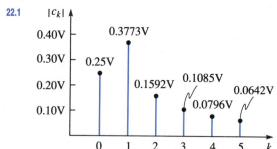

22.3

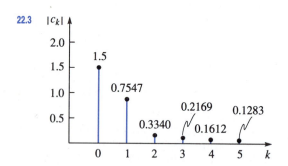

22.5

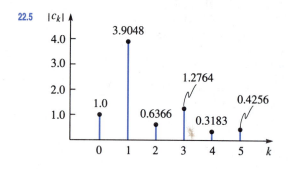

22.7

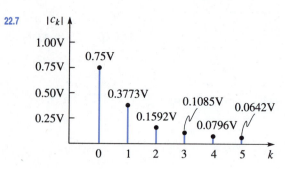

22.9

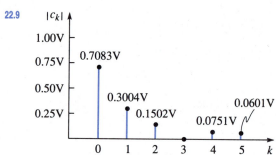

22.11 $F(\omega) = \dfrac{10}{j\omega}(e^{-j\omega} + 1) - \dfrac{20}{j\omega} e^{-j2\omega}$

22.13 $F(\omega) = \dfrac{1}{j2\omega}\left(e^{-j4\omega} - \dfrac{1}{2} e^{-j2\omega} + 1\right)$

22.15 $F(\omega) = \dfrac{10}{j\omega}(2 - e^{-j\omega} - e^{-j2\omega})$

22.17 $F(\omega) = e^{-j\omega t_0}$

22.19 $F(\omega) = \dfrac{1}{(j\omega + a)^2}$

22.21 $F(\omega) = \dfrac{b}{(a + j\omega)^2 + b^2}$

22.23 $F(\omega) = -\dfrac{1}{j\omega - 3}$

22.25 $v_0(t) = -4(|t| + e^{-2t})u(t)$
$- 8[|t - 0.5| - e^{-2(t-0.5)}]u(t - 0.5)$
$- 4[|t - 1| + e^{-2(t-1)}]u(t - 1)V$

22.27 $v_0(t) = 40(sgn(t) - 2e^{-2t})u(t)$
$- 40(sgn(t - 2) - 2e^{-2(t-2)})u(t - 2)V$

22.29 $v_0(t) = 8e^{-8(t-0.02)}u(t - 0.02)$
$- 16e^{-8(t-0.04)}u(t - 0.04) + 8e^{-8t}u(l)V$

22.31 $p = 50 \ W; \ percent = 37.89$

INDEX

KRAUS, CIRCUIT ANALYSIS, PROGRAMS, EE TOOLS, AND MATRIX.
WITH 5¼" DISKETTE BY ALLAN KRAUS.

IMPORTANT: PLEASE READ BEFORE OPENING THIS PACKAGE
THIS PACKAGE IS NOT RETURNABLE IF SEAL IS BROKEN.

West Services, Inc.
58 West Kellogg Boulevard
St. Paul, Minnesota 55164

LIMITED USE LICENSE

Read the following terms and conditions carefully before opening this diskette package. Opening the diskette package indicates your agreement to the license terms. If you do not agree, promptly return this package unopened to West Services for a full refund.

By accepting this license, you have the right to use this Software and the accompanying documentation, but you do not become the owner of these materials.

This copy of the Software is licensed to you for use only under the following conditions:

1. PERMITTED USES
You are granted a non-exclusive limited license to use the Software under the terms and conditions stated in this license. You may:

    a. Use the Software on a single computer.
    b. Make a single copy of the Software in machine-readable form solely for backup purposes in support of your use of the Software on a single machine. You must reproduce and include the copyright notice on any copy you make.
    c. Transfer this copy of the Software and the license to another user if the other user agrees to accept the terms and conditions of this license. If you transfer this copy of the Software, you must also transfer or destroy the backup copy you made. Transfer of this copy of the Software, and the license automatically terminates this license as to you.

2. PROHIBITED USES
You may not use, copy, modify, distribute or transfer the Software or any copy, in whole or in part, except as expressly permitted in this license.

3. TERM
This license is effective when you open the diskette package and remains in effect until terminated. You may terminate this license at any time by ceasing all use of the Software and destroying this copy and any copy you have made. It will also terminate automatically if you fail to comply with the terms of this license. Upon termination, you agree to cease all use of the Software and destroy all copies.

4. DISCLAIMER OF WARRANTY
Except as stated herein, the Software is licensed "as is" without warranty of any kind, express or implied, including warranties of merchantability or fitness for a particular purpose. You assume the entire risk as to the quality and performance of the Software. You are responsible for the selection of the Software to achieve your intended results and for the installation, use and results obtained from it. West Publishing and West Services do not warrant the performance of nor results that may be obtained with the Software. West Services does warrant that the diskette(s) upon which the Software is provided will be free from defects in materials and workmanship under normal use for a period of 30 days from the date of delivery to you as evidenced by a receipt.

Some states do not allow the exclusion of implied warranties so the above exclusion may not apply to you. This warranty gives you specific legal rights. You may also have other rights which vary from state to state.

5. LIMITATION OF LIABILITY
Your exclusive remedy for breach by West Services of its limited warranty shall be replacement of any defective diskette upon its return to West at the above address, together with a copy of the receipt, within the warranty period. If West Services is unable to provide you with a replacement diskette which is free of defects in material and workmanship, you may terminate this license by returning the Software, and the license fee paid hereunder will be refunded to you. In no event will West be liable for any lost profits or other damages including direct, indirect, incidental, special, consequential or any other type of damages arising out of the use or inability to use the Software even if West Services has been advised of the possibility of such damages.

6. GOVERNING LAW
This agreement will be governed by the laws of the State of Minnesota.

You acknowledge that you have read this license and agree to its terms and conditions. You also agree that this license is the entire and exclusive agreement between you and West and supersedes any prior understanding or agreement, oral or written, relating to the subject matter of this agreement.

THIS PACKAGE IS NOT RETURNABLE IF SEAL IS BROKEN